MILLER'S

ANTIQUES PRICE GUIDE

1991

(Volume XII)

Compiled and Edited by

Judith and Martin Miller

MILLERS PUBLICATIONS

An English original painted pine decoy pigeon, on a new stand, Suffolk, c1900, 14in (36cm) long.
£100-150 *UC*

MILLER'S ANTIQUES PRICE GUIDE 1991

Created and designed by
M.J.M. Publishing Projects for
Millers Publications Limited
The Mitchell Beazley Group
Sissinghurst Court, Sissinghurst
Cranbrook, Kent TN17 2JA
Telephone: (0580) 713890

Compiled and edited by
Judith & Martin Miller

Editorial co-ordinator: Jo Davis
Assistant Editor: Sue Boyd
Editorial Assistants: Marion Rickman, Sue Woodhouse
Production Assistant: Gillian Charles
Advertising Executive: Elizabeth Smith
Index compiled by: DD Editorial Services, Beccles
Additional photography by Robin Saker and Ian Booth

A CIP catalogue record for this book is available from the British Library

ISBN 0-905879-61-9

Typeset by Ardek Photosetters, St. Leonards-on-Sea
Colour origination by Scantrans, Singapore.
Printed and bound in England by William Clowes Ltd., Beccles and London

James Buckingham

COLLECTION OF ENGLISH PERIOD COPIES

TWIN PEDESTAL DESKS
4′ x 2″ Mahogany **£391** Yew **£431**
5′ x 3″ Mahogany **£578** Yew **£614**
Also available, L-shape Computer Desks with side returns.

SET OF 6 CHAIRS
(4 Single & 2 Carvers)
Mahogany **£488**
Yew **£506**

FILING CABINET
2 drawer mahogany **£295**
2 drawer yew **£331**
3 drawer mahogany **£378**
3 drawer yew **£424**

LOWBOY
Mahogany **£343**
Yew **£343**
Walnut **£378**

7′ DINING TABLE & CENTRE LEAF
Mahogany **£218**
Yew **£298**
8′ 8″ Mahogany **£303**
Yew **£399**

REVOLVING BOOKCASE
Mahogany **£179**
Yew **£202**
Walnut **£226**

BREAKFAST TABLE
in Mahogany & Yew.
Several sizes from **£216**

NEST OF 4 TABLES
Mahogany **£345**
Yew **£388**

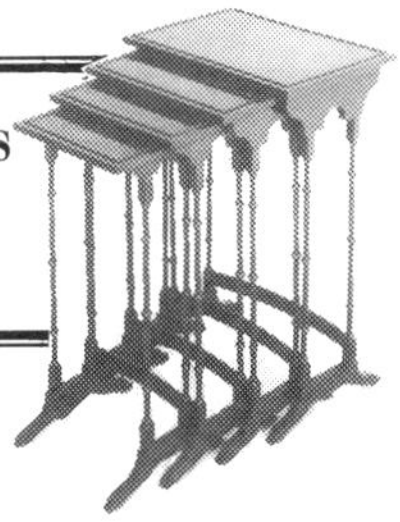

The above prices are inclusive of VAT
Prices are correct at time of going to publication but may be subject to change.

WHOLESALE **RETAIL** **EXPORT**

James Buckingham

Tel: (04 44) 245577
School Close, Queen Elizabeth Avenue
Burgess Hill, West Sussex (Nr. Brighton) RH15 9RX
Fax (04 44) 232014
ENGLAND

THERE ARE MANY ANTIQUE

... few, if any, who are as quality conscious as Norman Lefton, Chairman and Managing Director of British Antique Exporters Ltd. of Burgess Hill, Nr. Brighton, Sussex.

Nearly thirty years' experience of shipping goods to all parts of the globe have confirmed his original belief that the way to build clients' confidence in his services is to supply them only with goods which are in first class saleable condition. To this end, he employs a cottage industry staff of over 40, from highly skilled antique restorers, polishers and packers to representative buyers and executives.

Through their knowledgeable hands passes each piece of furniture before it leaves the B.A.E. warehouses, ensuring that the overseas buyer will only receive the best and most saleable merchandise for their particular market. This attention to detail is obvious on a visit to the Burgess Hill showrooms where potential customers can view what must be the most varied assortment of Georgian, Victorian, Edwardian and 1930s furniture in the UK. One cannot fail to be impressed by, not only the varied range of merchandise, but also the fact that each piece is in showroom condition awaiting shipment.

The Company have a very good selection but cannot stock everything (neither can anyone else). If they have not got the antique you require in stock they do know where to find it. This is one of their main strengths and for the 1990s they are also offering a new concept of buying on commission only. This enables the overseas dealer to have a resident buying office in the U.K. for as little as 10% commission for goods purchased and provides the non-resident dealer with his exact requirements to a precise specification.

As one would expect, packing is considered somewhat of an art at B.A.E. and the manager in charge of the works ensures that each piece will reach its final destination in the condition a customer would

BRITISH ANTIQUE EXPORTERS LTD,

SCHOOL CLOSE, QUEEN ELIZABETH AVENUE,
BURGESS HILL, WEST SUSSEX RH15 9RX, ENGLAND.

Telephone BURGESS HILL (04 44) 245577.

Fax (04 44) 232014.

Members of L.A.P.A.D.A. and Guild of Master Craftsmen

SHIPPERS IN BRITAIN BUT...

wish. B.A.E. set a very high standard and, as a further means of improving each container load, their customer/container liaison dept, invites each customer to return detailed information on the saleability of each piece in the container, thereby ensuring successful future shipments.

This feedback of information is the all important factor which guarantees the profitability of future containers. "By this method" Mr. Lefton explains, "we have established that an average £10,000 container will immediately it is unpacked at its final destination realise in the region of £15,000 to £20,000 for our clients selling the goods on a quick wholesale turnover basis."

When visiting the warehouses various container loads can be seen in the course of completion. The intending buyer can then judge for himself which type of container load would be best suited to his market. In an average 20-foot container B.A.E. put approximately 75 to 100 pieces carefully selected to suit the particular destination. There are always at least 10 outstanding or unusual items in each shipment, but every piece included looks as though it has something special about it.

In the unlikely event of the merchandise not being suitable for any reason whatsoever the Company offers a full money back guarantee less one-way freight.

B.A.E. have opened several new showrooms based at its 15,000 square feet headquarters in Burgess Hill which is 15 minutes away from Gatwick Airport, 7 miles from Brighton and 39 miles from London on a direct rail link, (only 40 minutes journey), the Company is ideally situated to ship containers to all parts of the world. The showrooms, restoration and packing departments are open to overseas buyers and no visit to purchase antiques for re-sale in other countries is complete without a visit to their Burgess Hill premises where a welcome is always found.

BRITISH ANTIQUE EXPORTERS LTD,

SCHOOL CLOSE, QUEEN ELIZABETH AVENUE,
BURGESS HILL, WEST SUSSEX RH15 9RX, ENGLAND.

Telephone BURGESS HILL (04 44) 245577.

Fax (04 44) 232014.

Members of L.A.P.A.D.A. and Guild of Master Craftsmen

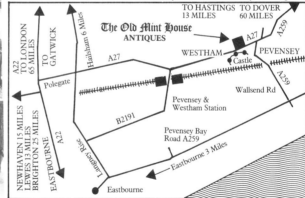

Hedleys
Humpers

DO YOU HAVE A LOAD ON YOUR MIND?

If you have a load to be transported abroad, whether it is antiques, household effects, or contemporary furniture, we can deliver it faster and more expertly than other transport companies, often at a lower cost.

For European destinations we offer a regular driver accompanied door to door service for either one piece or a truck load and for the rest of the world we operate through our network of experienced furniture carriers who can ensure the safe delivery of our especially packaged goods by air or by sea.

HEDLEY'S HUMPERS LTD

UNITS 3 & 4, 97 VICTORIA ROAD,
LONDON NW10 6ND
TEL:081 965 8733 FAX:081 965 0249
TELEX:25229

1 IMPASSE SIMON
RUE DES ROSIERS, PARIS, 93400 ST OUEN, FRANCE.
TEL:40109400 FAX:40100564

ANTIQUES WAREHOUSE

IAN F.VINCE 0245 400046

Members of LAPADA

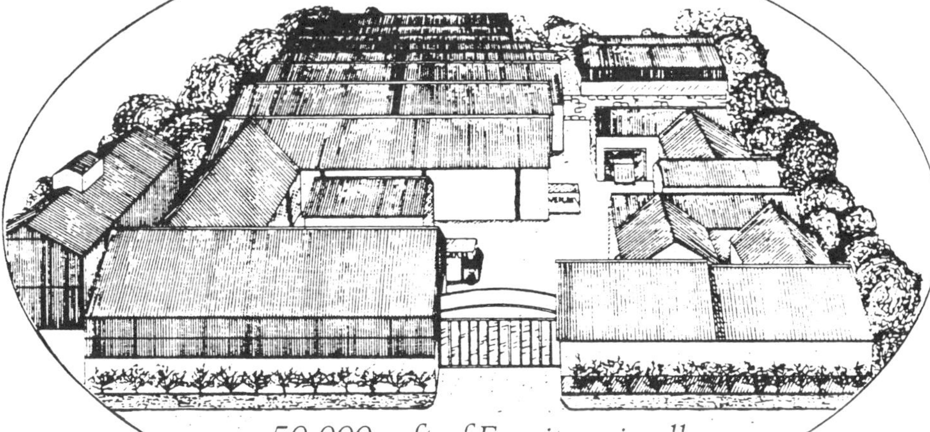

50,000sq ft of Furniture in all Styles and Periods

RAWLINGS FARM BUILDINGS,
(A130) RETTENDON, ESSEX

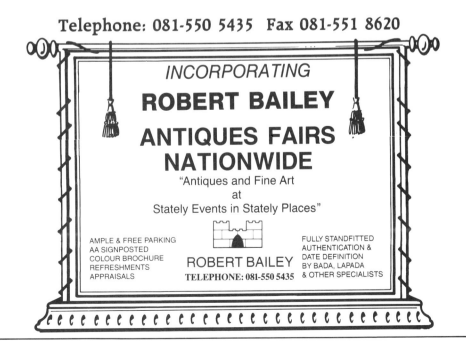

INDEX TO ADVERTISERS

Alfies Antique Market 707
Anderson & Garland 768
Antiques Trade Gazette ..... Inserts
Antiques Bulleting 323
Antique Leathercraft Company 381
Antique Desks 379
Antique Dolls 669
Anthemion 365
AS Antiques 565
Ascent Auctions 758
Ashburton Marbles 443
Architectural Antiques 455
Armstrongs Auctions 764
Atlantic Centres 619
Aylsham Salerooms 766
Bacchus Antiques 599
Robert Bailey 16, 17
Barn Full of Sofas & Chairs 343
Beehive Antiques 59
Bexhill Antique Exporters 12
Black Horse Agencies 770, 771
Bloomsbury Antiques 553
Andrew Spencer Bottomley 753
Boardman 765
Bonhams .... Back Cover
Bonhams West Country 757
Boulton & Cooper 768
Michael J Bowman 756
Roy W Bunn Antiques 37
Brighton Architectural Salvage 449
British Antique Exporters 2, 4, 8, 9, 10
William H Brown 765
W F Bruce 495
F G Bruschweiler 11
James Buckingham 7
Burlington Specialised Forwarding Ltd 295
Burston & Hewett 758
Butchoff Antiques 409
Gerard Campbell 497
Carless & Co 765
H C Chapman 768
Chancellors 560
Peter Cheney 560
Clevedon Salerooms 757
The Clock Clinic 497
The Clock Shop 511
The Clock Shop (Samuel Orr) 501
The Collector 547
Collins Antiques 417
Conquest House 311
Cooper Hirst 561
Cooper & Tanner 756
Coppelia Antiques 491
County Group 758
The Crested China Company .. 169
Cultural Exhibitions 23
Cumbria Auction Rooms 768
Julian Dawson 560
Denhams 762
Delvin Farm Galleries 739
Didier Antiques 541
R C Dodson 15
The Dorking Desk Shop 377
Dowell Lloyd & Co 560
A E Dowse & Son 768
Drummonds of Bramley 457
Dycheling Antiques 349
Halifax Antiques Centre 23
Halifax Property Services 758
Hampton Court Clocks 495
Andrew Hartley 769
David Harriman 507
J Hartley Antiques Ltd 277
Giles Haywood 764
Hedleys Humpers Ltd 14
Muir Hewitt 623
Robert I Heyes 768
Andrew Hilditch & Son 768
Bob Hoare Pine Antiques 734
Hobbs & Chambers 762
Hobbs Parker 759
Paul Hopwell 253
Jonathan Horne 35
Howards Antiques 41
Valerie Howard 51
Christopher Howarth 25
Hubbard Antiques 25
Hunts 757
Empire Antiques 737
Robin Elliott 561
Featherston Shipping 15
Alan Franklin 15
Furnace Mill 343
GA Fine Art & Chattels 763
F Le Gallais & Sons 757
Galleria Fine Arts Ltd 385
Thos W M Gaze & Son 767
George, Clocks 493
Gildings 766
Gorringes Auction Galleries ... 758
Goss & Crested China 167, 173
Grays Antique Market 707
Ibbett Mosely 758
Islington Artefacts 736
Its About Time 491
John Ives 24
Jazzy Art Deco 567
Arthur Johnson & Sons 764
James A Jordan 517
Key Antiques 637
G A Key 766
Kingsbridge Auction Sales 756
Lakeside Antiques 798, 799
Penny Lampard 16, 741
Garnet Langton 762
Lawrence Bletchingley 560
David Lay 756
Lewes Auction Rooms 560
Ann Lingard 735
Lithgow Sons & Partners 768
Brian Loomes 489
Lowe of Loughborough 345
Martel Maides & Le Pelley 757
Jamie Maxtone Graham 685
May & Sons 762
McBain Exports 25
McCartneys 764
Millers Auctions 756
Millers Collectables Price Guides 537
Millers of Chelsea Antiques Ltd 741
Millers Antiques Price Guides 595
Millers Pocket Fact File 39
Robert Mills 453
Mint & Boxed 703
William Morey & Sons 757
Morgan Evans & Co 766
Nationwide Fine Art & Furniture 759
Neales of Nottingham 767
D M Nesbitt 763
Michael Newman 756
B J Norris Auctioneers 759
Morris & Duval 764
Nostalgia 447
Old Bakery Antiques 255
Old Court Pine 743
The Old Cinema 285
Old Mint House 13
Oola Boola Antiques 279
Jacqueline Oosthuizen 43
Oxford Antique Trading Co 23
P A Oxley 503
J R Parkinson Son & Hamer ... 769
Janice Paull (Beehive Antiques) 59
Sue Pearson 675
Penman Antique Fairs 28
Pine Finds 740
Graham Price Antiques 331
David & Sarah Pullen 493
Retro Products 24
Riddetts 762
Ripley Antiques 413
Derek Roberts 462
Rochester Fine Arts 464
Rogers de Rin 103
Romsey Auction Rooms 757
Russell Baldwin & Bright 766
Scotts 53
Sheffco 577, 583
Shiners 445
Osward Simpson 249
Somervale Antiques 217
Somerville Antiques 743
South Bar Antiques 463
Southgate Auctions 561
Spencer Thomas & Woolland .. 756
Don Spencer Antiques 379
Henry Spencer & Sons 766
Spurrier-Smith Antiques 605
Studio Antiques 3
Swan Antiques 251
Sworders 767
Christopher Sykes 597
Teddy Bears of Witney 677
Teme Valley Antiques 139
Tennants 769
Thames Gallery 581
Thesaurus 26
Trace Publications 24
Up Country 331
Utopia Antiques Ltd 738
T Vennet-Smith 697
Victoria & Edward 16
Ian F Vince 14
Wallis & Wallis 751
Anthony Wakefield & Co Ltd . 24
Wakelin & Linfield 257
Walter's 767
Islwyn Watkins 49
Chris Watts Antiques 405
Thos Watson & Sons 769
Wealden Auction Galleries 759
West Street Antiques 755
A J Williams 15
Peter S Williams 758
Wingate & Johnson 12
Wright Manley 769
Robert Young Antiques 259

Acknowledgements

The publishers would like to acknowledge the great assistance given by our consultant editors:

POTTERY:	**Jonathan Horne,** *66b and c Kensington Church Street, London W8.*
	Ron Beech, *Victorian Staffordshire Figures and Pot Lids, No. 1 Brambledean Road, Portslade, Sussex BN41 1LP.*
PORCELAIN:	**Christopher Spencer:** *Greystones, 29 Mostyn Road, Merton Park, London SW19.*
	Nicholas Long, *Studio Antiques, Bourton-on-the-Water, Glos.*
WORCESTER:	**Henry Sandon,** *11 Perrywood Close, Worcester.*
GOSS & CRESTED WARE:	**Nicholas Pine,** *Goss & Crested China Ltd, 62 Murray Road, Horndean, Hants.*
FURNITURE:	**John Bly,** *50 High Street, Tring, Herts.*
	Richard Davidson, *Richard Davidson Antiques, Lombard Street, Petworth, Sussex.*
OAK:	**Victor Chinnery,** *Bennetts, Oare, Nr Marlborough, Wilts.*
LONGCASE CLOCKS:	**Brian Loomes,** *Calfhaugh, Pateley Bridge, N Yorks.*
GLASS:	**Wing Cdr R G Thomas,** *Somervale Antiques, 6 Radstock Road, Midsomer Norton, Bath, Avon.*
ART NOUVEAU & ART DECO:	**Eric Knowles,** *Bonhams, Montpelier Galleries, Montpelier Street, Knightsbridge, London SW7.*
LALIQUE:	**Russell Varney,** *Bonhams, Montpelier Galleries, Montpelier Street, Knightsbridge, London SW7.*
CARPETS & TEXTILES:	**Robert Bailey,** *1 Roll Gardens, Gants Hill, Essex.*
TOYS:	**Stuart Cropper,** *Grays Mews, 1-7 Davies Mews, London W1.*
ARMS & ARMOUR:	**Roy Butler,** *Wallis & Wallis, West Street Auction Galleries, Lewes, Sussex.*
PINE FURNITURE:	**Ann Lingard,** *Rope Walk Antiques, Rye, Sussex.*
JEWELLERY:	**Valerie Howkins,** *Peter Howkins, 39-40 and 135 King Street, Great Yarmouth, Norfolk.*
FISHING:	**Jamie Maxtone Graham,** *Lyne Haugh, Lyne Station, Peebles, Scotland.*
EPHEMERA	**Trevor Vennett-Smith, FRICS, FSVA, CAAV,** *11 Nottingham Road, Gotham, Nottinghamshire.*

A wooden toy horse and cart, c1920.
£60-80 *AL*

Key to Illustrations

Each illustration and descriptive caption is accompanied by a letter-code. By reference to the following list of Auctioneers (denoted by *) and Dealers (•), the source of any item may be immediately determined. In no way does this constitute or imply a contract or binding offer on the part of any of our contributors to supply or sell the goods illustrated, or similar articles, at the prices stated. Advertisers in this year's directory are denoted by †.

ABS •Abstract, 58/60 Kensington Church Street, London, W8. Tel: 071-376 2652.

AG †* Anderson & Garland, Marlborough House, Marlborough Crescent, Newcastle-upon-Tyne. Tel: 091-232 6278.

AH †* Andrew Hartley, Victoria Hall, Little Lane, Ilkley, West Yorkshire. Tel: (0943) 816363.

AI •Antiques & Interiors, 22 Ashford Road, Tenterden, Kent. Tel: (05806) 5462.

AJ •A. J. Partners, Alfies Stand F104, Church Street, Marylebone, NW8. Tel: 071-258 3602/723 5363.

AL †•Ann Lingard, Ropewalk Antiques, Ropewalk, Rye, Sussex. Tel: (0797) 223486.

ALL * Allen & Harris (Osmond Tricks), Regent Street, Auction Rooms, Clifton, Bristol, Avon. Tel: (0272) 737201 (see OT).

AnC •(Antique Connoisseur), now Pieces of Time, Grays Mews, 1-7 Davies Mews, London, W1. Tel: 071-629 2422.

ARC †•Architectural Antiques, West Ley, Alswear Old Road, South Molton, Devon. Tel: (07695) 3342.

ARF •Art Furniture (London) Ltd, 3B Prowse Place, 158 Camden Street, London, NW1. Tel: 071-267 4324.

ART •Artemesia Antiques, 16 West Street, Alresford, Hants. Tel: (0962) 732862.

ASA †•AS Antiques, 26 Broad Street, Pendleton, Salford 6, Lancashire. Tel: 061-737 5938/736 6014.

ASB †•Andrew Spencer Bottomley, The Coach House, 173A Huddersfield Road, Thongsbridge, Holmfirth, Huddersfield. Tel: (0484) 685234.

ASH †•Ashburton Marbles, London House, 6 West Street, Ashburton, Devon. Tel: (0364) 53189.

AW •Country Collectables, The Old Surgery, Hall Street, Long Melford, Sussex. Tel: (0787) 310140.

B †* Boardman, Station Road Corner, Haverh ., Suffolk. Tel: (0440) 703784.

Ba †•Butchoff Antiques, 233 Westbourne Grove, London, W11. Tel: 071-221 8174.

BAL •Sharon Ball, Unit 41, Stratford-upon-Avon Antique Centre, Ely Street, Warwickshire. Tel: (0789) 204180.

Bea * Bearnes, Rainbow, Avenue Road, Torquay, Devon. Tel: (0803) 296277.

BEB †•Judy Bebber Antique Dolls, Stand L14 Grays Mews, 1-7 Davies Mews, London, W1. Tel: 071-499 6600.

BEV •Beverley, 30 Church Street, London, NW8. Tel: 071-262 1576.

BH †•Bob Hoare Pine Antiques, Unit Q, Phoenix Place, North Street, Lewes, Sussex. Tel: (0273) 480557.

BHA •Beaubush House Antiques, 95 Sandgate High Street, Folkestone, Kent. Tel: (0303) 49099/51121.

BIZ •Bizarre, 24 Church Street, London, NW8. Tel: 071-724 1305.

BLO †•Bloomsbury Antiques, 58/60 Kensington Church Street, London, W8. Tel: 071-376 2810.

Bon †* Bonhams, Montpelier Galleries, Montpelier Street, Knightsbridge, London, SW7. Tel: 071-594 9161.

BWe * Biddle & Webb of Birmingham, Ladywood Middleway, Birmingham. Tel: 021-455 8042.

BL †•Brian Loomes, Calf Haugh, Pateley Bridge, N. Yorks. Tel: Harrogate (0423) 711163.

C * Christie's, Manson & Woods Ltd, 8 King Street, St. James's, London, SW1. Tel: 071-839 9060.

CA •Crafers Antiques, The Hill, Wickham Market, Woodbridge, Suffolk. Tel: (0728) 747347.

CAC •Cranbrook Antique Centre, High Street, Cranbrook, Kent. Tel: (0580) 712173.

CAm * Christie's Amsterdam, Cornelis Schuytstraat 571071 JG, Amsterdam, Holland. Tel: (020) 64 20 11.

CD •The China Doll, 31 Walcot Street, Bath, Avon. Tel: (0225) 465849.

CDC * Capes Dunn & Co, The Auction Galleries, 38 Charles Street, off Princess Street, Manchester. Tel: 061-273 6060.

CEd * Christie's & Edmiston's Ltd, 164-166 Bath Street, Glasgow. Tel: 041-332 8134/7.

CG * Christie's (International) SA, 8 Place de la Taconnerie, 1204 Geneva, Switzerland. Tel: (022) 28 25 44.

CLC †•The Clock Clinic Ltd, 85 Lower Richmond Road, Putney, London, SW15. Tel: 081-788 1407.

CNY * Christie, Manson & Woods, International Inc, 502 Park Avenue, New York NY 10022 USA. Tel: (212) 546 1000 (incuding Christie's East).

COB •Cobwebs (P. A. Boyd-Smith), 78 Northam Road, Southampton. Tel: (0703) 227458.

COG †* Country Group (formerly Butler Hatch Waterman), 102 High Street, Tenterden, Kent. Tel: (05806) 3233.

CoH †* Cooper Hirst, Goldlay House, Parkway, Chelmsford, Essex. Tel: (0245) 58141.

CS †•Christopher Sykes Antiques, The Old Parsonage, Woburn, Milton Keynes, Bucks. Tel: (0525) 290259/290467.

CSK * Christie's (South Kensington), 85 Old Brompton Road, London, SW7. Tel: 071-581 7611.

DDM * Dickinson, Davy & Markham, Wrawby Street, Brigg, South Humberside. Tel: (0652) 53666.

DDS †•Dorking Desk Shop, 41 West Street, Dorking, Surrey. Tel: (0306) 883327/880535.

DEN †* Denham's & Associates, Horsham Auction Galleries, Nr. Horsham, Sussex. Tel: (0403) 55699/53837.

DID †•Didier Antiques, 58/60 Kensington Church Street, London, W8. Tel: 071-938 2537/(0836) 232634.

DN * Drewett Neate, Donnington Priory, Donnington, Newbury, Berks. Tel: (0635) 31234.

DOW •Brian & Angela Downes Antiques, 9 Broad Street, Bath, Avon. Tel: (0225) 465352.

DRA †•Derek Roberts Antiques, 24/25 Shipbourne Road, Tonbridge, Kent. Tel: (0732) 358986/351719.

DRU †•Drummonds of Bramley, Birtley Farm, Horsham Road, Bramley, Guildford, Surrey. Tel: (0483) 898766.

DS †•Don Spencer Antiques, Unit 2, 20 Cherry Street, Warwick. Tel: (0926) 499857 & (0564) 775470.

DSA •Gallery Antiques (Derek Smith), Mill Street, Oakham, Leicester. Tel: (0572) 755094.

DY †•Dycheling Antiques, 34 High Street, Ditchling, Hassocks, West Sussex. Tel: (079 18) 2929.

EHA •Gloria Gibson, 2 Beaufort West, Bath. Tel: (0225) 446646.

FA ●Frank Andrews, 10 Vincent Road, London, N22. Tel: 081-889 3445.

FAL ●Falstaff Antiques, 63-67 High Street, Rolvenden (Motor Museum), Kent. Tel: (0580) 241234.

FF ●Fritz Fryer, 12 Brookend Street, Ross-on-Wye, Herefordshire. Tel: (0989) 67416.

FR * Fryer's Auction Galleries, Terminus Road, Bexhill-on-Sea, E. Sussex. Tel: (0424) 212994.

GA(W) †* GA Property Services, Canterbury, Kent. Tel: (0227) 763337.

GAK †* GA Key, Aylsham Saleroom, off Palmers Lane, Aylsham, Norfolk. Tel: (0263) 733195.

G&CC †* Goss & Crested China Ltd, Nicholas J. Pine, 62 Murray Road, Horndean, Hants. Tel: (0705) 597440.

GC †* Geering & Colyer, Highgate, Hawkhurst, Kent. Tel: (0580) 753181/753463.

GD * See DEN

GeC †●Gerard Campbell, Maple House, Market Place, Lechlade-on-Thames, Glos. Tel: (0367) 52267.

GH †* Giles Haywood, The Auction House, St. John's Road, Stourbridge, West Midlands. Tel: (0384) 370891.

GIL †* Gilding's, Roman Way, Market Harborough, Leicester. Tel: (0858) 410414.

GM * George Mealy & Sons, The Square, Castlecomer, Co. Kilkenny, Ireland. Tel: (010 353 56) 41229.

GSP * Graves, Son & Pilcher, 71 Church Road, Hove, East Sussex. Tel: (0273) 735 266.

HAR ●Patricia Harbottle, 107 Portobello Road, Geoffrey Vann Arcade, London, W11. Tel: 071-731 1972.

HCH †* Hobbs & Chambers, 'At The Sign of the Bell', Market Place, Cirencester, Glos. Tel: (0285) 4736. Also: 15 Royal Crescent, Cheltenham, Glos. Tel: (0242) 513722.

HF ●Lynne Hacking & Elizabeth Formby, 58/60 Kensington Church Street, London, W8. Tel: 071-326 0425.

HFG ●Habsburg, Feldman S.A., Geneva, 202 Route du Grand-Lancy, PO Box 125, 1213 Onex, Geneva, Switzerland. Tel: (022) 757 25 30.

HOL ●E. Hollander Ltd, The Dutch House, Horsham Road, South Holmwood, Surrey. Tel: (0306) 888921.

HOW †●Howards Antiques, 10 Alexandra Road, Aberystwyth, Dyfed. Tel: (0970) 624973.

HSS †* Henry Spencer & Sons, 20 The Square, Retford, Notts. Tel: (0777) 708633.

HUN ●Huntercombe Manor Barn, Nr. Henley on Thames, Oxon. Tel: (0491) 641349.

IM †* Ibbett Mosely, 125 High Street, Sevenoaks, Kent. Tel: (0732) 452246.

IW †●Islwyn Watkins, 1 High Street, Knighton, Powys, Wales. Tel: (0547) 520145/528940.

JD †* Julian Dawson, Lewes Auction Rooms, 56 High Street, Lewes, East Sussex. Tel: (0273) 478221.

JH * Jacobs & Hunt, Lavant Street, Petersfield, Hants. Tel: (0730) 62744.

JHo †●Jonathan Horne (Antiques) Ltd, 66B & C, Kensington Church Street, London, W8. Tel: 071-221 5658.

JL ●Joy Luke, The Gallery, 300 East Grove Street, Bloomington, Illinois 61701. Tel: (309) 828 5533.

JMG †●Jamie Maxtone Graham, Lyne Haugh, Lyne Station, Peebles, Scotland. Tel: (07214) 304.

JRP †* J. R. Parkinson, Son and Hamer Auctions, The Auction Rooms, Rochdale Road (Kershaw Street), Bury. Tel: 061-761 1612/761 7372.

K ●Keith, Old Advertising, Unit 14, 155a Northcote Road, Battersea, London, SW11. Tel: 071-228 0741/071-228 6850.

KEY †●Key Antiques, 11 Horse Fair, Chipping Norton, Oxon. Tel: (0608) 643777.

KOT ●Kotobuki (Stephen Joseph), Unit F100, Alfies Antique Market, 13/25 Church Street, London, NW8. Tel: 071-402 0723.

LAY †* David Lay, ASVA, Penzance Auction House, Alverton, Penzance, Cornwall. Tel: (0736) 61414.

LEW ●Jill Lewis, Geoffrey Vann Arcade, 107 Portobello Road, London, W11. Tel: 071-221 1806 (Sats only).

LRG * Lots Road Chelsea Auction Galleries, 71 Lots Road, London, SW10. Tel: 071-351 7771.

LS * Lacy Scott Auctioneers, 10 Risbygate Street, Bury St Edmunds, Suffolk. Tel: (0284) 763531.

M * Morphets of Harrogate, 4-6 Albert Street, Harrogate, N. Yorks. Tel: (0423) 502282.

MA ●Manor Antiques, 2a High Street, Westerham, Kent. Tel: (0959) 64810.

MAG * MacGregor, Nash & Co, Lodge House, 9-17 Lodge Lane, North Finchley, N12. Tel: 081-445 9000.

MAT ●Christopher Matthews, Heathcote House, Forest Lane Head, Harrogate, N. Yorks. Tel: (0423) 887296/883215/885732.

MAW ●M. Allen, Watch & Clock Maker, 76a Walsall Road, Four Oaks, Sutton Coldfield. Tel: 021-308 6117.

McC †* McCartney's, Portcullis Salerooms, Ludlow, Shropshire. Tel: (0584) 2636.

MGM †* Michael G. Matthews, ASVA, ARVA, The Devon Fine Art Auction House, Dowell Street, Honiton, Devon (now Bonham's West Country). Tel: (0404) 41872 and 3137.

MIN †●Mint & Boxed, 110 High Street, Edgware, Middlesex. Tel: 081-952 2002.

MJB †* Michael J. Bowman, 6 Haccombe House, Nr. Netherton, Newton Abbot, Devon. Tel: (0626) 872890.

MN †* Michael Newman, The Central Auction Rooms, Kinterbury House, St. Andrew's Cross, Plymouth, Devon. Tel: (0752) 669298.

N †* Neales of Nottingham, The Nottingham Salerooms, 192 Mansfield Road, Nottingham. Tel: (0602) 624141.

Nor ●Sue Norman, L4 Antiquarius, 135 Kings Road, London, SW3. Tel: 071-352 7217 and 081-870 4677.

O †* Olivers, Burkitts Lane, Sudbury, Suffolk. Tel: (0787) 880305.

OD ●Offas Dyke, Antique Centre, 4 High Street, Knighton, Powys, Wales. Tel: (0547) 528634.

OL * Outhwaite & Litherland, Kingsway Galleries, Fontenoy Street, Liverpool. Tel: 051-236 6561.

ONS * Onslows, Metrostore, Townmead Road, London, SW6. Tel: 071-793 0240.

OS †●Oswald Simpson, Hall Street, Long Melford, Suffolk. Tel: (0787) 77523.

OSc ●Simon & Penny Rumble, Old School Antiques, Chittering, Cambridge. Tel: (0223) 861831.

OT * (See ALL)

OX †●P. A. Oxley, The Old Rectory, Cherhill, Nr. Calne, Wiltshire. Tel: (0249) 816227.

P * Phillips, Blenstock House, 101 New Bond Street, London, W1. Tel: 071-629 6602.

PAR ●Park House Antiques, Park Street, Stow-on-the-Wold, Glos. Tel: (0451) 30159.

P(Ba) * Phillips, 1 Old King Street, Bath. Tel: (0225) 310609/310709.

PC Private Collection.

PCA ●Paul Cater Antiques, High Street, Moreton-in-Marsh, Glos. Tel: (0608) 51888.

PCh †* Peter Cheney, Western Road Auction Rooms, Western Road, Littlehampton, West Sussex. Tel: (0903) 722264/713418.

P(Ch) * Phillips of Chichester, Baffins Hall, Baffins Lane, Chichester, W. Sussex. Tel: (0243) 787548.

PHA †●Paul Hopwell Antiques, 30 High Street, West Haddon, Northamptonshire. Tel: (078 887) 636.

PLJ * Philip Laney & Jolly, 12a Worcester Road, Great Malvern. Tel: (0684) 892322.

P(M) * Phillips, Trinity House, 114 Northenden Road, Sale, Manchester. Tel: 061-962 9237.

P(R) * Phillips Rye, Rye Auction Galleries, Cinque Ports Street, Rye, E. Sussex. Tel: (0797) 225090.

P(S) * Phillips, 49 London Road, Sevenoaks, Kent. Tel: (0732) 740310.

P(Sc) * Phillips Scotland, 65 George Street, Edinburgh. Tel: (031) 225 2266.

PSG • Patrick & Susan Gould, Stand L17, Grays Mews, 1-7 Davies Mews, London, W1. Tel: 071-408 0129 or 081-993 5879 (home).

P(W) * Phillips of Winchester, The Red House, Hyde Street, Winchester, Hants. Tel: (0962) 62515.

RBB †* Russell Baldwin & Bright Inc Campbell & Edwards, Fine Art Saleroom, Ryelands Road, Leominster, Hereford. Tel: (0568) 611166.

RdeR †• Rogers de Rin, 76 Hospital Road, Paradise Walk, London, SW3. Tel: 071-352 9007.

RFA †• Rochester Fine Arts, 86 High Street, Rochester, Kent. Tel: (0634) 814129.

RID †* Riddets of Bournemouth, 26 Richmond Hill, The Square, Bournemouth. Tel: (0202) 25686.

RMC • Romsey Medal Centre, 101 The Hundred, Romsey, Hants. Tel: (0794) 512885.

RO • Roswith, Stand F103, Alfies Antique Market, 13-25 Church Street, London, NW8.

RTT • Rin Tin Tin, 34 North Road, Brighton. Tel: (0273) 672424/733689.

RWB †• Roy W. Bunn Antiques, 34/36 Church Street, Barnoldswick, Colne, Lancashire. Tel: (0282) 813703.

RYA †• Robert Young Antiques, 68 Battersea Bridge Road, London, SW11. Tel: 071-228 7847.

SAA †* Southgate Antique Auction Rooms, Rear of Southgate Town Hall, Green Lanes, Palmers Green, London, N13. Tel: 081-886 7888.

SAD • Old Saddlers Antiques, Church Road, Goudhurst, Kent. Tel: (0580) 211458.

SAI • Sailor Ceramics, Camden Lock Antique Centre, 248 Camden High Street, London, NW1. Tel: 081-981 1180.

SBA †• South Bar Antiques, Digbeth Street, Stow-on-the-Wold, Gloucestershire. Tel: (0451) 30236.

SO †• Samuel Orr, The Clock Shop, 36 High Street, Hurstpierpoint, West Sussex. Tel: (0273) 832081.

Som †• Somervale Antiques, 6 Radstock Road, Midsomer Norton, Bath. Tel: (0761) 412686.

SP †• Sue Pearson, 13 Prince Albert Street, Brighton, East Sussex. Tel: (0273) 29247.

SSD • Smith & Smith Designs, 58a Middle Street North, Driffield, E. Yorkshire. Tel: (0377) 46321.

Sto • Stockspring, 114 Kensington Church Street, London, W8. Tel: 071-727 7995.

SWa • Stephen Watson, Alfies Antique Market, 13/25 Church Street, London, NW8. Tel: 071-723 0678.

SWN †• Swan Antiques, Stone Street, Cranbrook, Kent. Tel: (0580) 712720.

SWO †* Sworders, G. E. Sworder and Sons, 15 Northgate End, Bishops Stortford. Tel: (0279) 651388.

TG †• Thames Gallery, Thameside, Henley-on-Thames, Oxon. Tel: (0491) 572449.

THA • The Tudor House Antiques, 11 Tontine Hill, Ironbridge, Shropshire. Tel: (095) 2453783.

TM * Thos. Mawyer & Son, The Lincoln Saleroom, 63 Monks Road, Lincoln. Tel: (0522) 24984.

TP †• Tom Power, The Collector, Alfies Antique Market, 13/25 Church Street, London, NW8. Tel: 071-883 0024.

TVA †• Teme Valley Antiques, 1 The Bull Ring, Ludlow, Shropshire. Tel: (0584) 874686.

UC †• Up Country, The Old Corn Stores, 68 St John's Road, Tunbridge Wells, Kent. Tel: (0892) 23341.

UP †• Utopia Pine & Country Furniture, Holme Mills, Burton-in-Kendal, Carnforth, Lancashire. Tel: (0524) 781739. (Shop) Utopia Pine & Country Furniture, Lake Road, Bownes on Windermere, Cumbria. Tel: (09662) 88464.

VH †• Valerie Howard, 131e Kensington Church Street, London, W8. Tel: 071-792 9702.

VS †* T. Vennett-Smith, 11 Nottingham Road, Gotham, Nottinghamshire. Tel: (0602) 830541.

Wai • Wain Antiques, Gallantry House, Chapel Lane, Stoke Heath, Market Drayton, Shropshire. Tel: (063 083) 620.

WAL †* Wallis & Wallis, West Street Auction Galleries, Lewes, Sussex. Tel: (0273) 480208.

WD * Weller & Dufty Ltd, 141 Bromsgrove Street, Birmingham. Tel: 021-692 1414/5.

WEL †• Wells Reclamation Co, The Old Cider Farm, Coxley, Nr. Wells, Somerset. Tel: (0749) 77087/77484.

WHB †* William H. Brown, Fine Art Auctioneers & Valuers, Olivers Rooms, Burkitt's Lane, Sudbury, Suffolk. Tel: (0787) 880305.

WIN • Winstone Stamp Co, Gt Western Antique Market, Bartlett Street, Bath, Avon. Tel: (0225) 310388.

WM • Ward & Morris, Stuart House, 18 Gloucester Road, Ross-on-Wye, Herefordshire.

WRe • Walcot Reclamations, 108 Walcot Street, Bath, Avon. Tel: (0225) 66291.

WW * Woolley & Wallis, The Castle Auction Mart, Castle Street, Salisbury. Tel: (0722) 21711.

YON • Yonna, B19 Grays Antique Market, 1-7 Davies Mews, London, W1. Tel: 071-629 3644.

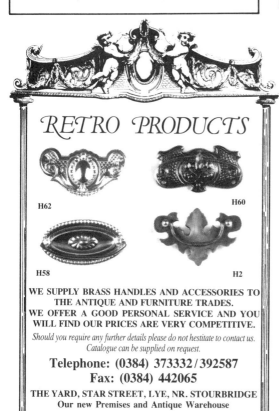

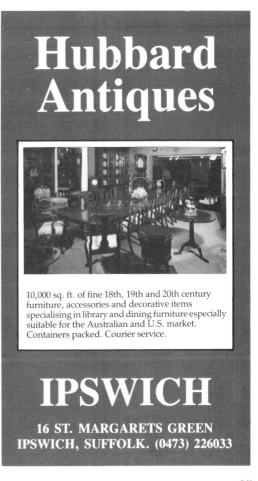

THESAURUS GROUP LTD. 24 TENNYSON ROAD, COWES, ISLE OF WIGHT, PO31 7QA.

CONTENTS

Pottery 29
Porcelain 118
Goss & Crested China 167
Oriental Pottery & Porcelain 176
Glass 211
Oak & Country Furniture . 242
Furniture 261
Architectural Antiques . . . 441
Clocks 489
Barometers 520
Scientific Instruments 522
Art Nouveau 534
Doulton/Royal Doulton . . . 544
Art Deco 557
Silver 574
Silver Plate 594
Wine Antiques 596
Metal 602
Ivory & Shell 639
Marble 640
Terracotta/Stone 642
Woodcarving 643
Antiquities 644
Rugs & Carpets 648
Textiles 650
Fans 659
Dolls 663
Toys 678
Models 681
Games 682
Musical 683
Leather & Luggage 684
Sport 685
Boxes 687
Transport 690
Crafts 691
Tribal Art 693
Ephemera 695
Oriental 700
Miniatures 732
Pine Furniture 734
Kitchenalia 744
Jewellery 746
Arms & Armour 749
Directory of Specialists . . . 772
Directory of Auctioneers . . 775
Index 790
Index to Advertisers 18

A dragonfly double overlaid and etched glass table lamp, by Emile Gallé, the domed shade overlaid in turquoise and brown etched to depict dragonflies, the base etched to depict irises and aquatic plants, cameo signatures on shade, 24in (61cm) high.
£60,000-80,000 CNY

1991 Penman Antiques Fairs FAIRS

January 17-20

WEST LONDON ANTIQUES FAIR
Kensington Town Hall, Hornton St, W.8.
(opposite Ken High St Tube Stn)
88 Stands on 3 floors, well vetted for quality
Furniture pre 1870, others pre 1890
Thurs/Fri 11-8. Sat/Sun 11-6. Adm: £4 inc Cata.

March 10-21

CHELSEA ANTIQUES FAIR
Chelsea Old Town Hall, King's Road, SW3
(Half a mile West of Sloane Square)
44 Top British Exhibitors
40 years' tradition of Excellence
Furniture pre 1830. most others pre 1860
Weekdays 11-8, Weekends 11-6. Adm: £6 inc Cata.

April 25-28

WESTMINSTER ANTIQUES FAIR
Royal Horticultural Hall, Vincent Square, SW1
(Half a mile E.S.E. of Victoria Station)
50 good quality Exhibitors.
Furniture pre 1840, most others pre 1860 or '90
Thurs/Fri 11-8, Sat/Sun 11-6. Adm: £4 inc Cata.

July 18-21

BRIGHTON ANTIQUES SHOW
Corn Exchange, Royal Pavilion Grounds, Sussex.
(Just under an hour by B.R. from Victoria)
Around 40 exhibitors, in Room Settings as well as tradional Stands, plus a Garden & "alfresco" Café
Thurs, Sat & Sun 11-6, Fri 11-9. Adm: £1.

August 15-18

WEST LONDON ANTIQUES FAIR
as in January, but with a few different exhibitors.

September 12-21

CHELSEA ANTIQUES FAIR
as in March

October 16-20

THE LAPADA SHOW
London & Provincial Antique Dealers' Assn
The first "Showcase" for LAPADA for a decade
Something Special.

Penman Antiques Fairs, P.O. Box 114, Haywards Heath, W. Sussex RH16 2YU
Tel: 0444 482514. Fax: 0444 483412

POTTERY

During the past two years, since the heady days of 1987, the market for pottery has stabilised. Auction hype would have us believe that the boom is continuing, but the fact is that prices for more common mid-18thC wares have slipped back a little. Would-be sellers have recognised this trend and it seems that the major auction rooms have found it more difficult to tempt good things onto the market. When they do appear, however, they make predictably high prices especially when dealers and auctioneers use their undoubted expertise in accurate, painstaking and detailed cataloguing.

Some of the most interesting pieces to appear on the market are those which appear correctly catalogued for the first time having just been discovered or previously unidentified. One such piece appeared at Phillips on November 22nd, 1989. The unglazed back was inscribed Clifton Dish, thus identifying it as a product of Clifton Potteries, Cumbria, rather than a Staffordshire product as was assumed. A combination of family provenance, rarity, good condition and the all important involvement of at least two determined bidders carried the dish to £21,000, a substantial price for a mid-18thC piece.

However, two years ago the dish would probably have made an even higher price when the market was prone to spectacular results for such rarities. A glance at the London catalogues reveals one area where sellers are confident and there is a consequent strength in the range and quality of wares offered. This area is maiolica. This market began to pick up at about the same time as that for English pottery though it did not boom in the same way. Rather it progressed steadily forward and it seems set to continue in 1991.

Baskets

A Staffordshire creamware basket and stand, c1770, stand 11½in (29cm) wide.
£475-500 *JHo*

A stand for a chestnut basket, with scene after Claude Lorraine, by John and Richard Riley, early 19thC, 11in (28cm) wide.
£130-160 *Nor*

Bottles

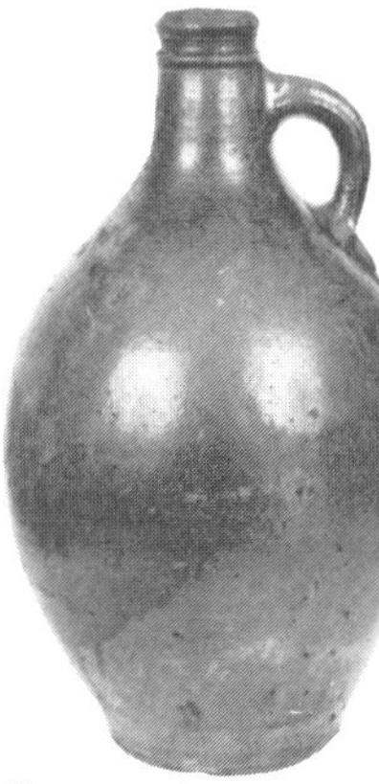

A German stoneware bottle, c1720, 14½in (37cm).
£120-150 *IW*

An earthenware bottle, probably Severn/Bristol Channel area, 14in (35.5cm).
£50-60 *IW*

An earthenware bottle, 19thC, 9in (23cm).
£40-50 *IW*

Bowls

A Jackfield teabowl, c1760.
£150-200 *Sto*

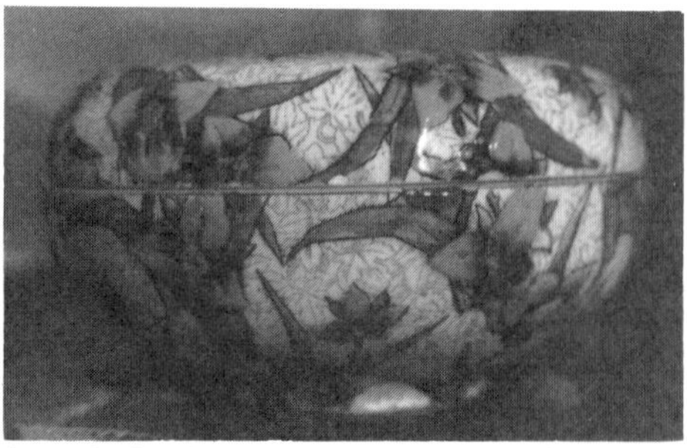

A powder bowl and cover, enamelled in relief in blue and green, Luneville-Keller & Guerin, mid-19thC, 6in (15cm) diam.
£75-100 *CA*

A Quimper soup bowl, 5in (12.5cm).
£20-40 *AI*

A Quimper blue and white bowl, 2in (5cm).
£15-25 *AI*

A Minton majolica jardinière and stand, the pink glazed basketweave moulded sides decorated in relief with trailing flowering and fruiting strawberries, with ochre rims and pale blue glazed interior, small chip to footrim of jardinière, impressed marks, pattern No. 811 and date code for 1870, 8½in (21cm).
£1,200-1,500 *C*

A Quimper bowl, signed, c1920, 5½in (14cm) square.
£45-55 *VH*

A Quimper bowl, 2in (5cm).
£15-25 *AI*

A Quimper soup bowl, 7in (18cm) wide.
£25-45 *AI*

A Wedgwood butter dish in glazed caneware, c1860, 7in (18cm) diam.
£200-250 *Sto*

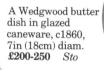

A Quimper bowl, signed, c1900, 6in (15cm).
£25-30 *VH*

A majolica dish with feet, c1880, 9½in (24cm) diam.
£60-75 *HOW*

A Staffordshire creamware bowl and cover, with flower finial and entwined rope twist handles, painted with scattered flowers, slight chips, c1780, 5in (12.5cm).
£150-200 *CSK*

A Wedgwood cream stoneware game pie dish, the cover with applied cabbage and carrot mounts, the sides with continuous fruiting vine decoration, 19thC, 8½in (22cm) diam.
£120-150 *DDM*

A Scottish porringer, with painted decoration, c1870, 3in (7.5cm) high.
£40-50 *IW*

A faience pedestal bowl, painted in bright colours in blue, green and yellow, 12in (30.5cm).
£250-350 *DDM*

Commemorative

A mug, issued for Wesley centenary celebrations, 1839, 5in (12.5cm).
£140-150 *IW*

GEORGE VI & QUEEN
HONI SOIT QUI MAL Y PENSE
DIEU ET MON DROIT

A Coronation mug, King George VI and Queen Elizabeth, 1937, some damage, 3in (7.5cm).
£8-10 *OD*

SILVER JUBILEE
LONG LIVE THEIR MAJESTIES
1910 1935

A Jubilee mug, King George V and Queen Mary, 4in (10cm).
£12-15 *OD*

LORD BYRON

A child's plate, Lord Byron, 6in (15cm) diam.
£150-160 *IW*

JUBILEE YEAR OF HER Majesty QUEEN VICTORIA COMMENCED TO REIGN

A Queen Victoria Jubilee tankard, some damage, 1887, 3in (7.5cm).
£35-40 *OD*

Miller's is a price Guide not a price List

The price ranges given reflect the average price a purchaser should pay for similar items. Condition, rarity of design or pattern, size, colour, provenance, restoration and many other factors must be taken into account when assessing values. When buying or selling, it must always be remembered that prices can be greatly affected by the condition of any piece. Unless otherwise stated, all goods shown in Miller's are of good merchantable quality, and the valuations given reflect this fact. Pieces offered for sale in exceptionally fine condition or in poor condition may reasonably be expected to be priced considerably higher or lower respectively than the estimates given herein

Cottages

A Staffordshire cottage pastille burner, with removable roof, c1820, 3½in (9cm).
£550-600 *BHA*

A model of a windmill, flanked by a boy and a girl holding sheaves of wheat, c1855, 11½in (29cm).
£150-200 *Bon*

A Staffordshire lilac ground pastille burner and detachable base, modelled as Warwick Castle, applied with coloured flowers and white moss, enriched in gilding, castle restored, minor chipping to flowers, c1840, 6½in (16.5cm).
£550-650 *C*

A Staffordshire cottage pastille burner, outlined in lavender, 5in (12.5cm).
£100-150 *CSK*

A Staffordshire lilac ground pastille burner, applied with coloured flowers and enriched in gilding, the base with gilt rim, slight hair cracks and some chipping to flowers, finial restored, c1840, 8in (21cm).
£400-600 *C*

Cow Creamers

A cow creamer, c1800, 8in (20cm) wide.
£800-850 *BHA*

A creamware cow creamer, late 18thC, 5in (13cm).
£2,500-3,000 *HSS*

Cups

A Quimper breakfast cup, 4in (10cm) diam.
£10-15 *AI*

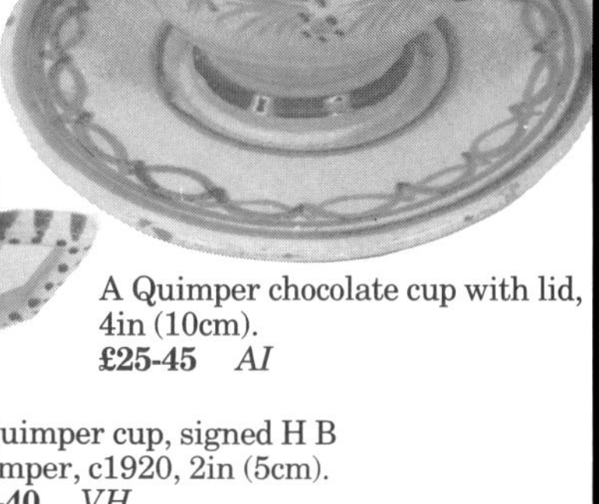

A Quimper chocolate cup with lid, 4in (10cm).
£25-45 *AI*

A Quimper cup, signed H B Quimper, c1920, 2in (5cm).
£30-40 *VH*

A Quimper cup and saucer, signed, c1930, cup 2½in (6cm).
£60-80 *VH*

A Jackfield loving cup, c1765, 4½in (11cm).
£135-145 *HOW*

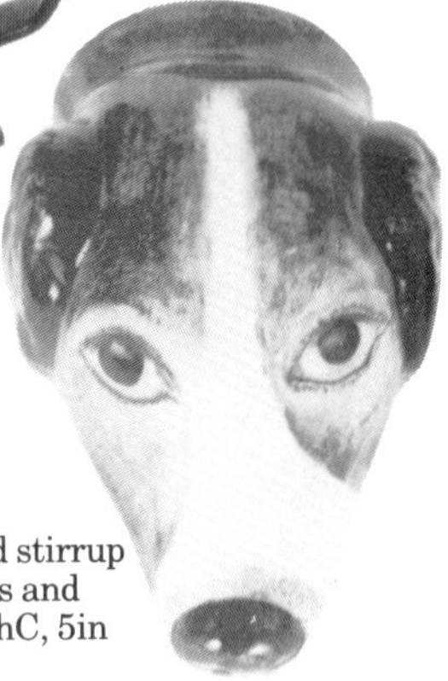

A pearlware hound's head stirrup cup, with brown markings and green collar, cracked, 19thC, 5in (12.5cm) long.
£350-450 *HSS*

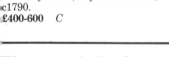

A pair of Wedgwood caneware teacups and saucers, the cups moulded in relief with putti at various pursuits above a fluted border, the undersides of the saucers similarly fluted, impressed marks, c1790.
£400-600 *C*

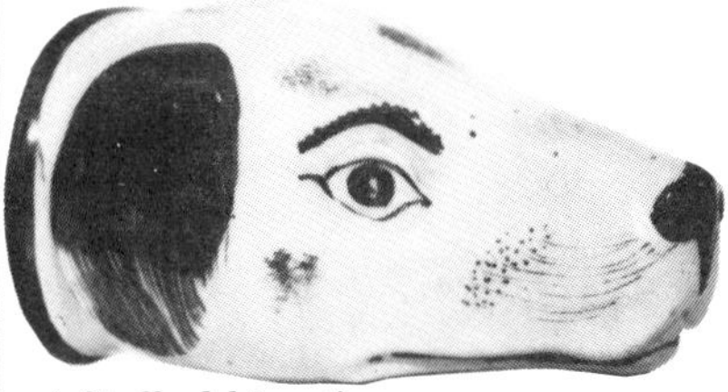

A Staffordshire stirrup cup, modelled as a hound's head, with painted details and brown rim, 5in (12.5cm).
£250-350 *CSK*

A pottery fox head stirrup cup, with red fur, yellow eyes and black collar, 5in (13cm).
£80-120 *HSS*

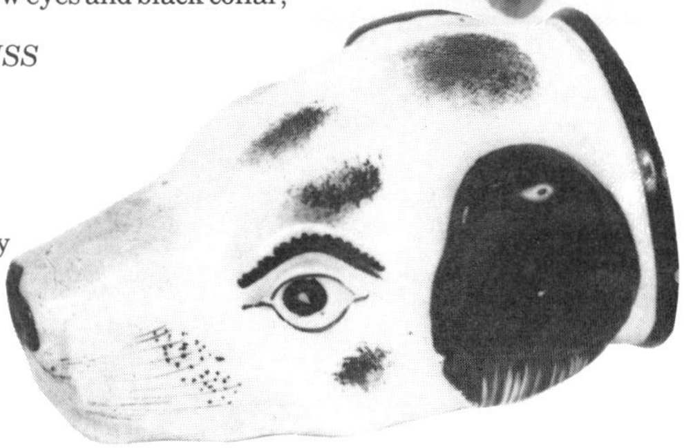

A stirrup cup, early 19thC, 5in (12.5cm).
£400-500 *JHo*

Figures – Animals

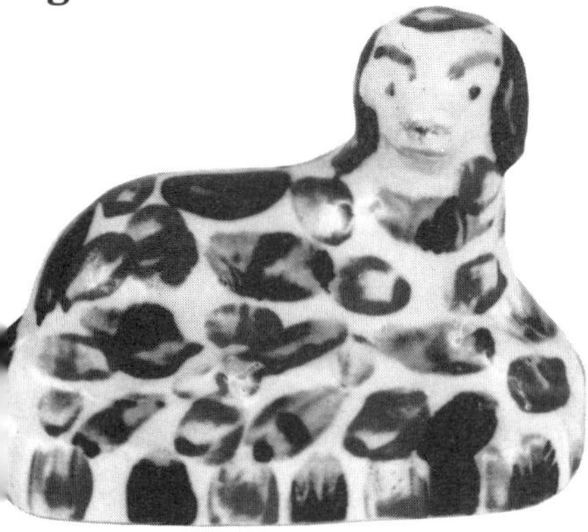

A Pratt ware hound, c1780, 4in (10cm) wide.
£750-850 *BHA*

A Staffordshire model of a recumbent dog, outside a house with a puppy to the side, 4in (10cm).
£150-200 *CSK*

A creamware model of a dog, wearing a yellow collar, the dark brown coat with scratched whiskers and hair markings, on green edged base, slight chip to base, c1835, 8½in (22cm).
£800-1,200 *C*

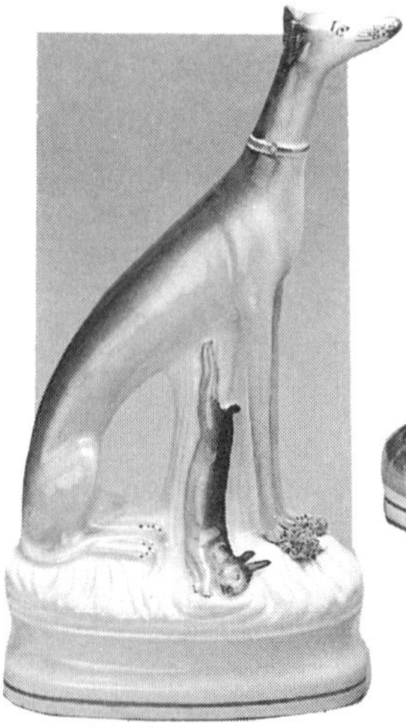

A model of a seated whippet, with separate moulded front legs, and gilt collar, a dead hare at his feet, on waisted gilt lined base, c1840, 13in (33cm).
£300-350 *Bon*

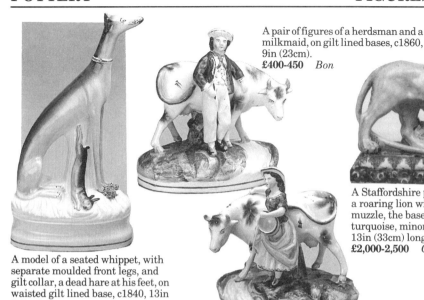

A pair of figures of a herdsman and a milkmaid, on gilt lined bases, c1860, 9in (23cm).
£400-450 *Bon*

A Staffordshire pearlware model of a roaring lion with brown mane and muzzle, the base enriched in turquoise, minor restoration, c1790, 13in (33cm) long.
£2,000-2,500 *C*

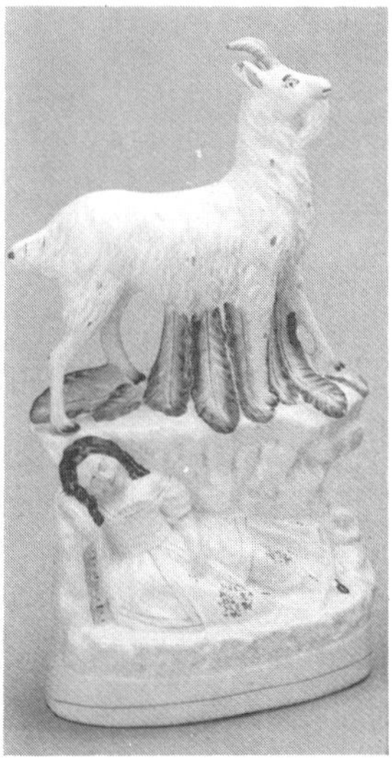

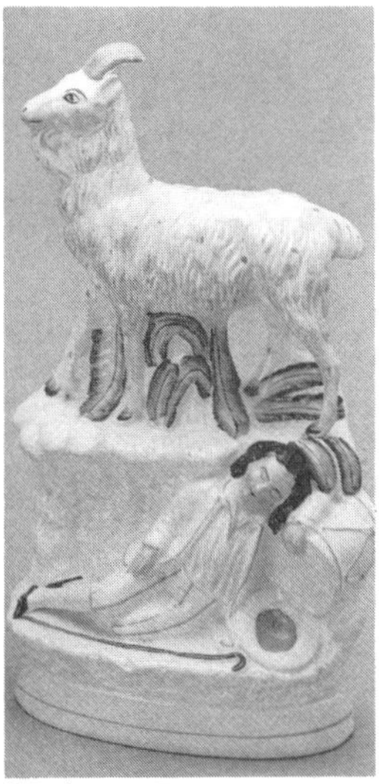

A pair of figures, depicting a girl and a boy sleeping with standing goats, on gilt lined bases, c1850, 12in (30.5cm).
£250-350 *Bon*

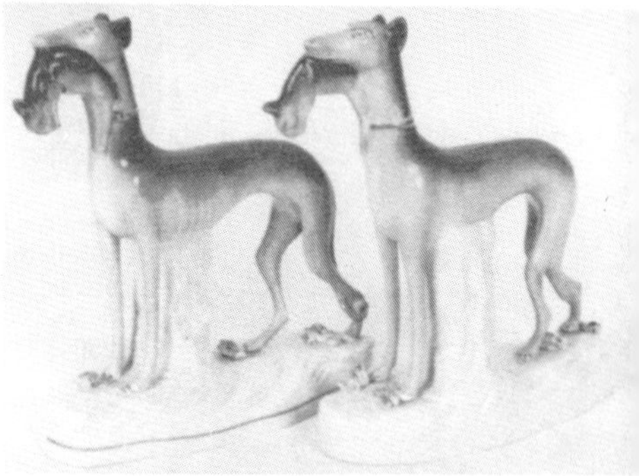

A pair of Staffordshire pottery figures of greyhounds, each with a rabbit in its mouth, painted in iron red, black, brown and gilt and raised on a rock moulded base applied with green painted tufts of grass, 19thC, 7½in (19cm).
£300-400 *HSS*

A pearlware cow, with a milkmaid and calf, decorated with sponged red, blue, black and ochre, Staffordshire or Yorkshire, restored, 5½in (14cm).
£750-850 *CSK*

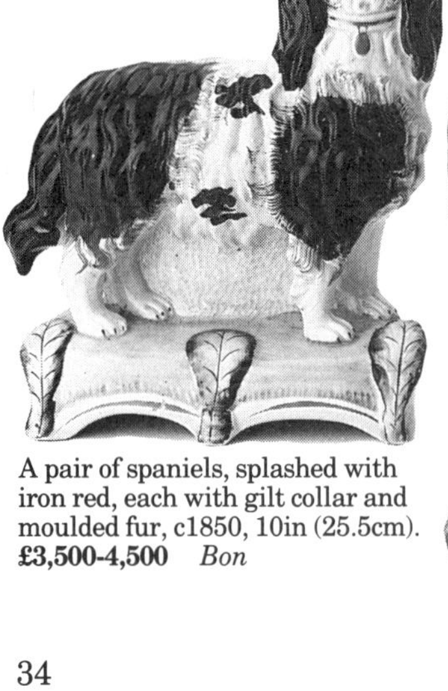

A pair of spaniels, splashed with iron red, each with gilt collar and moulded fur, c1850, 10in (25.5cm).
£3,500-4,500 *Bon*

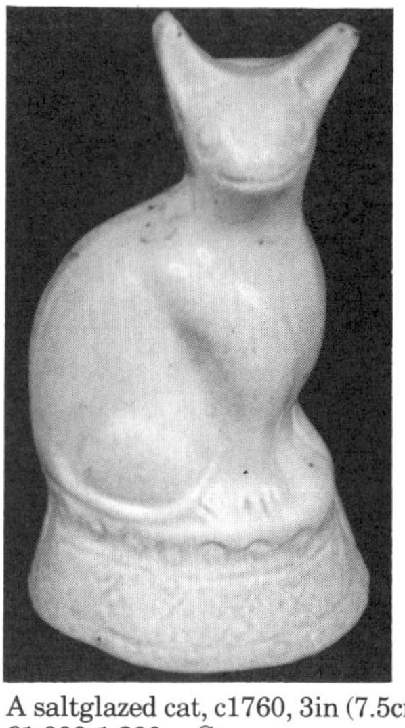

A saltglazed cat, c1760, 3in (7.5cm).
£1,000-1,200 *Sto*

A pair of Staffordshire figures of greyhounds, c1860, 11in (28cm).
£270-300 *RWB*

A pearlware model of a horse, with ochre saddle cloth and brown harness, his coat sponged in yellow, ochre and brown, perhaps Yorkshire or Staffordshire, ears restored, c1790, 6½in (16.5cm).
£2,500-3,000 *C*

A Staffordshire figure of a deer, early 19thC, 5in (12.5cm).
£350-400 *JHo*

A Pratt figure, 3in (7.5cm).
£1,600-1,800 *JHo*

A Staffordshire group of a bitch and her puppies, 9in (23cm) wide.
£600-700 *BHA*

A Staffordshire cow and milkmaid, c1850, 7in (18cm).
£250-280 *HOW*

A creamware model of a horse, with docked tail, splashed in manganese, with sponged brown mane and hoofs, Staffordshire or Yorkshire, ears restored, c1790, 6in (15cm).
£3,500-4,500 *C*

A Staffordshire Walton type figure group, early 19thC.
£550-650 *GIL*

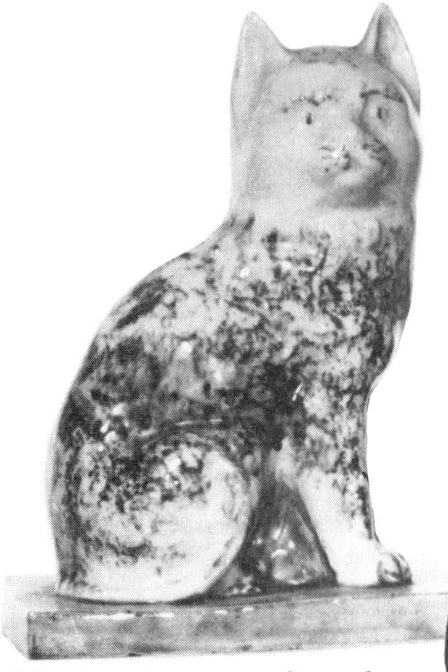

A Continental creamware figure of a cat, its fur sponged in black and yellow, on a green base, 5½in (14cm).
£200-250 *CSK*

A Staffordshire dog group, c1855, 7in (18cm).
£450-475 *HOW*

A Staffordshire bird whistle, early 19thC, 2in (5cm).
£400-500 *JHo*

A Staffordshire figure of an elephant, c1885, 9½in (24cm).
£450-500 *HOW*

A Staffordshire sheep, c1850, 5in (13cm).
£120-140 *HOW*

A Yorkshire buff pottery equestrian group, the rider wearing a brown hat, blue jacket and yellow breeches, damaged and chipped, c1790, 9in (23cm).
£3,000-3,500 *C*

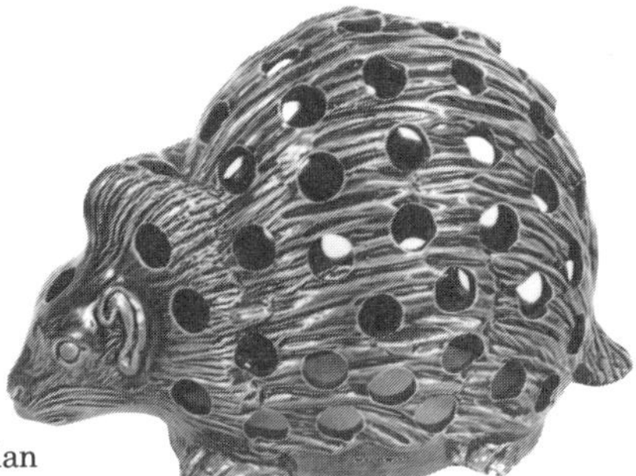

A Wedgwood green glazed hedgehog, 7in (18cm).
£600-650 *JHo*

Figures – People

A model of Auld Lang Syne, on gilt lined base, c1850, 8½in (22cm).
£250-350 *Bon*

A Staffordshire figure depicting Flora, emblematic of Spring, probably Enoch Wood, c1810, 13in (33cm).
£250-300 *RWB*

A Staffordshire figure, probably Sir Robert Peel, c1846, 8½in (22cm).
£250-300 *RWB*

A Staffordshire Pratt ware figure emblematic of Winter, decorated in blue, ochre and green glazes, the base sponged in similar colours, c1790, 9in (23cm).
£300-350 *RWB*

A Staffordshire Pratt ware figure, depicting Flora emblematic of Spring, decorated in brown, green, yellow and ochre washed glazes, c1790, 9in (23cm).
£300-350 *RWB*

An unidentified theatrical group, on gilt lined base, c1850, 6in (15cm).
£150-200 *Bon*

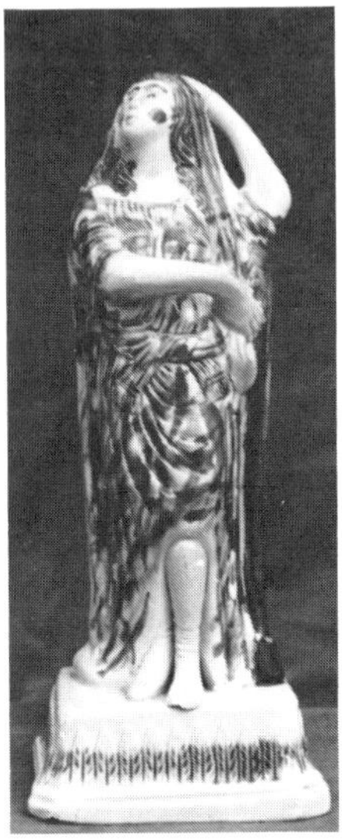

A Staffordshire Pratt ware figure depicting Hope, decorated in brown, green and ochre washed glazes, c1790, 8in (20.5cm).
£300-350 *RWB*

A pair of Staffordshire theatrical figures, depicting Selim and Zuleika in The Bride of Abydos, c1847, 7in (18cm).
£200-230 *RWB*

A Staffordshire figure, Obadiah Sherratt, c1820.
£350-400 *RWB*

Charity

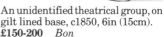

A Staffordshire group entitled Charity, c1810, 9in (23cm).
£300-350 *RWB*

An unidentified theatrical figure, on gilt lined base, c1850, 9½in (24cm).
£70-100 *Bon*

A Staffordshire group of the Princess Royal on a dog, c1850, 5in (13cm).
£180-200 *HOW*

A Staffordshire group of children playing marbles, c1860, 8in (20cm).
£280-300 *HOW*

A Staffordshire figure of Britannia, by Thomas Pan, c1840, 14½in (36cm).
£500-550 *HOW*

A portrait of Anne Boleyn and King Henry VIII, on gilt lined base, c1850, 10in (25.5cm).
£600-700 *Bon*

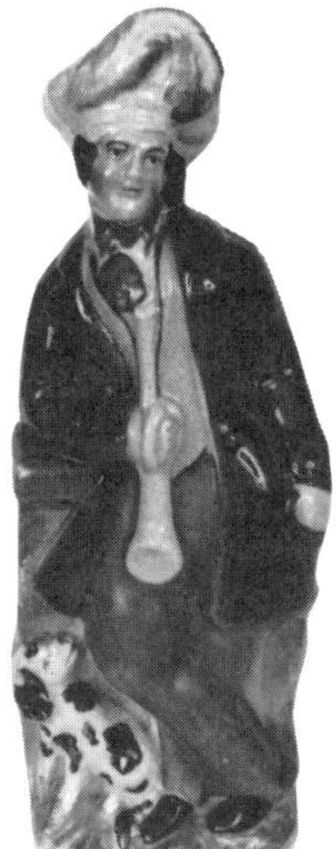

A Staffordshire musician with dog, c1860, 9in (23cm).
£140-160 *HOW*

A Staffordshire group of Samson and the Lion, 11½in (29cm).
£250-300 *HOW*

A Staffordshire woodcutter, c1840, 7½in (19cm).
£175-200 *HOW*

A Staffordshire boy with rats, c1840, 5½in (14cm).
£200-250 *HOW*

VIVANDIERE

A Staffordshire figure of Vivandiere, c1850, 13in (32cm).
£380-400 *HOW*

PRINCE OF WALES

A Staffordshire figure of the Prince f Wales, c1850, 11in (29cm).
200-260 *HOW*

A Staffordshire figure of Uncle Tom with Eva, c1852, 11in (28cm),
£240-260 *HOW*

A pair of Quimper figures, marked I B Quimper, 9in (23cm).
200-250 *VH*

Staffordshire umbrella group, 1850, 7in (18cm).
160-180 *HOW*

A Quimper figure of a piper, signed, c1920, 13in (33cm).
£300-350 *VH*

STE VIERGE

A Quimper figure of Virgin and Child, marked, c1920, 8½in (21cm).
£200-250 *VH*

An Austrian slip cast earthenware half length figure of a negro, playing a stained wood ukelele banjo, with cream shirt, red waistcoat and short green jacket, raised on a black base, some damage, 32in (81cm).
£2,000-2,500 *HSS*

A Staffordshire Welsh figure group, 10½in (26cm).
£450-500 *HOW*

A Staffordshire Whieldon type figure, c1765, 4½in (11cm).
£800-900 *JHo*

A Staffordshire flatback group, the lady balancing a bundle of sticks on her head, the man holding a pitcher, 12½in (32cm).
£60-100 *DDM*

A Staffordshire figure of Will Watch, c1860, 6½in (16cm).
£140-160 *HOW*

A Ralph Wood type figure, c1780, 9in (23cm).
£550-600 *JHo*

An Obadiah Sherratt tea-time group, modelled as a gallant and his companion before a yellow turreted building, with iron red table, some damage, c1830, 7½in (18.5cm) wide.
£3,000-4,000 *C*

Two Whieldon type figures of The Seasons, 7in (18cm).
£4,000-5,000 *JHo*

A Staffordshire figure, c1800, 5in (12.5cm).
£200-250 *JHo*

A Staffordshire pearlware group of The Parson and Clerk, wearing streaked brown clothes, supported by a green tree stump, on a green base, some restoration to hat, c1810, 10in (25cm).
£600-800 *C*

Four pale beige smear glazed stoneware figures of The Seasons, after the models by Pierre Stephan, restoration and repairs, probably Turner, c1800, 9½in (23.5cm).
£2,000-2,500 *C*

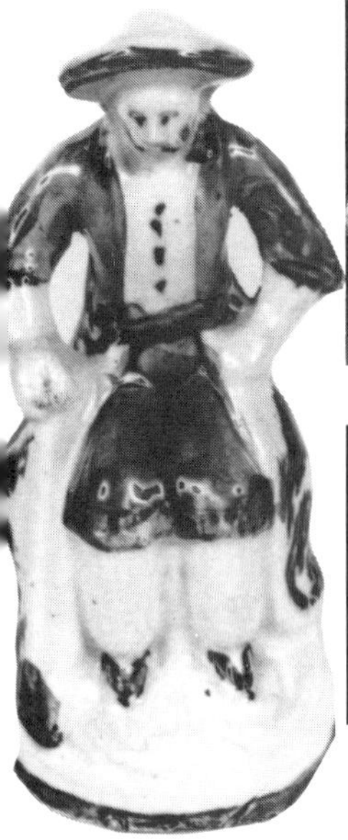

A Portobello figure of a gardener, c1790, 6in (15cm).
£400-450 *BHA*

Locate the source

The source of each illustration in Miller's can be found by checking the code letters below each caption with the list of contributors

HAMLET

GIN

A Staffordshire double-sided figure, 'Gin' and 'Water', 9in (23cm).
£150-250 *SBA*

A figure depicting Hamlet, titled in impressed gilt lettering, restored, c1852, 11in (28cm).
£200-250 *Bon*

A Staffordshire figure of a woman, perhaps emblematic of Peace, holding a bird, restored, 11in (28cm).
£75-100 *CSK*

A Staffordshire flute player, c1800, 8½in (22cm).
£400-500 *BHA*

An Enoch Wood figure, c1820, 6½in (16cm).
£600-700 *BHA*

A Thomas Parr type theatrical portrait of the Cushman sisters in the role of Romeo and Juliet, Charlotte Cushman dressed as Romeo, Susan Cushman dressed as Juliet, with black printed quotation, c1852, 10½in (26cm).
£650-750 *Bon*

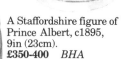

A Staffordshire creamware group of Venus and Cupid, of Ralph Wood type, the Goddess draped in a green robe with Cupid and a green dolphin at her side, the brown pedestal moulded with classical urns, restored, c1785, 10½in (27cm).
£400-500 *C*

A Staffordshire figure of Prince Albert, c1895, 9in (23cm).
£350-400 *BHA*

A figure of Falstaff, titled in raised gilt capitals on rococo moulded base, c1845, 16in (40cm).
£450-650 *Bon*

In the Ceramics section if there is only one measurement it usually refers to the height of the piece

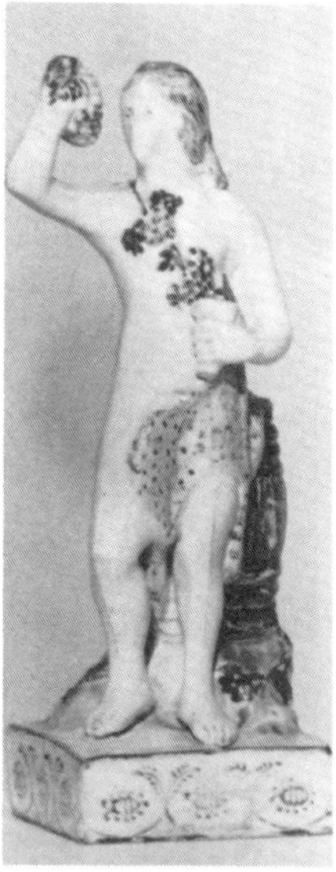

A pottery figure, emblematic of Autumn, scantily clad with fruiting vine beside a barrel on a square base, 7in (17.5cm).
£100-150 *CSK*

A Staffordshire pearlware figure of Neptune, of Ralph Wood type, scantily draped in green and holding a trident, repaired, c1785, 11½in (28.5cm).
£400-500 *C*

TAM-O SHANTER
SOUTER JOHNNY

An Obadiah Sherratt group of Tam O'Shanter and Souter Johnny, the former in tartan jacket and blue striped breeches, the latter in brown coat and yellow smock, seated on a red and yellow couch, base restored, c1825, 8in (20cm).
£3,500-4,500 *CSK*

A group of Tom Cribb and Molyneaux, in grey and yellow breeches on a red base, repaired and chipped, c1811, 6in (15cm).
£3,000-3,500 *CSK*

A pair of Staffordshire figures of Royal children, c1845, 6in (15cm).
£400-500 *BHA*

ɩn unrecorded figure of an officer in lumed hat and dark blue uniform, ıolding a sword, c1854, 11in (28cm).
900-1,200 *CSK*

A Staffordshire figure of the Prince of Wales, c1862, 10in (26cm).
£150-200 *IW*

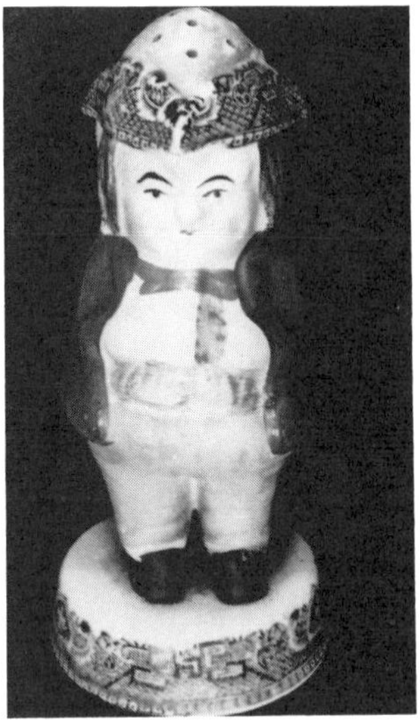

A Toby pepper pot, English/Scottish, restored, c1870.
£55-65 *Nor*

Refer to Miller's Collectables Price Guide 1990-91 for a selection of Staffordshire peppers.

A pair of Staffordshire figures of The Seasons, c1840, 5in (12.5cm).
400-500 *BHA*

PRINCE AND PRINCESS

A Staffordshire group of Royal children, c1860, 8in (20cm), (A,49).
£450-500 *BHA*

ɩ pair of Staffordshire figures of Royal children equestrian figures, 1845, 9in (23cm).
500-600 *BHA*

ɩ pair of Staffordshire figures, hought to be Queen Victoria and he Royal groom, c1845, 7½in 19cm), (A141,142).
250-300 *RWB*

Staffordshire Figures

A figure of Sir Robert Peel, in dark blue jacket and brown trousers, with scroll inscribed Repeal of the Corn Law, the base entitled in gilt Sir R. Peel, repairs to neck, c1846, 8in (20.5cm), (B1,2).
£400-500 *CSK*

A portrait of Dan O'Connell, wearing a black jacket enriched in gilt, green neckerchief and trousers, titled in gilt script on oval base, c1870, 17½in (44cm), (B,2).
£450-500 *Bon*

STAFFORDSHIRE FIGURES

The letters and figures in brackets refer to the book *Staffordshire Portrait Figures* by P. D. Gordon Pugh

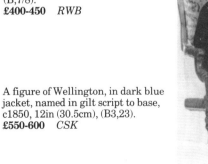

A figure of Gladstone, named in raised capitals to the base, c1882, 13½in (34cm), (B16,54).
£200-250 *CSK*

WELLINGTON

A Staffordshire figure of the Duke of Wellington as a politician, c1850, 13in (33cm), (B,17).
£150-180 *RWB*

A pair of Staffordshire figures, previously suggested as portraying Lord Shaftesbury and Elizabeth Fry, but now believed to portray the Royal tutors with the Royal children, c1848, 7½in (19cm), (B,7/8).
£400-450 *RWB*

WASHINGTON

A figure of Franklin in dark blue coat and floral tunic holding a letter and hat in his hands, mis-titled Washington in raised gilt capitals to the base, c1855, 16in (40.5cm), (B24,71).
£600-650 *CSK*

A figure of Wellington, in dark blue jacket, named in gilt script to base, c1850, 12in (30.5cm), (B3,23).
£550-600 *CSK*

A rare model of the Redan, a fortress near Sebastopol, painted mainly in grey and outlined with coloured flowers, flag restored, c1854, 8½in (21cm), (C70,189).
£1,500-2,000 *CSK*

A group representing France, England and Turkey, with Queen Victoria flanked by Napoleon III and Abd-ul-Medjid, c1854, 11½in (29cm), (C32,76).
£300-350 *CSK*

A figure of Raglan, in plumed hat and dark blue military uniform, named in raised capitals on base, c1854, 13in (33cm), (C53,132).
£2,500-3,500 *CSK*

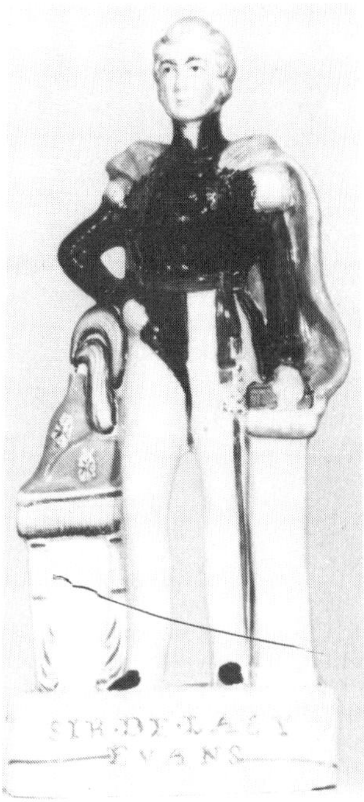
SIR DE LACY
EVANS

A figure of Sir George De Lacy Evans, in green cape and dark blue military uniform, named in raised gilt capitals, c1854, (C54,135).
£1,500-2,000 *CSK*

A figure of Canrobert, in iron red military uniform, named in raised gilt capitals, enamels worn, c1854, 12in (30cm), (C53,133).
£300-400 *CSK*

A figure of Florence Nightingale, with dark blue and gilt dress, named in raised gilt capitals, c1855, 10½in (26cm), (C54,139).
£1,200-1,500 *CSK*

A group of Louis Napoleon and Albert, in gilt uniforms below crossed flags and named in raised gilt capitals, c1854, 14in (36cm), (C77,225).
£200-250 *CSK*

EMPEROR
EMPRESS

A pair of Staffordshire equestrian figures of Emperor Napoleon III and Empress Eugénie, c1854, 10in (25.5cm), (C,82/83).
£400-450 *RWB*

Did you know
MILLER'S Antiques Price Guide builds up year by year to form the most comprehensive photo-reference system available

A figure of Havelock, in dark blue military uniform and named in gilt script to the base, c1857, 9in (23cm), (C90,268).
£800-1,000 *CSK*

A pair of Staffordshire equestrian figures of General Brown and General Simpson, c1854, 13in (33cm), (C,149/150).
£800-950 *RWB*

THE
SAILORS RETURN

A Staffordshire group depicting The Sailor's Return, c1855, 12½in (32cm), (C,197).
£400-450 *RWB*

A Staffordshire group depicting the Crimean War Victory, repairs to flags, c1856, 14in (36cm), (C,185).
£1,600-1,800 *RWB*

A Staffordshire figure of Omar Pasha, c1854, 13in (33cm), (C,130).
£350-400 *RWB*

NAPOLEON ALBERT

A Staffordshire group of Napoleon III and Prince Albert, c1854, 14in (36cm), (C,225).
£270-320 *RWB*

SOLDIER

A Staffordshire group depicting The Wounded Soldier, c1855, 10in (26cm), (C,194).
£220-250 *RWB*

A Staffordshire equestrian figure of Sultan Abd-ul-Medjid, c1854, 7½in (18cm), (C,167a).
£140-160 *RWB*

A Staffordshire figure of Maretta Alboni as Cinderella, wearing a blue dress, 9in (23cm), (E,20).
£350-400 *DDM*

A figure of Mlle Alboni as Cinderella, in dark blue and floral dress, c1848, 9in (23cm), (E20,43).
£1,000-1,500 *CSK*

GARIBALDI

A pair of Staffordshire equestrian figures of Victor Emmanuel II, King of Sardinia and Garibaldi, c1860, 11in (28cm), (C,298/9).
£400-450 *RWB*

A figure of Cardinal Manning, in typical robes, standing beside a dark blue draped column, c1870, 18in (46cm), (D4,8).
£300-500 *CSK*

A portrait of Nellie Chapman, c1845, 13in (33cm), (E,78).
£700-800 *Bon*

A figure of Jenny Lind, in green bodice and floral dress with a bag hanging from her wrist, named in gilt script, c1848, 8in (20cm), (D87,173).
£350-450 *CSK*

A portrait of Edmund Kean in the role of Richard III, on oval gilt lined base, c1850, 10in (25.5cm), (E14).
£150-200 *Bon*

OPHELIA

A figure depicting Ophelia, titled in impressed black lettering on base, c1852, 10in (26cm), (E,1A).
£200-250 *Bon*

A portrait of the famous lion tamer, Nellie Chapman, wearing a plumed hat, bodice and skirt, on gilt lined base, c1847, 12in (30cm), (E,78).
£500-600 *Bon*

A figure of John Elias, painted mainly in black, standing beside a grey column, named in gilt capitals Rev John Elies, c1850, 14in (36cm), (D23,45).
£650-750 *CSK*

A figure of Revd. Robert Trogwy Evans, in black coat and floral tunic standing beside a pink drape and named in raised letters, c1856, 11½in (29cm), (D24,49).
£1,200-1,500 *CSK*

A pair of Staffordshire figures of the Reverends Christmas Evans and John Elias, c1850, 14in (36cm), (D48 & D45).
£2,000-2,300 *RWB*

A figure of Luigi Lablanche as Dr. Dulcamara, in brown jacket and pink breeches, c1848, 8in (20cm), (E62,113).
£600-650 *CSK*

A group of Isaac Van Amburgh in Roman costume, with a leopard on his back and flanked by a lion, lioness and cub, named in script to the base, restored, c1839, 6in (15cm), (E100,200).
£700-800 *CSK*

A pair of figures of James Rush and Emily Sandford, the former in dark blue jacket and pink trousers, the latter in dark blue bodice and green dress, both named in gilt script, c1849, 10in (25.5cm), (G23,47/48).
£1,500-2,000 *CSK*

A group of Charles Kean, in mainly dark blue costume, c1856, 13in (33cm), (E78,152).
£200-250 *CSK*

A Staffordshire figure of Nellie Chapman, c1847, 12in (30.5cm), (E,150).
£750-900 *RWB*

A model of Stanfield Hall, with a blue roof, the building with white walls outlined with flowers and windows edged in puce, named in gilt script to the shaped base, c1849, 7in (17.5cm), (G25,52).
£550-650 *CSK*

A Staffordshire group of Smith and Collier, 13in (33cm), (G,27).
£500-600 *BHA*

A group featuring Shakespeare flanked by figures representing Hamlet and Lady Macbeth, c1855, 10in (25.5cm), (H5,14).
£350-400 *CSK*

A Staffordshire figure, possibly portraying Mr. Wood playing Atabarnes in Artaxerxes, maker Lloyd Shelton, c1840, 12in (30.5cm), (E,294).
£320-380 *RWB*

A Staffordshire figure of the Great Gate, Trinity College, Cambridge, c1860, 8in (20cm), (I,100).
£140-180 *RWB*

BRAIDWOOD

A figure of James Braidwood, with black helmet and iron red uniform, named in raised black capitals to the base, cracked and worn, c1861, 15in (38cm), (I1,1).
£600-700 *CSK*

A pair of figures in Eastern costume, standing with giraffes, before tree stump spill vases, one chipped, c1845, 9½in (24cm), (I18,44).
£900-1,200 *CSK*

A figure of James Braidwood, in white uniform with green trousers, named in raised black letters, restoration to neck and top of hat, c1861, 14in (35.5cm), (I1,1).
£750-850 *CSK*

A model of Caernarvon Castle, with salmon pink walls outlined in gilt and applied foliage, named in raised gilt capitals to the base, c1855, 7in (17.5cm), (I49,93).
£600-800 *CSK*

Flasks

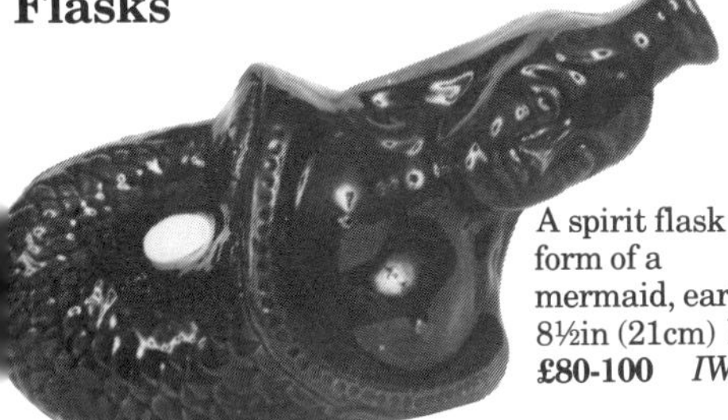

A spirit flask in the form of a mermaid, early 19thC, 8½in (21cm) long.
£80-100 *IW*

A Scottish 'tattie' flask, underglaze painted, early 19thC, 7in (17.5cm).
£80-100 *IW*

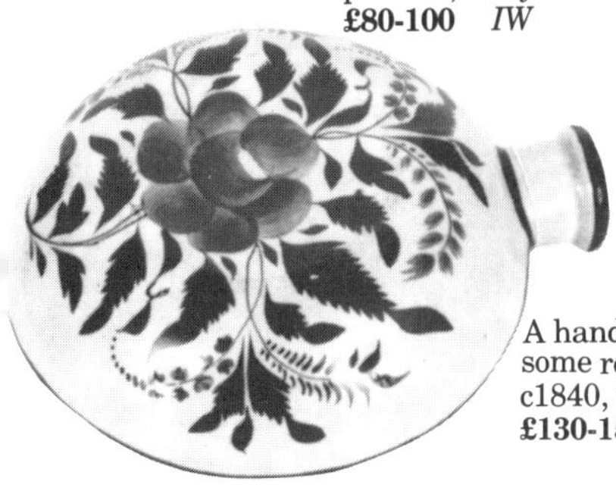

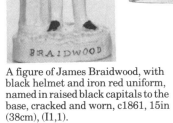

A hand painted flask, some restoration, c1840, 7½in (19cm).
£130-150 *IW*

Flatware

Use the Index!
Because certain items might fit easily into any of a number of categories, the quickest and surest method of locating any entry is by reference to the index at the back of the book.
This has been fully cross-referenced for absolute simplicity

A Bo'Ness plate, J. Marshall, c1865, 9½in (24cm).
£30-50 *OD*

A pair of English tin glazed chargers, painted with flowers in green, blue, yellow and mauve, rim chips, 13½in (34cm).
£800-1,000 *M*

A set of 5 Welsh slipware bowls, 9½ to 15½in (24 to 39cm) diam.
£850-1,000 *SBA*

A Brameld tureen stand, Woodman pattern, c1820.
£120-150 *CA*

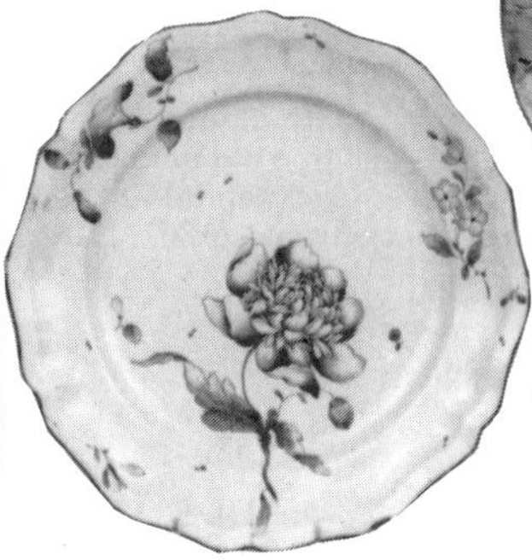

Two Strasbourg faience plates, painted in colours with botanical specimens, with puce line rims, rim chips, H39 in blue for Joseph Hannong, c1750, 9½in (24cm).
£650-750 *C*

A Liverpool polychrome dish, c1765, 14in (35cm).
£550-600 *JHo*

A Nevers blue and white dish, the centre with figures beside a fence within a border of birds, flowers and buildings, the underside with trailing flowering branches, minute rim flaking, blue dagger and dot mark, c1680, 12in (30cm).
£550-650 *C*

A pearlware patch stand, c1790, 2½in (6cm).
£90-120 *Sto*

A Turin blue and white armorial dish, the centre painted within a border of foliage and flowerheads, restored, c1700, 19in (48cm) wide.
£350-450 *C*

JOHN & SARAH ARTIS. YARMOUTH, 1769

A creamware transfer printed plate, by John Sadler, with The Sailor's Return, chipped, c1769, 9½in (24cm).
£1,800-2,500 *C*

An early Quimper plate, painted in red, yellow, blue and green, c1885, 8½in (21cm).
£110-130 *VH*

A Quimper plate, signed, c1910, 6in (15cm).
£45-55 *VH*

A Quimper plate, marked HB, c1880, 5½in (13.5cm).
£60-80 *VH*

Two Quimper plates, 9in (23cm).
£45-65 each *AI*

A pair of Malicone plates, damaged, PBX mark, c1875, 5in (12cm).
£40-50 *VH*

A Quimper dish, signed, c1910, 9in (23cm) wide.
£55-75 *VH*

An early Quimper dish of silver shape, unmarked, c1875, 11in (28cm).
£150-180 *VH*

A pair of Quimper plates, signed H B Quimper, c1829, 5in (12.5cm).
£55-75 *VH*

A Riley blue and white transfer printed plate, c1820.
£50-100 *CA*

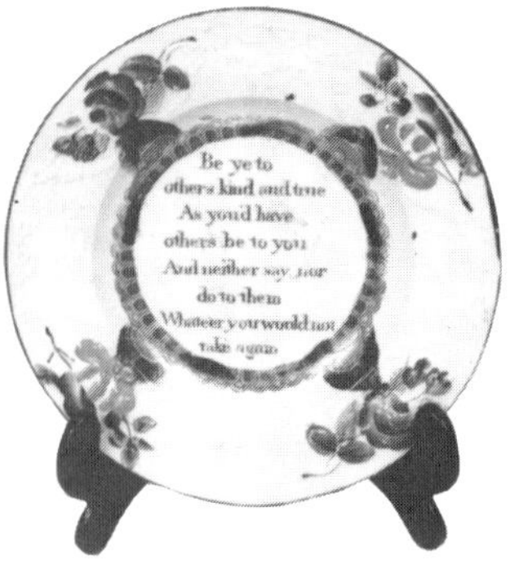
Be ye to
others kind and true
As you'd have
others be to you
And neither say nor
do to them
Whateer you would not
take again

A Swansea rhyme plate, c1820, 5½in (14cm).
£100-120 *HOW*

A Swansea teapot stand, 7in (18cm) wide.
£130-150 *THA*

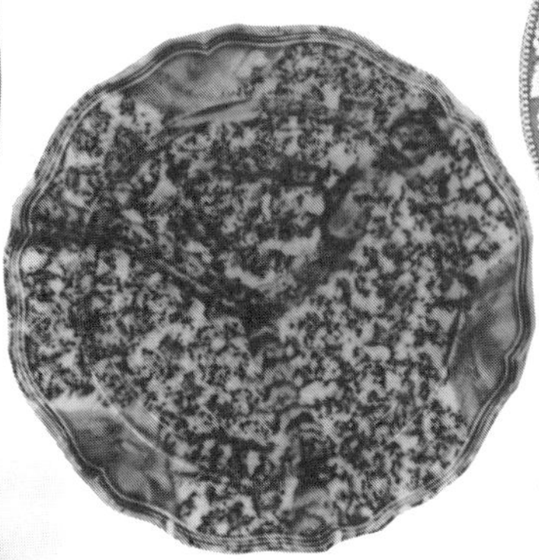

A Staffordshire Whieldon type plate, c1765, 10in (25.5cm).
£350-450 *JHo*

A Staffordshire plate, Clews & Co. Dr. Syntax series, Painting a Portrait, c1820, 10in (25cm).
£240-260 *HOW*

HR QUIMPER

HR QUIMPER

A pair of Quimper plates, 7½in (19cm).
£45-65 each *AI*

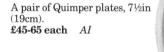

A Wedgwood earthenware fluted centre dish, with entwined double serpent handles, painted by Emile Lessore, the underside with a mottled tortoiseshell glaze, on short spreading foot, rim and handle restored, impressed mark, signed, c1865, 12½in (32cm) wide.
£800-1,000 *C*

HB Quimper

Two Quimper plates, 5½ and 6½in (14 and 16cm).
£45-65 each *AI*

A Swansea, Dillwyn, plate, showing woman with baskets, marked, c1825, 10in (25cm).
£250-300 *HOW*

A Glamorgan plate, c1820, 7½in 19cm) diam.
:90-100 *HOW*

A Staffordshire blue and white meat dish, printed with Eastern figures before a temple and the border reserved with panels of Oriental figures and flowers, 19in (48cm) wide.
£100-150 *CSK*

A slipware dish, the brown ground trailed in dark and pale cream slip, with geometric design of loops and blobs, within a piecrust rim, probably Staffordshire, rim chipped, the underside flaking, 18thC, 14in (34.5cm).
£900-1,200 *C*

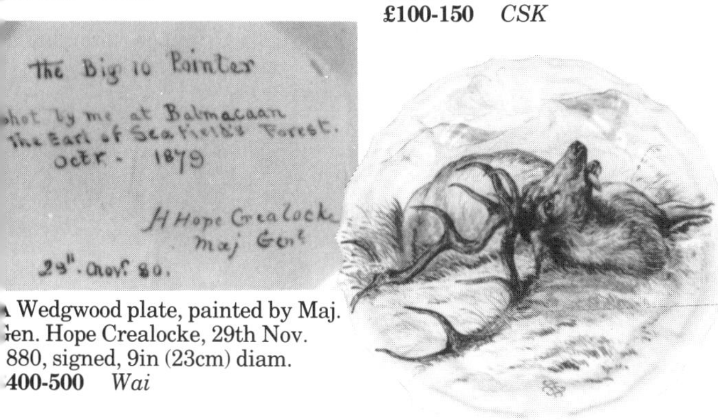
The Big 10 Pointer
hot by me at Balmacaan
The Earl of Seafield's Forest.
Octr - 1879
H Hope Crealocke
Maj Genl
29th Novr 80.

A Wedgwood plate, painted by Maj. Gen. Hope Crealocke, 29th Nov. 880, signed, 9in (23cm) diam.
400-500 *Wai*

A Quimper saucer, with yellow ground, 4in (10cm).
£40-65 *AI*

A Spode blue and white meat dish, printed with Shooting a Leopard in a tree from the Indian Sporting Series, chip to rim, impressed mark, c1815, 20in (50.5cm) wide.
£350-400 *CSK*

Mason's Ironstone dish, with ater lily pattern, c1815, 11in 8cm) long.
200-250 *VH*

A Spode blue and white printed dish, Buffalo pattern, c1790, 7in (17.5cm).
£25-30 *OD*

A Yorkshire creamware plate, c1770, 9in (23cm).
£350-400 *JHo*

A Faenza a quatieri crespina, painted with the figure of Mary Magdelene within alternating orange and blue ground panels reserved with groteschi and foliage the reverse with blue gadroons enriched with orange feathering, rim chips, c1540, 9in (24cm).
£10,000-12,000 *C*

A miniature Swansea plate, c1825, 4½in (11cm).
£65-75 *CA*

A chinoiserie plate, c1815.
£70-80 *Nor*

A Hispano-Moresque dish, with raised central boss, lustred with mock calligraphy, enriched in copper and blue, pierced for hanging, probably Manises, cracked, chipped and flaking, late 15th/early 16thC, 12½in (32cm).
£800-1,200 *C*

A Swansea plate, c1820, 7in (17cm).
£50-60 *IW*

A pair of pearlware blue and white plates, transfer printed with a Temple, c1790, 9½in (24cm).
£50-80 *OD*

A Hispano-Moresque copper lustre dish, with a central boss painted with lozenges enriched in blue on a ground of stylised foliage, pierced for hanging, 16th/17thC, 15½in (39cm).
£1,200-1,500 *C*

A Swansea meat dish, Bevington period, impressed 14 on reverse, 15½in (39cm) wide.
£300-350 *OD*

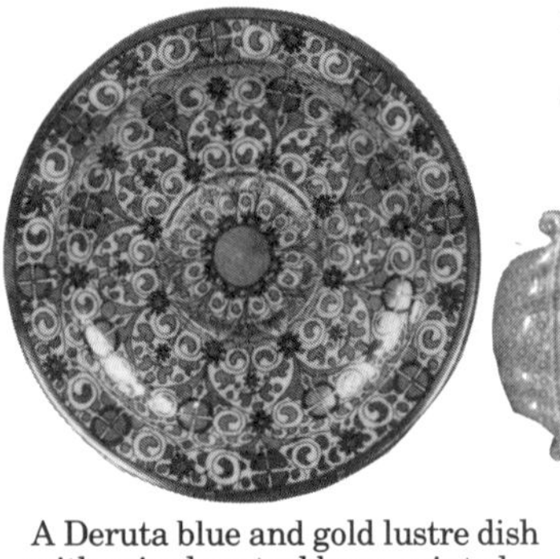

A Deruta blue and gold lustre dish with raised central boss, painted with concentric stylised flowering foliage, c1520, 13in (33cm).
£2,500-3,500 *C*

A blue and white transfer printed tureen stand, c1820, 14in (35.5cm) wide.
£150-200 *CA*

A Hispano-Moresque copper lustre dish, the central boss painted with a flowerhead, the outer border moulded with stylised palm leaves, damaged, mid-17thC, 15½in (39cm).
£700-1,000 *Bon*

A Montelupo fluted crespina, painted in colours within a yellow band, the borders with panels of exotic birds, flowers and foliate scrolls, yellow rim, minor rim chips, early 17thC, 10in (25cm).
£550-800 *C*

A Montelupo dish, painted in ochre and blue against a stylised landscape background with trees and blue mountains, small rim chips, c1640, 12½in (32cm).
£3,500-4,500 *C*

A pair of Italian pottery dishes, in the maiolica style, painted with classical figures among clouds within blue borders of mythical beasts and scrolling foliage, 24in (61cm).
£350-400 *CSK*

A Montelupo dish, painted with a pair of musketeers wearing green and orange striped doublet and trousers striding over hills, on a yellow and green ground, copper green rim, 3 brown concentric lines to the reverse, rim chip, c1650, 12½in (32cm).
£1,500-2,500 *C*

A Nevers Conrade dated blue and white dish, painted with a central galleon, surrounded by arches, trophies, castles and animals, one creature inscribed with the date 1644, the rim with trailing flowers, cracked and chipped, 16½in (42cm).
£5,000-6,000 *C*

Jars

S.Coriand.

A pair of Catalan blue and white albarelli, painted with the name of the contents S.QUICX and S.CORIAND, neck rim chips, one with crack to body, glaze flakes, probably Talavera, 17th/18thC, 12in (30cm).
£1,500-2,000 *C*

A creamware wet drug jar, c1780, 7½in (19cm).
£180-220 *Sto*

A Sicilian albarello, painted on one side with a portrait bust and the other with a lion, in green, ochre, yellow and blue enamels, cracked, c1700, 12in (30cm).
£2,000-2,500 *Bea*

C: RALEIGH

A pill pot, probably London, c1760, 3in (7cm).
£400-500 *JHo*

A Hispano-Moresque copper lustre and blue albarello, painted all over with concentric bands of stylised foliage between blue lines, rim chips, glaze flakes, blue retouched, late 15thC, 10½in (26.5cm).
£3,000-3,500 *C*

A Catalan coloured albarello, painted in the workshop of Francisco Niculoso in the Deruta style, in blue and manganese on a yellow ground, broken and riveted, 17thC, 12in (31cm).
£2,500-3,500 *C*

A Quimper pickle jar with lid, 6in (16cm).
£20-35 *AI*

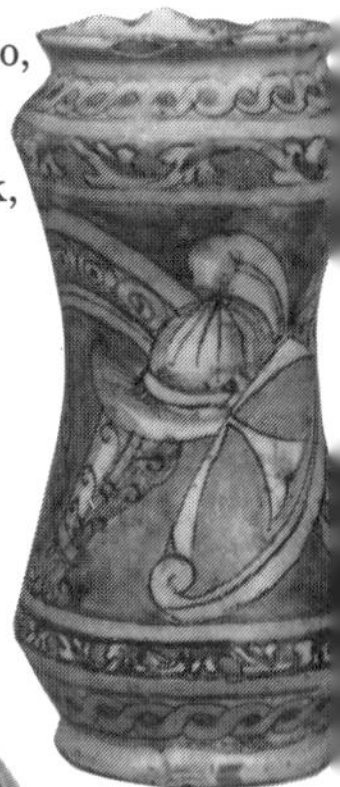

A Southern Italian dated albarello, painted in colours and inscribed S.P.Q.P. 1667 on a pale green ground, chips to neck, small crack, 9½in (23cm).
£900-1,200 *C*

A Southern Italian baluster pharmacy jar, painted in blue, green and yellow, the neck and waist with a band of green and yellow rope twist, minor chips to rims, restored, 17thC, 12in (31cm).
£1,500-2,000 *C*

An English wet drug jar, early 18thC, 7in (18cm).
£700-800 *JHo*

A Burmantofts faience jardinière and stand, cracked.
£200-300 *GIL*

A banded slipware jar, Northern England, 11½in (29cm).
£40-50 *IW*

A Venetian Berettino albarello, painted with an elaborate scroll inscribed with the name of the contents Mo Franda F, chip to base and rim, glaze flakes, 17thC, 13½in (34cm).
£3,000-4,000 *C*

An Italian maiolica albarello, painted in blue above a yellow band, the foot with vertical blue dashes, rim restored, 18thC, 8in (20cm).
£150-200 *CSK*

A pair of maiolica albarelli, painted in blue and yellow, damaged and restored, 10in (26cm).
£600-650 *CSK*

A Palermo maiolica albarello, painted with a yellow ground panel of a bishop saint, with patterns and stiff leaves painted in blue, yellow, brown and green between ribbon borders, glaze damaged, rim and foot chipped, 17thC, 11½in (29cm).
£1,200-1,500 *CSK*

A Ligurian blue and white waisted albarello, painted with a townscape and trees, with a crowned cartouche inscribed 'Charitas', the reverse with the date 1734, 9in (23cm).
£800-900 *C*

A Laterza squat waisted albarello, painted in blue with a seated figure among rockwork and trees, named in ochre, slight rim chip and crack, 1720, 8in (20cm).
400-500 *C*

\ pair of Caltagirone waisted lbarelli, painted with portraits vithin yellow scroll cartouches, eserved on a blue ground with crolling flowers and foliage in ellow and pale green, minor laking, one cracked, 17thC, 9in 24cm).
2,000-3,000 *C*

A waisted albarello, painted in blue and manganese, perhaps Savona, rim and footrim chips, c1700, 7½in (18cm).
£400-450 *C*

Jugs

A Derbyshire saltglazed stoneware jug, Brampton, possibly Oldfield, damage, c1840, 10in (26cm).
£80-100 *IW*

A Liverpool pearlware cream jug, with S-scroll handle, painted in iron red with 2 swans, the trefoil lip and flared rim with a band of scrolls, rim cracked and chipped, Samuel Gilbody's factory, c1758.
£3,000-3,500 *C*

A North Devon jug with yellow slip, c1880, 5in (13cm).
£60-80 *Sto*

A Jackfield jug, with gilt decoration, rubbed, 4in (11cm).
£250-300 *Sto*

A Jackfield jug with moulded decoration, 5in (12.5cm).
£100-120 *THA*

See page 104 in Miller's Collectables Price Guide 1990-91 for a further selection of Jackfield ware.

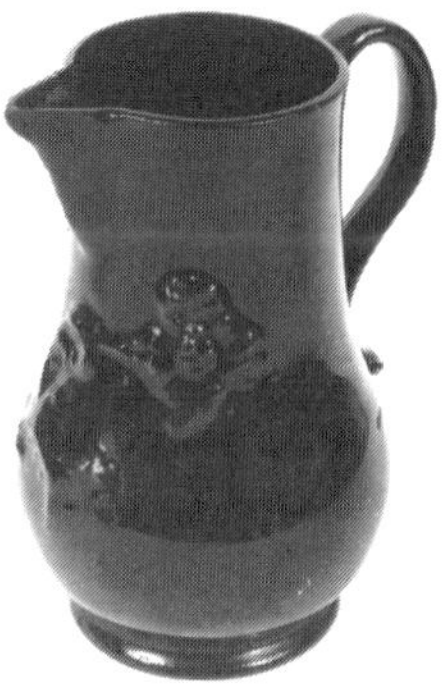

A Jackfield jug with moulded decoration, 4in (10cm).
£75-100 *THA*

A Liverpool creamware jug, printed in black with Masonic motifs and verse, early 19thC, 5½in (14cm).
£150-200 *HSS*

A pair of Rye Pottery owl jugs, with dark green glaze on a terracotta body, c1870, 7in (17.5cm).
£80-100 *CA*

A Pratt ware jug, c1800, 6in (15cm).
£300-350 *HOW*

A Bacchus mask jug, 4½in (11cm).
£75-100 *SBA*

A gaudy lustre jug, with lion head spout, c1835, 5in (13cm).
£80-100 *HOW*

A Quimper jug, c1920, 7in (17cm).
£100-120 *VH*

A Staffordshire pearlware Bacchus mask moulded jug, enriched in colours with puce, yellow and red dots, within brown lines, cracked and chipped, 5in (12.5cm).
£100-150 *CSK*

A Staffordshire enamelled saltglazed jug, c1765, 3½in (9cm).
£1,000-1,200 *JHo*

A silver lustre jug, c1814, 7½in (18cm).
£330-350 *HOW*

A pair of Spode jugs, printed and coloured in 'famille rose' style, printed marks, 12½in (32cm).
£1,200-1,500 *CSK*

A Quimper jug, marked H, c1890, 3½in (9cm).
£50-80 *VH*

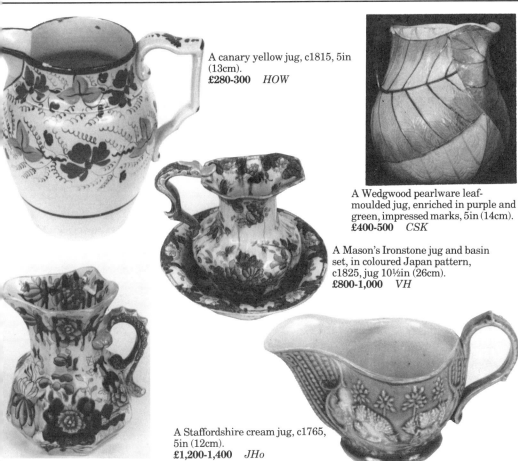

A canary yellow jug, c1815, 5in (13cm).
£280-300 *HOW*

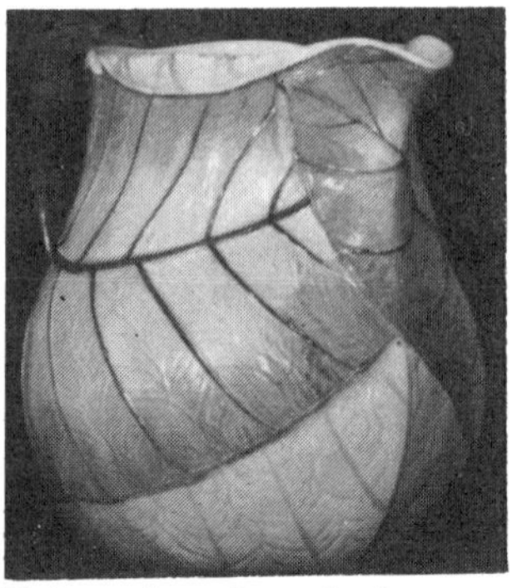

A Wedgwood pearlware leaf-moulded jug, enriched in purple and green, impressed marks, 5in (14cm).
£400-500 *CSK*

A Mason's Ironstone jug and basin set, in coloured Japan pattern, c1825, jug 10½in (26cm).
£800-1,000 *VH*

A Mason's Ironstone jug, marked, c1820, 7in (17cm).
£180-200 *VH*

A Staffordshire cream jug, c1765, 5in (12cm).
£1,200-1,400 *JHo*

An enamelled creamware jug, with Miss Piff design, c1775, 5in (13cm).
£1,200-1,500 *JHo*

An English whiteware shell pattern jug, c1900, ½in (19cm).
£50-100 *UC*

A Staffordshire blue and white jug, c1815, 11in (28cm).
£350-450 *CSK*

A Staffordshire whiteware and pewter covered wine jug, c1870, 8½in (21cm).
£125-175 *UC*

A Staffordshire jug and bowl set, c1900, jug 7½in (19cm).
£150-200 *UC*

A pottery jug, attributed to Swansea, early 19thC, 5½in (14cm).
£250-300 *HOW*

A Swansea gaudy lustre octagonal jug, c1835, 6½in (16cm).
£160-200 *HOW*

A jug with hand coloured enamel decoration, c1820, 6½in (16cm).
£180-200 *HOW*

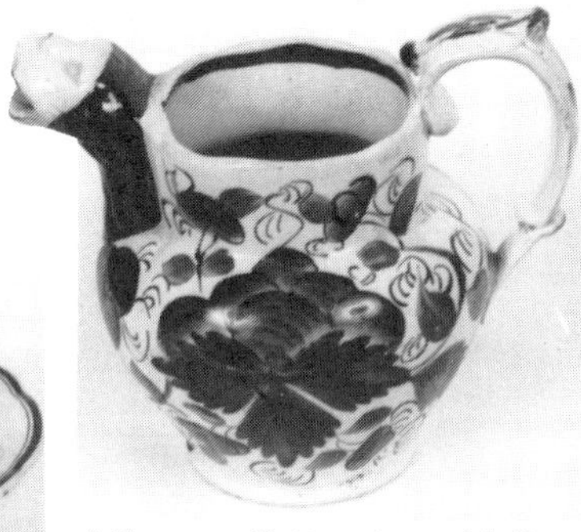

A Swansea Cottage jug, with lion head spout, c1845, 5½in (14cm).
£160-200 *HOW*

A creamware inscribed and dated jug, painted in colours, with inscriptions, perhaps Liverpool or Staffordshire, chipped, c1789, 10in (25cm).
£2,500-3,500 *C*

A saltglazed cream jug, c1755, 3in (8cm).
£700-800 *BHA*

A creamware baluster jug, the tortoiseshell ground applied with green swags of foliage, chips and cracks, interior staining, c1780, 6½in (16.5cm).
£400-500 *C*

A Leeds type creamware jug, handle restored, c1785, 4½in (11cm).
£200-250 *IW*

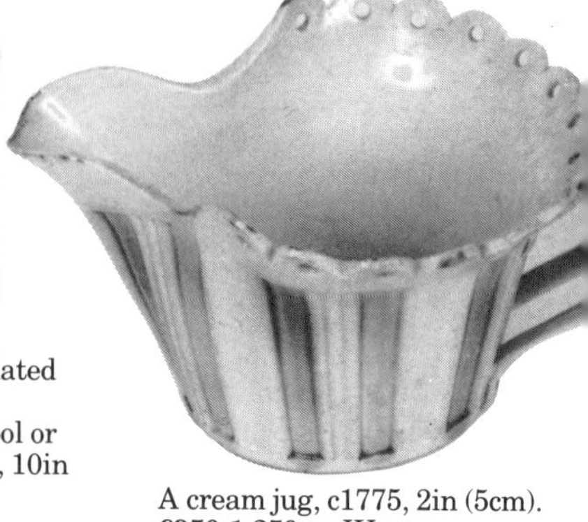

A cream jug, c1775, 2in (5cm).
£950-1,250 *JHo*

JOHN & HANNAH
WENT
1790
HANNAH

A creamware jug with scroll handle, decorated in blue with floral and foliate sprays, inscribed John & Hannah Went 1790, some damage, 8½in (21cm).
£250-350 *P(S)*

A gravel finished jug, with gadrooned band, c1830, 3in (7cm).
£30-40 *IW*

A creamware jug, handle restored, c1800, 8in (20cm).
£220-250 *IW*

A London saltglazed jug, with Sheffield plate cover, thumbpiece missing, c1830, 9in (23cm).
£100-120 *IW*

A pearlware jug with underglaze blue decoration, C mark under foot, slight damage, c1790, 5½in (14cm).
£150-200 *IW*

A pearlware baluster puzzle jug, with gilt inscription, flanked by 2 oval bat printed panels, the border painted with garden flowers, some flaking, c1827, 8½in (21cm).
£400-500 *CSK*

A mocha jug, c1850, 6in (15cm).
£100-140 *IW*

A blue transfer printed moulded jug, c1810, 5in (13cm).
£80-120 *IW*

A Herculaneum milk jug, depicting a hunter with 2 pointers, within stylised flower border, c1820, 4in (10cm).
£100-150 *Bon*

Locate the source

The source of each illustration in Miller's can be found by checking the code letters below each caption with the list of contributors

WILLIAM.
BALANTINE
KING

An earthenware masonic jug, printed in blue with chinoiserie lake views, figures in boats, within floral borders, the front with painted inscription in black, some chips and cracks, dated 1831, 9in (23cm).
£450-500 *P(S)*

A jug with printed allegorical figure of Europe and verse, on a canary yellow ground, silver lustre decoration, 19thC.
£250-300 *AH*

An English green glazed jug, 14th/15thC, 6in (16cm).
£250-300 *Sto*

A Quimper jug, 4½in (11cm).
£20-45 *AI*

A blue and white jug, 8in (20cm).
£45-85 *AI*

A Welsh jug made for the French market, c1840, 4½in (11cm).
£175-200 *BHA*

A French faience jug of fluted helmet shape, on spreading foot, painted in blue with a band of stylised scrolls, the handle with blue scrolling decoration, spout repaired, 8½in (21cm).
£100-150 *CSK*

Toby Jugs

A Staffordshire creamware Toby jug, with streaked brown jacket and shoes, white waistcoat and breeches, some restoration, c1760, 9½in (24cm).
£1,000-1,500 *C*

A Staffordshire creamware Toby jug of Ralph Wood type, in brown hat, pale brown jacket, green waistcoat, ochre breeches and dark brown shoes, a pipe between his feet, slight crack to base, c1775, 10in (25cm).
£900-1,200 *C*

A Staffordshire creamware Toby jug, in dark brown hat and blue streaked jacket, spotted waistcoat and dark brown shoes, some restoration, minor chipping, c1760, 9½in (24cm).
£1,000-1,500 *C*

A Staffordshire creamware 'village idiot' Toby jug, in streaked brown hat, blue jacket and breeches, pale green waistcoat and brown shoes, his eyes outlined in blue, with pale pink face and hands, hat restored, c1775, 9½in (24cm).
£1,500-2,000 *C*

Staffordshire creamware Toby
g, with blue baluster jug, dark
rown hat, grey jacket, white
aistcoat, brown breeches and dark
rown stockings and shoes, slight
acks and flaking, c1780, 10in
5cm).
700-1,000 *C*

A Staffordshire Toby jug, with a glass of ale and a globular jug, in brown hat, streaked yellow jacket, green waistcoat, blue breeches and brown shoes, on a green base, c1780, 14in (35.5cm).
£1,000-1,500 *C*

A Staffordshire pearlware Toby jug, holding a jug of ale, in lustrous brown hat, streaked brown jacket, patterned waistcoat, yellow breeches and brown shoes, c1785, 10½in (26cm).
£800-1,000 *C*

A Staffordshire creamware Toby jug, holding a brown baluster jug, in brown hat, green jacket, green waistcoat and blue breeches, a pipe at his side, on a blue washed base, c1780, 10in (25cm).
£1,000-1,200 *C*

Staffordshire Toby jug of Ralph
'ood type, in streaked blue hat and
at, base repaired, c1780, 10in
5cm).
400-500 *RWB*

A pearlware Toby jug, holding a jug of frothing ale, painted in a Pratt palette, in yellow-edged patterned jacket, blue waistcoat and ochre breeches, Yorkshire or Staffordshire, hat damaged, c1790, 10in (25cm).
£550-650 *C*

A pearlware Toby jug, with brown hat, sponged brown jacket, green breeches and brown shoes, hat cracked, probably Yorkshire, c1810, 8in (21cm).
£550-650 *C*

A Staffordshire creamware Toby jug and cover, with blue hands and eyebrows, wearing a striped brown, manganese, green and blue jacket, white waistcoat, green breeches and brown shoes, restored, some chips, c1785, 10½in (26cm).
£1,000-1,500 *C*

Staffordshire creamware Toby
g, holding a blue baluster jug of
e and a pipe, in white hat, green
cket, blue waistcoat and breeches,
id light brown shoes, handle
paired, c1780, 10in (26cm).
1,200-1,500 *C*

A pearlware Toby jug, wearing black hat, streaked brown jacket, yellow waistcoat and black breeches, some chipping and glaze flaking, probably Staffordshire, c1785, 10in (26cm).
£500-600 *C*

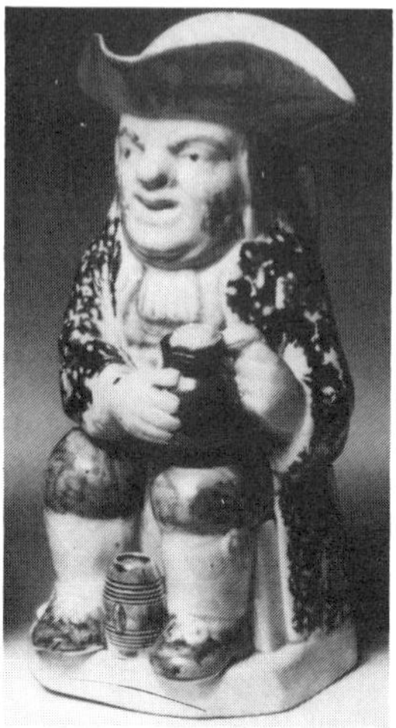

A Staffordshire pearlware Toby jug, holding a brown jug of ale, in grey hat, sponged blue jacket, yellow waistcoat, grey breeches and shoes, c1790, 10in (25cm).
£800-1,000 *C*

A Staffordshire pearlware sailor Toby jug, in opaque enamelled black hat, pink jacket, yellow waistcoat, white breeches and black shoes, hat restored, c1800, 11in (28cm).
£1,500-2,000 *C*

A pearlware Hearty Good Fellow jug, holding a pipe and striped jug of ale, in brown coat, patterned yellow blue and ochre waistcoat, green breeches and white shoes with yellow buckles, traces of impressed mark, perhaps Yorkshire, c1800, 11½in (29cm).
£1,500-2,000 *C*

A Staffordshire Pratt ware Toby jug, decorated in typical Pratt ware colours of yellow, blue and orange, hat repaired, c1790, 9½in (24cm).
£400-500 *RWB*

A Staffordshire Toby jug, in green coat and pink waistcoat, on a green circular base, c1800, 8in (19cm).
£200-250 *C*

A pearlware 'convict' Toby jug, in brown hat, patterned blue and brown jacket, white waistcoat, ochre cuffs, yellow breeches and brown shoes, hat restored, perhaps Yorkshire, c1785, 9½in (24cm).
£1,200-1,500 *C*

A pearlware sailor Toby jug, in brown hat, yellow-edged blue jacket, white waistcoat, striped blue and ochre breeches and brown shoes, hat restored, perhaps Yorkshire, c1800, 11in (28cm).
£2,000-2,500 *C*

A pearlware Toby jug and cover, in black hat, ochre jacket, striped ochre, black and blue waistcoat, green breeches and black shoes, on a D-shaped base, hat restored, perhaps Scottish, c1800, 8in (20cm).
£650-850 *C*

A pearlware Toby jug, holding a jug of ale, with brown hair, patterned brown, ochre and blue jacket, green waistcoat, yellow breeches, striped blue stockings and brown shoes, hat restored, perhaps Yorkshire, c1800, 10in (25cm).
£800-1,000 *C*

A pearlware Toby jug, with ruddy hands and complexion, in yellow-edged brown hat, green jacket, white waistcoat, yellow breeches, striped stockings and brown shoes, on a sponged yellow and blue base, base restored, perhaps Yorkshire, c1800, 10in (25cm).
£700-1,000 *C*

A creamware Toby jug, in dark brown hat, blue jacket, grey waistcoat and breeches and black shoes, c1775, 13½in (34cm).
£1,500-2,000 *C*

A pearlware Toby jug of Pratt type, with brown hair, ochre-collared blue coat, chequered waistcoat, ochre breeches and black shoes, hat chipped, perhaps Yorkshire, c1800, 8in (20cm).
£500-600 *C*

A squire Toby jug, of Ralph Wood type, decorated in coloured glazes, c1775, 11in (28cm).
£5,000-6,000 *JHo*

A Lord Howe Toby jug of the Ralph Wood school, c1775, 10in (25cm).
£3,000-3,500 *JHo*

A pearlware Toby jug, in green hat and jacket, brown breeches and grey shoes, restoration to hat and left shoe, c1800, 9½in (24cm).
£550-700 *C*

Mugs

Mary Ann
Bond
1801

A Liverpool creamware dated and named mug, 3in (7.5cm).
£250-300 *Sto*

GRACE AFTER MEAT
We thank thee LORD for this our food
But more because of JESUS Blood
Let Manna to our Souls be given
The Bread of Life sent down from Heav'n

A creamware mug with lustre decoration and verse, 2½in (6cm).
£60-70 *THA*

A Quimper mug, 5in (12cm).
£20-30 *AI*

A Staffordshire saltglazed mug, c1750.
£800-950 *Sto*

A Staffordshire slipware mug, early 18thC, 3in (8cm).
£1,800-2,000 *JHo*

A Westerwald saltglazed tankard, 5½in (14cm).
£200-300 *Wai*

An agate bodied earthenware beaker, possibly Sussex, early 19thC, 3in (8cm).
£70-100 *IW*

A Jackfield tankard, with original cold enamel decoration, c1780, 5in (12cm).
£280-300 *Wai*

A Staffordshire lead-glazed redware mug, c1750, 4½in (11cm).
£1,200-1,500 *JHo*

A copper lustre mug, with figure of a greyhound, c1840, 3in (7.5cm).
£120-150 *HOW*

A Jaco mug with blue transfer decoration, 4½in (11cm).
£250-270 *HOW*

A Shropshire Jackfield mug, c1750, 3½in (9cm).
£100-120 *THA*

Wood Street

A creamware tavern pot or tankard with inscription, late 18thC, 5½in (14cm).
£150-200 *IW*

This form of tavern pot is often found in white and grey stoneware, delftware, heavier earthenware and ironstone, as well as in pearlware.

Make the Most of Miller's

CONDITION is absolutely vital when assessing the value of an antique. Damaged pieces on the whole appreciate much less than perfect examples. However a rare, desirable piece may command a high price even when damaged

A transfer printed pink lustre and enamelled mug, chipped, c1850, 4in (10cm).
£100-150 *IW*

. yellow mug with silver lustre
ecoration, 2in (5cm).
40-60 *THA*

A pearlware dated and named mug, some damage, c1820, 3in (8cm).
£150-200 *Sto*

A pearlware beaker, 3in (8cm).
£550-600 *JHo*

. creamware tankard, c1775, 5in
.3cm).
1,000-1,200 *JHo*

A Mason's Ironstone harvest mug, impressed mark, c1815, 5in (13cm).
£400-450 *VH*

A creamware sporting mug, with coloured transfer printing, c1790, 5in (12cm).
£350-450 *Sto*

'laques

. Wedgwood and Bentley black
asalt portrait medallion of
'ldenbarneveld in high relief,
amed, within a self-moulded
'ame, rim chip, impressed lower
ase mark, c1780, 3in (7cm).
200-250 *C*

Three Wedgwood black basalt portrait medallions, of Egbert Kortenaer, Jacob Cats and Rombout Hogerbeets, two chipped, all inscribed on the reverses, impressed lower case marks, c1780, 4½in (11cm).
£450-550 *C*

Two Wedgwood black basalt portrait medallions of Peiter Hein and Gellers, inscribed on the reverses, one chipped, impressed lower case marks, c1787.
£550-650 *C*

Two Wedgwood black basalt portrait medallions, of Egbert de Vrij Temmink and Jan de Witt, both chipped, inscribed on the reverses, impressed lower case marks, c1785, 4in (10cm).
£500-550 *C*

An agateware Royal armorial plaque, moulded in high relief with the Royal Arms and supporters, flanked by mantling and scrolls within a foliage moulded surround, covered in cream, brown and grey simulated agate glazes, perhaps Staffordshire, rim chips, c1750, 7in (17.5cm) high.
£1,500-2,500 *C*

A Mettlach plaque, decorated after Stahl in white relief on a blue grey ground, incised I.S. monogram, impressed castle mark 7040, 20½in (52cm).
£800-1,200 *P(S)*

Pots

A Pratt ware pot, No. 402 'Uncle Tom', c1853, 4in (10cm).
£150-200 *CA*

A saltglazed shop pot, London, mid-18thC, 9½in (24cm).
£50-60 *IW*

A Quimper mustard pot, marked, c1925, 3in (7cm).
£35-45 *VH*

A Quimper jam pot, 2½in (6cm).
£35-45 *AI*

A Wedgwood basalt enamel ware sugar box, c1800, 4in (10cm).
£250-300 *BHA*

A Staffordshire blue chamber pot, gilded, 9in (23cm) diam.
£25-35 *THA*

Pot Lids

Sandringham
COLD CREAM

Sandringham Cold Cream, green print, c1880.
£75-100 *K*

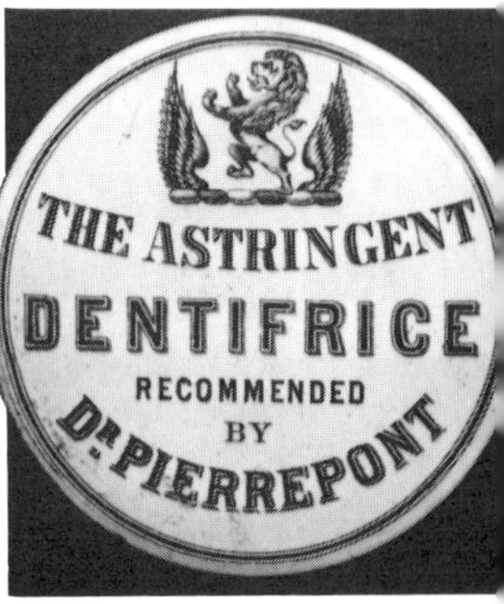
THE ASTRINGENT
DENTIFRICE
RECOMMENDED
BY
Dr. PIERREPONT

Dr. Pierrepont Dentifrice, late 19thC.
£50-75 *K*

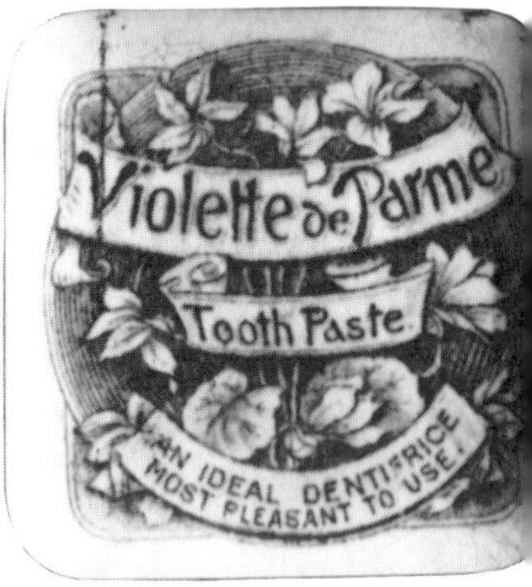
Violette de Parme
Tooth Paste
AN IDEAL DENTIFRICE
MOST PLEASANT TO USE

Violette de Parme Toothpaste, purple print, c1880.
£75-100 *K*

A pottery punchbowl, decorated with stylised flowerheads and gilt foliate painting, with gilt borders on circular flared foot, early 19thC, 11½in (29cm) diam.
£350-400 *HCH*

A Staffordshire creamware Whieldon type candlestick, cracked and chipped, c1750, 8in (21.5cm).
£12,000-15,000 *C*

A Faenza baluster famiglia gotica albarello, with bands of stylised leaves and flowerheads, footrim chip, c1480, 12in (30cm).
£40,000-45,000 *C*

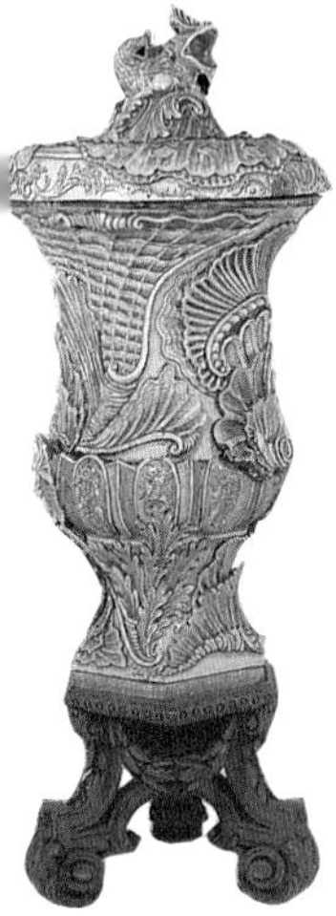

l. A rococo blue and white covered fountain, on later wooden stand, minor damage, mid-18thC, 49in (125cm).
£25,000-30,000 *C*

A Wemyss fruit bowl, 8½in (22cm) diam.
£100-150 *RdeR*

An enamel decorated figure of Summer, probably North of England, c1820, 9in (23cm).
£150-200 *IW*

A George Jones majolica cheese bell and stand with kingfisher finial, repaired, late-19thC, 13½in (35cm) high.
£300-400 *PCh*

A French Mosanic hand painted pug, c1900.
£500-600 *RdeR*

r. A Gallé cat with rare cream ground, signed Emile Gallé, c1900.
£4,500-5,000 *RdeR*

l. A creamware sauce-boat in the form of a duck, c1820, 8in (20cm) long.
£1,000-1,500 *ART*

A Staffordshire pearlware group of Obadiah Sherratt type, extensively damaged, c1820, 13in (33.5cm) wide.
£10,000-12,000 *C*

A Deruta gold lustre tondino with portrait bust of a lady, slight chips, c1530, 9in (23cm).
£4,000-5,000 *C*

A Deruta Istoriato dish with Salome holding the head of John the Baptist before Herod and four attendants, c1580, 13½in (34cm).
£17,000-20,000 *C*

A Hispano-Moresque faience lustre dish, 16th/17thC, 17in (43cm).
£1,000-1,200 *Wai*

A Southwark delft polychrome La Fécondité dish, cracked and repaired, minor chips, c1650, 17in (43cm) wide.
£20,000-25,000 *C*

M. P.

An Italian moulded dish with twin tailed mermaid, probably Angarano, late 17th/early 18thC, 18½in (47cm).
£3,500-4,500 *C*

MS·CEL

An Alla Candiana circular tazza painted in the Islamic style, the reverse with blue scrolling, minor rim chips, late 17thC, 13½in (34cm).
£3,000-4,000 *C*

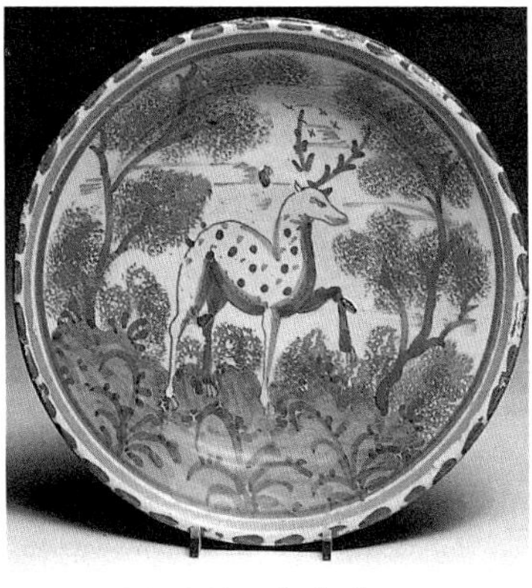

A Bristol delft blue dash charger painted with a deer, c1710, 11½in (30cm).
£25,000-30,000 *C*

Pray Gentlemen Pay
1716

l. A London delft barber's bowl, c1716, 10in (26cm).
£25,000-30,000 *C*

A Dutch Delft plate, c1720, 8½in (21cm).
£100-150 *IW*

l. A Castelli armorial plate painted by Aurelio Grue after a print from the 'Hunt Series' by Antonio Tempesta, c1725, 11½in (29cm).
£14,000-16,000 *C*

r. A Holics Istoriato plate in the Sienna style, with Neptune in a shell chariot drawn by a pair of hippocamp, HF and star mark, c1750, 10in (25cm).
£2,500-3,500 *C*

A French faience charger, Marseille factory of La Veuve Perrin, late 18thC, 14in (35.5cm) diam. **£400-500** *IW*

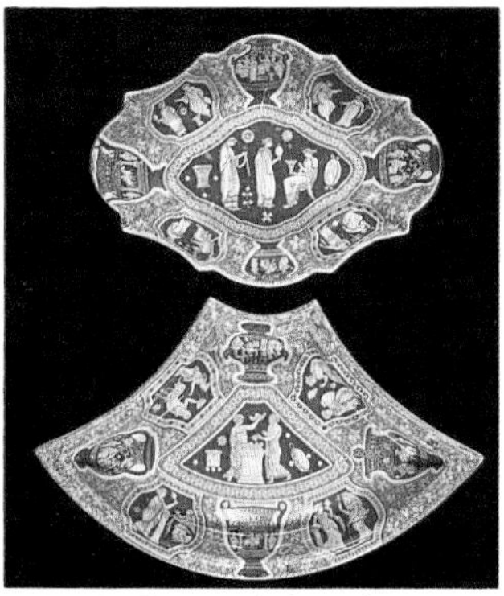

A Spode dessert dish and supper section, Greek patterns, c1805.
£80-140 each *Nor*

A Bathwell and Goodfellow soup plate, from the Rural Scenery series, Firewood pattern, c1820, 10in (25.5cm). **£75-125** *Nor*

A dinner plate, with Fruit and Flowers pattern, c1815, 10in (25.5cm) diam.
£75-100 *Nor*

A soup tureen stand, The Beemaster, maker unknown, c1820, 15in (38cm) wide. **£350-450** *Nor*

A Bathwell and Goodfellow dinner plate, The Reaper pattern, c1820, 10in (25.5cm). **£75-125** *Nor*

A Wemyss Gordon plate, with daisies and forget-me-nots, 8in (20cm) diam. **£200-250** *RdeR*

A Quimper teapot and cup and saucer set, teapot 5in (12.5cm) high.
£120-150 *VH*

A Staffordshire saltglazed soup tureen, cover and a stand, some damage, c1760.
£30,000-35,000 *C*

A pair of Berlin baskets, underglaze and impressed marks, c1755, 9in (23cm).
£4,500-5,500 *CG*

A pair of delft vases and covers, Liverpool or London, some damage, c1760, 8½in (21cm).
£5,000-6,000 *C*

Sir, Robert Peel

A Staffordshire figure of Sir Robert Peel, c1850, 12in (30.5cm), (B,31).
£750-1,000 *RWB*

A Wemyss pottery toilet set, with rose pattern and green border decoration, impressed and painted mark.
£4,000-5,000 *AH*

A Worcester armorial mug, with grooved loop handle, c1770, 5in (12cm) high.
£8,000-10,000 *C*

A Meissen Kakiemon tankard and cover, chip to cover, blue caduceus mark, c1723, 4in (10.5cm) high.
£16,000-20,000 *C*

A Worcester butter tub, painted with an Oriental, the interior with a flowering branch within a diaper and floral border, chip to footrim, c1754, 7½in (18.5cm) wide. **£18,000-20,000** *C*

A Frankenthal snuff box and cover, c1770, with contemporary gilt metal mount, 4in (10cm) wide.
£10,000-12,000 *C*

A Sèvres wine cooler, some damage, marked and letter H for 1760, 7½in (19.5cm) high.
£4,000-5,000 *C*

A Chelsea leveret box and cover, red anchor and 110 marks, c1756, 4in (9.5cm) wide. **£14,000-16,000** *C*

A Meissen tobacco box, painted in the manner of J. G. Horoldt, c1740, contemporary copper gilt mounts, 5½in (13cm). **£35,000-40,000** *CG*

A Worcester dish, rubbing and chips, blue square seal mark, c1770, 10½in (26cm) wide.
£6,000-8,000 *C*

A Böttger figure, damaged, marked, c1717.
£10,000-12,000 *C*

A Fürstenberg figure of Andromeda, restored, script and incised marks, c1774, later gilt chains, 11½in (28.5cm). **£1,500-2,500** *C*

A Bow group of Harlequin and Columbine, some damage, c1765, 6½in (16cm) high.
£5,000-7,000 *C*

l. A Doccia figure of a bearded Turk, chipped, c1765, 5½in (14cm).
£2,500-3,000 *C*

A Höchst arbour group allegorical of Autumn, chips and repairs, wheel and incised mark, c1760.
£9,000-12,000 *C*

A pair of Höchst figures of street vendors, repairs, red and puce wheel marks, c1760, 7½in (19cm).
£12,000-15,000 *C*

A Mennecy group, two arms restored, incised d,v to base, 5½in (14cm).
£1,500-2,000 *C*

A Meissen miner musician, damaged and restored, blue crossed swords mark, c1730, 6in (15cm).
£10,000-12,000 *C*

A Meissen model by J. J. Kändler, extensively restored, faint blue mark to base, porcelain c1740, later decoration, 6½in (16cm).
£6,000-8,000 *C*

A Fulda Commedia dell'Arte figure of Harlequin, damaged, blue cross mark, c1770, 6½in (16cm).
£13,000-15,000 *C*

A Meissen salt by J. J. Kändler, repaired, marked, c1737, 7½in (19cm). **£8,000-10,000** *C*

A French faience figure of an Oriental lady, repaired and damaged, c1730, 14½in (37cm).
£4,000-5,000 *C*

A Nymphenburg figure of Columbine from the Commedia dell'Arte, by Franz Anton Bustelli, repaired and chipped, impressed shield mark, c1762, 8in (20cm).
£12,000-15,000 *C*

A Sèvres biscuit figure of L'Abbé Fénélon after the sculpture by Lecomte, repaired and chipped, c1784, 19in (48cm).
£4,500-5,500 *C*

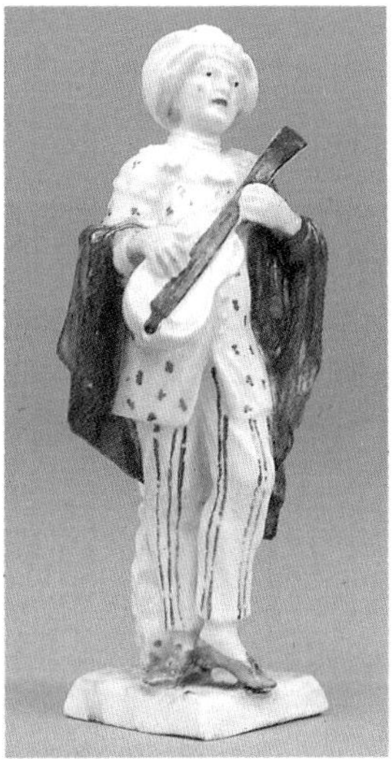

A Würzburg Commedia dell'Arte figure of Bagolin, possibly by Ferdinand Tietz, repaired, c1770, 5in (13cm). **£2,500-3,500** *C*

A Chelsea group of 2 goats, restored and damaged, raised red anchor mark, c1751. **£6,000-8,000** *C*

A pair of Meissen hunt groups, by J. J. Kändler, damage and repairs, crossed swords marks, c1755, decoration later, 9in (23cm) wide. **£7,000-8,000** *C*

A pair of Meissen ormolu mounted bears, restored, porcelain 18thC, 4in (10.5cm) high. **£5,000-6,000** *C*

A Meissen Hausmalerei plate, blue crossed swords mark, c1735, decoration later. **£25,000-30,000** *C*

A Chelsea spoon tray, painted in the Kakiemon palette with the Quail pattern, glaze crack, raised anchor mark, c1750, 6in (15cm). **£5,000-6,000** *C*

A Meissen plate, blue crossed swords mark, c1735, 15in (38cm). **£14,000-16,000** *C*

A Nymphenburg documentary tray, signed and dated 1813, impressed and incised marks, 15½in (39.5cm) wide. **£7,000-8,000** *C*

A German dish, probably Ottweiler, border damaged, c1765, 12½in (31.5cm) diam. **£1,000-1,500** *C*

A Meissen dish from The Red Dragon service, crossed swords and puce KHC mark, c1740, 11½in (29.5cm). **£2,500-3,500** *C*

l. A Dutch decorated Kakiemon dish, c1700, 7½in (18cm). **£5,000-6,000** *C*

A Sèvres plate from The Egyptian service, various marks, 9½in (24cm). **£28,000-30,000** *C*

A Vincennes 'bleu celeste' tray, with gilt dentil rim, interlaced L's enclosing date letter A for 1753, painter's mark, 11in (28cm) wide. **£5,000-6,000** *C*

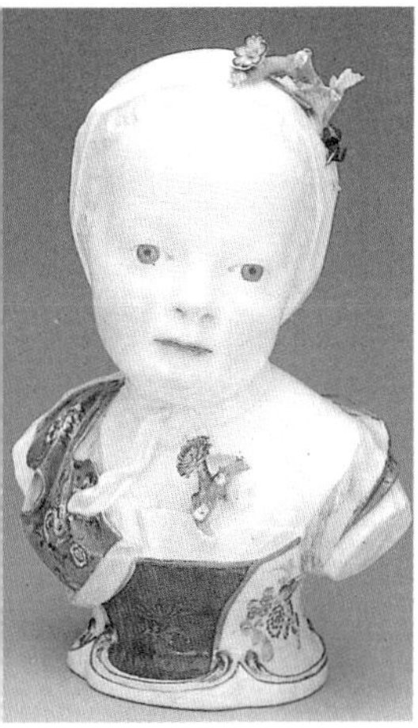

l. A Meissen portrait bust, by J. J. Kändler, some damage, crossed swords mark, c1755, 10in (25cm).
£9,000-12,000 *CG*

r. A Soviet porcelain propaganda plate, by the Imperial Porcelain Factory, 1921, 10in (25cm). **£5,000-6,000** *C*

A Berlin K.P.M. Terrassenmalerei tête-à-tête, blue sceptre marks and gilder's dot mark to all pieces, various incised marks, c1790, the tray 13in (33cm) wide.
£7,000-8,000 *CG*

A Coalport Imari pattern part dinner service, comprising 86 pieces, some damage, c1805.
£10,000-12,000 *C*

A Derby part dessert service, comprising 31 pieces, some damage, marked, c1800. **£40,000+** *C*

l. A Bayreuth faience Hausmalerei 'famille rose' teapot and cover, cracked and repaired, c1740, 7½in (18.5cm) wide. **£8,000-10,000** *C*

A Berlin K.P.M. part dinner service, comprising 43 pieces, sceptre marks and various gilder's marks, c1835.
£7,000-8,000 *CG*

A set of 8 Meissen plates, blue crossed swords marks and Pressnummer 16, c1745.
£5,000-6,000 *C*

A Meissen sauceboat from The Swan Service, modelled by J. J. Kändler and J. F. Eberlein, blue crossed swords mark, c1740, 10½in (25.5cm) wide.
£10,000-12,000 *C*

A Naples cabaret, damage and repairs, blue crowned N marks, c1785, tray 12½in (32cm) wide. **£10,000-12,000** *C*

r. A Bristol documentary sauceboat, Bristoll mark, incised mark, c1750, 8in (20cm). **£10,000-12,000** *C*

A Chelsea moulded teapot and cover, with bamboo moulded handle, chipped and cracked, incised triangle mark, c1745, 4½in (12cm) high.
£25,000-30,000 *C*

A Nymphenburg coffee pot and cover, minute chips, indistinct incised mark, c1760, 9in (23cm) high.
£2,500-3,000 *C*

A Meissen teapot and cover, by J. J. Kändler, repairs, marked, c1735.
£4,500-5,500 *CG*

A Meissen underglaze blue teapot and cover, chipped and repaired, marked, c1724, 6½in (16.5cm) wide.
£12,000-15,000 *C*

A Venice teapot and cover, repairs and chips, incised and iron red mark, c1725, 7in (17.5cm) wide.
£12,000-15,000 *C*

Two Chelsea eel tureens, their tails forming the handles, one restuck and crack to cover, red anchor marks, c1755, 7½in (18.5cm) wide.
£22,000-25,000 *C*

A Bow squat bowl and cover in a Kakiemon palette, incised R mark, c1750, 5½in (14.5cm) wide.
£20,000-25,000 *C*

A Meissen two-handled écuelle and cover, painted by Bonaventura Gottlieb Hauer, crossed swords marks, c1745, 8in (20cm) wide.
£16,000-18,000 *C*

A Longton Hall tureen and cover, modelled as open tulips, repairs and chips, c1755, 5in (12cm) wide.
£20,000-22,000 *C*

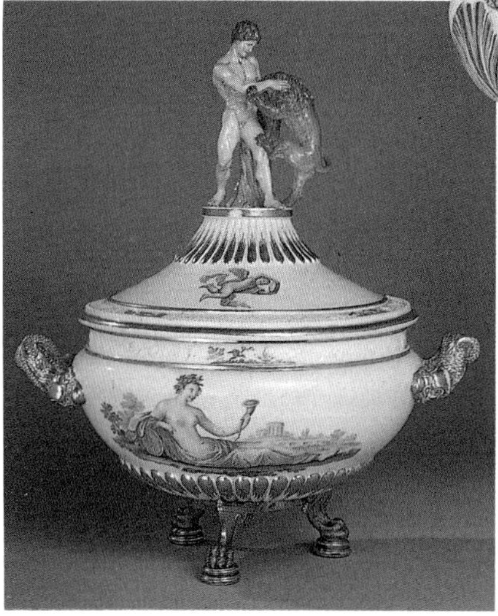

l. A Naples royal soup tureen and cover, from The Ercolanese Service, with inscription, repaired and gilding rubbed, c1781, on an almost contemporary gilt bronze mount, 14in (35.5cm) high.
£45,000-50,000 *C*

A Böttger tea caddy and cover, slight damage, c1725, 4in (9.5cm) high.
£2,000-2,500 *C*

\ Chantilly pot pourri, the pierced
:over with applied flowers, chips and
epairs, c1750, 7½in (19cm) high.
:6,000-8,000 *C*

A pair of Chelsea vases and covers, minor damage, gold anchor marks, c1763.
£10,000-12,000 *C*

A pair of Chelsea vases, painted within gilt cartouches, chip to footrim, c1765, 7in (17.5cm) high.
£4,000-5,000 *C*

A Sèvres caisse à fleurs, restored, marked, c1759, 7in (17.5cm) high.
£4,000-5,000 *C*

l. A Copenhagen vase, repaired, mark, c1810. **£25,000-30,000** *CG*

\ Coalport garniture, comprising 2 ice pails, covers and
iners and a fruit stand, some restoration, puce printed
:BD marks incorporating retailer's marks for Daniell,
·1855, ice pails 29½in (74cm) high. **£10,000-12,000** *C*

A Sèvres vase and pierced stand, some damage, marks, c1757, 8in (20cm) wide. **£6,000-8,000** *C*

\ porcelain vase, with ormolu
nounts and brass liner, the
rmolu c1830, 39in (99cm) high.
:2,000-4,000 *C*

A pair of Louis XV ormolu mounted Transitional blue and white vases, porcelain c1650, 19½in (49cm). **£25,000-30,000** *C*

A pair of ormolu mounted jars and covers, the porcelain probably 18thC, the mounts later, 15in (38cm) high.
£7,000-10,000 *C*

A Bow documentary ink pot, some damage, signed Ja. Welsh, c1758, 3½in (9cm) diam. **£14,000-16,000** *C*

A blue and white bottle vase, late Wanli, 7½in (18.5cm) high, wood box.
£10,000-12,000 *C*

A Kutani bottle, rim restored, c1670, 8in.
£7,000-10,000 *C*

An Arita blue and white bottle, c1680, 18½in (46cm) high.
£4,500-5,500 *C*

An Imperial 'famille verte' bowl, Yongzheng Yuzhi marks, 5½in (13.5cm) diam, box.
£50,000-60,000 *C*

A 'famille rose' mythological subject punchbowl, crackec Qianlong, c1750, 15½in (39cm) diam.
£9,000-12,000 *C*

A water pot, decorated with copper red and iron red flowerheads, rim chips, Kangxi six-character mark.
£22,000-25,000 *CNY*

An Imari bowl, decorate with a continuous scene, restored, Genroku perioc 15½in (39.5cm) diam.
£8,000-9,000 *C*

A ru-type bulb bowl, restored, underglaze blue Qianlong four-character seal mark and of the period, 9in (23cm). **£10,000-12,000** *CNY*

l. A 'famille verte' enamelled biscuit bowl, Kangxi mark in undergl blue within a double circle and of the period, 6½in (16.5cm).
£18,000-20,000 *CNY*

A Kakiemon blue and white bowl, kin mark, late 17thC, 8½in (22cm).
£5,500-6,000 *C*

r. A blue and white punchbowl, Kangxi, 15½in (40cm) diam.
£5,000-6,000 *C*

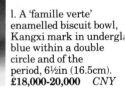

A pair of yellow glazed bowls, one cracked, Qianlong seal marks and of the period, 4½in (12cm).
£12,000-14,000 *C*

A 'famille rose' punchbowl, painted with figures, Qianlong, 15in (38.5cm).
£4,000-5,000 *C*

大明萬
曆年製

A blue and white bowl, encircled Wanli six-character mark and of the period, 6in (15cm).
£7,000-9,000 *C*

r. A Canton 'famille rose' punchbowl, early 19thC, 21in (52.5cm) diam.
£3,500-4,500 *C*

A Ming blue and white dragon bowl, star crack, Zhengde four-character mark in underglaze blue within a double circle and of the period, 6in (15cm) diam.
£25,000-30,000 *CNY*

大明嘉
靖年造

A pair of blue and white bowls, painted with flying phoenix, some damage, encircled Jiajing six-character marks and of late in the period, 5in (12cm) diam, 2 boxes.
£1,200-1,500 *C*

A copper red glazed bowl, with finely pitted glaze, rim chip, Yongzheng mark within a double circle and of the period, 6in (15cm). **£1,000-1,500** *CNY*

A Neolithic painted pottery basin.
£10,000-12,000 *CNY*

A blue and white incense burner and cover, formed as Liu Hai riding on the back of his mythical three-legged toad, chips, mid-17thC, 4½in (11cm).
£10,000-12,000 *C*

A pair of 'famille verte' dragon and phoenix bowls, Qianlong seal marks and of the period, 5½in (14.5cm), boxes. **£22,000-25,000** *C*

Three blue and white eggshell month cups, painted with various flowers for December, September and January, cracks, Kangxi mark and of the period, 3in (8cm). **£1,500-2,000** *CNY*

A doucai cup, painted with chickens, Kangxi, 3½in (8cm), wood stand, box. **£25,000-30,000** *C*

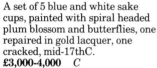

A set of 5 blue and white sake cups, painted with spiral headed plum blossom and butterflies, one repaired in gold lacquer, one cracked, mid-17thC.
£3,000-4,000 *C*

A set of 5 blue and white cups, rims fritted, encircled Jiajing six-character marks, Chongzhen, 3in (7.5cm) diam.
£2,500-3,000 *C*

A blue and white stem cup, painted in underglaze blue with a continuous scene, the interior with a central medallion surrounded by a foliate diaper border at the rim, 16thC, 5½in (14cm) diam.
£8,000-10,000 *CNY*

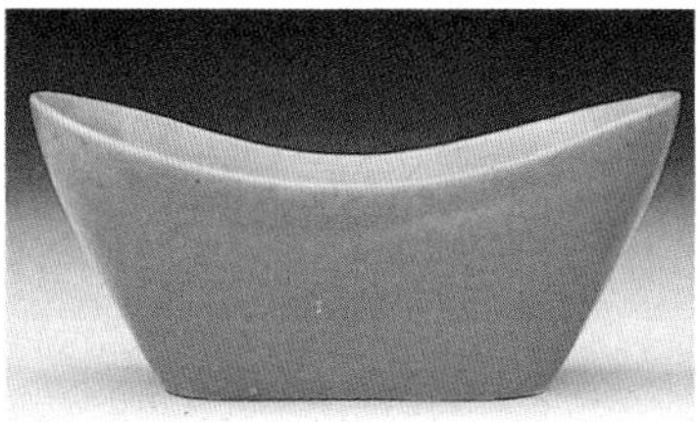

A pair of yellow and blue glazed wine cups, Daoguang, 4½in (11cm) wide, fitted cloth box.
£1,000-1,500 *CNY*

A pair of Ming blue and white saucer dishes, rim chip, Jiajing mark and of the period, 6in (15cm) diam.
£14,000-16,000 *CNY*

A blue and white serving dish, Chinese or Japanese, firing cracks, possibly 17thC, 9in (23cm), wood box. **£12,000-14,000** *C*

A set of 6 blue and white mukozuke, frits, one with underglaze blue Chenghua six-character mark, Chongzhen, 5½in (14cm), wood box.
£3,000-4,000 *C*

A set of 5 blue and white enamelled mukozuke, with scalloped borders and brown rims, rim frits, four-character seal marks, Chongzhen, 5½in (14cm), wood box. **£5,000-6,000** *C*

l. A 'famille verte' dish, some damage, Kangxi, 12½in (31.5cm) diam.
£4,500-5,500 *C*

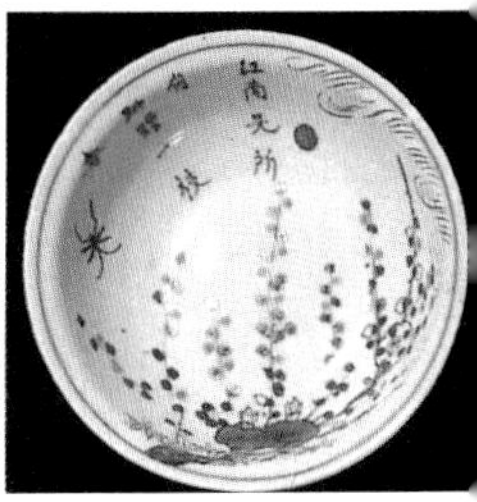

A set of 6 blue and white mukozuke, each painted with an underglaze blue Tang poem, rim frits, Tianqi, 5½in (14.5cm), wood box.
£4,500-5,500 *C*

A Kakiemon teabowl, decorated in enamels and gilt, the interior with a five-pointed floret, c1680, 3in (7cm). **£2,500-3,000** *C*

Two Ming red lacquer carved boxes and covers, 16th/17thC.
£5,000-6,000 each *C*

A Ming stem cup, the iron red enamel laid over a yellow enamel ground, rim crack, Jiajing six-character mark and of the period, 6in (15cm) diam.
£2,500-3,000 *C*

A blue and white display dish, rim chips, late Wanli, 13½in (34cm) diam, wood box.
£16,000-18,000 *C*

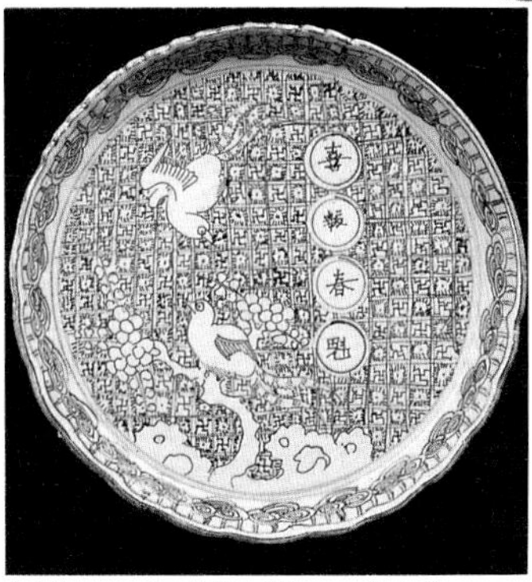

A blue and white Shonzui style serving dish, fu seal mark, Chongzhen, 8in (20cm), wood box.
£10,000-12,000 *C*

A blue and white Shonzui style serving dish, encircled Chenghua six-character mark, Chongzhen, 9in (23cm), wood box.
£7,000-10,000 *C*

A blue and white Shonzui style serving dish, rim frits, Tianqi, 8in (20.5cm), wood box.
£4,000-5,000 *C*

r. A 'famille verte' saucer dish, painted with the English coat-of-arms below a royal crown and inscription, some damage, Kangxi, 13½in (34cm).
£6,000-7,000 *C*

ENGELANDT

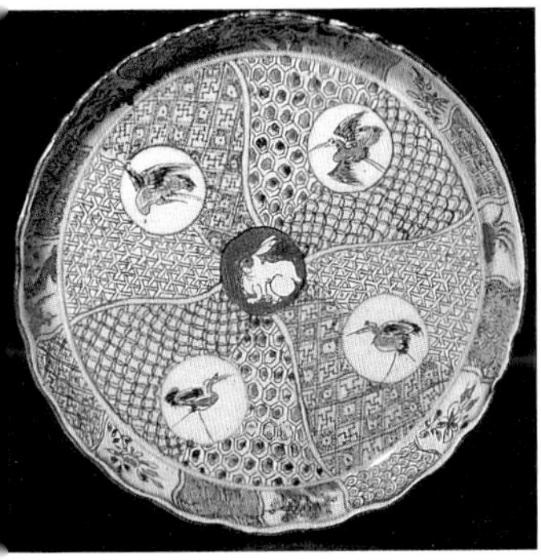

A blue and white enamel Shonzui style serving dish, fu mark within a double square, Chongzhen, 8in (19.5cm). **£15,000-18,000** *C*

r. A rare moulded dish, the veins in raised relief within line borders and reserved in white, footrim chip, Yongzheng mark in underglaze blue within a double circle and of the period, 13in (33cm).
£18,000-20,000 *CNY*

A pair of dishes, painted with a bust profile of Queen Anne, Qianlong, 14in (35.5cm).
£5,500-6,500 *C*

A pair of 'rose/verte' dishes, painted with court ladies and a young boy in a garden, rim frits, Yongzheng, 15in (38cm).
£12,000-15,000 *CNY*

Two 'famille rose' saucer dishes, Yongzheng mark and of the period.
£8,000-10,000 *CNY*

A pair of blue and white dishes, firing crack, Daoguang seal marks and of the period, 7in (18cm).
£2,000-3,000 *C*

A pair of 'famille verte' dishes, the centre of each pencilled in underglaze blue, rim crack, Kangxi, 13in (33cm).
£4,000-5,000 *CNY*

A Ming style saucer dish, Yongzheng mark and of the period, 8in (20cm).
£1,000-1,200 *C*

l. A pair of Chinese 'famille rose' saucer dishes, mid-19thC.
£1,000-1,200 *Wai*

A pair of Arita blue and white dishes, small chip, late 17thC, 12½in (32cm) diam.
£3,500-5,000 *C*

A Kakiemon type dish, in coloured enamels on underglaze blue with a lakeside landscape, late 17thC, 10in (25cm).
£4,000-5,000 *C*

A pair of Kakiemon dishes, decorated in enamels with a bridge scene, footrim chip, late 17thC, 7½in (19cm).
£10,000-12,000 *C*

A pair of Arita blue and white saucer dishes, marks, early 18thC, 6½in (16cm).
£2,500-3,500 *C*

A pair of 'famille verte' dishes, painted with an aquatic scene, early 18thC, 14½in (38cm).
£7,000-9,000 *C*

An Imari dish, decorated in coloured enamels and gilt, Genroku period, 12½in (32.5cm).
£3,000-4,000 *C*

A Kakiemon dish, decorated with the Shiba Onko story, slight damage, c1680.
£8,000-10,000 *C*

A pair of Arita sake ewers modelled as minogame, in iron red enamel and gilt, late 17thC/early 18thC, 7in (18cm) long. **£7,000-10,000** *C*

Two blue and white kendi for sake, l. late Wanli, 8in (20cm), r. rim frits, Chongzhen, 6in (15cm). **£4,000-6,000 each** *C*

A ewer and fixed cover for serving sake, with tall hollow pierced bracket handle, rim frits, mid-17thC, 9½in (24.5cm) high. **£10,000-12,000** *C*

l. A blanc de chine figure of Guanyin, cracks, incised and commendation marks, 18thC, 20in (51cm). **£15,000-18,000** *CNY*
r. A pair of 'famille rose' export candle holders, one cracked, Jiaqing, 16in (41.5cm). **£13,000-15,000** *C*

l. A painted pottery figure of a court lady, with traces of pigment and gilding, Tang Dynasty, 15½in (39.5cm). **£4,500-5,500** *CNY*
above r. A pair of export figures of ladies, their robes embellished with gilt restored, heads later, Qianlong, 11½in (29cm). **£7,000-9,000** *C*

The rear view of a Kakiemon model of a bijin, restored, damaged, c1680, 15½in (39.5cm). **£30,000-50,000** *C*
r. A figure of a matron, restored, Tang Dynasty, 18in (45cm). **£25,000-30,000** *C*

A Sancai guardian figure, both hands and head unglazed traces of black and red pigment, restored, Tang Dynasty, 18in (45cm). **£3,000-5,000** *C*

l. A pair of painted pottery figures of soldiers, traces of pigment, restored, Northern Wei Dynasty, 14in (36cm). **£8,000-10,000** *CNY*
c. A painted pottery figure of a kneeling lady, Han Dynasty, 18in (45.5cm). **£6,000-8,000** *C*
r. A pair of painted grey pottery figures of dancers, traces of white slip and earth encrustation, restored, Northern Qi Dynasty. **£5,000-6,500** *CNY*

A pair of Chinese warthogs, in green monochrome, restoration, c1820, 6½in (16cm) high.
£500-600 *Wai*

r. An Imari model of a cockerel, painted in underglaze blue, iron red, black, green enamel and gilt, restored, Genroku, 10in (26cm).
£8,000-10,000 *Bon*

A Chinese export hound in recumbent position, with iron red decoration, 9½in (24cm) wide.
£2,000-3,000 *Wai*

An amber glazed red pottery figure of a recumbent dog restored, Han Dynasty, 12½in (31.5cm) long.
£5,000-7,000 *CNY*

A painted red pottery figure of a dog, Han Dynasty, 10½in (26.5cm) high. **£4,000-5,500** *CNY*

A green glazed pottery dog, the glaze with shiny iridescent areas, some restoration, Han Dynasty, 13in (33cm) long. **£6,000-8,000** *C*

l. A pair of grey pottery mythical beasts, Six Dynasties, 11in (28.5cm) wide. **£10,000-12,000** *C*

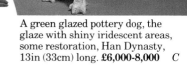

l. A Chinese green glazed cockerel, c1820, 8½in (21cm) high.
£600-800 *Wai*

A pair of 'famille verte' enamelled Buddhistic lions, restored, Kangxi, 17in (43.5cm) high.
£12,000-15,000 *CNY*

r. An Arita model of a seated horse, after a Dutch Delft original, damaged, c1700, 7in (18cm) long.
£8,000-10,000 *C*

. blue and white moon flask, ring cracks, Qianlong six-haracter seal mark, 19½in 19.5cm) high. **£25,000-30,000** *CNY*

A moon flask, painted in iron red with peony blossom and other flowers and leaves, Kangxi, 9in (23cm). **£15,000-18,000** *CNY*

A Sancai pottery flask, the flattened globular body moulded with a dense floral scroll beneath foliate loop handles, the glaze stopping irregularly at the spreading foot, enamel added to unglazed spots, Tang Dynasty, 6in (15.5cm). **£12,000-15,000** *C*

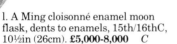

A 'famille rose' jardinière, Yongzheng/early Qianlong, 14½in (37.5cm) wide. **£8,000-10,000** *C*

l. A Ming cloisonné enamel moon flask, dents to enamels, 15th/16thC, 10½in (26cm). **£5,000-8,000** *C*

A doucai jardinière, restored, Qianlong seal mark and of the period, 13in (33cm) diam. **£15,000-18,000** *C*

pair of 'verte' Imari achepots, with lions' asks applied to the des at the shoulder, itting, mid-18thC, n (21cm) diam. **9,000-11,000** *CNY*

A large green glazed pottery lian, restored, Han Dynasty, 12in (31cm) diam. **£6,500-9,000** *CNY*

A blue and white jardinière, with gilt lacquered biscuit lions' masks, chips, Qianlong, 24½in (62cm) diam. **£12,000-15,000** *CNY*

. 'famille rose' jardinière, with ilt lacquered biscuit lions' masks, rack, fritting, Yongzheng/Qianlong, 5½in (64.5cm). **£12,000-15,000** *CNY*

A blue and white jardinière, kiln dhesion polish to one side, 19thC, 4½in (62.5cm) diam. **£5,000-8,000** *C*

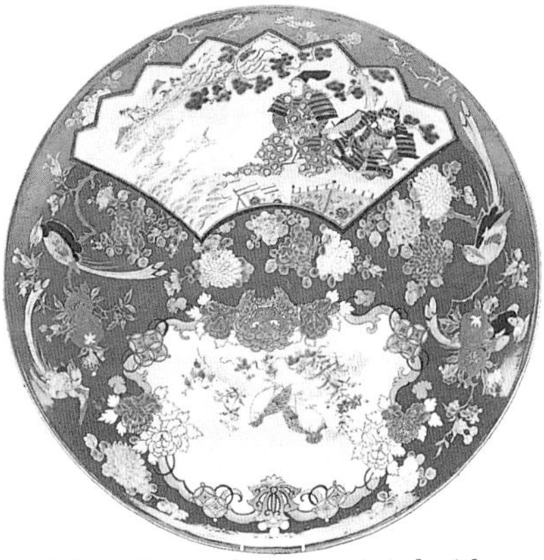

A large Imari charger, painted with a fan shape panel, late 19thC, 24in (62cm). **£1,200-1,500** *Bea*

A set of 5 blue and white serving plates, rim frits, Tianqi/Chongzhen, 6½in (16cm) diam, wood box.
£2,500-3,500 *C*

A set of 5 blue and white serving plates, chips and frits, Tianqi, 6in (15cm) diam, wood box.
£2,000-3,000 *C*

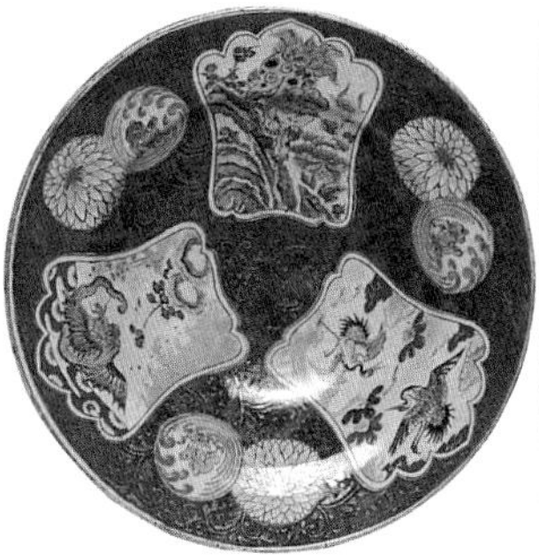

An Imari charger, Genroku period, 21½in (54.5cm).
£7,000-8,000 *C*

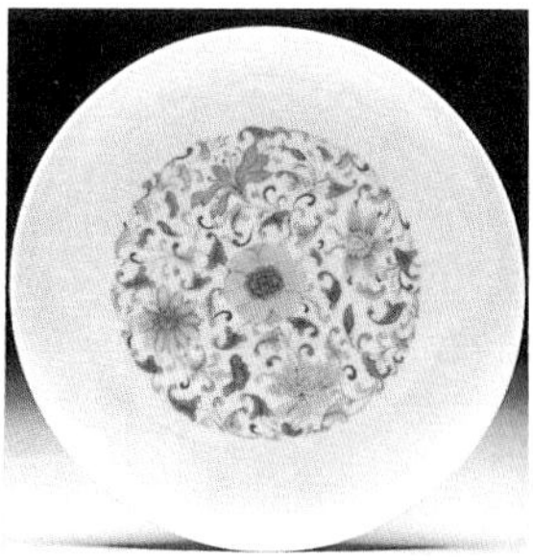

A pair of doucai dishes, enamels rubbed, 18thC, 6in (15cm), wood stands.
£12,000-15,000 *CNY*

A 'famille rose' eggshell deep plate, Yongzheng, 8½in (21cm) diam, box.
£15,000-17,000 *C*

A Ming blue and white cup stand, Wanli mark within a double circle and of the period, 6in (15cm) diam.
£3,500-4,500 *CNY*

A 'famille rose' five-piece garniture, decorated with Buddhist emblems, restoration and chips, iron red Qianlong six-character seal marks, 19thC, the beakers 11in (27cm). **£6,000-8,000** *C*

A 'famille rose' plaque, mid-18thC, 16½in (42cm)
£2,000-2,500 *AG*

r. A 'famille rose' dish, mid-18thC, 15in (38cm).
£2,500-3,000 *AG*

An Imari garniture, decorated in enamels and gilt c
underglaze blue, small cracks, Genroku period, the mounts later, vases 17in (43cm).
£10,000-12,000 *C*

ʌn Imari oviform jar and cover, ·ecorated in enamels and gilt on ınderglaze blue, cover damaged and estored, Genroku, 12in (31cm).
:4,000-5,000 *C*

A pair of Imari jars and covers, each decorated in iron red and black enamels and gilt, restored, late 17th/ early 18thC, 24in (62cm).
£25,000-30,000 *C*

A kettle and cover, after an archaic bronze prototype, rim and spout chips, body crack, Qianlong seal mark and of the period, 9½in (23.5cm) wide. **£6,500-7,500** *C*

A pair of 'famille rose' Mandarin pattern tureens, covers and stands, with animal head handles, covers with pomegranate finials, enamels rubbed, stands fritted, Qianlong, 15½in (39cm) wide.
£15,000-18,000 *C*

ʌ pair of Ko-Imari teapots, ·ecorated in enamels, epaired, late 17thC, ·½in (11.5cm) high.
:5,500-6,500 *C*

r. An Imari oviform vase, decorated in coloured enamels and gilt on underglaze blue, cracked base, c1700, 8½in (21cm). **£1,200-1,800** *C*

A pair of 'famille rose' tureens and stands, with dog finials, fritted, Qianlong, largest stand 16½in (42cm) wide.
£18,000-20,000 *C*

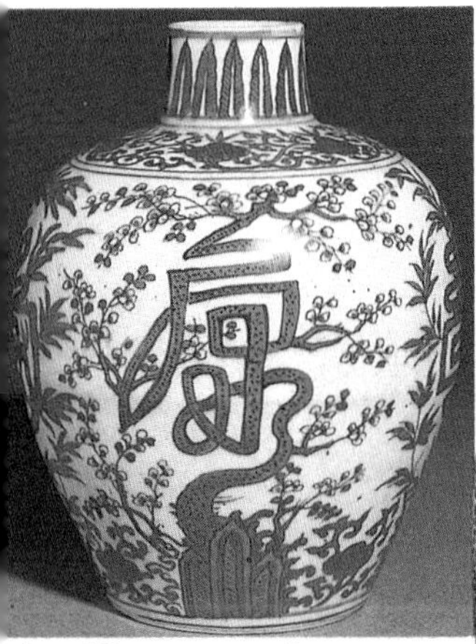

ʌ late Ming vase, cracks ınd frits, Wanli mark and ·f the period, 8in (20cm).
:3,000-5,000 *C*

r. A pair of Canton vases, restored, 19thC, 51½in (130cm). **£10,000-12,000** *C*

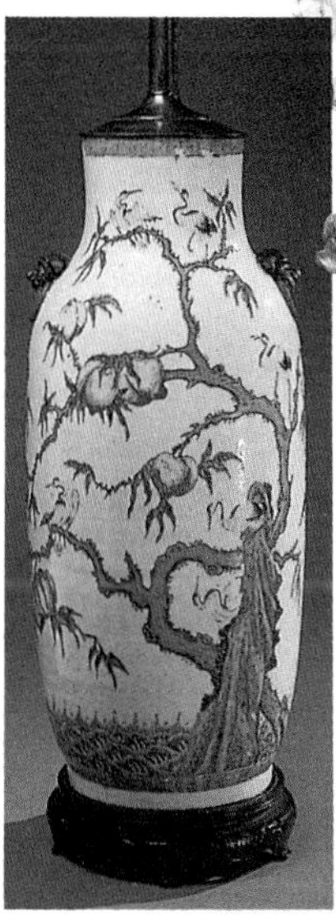

l. A Chinese export 'famille rose' baluster vase, mounted as a lamp, in the Ch'ien Lung style, 21½in (54.5cm) high.
£500-700 *CNY*

A 'famille rose' bottle vase, Qianlong seal mark and of the period, 20½in (52cm) high.
£20,000-25,000 *CNY*

A pair of 'famille rose' export tureens and covers naturalistically painted, one with some restoration, Qianlong, 13in (33cm) high.
£60,000-70,000 *C*

A pair of Satsuma baluster vases, some damage, unsigned, late 19thC.
£7,000-8,000 *C*

A Yabu Meizan vase, gilt rubbed, Meiji period, 9in (22.5cm) high.
£7,500-8,500 *C*

A 'famille verte' rouleau vase, 19thC, 14in (36cm) high.
£600-800 *ART*

An Imari vase, Genroku period, 21½in (54cm) high.
£13,000-15,000 *C*

An important oviform Kakiemon vase, decorated with coloured enamels in 3 panels, one crack, c1680, 15½in (39cm) high. **£250,000+** *C*

Above r. A pair of Canton 'famille rose' barrel-shaped garden seats, 19thC, 18in (45.5cm) diam.
£5,000-6,000 *C*

l. A pair of Canton 'famille rose' vases, the necks with lion handles, one wood stand, 35½in (90cm) high.
£4,500-5,500 *AG*

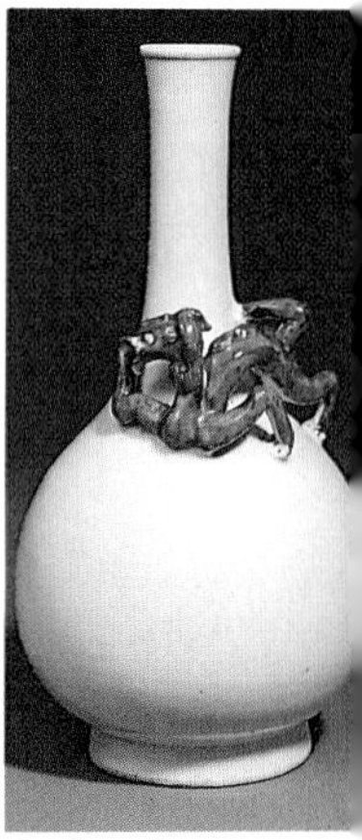

A glazed vase, 'lingzhi' mark, Kangxi, 9½in.
£2,000-3,000 *C*

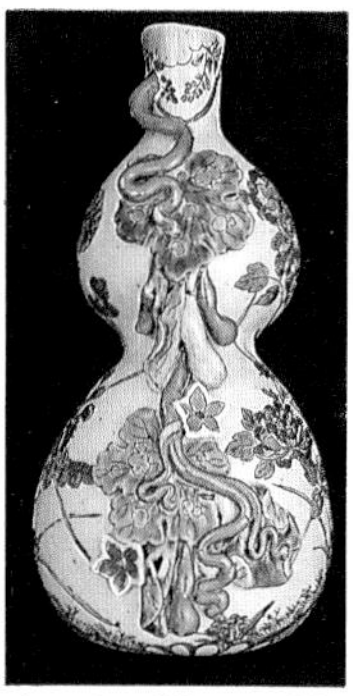

A pair of Imari Hanaike, some restoration, c1700, 8½in (21.5cm) high. **£6,000-7,000** *C*

Above r. A gilt decorated 'famille rose' rotating triple vase, Qianlong seal mark and of the period, some damage, 9in (23cm) wide. **£25,000-35,000** *CNY*

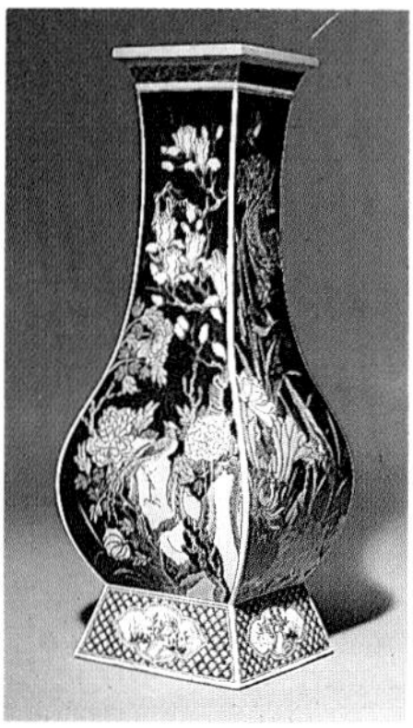

A 'famille noire' vase, base crack, porcelain Kangxi, 20½in (53cm).
£16,000-18,000 *C*

HOLLANDS

wo spirit decanters, c1780.
180-220 each
A wine glass cooler, c1800.
30-100 *Som*
r. A spirit decanter for 'Shrub', c1800. **£200-300** *Som*

SHRUB

B
H
R
S
BRANDY
HOLLANDS
RUM
SHRUB

A set of 4 spirit decanters, with gilt simulated wine labels and gilt lozenge stoppers, c1800, 7½in (18.5cm).
£900-1,200 *Som*

RUM

mallet shaped decanter, ngraved Rum and .F" above, c1800, 8½in 21.5cm). **£350-400** *Som*

An onion shaped carafe, c1830, 7½in (19cm).
£150-200 *Som*

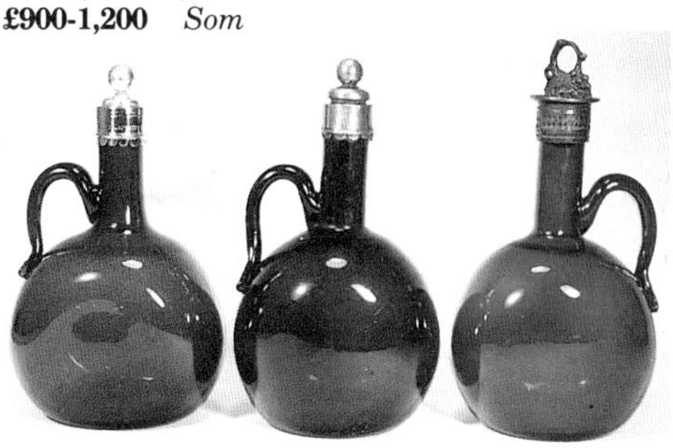

Three spirit flagons, with metal mounts and metal and cork stoppers, c1825, 8in (20cm).
£100-150 each *Som*

heavy engraved carafe, 1830, 8½in (21.5cm).
200-250 *Som*

A pair of broad flute decanters, with star cut bases and hollow cut mushroom stoppers, c1840, 9in (23cm).
£450-500 *Som*

A pair of decanters, with star cut bases and hollow mushroom stoppers, c1840, 9in (23cm).
£350-400 *Som*

Two onion shaped decanters, with cork/metal stoppers, 8in (20cm).
£175-200 each *Som*

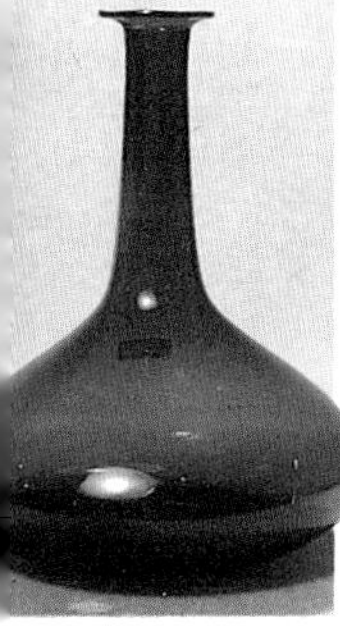

An onion shaped amethyst carafe, 840, 8½in (21cm). **£150-200** *Som*
A pair of engraved carafes, th cork/metal stoppers, c1840, n (23cm). **£350-400** *Som*

A pair of onion shaped blue opaline carafes, c1850, 8in (20.5cm).
£300-350 *Som*

A cut glass chandelier, part 18thC, fitted for electricity, 44in (112cm).
£5,000-6,000 *C*

Purple amethyst bottles with l. plated cork mount, r. loop handled Britannia/cork mount, c1830, 8in (20cm).
£180-220 each *Som*

l. Pair of blue spirit bottles with annulated mouth rims, c1830, 11in (28cm). **£300-350** *Som*

A Central European enamelled glass-blower flask, inscribed Johann Georich Hettne/anno 1767, 6½in (16cm) high
£12,000-13,000 *C*

Two flute cut amber spirit bottles with cut pouring lips and cut spire stoppers, c1840, 9 and 12in (23 and 31cm) high.
£120-150 each *Som*

A pair of blue spirit bottles with turnover rims and cork/metal stoppers, c1830, 12in (30cm).
£350-400 *Som*

Spirit bottles, amber wrythen with cork/metal stopper, plain amethyst with similar stopper, blue with plain lozenge stoppers, c1850, tallest 12in (30cm).
£150-250 each *Som*

A shell shaped satin glass dish, decorated with flowers, gilded branches and leaves in a silver plated figural stand, two reindeer pulling shell, 13½in (34cm) long.
£650-750 *JL*

RUM
BRANDY

A set of 3 Bristol blue decanters, c1790, 8in (20cm). **£1,200-1,500** *Som*

A cylindrical bowl on solid glass round foot, deeply engraved with design of fish amidst seaweed, engraved signature Keith Murray S & W Brierley, 6in (15cm).
£2,500-3,000 *C*
r. A Monart footed bowl, with blue and purple stripes and bubbles, damaged. **£90-100** If perfect **£400-500** *FA*

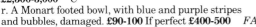

A Webb cameo glass bride's bowl, on metal stand, marked, 10in (25cm). **£800-1,000** *JL*

A blue bonnet glass, c1780, 3in (7cm). **£150-200** *Som*

l. A pair of green wines, with cup bowls, hollow knopped stems, c1850, 4½in (11.5cm). **£50-75** r. A set of 8 green wines, c1825, 5in (13cm). **£450-500** *Som*

ı emerald green wine glass, the ovoid body on a hexagon t facet stem, with plain conical foot, c1780, 5½in 3.5cm). **£500-550** *Som*

A wrythen moulded sugar basin and cream jug, c1800, bowl 3½in (8.5cm). **£120-150 each** *Som*

l. A set of 6 dimple moulded wine glasses, c1860, 5in (12cm). **£200-250** *Som*

A Nailsea bottle glass wine jug and carafe, with white marvered inclusions, c1810, jug 5½in (14cm). **£200-250** carafe **£150-200** *Som*

l. A black glass linen smoother, c1860. **£150-200** r. A Nailsea cream jug, c1810, 4½in (11cm). **£250-300** *Som*

& r. Clear glass scent bottles with silver/silver gilt ounts, c1850. **£150-200 each** A cut scent bottle, c1850, 4in (10cm). **£80-100** *Som*

Scent bottles, c1870, l. silver mount. **£80-100** c. Silver gilt and gilt brass holder. **£300-400** r. Diamond cutting. **£60-80** *Som*

ıree scent bottles, l. **£150-200** & r. With silver gilt mounts. **:50-300 each** *Som*

Three scent bottles with gilt brass or silver gilt mounts, c1870. l. **£75-100** c. & r. **£300-350 each** *Som*

A Louis XV gilt bronze, iron and rock crystal six-light chandelier, fitted for electricity, 38in (96.5cm) high.
£15,000-20,000 *C*

Three scent bottles, mid-19thC, l. with gilt metal mou
£120-150, c. with prism and star cut moulding **£250-3**
r. Bohemian with gold mount. **£250-300** *Som*

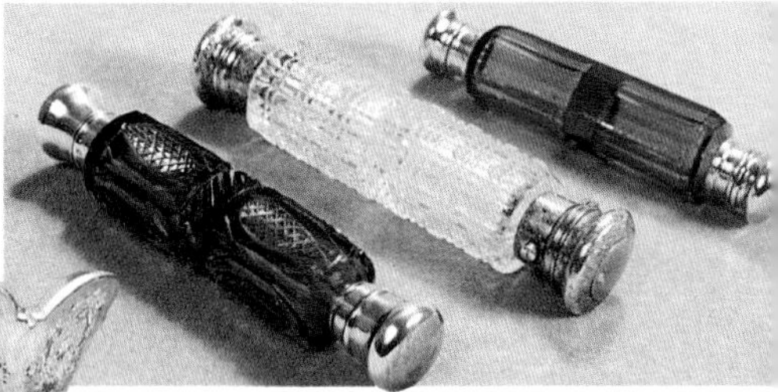

Three double-ended scent bottles, with hallmark
silver, silver gilt and gilt metal mounts, late 19th
5 to 6in (13 to 15cm). **£100-150 each** *Som*

l. A Bohemian vaseline glass vase, painted in enamel colours and gold, 19in (49cm) high.
£3,500-4,500 *Bea*

r. A blue glass pipe, c1860, 18½in (47cm).
£150-200 *Som*

A cut glass scent bottle, with silver and enamel top, Birmingham 1930, 6in (15cm) high.
£200-250 *PCh*

A pair of ormolu mounted cut glass vases, on bronze plinths mounted with military trophies, inscribed Napoleon, 25½in (65cm) high.
£14,000-16,000 *C*

An enamelled Kurfursten Humpen, perhaps Bohemia, c1600, 11in (27.5cm).
£8,000-10,000 *C*

AESCHYLVS

A set of 3 stained glass panels, entitled Sophocles, Aeschylus an
Homer, some damage, 19thC, 79
(200cm) high. **£4,000-5,000** *C*

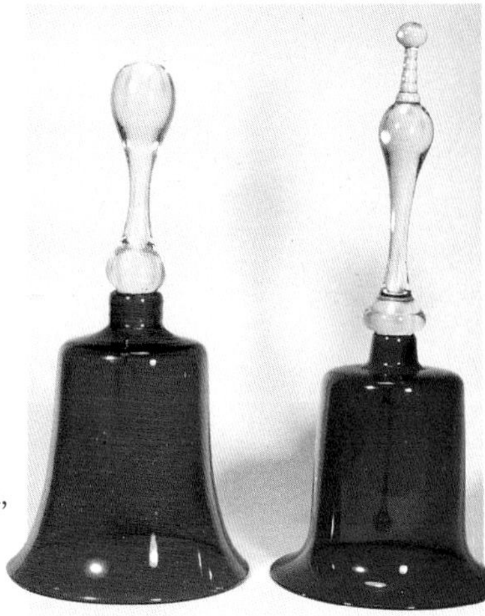

l. Two small bells with clear handles, c1860. **£120-150 each** *Som*

POMADE SYLPHIDES
Infallible cure for removing
Dandriff and all eruptions of the Skin
DIRECTIONS FOR USE
DIVIDE THE HAIR INTO PARTS APPLY THE
POMADE TO THE SKIN OF THE
HEAD AND BRUSH WELL AFTERWARDS
PREPARED ONLY AT THE
ARMY & NAVY TOILET CLUB
35. BUCKLERSBURY. E.C.

omade Sylphides, blue print, late
9thC.
50-75 *K*

ALMOND
SHAVING CREAM
ARMY & NAVY COOPERATIVE SOCIETY
LIMITED

Almond Shaving Cream, sepia
print, c1900.
£40-60 *K*

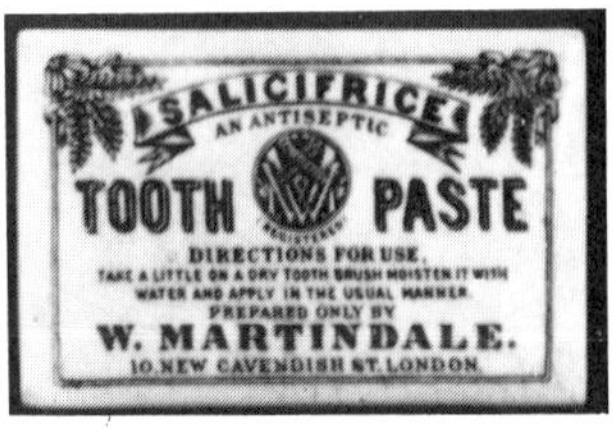
SALICIFRICE
AN ANTISEPTIC
TOOTH PASTE
DIRECTIONS FOR USE.
W. MARTINDALE.
10 NEW CAVENDISH ST. LONDON

W. Martindale Tooth Paste, black
print, 19thC.
£60-80 *K*

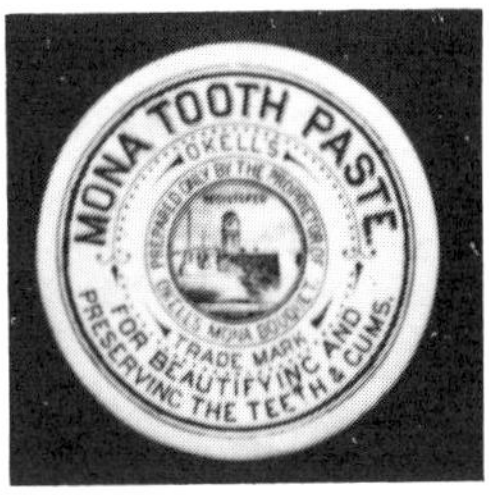
MONA TOOTH PASTE
OKELL'S
TRADE MARK
FOR BEAUTIFYING AND
PRESERVING THE TEETH & GUMS

Mona Tooth Paste,
black print,
c1890.
£80-100 *K*

JAMES ATKINSON'S BEARS GREASE
24 OLD BOND STREET
LONDON
Price 5s

ames Atkinson's Bears Grease,
lack print, c1890.
50-75 *K*

CIVIL SERVICE
ROSE
LIP SALVE
H. NEST
COOPERATIVE SOCIETY

Civil Service Rose Lip Salve, pink
print, late 19thC.
£40-60 *K*

THYMOL
TOOTH PASTE
for cleansing & preserving
THE
TEETH & GUMS

Thymol Tooth Paste,
black print,
c1880.
£20-30 *K*

Services

A Samuel Alcock tea service, decorated with leaves, scrolls and flowerheads on a pink ground, pattern No. 114, comprising 25 pieces, c1840.
£500-550 *WW*

A Victorian Keeling & Co. dinner service, in the Stirling pattern, comprising: soup tureen with cover, ladle and stand, 2 vegetable tureens with covers, 2 sauce tureens with covers and ladles, 2 open tureens, 4 graduated meat plates, 12 soup bowls, 35 plates and one sauceboat.
£450-550 *DDM*

A Davenport stone china part dinner service, painted in pink, iron red and lavender blue, comprising: a meat dish, 2 serving dishes, 2 vegetable dishes and covers, 5 soup plates, 16 dinner plates, 16 dessert plates, some damage, printed Davenport Longport Staffordshire marks within a garter and pattern No. 79, c1845.
£3,000-4,000 *C*

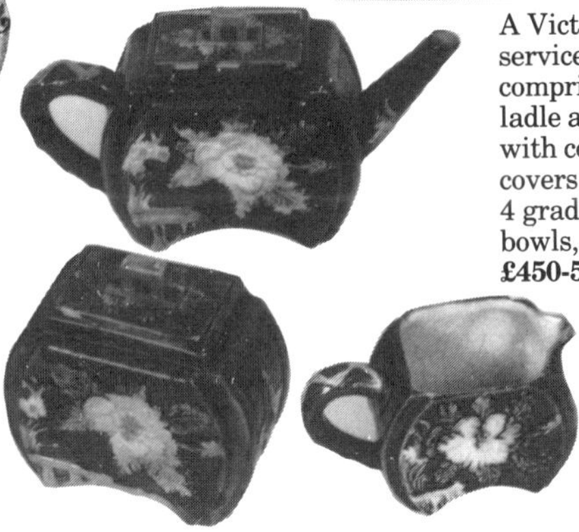

A majolica tea set, c1875, teapot 5in (12.5cm).
£200-250 *HOW*

A Mason's Ironstone complete dinner service, c1835.
£7,000-8,000 *VH*

A Sampson Hancock & Sons dinner service, in the Norman pattern, comprising: 4 tureens and covers, ladles and stands, a graduated set of 6 meat plates and 36 plates in 3 sizes, late 19thC.
£300-400 *DDM*

A Mason's Ironstone part dinner service, decorated in an Imari palette in blue, white, green and red, comprising: 13 soup bowls, 46 plates, 2 serving dishes, covers and stands, one soup tureen, cover and stand, 7 serving platters, 3 sauce tureens, covers and stands, and one separate stand, 19thC.
£3,500-4,500 *Bon*

A Spode pearlware part dessert service, printed in blue and coloured with a bird perched on flowering peony on a green printed cracked ice pattern ground, comprising 2 baskets and stands, a sauce tureen, cover, stand and ladle, 5 dishes and 12 plates, impressed and printed marks and pattern No. 3716, some damage, c1820.
£2,000-3,000 *C*

A Wedgwood pearlware blue and white part dinner service, transfer printed with The Blue Palisade Pattern, comprising 3 tureens and covers and a Spode ladle, 2 sauce ladles, 2 sauceboats, 2 vegetable dishes and covers, 9 serving dishes and 36 plates, impressed marks and various potter's marks, c1815.
£3,000-4,000 *C*

A creamware crested part dessert service, each piece painted in iron red with a crest, comprising: 2 sauce tureens, covers and fixed stands, 2 plain ladles, 2 shallow dishes and 12 square plates, perhaps Wedgwood, some damage and staining, c1800.
£1,500-2,000 *C*

Did you know
MILLER'S Antiques Price Guide builds up year by year to form the most comprehensive photo-reference system available

A Mason's patent ironstone china part dinner service, printed and decorated in the Imari style in iro red, blues, green and buff, comprising: 10 dishes, with covers and stands, some damage, and 36 plates, repaired and damaged, printed marks, pattern No. 1765, c1850.
£1,500-2,000 *C*

Tea Caddies

A Staffordshire tea canister, c1770, 4½in (11cm).
£550-650 *JHo*

A Staffordshire creamware cylindrical tea caddy, painted in colours, slight wear, 4in (10cm).
£50-100 *CSK*

An English tinglazed tea canister, c1780, 4in (10cm).
£600-700 *JHo*

Tea & Coffee Pots

A Brownfield earthenware novelty teapot in the form of a Chinaman, decorated in majolica type glazes, some damage, impressed registration mark.
£450-500 *HSS*

A chinoiserie pattern teapot, by William Greatbatch, c1755, 6in (15cm).
£900-1,200 *BHA*

A Staffordshire teapot and cover, splashed in manganese, green and yellow glazes, slight wear and chips, c1765, 7½in (18cm).
£500-700 *CSK*

A cauliflower teapot, by William Greatbatch, c1775, 6in (15cm).
£2,000-2,500 *JHo*

A Jackfield teapot, c1770, 5½in (14cm).
£350-450 *Sto*

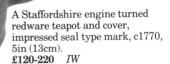

A Wedgwood type cauliflower moulded teapot and cover, the lower part covered in a bright green glaze, c1760, 11in (28cm) wide.
£1,200-1,700 *CSK*

A Staffordshire engine turned redware teapot and cover, impressed seal type mark, c1770, 5in (13cm).
£120-220 *IW*

A Staffordshire teapot, c1765, 5in (13cm).
£2,700-3,000 *JHo*

A Whieldon teapot and cover, with crabstock handle and spout, in mottled green and yellow glaze, spout and cover restored, 3½in (8cm).
£200-250 *CSK*

A Staffordshire saltglazed lobed teapot and cover, on 3 feet, some damage, late 18thC, 6in (15cm).
£2,000-2,500 *Bea*

A Whieldon type coffee pot, c1765, 7½in (19cm).
£3,000-3,500 *JHo*

A coffee pot and cover, decorated with a view of a Continental town enclosed by a mountainous landscape, cover cracked, minor restoration to spout, 10½in (26cm).
£100-150 *Bon*

A Quimper tea service, marked, c1930, teapot 7½in (19cm) high.
£250-300 *VH*

A pearlware teapot, c1800, 7in (18cm).
£250-300 *BHA*

A Quimper coffee pot, 8in (20cm).
£65-85 *AI*

An enamelled saltglazed coffee pot, c1765, 8½in (21cm).
£3,000-3,500 *JHo*

A Staffordshire teapot and cover, printed in black with bust portraits of Queen Caroline and inscribed 'Long Live Queen Caroline', some staining, c1820, 9½in (24cm).
£250-300 *CSK*

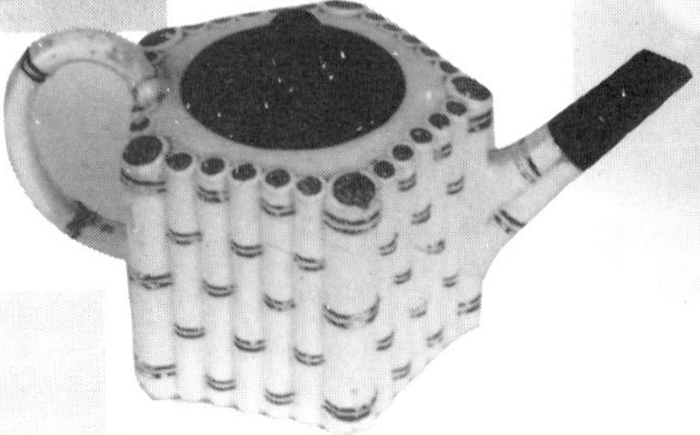

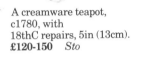

A creamware teapot, c1780, with 18thC repairs, 5in (13cm).
£120-150 *Sto*

A Yorkshire creamware coffee pot, c1775, 9½in (24cm).
£3,500-4,000 *JHo*

A pearlware teapot and cover, small chips, c1800, 7½in (19cm).
£200-250 *CSK*

A coffee pot and cover, printed with a scene of Gothic style ruins in an extensive landscape, spout damaged, cover cracked, 9½in (24cm).
£100-150 *Bon*

Tiles

A Bristol tile, restored, c1760.
£90-100 *Sto*
In perfect condition – £180-220

A Liverpool tile, restored, c1750.
£50-60 *Sto*

A Liverpool biblical tile, c1750.
£40-50 *Sto*

A Bristol polychrome tile, c1765.
£250-300 *JHo*

A Liverpool wood block printed tile, c1757.
£300-350 *JHo*

A Liverpool tile, damaged, c1760.
£45-55 *Sto*

A Liverpool tile, damaged, c1760.
£25-35 *Sto*

A Liverpool transfer printed tile, c1765.
£180-200 *JHo*

A Liverpool transfer printed tile, c1765.
£160-180 *JHo*

A Liverpool tile, c1770.
£100-150 *JHo*

A Liverpool polychrome tile, c1770.
£150-200 *JHo*

A Liverpool tile, c1770.
£50-100 *JHo*

A Liverpool tile, c1770, 5in (12.5cm) square.
£60-70 *Sto*

A Liverpool black transfer printed tile, John Sadler, c1770, 5in (12.5cm) square.
£120-150 *Sto*

A London tile, with manganese decoration, c1755.
£60-80 *Sto*

A Liverpool polychrome tile.
£150-180 *JHo*

A London biblical tile, c1720.
£45-55 *Sto*

A London tile, c1745.
£50-100 *JHo*

A London tile, damaged, c1740.
£30-40 *Sto*

A rare London tile, c1760.
£120-150 *JHo*

A London tile, c1775.
£40-60 *JHo*

A rare tile, possibly London.
£140-160 *JHo*

A London or Bristol tile.
£75-100 *JHo*

A Minton Shakespeare tile, 'Much Ado About Nothing', 6in (15cm) square.
£20-25 *Sto*

An English floor tile, 15thC, 4in (10cm) square.
£100-150 *Sto*
From a house in Chester.

A set of 10 Poole pottery nursery tiles, designed by Dora Batty, comprising: 8 tiles depicting characters from nursery rhymes and 2 spacer tiles, painted in colours on a crackled cream ground, damaged, each 5in (12.5cm) square.
£350-400 *CSK*

A set of 6 Austrian terracotta hand painted and tin glazed blue and white tiles, Linz, c1800, 5in (12.5cm) square.
£500-600 *UC*

A tin glazed flower tile, probably Flemish, 16thC.
£150-200 *JHo*

Locate the source

The source of each illustration in Miller's can be found by checking the code letters below each caption with the list of contributors

A Low Countries fireplace tile, with stylised sun, 17thC, 6½ by 5in (16 by 12.5cm).
£350-400 *IW*

A Dutch or German fireplace tile, a hound in relief, 16th/17thC, 5 by 3½in (12.5 by 8.5cm).
£350-400 *IW*

A Spanish floor tile, 16thC, 10in (25.5cm) square.
£30-40 *Sto*

A Low Countries relief fireplace tile, dated 1606, 6 by 4in (15 by 10cm).
£350-400 *IW*

Tureens

A Leeds creamware sauce tureen and cover, in the form of an oval melon, with branch handle, c1785, 9in (23cm) wide.
£1,000-1,500 *WW*

A tureen decorated with a dromedary pattern on a stippled ground, on rounded foot rim, 8½in (21cm).
£250-300 *Bon*

A Quimper tureen, 9½in (24cm).
£100-120 *AI*

A Minton basket weave pattern game pie dish, the cover with dead game in relief, with rustic pattern handle, impressed Minton, 13in (33cm) wide.
£600-1,000 *AG*

A Spode stone china tureen and cover, printed and painted with flowers in panel in Chinese style, 13½in (35cm) wide.
£200-250 *ALL*

A Continental faience quatrefoil tureen and cover, with pink and yellow scroll handles and naturalistic turkey's head finial, with an all over pattern of trellis with pink flowerheads and yellow fleur-de-lys, cracks restored, perhaps Buen Retiro, c1800, 17½in (44.5cm) wide.
£5,000-6,000 *C*

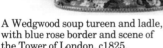

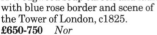

A Wedgwood soup tureen and ladle, with blue rose border and scene of the Tower of London, c1825.
£650-750 *Nor*

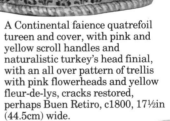

A Quimper tureen and cover with yellow background, 5½in (14cm).
£45-55 *VH*

An English yellow ground tureen and cover, with black printed children's scenes, early 19thC, 8in (20cm) diam.
£250-350 *P(S)*

A Milan (Clerici) maiolica partridge tureen and cover, the bird seated on a basket painted in colours, the plumage manganese, the wings black with yellow flashes, the breast iron red, cover repaired, 3 flanges missing, c1750, 6½in (17cm) wide.
£4,000-5,000 *C*

Vases

A Derbyshire stoneware vase, late 18thC, 9½in (24cm).
£350-400 *JHo*

A Wedgwood black basalt vase, with impressed marks, 10in (25cm).
£300-400 *CSK*

A Wedgwood baluster vase and cover, in white and gilt on a dark blue ground, cover cracked, gilding worn, impressed marks, 10½in (26cm).
£100-150 *CSK*

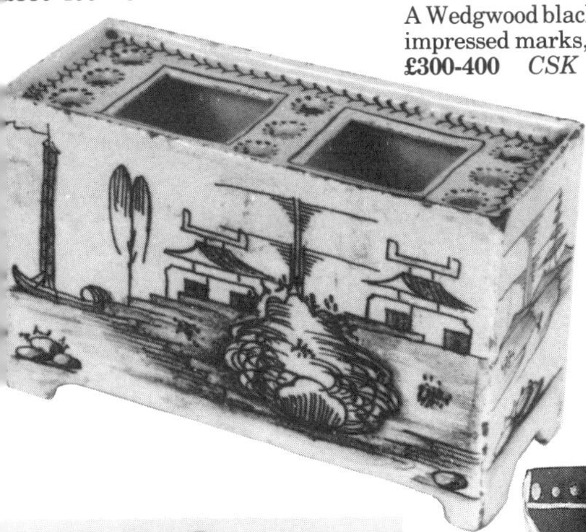

A Liverpool flower brick, decorated in manganese, c1760, 3½in (9cm).
£600-700 *JHo*

A Wedgwood & Bentley creamware two-handled vase and cover, applied with an oval medallion of the Three Graces, the handles moulded with leaves and female mask terminals, the foot with a circular laurel wreath, all with traces of gilding, plinth and cover chipped, c1770, 9in (23cm) high.
£900-1,200 *C*

A pair of Minton pot pourri vases, c1872, 15in (38cm).
£700-800 *BHA*

A Wedgwood black and white jasper vase, one rim ground, impressed mark Wedgwood, late 18thC, 10½in (26cm).
£500-600 *Bon*

A garniture of 3 Mason's vases, c1815, 4 to 5in (10 to 12.5cm).
£280-300 *VH*

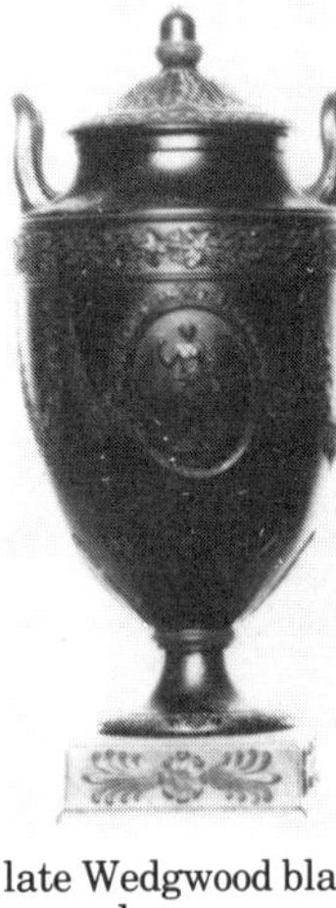

A pair of late Wedgwood black basalt vases and covers, one cover repaired, impressed marks, 11½in (29cm).
£350-450 *CSK*

An English blue ground majolica vase, c1860, 13in (33cm).
£400-500 *CSK*

A Quimper vase, handle repaired, c1920, 11in (28cm).
£170-200 *VH*

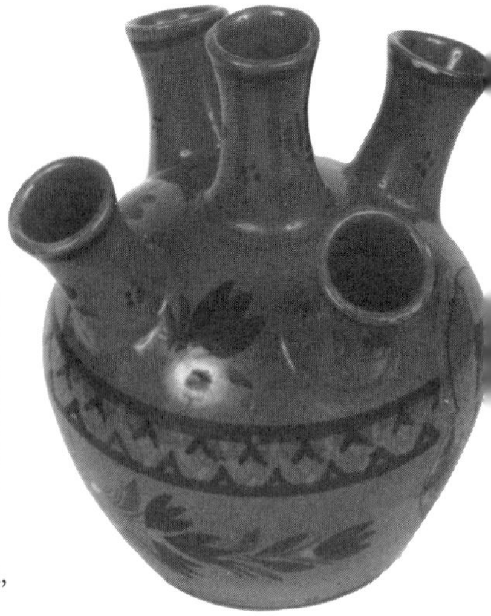

A Quimper tulip vase, c1930, 5½in (14cm).
£75-100 *VH*

A South Wales type clock vase in copper lustre, c1825, 7½in (19cm).
£175-200 *HOW*

A Mason's vase and cover, with Peacock pattern, c1830, 18in (46cm).
£750-850 *VH*

A Staffordshire castle spill vase, with 2 towers and outlined in coloured flowers, 5in (13cm).
£100-150 *CSK*

A sparsely coloured spill vase, c1860, 11in (28cm).
£200-250 *Bon*

A Staffordshire spill vase group, modelled as a boy seated and a girl standing, flanking a cauldron, 8in (20cm).
£50-100 *CSK*

A Worcester polychrome spill vase, toes restored, c1870, 5½in (14cm).
£250-300 *CA*

A pair of Portobello spill vases, with yellow birds on branches, c1770, 5½in (14cm).
£1,750-2,000 *BHA*

Wemyss

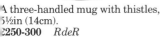

A three-handled mug with thistles, 5½in (14cm).
£250-300 *RdeR*

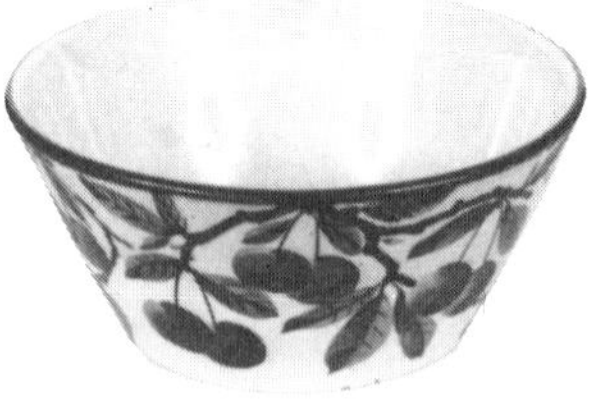

A fruit bowl decorated with cherries, 4in (10cm).
£100-150 *RdeR*

A Wemyss pottery tankard, decorated with peacock in rushes, 5½in (14cm).
£1,000-1,500 *AH*

A Wemyss basket, 12in (31cm) long.
£600-750 *RdeR*

A Wemyss loving cup with tulips, 7½in (19cm).
£500-600 *RdeR*

a little wealth
with freedom
a little friend
to need him

A Wemyss sampler tankard, 5½in (14cm).
£750-1,000 *RdeR*

A Wemyss three-handled loving cup, painted with wild roses, the handles, rim and foot edged in green, damaged and repaired, impressed mark, 9½in (24cm).
£500-700 *Bon*

Save yer braith tae cuil yer parritch.

A Wemyss porridge bowl, 6in (15cm) diam.
£300-350 *RdeR*

A bowl with violets, 3in (8cm).
£200-250 *RdeR*

A Wemyss tankard decorated with black fowl on green base, with green band decoration and ribbed loop handle, impressed mark, 5½in (14cm).
£450-500 *AH*

A Wemyss Gordon plate with Victoria plum design, 8in (20cm).
£100-150 *RdeR*

Gordon plates all have indented rims and are often sold for use as dessert plates.

A Wemyss Gordon plate, with blackcurrants, 8in (20cm).
£150-200 *RdeR*

A Wemyss pig with clover decoration, Scottish impressed mark, 7in (18cm) long.
£350-500 *RdeR*

A Wemyss Gordon plate with buttercup design, 8in (20cm).
£250-300 *RdeR*

A Wemyss Gordon plate with bramble design, 8in (20cm).
£150-200 *RdeR*

A pig with clover decoration, painted by Joseph Nekola, Bovey Tracey, 19in (48cm) long.
£2,000-3,000 *RdeR*

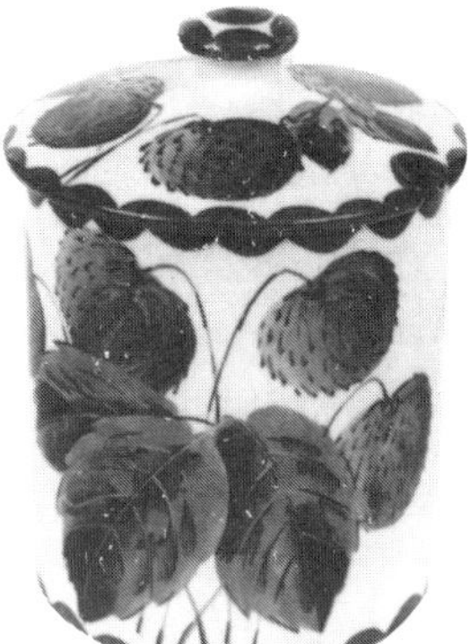

A preserve pot decorated with strawberries, 5in (13cm).
£75-100 *RdeR*

A Wemyss Gordon plate, with a honeysuckle design, 8in (20cm).
£250-350 *RdeR*

A Wemyss marmalade cat, Bovey Tracey, c1935, 13in (33cm).
£2,000-3,000 *RdeR*

A Wemyss early morning teaset.
£400-500 *RdeR*

A jam pot with dish, impressed Wemyss, 7½in (18cm).
£300-500 *RdeR*

A Wemyss Gordon plate, with a beehive, 8in (20cm).
£200-250 *RdeR*

A miniature gypsy pot, 1¼in (3cm).
£250-300 *RdeR*

An apprentice piece or travellers sample.

Locate the source

The source of each illustration in Miller's can be found by checking the code letters below each caption with the list of contributors

A Japan vase, painted with heather, 8in (21cm).
£400-600 *RdeR*

A Wemyss Gordon plate, with rare poppy design, 8in (20cm).
£200-300 *RdeR*

A Wemyss comb tray with plums, 9½ by 8in (24 by 20cm).
£100-150 *RdeR*

A small Stuart pot, 5in (13cm).
£400-500 *RdeR*

A bulb trough, decorated with apples, 11in (28cm) wide.
£600-1,000 *RdeR*

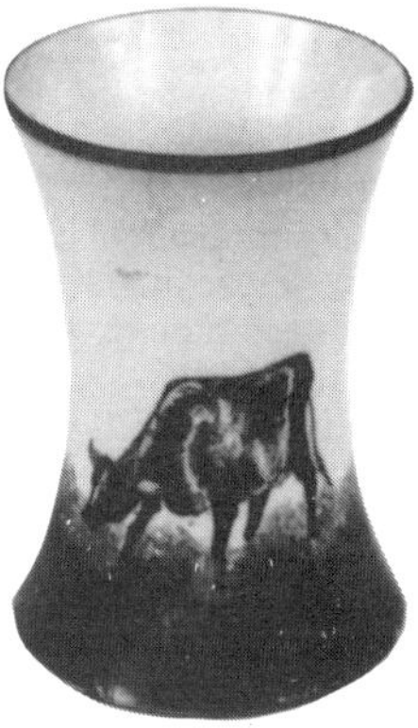

A brush vase with cow, 4½in (11cm).
£200-300 *RdeR*

A Wemyss preserve pot with moulded fruit, 3in (7cm).
£200-250 *RdeR*

No Rose without a thorn.

A Wemyss plaque, 5in (13cm) wide.
£100-150 *RdeR*

A Lady Eva vase, 11½in (29cm).
£300-400 *RdeR*

ENGLISH DELFTWARE

The use of the term delftware as a description of tin glazed English earthenware was adopted as an everyday term in the early part of the 18thC. Before this the standard terminology was gallyware or white earthenware.

Delftware is buff coloured earthenware coated with a wash of tin oxide and glazed with a lead glaze containing a proportion of tin oxide. Before this application the earthenware is fired so that the glaze application soaks into the body evenly. The ware is then fired for a second time.

Firing temperature is about 1000°-1050°C. Wares were rested on supports during the second firing and these left blemishes in the glaze.

Decoration is executed in colours made from mineral oxides finely ground and mixed with the basic glaze. The basic early colours were:–
Cobalt oxide — blue
Manganese oxide — purple
Iron oxide — brick red
Antimony — yellow
Copper oxide — green
Tin oxide — white
A combination of copper, manganese and cobalt oxides produced black.

Production of English delftware commenced in the 1560s when Flemish potters started work in Norwich. The Yarmouth clay was ideally suited to earthenware manufacture and there are records of its export to Rotterdam in 1597.

The first London delftware potteries were established at Aldgate by the Flemish potters who had worked in Norfolk. Clay was sent from Norfolk to London and mixed with local clays to improve its strength.

At least 19 separate delftware potteries were established in London, mainly along the banks of the Thames, between 1571 and 1757. Potteries were also established in other parts of Britain from 1640 and, of course, in America during the mid-17thC.

Production generally declined in the period 1760-1800 due to the introduction of improved pottery bodies which were both cheaper and more durable than delft.

The products of the English delftware manufacturers are very similar and not easily differentiated. Early London wares are very rare, are similar in form and decoration to wares of the same period from the Netherlands and both are difficult to tell from similar Italian wares. Amongst known pieces are small jugs, vases, dishes and apothecaries' pots. Main colours tend to be blue, ochre and green and designs feature geometric patterns, foliage, birds and animals.

In the early 17thC the first Chinese porcelains reached England and these had an almost immediate influence on styles of decoration. Although decoration tended to follow prevailing Chinese and European fashions, native forms of decoration did develop from the mid-17thC. Bottles coated with a creamy white glaze were simply decorated with the name of their contents in blue, and colourful large chargers decorated with pictures of the reigning monarch, national heroes, Adam and Eve, tulips or geometrical patterns seem to have been very popular. They are certainly eagerly collected today even when damaged.

A London delft blue and white dated armorial mug, with loop handle, painted with the arms of The Worshipful Company of Butchers, flanked by the initials I^{W}M and the date 1684, on a spreading circular foot, crack round base and rim repaired, foot chipped, minor glaze flaking, 1684, 5½in (13.5cm).
£7,000-9,000 *C*

Bristol wares can often be identified through the frequent use of sponged decoration. The palette of Liverpool polychrome wares has a distinctive lemon yellow, which is used in combination with orange, sage green, pale manganese, French blue and black. This palette is often termed the 'Fazackley' palette after a pair of mugs bearing an inscription in that name. However, a similar palette was in use at Bristol and it is often difficult to ascribe pieces to specific areas of production.

Ship bowls decorated with ships in sail and inscriptions were specialities at Bristol and, in particular, Liverpool which was also responsible for char dishes (for fish). Pill slabs painted with the arms of the Apothecaries Company, flower bricks, inkwells, double lipped sauceboats, wall pockets, posset pots and caudle cups are all essentially English shapes.

Delftware is such a soft material that damage is almost inevitable. Since the rise in value of English delft more and more damaged pieces are being restored. These restorations are very difficult to detect but they do affect value considerably so take care to study bargains very carefully.

The Market for English delft
The market remains strong though more predictable than in the past couple of years. Rare pieces can still exceed expectation but sales have been less volatile and prices exceeding double the top auction estimate are rare.

The market is particularly strong for early wares. If you have a few 17thC chargers hidden about your person it is still a good time to sell!

A Dutch Delft basket and cover, with a dog of Fo finial, hairline cracks, marked with 5, late 17thC, 9in (22cm).
£6,000-7,000 *CAm*

A pair of Delft butter dishes and covers, painted in 'petit feu' colours in the Kakiemon style, the covers with dog of Fo finials, dashed in pink, minor chips, one cover marked 3 in overglaze red, the other marked 4, early 18thC, 5in (13cm) wide.
£2,500-3,500 *CAm*

URY, HER MUG
THERE AT TO TUG
RE SHE PLEASE
N BREAD AND CHEE
SE IS EAT AND SPE
EXCELENT

A London delftware tankard, c1790, 6in (15cm).
£2,500-3,000 *JHo*

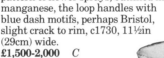

A delft blue and white broth bowl and cover, painted with an all-over pattern of flower sprays, outlined in manganese, the loop handles with blue dash motifs, perhaps Bristol, slight crack to rim, c1730, 11½in (29cm) wide.
£1,500-2,000 *C*

A delft blue and white bottle, Liverpool or London, rim chip, c1760, 9in (23cm).
£450-600 *C*

A Bristol delft blue and white bowl, repaired and restored, c1740, 12in (31cm) diam.
£2,000-3,000 *C*

A Liverpool delft blue and white tea caddy, the sides painted with classical figures by a stream, in an extensive mountainous wooded landscape with goats and hounds, between hatch-pattern borders, slight rim chips, c1760, 6in (15cm).
£3,500-4,000 *C*

An English delft blue and white bowl, Bristol or London, rim and foot chipped, c1725, 14in (35cm).
£1,700-2,500 *C*

A Dutch Delft cabbage leaf bowl, naturalistically moulded in relief, the exterior as a yellow veined green cabbage with shaped overlapping leaves, the interior with a chinoiserie scene, hairline crack, c1770, 10½in (26.5cm).
£2,000-2,500 *CAm*

A Dutch Delft tea caddy and stopper, decorated in the Persian style, chips to edges, marked 3 above AL and 5 for De Grieksche A, late 17thC, 11in (28cm).
£6,000-7,000 *CAm*

A Dutch Delft figural fountain jug, hat restored and chipped, marked PVDB above 6 for Pieter van der Briel, 't Fortuyn, 1747, 14in (35cm).
£5,000-5,500 *CAm*

A Dutch Delft sweetmeat dish, minor chips, marked GVS for Geertruy Verstelle, c1760, 5½in (14cm).
£2,000-3,000 *CAm*

A Dutch Delft sweetmeat dish, naturalistically modelled in relief as a male figure in period costume after German porcelain examples, minor repair and chips, marked GVS for Geertruy Verstelle, c1760, 5in (13cm).
£2,000-3,000 *CAm*

A Dutch Delft figure of a young gentleman, possibly a pilgrim, painted in colours, carrying a child on his back, head of child repaired, c1780, 7½in (19cm).
£700-1,000 *CAm*

An English delft tulip charger, repaired, c1680, 13½in (34cm).
£800-950 *Sto*

A pair of Dutch Delft mixed technique figural butter dishes and covers, modelled in relief after Meissen porcelain examples, damaged, marked for de drie astonnekens, c1750, 5½in (14.5cm).
£8,000-9,000 *CAm*

A Dutch Delft figure of a young woman, possibly a pilgrim, painted in colours, c1780, 7in (18cm).
£700-1,000 *CAm*

An English delft blue dash Adam and Eve charger, outlined in manganese, a green boughed tree with striped yellow fruit, with blue dash rim, Brislington or Bristol, cracked and repaired, c1680, 13in (33cm).
£1,500-2,000 *C*

A Dutch Delft figure of a putto, emblematic of Summer, painted in blue, yellow and iron red, head re-stuck, chips to ears of corn, c1750, 16in (40cm). **£900-1,200** *C*

A London delft pomegranate charger, the 3 fruits flanked by grey-green foliage edged in blue and divided by stylised blue flowerheads and foliage, within a green line rim, rim cracked, c1680, 13in (33cm).
£5,000-6,000 *C*

ₙn English delft blue dash tulip harger, the centre painted with a lue and yellow tulip and 2 buds, ʼithin a border of yellow and green eaves, with blue dash rim, probably ondon, crack repaired, c1680, 14in 35cm).
800-1,000 *C*

. London delft plate, painted in ıanganese and blue stylised vine ʼithin a border of pendant foliage, hips to rim, c1680, 8in (20cm).
600-800 *C*

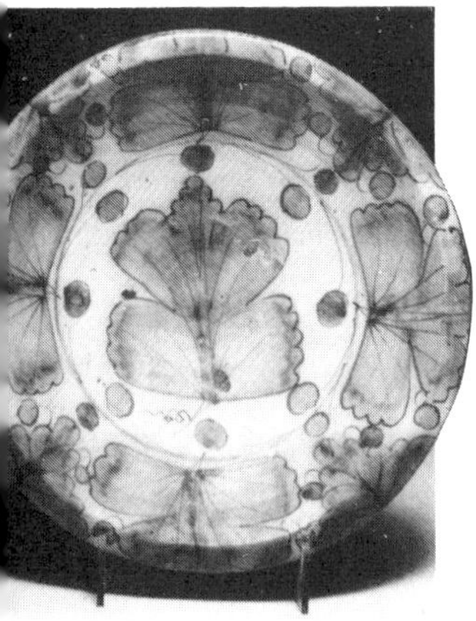

. London delft oak leaf charger, ith a central pale green oak leaf lged in manganese, with blue and ellow fruit within a slightly sloping ıallow rim, minute cracks to rim, 1690, 14in (35cm).
2,000-2,500 *C*

A Bristol delft polychrome dish, painted in blue, green and iron red, with a narrow iron red diaper border reserved with panels of flowerheads edged in blue, the underside with star and line under-rim markings, minor glaze flaking, c1730, 13in (33cm).
£1,000-1,200 *C*

A Bristol delft blue dash pomegranate charger, boldly painted in blue, iron red, yellow and green, within a double yellow line and blue dash rim, crack riveted, rim chips, c1690, 14in (36cm).
£2,000-2,500 *C*

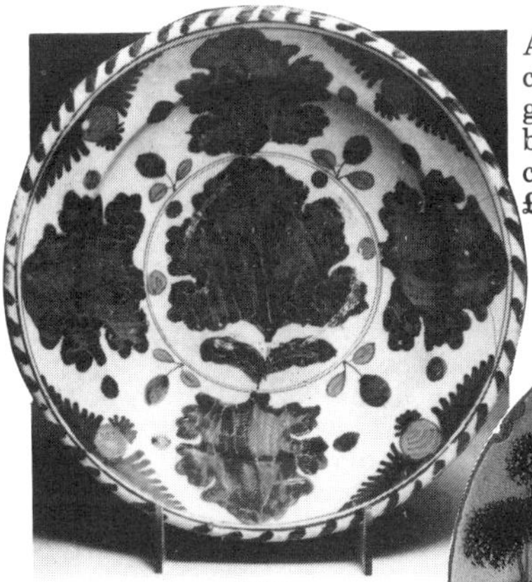

A Bristol delft polychrome plate, painted with a bird in flight, flanked by manganese and iron red trees within a triple blue line rim, chips to rim, c1740, 9in (23cm).
£700-1,000 *C*

A Bristol delft polychrome dish, painted predominantly in iron red, yellow, green and blue, minor glaze flaking, the underside with circle and line under-rim markings, c1730, 13in (33cm).
£700-1,000 *C*

A Bristol delft blue dash oak leaf charger, painted with radiating green oak leaves and fruit, within a blue dash rim, cracked and repaired, c1720, 13½in (34.5cm).
£2,500-3,000 *C*

A Bristol delft polychrome plate, painted in blue and yellow flanked by sponged manganese trees and bushes, rim chips, c1740, 8in (20cm).
£600-700 *C*

Two Bristol delft powdered manganese ground polychrome dishes, painted in blue, yellow and green, within a woolsack cartouche, the borders reserved with leaf shaped panels of flowers, chips to rim and foot rim, c1750, 13in (33cm).
£1,000-1,500 *C*

A Bristol delft polychrome dish, painted with bamboo and chrysanthemum issuing from stylised pierced blue rockwork, within a border of trailing flowers, slight rim chip, c1750, 13½in (34cm).
£400-600 *C*

An English delft powdered manganese ground polychrome dish, perhaps London, crack restored, c1750, 13½in (34.5cm).
£400-600 *C*

A Bristol delft blue and white dish boldly painted with an Oriental in shrubby landscape, c1760, 12½in (32.5cm).
£400-600 *C*

An English delft powdered blue ground dish, perhaps London, cracked and restored, c1750, 15in (38cm).
£400-600 *C*

A Bristol delft polychrome dish, boldly painted with flowering shrubs and insects, slight crack to rim and flaking, c1760, 13½in (34.5cm).
£400-600 *C*

A Lambeth delft polychrome dish, painted with a parrot perched on green, blue and yellow rockwork issuing with flowering shrubs, within a border of iron red pinecones and trailing flowers, slight flaking, c1760, 13½in (34cm).
£350-450 *C*

An English delft polychrome dish, painted with a bird flanked by shrubs within a leaf garland border, cracks and chips, c1755, 8in (20cm).
£300-500 *CSK*

A Lambeth delft dish, painted in iron red and blue, on a ground of radiating manganese lines, slight glaze flaking, c1760, 13½in (34.5cm).
£500-700 *C*

A Lambeth delft polychrome dish, pierced for hanging, rim chips, c1760, 13in (34cm).
£400-500 *C*

A Bristol delft polychrome dish, painted in the Fazackerly palette, with a boldly painted pink, yellow and blue flowering branch, slight rim chips, the reverse with X and 1 under rim markings, c1760, 13½in (33.5cm).
£600-800 *C*

. Bristol delft blue and white dish, ainted within a 'bianco-sopra-ianco' border of pinecones, flowers nd foliage, slight glaze flaking to im, c1760, 13½in (34cm).
350-450 *C*

Liverpool delft blue and white ıted shipping plate, painted with a ıip at full sail, the reverse ıscribed P 1770, minute rim aking, 1770, 9in (23cm).
2,000-2,500 *C*

Liverpool delft blue and white ıted plate, painted with a ship ınked by harbour walls, the verse inscribed P 1770, minute m chips, 9in (23cm).
,500-2,500 *C*

Use the Index!

Because certain items might fit easily into any of a number of categories, the quickest and surest method of locating any entry is by reference to the index at the back of the book.
This has been fully cross-referenced for absolute simplicity

A Liverpool delft polychrome dish, painted in the Fazackerly palette, slight rim chips, c1760, 13½in (34cm).
£2,000-2,500 *C*

A delft blue and white serving dish, perhaps Dublin, restoration to flaked rim, c1760, 21½in (54cm) wide.
£800-1,500 *C*

A Liverpool delft polychrome dish, sketchily painted, cracked, rim chip and flaking, c1760, 13in (33cm).
£1,000-1,500 *C*

A Liverpool delft blue and white dated shipping plate, painted with a sailing ship above an elaborate cartouche of flowers and foliage, inscribed J + S 1771, minute rim flaking, 9in (23cm).
£3,000-3,500 *C*

A London or Bristol delft plate, c1760, 7in (18cm).
£500-550 *BHA*

A Lambeth delft polychrome dish, boldly painted with flowering plants issuing from pierced blue and yellow rockwork, within a border of sunflowers flanked by flowers and blue foliage, c1770, 13½in (34cm).
£400-600 *C*

An English delft blue and white plate, probably London, c1770, 9in (23cm).
£250-350 *C*

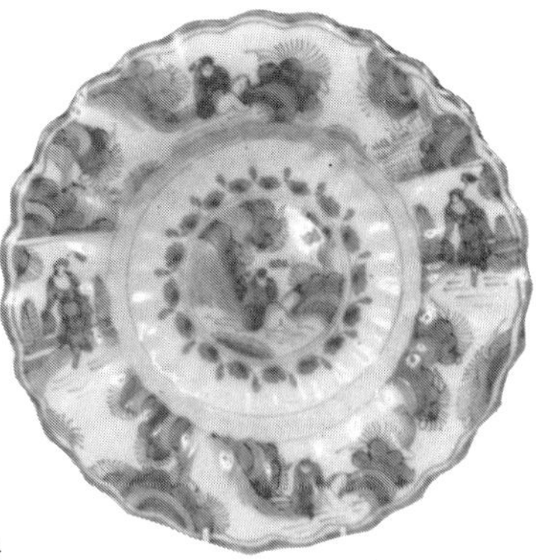

An early delft lobed dish, c1680, 13in (33cm).
£700-1,000 *PAR*

A Dutch Delft tripod herring-shaped dish, the concave border moulded with fins and tail, minor chips, marked for De Dissel, c1695, 11½in (29cm) wide.
£1,500-2,000 *CAm*

A Dutch Delft month dish, after an engraving by Jan van de Velde II, inscribed December, chipped, marked CK in underglaze blue for Cornelis Keyser, mid-17thC, 9in (24cm).
£500-550 *CAm*

This dish is one of the earliest examples from the month series.

A Dutch Delft charger, probably, crack and area of restoration, c1730, 14in (35.5cm).
£300-350 *IW*

S · MORO

A London delft blue and white wet drug jar, named for S. Mororv, rim chips and glaze flaking, c1670, 7½in (19cm).
£1,500-2,000 *C*

A London delft blue and white posset pot and cover, with strap handles and curved spout, perhaps Vauxhall, spout restored, chips and cracks to cover, c1710, 8in (19.5cm).
£1,000-1,500 *C*

ALBI · RHAS

A London delft blue and white named drug jar, damaged and repaired, late 17thC, 4in (9.5cm).
£500-700 *C*

S: SAMBU

A London delft wet drug jar, with waisted cylindrical spout and flared base, inscribed S: Sambuci 1699, some damage, 7½in (18cm).
£900-1,200 *HSS*

A London delft blue and white baluster posset pot, with curved spout and S-scroll handles, paintec with Orientals, edged in manganese, beneath a border of stylised lappets and manganese lines, spout and rim restored, sligh crack, c1680, 4½in (11.5cm).
£450-650 *C*

Æ.GYPTIA

A London delft blue and white named dry drug jar, top rim and foo restored, slight glaze flaking, c168 7½in (18.5cm).
£700-800 *C*

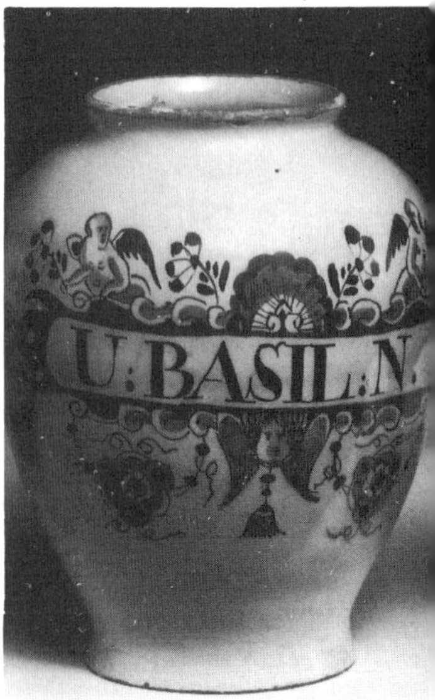
U:BASIL:N

A Bristol delft dry drug jar, named in manganese for U;Basil;N within a cartouche, c1740, 8in (19.5cm).
£900-1,200 *C*

STOM:CU

London delft blue and white
amed drug jar, large crack and
aze flaking, c1680, 4in (9.5cm).
400-500 *C*

Bristol delft polychrome
vo-handled jar of acorn shape,
ainted with panels of flowering
anches divided by shaped panels
scrolls and flowerheads, between
rders of scrolling foliage, glaze
aking, rim chips, c1730, 6in
4.5cm).
,000-1,500 *C*

S:PECTO

Bristol delft blue and white wet
ug jar, named for S: Pectoral on a
roll cartouche with winged
erubs holding flowers flanking a
ell above, and a winged angel's
ad suspending tassels and flowers
low, rim chips, c1730, 7in (17cm).
,000-1,500 *C*

S;BALSA

A Bristol delft blue and white wet drug jar, named in manganese for S;Balsam, rim chips, c1740, 7½in (19cm).
£500-600 *C*

ROB SAMB:

A Dutch Delft drug jar, painted in blue with a scrolling cartouche surmounted by a basket of fruit and twin birds above a cherub mask and swags of fruit, inscribed Rob Samb: rim and foot chips, 18thC, 7in (17.5cm).
£200-250 *CSK*

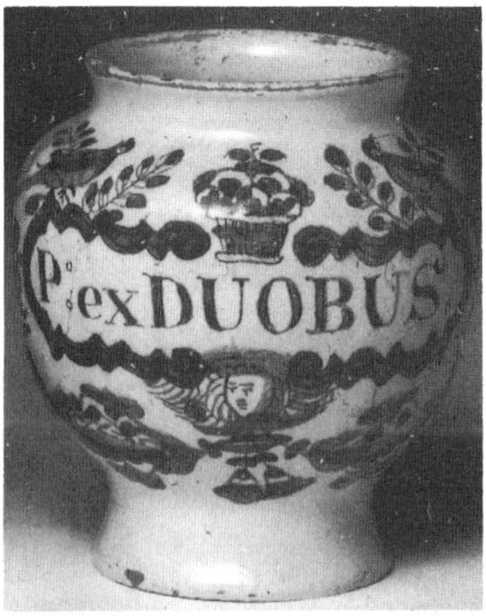
P: exDUOBUS

Two Bristol delft blue and white named drug jars, damage and repairs, c1740, 3½in (9cm).
£1,500-2,000 *C*

THER:AND:

A Lambeth delft blue and white named drug jar, foot chipped, c1760, 3in (8.5cm).
£500-600 *C*

CRAD:ALTHÆA

A Bristol delft blue and white named dry drug jar, chip to foot, c1740, 8in (19.5cm).
£400-500 *C*

POMPADOR

A pair of Dutch Delft tobacco jars, with brass covers, the bodies painted in blue, one inscribed Spaanse, the other Pompadoer, one body cracked, Three Bells factory marks, the jars 18thC, the covers later, 9in (23cm).
£1,200-1,600 *CSK*

ST DOMINGO

A pair of Dutch Delft blue and white named tobacco jars, chips to rims, marks of DE3 Klokken factory, c1750, 9½in (24cm).
£1,200-1,600 *C*

A Lambeth delft jug, c1760, 7½in (19cm).
£750-950 *Sto*

A Lambeth delft jug, with loop handle, restored and glaze flaking to rim, c1780, 8in (20cm).
£600-700 *C*

OPIFER·QUE·PER·ORBEM·DICOR

A London delft blue and white shield-shaped pill tile, painted in bright blue with the arms of The Worshipful Society of Apothecaries, with motto on a shaped cartouche, pierced for hanging, late 17thC, 12in (30cm).
£4,000-5,000 *C*

A Liverpool delft blue and white dated puzzle jug, with hollow loop handle connected to a cylindrical neck pierced with interlaced circles and with 3 short spouts, glaze flaking and re-touching to spout, dated 1766 on base, 9½in (24cm).
£4,500-5,500 *C*

A Liverpool delft blue and white inscribed and dated jug, with strap handle and mask spout, cracked body and repaired, crack to base of handle, 1773, 10in (25.5cm).
£2,000-2,500 *C*

A Liverpool delft blue and white puzzle jug, with hollow loop hand the neck and rim with 3 short spouts, the neck pierced with hea and ovals, with inscription, the interior with a cone-shaped strainer, spouts chipped, c1760, 8½in (21cm).
£1,500-2,000 *C*

A Lambeth delft tile, c1750, 5in (12.5cm) square.
£45-55 *IW*

A medallion polychrome tilefield, comprising 28 tiles, 'spaartechniek corners in blue, depicting various animals after engraving by Adriae Collaert, restored, early 17thC.
£6,000-6,500 *CAm*

. Lambeth delft blue and white eart-shaped pill tile, with the arms f The Worshipful Society of .pothecaries and motto, pierced for anging, cracked and restored, 1780, 12in (31cm).
1,500-2,000 *C*

A pair of Liverpool delft flower bricks, the tops pierced with circular holes, edged in blue and with a central square aperture, glaze flaking to rims, c1760, 6in (14.5cm) wide.
£3,000-4,000 *C*

A Liverpool delft flower brick, painted in a Fazackerly palette of blue and yellow, minute flaking to rims, c1765, 5½in (13cm).
£2,500-3,500 *C*

wo English delft blue and white ower bricks, Bristol or London, the ps pierced and with chequer- ttern, slight rim chips, one top ith piece missing by central erture, c1750, 6in (15.5cm) wide.
50-750 *C*

A Dutch Delft baluster money box, inscribed H.H., the arched cover with lambrequin motifs and rectangular slit, minor chips, marked for Geertruy Verstelle, Het oude Moriaenshooft, c1770, 9in (22cm).
£1,200-1,500 *CAm*

A Dutch Delft chinoiserie plaque, painted in iron red, yellow, green and blue, the rim modelled in relief, with dark blue ground to the outside and small floral cartouches alternating with stylised florets to the inside, minor chips, c1740, 13½in (34cm).
£4,500-5,000 *CAm*

A late Dutch Delft suite of furniture, comprising 5 pieces, painted in blue with landscapes, some restoration, blue marks, 3½ to 6in (9 to 15cm).
£250-350 *CSK*

pair of Dutch Delft lipières, minor damage, arked with Pieter driaenszoon Kocks, 700, 10½in (27cm).
0,000-25,000 *CAm*

A delft flower brick, probably London, c1730, 3½in (9cm).
£450-500 *JHo*

Miller's is a price Guide not a price List

The price ranges given reflect the average price a purchaser should pay for similar items. Condition, rarity of design or pattern, size, colour, provenance, restoration and many other factors must be taken into account when assessing values. When buying or selling, it must always be remembered that prices can be greatly affected by the condition of any piece. Unless otherwise stated, all goods shown in Miller's are of good merchantable quality, and the valuations given reflect this fact. Pieces offered for sale in exceptionally fine condition or in poor condition may reasonably be expected to be priced considerably higher or lower respectively than the estimates given herein

Miscellaneous

A bellarmine, possibly English, late 17th/early 18thC, 8in (20cm).
£600-700 *IW*

A Bates, Brown-Westhead and Moore parian bust of Apollo, after a model by Delpech, Art Union stamp and dated 1861, 14in (35cm).
£400-450 *CSK*

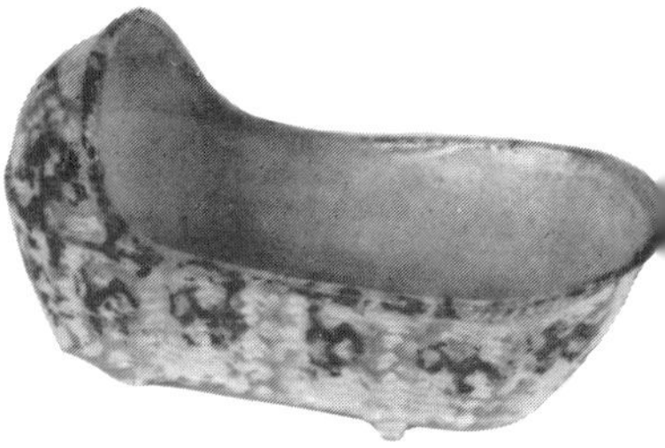

A Pratt ware cradle, c1800.
£250-300 *BHA*

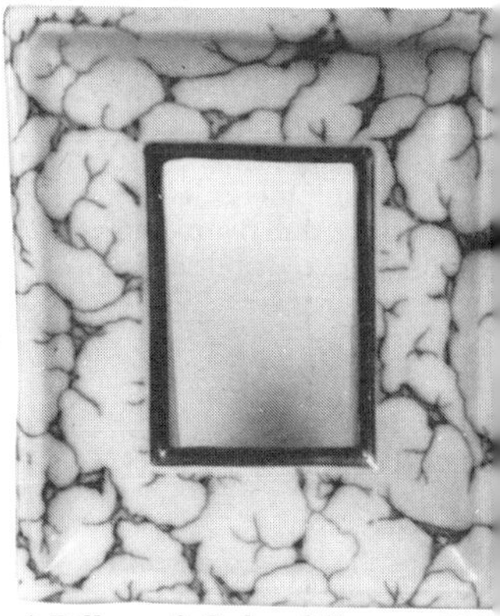

A Dillwyn & Co lazuli frame, c185 8 by 6in (20 by 15cm).
£250-350 *HOW*

A Pratt ware money box, c1830, 5in (12.5cm).
£500-600 *BHA*

A Mettlach saltglazed stoneware jardinière, impressed and incised marks, 9in (23cm) diam.
£350-400 *HSS*

A Wedgwood & Bentley blue and white jasper portrait medallion of Linnaeus, impressed lower case mark, contemporary stamped gilt metal frame, c1775, 3½in (8.5cm).
£1,200-1,700 *C*

A late Victorian cheese dish and cover, with floral decoration and gilded handle, 12in (30.5cm).
£50-100 *DDM*

An Italian maiolica ink stand, with large central aperture surrounded by 8 pen holders, the sides painted in blue, the upper surface inscribed, chipped, 18thC, 6½in (16cm) diam.
£250-350 *CSK*

A set of saltglazed furniture rests, depicting the Duke of Wellington, c1820.
£900-1,200 *BHA*

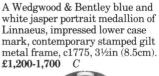

A Wedgwood black jasper-dip lamp base, 19thC, 9in (23cm).
£500-600 *Wai*

. Westerwald saltglazed stoneware esk set, 19thC, 7in (17cm) wide.
300-400 *Wai*

A Quimper pepper and salt, 4½in (11cm) wide.
£10-25 *AI*

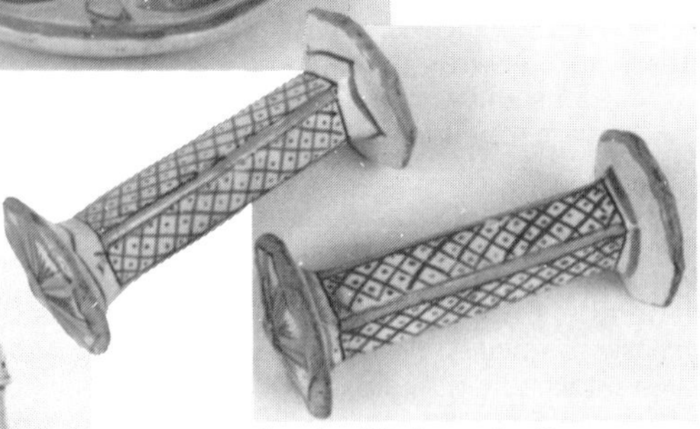

A pair of Quimper knife rests, c1870, 3in (7.5cm) long.
£70-80 *VH*

A Yorkshire creamware condiment stand and 5 bottles, chip and restoration, c1785, later turned wood handle.
£400-500 *CSK*

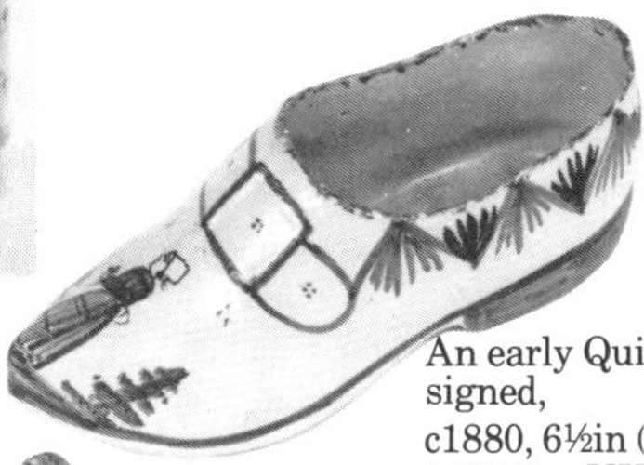

An early Quimper shoe, signed, c1880, 6½in (16cm).
£70-80 *VH*

n English brown saltglazed stern, c1800, 9½in (24cm).
00-1,200 *BHA*

robably used for gin.

A Quimper double salt, c1930, 7in (18cm) wide.
£45-55 *VH*

A Quimper finger plate, signed, 9in (23cm) long.
£100-120 *VH*

Quimper planter, signed on ttom and front, 12½in (32cm) de.
00-150 *AI*

A Quimper spice carrier or double salt, c1880, 4in (9cm) wide.
£80-100 *VH*

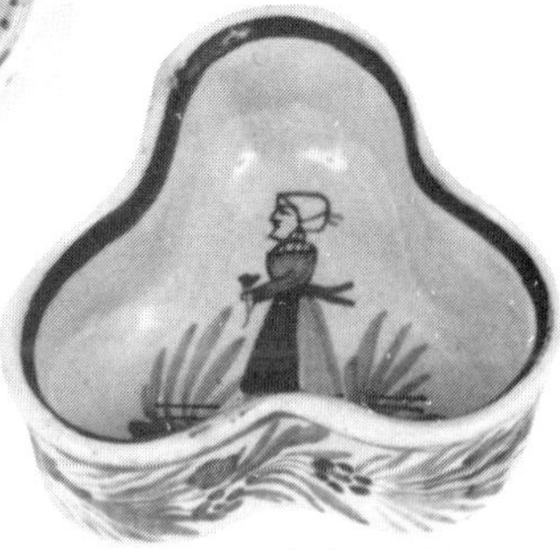

A Quimper dish, c1890, 3in (7.5cm) wide.
£30-50 *VH*

A creamware condiment stand, outlined in blue with star and oval pierced sides, on 3 low feet, the central stem with curved ring handle, containing 3 baluster pepper pots and 2 oil jugs, perhaps Leeds, chipped, cracked and stained, c1785, 8in (20cm) diam.
£500-600 *CSK*

ENGLISH PORCELAIN

During the past year good Chelsea figures and some decorative Bow rarities have come onto the market. Price levels achieved for these pieces were uniformly high. This increase in price levels was reflected in the prices asked for fine Chelsea wares at Fairs and Exhibitions and some superb pieces were tempted onto the market.

However, this trend has not been reflected in prices generally. Price levels in most areas remained stable and it has been noticeable that single rarities, often poorly catalogued appearing at country auctions, have fetched more than comparable pieces in London.

As usual prices of Worcester, Lowestoft and Plymouth remain higher than for comparable wares away from 'home' and this is a natural reflection of local collecting interest.

Interest in wares previously ascribed to William Ball, Liverpool, has been stimulated by archaeological research at Vauxhall in London where it seems these wares may have been made. However, the relatively small number of collectors and their sensible approach to buying seems to have offset any tendency for new discoveries to overstimulate prices.

EUROPEAN PORCELAIN

Sales of European porcelain both here and in America have been strong. Estimates of good Meissen and other major European factories have very frequently been exceeded, ofte about double the anticipated figure has been the going rate.

Sales tend to be carefully timetabled to coincide with major fairs to take advantage c dealers and collectors in attendance.

Early Meissen has sold strongl as have du Paquier wares and Sèvres. More interest has been shown in decorative tureens, te caddies, teapots and other domestic wares than in figures which have generally been more accurately estimated.

Baskets

A Belleek basket, with double entwined twig handles, the rim moulded and applied with lilies, slight damage, impressed ribbon mark, late 19thC, 11in (28cm) diam.
£350-400 *HSS*

A Lowestoft blue and white pierced basket of conventional type, transfer printed with The Pinecone and Foliage pattern, chip to one terminal, blue crescent mark, c1780, 9½in (24cm).
£550-650 *C*

A Spode basket and cover, c1820 5½in (14cm).
£1,600-1,800 *DOW*

A Davenport basket and stand, slight damage, c1810, stand 10in (25.5cm) wide.
£500-600 *Sto*

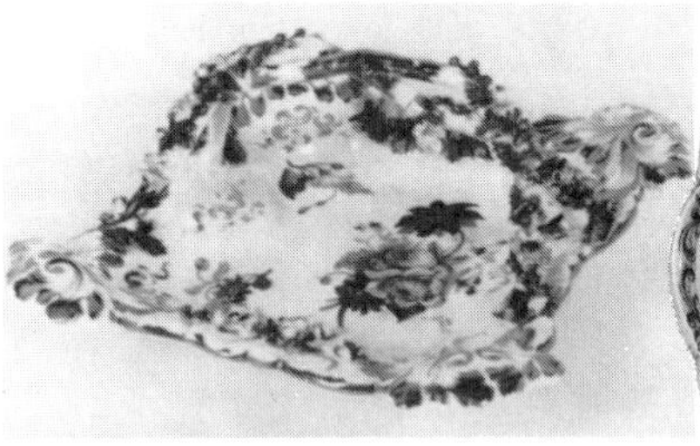

A Rockingham basket, painted in colours, encrusted with foliage and highlighted in gilt, slight damage and repair, puce griffin mark, 12in (30cm).
£1,000-1,500 *HSS*

A pair of Worcester baskets, both cracked, c1758, 8in (20cm) diam.
£2,000-2,500 *C*

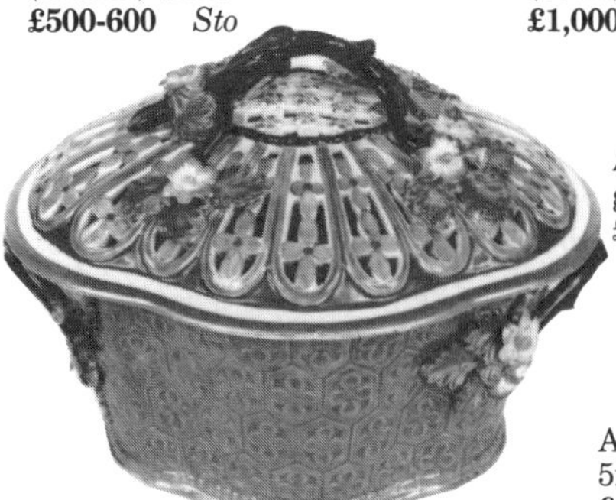

A Worcester chestnut basket, in pea green, c1800, 6½in (16cm) high.
£1,200-1,500 *BHA*

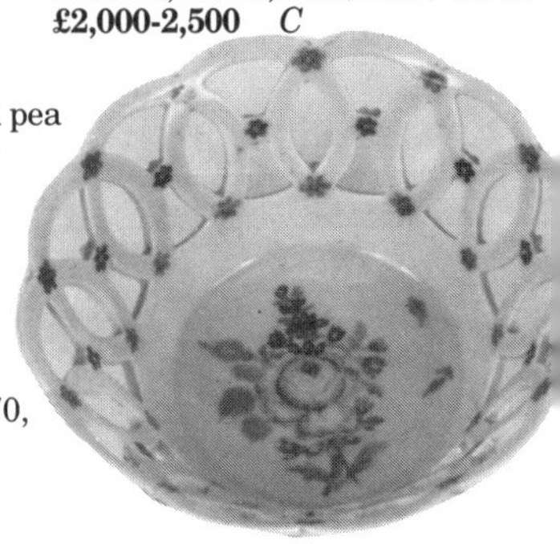

A Worcester pierced basket, c1770, 5in (12.5cm).
£400-500 *THA*

A pair of fruit baskets, unmarked but probably Spode, 11in (28cm).
£900-1,000 *BHA*

A Lowestoft blue and white bowl, painted in an inky blue with a musician standing on scrolls between wooded river islands, chip to footrim, indistinct painter's numeral, perhaps 17, c1765, 6in (15cm) diam.
£300-400 *C*

A Royal Crown Derby miniature cauldron shape bowl, in the Old Derby Witches pattern, c1917, 2½in (6cm) high.
£300-350 *TVA*

Spode two-handled botanical
›ntre dish, on spreading foot and
ith beaded rim, painted in bright
›lours with garlands of flowers,
amed on the underside, the branch
andles with moulded and coloured
uit and leaf terminals, c1825,
1½in (29cm).
,000-1,500 *C*

A Caughley patty pan, with the Island pattern, c1785, 4in (10cm) diam.
£250-350 *THA*

A Worcester sugar bowl and cover, painted with flowers, the cover with blue flower finial, restoration to finial, chips to footrim, c1758.
£500-1,000 *C*

Worcester blue and white pierced
uatrefoil chestnut basket and
›ver, with branch handles and
nial, painted with flowers,
›stored, crescent marks, 8in (20cm).
150-250 *CSK*

A Lowestoft blue and white flared patty pan, painted with trailing flowering branches, the centre with a butterfly, within a flowerhead rim, the exterior with trailing flowers, cracks to rim and base, c1765, 6in (15cm) diam.
£200-300 *C*

owls

pair of Coalport bowls, covers and
ands, decorated in the London
udio of Thomas Baxter, within gilt
rtouches, reserved on a gilt dot
d red trellis pattern ground,
tween gilt foliage and hatch
ttern borders, one stand with rim
ip repair, c1805, the stands 6in
5cm) diam.
,000-2,500 *C*

A Minton bowl, painted with fishing boats off the Dutch coast, signed by J. E. (Teddy) Dean, impressed date codes, printed factory marks, c1915, 8½in (21cm) diam.
£700-750 *TVA*

A Lowestoft sugar bowl and flat cover, painted with scattered cornflowers and gilt foliage between gilt line rims, the cover with faceted conical finial, piece missing from rim of cover, some minor staining, c1795, 4½in (11.5cm) diam.
£1,200-1,500 *C*

A Caughley blue and white bowl, hand painted with the Island pattern, c1780, 6in (15cm) diam.
£200-250 *THA*

A pair of Victorian Grainger's Worcester bowls, painted with finches and gilt leaf sprays on a cream ground, 3in (7.5cm).
£200-250 *GC*

A Wedgwood Fairyland lustre footed bowl, decorated after a desi by Daisy Makeig-Jones, the exter decorated on a shaded orange ground, some rubbing, printed Portland vase mark and pattern No. Z5360, c1920, 10½in (27cm) diam.
£2,000-3,000 *C*

A Worcester bowl, transfer printed in underglaze blue with uncommon European landscapes, c1780, 4½in (11cm) diam.
£200-250 *TVA*

A pair of ormolu mounted Vincennes bowls, painted with fruit, flowers and exotic birds with rich gilt and blue rims, on crisply cast scroll bases and foliage rims, cracked, 11in (28cm).
£900-1,200 *GSP*

A Caughley miniature teabowl and saucer, in the Island pattern, saucer 3in (7.5cm) diam.
£250-300 *THA*

A Meissen sugar bowl, painted in the manner of Bonaventura Gottlieb Hauer, with a continuous scene beneath a border painted in gilt with 'Laub-und-Bandelwerk', blue crossed swords mark, c1740.
£1,000-1,500 *C*

A Meissen bowl, pierced with scrolls, with ram mask handles an 4 paw feet, some regilding, cancelled blue crossed swords, c1880, 15in (38cm) wide.
£800-1,000 *CSK*

Boxes

A Rockingham metal mounted box, griffin mark, c1830, 3in (7.5cm) diam.
£600-700 *BHA*

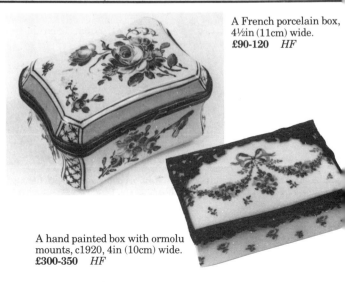

A hand painted box with ormolu mounts, c1920, 4in (10cm) wide.
£300-350 *HF*

A French porcelain box, 4½in (11cm) wide.
£90-120 *HF*

:addies

Meissen Marcolini yellow ground
a canister and cover, with apple
nial, reserved and painted in
lours with figures in landscapes,
riched with gilding, the sides with
uquets of flowers, the shoulders
plied with flowers, cancelled blue
oss swords and star mark, 7½in
9cm).
'50-1,000 *CSK*

A pair of Dresden five-light candelabra, enriched with gilt lines, one branch restored, some chipping, blue crossed swords and star marks, late 19thC, 20in (51cm).
£350-550 *C*

A Ridgway hand painted chamberstick and snuffer, slight restoration, c1820.
£75-100 *CA*

A Paris ware chamberstick, 6in (15cm) diam.
£100-120 *HF*

A Minton chamberstick, c1825, 8in (20cm) wide.
£750-850 *DOW*

andelabra

)air of Bow candlestick groups,
delled as canaries perched in
wering trees, the central nozzle
)ported on a 'tôle peinte' branch,
tored and repaired, nozzles with
pressed T mark, c1762, 8½in
:cm).
500-2,000 *C*

A pair of Minton rococo scroll moulded candlesticks, applied with trailing bouquets of garden flowers, enriched in pale green and gilding, small chips to flowers, c1835, 9½in (24.5cm).
£2,000-2,500 *C*

A Coalport chamberstick, c1830, 2½in (6cm).
£200-300 *DOW*

A pair of Derby figures of Mars and Venus, modelled as candlesticks, slight restoration, c1765, 10in (25.5cm).
£1,500-1,600 *Sto*

In the Ceramics section if there is only one measurement it usually refers to the height of the piece

A pair of Meissen chambersticks, restoration to one, damaged, underglaze blue mark, 8in (21cm).
£900-1,000 *CSK*

Centrepieces

A Coalport comport, c1840, 8½in (21cm).
£175-225 *THA*

A Crown Staffordshire centrepiece, modelled as a vase of flowers, realistically coloured and modelled, some with bees, 20thC, 11in (28cm).
£250-350 *Bon*

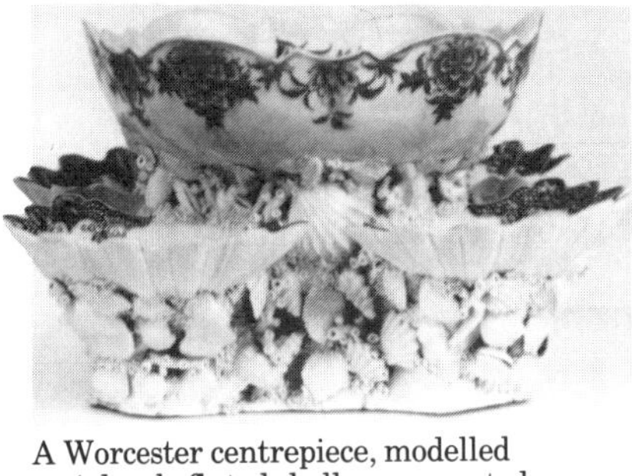

A Worcester centrepiece, modelled as 4 deeply fluted shells surmounted by a bowl, one shell restored, restored rim chips, c1770, 14½in (36.5cm) wide.
£2,000-3,000 *C*

A Berlin centrepiece, modelled as 2 maidens supporting a pierced basket, one maiden wearing a pink robe with gilt flowerheads, the other wearing scanty yellow robe lined in pink, rim damaged, gilding worn, blue sceptre and circular medallion mark, c1850, 15in (38cm).
£450-550 *CSK*

A German pierced tazza, painted in colours and enriched with gilding, damage to extremities, impressed numeral, 16in (40.5cm).
£400-500 *CSK*

A Meissen centrepiece and a pair of four-light candelabra, on shaped scroll moulded bases enriched with gilding, damaged, 19thC, centrepiece 11in (28cm).
£2,500-3,500 *Bon*

A Carl Thieme Potschappel centrepiece, decorated in coloured enamels and gilded, some damage, mark in underglaze blue, 21½in (55cm).
£950-1,200 *HSS*

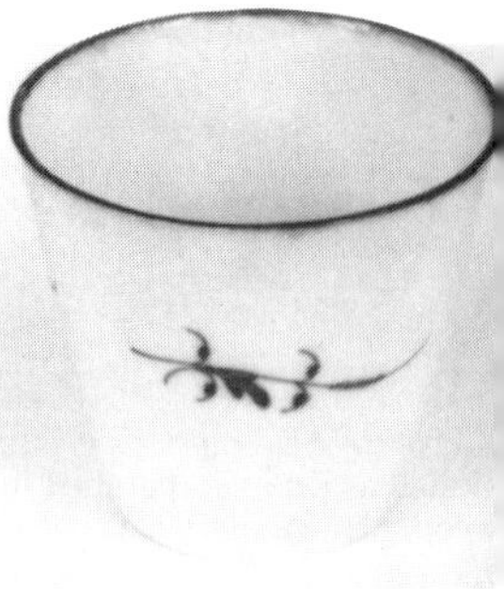

A Caughley beaker, hand painted in underglaze blue in the French style, blue painted S mark, c1785, 2½in (6cm).
£250-350 *TVA*

Cups

A Chamberlain trio, pattern No. 886, c1820, saucer 6in (15cm) diam.
£250-300 *TVA*

A Coalport cup and saucer, hand painted by Thomas Martin Randall, c1820.
£150-200 *CA*

Coalport teacup and saucer,
corated in the studio of Thomas
axter, c1805.
00-350 *C*

A Coalport coffee can and saucer, date code for 1929.
£70-100 *TVA*

A Davenport cup and saucer, c1825, 6in (15cm).
£250-350 *DOW*

Coalport miniature cup and
ucer in bamboo pattern, c1910,
p 1½in (3.5cm).
50-200 *TVA*

A Derby trout's head stirrup cup, naturally modelled and coloured, the rim inscribed The Angler's Delight, between gilt lines, Robt. Bloor & Co., slight crack to one side, c1820, 5in (13cm).
£1,500-2,000 *C*

A Spode blue and white printed coffee can, c1805, 2in (5cm).
£50-100 *TVA*

oalport cup and saucer, in Green
agon pattern, Empire shape,
20, 3½in (9cm).
-50 *THA*

A New Hall cup and saucer, bat printed with the Mother and Child pattern No. 1109, c1815, saucer 6in (15cm).
£150-200 *TVA*

A Coalport coffee cup and saucer, 1920.
£100-150 *TVA*

Five Lowestoft miniature teabowls and saucers, painted with a sailing boat between river islands with huts and trees, within loop and husk pattern borders, 2 teabowls with slight cracks, one chipped, traces of painter's numerals, c1765.
£1,200-1,500 *C*

A Lowestoft teabowl and saucer, painted with The Dragon pattern extending over the rim to the exterior, blue crescent mark, c1770.
£450-550 *C*

A Spode puzzle cup, containing an Oriental standing figure, with matching saucer, each piece painted with sprigs of flowers in enamel colours and gold on a deep blue ground within a gold line rim, pattern No. 3420, painted mark in red, early 19thC.
£350-450 *Bea*

A Worcester coffee cup, c1765, 2½ (6cm).
£300-350 *BHA*

Make the most of Miller's

Unless otherwise stated, any description which refers to 'a set' or 'a pair' includes a valuation for the entire set or the pair, even though the illustration may show only a single item

A Spode blue and sepia cup and saucer, c1810, saucer 5in (12.5cm).
£70-100 *Sto*

A Spode hand painted cup and saucer, c1825.
£70-100 *CA*

A Worcester peach-shaped wine taster, with entwined brown branch handle, pink and yellow flower terminals on a basketweave pattern ground, the interior with a border of flowers, minute chip to handle, c1765, 4in (9.5cm) wide.
£4,000-4,500 *C*

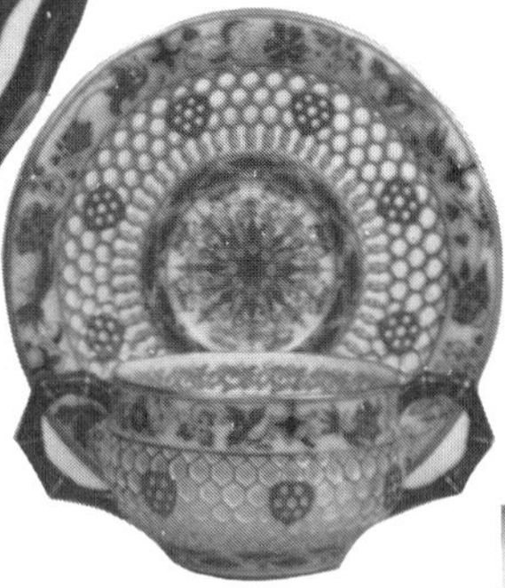

A Chamberlain's Worcester two-handled cup and saucer, pierce with gilt hexagons and iron red flowerheads between yellow borders, script marks, c1830.
£700-800 *C*

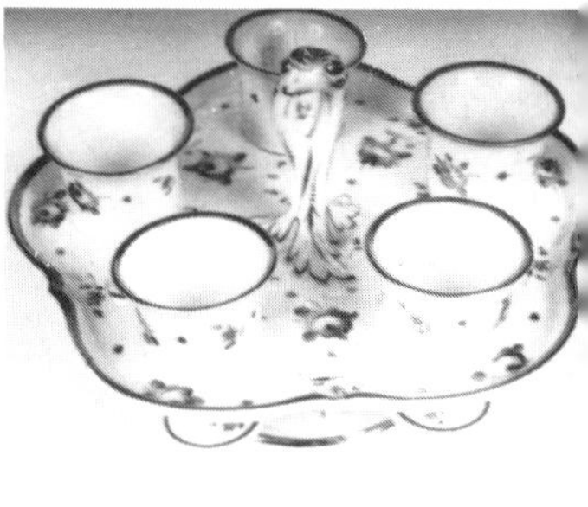

A Chamberlain's Worcester egg cup stand, one egg cup restored, 8in (20cm) diam.
£400-500 *Sto*

A Worcester First Period chocolate cup and saucer, with alternate panels of flowers, blue ground gilt trellis pattern and blue and white trellis pattern, scattered flowerhead motifs and prunus branches in the centre, the cup with branch handle, c1770. **£750-850** *WW*

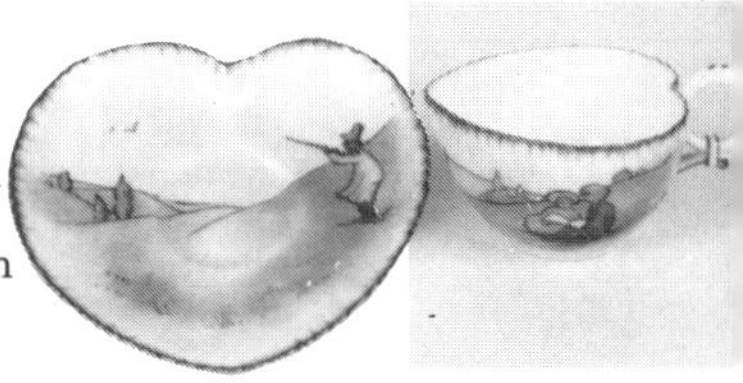

A Royal Worcester heart-shaped cup and saucer, painted in Kate Greenaway style, 1904, cup 1½in (4cm).
£300-350 *TVA*

\ Worcester fluted coffee cup, ›ainted in the Kakiemon palette, :1760.
:250-350 *CSK*

A Meissen Hausmalerei vine moulded coffee cup and saucer, painted in colours in the workshop of Mayor von Pressnitz, enriched with gilding, crossed swords marks, Pressnummer 17 to saucer, the porcelain c1740, the decoration a little later.
£2,000-2,500 *C*

A Sèvres cup and cover with flower finial, painted in pink monochrome, outlined in gilt and blue 'feuille de choux', with gilt dentil rims and gilt handle, rim chipped, blue interlaced L marks, date code indistinct but c1770, 4in (10cm).
£900-1,200 *CSK*

\ Doccia armorial beaker, painted n colours in the manner associated vith Klinger, chip to rim and 3 hair :racks, c1745, 3in (7.5cm).
'800-1,200 *C*

Ewers

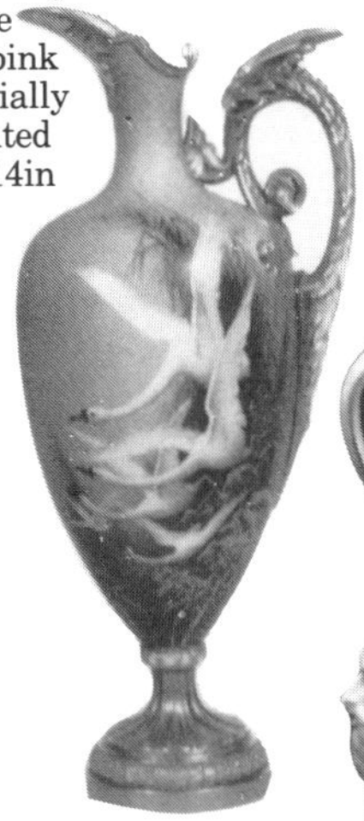

A Royal Worcester ewer, painted by C. Baldwyn, on a matt pale blue ground, heightened in salmon pink and enriched with gilding, partially indistinct signature, green printed marks and date code for 1902, 14in (35cm).
£4,500-5,000 *C*

A pair of Coalport royal blue ground ewers, c1840, 13in (33cm).
£1,000-1,200 *C*

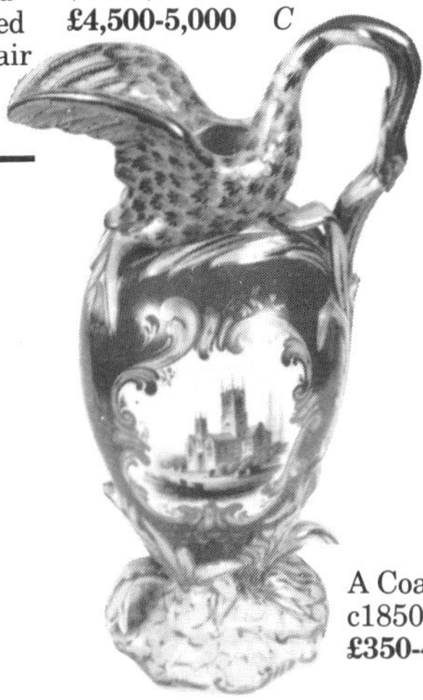

A Coalport hand painted ewer, c1850, 11in (28cm).
£350-400 *THA*

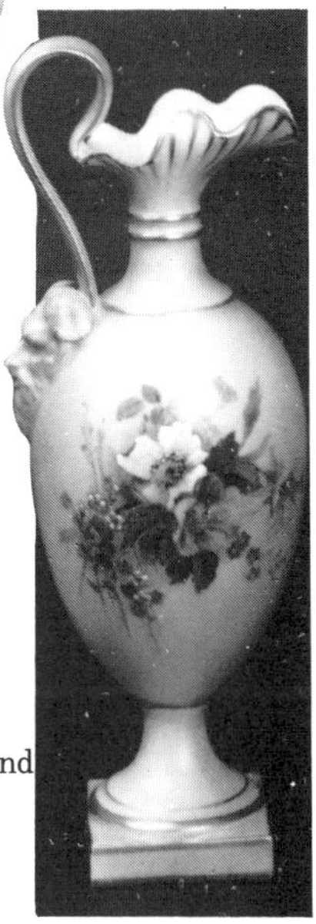

A Royal Worcester cream ground ewer, date code indistinct, 7in (17cm).
£200-250 *GC*

'igures – Animal

A Royal Worcester study of a group of young foxes, by Doris Lindner, shape No. 3131, introduced 1936, 12½in (32cm).
£300-400 *TVA*

A Bow model of a bull, with brown markings, standing on an oval base by a flowering tree stump and rockwork, restored, chipping, brown 2 mark, c1758, 5½in (14cm) long.
£1,200-1,500 *C*

A Bow group of a goat and kid, naturally modelled with shaggy brown coats, minor restorations, c1758, 4½in (12cm), wood stand.
£1,200-1,800 *C*

A Minton model of a cat, sponged in green and yellow, seated on a gilt and yellow fringed and tasselled purple cushion, ears restored, c1830, 5in (12.5cm).
£400-500 *C*

A Royal Worcester model of Red Rum, by Doris Lindner, on wood stand, limited edition No. 88 of 25[0] with framed certificate, 9½in (24cm).
£300-350 *GSP*

A Samson group of a Queen perhaps Cybele, mounted on a white charger, 7½in (18.5cm).
£200-300 *CSK*

A pair of Samuel Alcock seated spaniels, their coats with grey patches, seated on pale yellow rockwork bases edged with a gilt line, glaze slightly worn, impressed number 121, c1835, 5½in (13cm).
£650-750 *C*

An English pug dog, with brown coat and black muzzle, and with a green collar tied by a red rosette, on a green base, perhaps Lowestoft or Derby, ear chipped, tail lacking, some rubbing, c1775, 3½in (9.5cm).
£1,000-1,200 *C*

A Worcester, Grainger, Lee & Co., recumbent dog, with brown markings, moulded with gilt foliage, ears restored, impressed mark, c1835, 4½in (11cm).
£200-300 *C*

A Royal Worcester model of HRH The Princess Anne on Doublet, by Doris Lindner, limited edition No. 288 of 750, with framed certificate, 11in (28cm).
£600-650 *GSP*

A Royal Worcester miniature tortoise, date code for 1910, 2in (5cm) wide.
£250-300 *TVA*

A Meissen figure of a recumbent lion, modelled by J. J. Kändler, painted with a brown coat, restoration, one tooth chipped, traces of crossed swords mark, Pressnummer 45, c1745, the decoration later, 9in (22cm) wide.
£1,500-2,000 *C*

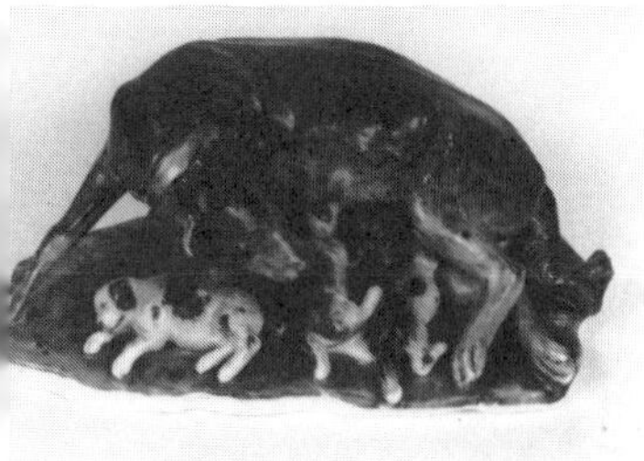

ıard paste dog group, c1865, 8in
).5cm) wide.
50-650 *BHA*

A Meissen carnary, c1820, 4in (10cm).
£450-500 *BHA*

A Meissen group of 3 pugs playing on a grassy mound, with blue ribboned collars and gilt bells, brown and beige markings, two tails restored, underglaze blue cross swords mark, 6in (15cm) wide.
£900-1,200 *CSK*

. English cow, 19thC.
)0-450 *BHA*

A Frankenthal hunting group, naturalistically painted in colours, hind legs of stag and base repaired, chips to leaves, blue rampant lion mark and impressed PH6, c1756, 8½in (22cm).
£1,500-2,000 *C*

A Sèvres group of a boar hunt, by Blondeau after Ouvri, modelled as a pair of hounds attacking a boar, tree stump broken and chips to extremities, late 18thC, 15in (38cm) wide.
£450-550 *CSK*

igures – People

3ow white figure of Apollo, by the
ıses Modeller, repaired and
pped, c1752, 7in (17cm).
000-3,000 *C*

A Bow group of a dancing Turk and companion, in blue and pink coats and flowered clothes, base enriched in puce and gilding, restorations and her right hand lacking, c1762, 8in (20cm).
£750-850 *C*

A Bow figure of a nun, in pink-lined black cowl and white habit, reading from the Bible, the text headed Vanitas Vanitatum, firing crack and restoration to hand, Bible and cowl, c1758, 6in (14.5cm).
£600-700 *C*

)air of Bow figures, c1760, 5½in
cm).
50-350 *Bon*

A Bow figure of Autumn, chipped, c1762, 7in (17.5cm).
£900-1,000 *Sto*

A Bow figure of a dancer, modelled as a girl in plumed hat, blue bodice and flowered apron and skirt, enriched in puce, turquoise and gilding, restoration to one hand, waist and tree, some chipping, c1762, 7½in (18.5cm).
£500-600 *C*

Two Bow arbour groups, each modelled as a sportsman and companion, in gilt flowered and patterned clothes standing before a pink, puce and iron red marbled wall fountain before flowering trees, the scroll moulded bases enriched in gilding, extensive restoration, anchor and dagger marks in iron red, c1770, 9in (23cm).
£2,000-2,500 *C*

A Bow figure of Mars, in plumed helmet, gilt and puce scale patter cuirass and moulded and striped pink and iron red chiton, the scro moulded base enriched in gilding restoration, some chipping, ancho and dagger mark in iron red, c17 12½in (31.5cm).
£750-1,000 *C*

Two Bow putti musicians, scantily draped in puce and turquoise, on pierced spreading marbled bases, one broken at base, both chipped and restored, c1762, 4½in (11cm).
£500-550 *C*

A Bow figure, emblematic of Autumn, late 18thC, 5½in (14cm
£750-850 *Bea*

A Chelsea figure emblematic of A modelled as a nymph in yellow lin pink cloak and turquoise blouse a skirt, slight restoration, c1760, 8½in (22cm).
£700-800 *C*

A Bow figure of Minerva, in black helmet, yellow-lined flowered pink cloak and gilt scale pattern turquoise cuirass, the scroll moulded base enriched in puce, owl a restored replacement, other restoration, c1760, 13in (33cm).
£600-800 *C*

A Bow white figure of a toper, leaning against a tree stump on a shaped rockwork base, restoration, crack to barrel, chips, c1753, 6in (15cm).
£500-800 *C*

A Chelsea Bacchanalian figure group, impressed C. Vyse, c1920.
£700-800 *GIL*

A Derby group, minor damag late 18thC, 5in (12.5cm).
£400-450 *Bea*

A very rare Coalport parian ware group of Beauty and the Beast, wearing cat and monkey masks, c1840, 8in (20cm).
£1,200-1,500 *Wai*

Illustrated in the Coalport Travellers Pattern Book belonging to the Chief Travelling Salesman, William Hedley, for John Rose & Co., List No. 44, costing 18/–.

A Derby sweetmeat figure, in a pink dress and flowered apron, on a mound base applied with flowers, Wm. Duesbury & Co., neck restored, c1760, 6½in (16cm).
£600-700 *C*

A pair of Derby figures of a shepherd and shepherdess, modelled as candlesticks, in pale pink, puce and turquoise, on scroll moulded gilt and turquoise bases, Wm. Duesbury & Co., restoration, the nozzles later Continental replacements, c1775, 8in (19.5cm).
£800-1,000 *C*

A Derby figure of Jupiter, the crowned god wearing a gilt flowered cloak and flowered pale yellow green lined robe, an eagle at his side, the scroll moulded base enriched in green, yellow and gilding, Wm. Duesbury & Co., firing cracks, damage to thunderbolt, c1765, 17in (43cm).
£3,000-3,500 *C*

Derby group of 2 macaroni ;ures, one wearing black bonnet, ange cape, yellow open robe, blue ›ral robe with her hands in a muff, e other with wig, pink open robe ıd petticoat with a fan, incised). 91, 8in (20cm).
50-200 *CSK*

A Derby group of dancers, slight restoration, marked with crossed swords and incised number, c1820, 6½in (16cm).
£1,400-1,600 *Sto*

A Derby figure of a gallant, in plumed hat, pink coat, turquoise jacket, white shirt and flowered yellow breeches, Wm. Duesbury & Co., restoration, c1765, 8½in (21cm).
£700-1,000 *C*

A pair of Derby figures of a sportsman and companion, wearing fur lined pale yellow and pink jacket and coat, a flowered waistcoat and dress and red breeches, he with a gun and standing before his dog, she holding a bird and with her dog at her side, both before flowering tree stumps, Wm. Duesbury & Co., his right hand and gun and her left hand and arm restored, chipped, c1765, 9in (22.5cm).
£1,800-2,500 *C*

Locate the source

The source of each illustration in Miller's can be found by checking the code letters below each caption with the list of contributors

A pair of Derby figures, in yellow robes, on rococo mound bases, applied with flowers, incised Nos. 63 and 65, late 18thC.
£500-600 *Bea*

A pair of Derby figures, Stevenson and Hancock, damage to her fingers and flowers, puce printed marks, 7in (17.5cm).
£400-500 *CSK*

A pair of Derby figures of a garder and companion, Stevenson and Hancock, both restored, puce mar 7in (17.5cm).
£250-300 *CSK*

A Derby figure of Dr. Syntax, on a green base, Robert Bloor & Co., restorations, crown, crossed batons and D mark in red and incised No. 7, c1820, 4½in (11cm).
£150-200 *C*

A Longton Hall figure of a milkman, wearing a black tricorn hat, white shirt, yellow and puce spotted neckerchief, puce coat and brown breeches, the base enriched in purple, slight chipping, c1755, 10½in (27cm).
£3,000-3,500 *C*

A pair of Derby figures of the Wel Tailor and companion, Stevenson and Hancock, restoration, puce marks, 5½in (14cm).
£350-450 *CSK*

A pair of figures of you women, the bases moulded with female masks and flowers, slight chipping, 24½in (62cm).
£1,500-2,000 *Bea*

A Derby figure of a young lady, in brightly painted 18thC costume, damage, some regilding, crossed swords marks, c1825, 10in (25.5cm).
£150-250 *CSK*

A pair of Derby figures of a boy and girl, Stevenson and Hancock, on bases outlined in gilt, his left hand missing, damage to extremities, girl restored, puce marks, 7in (17.5cm).
£200-250 *CSK*

A Minton flat back model of The Dutch Pedlar, on gilt enriched base, restored, c1825, 5½in (14cm).
£350-400 *Bon*

A Worcester crinoline figure, modelled as an unrecorded tea cosy top, colour scheme 2, shape No. 2620, c1916, 3in (7.5cm).
£450-500 *TVA*

The moulds were destroyed in 1920.

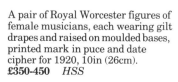

A pair of Royal Worcester figures of female musicians, each wearing gilt drapes and raised on moulded bases, printed mark in puce and date cipher for 1920, 10in (26cm).
£350-450 *HSS*

A Royal Worcester equestrian group, entitled 'At the Meet', with wood plinth, 9in (23cm).
£400-450 *Bea*

A Royal Worcester equestrian group, entitled 'Huntsman and Hounds', on wood plinth, 9in (23cm).
£400-450 *Bea*

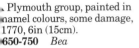

. Plymouth group, painted in namel colours, some damage, 1770, 6in (15cm).
650-750 *Bea*

A Worcester majolica figure, c1862, 8½in (21cm).
£600-700 *BHA*

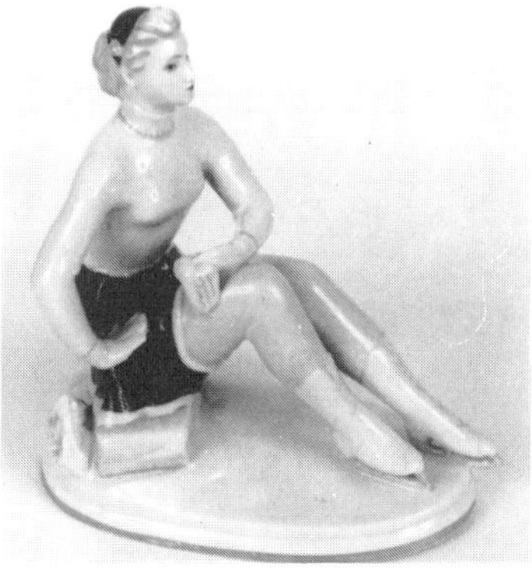

A European figure of a girl skater, c1930, 7in (17.5cm).
£60-100 *TVA*

Minton parian group entitled Jaomi and her daughters-in-law', ie base inscribed in indented ıpitals, minor damage, incised o. 183, 13½in (34cm).
200-250 *CSK*

A pair of Continental figures of a seated lady and gentleman with dogs, on circular bases, blue printed mark, 19thC, 6in (15cm).
£900-1,200 *AH*

A rare English parian ware figure of Venus, c1850, 9½in (24cm).
£400-500 *Wai*

pair of Royal Worcester figures of)y and Sorrow, modelled by James adley, Joy wearing pink robe, orrow wearing a green robe with ısted gilt highlights on coloured ıses, puce printed factory mark ıd model number 2/57, date code r c1933, 9½in (24cm).
500-600 *CSK*

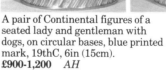

A Dresden group, painted in colours and enriched in gilding, the base heightened in pale pink and turquoise and enriched in gilding, minor chipping to flowers, blue crossed swords and dash marks, incised numeral marks, c1880, on a plush covered wood stand, 16½in (42cm).
£800-1,000 *C*

A Dresden group of a huntsman in 18thC costume and 2 leaping hounds, chips and restoration, 15in (38cm).
£600-700 *CSK*

A Meissen figure of St. Matthew, modelled by J. J. Kändler, with a long grey beard, wearing a long cloak with a purple and gilt scrolling border over a robe with scattered purple 'indianische Blumen' with gilt stems, an angel at his side, on a square chamfered base, crossed swords mark, c1740, 9½in (24cm).
£4,000-5,000 *C*

A Meissen group of The Hand Kiss, by J. J. Kändler, she wearing a puce crinoline with a flowered hem and yellow coat, he with a white coat enriched with gilding and purple revers, a black tricorn hat under his arm, damaged and repaired, c1740, 9in (23cm) wide.
£5,500-7,000 *C*

A Meissen figure of a bagpiper, modelled by J. J. Kändler, in black hat, green and yellow waistcoat and pink cloak with yellow stockings, on flower encrusted base, hair cracks to base, c1740, 9in (23cm).
£2,000-3,000 *C*

A Meissen rococo arbour group of lovers, modelled by J. J. Kändler and P. Reinicke, he in gilt trimmed jacket and waistcoat and black breeches, she in puce and gilt floral dress with black and blue bodice, the trellis modelled with trailing flowers, minor restoration, traces of crossed swords mark, c1745, 7½in (19cm).
£4,000-5,000 *C*

A Meissen figure of a Moor restraining a horse, modelled by J. J. Kändler, wearing a yellow striped turban, purple robe tied with a red striped sash and yellow boots, repair to the Moor, base and horse's fetlocks and ears, c1755, 9in (23cm).
£2,500-3,000 *C*

A late Meissen figure of Psyche seated on a tree stump, base cracked, some restoration, 21½in (54cm).
£1,300-1,500 *CSK*

A pair of Meissen figures of a Bulgar and Persian companion, from a series of Orientials modelled by J. J. Kändler and P. Reinicke, the man with fur-trimmed puce hat, buff lined pink cloak, cream coat reserved with sprays of flowers in puce and gold and with blue pantaloons, his companion dressed to match, his left arm, right sleeve and staff damaged, crossed swords mark at back, c1750, 9in (22cm).
£2,500-3,500 *C*

A Meissen equestrian figure, restored, 18thC, 8in (20cm).
£1,500-2,000 *BHA*

A Meissen figure of a monk carrying a young lady wrapped in a sheaf into his monastery, modelled as a double scent bottle, 18thC, 4in (10cm).
£1,500-2,000 *BHA*

A Meissen group, after Kändler, 19thC, 6in (15cm).
£750-1,000 *BHA*

A Meissen gardening group, painted in colours and enriched in gilding, minor chipping to flowers, blue crossed swords and incised numeral marks, late 19thC, 11½in (29cm).
£3,000-3,500 *C*

A Meissen figure of a moustached Saxon fusilier, wearing a black tricorn hat, buckled bandaliers, red trim to his waistcoat and jacket, black riding boots with spurs, the base enriched with puce, repairs, faint crossed swords mark to base, c1760, 9in (23cm).
£1,200-1,700 *C*

A Meissen group of children dressed as minstrels, 19thC, 8in (20cm).
£1,500-2,000 *BHA*

A set of 5 Meissen figures, emblematic of the Senses, modelled as ladies in 18thC dress, painted in colours and enriched in gilding, the bases moulded with pink flutes enriched in gilding, minor chipping, blue crossed swords, incised and impressed numerals, late 19thC, 5 to 6in (12 to 15cm).
£4,500-5,500 *C*

A Meissen figure of Cupid, kneeling beside a target centred with a pink heart adorned with a flower garland, on a mound base and waisted plinth, slight damage, blue crossed swords and incised and impressed numerals, late 19thC, 6½in (16cm).
£450-500 *CSK*

A Meissen group of The Rape of the Sabine Woman, modelled as a scantily clad man carrying a woman over his shoulder, the base edged with gilt scrolls, lower arm restored and minute chipping to hand, crossed swords in underglaze blue and incised 1919, 19thC, 7in (17.5cm).
£200-250 *Bon*

A Meissen figure of a harlequin with pug dog, after J. J. Kändler, wearing a brightly enamelled diamond pattern jacket and octagonal sided hat, crossed swords in underglaze blue, impressed 3043, 20thC, 7½in (18.5cm).
£400-600 *Bon*

A Meissen group of 3 figures, the base moulded and gilt with a band of lozenges, damage and restoration, blue crossed swords and incised numerals, c1880, 8in (20cm).
£600-700 *CSK*

A pair of Meissen groups, one in the form of a semi-naked boy sitting by a brazier, making tea, the other depicting 2 boys, one doing laundry, the other baking cakes, slight damage, 4in (10.5cm).
£900-1,200 *Bea*

A German group of 4 figures on a rocky base, damage to extremities, 13½in (34cm).
£250-350 *CSK*

A Meissen figure of a clown, wearing a miniature top hat and suit with sun and moon motifs, damaged and restored, 12½in (32cm).
£700-800 *HSS*

A pair of French coloured biscuit figures of a gallant and companion, he wearing a buff lined pale turquoise cloak, his striped and coloured clothes enriched in gilding, his companion in lilac lined pink cloak, her clothes painted in colours and enriched in gilding, on shaped tiled and marbled bases, perhaps Gille Jeune, he lacking one finger, c1865, 24½in (62cm).
£1,000-1,500 *C*

A pair of German figures of a youth and companion, some wear, 17½in (44cm).
£400-450 *CSK*

A pair of German coloured bisque groups of seated figures, one with lady playing the lute, slight chips, 8 and 9in (20 and 23cm).
£250-350 *CSK*

A pair of French blue glazed figures of a young boy and girl seated on rocky bases, scantily clad in drapes, she with a flower garland with gilt highlights, blue interlaced L marks, 8in (20cm).
£300-350 *CSK*

If youth knew

A German fairing, entitled 'If Youth Knew', 3½in (9cm).
£150-250 *DDM*

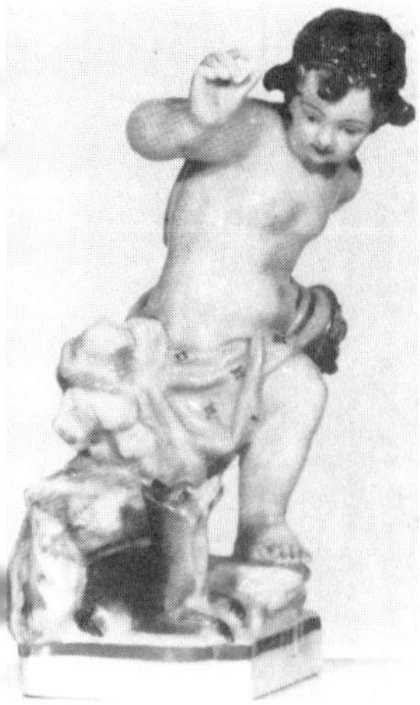

A Berlin figure of a putto, emblematic of Plenty, the base lined in gilt, slight chips to extremities, blue sceptre marks, 19thC, 7½in (19cm).
£200-250 *CSK*

A pair of Sitzendorf candle holder figures, modelled with a young man and woman, standing before stump supports on footed bases moulded with scrolls and applied and painted with flowers, slight chips, blue factory marks, 13in (33cm).
£400-450 *CSK*

A Würzburg figure, allegorical of Ceres, the scantily clad goddess holding a sheaf of corn and a scythe, her robe painted with scattered sprays of puce flowers, her hair and features naturalistically coloured, repaired, c1770, 6½in (16.5cm).
£2,000-3,000 *C*

Did you know
MILLER'S Antiques Price Guide builds up year by year to form the most comprehensive photo-reference system available

A Berlin figural group, modelled as a classical maiden wearing an orange robe lined in yellow, some damage, blue sceptre and iron red K.P.M. and globe mark, late 19thC, 16in (40.5cm).
£550-650 *CSK*

A pair of Sitzendorf figures of a young man and companion wearing 18thC style costume, the bases painted in predominantly pastel colours, damage to extremities, factory marks, 15½in (39cm).
£350-450 *CSK*

A Volkstedt figure of a female gardener, holding a watering can, in a black bonnet, yellow bodice and red dress, standing on a grassy mound base, restored, c1780, 7in (17cm).
£250-350 *CSK*

A pair of Doccia figures of Summer and Winter, she wearing a pink robe and blue cloak, Winter modelled as an old man draped in a fur lined cloak holding a cornucopia, both restored, c1780, 9in (23cm).
£900-1,200 *C*

A Vienna group, after a model by Anton Grassi, depicting a man and woman in 18thC costume, 11½in (29cm).
£1,000-1,500 *Bea*

Two Buen Retiro allegorical figures, Neptune standing with left arm raised, scantily clad and wearing a gilt crown, before a dolphin in blue and red, forearms missing, restored, and Laocoon loosely draped with a serpent entwined around his right arm, chipped, serpent's head missing and firing crack, c1770, 6in (15cm).
£1,200-1,500 *C*

A pair of Volkstedt groups of 2 children, holding fruit and with hens, geese and chickens feeding, slight damage to fingers, blue factory marks, 6in (15cm).
£150-200 *CSK*

A Ludwigsburg figure of the Chinese goddess Guanyin, with red decorated headdress in a green and floral headed cloak and a yellow dress, standing on a wavy base, 20½in (52cm).
£550-600 *WW*

A Lladro figure of Othello, 12in (30.5cm).
£75-100 *SAA*

Flatware

A Bow plate, enamelled with the Quail pattern, c1750, 8½in (21cm).
£500-600 *TVA*

A Bow blue and white plate, decorated with flowering shrubs, trailing flowers and a fence, the border with medallion and floral panels, the reverse with 3 trailing branches, mid-18thC, 9in (22cm).
£350-400 *AG*

A Bow dish, painted in a vibrant 'famille rose' palette, the well with yellow flowerheads and trailing branches, within a green cell-pattern rim, slight rim chip, c1758, 12in (31cm).
£3,000-3,500 *C*

A Bow dish, painted with a branch of trailing pink roses and scattered insects, within a brown line rim, c1758, 10½in (27cm).
£9,000-10,000 *C*

A Caughley shell-shaped blue and white pickle dish, with the Fisherman pattern, impressed Salopian, c1775, 6in (15cm) long.
£250-350 *THA*

A pair of Chelsea botanical plates, painted with specimen flowers, within moulded gilt scroll rims, one with minute rim chip, slight rubbing to enamels, gold anchor marks, c1760, 8½in (21cm).
£2,500-3,500 *C*

A Chelsea plate, painted with 3 exotic birds among flowers, within a leaf moulded border outlined in brown and turquoise, enamels rubbed and stained, red anchor marks, c1758, 8½in (21cm).
£250-350 *CSK*

A Coalport hand painted plate, with gilded decoration, c1845, 9in (23cm).
£125-175 *THA*

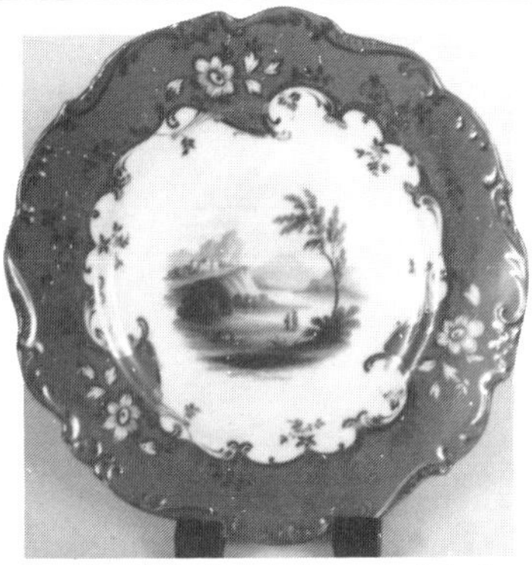

A pair of Coalport plates, painted with landscapes, c1840.
£300-350 *TVA*

A pair of Coalport plates, painted with floral bouquets, c1840.
£200-250 *TVA*

A Chelsea silver shaped moulded dish, with red anchor mark, c1756, 8½in (21cm).
£300-400 *Sto*

A Coalport dish, c1825, 9in (23cm).
£350-450 *DOW*

A Coalport dish, painted with a rare view of Ludlow Castle, by Doe & Rogers, Worcester, c1820, 12½in (33cm) wide.
£600-650 *TVA*

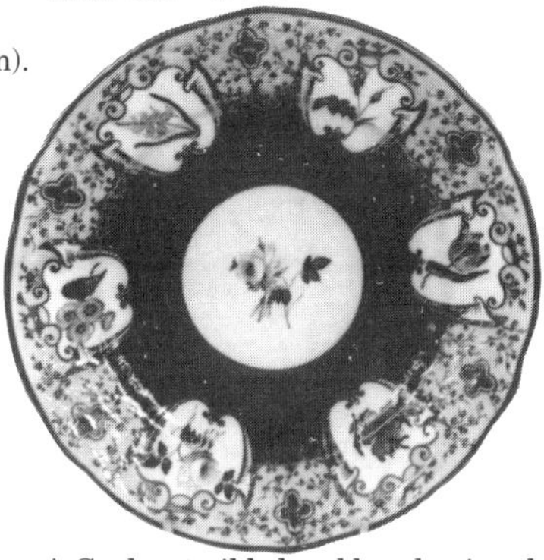

A Coalport gilded and hand painted plate, c1815, 9½in (23cm).
£200-250 *THA*

A Chelsea blue ground plate, the well gilt with the egg-and-dart pattern within an underglaze blue border gilt with swags of vine, rim chip, gold anchor mark, c1765, 8½in (22cm).
£300-350 *C*

A Coalport plate, painted with birds perched on a nest among flowers, on a salmon pink ground and with pink border, enamels rubbed, 8½in (21cm).
£150-200 *CSK*

A Coalport soup dish, hand painted with the Tiger pattern, c1805, 9½in (24cm).
£75-100 *THA*

A Coalport documentary crested plate, painted by John Duncombe Taylor, with The Exposure of Prince Bahman taken from Arabian nights, inscribed on the reverse, the gilt chequered pattern border reserved with an iron red crest, inscribed and dated July 1807, 8½in (21.5cm).
£400-800 *C*

A John Rose and Co. Coalport part dessert service, comprising: a comport, pedestal bowl and 8 plates, each piece finely painted with a flower within a pierced border, decorated in gold and turquoise, mid-19thC.
£3,500-4,000 *Bea*

A Coalport dish, with central painted landscape, c1900, 12½in (33cm).
£400-450 *TVA*

A Coalport plate, with a view of Windsor Castle within a pink border with gilt decoration, signed Arthur Perry, c1891.
£300-350 *THA*

A finely painted Coalport plate, attributed to F. H. Chivers, c1910, 9in (23cm).
£225-275 *TVA*

A Coalport plate, with a painting of Lago Di Garda within a green border, c1855, 9½in (24cm).
£150-200 *THA*

A Coalport soup plate, with heavy gilding, 10in (25cm).
£50-100 *THA*

A Derby dish, with the arms of Viscount Tamworth, Leicestershire, c1820, 10in (25cm).
£800-900 *DOW*

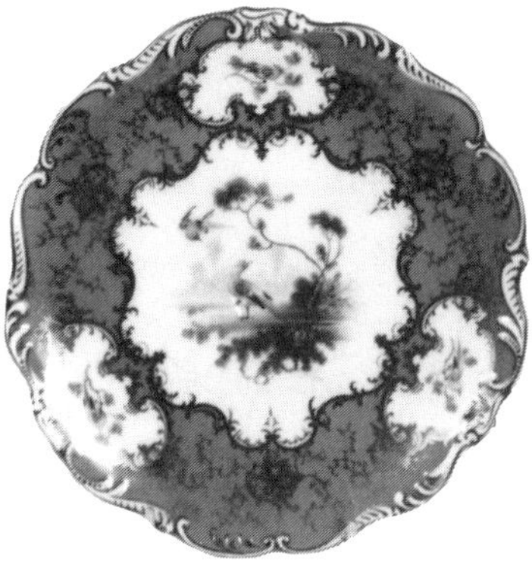

A Coalport plate, hand painted by Percy Simpson and signed, c1891, 8½in (21cm).
£280-320 *THA*

A Coalport dish, printed in dark blue with huntsman and dogs in gilt and silver, geometric border, 7in (17.5cm) wide.
£100-120 *P*

A Coalport cabinet plate, entitled Clear Springs Valley, signed Arthur Perry, c1900, 9in (23cm).
£375-400 *TVA*

A Davenport blue transfer ware plate, from the Rustic series, c1820, 10in (25cm).
£100-150 *HOW*

A set of 6 Davenport plates, with
ouce mark, c1880, 10in (25cm).
£650-700 *TVA*

A Derby plate enamelled with Chantilly sprigs, with red mark, c1810, 10in (25cm).
£60-80 *TVA*

A Minton pierced dish, applied with naturally modelled green peas, the border enriched in gilding, on 4 green and gilt foliage feet, restored, c1840, 6½in (16cm).
£600-700 *C*

A Derby botanical plate, painted
vith flowers within a spirally-
noulded border, gilt with foliage,
rown, crossed batons and D mark,
attern No. 141 in blue, Wm.
Duesbury & Co, c1790, 8½in
21.5cm).
550-650 *C*

A pair of Nantgarw plates, painted within a shaped gilt dentil rim, impressed Nant-Garw C.W. marks, c1820, 10in (25cm).
£3,000-4,000 *C*

A set of 6 Derby porcelain botanical plates, each decorated in gold with a crest in the form of a bird with open wings under a crown, the flower names in Latin and English on the reverse with the crown and baton mark in blue, one plate cracked, c1800.
£2,000-2,500 *Bea*

Lowestoft blue and white
eaf-shaped pickle dish, with a
euille de choux' rim, rim chips,
iveted, painter's numeral 8, c1765,
½in (11.5cm).
150-200 *C*

A Derby plate, hand painted with a vulture, c1820, 9½in (24cm).
£75-100 *TVA*

A Derby armorial dish, the centre with the arms of Pigott impaling Cope, within an iron red and gilt chain border, 10½in (27cm).
£350-450 *WW*

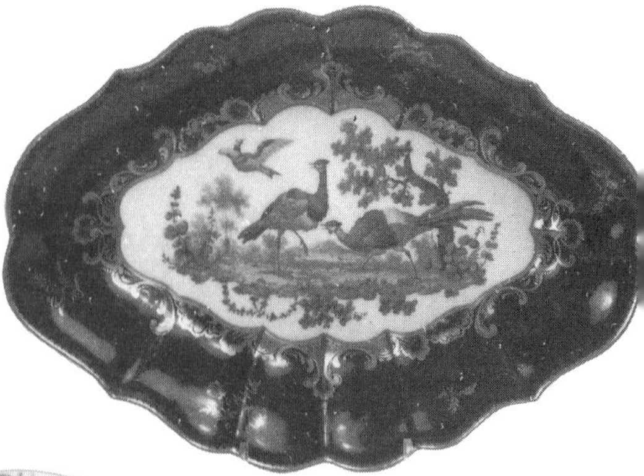

A Worcester blue ground lozenge shaped dish, the centre painted with exotic birds in a wooded landscape vignette, within a gilt scroll and diaper panelled cartouche, the border gilt with flowersprays, flakes to gilt rim, blue square seal mark, c1770, 10½in (27cm) wide.
£600-800 *C*

A Samson Imari deep dish, with everted rim, painted with a central river landscape, 18in (46cm).
£700-1,000 *CSK*

A Lowestoft blue and white fluted junket dish, painted in pale blue with flowers and insects, extended firing cracks, c1765, 9in (22cm).
£500-600 *C*

A Worcester leaf dish, the overlapping leaves with puce mid-ribs and raised veins, 2 small rim chips, c1760, 13in (35cm).
£900-1,200 *C*

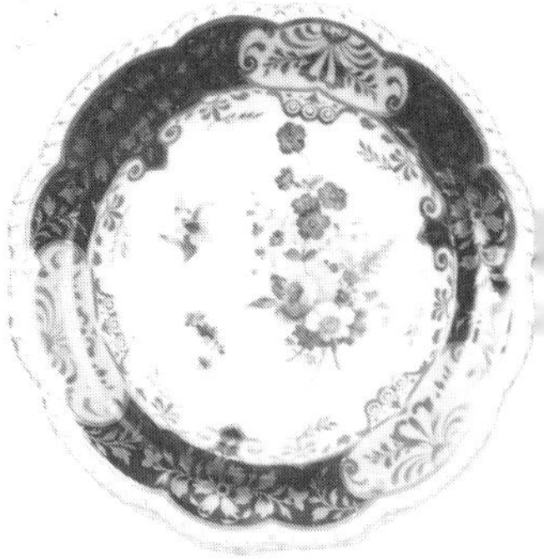

A set of 12 Ridgway dessert plates, with gadrooned gilt moulded border, with a blue and yellow alternate panel gilt decorated band, the centres with bouquet and sprigs of flowers, pattern No. 1385, double crest and ribbon motto in underglaze blue, 10in (25cm).
£1,200-1,500 *WW*

A Nantgarw lobed dish, with finely painted flowers, impressed mark, c1818, 11½in (29cm).
£750-800 *TVA*

A Spode dish, Hunting Buffalo pattern, marked, c1820, 12½in (33cm) wide.
£550-600 *HOW*

Two Worcester blue ground plates, the centres painted with exotic birds in wooded landscapes within gilt gadroon cartouches and lobed gilt dentil rims, one rim chipped, blue square seal and blue W marks, c1770, 7½in (18.5cm).
£600-800 *C*

A pair of Ridgway plates, with 3 polychrome flower decorated reserve panels, on deep blue and buff coloured ground with gilt vine scroll and flower decoration, early 19thC, 9in (22cm).
£350-400 *AH*

pair of Samson 'famille rose' deep
ɜhes, painted with peacocks
nong flowering shrubs and
ckwork, within a floral border and
›n red rim, 13in (33cm) diam.
50-450 *CSK*

ı early Spode dish, painted with
ll blown roses, c1815, 10in (25cm).
20-160 *TVA*

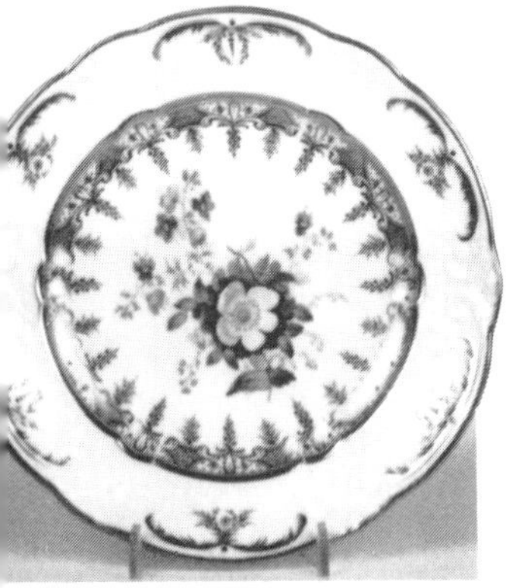

Swansea plate, painted by
illiam Pollard within an elaborate
t diaper and foliage well, reserved
th gilt green berried foliage,
thin a gilt line rim, red stencil
ırk, c1820, 8in (20cm).
,000-1,500 *C*

A pair of Chamberlain's Worcester armorial plates, red script mark, c1820, 10in (25cm).
£650-700 *TVA*

A pair of Worcester blue scale plates, of Lady Mary Wortley Montagu type, painted in the atelier of James Giles, with loose bouquets and flowersprays within gilt vase and mirror-shaped cartouches, minor rubbing, blue square seal marks, c1770, 8½in (22cm).
£1,700-2,000 *C*

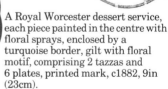

A Worcester green ground dish, c1775, 10in (25cm).
£900-1,000 *Sto*

A Barr, Flight & Barr, Worcester shaped armorial dish, with central arms and motto, flanked by gilt formal scrolling foliage, the border with a band of gilt anthemion, scrolls and foliage between gilt lines, slight wear, impressed and printed marks, c1816, 11in (28cm) wide.
£700-800 *C*

The Arms are those of Prendergast, 1st Viscount Gort.

A set of 6 Worcester plates, decorated within egg shell blue border, with ornate pierced latticed rim, lined in pink, with gilt moulded lambrequins, impressed mark, c1865, 9in (23cm).
£200-250 *Bon*

A Royal Worcester dessert service, each piece painted in the centre with floral sprays, enclosed by a turquoise border, gilt with floral motif, comprising 2 tazzas and 6 plates, printed mark, c1882, 9in (23cm).
£250-300 *Bon*

A pair of Barr, Flight & Barr dessert plates, painted with figures in the centre, the white borders with meandering scroll and anthemion motifs in gilt, printed and impressed marks, 8½in (21cm).
£1,200-1,500 *GSP*

A pair of Chamberlain's Worcester dishes, the centres decorated with polychrome flowers, pink border surround with flower decorated panels, 10in (25cm).
£350-400 *AH*

A Royal Worcester plate, signed by J. Freeman, c1950, 9in (23cm).
£70-100 *TVA*

A pair of Royal Worcester dessert dishes, the hand painted central panel by J. Stinton, with deep blu and gilt decorated border surroun with polychrome floral reserve panels, 9in (23cm).
£1,200-1,500 *AH*

A Chamberlain's Worcester plate, from the Princess Charlotte service, c1816, 10in (25cm).
£800-1,000 *DOW*

A Grainger's Worcester plate, painted with birds in the centre, signed by James Stinton, c1899, 8½in (21cm).
£450-500 *TVA*

A pair of Worcester blue and white dishes, decorated with butterflies and floral and fruit sprays, 13in (34cm) wide.
£1,000-1,200 *GC*

A pair of English porcelain 'jewelled' plates, c1880, 9in (23cm).
£350-400 *TVA*

A pair of Meissen plates, with a poppy, fritillary and insects, crossed swords marks, c1735, 9½in (24cm).
£1,500-2,000 *C*

An English dessert dish, with polychrome central reserve depicting Coniston Lake, in gilt scrolled border surround on pink ground, 11in (29cm) wide.
£400-450 *AH*

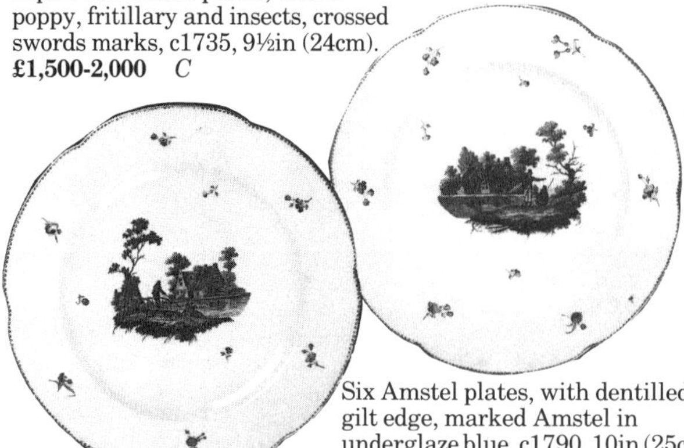

Six Amstel plates, with dentilled gilt edge, marked Amstel in underglaze blue, c1790, 10in (25cm).
£2,500-3,000 *CAm*

oyal Worcester comport raised
ow foot, the dish painted by
.ing, within a gilt border,
ited in coloured enamels in the
nese 'famille rose' style,
ressed marks, 9½in (24cm).
0-400 *CSK*

[eissen plate, painted in colours
gilt within a surround of flowers
insects, the border painted in
e and gilt with gilt scrolling rim
turquoise feather painted edge,
e crossed swords and dot mark,
ing worn, c1770, 8½in (21cm).
0-300 *CSK*

air of Meissen Schmetterling
cer dishes, painted in the
kiemon style, with chocolate
s, crossed swords marks, c1740,
(20cm).
00-1,500 *C*

Locate the source

The source of each illustration in Miller's can be found by checking the code letters below each caption with the list of contributors

A Sèvres pattern turquoise ground tray, reserved and painted with a central portrait of Henri IV, surrounded by portraits of Court beauties, named on the reverse, within gilt band and foliage scroll cartouches, with gilt rim, some rubbing, imitation interlaced L marks, late 19thC, 19in (48cm) diam, on a carved stand enriched in gilding, damaged.
£2,000-2,500 *C*

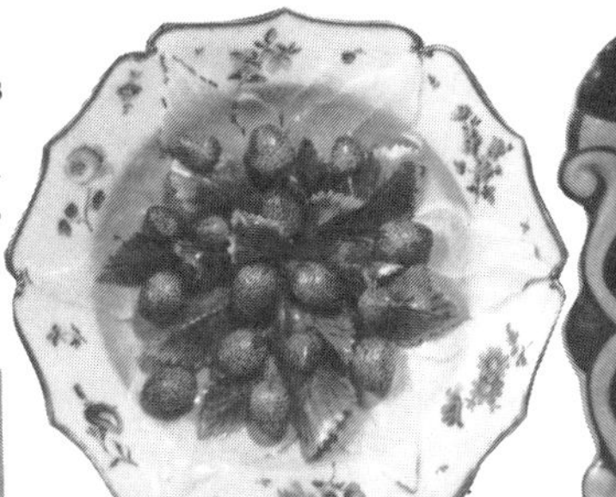

A German trompe l'oeil plate, with scattered flowers to the border, within a gilt rim, small chips to leaves, gilding rubbed, c1765, 9in (23cm).
£2,000-2,500 *C*

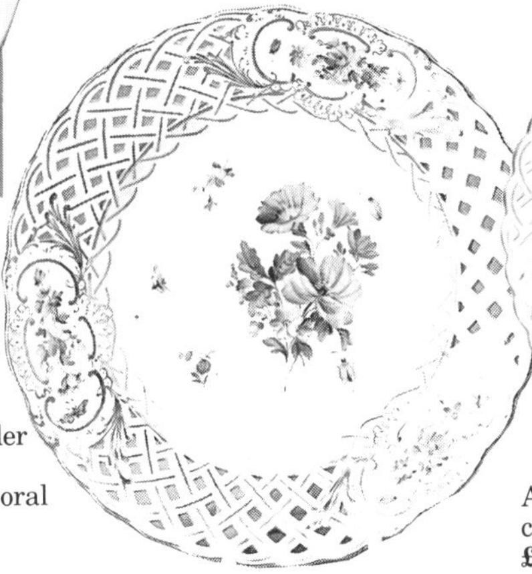

A set of 5 Meissen pierced border plates, the borders with gilt latticework with alternating floral panels, 19thC, 8in (20cm).
£650-750 *Bon*

A Vienna, Du Paquier, plate painted in the Oriental style, enriched with gilding, within an iron red diaper border, reserved with 4 panels of flowers, incised N, c1735, 9in (23cm).
£1,000-1,500 *C*

A Spode dish, c1815, 10½in (26cm) wide.
£350-450 *DOW*

A pair of Ridgway dishes, c1820, 8½in (21cm).
£350-450 *DOW*

A Meissen Marcolini pierced plate, c1763, 9½in (23.5cm).
£400-450 *BHA*

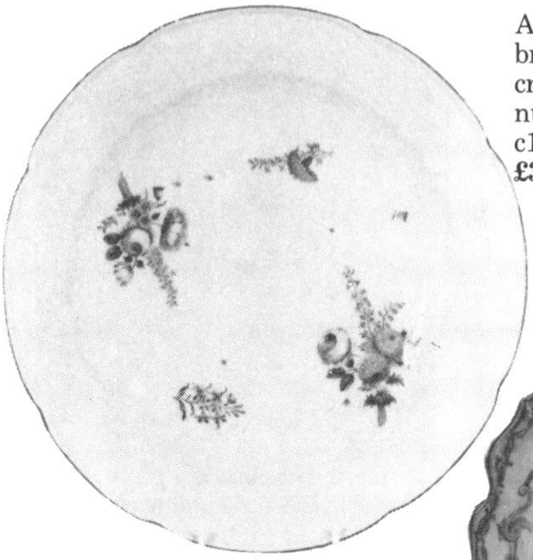

A Meissen dish with fluted sides and brown rim, minute rim chips, blue crossed swords and impressed numerals, impressed number 20, c1750, 12in (30cm).
£350-450 *CSK*

A 'Vienna' puce ground plate, tł puce border with classical heads flanked by figures and gilt scrol floral foliage beneath green and borders, imitation blue beehive mark, c1880, 10in (25cm).
£500-700 *C*

A Vienna, Du Paquier, dish painted in Schwarzlot, with a shepherd and companion, the border with trails of leaves enriched with gilding, the reverse with a band of continuous foliage, 3 chips and crack to rim, c1730, 13½in (34cm).
£1,000-1,500 *C*

A Sèvres rose ground tray, painted in colours with a landscape, enclosed by gilt scrolls and trails of flowers shaded in puce, gilt dentil rim, rim broken and repaired, interlaced L's enclosing date letter H for 1760, incised BP, the decoration possibly later, 11½in (29cm) wide.
£2,000-2,500 *C*

A pair of 'Vienna' plates, the r blue borders reserved with put within oval gilt beaded cartou with foliate and diaper ornam within lobed rims, imitation b beehive mark, 20thC, 9in (23c
£900-1,200 *C*

A 'Vienna' gold ground dish, the centre reserved and painted by H. Görner with Mercury descending from clouds, the richly gilt border with tooled ornament and reserved with 6 pale mauve roundels gilt with birds, the rim gilt, the reverse inscribed Mercur und Herse, signed, imitation blue beehive mark, late 19thC, 18½in (47cm).
£2,500-3,500 *C*

A Sèvres pattern turquoise ground tray, the centre painted by Paul Fortin, The Village Wedding by Greuze, within a gilt rim, signed, imitation interlaced L marks, late 19thC, 19in (50cm) diam, with plush and carved giltwood frame.
£1,700-2,500 *C*

A 'Vienna' dish, painted by Fale inscribed Coquetterie on the reverse, the young woman wear a mauve dress, a pink rose in he hair, the rim gilt, signed, imitat blue beehive mark, c1900, 13½i (34cm).
£550-650 *C*

A pair of 'Vienna' shallow dishes, painted by Elm, inscribed on the reverses, the rims gilt, the footrims pierced for hanging, signed, imitation blue beehive marks, late 19thC, 11½in (30cm). **£1,000-1,200** *C*

e Pails

air of Coalport ice pails, covers
. liners painted within seeded
e borders edged with gilt foliage,
liner and one stem repaired, rim
), some staining, c1820, 10½in
:m).
)00-3,500 *C*

air of Chamberlain's Worcester
ket shaped ice pails, covers and
rs, with gilt shell and foliage
dles and dolphin and cone
als, one body with crack to rim,
handle restored, enamel
:ing, 3 small rim chips, script
:ks in puce, c1800, 10½in (27cm).
)00-7,000 *C*

kwells

amuel Alcock inkstand in blue
gilt, c1840, 15in (38cm) wide.
0-800 *BHA*

) Coalbrookdale inkwells of
nion shape, painted with flowers,
e factory marks, 5in (13cm).
0-250 *CSK*

Jardinières

A Coalport flared flower pot and stand, decorated in the London studio of Thames Baxter, the stand with 3 gilt paw feet, gilding rubbed, c1805, 6½in (16.5cm) wide.
£650-750 *C*

A Sèvres bucket shaped jardinière, the blue and gold mosaic borders with 4 panels of flowers enclosed by gilt scrolls, gilt rim and footrim, gilding to footrim rubbed, blue interlaced L marks enclosing date letter H for 1760, painter's mark for Méreau jeune, incised 4, 9in (22cm) wide.
£2,000-3,000 *C*

A Minton leaf-shaped inkwell, with branch handle, applied with flowers and leaves, chips and small cracks, one cover restuck, c1835, 8½in (21.5cm).
£1,500-2,000 *C*

Two Chamberlain's Worcester inkwells, modelled as groups of coloured shells on seaweed and rockwork moulds and square canted bases, in underglaze blue enriched with gilding, c1840, 3½in (8.5cm) wide.
£900-1,000 *C*

Jugs

A Caughley jug with the Fisherman pattern, marked, c1780, 5½in (14cm).
£300-350 *THA*

A Davenport jug, c1825, 5in (14cm).
£200-300 *DOW*

A Lowestoft blue and white moulded jug, painted between borders of moulded pendant leaves and flowers, painter's numeral 5, c1765, 10in (26cm).
£900-1,200 *C*

A Christian's Liverpool creamer, with chinoiserie decoration, 3in (8cm).
£500-600 *BHA*

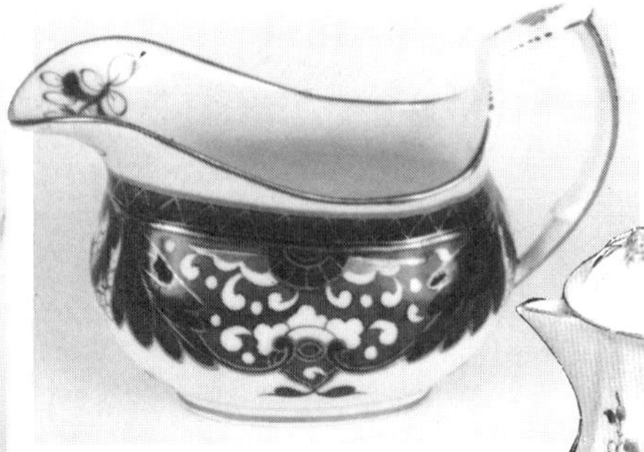

A Chamberlain's cream jug, decorated with the Japan pattern, c1820, 6in (15cm) wide.
£175-200 *TVA*

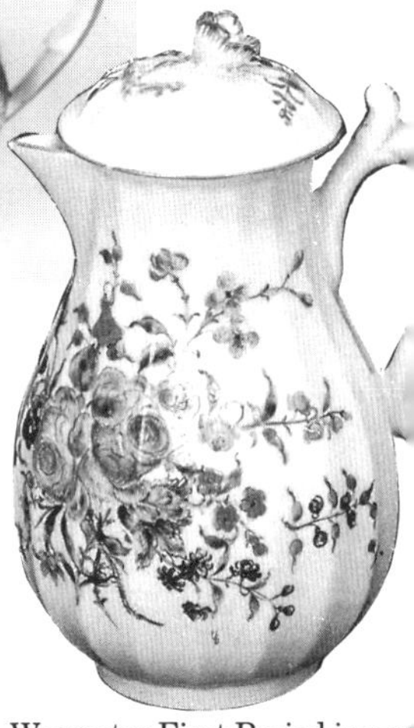

A Worcester First Period jug a cover, the domed cover with flo head finial, blue underglaze se mark, c1765, 5½in (13.5cm).
£500-600 *WW*

A Lowestoft cream jug, painted in a 'famille rose' palette, beneath a border of swags of flowers and an iron red line rim, minute crack to lip, c1790, 3in (8cm).
£200-250 *C*

A Derby crested oviform mask jug, with the motto An Droit Devant, flanked by bouquets and flowersprays 'en camaieu rose', Wm. Duesbury & Co, slight chip to lip, c1780, 9½in (23.5cm).
£800-900 *C*

The crest is that of Molyneux.

A Grainger & Co., Worcester oviform jug, with scroll handle, painted with huntsmen wearing pink and a squire within a gilt cartouche, rim crack and restoration, script mark, c1805, 1 (25cm).
£1,000-1,500 *C*

A Staffordshire porcelain baluster jug, painted with a view of Worcester within a gilt panel and flanked by flowersprays on an apple green ground, the wide gilt neck inscribed in script 'J F S & L A M', 8in (20cm).
£200-250 *CSK*

A Lowestoft baluster cream jug, cracked body, rim chipped, c1785, 3in (7.5cm).
£200-250 *C*

A Royal Worcester miniature jug, dated 1909, 1½in (4cm).
£100-150 *TVA*

Worcester jug, with chinoiserie
ecoration, c1760, 3½in (9cm).
300-850 *BHA*

Two miniature Spode jugs, c1820, 1½in (4cm). **£200-250** *DOW*

A Coalport mug, c1850, 3½in (8cm).
£50-70 *THA*

A Coalport mug, transfer printed with a view in Shrewsbury, c1880, (3in) 8cm.
£40-60 *TVA*

Royal Worcester miniature jug,
ated 1912, 2in (5cm).
100-150 *TVA*

baluster jug, with gilt angular
andle, slight cracks to base,
encilled Pardoe Cardiff mark
ithin a shaped rectangular
rtouche, c1820, 6in (15cm).
450-550 *C*

Mugs

A Bow baluster mug, with grooved handle and heart-shaped terminal, painted in the 'famille rose' palette with flowers issuing from pierced rockwork, the rim with flowers reserved on a narrow diaper, minute chip to rim, crack to base of handle, painter's numeral 10, c1755, 5in (12.5cm).
£600-700 *C*

A Coalport miniature mug, signed S. Schofield, 1½in (3.5cm).
£85-100 *THA*

A Lowestoft blue and white mug, transfer printed with an Oriental crossing a bridge, the interior with a diaper pattern rim, c1780, 6in (14.5cm).
£450-650 *C*

Use the Index!

Because certain items might fit easily into any of a number of categories, the quickest and surest method of locating any entry is by reference to the index at the back of the book.
This has been fully cross-referenced for absolute simplicity

A Coalport coffee can dated 1807, initialled J.V., 2½in (6cm).
£125-175 *THA*

A Derby bell-shaped mug, with grooved handle, painted in colours on either side, slight damage, mid-18thC, 5in (13cm).
£700-900 *Bea*

A Hancock bell-shaped mug, The Masons Company of Edinburgh, small restoration, c1765, 5in (14cm).
£900-1,000 *BHA*

A bone china bat-printed mug, c1820, 3in (8cm).
£60-80 *THA*

A Lowestoft blue and white baluster mug, with scroll handle, cracked, foot chipped, painter's numeral 4, c1765, 6in (15cm).
£300-350 *C*

A Pinxton mug, decorated with a yellow band, painted with stylised floral designs, letter P mark in gold, c1900, 4½in (11cm).
£450-550 *Bea*

A Worcester blue scale baluster mug, with grooved loop handle, reserved with mirror and vase shaped cartouches edged with gilt scrolls enclosing swags of garden flowers, the handle enriched in gilding, blue square seal mark, c1770, 6in (15cm).
£2,000-2,500 *C*

Three miniature mugs, 1½in (4cm). **£30-60 each** *THA*

A First Period Worcester tankard, painted with the Walk in the Garden pattern, open crescent mark, c1760, 6in (15cm).
£1,200-1,500 *TVA*

A Coalport mug, c1835, 3½in (8cm).
£40-60 *THA*

A Copeland hand painted mug, c1850, 3in (8cm).
£80-100 *THA*

Vorcester mug, painted in a
oical 'famille rose' palette, with
e Beckoning Chinaman pattern,
ck to top of handle, painter's
rk, c1758, 4in (11cm).
00-1,200 *C*

Vorcester mug, painted with a
iquet and scattered flowers,
nute crack to rim, c1760, 4½in
cm).
200-1,500 *C*

Vorcester blue and white
uster mug, printed with
terflies and flowersprays, handle
cked, crescent marks, c1770, 6in
cm). **£150-200** *CSK*

nug, c1825, 2½in (7cm).
-75 *THA*

A Worcester miniature mug, 1¼in (3cm).
£50-70 *THA*

An English matt blue ground mug, with moulded scroll handle, painted with baskets of fruit and flowers within gilt cartouches, gilt monogram 'EMK' within oval reserves, c1820, 5½in (13cm).
£1,500-2,000 *C*

Plaques

A Worcester white glazed wall pocket, moulded as a young girl supporting a basket, within ivory border, 10in (25cm) high, mounted on a plush wall plaque.
£250-300 *P(M)*

A pair of English plaques, painted with vases of flowers, one with hair cracks, both with restoration to decoration, mid-19thC, carved giltwood frames, 12½ by 9½in (32 by 24cm).
£3,000-4,000 *C*

A pair of small Fürstenberg rococo framed Imperial portrait plaques, painted in colours, of the Emperor Joseph II of Austria and the Empress Marie-Josephine of Austria, damaged and restored, marked to the glazed sloping sides with an underglaze blue F, late 1760s.
£15,000-18,000 *CAm*

A Berlin plaque, painted after the style of Guido Reni, with a portrait of the Virgin Mary wearing an ochre shawl and dark draped robes, impressed sceptre and KPM marks, c1880, 7½in (19cm) high, in carved giltwood frame.
£450-550 *C*

A Berlin plaque, impressed sceptre and KPM marks, late 19thC, 8½in (22cm) high, plush and giltwood frame. **£650-750** *C*

A Vienna hand painted plaque, wi underglaze blue beehive mark to base.
£650-750 *GIL*

A Berlin plaque, painted in bright colours, inscribed on the reverse, impressed KPM and sceptre marks, imitation beehive mark, late 19thC, 10in (25cm) high, carved giltwood frame.
£4,500-5,000 *C*

A German plaque painted in colours, c1880, 3in (7cm), gilt frame.
£200-300 *CSK*

A pair of Continental plaques of putti, 7 by 5½in (17.5 by 14cm), in gilt frames.
£600-700 *AH*

Pots

A Bow miniature flower p with 4 yellow fixed ring handles, painted with flov the body with raised brown ribs, the top rim wi alternating puce and yellc gadroons, chip to foot, incised 26, c1760, 1½in (4cm).
£450-550 *C*

A Derby bough pot of demi-lune form, with twin lion mask terminals, painted and coloured with sprigs of roses, divided by gilt foliage within gilt bands, restored, gilding worn, puce factory marks, 5in (13cm).
£100-150 *CSK*

A Coalport D-shaped bough pot pierced cover, the blue ground enriched in gilt with flowerheads reserved with cartouches of gard flowers, cracked and chipped, fee re-stuck, c1805, 7½in (18cm).
£600-800 *C*

In the Ceramics section if there is only one measurement it usually refers to the height of the piece

Sauceboats

A Caughley blue and white sauce boat, c1780, 6½in (16cm) wide.
£250-300 *THA*

Make the Most of Miller's

In Miller's we do NOT just reprint saleroom estimates. We work from realised prices either from an auction room or a dealer. Our consultants then work out a realistic price range for a similar piece. This is to try to avoid repeating freak results – either low or high

Scent Bottles

Coalport scent bottle, encrusted ith flowers, marked C.D., 3½in cm).
180-200 *THA*

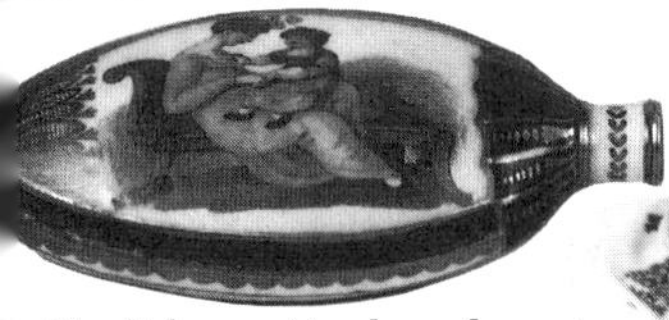

n English navette-shaped scent ttle, bat printed and coloured with gures, within blue and gilt borders, 810, 4in (10cm) long.
100-150 *C*

Services

n armorial part dinner service, ade as replacements to a Chinese rvice, comprising: 6 tureens, vers and stands, 7 oval meat shes, 2 dishes, perhaps Coalport, up tureen covers cracked, c1805.
,000-4,500 *CSK*

A Coalport part dessert service, painted with iron red bands with yellow scrolling foliage on a gilt and white diamond pattern ground, reserved with gilt navette shaped paterae between gilt line rims, comprising 22 pieces, gilding rubbed, some damage, c1810.
£2,500-3,500 *C*

A Coalport part tea and coffee service, comprising: 6 teacups and saucers, 6 coffee cups and saucers and 2 plates, c1860.
£500-600 *THA*

A Coalport blue and white cabaret set, in Pine Cone pattern, including 6 cups and saucers, c1850.
£500-550 *THA*

A Royal Crown Derby part coffee service, painted by W. E. J. Dean, comprising, a coffee pot and cover, a sugar bowl and cover, a box and cover, 2 trays and 6 cups and saucers, and a plate, yachts named on reverse, printed factory marks, 20thC.
£3,000-3,500 *CSK*

A Coalport blue ground part dessert service, painted with pink roses and vetch within pale yellow cartouches enriched with gilding, comprising 28 pieces, chips to stand, one dish repaired, c1820.
£5,000-6,000 *C*

A Derby Imari pattern composite part dinner, breakfast and coffee service, painted within gilt line rims, comprising 216 pieces, Robt. Bloor & Co., some staining, crown, crossed batons and D marks and printed crowned D marks in iron red, c1825.
£10,000-12,000 *C*

A Coalport composite gold ground part tea and coffee service, painted on a gold ground between bands of gilt scrolling foliage, diamond and loop pattern or anthemion, within gilt line rims, comprising 52 pieces, some minor rubbing to gilding, some pieces later replacements, c1810.
£5,500-6,500 *C*

A Royal Crown Derby fruit service, decorated in red on a white ground, bordered in deep blue and gilt, comprising: a pair of comports, 4 dishes and 12 plates.
£600-700 *DDM*

A Derby part dinner service, printed and painted in iron red and underglaze blue in the Imari pattern and enriched with gilding, comprising: meat dish, 2 vegetable tureens and covers, sauce tureen, cover, stand and ladle, a gravy boat and stand, 6 soup plates, and 21 plates, impressed and printed marks.
£1,000-1,500 *CSK*

A Copeland Imari pattern part dessert service, with flowers and foliage, enriched in gilding, comprising: 2 tazzas, 4 comports and 12 plates.
£1,000-1,500 *CSK*

A Derby armorial part tea service, painted in Smith's blue and gilt with a coat-of-arms and crest, within a shaped blue and gilt border, comprising: teapot, cover and stand, slop basin, 2 plates, sugar bowl cover, 12 teacups and 16 saucers, Wm. Duesbury & Co., some damage, crowned D marks in puce, c1785.
£2,000-2,500 *C*

The arms are possibly those of either the City or Bishopric of Durham.

A Derby part dessert service, the centres painted with urns and scattered bouquets within wide Smith's blue borders, gilt with scrolling anthemion between gilt and white dot pattern rims, comprising: a two-handled centrepiece, 3 dishes, 4 soup plates and 15 plates, some damage, Wm. Duesbury & Co., entwined anchor and D marks in gold, some pieces with crowned D mark in blue, c1775.
£1,500-2,000 *C*

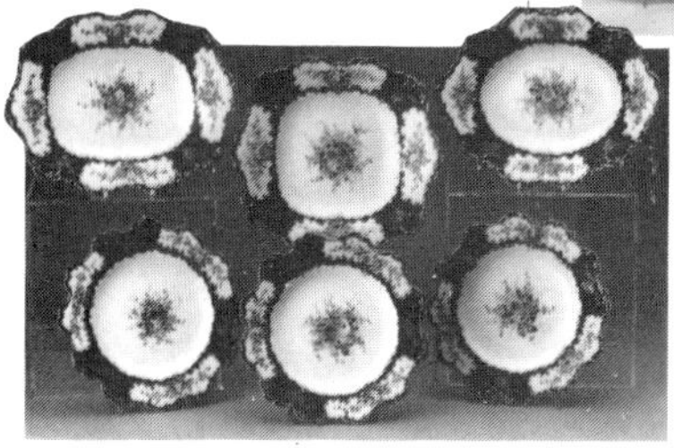

A Royal Crown Derby part dessert service, decorated with central flower bouquets within a wide blue border with floral reserves, enriched with gilt floral sprays, comprising 18 pieces.
£1,600-2,000 *Bon*

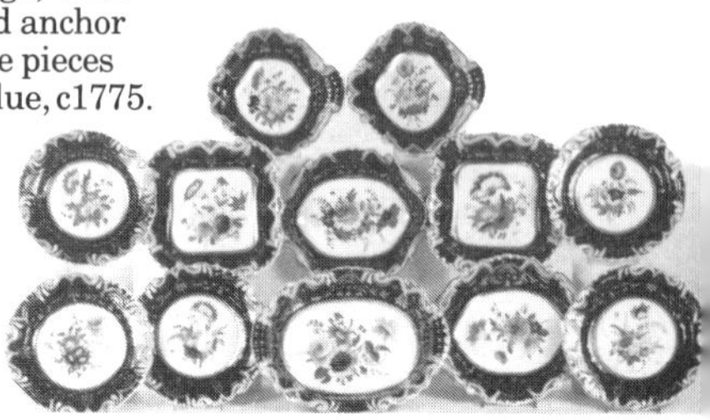

A Ridgway blue ground part dessert service, painted within a deep blue border gilt with foliage, within a moulded yellow scroll and gilt shell rim, comprising: 7 dishes, one riveted, some damage, and 12 plates, slight rubbing, pattern No. 733, c1830.
£2,000-3,000 *C*

A Derby part tea service, painted with the 'Imari' pattern in underglaze blue and iron red enriched in gilding, comprising: creamer, 9 teacups, 11 coffee cans and 11 saucers, the creamer and a coffee can cracked, gilding rubbed.
£600-800 *CSK*

A Staffordshire porcelain cabaret set, printed with panels of flowers in Imari colours comprising: teapot and cover, a sugar basin and cover, milk jug, 4 teacups and saucers and a tray, some damage.
£400-600 *CSK*

. Worcester blue and white part tea
ervice, painted with the Fence
attern and a Chinese pavilion on a
ocky island and 2 flying wild
ucks, the domed covers with
owerbud finials, comprising:
eapot and cover, milk jug and cover,
ugar pot and cover, cream pot and
over, broth bowl, basket with cover
nd stand, 12 cups and saucers and
cups, very minor chips, marked
ith an underglaze blue crescent,
ate 18thC.
2,000-2,500 *CAm*

A pair of Niderviller porcelain dishes, painted in colours within gilt rims, blue crowned interlaced C's, Custine period, c1775, and a matching dish.
£1,200-1,500 *CG*

A Meissen miniature tête-à-tête, each piece applied with coloured flowers beneath gilt rims, comprising: coffee pot and cover, milk jug, a sugar bowl and cover, 2 cups and saucers and a tray, some chipping to flowers, blue crossed swords marks, c1880, in fitted leather case, worn.
£3,000-4,000 *C*

A Victorian Royal Worcester china dinner service, with Chinese vase and floral decoration, comprising 44 pieces.
£400-500 *P(M)*

Chamberlain's Worcester apricot
ound part breakfast service, the
ntres with gilt paterae within a
order of gilt radiating diamond
attern and a band of gilt scrolling
liage and paterae, comprising 18
eces, pattern No. 305, some
amage, c1800.
3,000-4,000 *C*

A Jacob Petit porcelain neo-rococo tea service, comprising 32 pieces, some damage and repair, painted mark in underglaze blue.
£600-700 *HSS*

Worcester, Flight and Barr, part
a service, painted in the
akiemon palette with The Quail
ttern, within gilt line rims,
mprising: teapot, cover and stand,
gar bowl, milk jug, slop bowl, a
ucer dish, 8 teacups and saucers,
me damage, incised B marks,
805.
3,000-4,000 *C*

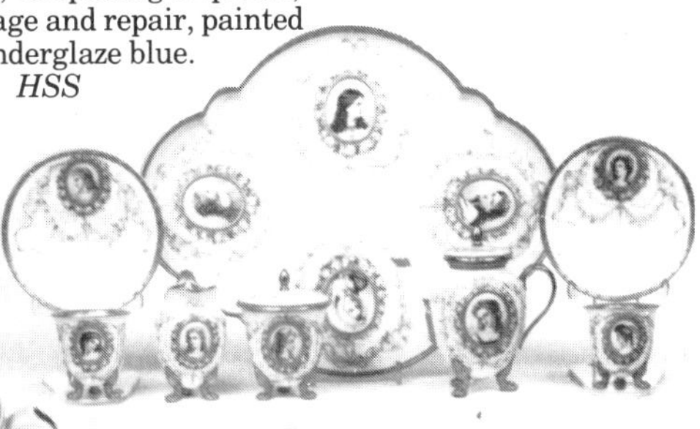

A Royal Worcester tête-à-tête, each piece painted within gilt band and beaded cartouche enclosed by pink roses and suspended from tied blue ribbon, on richly gilt claw feet, comprising 8 pieces, green and brown printed crown marks, c1865.
£2,000-2,500 *C*

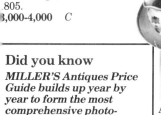

A Chamberlain's Worcester miniature teaset, including an egg cup, marked, tray 8in (20cm) diam.
£900-1,000 *Sto*

Did you know

MILLER'S Antiques Price Guide builds up year by year to form the most comprehensive photo-reference system available

Locate the source

The source of each illustration in Miller's can be found by checking the code letters below each caption with the list of contributors

A Copenhagen celadon ground tête-à-tête, reserved and painted with views, comprising: teapot and cover, a sugar bowl and cover, 2 cups and saucers, and an oval tray, the centre with crowned LC monogram and inscribed, some repairs, blue waved line marks, c1860.
£2,000-3,000 *C*

A Meissen part dinner service, painted within 'Neubrandenstein' moulded borders and shaped gilt rims, comprising: a two-handled soup tureen, cover and stand, 2 vegetable dishes and covers, 2 serving dishes, and 23 dinner plates, some damage, blue crossed swords marks, c1900.
£4,000-4,500 *C*

A Sèvres pattern turquoise groun tea service, decorated in colours within gilt band cartouches, the rims gilt, comprising: a teapot an cover, milk jug, two-handled suga bowl and cover, 12 teacups and saucers, and 14 plates, some damage, imitation interlaced L marks, late 19thC.
£2,000-3,000 *C*

An English porcelain part tea service, bat printed in grey with animals in their habitats, with chocolate rims, comprising: sugar bowl and cover, a miniature plate, one teacup, 6 coffee cans and 3 saucers, slight damage.
£500-550 *CSK*

A Rauenstein part tea service, moulded with wavy vertical ribs and painted in purple with landscape vignettes and scattered flowers, comprising: teapot and cover, tea caddy and cover, sugar box and cover, 3 teacups and saucers, puce crossed swords mark c1780.
£1,000-1,500 *CG*

Sucriers

A Wedgwood bone china sucrier and cover, painted in puce, marked, 5½in (14cm).
£200-250 *Sto*

A Samuel Alcock sucrier and cover, c1835, 6in (15cm).
£280-320 *DOW*

Tea & Coffee Pots

A Bow baluster chocolate pot and a Chinese cover, painted in a 'famille rose' palette with The Quail Pattern, the grooved loop handle with heart-shaped terminal, the cover with flowers, repaired and riveted, c1758, 6½in (16cm).
£300-400 *C*

A Coalport teapot, with the Japan/Imari pattern, 7½in (18cm).
£150-200 *THA*

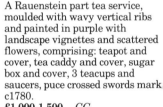

A Minton teapot, cover and stand c1825, 10in (25cm) wide.
£250-300 *DOW*

A Coalport teapot and stand, wit the Easter Lily pattern, John Ros & Co, c1805, 7½in (19cm).
£200-250 *THA*

›erby teapot and cover, with gilt
; handle and painted with
ıflowers, finial restuck, crossed
ons and D mark in puce,
›ressed initials BNP, c1795, 9in
.5cm) wide.
‹0-450 *CSK*

A Lowestoft blue and white transfer printed coffee pot and cover, slight crack to body, rim chip, c1780, 10½in (26.5cm).
£1,000-1,200 *C*

A Minton topographical part veilleuse, the teapot and cover with gilt borders of diaper pattern, trellis and dots, edged with gilt scrolls, the cover with gilt finial, base lacking, c1840, 7½in (19cm).
£350-450 *C*

owestoft teapot and cover,
ıted in a 'famille rose' palette
ı Orientals, the cover with
'ers and pink flower finial, the
y extensively repaired, cover
finial chipped, c1772, 4½in
5cm).
0-450 *C*

A coffee pot, possibly Grainger's Worcester, c1810, 10½in (26cm).
£200-250 *Sto*

A Worcester blue scale baluster coffee pot and cover, painted with flowers within cartouches, the cover with pink flower finial, chips to finial and footrim, blue square seal mark, c1768, 8½in (21.5cm).
£5,500-6,500 *C*

owestoft teapot and cover,
ıted in pink 'camaieu', perhaps
he Tulip Painter, with borders of
scrolling foliage, cracked body,
ıt repaired, gilding rubbed,
'5, 5½in (14cm).
:00-1,500 *C*

A Meissen Hausmalerei white ground chinoiserie gilt teapot with cover and 6 teacups and saucers, in the style of F. J. Ferners, painted in underglaze blue, with flowers painted in colours, minor chips to spout, the cups and saucers marked with crossed swords, dotted hilts and central dot, c1755.
£3,000-3,500 *CAm*

A Worcester teapot, with different raised pattern each side, c1765, 4in (10cm).
£1,250-1,500 *BHA*

A Lowestoft teapot and cover, painted in a 'famille rose' palette, hair crack beneath the spout, c1785, 6½in (16cm).
£450-550 *C*

A Meissen Watteauszehen 'camaieu' purple coffee pot and domed cover, with artichoke finial, painted to each side with Italian Commedia dell'Arte figures and scattered 'Holzschnitt Blumen', all enriched with gilding, crossed swords mark, c1745, with silver gilt chased mount to the spout, 9in (23cm).
£1,500-2,000 *CG*

A Worcester teapot, cover and hexafoil stand, enriched in dry b the centre of the stand with a dry blue flowerspray, within gilt den rims, spout restored, c1775, the stand 6in (15cm) wide.
£400-450 *C*

A Worcester teapot with chinoiserie pattern, crack to base, c1765, 6in (15cm).
£375-400 *BHA*

A Hochst teapot and a cover, painted in puce monochrome, wit pair of matching teacups and saucers, restored red wheel mark and impressed marks, c1750.
£100-150 *CSK*

Tureens & Butter Tubs

A Caughley polychrome tureen, c1780, 9in (23cm) wide.
£250-300 *THA*

A pair of Rockingham sauce tureens, covers and stands, paint with flowers within gadroon, she and foliage moulded rims, the gi handles extending to 4 branch fe with leaf and acorn terminals, cracked and some staining, patte No. 534, iron red griffin marks, c1830, 7in (17.5cm) wide.
£2,000-2,500 *C*

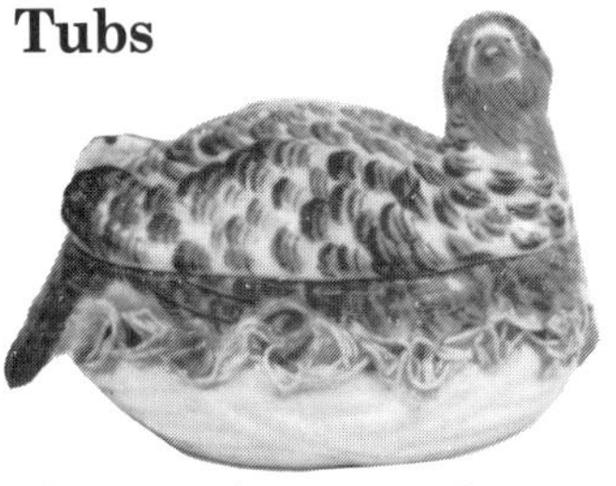

A Bow partridge tureen and a cover, naturally modelled in brown, yellow, blue and purple, the nest edged with yellow straw and green leaves, minor chipping to foliage, base crack, c1760, 5in (12.5cm) wide.
£900-1,200 *C*

A Derby two-handled sauce tureen and cover, the handles and paw feet terminating in lion heads, brightly painted on either side with sprays of flowers and gold scrolling foliage, painted mark in red, early 19thC, 7in (17.5cm).
£2,000-2,500 *Bea*

A Caughley blue and white butter dish and stand, c1785.
£300-350 *THA*

A pair of Derby tureens and stands, c1820, 8in (20cm).
£1,000-1,200 *DOW*

ɪair of First Period Worcester
ʼtridge-on-nest tureens and
ʼers, each bird with naturalistic
ımage, colour enamelled mainly
ıron red, c1760, 4½in (11cm).
500-3,500 *Bon*

A Chamberlain's Worcester armorial sauce tureen, ladle and stand, c1810, 7in (18cm).
£900-1,000 *Sto*

\ Worcester Royal armorial sauce
ureen and cover, from the service
nade to the order of the Duke of
ʼlarence, the Arms with the Garter
notto and with the Order of St.
\ndrew, the cover with entwined
ibbons of the Orders of the Garter
ınd Thistle, finial restored, crowned
cript Flight and crescent mark in
lue, c1789, 7in (17cm) wide.
:800-1,000 *C*

*Лade in 1789 when Prince William
vas created Duke of Clarence and St.
\ndrew; this was the first Royal
ervice made at Worcester.*

A Worcester quatrefoil tureen and cover, with branch handles and finial, painted with bouquets and scattered flowers, 11in (28cm) wide.
£200-300 *CSK*

A pair of Flight, Barr & Barr, Worcester pale blue ground sauce tureens and covers, with entwined gilt vinestock handles, painted with Malvern Abbey Church, and a church, the reverses with exotic birds in landscape vignettes, the bases edged in gilt and bronze, the covers with gilt cone finials, impressed marks, one with script marks and inscribed, c1815.
£4,000-5,000 *C*

A Chelsea vase, painted in the Kakiemon palette beneath a border of scrolling blue foliage, the neck with iron red panels, extensively riveted, raised anchor mark, c1750, 9in (22.5cm).
£2,000-3,000 *C*

The price would be £1,200-1,800 without the raised anchor mark.

ases

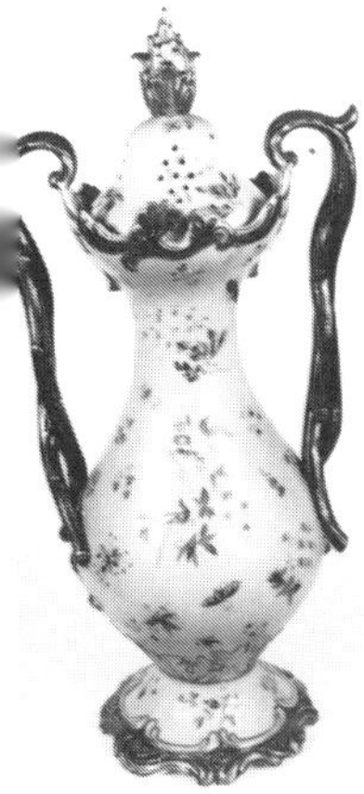

ɪair of Samuel Alcock porcelain
pourri vases, c1840, 25½in
:m).
200-1,500 *BHA*

A Bow flower vase, the top pierced with holes around a central aperture, the body applied with female masks surrounded by puce moulded scrolls and coloured flowers, some flowerheads and foliage lacking, indistinct painter's numeral in brown, c1762, 5in (12.5cm).
£800-900 *C*

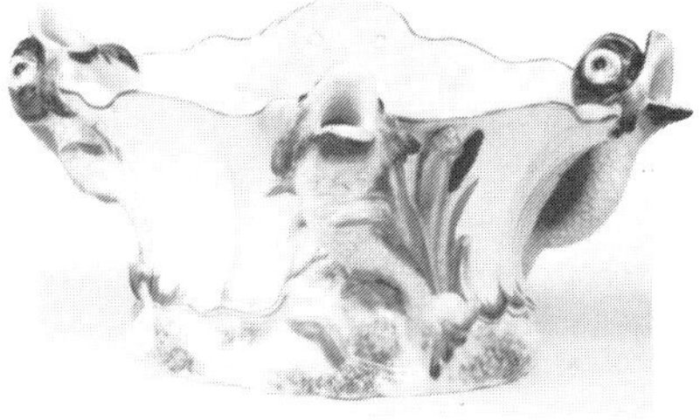

A Chelsea bough pot, the sides moulded and coloured with dolphins and bulrushes, the lower part with gilt 'feuille de choux' on a green rockwork base, restoration, red anchor mark, c1756, 13in (32cm) wide.
£2,000-2,500 *C*

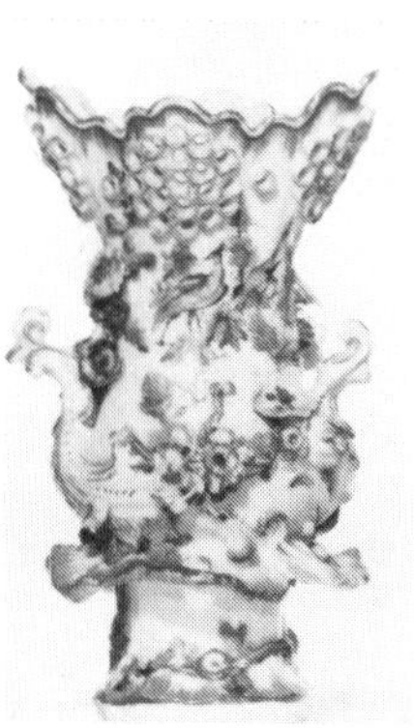

A pair of Chelsea vases of scrolling form, with spreading pierced necks, pierced frill, minor damage and restoration, gold anchor marks, 8in (20cm).
£550-650 *CSK*

A Chelsea mottled claret ground vase and cover, with gilt loop handles, painted in the manner of Richard Askew, crack to rim, restoration, c1765, 12in (30cm).
£1,000-1,200 *C*

A Coalport two-handled campana vase, the gold ground reserved with brown ground panels and painted 'en grisaille', perhaps in the Studio of Thomas Baxter, with Hercules slaying the Lernaean Hydra, flanked by vertical bands of purple foliage, handles restored, some re-gilding, impressed number 25, c1805, 10in (25cm).
£350-450 *C*

A Coalport documentary vase, decorated in the London studio of Thomas Baxter, painted in sepia within a gilt oval cartouche, reserved on a gilt and white chequered ground between bands of gilt scrolling foliage, the neck and foot painted with bands of coloured flowers, slight rubbing to gilding, signed T. Baxter, 1802, 11½in (29cm).
£1,200-1,500 *C*

A Coalport pot pourri and cover, c1820, 5½in (14cm).
£500-600 *DOW*

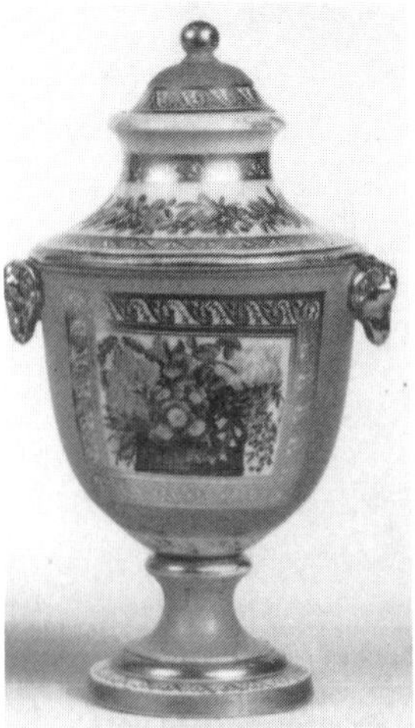

A Coalport sponged pale blue ground vase and cover, with gilt rams mask handles, painted in the studio of Thomas Baxter, slight rubbing to gilding, c1805, 10½in (27cm).
£600-700 *C*

A Coalport pot pourri vase, painted and signed by E. O. Ball, c1891, 7in (18cm).
£600-650 *THA*

A Coalport vase, with painted flowers attributed to Thomas Dixc c1830.
£240-270 *TVA*

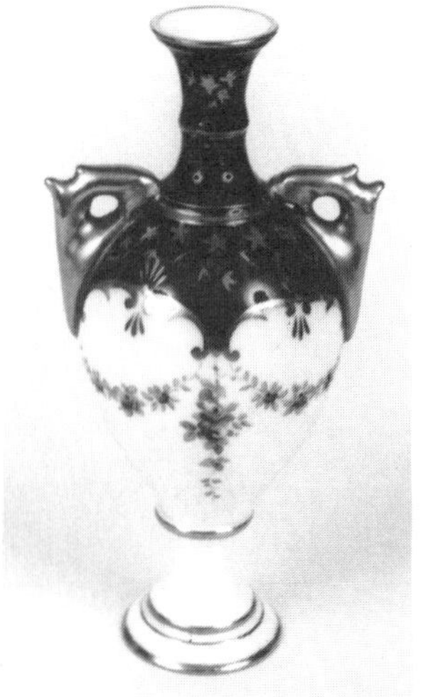

A pair of Coalport miniature vase c1900, 4½in (11cm).
£400-500 *TVA*

Coalport pot pourri vase and
ver, painted on a royal blue
ound, early 20thC, 7in (18cm).
50-300 *P(M)*

Derby vase and cover, decorated
h classical figures and birds,
ght restoration, c1760, 13in
cm).
00-900 *Sto*

e from a garniture. If complete
000+

air of Derby vases and covers,
h blue and gilt strapwork
ndles, painted in sepia with
nerva and Plenty and with
nerva and Juno, the covers with
e and gilt acorn finials, Wm.
esbury & Co., cracks, chips and
airs, incised No. 101 G and with
wn, crossed batons and D marks
gold, c1780, 10½in (26.5cm).
000-9,000 *C*

A Derby two-handled vase, with cracked ice ground, c1770, 6in (16cm).
£400-500 *Sto*

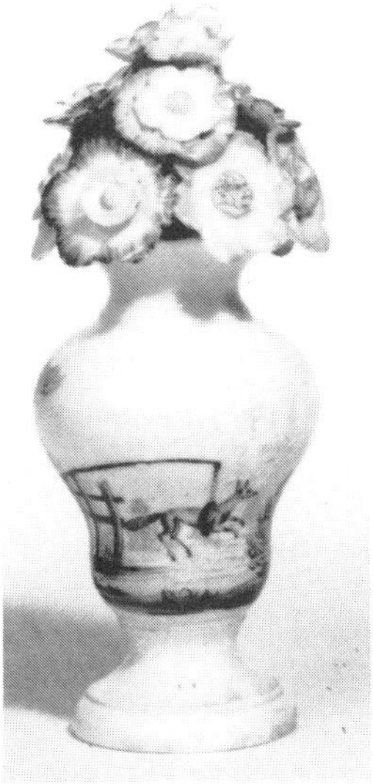

A Derby inverted baluster vase of flowers, painted with a continuous fable scene, the neck applied with flowerheads, Wm. Duesbury & Co., flowers chipped, some glaze fritting, c1760, 5½in (14cm).
£1,500-2,000 *C*

A Bloor Derby vase, painted by Richard Dobson, c1815, 10in (25cm).
£300-350 *BHA*

A Royal Crown Derby miniature vase, in the Old Derby Witches pattern, c1916, 3in (8cm).
£250-300 *TVA*

A Royal Crown Derby quatrefoil vase, in the Japan pattern, c1919, 3in (8cm).
£250-300 *TVA*

A Royal Crown Derby miniature vase, in the Japan pattern, c1918, 3in (8cm). **£250-300** *TVA*

A Royal Crown Derby miniature vase, in the Old Derby Witches pattern, dated 1820.
£300-350 *TVA*

A Longton Hall vase, moulded with scrolls and shell bosses, the rim applied with a band of flowerheads, the body painted in colours with bouquets of flowers within puce cartouches, restored, 5in (12cm).
£250-300 *CSK*

A pair of Minton 'pâte-sur-pâte' two-handled vases and covers, with richly gilt entwined snake handles, c1894, 9½in (24.5cm).
£1,000-1,200 *C*

A vase, painted with a wide continuous panel of garden flower within beaded and gilt borders, possibly Spode, minor cracks to fo c1815, 6½in (16cm).
£400-450 *CSK*

A pair of Hicks & Meigh vases, c1835, 8in (20cm).
£800-1,000 *DOW*

A Samson giltmetal mounted pot pourri vase and cover, the rim applied with a giltmetal band pierced with scrolls and with caryatid handles, on a shaped square giltmetal base, late 19thC, 23in (58cm).
£2,500-3,000 *C*

A Spode vase, c1810, 4½in (11cm).
£650-750 *DOW*

A pair of Minton vases, richly painted with birds on flowering boughs, on 3 gilt peg feet, impressed marks, 7in (18cm).
£300-400 *AG*

A pair of Samson armorial vases, painted in colours with scattered flowersprigs within bianco-sopra-bianco outlines, bases cracked, 12½in (32cm).
£450-550 *CSK*

A pair of Spode vases, painted wit fruit and flowers on a rich gold ground, between white beaded rim one vase with red mark and patte No. 711, c1815, 6½in (16.5cm).
£2,200-2,500 *C*

An English tulip vase, modelled as a red striped open yellow bloom, flanked by a tight bud and green leaves, restoration to 2 petals and 2 leaves, possibly Spode, c1820, 6in (15.5cm).
£2,000-2,500 *C*

ipode garniture of spill vases,
15, 5½in (14cm).
0-750 *Sto*

A pair of Grainger & Co., two-handled vases, painted in colours with birds, the pierced scrolling handles and leaf moulded rims enriched with gilding, 8in (20cm).
£400-500 *CSK*

air of Chinese blue ground
tened hexagonal vases, with gilt
st handles, gilt in the London
dio of Thomas Baxter, the key
tern border between gilt line
is, one vase restored, c1802, 11in
cm).
0-1,000 *C*

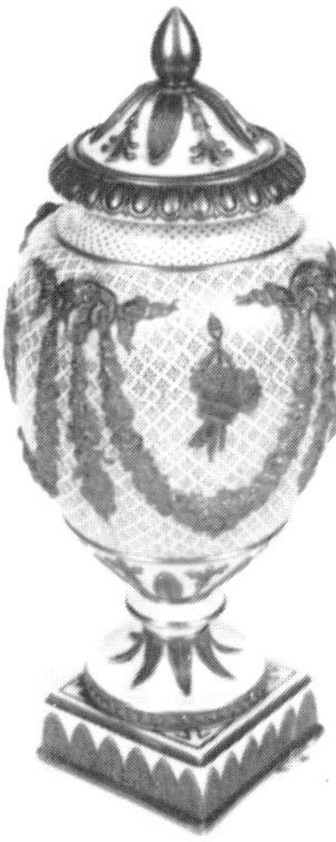

A Wedgwood lidded vase, finely gilded, c1895, 8½in (21cm).
£1,800-2,000 *Wai*

A pair of Royal Worcester vases, with gilt ring and scroll handles, the cream bodies printed in colours, puce printed marks and model number 1432, date code for c1892, 11½in (29cm).
£650-750 *CSK*

A Worcester, Flight, Barr & Barr, green ground vase, with entwined gilt serpent handles, painted with named views of Windsor Castle and the Straits of Menai, from Anglesey, one handle restored, script mark, c1820, 8in (20cm).
£2,000-2,500 *C*

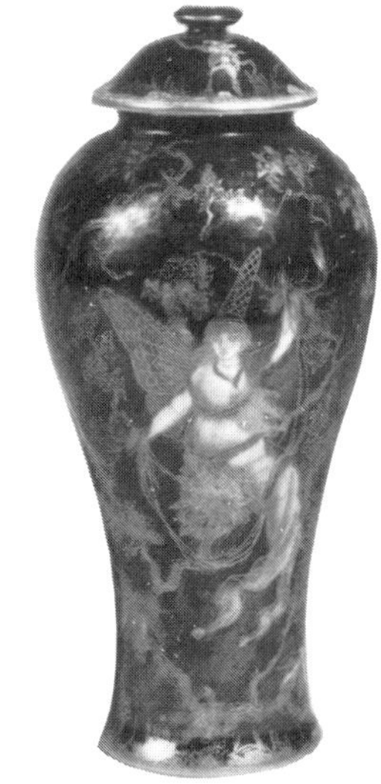

Vedgwood Fairyland Lustre vase
l cover, the iridescent black
und printed in gold and coloured
h fairies, gilt Portland vase
rks and numbers Z4968i to base
l cover, c1920, 8½in (21.5cm).
500-3,000 *C*

A Grainger's Worcester cream ground vase, painted with a linnet, dated 1902, 3in (8cm).
£225-250 *TVA*

A Worcester, Flight, Barr & Barr vase, with a painted view, c1820, 3½in (9cm).
£750-850 *DOW*

A Royal Worcester green ground vase, painted by Jas. Stinton, the neck moulded and gilt beneath a gilt rim, the foot with a band of lappets, the base enriched in gilding, signed, puce printed mark and date code for 1897, shape No. 1794, 13in (33cm).
£2,000-2,500 *C*

A Worcester, Flight, Barr & Barr vase, painted flowers by Baxter, c1820, 3½in (9cm).
£750-850 *DOW*

A garniture of 3 Staffordshire porcelain vases, c1830, 11in (28cm).
£1,600-1,800 *DOW*

> **Did you know**
> ***MILLER'S Antiques Price Guide builds up year by year to form the most comprehensive photo-reference system available***

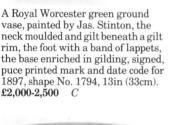

A Grainger's Worcester pot pourri and cover, with a view of Malvern, 2½in (6cm).
£600-650 *DOW*

A Royal Worcester posy vase, with Union Jack flag mark of 1914-18, shape No. G161, 3in (7.5cm) diam.
£150-200 *TVA*

A Royal Worcester vase, shape No. G957, 1916, 3in (7.5cm).
£150-200 *TVA*

A pair of Barr, Flight & Barr, Worcester pot pourri vases and pierced covers, with fixed gilt eagle's head and ring handles, the covers with gilt griffin finials, cracked, restored, wear to gilding, script marks, c1810, 7in (17.5cm).
£1,700-2,000 *C*

A Royal Worcester pierced vase, painted with a pheasant in a woodland setting, signed by Jame Stinton, dated 1908, 5in (14cm).
£400-450 *TVA*

A Barr, Flight & Barr, Worcester spill vase, painted with garden flowers, beneath a white beaded rim, the inner rim with a bronzed band of gilt 'caillouté', slight wear t gilding, c1810, 5½in (13.5cm).
£1,000-1,500 *C*

A pair of Royal Worcester posy vases, painted with a blue tit and robin, c1913.
£380-400 *TVA*

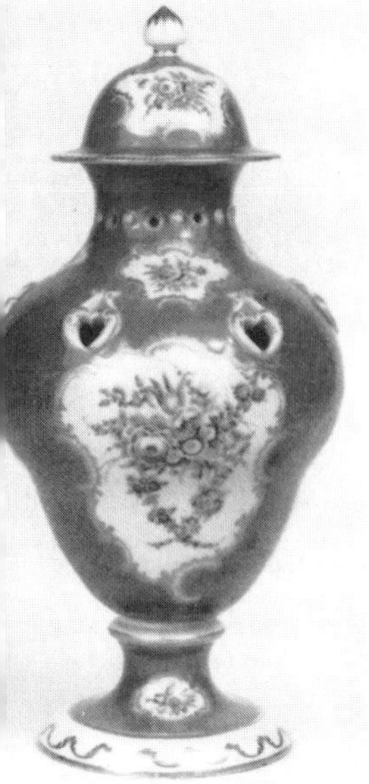

Vorcester pot pourri vase and
er, painted with flowers within
croll cartouches, the shoulder
rced with scroll moulded
rtures, restoration, chip to cover,
70, 13½in (34cm).
0-700 *C*

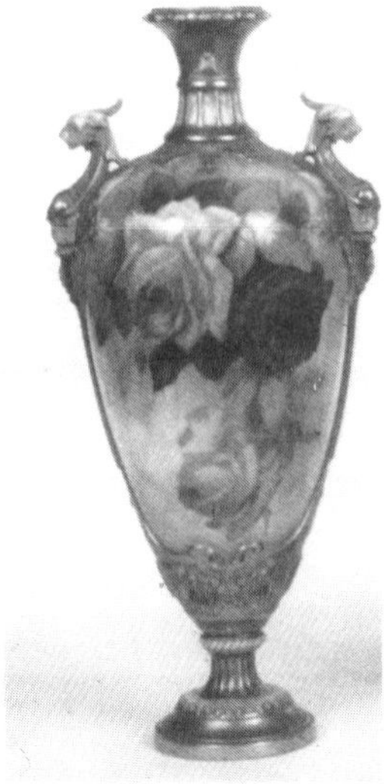

A Royal Worcester vase, the sides painted by Sedgley with red and pink roses pendant from the shoulder, the tinted ivory handles modelled as a griffin's head and enriched in gilding, signed, puce printed mark and date code for 1914, shape No. 1764, 14½in (36.5cm).
£700-900 *C*

A Royal Worcester pot pourri vase and cover, painted by J. Stinton, the handles covered in a rich bronzed and gilt patina, the foot and cover moulded with stiff leaves and enriched in similar patinas, signed, puce printed mark No. 1428 and date code for 1917, 12in (31cm).
£4,000-4,500 *C*

loyal Worcester vase, with twin
f moulded handles, painted by
man in colours on a shaded ivory
und, gilt highlights, puce printed
rks and model No. 1459, date
e for c1911, 12in (31cm) wide.
0-600 *CSK*

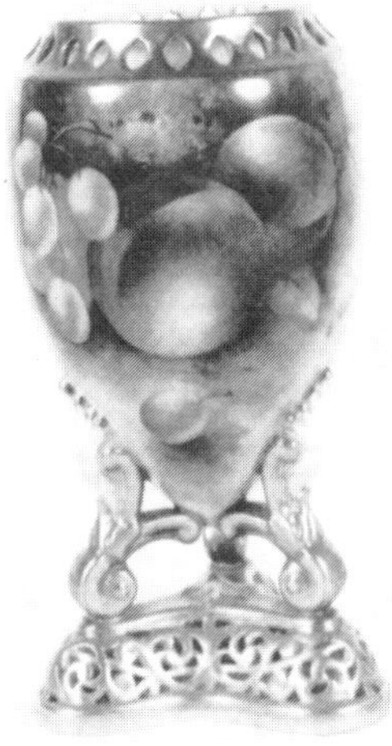

A Royal Worcester vase, painted in colours with peaches and grapes, the whole highlighted in gilt, signed by E. Townsend, printed mark in puce and date cipher for 1938, 6in (15cm).
£450-550 *HSS*

A Royal Worcester enamelled vase, decorated in colours and gilt with sprays of flowers on a yellow shading to pink ground, within pink and sky blue borders, printed mark in puce, 9in (23cm).
£250-350 *HSS*

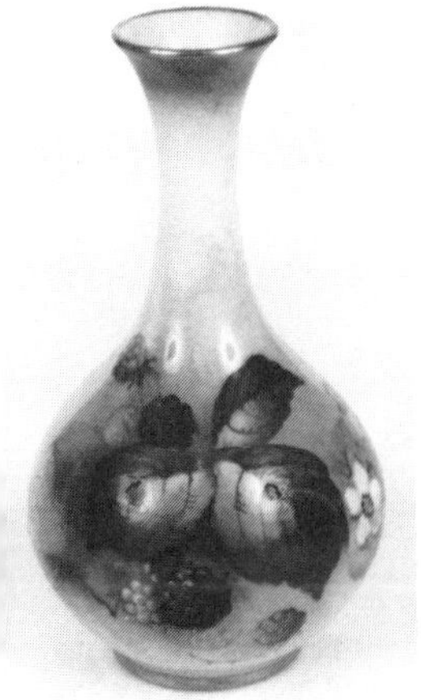

loyal Worcester miniature vase,
nted and signed by Kitty Blake,
ed 1931, 4½in (11cm).
0-300 *TVA*

An English bough pot and cover, painted with garden flowers, damaged, 8in (20cm).
£600-700 *CSK*

An English spill vase, painted on one side with exotic birds in a river landscape and on the other with an insect, reserved on a gold decorated semi-matt blue ground, early 18thC, 5½in (14cm).
£200-300 *Bea*

A pair of English vases and covers in Sèvres style, coloured in cobalt and white, with gilt highlights, pincecone finials, restoration and damage, 15in (39cm).
£800-1,000 *CSK*

A pair of English vases and covers, painted in colours, with all-over applied flower decoration, damaged, gilding rubbed, 17in (44cm).
£350-400 *CSK*

A garniture of 3 English vases, with gilt scrolling handles, the blue grounds with panels of birds and flowers within elaborate gilt outlines, 2 vases repaired at stems, one restored, 7 and 11in (18 and 27cm).
£600-700 *CSK*

An English vase, c1830, 8½in (21cm).
£450-500 *BHA*

A pair of Brussels gilt campana vases, manufactured by Frédéric Faber, painted in colours, possibly after J. B. Madou, the narrow pedestal foot on white square plinth, one rim restored, 1818-47, 12½in (32cm).
£2,500-3,000 *CAm*

A Copenhagen beige ground vase the body painted within gilt cartouches, with crowned F and C monograms, the rim and foot rich gilt, blue waved line marks, c186 17in (43cm), fitted for electricity.
£1,500-2,000 *C*

Two English spill vases, the pink grounds reserved with panels of flowers within gilt borders, hairline cracks, some wear, 5in (14cm).
£150-200 *CSK*

A Copenhagen pale pink ground vase, reserved and painted within a gilt band and scroll cartouche, blue waved line mark, late 19thC, 10½in (26cm), fitted for electricity.
£550-650 *C*

A pair of Jacob Petit cornucopia vases, the bodies painted with flowers and moulded with leafy scrolls, with orange and gilt highlights, blue JP monogram, gilding worn, 19thC, 9in (23cm).
£450-550 *CSK*

St. Clement bough pot, the bombé
les painted 'en camaieu' within
ce cartouches, the scroll feet and
mpartments enriched with puce
bons and blue trailing flowers,
ips to corners, one foot restuck,
785, 10in (25cm) wide.
00-1,000 *C*

Jacob Petit figural vase, modelled
a lady seated, wearing a spotted
b-cap, green shawl and flower
rigged gown, the pierced rococo
rolling base decorated in colours
d gilt, damaged, underglaze blue
ark, 11in (28cm).
50-450 *HSS*

pair of French gilt vases, probably
moges, painted in colours and
plied with flowers and scrolls in
e Second Rococo Revival style,
nor chips, marked with some
pressed numbers and figures,
rly 19thC, 20½in (52cm).
,500-2,000 *CAm*

A pair of assembled Sèvres pattern
gilt bronze mounted vases and a
pair of covers, the bodies decorated
after Fragonard, with gilt bronze
foliage moulded loose ring handles,
the bodies signed Jeanne, late
19thC, 38in (98cm).
£12,000-15,000 *C*

A pair of Sèvres pattern ormolu mounted vases and covers, the royal blue ground oviform bodies painted within gilt floral foliage cartouches, applied with ormolu caryatid handles, the domed covers reserved within gilt borders and with ormolu berried finials, c1865, 15in (38cm).
£2,500-3,000 *C*

A Sèvres pattern royal blue ground vase and cover, painted in colours and enriched with gilt, one handle and finial restored, imitation interlaced L marks, c1870, 20½in (52cm).
£1,500-2,000 *C*

A pair of Sèvres pattern jewelled pink ground gilt bronze mounted vases and covers, one cover restored, late 19thC, 14in (35cm).
£2,000-2,500 *C*

A pair of Sèvres pattern ormolu mounted turquoise ground vases and covers, decorated by Guillou, the waisted necks and domed covers enriched in gilding, the feet inscribed, signed, one rim repaired, late 19thC, 38in (98cm).
£9,000-12,000 *C*

A German vase modelled as an owl perched on a gnarled branch, naturalistically coloured plumage, leaves restored and chipped, blue factory marks, 12½in (32cm).
£300-350 *CSK*

A Sèvres pattern blue ground giltmetal mounted vase and cover, decorated by Poitevin within an oval gilt band cartouche, the reverse richly gilt on a blue ground, signed, c1900, 16in (40cm).
£3,000-4,000 *C*

A German pot pourri vase and pierced cover, painted in colours with gilt rims, finial chipped, impressed marks, 14½in (37cm).
£300-400 *CSK*

A pair of Meissen KPM vases, with pink and gilt pattern, one restored 18thC, 12in (31cm).
£2,500-3,000 *BHA*

A pair of Dresden yellow ground vases and covers, reserved and painted within shaped cartouches, edged with black lines, the covers similarly decorated and with gilt spire finials, both vases restored, blue AR marks, c1900, 25in (64cm).
£3,500-4,000 *C*

A pair of Meissen Marcolini royal blue ground vases and covers, with gilt satyrs mask handles, the bodies enriched in gilding, the domed covers with a border of white and gilt stiff leaves in relief and with acorn finials, cover repaired, handles damaged, footrim chipped, blue crossed swords and star marks, c1800, 12½in (31.5cm).
£2,500-3,000 *C*

A pair of late Meissen vases, applied in relief with spiralling bands of forget-me-nots, blue crossed swords incised and impressed numerals, 7½in (18cm).
£200-300 *CSK*

A Pottschappel vase and cover, the foot with encrusted floral garlands, small chip and crack to rim, blue crossed batons 'T' mark, 24in (61cm).
£600-700 *P(S)*

A white glazed vase, decorated in bright colours of red, green, blue and yellow, with gilt Greek key pattern border, late 19thC, 10½in (26cm).
£250-300 *DDM*

Make the Most of Miller's

Every care has been taken to ensure the accuracy of descriptions and estimated valuations. Price ranges in this book reflect what one should expect to pay for a similar example. When selling one can obviously expect a figure below. This will fluctuate according to a dealer's stock, saleability at a particular time, etc. It is always advisable to approach a reputable specialist dealer or an auction house which has specialist sales

·rested China

aving seen the success of the ' H Goss factory who invented ɜraldic porcelain during late ictorian and Edwardian times, ıany other manufacturers arted to produce their own ınges of crested ware. All ısed in Stoke-on-Trent, ɜtween 1880 and 1940, ıctories such as Arcadian, arlton, Grafton, Shelley and 'illow Art produced some),000 shapes bearing over 000 coats-of-arms.

hese products from other anufacturers were sold at ızaars, tea rooms, libraries, at ıe end of the pier and anywhere that a suitable outlet could be found.

The ranges made were more amusing than Goss, appealing to those with a sense of humour and a love of anything amusing, whilst products of the Goss factory tended to be more serious reproductions of historic shapes, for example, Roman, Greek and Ancient British urns and vases.

These other factories produced their wares (with the exception of Grafton) from pottery rather than porcelain. It is of poorer quality than Goss but its collectability has ensured a continuing rise in value during recent years.

Major themes collected include World War I, of which there are over 500 different pieces, animals, buildings, transport, seaside, countryside and home/nostalgic.

For further reading, collectors are recommended to *Crested China* by Sandy Andrews and *The Price Guide to Crested China* by Nicholas Pine, both published by Milestone Publications, 62 Murray Road, Horndean, Hants.

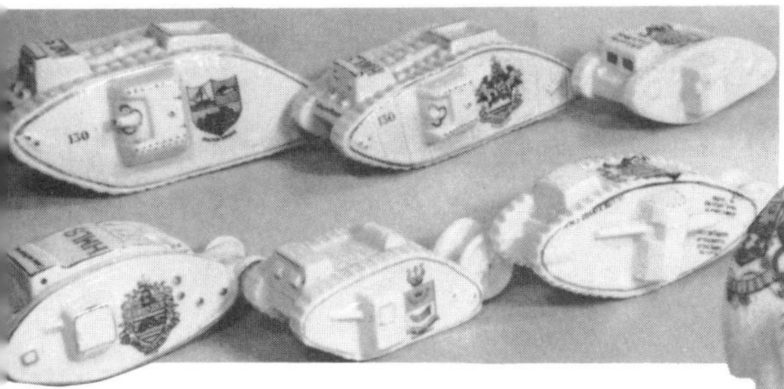

orld War I tanks.
5-50 each *G&CC*

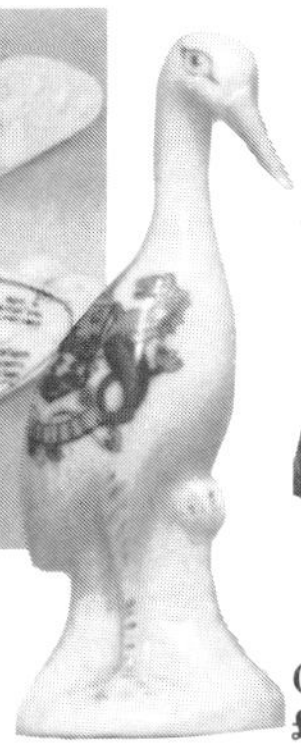

Carlton stork.
£30 *G&CC*

Arcadian series of black boys.
£85-125 each *G&CC*

ısorted animals.
0-40 each *G&CC*

on, donkey and teddy bear.
5-30 each *G&CC*

ɜvonia Drake statue, ymouth.
.5 *G&CC*

Carlton jockey on racehorse.
£80 *G&CC*

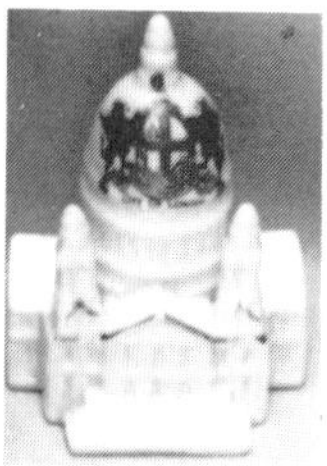

St. Paul's Cathedral by Arcadian.
£15-25 each *G&CC*

Domestic assortment.
£5-20 each *G&CC*

Willow ram with curly hor
£50 *G&CC*

Willow Art gateway, Monmouth.
£45 *G&CC*

Dreadnought

Grafton Dreadnought charabanc.
£55 *G&CC*

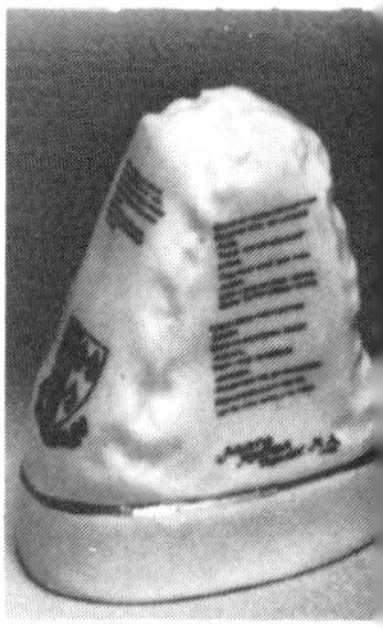

Rock of Ages by Arcadian.
£10 *G&CC*

Time
Glass

Timepieces.
£10-25 each *G&CC*

Willow Art Toby jug.
£7 *G&CC*

Black cat transfers.
£10 each *G&CC*

Owls.
£12 each *G&CC*

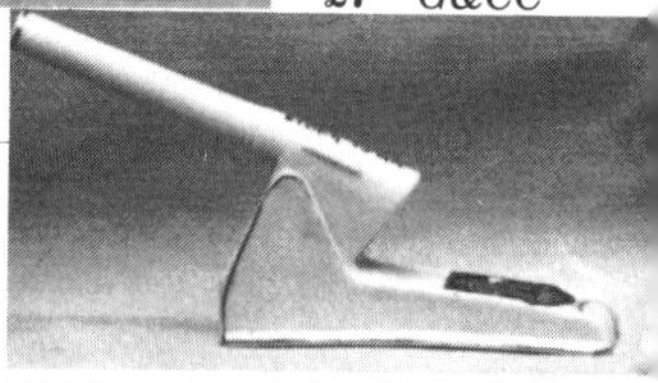

Field gun on sledge, inscribed 'French 75', by Grafton.
£50 *G&CC*

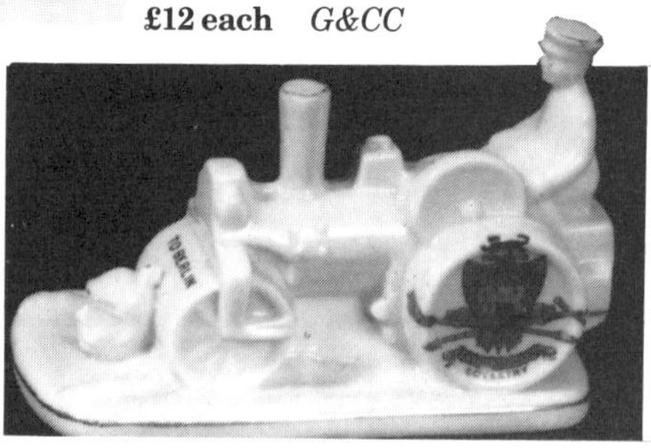

Rare Arcadian model, Tommy driving a steam roller over the Kaiser.
£450 *G&CC*

A TRUCK OF COAL FROM

Truck of coal by Willow Art.
£30 *G&CC*

Parian busts of Edward VII an Queen Mary.
£35-55 each *G&CC*

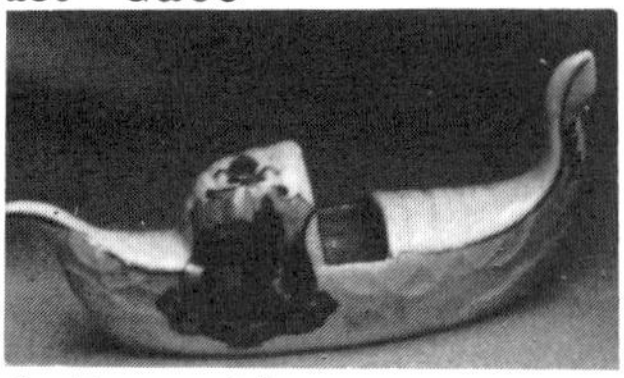

Carlton gondola.
£15 *G&CC*

MODEL OF THE FORTH BRIDGE

Forth Bridge by Arcadian.
£30 *G&CC*

Aynsley china military badges.
£30-50 each *G&CC*

DERRY'S CLOCK
PLYMOUTH

Clock Tower

Clock towers.
£10-20 each *G&CC*

Canterbury West Gate by Arcadian.
£30 *G&CC*

British Empire Exhibition, Wembley decorations, 1924.
£15-25 each *G&CC*

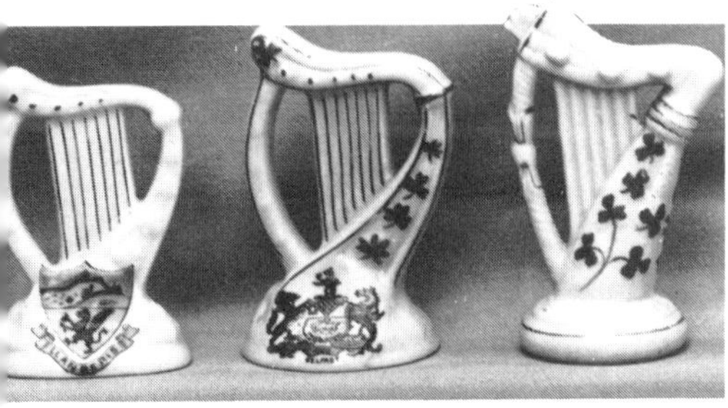

Harps.
£10 each *G&CC*

THERE'S NO PLACE LIKE HOME

German yellow/brown ware with lucky white heather transfers.
£10-20 each *G&CC*

Crested monoplanes.
£50-75 each *G&CC*

Assorted boats.
£10-20 each *G&CC*

OLD CROSS
BOVEY TRACEY

Buildings from assorted factories.
£30-75 each *G&CC*

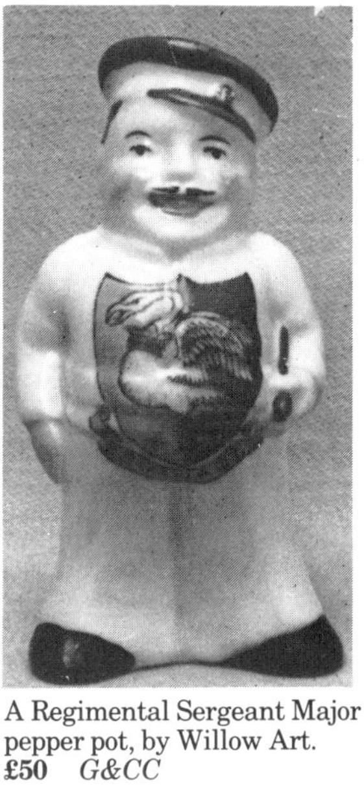

A Regimental Sergeant Major pepper pot, by Willow Art.
£50 *G&CC*

World War I nurses and sailor.
£75-120 each *G&CC*

Military hats.
£10-20 each *G&CC*

World War I submarines. **£18-45 each** *G&CC*

:OSS CHINA

ioss china collecting became a raze in late Victorian and dwardian times when, with ie advent of the railways and ay trips to the seaside, William Ienry Goss and his son, .dolphus, realized that there 'as a market for souvenirs.

'hey introduced a range of istoric models, mainly of ireek and Roman urns found a museums and applied the oats-of-arms of towns to these. .dolphus became the firm's rst commercial traveller and oured the country appointing gents, only one per town, and his would normally be the most nportant china shop in the own or a respectable ewsagency in smaller places.

3y 1914 some 1,600 agents vere appointed and over 2,500 hapes were available bearing no less than 8,000 different coats-of-arms.

The firm's early production comprised parian busts and figures, which were produced between 1858 and 1887, termed the First Period. From the late 1800s until 1930, the Second Period was the factory's largest period of production and it is estimated that some 90% of wares were manufactured during this time. This production comprised the range of historic models and shapes, cottages, fonts, crosses, lighthouses and shoes.

The family sold out around 1930 and under its new ownership, termed the Third Period which ended in 1939, heavy, more crude wares were produced in limited numbers before the 1930s slump ended the trade.

For further information collectors are recommended to read *The Concise Encyclopaedia and Price Guide to Goss China* and *The Price Guide to Arms and Decorations on Goss China*, both by Nicholas Pine, available from Milestone Publications, 62 Murray Road, Horndean, Hants. For those who wish to learn about the history of the factory and the family who produce Goss china, the definitive biography: *William Henry Goss, The Story of The Staffordshire Family of Potters Who Invented Heraldic Porcelain* by Lynda and Nicholas Pine is also available from Milestone Publications and is a fascinating vignette on the craze for crested china collecting which swept the country for 50 years and is now re-emerging.

A cottage butter dish and lid.
£30 *G&CC*

A preserve pot and lid, decorated with bees and clover.
£50-60 *G&CC*

Goss Rock of Ages, with verse.
£45 *G&CC*

Bust of Sir Moses Montefiore wearing hat.
£200 *G&CC*

ioss League model 1927, 'olchester Roman camp.
:160 *G&CC*

Charles Dickens house, Rochester, without porch windows.
£130 *G&CC*

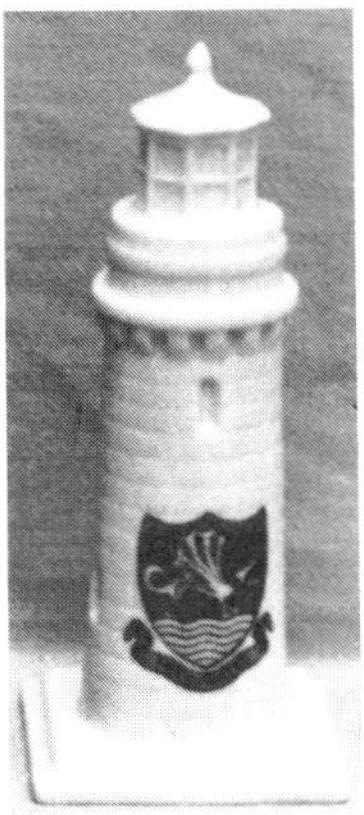

Teignmouth lighthouse.
£40-70 *G&CC*

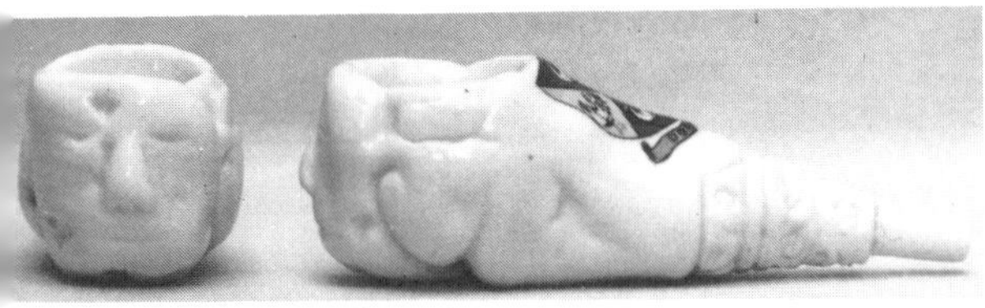

'wickenham Pope's antique pipe.
:40-65 *G&CC*

Bust of Beaconsfield.
£160 *G&CC*

.mersham leaden measure.
:30 *G&CC*

Green shamrock decorations.
£10-18 each *G&CC*

The Abbots Kitchen, Glastonbury Abbey.
£600 *G&CC*

Dr. Samuel Johnson's house, Lichfield.
£180 *G&CC*

Goss seaside selection.
£10-150 each *G&CC*

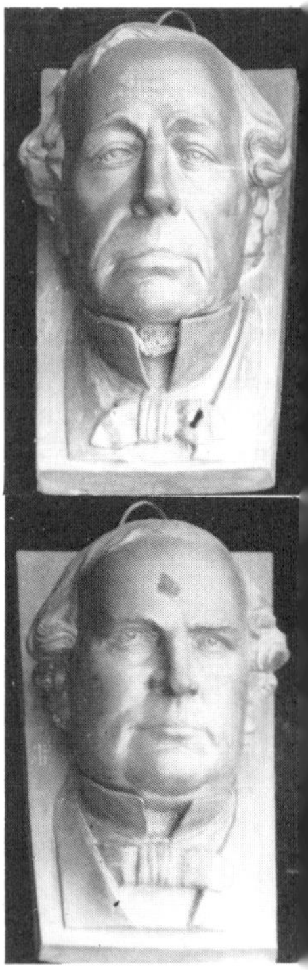

Goss terracotta keystone of the Kingdom, Lord Beaconsfield and Lord Derby.
£350-400 each *G&CC*

Southampton Bargate, in white, brown or grey.
£55-250 *G&CC*

Bristol puzzle cider cup.
£20-35 *G&CC*

Fox and prey on oval plinth.
£200-300 *G&CC*

Goss bust of Gladstone.
£165 *G&CC*

EDWARD VIII
CROWNED

Goss Third Period group, 1930-39.
£7-70 each *G&CC*

Goss cottages:
First and Last House, Land's End.
£120
Lloyd George's early home.
£160
Robert Burns' cottage, Ayrshire.
£120 *G&CC*

The Peace plate, 10in (25cm)
£350-450 *G&CC*

Cornish stile.
£40-90 *G&CC*

Teapot and cover.
£40-65 *G&CC*

Terracotta tobacco jar.
£50-75 *G&CC*

A rare Goss Trusty Servant, coloured.
£1,500 *G&CC*

Delicate Goss brooches.
£75-150 *G&CC*

Waterlooville soldier's bottle.
£30 *G&CC*

Avebury Saxon font.
£130-180 *G&CC*

Goss amphora vase with 3 butterfly handles.
£20 *G&CC*

Goss candle snuffers:
Monk. **£165**
Cone. **£10**
Welsh lady.
£85 *G&CC*

A selection of rarer models and decorations. **£20-400 each** *G&CC*

teapot stand with verse.
5 *G&CC*

Goss Winchester cathedral font, white or black.
£425-500 *G&CC*

Denbigh brick, in white, brown or red.
£65-250 *G&CC*

Goss Cardinal Beaufort's salt cellar.
£75-115 *G&CC*

Goss Chile spur.
£200-315 *G&CC*

Goss Herefordshire wall pocket.
£10-12 *OD*

A Goss Ludlow sack bottle Gloucester.
£15-20 *OD*

A Goss Welsh mil can, with Shrewsbury School crest.
£20-25 *OD*

A selection of Irish crests and models.
£10-30 each *G&CC*

Goss Windleshaw Chantry.
£165 *G&CC*

Old Market House, Ledbury.
£300-350 *G&CC*

A Goss Salopian ewer, with Bromley crest.
£9-12 *OD*

Goss Bath Roman ewe
£7-10 *OD*

A model of a Roman ewer found Bath now in a Dorset museum.

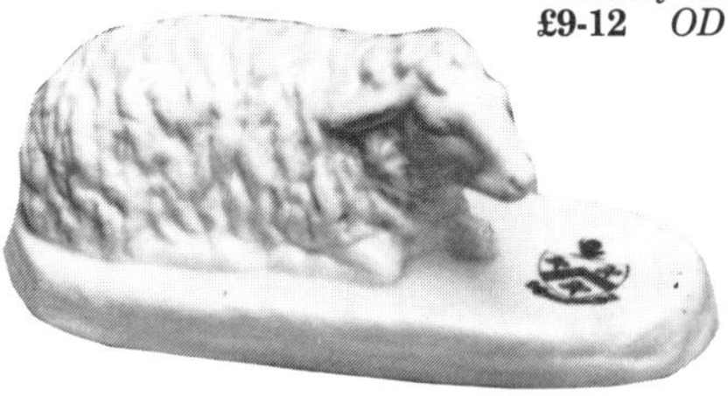

Goss sheep on plinth.
£200-250 *G&CC*

Tankard mug, commemorating 1911 coronation of George and Mary.
£45 *G&CC*

St. Buryan ancient cross, brown.
£65-130 *G&CC*

BUTTER

Butter dish with wooden surround.
£20 *G&CC*

'Iiscellaneous

Bow pierced stand, painted with
sects and moths, the feet with
oulded puce scrolls, the top with
llow, puce and blue marbling,
762, 2½in (6cm).
00-600 *C*

Thuringian eye bath, modelled as
e head of a man wearing a yellow
at, his buttoned waistcoast forms
e bowl, restored, late 18thC, 3in
cm) long.
00-600 *C*

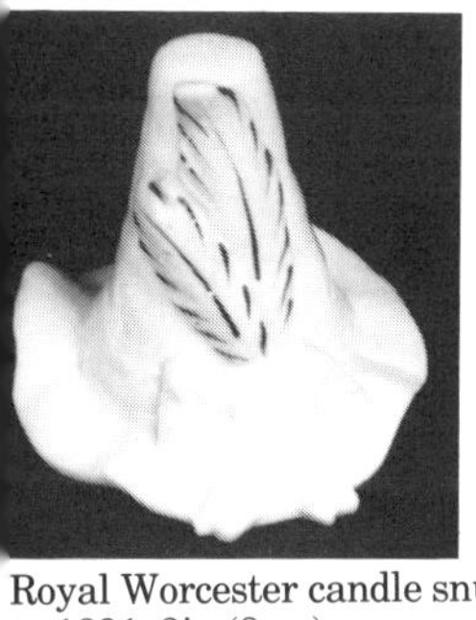

Royal Worcester candle snuffer,
te 1891, 3in (8cm).
25-150 *TVA*

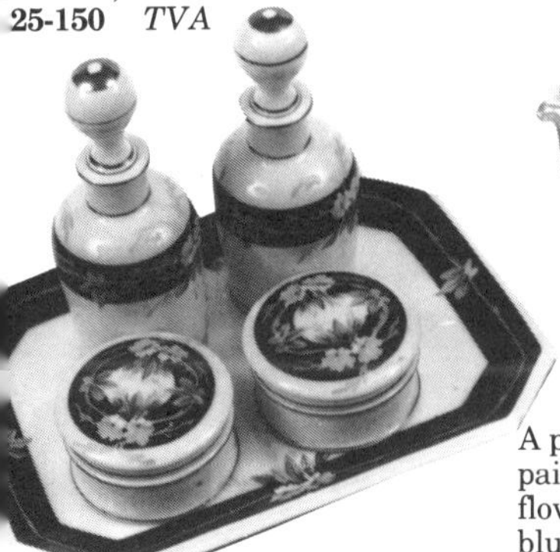

Victorian toilet set, bottles 6in
5cm).
0-100 *HF*

A Coalport pin tray, c1885, 4in (10cm) wide.
£80-100 *TVA*

A Coalport horseshoe shaped pin tray, c1885, 5in (12.5cm) long.
£150-170 *TVA*

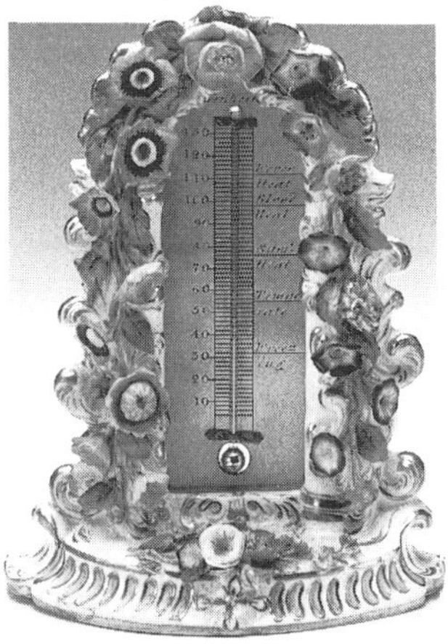

A thermometer in a Minton rococo frame, applied with flowers, on a semi-circular base, some damage, c1830, 7½in (18cm).
£170-250 *Bea*

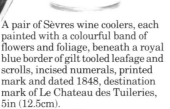

A pair of Sèvres wine coolers, each painted with a colourful band of flowers and foliage, beneath a royal blue border of gilt tooled leafage and scrolls, incised numerals, printed mark and dated 1848, destination mark of Le Chateau des Tuileries, 5in (12.5cm).
£1,000-1,400 *N*

A pair of openwork wall pockets, probably Coalport, slight damage, mid-19thC, 8½in (21cm).
£350-450 *Bea*

A pair of Spode wine coolers, covers and liners, from the Lubbock Family Services, decorated with garlands of blue flowers, the rims and bases with white jewelled and gilt bands, the pierced covers with finials, on flower moulded gilt bases, minor damage, early 19thC, 16in (41cm).
£4,000-4,500 *Bon*

A pair of Dresden table lamps, in the form of rose encrusted urns supported by 3 putti, 19thC.
£800-1,200 *LRG*

ORIENTAL POTTERY & PORCELAIN

Bottles

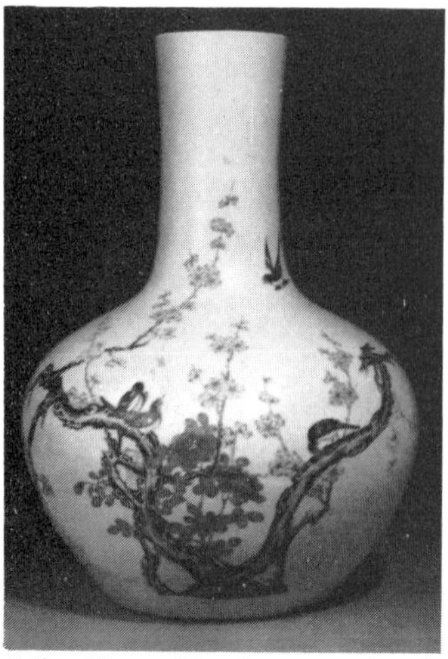

A 'famille rose' bottle vase, painted with magpies among flowering peony and bush peony, Qianlong seal mark, 19thC, 21½in (54cm).
£6,000-7,000 *C*

A 'famille verte' bottle, painted with alternate panels of vessels and emblems and flowering shrubs, above cell pattern at the foot and below lappets and trellis pattern at the shoulder, Kangxi, 9½in (24cm), wood cover.
£900-1,200 *CSK*

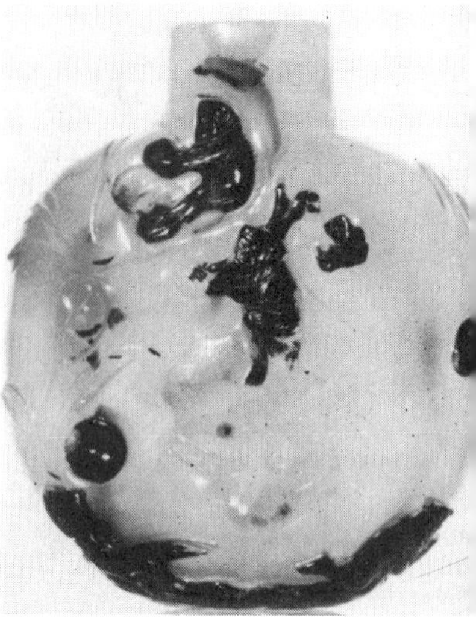

An agate flattened globular snuff bottle, carved in relief with 3 monkeys at play amongst pine and peach trees.
£300-400 *CSK*

A pair of Imari double gourd bottles, the upper sections with oval panels of ho-o, all on a ground of large stylised flowerheads and dense flowering shrubs, 17½in (44cm).
£3,000-4,000 *CSK*

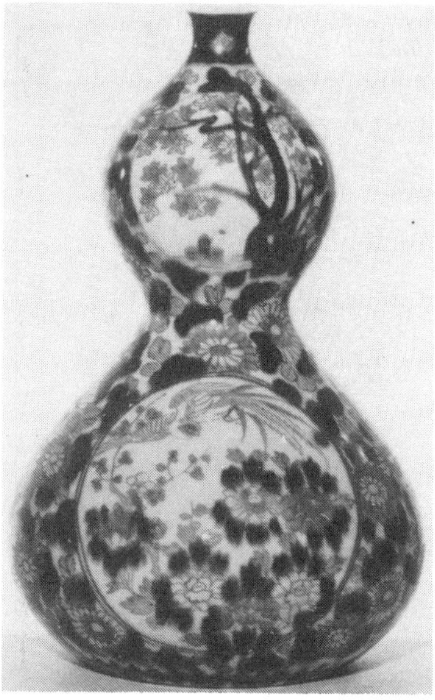

A pair of Imari double gourd bottles, with spreading bulbous lower halves, painted with roundels of ho-o above flowers below flowering trees, all on grounds of scrolling chrysanthemum, rims restored, 9½in (24cm).
£650-750 *CSK*

A Satsuma bottle vase, decorated i various coloured enamels and gilt, gilt rim, signed Tozan sei, 19thC, 4½in (10.5cm).
£900-1,000 *C*

A pair of late Ming blue and white pear-shaped bottles, painted with panels of flowering shrubs below hanging tassels and lappets, Wanli, 5½in (14cm).
£1,000-1,200 *CSK*

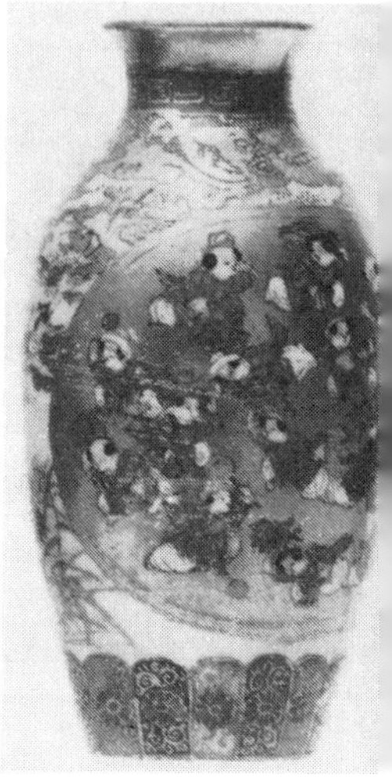

A Satsuma bottle, painted with a gold ground roundel of numerous children on a ground of cranes wading in water below gilt clouds, 3½in (9cm).
£200-300 *CSK*

:owls

Sancai water pot, the glaze
opping irregularly above the
attened base revealing the buff
•loured body, Tang Dynasty, 2½in
•cm).
2,000-2,500 *C*

A Sultanabad deep bowl, painted in the interior with concentric blue, turquoise and black bands, 12th/13thC, 8in (20cm) diam.
£100-150 *CSK*

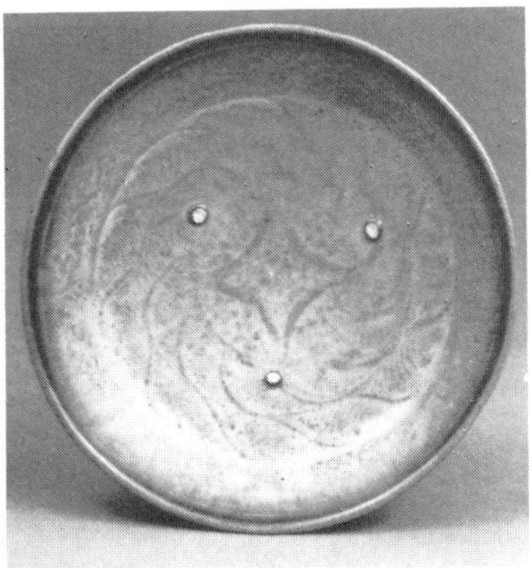

An amber glazed dish, moulded to the interior with scrolling foliage beneath a continuous floral garland in the well, all under a rich amber glaze deepening in tone at the rim and stopping unevenly above the buff pottery foot, the interior with 3 spur marks, Liao Dynasty, 5½in (13cm) diam.
£1,200-1,600 *C*

Yuan blue and white bowl, the
:terior with a band of lotus panels
•low a lingzhi scroll, the heavily
•tted sides resting on a thick solid
•ot, restored, c1340, 7½in (19cm)
am.
1,000-1,500 *C*

A Cantonese blue ground bowl for the Persian market, painted with panels of figures on terraces and gold ground panels of birds and flowers below a trellis pattern border, dated , 8in (20cm) diam.
£450-550 *CSK*

A Ming Imperial yellow glazed bowl, with slightly everted rim under a glaze of even tones thinning slightly at the rim, rim chip, glaze rubbed, encircled Jiajing six-character mark and early in the period, 8in (20cm) diam.
£5,000-7,000 *C*

blue and white foliate dish,
•inted in a pencilled style with an
•erall design of foaming and
virling waves, dotted with
•owerheads and an unusual double
•aded eel-form fish to the centre,
•nall rim chip and frits, Jiajing
ark, 17thC, 6½in (16cm) diam.
300-1,200 *C*

A large Swatow polychrome dish, painted to the centre below 6 ogival panels enclosing fruiting or flowering sprays on lozenge pattern grounds in the well, rim crack, 16thC, 16½in (42cm) diam.
£1,200-1,700 *C*

A pair of 'famille rose' yellow ground bowls, painted with birds, 5in (14cm) diam.
£1,000-1,200 *CSK*

A Longquan celadon dish, carved to the centre, all under an even glaze of bright olive tones, 14th/15thC, 13in (33cm) diam.
£1,200-1,600 *C*

A Satsuma fluted bowl, painted in colours and richly gilt with numerous small shaped panels of seated Immortals and ladies, 5in (12cm).
£600-700 *CSK*

A Kakiemon deep bowl, painted with a flowering plum tree and iron red and turquoise birds in flight, the interior with a single flowerhead, late 17thC, 4in (10cm) diam.
£1,800-2,200 *CSK*

A pair of Arita bowls, late 17thC, 6½in (16cm) diam.
£500-600 *Wai*

A Longquan celadon bulb bowl, on 3 feet, the exterior decorated with an incised floral band, wide firing crack across base, late Ming, 11in (28cm) diam.
£350-450 *Bon*

An Imari saucer dish, with gilt metal stand, cracked, the porcelain late 17thC, 15½in (39cm) wide.
£850-950 *CSK*

A Chinese Imari barber's bowl, painted at the centre with peony and lotus, below cartouches reserved on a band of scrolling lotus at the border, the reverse with iron red flowersprays, fritted, early 18thC, 11in (28cm) diam.
£1,000-1,500 *C*

Two Imari tripod bowls, with everted foliate rims, on mask feet, the interiors with central flowersprays, c1700, 6in (15cm) diam.
£600-700 *CSK*

An Imari barber's bowl, painted in underglaze blue, yellow, green and iron red enamels and gilt, late 17th/early 18thC, 11in (28cm) diam.
£2,500-3,000 *Bon*

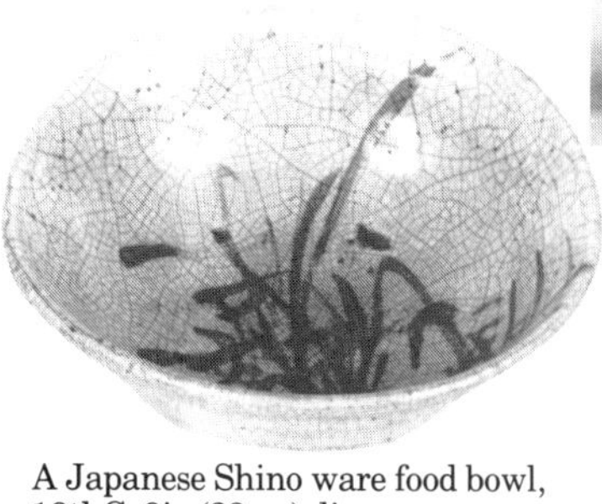
A Japanese Shino ware food bowl, 18thC, 9in (23cm) diam.
£1,800-2,000 *Wai*

A 'verte' Imari punchbowl, painted with sprays of chrysanthemum above a band of petals and whorl pattern at the foot, below a band of underglaze blue trellis pattern enriched with iron red and gilt, hairline crack, gilt slightly rubbed, foot rim chipped, base with square seal mark, early 18thC, 13½in (34.5cm) diam.
£1,500-2,000 *C*

A saucer dish, the exterior under a liver red glaze, the interior plain, encircled Yongzheng six-character mark and of the period, 6in (15cm) diam, with box.
£1,200-1,500 *C*

ｗo late Ming blue and white shes with everted rims, each ıinted to the centre with a ›werhead within panels of cell ıttern, swastika pattern and scale ıttern within rims of scrolling liage, Tianqi, 8½in (21cm) diam.
500-700 *CSK*

A blue and white bowl, painted on the exterior with ruyi lappets, the interior with a central peony roundel beneath a band of trellis and swastika reserved with cartouches, rim frits, the base with square seal mark, Kangxi, 14in (35cm) diam.
£1,500-2,000 *C*

A blue and white bowl and cover, mounted with metal rings, Kangxi, 9in (23cm) diam.
£1,000-1,200 *C*

pair of Imari bowls and covers, ınted and gilt with shishi lions, e interiors with flowersprays, the vers similarly decorated, minute ips, c1700, 6½in (16cm) diam.
'00-800 *CSK*

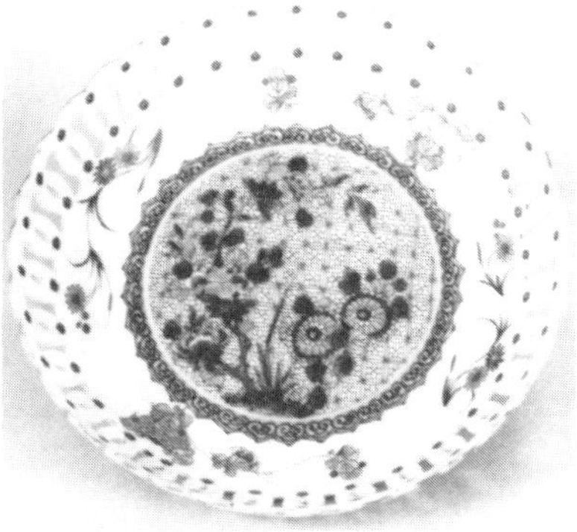

A Chinese Imari dish, with pierced border, painted with peony and chrysanthemum on a cell pattern ground, hairline cracks, early 18thC, 8½in (21cm) diam.
£800-1,000 *C*

Kyo-Satsuma deep bowl, painted colours and gilt, 6in (15cm) diam.
50-550 *CSK*

A 'famille rose' punchbowl, delicately painted with a continuous scene, restored, rim chipped, early Qianlong, 15½in (39cm) diam.
£3,000-4,000 *C*

A blue and white bowl, painted with flowers, fritted, chip restored, square seal mark to base, Kangxi, 13½in (34cm) diam.
£1,500-2,000 *C*

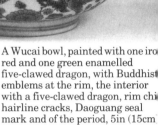

A Mandarin pattern 'famille rose' punchbowl, painted with figures reserved on a gilt scrolling ground above bands of cell pattern and iron red and gilt spear heads at the foot, cracked, Qianlong, 14in (35.5cm) diam.
£2,000-2,500 *C*

A Wucai bowl, painted with one iro red and one green enamelled five-clawed dragon, with Buddhist emblems at the rim, the interior with a five-clawed dragon, rim chi hairline cracks, Daoguang seal mark and of the period, 5in (15cm) diam.
£1,000-1,500 *C*

A Chinese blue and white pierced flared oval basket and stand, early 19thC, stand 10in (25.5cm) diam.
£750-850 *CSK*

A 'famille rose' punchbowl, painted with scenes of Chinese figures, within underglaze blue floral surrounds, restoration to one side, Qianlong, 16in (40.5cm) diam.
£1,000-1,500 *C*

A 'famille rose' bowl, paint with European hunting scenes, cracks, Qianlong, 11in (28cm) dian
£600-800 *CSK*

A Chinese porcelain blue and white pouring bowl, Qianlong, c1750.
£850-950 *ART*

These bowls with handles and spouts were possibly used to separate cream from milk. A rare item of salvage from the Nanking Cargo.

A pair of Canton enamel bowls and covers, painted with continuous scenes of European figures reclining at leisure in wooded and rocky landscapes, between bands of scrolling foliage, Qianlong, 4½in (11cm) diam.
£150-200 *CSK*

In the Ceramics section if there is only one measurement it usually refers to the height of the piece

Four blue and white square bowls with canted corners, variously decorated beneath broad bands at the rims, fritted, one base rim chipped, 2 cracked, late Qianlong, 10½in (25.5cm) wide.
£1,000-1,500 *C*

An Imari barber's bowl, painted with a large central vase of flowers on a table, the everted rim with buildings and flowers, restored, late 17thC, 11in (28cm).
£350-400 *CSK*

A 'famille rose' Rockefeller-type warming dish and cover, painted within a border of gilt tightly scrolling foliage reserved with sma panels of sepia landscapes and bird crack to base, chipped foot, one handle restored, Jiaqing, 14in (35.5cm) wide.
£1,500-2,000 *CSK*

. Cantonese punchbowl, painted
ith panels of ladies divided by
reen scroll gold ground bands, the
iterior rim with a gold ground
and, rim break restored,
)aoguang, 20in (50cm) diam.
4,000-5,000 *CSK*

. deep Imari bowl, decorated in
arious coloured enamels and gilt
n underglaze blue, bordered by a
and of various Buddhistic
mblems, the exterior with a similar
and above sprays of peony, the base
ith a pomegranate spray, late
9thC, 10in (25cm) diam.
1,800-2,500 *C*

Satsuma bowl, painted on the
iterior with ducks beneath plum
lossom and bamboo, the exterior
ith flowersprays on a dark blue
round, signed, 5in (12.5cm) diam.
300-500 *CSK*

A Satsuma bowl, decorated in various coloured enamels and gilt, with Yamato Takeru no Mikoto and his retainers, gilt rim, gilt rubbed and small chip, signed Choshuzan late 19thC, 9½in (24cm) diam.
£2,000-3,000 *C*

A pair of 'famille rose' fish bowls, each painted with a continuous scene, the interiors with fish among aquatic plants, 18in (46cm) diam.
£1,800-2,200 *CSK*

A set of 20 small Arita blue and white bowls, enriched with gilding, 3½in (8cm) diam, two tier inscribed wood box. **£1,000-1,500** *CSK*

A Cantonese flared punchbowl, painted with panels of figures on terraces and birds and butterflies among flowers on green scroll gold ground, rim chip restuck, 13in (33cm) diam.
£1,200-1,700 *CSK*

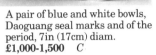

A pair of blue and white bowls, Daoguang seal marks and of the period, 7in (17cm) diam.
£1,000-1,500 *C*

A pair of 'famille rose' bowls and covers, one cover cracked, minor chips, blue enamel Xuantong six-character marks to cover and base and of the period, 8in (20cm) diam.
£1,200-1,700 *C*

CHINESE PORCELAIN – VALUE POINTS

- ★ about 80% of the marks that appear on Chinese porcelain are retrospective
- ★ if a piece bears a correct, as opposed to a retrospective, reign mark then its value compared to an unmarked but comparable specimen would probably be of the magnitude of 3 to 4 times more
- ★ a piece of a known date but bearing the mark of an earlier reign would be adversely affected and could possible fetch less than an unmarked piece of the same vintage
- ★ as a rule condition will adversely affect a readily available type of ware more than a very rare or early type
- ★ original covers or lids can raise the price considerably – especially if the vessel appears more complete with it. Hence a baluster vase, for example, would be less affected than a wine ewer

A Satsuma fluted bowl, painted in blue enamel, iron red, colours and gilt on the exterior with 5 figures seated among furniture, the interior with chrysanthemum growing on a fence, rim crack, 7in (18cm) diam.
£500-700 *CSK*

A Japanese spittoon, Genroku period, late 18thC, 5in (12.5cm) diam.
£800-1,000 *Wai*

A Japanese teabowl, with blue decoration, Genroku period, 4in (10cm) diam.
£600-800 *Wai*

A Satsuma pottery bowl, the interior decorated with a scene of a man and 3 ladies on a river bank, 10in (25.5cm) diam.
£150-250 *HCH*

Censers

An unglazed Shiwan pottery tripod censer and cover, on cabriole feet, the cover surmounted by a Buddhistic lion finial, the underside impressed with a hallmark Wunan Shitang, 19thC, 11in (27.5cm) high.
£1,800-2,200 *C*

Cups

A Transitional blue and white stem cup, 17thC, 3½in (8.5cm).
£800-1,000 *Wai*

Two London decorated Chinese porcelain coffee cups, painted with bouquets, flowersprays and a butterfly, showing 2 distinct styles of painting, c1760.
£200-250 *C*

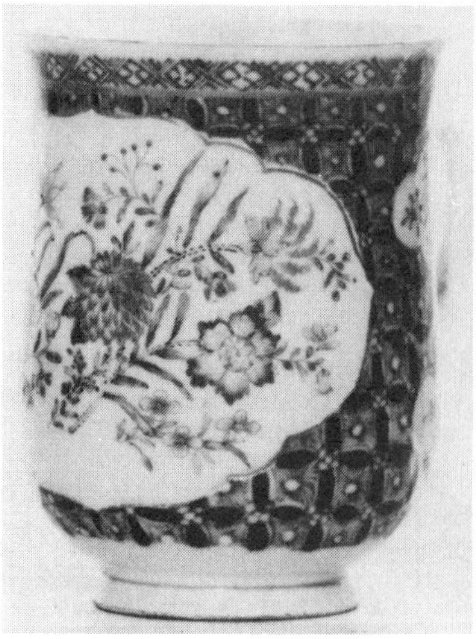

A set of 3 'famille rose' bell-shaped mugs, each painted with a large panel of flowersprays flanked by four smaller quatrefoil floral panels, on underglaze blue cell-pattern grounds, late Qianlong, 4½ to 5½in (11 to 13cm).
£1,000-1,200 *CSK*

A Transitional blue and white cup, on tall spreading foot, painted with a bird in flight beside pine, prunus and bamboo, incised collector's mark, c1650, 6in (15cm).
£800-1,200 *C*

A Japanese cup, probably Noritake, 2½in (6cm).
£10-30 *THA*

Chinese Imari ormolu mounted
p, the porcelain early 18thC, the
ounts later, 6in (15cm).
,000-2,500 *C*

A pair of 'famille rose' flared libation cups and stands, painted with panels of figures among furniture, on grounds of gilt scrolling foliage reserved with small pink panels, within borders of trailing flowers and bamboo, Qianlong, stands 6½in (16cm) wide.
£700-1,000 *CSK*

A pair of Doucai wine cups, painted on the exterior with phoenix among scrolling lotus, the interiors plain, Jiajing six-character marks, Kangxi/Yongzheng.
£2,000-2,500 *CSK*

wers

Yingqing ewer with short spout,
bed handle and 2 looped handles
low the flaring neck, the glaze at
e body and mouth with iron spots,
ng Dynasty, 4in (10cm).
,000-1,200 *C*

A late Ming blue and white kraak type kendi, painted with alternate panels of leaping horses and sprays of flowers, Wanli, 7½in (19cm).
£800-1,200 *CSK*

An Arita blue and white Kakiemon-type kendi, the neck and spout restored, c1700, 8in (20cm).
£500-800 *CSK*

A Shino ware ewer, 19thC, 4in (10cm).
£600-800 *Wai*

A set of 3 Imari pear-shaped jugs, covers and stand, painted with flowering shrubs, one handle repaired, one spout missing, late 17thC, 5in (12.5cm).
£1,500-2,000 *CSK*

TRANSITIONAL WARES

- ★ these wares are readily identifiable both by their form and by their style of decoration
- ★ forms: sleeve vases, oviform jars with domed lids, cylindrical brushpots and bottle vases are particularly common
- ★ the cobalt used is a brilliant purplish blue, rarely misfired
- ★ the ground colour is of a definite bluish tone, probably because the glaze is slightly thicker than that of the wares produced in the subsequent reigns of Kangxi and Yongzheng
- ★ the decoration is executed in a rather formal academic style, often with scholars and sages with attendants in idyllic cloud-lapped mountain landscapes
- ★ other characteristics include the horizontal 'contoured' clouds, banana plantain used to interrupt scenes, and the method of drawing grass by means of short 'V' shaped brush strokes
- ★ in addition, borders are decorated with narrow bands of scrolling foliage, so lightly incised as to be almost invisible or secret (anhua)
- ★ these pieces were rarely marked although they sometimes copied earlier Ming marks

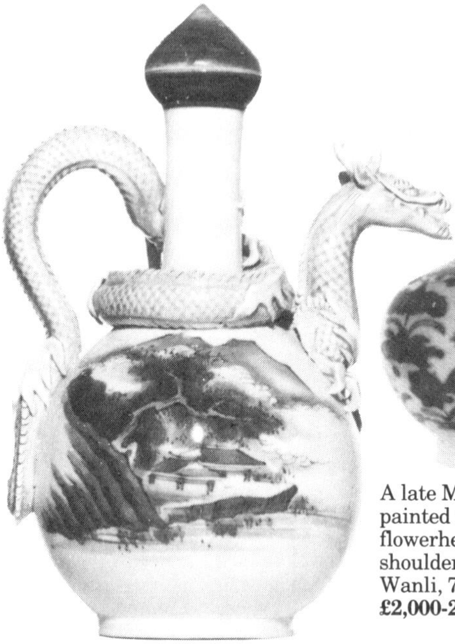

A Hirado blue and white ewer and stopper, modelled in high relief with a dragon coiled around the neck and forming the handle and spout, the body painted with mountainous river landscapes, 10in (25.5cm).
£600-1,000 *CSK*

A late Ming blue and white kendi, painted with fish below a band of flowerheads and lappets at the shoulder, chipped and cracked, Wanli, 7in (18cm).
£2,000-2,500 *CSK*

A blue and white oviform wine ewer, applied at the shoulder with 4 mask loop handles above large ogival panels, painted with the 2 laughing twins, 'hehe erxian', on a scale ground, small spout chip and fritting to handles, Kangxi, 7½in (19cm), wood cover.
£1,000-1,500 *C*

Figures – Animal

A Chinese buff pottery standing figure of a camel, modelled with simulated tufted hair, some traces of pigment remaining on details, Tang Dynasty, 17in (43cm).
£3,000-3,500 *CSK*

A red pottery equestrian figure, traces of painted pigment, some restoration, Tang Dynasty, 12in (31cm).
£2,000-2,500 *C*

A painted buff pottery figure of a camel, some traces of pigment remaining, Tang Dynasty, 14½in (37cm).
£5,000-6,000 *C*

A rare Hirado 'Hanaike' modelled as a hawk, its feather details in underglaze blue and brown enamels, slight crazing, late 19thC, 8½in (21cm).
£1,000-1,500 *C*

A large Chinese painted grey pottery horse torso, with traces of red strapwork on a white ground, Han Dynasty, 17½in (44cm) long.
£1,500-2,000 *CSK*

A Hirado blue and white candlestick, late 19thC, 7in (18cm) long.
£500-600 *Wai*

A pair of Arita goats, 19thC, 5½in (14cm) long.
£600-800 *Wai*

late Kutani moulded model of a ıg dog, decorated in iron red, een, blue, yellow and aubergine amels and gilt, chips to front ws, slight crack to tail, id-19thC, 10in (25cm) long.
,200-1,600 *C*

Two Cantonese candle holders, modelled as recumbent Buddhistic lions, with iron red and gilt fur markings and florally decorated saddle cloths, one candle holder missing, 4½ and 5in (11 and 12.5cm) long.
£1,000-1,200 *CSK*

'igures – People

A pair of late Ming blue and white figures of boys, wearing floral aprons, both on bases decorated with flowersprays, lotus leaf chipped, fritted, 17thC, 8½in (21cm).
£2,000-2,500 *C*

A pair of glazed buff pottery figures of warriors, their heads and clothes under an iridescent straw glaze with traces of red and green pigment remaining, Sui/early Tang Dynasty, 16in (41cm).
£2,500-3,500 *C*

Two Chinese glazed ridge tiles, modelled with striding demon figures, in ochre, green and cream, Ming Dynasty, 14 and 15in (36 and 38cm).
£1,000-1,200 *CSK*

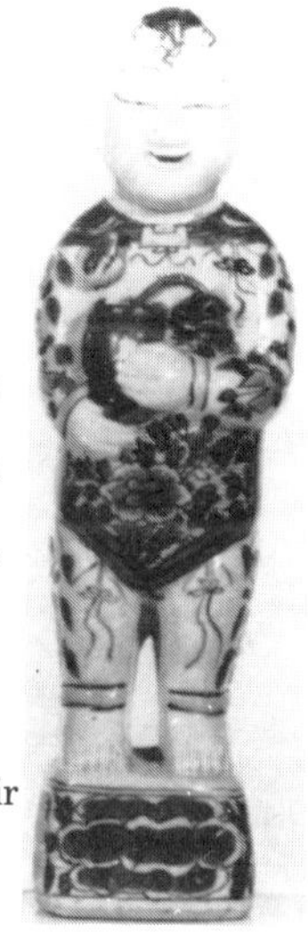

A pair of 'famille verte' figures of boys, painted with precious objects and with ruyi head collar, their hair tied in a bow at the front, minor damage, Kangxi, 11in (28cm).
£2,000-2,500 *CSK*

A 'famille verte' figure of a bearded smiling official, wearing a blue ground robe with 'famille verte' undergarment, holding a 'ruyi' in his right hand and a black hat, some fritting, firing line to sceptre, Kangxi, 8½in (22cm).
£1,000-1,200 *C*

A Wucai figure of a laughing boy, holding a lotus bud in his hands and wearing a floral apron over a chequered tunic, hand chipped, fritted, 17thC, 9in (23cm).
£1,500-2,000 *C*

A rare 'famille verte' group of 2 ladies, both wearing coats decorated with roundels of flowerheads over long skirts bordered with iron red bands, one head re-stuck, hands chipped, base cracked, Kangxi, 8½in (21.5cm).
£2,000-3,000 *C*

A blanc-de-chine group of Guanyin seated with a child on her knees, 18thC, 6½in (16cm).
£450-550 *CSK*

A Chinese figure of Guanyin, holding a scroll, wearing an elaborate necklace, her headdress, cloak and gown decorated with three-clawed dragon roundels in white, rose pink, yellow and grey on a green ground, with yellow undergarment, right hand broken off and in pieces, early 19thC, 29in (74cm).
£1,000-1,500 *P(S)*

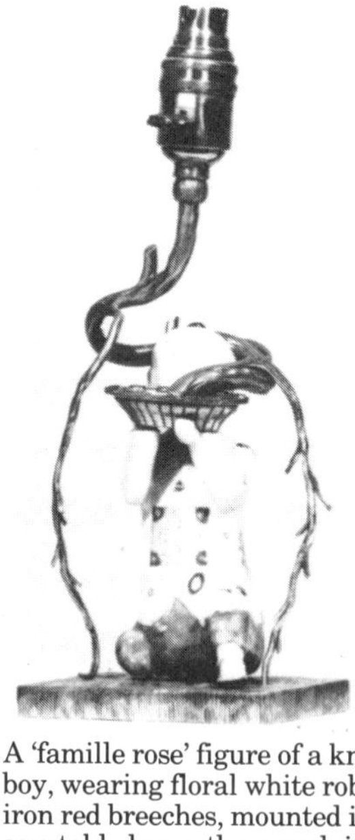

A 'famille rose' figure of a kneeling boy, wearing floral white robe and iron red breeches, mounted in brass as a table lamp, the porcelain 18th/early 19thC, 12in (30.5cm).
£600-700 *CSK*

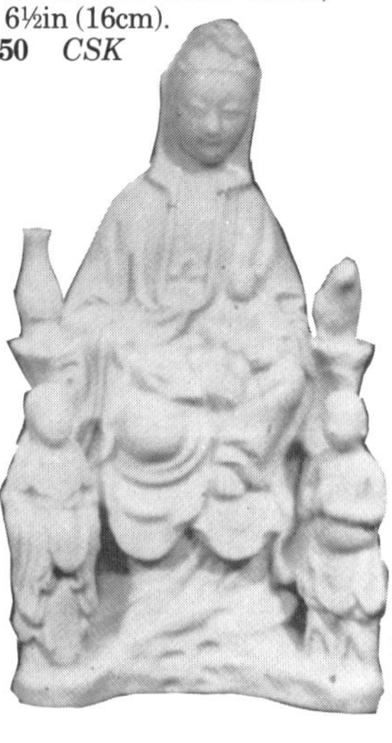

A blanc-de-chine group of Guanyin, 18thC, 7½in (19cm).
£450-550 *CSK*

Flasks

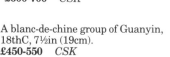

A pair of 'famille verte' moon flask each painted with flowers on a pal yellow ground, the neck decorated with scrolling peony on a pale gree ground, 18th/19thC, 11in (27.5cm)
£2,500-4,000 *C*

pair of 'famille rose' moon flasks, plied on the shoulder with gilt ıi' handles, the tall foot with a nd of trellis pattern, 19thC, ½in (29cm).
,200-1,700 *C*

Flatware

Three Ming blue and white dishes, with birds and foliage within panelled borders, repaired, 14 and 18in (35.5 and 46cm).
£700-800 *SWO*

A pair of late Ming blue and white saucer dishes, each decorated with geese beneath grasses on a river bank, fritted, Chongzheng, 6in (15cm) diam.
£800-1,000 *C*

A pair of Cantonese celadon ground shell-shaped dishes, with flattened gilt handles, 10½in (26cm).
£400-500 *CSK*

late Ming blue and white kraak ep dish, painted with birds below us on a river bank, the border th alternate panels of wersprays and emblems, Wanli, ½in (29cm).
00-800 *CSK*

A late Ming blue and white dish, painted within a well of trailing foliage, the border with alternate panels of travellers in landscapes and stylised foliage, minor frits, c1630, 14in (35.5cm) diam.
£2,000-2,500 *CSK*

A late Ming blue and white saucer dish, painted with a central roundel of a vase, the border with butterflies in flight among flowering and fruiting branches, fritted, Xuande mark, Wanli, 11in (28cm).
£600-800 *CSK*

Arita dish, modelled in the form n 'uchiwa', decorated in various ›ured enamels and gilt on lerglaze blue, the reverse with ›lling foliage, Chenghua character mark, early 18thC, ın (19cm) wide.
500-3,000 *C*

A late Ming blue and white 'kraak porselein' dish, painted in vivid blue tones at the centre, within a band of trellis and cell pattern divided by half flowerheads, the well decorated with quatrefoil lappets of flowers and fruit below the foliate rim, the exterior with similar lappets, fritted, Wanli, 18in (45cm) diam.
£4,000-4,500 *C*

A late Ming blue and white 'kraak porselein' dish, fritted, Wanli, 14in (35.5cm) diam.
£1,200-1,700 *C*

A Transitional blue and white saucer dish, painted with a ferocious 'qilin' breathing flames beside plantain, the exterior plain, the base with four-character 'yutang jiaqi' mark, fine vessel for the jade hall, c1650, 14in (35cm) diam.
£900-1,200 *C*

A 'famille verte' dish, painted wi chrysanthemum issuing from gr rockwork within a cell pattern border reserved with panels of emblems, fritted, small cracks, Kangxi, 14½in (37cm) diam.
£1,000-1,200 *CSK*

Five late Ming blue and white 'kraak' deep plates, each painted variously to the centres, minor chips, Wanli, 8½in (21cm) diam.
£600-800 *CSK*

A large Chinese blue and white saucer dish, with slightly flared rim painted, chipped, Kangxi, 15½in (40cm).
£500-600 *CSK*

A late Ming blue and white 'kraak porselein' dish, fritted and cracked c1620, 18½in (47cm) diam.
£2,000-3,000 *C*

A 'famille verte' dish, with a pierced ribbon border, painted within a rim of trellis pattern, hairline crack, Kangxi, 12½in (32cm) diam.
£2,000-2,500 *CSK*

An Arita blue and white dish, in Kakiemon style, decorated in the centre with cranes bordered by branches of plum, pine and bamboo, the exterior with scrolling flowerheads and foliage, late 17thC, 8in (20cm) diam.
£1,000-1,200 *C*

A pair of Chinese blue and white saucer dishes, Chenghua six-character marks, Kangxi, 6in (15cm) diam.
£1,000-1,200 *CSK*

A pair of 'famille verte' deep plates, minor frits, Kangxi, 8½in (21cm) diam.
£500-700 *CSK*

›lue and white dish, painted at › centre and reserved on a key ttern ground within a foliate rim, ›ted, Kangxi six-character mark ‹ of the period, 13½in (34.5cm) ›m.
,200-2,700 *C*

A set of 4 Chinese blue and white deep dishes, with everted rims painted to the centres with sprays of finger citrus, within borders of further fruit sprays, Kangxi, 7½in (19cm).
£1,000-1,500 *CSK*

An Arita blue and white 'kraak' style charger, the central roundel containing branches of pomegranates surrounded by alternate panels of Buddhistic emblems and stylised flowerheads and foliage, linked by narrower panels of a single flowerhead, late 17thC, 16½in (41cm) diam.
£1,600-2,000 *C*

A blue and white saucer dish, Kangxi, with a commendation mark, 9½in (24cm) diam.
£500-600 *Wai*

A 'famille verte' plate, Kangxi, 9in (23cm) diam.
£300-400 *Wai*

A 'famille verte' dish, painted in pencil underglaze blue to the centre with chrysanthemum sprays below enamelled flower panels, on an iron red and gilt flowerhead band at the well and flowersprays at the border, Kangxi, 15in (38cm) diam.
£2,000-2,500 *C*

A set of 5 Kakiemon foliate dishes, each painted in typical enamels with a bird perched in a plum tree above blue and green rockwork, damaged, late 17thC, 4½in (11cm) diam.
£1,500-2,000 *CSK*

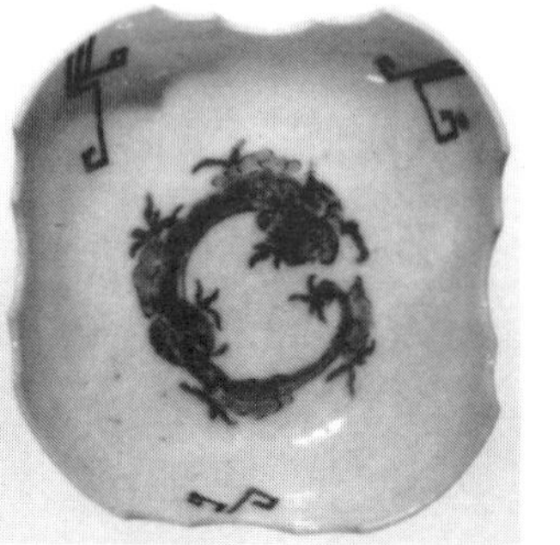

A pair of Kakiemon dishes with foliate rims, decorated in iron red, green, yellow, blue and black enamels with a dragon coiled beneath sheets of stylised lightning, ring feet, one with slight chip to rim, late 17thC, 3½in (8.5cm) wide.
£1,000-1,200 *C*

A pair of Arita blue and white saucer dishes, in the Kakiemon style, Fuku marks, late 17thC, 6i (15cm) diam.
£1,200-1,600 *C*

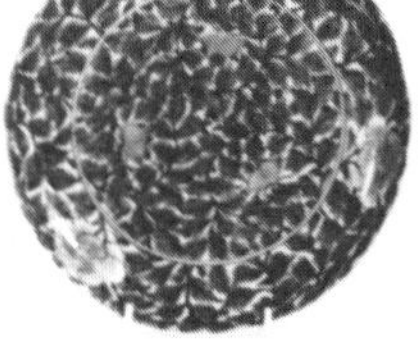

An Arita blue and white thickly potted dish, with slightly shaped rim, densely painted with scrolling flowers and leaves, c1700, 9½in (24cm) diam.
£400-500 *CSK*

A Chinese Imari charger, the broad rim with gold, iron red and blue chrysanthemum and peony decoration, 18thC, 14in (35.5cm) diam.
£350-450 *P(M)*

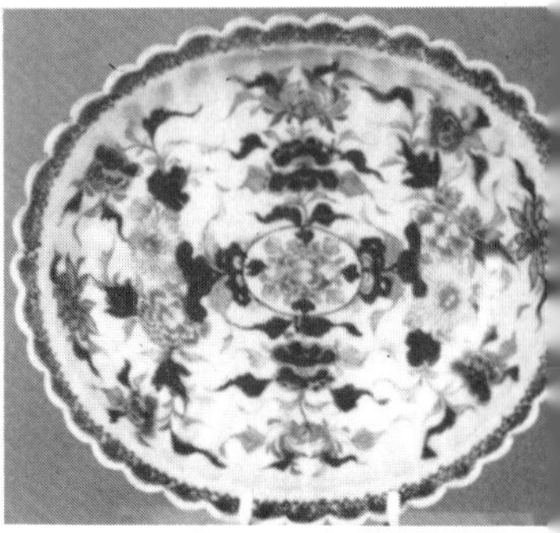

A Chinese Imari shallow bowl, painted within a border of blue a gilt tightly scrolling foliage, earl 18thC, 10½in (26cm) wide.
£1,200-1,500 *CSK*

A blue and white bowl, pencilled at the centre with scholars before pavilion on a terrace, rim slightly polished, seal mark on base, 18thC, 15½in (39cm) diam.
£1,500-2,000 *C*

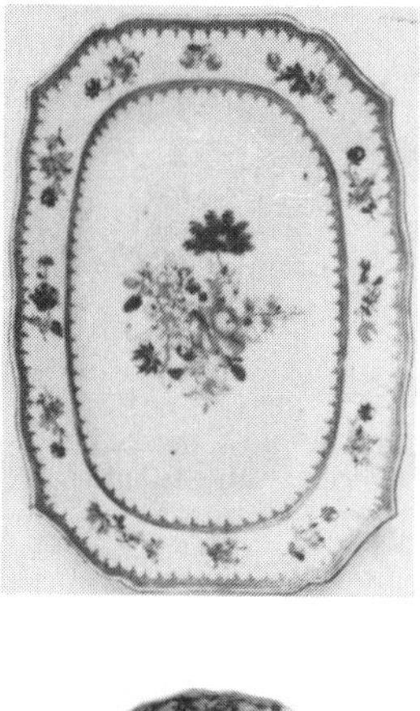

Two 'famille rose' meat dishes, painted with bouquets of flowers within iron red and gilt spearhead wells and rims, the borders with flowersprays, Qianlong, 10 and 12in (25.5 and 30.5cm) wide.
£2,000-2,500 *CSK*

An Arita blue and white painted dish, small rim chip, Fuku mark, late 17thC, 8in (20cm) diam.
£400-600 *CSK*

A pair of Arita foliate rimmed blue and white dishes, minor chip, late 17thC, 11in (27cm) diam.
£2,000-2,500 *C*

arge 'famille rose' and
derglaze blue decorated dish,
h everted foliate rim, painted
h a central panel of a river
dscape within a whorl pattern,
anlong, 15in (38cm) diam.
50-850 *CSK*

An Arita blue and white Kakiemon type dish, painted within a border of tightly scrolling flowers and leaves, rim chips, late 17thC, 8½in (21cm) diam.
£550-650 *CSK*

A pair of 'famille rose' dishes, each painted with a yellow and blue bird perched on blue rockwork, within pink swastika pattern wells, borders of flowersprays and rims of iron red and gilt foliage, one restored, Yongzheng, 15in (38cm) diam.
£2,500-3,000 *CSK*

A 'famille rose' dish, with barbed silver shaped rim, painted to the centre with peacocks amongst branches and peony, the rim with scattered floral sprigs, Qianlong, 13in (33cm) wide.
£500-700 *Bon*

amille rose' deep plate, painted
n yellow and black cockerels
ong flowering shrubs and pierced
kwork, the pale blue cell pattern
der reserved with panels of fruit
flowers, restored, Yongzheng,
n (21cm) diam.
0-300 *CSK*

A pair of rose/Imari plates, painted within a blue trellis pattern border reserved with panels of insects, Yongzheng, 8½in (21cm) diam.
£400-500 *CSK*

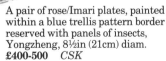

pair of 'famille rose' soup plates,
nted with elaborate gilt
nograms within chain pattern
lls and borders of flowersprays
d exotic birds, Qianlong, 9in
cm) diam.
)0-700 *CSK*

*e crest and cypher are those of
lliam Braund.*

A 'famille rose', iron red and gilt armorial plate, painted at the centre with a shield shaped coat-of-arms, the well with iron red and gilt flowersprays and a chain band below a leafy floral band, edge chips, Qianlong, c1765, 9in (23cm) wide.
£450-700 *C*

The arms are those of Bennet.

A blue and white armorial dish, painted at the centre with a gilt coat-of-arms with a sepia squirrel beneath a coronet, Qianlong, c1745, 15in (38.5cm) wide.
£4,000-5,000 *C*

The arms are those of Sichterman, the family of the Dutch Governor of Bengal between 1734 and 1744. These arms with a squirrel have often been confused with the arms of the French family Foucquet whose name was close to the old French word 'fouquet' or squirrel.

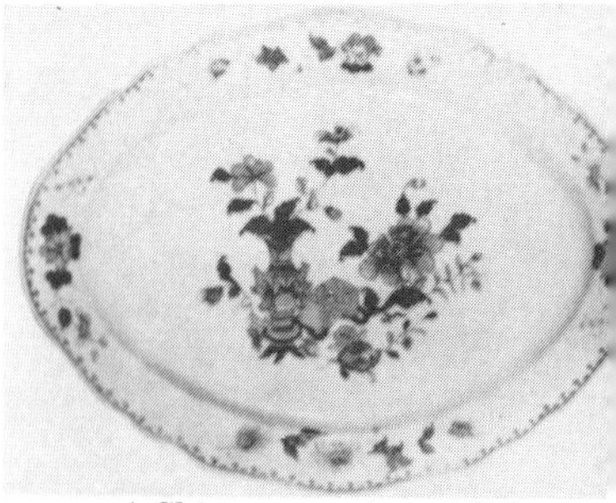

A Chinese export meat dish, pain 'en grisaille' and gilt with a vase among flowers and emblems wit 4 flowersprays and a gilt spearh rim, Qianlong, 16in (41cm) wide
£500-600 *CSK*

A set of 4 'famille rose' peacock pattern plates, each painted with peacocks perched among flowering chrysanthemum and rockwork, cracked and chipped, Qianlong, 9in (23cm).
£1,000-1,500 *CSK*

A 'famille rose' plate, painted with ducks swimming among water plants, the border with the 8 Immortals with attributes among breaking waves, Qianlong, 9in (23cm) diam.
£500-600 *CSK*

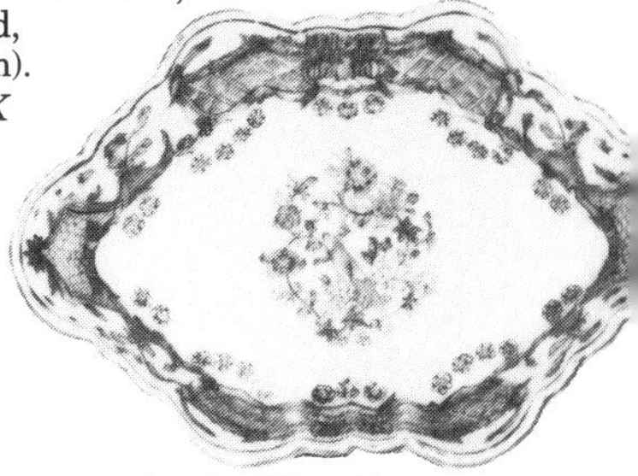

A pair of 'famille rose' fluted spo trays, painted with central medallions of exotic birds and flowers within borders of feathe and flowersprays, one with star crack, Qianlong, 5in (12.5cm) w
£450-500 *CSK*

A 'famille rose' armorial dish, painted at the centre with a coat-of-arms surmounted by a crest within a band of underglaze blue cell pattern at the well and Fitzhugh-pattern at the shaped border, slightly fritted, Qianlong, c1790, 16½in (41.5cm) wide.
£1,500-2,000 *C*

The arms are those of Canning.

A pair of 'famille rose' dishes, with sheep pattern, c1780, 10in (25.5cm) diam.
£800-1,000 *Wai*

A 'famille rose' plate, painted with central scene of the Czar's visit to Beijing, damaged, Qianlong, 15½ (39cm).
£300-400 *CSK*

Chinese blue and white meat
h, painted within a cell pattern
der reserved with panels of
wers, and later decorated iron red
l gilt, small rim chips, one
tored, Qianlong, 15in (38cm)
le.
50-550 *CSK*

An Arita blue and white dish, boldly decorated with sprays of tree peony issuing from swirling waters beneath cumulus clouds, late 18thC, 9in (23cm) diam.
£1,800-2,200 *C*

A 'famille rose' dish, painted and gilt with a central scene within a gilt spearhead border and peony sprays to the rim, Qianlong, 15in (38cm) wide.
£700-800 *CSK*

air of 'famille rose' meat dishes,
nted within underglaze blue
terfly, cell-pattern and floral
ders and iron red and gilt rims,
anlong, 13¼in (34cm) wide.
000-2,500 *CSK*

A 'famille rose' European subject dish, painted with a lady wearing puce dress with green bodice and a yellow wrap, and a boy in an orange coat, blue breeches and white leggings, c1820, 15in (38cm) wide.
£1,500-2,000 *C*

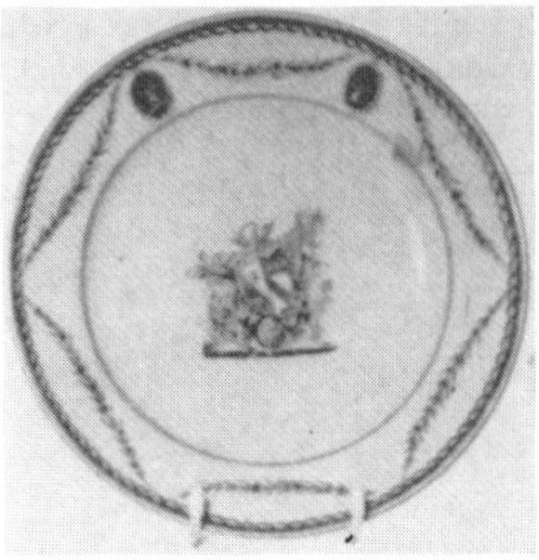

A set of 5 'famille rose' armorial plates, 2 cracked, Jiaqing, 7½in (19cm).
£1,000-1,500 *CSK*

A 'famille rose' Rockefeller-pattern dish, painted at the centre with a lady and a child peering out of the window watching a bearded gentleman leading a camel along a river bank, the camel with a banner, within a band of sepia trellis enriched with bird cartouches at the well, the curved border with further sepia cartouches on a rich gilt scrolling ground, rim repaired, c1800, 10in (25cm) diam.
£400-800 *C*

It appears from the large full beard and form of dress that the figure is a Middle Eastern, possibly Persian, quack advertising his medicinal services.

A pair of 'famille rose' soup plates, chipped, Daoguang, 10in (25cm).
£500-600 *CSK*

A large Imari dish, decorated in iron red enamel and gilt on underglaze blue, slight chip restored, late 19thC, 17in (43cm) wide.
£1,600-2,000 *C*

A Satsuma charger, decorated in various coloured enamels and gilt, with archers, warriors, standard bearers and horsemen in battle, a central roundel containing a 'kikugata' emblem bordered by a band of lappets, the border similarly decorated, late 19thC, 22½in (57cm).
£4,500-5,500 *C*

A Chinese blue and white shallow basin, painted to the centre with a standing lady among flowers, Xuande six-character mark, 18thC, 11½in (29cm) diam. **£2,000-2,500** *CSK*

A Cantonese meat dish, painted and gilt with alternating figures of warriors and ladies, 19in (48cm) wide. **£900-1,000** *CSK*

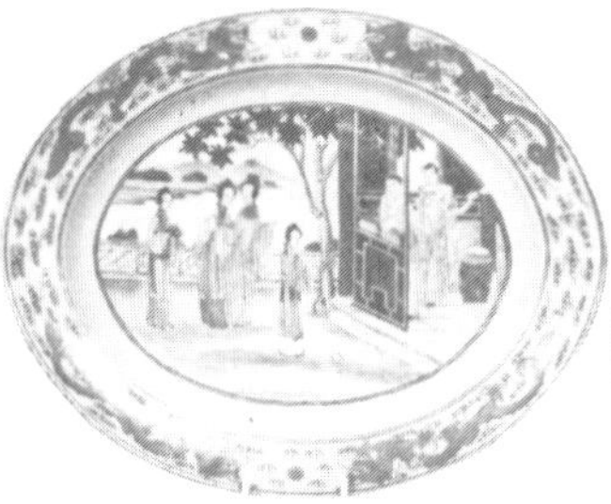

A Cantonese meat dish, painted in the centre with figures, the border with iron red and gilt dragons chasing flaming pearls, 14½in (37cm) wide. **£500-600** *CSK*

A Kinkozan dish, decorated in various coloured enamels and gilt on a deep blue ground, signed and impressed mark Kinkozan zo, painter's mark Hosui, late 19thC, 8½in (21cm) diam.
£1,000-1,500 *C*

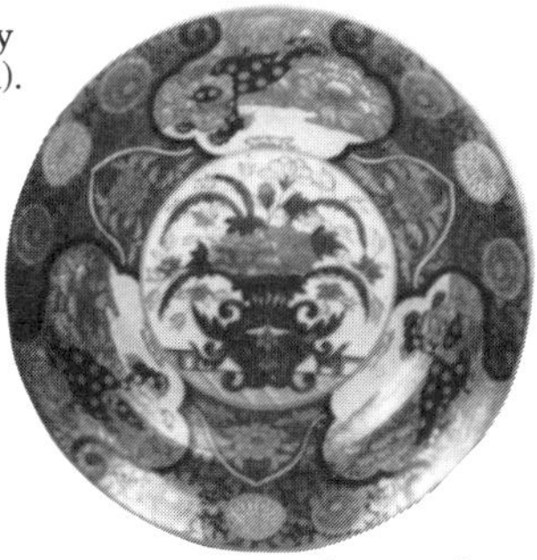

An Imari charger, decorated in iron red and black enamels and gilt on underglaze blue, restored, Genroku period, 21½in (55cm) diam.
£2,000-2,500 *C*

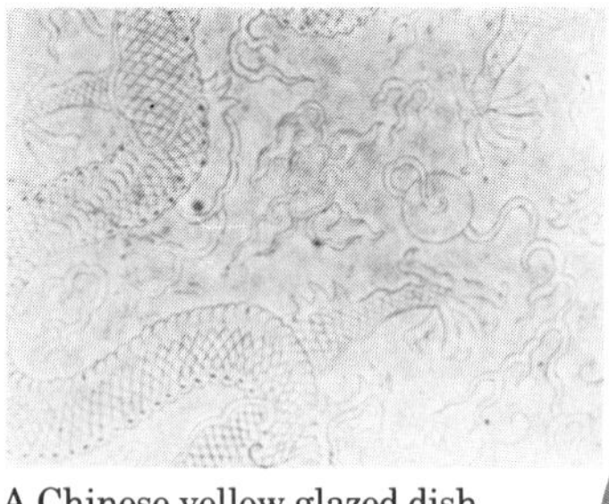

A Chinese yellow glazed dish, decorated to the centre with incised dragons chasing flaming pearls amongst cloud scrolls, Tongzhi six-character mark and of the period, 12½in (32cm) diam.
£4,000-4,500 *CSK*

A Satsuma dish, decorated in various coloured enamels and gilt with a winding 'daimyo' processio bearing a litter, standards and oth trophies, within a key pattern border, signed Fuzan, late 19thC, 7½in (18cm) diam.
£800-1,000 *C*

A foliate rimmed Imari dish, decorated in typical coloured enamels and gilt on underglaze blue, the central panel with 'kirin beneath branches of cherry blosso each corner with a ho-o roundel, minor chip to rim, late 19thC, 12i (30.5cm) wide.
£500-600 *C*

An Imari charger, decorated in ir red enamel and gilt on underglaz blue, restored, Genroku period, 21½in (54cm) diam.
£1,500-2,000 *C*

A Satsuma dish, painted and heavily gilt with a shaped panel bordered by a ho-o enclosing figure in a fenced garden, 12in (30.5cm) diam.
£800-1,000 *CSK*

t of 5 Japanese Nabeshima-style
cer dishes, with combed foot
s, painted in underglaze blue,
en and yellow enamels and iron
with sprays of daisies, 8in
m) diam.
0-600 *CSK*

An Imari colander and tray, both decorated in typical coloured enamels and gilt on underglaze blue, tray restored, the tray with Ming six-character mark, Genroku period, colander 10in (25cm) diam.
£2,500-3,000 *C*

A set of 12 Kutani plates, painted and gilt with central scenes of ladies at leisure, within borders of floral, ho-o and geometric roundels among cloud scrolls, 3 damaged, 9½in (24cm) diam.
£800-1,000 *CSK*

hinese blue and white saucer
, painted to the interior with
lling lotus, small rim chips,
guang seal mark and of the
od, 8in (20cm). **£300-400** *CSK*

An Arita Imari plate, late 17thC, 9in (23cm) diam.
£200-250 *Wai*

rdinières

ose/verte' jardinière, the interior
nted with iron red fish among
er plants, 19in (48cm) diam.
0-700 *CSK*

A blue and white low jardinière, painted with a band of scrolling lotus between pendent dot lappets at the foot and key pattern at the rim, 18thC, 21in (53cm) diam.
£3,000-5,000 *C*

A blue and white jardinière, base pierced, Kangxi, 9in (23cm) diam.
£900-1,200 *C*

A 'famille verte' jardinière, painted with 4 panels of warriors and an audience scene, all reserved on a dense scrolling foliage ground enriched with flowerheads and butterflies above a band of iron red stiff lappets at the foot, beneath a 'ruyi' collar and a band of key pattern below the rim, 19thC, 21½in (54cm) diam, wood stand.
£3,000-4,000 *C*

Jars

A Satsuma pottery globular jardinière and stand, painted in colours and gilt, with moulded green leaves around the foot rim, 39½in (100cm) high.
£900-1,200 *CSK*

A pair of blue and white jardinières, painted on the exterior in mirror image with scholars and young boys, above a band of stiff lappets at the foot and below a 'ruyi' collar, the flat rim with a continuous band of scrolling foliage, fritted, one base restored, 19thC, 18½in (47cm) high, wood stands.
£3,000-4,000 *C*

A green glazed impressed jar, the top half covered with an olive green glaze stopping just above the mid-body, Zhou Dynasty, 15½in (39cm) wide.
£3,000-4,000 *C*

A Ming Fahua baluster jar, moulded in a cloisonné technique, painted predominantly in yellow and turquoise on a deep blue ground, the interior green glazed, neck restored, foot replacement, c1500, 13in (32.5cm) high, wood stand.
£3,000-3,500 *C*

A Wucai baluster jar and domed cover with knop finial, painted with a continuous scene of boys at play, repaired, Transitional, 17in (43cm).
£700-800 *CSK*

A late Ming blue and white jar, painted with a bird perched on ro between peony and chrysanthemum, above a band of whorl pattern, Wanli, 8½in (21.5cm).
£900-1,200 *C*

A Chinese blue and white balust jar, painted with birds in flight, cracks, glaze chip to shoulder, ea Kangxi, later replacement cover, 19½in (49cm).
£3,000-3,500 *CSK*

A Transitional blue and white oviform jar, rim interior with shallow chip, c1650, 9½in (24cm).
£3,000-4,000 *C*

A Chinese blue and white oviform jar and domed cover, Yuan/early Ming Dynasty, 5½in (14cm).
£400-600 *CSK*

Ming blue and white baluster jar, ›inted with flowers below 'ruyi' ›ads and key-pattern at the ›oulder and short neck, 16thC, ¼in (11cm) high.
›00-600 *CSK*

A Transitional blue and white oviform jar, painted with two 'qilins' beside rockwork and plaintain on a terrace, rim crack, c1643, 10in (25cm) high, wood cover.
£2,000-2,500 *C*

A blue and white ginger jar and cover, with a cracked ice pattern ground enriched with prunus heads between bands of fret pattern at the foot and on the shoulder, the cover similarly decorated, Kangxi, 12in (30.5cm).
£1,000-1,500 *C*

Japanese jar and cover, with lion ›ask ring handles, some pitting ›d finial missing, 8½in (21cm).
›00-400 *CSK*

A Chinese Imari jar and cover, painted with a pheasant among flowering shrubs and pierced rockwork in a fenced garden, Qianlong, 9in (23cm).
£1,500-2,000 *CSK*

A blue and white oviform jar, decorated in vivid blue tones, foot with glaze flake, Kangxi, 7½in (19cm), wood cover.
£1,500-2,000 *C*

pair of Chinese blue and white iform jars and domed covers, ›inted with figures standing in ›ntinuous rocky landscapes below ›nds of leaves at the shoulders, ›an/early Ming Dynasty, 5in ›3cm).
›00-700 *CSK*

A 'famille rose' jar, painted with phoenix among flowering shrubs issuing from pierced blue rockwork, Qianlong, 8in (20cm), with gilt metal tripod stand and pierced wood jade mounted cover.
£700-800 *CSK*

›o late Ming blue and white iform jars, one painted with ›rolling flowers and leaves below ›yi' heads at the shoulder, the ›her with flowering shrubs and ›asses, Wanli, 5 and 5½in (13 and ›cm).
›00-600 *CSK*

An underglaze copper red and blue celadon ground jar of oviform shape, painted with peach sprays, the glaze pooling in places, some surface scratching, Kangxi, 6½in (16.5cm).
£1,000-1,500 *C*

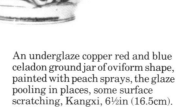

A 'famille verte' tea caddy, painted on 2 sides with cockerels, the smaller sides with butterflies and flowers, Kangxi, 3in (7.5cm), white metal cover.
£500-600 *CSK*

A pair of Chinese blue and white jars and covers, decorated in inky cobalt, Kangxi, 12in (30.5cm).
£4,000-5,000 *N*

A Chinese Imari oviform jar, painted with pheasants among flowering shrubs and rockwork in a fenced garden, Qianlong, 8½in (21cm).
£800-900 *CSK*

A Chinese blue and white square tea jar, painted with pagodas and boats in a rocky wooded river landscape, cracked, c1800, 12½in (32cm) high.
£1,200-1,500 *CSK*

A 'famille rose' pale blue ground oviform jar and domed cover, painted with gilt shou characters below yellow lappets to the shoulder, star crack, cover chipped, iron red Daoguang seal mark and c the period, 9½in (24cm).
£800-900 *CSK*

A 'famille rose' jar and domed cover, 10½in (26cm).
£800-900 *CSK*

An Arita polychrome oviform jar and cover, with shishi and ball finial, painted with scenes above black and iron red ground panels of scrolling foliage at the foot and iron red key pattern on the neck and cover rim, body cracks, 37in (94cm).
£3,000-3,500 *CSK*

A Fukagawa cylindrical jar and fla cover, painted with figures below hanging leaves on a black ground, with bamboo finial, 6½in (16cm).
£1,500-2,000 *CSK*

A pair of Chinese blue and white jars and domed covers, painted with panels of figures at leisure, 12½in (32cm). **£1,500-2,000** *CSK*

Satsuma oviform jar and cover, ith shishi finial, ring and ıssel handles, painted in colours ıd richly gilt with figures in ndscapes, below stylised floral orders, rim cracks, 45in (114cm), ood stand.
,200-1,700 *CSK*

Tea & Coffee Pots

An Imari coffee urn, on shaped feet, decorated in iron red enamel and gilt on underglaze blue, the loop handle with scrolling 'karakusa', the slightly domed cover with a knop finial, slight chipping to cover, Genroku period, the silver mounts by Annoldi & Wielick, Amsterdam, c1850, 12in (30cm).
£3,000-4,000 *CSK*

A Chinese blue and white barrel-shaped teapot and flat cover, with Buddhistic lion finial and rope twist handle and spout, painted with panels of vessels and emblems, Kangxi, 6½in (16cm) wide.
£200-300 *CSK*

A Yixing teapot and cover, decorated with squirrels, the handle and spout modelled as gnarled branches, the cover similarly decorated, cover chipped, 19thC, 14in (35.5cm), gilt metal mounts.
£1,200-1,500 *C*

ervices

Satsuma pottery tea service, served on a gold decorated deep ue ground, comprising: teapot and ver, sugar basin and cover, milk g and 6 cups and saucers.
00-500 *Bea*

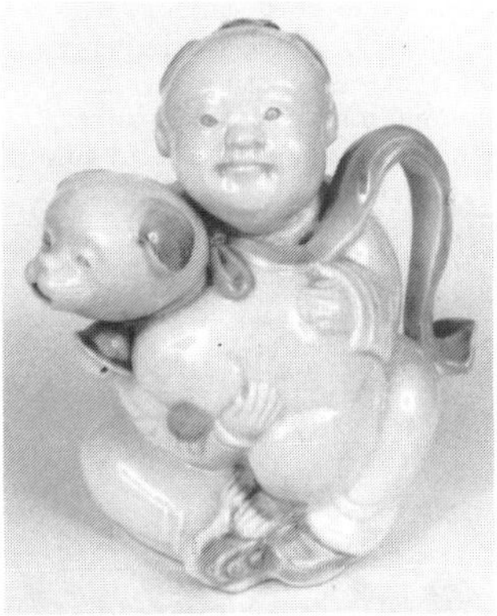

A Hirado teapot, late 19thC, 8in (20cm).
£500-600 *Wai*

ureens

A Chinese blue and white tureen and cover, with boar's head handles, with matching stand, decorated with peony and other flowersprays between scrolling borders, Qianlong, tureen 13½in (34cm) wide.
£2,000-2,500 *CSK*

blue and white tureen and cover, ith foliate knop and rabbit head ındles, knop repaired, Qianlong, in (35.5cm) wide.
00-400 *Bon*

A Cantonese soup tureen, domed cover and stand, with entwined gilt handles and gilt finial, painted on a green scroll gold ground, 14in (35.5cm) wide.
£2,000-2,500 *CSK*

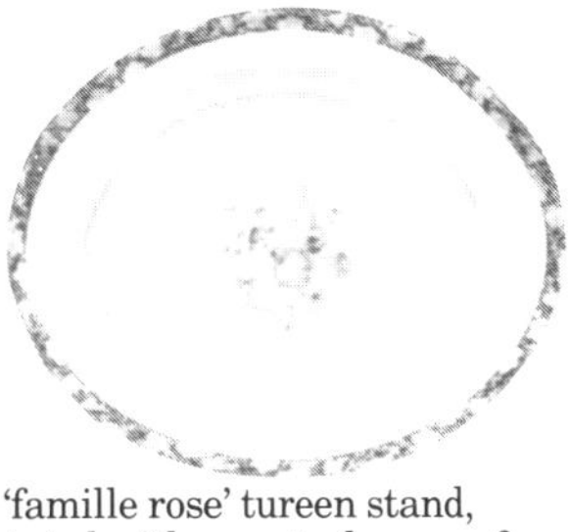

A 'famille rose' tureen stand, painted with a central spray of flowers within a blue enamel and gilt border of fruiting vine, c1800, 14½in (37cm) wide.
£500-600 *CSK*

Vases

A Chinese blue and white Fitzhugh pattern soup tureen, domed cover and stand, with flowerhead and leaf finial and entwined strap handles, enriched with gilding, inner cover restored, c1800, the stand 14in (35.5cm) wide. **£1,500-2,000** *CSK*

A Chinese red pottery hu-shaped vase, with ring handles and bands of horizontal ribbing, under a thin pale greenish yellow degraded glaze, Han Dynasty, 13½in (34cm). **£600-800** *CSK*

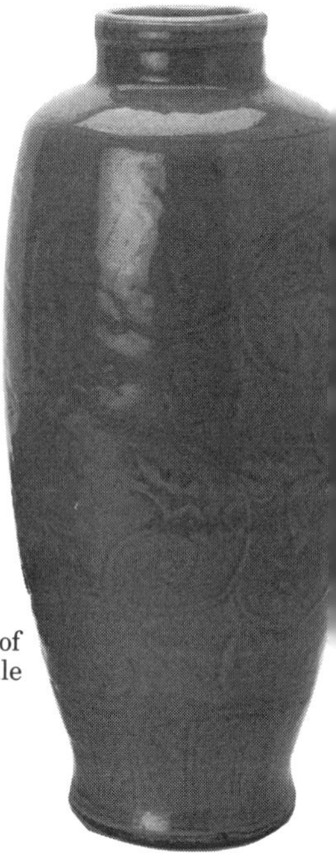

A celadon vase, the neck carved with scrolling peony stems above a band of stiff leaves, glaze cracks, firing crack in base, 15th/16thC, 10½in (26cm). **£700-1,000** *Bon*

A pair of Cantonese celadon ground oviform vases with gilt Buddhistic lion handles, painted in underglaze blue, iron red and gilt, and moulded in low relief, 24½in (62cm). **£2,000-2,500** *CSK*

A Chinese blue and white beaker vase, cracked, Transitional 18in (45.5cm). **£1,500-2,000** *CSK*

A green glazed red pottery baluster vase, with some iridescence, slight chips, Han Dynasty, 18½in (47.5cm). **£1,000-1,500** *C*

A Satsuma miniature conical two-handled tripod vase, painted in colours and gilt with figures in a continuous mountainous wooded landscape, 3½in (9cm). **£300-350** *CSK*

A 'famille rose' vase of quatrefoil cross section, painted with panels of figures in river landscapes within underglaze blue floral surrounds, on a ground of iron red, black and gilt Y-pattern, Qianlong, 11in (28cm). **£350-400** *CSK*

A moulded Yingqing vase and integral stand, Yuan Dynasty, 1280-1367 AD. **£750-1,000** *ART*

Make the most of Miller's

Unless otherwise stated, any description which refers to 'a set' or 'a pair' includes a valuation for the entire set or the pair, even though the illustration may show only a single item

. late Ming blue and white 'kraak' ottle, painted with panels of ›aping horses and flowering shrubs elow a band of lappets, glaze fault, Vanli, 11in (28cm).
1,000-1,200 *CSK*

A pair of Cantonese rouleau vases, painted in gilt with shaped panels of figures on terraces and birds and butterflies, on a green gold scroll ground, slight damage, 18in (45.5cm). **£1,500-2,000** *CSK*

An Arita blue, white and biscuit vase, painted with flowers reserved on an iron oxide washed biscuit ground, Persian silver neck and cover with niello decoration, late 17thC, 10in (25cm).
£600-700 *Bon*

Ming double gourd vase, painted underglaze blue with sprays of amellia and peony, body cracks, 6thC, the red enamel probably ter, 13½in (35cm).
1,000-1,500 *C*

A Wucai vase, painted with a band of shaped panels of buildings in mountainous river landscapes, on an iron red wave pattern ground, Transitional, 13½in (34cm).
£500-600 *CSK*

A blue and white five-piece garniture, painted with audience scenes in river landcapes, the covers surmounted with Buddhistic lion finials, some restoration, four-character Kangxi marks, 19thC, baluster vases 15in (38cm).
£4,000-5,000 *C*

Shoki Imari underglaze blue ›ttle vase, with everted rim, ecorated with a hatched design ›low double lines, late 17thC, 7in 8cm).
1,000-1,500 *C*

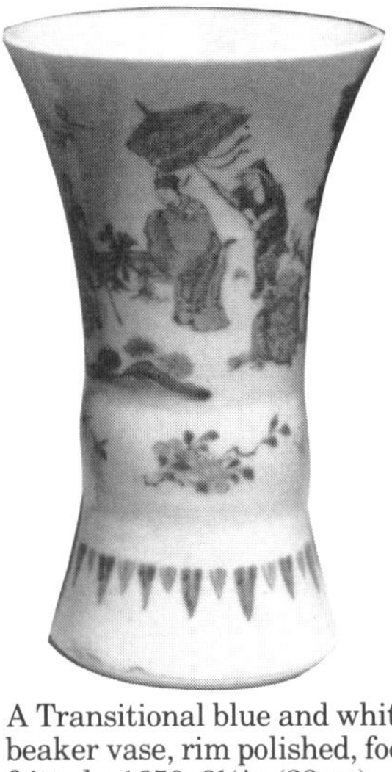

A Transitional blue and white beaker vase, rim polished, foot rim fritted, c1650, 8½in (22cm).
£800-1,200 *C*

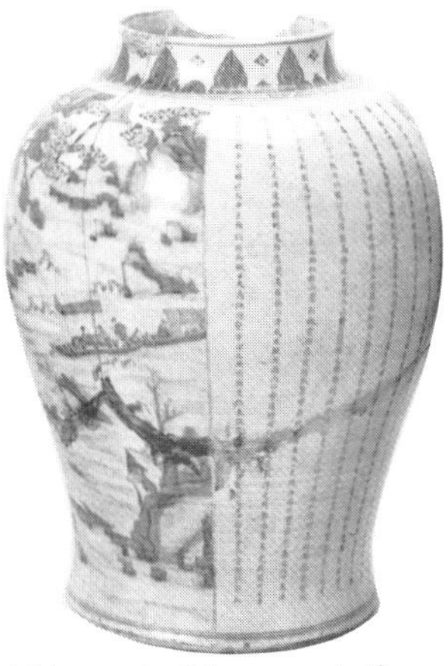

A blue and white presentation vase, damaged, Kangxi, 25½in (65cm).
£900-1,200 *Bon*

A Transitional blue and white vase, rim frit, c1650, 8in (20cm).
£1,200-1,500 *C*

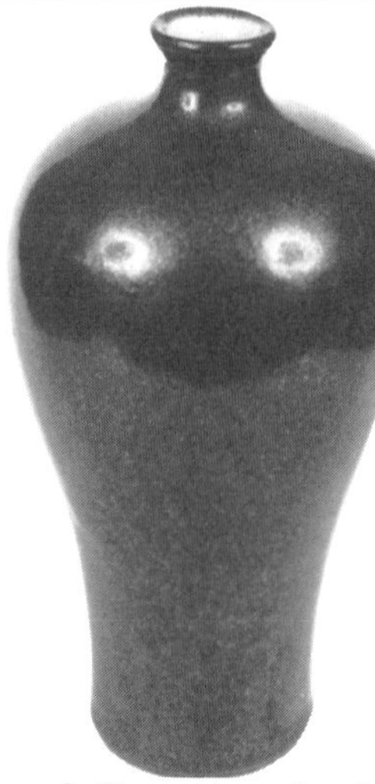

An early Kangxi iron glazed monochrome vase, 7in (17.5cm).
£450-550 *Wai*

A powder blue glazed rouleau vase gilt to one side, the other with a fain inscription below emblem cartouches at the shoulder and 'shou' characters dividing swastika at the neck, Kangxi, 18in (45cm).
£1,500-2,000 *C*

A 'famille verte' rouleau vase, painted with a continuous scene on a trellis pattern ground, gilt metal mounted, the cover with a recumbent elephant finial, body cracked, the porcelain Kangxi, the gilt metal mounts probably Qianlong, 17in (43cm).
£1,500-2,000 *CSK*

A pair of blue and white moulded vases, painted with flowers on a diaper ground, between moulded lotus leaves at the shoulder, one cracked, some fritting, Kangxi, 10½in (26cm).
£1,200-1,500 *C*

A blue and white vase, Kangxi, 9½in (24cm).
£600-700 *Wai*

A Chinese powder blue slender vase, decorated and gilt with shaped panels, 18thC, 18in (45.5cm).
£1,000-1,500 *CSK*

A blue and white yanyan vase, base pierced, Kangxi, 18in (45cm).
£1,400-1,700 *C*

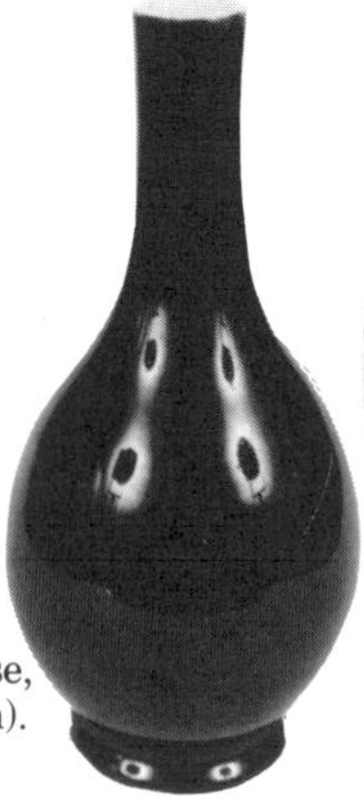

A Chinese black monochrome vase, 18thC, 9in (23cm).
£400-600 *Wai*

A pair of 'famille rose' square baluster vases, painted within iron red and gilt rococo borders on a gilt floral ground above and below smaller cartouches in iron red, sepia and 'grisaille' of birds and landscapes, chipped, gilt rubbed, Qianlong, 10½in (26cm).
£1,500-2,000 *C*

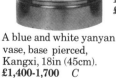

A blue and white baluster vase and cover, painted with flowers below blue ground lappets at the shoulder, heightened with gilding, Qianlong, 16½in (42cm).
£1,500-2,000 *CSK*

'famille verte'
ıse, fritted,
angxi six-
aracter mark,
❟½in (51cm).
,500-2,000 *C*

A pair of Chinese blue and white baluster vases, drawn with shaped panels of leafy branches above rockwork, the porcelain Kangxi, the silver Sheffield 1897, 9½in (24cm).
£1,800-2,200 *CSK*

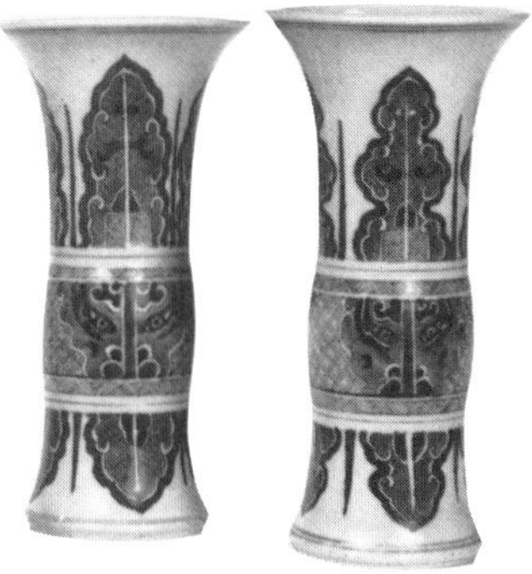

A pair of blue and white gu-shaped beaker vases, painted on the central section with 2 'taotie' masks on a trellis pattern ground, one rim with hairline crack, Kangxi, 10in (25.5cm). **£1,200-1,500** *C*

A blue and white vase, Kangxi, 6in (15cm).
£400-500 *Wai*

famille rose' beaker vase,
corated on a ground of gilt
olling foliage, rim fritted, base
ip, Qianlong, 16½in (42cm).
,500-2,000 *CSK*

A blue glazed hexafoil baluster vase, applied at either side of the long neck with 'kui' handles, all under a deep blue glaze thinning at the extremities, 18th/19thC, 16in (41cm).
£800-1,000 *C*

A 'famille rose' pear-shaped vase, painted with deer, applied at either side of the tapering neck with iron red and gilt scroll handles, Qianlong seal mark, 19thC, 18in (45.5cm).
£6,000-8,000 *C*

A Canton 'famille rose' vase, the sides decorated in enamels and gilt, the shoulders applied with pairs of 'chilong', the neck with confronting shishi, 19thC, 32in (81cm).
£2,000-2,500 *Bon*

ɔair of Cantonese vases, the
ɔulders and necks moulded with
shi, the bodies decorated in
ghtly coloured enamels, the
ɔunds with birds and flowers, one
shi fractured, 19thC, 18in (46cm).
00-700 *P(S)*

A pair of blue and white vases and covers, with knop finials, necks reduced, one with crack to rim, one cover cracked, Qianlong seal marks and of the period, 19in (48cm).
£5,000-6,000 *C*

A pair of 'famille rose' semi-eggshell slender tapering oviform vases with narrow necks, painted with figures on grounds of gilt scrolling foliage, crack to rim, Qianlong, 8½in (21cm).
£750-850 *CSK*

A Canton 'famille rose' celadon ground vase, decorated on a scattered peony, precious object and butterfly ground, the neck applied with 'chilong' handles, Daoguang, 18in (46cm).
£600-800 *Bon*

An Imari vase, painted in underglaze blue, iron red, green enamel and gilt, below a dense 'kiku' ground surrounded by further scrolling flowerheads, 19thC, 30in (76cm).
£2,000-3,000 *Bon*

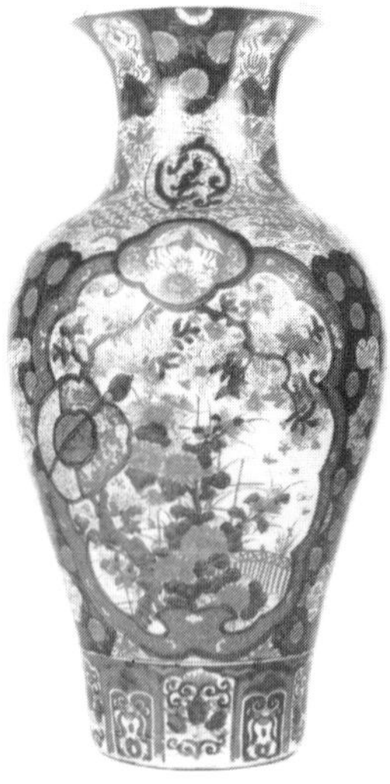

A Fukagawa Imari vase, decoratec in iron red enamel and gilt on underglaze blue, Fukagawa device 19thC, 29½in (75cm).
£3,000-3,500 *C*

A pair of late Kutani vases, decorated in iron red and gilt with black enamel detail, one with hairline crack, the other with chip and hairline to neck, signed Nihon Kutani sei Setsu do, late 19thC, 14½in (37cm).
£2,500-3,000 *C*

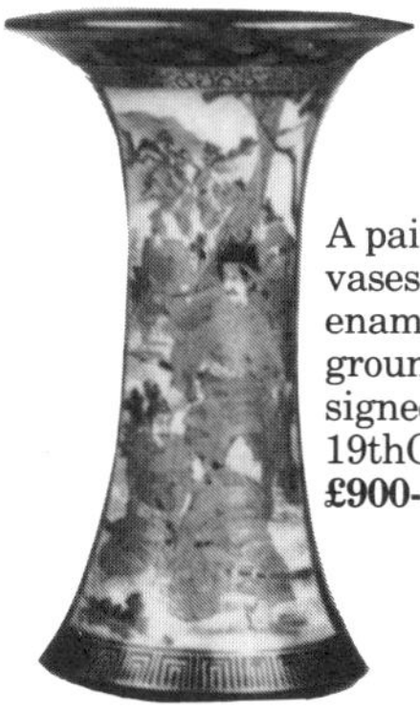

A pair of Satsuma trumpet shaped vases, decorated in various coloure enamels and gilt on a deep blue ground, one with crack and chip, signed Satsuma yaki Hotoda, late 19thC, 9½in (24cm).
£900-1,200 *C*

A pair of Satsuma bottle vases, decorated in various coloured enamels and gilt, the neck with a bulge featuring a party of cranes, signed Dai Nihon Yozan sei, late 19thC, 9½in (24cm).
£3,000-3,500 *C*

A pair of Satsuma vases, decorated in various coloured enamels and gilt with various irregularly shaped panels depicting archers, warriors and gentry, the foot decorated with a band of lappets, the neck similarly decorated above and below 4 quatrefoil decorative motifs, signed Hotoda, late 19thC, 20½in (52cm).
£5,000-6,000 *C*

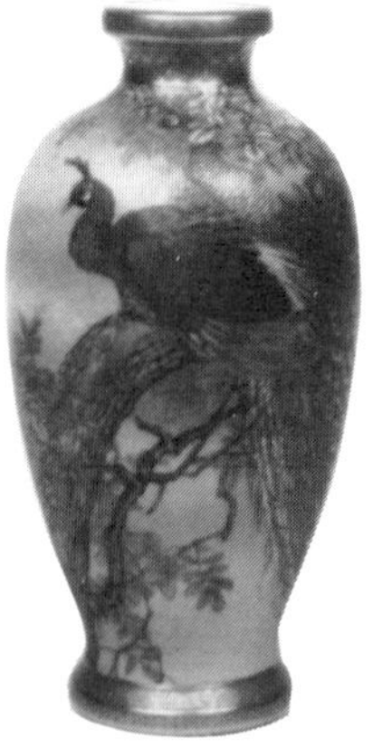

A Satsuma baluster vase, decorated in various coloured enamels and gilt, with a pair of peacocks against a yellow sky, gilt rim, sealed near to foot and on base Itsuzan, signed on the base Kinkozan sei, late 19thC, 7in (17cm).
£600-800 *C*

A Satsuma vase, decorated in various coloured enamels and gilt, the body with a continuous design o carp swimming underneath the boughs of a blossoming 'Queen of the night' jasmine tree, gilt rim, signed Kinkozan zo on the base an sealed Kisui on the foot, late 19thC 11½in (30cm).
£2,000-2,500 *C*

pair of Satsuma vases, with ring
ndles held in the claws of dragons,
corated in various coloured
amels and gilt with shaped
nels, crack, other damage and
nature rubbed, late 19thC, 37in
4cm).
,000-8,000 *C*

A pair of Chinese eggshell porcelain vases, early 20thC, 6in (15cm), in original box. **£200-300** *Wai*

A pair of Chinese eggshell porcelain vases, early 20thC, 7½in (19cm).
£200-300 *Wai*

pair of 'famille verte' squat vases
d covers, the cylindrical necks
th cloud scrolls and the pierced
med covers with fruit and foliage
neath the iron red scroll finial,
ghtly chipped, 19thC, 19in (48cm).
,000-5,500 *C*

An Imari oviform vase, decorated in various coloured enamels and gilt on underglaze blue, with a wide panel of ho-o birds amongst paulownia and peonies, the neck with iris sprays, restored, Genroku period, 16½in (42cm).
£2,000-2,500 *C*

An Arita vase, decorated in various coloured enamels and gilt on underglaze blue with a continuous band of ho-o birds amongst peonies and rockwork, slight cracks, Genroku period, 12in (30cm).
£2,000-2,500 *C*

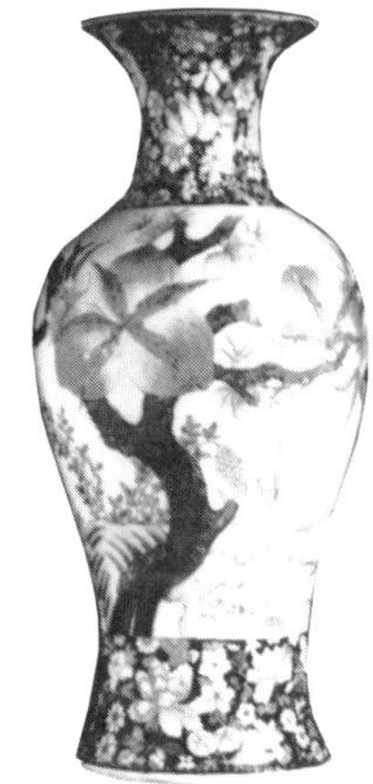

Chinese tapered vase, painted
th fruit and flowers on a black
ound, 18in (45.5cm), on wood
nd.
50-300 *AG*

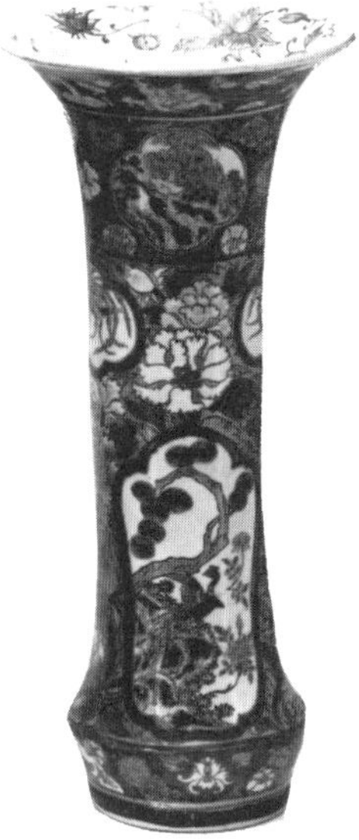

A pair of Imari beaker vases, painted in underglaze blue, iron red, green, aubergine enamels and gilt with panels of karashishi, ho-ho and other birds, on a dense 'kiku' and peony ground, both rims restored, Genroku period, 16½in (42cm).
£2,000-2,500 *Bon*

An Imari vase and cover, decorated in iron red and black enamels and gilt on underglaze blue, the rim with chrysanthemum flowerheads, a scrollwork ormolu mount, the vase pierced for electricity, karashishi finial missing, Genroku period, the mount later, 23½in (59cm).
£5,500-6,500 *C*

A pair of Cantonese vases, with gilt lion mask handles, 9in (23cm).
£800-1,000 *CSK*

A pair of Cantonese vases of quatrefoil cross-section, with gilt Buddhistic lion handles, painted on green scroll gold grounds, 1 cracked, 12in (31cm).
£800-1,000 *CSK*

A Japanese gold splashed ovoid vase, decorated in relief with hanging bean pods, signed Yoshimasa, 10in (25.5cm).
£300-400 *CSK*

A pair of 'famille verte' vases, painted on each side with a warri Immortal above yellow ground bands of scrolling foliage, 25in (63cm).
£1,700-2,000 *CSK*

A pair of Cantonese double gourd vases, painted with figures on green gold scroll grounds, 13in (33cm).
£700-800 *CSK*

A pair of Japanese cloisonné lacquered porcelain bottle vases, decorated in colours with birds amongst foliage on a brown ground, 8½in (22cm).
£300-400 *HSS*

A pair of Japanese Shibayama-sty white metal mounted vases with flowerspray handles, the mounts with enamelled stylised flowerheads, signed on raised tablets, 4in (10cm).
£900-1,200 *CSK*

Make the Most of Miller's

CONDITION is absolutely vital when assessing the value of an antique. Damaged pieces on the whole appreciate much less than perfect examples. However a rare, desirable piece may command a high price even when damaged

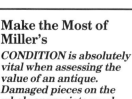

A pair of Satsuma vases, painted in colours and gilt with panels of bijin and rakan on dark blue grounds enriched with gilding, 9½in (24cm).
£1,000-1,500 *CSK*

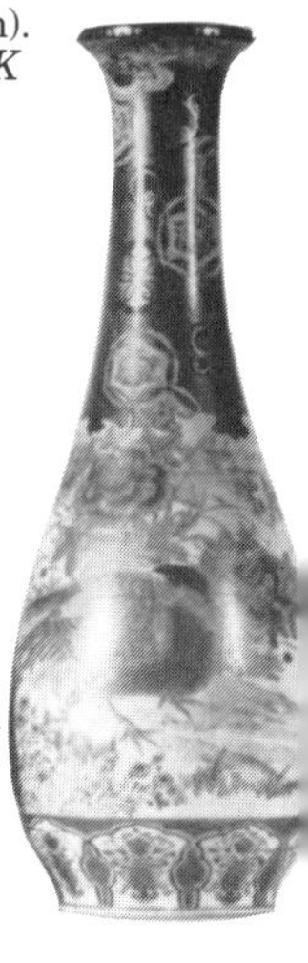

A pair of Kaga vases, painted in iron red, black and gilt with pheasants among flowers by a river, 15in (38cm).
£700-800 *CSK*

pair of Satsuma vases, painted in
lours and gilt on one side with
nels of ladies and children below
mboo in gardens, cracked, signed
ozan, 7½in (19cm).
,200-1,500 *CSK*

A Satsuma vase, painted in colours and gilt on a ground of geometric designs, 4in (10cm).
£150-200 *CSK*

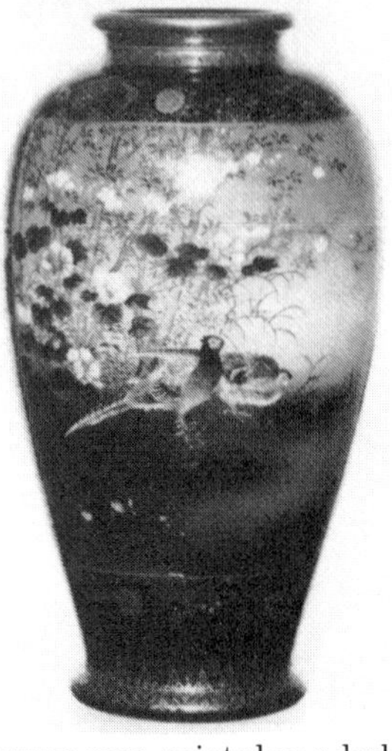

A Satsuma vase, painted on a dark blue gilt flowerhead ground and between bands of lappets, signed Kinkozan, 10½in (26cm).
£800-900 *CSK*

A pair of 'rose/verte' vases, with mask ring handles, 18in (45.5cm).
£850-950 *CSK*

air of Satsuma vases,
nted in colours and richly
t, on dense floral and
metric grounds, 9½in
cm).
0-750 *CSK*

A Satsuma pottery vase, with waisted neck heavily enamelled and gilt with panels of figures divided by geometric designs and flowers, 28in (71cm).
£400-450 *CSK*

A pair of Satsuma vases, moulded, painted and heavily gilt, signed, 9in (23cm).
£500-600 *CSK*

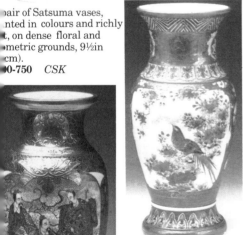

A pair of Kutani vases, painted with figures on one side and birds in a garden on the other, reserved on a gold decorated orange ground, 14in (35.5cm). **£600-700** *Bea*

A Satsuma vase, painted with figures reserved within a narrow decorative band, the neck and foot painted with flowers and geometric designs, 4½in (12cm).
£400-500 *Bea*

air of Satsuma vases, painted
th figures on a brocade ground, in
ical enamel colours and gold.
200-1,600 *Bea*

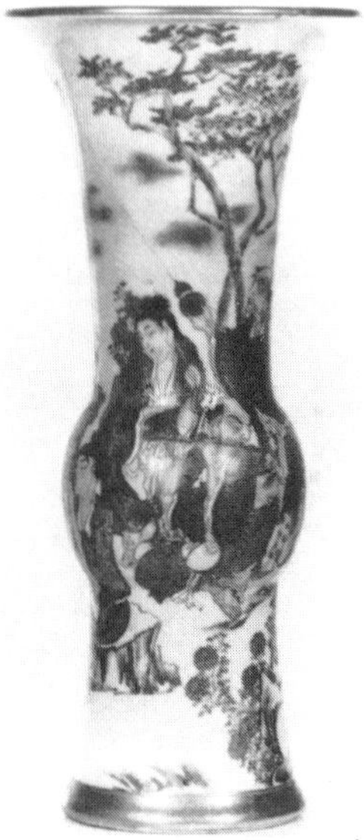

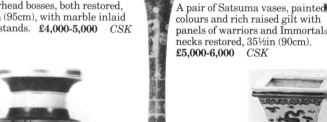

A pair of Kutani beaker vases, painted and heavily gilt with the 8 Buddhistic Immortals, one with a star cracked base, signed, 18in (45.5cm).
£1,500-2,000 *CSK*

A pair of Satsuma vases, with ring and tassel handles, each painted and gilt, the necks with panels of cell pattern, the rims with flowerhead bosses, both restored, 37½in (95cm), with marble inlaid wood stands. **£4,000-5,000** *CSK*

A pair of Satsuma vases, 8in (20cm)
£1,000-1,200 *CSK*

A pair of Satsuma vases, painted colours and rich raised gilt with panels of warriors and Immortals necks restored, 35½in (90cm).
£5,000-6,000 *CSK*

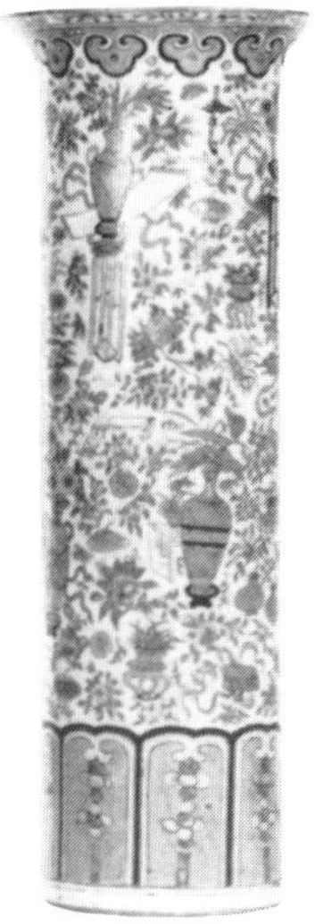

A pair of Cantonese vases, painted on a ground of flowerheads, fruit and butterflies between bands of lappets, all on a yellow ground, the interior with fruit sprays, some restoration, 24in (61cm).
£1,000-1,200 *CSK*

A pair of Satsuma vases, painted in colours and gilt on crackled cream grounds, 17in (43cm).
£2,500-3,000 *CSK*

A pair of 'famille rose' yellow grou beaker vases, 10½in (26cm).
£300-400 *Bon*

In the Ceramics section if there is only one measurement it usually refers to the height of the piece

A pair of 'famille verte' vases, with lion mask and ring handles, painted with warriors, the shoulders with trellis pattern and key pattern, 24in (61cm).
£2,500-3,000 *CSK*

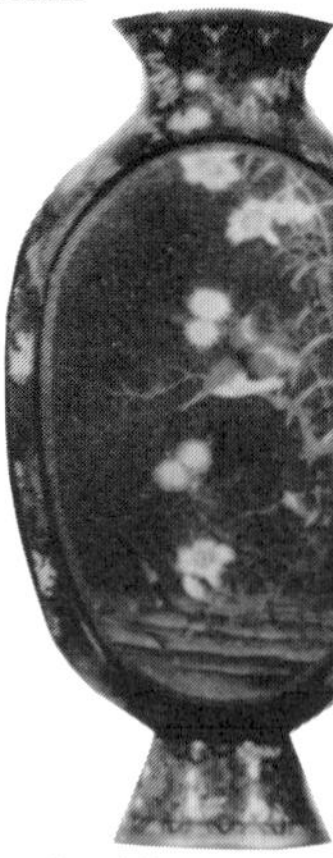

A pair of Japanese cloisonné vases, decorated on a gold stone ground, the ovals divided by a ground of ho-o roundels and foliage, 8½in (21cm).
£700-800 *CSK*

A pair of Cantonese vases, applie with Buddhistic lion and cub handles and gilt dragons, one riveted, 35in (89cm).
£4,000-5,000 *CSK*

Miscellaneous

pair of 'famille
se' pink ground
ıleau vases,
inted with dragons
ıong various
wering plants,
ns fritted,
½in (62cm).
,200-2,500 *CSK*

A pair of Satsuma vases, painted in colours and richly gilt, 12in (30.5cm).
£1,500-2,000 *CSK*

A blue and white box and cover, minutely fritted, Kangxi, 8½in (21.5cm) diam.
£2,000-2,500 *C*

A Chinese blue and white broad cylindrical squat brush pot, painted qilong among scrolling foliage, fritted, four-character hallmark, Kangxi, 7in (18cm).
£500-600 *CSK*

'famille rose' armorial pierced
.red basket with gilt handles, the
terior with raised iron red and gilt
werheads, restored, late
anlong, 10½in (26cm) wide.
00-1,200 *CSK*

A Satsuma two-handled squat bell-shaped tripod koro and domed cover with kiku finial, painted with scrolling chrysanthemum, 3½in (9cm) diam.
£500-600 *CSK*

pair of Chinese blue and white
allow butter tubs and flat covers,
inted with vases of flowers in
ıced rocky gardens, with fruit
ials, late Qianlong, 4¼in (11cm).
00-700 *CSK*

A late Kutani box and cover, decorated in various coloured enamels and gilt, damage to fingers, signed Takayama ga, late 19thC, 10in (25cm).
£3,000-3,500 *C*

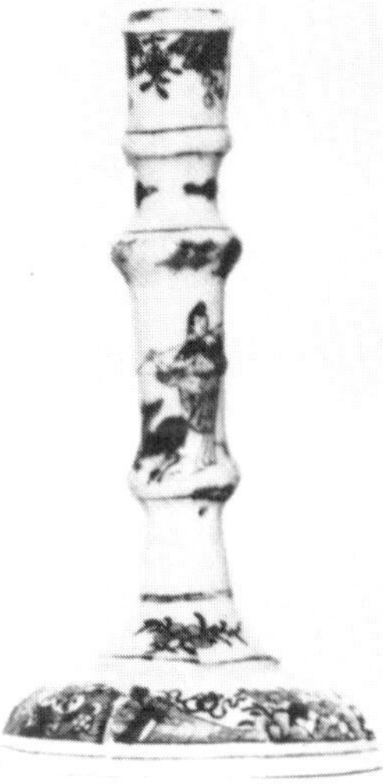

A pair of Chinese blue and white silver shaped candlesticks, the columns painted with ladies and deer in landscapes below pine, the tops and bases with borders of stylised foliage, one damaged, Qianlong, 9in (23cm).
£3,000-4,000 *CSK*

An Arita blue and white chamber pot, restored, late 17thC, 8½in (21cm).
£450-650 *CSK*

Chinese dynasties and marks

Earlier Dynasties

Shang Yin, c.1532-1027 B.C.
Western Zhou (Chou) 1027-770 B.C.
Spring and Autumn Annals 770-480 B.C.
Warring States 484-221 B.C.
Qin (Ch'in) 221-206 B.C.
Western Han 206 BC-24 AD
Eastern Han 25-220
Three Kingdoms 221-265
Six Dynasties 265-589
Wei 386-557
Sui 589-617
Tang (T'ang) 618-906
Five Dynasties 907-960
Liao 907-1125
Sung 960-1280
Chin 1115-1260
Yüan 1280-1368

Ming Dynasty

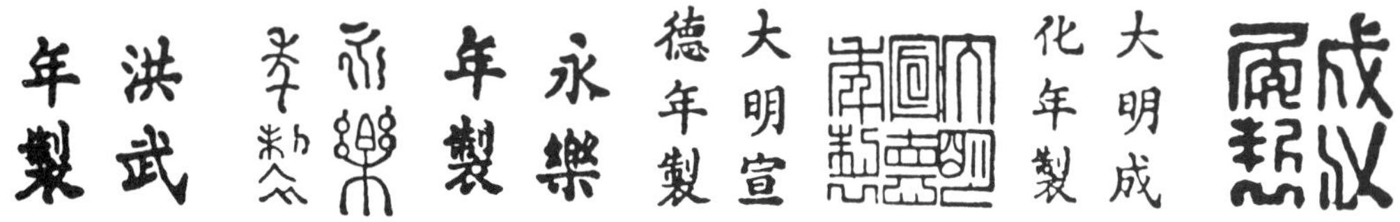

Hongwu (Hung Wu) 1368-1398

Yongle (Yung Lo) 1403-1424

Xuande (Hsüan Té) 1426-1435

Chenghua (Ch'éng Hua) 1465-1487

Hongzhi (Hung Chih) 1488-1505)

Zhengde (Chéng Té) 1506-1521

Jiajing (Chia Ching) 1522-1566

Longqing (Lung Ching) 1567-1572

Wanli (Wan Li) 1573-1620

Tianqi (Tien Chi) 1621-1627

Chongzhen (Ch'ung Chêng 1628-1644

Qing (Ch'ing) Dynasty

Shunzhi (Shun Chih) 1644-1661

Kangxi (K'ang Hsi) 1662-1722

Yongzheng (Yung Chêng) 1723-1735

Qianlong (Ch'ien Lung) 1736-1795'

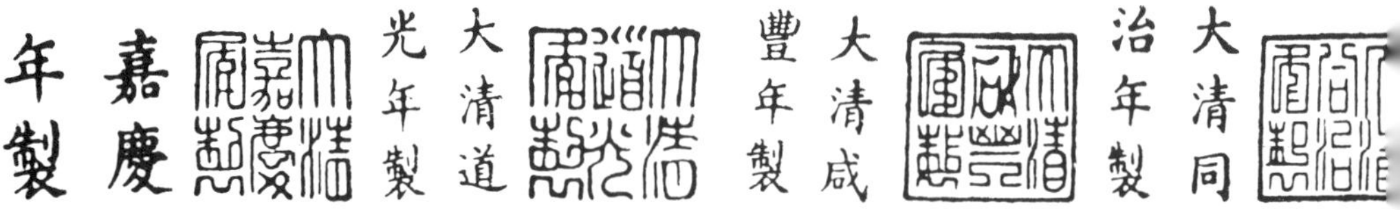

Jiaqing (Chia Ch'ing) 1796-1820

Daoguang (Tao Kuang) 1821-1850

Xianfeng (Hsien Féng) 1851-1861

Tongzhi (T'ung Chih) 1862-1874

Guangxu (Kuang Hsu) 1875-1908

Xuantong (Hsuan T'ung) 1909-1911

Hongxian (Hung Hsien) 1916

ASS – PRICE TRENDS

›r the past twelve months the ·ked increase in the price of all ectable glass has continued and, in ›e categories, accelerated and, lst the present dearth of good glass ›ing onto the market continues, situation is likely to remain. ›ing said that, this situation has ıght a number of small collections ariable quality into the salerooms; ›e insufficient, however, to satisfy ›and.

› type of glass seldom seen on the ·ket is Davenport. Better known ts pottery and porcelain in the ıC, this firm made large ntities of run-of-the-mill table ›s. Amongst this is a group of early ıC glassware, mainly rummers ı what appear to be acid etched ›ration usually in the form of ·ting activities and landscapes.

se pieces have a small etched angle marked 'Patent' under the › of the article, with no other mark. nall quantity appeared in the rooms during the past year but did go unnoticed: in one sale two lets with very patchy decoration le £1,650. In another saleroom, where a small collection was on offer, two more goblets, or rummers, with, once again, patchy decoration made £968, whereas a ewer, a rare item, made £1,875.

Pressed glass, both clear and vitro porcelain (commonly called slag glass) continues to excite a lot of interest. Vitro porcelain has probably appreciated two- and three-fold over the past two years, however the type of decoration governs the price realised: pieces with inscriptions, nursery rhymes, etc., command high prices. In the Midlands last year, a very large private collection came onto the market. It was highly publicised, with a catalogue of its own, and some exceptional prices were realised.

Decanters are still appreciating strongly and any decanters with marked labels, Masonic decoration, etc., will easily make £500 or more at auction. Recently three fine decanters with cut spiral neck rings and engraved with the Beckford of Fonthill crest, made a hammer price of £6,000.

Early coloured glass is now very expensive and scarce as illustrated by a hammer price of £13,000 for a wine glass with blue bowl and foot and opaque twist stem. This is the only one recorded, but is probably from the same stable as similar glasses with green bowls and feet. As for colour twists, three garish wines, probably Victorian, made £1,000, £3,600 and £4,800.

As for clear glass, a reasonable cylinder knop wine glass made £3,800, and for the more ordinary examples, a good opaque twist wine glass c1760, that one could expect to get under the hammer for £70-100 two years ago, will now make about £140-200.

Continental glass hasn't appreciated as fast as English glass. A lovely Venetian gadrooned dish, c1500, with the usual enamelled dots and gilt scale decoration made £14,300. Also, a rare German 17thC amber coloured Rhine beaker, with conical bowl, three suspended rings and trailed decoration made £8,800.

R. G. Thomas

›akers

›nical tumbler, engraved with a ›herd playing his pipe, his dog sheep around, engraved on the ›rse John and Anne Saxon, 30, 4in (10cm).
0-350 *Som*

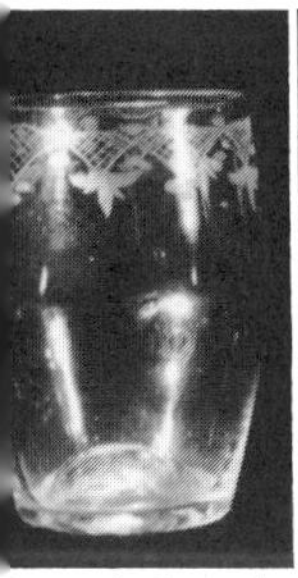

barrel-shaped tumbler, with a d of hatched decoration, c1800, (10cm).
-100

tapered tumbler, with a band of ·hed rose decoration and ription 'George & Mary Owen 5', 4in (10cm).
-100 *Som*

A North Bohemian Lithyalin beaker, attributed to Friedrich Egermann, the marbled iron red and dark blue sides cut with vertical flutes, Blottendorf, chipped, c1835, 4½in (11.5cm). **£2,000-3,000** *C*

A Bohemian transparent enamelled beaker, with raised panels painted in bright colours with chinoiserie figures, in the manner of C. von Scheidt, the underside of the foot flashed in pink, chipped footrim, c1840, 5in (12.5cm).
£2,000-2,500 *C*

A North Bohemian Lithyalin beaker, from the workshop of Friedrich Egermann, in dark grey marbled glass, cut with wide flutes, Blottendorf, chips to rim, c1835, 4½in (11cm). **£800-1,000** *C*

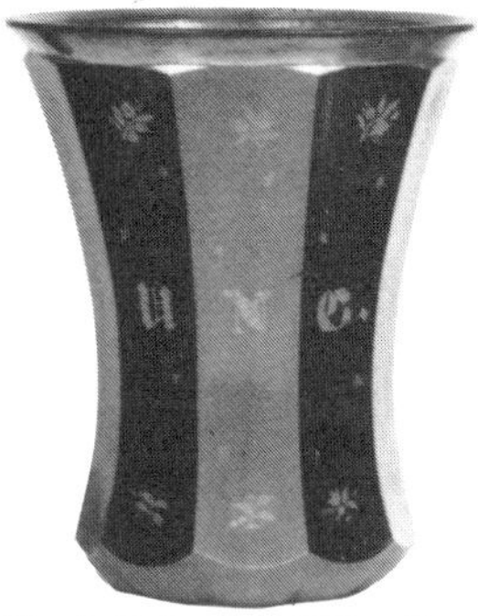

A North Bohemian Lithyalin beaker, attributed to Friedrich Egermann, the marbled olive green exterior cut with wide flutes to reveal a translucent iron red ground with striated inclusions, each flute gilt with a letter spelling 'Erinnerung', gilt rim, Blottendorf, chipped and gilding rubbed, c1835, 4in (10.5cm).
£3,000-3,500 *C*

Bottles

An early sealed and dated dark green tint wine bottle, applied with a seal inscribed 'John Lovering Bidiford 1695', minor chipping to edge of seal and slight chip to rim, 5in (12.5cm).
£3,000-3,500 *C*

An armorial wine bottle, applied with a seal bearing a coat-of-arms, the neck with string ring and with kick-in base, damage and burial discolouration, c1680, 7in (17cm).
£900-1,200 *C*

The arms are those of Lowther.

A sealed green tint wine bottle, applied with an inscribed seal, the neck w modern silver replaceme string ring and rim, c1660, 8½in (22cm).
£2,000-3,000 *C*

An early green tint wine bottle, the neck with string ring and with kick-in base, burial discolouration, c1660, 7in (17.5cm).
£2,000-3,000 *C*

Found in Stamford, Ct., U.S.A.

A Netherlands serving bottle with a silver gilt stopper, late 17th/18thC, the stopper mid-18thC, 6in (15cm).
£900-1,200 *C*

A sealed and dated green tint win bottle, the shoulder applied with a seal inscribed 'Francis Young; de Rye 1700', the neck with a string ring and with a kick-in base, rim reduced and damage to string ring 5½in (14cm).
£2,000-2,500 *C*

A sealed green tint wine bottle, with inscribed applied seal, the neck with string ring and with kick-in base, chipped, c1670, 8in (20cm).
£7,000-8,000 *C*

This bottle probably belonged to a member of the Loupe family.

A dark olive tint serving bottle, the slender neck with a pouring lip and applied loop handle with pincered thumbpiece, crack to base of handle, c1725, 6½in (17cm).
£1,000-1,200 *C*

A sealed olive green tint wine bott the shoulder applied with a seal marked 'VI', the neck with a strin ring and with kick-in base, damag to string ring and some surface wear, c1690, 6in (15cm).
£500-750 *C*

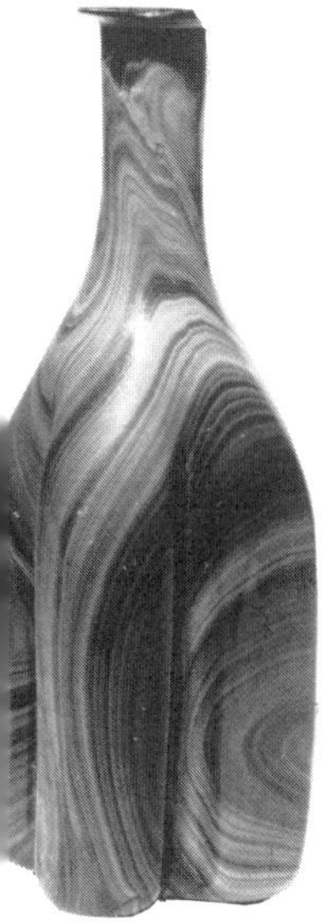

Venetian Calcedonio moulded
ttle, of olive green, purple, blue
d brown striated glass, the neck
ith everted lip, 17th/18thC, 8½in
1cm).
50-550 *C*

LIN:SAPO
OPII

A pair of amethyst glass apothecary bottles and covers, with gold and red inscriptions, 14in (35cm) high, and a blue glass jar and stopper, with inscription on an orange and gilt label, 19thC, 9in (23cm).
£250-300 *HSS*

A sealed olive green tint tavern bottle, the shoulder applied with an inscribed seal, with string rim to neck and with kick-in base, internal crack and damage, late 17thC, 9in (23cm).
£900-1,200 *C*

Found on the site of the Cupps Hotel, Colchester, demolished in 1969.

sealed olive green tint wine bottle,
plied with an inscribed seal, the
ck with a string rim and with
ck-in base, damage, dated 1740,
n (20cm).
50-550 *C*

A sealed dark olive green wine bottle, applied with a seal inscribed 'R S 1739', the neck with string ring and with kick-in base, 10in (25.5cm).
£3,500-4,000 *C*

Two tazzas, with baluster stems and domed folded feet, c1740:
Top. 10in (25cm) diam.
£220-250
Bottom. 12in (32cm) diam.
£250-300 *Som*

owls

tazza, with ribbed rim to platform,
a moulded Silesian stem, folded
nical foot, c1750, 10in (25cm)
am.
250-300 *Som*

A pair of early tazzas, the saucer platforms with gadrooned moulding, on balustroid stems and folded conical feet, c1720, 3in (8cm).
£500-600 *Som*

l. A pair of bowls, with slant cutting, notched rims and diamond shaped lemon squeezer feet, c1800, 3½in (8.5cm).
£70-100
r. A pair of cut bowls on lemon squeezer feet, c1810.
£70-100 *Som*

A butter dish with fan cut handles, the body with diamond and flute cutting, star cut base, c1810, 8in (20cm).
£400-450 *Som*

A dish cut with panels of small diamonds and stars, scalloped rim, star cut base, c1820, 8in (20cm) diam.
£90-120 *Som*

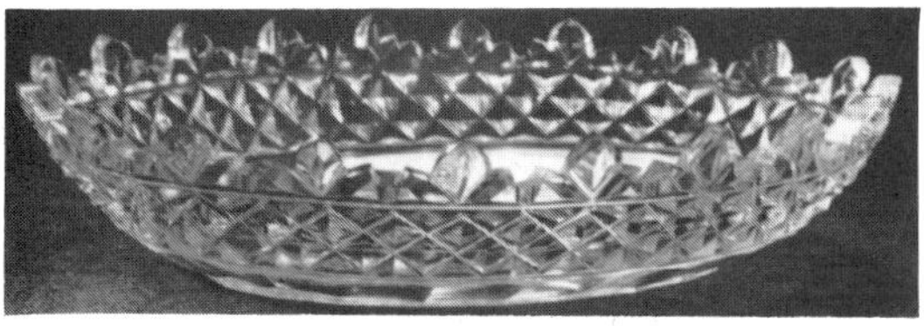

A dish with diamond and flute cutting, star cut base, c1810, 10½in (27cm) diam.
£180-220 *Som*

A tazza with rimmed platform, on a hollow conical foot with folded rim, c1720, 3in (7.5cm).
£300-350 *Som*

A tazza, on hollow moulded Silesian stem, domed folded foot, c1780, 12in (30cm) diam.
£250-300 *Som*

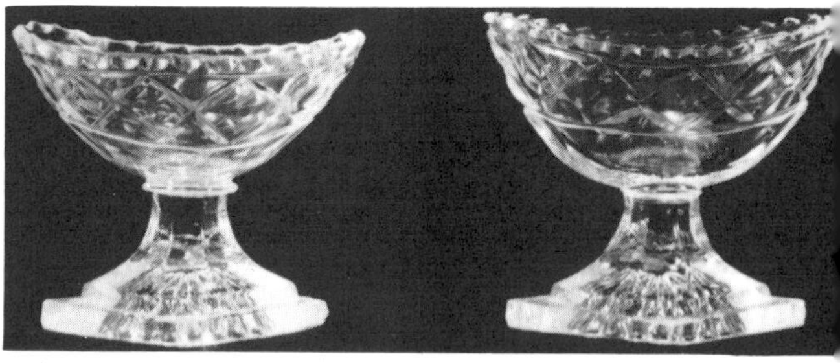

A pair of salts, cut with flutes and a band of diamonds, notched rims, c1810, 3in (8cm).
£120-160 *Som*

An Irish fruit bowl, with turnover rim and geometric cutting, on a bobbin knopped stem and lemon squeezer foot, c1800, 8in (20cm).
£900-1,000 *Som*

An Irish fruit bowl, with turnover rim, on a knopped stem, c1790, 8in (20cm).
£1,500-1,800 *Som*

Bohemian green tinted
-eetmeat dish, with all-over gilt
-coration, and alternate overlaid
-nels of portraits and gilt motifs,
-nall chip, 19thC, 8in (20cm).
-50-550 *GC*

A pair of comports and covers, cut with bands of diamonds, the bodies with French silver gilt hallmarked rims, on square pedestal lemon squeezer feet, c1830, 10½in (26cm) high overall.
£1,600-1,800 *Som*

Lynn green finger bowl, late
-thC, 4½in (11.5cm) diam.
-00-600 *C*

A bowl on detachable stand, the collared pedestal base cut underneath with hobnailing, early 19thC, 10½in (27cm) diam.
£300-400 *ALL*

-moulded and cut butter dish and
-ver, with looped band in relief,
-obably Irish, c1830, 6½in (17cm).
-80-550 *Som*

l. An Irish sugar basin, with prism and flute cutting, everted notch cut rim, and plain foot, star cut, c1820, 4in (10cm).
£100-130

r. A comport and cover, the body cut with strawberry diamonds fluting and prisms, star cut foot, notched rim and domed cover similarly cut, with mushroom finial, c1825.
£230-250 *Som*

A cut piggin and stand, the bowl with alternate panels of small diamonds and flutes, fan cut stave handle, the stand similarly cut and with lobed rim, c1810, stand 7½in (18.5cm) diam.
£600-650 *Som*

An Irish cut bowl, with a band of shallow diamond-within-lozenge ornament beneath bevelled rim, the stem with swelling waist knop above an oval foot, moulded with flutes and with lemon squeezer base, minor rim chips, c1800, 15½in (39cm) wide.
£1,500-2,000 *C*

A cut bowl, with turnover rim, on a square stepped base, c1820, 7in (18cm).
£250-300 *BAL*

Candlesticks

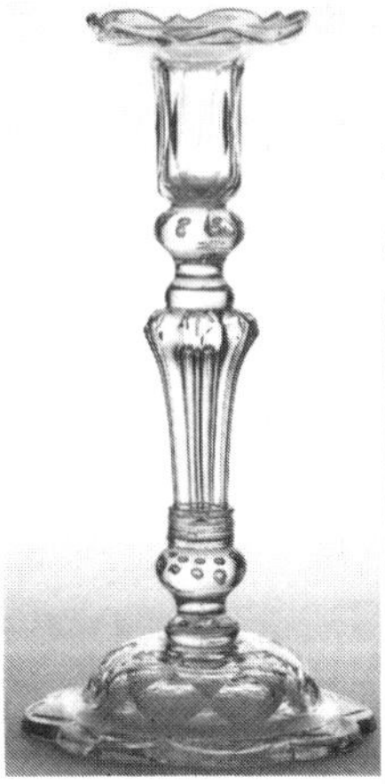

A cut pedestal stemmed candlestick, the domed foot with facet and geometric ornament and with waved rim, mid-18thC, 10in (25cm).
£550-600 *C*

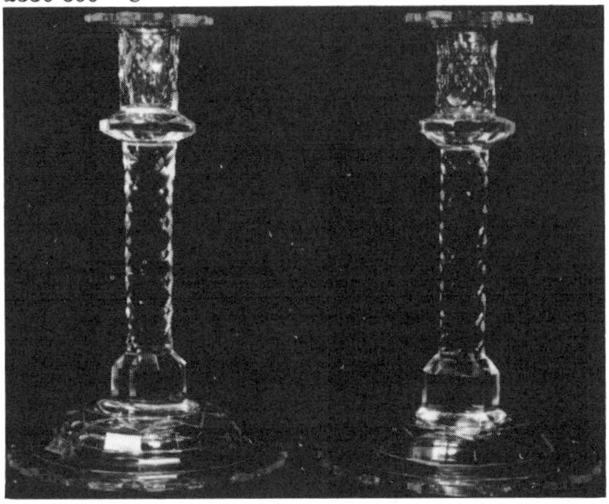

A pair of diamond cut candlesticks, with scalloped candle sockets and knopped stems, with domed diamond cut feet, c1830, 10in (25cm).
£900-1,000 *Som*

A baluster candlestick, the cylindrical nozzle with everted rim, on a domed foot, c1750, 9½in (23.5cm).
£1,000-1,500 *C*

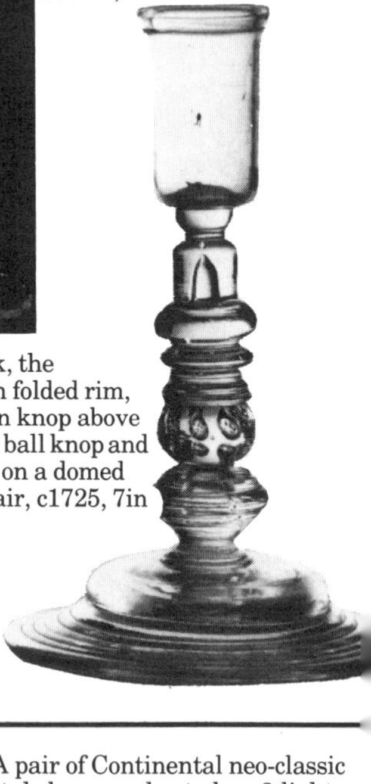

A baluster candlestick, the cylindrical nozzle with folded rim, supported on a cushion knop above an acorn knop, beaded ball knop and an annulated section, on a domed and terraced foot, repair, c1725, 7in (17.5cm).
£1,000-1,500 *C*

Chandeliers

A pair of Continental neo-classic style brass and cut glass 8-light chandeliers, 32in (81cm) diam.
£7,000-8,000 *CNY*

A giltmetal 18-light chandelier, with foliate scrolled branches, each supporting 2 nozzles hung with faceted drops, fitted for electricity, 26in (66cm) wide.
£800-1,200 *C*

Make the Most of Miller's

CONDITION is absolutely vital when assessing the value of an antique. Damaged pieces on the whole appreciate much less than perfect examples. However a rare, desirable piece may command a high price even when damaged

An Empire ormolu and cut glass 8-light chandelier, with later cut glass nozzles and drip pans, 21in (53cm) diam, adapted for electricity.
£6,000-7,000 *CNY*

·ecanters

An armorial decanter, engraved with a coat-of-arms within an elaborate cartouche and inscribed below 'William Kingdon', chip to rim, 9in (23cm), and a matching armorial cylindrical mug with scroll handle, 3½in (8.5cm), c1775.
£700-800 *C*

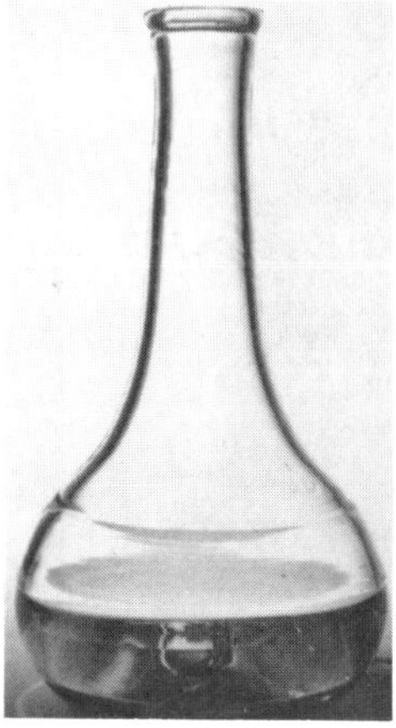

A Lynn carafe, the body with horizontal ribbing, the neck with slightly everted folded rim, c1765, 9½in (24cm).
£1,000-1,500 *C*

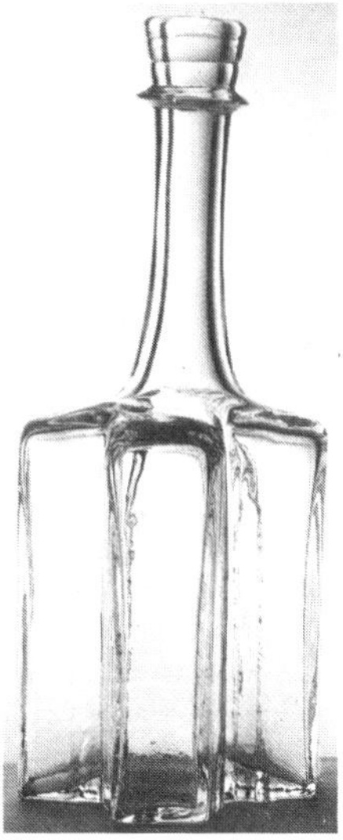

·moulded cruciform bottle-
·canter, the body of deeply
·lented rectangular section, slight
·ipping to collar, footrim bruised,
·725, 11½in (29cm).
·50-550 *C*

A set of 3 octagonal spirit decanters, with pouring lips and cut ball stoppers, c1810, 6in (15cm).
£300-400 *Som*

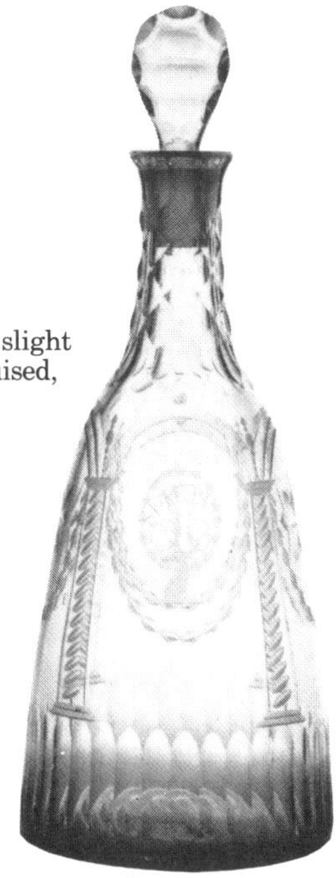

A cut decanter and stopper, engraved with a crest and motto beneath, the drop stopper with facet cut edges, minor rim chips, c1790, 12in (30cm).
£800-900 *C*

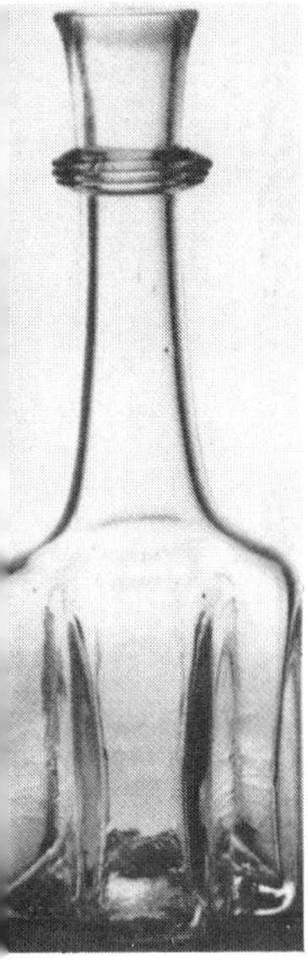

A decanter, the neck with an applied collar beneath an everted rim, c1735, 8in (20cm).
£350-450 *C*

A pair of cut mallet shaped decanters and ball stoppers, the facet necks above strawberry diamonds and prisms, 10in (25cm).
£400-500 *CSK*

Three barrel shaped spirit decanters, with flute, prism and diamond cutting, cut mushroom stoppers, c1810, 6½in (16.5cm):
l. & r. **£100-150**
c. **£50-100** *Som*

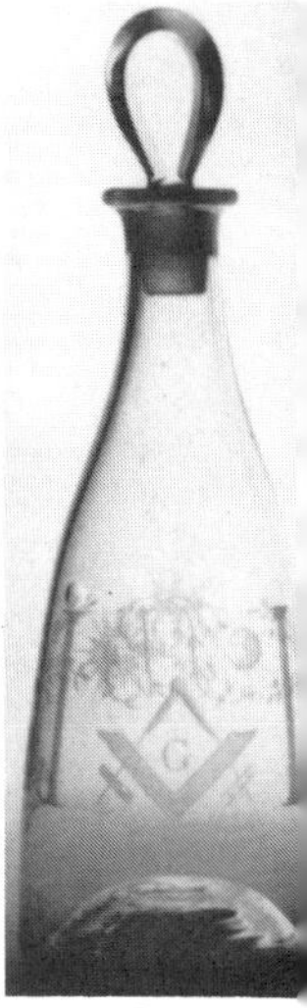

A Masonic decanter and stopper, engraved with emblems flanked foliage, c1800, 12in (30cm).
£600-700 *C*

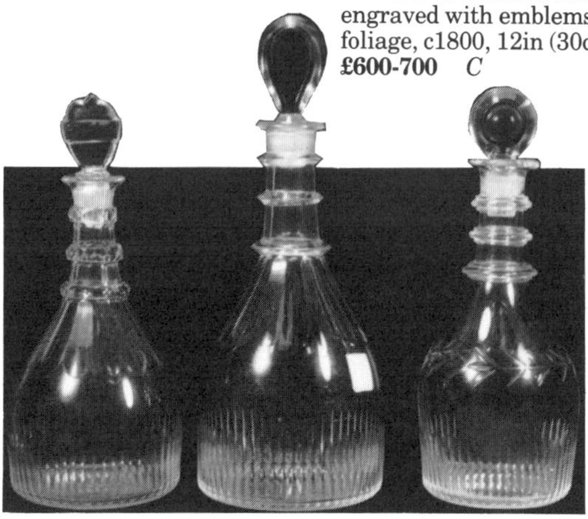

Three spirit decanters with flute cutting, c1810:
l. With diamond cut neck rings, 7½in (19cm).
£100-120
c. With angular neck rings and lozenge stopper, 8½in (22cm).
£150-200
r. With sprig decoration and target stopper, 8in (20cm).
£100-120 *Som*

Two ovoid body spirit decanters, with base and neck fluting, 3 neck rings and cut lozenge stoppers, c1810, 7½in (19cm).
£100-150 each *Som*

A pair of heavy Irish cut decanters, with flute and diamond cutting, 3 annulated neck rings and cut mushroom stoppers, c1810, 8in (21cm).
£550-650 *Som*

l. & r. A pair of ovoid flute cut spirit decanters, with cut neck rings and target stoppers, c1830, 7½in (18.5cm).
£300-350
c. A decanter with flute and diamond cutting, 2 diamond cut neck rings, and mushroom stopper, c1820, 8in (20cm).
£150-200 *Som*

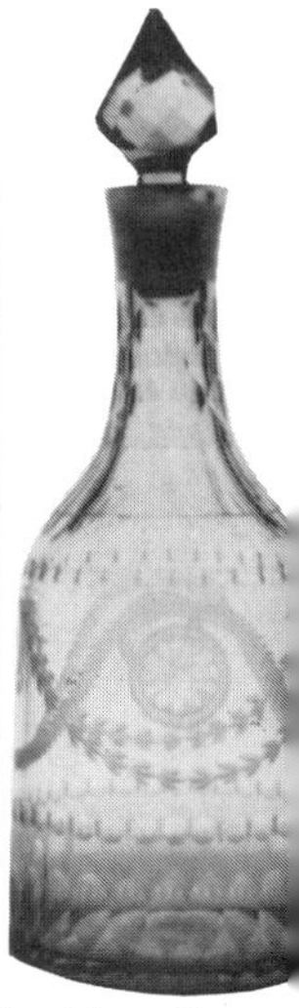

An engraved and cut decanter an stopper, the body engraved with garlands of foliate and husk ornament between dot and star borders, with a faceted spire stop c1780, 12in (30.5cm).
£600-700 *C*

;underland Bridge decanter and
topper, engraved with a sailing
p passing beneath the Iron
idge and inscribed 'Sunderland
idge Span 236 feet Ht 100', early
:hC, 9in (23cm).
,000-1,500 *C*

l. A decanter with 3 annulated neck rings and target stopper, c1800, 8½in (22cm).
£200-250
c. A decanter with broad flute cut body, prism cut neck and target stopper, c1830, 7in (18cm).
£100-150
r. A decanter with bladed neck rings, c1800, 9in (22.5cm).
£200-250 *Som*

An Irish decanter, with engraved ship and floral decoration, moulded mushroom stopper, c1810, 8½in (22cm).
£350-400 *Som*

l. & r. A pair of decanters with blaze, printy, diamond and flute cutting, cut mushroom stoppers, c1815, 8in (20cm).
£600-700 *Som*
c. A tapered decanter, with 3 bladed neck rings and cut lozenge stopper, c1780, 7½in (19cm).
£80-100 *Som*

SOY

ree miniature green bottles and
opers, named in gilt, enriched in
ling, with leather and metal
nd, slightly damaged, early
hC, the bottles 5½in (14cm).
000-1,500 *C*

A mallet shaped decanter, with annulated neck ring and lip, c1730, 8in (21cm).
£300-350 *Som*

air of Anglo-Irish cut glass
anters, each with cylindrical
k and rings, the oval stoppers
h sawtooth edges, the body cut
h flowers and leaves, the bottom
h a sunburst, c1825, 10½in
cm).
200-1,500 *CNY*

A Georgian decanter, with triple neck rings and mushroom stopper, c1800, 10in (25cm).
£250-300 *TVA*

A blue decanter and stopper for Rum, named in gilt within a pendant fruiting vine cartouche, stopper damaged, early 19thC, 10½in (26cm).
£300-400 *C*

A club shaped clear decanter, with gilt wine label for Rum, gilt lozenge stopper, c1790, 8in (20cm).
£180-220 *Som*

A pair of cut glass decanters, wit single neck ring, c1835, 10in (25c
£180-200 *BAL*

A pair of flute cut decanters, with 3 plain neck rings and cut hollow mushroom stoppers, c1840, 9in (23cm).
£250-300 *Som*

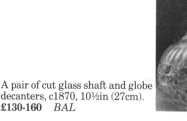

A set of 3 spirit decanters, with panel cut sides, 2 neck rings and hollow cut mushroom stoppers, in a Sheffield plated frame, c1840, bottles 6½in (17cm) high.
£500-550 *Som*

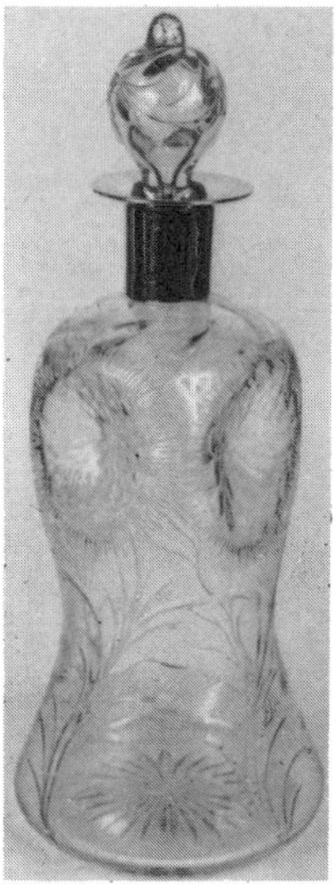

A silver mounted glass decanter, mount by Mappin & Webb, London, 1922, 11in (29cm).
£300-350 *TVA*

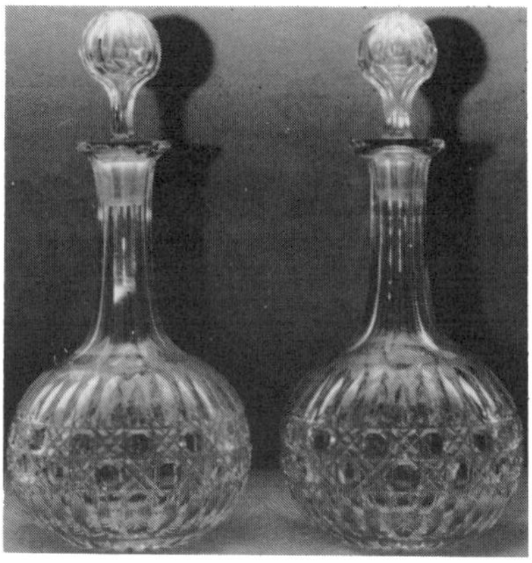

A pair of cut glass shaft and globe decanters, c1870, 10½in (27cm).
£130-160 *BAL*

A pair of Bohemian wine dec 13in (33cm).
£120-160 *THA*

rinking Glasses

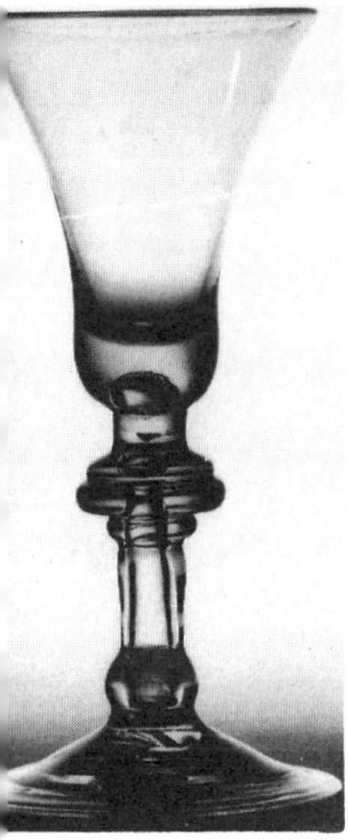

aluster wine glass, the bell bowl
h a tear to the lower part, the
n with a triple annulated
ulder knop and basal knop and
losing an elongated tear, on
ed conical foot, c1720, 6in
cm).
0-500 *C*

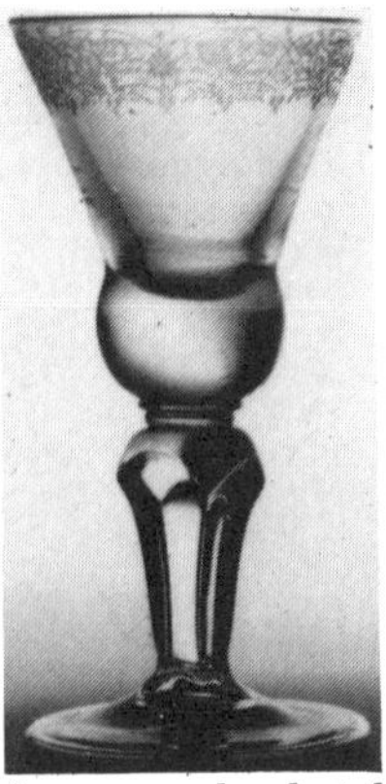

An engraved pedestal stemmed wine glass, the thistle shaped bowl engraved with a foliate border and with solid lower part, with folded conical foot, c1725, 6½in (16cm).
£600-700 *C*

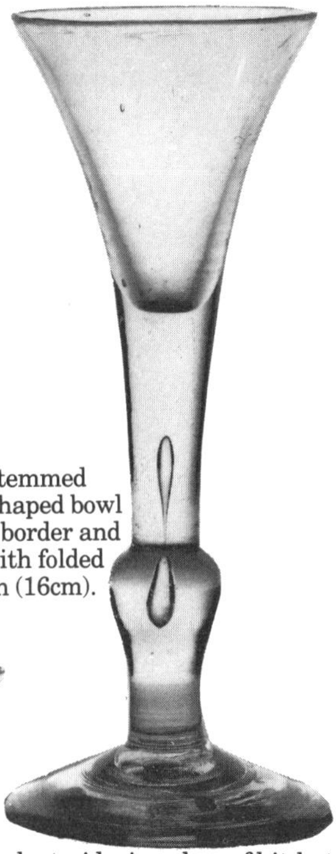

A balustroid wine glass of kit-kat type, on conical foot, c1720, 6½in (16.5cm).
£450-500 *C*

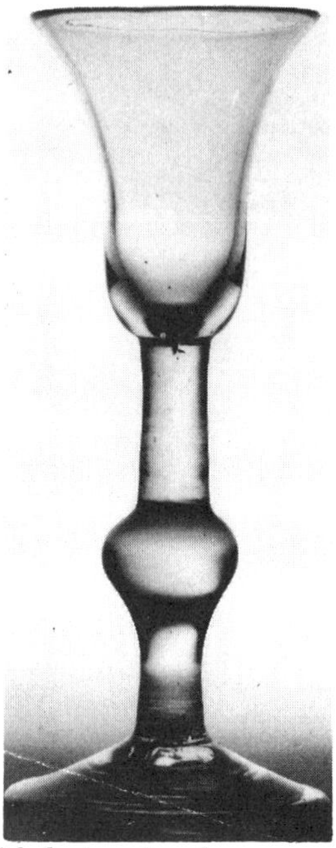

A baluster wine glass, on conical foot, c1725, 6½in (16cm).
£300-400 *C*

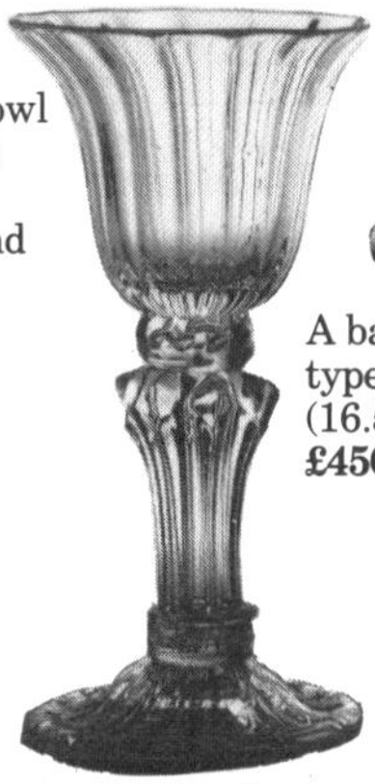

A pedestal stemmed wine glass, with vertically ribbed bowl supported on a beaded knop above an octagonal pedestal stem and radially ribbed domed and folded foot, c1750, 6in (15cm).
£500-600 *C*

An ale glass, the extended funnel bowl with hops and barley engraving, on a plain stem and conical folded foot, c1740, 7½in (18cm).
£250-300 *BAL*

ylinder knopped baluster goblet,
flared funnel bowl with a solid
er part enclosing a tear, on a
ed conical foot, c1715, 7in
cm).
00-4,500 *C*

A Bohemian goblet, the fluted funnel bowl with 4 medallions reserved on an elaborately engraved ground, the knopped and inverted baluster stem cut with facets and filled with spiral red and gilt threads, c1725, 11½in (28.5cm).
£7,000-8,000 *C*

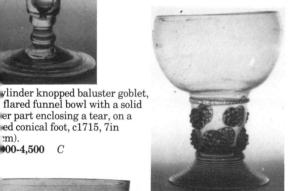

A light green tint roemer, the stem applied with raspberry prunts, The Netherlands or Rheinland, 17thC, 5in (12cm).
£1,000-1,200 *C*

A Nuremburg armorial goblet, the round funnel bowl engraved with 2 coats-of-arms within berried foliage cartouches, the conical foot with folded rim, foot detached and damaged, c1690, 11½in (29cm).
£1,000-1,500 *C*

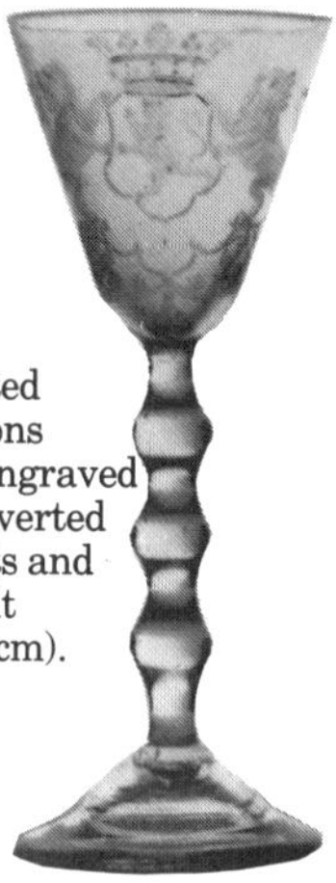

A Dutch engraved armorial baluster goblet, the funnel bowl with crowned arms of Holland flanked by lion supporters above foliage scrolls, on a multi-knopped stem and domed foot, c1740, 8in (20cm).
£1,000-1,200 *C*

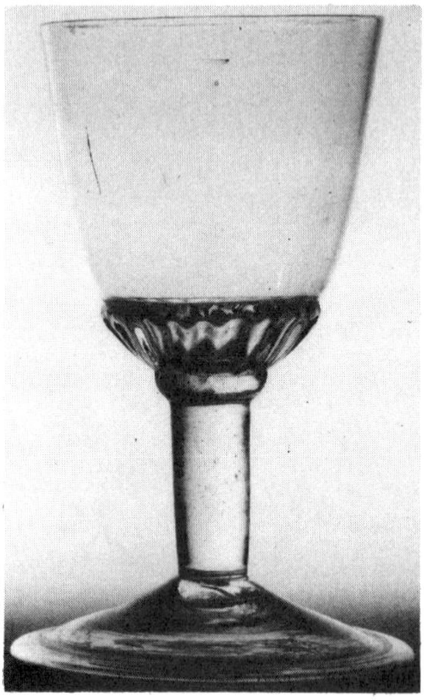

A Dutch engraved armorial baluster goblet, engraved with the crowned arms of the Province of Utrecht, the reverse with a stylised flowerspray, on a conical foot, c1750, 7in (17.5cm).
£900-1,200 *C*

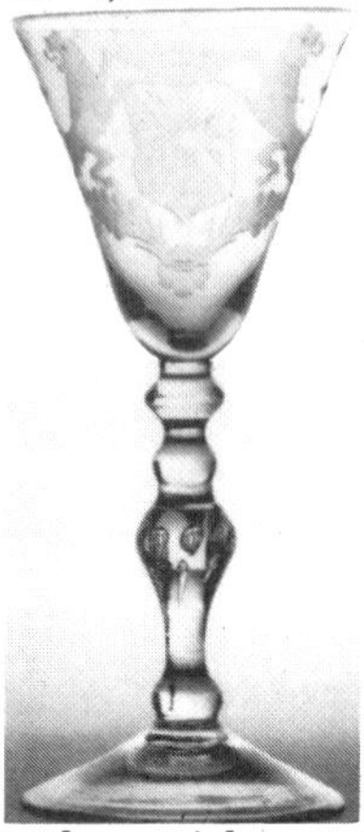

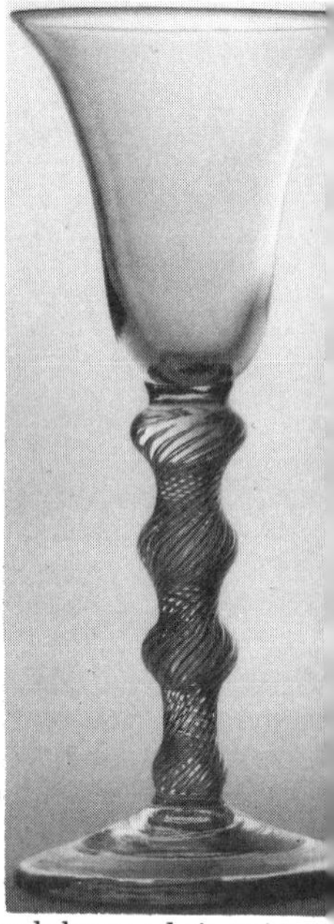

A plain stemmed goblet, the funnel bowl with gadrooned lower part, supported on a shoulder knopped stem and folded conical foot, c1740, 6in (15cm).
£800-900 *C*

A Dutch engraved armorial baluster goblet, engraved with the arms of Utrecht, the multi-knopped stem including a beaded inverted baluster section, on a conical foot, mid-18thC, 7½in (19cm).
£1,000-1,500 *C*

A quadruple knopped air-twist w glass, on conical foot, c1750, 7in (17.5cm).
£1,600-2,000 *C*

A mercury cordial glass, the bowl with honeycomb moulded lower part, the stem with a spiral air-core within a seven-ply spiral, on conical foot, c1750, 6½in (16.5cm).
£450-550 *C*

A Newcastle engraved baluster wine glass, the funnel bowl with a border of 'Laub-und-Bandelwerk', supported on a multi-knopped stem on a conical foot, c1750, 6in (15cm).
£500-600 *C*

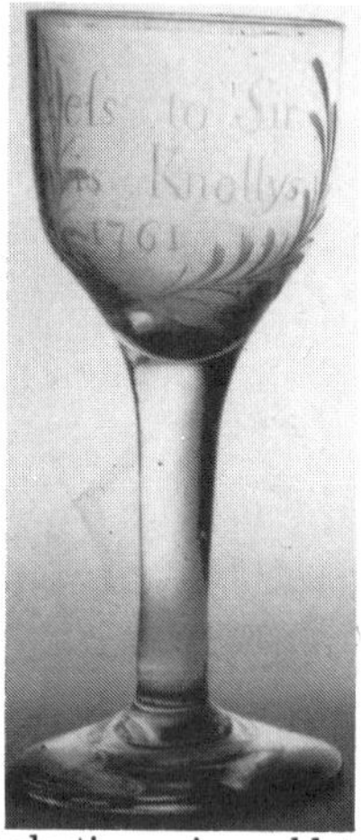

Knollys

An electioneering goblet, inscribed and dated, on pla stem and conical foot, 1761 7in (17cm).
£750-1,000 *C*

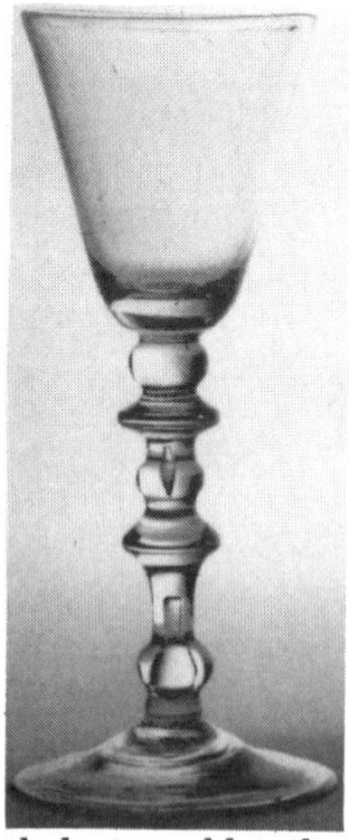

A Newcastle baluster goblet, the funnel bowl supported on a multi-knopped stem enclosing tears, above a conical foot, c1750, 7½in (18cm).
£900-1,200 *C*

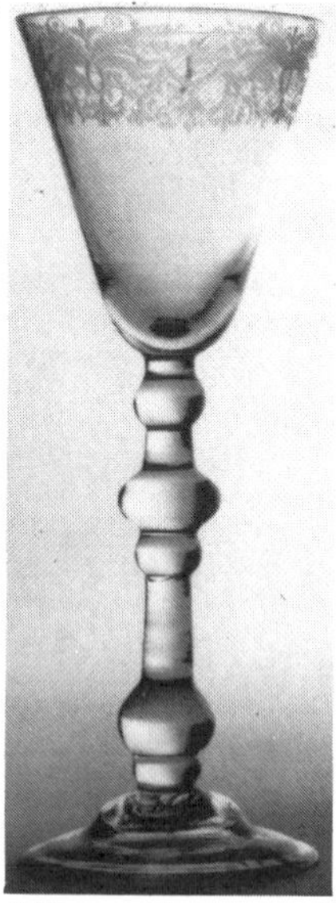

A Newcastle engraved baluster goblet, the funnel bowl supported on a multi-knopped stem including a beaded inverted baluster section with basal knop, above a conical foot, c1750, 7½in (18cm).
£1,000-1,500 *C*

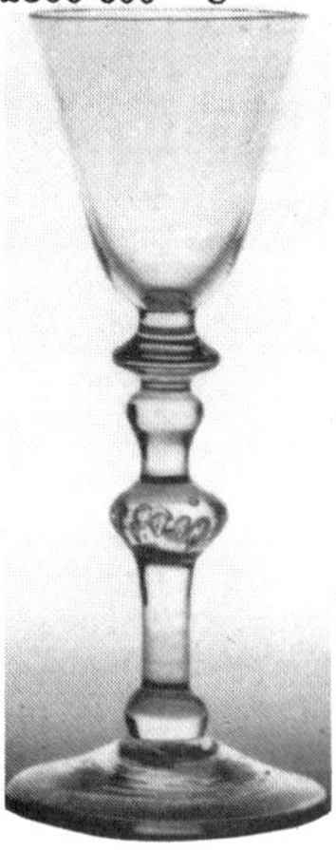

A Newcastle baluster goblet, the funnel bowl supported on a knopped section above a beaded inverted baluster stem with basal knop, on a conical foot, c1750, 7in (17.5cm).
£600-700 *C*

An ale glass, engraved with hops and barley motif, on a stem with a double series air-twist, thick plain foot, c1750, 7½in (18.5cm).
£400-450 *Som*

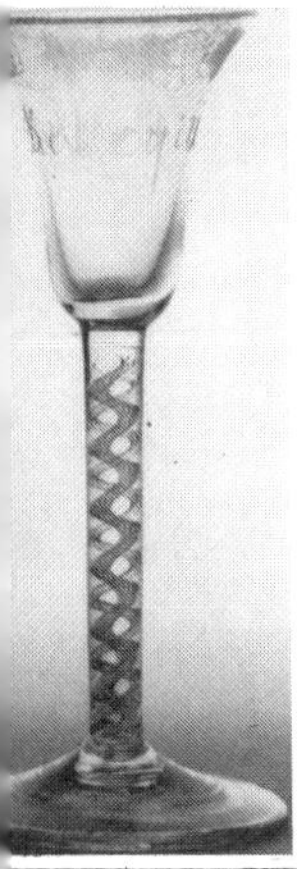

Three plain conical dwarf ales, with conical feet, c1810, 5in (12.5cm).
£40-60 each *Som*

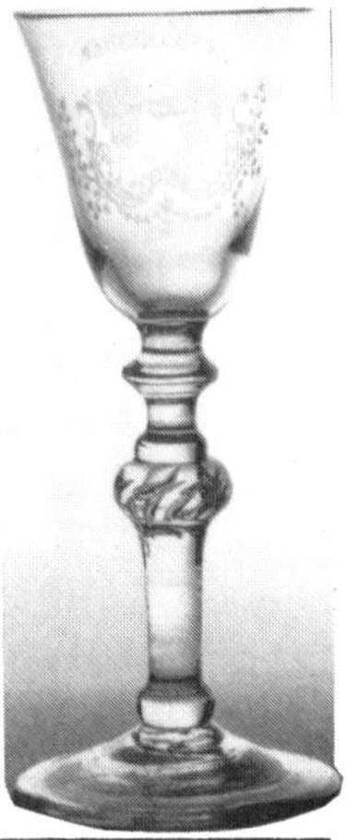

An engraved and dated air-twist wine glass, inscribed 'Jno. Keltey, 1754', beneath a border of engraved and polished fruiting vine, the stem with 2 entwined gauze spirals, on a conical foot, 6½in (16.5cm).
£600-700 *C*

A Dutch baluster goblet, the funnel bowl engraved with 2 clasped hands, inscribed 'Ametitia', on a beaded multi-knopped stem terminating in a basal knop on a conical foot, c1750, 7in (17cm).
£1,000-1,200 *C*

GLASS APPENDIX

Drinking glasses

STEM FORMATIONS

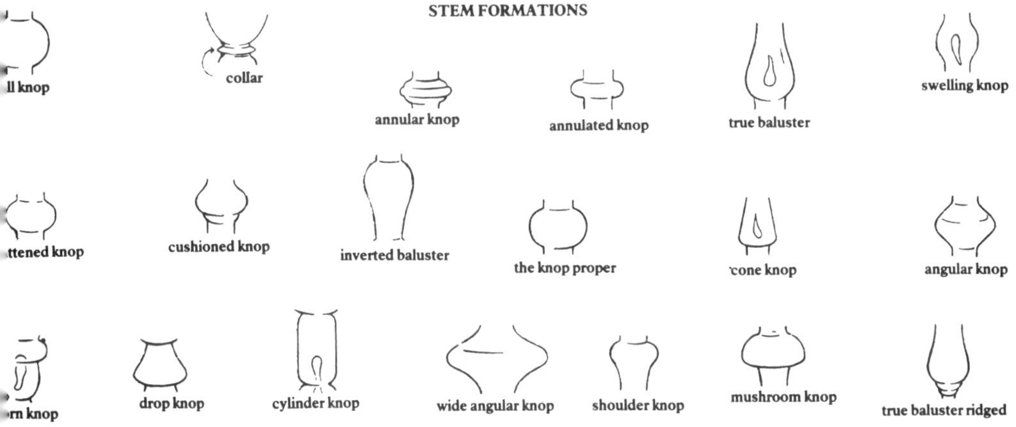
ll knop
collar
annular knop
annulated knop
true baluster
swelling knop
ttened knop
cushioned knop
inverted baluster
the knop proper
cone knop
angular knop
rn knop
drop knop
cylinder knop
wide angular knop
shoulder knop
mushroom knop
true baluster ridged

BOWL FORMS

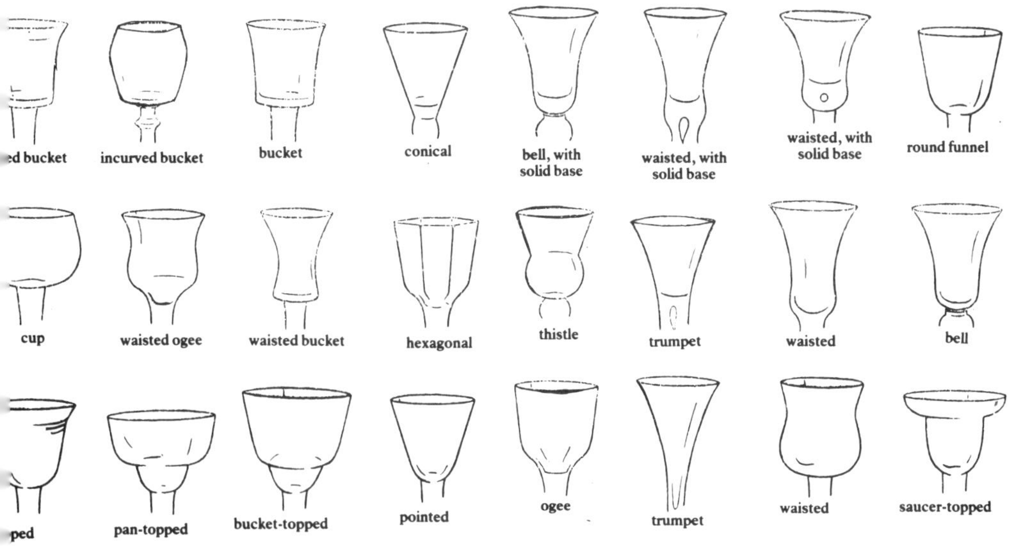
ed bucket
incurved bucket
bucket
conical
bell, with solid base
waisted, with solid base
waisted, with solid base
round funnel
cup
waisted ogee
waisted bucket
hexagonal
thistle
trumpet
waisted
bell
ped
pan-topped
bucket-topped
pointed
ogee
trumpet
waisted
saucer-topped

FOOT FORMS

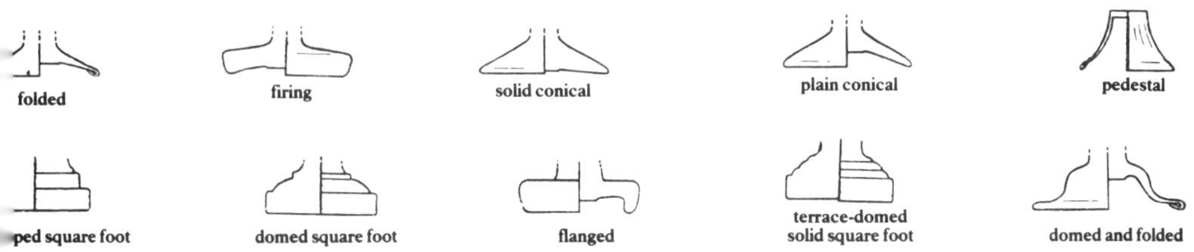
folded
firing
solid conical
plain conical
pedestal
ped square foot
domed square foot
flanged
terrace-domed solid square foot
domed and folded

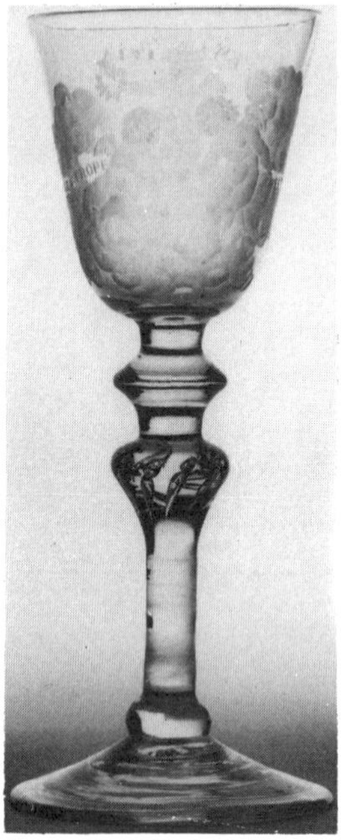

An engraved baluster goblet, engraved by a German hand with winged putti, inscribed, the stem with wide angular knop above a beaded inverted baluster section with basal knop, on conical foot, slight chip, c1760, 7½in (18.5cm).
£2,500-3,000 *C*

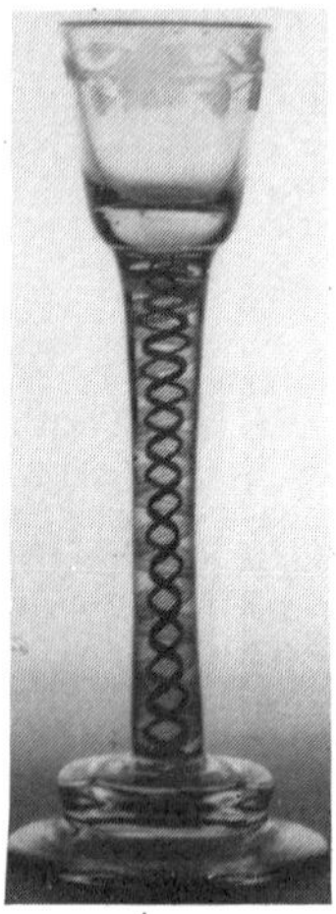

An engraved opaque-twist cordial glass of Jacobite significance, the funnel bowl with flowersprays, the stem with an entwined double thread core within a multi-ply spiral, on domed foot, c1770, 6½in (16.5cm).
£600-700 *C*

A mug with base gadrooning and trailed rim, the foot containing a silver coin, the body engraved with monogram 'AM', applied strap handle, c1760, 5in (13cm).
£350-400 *Som*

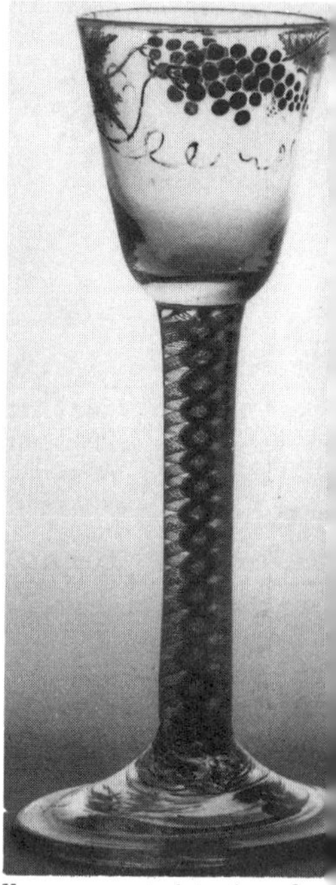

A Beilby opaque-twist wine glas the funnel bowl enamelled in wh with a border of fruiting vine, or double series stem and conical fo c1770, 5in (15cm).
£1,000-1,500 *C*

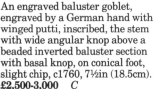

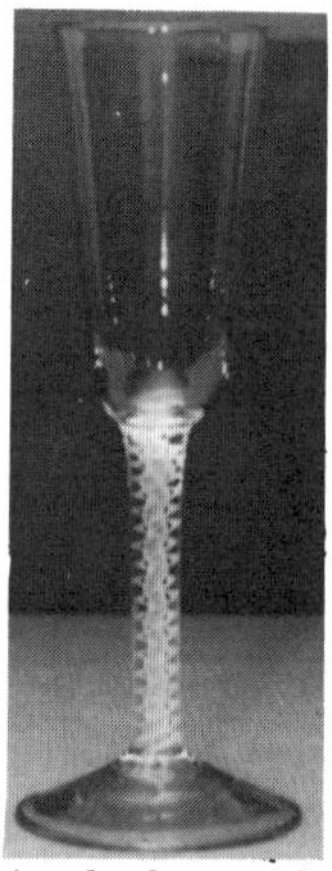

An ale glass, with deep round funnel bowl on double series opaque twist stem, c1765, 8in (20cm).
£200-250 *BAL*

A mug with base gadrooning and trailed rim, applied strap handle, damaged handle, c1760, 5in (13cm).
£150-200 *Som*

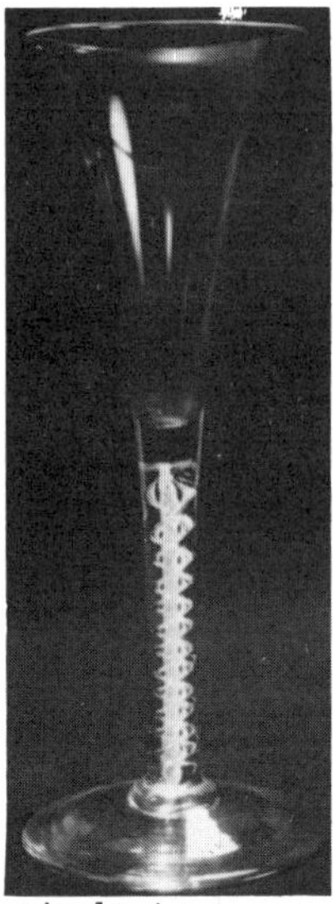

A flute with mixed twist stem, on a plain conical foot, c1760, 7½in (18.5cm).
£550-600 *Som*

A South Bohemian Lithya goblet of marbled brown glass, inscribed, with trace of gilding to the rim, rim chip, c1840, 5½in (14cm).
£500-600 *C*

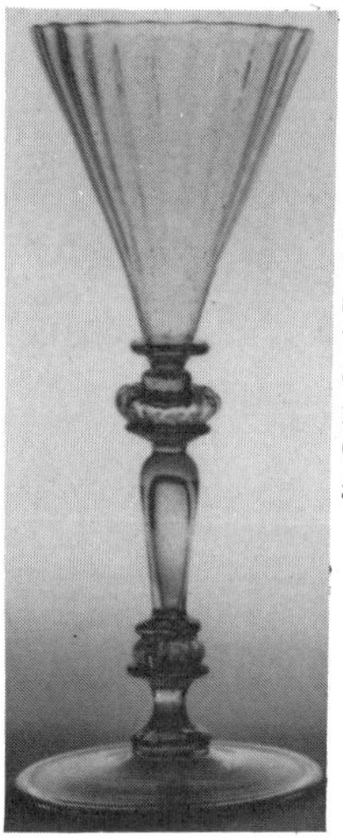

A façon de Venise goblet, with flared vertically ribbed funnel bowl, the stem with a central almost hollow tapering section set between ribbed cushion knops and divided by mereses, on folded conical foot, Low Countries, mid-17thC, 8in (20cm).
£2,000-2,500 *C*

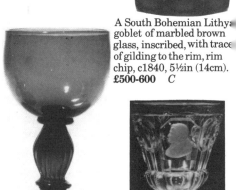

A green tinted wine glass, the bowl supported on a swelling knop moulded with vertical ribs between collars, on a conical foot applied with trailed thread, slight damage, early 19thC, 5½in (13cm).
£350-400 *C*

A French goblet, with sulphide portrait of Pope Pius IX, mid-19t 6½in (15.5cm).
£200-300 *C*

A dwarf ale, the bowl with a translucent green rim and band of hatched rose engraving, bladed knop stem, on a plain conical foot, c1825, 5½in (14cm).
£250-300 *Som*

A South Bohemian Lithyalin goblet, of marbled pale green/grey opalescent glass, the faceted bowl outlined in gilt, Buquoy Glasshouse, c1840, 5in (12.5cm.
£2,500-3,000 *C*

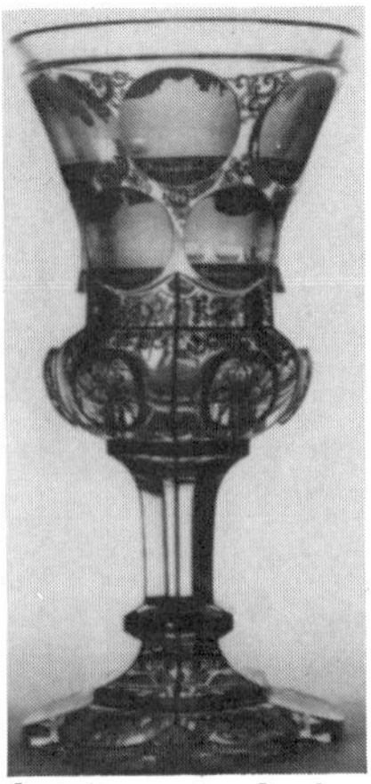

A Bohemian stained ruby spa goblet, engraved with named views, on fluted shaped stem and hexafoil foot, c1865, 10½in (26.5cm).
£2,000-2,500 *C*

A heavy baluster goblet, the stem enclosing a large tear above a basal knop, on a folded conical foot, c1705, 7in (17cm).
£700-800 *C*

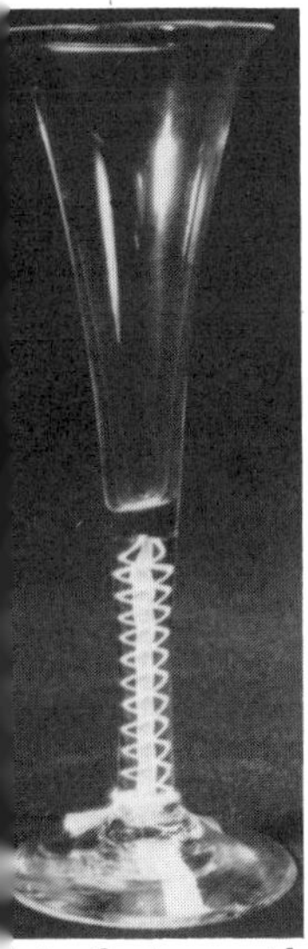

ute, the trumpet bowl on a
ıder stem with a double series
que twist, plain conical foot,
60, 8in (20cm).
0-350 *Som*

A set of 6 flutes, with trumpet bowls and drawn flute cut stems, on plain conical feet, c1830, 6in (15cm).
£250-350 *Som*

A set of 6 flutes, with drawn flute cut stems, plain feet, c1840, 6½in (16cm).
£250-300 *Som*

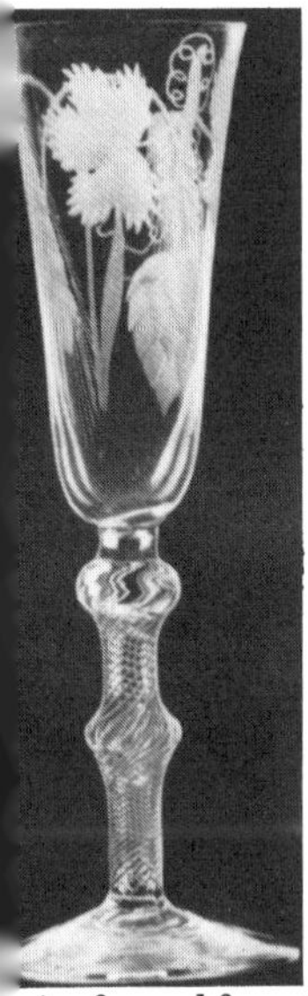

air of round funnel bowl ale
sses, engraved with hops and
ley, on angular knopped
twist stems and flattened feet,
chipped, 8in (20cm).
0-500 *CSK*

Three flutes, c1840, 6 to 7in (15 to 17cm).
£40-60 each *Som*

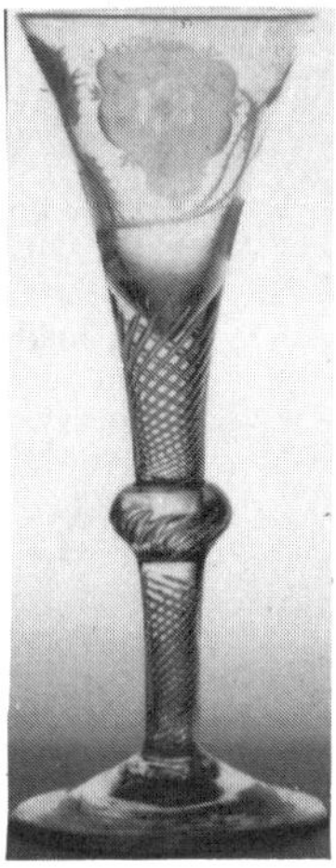

A Jacobite air-twist wine glass, engraved with roses and the motto 'Fiat', the stem filled with spiral threads and set into a beaded and air-twist inverted baluster section, on a conical foot, small chip to footrim, mid-18thC, 7in (17.5cm).
£1,000-1,200 *C*

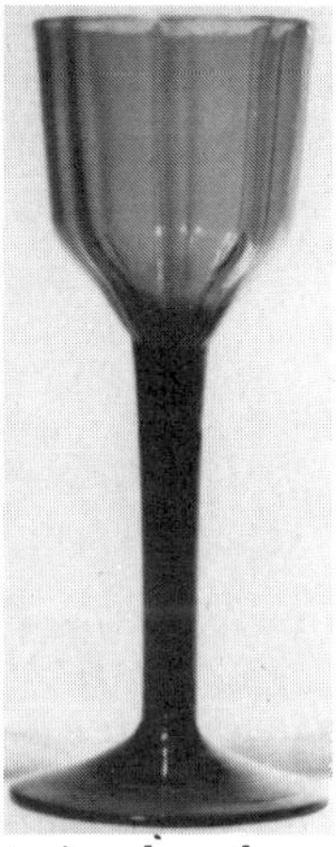

A green air-twist wine glass, the ribbed ogee bowl supported on a stem enclosing spiral air threads, on conical foot, c1765, 7½in (18.5cm).
£1,500-2,000 *C*

A pedestal stemmed goblet, c1740, 7in (17cm).
£350-450 *C*

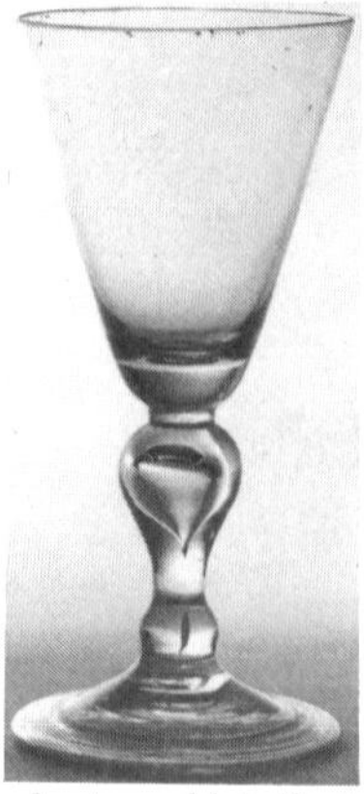

A baluster goblet, the inverted baluster stem enclosing a tear, and with a basal knop, above a folded conical foot, c1720, 6in (15cm).
£250-350 *C*

An armorial air-twist goblet, the funnel bowl engraved by a German hand, on a double knopped air-twist stem above a conical foot, the upper knop with inscription, c1750, 8in (20cm).
£2,500-3,000 *C*

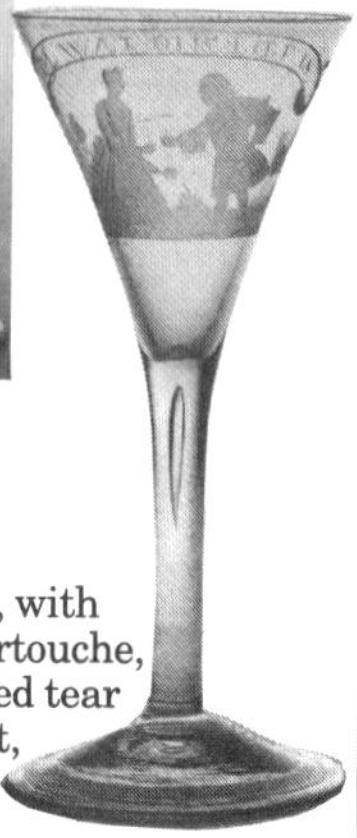

A Dutch engraved goblet, with inscription in a ribbon cartouche, the stem with an elongated tear above a folded conical foot, mid-18thC, 8in (20cm).
£700-800 *C*

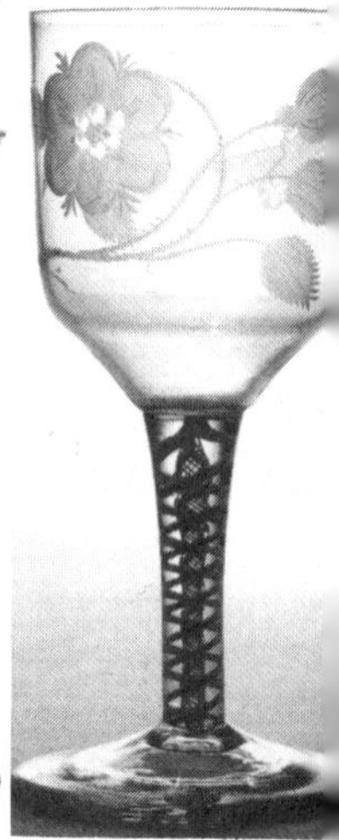

A Jacobite opaque-twist goblet, t ogee bowl engraved with a rose a buds, the stem with 2 ribbon spir on a conical foot, c1770, 8in (20c
£450-550 *C*

A pair of large goblets, the trumpet bowls on drawn stems with air tears, on folded conical feet, c1740.
£600-650 *Som*

A Middle German engraved goblet, the flared ogee bowl on a teared multi-knopped stem divided by mereses, the conical foot with a band of foliage, perhaps Thuringia, c1735, 9½in (24cm).
£1,000-1,500 *C*

A Dutch engraved baluster goblet, with inscription beneath the rim, the slende inverted baluster stem on a conical foot, c1750, 7½in (18cm).
£1,200-1,600 *C*

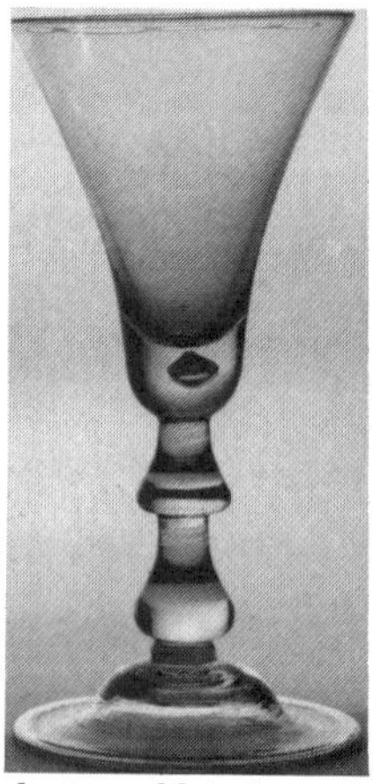

A baluster goblet, the wais funnel bowl with a tear to t solid lower part, on a doubl drop knop stem, above a on domed and folded foot, c172 8in (21cm).
£1,200-1,500 *C*

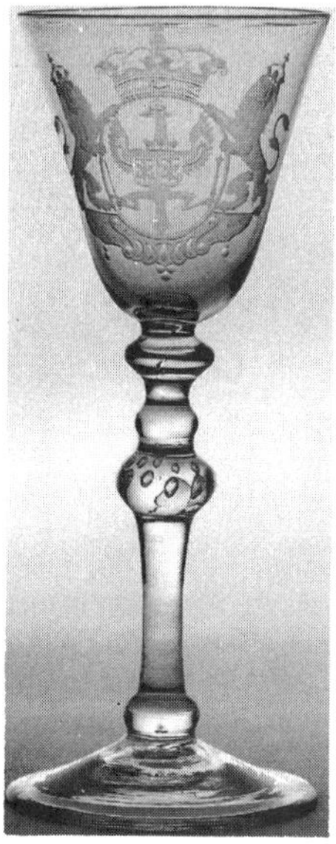

A Dutch engraved armorial baluster goblet, engraved with the arms of Princess Frederika Wilhelmina Sophia of Prussia, supported on a beaded multi-knopped stem above a conical foot, c1767, 7½in (18cm).
£2,500-3,000 *C*

A Dutch engraved dated baluster goblet, with inscription and date 1765, the stem with an angular knop, beaded inverted baluster section and flattened basal knop, the foot with a foliate band, signed with initials 'I F' on the cartouche, 8in (20cm).
£4,000-4,500 *C*

Two rummers with ovoid bowls a square feet, c1810:
l. Bowl with engraved decoration and solid stepped foot, 5½in (13.5cm).
£70-90
r. Plain bowl, 4½in (12cm).
£60-80 *Som*

A set of 7 flutes, with trumpet bowls, with diamond cut knop and plain conical feet, c1850, 6in (16cm).
£450-500 *Som*

A German engraved goblet, the lower part cut with flutes, on a facet cut inverted baluster stem, the domed and folded foot with a foliage spray, perhaps Saxony, mid-18thC, with a domed cover, 8in (20cm).
£600-700 *C*

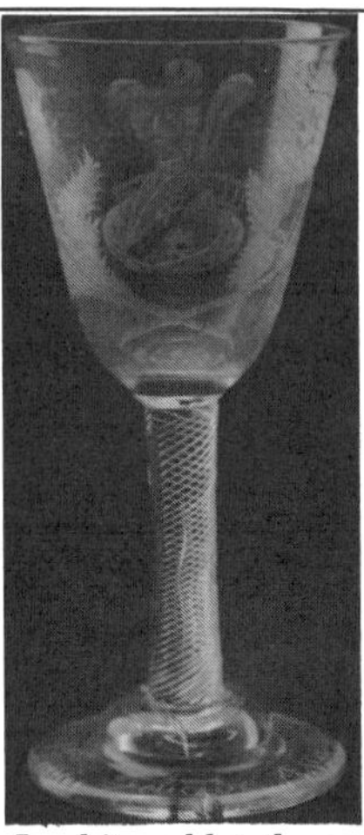

A rare Jacobite goblet, the ogee bowl engraved on one side with the portrait of Prince Charles Edward, flanked by rose and thistle motifs, and the reverse with the Prince of Wales feathers and motto 'Ich Dien', the stem with multiple spiral air-twist and central cable tear extending from the domed circular foot, foot damaged and repaired, c1750, 8in (20cm).
£1,000-1,500 *Bon*

ummer engraved with the
derland Bridge, the reverse
n a basket of flowers and initials
C, within an octagonal
ouche, c1820, 5½in (14cm).
0-450 *Som*

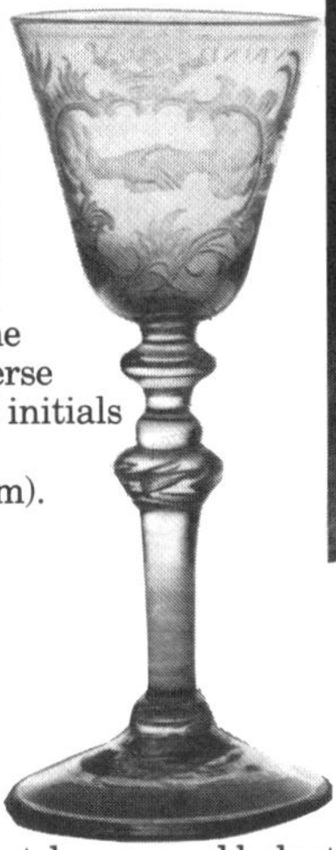

A rummer engraved with 'No Grumbling', with fruiting vine decoration and monogram, on a short knopped stem and plain conical foot, c1820, 8in (20cm).
£400-450 *Som*

A Dutch engraved baluster goblet, the funnel bowl engraved with clasped hands, the reverse inscribed 'Vrindschap', on a knopped section above a beaded inverted baluster stem with basal knop, on a conical foot, c1750, 7½in (17.5cm).
£1,000-1,500 *C*

l. A set of 8 ovoid bowl rummers, with capstan stems and plain feet, c1830, 5in (13cm).
£500-550
r. A single rummer, with capstan stem.
£60-80 *Som*

eavy baluster goblet, the conical
l with a solid section, on a stem
inverted baluster knop with air
, on folded conical foot, c1710,
(20cm).
00-1,800 *Som*

t of 6 matching panel-moulded
mers, with ovoid bowls and
n conical feet, c1810, 4½in
m).
0-350 *Som*

A rummer engraved J.H. 1846, the knopped stem containing a damaged coin for 1846, on star cut foot, 7in (18cm).
£250-300 *Som*

Use the Index!

Because certain items might fit easily into any of a number of categories, the quickest and surest method of locating any entry is by reference to the index at the back of the book.
This has been fully cross-referenced for absolute simplicity

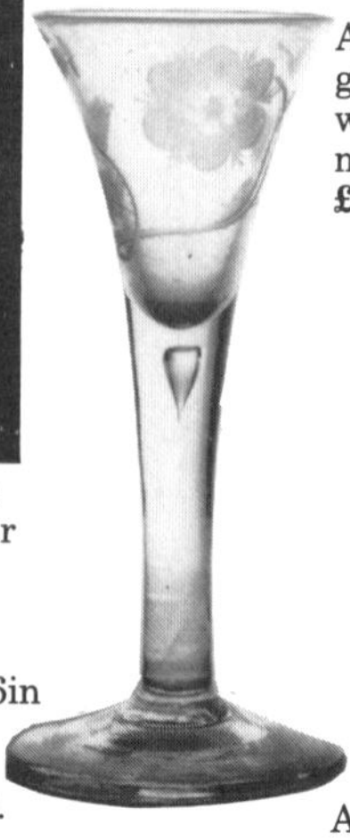

A Jacobite drawn trumpet wine glass, engraved with roses, the st with a small tear, on a conical fo mid-18thC, 6½in (16cm).
£600-800 *C*

A pair of heavy baluster wine glasses, the bowls with solid sections, on stems with inverted baluster air-teared knops and ba knops, on domed folded foot, c172 7in (17.5cm).
£2,000-2,500 *Som*

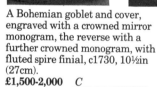

Ovoid bowl rummers on capstan stems and square lemon squeezer feet, c1800:
l. 5½in (13.5cm).
£150-170 a pair
c. Engraved monogram 'JASC', 6in (15.5cm).
£75-100
r. Engraved TBF, 5½in (13.5cm).
£90-120 *Som*

l. A bucket rummer with flute cut body, knopped stem and plain foot, c1825, 5in (13cm).
£60-80
r. A pair of similar rummers, c183 5in (13cm).
£120-150 *Som*

A Bohemian goblet and cover, engraved with a crowned mirror monogram, the reverse with a further crowned monogram, with fluted spire finial, c1730, 10½in (27cm).
£1,500-2,000 *C*

Three rummers:
l. With capstan stem, c1810, 5in (12.5cm).
£40-60
c. With bowl engraved with hops and barley, c1810, 5in (12.5cm).
£90-120
r. Cup shaped bowl with cut printies, c1840, 5½in (14cm).
£40-60 *Som*

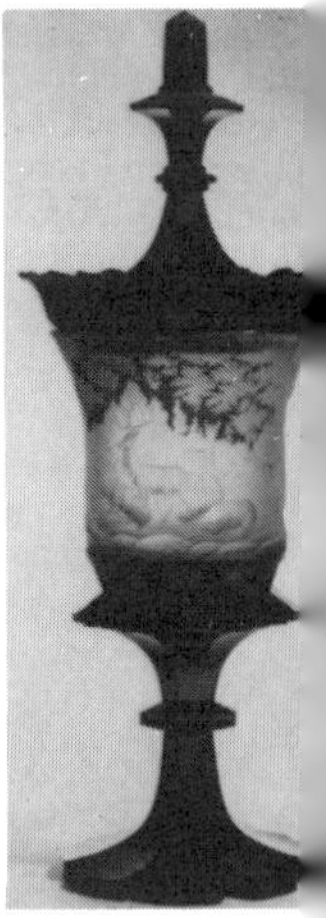

A large Bohemian ruby flash gob and cover, engraved with a stag a numerous hind in a landscape, above an everted scalloped collar, a knopped spreading octagonal st with waved footrim, cover damag c1865, 21in (53cm).
£7,000-8,000 *C*

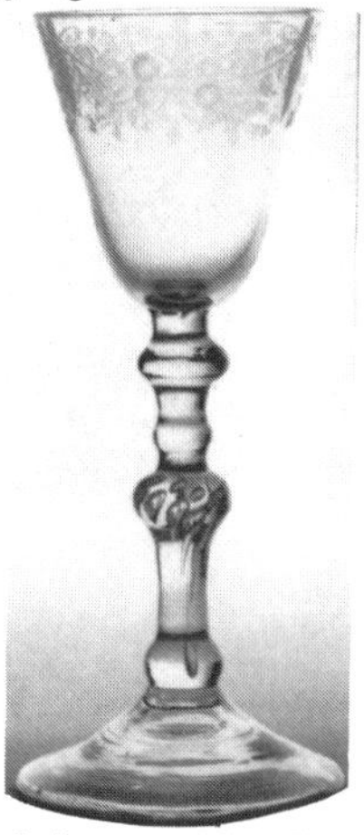

A Newcastle baluster goblet, the funnel bowl engraved with a border of birds perched among 'Laub-und-Bandelwerk', on a knopped section above a baluster stem with basal knop, on domed foot, c1750, 7in (17.5cm).
£750-1,000 *C*

A heavy baluster wine glass, the pointed round funnel bowl on a stem with an inverted baluster knop and air tear, on folded conical foot, c1710, 8in (20cm).
£900-1,000 *Som*

A baluster cordial glass, the waisted bucket bowl supported on an annular knop, the stem with swelling waist knop enclosing a tear, on conical foot, c1725, 6in (15cm).
£550-600 *C*

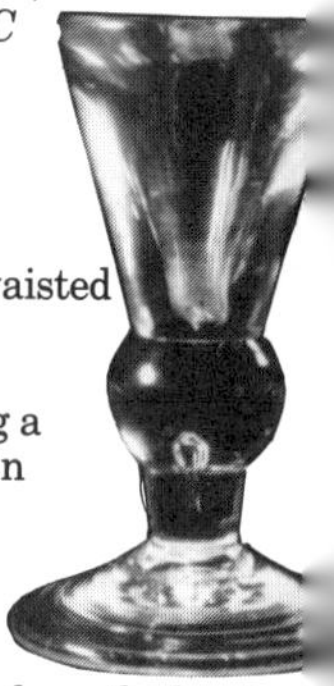

A toastmaster's glass, the bowl se on a stem with an inverted balust knop, on folded conical foot, c171C 4½in (11cm).
£500-550 *Som*

A baluster wine glass, on a stem with air beaded knop and base knop, on plain domed foot, c1730, 6½in (16cm).
£700-800 *Som*

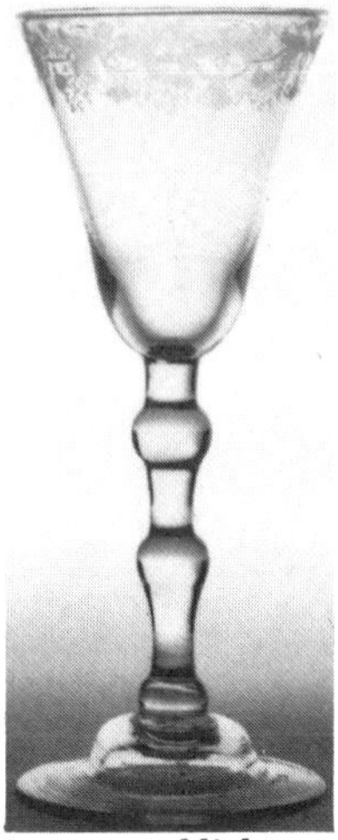

reen tinted wine glass, the -shaped bowl with a tear to the ering lower part, set on a hollow ulder knopped stem, on a conical , possibly English, possibly late hC, 6½in (16cm).
0-400 *C*

A Newcastle engraved light baluster goblet, the funnel bowl decorated with a border of birds perched among 'Laub-und-Bandelwerk', on a multi-knopped stem above a domed foot, c1750, 8in (20cm).
£800-1,000 *C*

l. A wine glass, the bell bowl engraved with a band of fruiting vine, with shoulder inverted baluster and base knops, folded conical foot, c1750, 6in (15cm).
£500-550
r. A baluster wine glass, the trumpet bowl with solid section ball knop and plain section conical foot, c1750, 7½in (17.5cm).
£300-350 *Som*

A Georgian glass with plain bowl and knopped stem, c1810, 4in (11cm).
£50-60 *TVA*

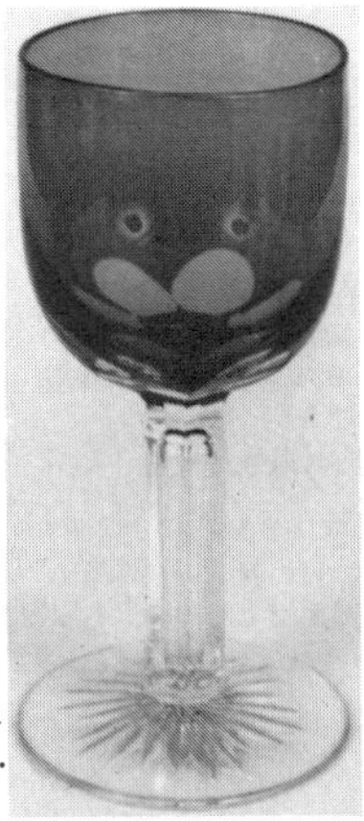

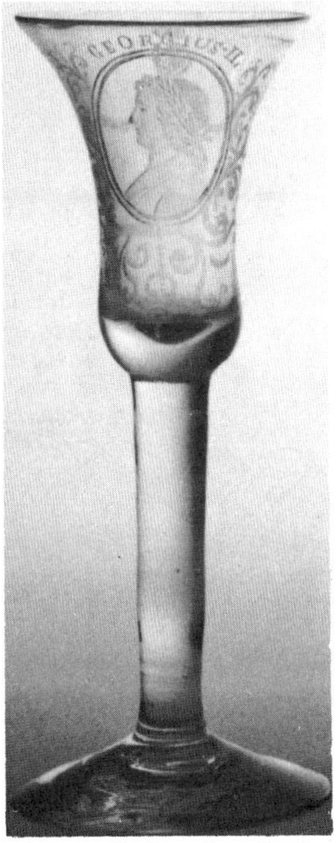

utch engraved dated armorial ıster goblet, with inscription and e 1776, on a multi-knopped and ded stem above a domed foot, 8in m).
)00-3,500 *C*

An engraved baluster wine glass, on domed folded foot, c1730, 7in (17cm).
£800-1,000 *Som*

A Victorian ruby glass port, with long tear drop faceted stem, c1870, 5in (14cm).
£60-80 *TVA*

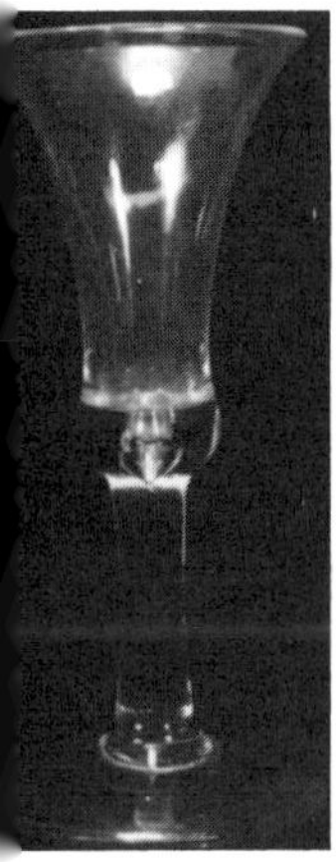

A wine glass, with wrythen moulded round funnel bowl, on a plain stem, folded conical foot, c1750, 6in (15cm).
£140-160 *Som*

A Royal portrait glass, inscribed 'Georgius II', on a plain stem and conical foot, footrim slightly chipped, mid-18thC, 6½in (16cm).
£600-800 *C*

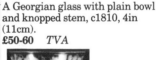

A wine glass, with pan topped round funnel bowl, on air-twist stem, c1750, 6in (15cm).
£200-250 *BAL*

ine glass with air tear in the e of the bowl, on plain stem and n conical foot, c1750, 7in 5cm).
0-150 *Som*

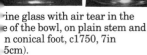

Locate the source

The source of each illustration in Miller's can be found by checking the code letters below each caption with the list of contributors

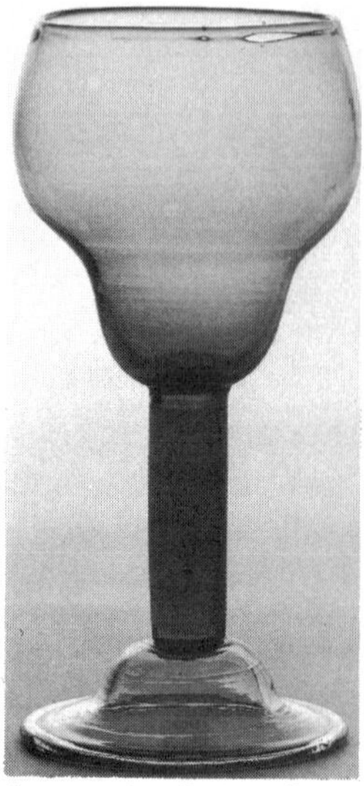

A pair of facet stem wine glasses, on plain feet, c1780, 4½in (11cm).
£120-150 *Som*

A green tinted wine glass, the double ogee bowl on a plain stem above a domed and folded foot, perhaps for export, c1765, 6in (15cm).
£400-500 *C*

A green plain stemmed wine gla the ovoid bowl with hammered flutes to the lower part, on a coni foot, c1765, 6½in (16.5cm).
£500-700 *C*

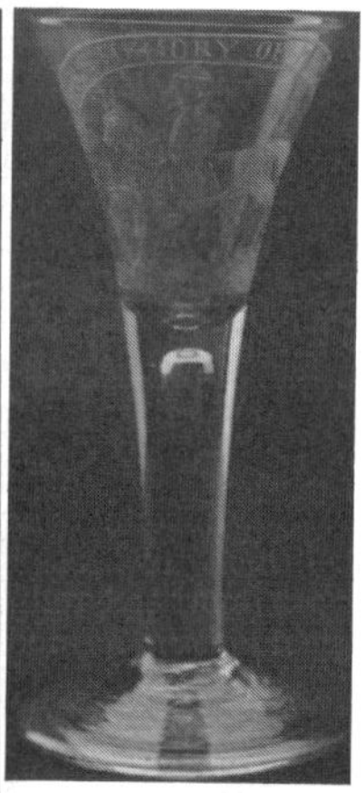

A Newcastle wine glass, engraved with the hands of friendship, the stem with bladed ball, air-beaded inverted baluster and base knops, on plain conical foot, c1750, 8in (20cm).
£2,000-2,500 *Som*

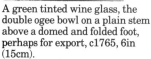

A rare Williamite portrait glass, the trumpet bowl engraved with the monarch on horseback and inscribed 'The Glorious Memory of King William III', the plain stem enclosing a single tear and on circular foot with fold under rim, c1740, 6in (15cm).
£1,700-2,500 *Bon*

A Royal armorial baluster goblet, the funnel bowl engraved with the Royal Arms of England above scroll ornament, on a multi-knopped teared and beaded stem with basal knop, above a conical foot, c1750, 8in (20cm).
£2,500-3,000 *C*

A trumpet bowl wine glass, on plain drawn stem with air tear and folded conical foot, c1740, 6in (15cm).
£150-180 *Som*

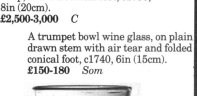

An engraved air-twist wine gla perhaps Jacobite, inscribed 'Bi Venue', the double knopped ste filled with spiral threads above conical foot, with a band of flor foliage, c1750, 6in (15cm).
£1,500-2,000 *C*

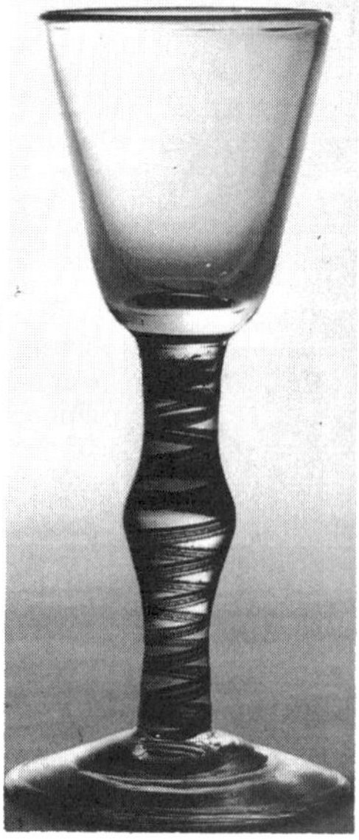

A colour twist wine glass, the swelling waist knopped stem with a spiral of multi-coloured threads including brick red, yellow, blue, white and pink, on a plain foot, late 18thC, 6in (15cm).
£700-800 *C*

A baluster wine glass, with air te in base, straight stem and cushio knop, on folded conical foot, c175 5½in (14.5cm).
£150-200 *Som*

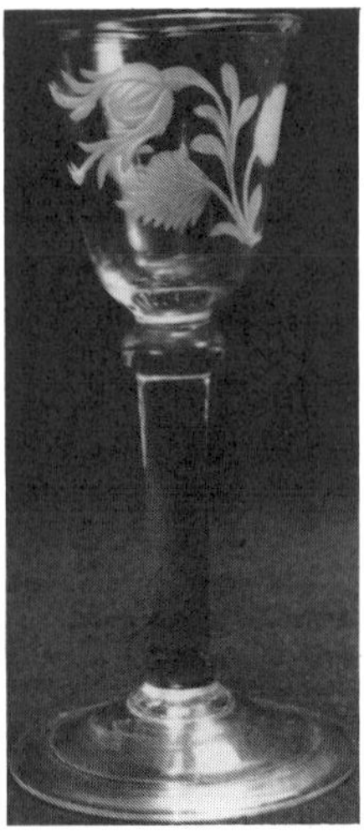

A baluster wine glass, engraved with a Jacobite rose, on a plain stem on folded conical foot, c1750, 6in (15cm).
£200-250 *Som*

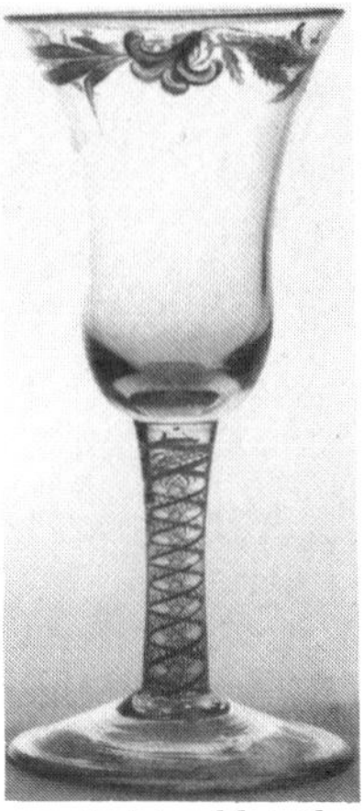

ine glass with trumpet bowl on nposite stem, plain inverted uster over multi-series air-twist, 50, 6in (16cm).
0-350 *BAL*

A Beilby opaque-twist goblet, the bowl enamelled in white, the rim with traces of gilding, on a double series stem and conical foot, footrim chipped, c1770, 8in (20cm).
£3,000-3,500 *C*

A wine glass with round funnel bowl, on a stem with knopped multiple spiral air-twist, plain conical foot, c1750, 6in (16cm).
£350-400 *Som*

air of ogee bowl drinking glasses, h multiple spiral opaque twist ns on conical feet, 5½in (14cm).
0-350 *CSK*

A rare Jacobite glass, engraved with a portrait of Prince Charles Edward, on a double air-twist and plain circular foot, c1750, 6in (15cm).
£3,000-3,500 *Bon*

A Jacobite air-twist wine glass, supported on a shoulder knopped stem filled with spirals above a conical foot, c1750, 6in (15cm).
£500-600 *C*

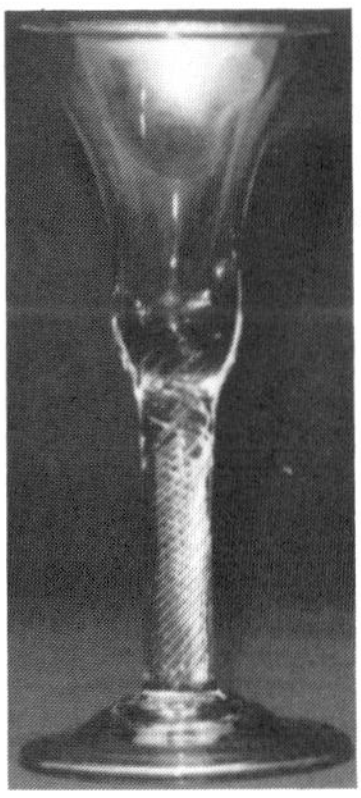

A wine glass with waisted bucket bowl, on multi-series air-twist stem with folded foot, c1745, 7½in (18.5cm).
£200-250 *BAL*

l. A baluster wine glass, the bowl with solid base and air tear stem with shoulder collar and baluster knop, folded conical foot, c1730, 6½in (17cm).
£650-700
r. A trumpet bowl glass, with shoulder knop and multiple spiral air-twist, plain conical foot, c1750, 7½in (18.5cm).
£350-400 *Som*

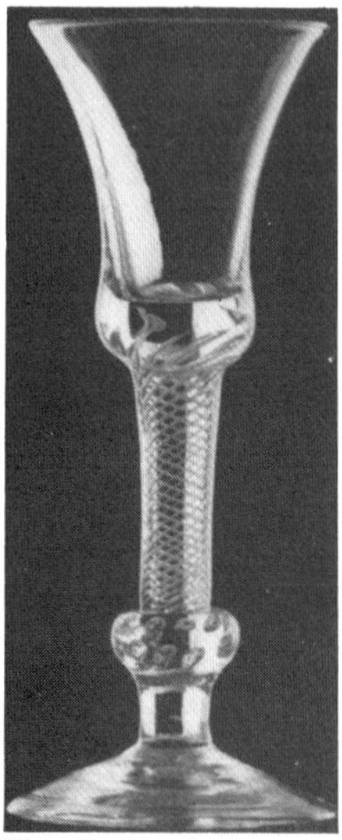

A bell bowl wine glass, on composite multiple air-twist stem over teared inverted baluster and conical foot, foot chipped, 6½in (16cm).
£150-200 *CSK*

l. A wine glass on a drawn stem, with multiple spiral air-twist, folded conical foot, c1745, 7in (18cm).
£200-250
r. A wine glass with bell bowl, on a plain stem domed foot, c1750, 8in (21cm).
£100-150 *Som*

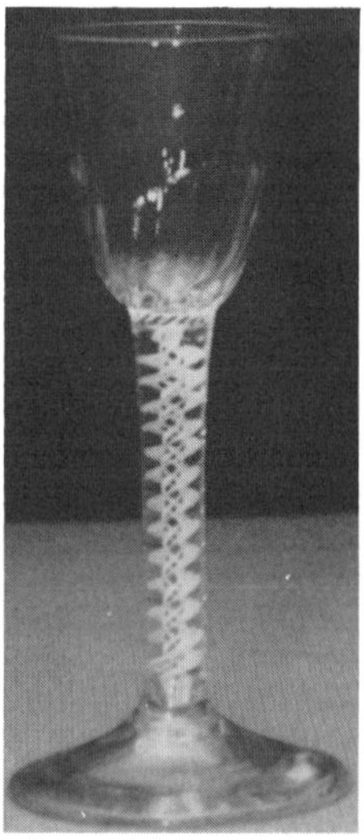

A wine glass, with round funnel bowl and wrythen base, on a dou series opaque twist stem, c1760, 5½in (14cm).
£140-180 *BAL*

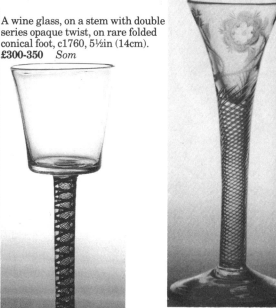

A Jacobite wine glass, on a drawn multiple spiral air-twist stem, folded conical foot, c1750, 6½in (16cm).
£800-850 *Som*

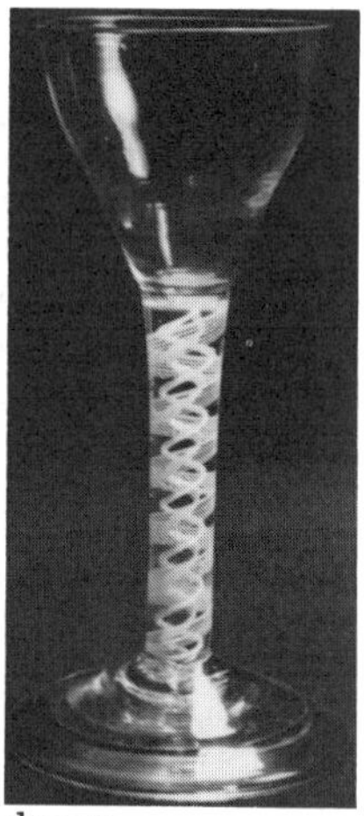

A wine glass, on a stem with double series opaque twist, on rare folded conical foot, c1760, 5½in (14cm).
£300-350 *Som*

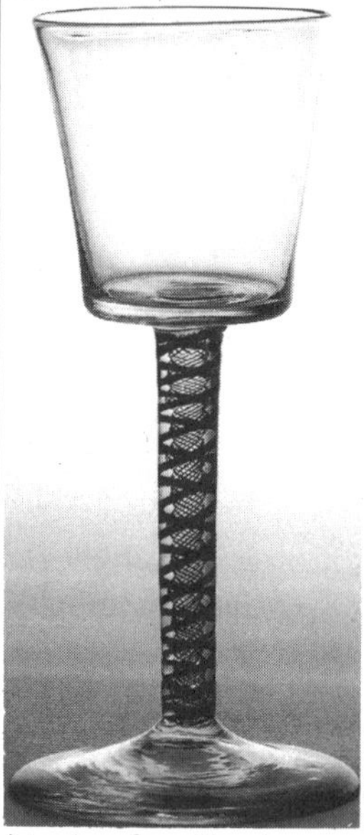

A colour twist wine glass, the stem with an opaque gauze core entwined by 2 blue/black ribbons, on a conical foot, c1765, 7in (17.5cm).
£2,500-3,000 *C*

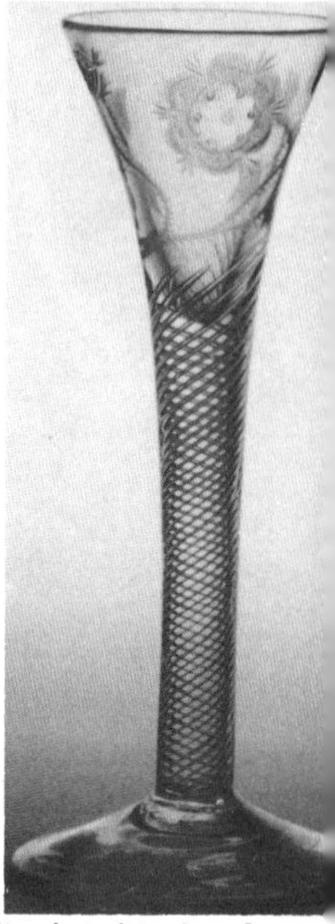

A Jacobite air-twist wine glass, inscribed with the motto 'Redi', t stem filled with spiral threads abc a conical foot, c1750, 6in (15cm).
£750-850 *C*

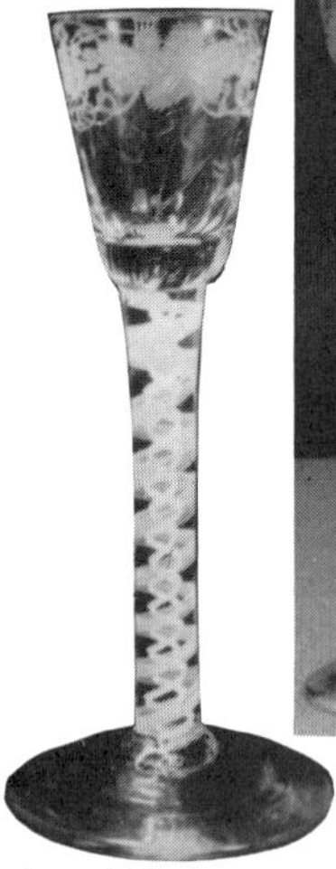

A cordial glass, engraved with fruiting vine motif, double series opaque twist stem, plain conical foot, c1760, 6½in (16.5cm).
£350-450 *Som*

A wine glass, with pan topped round funnel bowl and floral engraving, on a mercury twist stem, c1750, 6in (15cm).
£350-400 *BAL*

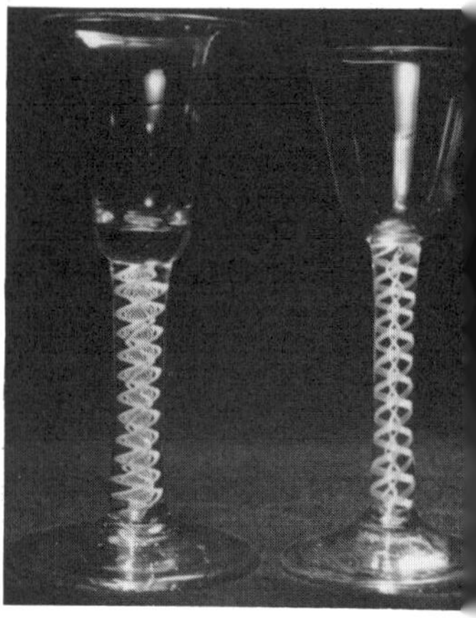

l. A mixed twist wine glass, the bell bowl on a stem with a double series opaque twist and following air-twist thread, c1760, 6½in (16cm).
£300-350
r. A wine glass, the round funnel bowl on a stem with double series opaque twist, plain conical foot, c1760, 6in (15cm).
£150-200 *Som*

\ wine glass, on a stem with
ıltiple spiral opaque twist with
elling centre knop, plain conical
t, 6in (15cm).
25-175
\n ale glass, on a stem with
ıble series opaque twist, plain
ıical foot, c1760, 6½in (16cm).
25-175 *Som*

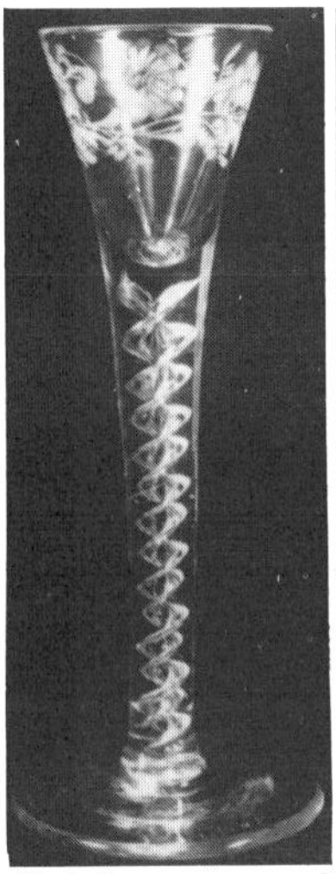

A cordial glass, engraved with a band of roses, on a drawn stem, with corkscrew mercury air-twist, on plain conical foot, c1745, 6½in (16.5cm).
£500-550 *Som*

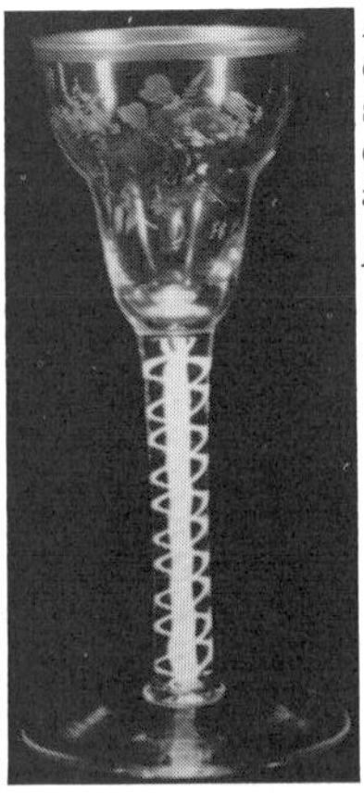

A wine glass, with pan top bowl decorated with gilt, on a double series opaque twist stem, plain conical foot, c1760, 6in (15cm).
£750-800 *Som*

In pristine condition.

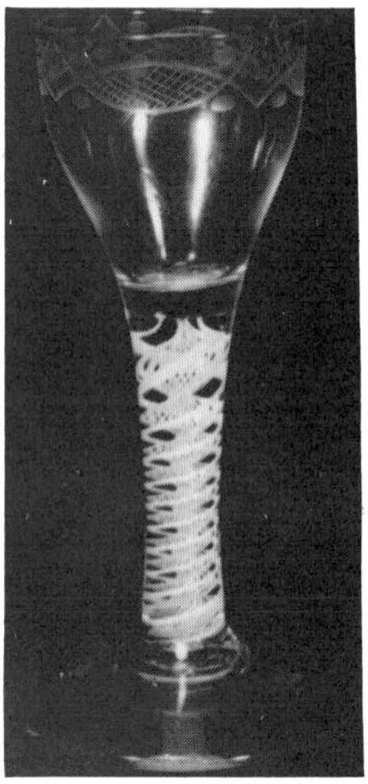

A wine glass, on double series opaque twist stem, plain conical foot, c1760, 5½in (14cm).
£150-200 *Som*

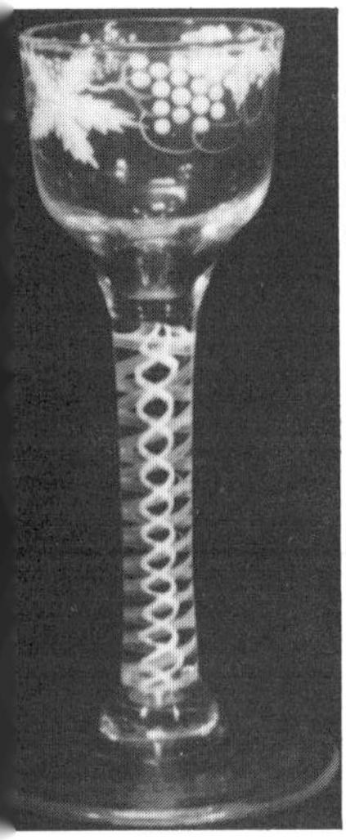

A Beilby wine glass, engraved in white enamel, on double series opaque twist stem, plain conical foot, c1765, 5½in (14cm).
£1,400-1,800 *Som*

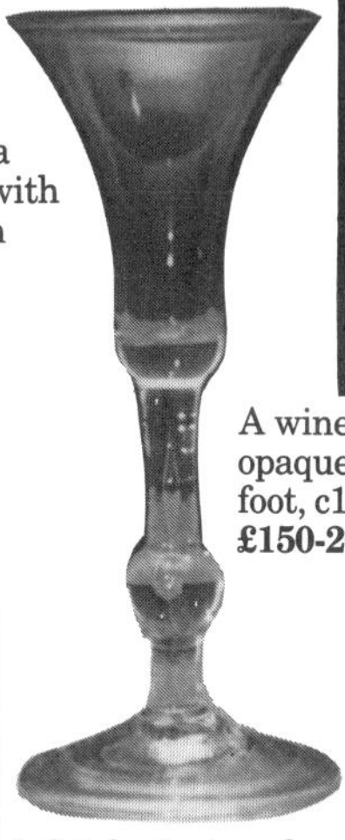

A 'kit-kat' wine glass, the bell bowl on an air-tear stem, with inverted baluster knop and conical folded foot, c1740, 6½in (16cm).
£350-400 *BAL*

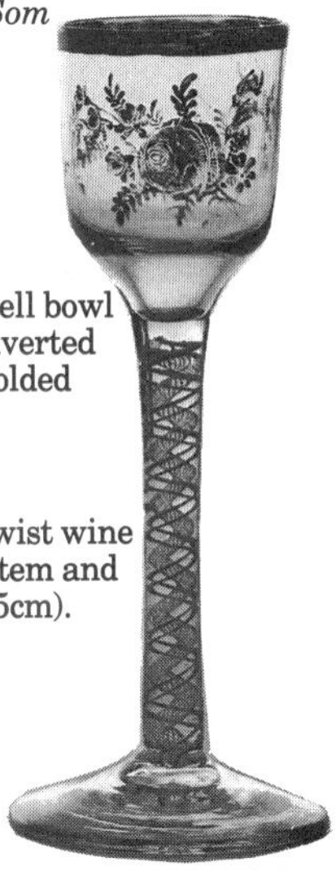

A gilt decorated opaque twist wine glass, on a double series stem and conical foot, c1765, 6in (15cm).
£450-500 *C*

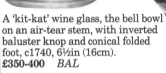

l. An ale glass, with double series opaque twist stem, plain conical foot, c1760, 8in (20cm).
£250-300
r. A wine glass on a plain stem, folded conical foot, c1750, 6½in (16.5cm).
£120-180 *Som*

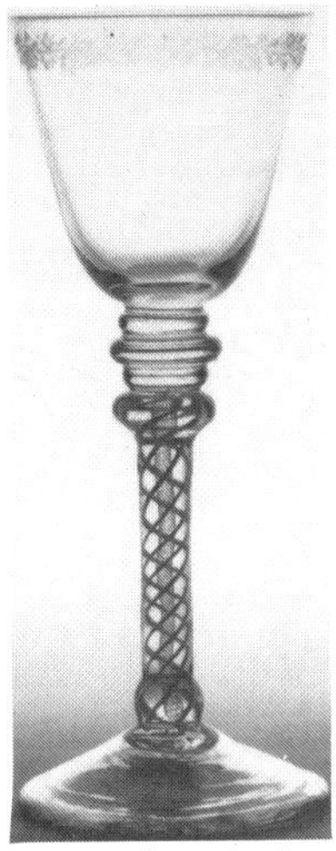

engraved composite stemmed
ıe glass, the funnel bowl
ported on a triple annulated
ɔp above a shoulder knopped
m, with on opaque gauze core
wined by 4 threads, on a conical
t, c1775, 7½in (18.5cm).
500-2,000 *C*

A large engraved and monogrammed stirrup glass in the form of a boot, c1760, 6½in (16cm).
£250-300 *BAL*

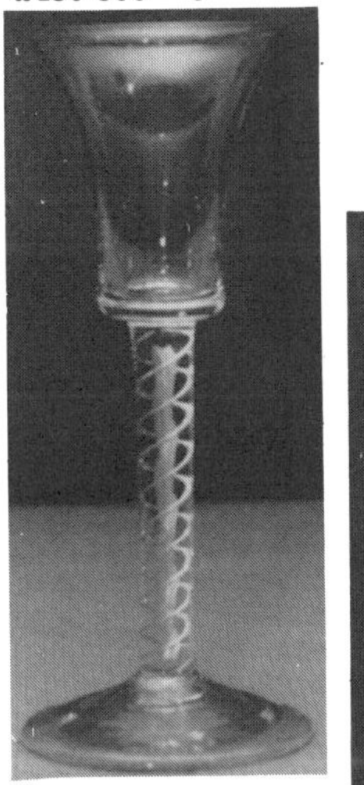

A wine glass with waisted bucket bowl, on a double series air-twist stem, c1750, 6in (15cm).
£250-300 *BAL*

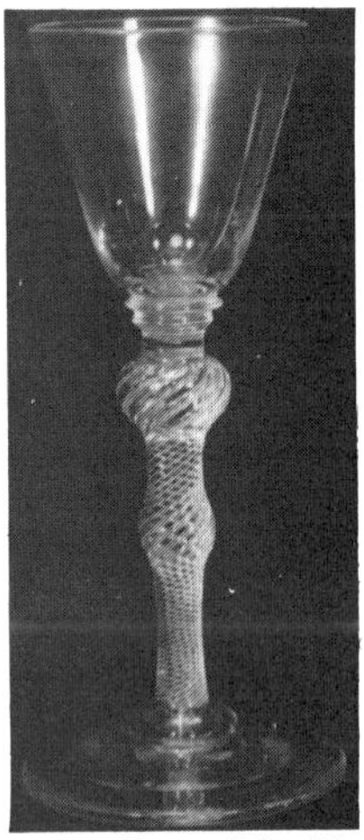

A wine glass, with collar and double knop multiple spiral air-twist stem, on plain conical foot, c1750, 6in (15cm).
£350-400 *Som*

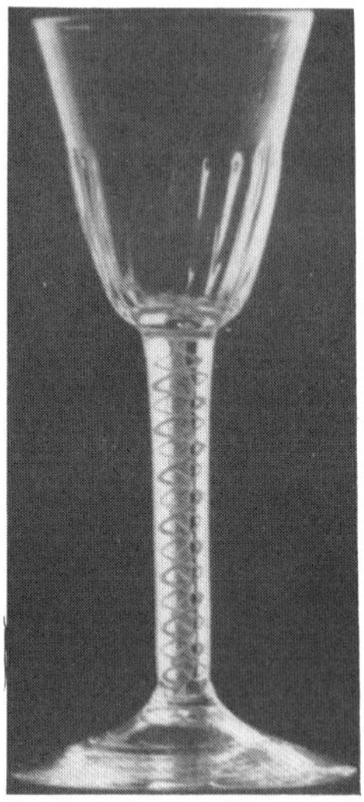

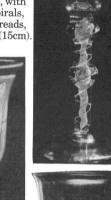

A wine glass, with round funnel bowl and basal flutes, on a double series opaque twist stem, 6½in (16cm).
£150-200 *CSK*

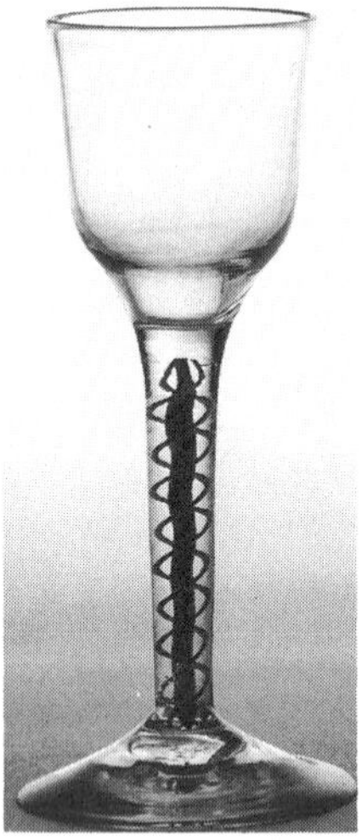

A colour twist wine glass, the stem with a solid white core incorporating a single yellow thread, within 2 white spiral threads, on a conical foot, c1765, 6in (15cm).
£1,300-1,700 *C*

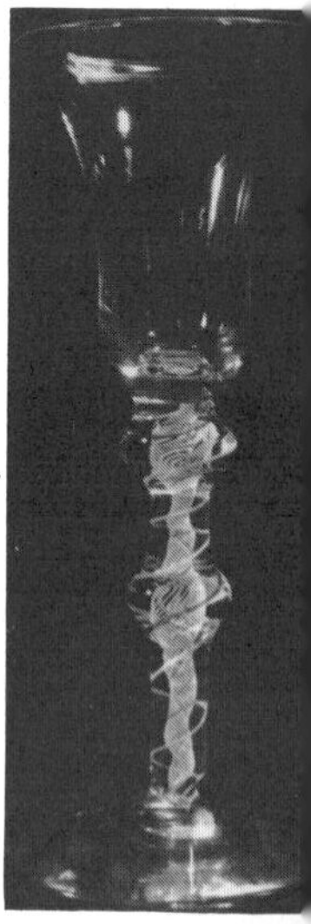

A colour twist wine glass, the bell bowl on a stem with 2 knops, with inner opaque white gauze spirals, and outer white and pink threads, plain conical foot, c1770, 6in (15cm).
£1,800-2,000 *Som*

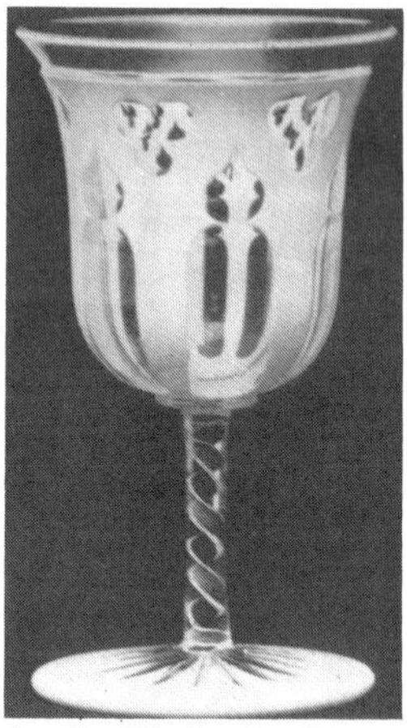

A pair of St. Louis white overlay goblets, on red and blue twist stems and sunray cut feet, the bowls cut with tapering panels, 7in (18cm).
£600-700 *CSK*

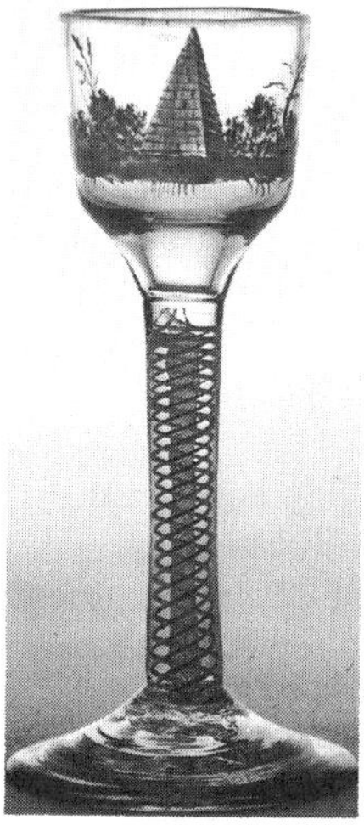

A Beilby opaque twist wine glass, enamelled in white with a pyramid flanked by trees and shrubbery, the rim with traces of gilding, on a double series stem and conical foot, c1765, 6in (15cm).
£2,700-3,000 *C*

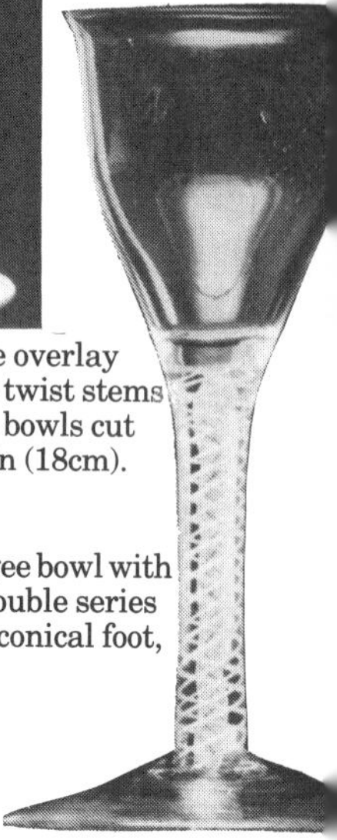

A drinking glass, the ogee bowl with slight flaring rim, on double series opaque twist stem and conical foot, 6in (15cm).
£50-100 *CSK*

Two wine glasses, the ogee bowls on stems with double series opaque twists on plain conical feet, c1770, 5½in (14cm).
£650-750 each *Som*

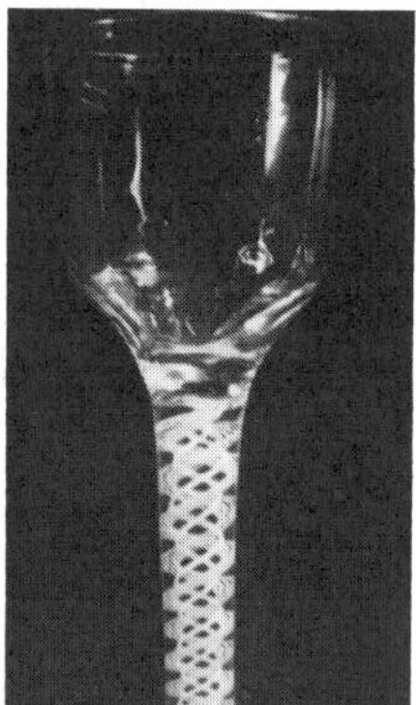

A wine glass, the stem with double series opaque twist, on plain conical foot, c1760, 5½in (14cm).
£150-170 *Som*

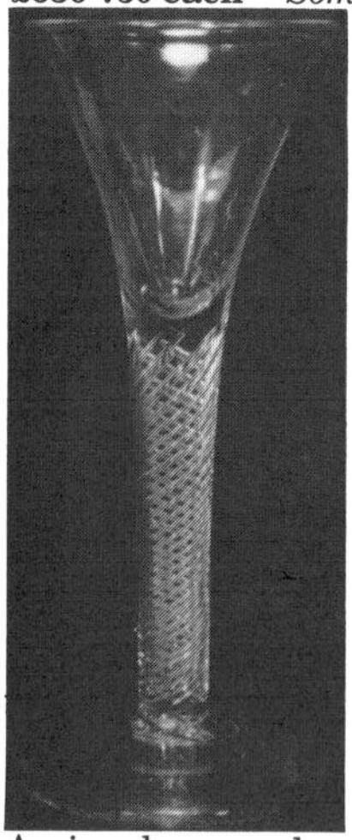

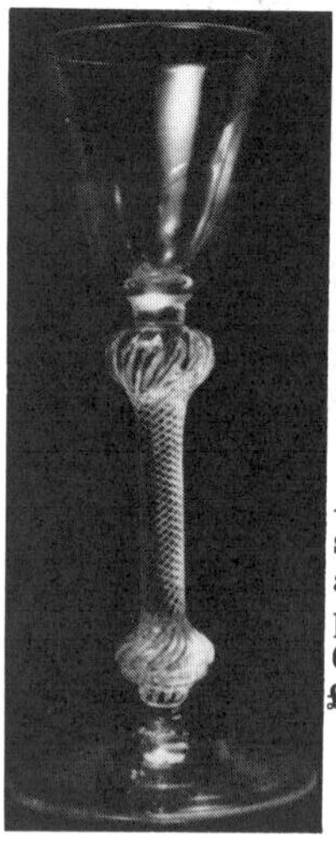

A wine glass on a multiple spiral air-twist, shoulder knop and annulated base knop, plain conical foot, c1750, 6½in (16.5cm).
£500-550 *Som*

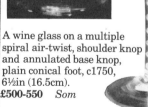

An air-twist wine glass, the bell bowl on a stem with single air-twist corkscrew, plain conical foot, c1745, 7½in (18.5cm).
£250-300 *Som*

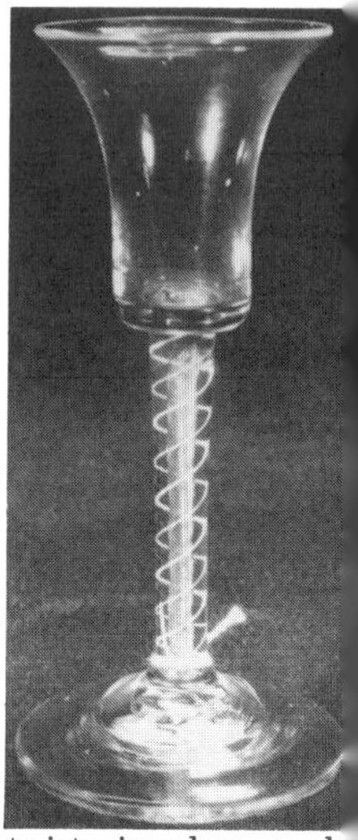

A mixed twist wine glass, on pla conical foot,c 1765, 6in (15cm).
£550-650 *Som*

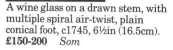

A wine glass on a drawn stem, with multiple spiral air-twist, plain conical foot, c1745, 6½in (16.5cm).
£150-200 *Som*

lasks

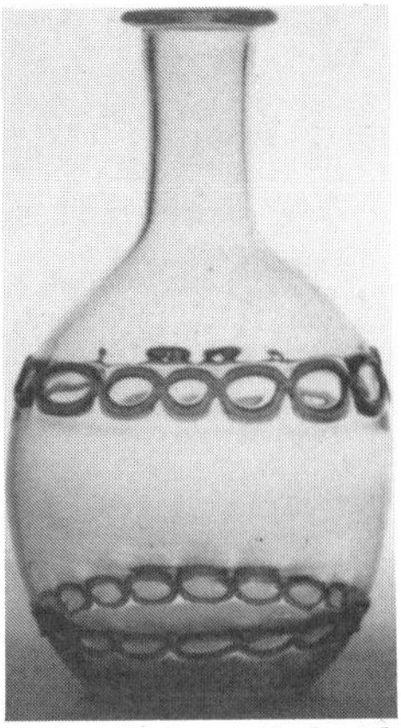

/enetian flask, applied with
ıds of turquoise chain ornament,
: neck with everted turquoise
gree rim, 17thC, 8½in (22cm).
)0-700 *C*

A pair of engraved moon flasks, painted in colours, on gilt metal bases and Buddhistic lion feet, 9½in (24cm) high.
£650-750 *CSK*

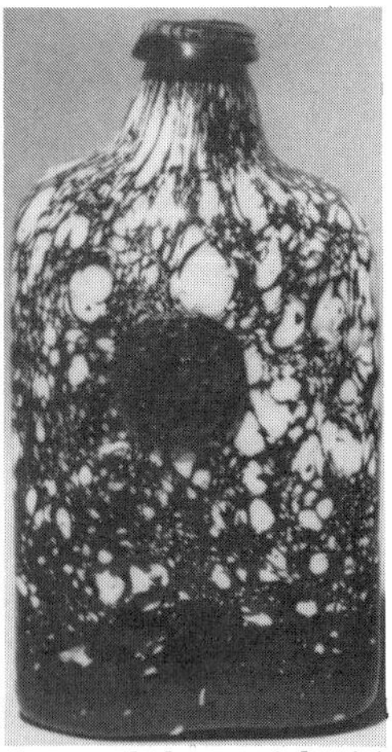

A Nailsea sealed armorial spirit flask, in olive green tint with spattered white inclusions, the neck with string ring, early 19thC, 6½in (16cm).
£1,500-2,000 *C*

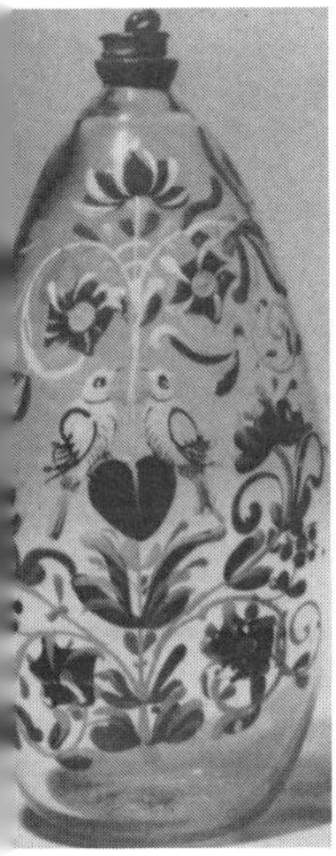

A Central European spirit flask, enamelled in iron red, blue, yellow and green, with pewter mount and screw cover, late 18thC, 7½in (19cm).
£350-450 *C*

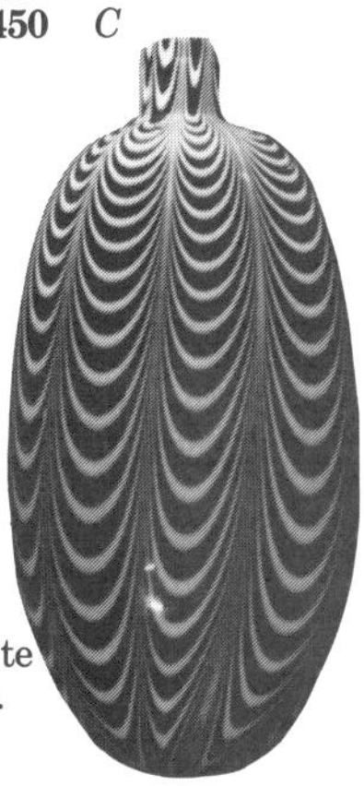

'uby flask with combed white
ping, c1860, 7½in (18.5cm).
)-100 *BAL*

l. A jelly glass with waisted body and applied handles, plain domed foot, c1800, 4in (10cm) high.
£160-200
c. A hexagon shaped jelly glass with scalloped rim, plain domed foot, c1760, 4in (10cm).
£150-180
r. A jelly glass, the conical bowl with applied handle, plain conical foot, c1820, 4½in (11cm).
£100-150 *Som*

·lly Glasses

Four jelly glasses with trumpet bowls and rudimentary stems, c1800, 3½ to 4in (9 to 10cm).
£30-50 each *Som*

l. A jelly glass with trumpet bowl on a domed foot, applied loop handle, c1760, 4½in (11cm).
£160-200
c. A hexagon shaped jelly glass with wrythen moulded bowl, domed foot, c1760, 4in (10.5cm).
£160-200
r. A jelly glass with trumpet bowl, domed foot, applied loop handle, c1780, 4½in (11cm).
£160-200 *Som*

Jugs

A rock crystal jug, engraved with flowering prunus, Stourbridge, c1885, 7½in (19cm).
£800-1,000 *C*

The engraving was possibly executed by John Orchard at Stevens & Williams, Brierley Hill.

A two-handled posset pot, with 2 applied scroll handles, chip to spout, mid-18thC, 7½in (18.5cm).
£1,000-1,500 *C*

A baluster jug, with applied scroll handle, early 18thC, 5½in (14cm).
£400-450 *C*

A clear glass claret jug, with cut a etched fruiting vine and trellis decoration, with plated mount, hi domed hinged cover and scrolling handle, 9½in (24cm).
£300-400 *HSS*

A magnum claret jug, with flute c body, 2 neck rings and applied str handle, star cut base, cut ball stopper, c1840, 10½in (27cm).
£1,000-1,500 *Som*

Paperweights

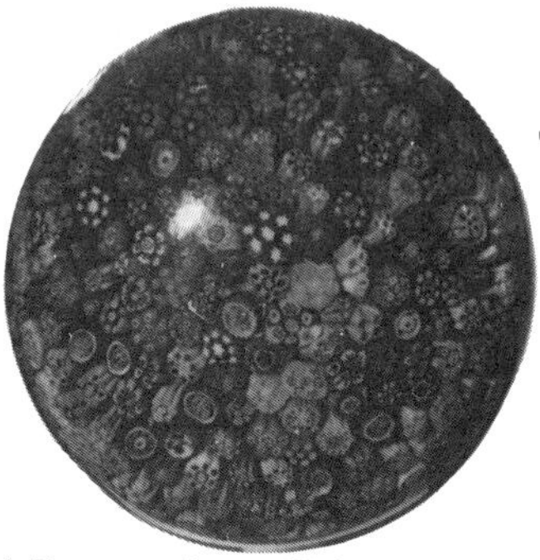

A Baccarat close millefiori weight, with closely packed brightly coloured canes including one inscribed 'B 1847', 3in (7.5cm) diam.
£500-700 *C*

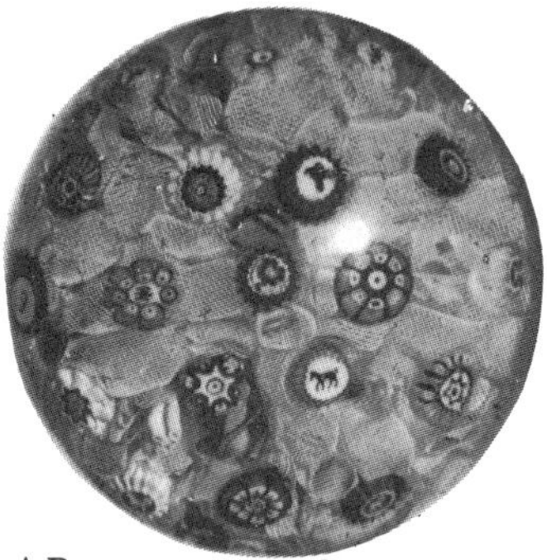

A Baccarat scattered millefiori weight, the brightly coloured canes set among short lengths of latticinio cable and coloured ribbon, one cane inscribed 'B 1848', scratched, 3in (7.5cm) diam.
£600-700 *C*

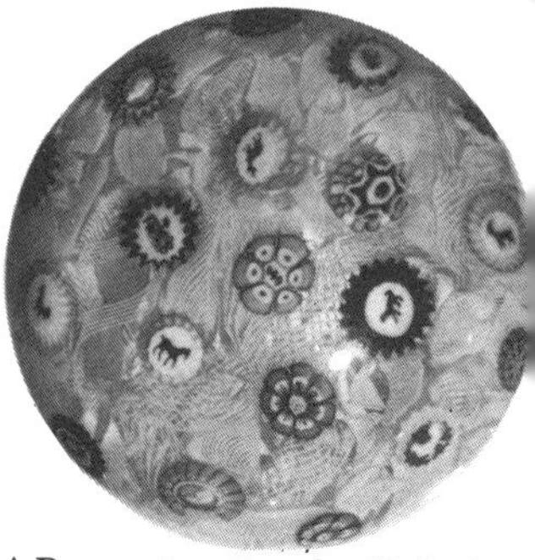

A Baccarat scattered millefiori weight, a cane inscribed 'B 1848', s among short lengths of latticinio cable and coloured ribbon, 3in (7.5cm) diam.
£600-700 *C*

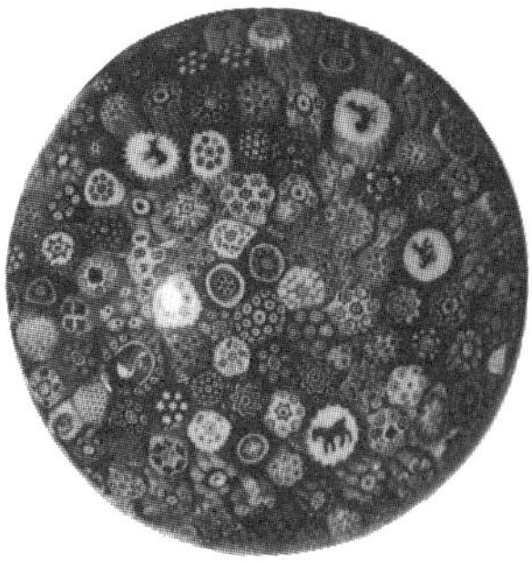

A Baccarat close millefiori weight, including 5 silhouette canes, revealing in places short lengths of latticinio ribbon, one cane inscribed 'B 1848', 3in (7.5cm) diam.
£600-800 *C*

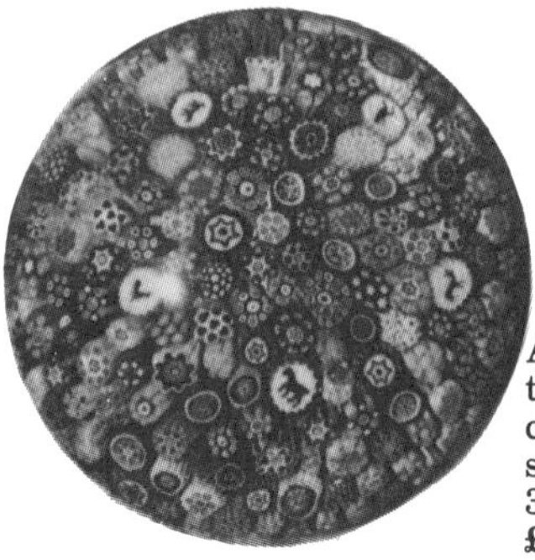

A Baccarat close millefiori weight, the closely packed brightly coloured canes with numerous animal silhouettes, one inscribed 'B 1848', 3½in (8cm) diam.
£700-800 *C*

. Baccarat scattered millefiori
eight, one cane inscribed 'B 1848',
ruised, 3½in (8cm) diam.
500-600 *C*

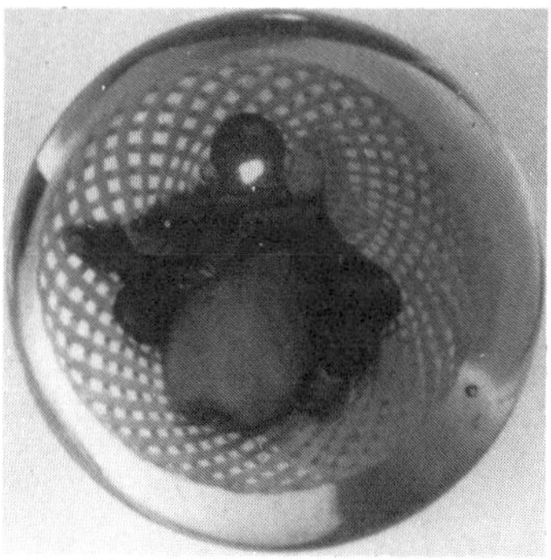

A St. Louis weight, with fruit on a cushion of opaque spiral latticinio thread, mid-19thC, 3in (7.5cm) diam.
£800-1,000 *C*

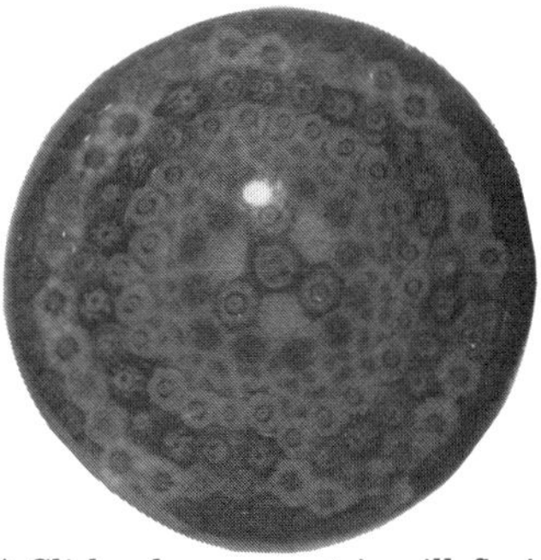

A Clichy close concentric millefiori weight, in pink, green, yellow, white and turquoise, mid-19thC, 3in (7cm) diam.
£400-500 *C*

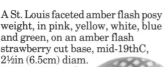

A St. Louis faceted amber flash posy weight, in pink, yellow, white, blue and green, on an amber flash strawberry cut base, mid-19thC, 2½in (6.5cm) diam.
£1,000-1,200 *C*

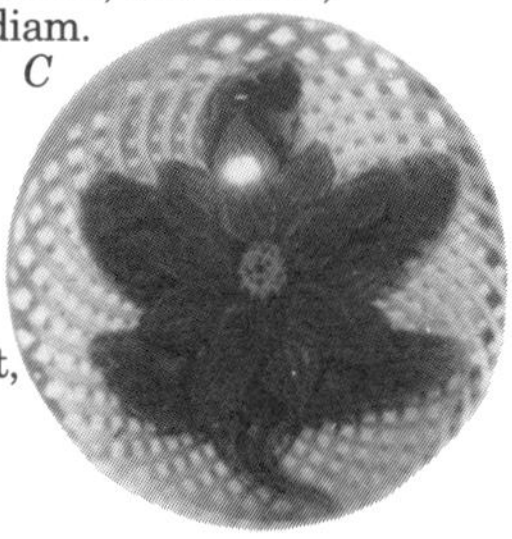

A St. Louis double clematis weight, in salmon pink, green and white, mid-19thC, 2½in (6cm) diam.
£800-1,000 *C*

A St. Louis fruit weight, surface wear, mid-19thC, 3½in (8cm) diam.
£800-1,000 *C*

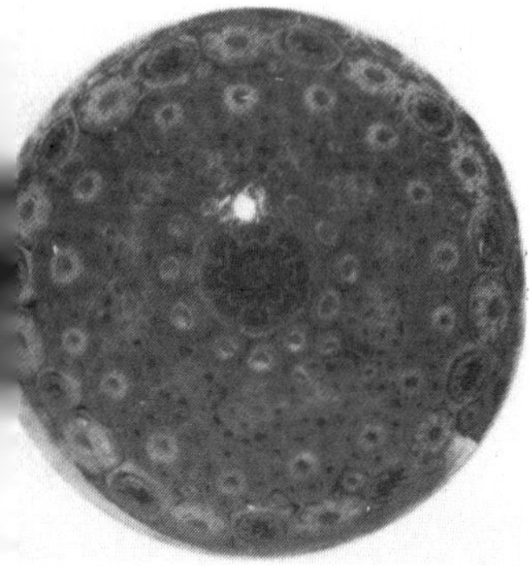

Bacchus close concentric
illefiori weight, in pink, mauve,
ue, green, white and yellow about
iron red and white petal-shaped
ne, mid-19thC, 3½in (8.5cm)
am.
00-500 *C*

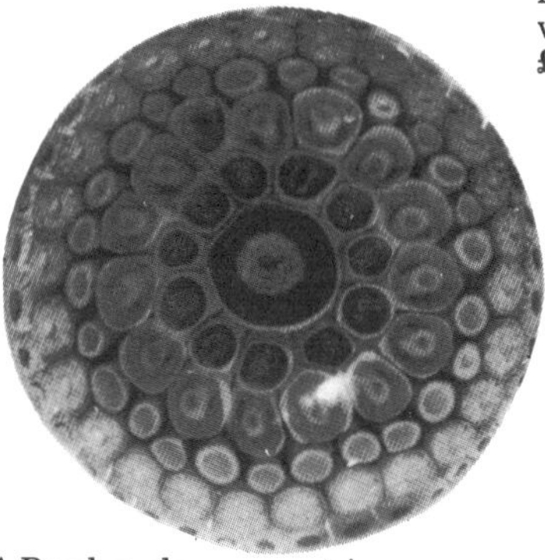

A Bacchus close concentric millefiori weight, in iron red, pale blue, cobalt blue, green and white, mid-19thC, 3½in (8.5cm) diam.
£800-1,000 *C*

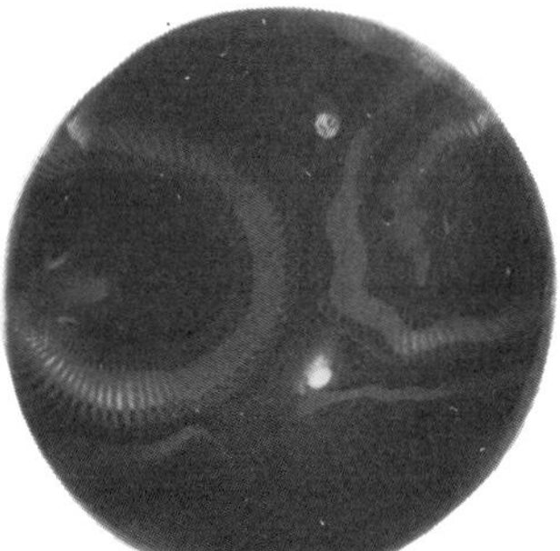

A Paul Ysart double snake pedestal weight, inscribed 'PY', on a black base, 20thC, 3in (7.5cm) diam.
£700-800 *C*

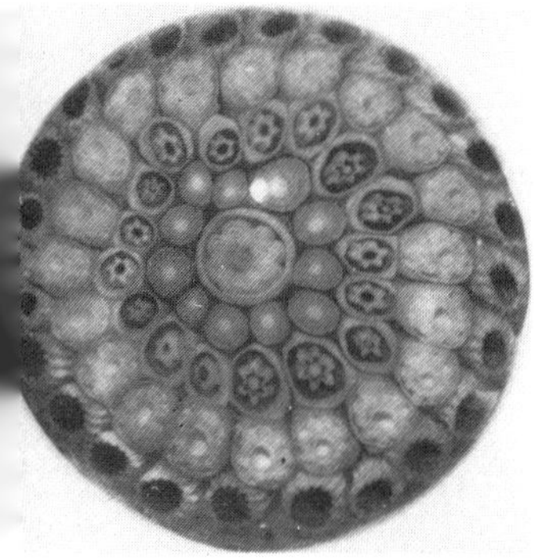

Bacchus close concentric
illefiori weight, in iron red, pale
een, blue, pink and white,
d-19thC, 3½in (8.5cm) diam.
00-400 *C*

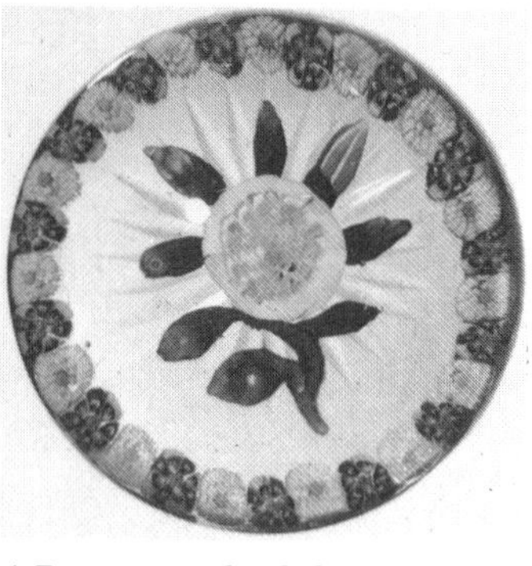

A Baccarat garlanded pompom weight, with white flower, yellow stamen, green leaves and a green and white bud, on a star cut base, mid-19thC, 3in (7.5cm) diam.
£400-600 *C*

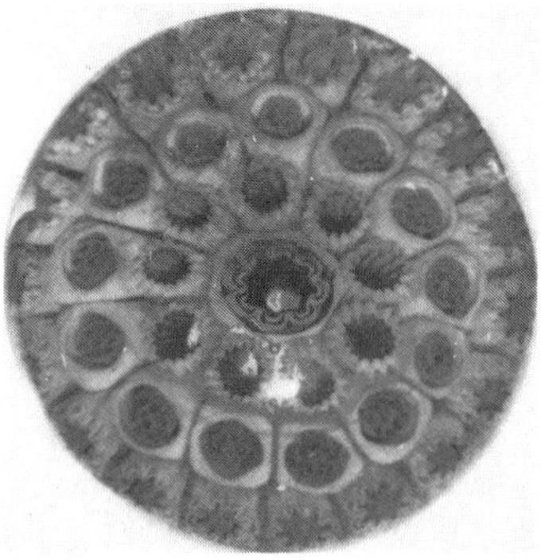

A Bacchus close concentric millefiori weight, in green, white, red, blue and mauve, mid-19thC, 3½in (8.5cm) diam.
£400-500 *C*

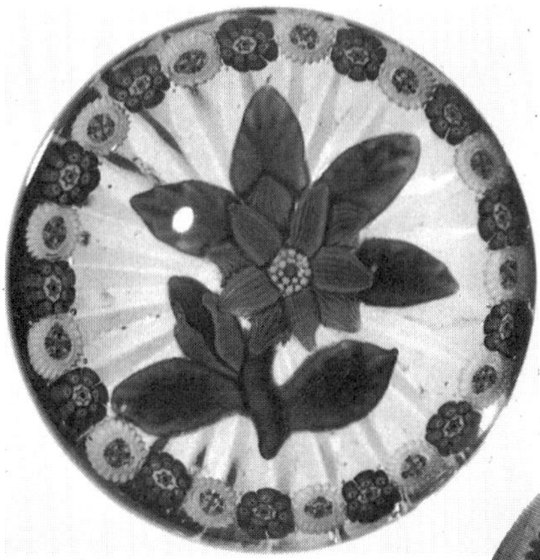

A Baccarat garlanded double clematis weight, the flower with ribbed pale mauve petals about a red and white star centre, set within a garland of alternate red and white canes, on a star cut base, mid-19thC, 2½in (6.5cm) diam.
£600-800 *C*

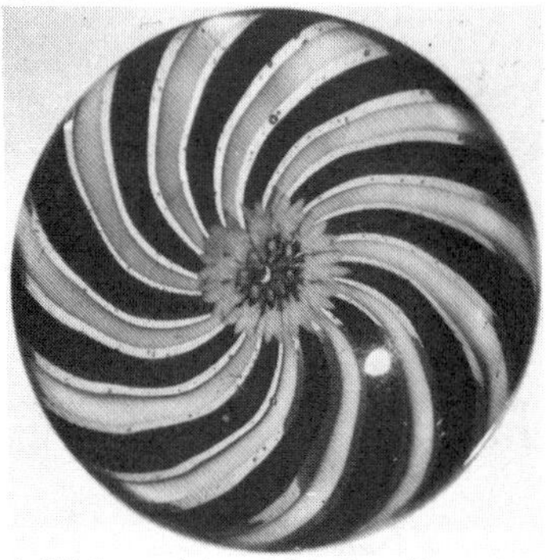

A Clichy swirl weight, the alternate dark green and white staves radiating from a central set-up of yellow rods and white star canes, mid-19thC, 3in (7cm) diam.
£400-700 *C*

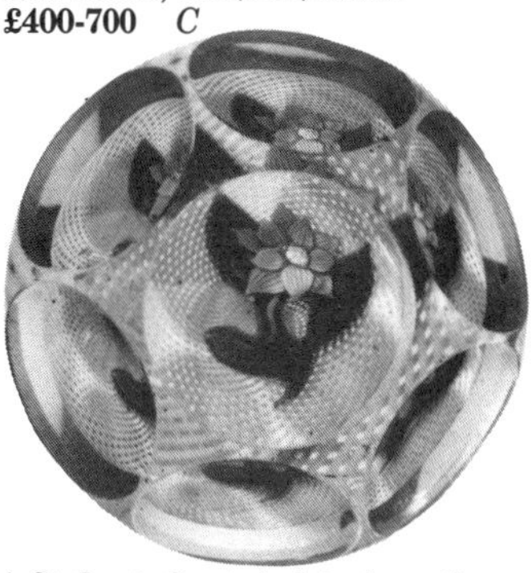

A St. Louis faceted pink clematis weight, set on a cushion of white swirling latticinio thread, cut with a window and 6 printies, mid-19thC, 3in (7.5cm) diam.
£400-600 *C*

A Bacchus close millefiori weight, the tightly packed large canes in shades of turquoise, white, pale green, pink and brick red and including numerous portrait silhouette canes, mid-19thC, 3½in (8.5cm) diam.
£500-600 *C*

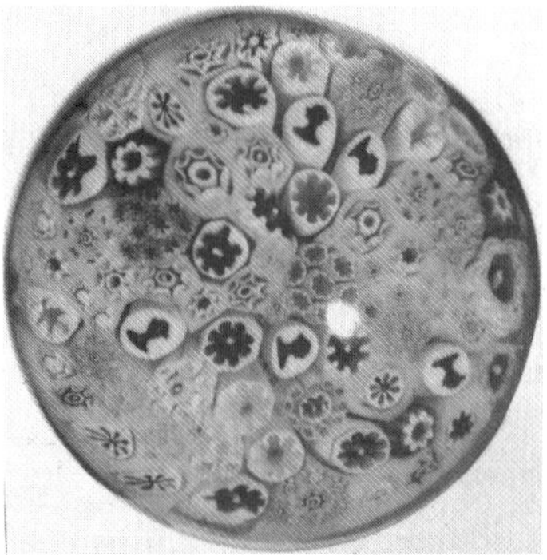

A Baccarat miniature primrose weight, inscribed on the base 18 4/72, mid-19thC, 2in (5cm) diam.
£800-1,000 *C*

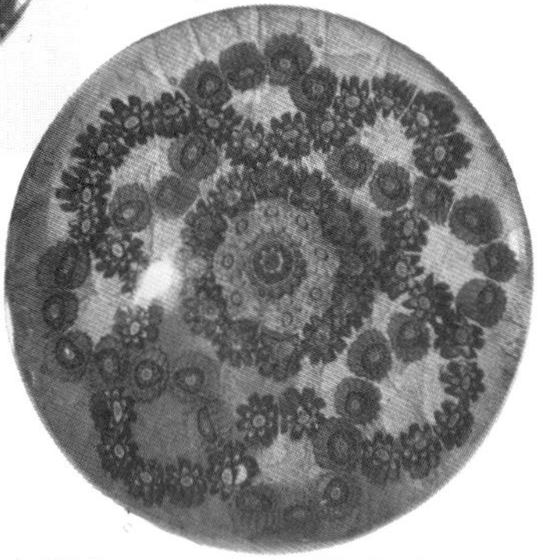

A Clichy patterned millefiori weight, in pale green, shades of dark blue and pink, on a muslin ground above a bed of horizontal cable, mid-19thC, 3½in (8cm) diam.
£400-700 *C*

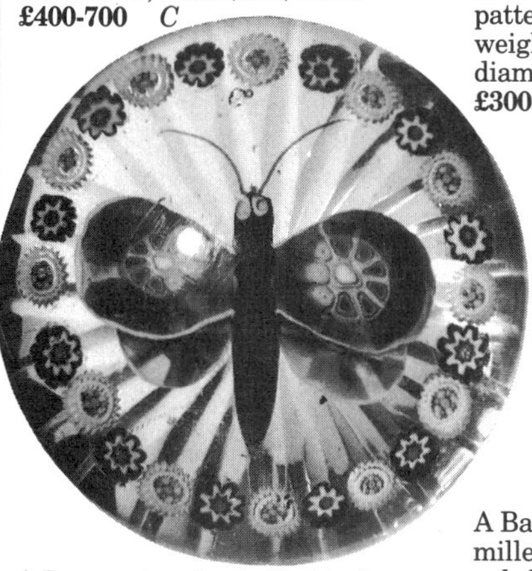

A Baccarat garlanded butterfly weight, the insect with translucent purple body and marbled wings, set within a garland of alternate pink, green and white canes, on a star cut base, chipping to footrim, mid-19thC, 2½in (6.5cm) diam.
£800-1,000 *C*

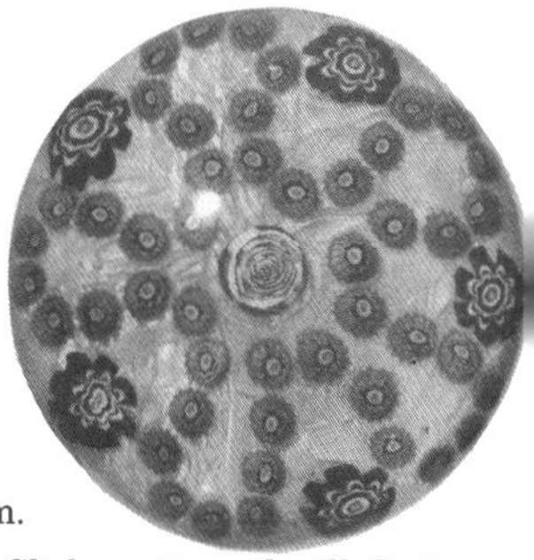

A Clichy patterned millefiori weight, with a tossed muslin ground above a bed of horizontal cable, mid-19thC, 3in (7cm) diam.
£700-900 *C*

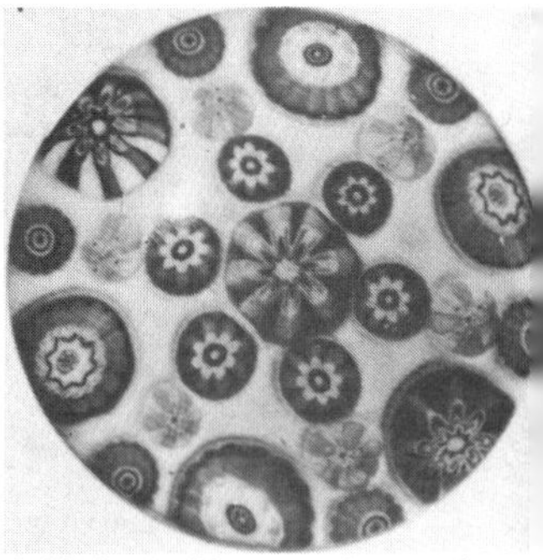

A Clichy 'sodden snow' ground patterned concentric millefiori weight, mid-19thC, 3½in (8.5cm) diam.
£300-400 *C*

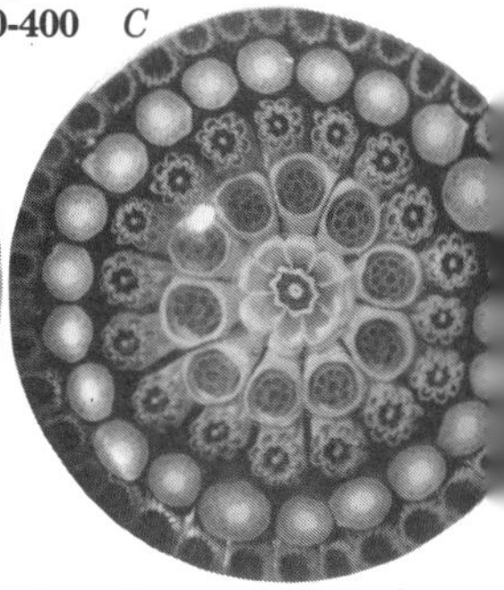

A Bacchus close concentric millefiori weight, in shades of pink, pale blue, dark blue, green and white within an outer circle of pale green lined white crimped tubes, mid-19thC, 3½in (8cm) diam.
£700-800 *C*

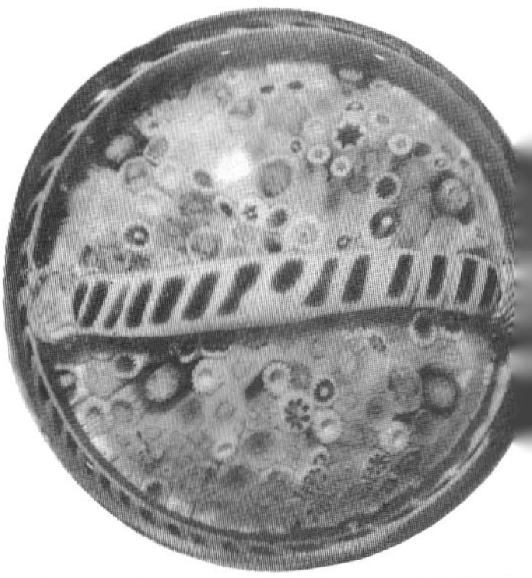

A Bacchus encased close millefiori basket weight, the tightly packed canes in predominant pale shades white, red, turquoise and blue, mid-19thC, 4in (10cm) diam.
£1,500-2,000 *C*

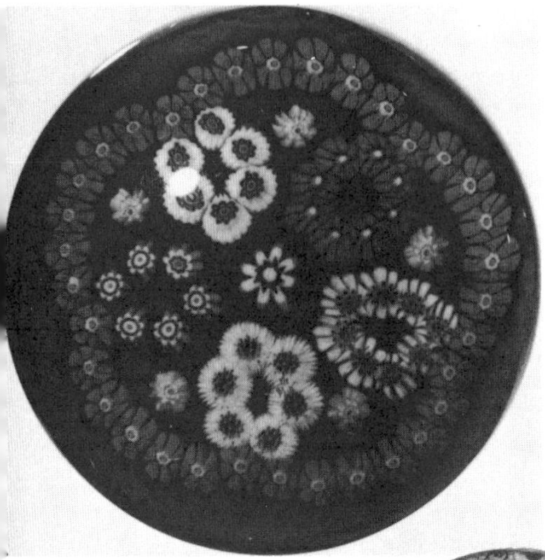

Clichy blue ground patterned millefiori weight, in pink, white, blue and green, set on a bright blue ground, bruised, mid-19thC, 3½in (8.5cm) diam.
300-400 *C*

A Baccarat garlanded double clematis weight, in rust red, white green and claret, on a star cut base, mid-19thC, 2½in (6.5cm) diam.
£500-800 *C*

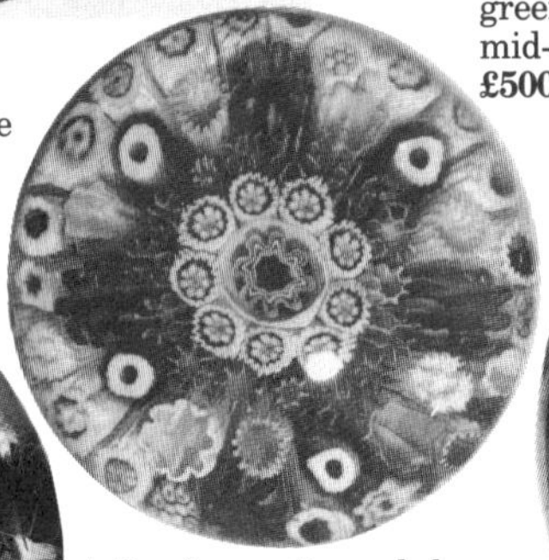

A Bacchus patterned close concentric millefiori weight, in pink, blue, white, pale turquoise and yellow, with an outer circle of pale green lined crimped tubes, mid-19thC, 3½in (8cm) diam.
£500-700 *C*

St. Louis crown weight, the lternate orange and green twisted ibbon and latticinio spirals adiating from a central lime green, ink and white set-up, mid-19thC, ½in (6cm) diam.
700-1,000 *C*

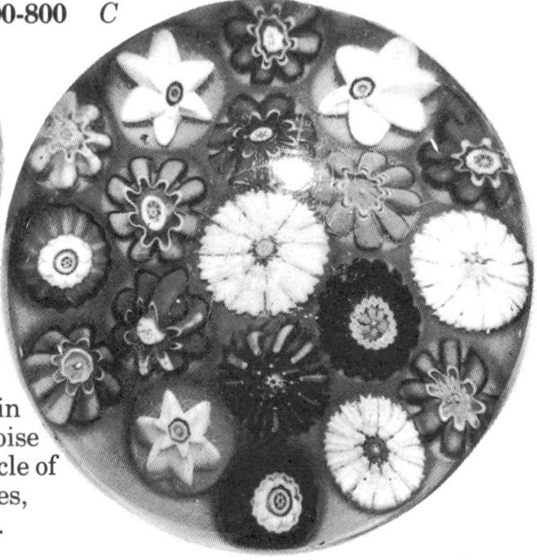

A Clichy pink ground scattered millefiori weight, the brightly coloured canes set on an opaque dark pink ground, mid-19thC, 2½in (6.5cm) diam.
£350-550 *C*

A Clichy pink ground patterned millefiori weight, in shades of pale green, pink, white and blue canes, set on an opaque pink ground, mid-19thC, 3in (7.5cm) diam.
£400-500 *C*

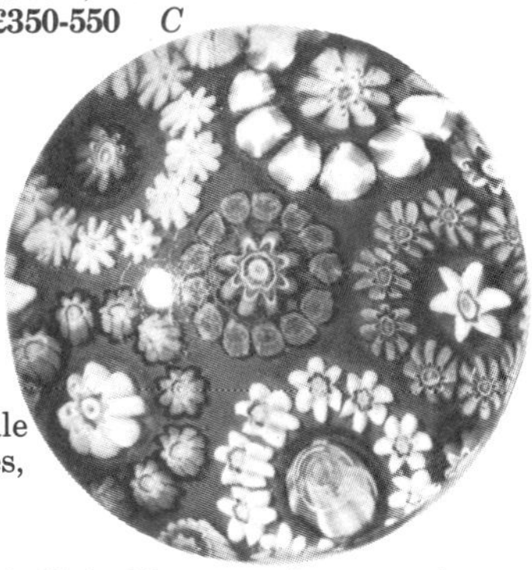

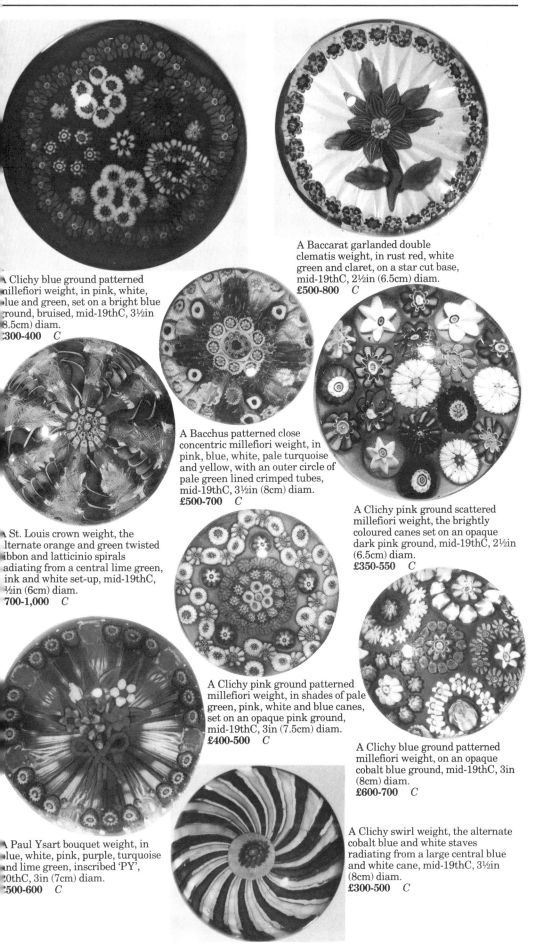

A Clichy blue ground patterned millefiori weight, on an opaque cobalt blue ground, mid-19thC, 3in (8cm) diam.
£600-700 *C*

Paul Ysart bouquet weight, in lue, white, pink, purple, turquoise nd lime green, inscribed 'PY', 0thC, 3in (7cm) diam.
500-600 *C*

A Clichy swirl weight, the alternate cobalt blue and white staves radiating from a large central blue and white cane, mid-19thC, 3½in (8cm) diam.
£300-500 *C*

Scent Bottles

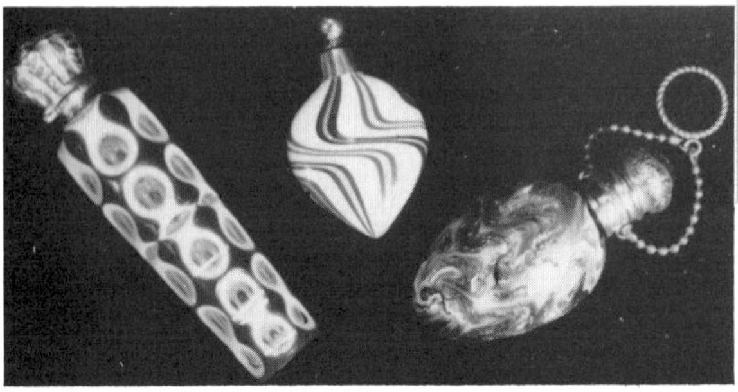

l. A clear scent bottle, with white and blue overlay, embossed white metal mount, c1860, 4in (10.5cm).
£300-350
c. A Nailsea type white opaque scent bottle, with red and blue swirls, gilt brass mounts, c1860, 2½in (6cm).
£70-100
r. A Venetian style scent bottle, with spangled inclusions, gilt brass mount and finger ring, c1820, 3in (7.5cm).
£60-100 *Som*

A Victorian cut glass scent bottl with gold cased mount.
£30-60 *AD*

An Apsley Pellatt anti-slavery sulphide scent bottle and stopper, allover with hobnail within diamond cutting, slight bruising to rim and stopper, c1830, 6in (15cm).
£1,200-1,500 *C*

A Bohemian double overlay scent bottle, 3½in (9cm).
£120-150 *AD*

A scent bottle, Birmingham, c1904, 2½in (6.5cm).
£80-100 *HF*

l. A blue double-ended scent bottle, with gilt metal mounts, c1870, 4in (10cm).
£70-100
c. A red single-ended scent bottle, with embossed silver mount, hallmark 1876, 2½in (6.5cm).
£60-100
r. A red double-ended scent bottle, with embossed silver mounts, c1880, 4¼in (10.5cm).
£70-100 *Som*

A Victorian green double overlay scent bottle, 7in (17.5cm).
£125-150 *AD*

A cut glass perfume bottle, with gilt top, 6½in (17cm).
£30-60 *THA*

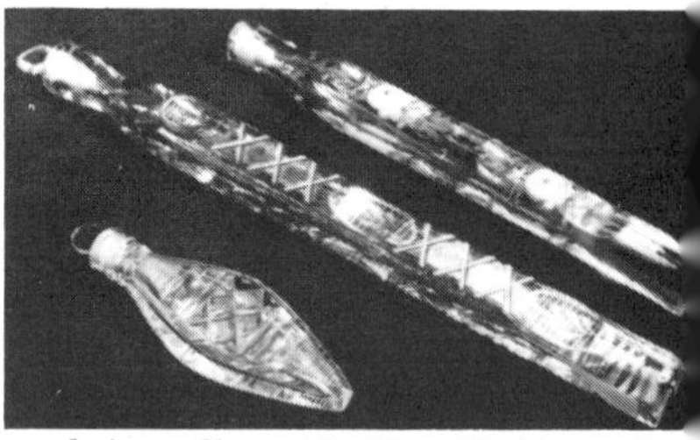

l. A small scent bottle with diamond and flute cutting, c1820, 3in (8cm).
£70-90
c. An Oxford lavender or throw-away scent bottle, with cut and gilt decoration, c1880, 8½in (21.5cm).
£50-70
r. A small scent bottle with enamelled floral decoration, c1880, 6in (15cm).
£50-70 *Som*

A French blue opaque glass scent bottle, decorated in gilt with berried foliage, gilt metal hinged cover and chain, 3in (7.5cm).
£60-80 *P(S)*

A French glass and gold mounted perfume flask, the shoulders engraved with rococo scrolls and flowers, the gold jacket and domed hinged cover embossed and chased in rococo style and with engraved monogram, 4½in (11.5cm).
£350-450 *P(S)*

Vases

clear glass vase, designed by lyne Farquharson, the body ecorated in the Leaf pattern of cut eaves on engraved sinuous stems, ngraved Clyne Farquharson RD 39, 10in (25cm).
250-350 *CSK*

pair of Bohemian lustre vases, ach with enamelled floral panels to he top, white overlaid bases and llover scrolling gilt decoration and ung with prism drops and zenges, late 19thC, 13in (34cm).
700-800 *DDM*

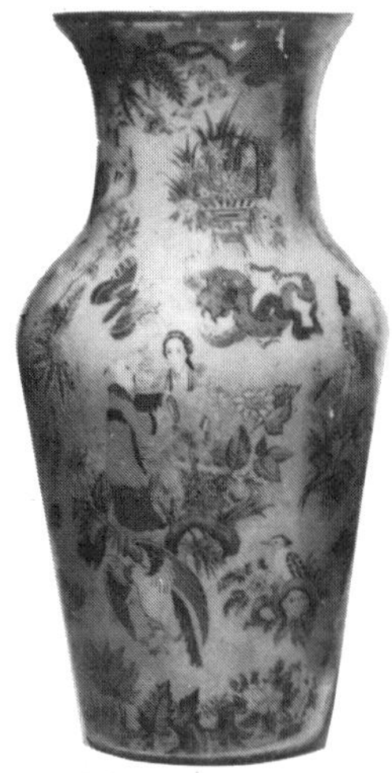

pair of decalomania vases, ecorated with coloured transfers, shades of blue, yellow and green buff grounds, some repainting to e interior, mid-19thC, 12in 0.5cm).
3,500-4,500 *C*

A decalomania vase and cover, decorated with coloured transfers on a bright blue ground, one transfer lacking to cover and damage to decoration, mid-19thC, 9in (23cm).
£500-600 *C*

A pair of Victorian pink opaque glass lustre vases, with white enamelled decoration, bordered in gilt, 14in (36cm).
£550-650 *DDM*

An opaque white vase, with enamelled decoration of exotic birds in a chinoiserie scene, South Staffs. or London, c1760, 5in (13.5cm).
£1,000-2,000 *Som*

Miscellaneous

A pair of Bohemian enamelled and gilt overlay vases, in dark cranberry glass overlaid in opaque white, the panels painted in colours, damaged, 17in (43cm).
£550-650 *HSS*

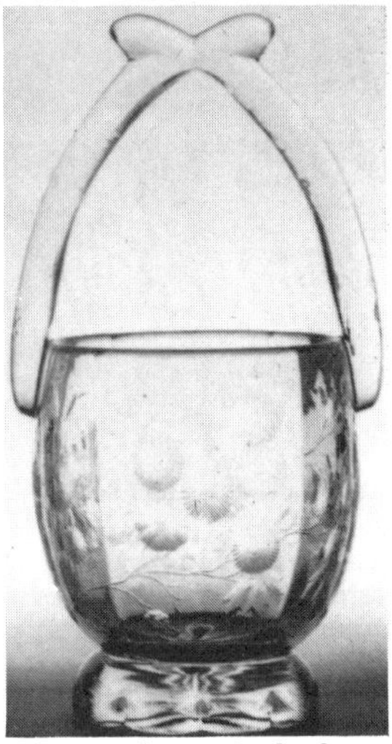

A rock crystal vase, in the form of a basket, Stourbridge, c1885, 9in (23cm).
£750-1,000 *C*

A Bohemian chinoiserie reverse painted and cut plate, the centre painted in colours with a youth standing holding an apple in one hand beside an exotic bird on a perch, possibly Buquoy Glasshouse, South Bohemia, border crazed, rim damaged, c1835, 8½in (21cm) diam, wood frame.
£400-600 *C*

A pair of Regency cut glass inkwells, c1820, 2½in (6cm) high.
£85-100 *CA*

OAK & COUNTRY FURNITURE

Beds

An oak cradle, with shaped hood and sides, basically 17thC, 36½in (92cm) long.
£600-800 *CSK*

An oak four-poster bed of panelled construction, the headboard with inlaid arched architectural panel, the tester carved with lozenges and foliage with foliate cornice, on bulbous turned posts, the footboard carved with lozenges, with box spring, 76in (193cm) long.
£3,500-4,500 *C*

Bureaux

A George III oak bureau bookcase, with mahogany frieze, the hinged slope enclosing a fitted interior, on bracket feet, 50½in (128cm).
£1,000-1,500 *CSK*

A George II oak bureau, with engraved brass plate handles and escutcheons, the interior fitted with stepped drawers, a centre cupboard and sunken well, on bracket feet, 36in (91.5cm).
£1,600-2,000 *MAT*

A George III oak bureau, with fitted interior, 2 short and 3 graduated long drawers, on bracket feet, adapted, 32in (81cm).
£1,200-1,500 *CSK*

A Queen Anne oak bureau, c1710.
£2,500-3,500 *PHA*

A George III oak bureau bookcase, c1760.
£6,000-9,000 *PHA*

A small Queen Anne oak burea bookcase, c1700.
£8,000-12,000 *PHA*

Cabinets

A Flemish cabinet-on-stand, heavily carved, the stand with dee frieze centred by a roundel of a trumpeting angel flanked by putti on bulbous turned sectional legs an ebonised feet, legs restored, early 17thC, 29½in (75cm).
£3,000-4,000 *C*

A fruitwood bureau cabinet, the sloping flap enclosing 6 small drawers, 2 short and 2 long drawers below, on bracket feet, 18th/19thC, 37in (94cm).
£2,500-3,500 *Bea*

:hairs

.n oak open armchair, the toprail
/ith foliate scrolls, solid seat, on
ırned legs, with stretchers, 17thC.
2,500-3,500 *C*

An oak open armchair, carved with a lozenge, with solid seat on turned legs with stretchers, lacking cresting, restored, 17thC.
£1,200-1,700 *C*

A Charles II carved oak wainscot chair, c1680.
£3,000-4,000 *PHA*

.n oak wainscot chair, the square
ack with carved shaped arched
resting rail flanked by scroll ears,
arved with the initials 'H.F.'
.anking the date '1612', raised upon
arrel turned and block supports
nd plain stretchers.
250-300 *HSS*

A set of 6 Charles II style Derbyshire elm and oak dining chairs, the foliate waved rail backs above leather seats on baluster legs with stretchers.
£600-1,000 *CSK*

A Queen Anne oak armchair, the frieze initialled JL, dated in numerals 1710, the arms with S-scroll supports, with solid seat and shaped seat rail on S-scroll and squared legs, with stretchers, back legs replaced.
£900-1,200 *C*

Charles II oak child's chair, the
prail with scrolled ends and the
itials RT, the arms with turned
ipports, with solid seat on squared
ıd turned legs with moulded
retchers.
',500-8,500 *C*

A pair of oak dining chairs, the canework seats on turned baluster and block supports, ending in tassled toes, joined by turned baluster stretchers, each chair initialled IP, late 17thC and later.
£1,500-2,000 *CEd*

A pair of oak hall chairs, with barley twist supports, upholstered seats, plain front legs with scrolling front stretchers, 18thC.
£350-450 *DDM*

A set of eight 17thC style oak dining chairs, including a pair of armchairs, with leaf and scroll carved pierced top rails, splat backs, panel seats on turned front supports.
£1,200-1,600 *P(M)*

An oak side chair, c1700.
£600-750 *PHA*

A set of 9 Restoration style carved oak chairs, with ornate leaf scroll and flower decorated high backs, overstuffed seats, raised understretchers and cabriole legs with paw feet, 19thC.
£2,000-3,000 *AH*

A pair of George I oak side chairs, c1725.
£800-1,200 *PHA*

A comb back Windsor armchair, with scrolled arms above a shaped seat, on baluster turned splayed legs joined by a bulbous turned H-stretcher, Pennsylvania, loss to bottom of one arm, c1800.
£2,700-3,200 *CNY*

A William and Mary painted maple side chair, on cylinder and ring turned front legs joined by a double arrow and ring turned stretcher, Essex County, Massachusetts, c1745.
£650-1,000 *CNY*

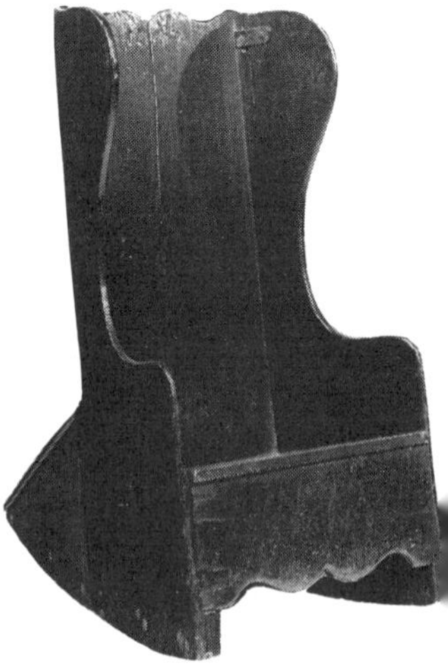

A George III child's oak rocking chair, of plain plank construction with shaped sides.
£300-350 *Bon*

A pair of bow back Windsor side chairs, each with bowed crest above bamboo turned spindles, ov a shaped seat on bamboo turned le joined by an H-stretcher, one branded Sanborn, Boston, Massachusetts, c1799, 37in (94cm
£1,000-1,500 *CNY*

A cherrywood comb back Winds armchair, c1760.
£1,500-2,500 *PHA*

Welsh elm child's chair, with ıaped top rail over spindle back, all ıised on splay supports, ıid-18thC, 14in (36cm) high.
650-750 *P(M)*

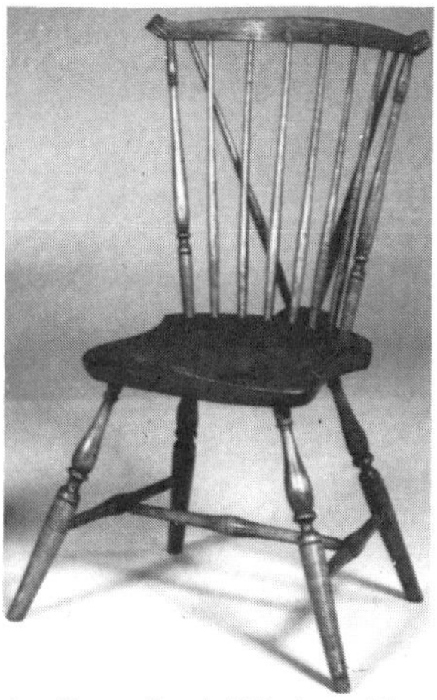

A pair of brace back Windsor side chairs, on baluster and ring turned legs joined by swelled stretchers, New England, late 18th/early 19thC.
£2,000-3,000 *CNY*

A slat back maple armchair, with ball and ring turned finials and flat arms, above a rush seat, on cylinder-and-ball turned legs joined by a double turned stretcher, New York or Connecticut, late 18thC.
£2,200-2,700 *CNY*

George III elm armchair, c1780.
'50-1,200 *PHA*

A fan back Windsor armchair, with curved and scalloped crest rail over 7 spindles flanked by baluster turned stiles, above a shaped seat on splayed baluster turned legs, joined by a bulbous turned H-stretcher, Massachusetts, feet reduced, c1800.
£450-700 *CNY*

A set of 6 elm spindle back chairs, c1820.
£1,500-2,000 *PCA*

Did you know

MILLER'S Antiques Price Guide builds up year by year to form the most comprehensive photo-reference system available

Windsor sack back armchair, on ıluster and ring turned legs joined ' turned stretchers, New England, ·thC.
,000-1,500 *CNY*

An 18thC style ladder back carver chair, with rush seat, on turned legs and stretcher.
£150-200 *DDM*

A Windsor bench, with incised arched crest above bamboo spindles over scrolled walnut arms, on bamboo turned legs joined by bamboo turned stretchers, Philadelphia, late 18th/early 19thC.
£7,500-8,500 *CNY*

A low bow armchair, with stick and fiddle back, on turned legs.
£300-400 *MGM*

A set of 6 ash matched ladderback chairs, c1810.
£3,000-3,500 *OS*

A set of 6 elm Windsor wheelback chairs, c1830.
£1,500-2,000 *PCA*

An Irish ash and elm famine chair, in original colour, Kerry, c1840, 21in (54cm).
£300-400 *UC*

A large oak elbow hall chair and matching set of 4 single chairs, carved in Jacobean style, supported on turned and carved feet with barley twist stretchers, each upholstered and covered to the back and seat with brown leather, 19thC.
£550-600 *DDM*

A pair of elm Windsor chairs, with crinoline stretchers, early 19thC.
£450-500 *PCA*

An English beech and elm child's bow armchair, c1920.
£100-150 *UC*

A set of 6 Windsor wheelback kitchen chairs, 19thC.
£550-600 *HCH*

A Lincolnshire yew and elm Windsor chair, the high hoop back with pierced splat flanked by dowels, on baluster turned supports terminating in stylised hoof feet, tied by a crinoline stretcher.
£550-650 *HSS*

A primitive child's chair, with original red paint, 19thC, 18in (46cm).
£180-250 *PCA*

An elm chair, late 18thC.
£120-160 *PCA*

A set of 4 black-painted fan-back Windsor chairs, on splayed bamboo urned legs joined by a bulbous H-stretcher, New England, 19thC.
:1,500-2,000 *CNY*

black painted Windsor child's rmchair, with shaped n-back above 7 spindles and at-shaped set back arms over a addle seat, on splayed baluster urned legs joined by a bulbous urned H-stretcher, 19thC.
400-700 *CNY*

yew wood bow arm high back 'indsor chair, with pierced splat, lid seat, turned legs and stretcher.
500-800 *DDM*

An English beech and elm carver chair, Sussex, c1870.
£225-275 *UC*

An Irish stripped beech and elm smoker's chair, c1875.
£230-270 *UC*

A set of 5 Irish beechwood penny seat and stick back chairs, c1890.
£400-500 *UC*

Locate the source

The source of each illustration in Miller's can be found by checking the code letters below each caption with the list of contributors

A set of 4 beech and elm children's stick back chairs, c1880, 26in (66cm).
£400-500 *UC*

A yew wood low back Windsor chair, on turned supports with crinoline stretcher, early 19thC.
£500-600 *DDM*

An English beech and elm spindle back Windsor rocking chair, Lancashire, c1860.
£450-500 *UC*

A Continental parcel gilt oak throne, the upholstered back with crowned fleur-de-lys crest, the sides with foliate fretwork panels, on X-frame supports, 19thC.
£1,200-1,500 *Bon*

A Charles II oak panelled box settle, c1680.
£2,500-4,000 *PHA*

An oak coffer with panelled top and front, shaped cornice and the legs formed from the reeded side stiles, 17th/18thC, 42in (106.5cm).
£600-700 *GAK*

An oak chest, the hinged top above an angled, panelled front with 2 short and one long drawer, on hig[h] bracket feet, early 18thC, 34in (86cm).
£1,500-2,000 *Bon*

A small oak panelled box settle, c1760.
£2,500-3,500 *PHA*

A small Charles I oak arcaded and inlaid coffer, c1625.
£2,000-3,500 *PHA*

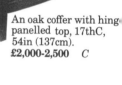

An oak coffer with hing[ed] panelled top, 17thC, 54in (137cm).
£2,000-2,500 *C*

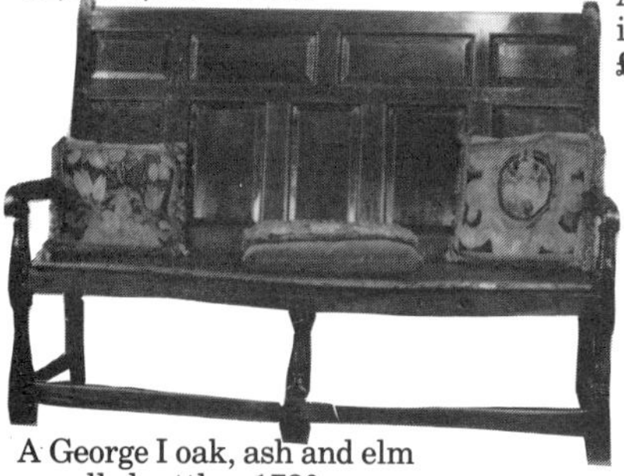

A George I oak, ash and elm panelled settle, c1720.
£1,500-2,000 *PHA*

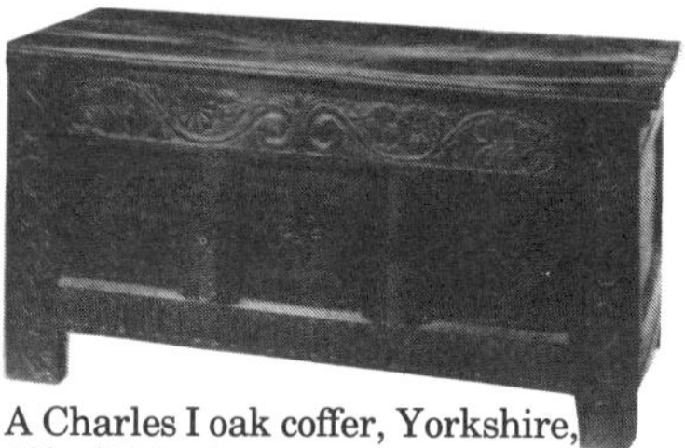

A Charles I oak coffer, Yorkshire, 49in (124cm).
£650-700 *Bon*

An oak chest-on-stand, with two short and 3 graduated long drawe[rs], the stand with 3 small drawers, o[n] inverted cupped baluster legs and cross stretchers, basically 18thC, 40in (101.5cm).
£1,200-1,600 *CSK*

An oak high wing back settle, of concave form, the seat with 2 drawers, 18thC, 50in (127cm).
£1,000-1,500 *DDM*

A carved oak arcaded coffer, c1660.
£2,500-3,500 *PHA*

A German metal bound oak coffer, with embossed bands, enclosed by a domed lid, with intricate lock mechanism and side carrying handles, on later turned feet, 18thC, 60in (152cm).
£750-1,000 *CSK*

Chests

An oak chest, with moulded hinged lid, on square channelled legs, West Country, early 17thC, 57in (145cm).
£2,000-2,500 *C*

A George III oak chest, with 2 short and 3 long graduated drawers, on bracket feet, altered, 36in (91cm).
£500-600 *MGM*

n oak coffer, late 17thC.
,200-1,500 *OS*

A Welsh oak coffer bach with drawer, c1750.
£1,500-2,500 *PHA*

n oak coffer, the carved panelled p above an S-scroll carved frieze d 3 lozenge carved panels, the ron bearing the date 1659, 47in 20cm).
00-600 *Bon*

An oak mule chest, with arched fielded panels to front and 2 drawers below.
£350-450 *MGM*

A Jacobean oak chest, in 2 sections, fitted with 4 panelled drawers, on later bun feet, 39½in (100cm).
£800-1,200 *CSK*

A Charles II carved oak boarded chest, c1670, 50½in (128cm).
£1,600-2,200 *PHA*

A Charles II oak mule chest, with hinged top above 3 arched panels and a long triple-panelled drawer, on later bun feet, 56in (142cm).
£800-1,200 *C*

n oak and alnut chest th 4 drawers, te 17thC, 36in 1.5cm).
00-1,200 *SWO*

A Jacobean oak chest, in 2 sections with plain top and 4 drawers, brass escutcheons and drop handles, on bun feet, 42in (106.5cm).
£650-750 *DDM*

A Charles II carved oak panelled coffer, c1680.
£1,500-2,500 *PHA*

A William and Mary burr oak chest of drawers, inlaid with fruitwood, c1695.
£3,500-5,000 *PHA*

A small oak chest of 4 drawers, with original brasses, c1745.
£1,500-2,500 *PHA*

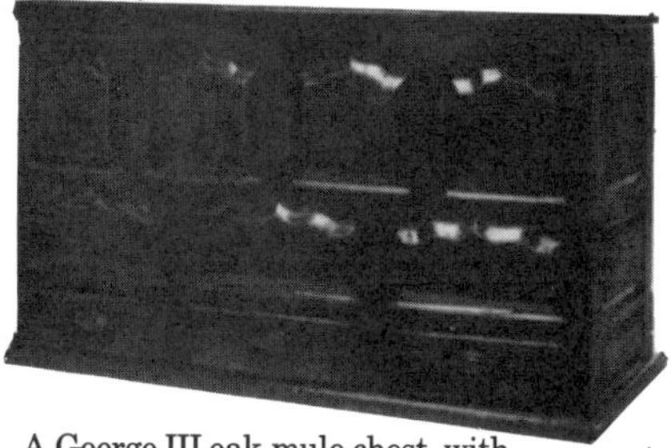

A George III oak mule chest, with hinged moulded top, above a panelled front filled with ogee arches and fitted with 3 short drawers, distressed, 59½in (150cm).
£800-1,200 *CSK*

An oak chest, with moulded top above 3 geometrically panelled graduated long drawers, on bun feet, restorations, late 17thC.
£1,500-2,000 *CSK*

Cupboards

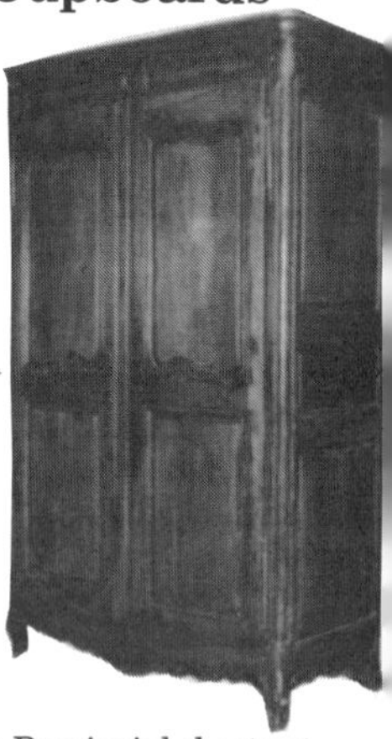

A French Provincial chestnut armoire, the shaped apron carved with a heart, on cabriole feet, 18th(later moulded cornice, 62in (157cm
£1,500-2,000 *C*

A French Provincial oak bas armoire, with frieze drawer, arche panel cupboard door, on square fee some restoration, late 18thC.
£600-700 *Bon*

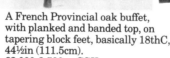

A small Jacbobean oak chest, with moulded drawer fronts, on bunfeet, 33in (84cm).
£400-450 *DDM*

A French Provincial oak buffet, with planked and banded top, on tapering block feet, basically 18thC, 44½in (111.5cm).
£2,000-2,500 *CSK*

A carved oak blanket box, on stum feet, 50½in (128cm).
£300-400 *OL*

An oak coffer, some restoration required, 53in (134.5cm).
£900-1,000 *DRU*

An oak blanket box, the lid with a moulded edge above a 3 panelled front carved with the initials E.D., 48in (122cm).
£400-450 *OL*

A French Provincial fruitwood buffet, with serpentine moulded to on squat cabriole legs, late 18thC, 52in (132cm).
£1,000-1,500 *CSK*

ı oak press, the panelled top above
noulded and carved frieze centred
 the initials 'AR' and the date
707', the base fitted with
lrawers above a pair of panelled
pboard doors, on moulded square
pports, basically 18thC, 75in
90cm).
,000-3,000 *CEd*

A French Provincial oak armoire, with moulded cornice, on rounded block feet, the interior with shelves and 2 drawers, 18thC, 62in (157cm).
£3,500-4,500 *C*

An oak cupboard, carved with tracery and foliage, on square uprights joined by an undertier, 17thC and later, 45in (114cm).
£3,000-3,500 *CSK*

A George II oak press, with moulded cornice, the base with 3 short and 2 long drawers, on block feet, the top and base possibly associated, 55in (140cm).
£1,500-2,000 *C*

An oak cupboard with moulded top, on square feet, mid-17thC, 62½in (158cm).
£3,000-3,500 *AH*

'rench Provincial chestnut
noire, with arched cornice,
oors each with pierced brass
utcheons, 3 drawers below, on
ıat cabriole legs, early 19thC,
n (157cm).
000-2,500 *CSK*

An oak court cupboard, the slight projecting base with moulded edge, the frieze carved with leaves and arcading, over cupboards enclosed by a pair of 3 panelled doors with later steel hinges, raised upon fluted extended stile supports, married, 17thC, 55in (139cm).
£1,500-2,000 *HSS*

An oak court cupboard, South Wales, c1690.
£5,000-8,000 *PHA*

An oak court cupboard, ornately carved in flind fret style, with scrolling leaves and motifs, late 17th/early 18thC, 52in (132cm).
£800-1,000 *DDM*

An oak cupboard, with moulded cornice above 2 panelled doors, on moulded plinth and later bun feet, reduced in depth, mid-17thC, 58½in (148cm).
£4,000-5,000 *C*

A bowfront corner cupboard with double doors, 19thC.
£500-550 *JH*

A Flemish oak cupboard, with moulded cornice, 2 pairs of ebony-set panelled doors divided by stop-fluted uprights and on later massive bun feet, 17thC, 52in (132cm).
£2,200-2,600 *Bea*

An oak court cupboard, with strapwork panels, the canopy top with 2 doors above 3 fielded cupboard doors, on block feet, c1668, 55½in (140cm).
£1,200-1,500 *CSK*

A Flemish oak cupboad, with a moulded cornice above a frieze applied with split bobbin turnings and roundels, the 2 geometrically panelled doors centred by roundels, a panelled front below, 17thC, 59in (149.5cm).
£800-1,000 *Bea*

An oak linen cupboard, the upper section with ogee moulded cornice, over hanging compartments, enclosed by a pair of arched double fielded panelled doors with brass hinges, knob handles and shaped escutcheons, over 3 drawers with later brass handles, flanked by quadrant stiles and raised upon ogee bracket feet, 18thC, 68in (172cm).
£2,000-2,500 *HSS*

A Georgian oak hanging corner cupboard, with stepped and dentil pediment, over 2 panel doors, enclosing 3 shelves, 34in (86cm).
£250-300 *DDM*

An oak press style cabinet, with 3 short and 4 long drawers, brass drop handles and escutcheons, bracket feet, 69in (175cm).
£1,500-2,000 *PLJ*

Paul Hopwell Antiques

Early English Oak

A set of six 19th Century ash spindle back chairs.
English c1840

A small mid 18th Century oak dresser and rack with spoon slots. Excellent colour and patination.
N. Wales c1750

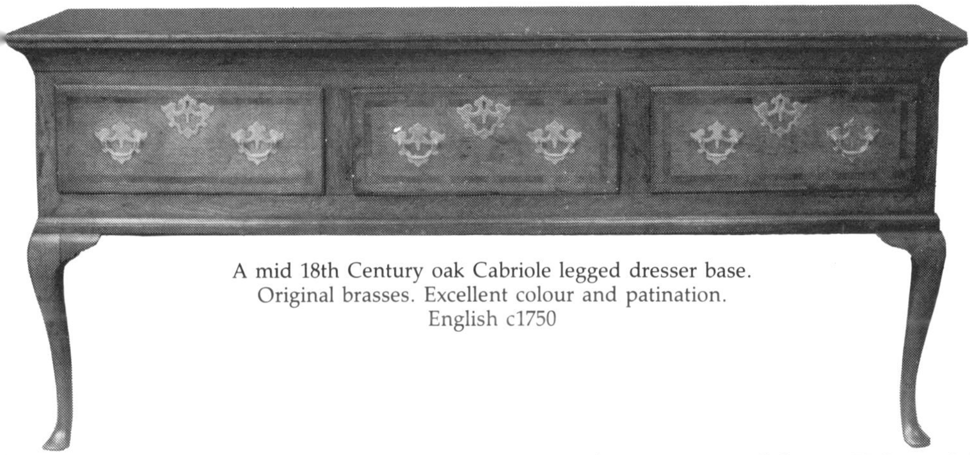

A mid 18th Century oak Cabriole legged dresser base.
Original brasses. Excellent colour and patination.
English c1750

30 High Street, West Haddon, Northamptonshire NN6 7AP
Tel: (078 887) 636

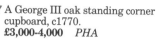

A French oak armoire, with ornate brass escutcheons, full length base drawer with shaped sunk panel front with raised and fielded panel ends, 18thC, 65in (166cm).
£550-750 *P(W)*

A George III oak standing corner cupboard, c1770.
£3,000-4,000 *PHA*

A Georgian North Country oak corner cupboard.
£900-1,200 *GIL*

An oak standing corner cupbo profusely carved, on bracket f late 19thC, 46in (116.5cm).
£600-900 *CSK*

An oak press cupboard, the top with moulded cornice and frieze dated '1733' and initialled 'P.E.K.', above a pair of fielded panelled doors, on a base of two similar short drawers, on block feet, 18thC, 53in (135cm).
£2,500-3,000 *MGM*

A George III oak hanging corner cupboard, with original brasses and secret drawers to interior, c1770.
£2,500-3,500 *PHA*

An oak court cupboard, carved with foliage and strapwork bands, initialled 'W.R.B.' and dated '1715', 47in (119cm).
£3,000-4,000 *CSK*

A Georgian oak hanging corner cupboard, with mahogany crossbanding, dentil pediment over 2 panel doors enclosing 3 shaped shelves, 30in (76cm).
£250-300 *DDM*

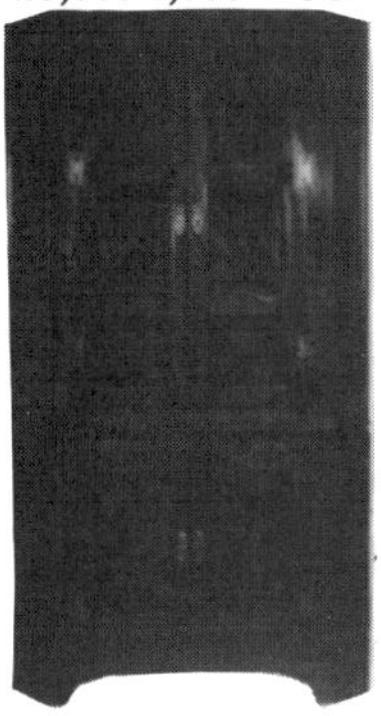

A George III mahogany standing corner cupboard, with a bolection moulded cornice, above a pair of fielded arched doors and a pair of panelled cupboard doors with canted angles on bracket feet, 48in (122cm). **£2,500-3,000** *CSK*

Dressers

An oak dresser, inlaid with ivor and chequer bands, on turned bu feet, 55½in (140cm).
£1,500-2,000 *CSK*

A late Georgian III oak dresser, t top section with a bolection corn and open shelves above an arcad base with 3 frieze drawers on baluster column supports and po board with block feet, 73in (185c
£3,000-4,000 *CSK*

A George III oak cupboard dresser, the rack with spice drawers and shaped ends, the base with canted reeded corners on ogee feet, North Wales, c1785.
£8,000-12,000 *PHA*

oak breakfront dresser base,
h moulded edge top, pierced drop
ndles, on stile supports, 18thC,
½in (194cm).
500-3,000 *AH*

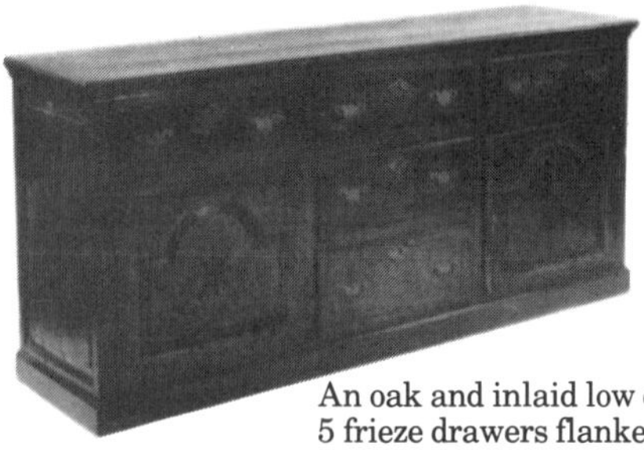

An oak and inlaid low dresser, with 5 frieze drawers flanked by a pair of panelled doors, on plinth base, late 18thC and later, 72in (182.5cm).
£3,500-4,500 *CSK*

nid-18thC style oak Welsh
sser, raised on turned baluster
pports with pot board, distressed,
n (137cm).
)0-1,000 *P(M)*

An oak dresser and rack, North Yorkshire, c1760.
£8,000-10,000 *PHA*

An oak dresser with moulded cornice, brass drop handles, 6 square supports and planked pot board, 18thC, 58in (147cm).
£3,000-3,500 *AH*

oak dresser, on
ned legs with
lertier, early 19thC,
n (157cm).
,500-4,500 *C*

Welsh oak dresser, the associated
with arched niches and shelves,
a base of 3 short drawers,
luster legs and a pot board, early
thC, 80in (203cm).
,000-8,000 *MGM*

An oak dresser, the top section with a cavetto moulded cornice and open shelves, above 3 frieze drawers and twin false drawers, on baluster columns, 71½in (180cm).
£4,500-5,500 *CSK*

A George III oak, mahogany crossbanded and ebony lined dresser, the moulded top above 3 frieze drawers and 2 short drawers, flanked on either side b pair of panelled cupboard doors, flanked by turned and fluted demi-column angles, on bracket feet, 72in (182.5cm).
£6,000-7,000 *CEd*

A Georgian oak dresser, the plate rack with moulded cornice and arcaded frieze, above 2 shelves fitted with iron books, the rounded top above 2 drawers and shaped apron, on square legs with rectangular undertier, 57in (145cm).
£3,500-4,500 *C*

Make the most of Miller's

Unless otherwise stated, any description which refers to 'a set' or 'a pair' includes a valuation for the entire set or the pair, even though the illustration may show only a single item

Stools

An oak and elm joint stool, with moulded seat, ring turned legs and squared stretchers, 17thC, 18in (46cm). **£2,000-2,500** *C*

An English beech and elm Windsor stool, c1860, 17in (43cm) high.
£55-70 *UC*

An oak joint stool, with moulded seat, the seat rail carved with foliate lunettes, on ring turned legs with carved stretchers, 17thC with later top and restorations, 18in (46cm).
£700-800 *C*

Tables

An oak side table, on bobbin turned legs joined by stretchers, late 17thC, 36in (91.5cm).
£1,000-1,500 *CSK*

An oak side table, with moulded top and frieze drawer, on baluster legs and conforming H-stretcher, one foot replaced, late 17thC, 34½in (88cm).
£800-1,200 *C*

A chestnut and polychrome-paint gateleg table, the top with single flap, on turned legs with turned a squared stretchers, restorations, 17thC.
£2,500-3,000 *C*

An oak lowboy, 18thC, 42in (106.5cm).
£700-1,000 *PCA*

ieorge II fruitwood lowboy, on
in turned tapered legs with pad
;, 30in (77cm).
0-900 *Bon*

A William and Mary oak credence table, c1690.
£2,500-4,000 *PHA*

A Georgian oak cricket table, with planked top, on moulded square legs with stretchers, 28½in (72cm) diam.
£500-800 *C*

ieorge II oak lowboy, the top and
ieze drawers crossbanded, with
ped apron, on 4 cabriole pad
ports, 32in (81cm).
500-2,000 *P(M)*

A George II oak lowboy, with moulded plank top, above one long and 2 short drawers, the brass drop handles with pierced back plates and escutcheons, above wavy frieze, on cabriole supports and pad feet, 30½in (77cm).
£1,200-1,600 *P(M)*

An oak gateleg table, the top with 2 drop flaps, raised upon baluster turned and block supports and stretchers, 18thC, 48in (122cm).
£700-1,000 *HSS*

A George I oak lowboy, with chased brass loop handles, cabriole legs with pad feet joined by cross stretchers, c1725, 31½in (80cm).
£1,500-2,000 *N*

A William and Mary oak side table with shaped drawer, c1695.
£2,000-3,000 *PHA*

oak side table
n a drawer, c1790.
0-600 *PCA*

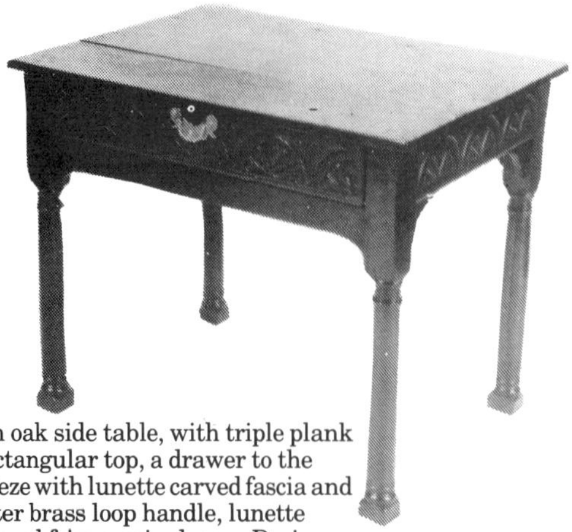

An oak side table, with triple plank rectangular top, a drawer to the frieze with lunette carved fascia and later brass loop handle, lunette carved frieze, raised upon Doric column supports, early 18thC, 34½in (87cm).
£450-550 *HSS*

A French Provincial chestnut table, on turned legs with moulded stretcher and later bun feet, 18thC, 57in (145cm).
£4,000-4,500 *C*

An oak gateleg table, the twin f top and 2 frieze drawers, on balu turned legs with stretchers, 78i (198cm).
£6,000-6,500 *CSK*

An Austrian elm work table with drawer, reduced in height, Tyrol, c1850, 33in (84cm).
£750-850 *UC*

A Spanish oak and fruitwood serving table, the plank top abov 3 frieze drawers on turned legs, t by moulded stretchers, part 17th 73in (186cm).
£1,500-2,000 *Bon*

Miller's is a price Guide not a price List

The price ranges given reflect the average price a purchaser should pay for similar items. Condition, rarity of design or pattern, size, colour, provenance, restoration and many other factors must be taken into account when assessing values.
When buying or selling, it must always be remembered that prices can be greatly affected by the condition of any piece. Unless otherwise stated, all goods shown in Miller's are of good merchantable quality, and the valuations given reflect this fact. Pieces offered for sale in exceptionally fine condition or in poor condition may reasonably be expected to be priced considerably higher or lower respectively than the estimates given herein

A Charles II style yew wood g dining table, on a bobbin and baluster twin double gated underframe, joined with cross stretchers, 81in (205.5cm).
£2,500-3,000 *CSK*

An oak gateleg dining table, with plain plank top supported on barley twist legs and plain stretchers, 18thC, 47in (119cm).
£700-800 *DDM*

, oak and fruitwood tripod table,
:hC, 22in (56cm).
50-450 *PCA*

mall oak refectory table, with
nked top and moulded frieze, on
are sectioned legs joined by
etchers, 55in (140cm).
0-650 *C*

An oak drawleaf refectory table, with cup and cover trestle supports, 68in (172.5cm).
£700-1,000 *CSK*

An oak candlestand, early 18thC.
£500-600 *PCA*

An Austrian walnut farmhouse table, with peg stopped substantial sliding top, shaped corners and deep drawer under, reduced in height, Linz, c1830, 41½in (105cm).
£900-1,200 *UC*

An elm gateleg table, with oval twin flap top, on carved trestle ends, with a single drawer and undertier, 43in (109cm).
£1,200-1,800 *C*

A tripod table, 18thC.
£300-400 *PCA*

A Victorian oak hall table, the marble top above 2 frieze drawers carved with foliage, on bulbous foliate carved square tapering legs, 66in (168cm).
£2,000-2,500 *CSK*

A Charles II oak side table, the plank top above a frieze drawer and wavy apron, on baluster turned legs, some restoration, 34in (86cm).
£1,200-1,700 *Bon*

Make the Most of Miller's

CONDITION is absolutely vital when assessing the value of an antique. Damaged pieces on the whole appreciate much less than perfect examples. However a rare, desirable piece may command a high price even when damaged

An oak Jacobean style refectory table, with thick 2 plank top, on 6 square baluster supports, 139 (353cm) long.
£13,000-17,000 *RBB*

An 18thC style oak oval gateleg dining table, with single frieze drawer, supported on ring turned legs with plain stretchers, 40in (101.5cm).
£250-300 *DDM*

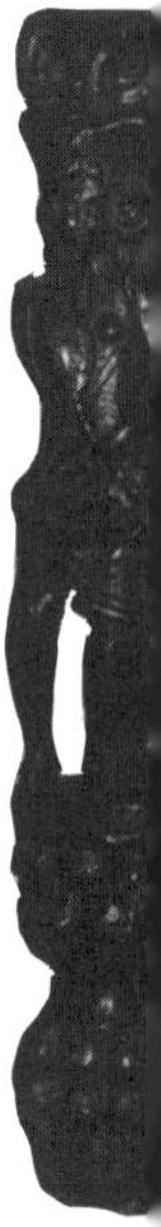

An oak carving, 17th(
£250-300 *PCA*

Miscellaneous

An oak and fruitwood hanging shelf, the 3 shelves with turned supports, the central shelf with guilloche carved front and arcaded sides, 28in (71cm).
£2,000-2,500 *C*

A Queen Anne oak bookcase top, with moulded double arched corn above 2 panelled doors, lacking lower section, 45in (114cm).
£500-800 *C*

An English iron bound oak wash tub on legs, Lincolnshire, c1890, 21in (53cm) diam.
£150-200 *UC*

An Irish rustic pearwood turf or pe box, Connemara, c1840, 36in (92cm).
£550-650 *UC*

RNITURE

ɘds

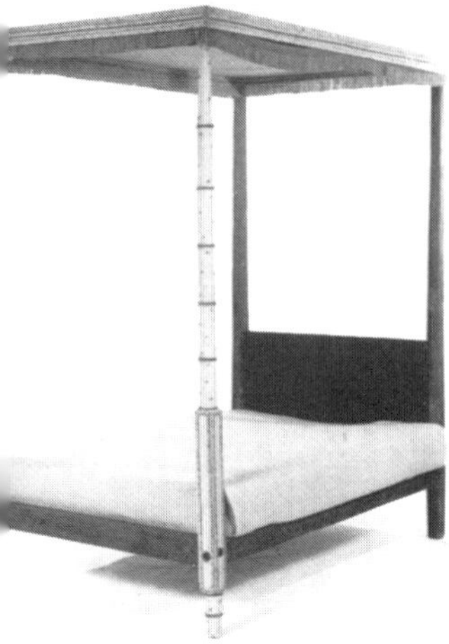

Regency painted four-poster bed, h moulded cornice, supported on nboo turned columns, 52in 2cm) wide.
)00-2,500 *Bon*

A Regency mahogany and cane panelled cradle, with ogee arched canopy and swing between acorned finialled turned uprights, joined by stretchers, 42in (106.5cm) long.
£900-1,200 *CSK*

A mahogany and pine four-poster bed, with carved canopy and fluted posts applied with acanthus scrolls on claw-and-ball feet, 18thC and later, 85in (216cm) long.
£2,000-3,000 *C*

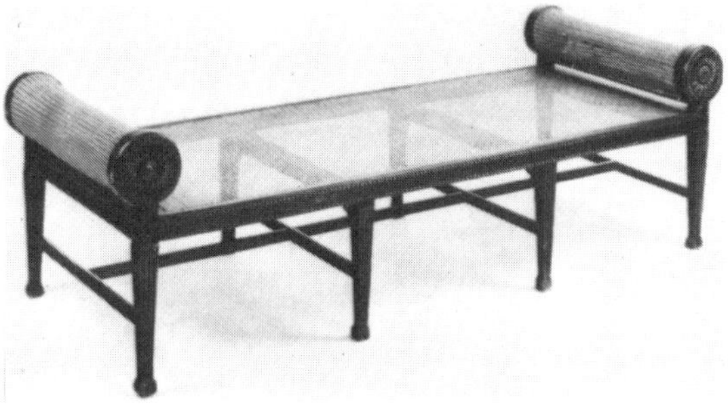

A mahogany and cane panelled daybed, the seat with bolster ends in a frame beaded and carved with paterae, on square tapered fluted legs joined by stretchers, with loose upholstered squab and 2 bolsters, late 18thC and later.
£1,500-2,000 *CSK*

ouis XV walnut daybed, with forming crisp carving on carbiole carved with flowerheads and age, possibly Liège, later blocks, orations, one foot missing, 83in m) long.
i00-2,000 *C*

A mahogany four-poster bed, the frieze with blind fret decoration supported on stop-fluted turned posts and shaped headboard, with pleated blue silk canopy and floral print chintz drapes, with box-spring and mattress, 86in (218cm) long.
£2,000-2,500 *C*

A late Federal carved mahogany high post bedstead, the footposts spiral turned with carved inverted balusters on inverted baluster and ring turned feet, Massachusetts, c1815, 58in (147cm).
£2,000-3,000 *CNY*

Italian parcel-gilt, walnut and ised bed, with shaped foot rest sides with turned finials and ılded columns headed by metal capitals, on claw and block , distressed padded solid dboard, 70in (177.5cm).
)00-4,500 *C*

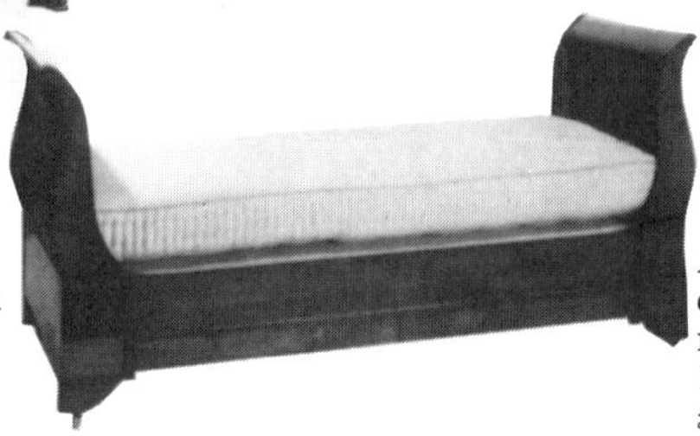

A French Provincial fruitwood daybed, with outscrolled ends and moulded rail, on bracket feet, 19thC, 78in (198cm).
£800-1,000 *CSK*

A Venetian rococo giltwood headboard, with cartouche-shaped padded back and pierced scrolling foliate crest issuing leafy scrolls, with vine leaves and grape clusters, upholstered in pale blue floral silk, 76in (193cm).
£4,000-5,000 *CNY*

Bonheur du jour

A Regency rosewood bonheur du jour, the mirrored shelf superstructure on S-scroll supports, with a subsidiary shelf on brass columns, the lower section with a frieze drawer, on turned and lobed legs headed by lotus carved capitals, 28in (71cm).
£5,000-6,000 *Bon*

An inlaid burr walnut bonheur d jour, with central mirror and dra between two glazed cupboards, t fall enclosing fitted interior and well, with ormolu mounts, on cabriole legs, 19thC, 33in (84cm)
£2,000-2,500 *SWO*

A neo-classical style satinwood bonheur du jour, painted and decorated, the 3 frieze drawers and concave undertier on square splayed tapering legs, 24in (62cm).
£4,000-5,000 *CSK*

An Edwardian mahogany bonheur du jour, on tapered legs with brass casters, with satinwood banding and boxwood stringing, 31in (79cm).
£1,500-2,000 *O*

A Louis XVI style kingwood and amaranth breakfront bonheur du jour, the tambour shutter enclosi a fitted interior, with a brass galleried undertier, on cabriole le with sabots and trophy mounted capitals, 26½in (68cm).
£2,000-2,500 *CSK*

Breakfront Bookcases

A William IV mahogany breakfront secretaire bookcase, the later moulded cornice applied with foliate motif above open shelves between moulded uprights, 112in (284.5cm).
£4,500-5,500 *CSK*

A George III style mahogany breakfront bookcase, with dentilled cornice, above glazed astragal doors and panelled doors on bracket feet, 80½in (204cm).
£4,500-5,500 *CSK*

A George III mahogany breakfron bookcase, with later moulded cornice, the base with a fitted interior, above a pair of panelled cupboards enclosing 3 graduated long drawers and with conforming cupboard doors, on later plinth, 90i (229cm).
£8,000-10,000 *C*

Jeorge III mahogany breakfront
:retaire bookcase, with central
:ed writing drawer, above a pair
panelled doors flanked by 2 other
ors, on platform base, 68in
'2.5cm).
,500-7,500 *CSK*

/ictorian mahogany breakfront
•kcase, the cavetto moulded
nice above 4 glazed astragal
•rs and a pair of radial moulded
nelled doors flanked by 8 side
wers, on plinth base, 98½in
0cm).
000-6,000 *CSK*

ate Victorian oak breakfront
rary bookcase, on plinth base,
elled Sopwith & Co., Newcastle-
Tyne, 98in (249cm).
500-2,000 *CSK*

. mahogany breakfront bookcase,
n plinth base, 142in (360cm).
5,500-6,500 *CSK*

An early Victorian mahogany breakfront library bookcase, with 5 glazed and 5 panelled doors, the whole raised upon a cushion moulded plinth, 139in (350cm).
£6,000-7,000 *HSS*

An Edwardian mahogany and satinwood banded breakfront bookcase, the lower section with 3 panel cupboard doors, on a plinth base, 72in (182.5cm).
£3,500-4,500 *Bon*

A mahogany breakfront bookcase, with moulded cornice above 4 glazed doors and 4 radial panelled cupboard doors, on plinth base, 64in (162.5cm).
£1,500-2,000 *CSK*

A Regency mahogany breakfront bookcase, the moulded cornice above 4 glazed doors, 4 drawers and 4 panelled doors on bracket feet, 102in (259cm).
£6,000-7,000 *CSK*

A Victorian mahogany library bookcase, the panelled doors flanked by 10 drawers, on plinth base, 96in (244cm).
£2,000-3,000 *CSK*

A Georgian style mahogany and line inlaid breakfront library secretaire bookcase, 92in (233cm).
£22,000-25,000 *GC*

Locate the source

The source of each illustration in Miller's can be found by checking the code letters below each caption with the list of contributors

A mahogany breakfront bookcase, with Greek key cornice, above inlaid fluted frieze and Gothic arch astragal glazed doors, the lower section with a kingwood crossbanded drawer above oval veneered cupboards, the sides with further drawers above cupboards, 98in (249cm).
£6,000-8,000 *Bon*

A Queen Anne style walnut bureau bookcase, with hinged fall front, the bookcase with 2 glazed doors and a broken arched pediment.
£2,200-2,600 *LRG*

A Georgian mahogany secrétaire bookcase, 42in (106.5cm).
£3,500-4,000 *JD*

A mahogany inverted breakfront bookcase, with additional later panelled mahogany and arched top, 180in (457cm).
£1,800-2,200 *DDM*

A George III mahogany bureau bookcase, with a fall flap revealing a fitted interior, the 4 long graduated drawers with brass and swan neck handles, on ogee bracket feet, 49in (124.5cm).
£2,700-3,000 *WW*

A George III mahogany bureau bookcase, the fall flap opening to reveal a fitted interior of pigeonholes, drawers and a cupboard, with 4 long graduated drawers under, on bracket feet, 44in (111.5cm).
£3,500-4,000 *AG*

Bureau Bookcases

A mahogany bureau bookcase, with fitted interior, brass drop handles and escutcheons, fluted pilasters and ogee bracket feet, mid-18thC, 42½in (106.5cm).
£10,000-12,000 *AH*

A George II style walnut and featherbanded bureau bookcase, with a pair of candle slides, above hinged sloping flap enclosing a fitted interior, on bracket feet, modern, 38in (96.5cm).
£2,000-2,500 *CSK*

A George III mahogany bureau bookcase, the fall front enclosing small drawers and pigeonholes, with 4 graduated long drawers below, bracket feet, 47in (119cm).
£2,500-3,000 *P(S)*

ɜeorge III oak bureau bookcase, bracket feet, 50½in (128cm).
,200-1,600 *CSK*

ι early George III red walnut ıreau bookcase, the fall enclosing ;eonholes, small drawers and a ›inet, with 4 graduated long ıwers below, bracket feet, 39in ›cm).
,500-4,500 *P(S)*

ı Edwardian mahogany and tinwood crossbanded bureau ɔkcase, on bracket feet, 32in ɩcm).
,200-1,500 *P(W)*

A George III mahogany bureau bookcase, the desk with hinged flap, the interior with drawers and pigeonholes, the drawer inlaid with Prince of Wales feathers, shaped bracket feet, top and bottom possibly associated, 48in (122cm).
£2,500-3,500 *C*

A Victorian walnut cylinder bureau bookcase, the cylinder enclosing a sliding lined and ratcheted writing slope and fitted interior, above 2 cupboard doors, on plinth, 50½in (128cm).
£2,000-2,500 *CSK*

An Edwardian inlaid mahogany bureau bookcase, with shell inlay and satinwood stringing decoration, the top with swan neck pediment, 33in (84cm).
£900-1,200 *DDM*

A George III mahogany bureau cabinet, with later broken pediment and dentilled cornice, above 2 glazed doors, on bracket feet, top and base probably associated, 43in (109cm). **£4,500-5,000** *C*

An Edwardian mahogany bureau bookcase, with inlaid shell scroll and leaf decoration to the fall flap, the whole with satinwood stringing, 36in (91.5cm). **£1,200-1,600** *DDM*

An Edwardian mahogany satinwood crossbanded and marquetry bureau bookcase, on bracket feet, 37in (94cm).
£2,000-2,500 *CSK*

An Edwardian mahogany bureau bookcase, the shell inlaid flap opening to reveal plain interior, over 3 graduated drawers, raised on bracket feet, 24in (61cm).
£900-1,200 *P(M)*

An Edwardian mahogany and satinwood banded bureau bookcase, the fall front with an inlaid oval enclosing a fitted interior, above 4 long graduated drawers, on bracket feet. **£1,500-2,000** *Bon*

An Edwardian inlaid mahogany bureau bookcase, with astragal glazed door, fall front and 3 drawers below with brass swan neck handles, on bracket feet, 93in (236cm) high.
£600-700 *HCH*

An Edwardian mahogany and satinwood banded bureau bookcase, with a bolection moulded cornice, 37in (94cm).
£1,500-2,000 *CS*

A Sheraton mahogany revival period bureau bookcase, with satinwood crossbandings and swan neck cornice, 24in (61cm).
£1,200-1,600 *GAK*

A walnut bureau bookcase, with arched top above 2 glazed doors, a featherbanded slope, 2 short and 2 long drawers, on bracket feet, 36in (91.5cm).
£2,000-2,500 *CSK*

A Victorian walnut dwarf breakfront open bookcase, with fitted adjustable shelves, on a plinth base, 72in (183cm). **£1,200-1,500** *P(W)*

Dwarf Bookcases

A set of Regency mahogany open bookshelves, with swan neck pediment, on splay feet, 34in (86cm).
£450-550 *OL*

A Regency rosewood open dwarf bookcase, with 3 stepped shelves, baluster turned columns, turned legs and brass casters, 35in (89cm).
£1,500-2,000 *AH*

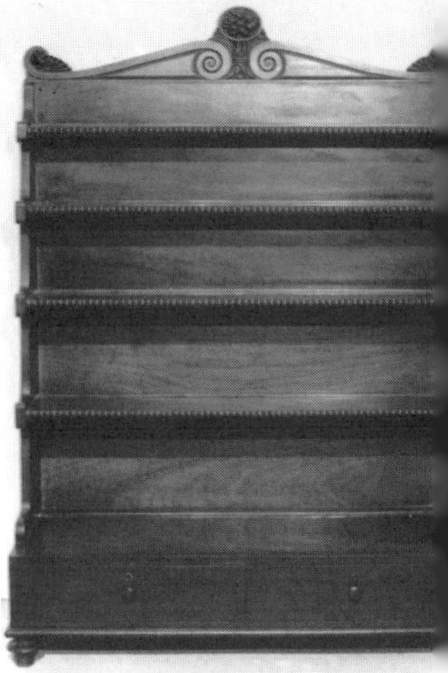

A rosewood open bookcase, with scrolled surmount, 5 graduated shelves with shaped sides and bead-and-reel moulding, 2 drawer below with turned knob handles, c 4 turned supports, early 19thC, 42i (106.5cm). **£1,000-1,500** *AH*

Regency mahogany bookshelf, the stepped shelves, with shaped sides ɔove a drawer on turned legs, 27in 9cm). **£2,000-2,500** *C*

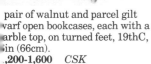

pair of walnut and parcel gilt varf open bookcases, each with a arble top, on turned feet, 19thC, ;in (66cm). **,200-1,600** *CSK*

,ibrary Bookcases

George III style mahogany okcase, with dentilled cornice ove a fluted frieze and a pair of tragal glazed doors, the base with ıted frieze and enclosed by a pair panelled doors, on bracket feet, ;in (142.5cm). **;,000-2,500** *CSK*

A mahogany dwarf open bookcase, the shelves with bobbin-turned fronts, clustered column supports, turned X-roundel side panels, with 2 drawers below, brass handles and turned feet, 18thC, 61in (155cm). **£2,500-3,000** *AH*

A pair of Victorian walnut open front dwarf bookcases, fitted with adjustable shelves, with parquetry Greek key pattern borders, on plinth bases, 33in (84cm). **£600-800** *P(W)*

A mid-Victorian mahogany bookcase, with pierced cartouche cresting above 4 glazed doors, the base with 4 convex strapwork drawers and 4 mirrored doors, on plinth base, 146in (370.5cm). **£5,000-6,000** *CSK*

A pair of painted satinwood dwarf bookcases, on tapered feet, 19½in (49cm). **£1,000-1,200** *CSK*

A George IV mahogany bookstand, the top with three-quarter spindle gallery, above a single frieze drawer fitted with a pen tray and inkwell, on turned feet, 17in (44cm). **£1,000-1,500** *C*

A William IV rosewood bookcase, with moulded cornice, the lower section with 2 frieze drawers and 4 panelled doors, on plinth, stamped T. Willson, 68 Great Queen Street, London, 72in (182.5cm). **£4,500-5,500** *CSK*

A Regency mahogany library bookcase, the frieze inlaid with key pattern, the lower part with a drawer above 2 panelled doors, both with carved roundels and inlaid string lines, the canted corners with reeded and panelled mouldings, 43½in (110cm).
£4,000-5,000 *P(S)*

A Victorian mahogany library bookcase, the upper part with a moulded cornice and 4 glazed doors enclosing adjustable shelves, the lower part with 4 panelled doors enclosing 9 drawers and shelves, 95in (240cm).
£9,000-10,000 *P(S)*

A mid-Victorian oak bookcase, th arched cornice above 6 glazed doo carved with scallops, the base wit 6 drawers and 6 doors, 162in (411cm).
£12,000-15,000 *CSK*

A Victorian walnut bookstand, the 2 hinged ends each with 4 columns surmounted by a broken pediment, on rusticated base, 33½in (85cm).
£4,000-5,000 *C*

An Edwardian mahogany and inlaid bookcase, on bracket feet, 37in (94cm).
£2,200-2,500 *P(W)*

A Georgian mahogany secrétaire bookcase, decorated with inlaid crossbanding and stringing, the secrétaire drawer below, fitted wit brass handles, a pair of panel door below, raised on bracket feet, 47in (119cm).
£3,000-3,500 *AG*

Secrétaire Bookcases

A George III mahogany secrétaire bookcase, with boxwood strung drawers, brass drum handles, 32in (81cm). **£52,000-55,000** *N*

A late George III mahogany secrétaire bookcase, the tambour roll front enclosing small drawers, pigeonholes and a pull-out writing slide, the writing surface adjustable for height on a ratchet, 4 graduated long drawers below with ebony string lines, shaped aprons, splay bracket feet, 42½in (106.5cm).
£3,500-4,500 *P(S)*

A George III mahogany secrétaire bookcase, with dentilled moulded cornice, above a pair of geometrically glazed doors, deep fitted drawers and a pair of panelle cupboard doors, on plinth base, adapted, 48in (122cm).
£3,000-4,000 *CSK*

. George III mahogany secrétaire ›okcase, the fascia hinged and .lling to reveal pigeonholes and nall drawers flanked by ıpboards, enclosed by oval ınelled doors, and with 3 long ·aduated drawers below, all with ırned rosewood handles, flanked ı cluster column stiles and raised ›on shallow French bracket feet, ›in (138cm). **£4,000-4,500** *HSS*

A George III mahogany secrétaire bookcase, the upper section with Greek key cornice, 44in (112cm).
£2,200-2,600 *Bon*

A George III mahogany secrétaire bookcase, with moulded cornice, a pair of glazed cupboard doors above a fitted secrétaire drawer, 3 graduated long drawers, on splayed feet, 50in (127cm).
£3,000-4,000 *C*

A Regency mahogany secrétaire bookcase, on splayed bracket feet, 44½in (112cm).
£4,000-5,000 *CSK*

A George III mahogany secrétaire bookcase, the base with fitted leather lined secrétaire drawer, above 2 short and 2 long drawers, on later blind fret carved bracket feet, 50in (127cm). **£3,000-5,000** *C*

A late George III mahogany secrétaire bookcase, with a ball studded moulded cornice, a pair of glazed astragal doors, a deep writing drawer, and pierced panelled doors on bracket feet, 48½in (123cm).
£1,500-2,500 *CSK*

mahogany secrétaire bookcase, .th rosewood banded writing awer and panelled cupboard ors, on splayed bracket feet, apted, early 19thC, 44½in 12cm). **£2,000-2,500** *CSK*

A late Georgian mahogany secrétaire bookcase, with shelved interior, the base with fully fitted secrétaire drawer and double cupboard below, on French bracket supports, 44in (111.5cm).
£2,500-3,000 *DEN*

A Regency mahogany secrétaire bookcase, with beaded glass doors, fitted drawer and enclosed cupboard under, 44in (111.5cm).
£1,000-1,500 *JH*

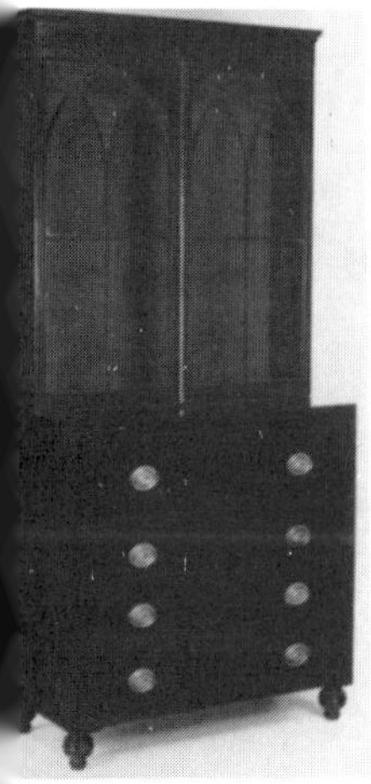

Regency mahogany secrétaire ›kcase, the top section with an aid frieze, 42in (106.5cm).
,500-2,000 *CSK*

An early Victorian walnut secrétaire bookcase, the lower section with a deep secrétaire drawer enclosing a fitted interior, above 2 cupboard doors, on plinth, 52in (132cm).
£2,000-2,500 *CSK*

A Victorian mahogany secrétaire bookcase, the top section with dentilled cornice and a pair of glazed doors, above a deep secrétaire drawer and 3 graduated long drawers, on bracket feet, 44in (111.5cm).
£3,000-4,000 *CSK*

A Regency mahogany secrétaire bookcase, with bowed eared base fitted with panelled secrétaire drawer, above 3 long drawers, th angles with reeded columns, on turned feet, 51in (130cm).
£3,000-4,000 *C*

A mahogany secrétaire bookcase, of stepped form, on plinth, restorations, inscribed in pencil T.F. King, America, 1857.
£4,000-5,000 *CSK*

A mahogany secrétaire bookcase, inlaid with boxwood and ebonised lines, 42in (106.5cm).
£2,500-3,000 *CSK*

A Victorian mahogany veneered secrétaire bookcase, with arched glazed panels, fitted drawer, cupboards under and carved deta
£2,000-2,500 *MGM*

Buckets

A George III brass bound mahogany bucket, with brass liner and carrying handle, 14in (36cm) high.
£700-1,000 *C*

A Dutch cherry and ebonised bucket, with brass swing handle and liner, with ball feet, mid-19thC, 15in (38cm) high.
£500-600 *C*

A Dutch ebonised and fruitwoo bucket, with detachable tin line and ribbed tapering body, with brass carrying handles, 11½in (29cm) diam.
£350-450 *C*

. brass bound bucket, with shaped
andle, brass liner and shovel,
3½in (35cm) diam.
1,500-2,000 *C*

A Georgian staved mahogany plate bucket, with 2 wide brass bands and overhead swing handle, 14in (36cm) high. **£550-650** *HSS*

Bureaux

A small William III walnut veneered bureau, with herringbone band inlay, oak lined drawers with engraved brass batswing plate handles and escutcheons, on replacement bun feet, 32½in (82cm).
£8,500-9,000 *WW*

walnut bureau, inlaid with
atherbands, the hinged slope
nclosing a fitted interior, basically
arly 18thC, 36in (91.5cm).
2,500-3,000 *C*

A walnut and pine bureau, with hinged sloping front enclosing a fitted interior, early 18thC, 36in (92cm).
£2,000-2,500 *CSK*

A Queen Anne walnut veneered bureau, with feather and cross banding, the fall front revealing a well, drawers and pigeonholes, with oak lined drawers double moulded outlined, on bracket feet, 34in (86cm).
£10,000-12,000 *WW*

walnut and featherbanded
ureau, with hinged sloping front
nclosing a fitted interior, on
racket feet, basically early 18thC,
6in (92cm).
2,500-3,500 *CSK*

A walnut kneehole bureau, the fall front enclosing small drawers, pigeonholes, pillar drawers and a cabinet, the top, fall and drawer fronts all feather and crossbanded, bracket feet, early 18thC, 36in (91.5cm).
£3,000-4,000 *P(S)*

A mahogany bureau, with fitted interior, on bracket feet, distressed, early 19thC, 32in (81cm).
£1,500-2,000 *DEN*

A Dutch marquetry bombé bureau, the curved writing fall revealing a fitted interior, with ornate brass handles and escutcheon, profusely marquetry decorated within leafy scroll borders, early 19thC, 34in (87cm).
£2,500-3,000 *P(W)*

A walnut marquetry bureau with shaped writing flap, stepped interior, single drawer under, on cabriole legs, 18thC, 34in (86cm).
£3,000-4,000 *IM*

BUREAUX

- ★ Bureaux were not made in this country until after the reign of Charles II
- ★ this writing box on stand was initially produced in oak and then in walnut
- ★ these were originally on turned or straight legs but cabriole legs became popular in the last decade of the 17thC
- ★ note the quality and proportion of the cabriole legs – good carving is another plus factor
- ★ always more valuable if containing an *original* stepped interior and well
- ★ also the more complex the interior – the more expensive
- ★ from about 1680 most bureaux made from walnut, many with beautiful marquetry and inlay
- ★ from about 1740 mahogany became the most favoured wood, although walnut was still used
- ★ the 'key' size for a bureau is 38in (96.5cm), as the width diminishes so the price increases dramatically
- ★ original patination, colour and original brass handles are obviously important features for assessing any piece of furniture, but these are crucial when valuing bureaux and chests

A Provincial walnut bureau, with banded top and hinged sloping flap, enclosing a fitted interior, adapted, late 18thC, 45in (114cm).
£1,500-2,000 *CSK*

A Dutch marquetry mahogany bureau of bombé form, on block feet, 18thC, 49½in (126cm).
£5,500-6,500 *HSS*

A George I featherbanded walnut bureau, the hinged slope enclosing a fitted oak interior, on bracket feet, the drawers relined, 42in (106.5cm).
£5,000-6,000 *CSK*

A walnut bureau, with stepped and fitted interior, 3 short and 3 long graduated drawers with brass handles and escutcheons, on bracket feet, 18thC, 38in (96.5cm).
£8,500-9,500 *IM*

A burr walnut herringbone crossbanded bureau, with one simulated and 3 long drawers below, brass drop handles and bun feet, early 18thC, 38in (96.5cm).
£6,000-7,000 *AH*

A mahogany bureau, the hinged sloping flap enclosing a fitted interior, on bracket feet, early 19thC, 47½in (120cm).
£1,000-1,500 *CSK*

A George I olivewood bureau, banded in walnut, restorations, 36i (91.5cm). **£2,500-3,500** *C*

. George I walnut bureau, with
erringbone banded and
rossbanded fall, enclosing a fitted
nterior, c1720, 36in (92cm).
4,200-4,600 *Bon*

George III fruitwood bureau, the
nged slope enclosing pigeonholes
d drawers, above 4 graduated
awers, on bracket feet, 36in
1.5cm).
,500-3,500 *C*

George III mahogany bureau,
th hinged slope and fitted
erior, the 3 graduated long
awers on bracket feet, 44in
1.5cm).
,200-1,700 *CSK*

George III mahogany writing
reau, with boxwood inlaid slope
closing a secret drawer and
ther inset, the drawers with
ginal handles, raised on bracket
t, 46½in (117cm).
,200-1,500 *P(M)*

A George I style burr walnut and featherbanded bureau, on bracket feet, 37in (94cm).
£900-1,200 *CSK*

A George III mahogany and marquetry inlaid bureau, with satinwood banded front enclosing a fitted interior, veneer distressed, 36in (91.5cm).
£1,500-2,000 *CSK*

A George III mahogany bureau, on ogee bracket feet, 44½in (112cm).
£900-1,200 *OL*

A George II walnut bureau, feather and crossbanded, the drawers with brass drop handles and butterfly backplates, on bracket feet, 39in (98cm).
£3,500-4,000 *P(W)*

A George III inlaid mahogany bureau, 46½in (117cm).
£1,500-2,000 *OL*

A George III mahogany bureau, the drawers with brass drop handles, flanked by reeded cylindrical columns, on bracket feet, 57in (114cm).
£1,200-1,700 *P*

A George II mahogany bureau, with shaped, stepped and fretted interior, original brass handles, c1750, 38in (96.5cm).
£4,000-5,000 *OS*

A George III inlaid mahogany bureau, fitted with 4 graduated drawers, and standing on bracket feet, 36in (91.5cm).
£1,200-1,700 *OL*

A George III mahogany bureau, the fall above 4 graduated long drawers, on bracket feet, restorations, 39in (99cm).
£800-1,200 *MGM*

A Georgian mahogany bureau, fitted with 4 graduated drawers an standing on ogee bracket feet, 37in (94cm).
£700-1,200 *OL*

A George III mahogany bureau, with elaborately fitted arcaded interior, on ogee bracket feet, 48in (122cm).
£2,000-2,500 *CSK*

A George III mahogany bureau, with brass drop handles and butterfly back plates, on bracket feet, 36in (92cm).
£2,000-2,500 *P(W)*

A George III mahogany bureau, th hinged sloping flap enclosing a fitted interior and well, above 4 graduated long drawers, on bracket feet, 39in (99cm).
£600-900 *CSK*

A Georgian mahogany bureau, with 4 long graduated drawers, brass loop handles and pierced back plates, on bracket feet, 30in (76cm).
£2,500-3,000 *JD*

A Georgian mahogany bureau, with fitted interior, over 4 long graduated drawers with knob handles, on splayed supports, 38in (96.5cm).
£900-1,200 *DDM*

A burr elm bureau, inlaid with chequered lines, the interior with arcaded drawers and pigeonholes flanking columns and a drawer, above 2 short and 3 long drawers on bracket feet, 28in (71cm).
£2,000-3,000 *C*

A late Victorian rosewood bureau inlaid with ivory and marquetry panels, with fitted interior above 3 long drawers, on bracket feet, 31 (79cm).
£1,500-2,500 *CSK*

. Georgian mahogany bureau, with
lain interior, over long graduated
rawers with brass handles, on
racket feet, 39in (99cm).
:700-900 *DDM*

. George III mahogany bureau, the
ill front enclosing central cupboard
nd secret compartments, with
rass drop handles and escutcheons,
racket feet, 46½in (117cm).
1,200-1,600 *AH*

walnut bureau, with hinged slope
nd fitted interior, on ogee bracket
et, 42½in (107cm).
1,800-2,200 *CSK*

An ormolu mounted kingwood and marquetry cylinder bureau, with fitted interior, and sliding writing surface above 2 drawers, on clasp headed cabriole legs and sabots, 29½in (75cm).
£900-1,200 *CSK*

A late Victorian or Edwardian mahogany and satinwood inlaid cylinder front bureau, one drawer stamped and with label for Edwards & Roberts, on square tapering legs and spade feet, 40in (101.5cm).
£3,500-4,500 *GC*

A Dutch mahogany and inlaid bureau, with a fitted interior, with 4 drawers with brass drop handles, shaped backplates and escutcheons, with fluted canted corners, early 19thC, 38in (98cm).
£2,000-2,500 *P(W)*

A Dutch marquetry miniature bureau, 18thC, 16½in (42cm).
£5,000-6,000 *BHA*

A late Victorian mahogany pedestal bureau, with a carved and panelled fall and drawers, on cabriole feet, stamped Maple & Co. Ltd., 48in (121cm).
£1,000-1,500 *MGM*

A mahogany bureau, the crossbanded fall front revealing a basic interior, 4 drawers to the base with turned knobs, bracket feet, mid-19thC, 36in (91.5cm).
£500-600 *GAK*

An inlaid mahogany bureau, the fall with tulipwood border band, brass carrying handles at the sides, bracket feet, Edwards & Roberts ivory label and stamps, 36in (91.5cm).
£2,000-3,000 *P(S)*

A Dutch walnut and marquetry bombé bureau, with fitted interior, on splayed feet, 42in (106.5cm).
£6,000-7,000 *CSK*

A mahogany bureau, with satinwood inlay and banding, 3 drawers, 36in (91.5cm).
£500-1,000 *JH*

A neo-classical style satinwood and rosewood banded cylinder bureau, the top enclosing an adjustable leather lined writing plateau, the base with a knee-hole flanked by 3 drawers, on square tapering legs, 32½in (82cm).
£3,500-4,500 *CSK*

A lady's French rosewood and marquetry writing desk, the top with three-quarter cast gilt metal galleries, 32in (82cm).
£1,500-2,000 *P(S)*

A Chippendale carved cherrywood reverse serpentine desk, with thumb moulded slant lid enclosing a fitted interior, on short cabriole legs with claw-and-ball feet, repair to hinge portion of desk interior, Massachusetts, c1780, 44in (111.5cm).
£7,500-9,500 *CNY*

A Chippendale mahogany reverse serpentine slant front desk, with 4 blocked and cockbeaded moulded long drawers over a conforming base with central fan carved pendant, on ogee bracket feet, side carrying handles, Salem, Massachusetts, c1780, 45in (114cm).
£12,000-15,000 *CNY*

A Chippendale figured maple slant front desk, on shaped bracket feet, one interior short drawer restored, New England, c1770, 37in (94cm).
£7,500-9,500 *CNY*

A French kingwood and rosewood banded bureau de dame with three-quarter pierced brass gallery top, the gilt metal mounted convex fall with Vernis Martin panel, enclosing drawers and a well, on gil metal mounted cabriole supports and sabots, late 19thC, 26in (67cm
£1,000-1,500 *P(M)*

A Continental walnut and marquetry bureau, the fall front enclosing fitted interior, the fall ar drawer fronts inlaid with floral ar foliate swags and formal foliate spandrels, the sides with decorati bandings, bracket feet, 36in (91.5cm).
£2,000-2,500 *P(S)*

Bureau Cabinets

A Dutch yew secrétaire à abattant, with moulded frieze drawer, above a fall front, 38½in (97cm).
£2,500-3,500 *CSK*

walnut and feather banded
critoire, with a cavetto moulded
rnice, long frieze drawer above a
ll writing panel enclosing a fitted
terior, on turned bun feet, part
thC, 33½in (85cm).
,000-2,500 *CSK*

A Louis Philippe mahogany secrétaire à abattant, with marble top and bolection frieze drawer, above a fall-front enclosing a maple lined fitted interior and 2 panelled doors on bracket feet, 42in (106.5cm).
£2,000-2,500 *CSK*

A Dutch walnut and floral marquetry bombé secrétaire, the secrétaire drawer with baize lined writing panel, with pierced floral-cast handles and escutcheons, on a deep apron and shaped feet, 19thC, 38½in (97cm).
£6,000-8,000 *N*

A gilt metal mounted walnut and parquetry secrétaire à abattant, after Riesener, with chamfered and moulded rectangular Louis XVI breccia marble top, bearing the indistinct stamp L.BOUDIN, JME twice, 32in (81cm).
£4,500-5,500 *C*

ourr walnut and seaweed
arquetry inlaid
reau cabinet, with a
lection moulded cornice
ove a pair of
velled mirrored
ors, on bracket feet,
sically late
thC, 37½in (95cm).
,000-6,000 *CSK*

A French ebony secrétaire à abattant, with gilt brass inlaid decoration, applied mounts and handles, late 19thC, 33in (84cm).
£500-600 *DDM*

early George III mahogany
reau cabinet, the mirror doors
closing adjustable shelves, the
erior with a door inlaid with a
ghlander flanked by inlaid
asters, on ogee bracket feet, 39in
cm). **£3,000-5,000** *C*

A South German walnut and ebonised bureau cabinet, inlaid with stars and geometric bands, the concave elm and yew base with 3 long drawers between canted angles, on turned tapering bun feet, basically 19thC, 51in (129.5cm).
£2,500-3,500 *CSK*

A German mahogany escritoire, with an applied carved cresting piece above on long drawer, the fall flap below enclosing a fitted interior of short drawers and a recess, 3 long graduated drawers under, flanked by reeded pilasters raised on turned feet, 19thC, 40in (101.5cm).
£1,500-2,000 *AG*

A mahogany secrétaire cabinet, th top section with a dentilled moulde cornice, above a geometrically glazed mirrored door enclosing adjustable shelves, the base with secrétaire drawer lined in green baize, above 9 drawers, on square chamfered legs and block feet with scroll brackets, 33in (84cm).
£4,500-6,500 *C*

Display Cabinets

A George III satinwood display case, adapted, 18in (46cm).
£700-1,000 *CSK*

A mahogany and satinwood banded side cabinet and associated bookcase top, early 19thC, 55in (139.5cm).
£900-1,200 *CSK*

An Edwardian Sheraton style mahogany display cabinet, 56 (142cm).
£2,000-2,500 *P(M)*

An early Victorian rosewood display cabinet, on cabriole legs with claw-and-ball feet, 64in (162.5cm).
£3,000-4,000 *CSK*

An Edwardian mahogany china cabinet with marquetry inlaid back piece, single lead glazed front door, line inlays to pilasters and feet, 24in (62cm).
£400-500 *GAK*

A Victorian inlaid rosewood drawing room cabinet, 54in (137cr
£2,000-2,500 *OL*

ın Edwardian inlaid mahogany
ow fronted display cabinet, 48in
122cm).
1,500-2,000 *OL*

An Edwardian mahogany china cabinet in the Sheraton manner, with mirrored back, on four tapering legs with line inlay, 25in (64cm).
£350-450 *GAK*

An Edwardian inlaid mahogany bow front display cabinet by Warings, on square tapering supports with stop feet, 54in (137cm).
£900-1,200 *OL*

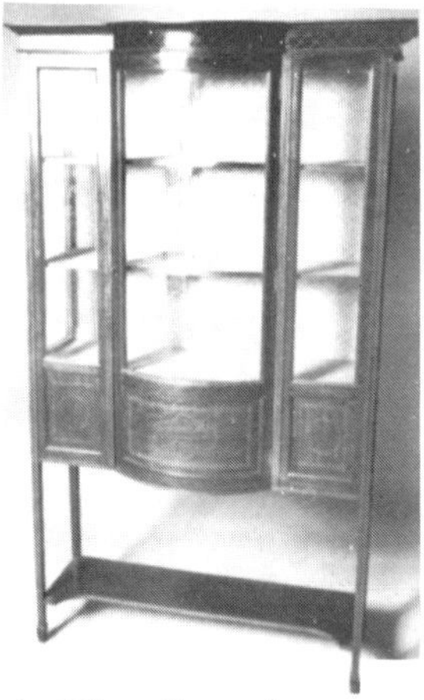

An Edwardian mahogany serpentine front china cabinet, with hatch inlay, tapering legs with spade feet, 45in (114cm).
£800-1,000 *GAK*

An Edwardian mahogany china cabinet, the 2 pairs of doors about a fixed bowed centre section, the square section legs with Chinese fret brackets, 47in (119cm).
£600-700 *MJB*

An Edwardian rosewood display cabinet by Hindley & Sons, London.
£3,000-4,000 *GIL*

An Edwardian inlaid mahogany shaped front corner display cabinet, with cupboard under enclosed by door, on square tapered legs, 30in (76cm).
£500-600 *PCh*

An Edwardian mahogany display cabinet, with satinwood stringing decoration, supported on an Art Nouveau style base and feet, 57in (144.5cm).
£1,500-2,000 *DDM*

An Edwardian Art Nouveau mahogany bowfronted display cabinet, with satinwood banding and ebony and boxwood stringing, the frieze and cornice inlaid in various woods with urns and foliate scrolls, 48in (122cm).
£1,500-2,000 *O*

An Edwardian mahogany display cabinet, with velvet lined shelves, with marquetry inlaid decoration c urns, swags, flowerheads and scrolling leaves and outlined with satinwood stringing, 48in (122cm).
£1,000-1,500 *DDM*

An Edwardian mahogany and inlaid display cabinet, with marquetry panels, shaped apron and raised on 4 splayed supports, 41in (104cm).
£800-1,000 *AH*

A Victorian walnut dwarf breakfront display cabinet, inlaid with symmetrical scrolling foliage and stringing, with velvet lined shelved interior, gilt metal beadin on a plinth base.
£1,500-2,000 *P(W)*

Cabinets-on-Stands

ate Victorian mahogany and
inwood banded pedestal display
inet, on square tapering legs
h spade feet, 42½in (106.5cm).
0-600 *CSK*

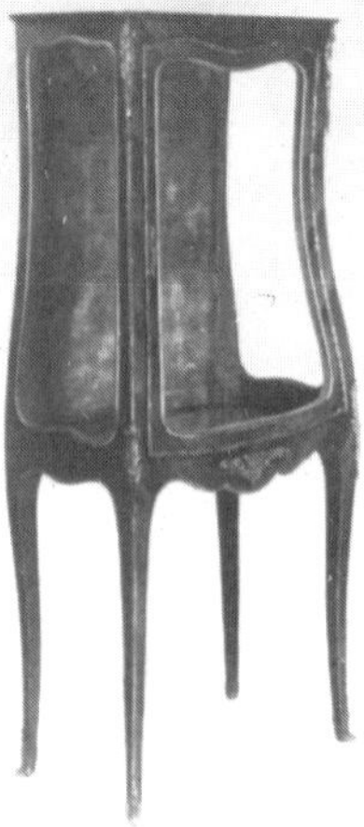

A gilt metal mounted kingwood bombé vitrine, with a glazed door and side panels, on cabriole legs with sabots, 29in (74cm).
£900-1,200 *CSK*

A Queen Anne oyster walnut cabinet, with ogee frieze drawer, above 2 panel doors with geometric boxwood star and line inlays, enclosing a fitted interior, on later stand fitted with 3 drawers, on square cabriole supports and pad feet, 29½in (75cm).
£2,000-2,500 *P(M)*

A black lacquer cabinet-on-stand, decorated in red and gilt, with 2 doors enclosing 11 drawers, the stand with waved apron on square legs, distressed, 18thC, 37in (94cm).
£1,500-2,000 *CSK*

A Regency lacquered collector's cabinet-on-stand, the stand with scroll frieze centered with lion's mask, on ring turned rear and cabriole front supports, containing the remains of the original collection of minerals, shells, seals and plaster casts, damaged, 42in (106.5cm).
£2,000-3,000 *RBB*

A Georgian mahogany toilet cabinet, with crossbanding, ebony and boxwood string inlays, single drawer, cupboard and X-stretcher.
£500-600 *MGM*

eather upholstered pedestal
inet, painted and decorated with
mals and foliage, the platform
e applied with gilt metal
erae, on turned bun feet,
pted, basically early 19thC, 31in
m).
0-1,000 *CSK*

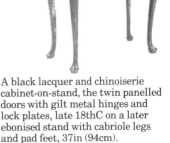

Charles II style black lacquer and
arcel gilt cabinet-on-stand, the
chinoiserie decorated panelled
ors with brass hinges and lock
ates, on hipped spiral cabriole legs
ith flowerheads and mask
eadings, 42in (106.5cm).
2,500-3,000 *CSK*

A black lacquer and chinoiserie cabinet-on-stand, the twin panelled doors with gilt metal hinges and lock plates, late 18thC on a later ebonised stand with cabriole legs and pad feet, 37in (94cm).
£2,000-2,500 *CSK*

An Edwardian satinwood lady's cabinet-on-stand, opening to reveal a fitted manicure set, raised on slender square tapering, outswept supports, united by a crossed stretcher, 12in (31cm).
£300-500 *GD*

An Edwardian rosewood salon cabinet, on slender turned and block supports tied by an undertier with balustraded gallery, the whole inlaid with neo-classic urns, swags of husks and foliage, in coloured woods, and strung with box, 48in (122cm). **£600-800** *HSS*

A French rosewood and satinwood inlaid bedside commode inlaid with marquetry, fitted 3 drawers, 19thC, 20in (51cm). **£800-1,000** *RID*

A Dutch Colonial ebony and rosewood cabinet-on-stand, applied with ripple mouldings, with 16 false drawers, the later stand with faceted graduating legs and block feet, 19thC and later, 39in (99cm).
£1,000-1,500 *CSK*

A satinwood and marquetry cabinet-on-stand, inlaid with berried foliate sprays, the stand with a frieze drawer on tapering legs, joined by a shaped platform, 27in (35cm).
£2,000-3,000 *C*

An Edwardian mahogany salon cabinet, of reverse break bow front form, inlaid with ribbon bows and swags of husks and pendant medallions, and crossbanded in satinwood and strung with ebony and box, raised upon square tapering supports terminating in spade feet, 48in (122cm).
£1,200-1,600 *HSS*

An Edwardian mahogany and satinwood surprise cocktail cabin[illegible] the hinged top with telescopic platform interior, above a spindle[illegible] undertier, on splayed tapering leg[illegible] 24in (61cm).
£500-800 *CSK*

A Dutch East Indies, Sri Lanka, jackwood and ebony brass mount[illegible] cabinet-on-stand, with moulded cornice above 2 panelled doors, on turned and reeded legs, early 19th[illegible] 40in (102cm).
£1,000-1,500 *C*

An Italian ebonised breakfront si[illegible] cabinet, applied with finials and gi[illegible] metal figurines, on a stand with spirally turned legs and cross stretcher, 19thC and later, 50½in (128cm).
£3,000-4,000 *CSK*

. Dutch East Indies, Sri Lanka, rass mounted jackwood, kaliatur nd ebony cabinet-on-stand, the :roll hinges engraved with fish, the :and with 2 frieze drawers, on ulbous baluster legs joined by :retchers, restorations, labelled utch Cabinet No. 1 His xcellency's Sitting Room, Queen's Iouse, Colombo, 45in (115cm).
2,000-3,000 *C*

rosewood and parcel gilt dwarf pen bookcase, with verde antico arble top, basically early 19thC, 6in (117cm).
1,500-2,000 *C*

scarlet boulle ebonised and gilt etal mounted side cabinet, applied ith acanthus clasps, with shaped inth on block feet, distressed, id-19thC, 76in (193cm).
1,200-1,600 *CSK*

walnut and inlaid side cabinet, ith gilt metal mounts and Sèvres yle porcelain plaques, the centre upboard flanked by a pair of bowed oors, on turned feet, mid-19thC, 6in (167.5cm). **£2,000-3,000** *PCh*

Side Cabinets

A pair of rosewood console side tables, applied with gilt metal mounts, Carrara marble tops, with silk sunburst upholstered panelled interior, on plinth platform bases, parts early 19thC, 25in (64cm).
£1,200-1,500 *CSK*

An ormolu mounted boulle red tortoiseshell and ebonised side cabinet, the cupboard doors enclosing red velvet-lined shelves, the sides with Bérainesque panels, the top and side panels 18thC, 49½in (126cm).
£3,000-4,000 *C*

A pair of breakfront amboyna wood and walnut side cabinets, each with heavy ormolu beading and mounts, Sèvres style plaques to the doors, with interior shelves and cupboards, and marble tops, 19thC, 27in (69cm).
£8,000-10,000 *RID*

A George IV rosewood chiffonier, the frieze drawer flanked by roundels, the 2 panelled doors flanked by columns and on a plinth base, 39in (99cm).
£700-900 *Bea*

A burr ash side cabinet, with galleried back and panelled doors applied with gilt metal crowned garter mounts, on gilt acanthus carved feet, early 19thC, 42in (107cm).
£2,500-3,000 *Bon*

A Victorian mahogany serpentine fronted chiffonier, with a dummy drawer, 2 fielded panel doors, carved decoration to the sides, on a platform base, 46in (116.5cm).
£900-1,200 *DDM*

A William IV mahogany chiffonier, with cushion fronted drawer and 2 cupboard doors, supported on lion paw front feet, 42in (106.5cm).
£500-700 *DDM*

A Victorian walnut serpentine side cabinet, with eared Carrara marble top below a mirrored back, on plinth base, 60in (152cm).
£700-1,000 *CSK*

A Regency ormolu-mounted rosewood chiffonier, the frieze with central plaque, the glazed doors backed with pleated green silk between turned columns on plinth base, 43in (109cm).
£4,000-5,000 *C*

A Regency mahogany and satinwood side cabinet, with crossbanded top, 2 frieze drawers above a pair of panelled cupboards, inlaid with ovals, with waved apron, and splayed feet, adapted, 36½in (93cm).
£1,000-1,500 *C*

An early Victorian mahogany chiffonier, with turned supports above 2 concave frieze drawers, above a pair of panelled doors between lappeted column uprights, on plinth base, 39½in (99cm).
£1,000-1,500 *CSK*

A George IV Irish mahogany chiffonier, the top with raised superstructure of one shelf with scrolled cresting, panelled back ar S-scroll supports, the frieze with a concave drawer, on Ionic column supports, the panelled back flanke by pilasters on a concave-fronted plinth base, 42in (106.5cm).
£2,000-2,500 *C*

A Victorian gilt metal mounted bu walnut and marquetry side cabine with a central painted porcelain plaque, 2 bowed glazed doors and Corinthian pilaster columns, on bu feet, 68in (172.5cm).
£4,000-4,500 *CSK*

A Victorian carved mahogany chiffonier, standing on bun feet 48in (122cm).
£500-600 *OL*

THE OLD CINEMA
ANTIQUES

A Spanish oak armchair, early 17thC.
£2,000-2,500 *C*

A set of 6 yew and elm Windsor armchairs, 19thC, Yorkshire. **£8,000-10,000** *C*

A William and Mary carved oak co
1691, English. **£1,000-2,000** *PHA*

A Welsh oak tridarn, mid-18thC
£4,000-6,000 *PHA*

A harlequin set of 6 yew and elm Windsor chairs, c1810. **£5,000-7,000** *C*

An English oak cofferbach, c1790.
£1,000-2,000 *PHA*

r. A George III elm table, c1790. **£2,500-3,000** *PHA*

A Charles II oak child's coffer, c1680. **£1,500-2,500** *PHA*

An English oak box on cabriole legs, c1760.
£2,000-3,000 *PHA*

l. An oak carved coffer, c1695.
£1,000-1,500 *PHA*

r. An English oak plank coffer, c1580.
£3,000-4,000 *PHA*

oak four-poster bed, basically
thC, with restorations and
ditions.
,000-8,000 *C*

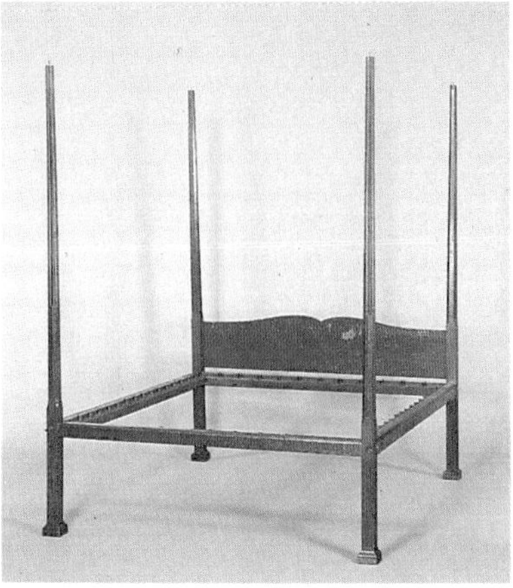

A Chippendale carved mahogany highpost bedstead, Newport, Rhode Island, c1770, 61in (155cm) wide.
£55,000-60,000 *CNY*

A George III painted parcel-gilt four-poster bed, 66in (168cm) wide.
£20,000-25,000 *C*

An Empire mahogany ormolu mounted lit en bateau.
£2,000-3,000 *C*

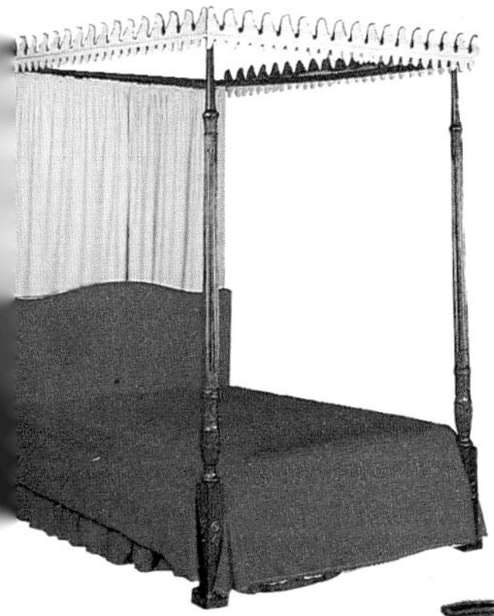

George III mahogany
d, 70in (178cm) wide.
,500-6,500 *C*

An Empire mahogany ormolu mounted lit d'alcove.
£12,000-15,000 *CNY*

A George III mahogany double breakfront bookcase, 145½in (369cm). **£20,000-25,000** *C*

A Regency mahogany breakfront bookcase, with central oak lined slides, probably reduced, 96in (244cm). **£3,000-5,000** *C*

ate Regency
hogany
kcase, the
rs fitted with
mah locks,
½in (151cm).
,000-12,000 *C*

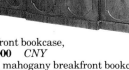

A George III
hogany
akfront
kcase,
n (173cm).
,000-16,000 *C*

A Federal inlaid walnut breakfront bookcase, c1810, 76in (193cm). **£4,000-6,000** *CNY*

Above r. A George III mahogany breakfront bookcase, 97in (246cm). **£6,000-9,000** *C*

A walnut bookcase, with moulded cornice above geometrically glazed doors and cupboard doors, on bracket feet, 38in (97cm).
£4,000-6,000 *C*

A George II mahogany bookcase, with moulded cornice above 2 glazed doors and 2 panelled doors, cornice cut, 104in (264cm) high.
£4,000-6,000 *C*

A George III mahogany bookcase, with pierced fretwork broken scroll pediment, the 2 panelled doors enclosing oak slides, inscribed George Shedden Esq., 60in (153cm).
£24,000-26,000 *C*

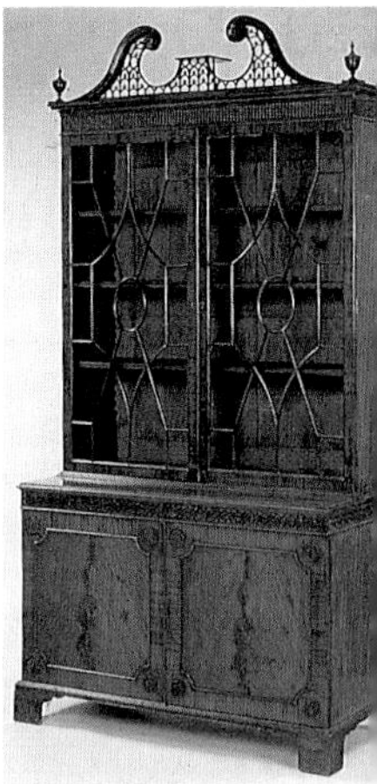

A George III mahogany bookcase, with pierced fretwork pediment, a pair of panelled doors enclosing 2 drawers an 2 slides, 49in (124cm).
£12,000-15,000 *C*

A George III mahogany bookcase, crossbanded with rosewood, 50½in (128cm). **£8,000-12,000** *C*

A Regency mahogany breakfront bookcase, 103in (262cm).
£12,000-15,000 *C*

A Regency ormolu moun rosewood breakfront bookcase, 81½in (207cm)
£14,000-16,000 *C*

A George III mahogany knee-hole secrétaire, 46in (117cm).
£10,000-12,000 *C*

A Federal inlaid mahogany secrétaire bookcase, in 2 parts, 40in (101.5cm).
£7,000-8,000 *CNY*

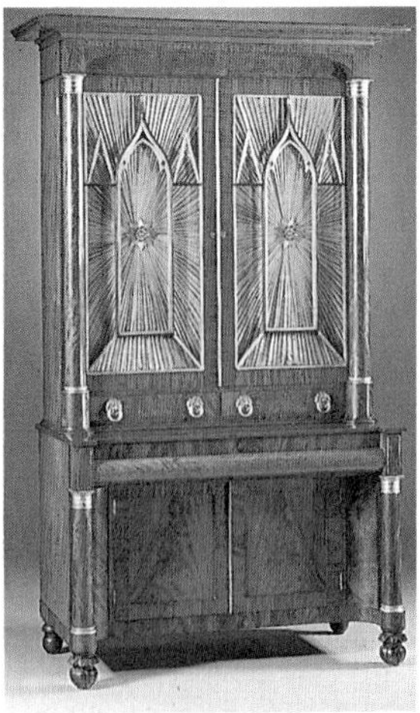

A Classical secrétaire bookcase, New York, c1830, 58in (147cm).
£25,000-30,000 *CNY*

A Regency rosewoo parcel gilt and bron inlaid bookcase, 30½in (77.5cm).
£10,000-12,000 *C*

ı Anglo-Indian padouk bureau
binet, with fitted interior,
ıer bun feet, 41½in (105cm).
5,000+ *C*

A Dutch East Indies,
Sri Lanka, kaliatur and
calamander bureau cabinet,
the hinged flap enclosing a
fitted interior, above
6 drawers, on bun feet,
18thC, 57in (144.5cm).
£2,500-3,000 *C*

A George I walnut bureau cabinet,
with fitted interior, later feet,
43in (109cm). **£30,000-35,000** *C*

William and Mary
lnut bureau cabinet,
later feet, restored,
½in (93cm).
5,000-30,000 *C*

A George III mahogany
bureau cabinet, fitted
interior, on bracket
feet, 30in (75.5cm).
£3,500-4,500 *CNY*

A North Italian walnut
bureau cabinet, partly
fitted interior, 44in
(111.5cm).
£50,000-55,000 *C*

A red and gold japanned
bureau cabinet, fitted
interior, restorations,
40½in (103cm).
£45,000-50,000 *C*

l. A George III
mahogany bureau
cabinet, late
18th/early 19thC,
35in (89cm).
£11,000-13,000 *CNY*

r. An Anglo-Indian
bureau cabinet,
distressed, 18thC,
25in (63.5cm).
£9,000-10,000 *C*

A red lacquer bureau
cabinet, with fitted
interior, 40in (102cm).
£8,000-10,000 *C*

A Napoleon III ormolu mounted vitrine cabinet, 41in (104cm) wide.
£4,000-6,000 *C*

An inlaid Flemish cabinet-on-stand with later top and stand, 53½in (135cm) high.
£6,000-7,000 *C*

A William and Mary parquetry inlaid tulipwood 2-stage cabinet, the upper section with doors concealing 10 drawers, 69in (175cm) high.
£18,000-20,000 *AH*

A Federal inlaid cherrywood linen press, c1800, 81½in (207cm) high.
£12,000-15,000 *CNY*

A Regency pollard elm clothes press, 83in (210cm) high.
£4,000-6,000 *C*

A Régence ormolu mounted kingwood armoire, c1720.
£30,000-33,000 *CNY*

A Federal inlaid mahogany sideboard an cabinet, possibly New Hampshire, possible old restoration, c1800, 70½in (178cm) high.
£6,500-9,500 *CNY*

A Federal grain painted step-back cupboard, some restoration, Vermont, early 19thC, 63½in (160cm).
£25,000-30,000 *CNY*

A pair of Louis XV kingwood and tulip wood parquetry encoignures, by RVLC, one with later marble top, 23½in (60cm) wide. **£12,000-15,000** *C*

A pair of Louis XVI ormolu mounted tulipwood, mahogany, marquetry and parquetry corner cabinets, c1775, 30½in (78cm).
£14,000-16,000 *CNY*

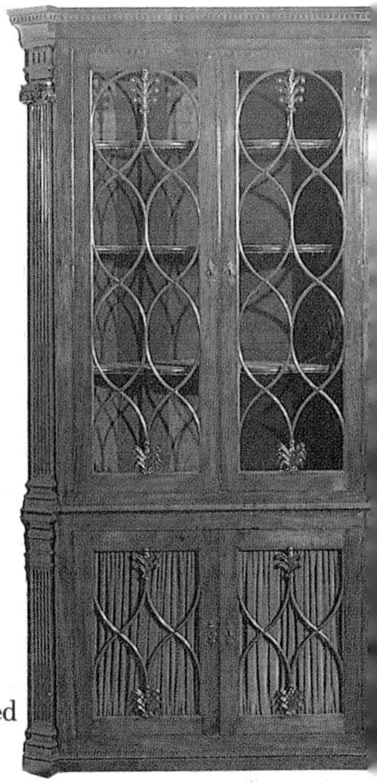

A George III double corner cupboard, 93in (236cm) high.
£10,000-12,000 *AG*

ɟeorge III mahogany
rétaire bookcase,
: base with
:ed interior and
:losed slides, 42½in
⁊8cm). **£7,000-9,000** *C*

A George III
style mahogany
secrétaire
cabinet,
31in (79cm).
£4,500-5,500 *CNY*

A Classical mahogany
and bird's-eye maple
secrétaire a abattant,
Philadelphia, c1825,
36½in (92cm).
£30,000-35,000 *CNY*

A Classical rosewood
and gilt-stencilled
ladies secrétaire,
in 2 sections, the
glazed doors enclosing
2 shelves, the lower
section with pull-out
writing slide, New York,
c1820, 37in (94cm).
£3,500-4,500 *CNY*

:lassical rosewood
k and bookcase,
wo parts,
bably Boston, c1830,
n (127cm).
000-10,000 *CNY*

A Louis XV ormolu mounted
tulipwood and marquetry
secrétaire a abattant,
stamped C. C. Saunier JME
twice, late 18thC, 29½in
(75cm). **£11,000-13,000** *CNY*

A green and black japanned and
giltwood cabinet-on-stand, painted
with chinoiserie scenes, the
panelled cupboard doors enclosing
13 drawers around a cupboard door,
41½in (105cm).
£3,000-5,000 *C*

panish parcel gilt and ebony
akfront cabinet-on-stand, the
s with carrying handles,
(195.5cm).
,000-12,000 *C*

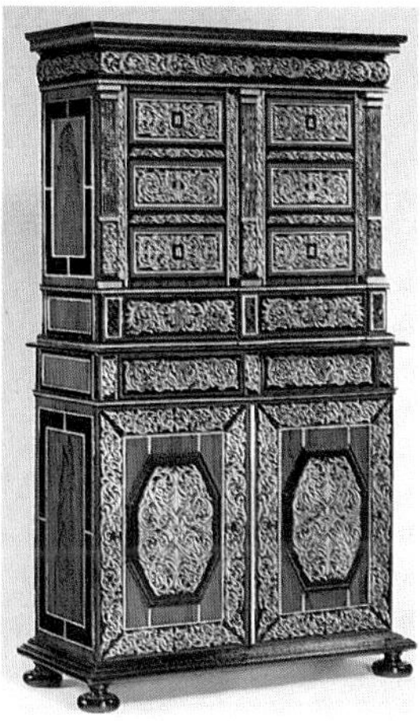

A Louis XVI boulle
cabinet en armoire,
42½in (108cm).
£9,000-12,000 *C*

A William IV mahogany library
cabinet, with leather lined
articulated rounded rectangular
top, the frieze with a brushing
slide to either side, the sides
with foliate bronze handles,
on plinth base, 54in (137cm).
£18,000-20,000 *C*

A Louis XVI Provincial mahogany bureau cabinet, with marble top and fitted interior, late 18thC, 44in (111.5cm) wide.
£6,500-9,500 *CNY*

A Louis XV tulipwood and marquetry secrétaire à abattant, restorations, 32in (81.5cm) wide.
£7,500-9,500 *CNY*

A Louis XVI ormolu mounted marquetry secrétaire à abattant, with Carrara marble top, fitted interior, stamped M. Ohneberg Jme, 38in (96.5cm) wide.
£15,000-20,000 *C*

A Regency secrétaire à abattant, 44in (111cm).
£3,000-5,000 *C*

A Flemish gilt metal mounted and kingwood strongbox-on-stand, the strongbox 17thC, 28in (71cm) wide.
£4,000-5,000 *C*

A Goanese inlaid cabinet-on-stand, 40in (101.5cm) wide.
£20,000-25,000 *C*

A walnut cabinet-on-chest, the top late 17thC, base 18thC. **£8,000-10,000** *C*

A Charles II japanned cabinet-on-stand, regilded, 46in (117cm) wide. **£20,000-25,000** *C*

Queen Anne burr walnut bureau,
e sloping flap enclosing a
ted interior of drawers and
cret drawers, on later bun feet,
½in (95cm).
7,000-20,000 *C*

Queen Anne cherrywood desk-on-
ame, the upper part with fitted
terior, on cabriole legs with
d feet, sliding lid supports
placed, Connecticut, c1750,
in (89cm).
0,000-35,000 *CNY*

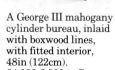

Chippendale carved mahogany
ock front desk, with
ted interior, on claw-and-
ll feet, damage and
storation, c1780, 45in (114cm).
8,000-20,000 *CNY*

A George I walnut bureau, the crossbanded fall enclosing a fitted interior, 31½in (80cm).
£7,000-9,000 *Bon*

A Chippendale mahogany desk, with fitted interior, some damage, Connecticut, c1770, 47in (119cm).
£7,000-10,000 *CNY*

A Dutch marquetry and mahogany bombé cylinder bureau, with fitted interior, late 18thC, 45in (114cm).
£6,000-8,000 *C*

A George I walnut bureau, the hinged flap lined with green baize, with fitted interior, on bracket feet, 26in (66cm).
£10,000-12,000 *C*

A cherrywood slant front desk, with fitted interior, labelled by Joseph Rawson, Providence, Rhode Island, feet damaged, c1790, 44in (111.5cm).
£12,000-15,000 *CNY*

A George III mahogany cylinder bureau, inlaid with boxwood lines, with fitted interior, 48in (122cm).
£4,000-6,000 *C*

l. An ormolu mounted kingwood, amaranth and parquetry bureau, 46in (117cm) high.
£6,000-8,000 *C*

A Flemish ebony, ivory and tortoi
shell table cabinet, the central doo
enclosing 5 drawers, the sides wit
carrying handles, late 17thC,
35½in (91cm).
£4,000-5,000 *C*

l. A George IV bird's-eye maple reading cabinet, 19in (48.5cm).
£14,000-16,000 *C*

A mahogany dwarf cabinet, early 19thC, the superstructure possibly later, 30½in (77cm).
£5,000-6,000 *GSP*

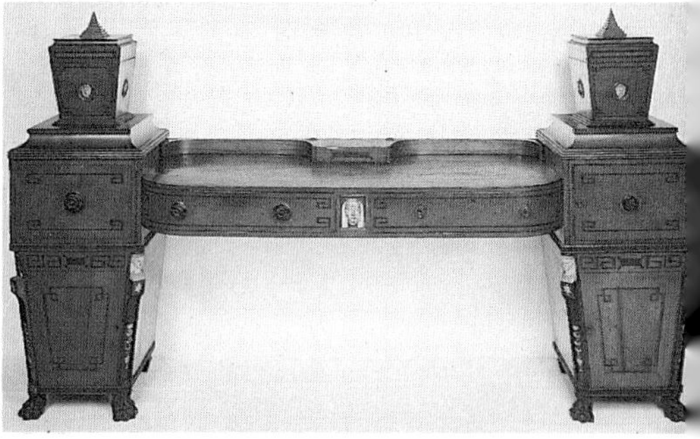

A Regency mahogany pedestal sideboard in the Egyptian style, formerly with a gallery, 109in (276.5cm). **£20,000-22,000** *C*

A Regency mahogany, ebonised and parcel gilt dwarf breakfront side cabinet, with later marble top, restored, 74in (188cm). **£9,000-10,000** *C*

A George III mahogany sideboard, with a central drawer above an arched kneehole, with 2 drawers to the left and deep drawer to the right, on block feet, 58in (147cm).
£7,000-9,000 *C*

A mid-Victorian ormolu mounted and marquetry side cabinet, with cross-banded breakfront top, 90in (229cm).
£4,000-6,000 *C*

A Federal inlaid cherry-wood sideboard with serpentine top, repairs, c1800, 61in (155cm).
£15,000-17,000 *CNY*

A late George III mahogany bow-fronted sideboard, 66in (168cm).
£14,000-16,000 *C*

A Regency mahogany serpentine sideboard, 48in (122cm).
£6,000-8,000 *C*

r. A late George III mahogany sideboard, crossbanded and inlaid, 69in (175cm).
£6,000-9,000 *C*

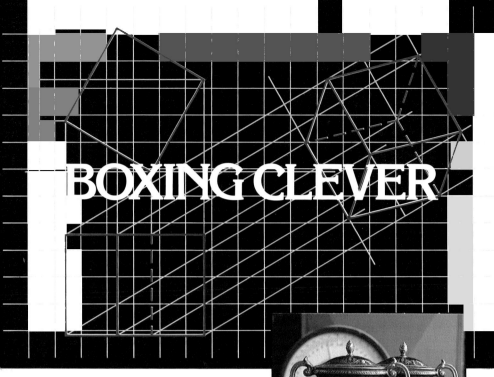

A George III ormolu mounted and brass inlaid mahogany, rosewood and satinwood breakfront table cabinet, with fitted interior. **£20,000-30,000** *C*

A Louis XVI mahogany console desserte, late 18thC, 56½in (143cm) wide. **£25,000-30,000** *CNY*

A Regency penwork breakfront side cabinet, with later slate top and some redecoration, 48½in (123cm) wide. **£15,000-20,000** *C*

An ormolu mounted ebo and boulle meuble d'appui. **£3,000-4,000** *C*

A Victorian inlaid burr walnut credenza with serpentine doors and gilt mounts. **£3,500-4,000** *SWO*

A pair of American brass inlaid ebonised side cabinets, late 19thC, 95½in (242cm) wide. **£24,000-26,000** *C*

A pair of Victorian walnut display cabinets with glazed doors, 34½in (87cm). **£2,000-3,000** *SWO*

r. A George III mahogany sideboard with bowfronted top, 73in (185cm) wide. **£10,000-12,000** *C*

A George III mahogany sideboard edged with boxwood, 71in (180cm) wide. **£13,000-15,000** *C*

r. A late George III mahogany sideboard, the ledgeback probably later, 72in (182.5cm). **£3,000-5,000** *C*

:eorge I walnut wing armchair
:h early 18thC upholstery, the
edlework restored, later blocks
feet.
5,000-50,000 *C*

An early George II walnut wing armchair with shaped sides, carved cabriole front legs on claw-and-ball feet, swept back legs.
£6,000-8,000 *C*

A rare Chippendale carved mahogany easy chair on cabriole legs with ball-and-claw feet, rear legs spliced to chair frame, Boston, Massachusetts, c1775.
£30,000-35,000 *CNY*

air of Irish
orge III
gères in the
nch taste.
000-10,000 *C*

A mahogany armchair with serpentine top, the arms, seat rail and cabriole legs carved, restorations.
£9,000-12,000 *C*

A pair of Louis XVI walnut bergères with possibly matching tabouret, late 18thC.
£6,500-9,500 *CNY*

air of Louis XVI giltwood
gères by Georges Jacob
l stamped, restored.
,000-30,000 *C*

A George I walnut open armchair with carved top-rail and drop-in seat, on cabriole legs with pointed pad feet, one later angle bracket and some restoration.
£12,000-15,000 *C*

A William IV mahogany tub armchair.
£10,000-15,000 *C*

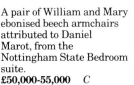

A pair of William and Mary ebonised beech armchairs attributed to Daniel Marot, from the Nottingham State Bedroom suite.
£50,000-55,000 *C*

A pair of George II mahogany library armchairs, with contemporary needlework upholstery.
£125,000+ *C*

A George III mahogany open armchair, covered in leather.
£6,000-8,000 *C*

A matched pair of George III mahogany library armchairs.
£14,000-16,000 *C*

A pair of George III mahogany armchairs, with buttoned backs and seats.
£8,000-12,000 *C*

A set of 4 George III painted armchairs, restored.
£3,000-5,000 *C*

A set of 8 George III mahogany open armchairs.
£35,000-40,000 *C*

A set of 4 George III giltwood open armchairs, some restoration.
£15,000-20,000 *C*

A suite of Louis XVI giltwood furniture, by Georges Jacob.
£15,000-20,000 *C*

A pair of Regency parcel gilt and painted armchairs.
£5,000-6,000 *C*

l. A set of 10 Regency mahogany dining chairs, with minor restorations.
£10,000-12,000 *C*

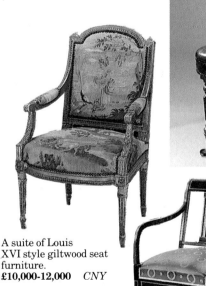

A Regency mahogany reading chair, with some restoration.
£8,000-10,000 *C*

A suite of Louis XVI style giltwood seat furniture.
£10,000-12,000 *CNY*

l. An Empire mahogany fauteuil-de-bureau with swivel seat, restored.
£1,500-2,000 *C*

l. A Russian brass mounted mahogany armchair with silk upholstered seat, late 18thC.
£6,000-8,000 *C*

eorge II walnut
lining wing armchair,
th raked adjustable
ck.
,000-8,000 *C*

A pair of George III mahogany tub chairs, covered in green leather, one reduced.
£9,000-11,000 *C*

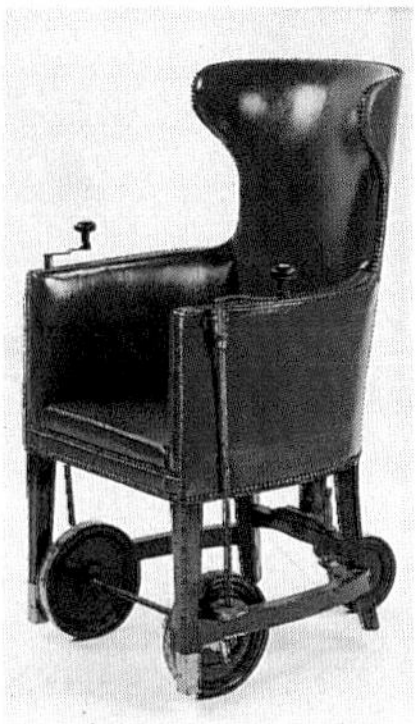

A George III mahogany invalid's chair, attributed to John Joseph Merlin.
£2,000-2,500 *C*

An Empire mahogany bergère.
£6,500-7,500 *C*

air of Louis XVI grey
nted marquises, with
ded legs headed by
erae, late 18thC,
½in (82cm).
,000-15,000 *CNY*

A pair of Louis XIII walnut fauteuils, with scrolled moulded arms.
£11,000-13,000 *C*

Two Transitional painted fauteuils, redecorated.
£3,000-4,000 *C*

A pair of giltwood fauteuils, stamped Bauve.
£32,000-35,000 *C*

l. A pair of George III grained rosewood open armchairs.
£4,000-6,000 *C*

arge George II
hogany open
nchair, lacking
ne angle
cks, 32½in
cm).
000-4,000 *C*

A pair of George II mahogany library armchairs.
£120,000+ *C*

A pair of George III armchairs.
£3,000-5,000 *C*

Two George II
ahogany master's
airs, one with
inted label
rt Treasures
xhibition 1928',
storations.
,000-12,000 *C*

l. A pair of Louis XV fauteuils, some restoration.
£15,000-20,000 *C*

A Regency mahogany reading chair, one arm with swing pen drawer, inscribed in ink A.S. twice, c1810.
£10,000-12,000 *C*

A Regency mahogany reading chair, repairs to back legs, stamped IO. **£6,000-8,000** *C*

A Regency simulated rosewood bergère, with cane seat and carved scroll legs.
£3,000-4,000 *C*

A Federal fancy painted side chair, attributed to Samuel Gragg, Boston, U.S.A., some damage, c1820.
£3,000-4,000 *CNY*

A pair of Regency rosewood tub bergères.
£15,000-20,000 *C*

Below. A pair of Regency mahogany armchairs.
£8,000-10,000 *C*

A Regency parcel gilt and ebonised armchair.
£8,000-12,000 *C*

Below. A set of 8 Regency mahogany dining chairs, including 2 armchairs, some damage and repairs.
£14,000-16,000 *C*

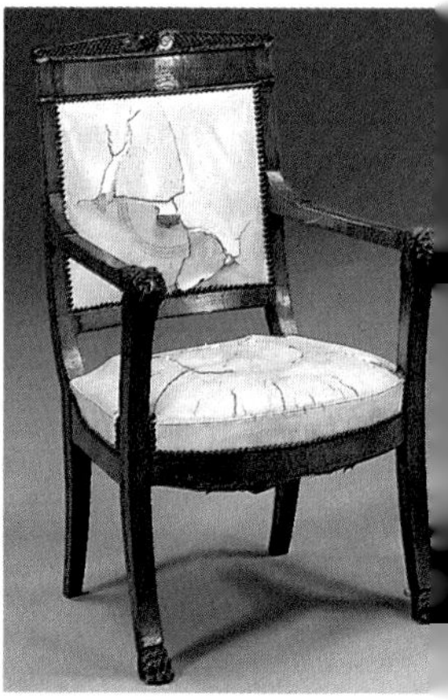

A pair of Empire mahogany fauteuils, c1810.
£9,000-10,000 *CNY*

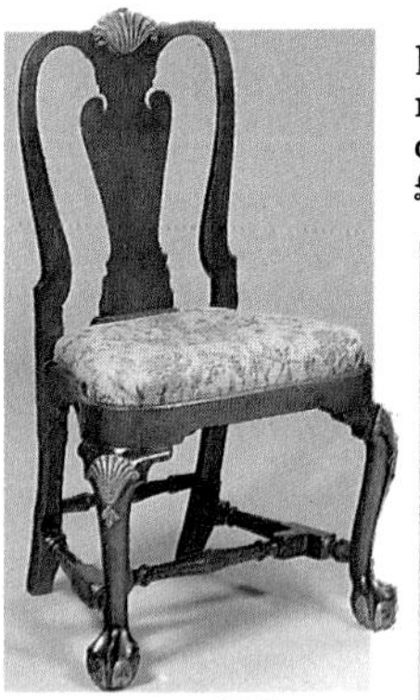

l. A pair of mahogany side chairs, c1760.
£60,000-70,000 *CN*

A Queen Anne painted carved side chair, attributed to John Gaines, c1730.
£20,000-25,000 *C*

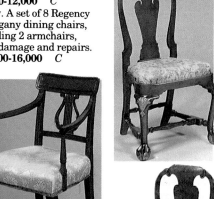

l. A pair of early Victorian mahogany armchairs. **£5,000-6,000** *C*

r. A set of 4 George I walnut chairs, 3 stamped ID, 1 stamped TM, restored. **£5,000-7,000** *C*

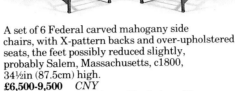

A set of 6 Federal carved mahogany side chairs, with X-pattern backs and over-upholstered seats, the feet possibly reduced slightly, probably Salem, Massachusetts, c1800, 34½in (87.5cm) high.
£6,500-9,500 *CNY*

l. A set of 6 George I walnut side chairs with caned panels and drop-in seats. **£10,000-12,000** *C*

A set of 4 Regency oak side chairs in the Gothic style.
£4,000-5,000 *C*

Regency simulated)sewood bergère with rched spoon-shaped back nd caned seat, on reeded abre legs.
4,000-5,000 *C*

An Empire giltwood chair with carved arched cresting.
£5,000-7,000 *C*

A set of 7 Regency brass inlaid mahogany dining chairs, including 2 open armchairs.
£20,000-22,000 *C*

A set of 6 William IV rosewood dining chairs with upholstered drop-in seats, curved toprail and scroll carved crossbar.
£1,500-2,000 *C*

set of 4 George IV vory-mounted rosewood ide chairs, with some estoration.
10,000-12,000 *C*

A set of 8 George IV mahogany dining chairs with broad curved toprails and buttoned seats.
£6,000-10,000 *C*

A set of 8 William IV balloon-back dining chairs.
£2,500-3,000 *SWO*

A set of 12 mid-Victorian dining chairs, stamped 'Gillows Lancaster L23097'.
£17,000-20,000 *C*

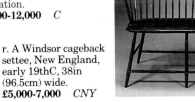

r. A Windsor cageback settee, New England, early 19thC, 38in (96.5cm) wide.
£5,000-7,000 *CNY*

l. A suite of Empire white painted and parcel gilt furniture, some restoration to decoration, possibly Italian, early 19thC.
£80,000-85,000 *CNY*

A George III mahogany open armchair, with serpentine toprail and suede seat.
£2,000-3,000 *C*

A George III fruitwood library armchair, with serpentine padded back, armrests and seat.
£3,000-4,000 *C*

A pair of mahogany open armchairs, with padded backs and bowed seats.
£5,000-6,000 *C*

A pair of Louis XVI fauteuils, c1780.
£10,000-12,000 *CNY*

A set of 10 late Regency mahogany dining chairs, including 2 armchairs.
£8,000-12,000 *CEd*

A pair of early Victorian rosewood open armchairs with shaped curved backs.
£6,000-7,000 *C*

A pair of Queen Anne red stained maple side chairs, some restoration.
£7,000-8,000 *CNY*

A Queen Anne carved maple side chair, possibly New Hampshire, c1735.
£6,000-8,000 *CNY*

A set of 6 Dutch walnut and marquetry chairs, c1730.
£20,000-25,000 *Bon*

A Queen Anne carved walnut side chair, attributed to John Goddard, Newport, Rhode Island, c1760.
£20,000-25,000 *CNY*

l. A set of 5 Queen Anne walnut dining chairs and 3 of later date, with drop-in seats on cabriole legs.
£24,000-25,000 *C*

A pair of George II walnut side chairs, with padded backs ane seats.
£11,000-12,000

l. A set of 8 George II walnut side chairs with padded backs and seats, on cabriole legs and pad feet, some restoration.
£20,000-22,000 *C*

l. A set of 10 German walnut side chairs, c1750.
£4,000-5,000 *C*

Chippendale carved
ıhogany side chair,
repair to top of
strail.
0,000-25,000 *CNY*

A pair of early George
III mahogany side
chairs. **£50,000-55,000** *C*

A set of 6
George III dining
chairs. **£5,000-6,000** *C*

A set of 4 George
III mahogany
dining chairs,
restored.
£2,500-3,000 *C*

A pair of early George
III walnut side chairs,
the legs cut and
rejoined.
£4,000-5,000 *C*

ɔair of George III
ıhogany side chairs,
ɔairs, late 18thC.
000-5,000 *CNY*

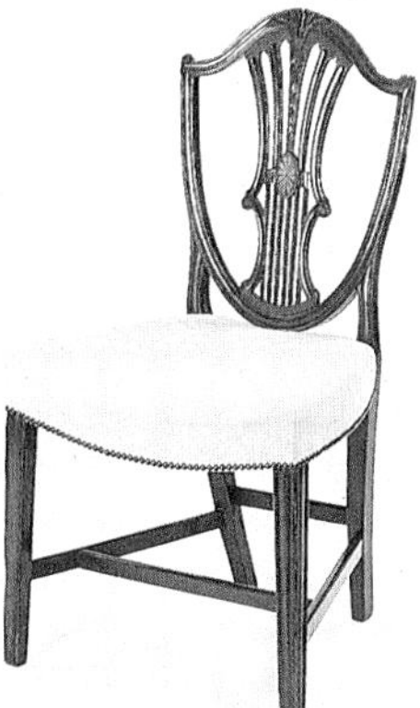

A pair of George
III mahogany
dining chairs,
each with pierced
shield back, and
central fan
medallion.
£1,500-2,000 *C*

Six George III
mahogany dining
chairs, repairs.
£3,500-4,500 *C*

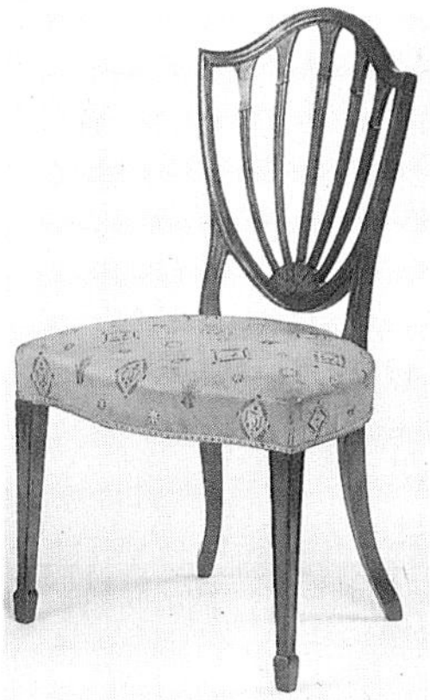

Eight George III
mahogany chairs.
£12,000-15,000 *C*

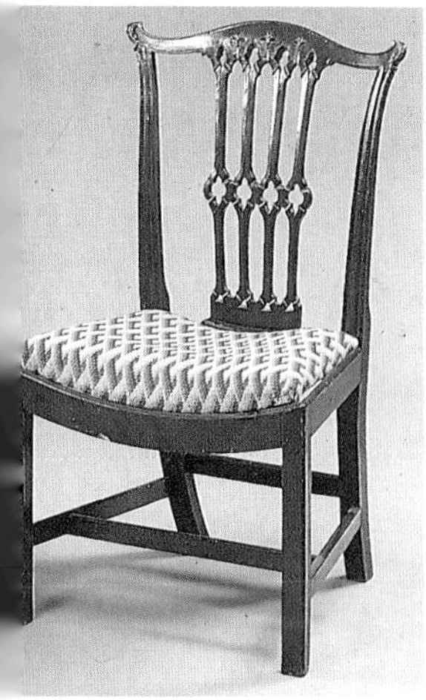

et of 4 George III
hogany dining chairs,
with slight
iations.
000-5,000 *C*

A pair of George III
giltwood chairs.
£6,500-7,500 *C*

A set of 4 mahogany
chairs, 19thC.
£850-900 *PCA*

l. A set of 6 George
III mahogany dining
chairs, including a
pair of open
armchairs, some
restoration.
£4,000-6,000 *C*

A set of 7 Federal carved mahogany dining chairs, some damage, Salem, Massachusetts, c1800.
£15,000-25,000 *CNY*

A set of 10 Chippendale mahogany dining chai comprising 2 armchairs and 8 side chairs, Massachusetts, one repaired, c1770.
£35,000-40,000 *CNY*

A set of 12 George III style mahogany dining chairs, including 4 armchairs, with waved crest rails and pierced splats. **£9,000-12,000** *CNY*

A set of 6 George III mahogany dining chairs, including a pair of open armchairs, with later blocks. **£8,000-11,000** *C*

A pair of Louis XV giltwood fauteuils, stamped Tilliard, mid-18thC.
£50,000-60,000 *CNY*

A pair of Louis XVI giltwood fauteuils en cabriolet, stamped G. Jacob.
£15,000-25,000 *CN*

A set of 6 Federal carved mahogany side chairs and an armchair, each with carved and reeded bowed rectangular back with 4 square reeded vertical splats, each branded 'MB', various repairs to legs, Philadelphia, c1800.
£3,500-5,000 *CNY*

A set of 8 Classical mahogany Klismos chairs, comprising 2 armchairs and 6 side chairs, each with a panelled tablet crest rail with a reeded and scrolled crest, the horizontal back rail with rope-twist and baluster turnings, the armchairs with open scrolled arms, Boston, c1820.
£20,000-25,000 *CNY*

A Louis XVI giltwood fauteuil a la reine, the frame and downswept arm supports carved with flowers and acanthus, upholstery distressed, c1780. **£9,500-11,000** *CNY*

A pair of Regency simulated bronze and parcel gilt bergères, after a design by George Smith, each with a scrolled back and deep toprail, centred by a Medusa mask, with double caned sides, redecorated.
£90,000-100,000 *C*

An Empire giltwood fauteuil, the frame and seat rail carved with laurel leaves, re-gilded, stamped Jacob.D.R.Meslee, early 19thC.
£13,000-16,000 *CNY*

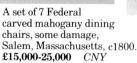

walnut sofa, upholstered
early 18thC needlework,
in (144.5cm).
7,000-20,000 *C*

A George I walnut double chairback settee, 50in (127cm).
£10,000-12,000 *CNY*

A Georgian walnut sofa.
£8,000-10,000 *C*

ı Irish George III giltwood
fa, with a carved moulded
at rail, 83in (210.5cm).
,000-7,000 *C*

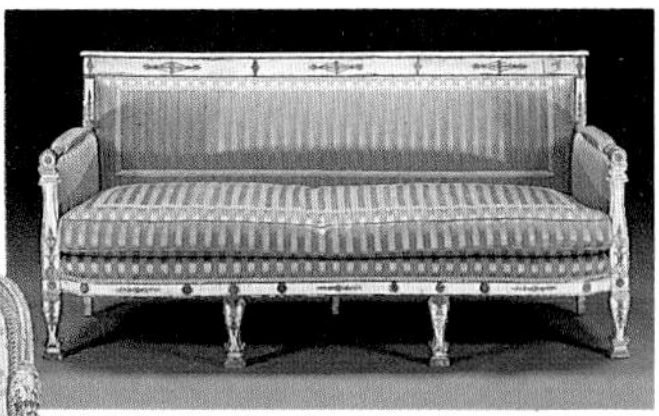

A suite of Empire white painted and parcel gilt furniture, possibly Italian, early 19thC.
£80,000-90,000 *CNY*

A Louis XV style marquise.
£4,000-5,000 *CNY*

Federal mahogany sofa, one front
ɔt pieced, c1800, 40in (101cm).
0,000-12,000 *CNY*

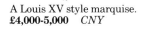

r. A George III mahogany window seat, 37½in (70cm). **£3,000-4,000** *C*

A pair of George IV oak window seats, some damage.
£17,000-20,000 *C*

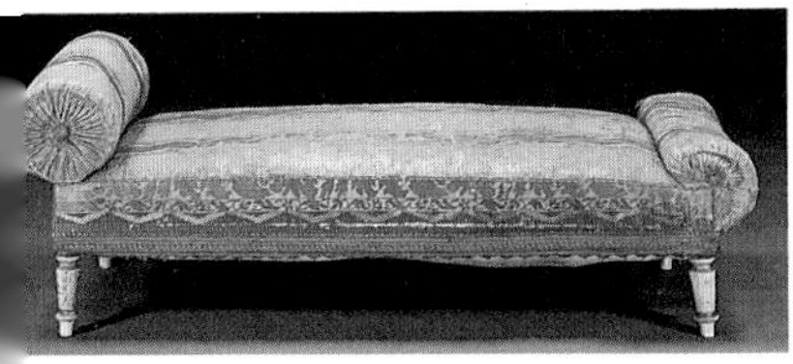

Neo-classic style white painted day
ł, 74in (188cm). **£1,000-2,000** *CNY*

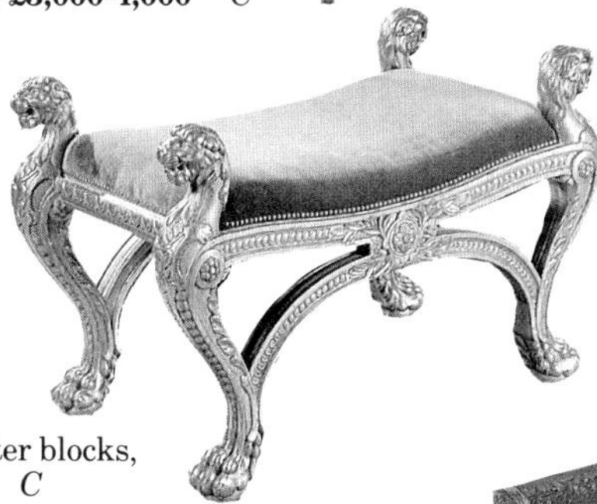

r. A giltwood stool, with later blocks, 39in (99cm). **£7,000-8,000** *C*

A pair of Regency window seats.
£23,000-25,000 *C*

early Victorian maple sofa,
in (195.5cm). **£7,000-9,000** *C*

r. A Victorian adjustable music stool. **£1,000-1,500** *MAG*

A pair of George IV mahogany window seats.
£9,000-10,000 *C*

A Directoire brass inlaid mahogany and amaranth gueridon, late 18thC, 29in (74cm) diam.
£5,000-6,000 *CNY*

A George III mahogany writing table, fitted with 2 drawers, the reverse with 2 slides, 48in (122cm).
£8,000-9,000 *C*

A George III ormolu mounted satinwood writing table, 34in (86cm).
£25,000-30,000 *C*

l. A Regency mahogany writing table, with 6 drawers, 74½in (189cm).
£20,000-25,000 *C*

r. A Regency ormolu mounted amboyna writing table, restored, 45in (114cm).
£15,000-20,000 *C*

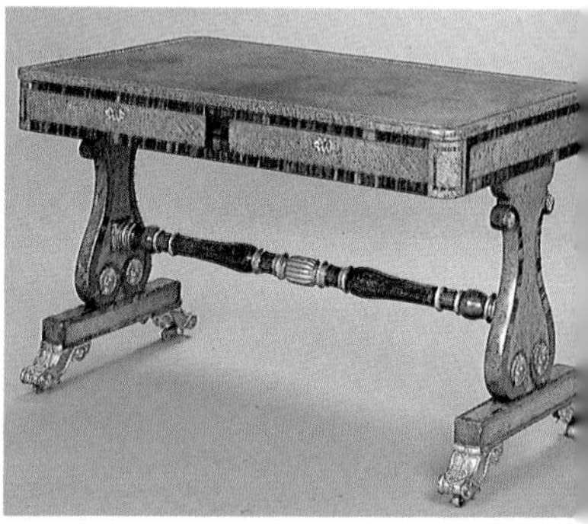

A Regency mahogany writing table, with moulded top and a drawer, on solid waisted end supports, labelled James Newton, 37in (94cm).
£5,000-6,000 *C*

A George IV mahogany writing table, by Gillows of Lancaster, the frieze with 6 drawers on reeded end standards and downswept legs with paw caps, 72in (182.5cm). **£12,000-15,000** *C*

A William IV plane writing table, with leather-lined rounded rectangular top, the frieze with 3 drawers, on turned legs, 54in (137cm). **£4,000-6,000** *C*

l. A William IV brass inlaid rosewood library table.
£30,000-35,000 *C*

r. An early Victorian parcel gilt ash writing table, by Holland & Sons.
£10,000-12,000 *C*

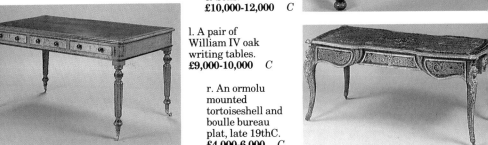

l. A pair of William IV oak writing tables.
£9,000-10,000 *C*

r. An ormolu mounted tortoiseshell and boulle bureau plat, late 19thC.
£4,000-6,000 *C*

Queen Anne walnut bachelor's
.est, with folding top,
storations, 29in (74cm).
.4,000-16,000 *C*

A George III mahogany chest, with original moulded handles and lock escutcheons, c1775, 36in (92cm). **£7,000-8,000** *AG*

A George III mahogany secrétaire chest, with stepped fretwork superstructure, 31½in (80cm). **£12,000-15,000** *C*

George I walnut chest, the sides
.th brass carrying handles,
storations to the feet,
.in (81cm).
5,000-18,000 *C*

A Federal figured maple chest of drawers, on modified French feet, c1810, 43in (109cm). **£3,500-4,500** *CNY*

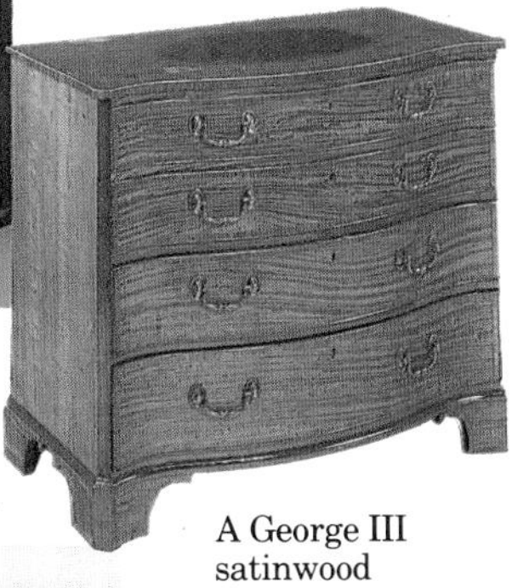

A George III satinwood serpentine chest of 4 long drawers, banded with tulipwood and inlaid with lines, on bracket feet, 37in (94cm). **£8,000-10,000** *C*

A Régence ormolu mounted ebony and marquetry commode, the rectangular brass bordered top centred by a vase of flowers, above a mask flanked by scrolling foliage, restorations, 47in (119cm). **£40,000-45,000** *C*

Jeorge I walnut bachelor's
.st, on later bracket feet,
torations, 27½in (70cm).
000-10,000 *C*

A North Italian walnut bombé commode, the sides with cupboards, on cabriole legs carved with flowerheads, with trefoil feet, 41in (104cm). **£5,000-7,000** *C*

r. A Louis XV/XVI ormolu mounted tulipwood and marquetry commode, late 18thC, 44in (112cm). **£14,000-16,000** *CNY*

A bronze mounted kingwood and parquetry bombé commode, 39in (99cm).
£7,000-9,000 *C*

A Restoration ormolu mounted mahogany commode with mottled grey marble top and decorated frieze drawer above 3 drawers, 50in (127cm).
£2,000-3,000 *C*

A German walnut and marquetry commode, top inlaid with geometr strapwork, on later bun feet, 18thC, 47½in (120.5cm).
£6,000-7,000 *C*

A Transitional ormolu mounted marquetry commode, the inlaid breakfront top possibly later, 57½in (146cm). **£70,000-80,000** *C*

A George III mahogany serpentin commode, the doors enclosing slid above 2 short and 1 long drawer, o ogee bracket feet, 49in (124.5cm).
£9,000-12,000 *C*

A George III style mahogany and marquetry commode, 48in (122cm).
£7,500-8,500 *Bea*

A George III mahogany commode, with eared serpentine top, restorations, the stand possibly later, 48in (122cm).
£8,000-12,000 *C*

A Regency mahogany pedestal cupboard, with moulded square top above a cupboard door and drawer fitted with removable bin, on plinth base, early 19th 13in (38cm), together with a later brass-bour mahogany jardinière, 15in (38cm) diam.
£3,500-4,500 *CNY*

A Charles X bois satine commode with marble top, 52in (132cm).
£5,000-6,000 *C*

A late Victorian satinwood and marquetry commode, by Edwards & Roberts, with 3 panelled doors, on square tapering feet, 60in (152cm).
£11,000-13,000 *C*

ı Italian rococo walnut commode,
cabriole legs with toupie feet,
d-18thC, 56½in (143cm) wide.
0,000-40,000 *CNY*

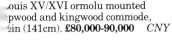

A Louis XV/XVI ormolu mounted kingwood, bois satiné and tulipwood parquetry commode, c1775.
£70,000-80,000 *CNY*

Above l. A Transitional ormolu mounted, tulipwood, harewood, amaranth and ebony parquetry commode, with later top, 56½in (143.5cm). **£18,000-20,000** *C*

ouis XV/XVI ormolu mounted
ipwood and amaranth commode,
mped N.Grevenich Jme, c1770,
n (127cm). **£40,000-50,000** *CNY*

ouis XV/XVI ormolu mounted
pwood and kingwood commode,
½in (141cm). **£80,000-90,000** *CNY*

A Swedish rococo ormolu mounted, tulipwood and walnut parquetry commode, the serpentine moulded crossbanded top inlaid with a lozenge panel, mid-18thC, 41in (104cm) wide.
£10,000-12,000 *CNY*

A Transitional ormolu mounted kingwood and marquetry commode, with later shaped breakfront marble top, stamped P.A. Foullet Jme. **£60,000-70,000** *C*

ransitional ormolu mounted marquetry commode,
ded in tulipwood and amaranth, with later top,
mped P.A. Foullet Jme, 57in (145cm) wide.
0,000-200,000 *C*

A George III mahogany commode, with gilt tooled leather lined slide, the doors and drawers edged with ebony, 47in (119cm) wide.
£70,000-80,000 *C*

A pair of ormolu mounted kingwood and amaranth petites commodes, with marble tops and frieze drawers above 2 drawers, 32½in (82cm) wide.
£9,000-10,000 *C*

A Louis XVI commode, late 18thC, 50in wide.
£9,500-12,000 *CNY*

A pair of South Italian walnut commodes, with composition marbl tops above banded and inlaid drawers, 18thC, 23in (58.5cm) wide.
£7,000-10,000 *C*

A William and Mary oyster veneered chest, originally on bun feet, now on later stand, 37in (94cm) wide.
£8,000-10,000 *Bon*

An Empire ormolu mounted mahogany commode, with marble top above 2 panelled doors enclosing 3 drawers, later bun feet, adapted, 51in (129.5cm) wide. **£10,000-12,000** *C*

A pair of George III mahogany dining pedestals, one fitted as a plate warmer, on with lead-lined compartments, 38in (96cm) high
£7,000-10,000

r. A Queen Anne mahogany high chest of drawers in 2 sections, Boston area, Massachusetts, c1760, 86in (218.5cm) high.
£30,000-36,000 *CNY*

l. A Chippendale carved mahogany high chest of drawers in 2 sections, probably West Chester, Pennsylvania, c1775, 92½in (234cm) high.
£30,000-35,000 *C*

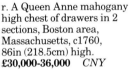

An early Georgian walnut tallboy on bracket feet, the drawers re-lined, restorations, 42in (106.5cm) wide.
£3,000-5,000 *C*

A Queen Anne carved cherrywood high chest of drawers, c1760, 73in (185cm) high.
£10,000-12,000 *CNY*

A Chippendale figured maple chest, adapted, c1785, 76in (193cm).
£15,000-20,000 *CNY*

A William and Mary walnut chest on-stand, on later bun feet, c1690, 42½in (107cm) wide.
£4,000-5,000 *Bo*

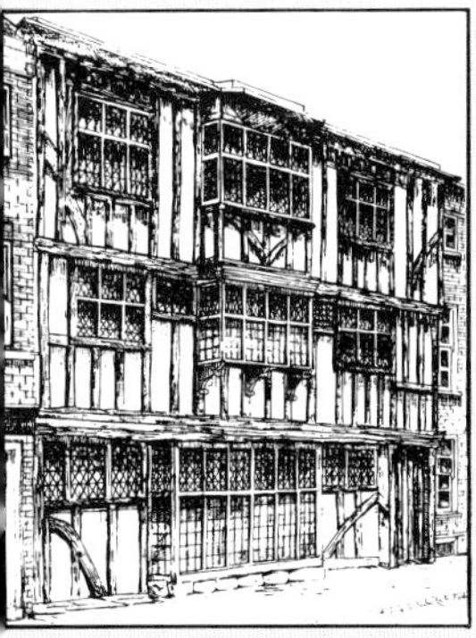

Conquest House

17 Palace Street, Canterbury,
Kent, CT1 2DZ
Telephone: (0227) 464587 Fax: (0227) 451375
From USA: (011-44-227)

LAPADA
London and Provincial Antique Dealers Association

An extensive collection of Antiques in a fascinating historic building

Open 9am-5.30pm Monday-Saturday 5 Showrooms

ISLINGTON ARTEFACTS
ORIGINAL PINE FURNITURE
12 & 14 Essex Road
Islington
London N1 8LN
071-226 6867
Delivery arranged worldwide

Empire Antiques

The Old Council Yard
Strand Street
Sandwich
Kent

Telephone: (0304) 614474/612395
From USA (011-44-304)

Fax (0227) 451375
From USA (011-44-227)

12,000 sq. ft. of warehouse space

Enormous range of antique stripped
Pine Furniture
and English Shipping Furniture

New stock arriving daily from Great Britain
and Europe. Realistic Trade Prices
Courteous service and expert advice

Shipping arranged Worldwide
Containers packed and shipped

8.00 am to 5.00 pm

he proprietors Desmond Magee and Caroline Hill, welcome you personally to come and visit ur shops in London and Canterbury and our trade warehouse in Sandwich, please ring us for n appointment, or just call in.

A George I burr walnut tallboy, the base with a slide, 41in (104cm) wide.
£25,000-30,000 *C*

A George I burr walnut secrétaire tallboy, crossbanded and inlaid, 40in (101.5cm) wide.
£25,000-30,000 *C*

A Chippendale carved mahogany chest-on-chest, some damage, c1775, 45in.
£100,000+ *CNY*

A William & Mary waln veneer high chest of drawers, some restoration, c1725, 37in (94cm) wide.
£7,000-8,000 *CNY*

A Queen Anne maple high chest of drawers, Massachusetts, c1750.
£15,000-20,000 *CNY*

A Queen Anne carved cherrywood high chest of drawers, some restoration, c1750, 41in (104cm) wide.
£12,000-15,000 *CNY*

A carved maple high chest of drawers in 2 sections, c1750, 40in (101.5cm) wide.
£20,000-25,000 *CNY*

A Queen Anne burr walnut kneehole desk on later bun feet, 37in (94cm) wide.
£6,000-9,000 *C*

r. A Louis XIV ormolu mounted scarlet boulle bureau mazarin, with later turned feet, 38in (96.5cm) wide.
£15,000-20,000 *C*

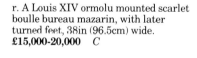

A William & Mary walnut and marquetry chest-on-stand. **£17,000-20,000** *A*

A George II mahogany kneehole desk with crossbanded top, 54½in (138cm) wide. **£20,000-25,000** *C*

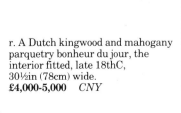

r. A Dutch kingwood and mahogany parquetry bonheur du jour, the interior fitted, late 18thC, 30½in (78cm) wide.
£4,000-5,000 *CNY*

A George III satinwood a rosewood inlaid desk.
£12,000-15,000 *C*

A mid-Georgian mahogany kneehole secrétaire desk.
£4,000-5,000 *C*

A George III style mahogany writing desk, with a writing slide and recessed kneehole cupboard, 35½in (90cm). **£3,000-4,000** *ALL*

George I walnut
eehole desk,
th one long
awer, 6 short
awers and a
eehole drawer
ound a recessed
pboard door, on
acket feet,
in (76cm).
,000-8,000 *C*

A George III partners' desk, with leather lined top, 60in (152cm).
£18,000-20,000 *C*

A George IV mahogany Carlton House desk, 64in (162.5cm).
£15,000-20,000 *C*

l. A George III mahogany partners' desk, the drawer fronts restored, 55in (139.5cm).
£8,000-9,000 *C*

l. A mahogany roll-top desk, possibly by Edwards and Roberts, c1900, 70½in (179cm).
£12,000-15,000 *C*

A George III mahogany roll-top desk, restored, 44in (112cm).
£12,000-15,000 *C*

ieorge II mahogany kneehole desk,
h later moulded top,
n (125cm). **£10,000-15,000** *C*

r. A Louis XV tulipwood bonheur du jour, stamped G.Cordie, late 18thC, 25½in (65cm). **£3,000-6,000** *CNY*

A Regency satinwood secrétaire and dressing chiffonier, crossbanded with rosewood, 21in (53cm).
£40,000-45,000 *C*

An Empire rosewood toilet mirror, the base inset with Paris porcelain plaques, 19½in (49.5cm) wide.
£3,000-4,000 *C*

An Italian carved and gilded tabernacle frame, with glass, 17thC, 41in (104cm) high.
£3,000-3,500 *CSK*

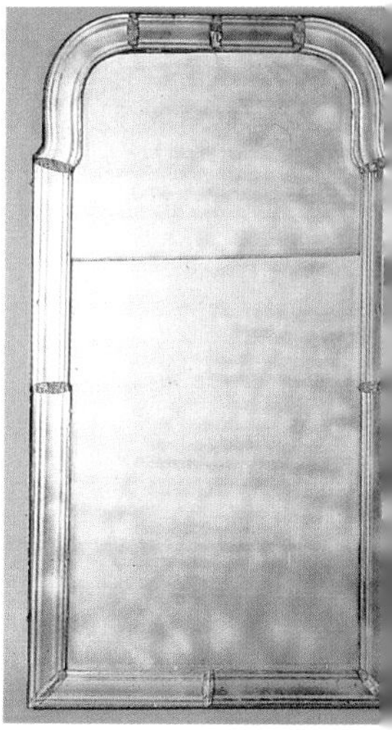

A pair of Queen Anne pier glasses, 58½in (148cm) high.
£50,000-60,000 *C*

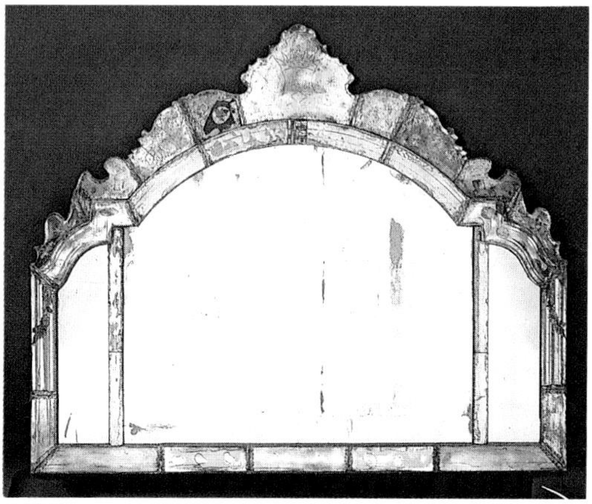

A William and Mary overmantel mirror, with restorations and replacement glass, 60 by 74in (152 by 188cm).
£10,000-15,000 *C*

A Scandinavian lead-framed mirror, early 18thC, 60in (152cm).
£9,000-12,000 *C*

A George II giltwood mirror, 68in (173cm) high.
£15,000-20,000 *C*

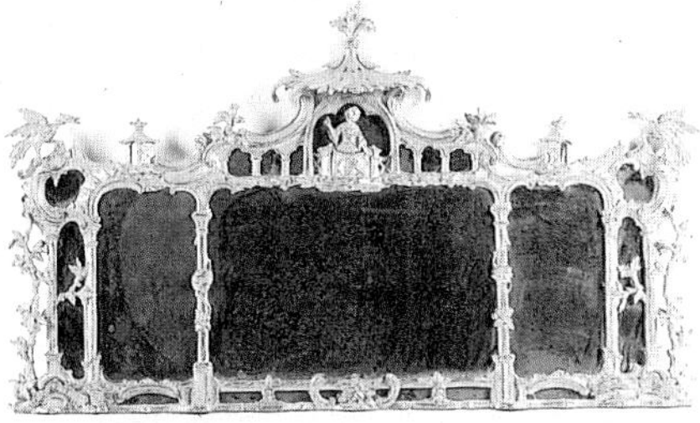

An early George III giltwood overmantel, later plates and re-gilt, 36in (92cm) high. **£10,000-15,000** *C*

A pair of Louis XV style giltwood mirrors, 39in (99cm) high.
£7,500-11,000 *CNY*

A George III giltwood mirror, restored, 80in (203cm) high.
£10,000-15,000 *C*

A pair of George II giltwood girandole restored, 51in (130 high.
£15,000-20,000 *C*

l. A George III style mirror. **£3,000-4,000** *CNY*

walnut and parcel gilt
ılet mirror, with 3
awers, 31½ by 19in
) by 48cm).
,000-1,500 *C*

A Queen Anne parcel gilt and lacquer toilet mirror, on later ogee bracket feet, 19in (48cm). **£3,000-4,000** *C*

A Queen Anne japanned toilet mirror.
£2,500-3,000 *C*

A Charles II giltwood mirror, with a carved frame, re-gilded, 39½ by 29in (100 by 74cm).
£2,000-3,000 *C*

Charles II black,
t and red japanned
rror, lacking cresting,
by 40in (127 by 102cm).
000-5,000 *C*

A Federal giltwood and eglomisé panel mirror, some damage, New York or Albany, c1800, 60 by 27½in (152 by 70cm).
£8,000-9,000 *CNY*

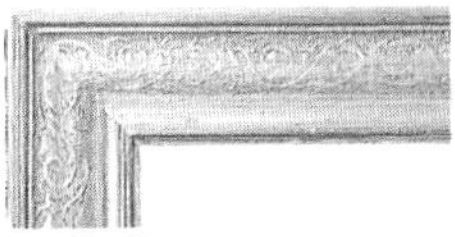

An Italian carved and gilded frame, 17thC, 41in (104cm) high.
£4,000-5,000 *CSK*

A Spanish carved, gilded and painted frame, 17thC, 59in (150cm) high.
£6,000-7,000 *CSK*

l. An Italian carved and gilded frame, 17thC.
£1,500-2,000 *CSK*

r. A Louis XIV carved and gilded frame, 47 by 39in (119 by 99cm).
£7,000-8,000 *CSK*

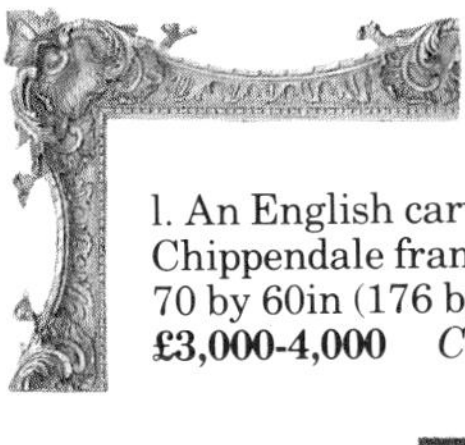

l. An English carved and gilded Chippendale frame, 18thC, 70 by 60in (176 by 151cm).
£3,000-4,000 *CSK*

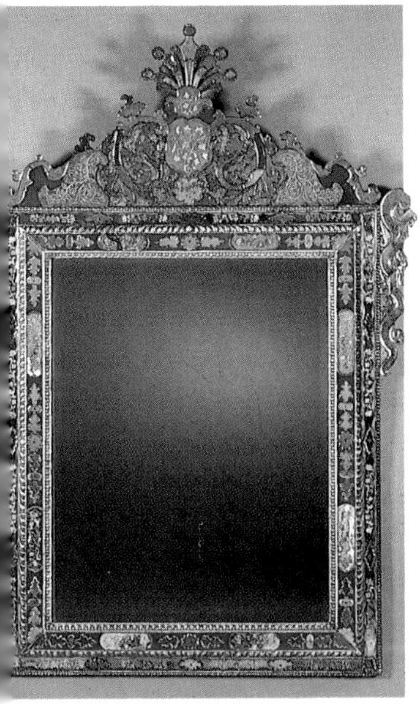

Italian blue and etched
ıss giltwood mirror,
ly 18thC, 62 by 44in
7 by 112cm).
0,000-40,000 *CNY*

A George III giltwood mirror, 56 by 24in (142 by 61cm).
£3,000-4,000 *C*

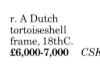

r. A Dutch tortoiseshell frame, 18thC.
£6,000-7,000 *CSK*

l. A Louis XIV style carved and gilded frame, 89in high.
£4,000-5,000 *CSK*

An Italian carved and gilded frame, early 17thC.
£5,000-6,000 *CSK*

l. A Regency mahogany and rosewood breakfast table, 63in (160cm) wide.
£3,000-5,000 *C*

A William and Mary black and gold japanned card table, some damage and repair, 31in (78cm) wide.
£10,000-12,000 *C*

A William IV mahogany breakfast table, lacking bolts, 46in (116.5cm) wide.
£2,000-3,000 *C*

A Queen Anne burr walnut card table, fitted interior, mid-18thC, 40in (101.5cm) wide.
£6,000-8,000 *C*

r. A George I burr walnut concertina-action card table, fitted interior, 33in (83.5cm) wide.
£40,000-50,000 *C*

A Chippendale carved walnut card table, repairs, c1770, 36in (92cm). **£12,000-15,000** *CN*

A George III mahogany card table, with inlaid D-shaped folding top, 42in (106.5cm) wide.
£5,000-6,000 *C*

A pair of George IV rosewood card tables, one with restorations, 36in (91.5cm) wide.
£4,000-5,000 *C*

A satinwood and painted card table, the D-shaped folding top and frieze inlaid, and with baize-lined interior, 36in (91.5cm) wide.
£5,000-6,000 *C*

A pair of early Victorian card tables, 36in wide. **£15,000-20,000** *C*

r. A Dutch marquetry card table/dumb waiter, 19thC. **£3,000-4,000** *MAG*

An early George III mahogany centre table, the top with moulded edge, 35in (89.5cm) wide.
£10,000-12,000 *C*

\ George III mahogany drum table,
he frieze inlaid with boxwood
ines, with turned pedestal,
ossibly reduced, 54in (137cm)
iam. **£7,000-10,000** *C*

A Regency simulated calamander drum table, redecorated, 48in (122cm) diam.
£5,000-6,000 *C*

A Regency brass inlaid rosewood centre table, 48in (122cm) diam.
£18,000-20,000 *C*

A Regency rosewood and parcel gilt centre table, with inlaid marble panel, 47in (119cm) diam.
£20,000-25,000 *C*

A Regency bird's-eye maple and rosewood centre table, top adapted, 29in (74cm) high. **£3,000-5,000** *C*

A Regency rosewood centre table with inset marble top, on bun feet, 34in (86cm) diam.
£13,000-15,000 *C*

A Regency mahogany drum table, with leather-lined top above 4 drawers, on turned shaft, 33in (84cm) diam.
£4,000-6,000 *C*

A Dutch marquetry, ebony and bone inlaid centre table, late 19thC, 46½in (118cm).
£4,500-5,500 *C*

A Regency brass inlaid and ormolu mounted rosewood reading, writing and games table, with fitted drawers, 30in (76cm).
£10,000-12,000 *C*

n ormolu mounted kingwood and tulip-
ood centre table, with oval leather-
ned top and 4 drawers,
5in (139.5cm).
,000-8,000 *C*

A Regency mahogany twin-pedestal dining table with rounded rectangular end sections, each with a frieze drawer, on baluster shafts and splayed quadripartite bases, 67in (170cm) including one leaf.
£7,000-10,000 *C*

An early Georgian walnut rectangular chest of drawers, with brushing slide, 31in (79cm).
£6,500-7,000 *C*

A George II mahogany chest, with brushing slide above 4 graduated drawers on bracket feet, 31in (79cm).
£6,000-7,000 *C*

A George III mahogany serpentine chest of 4 long drawers, on splayed feet, 36½in (92cm).
£7,000-8,000 *C*

A Chippendale inlaid walnut blanket chest, c1755.
£7,000-8,000 *CNY*

A Chippendale cherrywoc chest of drawers, c1775.
£14,000-16,000 *CNY*

A Chippendale cherrywood chest of drawers, c1790.
£13,000-14,000 *CNY*

A Federal carved mahogany bowfront chest of drawers.
£9,000-11,000 *CNY*

r. A George III chest of drawers, 40½in (103cm).
£5,500-6,500 *C*

A painted 2-drawer blanket chest, c1820, 51in (129.5cm). **£4,000-5,000** *CNY*

l. A Chippendale cherrywood chest of drawers, c1790, 40in (101.5cm). **£4,000-5,000** *CNY*

Regency mahogany serving table, with 4 frieze
awers centred by a lion's mask, 78½in (199.5cm).
.3,000-15,000 *C*

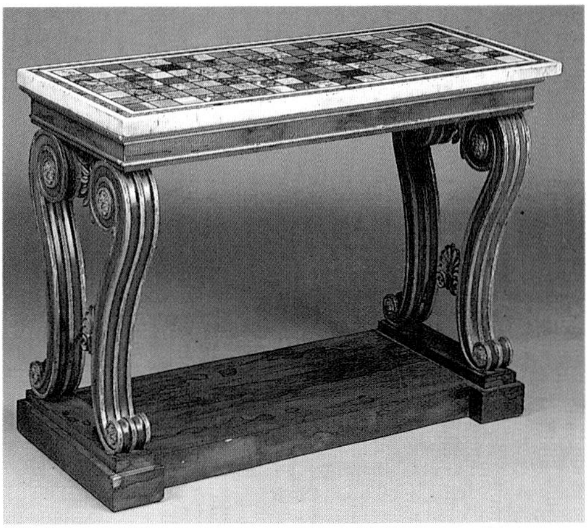

r. A Regency parcel gilt rosewood and simulated rosewood side table, the specimen marble top inlaid with squares of various marbles and semi-precious stones, 43in (109cm). **£23,000-25,000** *C*

George III satinwood and
sewood crossbanded sofa table,
laid with brass, the drawers
ith turned ebonised handles,
in (147cm) wide.
1,000-14,000 *AG*

r. A Regency mahogany sofa table, with crossbanded top, 60in (152cm). **£5,000-6,000** *C*

l. A Regency fiddleback mahogany sofa table, the frieze with 2 cedar-lined drawers, 48½in (123cm). **£5,000-7,000** *C*

George IV mahogany sofa table,
laid with satinwood,
plied with roundels on spreading
aft, one leg replaced, 60in
52cm). **£3,000-5,000** *C*

A George III mahogany library table, the top lined with gilt-tooled green leather, the frieze fitted with 6 drawers and 4 dummy drawers, 107in (272cm). **£30,000-35,000** *C*

late George III mahogany writing
ble, the frieze fitted with 3
awers, 44in (111.5cm).
,000-10,000 *C*

A Chippendale mahogany tilt-top tea table, attributed to John Goddard, Rhode Island, repaired, c1775. **£17,000-25,000** *CNY*

A George III padoukwood secrétaire table, with rectangular crossbanded twin-flap top, the deep frieze fitted with a fall flap simulated as 2 long drawers enclosing small drawers, 59½in (151cm) wide open. **£4,000-6,000** *C*

A pair of Louis XVI style ormolu mounted marble console tables, 19thC, 41½in (105cm) wide.
£20,000-25,000 *CNY*

A William IV mahogany serving table, 91in (231cm) wide.
£4,000-5,000 *CSK*

Below. A giltwood pollard oak and painted side table, 44½in (113cm) wide. **£4,500-5,000** *C*

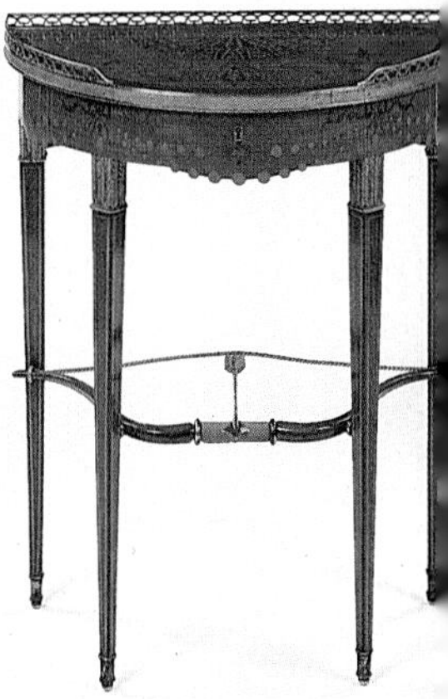

An ormolu mounted rosewoo and marquetry side table, the frieze fitted with a drawer, 24in (61.5cm) wide.
£6,000-7,000 *C*

Above l. A Regency ormolu mounted rosewood side table with mirror-glazed top, formerly marble, possibly Continental, early 19thC, 53in (134.5cm). **£12,000-15,000** *C*

r. A George II mahogany tripod table in the manner of John Channon, with brass and mother-of-pearl inlay, repaired, 25in (63cm) wide.
£10,000-15,000 *C*

A Regency rosewood sofa table in the manner of John Maclean, with cedar lined drawers, 65in (165cm) open.
£8,000-12,000 *C*

A Regency rosewood sofa table with leather-lined top and central easel, 58in (147cm) wide.
£8,000-10,000 *C*

A figured mahogany vene sewing table, school of Thoma Seymour, Bosto c1812, 21½in (54cm) wide.
£7,000-9,000

A Regency brown oak writing-table attributed to George Bullock, the top with inlaid ebony band, 36in (91.5cm) wide.
£4,500-5,500 *C*

A Regency brass-inlaid rosewood writing table, 44½in (113cm).
£5,000-6,000 *C*

George II gilt gesso stand, with
.ter grey and blue marble top,
.e pierced frieze carved with
rolling foliage, 52in (132cm).
4,000-18,000 *C*

A George III mahogany serving table, with serpentine fronted top, 47½in (121cm). **£4,000-6,000** *C*

A Louis XVI giltwood console table, with breakfront demi-lune black and white marble top and entrelac frieze, c1780, 34in (86.5cm). **£3,500-5,000** *CNY*

pair of George III style mahogany
rving tables, with crossbanded
eze drawers, 50½in (128.5cm).
,500-6,000 *CNY*

A George III mahogany serving table, the eared crossbanded serpentine top inlaid in a geometric pattern, legs probably shortened, 61in (155cm). **£6,000-8,000** *C*

A Régence kingwood side table, with breccia marble top, the shaped frieze fitted with drawers mounted with ribbed handles and cartouche lockplates, 49½in (126cm). **£14,000-16,000** *C*

Louis XVI grey painted and
rcel gilt console table, with
er Siena marble top, c1780,
½in (146cm). **£10,000-12,000** *CNY*

l. A Classical carved mahogany pier table, with marble top, Baltimore, c1820, 48½in (123cm). **£4,000-5,000** *CNY*

George III grained pier table,
th semi-eliptical mahogany top,
rly 19thC, 76½in (194cm).
,000-6,000 *C*

l. A Classical mahogany marble top pier table, with a mirrored backboard, New York, c1830, 42in (106.5cm). **£2,500-4,000** *CNY*

A William IV Irish pier table, 52in (132cm). **£10,000-15,000** *C*

George III serving table,
: frieze centred by a tablet
d fitted with a drawer, 72in
32.5cm). **£3,000-6,000** *C*

A George IV mahogany side table, 52in (132cm). **£9,000-11,000** *C*

r. A Regency rosewood side table, 69½in (176.5cm). **£12,000-15,000** *C*

An Empire style ormolu and malachite centre table, after Jacob-Desmalter, 50in (127cm) wide.
£25,000-30,000 *CNY*

An early Victorian ormolu mounted satinwood, amboyna and marquetry centre table, 55in (139.5cm).
£27,000-30,000 *C*

A Regency grained oak centre table, on S-scroll legs applied with flower-head roundels, 54in (137cm) wide.
£4,500-5,500 *C*

A Victorian inlaid burr walnut loo table.
£4,000-5,000 *SWO*

A pair of early Victorian giltwood and rosewood centre tables, 36in (92cm) wide. **£9,000-10,000** *C*

An early Victorian oak centre table, attributed to A. W. N. Pugin, 66in (167.5cm) wide.
£10,000-12,000 *C*

A George III mahogany pillar dining table with 2 leaves, 142in (360cm) open.
£9,500-10,000 *C*

A Louis XVI mahogany dining table, 1 contemporary and 3 later leaves, 149in (377.5cm) long open.
£15,000-18,000 *CNY*

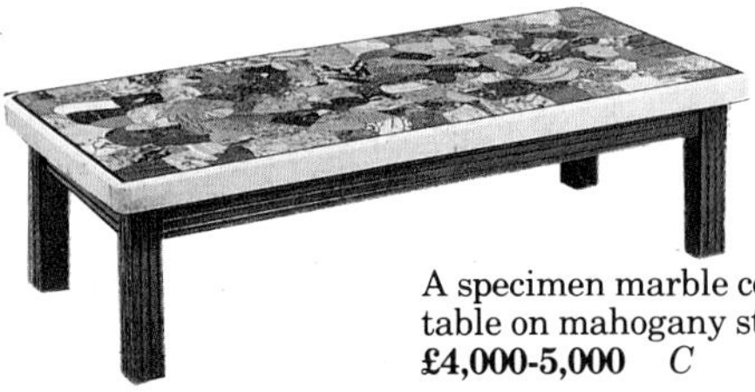

A specimen marble coffee table on mahogany stand.
£4,000-5,000 *C*

A late Regency mahogany triple pillar dining table, with alterations, 184in (467cm) open. **£15,000-20,000** *CEd*

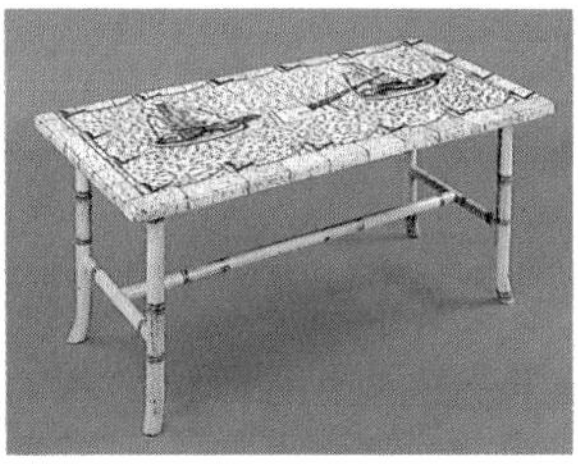

l. A decorated steel coffee table, by Piero Fornasetti, labelled, 17½in (45cm) high.
£2,000-3,000 *C*

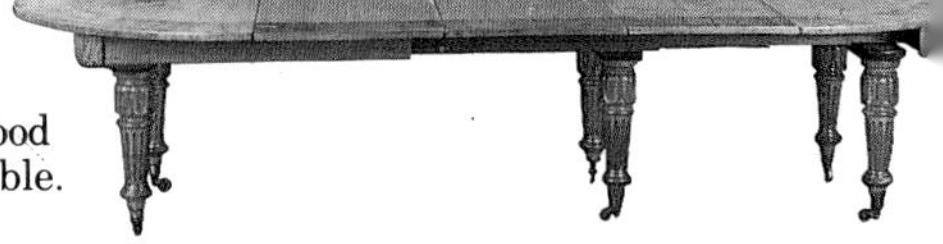

A Victorian satinwood extending dining table.
£9,000-10,000 *C*

A mahogany twin pedestal dining table, Boston, c1825, 95in (241cm).
£17,000-20,000 *CNY*

A Queen Anne carved mahogany dressing table, Massachusetts, c1750.
£40,000-45,000 *CNY*

A Queen Anne figured maple dressing table, Delaware River Valley, c1760.
£25,000-30,000 *CNY*

A George III mahogany and marquetry dressing table with fitted interior.
£3,000-4,000 *C*

A George III ormolu mounted tulipwood and marquetry dressing table, with fitted interior, 32in (81cm).
£30,000-50,000 *C*

A Louis XV kingwood and marquet table de toilette, with fitted interior, restorations, 34in (87cm).
£4,000-6,000 *C*

A George III mahogany dressing table, with divided interior, 26in (66cm).
£8,000-9,000 *C*

A Regency mahogany dressing table, with fitted interior, 48in (122cm).
£5,000-6,000 *C*

A George III mahogany Pembroke table. **£5,000-7,000** *C*

A Federal inlaid mahogany Pembroke table, c1805.
£5,000-7,000 *CNY*

A Sicilian giltwood console table, c1700. **£20,000-25,000** *CNY*

A pair of George I black and go japanned side tables, 36in (92c
£20,000-30,000 *C*

George III white painted and parcel
t mahogany console table, some
eration. **£3,000-4,000** *C*

A pair of late George III satinwood and marquetry console tables, with some alteration, 26in (66cm).
£17,000-20,000 *C*

A marquetry and rosewood table, with pierced brass gallery, late 18thC, 19½in (49cm).
£2,000-3,000 *C*

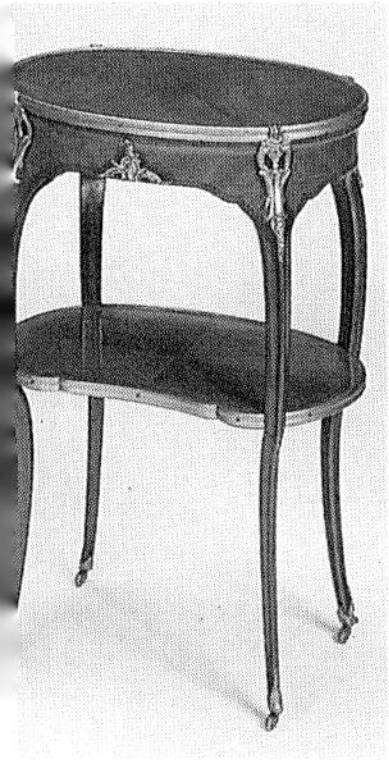

Louis Philippe gilt metal mounted,
ahogany and amaranth gueridon.
,**000-2,500** *C*

ove r. A George III small table,
½in (51.5cm). **£3,500-4,000** *C*

A Regency rosewood work table, 20in (51cm).
£2,500-3,000 *C*

ieorge III
hogany dumb-
iter, 45½in
5cm) high.
000-2,500 *C*

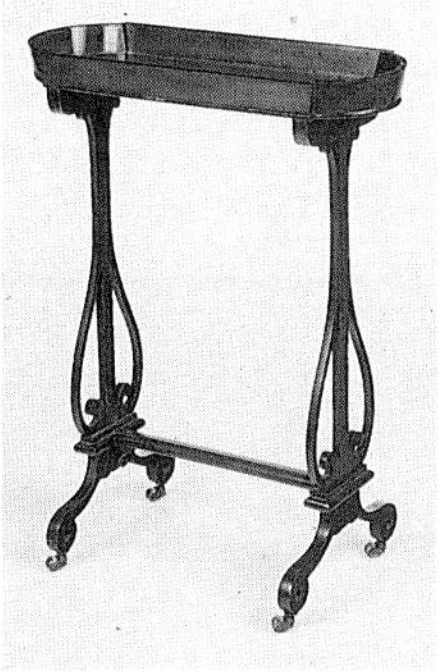

A mahogany vide poche, late 18thC.
£1,200-1,500 *C*

A Transitional ormolu mounted tulipwood gueridon, 22½in.
£4,500-5,500 *C*

A red lacquer low table, some damage, c1700.
£5,000-6,000 *C*

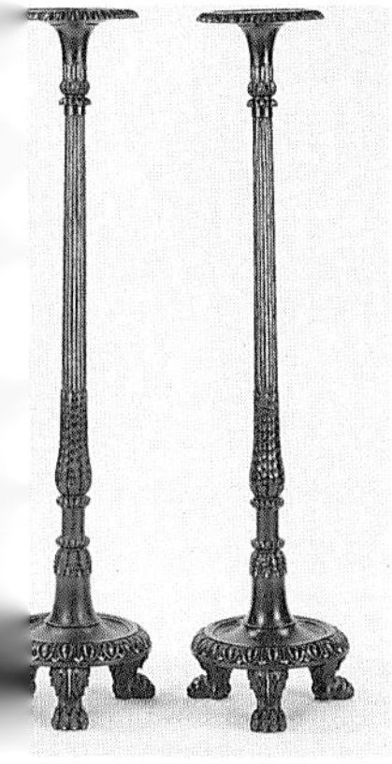

air of torchères.
000-8,000 *C*

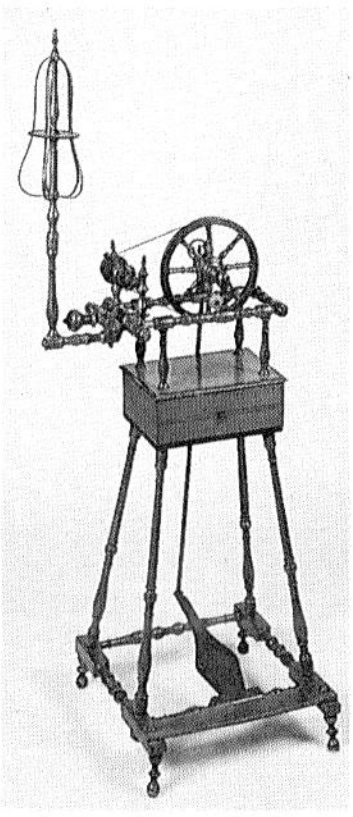

A George III spinning wheel.
£1,500-2,000 *C*

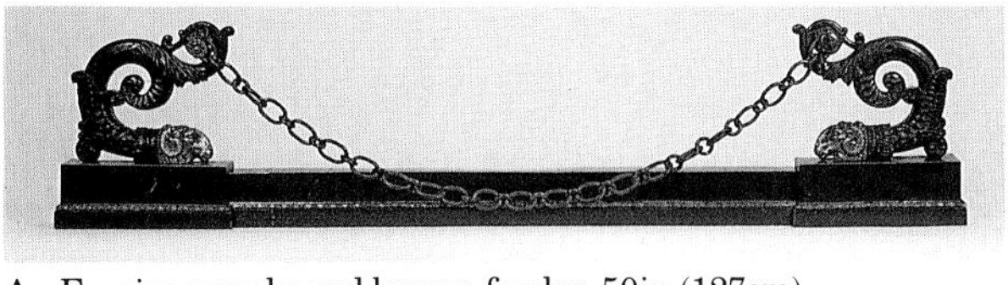

An Empire ormolu and bronze fender, 50in (127cm).
£1,500-2,000 *C*

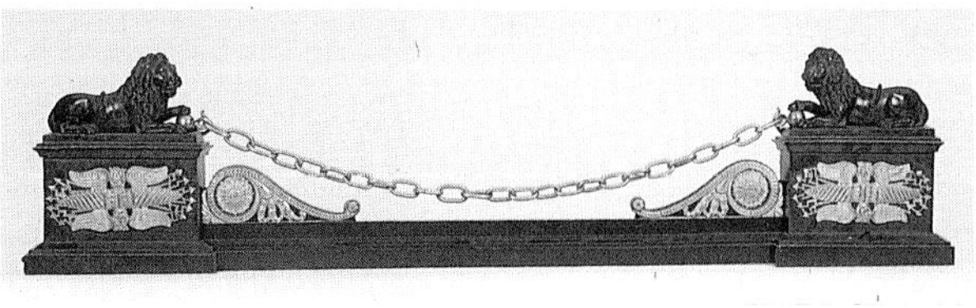

An Empire ormolu and bronzed adjustable fender, 59in (150cm). **£3,000-3,500** *C*

A large Chinese mirror painting, decorated with a hilly river landscape, including figures, with a black and gold chinoiserie frame, 28½ by 46in (72 by 117cm). **£30,000-40,000** *C*

A Dutch embossed leather four-leaf screen, 17thC. **£1,000-2,000** *C*

A Dutch painted leather four-leaf screen, the leather 18thC. **£4,500-5,500** *C*

A George III mahogany breakfast table, with later bun feet and restoration to one leg, 64in (162.5cm) diam. **£12,000-14,000** *C*

A Federal inlaid mahogany card table, Massachusetts, c1800. **£9,000-11,000** *CNY*

A Regency faded mahogany breakf table, 61in (155cm) wide. **£4,000-5,000** *C*

An early George III mahogany concertina-action tea table, with moulded folding top, 36in (91.5cm). **£7,000-8,500** *C*

A giltwood stand, with later marble top and bun feet, 17thC, restorations, 38½in. **£5,000-7,000** *C*

A George III mahogany centre table, 48in (122cm) diam. **£8,000-10,000** *C*

A Chinese export scarlet and gilt lacquer centre table, the top inlaid in polychrome mother-of-pearl, 19thC, 44in (111.5cm) diam. **£23,000-25,000** *C*

A Swedish mahogany centre table, the frieze fitted with 3 drawers, early 19thC, 55½in (141cm) diam. **£8,000-12,000** *C*

An early Victorian amboyna centre table, by Jerome Denny Bright & Co., 36in (91.5cm) diam. **£9,000-11,000** *C*

An eight-leaf screen with Chinese decoration, each leaf 105in (266.5cm) high. **£4,000-6,000** *C*

l. A painted leather chinoiserie five-leaf screen, 18thC, each leaf 86in (218cm) high. **£3,000-5,000** *C*

mahogany cheval fire-
-een with needlework
-nel, 25½in (64cm) wide.
,200-1,500 *C*

A pair of mahogany and parcel gilt pedestals, 45in (115.5cm) high. **£5,000-6,000** *C*

A mahogany pedestal, after a Thomas Chippendale design, 44in (112cm) high. **£8,000-10,000** *C*

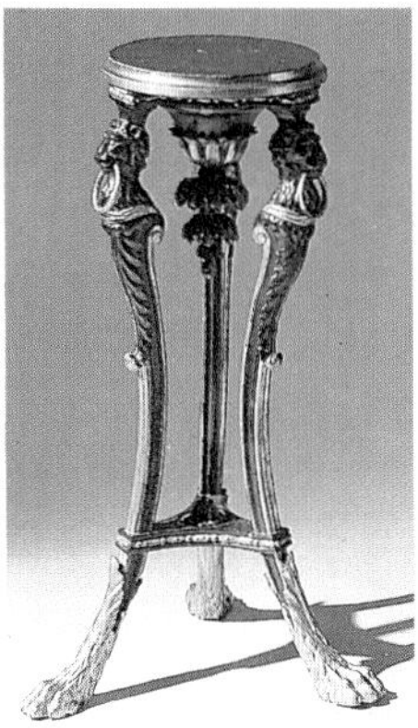

A pair of Regency ebonised and gilt torchères with circular tops, 30in (76cm) high. **£8,000-12,000** *C*

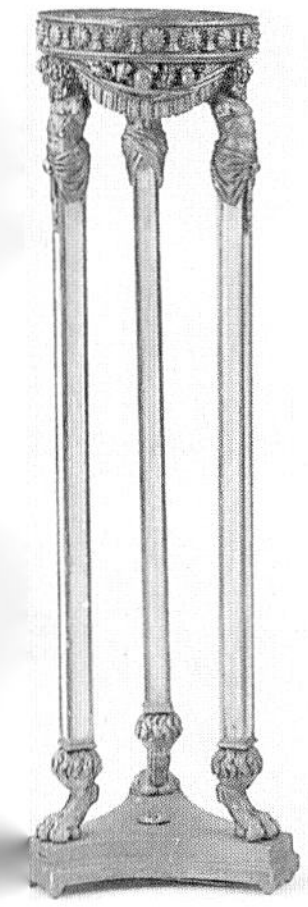

-pair of Regency
-rcel gilt and
-ite-painted
-chères,
-½in (125.5cm).
1,000-12,000 *C*

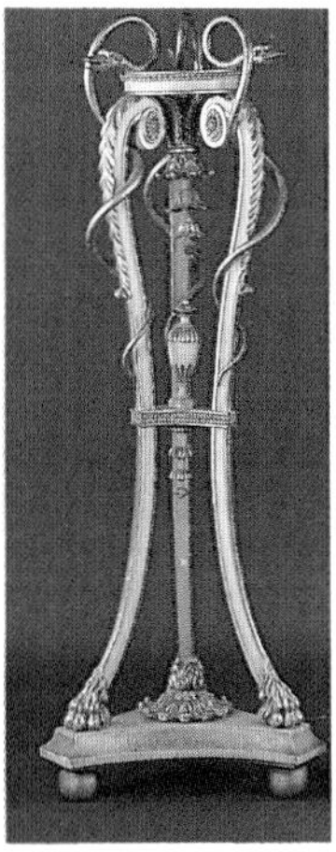

A pair of Regency parcel gilt and white painted torchères, 65½in (166.5cm). **£28,000-30,000** *C*

An ormolu gueridon with blue-stained pink marble top, 32½in (82.5cm) high. **£20,000-25,000** *C*

A Charles X ormolu, cut glass and scagliola gueridon, 23½in (59.5cm) diam. **£30,000-35,000** *CNY*

l. A Louis XIV brass mounted boulle casket, 12½in (32cm). **£5,500-6,500** *C*

r. A German ormolu mounted mahogany casket encrier, late 18thC, 10½in (26.5cm). **£3,000-5,000** *C*

A Régence giltwood side table, with green and white veined marble top, carved frieze, apron, legs and X-stretcher, 63in (160cm).
£26,000-28,000 *C*

A Régence giltwood side table, with mottled red marble top, carved frieze, scrolled legs and stretchers, 64in (163cm). **£27,000-30,000** *C*

A Louis XIV style side table, 19thC, 23½in (60cm wide. **£2,500-3,500** *CNY*

l. A George III paperwork tea caddy, 6in (15cm) wide.
£1,500-2,000 *Bea*

A George III ormolu mounted mahogany wine cooler, design attributed to Robert Adam, 34in (86cm) wide.
£50,000-60,000 *C*

A figured mahogany veneer cellaret, with fitted interior, attributed to Duncan Phyfe, New York, c1820, 25in (64cm) high.
£8,000-9,000 *CNY*

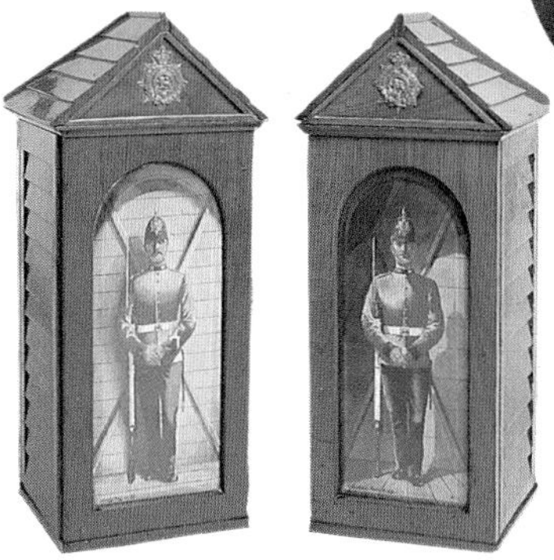

A pair of late Victorian walnut miniature sentry boxes, with badge of Royal Lancaster Regiment, 22in (56cm) high.
£4,000-4,500 *C*

An ormolu mounted harewood, bois clair and mahogany marquetry over-strung grand piano by Steinway, c188 recently reconditioned.
£72,000-75,000 *C*

A William IV mahogany wine cooler of sarcophagus shape with stepped cover, 36in (92cm) wide.
£2,000-2,500 *SWO*

l. A pair of white marble urns on pedestals, ovoid shape, on turned bases, c1800, 82in (208cm) high.
£90,000-110,000 *C*

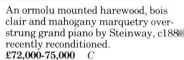

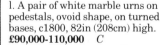

A pair of terracotta lions after the Antique, stamped Virebent Fres Toulouse, 44½in (113cm) wide.
£30,000-35,000 *C*

A Norwegian carved marriage box, wi original metalwork and some original paint, mid-18thC.
£800-900 *RYA*

Regency mahogany plate and
tlery stand on removable legs,
e leg restored, 34in (86cm) wide.
,000-10,000 *C*

An Italian Empire ormolu mounted and blue tôle jardinière, 24in (56cm).
£20,000-25,000 *C*

A Charles II oyster veneered olivewood, ebony and marquetry box on later feet, 11in (28cm) wide.
£1,800-2,000 *C*

Napoleon III ormolu
ounted corne verte, boulle
d agate casket,
in (41cm) wide.
,500-3,000 *C*

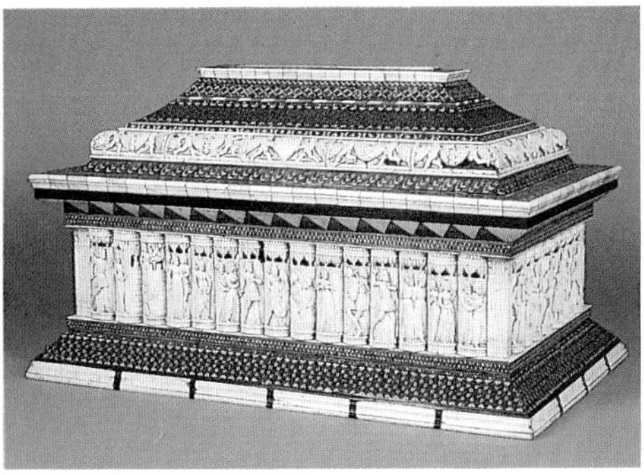

An Embriachi style bone casket, slight damage to interior trays, in wooden travelling case, 27in (69cm) wide. **£6,000-7,000** *C*

A pair of George III brass bound mahogany buckets, restored, 12½in (32cm) wide.
£2,500-3,500 *C*

Above l. A George III brass bound mahogany wine cooler, 13½in (35cm). **£6,500-7,500** *AG*
ove r. A George III oval mahogany brass bound wine cooler,
½in (32cm). **£4,000-5,000** *AG*

Below. A pair of George III mahogany dining room pedestals and lead lined urns, 68in (173cm) high.
£15,000-20,000 *C*

Regency mahogany wine cooler with
ided interior, 34in (86cm) wide.
,000-6,000 *C*

A set of Regency mahogany library steps with column supports, 72in (182.5cm) high. **£12,000-15,000** *C*

A pair of elm kitchen chairs, c1880.
£100-150 *SSD*

A hand stripped oak dressing chest, c1910, 42in (106.5cm). **£300-350** *SSD*

A hand stripped oak 4-drawer chest, c1895, 39in (99cm).
£200-250 *SSD*

An Austrian painted pine chest, c1854, 53in (134.5cm).
£850-1,000 *UC*

A pine and walnut settle with shepherd's crook arms, c1800, 48in (122cm).
£650-700 *OSc*

A hand stripped ash dressing table, c1890, 42in (106.5cm).
£300-350 *SSD*

A Lancastrian pine chest with original decoration, c1850.
£700-800 *UC*

A Danish pine chest of drawers, some restoration, c1820.
£700-750 *UC*

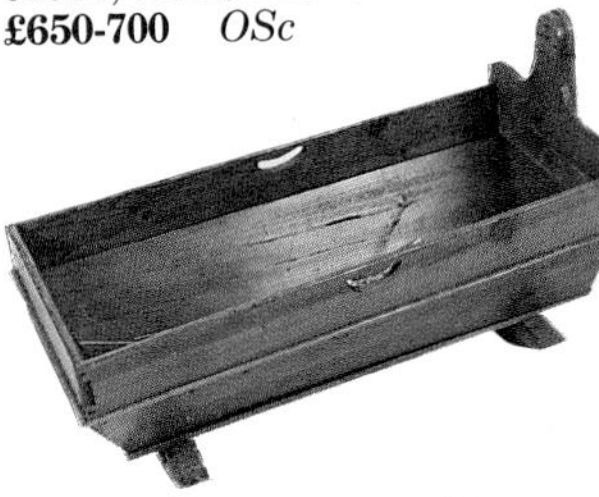

A Spanish pine rocking crib, c1870, 39in (99cm) long. **£300-350** *UC*

An Irish pine farmhouse dresser, Galway, c1830.
£1,000-1,500 *UC*

A French beech and lime vitrine in original condition. **£4,000-5,000** *UC*

An Irish astragal gl
corner cupboard, c1
£2,500-3,000 *UC*

A Suffolk pine open bookcase with drawers under, c1900, 49½in (126cm) wide.
£750-850 *UC*

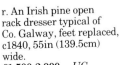

A Lancashire pine wash
c1860. **£500-600** *UC*

r. An Irish pine open rack dresser typical of Co. Galway, feet replaced, c1840, 55in (139.5cm) wide.
£1,500-2,000 *UC*

l. A pine corner cupboard, c1860. **£1,000-1,500** *UC*

A finely carved Norwegian birch wood spice/tobacco jar, 19thC.
£250-300 *RYA*

A distinguished 'Folk Art' model of a pony and trap, in original condition.
£800-900 *RYA*

A Georgian yew wood veneered work box, in the form of a house, c1820.
£2,000-3,000 *RYA*

A Norwegian pudding box, carved and painted, c1800.
£800-1,500 *RYA*

A 'Folk Art' hand carved and painted model of a carthorse, c1860.
£350-500 *RYA*

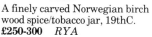

A Georgian child's money box, in the form of a bowfronted house, c1820.
£500-700 *RYA*

Three Norwegian hand carved and polychrome painted ceremonial drinking vessels, 18th and 19thC.
£550-850 each *RYA*

An English hand carved and painted wood pigeon decoy, 19thC.
£150-200 *RYA*

A rare English 'blackamoor' tobacc shop sign, with orig decoration, 18thC.
£1,000-1,500 *RY*

A French provincial watch hutch, carved in solid fruitwood, c1830.
£800-1,000 *RYA*

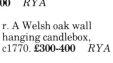

r. A Welsh oak wall hanging candlebox, c1770. **£300-400** *RYA*

Two tea caddies, in pear and apple woods, c1800, 5in (12.5cm).
£2,000-2,500 each *RdeR*

Villiam IV rosewood chiffonier,
h mirrored back, 60in (152cm).
0-900 *Bea*

A Victorian gilt metal walnut and ebonised credenza, with glazed door flanked by bowed doors divided by pilasters, on plinth, 66in (167.5cm).
£1,500-2,000 *CSK*

A Victorian inlaid walnut vitrine.
£1,500-2,000 *GIL*

'ictorian ormolu mounted
nut and marquetry display side
inet, with shaped glazed door
clasp headed uprights on
ped plinth, 33in (84cm).
0-1,000 *CSK*

A Victorian satinwood side cabinet, inlaid with paterae and foliate scrolls, 52in (132cm).
£3,000-4,000 *GSP*

A mid-Victorian walnut and marquetry inlaid dwarf serpentine side cabinet, applied with gilt metal mounts, the yew wood crossbanded top with a pierced three-quarter gallery, on turned tapering legs, 72in (182.5cm).
£4,000-5,000 *CSK*

air of Victorian ebonised and
oyna banded dwarf side
nets, with gilt metal mounts,
eared tops with marquetry
ded friezes, on turned tapering
feet, labelled Frederick Gwilt,
Iigh Oak, Pensnett, 32in (81cm).
00-2,500 *CSK*

A Victorian walnut dwarf side cabinet, inlaid with marquetry and rosewood bands, applied with paterae, on plinth base, 36½in (92cm).
£1,200-1,500 *CSK*

A Victorian walnut and inlaid dwarf side cabinet, with concave top above 3 glazed doors, with gilt metal mounted pilasters, on plinth base, 55in (139.5cm).
£1,500-2,000 *CSK*

A Victorian ebonised and inlaid dwarf side cabinet, with gilt metal mounts, painted and decorated porcelain plaques, and on turned bun feet, 60in (152cm).
£900-1,200 *CSK*

/ictorian walnut and boxwood
ing breakfront side cabinet, the
ulded top above scroll carved
es flanking 3 glazed doors, on a
ith base, 74in (188cm).
0-1,200 *MGM*

A Victorian burr walnut and inlaid credenza, with moulded top, and beaded gilt metal stringing, on a plinth base, 66in (168cm).
£3,000-3,500 *P*

A Victorian burr walnut dwarf pedestal side cabinet, the velvet lined shelved interior enclosed by a single panel door, inlaid with symmetrical leafy scrolls, gilt metal bordered and mounted pilasters, on a plinth base, 36in (92cm).
£1,200-1,700 *P(W)*

An Edwardian music cabinet in rosewood, with satinwood inlay a mirror panel front, 22in (56cm).
£250-300 *JH*

A late Victorian walnut, foliate marquetry and gilt metal mounted breakfront side cabinet, with ebonised panel centred by a ribbon-tied tulip motif, on a shaped plinth with trade label Druce & Co. Upholsterers and Cabinet Makers, Baker Street, Portman Square, 71½in (180cm).
£2,000-2,500 *CSK*

An Adam design inlaid satinwood cabinet, with brass gallery, crossbanded in kingwood and inlaid with rosewood, on tapered legs, 42in (106.5cm).
£5,000-6,000 *GSP*

An Edwardian satinwood cabine decorated with inlaid rosewood crossbanding and ebony stringin raised on turned tapering legs, 49½in (125cm).
£4,000-4,500 *AG*

A Dutch mahogany side cabinet, with broken pediment, on square tapering block feet, basically late 18thC, 68in (172.5cm).
£5,000-6,000 *CSK*

A green marblised and parcel gilt breakfront side cabinet, with four doors, each with a yellow silk pleated panel, 68in (172.5cm).
£800-1,200 *CSK*

A Louis XV style walnut and marquetry inlaid meuble d'appui, applied with gilt metal mounts, on an undulating plinth base, 35in (89cm).
£2,000-3,000 *CSK*

A Spanish painted pine cupboard, late 18thC, 46i (116.5cm) high.
£2,500-3,000 *SBA*

 French walnut credenza, of
rpentine form with ormolu
ıdroon and beaded mounts, the
ieze with marquetry inlaid panels,
ıe doors and column stems with
laid stringing and crossbanded
ecoration, mid-19thC, 63in
60cm).
2,500-3,000 *DDM*

A French gilt metal mounted mahogany breakfront side cabinet, with eared Carrara marble top, 75in (190.5cm).
£2,000-3,000 *CSK*

A Louis Philippe cartonniere, in gilt metal mounted quartered kingwood with rosewood banding, the door with Sèvres floral medallion enclosing velvet interior with shelf, 28in (71cm).
£1,700-2,000 *GSP*

anterburies

George IV mahogany music
nterbury, the front, back and two
visions, of butterfly shape and
plied with draught-turned
ouldings, on splayed legs with
ass acanthus cast sockets with
sters, drawer stamped 27006,
825, 22½in (56cm).
,500-2,000 *N*

A Regency mahogany canterbury, the top with 4 dished dividers, on square supports above a divided drawer, on square tapering legs, 18in (46cm).
£2,500-3,000 *C*

A Regency rosewood canterbury, with cross shaped divisions joined by turned grips, scroll edged base with single drawer, turned knobs, and turned feet with brass casters, 19in (48cm).
£1,200-1,700 *AH*

ate Georgian mahogany
ıterbury, with plain railed
isions, single frieze drawer on
ned supports, 19in (48cm).
200-1,500 *DDM*

A Regency rosewood canterbury with 4 slatted divisions, baluster turned corner supports, on turned legs, with brass casters, 19½in (49cm). **£1,800-2,200** *Bea*

A George IV mahogany canterbury by L. W. Collmann, with an asymmetrical arrangement of 4 slatted divisions, turned corner supports with knob finials, on tapering turned feet with brass casters, 26in (66cm).
£800-1,200 *Bea*

A George IV mahogany canterbury of X-framed form, united by baluster turned spindles, on tapering turned legs with brass casters, 19in (48cm).
£1,000-1,500 *Bea*

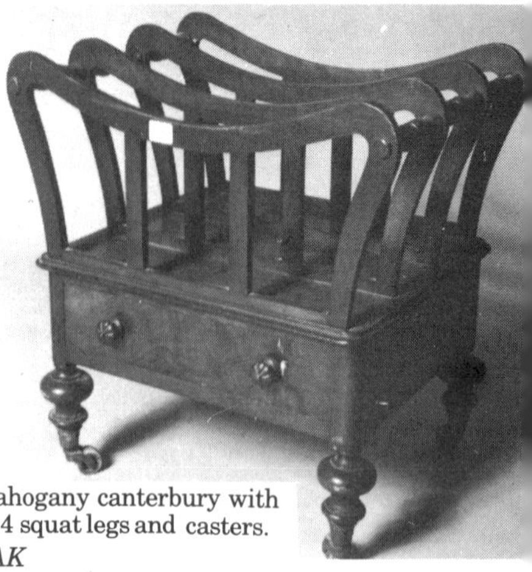

A Victorian mahogany canterbury with single drawer, 4 squat legs and casters.
£550-650 *GAK*

A Regency mahogany canterbury, on ring turned and fluted tapering supports, the base fitted with a drawer above a rosewood crossbanded apron, 19in (48cm).
£2,000-2,500 *CEd*

A mahogany music canterb with 4 divisions, drawer and turned ringed supports, fitt with casters, 19thC, 17½in (44cm).
£1,500-2,000 *GSP*

A William IV mahogany music canterbury, with pierced division above a drawer.
£700-1,000 *LRG*

A mid-Victorian walnut and crossbanded low music cabinet, the open shelves between canted angles, on turned feet, 20in (51cm).
£500-600 *CSK*

A mahogany canterbury, with o drawer, raised on turned suppor with casters, early 19thC.
£1,500-2,000 *P(M)*

A William IV rosewood canterbury, with 4 divisions formed as pierced scrolls and leaves, on a base with a single frieze drawer, on turned legs, 20in (51cm).
£750-850 *DDM*

A mahogany canterbury with plain turned divisions and baluster side rails, above a shelf and brass casters, 19thC.
£300-400 *LAY*

A Sheraton period mahogany mu canterbury, outlined with ebony stringing, the tapering square le with brass sockets and casters, 17½in (44cm). **£5,500-6,500** *N*

›pen Armchairs

valnut open armchair,
nolstered in close-nailed gros and
it-point needlework, the
scrolled arms carved with foliage
scrolling supports, the front
etcher carved with a flowerhead
l foliage, on scrolling legs with
er paw feet and waved stretchers,
t late 17thC.
500-4,000 *C*

. George III mahogany open
rmchair, the channelled arms on
ownswept supports, above a
added seat covered in pink and
ream trellis pattern material, on
quare tapering panelled legs and
lock feet headed by stiff leaves.
600-700 *C*

early George III style mahogany
a armchair, with shaped toprail
pierced interlaced splat, the
s carved with acanthus, the
-in seat upholstered in green
her, on cabriole legs and hairy
feet carved with C-scroll
chons. **£600-900** *C*

A George III mahogany carver chair, with reeded and carved decoration, on turned legs.
£250-300 *MGM*

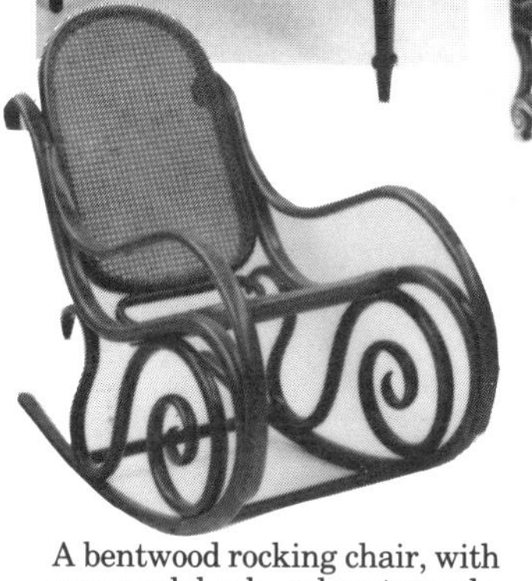

A bentwood rocking chair, with canework back and seat panels, together with a similar rocking foot stool. **£200-250** *DDM*

CHAIRS

- ★ check seat rails are the same, with equal patination
- ★ top rail should never overhang sides
- ★ carving should not be flat
- ★ if stretchers low, chair could have been cut down
- ★ the height from floor to seat should be 18in (45.5cm)

A Venetian carved giltwood grotto chair, with shell seat and back, serpent arms, sea horse supports and serpent rockers, mid-19thC.
£2,500-3,000 *P(M)*

A pair of walnut open armchairs, upholstered in 17thC tapestry, with foliate carved arm rests, on turned legs and stretchers.
£2,000-3,000 *CSK*

A pair of 17thC style walnut open armchairs, upholstered in embossed leather and decorated with flowers and scrolls, the arms terminating in acanthus scrolls, on conforming legs joined by stretchers.
£2,000-2,500 *CSK*

A George III cream and pink painted open armchair, the padded back and seat with moulded frame and ribbon-tied cresting, the fluted seat rail on ribbed tapering legs with foliage bands.
£1,500-2,000 *C*

A George III style mahogany open armchair, with shaped toprail and pierced interlaced splat carved with foliage and scrolls, the shaped arms with scrolled ends, the padded seat upholstered in floral needlework, on square chamfered legs joined by stretchers.
£600-900 *C*

A George IV mahogany commode armchair, the solid hinged seat with brass recessed handle above 2 panelled doors, with buttoned green leather cushion, 25in (63.5cm).
£700-1,000 *C*

A pair of Regency mahogany open armchairs, each with scrolling curved toprail, pierced foliate horizontal splat, downswept reeded arms on baluster supports, with padded seats and turned legs, later blocks.
£1,500-2,000 *C*

A pair of George III beech framed open armchairs, with fluted oval frames to the padded backs, padded arms with acanthus terminals and upholstered bow front seats, on fluted leaf carved legs.
£2,000-2,500 *Bea*

A pair of Regency yew wood open armchairs, each with a spindle filled back, down curved arms and solid bowed seat, on square tapered legs.
£600-700 *CSK*

A set of 3 Regency ochre-painted beechwood open armchairs, the pierced back with crossed arrows joined by an oval medallion decorated with Prince of Wales feathers, with serpentine rush seat, on turned legs and conforming stretchers.
£2,000-2,500 *C*

Two George III mahogany librar armchairs, with padded arms an seats upholstered in white floral damask, with downswept arm supports and square legs joined b stretchers, restorations and replacements. **£5,000-7,000**

A George IV mahogany framed open armchair, with overscrolled upholstered back and conforming padded arms, serpentine seat and baluster legs. **£800-1,000** *B*

An early Victorian mahogany library armchair, with upholster panelled back and slightly bowed seat, the arms carved with acanth and paterae, on turned tapered fluted legs with ribbed collars.
£800-1,000 *CSK*

Use the Index!

Because certain items might fit easily into any of a number of categories, the quickest and surest method of locating any entry is by reference to the index at the back of the book.
This has been fully cross-referenced for absolute simplicity

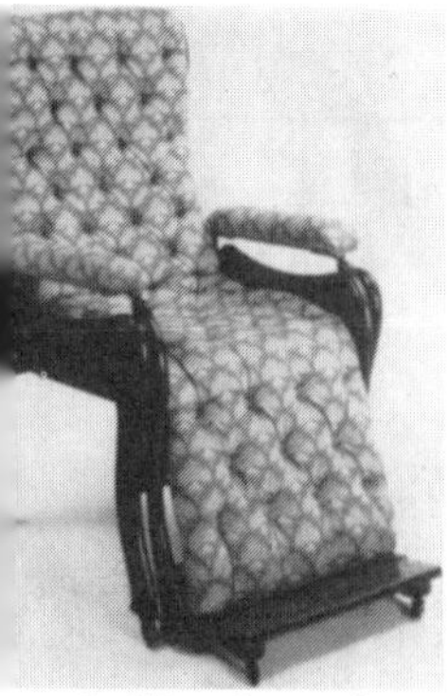

. early Victorian mahogany
:lining chair, with buttoned panel
:k and adjustable seat
holstered in tapestry, on curved
s. **£800-1,000** *CSK*

A Victorian walnut gentleman's armchair, the acanthus carved scrolling frame with buttoned back, circular seat and arms on cabriole legs; and the lady's chair en suite.
£1,500-2,000 *CSK*

A Victorian walnut framed buttonback armchair, with carved decoration on cabriole legs.
£400-500 *MGM*

'ictorian carved walnut
›nback open armchair.
500-2,000 *GIL*

A set of 6 Victorian carved oak dining chairs, with barleytwist supports, carved grape and vine leaf decoration and leather seats.
£1,000-1,500 *MGM*

A pair of Victorian lady's and gentleman's armchairs, with floral carved toprails, upholstered spoon shaped backs, scroll hand grips on floral carved cabriole supports and bowed seat rails, requiring restoration.
£3,000-3,500 *P(M)*

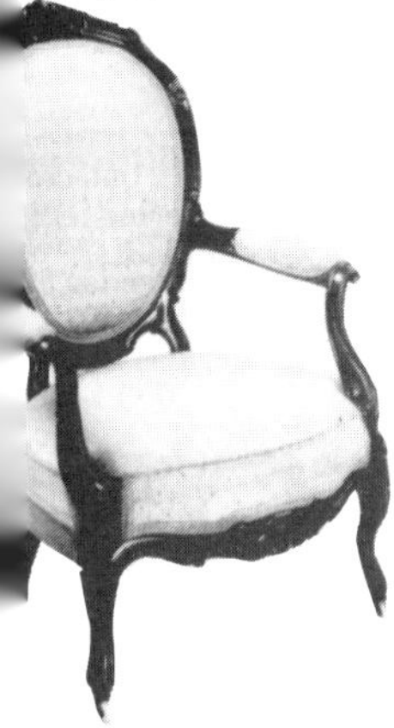

A Victorian walnut gentleman's armchair, with C-scroll frame, upholstered seat, arms and spooned back with acanthus cresting, on cabriole legs; and a similar lady's chair.
£900-1,200 *CSK*

A late Victorian 5-piece rosewood drawing room suite, inlaid with marquetry and boxwood lines, on square tapering legs with spade feet.
£1,500-2,000 *CSK*

A late Victorian rosewood and foliate marquetry drawing room suite, with two tub chairs, each with an upholstered toprail and a pierced splat above a bowed seat, on turned legs, and a sofa with outscrolled end and pierced back, the arms carved with acanthus.
£1,200-1,600 *CSK*

A Victorian walnut open armchair, with waisted buttoned back, armpads and serpentine seat upholstered in green silk rep.
£1,500-2,000 *CSK*

An Empire mahogany and parcel gilt open armchair, applied with gilt metal mounts, the upholstered back and bowed seat with dolphin's head arm terminals, on sabre legs.
£1,000-1,200 *CSK*

A pair of Louis XIV style giltwood fauteuils, upholstered in blue silk damask, the frame carved with husks, C-scrolls and acanthus, on cabriole legs and scroll feet.
£1,200-1,600 *CSK*

A Scandinavian mahogany veneered elbow chair, with open scroll arms, cane panel seat, on sabre supports, the frame decorated with stringing, scrolling foliage, garlands, leaves and classical motifs, early 19thC.
£600-800 *P*

A beechwood fauteuil, with cartouche shaped padded back and seat, cabriole legs with conforming carving on pad feet, basically mid-18thC, possibly German.
£800-1,200 *C*

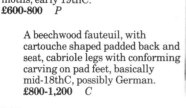

A French walnut open armchair, with raked back and padded seat upholstered in silver blue velvet, with scrolled arms, on turned and squared legs with turned stretchers, 17thC. **£800-1,000** *C*

An Anglo-Indian rosewood planter's chair, the splayed rear legs of shell carved paw-and-ball form, mid-19thC. **£1,500-2,000** *N*

A Federal mahogany armchair, the back with reeded crest, stiles and three vertical bars flanked by reeded arms, above an upholstered seat, on reeded tapering legs with turned feet headed by oval carved rosettes, 32in (81cm).
£2,000-3,000 *CNY*

An Austrian beechwood and press board bentwood rocking chair, Vienna, c1895, 36in (91.5cm) high
£600-700 *UC*

A Venetian parcel gilt, silvered ar painted grotto chair, with scallope shell back and seat with dolphin arms, on naturalistic rockwork leg
£4,500-5,500 *C*

Grotto furniture was keenly sough after in the 1920s and 1930s by members of the Magnesco Society, founded in 1924 to restore interest baroque art.

An Anglo-Indian ebony bergère, with buttoned back and padded se upholstered in cut velvet, the toprai carved with a plumed coronet, the arms with gadrooned supports, wit reeded seat rail and tapering legs.
£1,000-1,500 *C*

rmchairs – pholstered

nahogany wing armchair, holstered in tapestry, on square ulded legs joined by stretchers, sically 18thC.
)0-1,000 *CSK*

A walnut wing armchair, with padded back, outscrolled arms and bowed seat, on cabriole legs and pad feet, early Georgian and later.
£3,500-4,000 *CSK*

A walnut framed wingback armchair, with scrolled arms, on plain cabriole legs with pad feet, basically early 18thC.
£1,500-2,000 *Bon*

A George I walnut wing armchair frame, with rectangular back, scrolled arms and bowed seat, on cabriole legs and claw-and-ball feet carved with shells, upholstery lacking.
£5,500-6,500 *C*

Villiam IV mahogany framed gère, with scoop-shaped back, on ned and lappet carved legs.
)0-1,200 *Bon*

air of William IV mahogany med library armchairs, on turned l reeded front supports and ters, upholstered in beige hide, ters missing on one.
000-3,500 *GA(W)*

ANTIQUE UPHOLSTERY

- ★ Condition is all-important. An early piece with sagging seat but with original or early needlework which is still largely intact will attract a higher value for its originality, but generally speaking an authentically re-upholstered item in good condition is clearly more valuable than an item requiring attention. Quality re-upholstery work is not cheap
- ★ Re-upholstery is acceptable provided it has been restored authentically with hand sewn hair borders, and hair padding, to the original contours of the design. Test the upholstery by prodding with one finger. Hair will crackle. Cotton flock and foam will not!
- ★ Pre-Regency furniture was not sprung, but was webbed on top of the seat rails and the upholstered pad invariably had a firm hair roll at the outer edge, and all hair stuffing. Later sprung upholstery is webbed beneath the seat rails to accommodate the springs
- ★ Originality of the cover fabric is immediately questionable if it is out of period. Textiles is a wide field but a study of fabric history and types, damasks, chintzes, crested, turkey-work, hand tapestry, brocades, etc, is well worthwhile to date an item
- ★ The use of dralon modern acrylic velvets will devalue an item in the same way as foam fillings, or similar low-grade upholstery work
- ★ The general quality of upholstery work is another pointer to value

A George IV mahogany tub armchair, with shaped leather upholstered back, outscrolled arms and buttoned squab-seat with moulded arm supports and ring turned legs.
£2,000-2,500 *C*

A George III armchair, upholster in green hide, with serpentine se and on mahogany moulded squa legs joined by stretchers.
£500-600 *Bea*

A Regency brass inlaid simulated rosewood bergère, upholstered in peach cotton, the arms inlaid with foliage and paterae on reeded tapering legs, restorations.
£800-1,200 *C*

A Regency partially reeded mahogany frame tub shape librar chair, upholstered in studded gre hide, the arms with inverted tapering reeded supports, on tur tapering legs.
£2,000-2,500 *GC*

A Victorian walnut framed gentleman's button back armchair, having carved detail and cabriole legs.
£600-800 *MGM*

A George IV mahogany framed wing armchair, the carved arm fronts over large lion's paw front supports and sabre rear supports.
£1,500-2,000 *P(M)*

A Regency mahogany bergère, w curved back, scrolled arms and padded seat upholstered in crims velvet, on reeded tapering legs w lambrequin capitals.
£4,500-5,000 *C*

Victorian walnut armchair, the
ved buttoned back continuing to
dded and florally carved arms and
ved cabriole legs with knuckle
t, on casters.
50-850 *Bon*

A Victorian mahogany spoon back armchair, with buttoned gold dralon upholstery, serpentine seat and carved scrolling front supports.
£350-400 *DDM*

A Victorian walnut framed gentleman's button back armchair, with carved decoration and standing on cabriole legs.
£800-1,000 *MGM*

ream painted armchair,
holstered in green and silver silk
nask, the seat rail hung with
sels, on cabriole legs and hoof feet
h shaped stretchers.
0-500 *C*

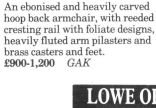

An ebonised and heavily carved hoop back armchair, with reeded cresting rail with foliate designs, heavily fluted arm pilasters and brass casters and feet.
£900-1,200 *GAK*

A giltwood bergère, in the manner of Louis XVI, upholstered in a cherry pattern silk rep, the arms terminating in ram's masks, on turned tapered fluted legs.
£900-1,200 *CSK*

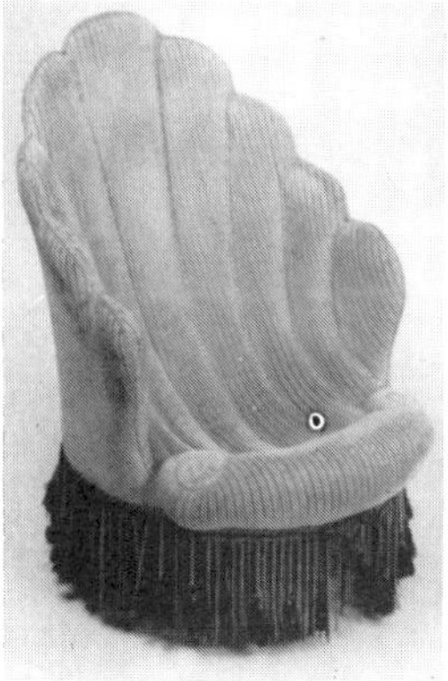

eechwood
gère, in the shape of
ell, covered in faded pink
uroy, edged with pink and
ow rope with black and
ow deep tasselled
e, on turned legs.
000-1,500 *C*

A pair of Louis XV white painted bergères, each with cartouche shaped back and bowed seat with a cushion upholstered in beige velvet, the moulded seat rails carved with flowerheads on cabriole legs, mid-18thC.
£3,500-4,000 *CNY*

A Chippendale mahogany easy chair, on square corner moulded legs joined by a moulded H-stretcher, upholstered in rose fabric with needlework floral and animal motifs, Salem, Massachusetts, c1780.
£5,000-6,000 *CNY*

A Federal mahogany easy chair, with arched crest flanked by shar wings over horizontally scrolled arms, on square tapering legs join by an H-stretcher, feet pieced, American, c1800.
£1,000-2,000 *CNY*

A Federal mahogany easy chair, on turned tapering legs with casters, Philadelphia, c1800.
£3,500-4,000 *CNY*

A George IV rosewood bergère, the curved back, arms and seat filled with cane, the seat cushion upholstered in floral cotton, on ribbed tapering legs.
£1,500-2,000 *C*

A Regency mahogany library armchair, with caned back, arms and seat, the padded arm rests, buttoned back and seat cushions upholstered in wine red hide, on ring turned legs.
£1,500-2,000 *C*

A Regency mahogany and caned bergère, the back with moulded frame and overscrolled arms, on sabre legs with brass casters.
£3,500-4,000 *Bon*

A Regency mahogany bergère, with caned back, arms and seat in a reeded frame, the scrolled arms on lion's paw supports, with padded seat cushion, on turned legs, back legs replaced.
£1,700-2,000 *C*

A Regency mahogany and caned bergère, the back with reeded fram and turned arm supports continuin to turned tapered legs.
£2,000-2,500 *Bon*

Regency mahogany bergère, the
rved arched buttoned back and
dded seat upholstered in red
ather, with turned arm supports
d turned tapering legs.
,500-2,000 *C*

A William IV mahogany bergère, with caned back, arms and seat, the arms with scrolled ends, fitted to the right with brass swivel attachment for a reading arm, on reeded tapering legs.
£1,000-1,500 *C*

A mahogany bergère, with scrolled back, padded arms and bowed seat, upholstered in green velvet, with guilloche moulded and fluted frame, the arms with spirally turned fluted supports on tapering legs.
£1,500-2,000 *C*

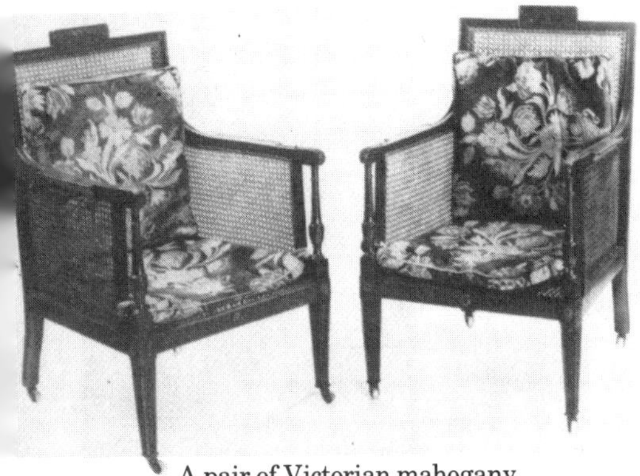

A pair of Victorian mahogany library armchairs, the cane filled backs, side and seats above a fluted frieze applied with paterae, on square tapering legs with bellflower headings, with loose cushions.
£1,000-1,500 *CSK*

Dining Chairs

A set of 4 George I style walnut dining chairs, including 2 armchairs, the arms with eagle head terminals, on shell carved cabriole legs with claw-and-ball feet.
£1,200-1,500 *CSK*

set of 8 late George III mahogany
ing chairs, including 2 carvers,
ring turned tapered legs,
torations.
,000-6,000 *CSK*

A set of 8 George III style dining chairs, including a pair of armchairs, with moulded bar backs and bowed seats on square tapered legs and spade feet, by Jas. Shoolbred, c1900.
£2,000-2,500 *Bon*

A set of 8 George III mahogany dining chairs in the Hepplewhite style, including 2 armchairs, upholstered in green and pink floral brocade, raised on square tapering supports and plain stretchers.
£7,000-8,000 *HSS*

A George III mahogany dining chair, with shield shaped back and pierced splat carved with wheat ears, upholstered seat, on square legs.
£300-500 *C*

A pair of George III mahogany shield back dining chairs, with pierced Gothic pattern baluster splats, drop-in seats, and square legs.
£900-1,200 *C*

A set of 6 mahogany chairs, including a pair of armchairs, on square tapered legs with spade fee 3 chairs, c1790, 3 later copies.
£2,000-2,500 *Bon*

A set of 8 mahogany dining chairs, including 2 armchairs, with upholstered seats, on square tapering legs, part George III.
£2,500-3,500 *CSK*

A pair of George III mahogany chairs, the backs with cable carvec edges and foliate carved splats, the seat rails centred by a rocaille carved clasp, on square chamfered legs, c1760. **£2,000-2,500** *Bon*

A set of 4 George III mahogany dining chairs, including one elbow chair, with stuff-over seats, on turned supports.
£750-850 *P(W)*

A set of 12 George III design mahogany dining chairs, including 2 armchairs, on square tapering legs with Marlborough block feet joined by stretchers.
£5,000-5,500 *CSK*

A set of 8 George III style mahogany dining chairs, including 2 armchairs, on square moulded legs joined by stretchers, 19thC.
£4,000-4,500 *CSK*

A set of 6 George III style mahogany dining chairs, with leather upholstered seats, on chamfered square moulded legs joined by cross stretchers.
£900-1,200 *CSK*

Make the most of Miller's

Unless otherwise stated, any description which refers to 'a set' or 'a pair' includes a valuation for the entire set or the pair, even though the illustration may show only a single item

set of 10 mahogany dining chairs,
ith scroll toprails, on ringed
ırned tapering legs, early 19thC.
),000-3,500 *GSP*

A set of 6 George III style mahogany dining chairs, the rounded backs with pierced splats and wheatsheaf and pendant husk motifs, on square tapered legs, c1900.
£1,000-1,500 *Bon*

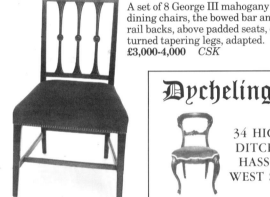

set of 8 George III mahogany
ning chairs, including 2 later
atching armchairs, the pierced
ıaped ladder backs above padded
ats, on chamfered square moulded
gs with cross stretchers, adapted.
,000-6,000 *CSK*

A set of 8 George III mahogany dining chairs, the bowed bar and rail backs, above padded seats, on turned tapering legs, adapted.
£3,000-4,000 *CSK*

A set of 8 Georgian mahogany dining chairs, with vertical splat backs with central roundels, on square tapering legs.
£2,000-2,500 *LRG*

A set of 8 George III style mahogany dining chairs, including 2 carvers.
£2,500-3,500 *CSK*

A set of 8 George III mahogany dining chairs, the reeded bar and tablet backs above velvet seats, on ring turned tapering legs.
£4,500-5,000 *CSK*

A set of 8 George III mahogany dining chairs, including 2 carvers, with pierced splat backs with serpentine crests, the drop-in seats on front square tapering legs with H-stretchers.
£8,000-10,000 *WW*

A set of 6 George III mahogany dining chairs, the shaped toprails and pierced latticed splats above padded drop-in seats, on square tapering legs.
£1,500-2,500 *CSK*

A set of 8 mahogany dining chairs, including 2 armchairs, the pierced shield backs carved with the Prince of Wales' feathers, above leather seats, on square tapering legs with spade feet and bellflower headings, 19thC.
£3,000-4,000 *CSK*

A set of 6 mahogany dining chairs, with bowed bar toprails and cross bars pierced with roundels between reeded uprights, the padded drop-in seats on square moulded legs, late George III and later.
£2,500-3,500 *CSK*

A set of 4 late George III mahogany dining chairs, the bowed bar and latticed rail backs applied with roundels, above upholstered seats, on turned tapering legs.
£1,000-1,200 *CSK*

A set of 6 George III mahogany dining chairs, with serpentine toprails and pierced splats, above padded seats, on square chamfered legs joined by stretchers, restorations.
£2,500-3,500 *CSK*

A set of 6 late George III mahogany dining chairs, including 2 carvers, restorations.
£2,000-2,500 *CSK*

A set of 8 mahogany dining chairs including a pair of open armchairs the drop-in seats upholstered in aquamarine silk, on moulded sabre legs, early 19thC.
£5,000-6,000 *C*

set of 8 mahogany dining chairs, ith foliate carved serpentine prails and formerly upholstered lats above padded seats, on square gs joined by stretchers.
2,500-3,000 *CSK*

A pair of late George III mahogany dining chairs, each with a pierced lattice back and padded seat, on turned tapered reeded legs.
£1,000-1,500 *CSK*

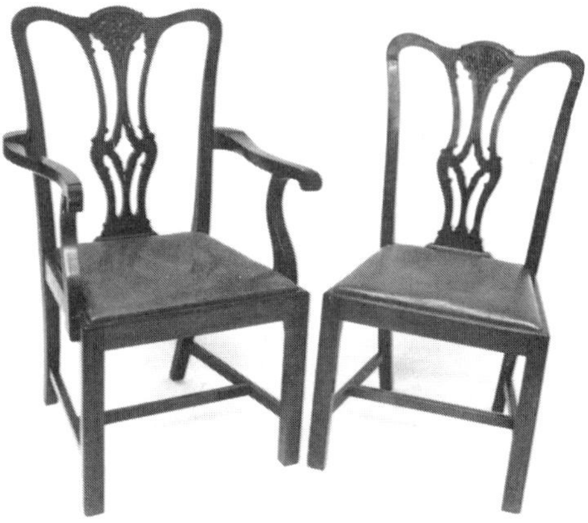

A set of 6 Chippendale style mahogany dining chairs, 19thC.
£1,200-1,500 *GIL*

set of 8 mahogany dining chairs, ith bowed bar toprails centred by a blet, above pierced cross bars tween reeded uprights, the dded drop-in seats on square pered legs joined by stretchers, thC.
,500-5,500 *CSK*

A set of 6 mahogany dining chairs, with bowed bar toprails and padded seats on square tapered legs joined by stretcher; and a similar armchair, 19thC.
£600-900 *CSK*

A set of 3 Regency dining chairs, with brass inlaid decoration cane seats and standing on sabre legs.
£250-300 *MGM*

et of 6 Regency mahogany dining airs, with anthemion and scroll ved curved cresting rails, etwist uprights pierced reeded uble tie rails centred by foliate ettes, raised upon reeded sabre nt supports.
,000-3,500 *HSS*

A set of 6 rosewood dining chairs with fluted legs, c1825.
£2,500-2,800 *DY*

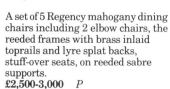

A set of 7 Regency beechwood dining chairs, the bowed toprails carved with rosettes, the reeded seat rails on sabre legs, the parcel gilt decoration distressed.
£900-1,200 *Bon*

A set of 5 Regency mahogany dining chairs including 2 elbow chairs, the reeded frames with brass inlaid toprails and lyre splat backs, stuff-over seats, on reeded sabre supports.
£2,500-3,000 *P*

A set of 5 late Regency mahogany and brass strung dining chairs, with bowed toprails and bar splats, on ring turned tapered legs.
£900-1,200 *Bon*

A set of 6 Victorian mahogany spoon back dining chairs, upholstered in brown hide, standing on leaf capped cabriole supports.
£1,700-2,000 *OL*

A set of 6 Regency period mahogan dining chairs, the backs with panelled fluted crests and hobnail cut turned rails, with cane seats, o sabre legs.
£3,000-3,500 *WW*

A set of 3 Regency mahogany dining chairs, inlaid with brass rings and a shell scroll, the carved cross bar above a drop-in seat upholstered in green silk, on sabre legs; and 3 similar chairs, minor variations, partly early 19thC.
£2,000-3,000 *CSK*

A set of 9 George IV mahogany dining chairs including 2 elbow chairs, with reeded toprails and frames, open X-shape splat backs, stuff-over seats, on turned supports.
£10,000-12,000 *P*

A set of 8 Regenc mahogany dinin chairs, upholste in wine rexhide and standing on turned taper supports.
£3,500-4,000

A set of 10 mahogany and parcel gilt dining chairs, including 2 carvers, the seats upholstered in red needlecord, on turned tapered fluted legs, each with a stiff leaf collar, stamped Gillow, late 19thC.
£5,000-8,000 *CSK*

A set of 6 Regency beechwood dining chairs, including an armchair, with brass inlaid bowed and reeded rail backs, above upholstered drop-in seats, on sabre legs.
£2,000-3,000 *CSK*

A set of 6 Regency black painted a parcel gilt dining chairs, each wi curved eared toprail and X-shape splat, centred by a cane filled ova and rounded cane filled seat, on turned tapering legs all stamped GJ, 2 with additional K, and 3 wi JS.
£2,500-3,000 *C*

A set of 4 Victorian mahogany balloon back chairs, each with shaped backs and carved rails over drop-in seats, on turned front supports.
£500-600 *DDM*

A set of 10 Victorian mahogany balloon back single dining chairs, each with upholstered seats, on turned front legs, some in poor condition.
£1,800-2,000 *DDM*

A set of 8 Hepplewhite style mahogany dining chairs including 2 elbow chairs, with pierced channelled splat backs, carved beaded borders, and slip-in seats, on square chamfered supports united by stretchers, late 19thC.
£3,500-4,000 *P*

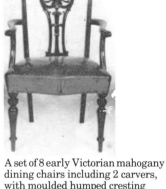

A set of 8 early Victorian mahogany dining chairs including 2 carvers, with moulded humped cresting rails, pierced anthemion and urn carved inverted baluster splats, overstuffed seats with serpentine seat rails upholstered in red leather, raised upon melon fluted knop and baluster turned tapering front supports terminating in peg feet.
£3,000-3,500 *HSS*

set of 4 Victorian mahogany alloon back dining chairs, pholstered in brown moquette and anding on flower capped cabriole apports.
700-800 *OL*

A set of 4 Continental oak dining chairs, with ornate carved and pierced backs with scroll, mask and leaf designs, over upholstered seats, on turned front legs, late 19thC.
£400-500 *DDM*

A set of 6 Victorian rosewood dining chairs, the scrolling railed semi-balloon backs above upholstered seats, on cabriole legs.
£2,500-3,000 *CSK*

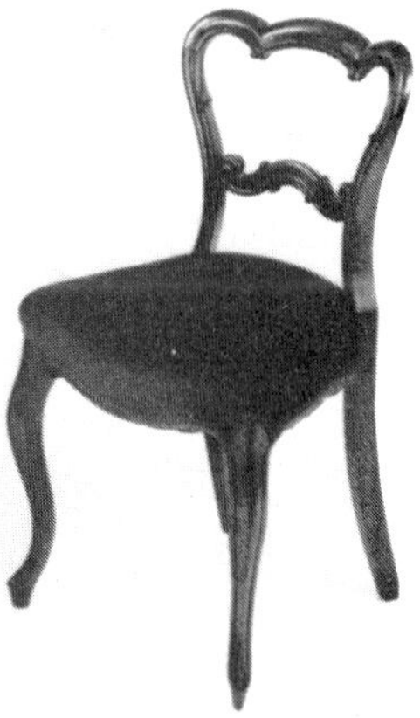

A set of 6 Sheraton period reeded mahogany dining chairs, with cross and lozenge pattern backs, having studded upholstered stuff-over seats, on turned tapering reeded legs.
£3,000-4,000 *GC*

A set of 8 mahogany dining chairs, including 2 armchairs, the acanthus carved backs with padded seats and gadrooned aprons, on cabriole legs with claw-and-ball feet, labelled S.S. & H. Jewell, 229-231 Little Queen Street, Holborn, WC.
£4,000-5,000 *CSK*

A set of 6 rosewood dining chairs, upholstered in neo-classical manner in red velvet, the shell carved toprail with lion finials above a frame carved with acanthus, on square legs with lion's paw feet joined by a cross stretcher, stamped Maples.
£2,500-3,000 *CSK*

A set of 6 mahogany dining chair carved with foliage above a slight bowed padded seat on square tapered legs and spade feet, with trade label Edwards & Roberts, Wardour Street.
£2,000-2,500 *CSK*

A set of 12 mahogany dining chairs, including 2 carvers, with serpentine toprails carved with acanthus above pierced splats and padded drop-in seats, with gadrooned seat rails, on acanthus carved cabriole legs and claw-and-ball feet, labelled S. & H. Jewell.
£5,000-6,000 *CSK*

A set of 10 mahogany dining chai including 2 carvers, with serpenti toprails and pierced splats above drop-in seats upholstered in leathe the gadrooned seat rails on cabriol legs and claw-and-ball feet.
£4,000-5,000 *CSK*

A set of 4 bamboo framed dining chairs, with cane seats and backs, on stretcher frames.
£250-300 *PCh*

A set of 15 mahogany dining chairs, including an armchair, with serpentine crestings and pierced splats above upholstered drop-in seats, on square chamfered legs joined by stretchers, labelled Maples.
£2,500-3,500 *CSK*

A set of 6 mahogany dining chairs, with pierced interlaced splats, padded seats and chamfered moulded square legs joined by stretchers.
£2,000-2,500 *C*

A set of 6 mahogany Chippendale style dining chairs, with pierced splats above upholstered drop-in seats, on claw-and-ball supports.
£1,000-1,200 *OL*

set of 8 reproduction Chippendale yle mahogany dining chairs cluding 2 elbow chairs, with erced arched ladder backs, uff-over floral wool tapestry seats, moulded square chamfered pports united by stretchers.
,500-2,000 *P(W)*

A set of 8 Hepplewhite style mahogany dining chairs, including 2 armchairs, with velvet upholstered seats, on square splayed tapering legs.
£3,000-3,500 *CSK*

A pair of Anglo-Indian Italian walnut dining chairs, the scrolled toprails over pierced carved splats incorporating foliage relief, over-stuffed seats raised on cabriole supports with carved knees and claw-and-ball feet.
£300-600 *P(M)*

A pair of Portuguese fruitwood chairs, with shaped pierced toprails carved with foliage, the drop-in seats upholstered in floral material, on cabriole legs with claw-and-ball feet, back legs restored, mid-18thC.
£1,500-2,000 *C*

Three Federal carved mahogany side chairs, with arched and moulded crestrails, vertically pierced with splats over slip-in seats, on square legs with moulded corners, Salem, Massachusetts, c1800.
£2,500-3,000 *CNY*

[H]all Chairs

nahogany hall chair, with leaf ved back on turned supports, ly 19thC.
0-150 *DEN*

et of 6 George III mahogany hall irs, with octagonal panelled ks, panel seats, turned front ports and rear sabre supports.
00-2,000 *P(M)*

A pair of mahogany hall chairs, late 18thC.
£5,000-6,000 *McC*

A pair of early George III mahogany hall chairs, the cartouche shaped solid backs painted with the Royal Arms, within roundels, with moulded seats and shaped legs, the Arms possibly later.
£2,000-2,500 *C*

A pair of George III mahogany hall chairs, each with pierced shield-shaped back and solid seat, on square tapering legs with stretchers.
£700-900 *C*

A pair of late George III mahogany hall chairs, with a balloon shaped waisted back, painted with a coat-of-arms, with crossed spears within a garter inscribed with a motto, with solid seats on square tapering legs.
£600-800 *C*

A pair of George IV mahogany hall chairs, each with waisted arched back with gadrooned top and oval panel, on reeded tapering legs.
£900-1,200 *C*

A pair of Regency mahogany hall chairs, each with shield shaped crest painted with a stag's head on a green ground, with solid seats on turned legs, one stamped EP.
£650-750 *C*

Side Chairs

A set of 6 mahogany tub shape side chairs, the caned seats with buttoned squab cushions, the front turned legs on brass casters, early 19thC.
£1,500-2,000 *WW*

A William and Mary walnut side chair, the caned seat with a shaped frieze and turned capped cabriole legs, with turned and block back legs and H-stretcher, old worm.
£800-1,000 *WW*

A pair of William and Mary walnut side chairs, upholstered in striped pink cloth, on knopped legs and H-shaped stretchers, restored.
£800-1,200 *C*

A set of 4 walnut chairs, upholstered in brown velvet with scrolling legs joined by waved stretchers, on later ball feet, with restorations, early 18thC. **£2,500-3,000** *C*

A set of 8 George III mahogany side chairs, with pierced splat domed backs and drop-in seats, the front square tapering legs with H-stretchers.
£2,500-3,000 *WW*

George III mahogany high chair, ıe shield shaped back with pierced ılat set below with a medallion, the ıtswept arms on reeded supports ıd the drop-in seat on tapering ıuare legs joined by stretchers.
2,000-2,500 *Bea*

A set of 6 George IV mahogany Norfolk chairs, with horizontal curved splats, saddle seats and on turned legs.
£700-800 *MAT*

An early Victorian oak Glastonbury chair, the panelled back with shaped finials, the solid seat on X-legs inscribed below the seat Thomas Shepp...d(?) maker February 21, 1846 no.28.
£400-500 *C*

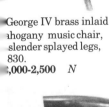

George IV brass inlaid ıhogany music chair, slender splayed legs, 830.
2,000-2,500 *N*

A set of 5 Regency black painted and parcel gilt side chairs, with trellis-painted toprail, the back posts painted with acanthus, with caned seats, the seat rails centred by flowerheads, on ring turned tapering legs.
£2,000-2,500 *C*

A Regency mahogany music chair.
£1,000-1,500 *GIL*

A set of 6 French walnut salon chairs, the spoon backs with rococo scroll carved cresting and tie rails, over-stuffed seats upholstered in green velour, with serpentine seat rails carved with diapering and foliage, terminating in peg feet, labels to inside of seat rail, dated 1906.
£700-1,000 *HSS*

A pair of mid-Victorian oak side chairs, in the Gothic style, with pierced back carved with arches and scrolling foliage, and moulded seats, the seat rail carved with scrolling foliage on square channelled legs and block feet.
£600-800 *C*

et of 6 George IV rosewood side ıirs, the seats covered in dralon, front turned reeded tapering legs.
000-2,500 *WW*

A set of 4 Regency rosewood single chairs, each with a concave back and foliate carved rail, above a bergère cane seat and standing on sabre legs, with loose seat cushions.
£1,000-1,500 *OL*

A Victorian papier mâché occasional chair, with inset mother-of-pearl surrounding a central panel, painted with fruit above a bergère cane seat and standing on cabriole supports, by H. Jenning of London, damaged.
£100-150 *OL*

A Victorian pale walnut wood spoon back nursing chair.
£450-550 *GD*

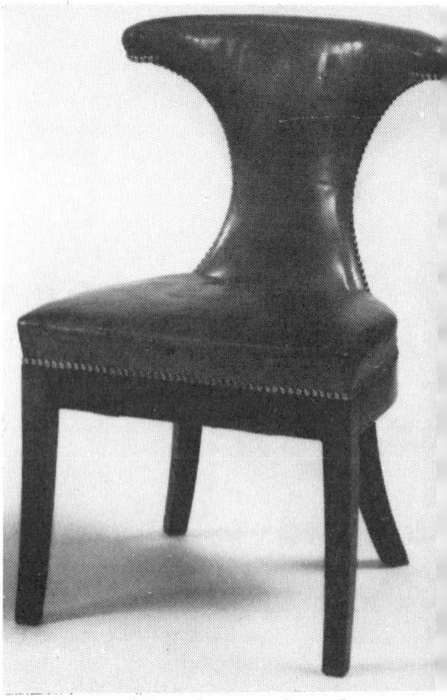

A set of 8 mahogany boardroom chairs, each with a waisted back an seat, close nailed upholstered in brown leather, on sabre legs.
£2,000-3,000 *CSK*

A Victorian mahogany nursing chair, with curving back and carved decoration, on cabriole front legs.
£300-400 *DDM*

A pair of Victorian ormolu mounted marquetry side chairs, each with shaped pierced splat inlaid with a musical trophy flanked by fluted columns, the circular seats upholstered in green cotton, on fluted tapering legs.
£1,500-2,000 *C*

A pair of Louis XV style carved giltwood fauteuils, with tapestry upholstered channelled frames, below a foliate shell carved crestin on cabriole legs, with scroll knob feet; and 3 matching side chairs.
£1,000-1,500 *CSK*

A late Victorian lady's walnut chair.
£300-400 *DDM*

A Victorian walnut chair, with ornate carved top, the back and seat with upholstered needlework panels, supported on turned front legs. **£400-500** *DDM*

A lady's Victorian walnut framed chair, with tapestry seat and back, on front cabriole type legs.
£450-550 *IM*

A set of 4 French wickerwork side chairs, Burgundy, c1920.
£600-700 *UC*

A Victorian walnut spindle back captain's chair, with hide seat and back, c1870.
£400-600 *DDS*

A Victorian mahogany revolving chair, with upholstered hide seat and adjustable height and tilt. **£300-450** *DDS*

Victorian rosewood
ımed chair with spiral
ist side supports, top
ials, tapestry seat
d back, on
briole front legs.
70-350 *IM*

A Queen Anne maple side chair, with moulded shaped crest above a leather upholstered back and seat, on block and baluster turned legs with baluster feet, joined by a ring turned stretcher, Boston, c1740, feet pieced.
£1,200-1,700 *CNY*

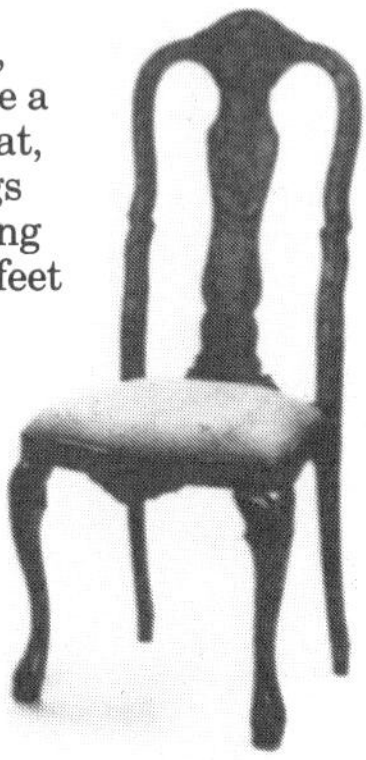

A pair of Dutch walnut and marquetry inlaid side chairs, with bar shaped splat backs above upholstered tapestry drop-in seats, on etched cabriole legs with claw-and-ball feet.
£1,200-1,600 *CSK*

A pair of Louis XV caned beechwood chairs, with cartouche shaped caned back crested by a flowerhead, on cabriole legs headed by flowerheads and ending in scroll toes, mid-18thC.
£2,200-2,500 *CNY*

et of 6 bamboo chairs,
h with spindle back
l paling toprail, the
ed seats with grey
hions, the legs with
ckets and stretchers.
000-1,500 *C*

A Queen Anne red stained maple side chair, with carved yolk crest above a solid vase shaped splat flanked by moulded stiles, over a slip-seat with a shaped skirt, New England, c1740.
£1,000-1,500 *CNY*

A Queen Anne leather back maple side chair, with moulded and shaped crest above an upholstered leather back flanked by moulded stiles above a slip-seat, on square cabriole legs with incised decoration and paint brush feet joined by a ball and ring turned stretcher, Massachusetts, c1740.
£1,200-1,700 *CNY*

ueen Anne black painted maple
chair, with carved yolk crest
ve a solid vase shaped splat
ked by moulded stiles over a
seat with a shaped skirt, New
land, c1740.
00-1,500 *CNY*

A Chippendale carved walnut slipper chair, with incise-moulded serpentine crest centering a carved shell, above a solid vase-shaped splat, over a slip-seat, on short cabriole legs with trifid feet, Philadelphia, c1750. **£2,500-3,500** *CNY*

Small Chests

A William and Mary walnut and crossbanded chest, with marquetry inlaid brass pear drop handles and escutcheons, moulded apron and later bun feet, 40½in (104cm).
£7,000-8,000 *AH*

A mahogany chest, on bracket feet, basically 18thC, 37½in (94cm).
£750-1,000 *CSK*

An early Georgian padouk bachelor's chest, the hinged moulded top lined in velvet above 2 short and 3 long pine-lined drawers, on ogee bracket feet, fee possibly replaced, restorations, 31½in (80cm).
£2,500-3,000 *C*

A Queen Anne walnut chest, on turned tapering bun feet, adapted, 37in (94cm).
£3,000-4,000 *CSK*

A walnut straight front chest, with inlaid decoration, reeded edge to the top, 2 short and 3 long drawers, with brass drop handles on bracket feet, 18thC, 37in (94cm).
£750-1,000 *DDM*

An early Georgian walnut and o chest, with moulded quarter veneered top, above 2 short and 3 long drawers, on bracket feet, 3 (99cm).
£2,000-3,000 *C*

A walnut veneered chest of drawers, the top quarter veneered, feather and crossbanded, bracket feet, early 18thC, 34½in (87cm).
£2,500-3,000 *P(S)*

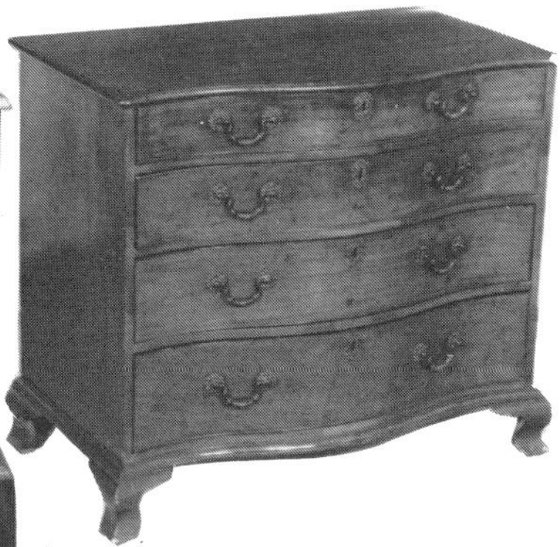

A mahogany serpentine dressing chest, with 4 graduated drawers fitted bronze drop handles and escutcheons, on pointed ogee bracket feet, the top drawer missing fittings, mid-18thC, 37in (94cm).
£4,000-5,000 *GSP*

A walnut and yew dwarf chest, w featherbanded inlay, on bracket feet, basically 18thC, 28½in (72cr
£3,000-4,000 *CSK*

A Queen Anne burr walnut chest, the later quarter veneered top above 2 short and 3 long herringbone banded drawers, on later bun feet, c1715, 38in (97cm).
£1,500-2,000 *Bon*

A walnut chest, with 3 small and 3 long drawers between fluted canted angles, on bracket feet, basically 18thC, 40½in (102cm).
£1,200-1,700 *CSK*

A walnut and mahogany chest, wit crossbanded top and herringbone inlay, with brass handles, cushione dividers between the drawers, bracket feet, 18thC, 39in (99cm).
£1,500-2,000 *GAK*

walnut and marquetry chest, the
› inlaid with foliate scrolls, above
short and 3 long similarly inlaid
awers, on bracket feet, feet
rtially replaced early 18thC, the
arquetry later, 28in (96cm).
,000-5,000 *C*

walnut and featherbanded chest,
:h baize lined brushing slide,
hort drawers and 3 graduated
ıg drawers between stop fluted
ıted angles on bracket feet,
sically 18thC, 42in (106.5cm).
,500-2,000 *CSK*

ıahogany chest, with string inlay
l crossbanding, moulded edged
, with concaved front and sides,
ıted inlaid corners, brass ring
ıdles and bracket feet, late
hC, 38in (96.5cm).
000-10,000 *AH*

eorge III mahogany bachelor's
est, with brushing slide, 2 long
l 2 short drawers with brass drop
ıdles, on bracket feet, 39in
cm).
0-450 *HCH*

A mahogany chest of 4 graduated drawers, with brushing slide, mid-18thC, 33in (84cm). **£3,500-4,000** *OS*

A George I walnut chest, with burr walnut veneered quarter panel top, with brass drop handles and butterfly backplates, on bracket feet, 39in (99cm).
£700-900 *P(W)*

A George I style burr walnut and banded bachelor's chest, with foldover top above four graduated long drawers with fluted canted angles, on bracket feet, 29½in (75cm).
£900-1,200 *CSK*

A Georgian style figured walnut chest, with herringbone inlay and ogee moulded edge to top, the drawers crossbanded and herringbone inlaid, on bracket feet, 37in (94cm). **£500-600** *HCH*

A George II mahogany serpentine chest, with baize lined slide and 4 graduated drawers, the canted angles carved with ribbon tied drapery, on bracket feet, 41½in (105cm).
£10,000-12,000 *C*

A Georgian style mahogany crossbanded serpentine chest, with moulded brass handles, raised on bracket feet, 36in (91.5cm).
£1,200-1,500 *AG*

A George III mahogany chest, on ogee bracket feet, 35½in (90cm).
£700-800 *CSK*

A George III mahogany chest, with moulded edge, the drawers with brass drop handles, on bracket feet, 37in (94cm).
£700-1,000 *P*

A George III mahogany veneered chest, the rectangular top above 2 short and 3 long graduated drawers, on bracket feet, 36in (92cm).
£300-400 *MGM*

A George III mahogany bow front chest, the frieze inlaid with a satinwood banding, on splayed bracket feet, 35in (89cm).
£1,200-1,500 *GA(W)*

A George III mahogany chest, with figured crossbanded top above a brushing slide and 4 graduated long drawers, c1770, 37½in (95cm).
£2,000-2,500 *Bon*

A George III mahogany bowfront chest, with 2 short and 3 long graduated drawers, waved apron and splayed feet, 38in (96.5cm).
£1,200-1,600 *C*

A George III mahogany bowfront chest, with 2 short and 3 graduated long drawers on splayed feet, 52in (132cm).
£1,000-1,500 *CSK*

A Georgian mahogany bowfront chest, with 2 short and 3 graduated drawers and standing on splay feet, 41in (104cm).
£500-700 *OL*

A George III mahogany chest, the later top above a brushing slide and 4 graduated long drawers with brass swan-neck handles, on bracket feet, 31in (79cm).
£1,200-1,500 *CSK*

A George III mahogany chest, with moulded top above a slide and 4 graduated drawers, on splayed bracket feet, 35in (89cm).
£4,000-4,500 *C*

A late George III bowfronted satinwood chest, with mahogany top edge moulding, the drawers with inlaid narrow bands, shaped aprons, and splay bracket feet, 36½in (92cm).
£2,500-3,000 *P(S)*

A late George III mahogany bowfront chest, with 4 graduated long drawers, shaped apron and splayed bracket feet, 37½in (95cn
£900-1,200 *CSK*

A George III mahogany dwarf che with a brushing slide, 2 short and 3 graduated long drawers on bracket feet, adapted, 35½in (90cr
£1,200-1,700 *CSK*

A George III mahogany Lancash chest, with hinged top, above a frc fitted with 5 false drawers and 4 drawers between rounded flute angles, on ogee bracket feet, 68½ (173cm).
£2,000-2,500 *CSK*

. teak military chest of drawers, on
un feet, with casters, early 19thC,
7in (94cm).
300-1,000 *P(M)*

A mahogany serpentine fronted chest of drawers, 19thC, 39in (99cm).
£1,500-2,000 *P(M)*

A George III mahogany serpentine chest with eared moulded top above 4 graduated drawers, with fluted angles, on bracket feet, 45½in (116cm).
£3,500-4,500 *C*

George III mahogany chest, on
racket feet, 42in (106.5cm).
,500-2,000 *OL*

A George III mahogany serpentine chest, the top with later satinwood inlay with 4 graduated long drawers, the top drawer formerly fitted, on later front feet, 46½in (117cm).
£2,000-2,500 *CSK*

A small George III red walnut chest, with a brushing slide, above 4 long drawers, bracket feet, 28in (71cm).
£3,500-4,000 *P(S)*

George III mahogany and inlaid
wfront chest, with rosewood and
tinwood crossbanded top, oval
ass drop handles and embossed
ckplates, on later turned
pports, 39in (99cm).
,200-1,500 *P(W)*

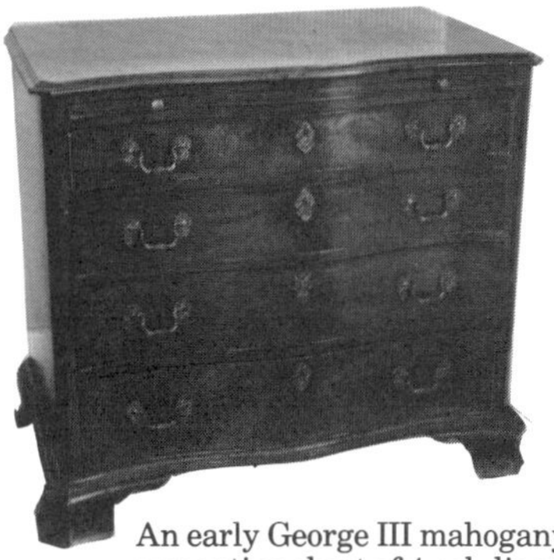

An early George III mahogany serpentine chest of 4 oak-lined drawers, with chased gilt drop handles and escutcheons, on ogee bracket feet, 37½in (95cm).
£7,500-8,000 *GSP*

A pair of mahogany chests, each with 4 graduated drawers, on bracket feet, 17in (43cm).
£4,500-5,000 *C*

ate Georgian mahogany small
crétaire chest, the fall front
vealing a fitted interior of small
awers and pigeonholes, 3 long
awers below with brass drop
ndles, and bracket feet, 31in
cm).
,500-2,000 *MAT*

A George III mahogany chest, the top inlaid with a satinwood shell medallion and boxwood and ebony stringing, brass swan neck handles and escutcheons, and on bracket feet, 36in (91.5cm).
£900-1,200 *MAT*

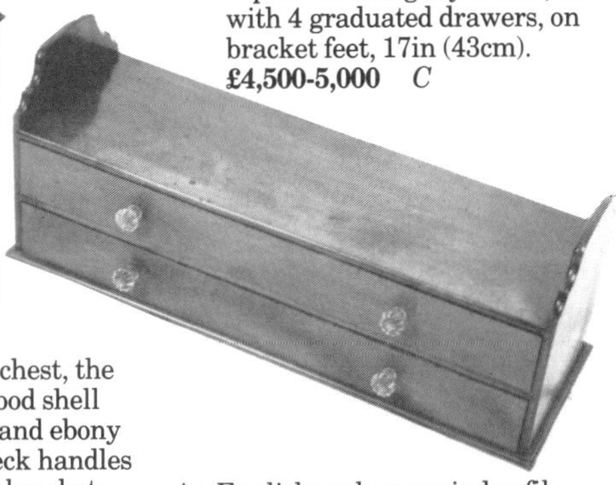

An English mahogany index file with 2 drawers, c1820, 30in (76cm).
£300-400 *UC*

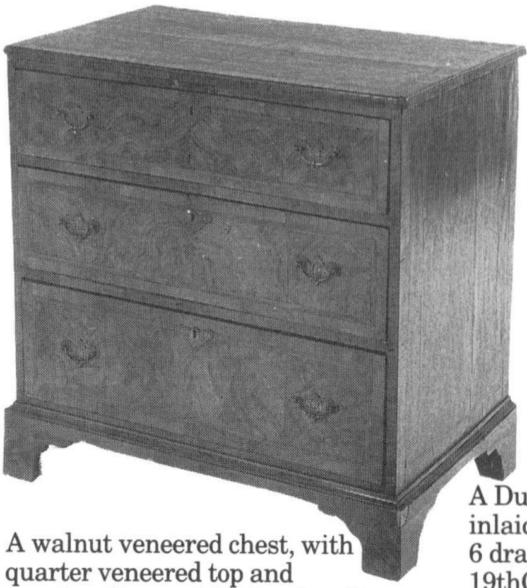

A walnut veneered chest, with quarter veneered top and crossbanding and feather banding throughout, on bracket feet, 34in (86cm).
£1,200-1,500 *Bea*

A Regency mahogany and boxwood inlaid dwarf chest, the top above 4 graduated long drawers and a bowed apron, on splayed bracket feet, 33in (84cm).
£900-1,200 *CSK*

A Regency mahogany bachelor's chest, with hinged top and 4 long drawers, on turned tapering feet, the sides with carrying handles, 33in (84cm).
£1,500-2,000 *C*

A veneered walnut chest of drawers, with bracket feet, in need of restoration, 36in (91.5cm).
£3,500-4,000 *PLJ*

A Dutch mahogany upright chest, inlaid with chequered bands, with 6 drawers, on square tapered legs, 19thC, 42in (106.5cm).
£1,000-1,500 *CSK*

A North Italian walnut and fruitwood chest, the top and sides inlaid, on later square legs, late 18thC, 49in (124cm).
£1,500-2,000 *C*

An oyster veneered walnut chest, on bracket feet, 31½in (80cm).
£1,200-1,500 *CSK*

A William IV mahogany chest, with moulded top, above drawers flanked by fluted columns, on reeded bulbous supports, 48½in (123cm).
£2,000-2,500 *CEd*

A Regency mahogany and inlaid bowfront chest, the rosewood crossbanded top with parquetry bandings, with brass lion mask ri handles, and diamond pattern pilasters headed by brass and ebo floral motifs, on bun feet, 39in (100cm).
£1,500-2,000 *P(W)*

A Victorian brass mounted walnut secrétaire military chest, with 5 drawers flanking a central fitted drawer, on turned tapering legs, 7 Duncannon Street, London, 39in (99cm).
£1,000-1,500 *CSK*

A Victorian teak military chest, in 2 sections, with 2 short and 3 long graduated drawers with inset bras handles and corners, on turned bu feet, 41in (104cm).
£1,200-1,500 *CSK*

A Victorian mahogany bowfront chest, with 2 short and 4 graduate long drawers on bracket feet, 45in (114cm).
£600-700 *CSK*

ed lacquer chest, decorated
erall with chinoiserie figures,
vilions and foliage, on later
acket feet, 36½in (93cm).
,000-2,500 *C*

nahogany chest, with 2 short and
raduated long drawers, on
acket feet, restorations, 30in
cm).
,500-3,000 *CSK*

Dutch walnut and crossbanded
est of drawers, with moulded
ged top, broken serpentine shaped
nt, brass drop handles and
utcheons, moulded apron and
acket feet, early 18thC, 37½in
cm).
500-4,000 *AH*

A Dutch walnut and foliate marquetry chest, decorated overall with flower-filled vases and trailing foliage, 19thC, 40in (101.5cm).
£3,000-4,000 *CSK*

Chests-on-Chests

An early Georgian walnut tallboy, with moulded cornice and convex frieze drawer, above 3 short and 3 long featherbanded drawers, the base with 2 short and 2 long drawers on bracket feet, 41in (104cm).
£6,000-7,000 *C*

A mahogany tallboy, with moulded dentilled cornice above 2 short and 3 long drawers, the base with 3 long drawers flanked by stop fluted chamfered angles, on bracket feet, 46in (117cm).
£3,500-4,500 *C*

A George III mahogany tallboy, on bracket feet, adapted, 42½in (107cm).
£1,500-2,000 *CSK*

A mahogany tallboy, with dentilled and cavetto moulded cornice above 2 short and 6 graduated long drawers, between fluted canted angles, on bracket feet, late 18thC and later, 42in (107cm).
£1,500-2,000 *CSK*

A walnut tallboy, with featherbanded inlaid borders, on bracket feet, early 18thC, 43in (109cm).
£3,000-4,000 *CSK*

A George III mahogany chest-on-chest, the upper section with dentil cornice above 2 short and 3 long drawers, with canted angles, on a base of 3 long drawers and bracket feet, 42in (107cm).
£2,000-2,500 *MGM*

A walnut and oak tallboy, with moulded cornice, brushing slide and on bracket feet, basically mid-Georgian, 41½in (104cm).
£4,500-5,500 *CSK*

An early George III mahogany chest-on-chest, with blind-fret carved frieze on later reduced bracket feet, 44½in (112cm).
£2,000-2,500 *CSK*

A George III mahogany chest-on-chest, with moulded Greek key pattern cornice, ornate brass drop handles and escutcheons, on bracket feet, 46in (117cm).
£1,200-1,500 *P(W)*

A burr walnut tallboy, inlaid wit stars and chequered boxwood lin on bracket feet, 42in (106.5cm).
£2,000-2,500 *CSK*

A George III mahogany tallboy, th top section with a dentilled cornic and canted angles, the lower secti with a brushing slide and 3 drawer on later bracket feet, 44½in (112cm
£2,000-2,500 *CSK*

A George III mahogany tallboy, with moulded Greek key pattern cornice, above 2 short and 3 long drawers, the lower section with slide above 3 graduated long drawers on bracket feet, 44in (112cm).
£1,500-2,000 *C*

A George III mahogany tallboy, with moulded cornice above 2 short and 6 graduated long drawers, on bracket feet, 43½in (109cm).
£900-1,200 *CSK*

:hests-on-Stands

William and Mary style burr
alnut chest-on-stand, with floral
arquetry panels, 19thC, 38in
6.5cm).
:,500-3,000 *SWO*

Queen Anne figured maple
est-on-stand, in 2 sections, on
briole legs with padded disc feet,
storation to frame, New England,
760, 40in (101.5cm).
,000-6,000 *CNY*

Queen Anne walnut high chest of
awers, in 2 parts, on cabriole legs
th pad feet, the rear legs of maple,
tch to lower case, apron sides
shaped, Massachusetts, c1750,
½in (105cm).
,500-7,500 *CNY*

A Queen Anne carved cherrywood high chest of drawers, in 2 sections, the centre panel fan carved over an arcaded skirt centering 2 pendant acorn drops, on cabriole legs with pad and disc feet, brasses original, one drop restored, North Shore, Massachusetts, c1760, 38in (96.5cm).
£7,500-9,000 *CNY*

A Queen Anne walnut chest-on-stand, with later veneered moulded top above 2 short and 3 graduated long drawers, the reduced stand with 3 drawers, with shaped apron and later bun feet, the chest in 2 parts, 38in (96.5cm).
£2,000-2,500 *C*

A Dutch walnut and featherbanded chest-on-stand, with arcaded apron, on turned bun feet, parts 18thC, 38in (96.5cm).
£1,500-2,000 *CSK*

A walnut chest-on-stand, with fluted canted angles, the stand fitted with 3 short drawers, on cabriole legs and pad feet, 40in (101.5cm).
£2,000-2,500 *CSK*

An early Georgian walnut chest-on-stand, on cabriole legs with pad feet, 38½in (97cm).
£3,000-3,500 *CSK*

An early Georgian walnut chest-on-stand, on cabriole legs with pad feet, 38½in (97cm).
£3,000-3,500 *CSK*

A walnut and featherbanded chest-on-stand, on cabriole legs with pad feet, parts 18thC, 39in (99cm).
£1,000-1,500 *CSK*

A walnut chest-on-stand, with moulded top above 2 short and 2 graduated long drawers, the stand on spiral twist legs joined by an undulating flat stretcher, on bun feet, 38in (96.5cm).
£2,000-3,000 *CSK*

A Queen Anne design walnut and featherbanded chest, on a stand with cabriole legs and pad feet, 42in (106.5cm).
£600-700 *CSK*

A walnut and banded chest-on-stand, on turned legs joined by a stretcher, 39in (99cm).
£1,200-1,700 *CSK*

A George I walnut chest-on-stand, the upper section with moulded edge, above 2 short and 3 long banded drawers, the stand with 3 small drawers above a shaped apron, on later turned club legs, c1730, 42½in (107cm).
£2,000-2,500 *Bon*

A George I walnut chest-on-stand, with featherbanded drawers with brass drop handles and engraved backplates, shaped apron, on later cabriole supports, 39in (98cm).
£1,000-1,500 *P*

Wellington Chests

A Victorian mahogany Wellington chest with 7 drawers, with turned knob handles, a locking bar to one side, raised on a plinth base, the top drawer stamped from S. & H. Jewells Furniture Warehouse, 29, 30 and 31 Little Queen Street, Holborn, 27in (69cm).
£1,500-2,000 *AG*

A mahogany Wellington chest, wit pierced brass gallery, over 7 graduated drawers with turned wooden handles, 19thC, 27in (69cm
£600-1,200 *MN*

A Victorian rosewood Wellington secrétaire chest, with fitted interio of small drawers and pigeonholes faced in maple wood, 22in (56cm).
£1,800-2,000 *MAT*

A Victorian Wellington chest, wit turned handles and scrolled capita to the front supports, 32in (81cm).
£800-1,000 *DEN*

;offers

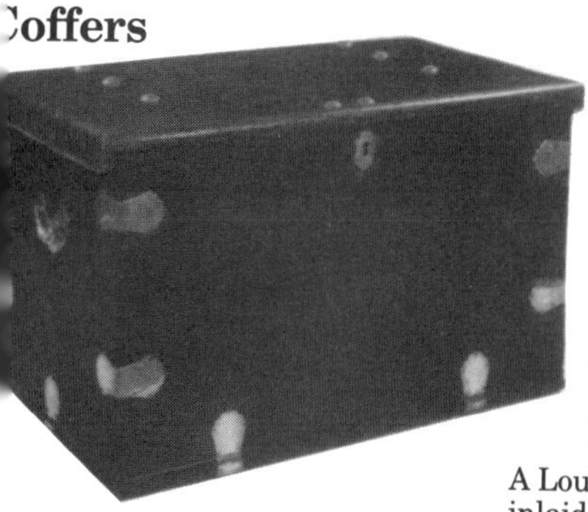

. Dutch East Indies camphor coffer,
ıe top with brass studs, the angles
ith lotus-shaped straps, the sides
ith carrying handles, 18thC, 45in
.14cm).
400-600 *C*

A Louis XV style tulipwood and inlaid serpentine commode, with rouge royale marble top, above 3 long drawers between volutes mounted with cabochon claps and sabots, early 19thC, 46in (116.5cm).
£3,500-4,500 *CSK*

A George III mahogany commode, inlaid with boxwood lines, with shaped apron, on bracket feet, adapted, 26½in (67cm).
£1,500-2,000 *C*

ommodes

.ouis XV style kingwood and
ırquetry bombé commode,
plied with gilt brass mouldings
d with mottled marble top, with
aid drawers and frieze, on
ayed feet, 26in (66cm).
500-2,000 *Bea*

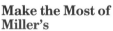

A South German walnut parquetry commode, with crossbanded overhung top inlaid with wide bands on an oysterwood ground, the drawer fronts and sides with walnut panels divided by ebonised lines, 18thC, 48in (122cm).
£13,000-15,000 *GSP*

A George III mahogany breakfront commode, the top enclosing fitted interior and concave sided fascia with one dummy and 3 drawers with turned wood handles and brass escutcheons, on 4 square tapered legs, 19½in (49cm).
£700-900 *AH*

An ormolu mounted tulipwood and end-cut marquetry bombé commode, with eared serpentine 'breche violette' marble top above inlaid drawers, on tapering legs with sabots, stamped R. Roessle, 56in (142cm).
£1,700-2,500 *C*

rench kingwood and marquetry
ɔentine fronted 2 drawer
ımode, with marble top and
ıolu mounts, on shaped legs,
ɦC, 29in (74cm).
900-1,500 *JD*

Make the Most of Miller's

CONDITION is absolutely vital when assessing the value of an antique. Damaged pieces on the whole appreciate much less than perfect examples. However a rare, desirable piece may command a high price even when damaged

A pair of George III mahogany night commodes, with pierced gallery tops above tambour shutter compartments, pull out pot holders with ebony stringing and brass swan neck handles, on square legs, 19in (48cm).
£8,000-9,000 *WW*

A South German walnut commode, the crossbanded top inlaid with strapwork designs above two inlaid drawers highlighted with bone husk motifs, on later bun feet, c1740, with later back, 46in (117cm).
£3,000-4,000 *Bon*

A Louis XVI style commode, veneered in exotic woods, with metal mounts and marble galleried top.
£1,500-2,000 *LRG*

A George III mahogany crossban and inlaid commode, with origin brass drop handles, on 4 square supports, 33in (84cm) high.
£700-900 *AH*

A Continental marble top commode, with serpentine front, 3 drawers and cast metal handles and mounts.
£1,500-2,000 *MGM*

A North Italian walnut commode, the quarter-veneered top inlaid with a lobed medallion and broad barber's pole stringing, the serpentine front fitted with 3 long drawers, on short tapered legs, late 18thC, 55in (140cm).
£6,000-7,000 *Bon*

A Dutch oak bombé commode, wi 4 graduated long drawers betwee canted volutes, on block feet, 19th 33in (84cm).
£1,200-1,500 *CSK*

A South German kingwood and ormolu mounted commode, the bracket feet with sabots, lacking marble top, distressed, mid-18thC, 38½in (97cm).
£5,000-6,000 *CSK*

An ormolu mounted marquetry, mahogany and harewood commode, after Leleu, with drawers inlaid 'sans travers' with a lozenge, the sides inlaid with a trellis of fleur-de-lys, on turned tapering legs with acanthus capital, 34in (86cm).
£2,000-3,000 *C*

A pair of gilt metal mounted marquetry and parquetry commodes of transitional style, w green veined marble top, on cabri legs with paw sabots, 46in (117cn
£6,000-7,000 *C*

An Empire ormolu mounted mahogany commode, with black fossil marble top, on turned feet, 50in (127cm).
£1,500-2,000 *C*

In the Furniture section if there is only one measurement it usually refers to the width of the piece

North Italian fruitwood and
nded serpentine commode, with
ong drawers and a shaped apron,
bracket feet, late 18thC, 48in
2cm).
,000-2,500 *CSK*

Italian blue painted and parcel
t commode, decorated with a
iling flower-filled urn, and with
rawers, shaped apron on cabriole
s, 41in (104cm).
)0-900 *CSK*

Empire ormolu mounted
hogany commode, with black
rble top, above 3 graduated long
wers mounted with lion's mask
handles, and flanked by
sters headed by classical busts,
bonised paw feet and later
forms, early 19thC, 50½in
3.5cm).
)00-5,000 *CNY*

Bedside Cupboards

An early George III mahogany bedside cupboard, with pierced galleried top, open cupboard and chamfered square legs, 16in (40.5cm).
£1,000-1,500 *C*

A pair of late Georgian mahogany square pot cupboards with single door with satinwood stringing, on square tapered legs, 10in (25cm).
£900-1,200 *RBB*

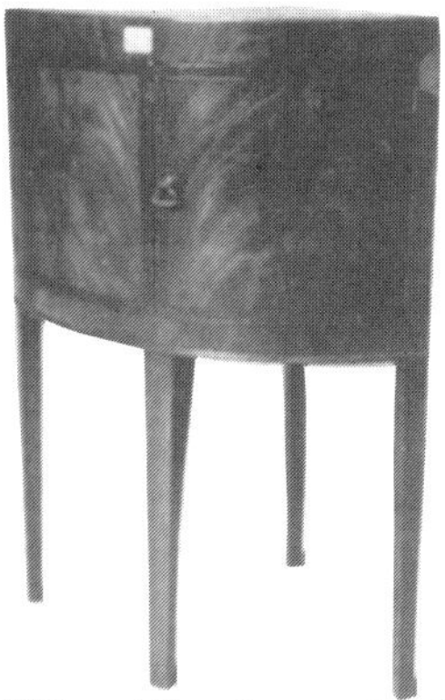

A William IV mahogany bowfront corner pot cupboard, with 2 doors, crossbanding and tapering legs, 20in (51cm).
£500-600 *GAK*

A Louis XVI style gilt metal mounted mahogany commode, with mottled liver marble top, with false frieze drawer, on toupie feet with gadrooned collars, bearing label Charles Jenner & Co., Princes Street, Edinburgh, 52in (132cm).
£1,000-1,500 *CSK*

Corner Cupboards

A Georgian mahogany large bowfront hanging corner cupboard, inlaid stringing and crossbanding to the 2 doors, enclosing 3 shelves over one real and 2 dummy drawers, 35in (89cm).
£500-700 *DDM*

A Georgian oak and mahogany banded hanging corner cupboard, the cavetto cornice above a moulded panel door, enclosing 3 shelves, 46in (116.5cm) high.
£200-400 *OL*

A George III mahogany corner cupboard, crossbanded with satinwood, with green painted 2-tiered interior, the base with 2 short and one long drawer and 2 cupboard doors, 48in (122cm).
£2,500-3,000 *C*

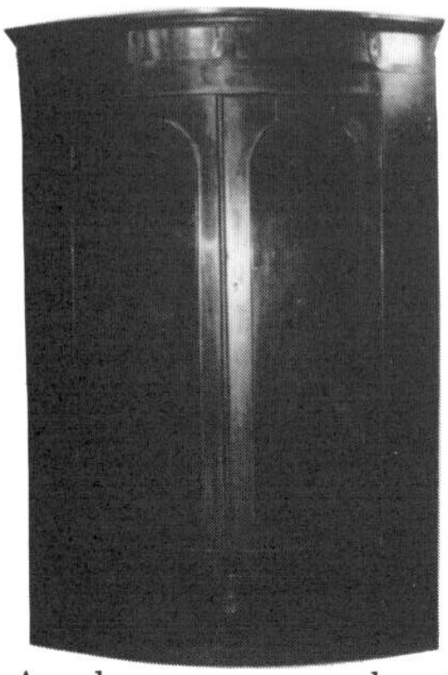

A mahogany corner cupboard, with double panel doors and small centre drawer, 19thC.
£250-400 *JH*

A Georgian inlaid mahogany bowfront hanging corner cupboard, with a pair of doors enclosing 3 shelves and 3 spice drawers, 43in (109cm) high.
£1,000-1,500 *OL*

A mid-18thC oak bowfront hanging corner cupboard.
£650-850 *P(M)*

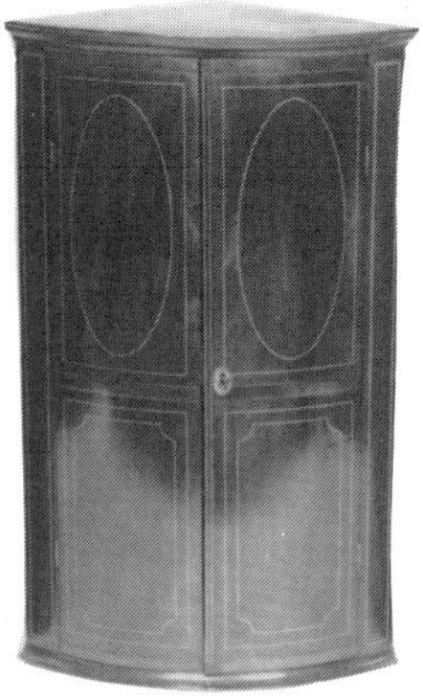

An early 19thC mahogany bowfront corner cupboard.
£550-800 *P(M)*

A George II mahogany bowfront hanging corner cupboard.
£500-700 *P(M)*

A George III mahogany bowfronted corner cupboard with boxwood stringing and boxwood, ebony, satinwood and harewood inlay, with fitted interior, 30in (76cm).
£800-1,000 *HCH*

An Empire period mahogany corner cupboard, with ebonised pilasters with ormolu mounts, standing on a plinth form base, 41½in (105cm).
£300-400 *OL*

Make the most of Miller's

Unless otherwise stated, any description which refers to 'a set' or 'a pair' includes a valuation for the entire set or the pair, even though the illustration may show only a single item

A Regency mahogany corner cupboard, with blind fret carved frieze, above 4 panelled doors flanked by reeded uprights, on plinth, 45½in (115cm).
£1,000-1,500 *CSK*

A Louis Philippe ormolu mounte kingwood and tulipwood corner cabinet of serpentine outline, wi quarter-veneered doors, a shelf above and below, 37½in (95cm) h
£600-800 *C*

A late Victorian mahogany corr standing display cabinet, inlaid with satinwood and boxwood lir the dentilled cornice above a gla lancet astragal door and a pane cupboard door between canted angles, on square tapering legs v spade feet, 27½in (70cm).
£700-900 *CSK*

'ictorian Gothic mahogany
ner cabinet, with arched ledge
:k, above a diagonally planked
r carved with monogram EA
hin a quatrefoil, on chamfered
are legs with pierced brackets,
h Chubb lock number 673310,
½in (67cm).
0-500 *C*

is lock was supplied c1872.

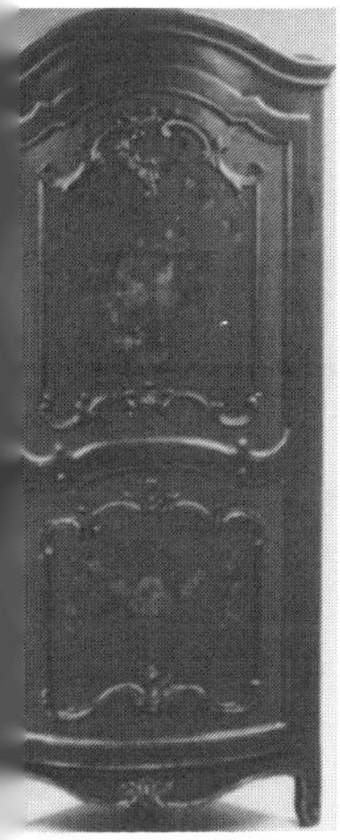

'rench green painted and parcel
: bowfront corner cupboard, with
ulded arched cornice, above a
r applied with acanthus scrolls
l rockwork motif, painted in
ychrome with flowersprays, with
ped apron on bracket feet, late
hC, 39in (99cm).
0-1,000 *CSK*

ıpboards – Linen 'esses

A George III mahogany and boxwood strung linen press, the dentil and cavetto moulded cornice above a pair of crossbanded doors, enclosing shelves, with 2 short and 2 long graduated drawers, on bracket feet, 50½in (128cm).
£1,200-1,500 *Bon*

A mahogany gentleman's press, the breakfront top section with 2 panelled doors enclosing folio trays.
£3,000-4,000 *CSK*

A George IV mahogany double wardrobe, with triangular pediment, 2 panelled doors enclosing sliding trays, 2 short and 2 long drawers below, a full-length panelled door to each side, on ring turned feet, 98in (249cm).
£600-900 *Bea*

A George III mahogany clothes press, the pediment with Gothic arches, above a pair of panelled doors crossbanded with rosewood and centred by ovals, the base with 2 short and 3 long drawers, with a waved apron on splay feet, 48in (122cm).
£2,000-3,000 *CSK*

A mahogany linen press, adapted as a wardrobe, with moulded and carved key pattern cornice, oval inlaid doors, with rosewood crossbanding, 2 short and 2 long drawers below, brass drop handles, bracket feet, late 18thC, 51in (129.5cm).
£3,000-4,000 *AH*

A George III mahogany clothes press, on splayed bracket feet, 41in (104cm).
£1,200-1,800 *C*

A George III period figured mahogany linen press with boxwood marquetry line inlay, 50in (127cm).
£1,500-2,000 *P(M)*

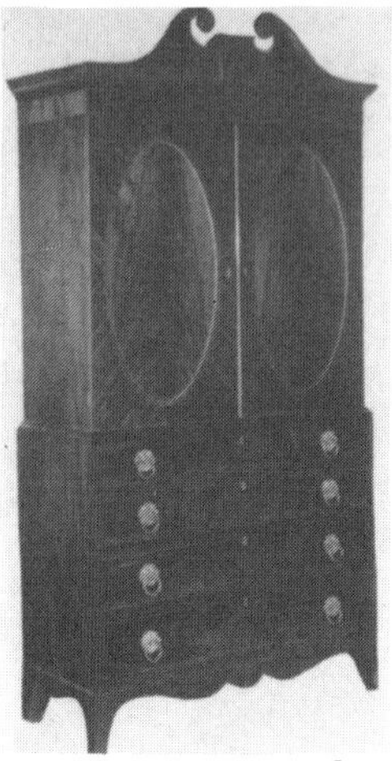

A Regency mahogany linen press, with broken pediment applied with metal gilt paterae, the 2 oval panel doors above 4 graduated long drawers, on splayed bracket feet, 52in (132cm).
£2,000-2,500 *CSK*

A Dutch mahogany linen press, with fret carved cresting, the lower section with 3 graduated long drawers between bellflower and acanthus carved canted angles, on square tapered fluted legs, early 19thC, 67in (170cm).
£4,000-4,500 *CSK*

A late Regency mahogany linen press, inlaid with geometric boxwood lines, with a dentilled moulded cornice, a pair of panelled doors with inset sliding trays above 2 short and 2 graduated long drawers on bracket feet, 54½in (138cm).
£1,000-1,500 *CSK*

A Regency mahogany bowfront linen chest, with moulded cornice, and 2 moulded panel doors, with 2 short and 2 graduated long drawers, on bracket feet, 56in (142cm).
£1,500-2,000 *CSK*

A Victorian mahogany and inlaid linen press, with cavetto cornice above a pair of moulded panelled doors, 2 short and 2 graduated long drawers, on splayed bracket feet, 52in (132cm).
£1,500-2,000 *CSK*

A mahogany clothes press, with plain stepped pediment over 2 cupboard doors with Gothic panels, pillar sides, over a base with one long cushion fronted drawer and 3 further graduated drawers, on a platform base, 19thC, 58in (147cm).
£500-700 *DDM*

Cupboards – Wardrobes

A Sheraton style satinwood wardrobe, the pediment cornice with urn finials above a pair of fielded panel doors, the whole wit tulipwood crossbanding, on brack feet, c1880, 55in (140cm).
£3,000-3,500 *Bon*

Davenports

A George IV pollard oak davenpo in the manner of Richard Bridger the top with undulating three-quarter gallery, 26in (66cm).
£2,000-2,500 *C*

An early Victorian rosewood davenport, the sliding top with brass balustrade and hinged leather-lined slope, 26in (66cm).
£1,200-1,500 *C*

William IV mahogany davenport, th bobbin and reel beaded ıtlines, the hinged sloping flap low a galleried lidded mpartment, on reeded baluster lumns, flanking twin side nelled doors enclosing drawers on ncave platform base, 30in (76cm).
,500-2,000 *CSK*

A Victorian walnut davenport, with fretwork gallery, the drawers with locking bars, on china casters, 20½in (52cm).
£1,500-2,000 *GSP*

A walnut veneer and mahogany davenport.
£800-1,000 *M*

William IV rosewood davenport, in (51cm).
,500-3,500 *MGM*

A Victorian burr walnut davenport, with inset leather-lined hinged sloping front, below a galleried lidded stationery compartment, on foliate carved cabriole supports flanked by 4 side drawers on turned bun feet, 21in (53cm).
£1,500-2,000 *CSK*

A Victorian walnut davenport.
£1,000-1,200 *PLJ*

An early Victorian rosewood davenport, with sloping flap enclosing real and false drawers, on shaped plinth with casters, 28in (71cm).
£1,000-1,500 *Bea*

Victorian figured walnut venport, with brass galleried t-up stationery compartment, ınt and 4 real and 4 dummy awers, on china casters, 22in 3cm).
,500-2,000 *GSP*

A Victorian walnut davenport, the back with galleried hinged stationery compartment, above a leather-lined sloping front on turned feet, 22in (56cm).
£800-1,000 *CSK*

Use the Index!

Because certain items might fit easily into any of a number of categories, the quickest and surest method of locating any entry is by reference to the index at the back of the book.
This has been fully cross-referenced for absolute simplicity

A Victorian walnut davenport, with hinged stationery compartment, pen trays, and a lined slope, enclosing a bird's eye maple interior, above 4 short drawers opposed by false drawers, on a plinth, 21in (53cm).
£1,000-1,500 *CSK*

A Victorian walnut davenport, with inset brown hide panel enclosing fitted interior, 4 short and 4 dummy drawers to the side, on turned and carved knopped supports, plinth feet, 22in (56cm).
£1,000-1,500 *HCH*

A Victorian marquetry and inlaid rosewood davenport, on carved foliate cabriole front supports, flanking 4 small side drawers and pen drawers, on bar and turned b feet, 22in (56cm).
£3,000-4,000 *CSK*

A Victorian figured walnut and marquetry inlaid davenport, the lined surface enclosing a well, with 4 drawers, knob handles, and carved scrolled brackets, 22in (56cm).
£2,000-2,500 *GC*

A Victorian inlaid figured walnut davenport, with fitted stationery compartment, slant and 4 real and 4 dummy drawers, carved scroll front supports and bun feet, 21½in (54cm).
£1,500-2,000 *GSP*

A Victorian burr walnut veneere pop-up piano front harlequin davenport, with fitted interior, cabriole supports and gallery.
£3,500-4,000 *MGM*

A Victorian walnut piano top davenport, with sprung stationery compartments, the interior fitted with a lined sliding writing surface and pen trough, with 4 short drawers to the right on bar feet and casters, 22in (56cm).
£2,500-3,500 *CSK*

A Victorian walnut davenport, the serpentine front with fall flap inset with leather, with sandalwood fitted interior, the top with an ogee sided lidded stationery compartment with brass gallery, the sides with drawers and dummy drawers, knob handles, on leaf carved cabriole supports, bun feet and casters, 21in (53cm).
£1,600-2,000 *WW*

A Victorian burr walnut veneerec davenport, with boxwood and ebo string inlays and central inlaid panel.
£1,500-2,000 *MGM*

esks

Carlton House style mahogany
d satinwood banded desk, inlaid
th radial boxwood lines, with a
rced brass gallery, on reeded
rned tapering legs, 61in (155cm).
,000-3,000 *CSK*

A mahogany inlaid tambour roll-top desk, with writing slide, c1880, 29in (72cm).
£1,400-1,600 *DDS*

A Victorian cylinder front kneehole desk with tray top, the drawers with turned handles, on plinth bases, labelled from Mart & Co., Cannon Street, London, EC., 48in (122cm).
£1,200-1,500 *P(W)*

Sheraton design mahogany
inder writing desk, with tambour
, fitted interior, 2 drawers and
are tapered legs.
000-1,500 *MGM*

A walnut cylinder top desk, the writing drawer with reading slope and satinwood interior drawers, c1880, 48in (120cm).
£1,600-2,000 *DDS*

A Dutch mahogany and brass mounted cylinder roll-top desk, on square tapering legs, 19thC, 50in (127cm).
£2,000-2,500 *CSK*

A Victorian mahogany cylinder front pedestal desk, with plain gallery, fitted interior, 54in (137cm).
£1,000-1,500 *DDM*

An oak roll-top desk, with fitted interior, on plinth base and casters, 50in (127cm).
£700-900 *HCH*

A lady's Edwardian mahogany escritoire, with brass gallery above an inset leather top, on square tapering supports.
£800-1,000 *OL*

An Edwardian mahogany lady's cylinder desk.
£900-1,200 *GIL*

A mahogany kneehole writing de: with frieze drawer and 6 side drawers with brass drop handles, recessed cupboard with interior shelf, 18thC, 27½in (70cm).
£2,000-3,000 *GSP*

A Victorian mahogany partners' desk, with lined top and 6 frieze drawers, on pedestals each with 3 short drawers opposed by a cupboard door, on plinth, 72in (182.5cm).
£2,500-3,000 *CSK*

A Victorian mahogany partners' desk, with leather lined top, on plinth bases, 60in (152cm).
£1,500-2,500 *CSK*

A mahogany kneehole desk, the frieze with brushing slide and lor drawer, on bracket feet, 31½in (80cm).
£1,000-1,500 *C*

A walnut and featherbanded desk, the crossbanded rectangular top above 9 drawers, flanking a central kneehole panelled door, on bracket feet, 18thC, 33in (84cm).
£1,000-1,500 *CSK*

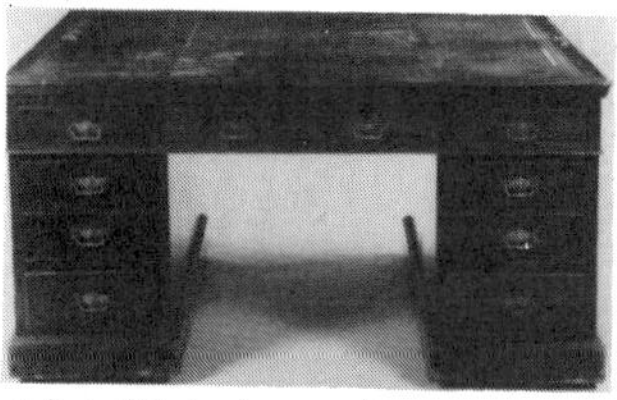

A late Victorian mahogany partners' kneehole pedestal desk, with inset leather lined top, on plinth bases, 60in (152cm).
£1,500-2,000 *CSK*

A mahogany roll-top desk, crossbanded and with string inlay, the fitted interior with satinwood faced small drawers, pigeonholes, ink pot and pen stands, fitted with 2 slides and 9 drawers surrounding the kneehole, bracket feet, veneered back, Maple & Co., metal label, 54in (137cm).
£3,500-4,000 *P(S)*

An Irish mid-Victorian mahogany partners' desk, with 2 silver plaques, one in Irish, the other inscribed 'Presented to William T Cosgrave Esq Ltd President Executive Council Saorstat Eireann by Wm and P Thomson Ltt as an expression of their deep appreciation of the invaluable services rendered by him to the Saorstat during the critical period of its history', stamped J J Burne and Sons, Cabinet Makers and Upholsterers Henry Street Dublin, 75in (190.5cm).
£3,000-4,000 *C*

A child's mahogany desk, the adjustable 2 sided writing slope with baize lining and well under, brass drop handles, on stand witl drawer and square tapered legs, l 18thC, 19in (49cm).
£2,500-3,000 *AH*

n early George III mahogany
ieehole desk, with moulded edge,
ove a long drawer and columns of
drawers flanking a cupboard, with
ılded panel door, 36in (91cm).
,700-2,000 *Bon*

nid-Georgian mahogany
eehole desk, on ogee bracket feet,
torations, 34in (86cm).
500-2,000 *CSK*

ieorgian design mahogany
tners' desk, with blind tooled
her top, 2 pull slides, raised on
n pedestal, the drawers mounted
h swan neck drop handles,
hC, 60in (152cm).
00-5,500 *MN*

'ictorian double-sided pedestal
k, the top with later gilt tooled
her inset, fitted with 9 drawers
ne side, 3 drawers and
pboards on the other, 65½in
cm).
00-2,500 *P(S)*

A Victorian burr walnut pedestal desk, with lined kidney-shaped top, above 3 frieze drawers and 8 pedestal drawers, stamped W. Williamson & Sons, Guildford, 51in (129.5cm).
£8,000-9,000 *CSK*

A mahogany partners' kneehole pedestal desk, with leather lined top above 6 drawers and a panelled door, the same to the reverse on plinth bases, 19thC and later, 62½in (158cm).
£3,000-3,500 *CSK*

A mid-Victorian mahogany partners' desk, the top with 2 hinged writing slopes enclosing drawers, with 5 drawers and a door to each side, 66in (167.5cm).
£2,000-2,500 *CSK*

An elm and mahogany banded desk, the top above a long frieze drawer and 6 small drawers, flanking a central kneehole panelled cupboard door, on plinth base, part 18thC, 40½in (102cm).
£700-1,000 *CSK*

A walnut roll-top desk, with hand dovetailed drawers, panelled and having side hinged supports and well fitted interior, c1910, 60in (152cm).
£1,400-1,600 *DDS*

A Sheraton revival period mahogany ladies desk, with satinwood line inlays, on tapering legs with casters, 27in (69cm).
£900-1,200 *GAK*

An oak roll-top desk, the tambour slide enclosing a fitted interior of pigeonholes and drawers over a central frieze drawer, with further drawers to each pedestal, 50in (127cm).
£600-800 *DDM*

A Victorian mahogany roll-top desk, the cylinder shutter enclosing a fitted interior, above 6 pedestal drawers on plinth base, 60in (152cm).
£1,500-2,000 *CSK*

A Victorian mahogany cylinder roll-top desk, with three-quarter gallery above a shutter fall, enclosing a fitted interior, 6 drawers to the pedestals, 53in (134.5cm).
£1,200-1,600 *CSK*

A Victorian mahogany cylinder roll-top pedestal desk, the three-quarter gallery above a shutter fall, enclosing a fitted interior and writing slide, above 6 small base drawers, 47in (119cm).
£900-1,200 *CSK*

A Victorian mahogany cylinder roll-top pedestal desk, with galleried elevated shelved back, on pierced C-scrolling carved supports, above a shutter fall enclosing a maple lined fitted interior, with 6 drawers to the pedestals, 49in (124.5cm).
£1,500-2,000 *CSK*

An oak roll-top kneehole desk, with fitted interior and tambour shutter, with 8 drawers, on plinth base, 48in (122cm).
£550-600 *HCH*

A lady's ebonised writing desk, in the French manner, supported on carved cabriole legs, late 19thC, 39in (99cm).
£300-400 *DDM*

A French burr and figured walnut lady's writing desk, with satinwoo interior, Sèvres plaque and ormolu mounts, on cabriole legs with galleried stretcher, 19thC, 25in (64cm).
£3,000-3,500 *GSP*

A mahogany roll-top desk, c1910, 60in (152cm).
£1,000-1,200 *DS*

A George I style featherbanded walnut kneehole desk, with brass drop handles and butterfly backplates, on bracket feet, stamp From W Williamson & Sons, Guildford, 32in (81cm).
£1,000-1,500 *P(W)*

A Victorian mahogany cylinder desk, with fitted interior, the drawers faced in satinwood, including a writing slope, 48in (122cm).
£1,500-2,000 *IM*

A carved and decorative oak writing desk, with drawers and compartments over a hide writing inset, c1880, 54in (137cm).
£2,200-2,500 *DDS*

An Edwardian mahogany cylinder bureau, the top crossbanded in satinwood, the cylinder enclosing drawers and pigeonholes and a leather lined slide above a kneehole drawer and 8 pedestal drawers, on square tapering legs, 45in (114cm).
£2,000-2,500 *C*

A mahogany partners' desk, with gilt-tooled leather lined and moulded top, on cabriole legs and scroll feet, 72in (182.5cm).
£2,000-3,000 *CSK*

A George II mahogany kneehole desk, on later bracket feet, 29½in (74cm).
£2,000-2,500 *P(M)*

A George III style mahogany pedestal desk, the leather lined top above 6 drawers and a panelled door, the same to the reverse, on plinth bases, 72in (182.5cm).
£2,000-2,500 *CSK*

A Victorian mahogany partners' desk, with lined top above 8 frieze drawers and 12 pedestal drawers, on plinth bases, 68in (172.5cm).
£6,000-7,000 *CSK*

walnut and featherbanded
eehole desk, with crossbanded
p, above 8 drawers with a star
laid door on bracket feet, modern,
in (91.5cm).
,000-1,500 *CSK*

A George III mahogany partners' desk, with brown leather lined top, the reverse with a panelled door on a plinth base, restorations, 59½in (152cm).
£6,000-7,000 *C*

A Victorian mahogany partners' desk, with leather lined top above 9 drawers, the reverse enclosed by a pair of panelled doors, on plinth bases, 48in (122cm).
£2,000-3,000 *CSK*

A Georgian clerk's desk, with 4 interior drawers and reading mould, c1820, on later stand, 48i (120cm) high.
£500-700 *DDS*

A Victorian walnut and elm kneehole pedestal desk, the inset leather lined top above 9 drawers between quadrant angles, on plinth bases, adapted, 54in (137cm).
£1,700-2,200 *CSK*

A Victorian larch and satinwood kneehole desk, the lined top above 9 drawers, on undulating plinth base, 54in (137cm).
£1,200-2,000 *CSK*

A Flemish walnut and marquetry desk, the top with gadrooned edge depicting an episode from classical mythology, also carved back, 67½in (171cm).
£4,000-5,000 *C*

An oak partners' desk, c1860, 60in (152cm).
£2,000-2,500 *DS*

An Edwardian mahogany kidney-shaped pedestal desk, wi green inset tooled leather, crossbanded with brass ring handles, the plinth bases on cast 48in (122cm).
£1,500-2,000 *WW*

A Victorian mahogany partners' pedestal desk, with leather lined top, on plinth bases, 60in (152cm).
£2,000-2,500 *CSK*

A Victorian oak desk, 72in (182.5cm).
£1,000-1,200 *DS*

A mahogany pedestal desk, with leather lined top above 9 drawers, the reverse with simulated drawers, on plinth bases, 19thC and later, 49in (124.5cm).
£4,000-4,500 *CSK*

An ebony veneered and amboyna banded pedestal desk, fitted with 3 frieze drawers, each pedestal fitted with a further 3 drawers, stamped Edwards & Roberts, 48in (122cm).
£1,500-3,000 *MGM*

An Edwardian walnut kneehole pedestal desk, with inset leather lined top, below a galleried elevat cabinet back fitted with 4 small drawers, above 9 graduated drawers to the pedestals, on plint bases, stamped Jas. Shoolbred & Co., 48in (122cm).
£900-1,200 *CSK*

A mahogany pedestal desk, the top with rail turned gallery, 6 small drawers and pigeonholes over 3 frieze drawers and 3 drawers to each side, late 19thC, 54in (137cm).
£900-1,200 *DDM*

late Victorian lady's mahogany heval screen writing desk, inlaid vith butterflies, ribbon bows, griffin nasks, putti and foliate motifs, and trung with box, on a double aluster turned stretcher with brass asters, 22in (56cm).
'2,000-2,500 *HSS*

A Louis XVI style plum pudding nahogany portable writing desk, nlaid with brass arabesques with gilt mounted border, the box top enclosed by a hinged pierced galleried lid, above a fall front panel enclosing a stationery fitted nterior, on end standards and scrolling down curving legs, joined by flat cross stretchers, 23in (59cm).
£2,000-3,000 *CSK*

Lowboys

A William and Mary style walnut featherbanded lowboy, with brass drop handles, double arched apron, on turned inverted cup form legs, united by a concave shaped stretcher, 19thC, 38in (69cm).
£650-800 *P*

A Queen Anne walnut lowboy, the quarter veneered top with narrow inlaid herringbone bandings, above one long and 3 short similarly banded drawers, on cabriole legs with pad feet, 30in (76cm).
£3,000-4,000 *Bon*

A walnut lowboy, with canted top above 4 frieze drawers, on cabriole legs with pad feet, part 18thC, 31in (79cm).
£1,500-2,000 *CSK*

A George I walnut lowboy, with a quarter veneered crossbanded top, canted fluted corners and a single drawer to the frieze, fitted with brass handles and pierced lock escutcheon, raised on cabriole legs with pad feet, 30in (76cm).
£700-900 *AG*

Mirrors & Frames

A Regency giltwood convex mirror, in an ebonised fluted slip and sphere encrusted cavetto frame with displayed eagle cresting and later foliate base, regilt, 33½ by 19½in (84.5 by 49cm).
£600-800 *C*

A Regency period convex mirror, surmounted by a sea horse, the base with sprays and an artichoke drop, 25in (64cm) wide.
£2,200-2,500 *WW*

A late Regency ebonised and gilt mirror, with convex plate in a ball encrusted moulded frame with eagle and scroll cresting, and gadrooned foliate apron, 38 by 25in (97 by 64cm).
£600-800 *C*

A Victorian gilt mirror, with ebonised reeded slip in an acanthus carved and ball mounted cavetto frame with eagle cresting, 56 by 31in (142 by 79cm).
£1,500-2,000 *CSK*

A George I walnut dressing glass, with later bevelled mirror plate, the stepped plateau with 3 short drawers over a long cushion drawer, on bracket feet, the whole with herringbone banding, 16½in (42cm).
£2,500-3,500 *HSS*

An early Georgian walnut mirror, the plate with re-entrant top corner and moulded frame, shaped archec cresting and conforming apron, 33 by 19in (85 by 48cm).
£500-700 *C*

A gilt girandole mirror, with two candlearms, damages and cracks, c1825, 38 by 22½in (97 by 57cm).
£2,500-3,000 *CNY*

A Regency mahogany toilet mirror, inlaid with ebonised lines on ring turned supports, the serpentine base with 2 drawers, on turned legs, 22in (56cm).
£700-900 *C*

A George III style satinwood toile mirror, with shield shaped bevelle plate on scrolled supports, with crossbanded serpentine base, on bracket feet, 18in (46cm).
£600-800 *C*

A George III style giltwood mirror, with pierced frame carved with scrolls, acanthus flowers and fruit, the cresting with a foliate plume with flowers, 19thC, 26in (66cm) wide.
£1,500-2,000 *C*

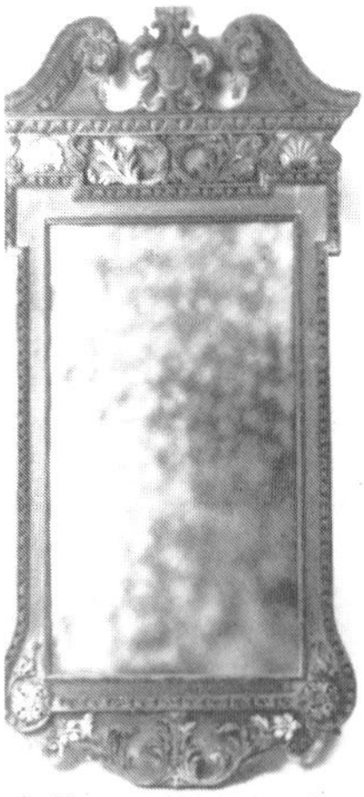

A George II style pine wall mirror, with an eared frame carved with egg-and-dart, the frieze applied with shells and acanthus beneath a broken pediment, 72 by 37in (182.5 by 94cm).
£2,000-2,500 *CSK*

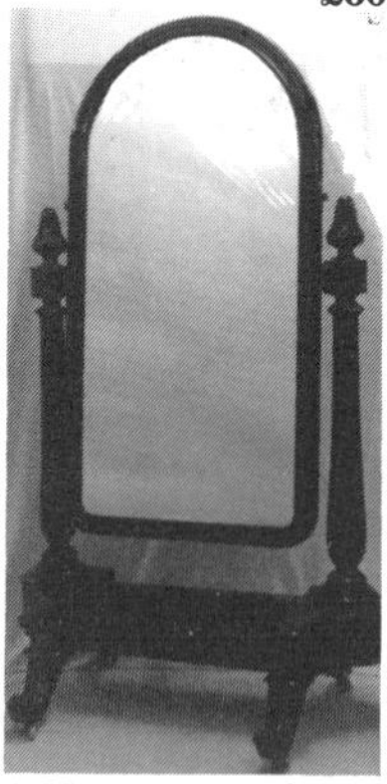

A Victorian mahogany cheval mirror, on turned reeded supports, the box top base with scroll legs and casters, 42in (106.5cm).
£250-300 *PCh*

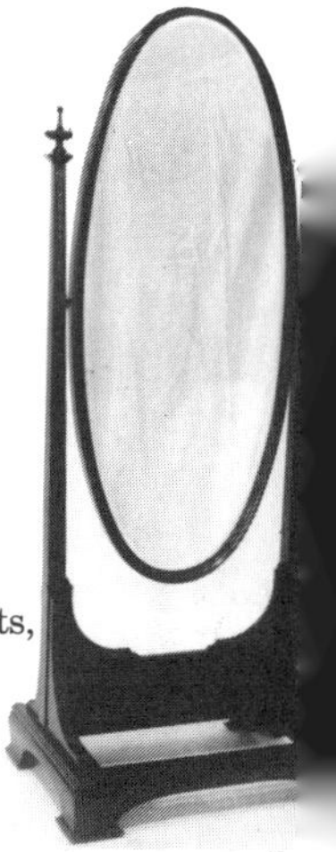

An Edwardian inlaid mahogany cheval mirror, with harebell inlay on rectangular base with bracket feet, 69½in (176cm) high.
£400-500 *HCH*

, George III satinwood toilet ıirror, with canted corners on nialled supports, the boxed base ·ith hinged lid inlaid with husks, wags and a circle, enclosing a silk ned interior with 2 lidded ompartments, 24in (36cm).
1,000-1,500 *C*

A William and Mary oyster veneered walnut mirror, with later plate in cushion moulded frame, lacking cresting, 30 by 25½in (76 by 65cm).
£1,000-1,500 *C*

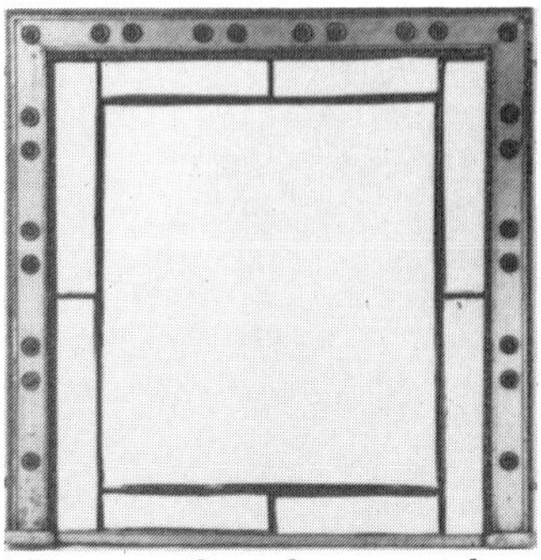

A Regency giltwood overmantel, with chanelled frame with acorn and oak leaf border applied with rosettes, 54in (137cm) high.
£2,500-3,000 *CSK*

Queen Anne style giltwood ırror, with bevelled plate, the ·olling strapwork frame with ılloped cresting and scrolling se, lacking candle sconces, 36 by ½in (91.5 by 52cm).
,000-2,500 *C*

An early Georgian walnut and parcel gilt mirror, with scrolling flowerheads and foliage with shaped apron, lacking cresting.
£2,000-2,500 *CSK*

An English Chippendale carved and gilded frame, with pierced C-scroll corners and centres, trailing foliage and flowers and a foliate sight edge, 18thC, 37 by 33in (94 by 84cm).
£1,200-1,500 *CSK*

ɜeorge III gilt and composition ·r glass, the frieze applied with ·werheads within beaded ındels.
,500-2,000 *C*

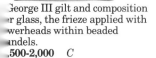

A George III style giltwood mirror, possibly Irish, 52 by 30in (132 by 76cm).
£1,500-2,000 *C*

A George III giltwood mirror, in a pierced C-scrolling frame carved with foliage below a cabochon and classical pediment, 39½ by 26in (100 by 66cm).
£1,000-1,500 *CSK*

A Regency carved and gilded frame, with anthemia corners flanked by opposed C-scrolls, trailing foliage on a cross hatched ground, cartouche centres and a foliate sight edge, 53 by 58½in (134 by 148cm).
£4,000-5,000 *CSK*

A Flemish walnut mirror, in plain chamfered frame, restorations, la 17thC, 21½in (55cm) wide.
£1,000-1,500 *C*

A George III parcel gilt wall mirror, the pine frame carved with an Adam urn and swags and having an arched pediment, 62 by 26in (157 by 66cm).
£700-1,000 *MAT*

A Regency giltwood and composition pier glass, in a beaded and leaf moulded frame, the angles with honeysuckle, 67 by 35in (170 by 89cm).
£2,000-2,500 *C*

A pair of Empire style gilt metal mounted mahogany pier glasses, applied with rosettes and foliate clasps, 66 by 42½in (167.5 by 107cm).
£2,500-3,000 *C*

A cream painted and parcel gilt p glass, late 19thC, 89 by 42in (226 b 107cm).
£1,500-2,000 *C*

A George III red, white and green-painted mirror, with oval plate in moulded frame with flaming urn and foliate cresting, the base with scrolling foliage, redecorated, 46 by 21in (116.5 by 53cm).
£2,000-2,500 *C*

A George III giltwood mirror, in moulded beaded frame with anthemion and scrolling foliate cresting, the base with scrolling foliage, 45 by 18½in (114 by 47cm).
£1,000-1,500 *C*

A giltwood pier glass, with mould pounced foliate frame, the crestin carved with a lambrequin flanke by eagles' heads, the apron with scallop shells, 62 by 25in (157 by 64cm).
£1,500-2,000 *C*

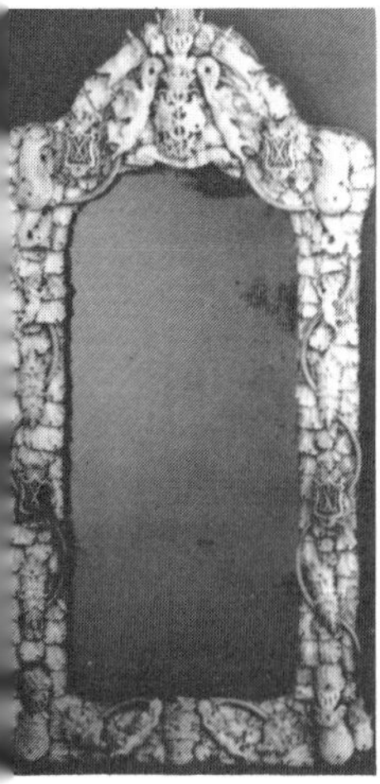

. Dieppe ivory mirror, the surround
›ntred by a coat-of-arms, with
pplied masks, dolphins and foliage,
9thC, 40in (101.5cm) high.
350-400 *CSK*

A pair of English carved and gilded landscape frames, with a shell cresting and opposed C-scroll corners, 18thC, 36½ by 49in (93 by 125cm).
£600-1,000 *CSK*

A giltwood overmantel, the triple plate with acanthus scroll frame below an urn cresting, mounted on claw feet, basically early 19thC, 32 by 51in (81 by 129.5cm).
£900-1,200 *CSK*

›air of William IV giltwood
rrors, each plate within a glazed
›ulded frame carved with
›olling leaves and flowerheads
th ribbon tied cresting and
›olled base, crestings damaged
d one piece deficient, 56 by 24in
‹2 by 61cm).
,000-8,000 *C*

A gilt gesso rococo wall mirror, with bevelled plate, 45in (114cm).
£600-700 *HCH*

An English carved and gilded frame, foliate sight edge, 18thC, 35 by 30in (89 by 76cm).
£500-550 *CSK*

iltwood overmantel, the plate
ıked by fruiting foliate uprights,
cresting with confronting
gons and an urn, the frieze with
›and tied flowerswags, 83 by
ı (210 by 109cm).
0-1,000 *CSK*

A carved giltwood frame wall mirror of asymmetric form, 18thC, 25½in (65cm).
£1,500-2,000 *GSP*

A Venetian engraved and moulded glass mirror, with arched bevelled plate, the shaped apron and cresting framed with C-scrolls and applied with flowers, mid-19thC, 72 by 37in (182.5 by 94cm).
£1,600-2,000 *C*

An English carved and gilded frame, the corners with rosettes flanked by pierced opposed C-scrolls and scrolling foliage and flowers, foliate sight edge, 18thC, 37 by 32in (94 by 81cm).
£900-1,200 *CSK*

A pair of Chippendale style giltwood mirrors, the plates surmounted by foliate and C-scroll crests with ho-ho birds, the sides with elongated C-scrolls, the aprons with C-scrolls and icicles, 50 by 26in (127 by 66cm).
£3,500-4,000 *Bon*

A Dutch carved ebonised frame, with various ripple and wave mouldings, 17thC.
£1,800-2,000 *CSK*

A pair of giltwood pier glasses, each with an arched bevelled plate in a gilt églomisé frame incorporating C-scrolls, distressed, 51 by 31in (130 by 79cm).
£2,500-3,000 *CSK*

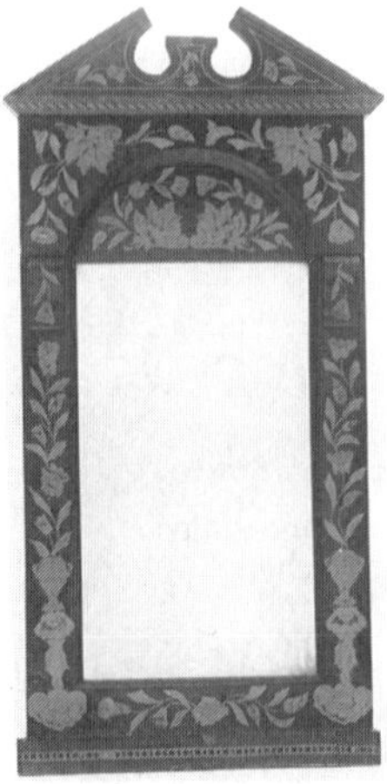

A walnut and floral marquetry wall mirror, with rectangular plate, the broken pediment above an arched recessed frieze, 36 by 17½in (91.5 by 44cm).
£600-700 *CEd*

A giltwood mirror, with bevelled plate, the frame with flowerhead and ribbon entwined border within pierced acanthus scrolls, the cresting with flowerheads, part 18thC, 44 by 34½in (112 by 87cm).
£1,500-2,000 *C*

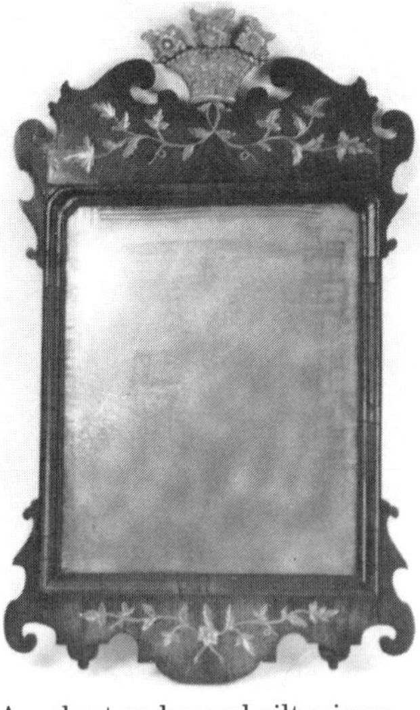

A walnut and parcel gilt mirror, with bevelled plate in a narrow moulded frame with shaped base and cresting, incised with foliage and with basket of flowers cresting, 33 by 19½in (84 by 49cm).
£1,200-1,500 *C*

An English carved and gilded frame, with foliate outer edge and scrolling foliage and flower inner edge, mid-18thC, 47 by 43in (119 109cm).
£800-1,000 *CSK*

A giltwood mirror, the bevelled plate engraved with a chinoiserie scene, in a moulded frame applied the corners with leaves, 33 by 26i (84 by 66cm).
£1,500-2,000 *C*

An English carved and gilded frame, 18thC, 38 by 30½in (96.5 77cm).
£500-600 *CSK*

A North Italian giltwood wall mirror, with waisted bevelled pla in a frame carved with C-scrolls foliage, pierced C-scroll and folia surmount and similar apron, 36 24in (92 by 61cm).
£800-1,000 *CEd*

. giltwood mirror, basically 18thC, 5 by 31½in (114 by 80cm).
2,000-2,500 *CSK*

An Italian painted and giltwood wall mirror, of cartouche form, later mirror plate and repaired, 19thC, 57 by 35½in (144 by 90cm).
£2,000-2,500 *HSS*

A French Regency carved and gilded frame, foliate sight edge, 34 by 38½in (86 by 97cm).
£1,000-1,500 *CSK*

n Italian giltwood mirror, with rched inset plate in a fish scale adrooned carved frame, decorated ith masks and acanthus scrolls elow a twin eagle and fruit stooned cresting, 19thC, 79 by in (200 by 127cm).
,500-3,000 *CSK*

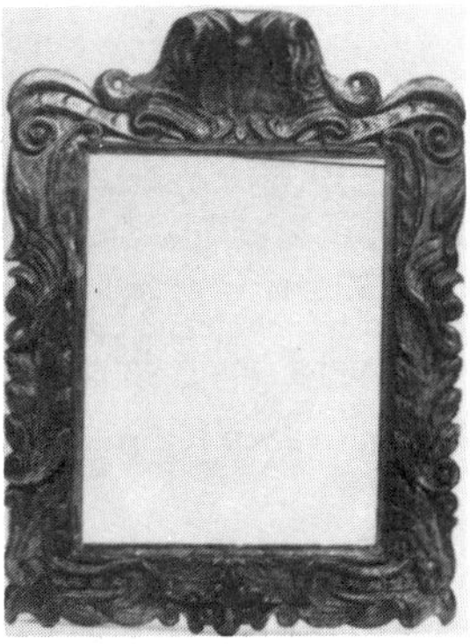

An English carved and gilded Sunderland frame, with scrolling foliage and flowers centred by a cartouche, the base carved with a lion's mask, 17thC, 12½in (32cm) wide.
£700-800 *CSK*

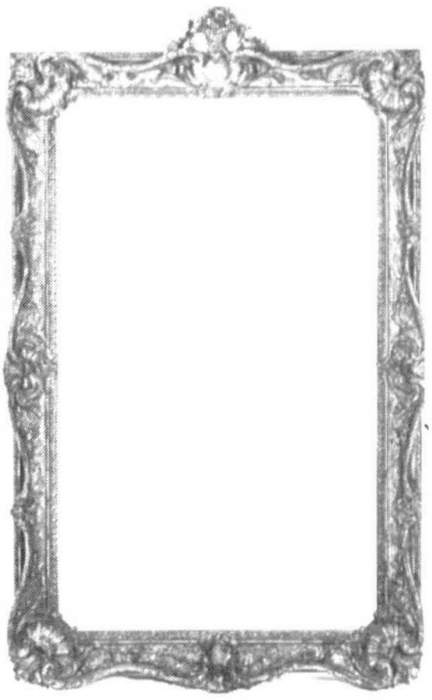

A French rococo carved and gilded frame, 31 by 19in (78 by 48cm).
£2,500-3,000 *CSK*

A Dutch tortoiseshell and ebonised frame, with ripple moulding, 19thC, 24 by 20½in (61 by 52cm).
£2,500-3,000 *CSK*

A Louis XIV style carved and gilded frame, 35in (90cm) wide.
£3,000-4,000 *CSK*

. Italian carved, gilded and inted tabernacle frame, with an ched pediment, early 17thC, ½in (37cm) wide.
,000-2,500 *CSK*

An Italian carved and gilded frame, with foliate outer edge, ribband central panel and an overlapping leaf design running to the corners, 17thC, 29½ by 26in (75 by 66cm).
£700-1,000 *CSK*

A fine Louis XIII carved and gilded frame, with a holly leaf pattern running from flowered centres to acanthus leaf corner, a foliate sight edge, 32 by 45in (81 by 114cm).
£5,000-6,000 *CSK*

A Louis XIV carved and gilded frame, with scrolling foliage and flowers and anthemia centres, foliate sight edge, 43in (109cm) high
£1,500-2,000 *CSK*

A Louis XIV carved and gilded frame, on a cross hatched ground, sand work and a foliate sight edge, 37 by 35in (94 by 89cm).
£1,000-1,500 *CSK*

An English carved and gilded frame, with an egg-and-dart outer edge and a stiff leaf inner edge, 18thC, 46 by 35in (116.5 by 89cm).
£1,000-1,200 *CSK*

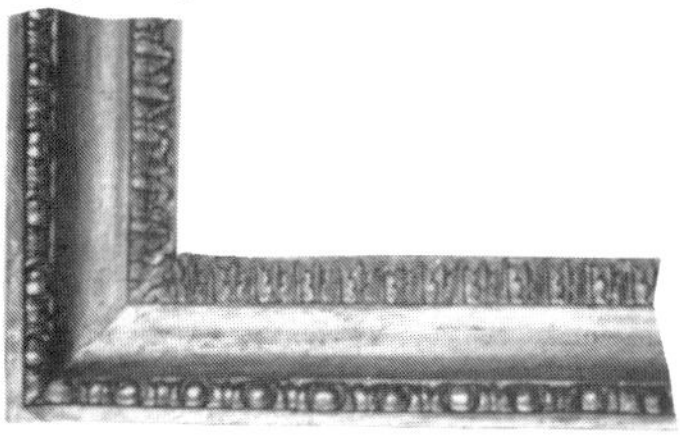

A Louis XIV carved and gilded laurel leaf corner frame, with anthemia and flower corners and a foliate sight edge, 15 by 20in (38 by 50.5cm).
£400-500 *CSK*

A Louis XIV style carved and gilded frame, on a cross hatched ground, sandwork and a foliate sight edge, 36½in (93cm) wide.
£1,500-2,000 *CSK*

A Louis XV carved and gilded frame, with scrolling acanthus leaves, on a cross hatched ground and a fluted sight edge, 19in (48cm) high.
£600-800 *CSK*

An Italian carved and gilded plate frame, 17thC, 28½in (72cm) wide.
£1,000-1,500 *CSK*

An Italian carved and gilded frame with a stiff leaf outer and sight edge, scrolling foliage and flowers, the raised inner edge carved with a running acorn pattern, 17thC, 55in (139cm) wide.
£2,500-3,000 *CSK*

An Italian carved and gilded tabernacle frame, with a broken pediment centred by a cherub's head, 17thC, 22 by 18½in (56 by 47cm).
£1,200-1,500 *CSK*

An Italian carved and gilded fram the inner edge carved with berries flowers and fruit running from the centres to the corners, 17thC, 61 b 44in (155 by 112cm).
£5,000-5,500 *CSK*

A Louis XIV carved and gilded frame, on a cross hatched ground, and a fluted sight edge, 28 by 24in (71 by 61cm).
£450-500 *CSK*

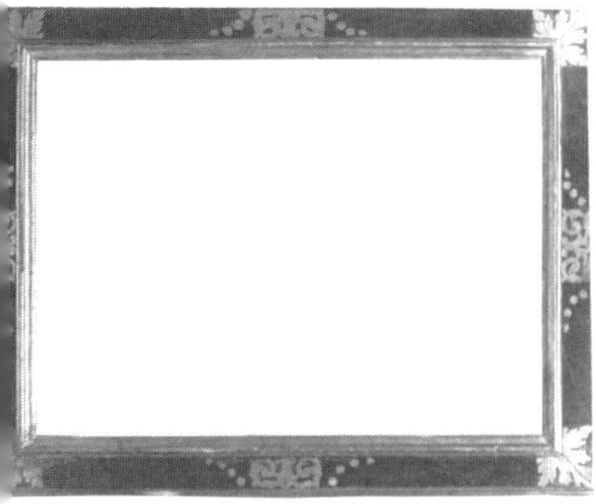

n Italian carved and gilded frame, ith leaf corners and stylised foliate ntres, 17thC, 40 by 53in (102 by 35cm).
,500-2,000 *CSK*

Italian carved and gilded frame, th pierced scrolling acanthus ves, cherubs' heads, bunches of it and a bar-and-treble-bead er edge, 27½ by 20½in (70 by 5cm).
,000-2,500 *CSK*

Italian carved gilded and nised frame, with bar-and-ble-bead outer edge and a foliate nt edge, 18thC, 14in (35cm) high.
0-450 *CSK*

ouis XIV carved and gilded el leaf corner frame, anthemia flower corners and engraved ses, 39 by 33in (99 by 84cm).
'00-2,000 *CSK*

A Spanish carved and gilded frame, with scrolling foliage and flowers and a notched ovolo sight edge, 17thC, 68 by 55½in (172.5 by 140cm).
£2,500-3,000 *CSK*

An Italian carved and gilded frame, with anthemia corners and pierced scrolling acanthus leaves running to foliate clasp centres, 17thC, 32 by 29in (81 by 74cm).
£1,000-1,500 *CSK*

A Florentine giltwood frame, carved with strapwork amid scrolling foliage, 16 by 15in (40.5 by 38cm).
£750-850 *C*

A Louis XV carved and gilded frame, with pierced opposed C-scroll corners centred with a shell, c1740, 28½in (73cm) square.
£1,600-2,000 *CSK*

An Italian carved and gilded frame, with scrolling acanthus leaves, shells and female masks at the corners, 19thC, 60 by 50in (152 by 127cm).
£900-1,200 *CSK*

An Italian carved gilded and painted frame, with cresting outer edge, flowerhead corners and a beaded inner edge, 19thC, 16 by 12in (40.5 by 30.5cm).
£500-600 *CSK*

A William IV giltwood mirror, in the rococo style, the pierced frame carved with C-scrolls, rockwork, acanthus and flowerheads, 69 by 55in (175 by 140cm).
£1,000-1,500 *C*

Screens

A Victorian ebonised and parcel gilt screen, the 4 Gothic folding leaves inset with scrapwork panels in etched and fluted banded borders, 84½in (214cm) high.
£1,000-1,500 *CSK*

A Dutch four-leaf screen decorated with 3 panels of parrots and exotic birds within studded leather borders, the reverse plain, 81in (206cm) high. **£2,000-2,500** *C*

A Spanish leather screen, with embossed panels depicting putti, acanthus scrolls and fruiting vines, on a gilt ground, the leather late 17thC, distressed.
£1,200-1,500 *CSK*

A pair of French painted two-leaf screens, each leaf inset with a coloured architectural engraving surrounded by flowers and scrolls hung with swags, 54in (137cm) high.
£1,500-2,000 *C*

A Victorian giltwood fire screen, with bellflower festooned headings joined by a fluted tablet cross stretcher, stamped V.R. 1886 Windsor Castle, Rm 507, 49½in (125cm). **£800-1,200** *CSK*

Miller's is a price Guide not a price List

The price ranges given reflect the average price a purchaser should pay for similar items. Condition, rarity of design or pattern, size, colour, provenance, restoration and many other factors must be taken into account when assessing values. When buying or selling, it must always be remembered that prices can be greatly affected by the condition of any piece. Unless otherwise stated, all goods shown in Miller's are of good merchantable quality, and the valuations given reflect this fact. Pieces offered for sale in exceptionally fine condition or in poor condition may reasonably be expected to be priced considerably higher or lower respectively than the estimates given herein

A Dutch painted leather chinoiser four-leaf screen, the border painte with flower filled vases, late 19th(72in (183cm) high.
£1,500-2,000 *C*

A Victorian mahog pole screen, with needlework p turned and baluster stem on a circular base and bun feet.
£100-120 *DDM*

A Victorian giltwood firescreen, t arched tufted beadwork panel depicting The Royal Pets with Osborne House in the backgroun after Landseer, 37½in (95cm).
£750-1,000 *C*

Sir Edwin Landseer, R.A., painte the picture on which this panel is based in 1839 as a commission fo Queen Victoria.

ettees

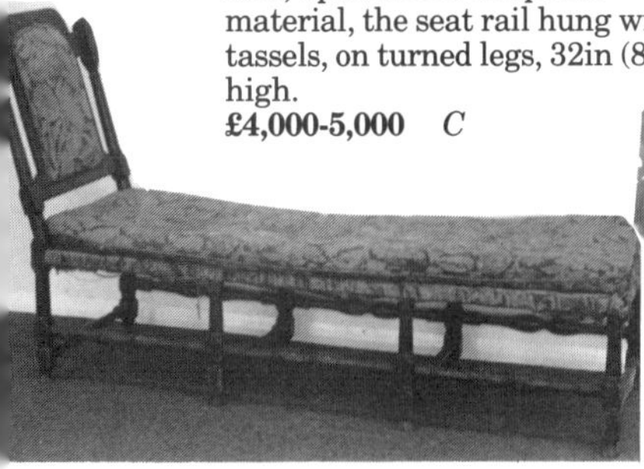

Charles II oak day bed, with
scan column supports and double
uster stretchers.
0-1,200 *MGM*

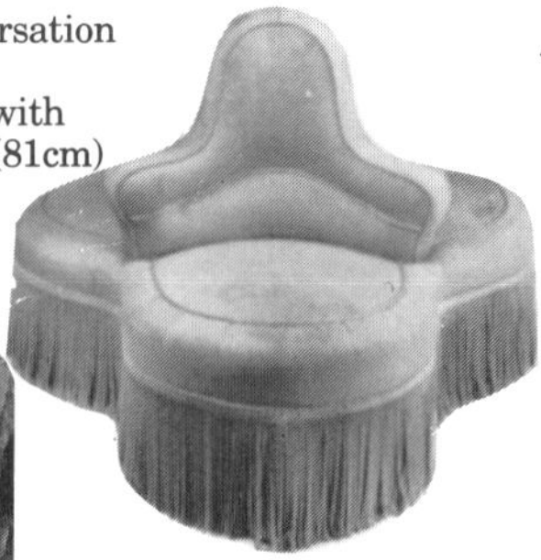

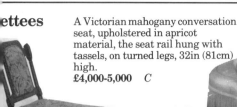

A Victorian mahogany conversation seat, upholstered in apricot material, the seat rail hung with tassels, on turned legs, 32in (81cm) high.
£4,000-5,000 *C*

A George III mahogany sofa, upholstered in striped floral damask, on square chanelled tapering legs headed by inlaid paterae, 53½in (136cm).
£4,000-4,500 *C*

Villiam and Mary design walnut
a, tassled and upholstered in gros
nt tapestry, on scrolling legs
ed by stretchers carved with
age and C-scrolls, 87in (221cm).
000-2,500 *CSK*

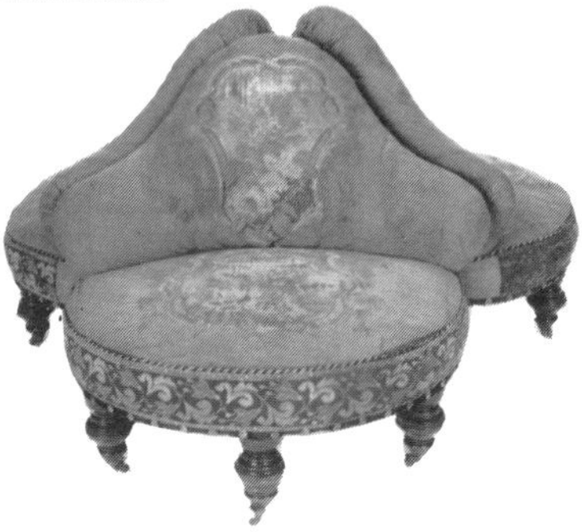

A Victorian metamorphic island sofa, upholstered in the original rose ground floral tapestry, the turned legs fitted with casters, late 19thC, 51in (129.5cm) diam.
£1,800-2,500 *N*

A Victorian walnut sofa, with buttoned upholstered arched back, bowed ends and seat, on fluted turned tapering legs with acanthus carved headings, 72in (182.5cm).
£700-1,000 *CSK*

George III mahogany sofa,
olstered in red damask, on
mfered legs carved with blind
work, later central back leg,
n (296cm).
500-4,000 *C*

A Victorian walnut trefoil conversation seat, upholstered in red velvet, on turned tapered legs, restorations, 44in (112cm).
£800-1,000 *Bon*

A Regency olive green painted triple back settee, the toprail painted with ribbon tied swags of flowers and a central classical urn, with cane filled seat, green velvet squab on ring turned tapering legs, 59in (149.5cm).
£2,000-3,000 *CSK*

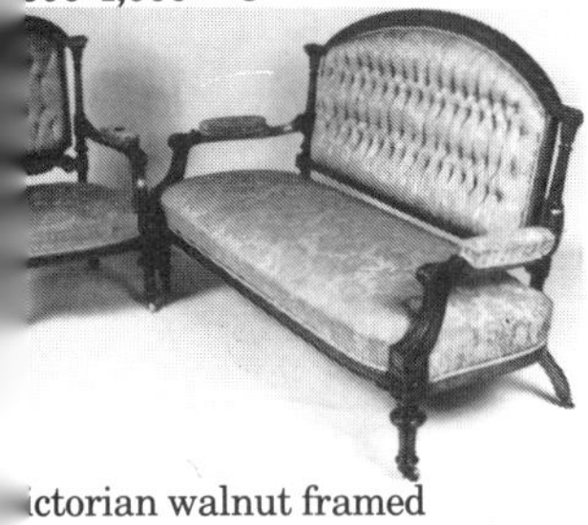

ictorian walnut framed
e-piece part lounge suite, the
back rails with carved laurel
ldings, the arms and uprights
ed, carved with acanthus leaves.
00-1,500 *SWO*

a, with deep seat, low back,
led arms and bolster cushions
lstered in tartan with tasselled
rail, 132in (335cm).
0-2,000 *C*

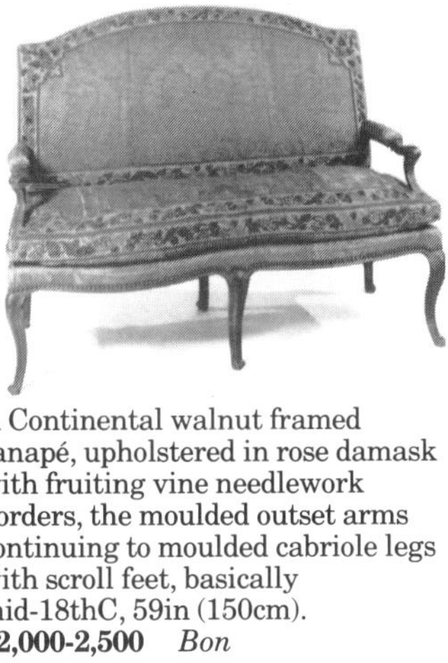

A Continental walnut framed canapé, upholstered in rose damask with fruiting vine needlework borders, the moulded outset arms continuing to moulded cabriole legs with scroll feet, basically mid-18thC, 59in (150cm).
£2,000-2,500 *Bon*

A Louis XVI style giltwood settee, with carved back and seat and elaborate foliate back panel and seat rail.
£1,500-2,000 *LRG*

A Regency beechwood open arm sofa, with simulated bamboo frame, on turned splayed tapering legs joined by abacus mounted cross stretchers, with loose upholstered seat squab, 74in (188cm).
£2,000-3,000 *CSK*

An Edwardian inlaid mahogany drawing room settee, with double arched back and bow fronted seat, upholstered in floral silk damask, and standing on square tapering supports with spade feet.
£600-700 *OL*

A Victorian mahogany 3 seater sofa, with upholstered buttoned bowed back and seat, on cabriol legs with foliate knob feet, 82in (208cm).
£1,000-1,200 *CSK*

A Louis XVI giltwood salon suite, comprising a canapé, a pair of fauteuil and 4 single chairs with foliate carved serpentine seat rails, raised upon slender fluted cabriole front supports carved at the knees with flowerheads, and terminating in peg feet and casters.
£3,500-4,000 *HSS*

A three-piece mahogany bergère suite with upholstered backs, carved side panels with armrests ending in carved eagles heads, overstuffed seats, blind fret frieze, and carved cylindrical front legs with claw-and-ball feet, early 20thC.
£2,500-3,000 *AH*

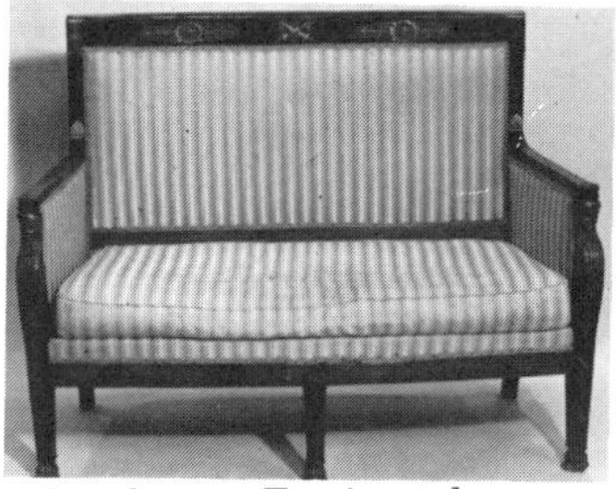

A mahogany Empire style two-seater settee, with cast brass plaques and carved Egyptian head, on cast brass claw feet.
£750-900 *MGM*

A Louis XVI style giltwood suite comprising 4 fauteuils and a canapé, upholstered in 18thC tapestry, on turned fluted taperi legs, the upholstery with restorations, canapé 67in (170cm
£2,500-3,500 *C*

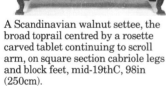

A Scandinavian walnut settee, the broad toprail centred by a rosette carved tablet continuing to scroll arm, on square section cabriole legs and block feet, mid-19thC, 98in (250cm).
£400-600 *Bon*

A pair of settees with double scr ends, finely carved frames with anthemion, acanthus scrolls an paterae, 96in (243.5cm).
£15,000-20,000 *RBB*

A Victorian walnut daybed, with scroll panelled head, rectangular seat and side panels upholstered in figured damask, on turned tapering legs, on casters, labelled Howard & Sons, London and numbered 2124 4360, 70in (177.5cm) long.
£1,200-1,500 *CSK*

A settee and a pair of bergères, with original flowered silk upholstery, with plaques, swags and flowers in the French taste, 19thC.
£3,000-3,500 *LRG*

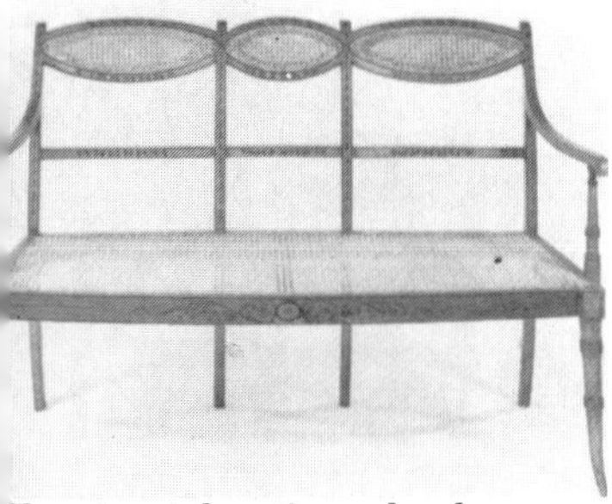

;heraton style satinwood and
:al painted settee, the toprail
:h 3 oval cane panels, on ring
ned tapered legs, late 19thC,
n (125cm).
.000-1,500 *Bon*

An Edwardian inlaid mahogany Hepplewhite style occasional settee, with double concave back above arched and reeded pilasters and floral upholstered seat, on slender turned supports, 42in (106.5cm).
£900-1,200 *OL*

;heraton design painted
inwood settee, with radiating
e work centred by painted panel,
n (109cm).
500-3,000 *P(S)*

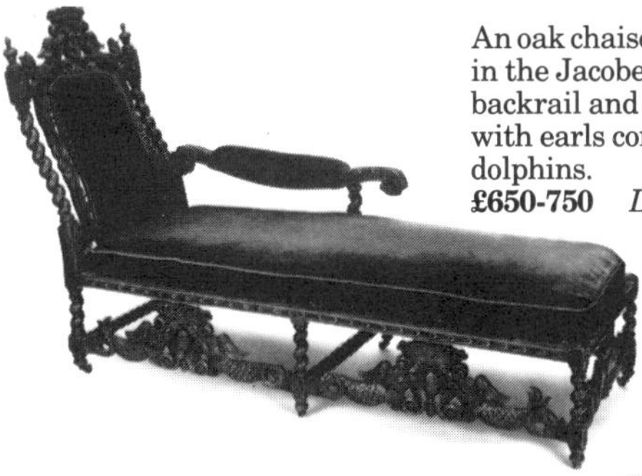

An oak chaise longue, highly carved in the Jacobean manner, the backrail and stretchers embellished with earls coronets supported by dolphins.
£650-750 *LRG*

18thC style walnut chair-back
e, upholstered in brown floral
ade and raised on 3 cabriole
t supports carved at the knees
acanthus leaves, terminating
aw-and-ball feet and 3 outward
yed back supports, terminating
d feet.
00-2,500 *HSS*

A Louis XVI style giltwood window seat, with lyre shaped ends, and carved bead and leaf mouldings, on fluted legs.
£700-900 *LRG*

A Biedermeier satin birch sofa, upholstered in green and cream silk, the scrolled toprail centred by an oval paterae, the scrolled ribbed arms with turned roundels, the seat rail with leafy paterae, on sabre legs, 89in (226cm).
£3,500-4,500 *C*

e George III cream painted and
orner sofa, with triple panelled
back, the toprail painted with
rs, the seat curved at one end,
rned tapering legs, 62½in
5cm).
0-1,500 *C*

An early Victorian rosewood sofa, with acanthus carved showframe and upholstered toprail, the twin bowed ends and serpentine seat upholstered in striped brocade, on scroll feet, 70in (177.5cm).
£800-1,000 *CSK*

A Dutch East Indies, Sri Lanka, hardwood and ebony sofa, with shaped toprail, spindle back and scrolled arms, the caned seat on square bobbin turned legs joined by an H-stretcher, 17thC, 44in (112cm).
£800-1,200 *C*

Sideboards

A George III mahogany bowfront sideboard, on square tapering legs, 36in (92cm).
£1,500-2,000 *CSK*

A mahogany and inlaid breakfront sideboard, with cellaret drawers, on square tapering legs, with spade feet, basically early 19thC, 48in (122cm).
£2,500-3,000 *CSK*

A George III mahogany sideboar with D-shaped breakfront top, above a central drawer and arche kneehole drawer with 2 drawers below and cellaret drawer to the right, on square tapering legs an spade feet, 67in (179cm).
£1,500-2,500 *C*

A reproduction George III style mahogany and inlaid sideboard, crossbanded in rosewood, with brass ring handles, raised on 6 square tapered legs, 54in (137cm).
£1,000-1,500 *P(W)*

A George III mahogany demi-lune sideboard, the crossbanded top above a napery drawer flanked by cellaret drawers and further shallow crossbanded drawers, on square tapered legs inlaid with oval fan paterae and husk chains, c1780, 72in (183cm).
£4,500-5,000 *Bon*

A mahogany sideboard, with serpentine top inlaid with box lines, on square tapering legs a spade feet, 47in (119cm).
£3,000-4,000 *CSK*

A mahogany and marquetry bowfront sideboard, with short drawer and 2 panelled doors with swag hung urns and stylised foliage, on square tapered legs, 72in (182.5cm).
£800-1,200 *CSK*

A Regency mahogany and inlaid pedestal sideboard, on reeded turned tapering legs, 74in (188cm).
£1,000-1,500 *CSK*

A late George III mahogany sideboard, inlaid with boxwood lines, the crossbanded serpentine top above a drawer and central a with recessed tambour shutter, 7 (181cm).
£4,000-5,000 *C*

A George III mahogany breakfront sideboard, the apron drawer with fan spandrels, tapering square stop fluted supports with spade feet, some alterations, 49½in (125cm).
£2,500-3,000 *Bea*

A serpentine front mahogany sideboard banded in boxwood and ebony, on square tapering supports, early 19thC, 56in (142cm).
£700-900 *P(M)*

A Sheraton design serpentine fronted mahogany sideboard, th top banded in satinwood and wi brass rail, with inlaid satinwood bands, shell quadrants and oval panels, string inlaid, and angled square tapering legs, spade feet, 48½in (123cm).
£2,500-3,000 *P(S)*

Georgian mahogany bowfront
eboard, the top with boxwood
ging, raised on inlaid square
pering legs ending in vase feet,
in (180 cm).
,500-3,000 *DDM*

A Regency mahogany and satinwood breakfront sideboard, on turned tapered ribbed legs, 66in (167.5cm).
£7,500-8,000 *CSK*

A Regency mahogany and inlaid sideboard, with shaped concave front, brass lion mask ring handles, on turned and reeded tapered feet, 90in (228.5cm).
£2,500-3,000 *AH*

A Regency mahogany sideboard, the brass finialled back with candle sconces, above 2 central drawers flanked by bowed doors and drawers, on turned reeded legs.
£2,000-3,000 *CSK*

Sheraton style mahogany and
inwood banded sideboard, the
aped top above 2 frieze drawers
nked by bowed cupboard doors,
square tapered legs and spade
t, late 19thC, 65in (165cm).
00-1,200 *Bon*

Use the Index!

Because certain items might fit easily into any of a number of categories, the quickest and surest method of locating any entry is by reference to the index at the back of the book. This has been fully cross-referenced for absolute simplicity

Sheraton style mahogany
vfronted breakfast board, with
ssbanded and inlaid top, the
awers with decorated octagonal
ass drop handles, arched apron
d square tapered legs with spade
t, late 18thC, 44in (111.5cm).
),000-11,000 *AH*

A Regency mahogany and marquetry bowfront sideboard, the tablet applied three-quarter gallery above 4 frieze drawers and 4 panelled cupboard doors, on square tapering legs, restored, 93in (236cm).
£2,500-3,000 *CSK*

A George IV mahogany bowfront sideboard, outlined with corded stringing, the crossbanded top above 2 central drawers, a cellaret and a door, on tapering square legs with spade feet, legs replaced, 72in (182.5cm).
£2,000-2,500 *Bea*

Sheraton style crossbanded
hogany shaped front sideboard,
h centre drawer flanked by
rawers and a deep drawer, on
are tapering legs with spade
t, 69in (175cm).
500-7,000 *GC*

A Regency mahogany pedestal sideboard, the galleried centre section fitted with 3 drawers, on outswept bracket feet, the whole inlaid with ebony stringing and fleur-de-lys, 81in (206cm).
£1,500-2,000 *Bon*

A mahogany sideboard, the top with a pair of brass curtain rails, the inverted breakfront lower section with 3 panel doors, one enclosing drawers, on a plinth base, 59in (149cm).
£900-1,200 *Bon*

A Regency mahogany and marquetry bowfront sideboard, the top with 2 frieze drawers flanked by 2 cellaret drawers, on square tapering legs, adapted, 79in (200.5cm).
£2,500-3,000 *CSK*

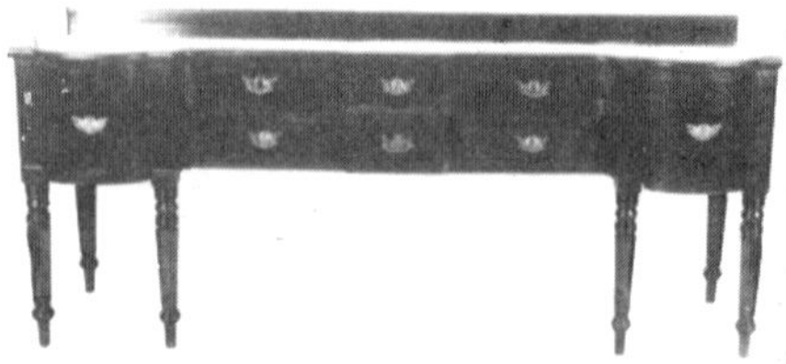

A mahogany sideboard, tl reverse breakfront top wi brass fan shaped loop handles and shaped back plates, raised on octagon: tapering supports terminating in peg feet, early 19thC, 95in (241cm
£1,200-1,500 *HSS*

A mid-Victorian walnut sideboard, the back carved with boars heads above an open centre flanked by 2 panelled doors inset with carved game trophies, mirror-back missing, 150in (381cm).
£3,000-5,000 *CSK*

A mid-Victorian oak, sycamore a alder sideboard, by Charles Beva inlaid with dots, chevrons and stylised flowers, labelled Marsh a Jones, late Kendall & Co, 84½in (215cm).
£2,000-2,500 *C*

A late Victorian oak mirror-back sideboard, ornately carved with shells, scrolls, flowerheads and acanthus leaves, on ornate bracket feet, 84in (213cm).
£1,000-1,500 *DDM*

A William IV mahogany pedestal mirror-back sideboard, the crossbanded mahogany top over 4 frieze drawers with sunken half round fronts, the right hand pedestal with lead lined cellaret drawer, 89in (226cm).
£400-500 *MJB*

Stands

An early Victorian mahogany three-tier dumb waiter, with moulded edges and rounded corners, the graduated sides joined by a stretcher, and the upper and lower tiers adjustable, 36in (91.5cm).
£400-450 *GC*

An early Victorian walnut folio stand, on shallow scroll legs and turned feet, some damage, c1840, 30in (76cm).
£2,000-2,500 *N*

A Victorian carved mahogany hallstand, with foliate cresting, shaped marble slab and glove drawer below, standing on cabrio supports, 50in (127cm).
£900-1,000 *OL*

A Victorian free standing display stand, with moulded edge top, on turned fluted and reeded supports, the centre circular undershelf raised on 4 leaf carved supports, rectangular shelves on either side with shaped frieze, 65in (165cm). **£2,500-3,000** *AH*

·eorgian design lyre-shaped
sic stand, having brass rods and
ınts, decorated with boxwood
ng inlay.
0-450 *MGM*

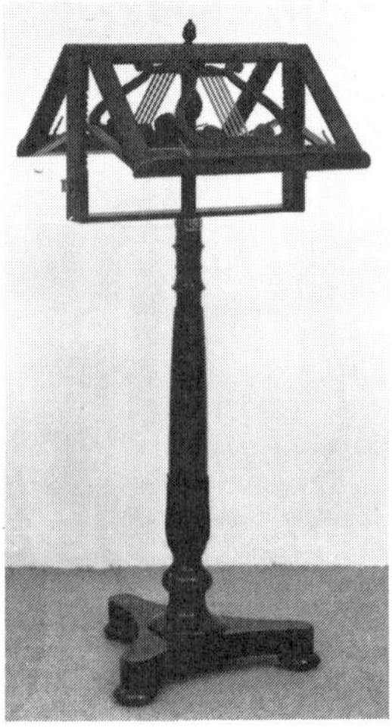

An early Victorian rosewood duet stand, the lyre inset flaps raised on ratchets, supported on a turned column with leaf carved stem and tripod platform base.
£800-900 *MAT*

A Victorian oak shaving stand, on an arched tripod support ending in pad feet, 17in (44cm) diam.
£300-500 *CEd*

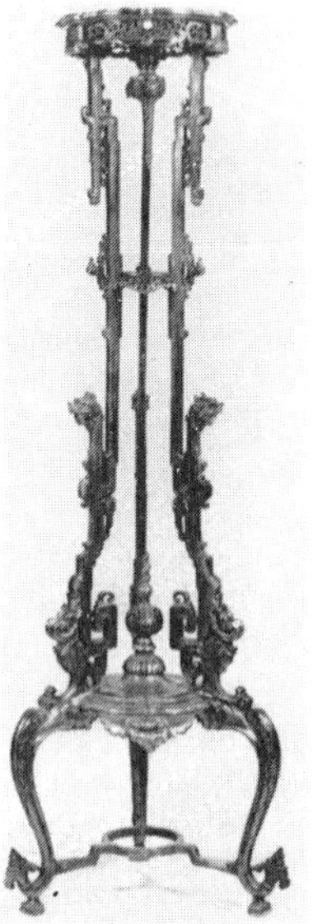

A pair of Victorian brass pedestals, in the Japanese style, c1880, 49in (125cm).
£2,500-3,000 *Bon*

air of mahogany bust stands,
ı partial fluted and wrythen
ıed columns to triple splay bases.
0-600 *GAK*

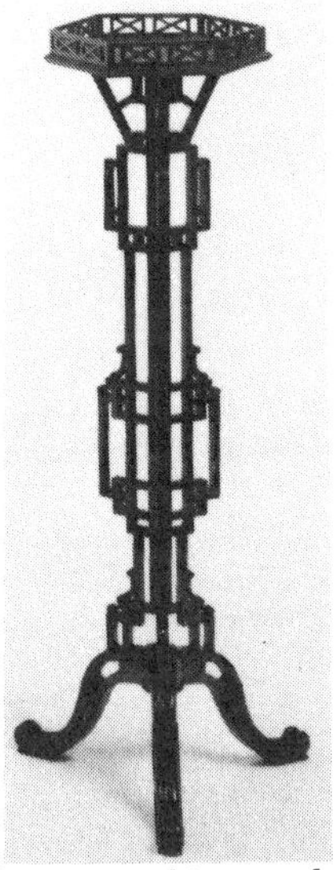

A pair of mahogany torchères, each with an hexagonal top with pierced gallery, on fretwork support and tripod base carved with foliate scrolls, 39in (99cm) high.
£800-1,200 *CSK*

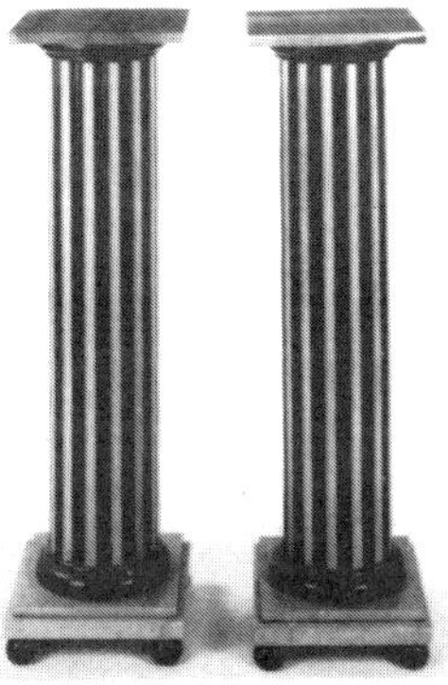

A pair of fruitwood and ebonised fluted columns, with square capitals and plinths, 40in (101.5cm) high.
£900-1,200 *CSK*

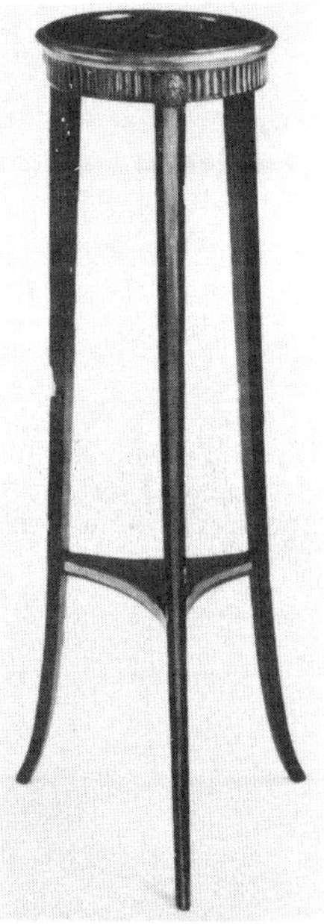

A pair of ebonised and gilded plant stands, with fluted friezes on square tapering splayed legs joined by triform stretcher, early 19thC, 34½in (87cm) high.
£800-1,200 *CSK*

Italian polychrome blackamoor
·hère, on tripod supports, late
ıC, 36½in (92cm) high.
0-500 *CSK*

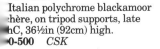

Make the Most of Miller's

CONDITION is absolutely vital when assessing the value of an antique. Damaged pieces on the whole appreciate much less than perfect examples. However a rare, desirable piece may command a high price even when damaged

A Victorian brass church lectern, the eagle crested rest mounted on an orbed baluster column decorated with cusps and cabochons, on a tiered platform base with claw feet, 67½in (171cm) high.
£2,000-2,500 *CSK*

A Louis XVI style satinwood and ormolu mounted pedestal, inlaid with boxwood lines, on paw feet, 50½in (128cm) high.
£2,000-2,500 *CSK*

A French carved beechwood and caned hall stand, c1900, 46½in (117cm).
£700-800 *UC*

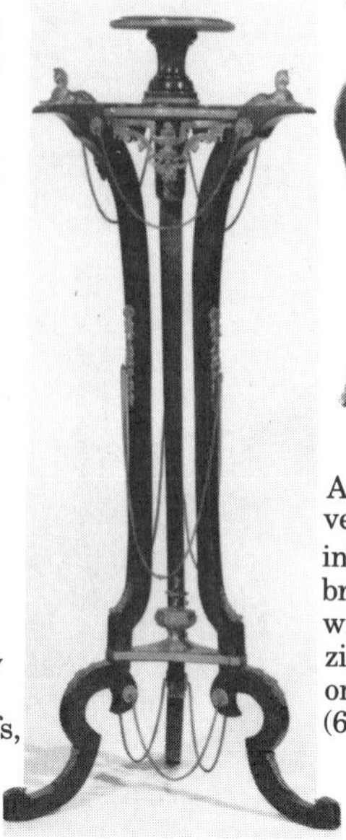

A French empire style mahogany jardinière stand, decorated with ormolu bands and 3 Sphinx motifs, with an urn below on tripod feet, 47in (119cm) high.
£450-500 *AG*

A French rosewood veneered jardinière stand, wit inlaid floral marquetry and gil bronze mounts, the galleried t with a lidded interior revealin zinc liner, serpentine edge frie on cabriole legs, 19thC, 26½in (67cm). **£1,200-1,600** *WW*

Steps

A set of William IV mahogany steps, lined in green leather, the top hinged, with pull-out middle, on turned legs, 16½in (42cm).
£1,500-2,000 *C*

Stools

An Irish mahogany stool, the seat upholstered in floral needlework, on cabriole legs and paw feet carved with foliage, restorations, 18thC, 28½in (72cm).
£1,500-2,000 *C*

A walnut stool, the needlework se on shell carved cabriole legs with carved and pierced claw-and-ball feet, part early 18thC, 22in (56cm
£700-800 *Bon*

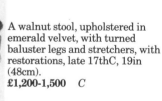

A walnut stool, upholstered in emerald velvet, with turned baluster legs and stretchers, with restorations, late 17thC, 19in (48cm).
£1,200-1,500 *C*

An early George III mahogany dressing stool, with slip in seat, 16½in (42cm).
£300-500 *GSP*

A George III mahogany stool, with drop-in seat on chamfered square legs and stretchers, 21in (53.5cm).
£450-700 *C*

ieorge III mahogany stool, with
cave sided drop-in seat, on
are legs and cross stretchers,
n (43cm).
0-1,200 *C*

A George III beechwood window seat, with outscrolled arms, upholstered in peach rep, the waved frieze carved with a shell on cabriole legs, headed by foliage, restorations, 41in (105cm).
£900-1,200 *C*

A Regency ormolu mounted ebonised window seat, upholstered in floral cotton, the arms applied with flowerheads, the seat rail with anthemion and flowerhead plaques, on reeded legs with turned stretchers, stamped IM, 47in (119cm).
£1,500-2,000 *C*

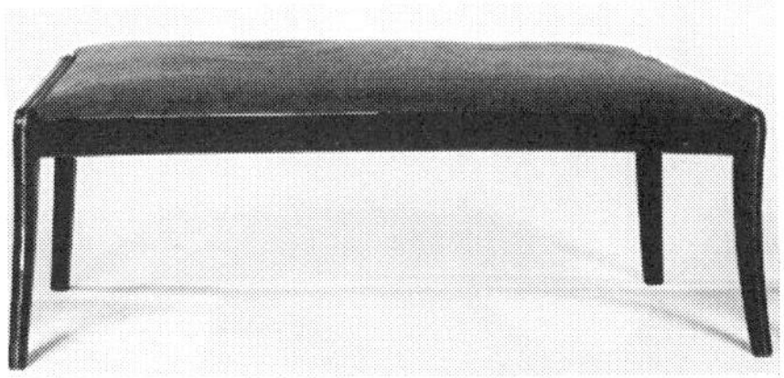

A Regency ebonised window seat, with a concave reeded seat rail, on sabre legs.
£500-700 *Bon*

ahogany stool, the top
olstered in close nailed dark
wn leather, on 6 fluted and
led legs, 35in (89cm).
00-1,500 *C*

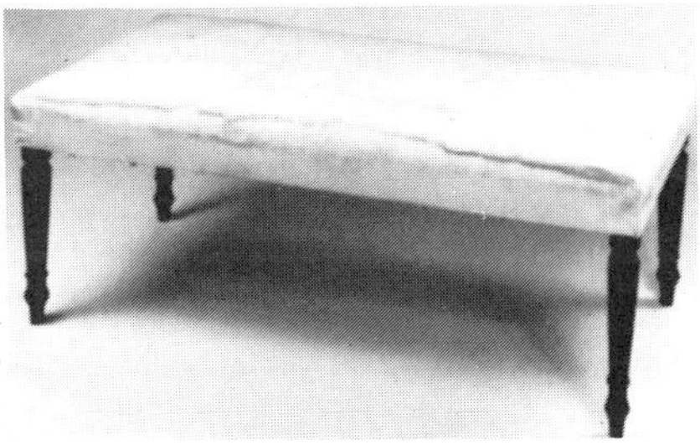

A mahogany fender stool, the padded seat upholstered in cream calico, on reeded legs, 49in (124cm).
£2,000-2,500 *C*

air of Regency rosewood dressing
ls, the drop-in seats upholstered
reen floral sculptured moquette,
ed on inverted X-frame supports
by a baluster turned stretcher.
700-2,000 *HSS*

A Regency mahogany window seat, the padded seat covered in green damask, the scrolling X-frame applied with paterae and joined by spirally reeded arms and stretchers, the legs with restorations, 64½in (164cm).
£9,000-11,000 *C*

A William IV rosewood window seat, with padded seat on turned and ribbed tapering legs, 35½in (90cm).
£800-1,000 *C*

A Classical carved mahogany footstool, with scrolled ends joined by turned balusters, above a straight skirt, on reeded baluster feet, with a padded slip seat, English, c1820, 17½in (45cm).
£400-600 *CNY*

A Victorian walnut two-seater stool, with woolwork tapestry seat, scroll end supports and turned cross stretcher.
£300-600 *HCH*

An early Victorian mahogany footstool, upholstered in floral patterned needlework, the sides carved with foliage, on turned f one foot replaced, 17½in (45cm)
£500-800 *C*

A mid-Victorian mahogany window seat, with padded drop-in seat between outcurved arms each applied with a patera and incised with bellflowers, the arcaded seat rail on an X-form support with hairy paw feet, the seat stencilled John W Small, 40in (101.5cm).
£1,500-2,000 *CSK*

An ormolu mounted satinwood stool, upholstered in green velvet, on turned legs applied with anthemia and shaped ends applied with torches, the bar feet joined by a moulded stretcher, 22½in (57cm).
£900-1,200 *C*

A Regency rosewood footstool, a a design by George Smith, the S-scroll padded top upholstered striped rep, carved on both sides with roundels and scrolling lotus ribbed bun feet, 15½in (39cm).
£1,200-2,000 *C*

A pair of Victorian walnut stools, each with a distressed upholstered top, on hipped cabriole legs carved with stylised foliage, on lion's paw feet, 17½in (45cm).
£2,000-2,500 *CSK*

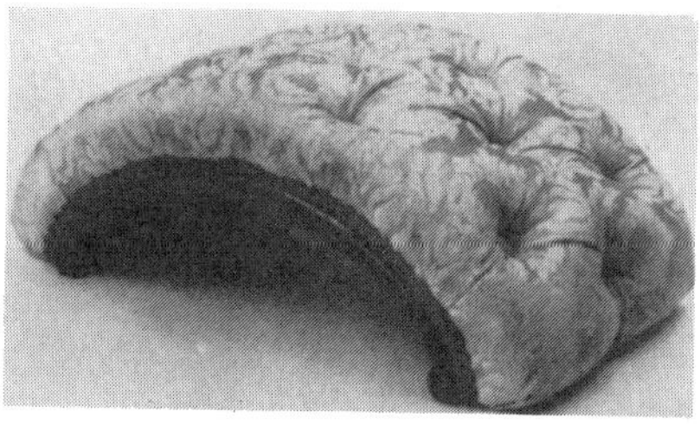

A pair of Victorian walnut C-scroll footstools, with buttoned green damask covers, 18in (46cm).
£400-600 *CSK*

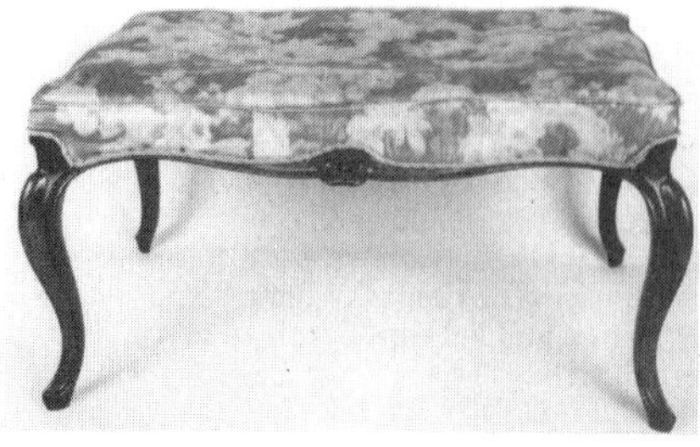

A Victorian rosewood dressing stool, of serpentine outline, having a stuff-over seat, on slender cabriole supports, 34in (86cm).
£700-900 *P(W)*

A Bavarian revolving piano stool, the seated bear with brown glass eyes, open snarling mouth, holding a toadstool above his head.
£2,500-3,500 *HSS*

rchitects Tables

ı early George III mahogany
:hitect's table, with crossbanded
ıged and ratcheted top, above a
eze drawer with lined writing
rface, on square chamfered legs,
in (86cm).
,000-7,000 *C*

An early George III mahogany architect's table, the frieze with pull-out drawer, on chamfered legs with turned inner legs, adapted, top fixed down, 36in (91.5cm).
£1,000-1,500 *C*

A Georgian architect's mahogany table, with adjustable top and 2 slides, fitted with a drawer, on square chamfered legs, 34in (86cm).
£1,500-2,000 *GC*

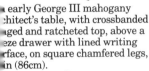

A George III mahogany secrétaire architect's table, with adjustable top with rests, above a writing drawer, on reeded turned tapering legs, with side carrying handles, 43in (109cm).
£5,000-5,500 *CSK*

A Georgian mahogany architect's desk.
£4,500-6,000 *GIL*

ìeorge III mahogany architect's
ıle, inlaid with satinwood fanned
ındrels and geometric bands, the
ustable coffered top above a
eze drawer, on baluster column
ports, adapted 39in (99cm).
000-3,000 *CSK*

ìeorge IV mahogany artist's
le, the ratcheted top with a book
t on adjustable side supports,
h double turned stretchers, the
ıy legs on brass sabots with
ters, 27in (69cm).
500-2,000 *WW*

Billiards Tables

A mahogany slate bed bar billiards table, of plain design with heavy chamfered supports, together with scoreboard, balls and cue, 73in (185cm) long.
£300-350 *DDM*

A mahogany slate bed bar billiards table, with heavy chamfered supports, together with scoreboards, cues and balls, 78in (198cm).
£700-900 *DDM*

Breakfast Tables

A George III mahogany breakfast table, on a quadripartite support with splayed reeded legs, 58½in (148cm).
£2,000-2,500 *CSK*

A Georgian mahogany breakf table, with reeded edge to the tilt-top over a ring turned stem on 3 splayed part flut legs, ending in brass cap casters, 51in (129.5cm).
£500-600 *DDM*

A George III mahogany breakfast table, on a quadripartite support with reeded legs, 52in (132cm).
£1,000-1,500 *CSK*

A George III mahogany pedestal breakfast table, with rosewood banded top and rounded ends, on a turned tapering shaft and quadripartite splayed legs with brass paw feet, 47in (119cm).
£900-1,200 *CSK*

A mahogany breakfast table, the tip-up top on a turned shaft with reeded splayed legs and lion's paw caps, Regency and later, 53in (134.5cm).
£1,200-1,600 *CSK*

A late Victorian walnut breakfast table, the moulded tip-up top on a turned quadripartite support with foliate carved splayed legs, restorations, 54in (137cm).
£700-1,000 *CSK*

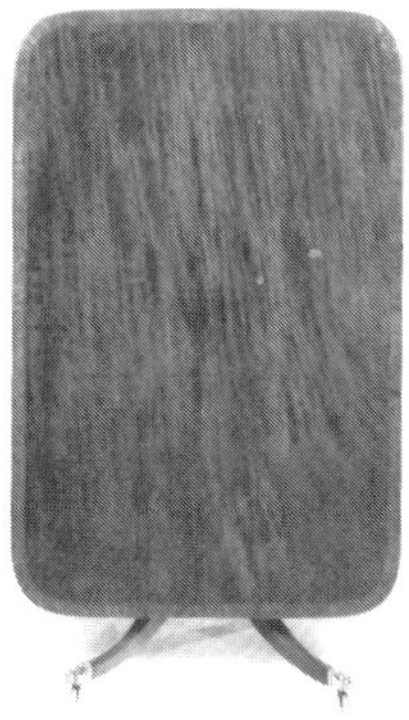

A Regency figured mahogany breakfast table, the satinwood banded top on a ring turned column and quadripartite outswept legs, restorations to frame, 55½in (141cm).
£700-800 *Bon*

A Regency mahogany breakfast table with tip-up top, reeded edge and fluted frieze, the turned and reeded column on concave quadruple support and brass paw feet, 54in (137cm).
£1,500-2,000 *AH*

A Regency mahogany tilt-top breakfast table, with wide zebrawood crossbanding, on turr shaped column and reeded quadruple splay support having brass terminals and casters, 52i (132cm).
£5,000-6,000 *GC*

A George IV rosewood breakfast table, on a faceted column, concave platform and bun feet.
£5,000-6,000 *CSK*

A Regency mahogany tilt-top breakfast table, with egg-and-tongue-moulded edge, on a turned palm tree trunk column with ball decoration, terminating in brass acanthus leaf decoration caps and casters, 45½in (115cm).
£2,200-2,500 *GC*

A mid-Victorian burr walnut breakfast table, the tip-up top inlaid with Tunbridgeware diamonds within boxwood line borders, on 4 column supports and foliate carved scrolling base with central finial, 56in (142cm).
£1,700-2,000 *CSK*

William IV mahogany breakfast
ole, the D-end tilt-top on a
lestal carved with lotus leaves,
e concave sided platform on
rned feet, 61in (155cm).
000-2,500 *CSK*

An early Victorian oak breakfast table, the tip-up top geometrically inlaid and centred by a sunburst design outlined in ebony, 49½in (125cm). **£900-1,200** *Bea*

A calamander breakfast table, with crossbanded top, on chamfered stepped triangular shaft with concave platform, scrolled legs and brass foliate caps, 48in (122cm). **£2,500-3,000** *CSK*

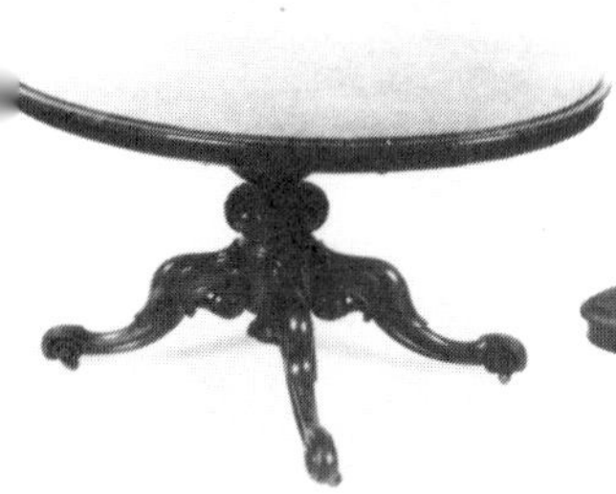

'ictorian figured walnut
akfast table, the snap-top
arter veneered, with thumb
ulded edge, raised upon a boss
l strapwork carved double
uster stem and cabriole
adruple support carved at the
ees and scroll feet with stylised
age, on casters, 59½in (150cm).
200-1,500 *HSS*

A rosewood breakfast table, the moulded tip-up top on a turned shaft with 4 splayed legs carved with acanthus, on flattened bun feet, 19thC, 54½in (138cm). **£2,000-2,500** *CSK*

A rosewood and brass inlaid pedestal breakfast table, with crossbanded tip-up top, the splayed legs with brass paw feet, basically early 19thC, 50½in (128cm). **£2,000-3,000** *CSK*

A William IV rosewood breakfast table, with knopped feet and casters, 49½in (125cm). **£1,500-2,000** *P(M)*

Anglo-Indian rosewood
kfast table, the base
a circular
ed paterae,
on bold lion's paw feet,
aC, 60in (152cm).
00-5,000 *GA(W)*

ictorian
estal table,
veneered and
sbanded top, brass
feet, 48in (122cm).
-1,200 *PLJ*

Card Tables

A George II Virginia walnut fold-over card table, with frieze drawer, brass drop handle, and cabriole legs with scroll carved knees and pad feet, 29in (74cm).
£2,000-2,500 *AH*

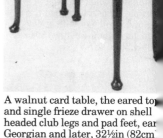

A mahogany fold-over card table, with single frieze drawer supported on cabriole legs and pad feet, 18thC, 30½in (77cm).
£800-1,500 *DDM*

A George II mahogany card table, with eared folding top lined in green baize, the plain frieze on cabriole legs carved with foliage, and claw-and-ball feet, 31½in (80cm).
£1,500-2,000 *C*

A George III mahogany and inlaid demi-lune card table, with a fold-over top, crossbanded in tulipwood, raised on tapered supports, headed by oval burr walnut panels, 36in (91cm).
£2,200-2,600 *P(W)*

A George II mahogany D-shaped card table, with fold-over top enclosing a well, on turned tapering legs and pad feet, 31in (79cm).
£1,700-2,000 *GC*

A George III mahogany card table, the fold-over top with canted corners and kingwood crossbanding, the tapering square legs headed by oval fan medallions, some restoration, 36in (91.5cm).
£2,000-2,500 *Bea*

A mahogany card table, applied with urns, bellflower festoons and paterae carved in the Adam manner, on tapering legs with spade feet, 18thC and later, 34in (86cm).
£1,500-2,000 *CSK*

A Chippendale style mahogany fold-over card table.
£500-700 *HCH*

A George III mahogany veneered D-shape card table, with inlaid stringing, the flap top baize lined with later brass knob handles, th square tapering legs on casters, c1800, 37in (94cm).
£700-1,200 *WW*

A walnut card table, the eared to and single frieze drawer on shell headed club legs and pad feet, ear Georgian and later, 32½in (82cm
£1,200-2,000 *CSK*

A pair of Sheraton style satinwoo card tables, each with a hinged t decorated with inlaid rosewood crossbanding and stringing, raise on square tapering legs, 36in (91.5cm). **£3,000-3,500** *AG*

A George III satinwood card tabl with mahogany crossbanded top, 36in (91cm). **£3,500-4,000** *Bo*

George III satinwood card table, ıe tulipwood crossbanded top ɔove a similarly banded frieze, on ıuare tapered legs, 37in (94cm).
,000-3,500 *Bon*

A Georgian mahogany fold-over top card table, by A. Blain & Son of Liverpool, 36in (91.5cm).
£1,200-1,500 *OL*

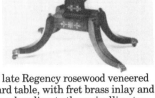

A late Regency rosewood veneered card table, with fret brass inlay and crossbanding to the swivelling top, with brass paw sabots on casters, 36in (91.5cm).
£1,700-2,000 *WW*

mahogany and satinwood ɔssbanded inlaid D-shape ld-over top card table, on square pered legs and spade feet, top ırped, early 19thC, 36in (91.5cm).
00-900 *PCh*

A Regency rosewood and brass inlaid card table with D-shaped fold-over top, turned column terminating in gadrooned pediment with quadruple support and brass paws and casters, 36in (91.5cm).
£1,500-1,700 *AH*

A Regency mahogany and rosewood banded card table, inlaid with ebonised geometric lines, with baize lined top on turned shaft and 4 downswept legs with brass paw caps, 34½in (88cm).
£1,500-2,000 *C*

Regency rosewood and brass ıaid card table, on a solid lyre ɔport faced within brass foliate signs, on a concave platform and :swept legs, 35½in (90cm).
000-3,500 *Bon*

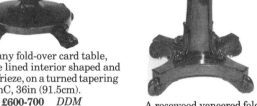

A mahogany fold-over card table, with baize lined interior shaped and moulded frieze, on a turned tapering stem, 19thC, 36in (91.5cm).
£600-700 *DDM*

A rosewood veneered folding card table, with carved supporting column and platform base with scrolled feet, 19thC.
£700-1,000 *MGM*

osewood breakfront folding card ıle, baize lined and raised on a ıcave tapering column, with ved paw feet, early 19thC, 36in .5cm).
200-1,700 *DEN*

A Regency brass inlaid rosewood card table, the baize lined top banded in mahogany, 36in (91.5cm).
£2,000-2,500 *C*

A Georgian inlaid maple folding top card table, on square tapering splayed legs with collars, 36in (91.5cm). **£800-1,000** *JD*

A Regency brass inlaid mahogany card table, with D-shaped folding top inlaid with a band of quatrefoils, two legs repaired, 36in (91.5cm).
£2,500-3,000 *C*

A mahogany and inlaid pedestal card table, with rosewood crossbanded top, brass paw feet, early 19thC, 38in (96.5cm).
£400-450 *CSK*

An early Victorian mahogany card table, on leaf scroll feet, 36in (91.5cm). **£1,000-1,500** *CSK*

A mahogany card table, with canted fold-over top banded in satinwood, with concave platform on splayed legs, early 19thC, 36in (91.5cm).
£2,000-2,500 *CSK*

A George IV rosewood card table, the rounded hexagonal stem with spreading base and on concave sid platform with lotus carved bun fe 36in (91.5cm).
£500-600 *Bea*

A Victorian walnut card table, the serpentine top on cabochon tapering shaft and scrolling quadruple supports, 36in (91.5cm).
£1,200-1,600 *CSK*

A Victorian walnut folding card table, with turned and reeded supports and carved scrolled splay feet. **£500-600** *MGM*

A Victorian demi-lune fold-o card table.
£300-400 *HCH*

A Victorian walnut and marquetry inlaid serpentine card table, with quadruple splayed legs, adapted, 35in (89cm).
£700-900 *CSK*

A calamander and gilt metal card table, with a baize lined playing surface and counter wells above a bead moulded frieze, on turned tapered fluted legs each with a foliate collar, late 19thC, 36in (91.5cm).
£700-1,000 *CSK*

An Edwardian rosewood envelope card table decorated with inlaid floral scrolls and stringing, openir to reveal a green baize lining and counter wells, an undertier below raised on turned and square legs with splay feet, 23in (59cm).
£1,700-2,000 *AG*

A Dutch walnut card table, inlaid with urns, flowerheads and foliate marquetry, the concave arched rectangular fold-over top enclosing a chessboard, with 2 frieze drawers, on cabriole legs with pad feet, part late 17thC, 30½in (77cm).
£1,700-2,000 *CSK*

An ormolu mounted ebonised and scarlet boulle serpentine card table, the shaped frieze centred by a mask clasp, on cabriole legs and sabots, 19thC, 35in (89cm).
£1,000-1,500 *CSK*

A burr walnut serpentine fold-ove card table, veneered on mahogany with ormolu mounts, inlaid with boxwood and amboyna stringing and on cabriole legs, 19thC, 38in (96.5cm).
£2,500-3,000 *MAT*

An Italian burr yew card table, the banded top centred by an inlaid geometric motif on square tapered legs, 33in (84cm).
£1,500-2,000 *CSK*

A Queen Anne design giltwood and black lacquer table, on cabochon headed cabriole legs joined by a stretcher, part 18thC, 36in (92cm).
£2,500-3,000 *CSK*

A George II design giltwood table, with verde antico marble top, the pierced apron carved with scrolling foliage and fruit, on cabriole legs headed by shells, on hairy claw-and-ball feet, redecorated, restorations, 60in (152cm).
£19,000-22,000 *C*

Centre Tables

A Regency rosewood centre table, with inlaid brass stringing, 2 frieze drawers, stained beech column and sabre legs with brass paw casters, 48in (122cm). **£1,200-1,700** *SWO*

A George III style mahogany cent table, with crossbanded and boxwood strung top inlaid to the corners, on square tapered legs ar spade feet, 66in (168cm).
£1,000-1,500 *Bon*

A Victorian walnut salon table, with figured top, supported on 2 turned stems and splayed legs with turned stretcher, the legs carved with fruit and scrolls, 53in (134.5cm). **£2,500-3,000** *DDM*

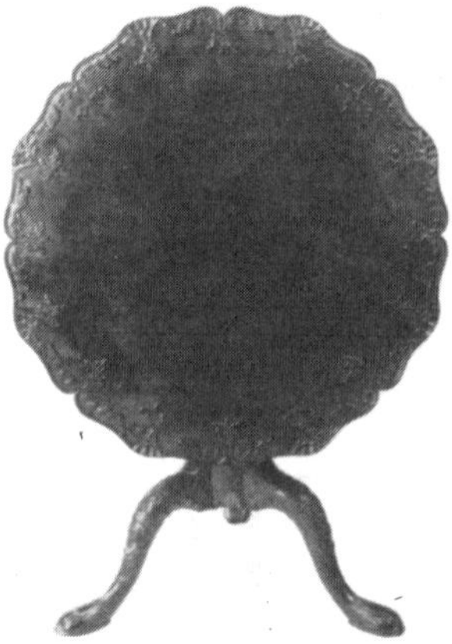

A mahogany centre table, with tip-up top on foliate carved splayed legs with dolphin head pad feet, part 18thC, 34in (86cm).
£1,500-2,000 *CSK*

A Victorian oak centre table in th Jacobean style, on 4 turned stems splayed legs and reeded stretcher, the whole with carved flutings, masks and lines, 46in (116.5cm).
£450-550 *DDM*

Regency rosewood centre table, ith brass inlaid wirework ringing gilded brass edging and lt painted decoration, the plain ipports with scroll mounts, ipported on scrolling feet with irned stretcher, 45in (114cm).
,000-3,500 *DDM*

A rosewood centre table, with pendant finials to the frieze, twist turned end supports joined by a stretcher and on downturned splayed feet with brass casters, mid-19thC, 52in (132cm).
£700-900 *Bea*

A Dutch walnut centre table, inlaid with marquetry with boxwood line borders, the coffered top with 2 frieze drawers, on spiralled baluster legs with latticed cross stretchers, labelled W. & J., Sloane Furniture, 5th Avenue, New York, 53in (134.5cm).
£2,000-2,500 *CSK*

A rosewood centre table, 36in (92cm).
£300-400 *Bea*

Louis Philippe walnut centre ole, with grey marble slab top, on ibbed vase shaped shaft and icanthus carved splayed legs with oll feet, some moulding missing, ½in (100cm) diam.
,500-2,000 *CSK*

A French kingwood, tulipwood and foliate marquetry centre table, on square supports joined by an undertier on cabriole legs with gilt metal sabots, 20in (51cm).
£800-1,200 *CSK*

A Victorian faded walnutwood centre table, the top with inset leather, raised on a well turned column with cabriole tripod carved with acanthus leaves, 30in (76cm).
£1,200-1,700 *DEN*

Louis XVI design giltwood centre ole, the top inset with a porcelain aque surrounded by 12 plaques in g-and-dart borders, above a iate composition frieze on anthus carved C-scrolling pports with cabochon headings d arched stretchers, labelled omline di Roma, Scalo Termini, ½in (68cm) diam.
,500-3,500 *CSK*

An ebonised parcel gilt and gilt metal mounted centre table, the top of serpentine outline centred by a porcelain plate within a border of portrait medallions, on foliate carved cabriole legs joined by a similarly mounted stretcher, late 19thC, 26in (67cm).
£2,000-2,500 *CSK*

A pair of rosewood snap-top centre tables, the supports carved with 3 entwined dolphins, the leaf carved concave sided triangular platform bases on 3 carved turtles, 19thC, 29in (73cm) diam.
£4,000-5,000 *P(S)*

A Dutch walnut centre table, with quart veneered tray top above one convex frieze drawer, on cabriole legs and claw-and-ball feet 35in (89cm).
£800-1,000 *C*

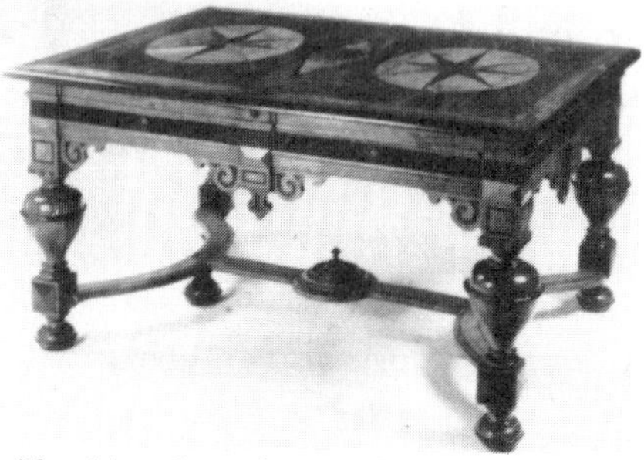

A Flemish walnut ebony and ebonised centre table, the top inlaid with stars, the shaped frieze on bulbous baluster legs joined by a finialled stretcher, the top with trade label, 60in (152cm).
£1,500-2,000 *CSK*

A French grey painted and parcel gilt centre table, the top lined in watered silk, 52in (132cm).
£1,000-1,500 *CS*

A French rosewood and marquetry centre table, with brass mounts to the serpentine sides, the top and frieze with floral and scroll marquetry, the whole supported on cabriole legs ending in brass mounted feet, late 19thC, 40in (101.5cm).
£1,500-2,000 *DDM*

An Italian walnut ebonised and bone inlaid centre table, decorated overall with stylised foliage, the top with bowed ends centred by a pewter tablet, on finialled pedestals, each with a square plinth joined by a flat stretcher on turned feet, 19thC, 49½in (125cm).
£1,000-1,500 *CSK*

A Portuguese walnut centre table, with geometrically carved frieze fitted with 2 drawers, on baluster turned legs joined by an H-stretcher, early 18thC, 57in (144.5cm).
£2,500-3,000 *CSK*

Console Tables

A rosewood console table, applied with gilt flowerheaded paterae, with a platform base on turned bun feet, early 19thC, adapted, 23½in (60cm).
£700-1,000 *CSK*

A carved giltwood rococo console table, the top inset with flecked marble, on 2 cabriole legs, with carved cartouches and leaf scrolls late 18thC, 35½in (89cm).
£4,000-4,500 *WW*

An early Victorian mahogany console table, with a frieze applied with foliate mouldings on 2 acanthus carved S-scroll supports backed by a mirror plate on a concave plinth, 54in (137cm).
£1,200-1,500 *CSK*

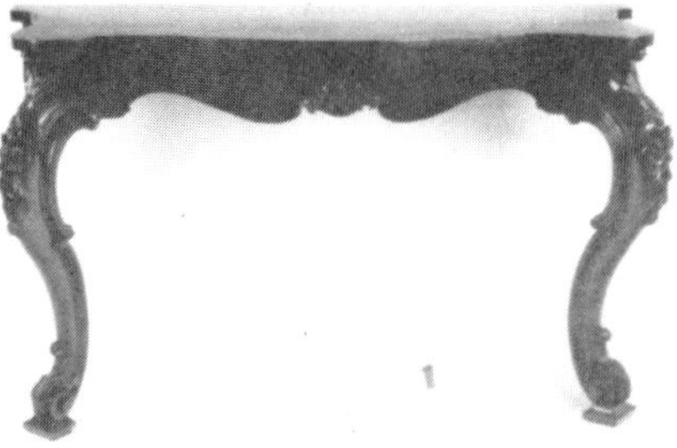

A Victorian rosewood serpentine console table, with crossbanded top and undulating frieze applied with mouldings on C-scrolling cabriole supports, adapted, 60½in (153cm).
£1,000-1,200 *CSK*

A Louis XV style giltwood console table, with marble top, on shell headed scrolling legs with finialled stretcher, 47½in (120cm).
£1,000-1,500 *CSK*

A Louis XVI style tulipwood and gilded serpentine console table, applied with gilt metal mounts, the velvet lined top with foliate tongue-and-dart borders, the frieze inset with painted foliate and Sèvres plaques, on shell and acanthus compositioned cabriole legs joined with a scrolling stretcher, 55in (139.5cm).
£3,000-5,000 *CSK*

A Victorian giltwood console table, with serpentine white marble top, on foliate carved scrolling legs with bowed undertier and mirrored back, 58½in (148cm).
£3,000-3,500 *CSK*

A French bowed giltwood console table, with eared marble top, on fluted and tapering legs with an urn finialled and festooned cross stretcher, 19thC, 50in (127cm).
£5,000-6,000 *CSK*

n Italian giltwood and composition
rpentine console table, with
arble top, on a pierced frieze and
stic cabriole supports entwined
ith fruiting vines, joined by a
retcher, early 19thC, 38in
6.5cm).
,500-2,000 *CSK*

A late Empire mahogany console table applied with ormolu mounts, with Carrara marble top and a mirror lined back and platformed base, stamped P. Lehaene, 35in (89cm).
£4,000-4,500 *CSK*

Dining Tables

A George II mahogany gateleg dining table, the top with a bevelled edge, on cabriole legs and claw-and-ball feet, 58in (147cm).
£3,000-3,500 *Bon*

An Irish mahogany drop-leaf dining table, with twin flap top on club legs with claw-and-ball feet, 18thC, 70in (177.5cm).
£2,500-4,000 *CSK*

A Georgian design mahogany 2 flap dining table, with carved scroll and leaf decoration to kne cabriole legs and hoof feet.
£600-700 *MGM*

A figured walnut D-end extending dining table, with 2 winding handles and a turned central leg, including 4 extra leaves, extendin to 144in (369.5cm).
£3,500-5,500 *CSK*

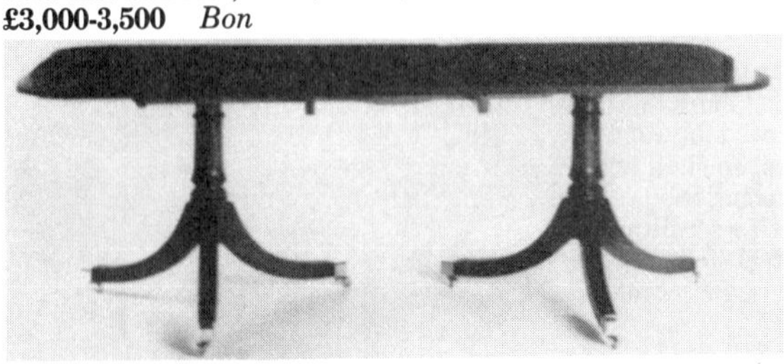

A Georgian style mahogany D-end dining table, on twin turned shafts and splayed legs with brass caps, with 2 leaves and rails, 106in (269cm).
£900-1,200 *CSK*

A George III mahogany extending dining table, on 4 baluster turned columns with a concave plinth and 4 foliate carved outswept legs, c1815, 2 later leaves, 86in (218cm) extended.
£6,500-7,500 *Bon*

A Regency mahogany dining tal the folding top on ring turned tapering legs, including an extra leaf, 55in (139.5cm).
£1,000-1,500 *CSK*

A late George III mahogany D-end dining table, on square tapered fluted legs headed by a fanned oval, associated, including an extra leaf, 84½in (214cm).
£1,800-2,000 *CSK*

A mahogany twin pedestal dinin table, with reeded edge, each pedestal with turned shaft and 3 moulded downswept legs, the pedestals early 19thC, 89in (226c extended.
£3,000-4,000 *C*

A Georgian style mahogany triple pedestal dining table, with plain top, reeded edge, supported on turned stems, splayed legs and brass cap casters, including 2 leaves, 144in (369.5cm) extended.
£2,000-3,000 *DDM*

A George III mahogany dining table, with ribbed tapering legs, later rails, the feet restored, including 2 leaves, 84in (213cm) extended.
£2,500-3,500 *C*

A mahogany and inlaid 3-part D-end dining table, on 14 square tapering legs, basically early 19thC, 94in (238cm) extended.
£3,000-4,000 *CSK*

George III
:yle mahogany
-end dining table,
n triple ring turned
ıpering shafts and
eeded down curving
gs with brass
ıw feet, including
extra leaves, 140in
59.5cm) extended.
,000-4,000 *CSK*

A George III style mahogany D-end dining table, with satinwood banded top, on triple turned tapering columns and reeded splayed legs with brass paw feet, including 2 extra leaves, 144in (369.5cm) extended.
£2,500-3,000 *CSK*

mahogany twin pedestal dining
ble, with rounded end sections on
rned shafts and splayed legs,
4in (264cm).
,000-4,000 *C*

A George III mahogany D-end dining table, with plain veneered arched friezes and on square legs, 114in (289.5cm).
£3,500-4,500 *Bea*

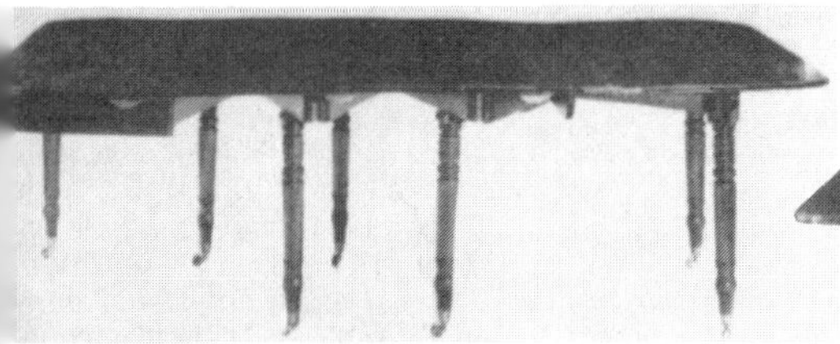

Regency mahogany D-end dining
le, with concertina action, on
g turned tapered legs, including
nodern leaves, 132in (335cm).
,000-6,000 *CSK*

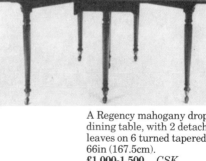

A Regency mahogany drop-leaf dining table, with 2 detachable leaves on 6 turned tapered legs, 66in (167.5cm).
£1,000-1,500 *CSK*

A mahogany D-end 3-pillar dining table, with moulded top on turned supports, basically 19thC, including 2 leaves, 118in (300cm) extended.
£2,000-2,500 *CSK*

A Regency mahogany twin pillar dining table, on turned baluster shafts and splayed quadripartite supports, 102in (259cm).
£17,000-20,000 *CEd*

A Regency mahogany extendir dining table, with panelled frie and ring turned legs, opening t include 3 further leaves, 94in (239cm) extended.
£4,000-4,500 *C*

A Regency mahogany extending dining table, on ring turned legs headed by roundels, the action stamped Wilkinson Patent Moorfields and Patent 483, opening to include 3 further leaves, including 3 leaves stamped 483, 96in (244cm).
£5,000-6,000 *C*

William and Thomas Wilkinson of 9 and 10 Broker Row, Moorfields, London (1790-1811), specialised in extending tables.

A mahogany pedestal dining table, the top on triple faceted tapering shafts with reeded collars above concave platform bases with scroll feet, adapted early 19thC, including 2 extra leaves, 12in (284.5cm) extended.
£5,500-6,500 *CSK*

A mahogany dining table, expanding by means of a band of extra leaves on 4 ring turned supports joined by a circular stretcher on splayed legs, including a leaf cabinet, 84in (213cm) extended.
£900-1,200 *CSK*

A William IV mahogany extending dining table, on turned tapered legs, each with a lotus leaf carved collar on brass caps and spooned casters, including 3 extra leaves, 135in (244cm) extended.
£3,000-4,000 *CSK*

A mahogany D-end dinin table, with fluted edge, de frieze, raised upon reede turned and tapering supports terminating in brass caps and casters, 19thC, 54in (134cm).
£900-1,200 *HSS*

A George IV mahogany 2 pillar dining table, the frieze with tablets at each end, each pedestal with turned shaft lappeted with lotus leaves and 4 downswept legs carved with acanthus, including one leaf, 75in (191cm) extended.
£4,000-4,500 *C*

A George IV mahogany 3 part dining table, the top with rounded ends and folding central section, on ring turned tapering legs, 81½in (206cm) extended
£2,000-3,000 *CSK*

Victorian mahogany xtending dining table, turned supports, cluding 3 leaves, 3in (249cm) extended.
2,000-2,500 *DDM*

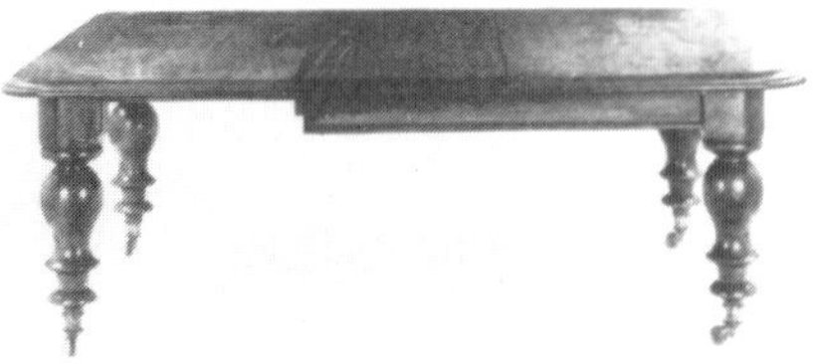

A Victorian mahogany dining table, on turned tapering bulbous legs, including 4 extra leaves, 142in (360.5cm) extended.
£3,000-4,000 *CSK*

A mahogany dining table, including 4 leaves, labelled, 19thC, 127in (322.5cm) extended.
£5,500-6,000 *CSK*

A Victorian mahogany dining table, with coffered top and rounded ends on ring turned tapering legs, including 2 extra leaves, 97in (246cm) extended.
£3,000-3,500 *CSK*

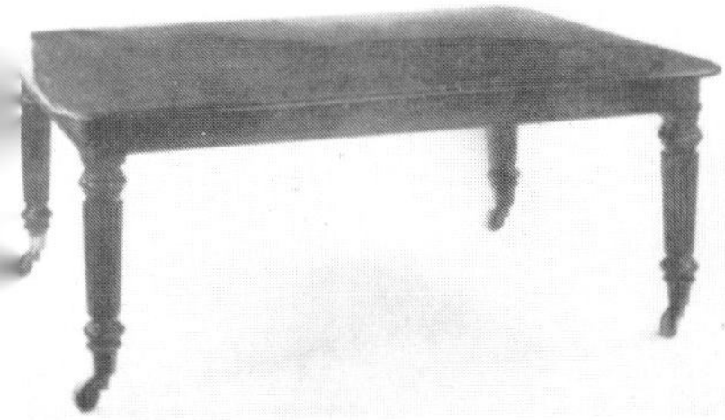

An early Victorian mahogany dining table, winding mechanism labelled Joseph Fitter, Patentee, Britannia Works, 210 Cheapside, Birmingham, including 3 extra leaves, 134in (340cm) extended.
£5,500-6,500 *CSK*

A Victorian 3-part D-end dining table, the centre section with a rectangular fold-over top, on 12 reeded turned tapering legs, adapted, 88½in (224cm) extended.
£1,000-1,500 *CSK*

A mahogany dining table, on turned tapered legs, including 3 extra leaves, 95in (241cm) extended.
£1,500-2,000 *CSK*

An early Victorian extending dining table, with a bevelled edge, on 6 lappet turned tapered legs, including a mahogany cabinet with 3 additional leaves, 120in (305cm) extended.
£4,000-4,500 *Bon*

Display Tables

A mahogany bijouterie table, with a velvet lined fully glazed interior, supported on cabriole legs with undertier, early 20thC, 23in (59cm).
£350-400 *DDM*

A Louis XV style ormolu mounted tulipwood vitrine table, enclosed by a hinged lid, on cabriole legs with sabots, 32in (81cm).
£1,500-2,000 *CSK*

Drawleaf Tables

A mahogany drawleaf breakfast table, with boxwood stringing, one side inlaid to simulate 2 drawers, the other fitted a single drawer flanked by simulated drawers, on square section tapering legs with brass casters, 45½in (115cm) extended.
£1,000-1,500 *LAY*

Dressing Tables

A Regency mahogany dressing table, inlaid with boxwood lines, with mahogany lined divided drawer, on turned tapering reeded legs with foliate carved feet, 32in (81.5cm).
£900-1,500 *C*

A parquetry and marquetry dressing table, part lined in maroon leather and enclosing 3 compartments, the shaped frieze fitted with 2 end drawers, on cabriole legs, 35in (89cm).
£1,700-2,000 *C*

A Victorian walnut dressing tabl with swing mirror, on platform ba with 3 small drawers, 39in (99cm
£700-900 *JH*

A George IV mahogany dressing table, the top above frieze drawers and a simulated panelled door flanking a kneehole on ring turned tapering legs, 45½in (115cm).
£900-1,200 *CSK*

Dropleaf Tables

A French ashwood circular drop-leaf table, Burgundy, c1820, reduced in height, 41in (104cm).
£500-600 *UC*

A mahogany dining table, with folding top above a frieze draw on cabriole legs with pointed feet, basically 18thC, 48in (122cm) extended.
£900-1,200 *CSK*

An Italian walnut table, the drop-leaf top with foliate moulde border, above 2 end drawers on shaped trestles carved with cartouches and scrolls joined by a stretcher, 41in (104cm).
£1,200-1,800 *C*

. mid-Georgian mahogany rop-leaf dining table, the twin-flap op on club legs and pad feet, 55in 139.5cm).
.1,000-1,500 *CSK*

A Regency mahogany Cumberland action drop-leaf supper table, with twin-flap top, on turned gatelegs with reeded downswept legs, 48in (122cm).
£2,000-3,000 *C*

Drum Tables

. George IV mahogany drum brary table, with gilt tooled red eatherette inset top, 4 fitted frieze rawers with brass ring handles, on ring turned centre pillar and eeded quartet base, 48in (122cm).
4,000-5,000 *P(W)*

A Regency style yew wood drum table, the inset leather lined top above a simulated frieze fitted with 2 drawers, on a fluted tapering shaft and scrolling triform base joined with flat cross-stretchers, 24in (62cm).
£500-800 *CSK*

A George IV mahogany veneered drum top library table, the border crossbanded in zebrawood, the frieze with alternate drawers and false drawers with replacement gilt brass ring handles, revolving on a turned vase stem with 4 moulded splay legs with brass sabots on casters, 49in (124.5cm).
£3,000-4,000 *WW*

. Regency walnut drum table, with egmented top and carved border, n cluster column and triform latform support, with claw feet and asters, 29in (74cm).
2,000-2,500 *JD*

Games Tables

A William IV amboyna games/work table, with a writing easel and an upholstered bowed well, on trestle supports and turned feet, 30½in (80cm).
£1,500-2,000 *Bon*

A coromandel and ebony games table, with half balustrade, the reversible centre inlaid with a chequerboard and enclosing a backgammon board, on ring turned legs joined by stretchers with downcurved feet, 37½in (95cm).
£1,500-2,000 *C*

Make the Most of Miller's

In Miller's we do NOT just reprint saleroom estimates. We work from realised prices either from an auction room or a dealer. Our consultants then work out a realistic price range for a similar piece. This is to try to avoid repeating freak results – either low or high

An Edwardian mahogany roulette table, the lift-off top revealing a fitted baize lined interior with roulette wheel and scoop, the shell and scroll carved aprons on leaf carved slender cabriole supports, 38in (96cm).
£700-900 *P*

A George III oak games table, with a reversible sliding chequer top enclosing a backgammon board, decorated with inlaid ebony stringing and star motifs, raised on square tapering legs, 22in (56cm).
£1,500-2,000 *AG*

A late Victorian ebonised games pedestal table, with plain circular top over a trefoil shaped revolving undertier with baluster gallery, on a turned stem and splayed supports, 27in (69cm). **£150-200** *DDM*

A George IV penwork and ebonised games table, the tip-up top decorated within a border of scrolling foliage, on a reeded shaft with concave sided ivory inlaid platform and scrolled feet, 21in (53cm).
£4,000-5,000 *C*

PATINATION

- ★ means layers of polish, dirt, dust, grease, etc, which have accumulated over the years — really the whole depth of surface of a piece of antique timber
- ★ the patination on different woods varies considerably but the same piece of wood will basically colour to the same extent (always allowing for bleaching by sunlight, etc)
- ★ walnut furniture often had an oil varnish applied to give it a good base to take the wax polish — this has led to the lovely mellow patina which is virtually impossible to fake
- ★ dirt and grease from handling are important guides (especially under drawer handles, on chair arms, etc) — these areas should have a darker colour — if they don't beware!
- ★ pieces which have carving or crevices will have accumulated dirt giving dark patches
- ★ colour and patination are probably the most important factors when valuing a piece of furniture
- ★ by repolishing a piece of furniture and removing evidence of patination, a dealer can conceal replacement or conversion

Library Tables

A Regency mahogany library table, in the manner of Thomas Hope, with green leather inset writing surface, on a tapered square section column inlaid with ebony anthemia, on bronzed winged lion's paw feet, 36in (91cm). **£8,000-8,500** *Bon*

A George II style mahogany library table, with gilt tooled leather inset, 3 frieze drawers opposing 2 real and one false drawer, above a gadrooned moulding, and on shell and acanthus carved cabriole legs with hairy paw feet, legs cut, 52in (132cm). **£2,700-3,000** *Bea*

An early Victorian rosewood library table, with frieze carved with scroll and fitted with 2 drawers opposed by false drawers, on solid end standards joined by a turned stretcher, on lotus leaf carved bar and ribbed bun feet, 60in (152cm).
£1,500-2,000 *CSK*

A Regency mahogany library table with leather lined double hinged top, the frieze inlaid with rosewood panels, on a turned shaft and 4 reeded downswept legs with brass caps, 54in (137cm). **£1,500-2,000** *C*

Manufacturers
To Her Majesty.
T. & G. SEDDON,
No. 4826
GRAY'S INN ROAD,
London.

An early Victorian burr walnut library table, on turned and tapering gilt embellished lotus carved trestle end supports and ba feet, ending in gilt scrolled toes headed by shells, bearing the label of T & G Seddon, Manufacturers to Her Majesty, Grays Inn Road, London, No. 4826, 63in (160cm).
£10,000-12,000 *CEd*

NB. The firm of George Seddon in Aldersgate Street was the largest cabinet maker in London during th late 18thC. When Seddon died in 1801, the family firm went into a short period of decline but in 1827 his nephews George and Thomas went into partnership with Nicholas Morel who had been chosen by King George IV as furniture maker in charge of refurbishing Windsor Castle. The firm of Morel and Seddon used Morel's address but the work was produced at the Seddon workshops in Aldersgate Street. Windsor Castle was the main commission but work was also done for other Royal Houses and Palaces. Morel's name disappeared from the Royal accounts in 1831 and the work passed to George and Thomas Seddon, although they were not given a Royal Warrant until 1832.

. Regency mahogany secrétaire
brary table, the top with reeded
dge, the deep secrétaire drawer
vith partly hinged front enclosing a
ather lined writing slide with
alphabetically inlaid
ompartments below, with panelled
ngles on reeded tapering legs and
rass socket casters, the casters
amped Rotary No. 7168, 43in
.09cm).
4,000-5,000 *C*

A late Victorian mahogany and inlaid library table, with an inset top, 4 fitted drawers each side with brass handles, raised on 5 shaped square tapering supports.
£1,300-1,700 *P(W)*

A Victorian mahogany library writing table, with inset lined coffered top above 6 frieze drawers, on lotus leaf lappeted turned tapering bulbous legs, 72in (182.5cm).
£2,000-3,000 *CSK*

An early Victorian oak library table, with parquetry top, the frieze carved with lunettes and 16thC style portrait roundels and fitted with a drawer, the turned legs with foliate bases and capitals on plinth feet, 54½in (138cm).
£1,000-1,500 *C*

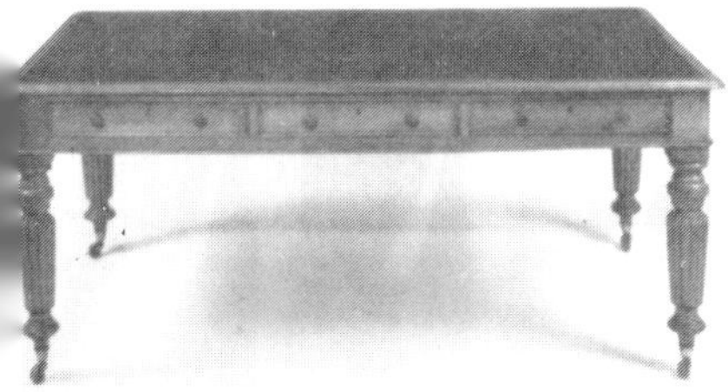

A Victorian oak library table, with leather lined top with 6 frieze drawers, on fluted turned tapering legs, 72in (182.5cm).
£800-1,200 *CSK*

A Victorian walnut library table, on heavily scrolled and carved supports with decorative stretcher, 54in (137cm).
£1,000-1,500 *GD*

A Victorian library table, the inset leather lined top above 6 frieze drawers, on square tapering legs, 48in (122cm).
£4,000-4,500 *CSK*

oo Tables

Victorian rosewood loo table, the
-top with crossbanded decoration
pported on a plain hexagonal
m, trefoil base and bun feet, 51in
9.5cm).
00-800 *DDM*

A Victorian rosewood loo table, with plain tilt top on an octagonal baluster stem, trefoil base ending in lion paw feet, 50in (127cm).
£500-700 *DDM*

Nests of Tables

A nest of 3 mahogany tables, with crossbanded tops on ring turned legs and shaped feet, 19in (48cm).
£900-1,200 *C*

A nest of Regency burr walnut tables, with inlaid chevron borders, on slender bulbous supports, smallest 13in (33cm).
£2,000-2,500 *GSP*

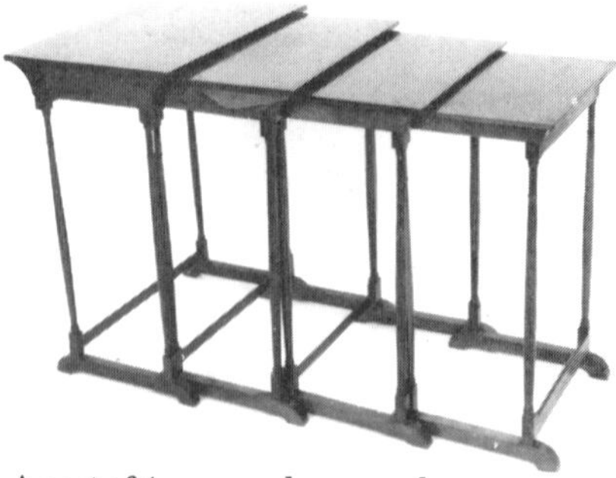

A nest of 4 rosewood veneered occasional tables, the tops with inlaid stringing on turned block legs with stretchered feet, restorations, early 19thC, smallest 15½in (39cm).
£900-1,200 *WW*

A nest of 3 rosewood tables, with moulded top banded in satinwood on ring turned supports and shape bar feet, 21½in (54cm).
£700-1,000 *C*

A nest of 3 French walnut occasional tables, the tops etched with roundels and with shaped borders, on end standards with turned bun feet, 20in (51cm).
£400-500 *CSK*

A nest of 4 rosewood tables, each top with a beaded rim, on turned supports and bar feet carved with acanthus scrolls, 19½in (49cm).
£2,000-2,500 *C*

A set of 3 rosewood tables, on tw turned tapering column end standards with down curving le joined by bowed cross stretchers 23in (59cm).
£1,200-1,500 *CSK*

A nest of 3 Edwardian bowfront mahogany and satinwood crossbanded tables.
£450-500 *LAY*

A nest of Edwardian mahogany occasional tables, decorated with inlaid satinwood crossbanding and boxwood stringing, raised on square tapering legs and understretchers, 25in (64cm).
£600-650 *AG*

A nest of 4 mahogany tables.
£450-550 *LAY*

)ccasional Tables

. mahogany occasional table, the
)p with a turned baluster gallery,
n a cluster column and fluted shaft
arved with swags, on an acanthus
arved arched tripod support ending
ı pad feet, 26½in (67cm).
2,000-2,500 *CEd*

A Regency kingwood occasional table, the top with Greek key pierced gallery, on a parcel gilt lotus carved column and outswept legs, 21in (53cm).
£2,000-2,500 *Bon*

A George IV burr elm pedestal table, the top inlaid with specimen wood segments centred by a boxwood star, on a faceted shaft carved with lotus and concave triangular platform with scroll feet, 20in (51cm).
£1,500-2,000 *C*

n occasional table, of bois clair
ıd ebony, the top with rosewood
ınding, the support column of
.ceted tapering form, early 19thC.
300-700 *LRG*

A crossbanded satinwood drum top occasional table, with lift-up lid and undershelf, on tapering splayed supports, 16½in (42cm).
£450-550 *HCH*

A Regency brass inlaid rosewood table, the tip-up top inlaid with flowerheads in the crossbanding, on a square stepped shaft and concave sided platform with scroll feet, 48in (142cm).
£3,000-5,000 *C*

'edestal Tables

yew wood pedestal breakfast
ble, the segmented veneered
-up top on a lappeted lotus leaf
.d beaded shaft and triform base,
.th turned bun feet, basically early
thC, 53½in (134.5cm).
,500-6,500 *CSK*

A flambé mahogany tilt-top dining table, the top with segmented veneers, on heavy turned column with foliate collar, plateau base and squat feet, early 19thC, 48in (122cm).
£850-950 *GAK*

A George IV brass inlaid rosewood centre table, with tip-up top, the frieze with foliate boulle panels flanked by plain panels, with gadrooned and baluster shaft, concave sided tripartite platform and foliate scrolling claw feet, 42½in (108cm).
£6,000-7,000 *C*

A William IV mahogany breakfast table, the tip-up top with gadrooned edge and bead moulded frieze, on ribbed shaft with foliate carved socle, the concave sided platform on turned feet, associated, 48in (122cm).
£2,000-3,000 *CSK*

A Victorian walnut salon table, the tilt-top with quarter-veneered decoration, on a carved bulbous stem and 4 carved scrolling supports, 59in (149.5cm).
£2,000-2,500 *DDM*

A Victorian mahogany pedestal table, with feathered and carved edge and carved triangular pedestal, 31in (79cm).
£1,500-2,000 *PLJ*

A Victorian burr walnut pedestal dining table, the crossbanded moulded tilt-top inlaid with amaranth bands, on a carved tapering bulbous column and quadripartite base with scrolled feet, 53in (134.5cm).
£1,500-2,500 *CSK*

A Victorian walnut salon table, the tilt-top with figured quarter-veneer design, bordered with floral marquetry, stringing and crossbanded decoration, bears label for Constantine & Co's. Cabinet & Upholstery Warehouse, 40in (101.5cm).
£2,000-3,000 *DDM*

Pembroke Tables

A George III mahogany Pembroke table, the folding top above 2 frieze drawers, on square tapering legs joined by a platform cross stretcher, adapted, 33in (84cm).
£600-700 *CSK*

A George III mahogany butterfly Pembroke table, the twin flap top and frieze drawer on square moulded legs and spade feet, 38½in (97cm). **£1,500-2,000** *CSK*

A yew Pembroke table, the top inlaid with batswing stringing and a batswing medallion, with frieze drawers and false drawer, 18thC, 37in (94cm) extended.
£22,000-24,000 *GSP*

A George III satinwood Pembroke table, banded in rosewood, the twin-flap top with later fanned oval panel flanked by lunettes, restorations, stamped from W. Williamson & Sons, Guildford, 38in (96.5cm).
£2,500-3,000 *C*

A Sheraton design satinwood Pembroke table, with rounded fall flaps, the top with broad rosewood band within ebony string lines, 36½in (93cm).
£2,000-2,500 *P(S)*

A satinwood and polychrome painted Pembroke table, with twin-flap top banded in trailing foliage and centred by an oval depicting 3 fishing putti, with a frieze drawer, on square tapered legs, 40½in (102cm).
£3,000-3,500 *CSK*

PEMBROKE TABLES

- ★ became popular in the mid to late 18thC, possibly designed and ordered by Henry Herbert, the Earl of Pembroke (1693-1751)
- ★ on early examples the legs were square which are by far the most desirable
- ★ later tables had turned legs
- ★ the turned and reeded legs are much less popular
- ★ those with oval or serpentine tops more desirable
- ★ flaps should have three hinges
- ★ rounded flaps and marquetry again increase desirability
- ★ satinwood was greatly favoured, particularly with much crossbanding and inlay
- ★ many 18thC Pembroke tables have chamfering on the insides of the legs
- ★ the Edwardians made many fine Pembroke tables which have been known to appear wrongly catalogued at auction
- ★ Edwardian tables now in great demand

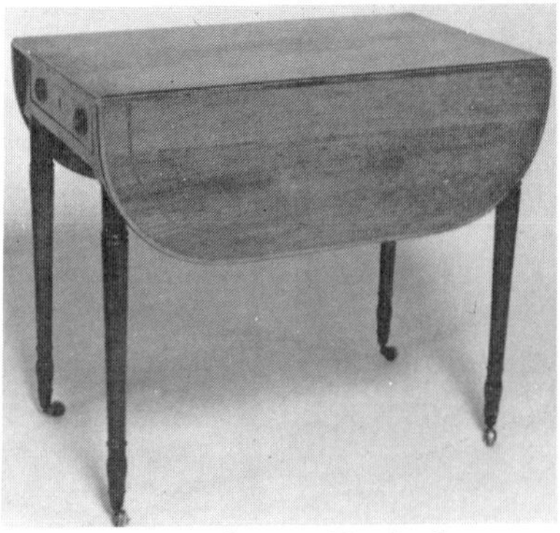

A Georgian mahogany Pembroke table, with ebony stringing inlay and satinwood crossbanding, single drawer and cylindrical tapered legs.
£500-1,000 *MGM*

A Dutch oak and marquetry Pembroke table, with folding top above a frieze drawer, on cabriole legs with pointed pad feet, early 19thC, 27in (69cm).
£1,500-2,000 *CSK*

A mahogany crossbanded Pembroke table, with drawer, late 19thC.
£550-600 *JH*

ı Edwardian Sheraton inlaid ahogany Pembroke table, with ıgle drawer, on tapered legs with ade feet, 27in (69cm).
'50-1,000 *JD*

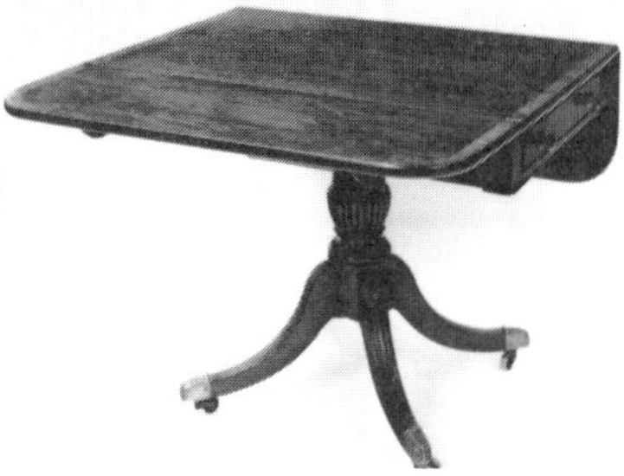

A Georgian mahogany pedestal Pembroke table, with crossbanded top, single frieze and dummy drawers, on a turned baluster and fluted stem ending in 4 curving legs and brass cap casters, 36in (92cm).
£500-600 *DDM*

A Regency inlaid mahogany Pembroke table, with rosewood banded top, above a frieze drawer, on square tapering legs with casters, 32in (81cm).
£2,500-3,000 *CSK*

:eading Tables

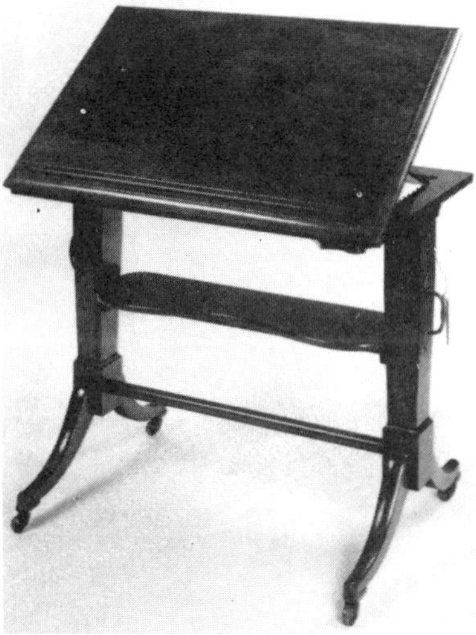

. Regency mahogany reading table, ·ith ratcheted adjustable top on end :andards joined by a shaped ndertier and turned stretcher, ·ith downswept feet, 36in (91cm).
1,000-1,500 *C*

A George IV mahogany reading table, with adjustable ratchet, on a baluster turned centre pillar and tripod base, 17½in (45cm).
£1,000-1,500 *P*

An early Victorian mahogany adjustable reading stand, with baluster support on concave trefoil base and bun feet.
£400-450 *CSK*

A mahogany tripod reading table, with adjustable tip-up top on a bulbous turned shaft with splayed legs and pad feet, 36in (92cm).
£1,000-1,500 *CSK*

Serving Tables

A mahogany serving table, with chamfered square legs headed by pierced brackets, 54in (137cm).
£900-1,200 *CSK*

An Irish mahogany serving table, with rope carved borders, on rope carved tapering legs with paw feet, parts early 19thC, 72in (182.5cm).
£3,500-4,000 *CSK*

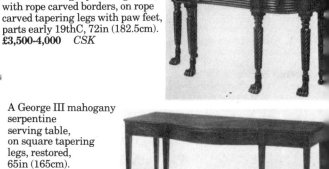

A George III mahogany serpentine serving table, on square tapering legs, restored, 65in (165cm).
£2,000-2,500 *CSK*

A George III mahogany bowfront serving table, with boxwood stringing, on square tapering legs inscribed in pen 'This sideboard belongs to Miss Florisida Norman Foyle Cottage, Vicarage Gardens Clacton-on-Sea', 72in (182cm).
£3,500-4,000 *C*

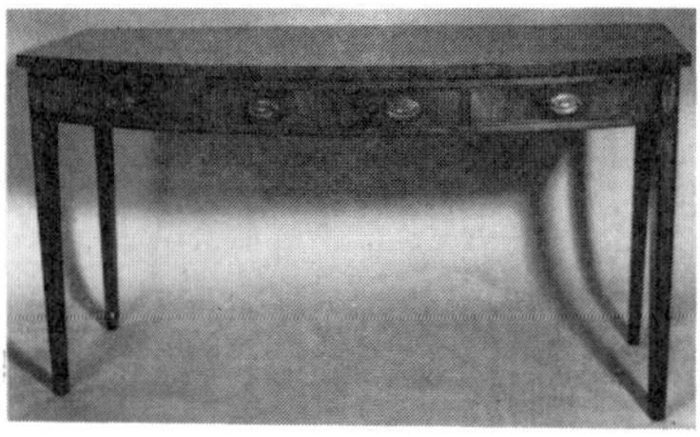

A mahogany serving table, with inlaid panels, late 18thC, 63in (160cm).
£1,500-2,000 *SWO*

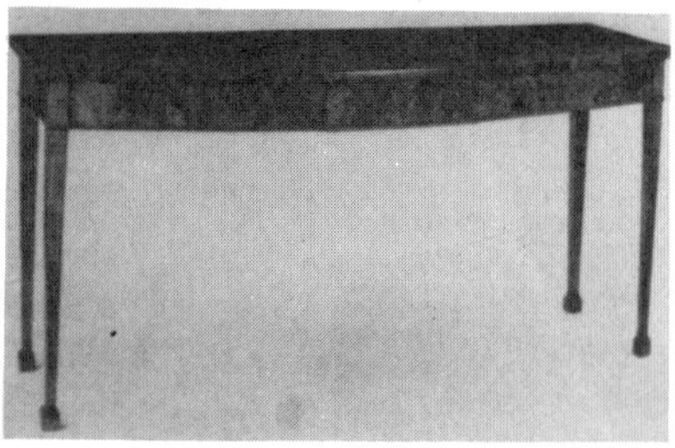

A George III mahogany bowfront serving table, with tablet centred frieze, on square tapering legs and block feet, the brass plaque on back inscribed Humphrey W. Cook Collection, 76½in (194cm).
£3,000-4,000 *CSK*

A Victorian carved mahogany serving table, decorated with a lion mask, supported on a pair of twin reeded legs joined by a platform and standing on acanthus capped scroll feet, by Fras & Jas Smith of Glasgow, 40½in (102cm).
£600-700 *OL*

A William IV mahogany D-shaped serving table, with beaded border and frieze carved with vine leaves, on 8 ribbed baluster legs, 141in (358cm).
£5,000-5,500 *CSK*

mahogany serving table, with
ain top, 3 frieze drawers with lion
ng brass handles, supported on
rved turned and fluted front legs
iding in lion paw feet, early 19thC,
in (216cm).
:,000-2,500 *DDM*

A Victorian pollard oak serving side table, the serpentine top with an oak leaf carved border, above a shaped frieze carved with rockwork scrolls and centred by an armorial motif, on cabochon headed cabriole legs, 93in (236cm).
£1,500-2,000 *CSK*

;ide Tables

pair of neo-classical style
tinwood pier tables, painted and
corated with foliate scrolls and
llflower festoons, the elliptical
oulded tops on square tapering
gs, 45in (114cm).
,200-1,500 *CSK*

A walnut side table, the crossbanded top above 2 short and a long frieze drawer, on later cabriole legs with pad feet, 38in (96.5cm).
£400-700 *CSK*

A George III mahogany D-shaped side table, crossbanded in rosewood and inlaid with boxwood and ebony lines, on turned tapering legs, 39in (99cm).
£2,500-3,000 *C*

George III mahogany serpentine
nt side table, the top with
ulded edge, 3 drawers to the
eze and raised upon square
ering supports, 31in (79cm).
,500-2,000 *HSS*

A George III mahogany and inlaid side table, the crossbanded top above a single frieze drawer flanked by mock drawers with brass ring handles, with canted corners, on square tapered supports with block feet, 43in (110cm).
£2,000-2,500 *P*

An Adam style mahogany side table, with harewood inlaid and kingwood crossbanded top, carved fluted frieze, square tapered and fluted legs and moulded feet, 60in (152cm).
£3,000-3,500 *AH*

Adam pine side table, with an
:hed foliate and fleur-de-lys
ved frieze on all sides with
:erae corners, the fluted square
ered legs carved with floral
toon, 42in (106.5cm).
)0-500 *MAT*

A mahogany, sycamore and marquetry side table, the elliptical top on square tapering legs, basically late 18thC, 48in (122cm).
£700-1,000 *CSK*

A late George III satinwood side table, inlaid with ebony lines, the D-shaped top crossbanded with tulipwood, with plain frieze on square tapering legs, 40in (102cm).
£3,000-4,000 *C*

A Regency mahogany secrétaire side table, the later top above a long writing drawer and 5 small drawers with inset brass handles, flanking a kneehole between quadrant angles on ring turned tapering legs, 39in (99cm). **£1,000-1,500** *CSK*

A Regency mahogany side table, crossbanded in rosewood, with 2 drawers, on spirally reeded tapering legs, previously fitted wit a work basket, 26in (66cm).
£1,000-1,500 *C*

A George IV mahogany side table, on plain end standards united by a turned centre stretcher, on reeded splayed supports, 31in (79cm).
£500-1,000 *P(W)*

A Dutch walnut and foliate marquetry side table, decorated with birds and a flower-filled urn, with later mirror fitments, the frieze with 2 drawers with a shaped apron, on shell carved cabriole legs and claw-and-ball feet, 18thC, 27in (69cm).
£3,000-4,000 *CSK*

A Louis XVI mahogany and kingwood side table, with crossbanded top centred by a lat floral marquetry oval, the panel frieze fitted with a drawer, on square tapering legs, Franco Flemish, 25½in (64.5cm).
£2,000-3,000 *C*

A Victorian rosewood and walnut side table, with segmented veneered top decorated with mother-of-pearl and inlaid with harewood and satinwood marquetry, above an acanthus banded frieze, fitted with 2 small drawers, on guilloche and foliate carved tapering bulbous end standards with scrolling splayed legs, 53in (134.5cm).
£4,000-5,000 *CSK*

A gilt metal and rosewood side table, with acanthus banded supports, mirror back and plinth base, 45in (114cm).
£1,500-2,000 *CSK*

A white painted and brass mounted bowfront side table, with green speckled scagliola top and plain frieze, on 5 square conforming marbled legs and block feet, 63½in (162cm).
£1,000-1,500 *C*

Silver Tables

A mahogany silver table, with fr blind outlines, with galleried top chamfered square moulded legs with Marlborough block feet, 32 (82cm).
£600-900 *CSK*

Sofa Tables

)utch walnut and foliate rquetry silver table, the dished decorated with spandrels and ds amongst foliage, the frieze h a single drawer, on cabriole s and pointed pad feet, 19thC, n (92cm).
500-3,000 *CSK*

A George III mahogany sofa table, crossbanded in rosewood, above 2 crossbanded drawers to either side, on 4 ring turned columns and concave plinth with outswept legs, 57in (145cm) extended.
£5,000-6,000 *Bon*

A mahogany and rosewood crossbanded sofa table, with moulded apron drawers, on twin turned columns and moulded quadruple supports, brass toes and casters, late 18thC, 66in (167.5cm).
£4,000-4,500 *AH*

A mahogany and inlaid sofa table, with folding top and 2 frieze drawers, on solid end standards and C-scrolling splayed legs with brass block terminals, part early 19thC, 57in (144.5cm) extended.
£2,000-2,500 *CSK*

›sewood sofa table, with inlaid nging decoration, 2 real and ımmy drawers, supported on a ; turned stem, ending in ›layed legs and brass paw ›ers, early 19thC, 71in (182.5cm).
›00-3,000 *DDM*

A rosewood sofa table, inlaid with brass, on quadruple baluster shaft with paw feet, early 19thC.
£5,000-6,000 *CSK*

A Regency mahogany sofa table, on later solid end standards with splayed feet, 70in (177.5cm).
£2,000-3,000 *CSK*

ɡured mahogany sofa table, with ıy line inlay and wide sbanding, 2 frieze drawers with ɩed brass handles, on 4 splay feet ı brass paw casters, 58in cm).
›00-6,000 *P(M)*

A red lacquer and gilt chinoiserie sofa table, with 2 frieze drawers, opposed by false drawers, on end standards joined by a turned stretcher on down curved legs, 46in (116.5cm).
£2,000-2,500 *CSK*

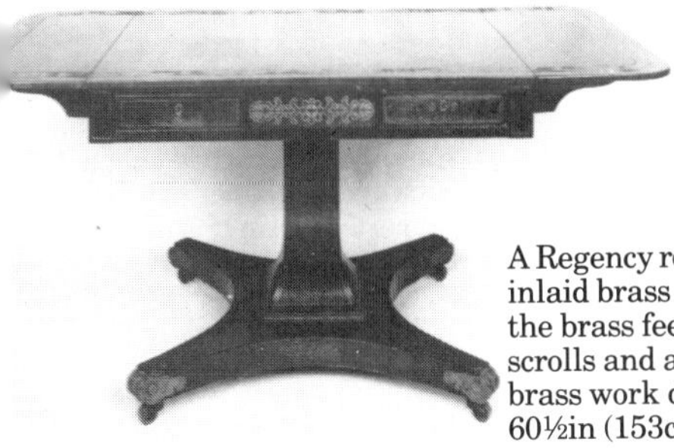

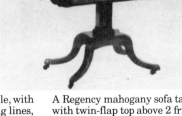

A Regency rosewood sofa table, with inlaid brass motifs and string lines, the brass feet with moulded florets scrolls and anthemia, casters, inlaid brass work defective in places, 60½in (153cm). **£3,000-4,000** *P(S)*

A Regency mahogany sofa table, with twin-flap top above 2 frieze drawers, on a square shaft with 4 splayed legs, distressed, 58in (147cm).
£1,500-2,000 *CSK*

A Regency rosewood games and sofa table, with wide burr walnut crossbanding, the underside with chequered games board, with brass handles and moulding, the lyre end standards gilt metal acanthus and roundel mounted, on swept supports terminating in brass claw casters, united by a later arched stretcher, 42in (107cm) extended.
£7,000-8,000 *P(W)*

A Regency rosewood sofa table, with interlaced lozenge boxwood stringing, raised on ring turned double pillar end standards and outward splayed square tapering supports terminating in peg feet and brass casters, 62½in (159cm) extended.
£2,000-2,500 *HSS*

A Regency mahogany sofa table, with solid trestle ends and splaye legs, 66in (168cm) extended.
£2,000-3,000 *C*

A late Regency mahogany sofa table, with moulded twin flap top and 2 frieze drawers, joined by a stretcher with splayed legs, restorations, 59in (149.5cm).
£2,000-3,000 *CSK*

Sutherland Tables

A George III mahogany Sutherland table, with twin-flap top and turned gateleg supports on turned feet, restored, 32½in (85cm).
£1,000-1,500 *C*

A Victorian burr walnut and inlaid Sutherland tea table, with an inlaid scrolling foliate border and stringing, on turned and whorled end standards, united by a centre stretcher, on leaf carved scrolled supports, 35in (90cm).
£700-1,000 *P(W)*

An early Georgian walnut tea table, with rectangular folding top and a drawer, on club legs and pad feet, 24in (61cm).
£1,500-2,000 *C*

A Victorian figured walnut pede Sutherland table, the top quarter-veneered and with 2 sha flaps, the frieze with 2 drawers, o turned fluted shaft and 3 splaye legs, 30in (76cm).
£750-850 *CSK*

Tea Tables

A George II red walnut and mahogany serpentine tea table, the top enclosing a boxwood lined interior above a banded frieze, on chamfered square moulded legs with acanthus carved wings, adapted, 33in (84cm).
£1,500-2,000 *CSK*

A Victorian burr walnut Sutherl table, with shaped leaves and standing on a turned cheval base with quadruple carved spreading supports, 39½in (99cm).
£1,500-2,000 *OL*

mahogany tea table, with
ossbanded serpentine folding top
ı chamfered legs with block feet,
⅜½in (85cm).
,000-2,500 *C*

Regency rosewood fold-over top
ı table, with segmented ball feet,
ın (92cm).
00-1,000 *OL*

George IV figured mahogany
l-over top tea table, of D-form
h black line inlays, on 4 turned
s with ring detail and brass
ters, 36in (92cm).
)0-1,200 *GAK*

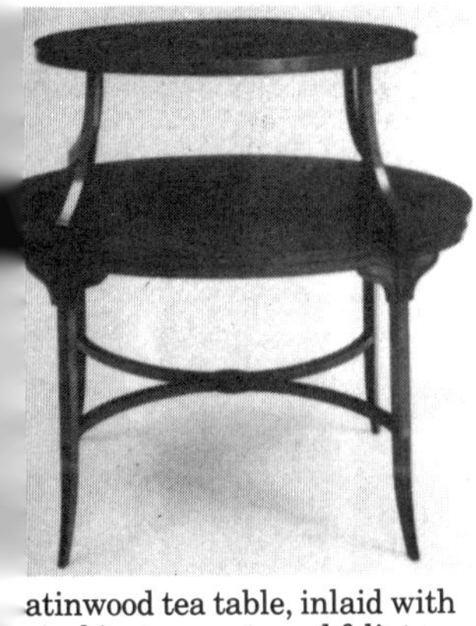

atinwood tea table, inlaid with
sical instruments and foliate
rquetry arabesques, with square
ayed tapering legs joined by
crolling cross stretchers, 35in
cm).
000-1,500 *CSK*

A late George III mahogany tea table, with D-shaped fold-over top above a frieze drawer with a gilt metal border, on turned tapering reeded legs, 40in (101.5cm).
£1,500-2,000 *CSK*

A Regency mahogany fold-over tea table, on turned and fluted column, on quadruple base and casters, 36in (92cm) extended.
£700-900 *HCH*

A pair of William IV rosewood pedestal tea tables, with swivelling fold-over tops, on faceted tapering shafts and concave sided platform bases with turned bun feet, stamped Gillows Lancaster, 36in (92cm).
£3,000-4,000 *CSK*

Tray Tables

A mid-Georgian mahogany tea table, with folding top, fitted with a drawer concealed by the gateleg, on square chamfered legs, 28½in (72cm).
£700-1,000 *C*

A rosewood veneered folding tea table, having leaf carved and fluted column on splay legs, 19thC.
£700-900 *MGM*

An Edwardian mahogany and marquetry veneered stand with 2 tray shelves.
£600-700 *LAY*

A George III mahogany and satinwood tray, inlaid with a fanned oval and leafy bands with waved rim and 2 brass handles, on a later stand with square legs, 27in (68cm).
£1,700-2,000 *C*

A George III mahogany butler's tray, the galleried top pierced with carrying handles, on a turned beech folding stand, 26in (66cm).
£1,200-1,500 *CSK*

A Victorian mahogany two-tier etagere with detachable tray top.
£600-700 *LAY*

A William IV black japanned papi mâché tray, decorated in gilt and colours with a spray of flowers within a leafy border, the later stand with ring turned legs and X-stretcher, 30½in (77cm).
£600-900 *C*

Tripod Tables

A Chippendale mahogany tripod table, on later well carved blind fret and floral stem and supports, 20in (51cm).
£1,500-2,000 *GSP*

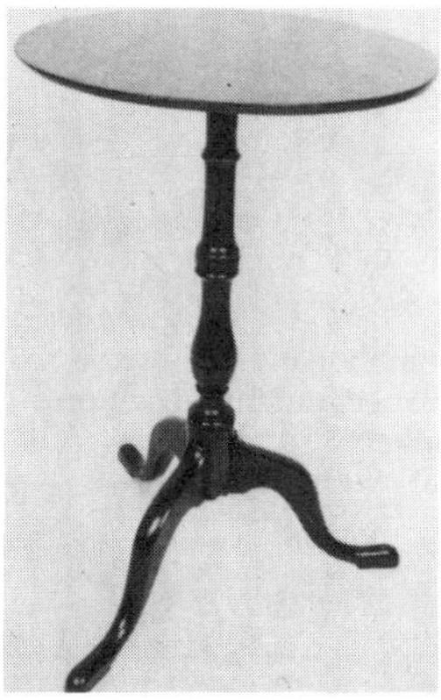

A George III mahogany tripod table, with snap-top, the ring turned baluster centre pillar, on a tripod base, 16½in (41cm).
£700-900 *P*

An Irish mahogany tripod table, each cabriole leg differently carv on shaped pad feet, mid-18thC, 3 (91cm). **£2,000-3,000** *C*

A George III mahogany and inlaid tripod table, the snap-top with canted corners and kingwood crossbanding, the ring turned centre pillar on a tripod base, 20in (51cm).
£600-700 *P*

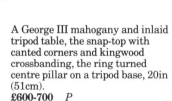

A mid-Georgian mahogany tilt-top table, on spiral fluted round tapering column to tripod cabriole supports, 31in (79cm).
£500-600 *MJB*

A mahogany tripod table, the top with spindled gallery, on turned shaft and arch splayed legs with paw feet carved with foliage, 28½in (72cm). **£800-1,000** *CSK*

A George III mahogany table, w dished snap-top, on a baluster turned centre pillar and tripod b 17½in (44cm).
£700-900 *P*

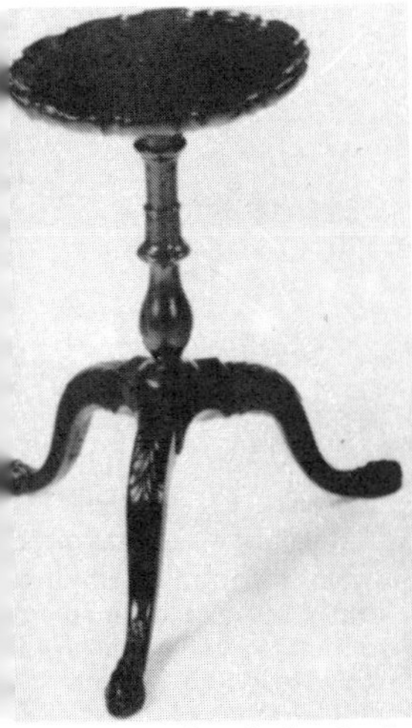

ıahogany and padouk tripod
le, with pie crust top and
uster shaft, the splayed base
ved with foliage on claw-and-ball
:, 14in (36cm).
200-1,500 *C*

A George III tilt-top table, the top above a bird cage base, with vase turned column and triple spreading supports, 31½in (80cm).
£900-1,200 *OL*

An early George III mahogany tripod table, the top on a birdcage action and a baluster turned and spiral fluted column hipped outswept legs and pointed pad feet, 36in (91cm).
£900-1,200 *Bon*

ıahogany pedestal table, the
ıp top with an undulating pie
ıt border, on a fluted tapering
ımn and splayed legs with
v-and-ball feet and acanthus leaf
dings, 29in (74cm).
0-700 *CSK*

An early George III mahogany occasional table, the tilt-top with a moulded edge, the fluted stem with ribbon paterae moulded edge, the fluted stem with ribbon paterae moulding on tied leaf spray carved cabriole legs, with claw-and-ball feet, 26in (66cm).
£5,500-6,000 *WW*

A mahogany tripod table, the tip-up top with a waved border carved with shells and husks, on a turned foliate carved shaft and splayed legs, 31in (79cm).
£600-800 *CSK*

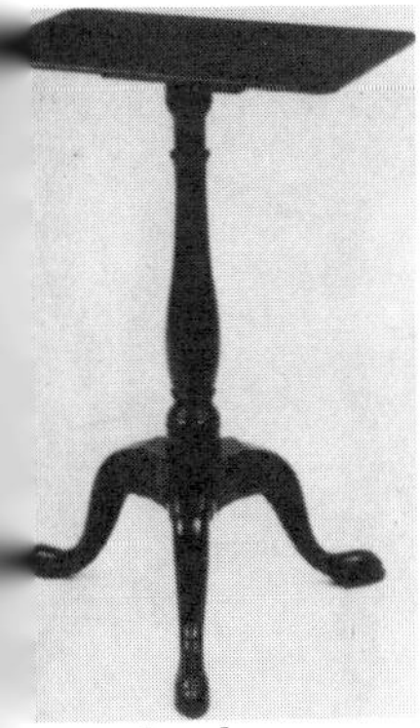

ew and mahogany
od table, the top on a
ıed shaft and
layed legs with
ıted pad feet,
ciated, mid-18thC,
ı (48cm).
0-800 *CSK*

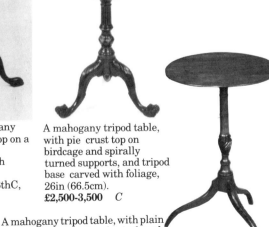

A mahogany tripod table, with pie crust top on birdcage and spirally turned supports, and tripod base carved with foliage, 26in (66.5cm).
£2,500-3,500 *C*

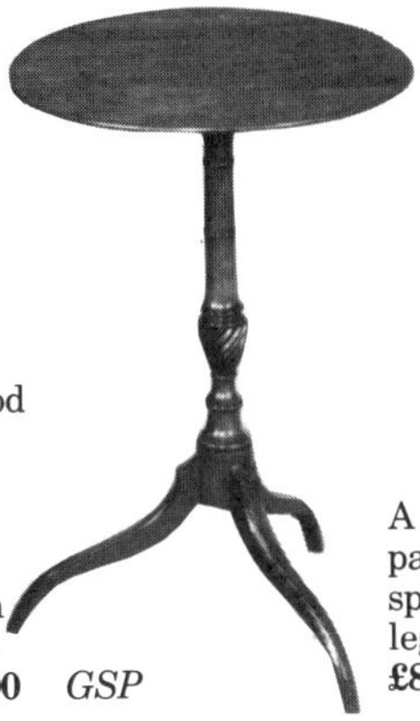

A mahogany tripod table, with plain fixed top, on turned and spiral reed stem, 19thC, 18in (46cm). **£300-400** *GSP*

A Regency rosewood grained and parcel gilt tripod table, the top on spirally fluted column and scrolled legs, 18in (46cm).
£800-1,200 *Bon*

A mahogany tripod table, the moulded pie crust tip-top with birdcage action on a spirally fluted baluster shaft, the cabriole legs carved with cabochons, C-scrolls, acanthus and rockwork with claw-and-ball feet, 27in (69cm).
£2,000-3,000 *C*

A mahogany snap-top tea table, on ring turned column to a triple splay base, with cabriole legs and casters, early 19thC, 39in (99cm).
£600-700 *GAK*

A Regency mahogany tripo table, the rounded tip-up to and baluster shaft on moul arched downswept legs wit spade feet, 31in (79cm).
£500-800 *C*

A George III rosewood tripod table, the tilt-top crossbanded and inlaid with narrow satinwood bands, on tapered reeded and fluted stem, the legs inlaid with satinwood bands, on peg supports, 20in (51cm).
£2,500-3,000 *GSP*

An Austrian fruitwood, yew and specimen wood tripod table, the top inlaid with various woods in a radiating pattern, on 3 shaped supports and downswept legs applied with turned roundels, 27½in (70cm).
£1,500-2,500 *C*

A Dutch painted and ebonised tripod table, the shaped oval tip-top painted with figures in front the Town Hall, Amsterdam, on turned shaft and cabriole legs wi pad feet, 18thC, 43in (109cm).
£3,000-4,000 *C*

Wine & Lamp Tables

A Regency mahogany lamp table, on a turned ribbed shaft with gadrooned socle and 4 scrolled feet, the top and bottom possibly associated, 22in (56cm).
£1,000-1,200 *C*

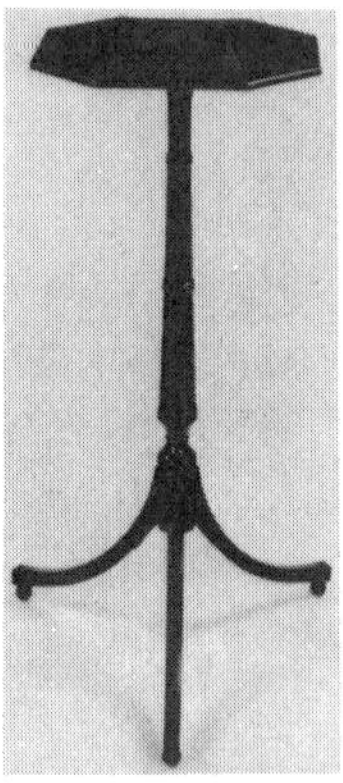

A pair of mahogany lamp tables, with ring turned shaft and 3 downswept legs with ball feet, 31in (79cm) high.
£2,000-3,000 *C*

A pair of brass mounted rosewood and satinwood lamp tables, each with octagonal top, square spreading shaft and tripod base with bun feet, 17in (43cm).
£2,000-2,500 *C*

Work Tables

A Regency rosewood sewi table, with crossbanded to and frieze drawer on ope lyre supports and gilt me claw feet, re-veneered, 19in (48cm).
£1,200-1,500 *CSK*

ieorgian mahogany writing work
le, with 2 drawers, one fitted
h a writing slide, on refectory
ports with splayed legs and
ters, 21in (53cm).
000-2,500 *MAT*

Regency satin birch work table,
top above a partially fitted frieze
wer and work basket on
haped support, the faceted shaft
h concave platform and scroll
, adapted, 18in (46cm).
500-2,000 *CSK*

ictorian walnut sewing table,
h single drawer and sliding well
partment, with shaped end
ports joined by turned stretcher
brass casters, 21in (53cm).
0-500 *IM*

A Georgian mahogany work table, with an oval crossbanded panel and inlaid stringing, fitted with brass knob handles, a sliding wool box below, raised on turned tapering legs, 21in (53cm). **£1,500-2,000** *AG*

A rosewood veneered sewing table, with segmented column, platform base and decorated with half bead moulding, early 19thC.
£1,300-1,700 *MGM*

A mahogany work table, with twin-flap top banded in kingwood, above 2 frieze drawers opposed by false drawers with a sliding well below, on lion's paw feet joined by a pierced stretcher, 32½in (82cm).
£1,200-1,700 *CSK*

A Regency mahogany Pembroke work table, the twin flap top with rounded angles above 2 frieze drawers, on ring turned tapering supports, 33in (84cm) extended.
£1,000-1,500 *CEd*

A George IV amboyna veneered work table, with a frieze drawer, sliding work compartment, tapering end standards joined by a pole stretcher and on trestle feet, 18½in (47cm). **£1,000-1,500** *Bea*

A Regency rosewood work table, the ridged top above a frieze fitted with a sewing basket, on lappeted tapering supports and turned feet, 16½in (42cm).
£1,200-1,500 *CEd*

A Victorian kingwood pedestal work table, with crossbanded top, frieze drawer and work basket, supported on an octagonal tapering stem, ending in a quatrefoil base and scroll feet, 20in (51cm).
£500-600 *DDM*

A Victorian burr walnut work table, the hinged top with marquetry inlaid and fret carved interior above an upholstered well, on scrolling end standards, 22in (56cm).
£1,000-1,500 *CSK*

An early Victorian rosewood sewing table, with upholstered basket on pierced scrolling end standards joined by conforming stretcher, 27in (69cm).
£1,200-1,700 *CSK*

An Edwardian inlaid mahogany sewing table, with fitted interior, raised on slender square outswep supports, 16in (41cm).
£500-600 *GD*

A Victorian rosewood sewing table, opening to reveal fitted compartments and a central sewing well, on cabriole tripod carved at the knees with flowerheads terminating in scroll feet, 20½in (52cm).
£400-500 *HSS*

A Victorian burr walnut work table, the top enclosing a fitted interior, on a conforming tapered stem and cabriole tripod feet, 18in (46cm).
£450-500 *MGM*

Writing Tables

A Regency mahogany writing table, with hinged flap to the rear, the frieze with a drawer, on ribbed turned tapering legs, the top lacking leather, stamped Gillow, 36in (92cm).
£1,800-2,200 *C*

A George III mahogany harlequin action writing the fold-over kingwood crossbanded top opening to reveal a baize lined interior, on square tapere legs, brass carrying han to the sides, c1790, 26in (66cm).
£1,800-2,200 *Bon*

A late George III mahogany writing table, the top with a 19thC superstructure, 36½in (93cm).
£800-900 *HSS*

A Regency mahogany writing table, in the manner of Gillows, the top containing an ink well with hinged flap, with 2 frieze drawers, on ring turned legs, 36in (92cm).
£2,000-3,000 *C*

A late Regency mahogany writi table, the green leather lined to with three-quarter gallery and central hinged panel, the frieze w 3 drawers, on square tapering le 48in (122cm).
£2,000-2,500 *C*

A George IV mahogany writing table, with leather lined sliding top above 4 frieze drawers, the ends each with a false drawer, on turned tapering legs, 58in (127cm).
£4,000-5,000 *C*

William IV mahogany writing
.ble, the top inset with later green
ather, raised upon melon fluted
ırned and tapering supports
rminating in brass caps and
ısters, one drawer stamped with
aker's name, by T. Wilson of
3 Great Queen Street, London,
7in (94cm).
100-500 *HSS*

Victorian bird's eye maple and
ıhogany writing table, with
rieze drawers, on foliate scrolling
d standards with bar stretchers
d bun feet, 48in (122cm).
,000-2,500 *CSK*

Victorian walnut writing table,
aid with foliate marquetry and
plied with gilt metal mounts, on
briole legs with sabots and
ochon headings, 46in (116.5cm).
000-6,000 *CSK*

.ouis XV style kingwood bureau
t, applied with gilt metal borders
l mounts, with inset leather lined
, on cabriole legs with sabots and
ochon headings, late 19thC, 59in
9.5cm).
)00-4,000 *CSK*

A William IV mahogany partners' writing table, with lined top, above 6 frieze drawers with false drawers to the sides, on solid end standards terminating in paterae on bar and lotus leaf feet, the locks labelled T Parsons patent, 63in (160cm).
£6,000-7,000 *CSK*

A Victorian satin birch writing/reading table, the top with a leather lined adjustable and sliding centre panel, above 2 frieze drawers and 2 pen drawers, on fluted turned tapering legs, stamped C. Hindley & Sons, 134 Oxford Street, London, No. 44435, 44in (111.5cm) extended.
£800-1,000 *CSK*

C. Hindley & Sons, 19thC furniture manufacturers becoming later Hindley & Wilkinson in 1899.

A William IV mahogany partners' writing table, the leather lined top above 6 frieze drawers, each fitted with a Bramah patent lock, on turned tapered ribbed legs, 60in (152cm).
£3,500-4,000 *CSK*

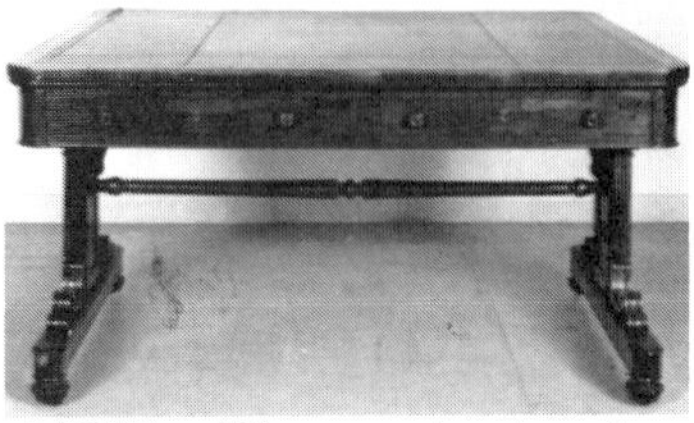

A William IV rosewood partners' writing table, with inset leather top, fitted with 2 drawers each side, on cheval frame with solid panelled ends applied with roundel motifs, joined by turned stretcher, on fluted bun feet, 57in (145cm).
£3,500-4,500 *RBB*

A William IV mahogany writing table, with crossbanded top and 2 concave frieze drawers, on trestle ends carved with bands of egg-and-dart with scrolling feet, 63½in (162cm).
£4,500-5,000 *C*

A Victorian mahogany writing table, fitted with 6 frieze drawers, on faceted turned tapering legs, stamped Webbs, 323 Grays Inn Road, 72in (182.5cm).
£1,500-2,000 *CSK*

A Victorian burr walnut and marquetry writing table, with tulipwood banded waved top with a frieze drawer, on cabriole legs mounted with sabots and gilt metal foliate headings, 44½in (112cm).
£2,000-2,500 *CSK*

An Edwardian mahogany and satinwood bowfront writing table, the elevated back with 4 small drawers above a leather lined plateau and 5 frieze drawers, on square tapering legs, 36½in (92cm).
£700-1,000 *CSK*

A mahogany writing table, maker's label in drawer, J. Batten, Rochester, Kent, late 18thC, 36in (92cm).
£1,800-2,000 *OS*

A Victorian mahogany writing table, with inset leather lined top and 2 frieze drawers, the reverse with simulated drawers, on lyre er standards and lappeted scroll feet joined by stretchers, adapted, 41in (104cm).
£500-800 *CSK*

A mid-Victorian mahogany writing table, the lined moulded top above a frieze fitted with 8 drawers, on turned reeded legs and casters, 121in (307cm).
£2,500-3,000 *CSK*

A mid-Victorian walnut writing table, with lined moulded top above a waved frieze fitted with a drawer, on cabriole legs, 42in (106.5cm).
£900-1,200 *CSK*

An Edwardian rosewood writing table, with floral inlay and satinwood stringing, 42in (106.5cm).
£850-1,000 *SWO*

A Louis XV style kingwood and marquetry inlaid bureau plat, applied with gilt metal mounts an borders, on cabriole legs and sabot 19thC, 45½in (115cm).
£3,500-4,000 *CSK*

A Louis XV style bureau plat, veneered in tulipwood with elaborate gilt metal mounts and leather top.
£4,000-5,000 *LRG*

A burr walnut wr table, with kingw crossbanding and ormolu mounts, shaped galleried shelf, a drawer and on 4 cabriole legs, 19tl
£4,000-5,000 *L*

A mahogany table, with painted X-trestle ends and turned stretcher, early 19thC, 49in (124.5cm).
£1,200-1,800 *WW*

A walnut and gilt metal mounted writing table, the lined top of serpentine outline, on clasp heade cabriole legs with sabots, restorations, late 19thC, 24½in (62cm).
£900-1,200 *CSK*

mahogany burr elm and gilt etal mounted bureau plat, the ıed top with a brass edge, above a ıaped frieze with 5 drawers, and ›plied with acanthus and female ask clasps, on cabriole legs with ıiry paw sabots, 71in (180cm).
,000-5,000 *CSK*

A Louis XVI design walnut and brass bureau plat, the top lined in gilt tooled green leather, on turned tapered fluted legs each with a brass capital and cap, 67½in (171cm).
£7,000-9,000 *CSK*

Teapoys

A Regency specimen wood parquetry pedestal teapoy, the octagonal top with a hinged lid enclosing 2 caddies and bowl apertures, the concave sided platform on gilt metal hairy paw feet.
£2,000-2,500 *CSK*

A late Regency rosewood pedestal teapoy, enclosing 2 caddies and mixing bowl apertures, on ribbed shaft and concave sided platform with bun feet, 18in (46cm).
£800-1,200 *CSK*

A William IV rosewood teapoy, with hinged slightly domed panelled top enclosing a fitted interior, 16in (41cm).
£2,000-2,500 *CEd*

ı Anglo Indian rosewood ›rcophagus teapoy, with fitted terior, on stepped square shaft ›rved with stylised foliage with ›ncave sided platform base and ›olling foliate feet, mid-19thC, ½in (47cm).
00-1,000 *C*

An early Victorian mahogany teapoy, of sarcophagus form, on an octagonal tapered column with lotus collar on concave base with scroll feet, 20½in (52cm).
£400-500 *MGM*

A Regency mahogany tea chest, with hinged domed lid enclosing a fitted interior, above a pair of panelled doors, with side carrying handles, on bracket feet, 22½in (57cm).
£700-1,000 *CSK*

'ashstands

Georgian mahogany washstand, ›th folding top, fitted interior, ›uble doors, on square tapered legs.
50-550 *MGM*

A Dutch mahogany washstand, with hinged top enclosing an interior fitted with 2 flaps, shelves and a bowl aperture, with 2 cupboard doors below, between canted angles, on square tapered legs, early 19thC, 48in (122cm).
£1,500-2,000 *CSK*

A pair of Regency mahogany washstands, in the manner of Gillows, each with three-quarter gallery, above a panelled frieze on turned tapering legs, 38½in (98cm).
£3,000-4,000 *C*

A Georgian mahogany corner washstand, with boxwood string inlay and satinwood crossbanding, lion head loop handles.
£400-500 *MGM*

Whatnots

A late Regency mahogany four-tier whatnot, each tier with concave sides, on ring turned finialled uprights, 53in (134.5cm) high.
£1,500-2,000 *CSK*

A Regency mahogany three-tier whatnot, each tier with a three-quarter gallery and rosewo banded drawer with turned handles, the frieze with a gadroon moulding, spiral turned intermediate supports and graduated bead mouldings, on turned feet, 23in (59cm).
£2,500-3,000 *P(S)*

A pair of three-tier rosewood etageres, with baluster turned supports, turned and lobed finials, the legs with casters, 19thC, 13½in (34cm).
£4,000-4,500 *P(S)*

An Irish mid-Victorian walnut three-tier buffet, with arched back on double fluted column supports, with turned bun feet, labelled R. Strahan, Dublin, 43½in (110cm).
£700-900 *CSK*

Miscellaneous

A Victorian mahogany two-tier lazy Susan, on turned column and base.
£200-300 *HCH*

A Regency rosewood table cabinet, with tablet mounted coffered top, above twin panelled doors enclosing 4 graduated drawers on turned bun feet, 14½in (37cm).
£500-600 *CSK*

A Regency mahogany boot-jack, with turned handles and supports, 33in (84cm) high.
£450-600 *C*

A mid-Victorian oak tabernacle of architectural form, the fluted superstructure with pepperpot finials, 39in (99cm).
£1,700-2,000 *CSK*

A George III brass bound mahogany tray, with scrolled carrying handles, 22in (56cm).
£800-1,000 *C*

ɪRCHITECTURAL ɪNTIQUES

'ire Irons

ɪset of 3 William IV ormolu ɔunted fire irons, comprising: a ɛrced shovel, tongs and a poker ɪth foliate handles, restoration to ɪgs, 30in (76cm).
ɪ00-900 *C*

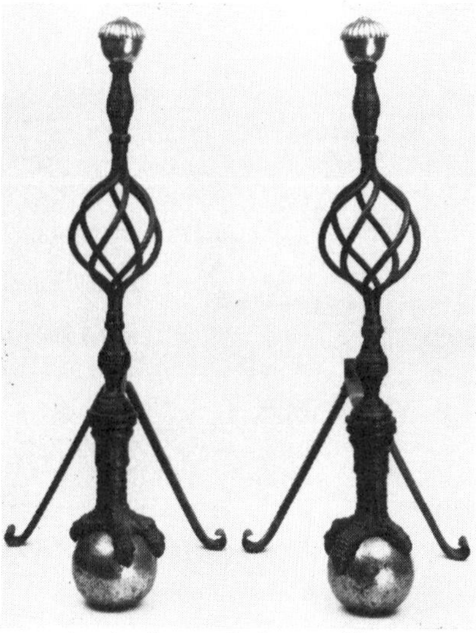

A pair of wrought iron and brass andirons, the ring turned uprights centred by spiral open twist knops, on claw-and-ball bases, late 18th/19thC, 25½in (65cm).
£600-800 *CSK*

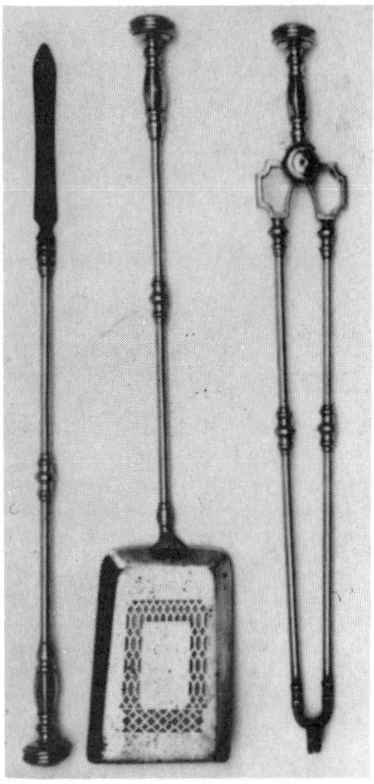

A set of 3 Georgian paktong fire irons, comprising: shovel, poker and tongs, the polygonal grips ring turned and with mushroom knops.
£2,500-3,500 *CSK*

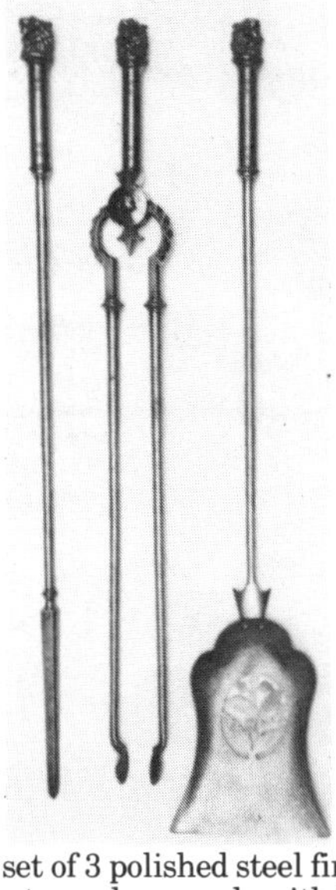

A set of 3 polished steel fire irons, the turned pommels with lion mask bosses comprising: a poker, a pair of tongs and a pierced shovel, the shovel 32in (81.5cm) long.
£900-1,200 *C*

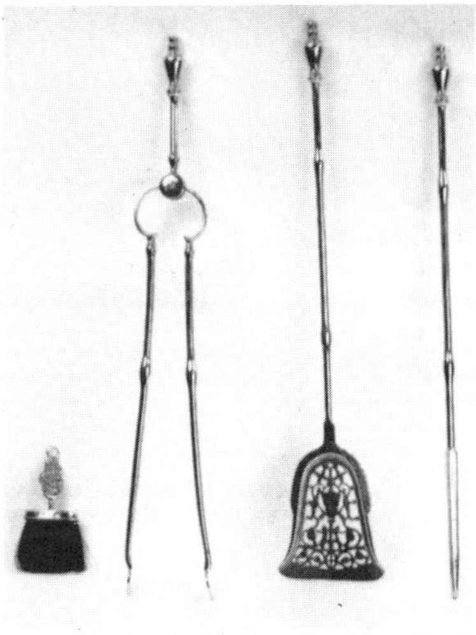

A set of 3 Georgian brass fire irons and a firebrush, with urn finials, the shovel 31in (79cm) long.
£800-1,000 *C*

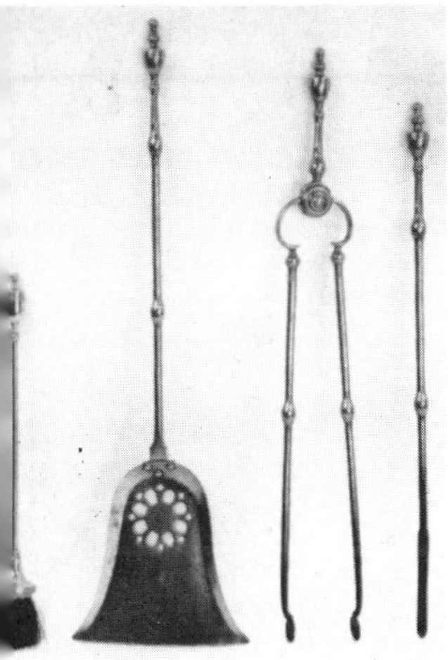

ɛt of 3 George III steel fire irons ɪ associated brush, with pommel ɪals, 31in (79cm).
ɪ0-800 *C*

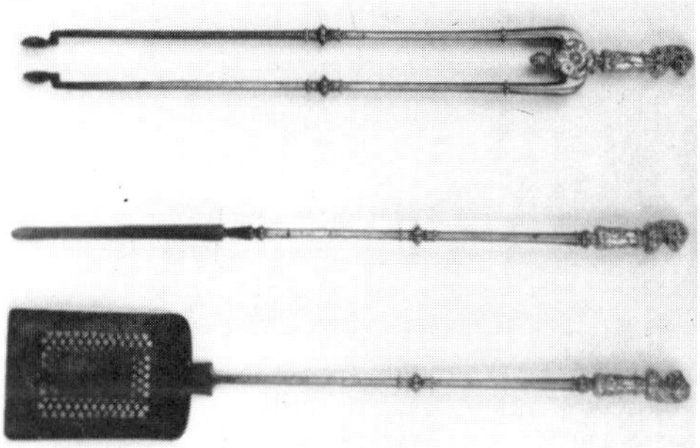

A set of 3 mid-Victorian steel and brass fire irons, with shovel, tongs and poker, each with lion and acanthus handles, and a pair of andirons, with lion mask finials, baluster stems and circular bases, 13½in (34cm) high.
£700-1,000 *C*

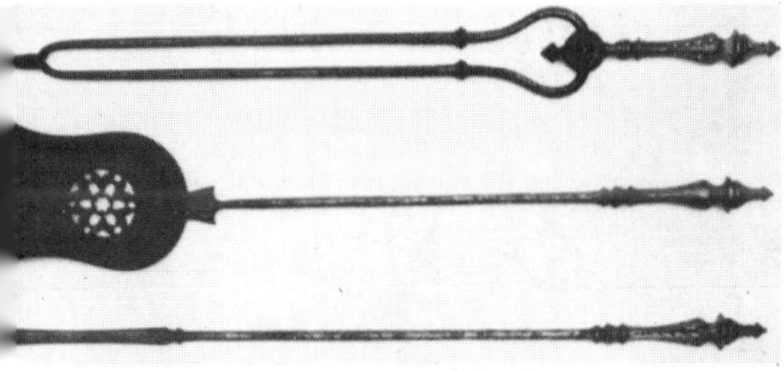

A set of 3 Georgian steel fire irons, the baluster brass grips chased with foliage.
£300-400 *CSK*

Fenders

A French gilt bronze pierced fender, decorated with shell leaf sprays and hatched panels, 19thC, 67½in (171cm).
£900-1,200 *WW*

A George III serpentine brass fender, the frieze pierced and engraved with linked lozenges and flowerheads, 44in (111.5cm).
£700-900 *CSK*

A George III serpentine brass fender, the frieze pierced and incised with foliate ornament, 48in (122cm).
£1,200-1,500 *CSK*

A serpentine brass fender, the frieze pierced and incised with an urn of flowers, dragons and scrolling foliage, flanked by applied coats-of-arms, late 19th/early 20thC, 90½in (229cm).
£1,200-1,600 *CSK*

A steel and brass fire kerb, with bead and Greek key border, with floral rectangular porcelain moun and ropework twist rail over, 63in (160cm).
£600-700 *AG*

A George III brass serpentine fender, pierced with urns, 49in (124.5cm) wide.
£500-700 *C*

A George III brass serpentine fender, pierced with flutes, patera and entrelacs, 46in (117cm).
£400-600 *C*

A bronze, steel and brass adjustable fender, with turned brass rail flanked by recumbent greyhounds with moulded plinth, 32in (91cm).
£400-600 *C*

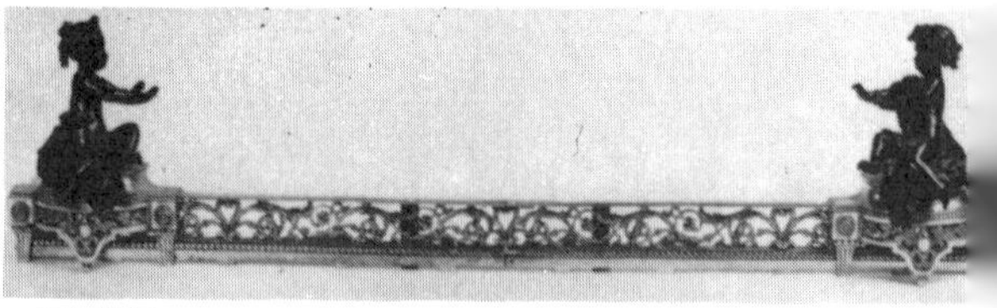

An ormolu and bronze adjustable fender, of Louis XVI style, the pierced front and sides cast with scrolling foliage, with a cherub to each side warming their hands, stamped BFP 1681 twice, 71in (180cm) wide.
£1,000-1,500 *C*

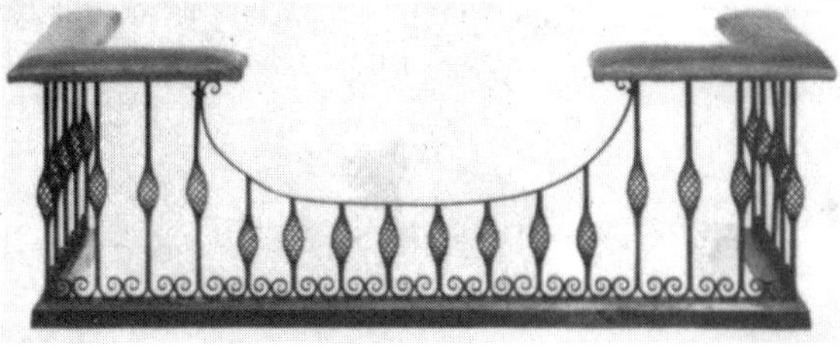

A black painted wrought iron club fender, the square uprights with central open spiral twist knops, terminating in scrolls, with green leather upholstered seats, 75½in (191cm).
£800-1,000 *CSK*

A George IV brass fender, the body pierced with anthemia, on claw feet, 35in (89cm).
£400-600 *C*

A William IV cast and polished steel and brass fender, with a frieze of stylised acanthus leaves and tulip motifs, on ball feet, 51in (129.5cm).
£300-400 *CSK*

A late Georgian steel fender, the lattice work frieze with applied lozenges, on ball feet, 48in (122cm).
£100-200 *CSK*

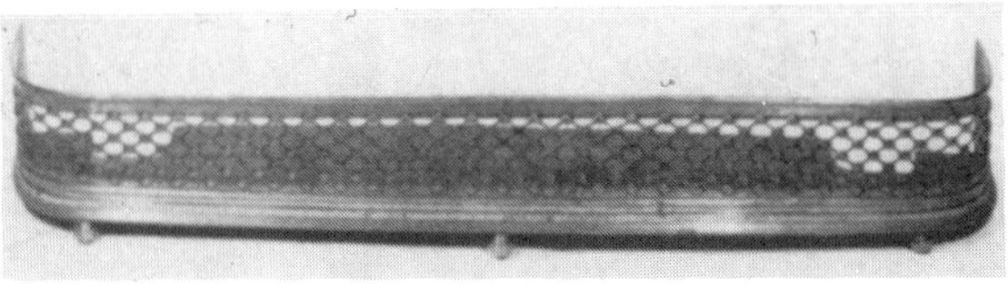

Fireplaces

An oak overmantel with carved decoration enclosing and surrounding needlework panels of the 4 elements, early 20thC, 65in (165cm) wide.
£650-700 *DDM*

An original fireplace, c1780.
£550-700 *WEL*

A carved wood and gesso overmantel, painted in green and highlighted in white, the top with acanthus leaf border above a frieze centred by a stylised classical urn, flanked by foliate arabesque and oval rosettes, the bevelled rectangular mirror plate flanked by fluted shelves, early 19thC, 67in (170cm). **£900-1,200** *C*

A Georgian decorated cast iron fireplace.
£450-500 *WEL*

A Victorian white painted pine and gesso chimneypiece in the Adam taste, the inverted breakfront shelf with stiff leaf moulding above an egg-and-dart cornice, the centre tablet to the frieze depicting a classical hunting scene, flanked by swags and urns with conforming jambs, 70½in (178cm).
£1,000-1,200 *CSK*

A white painted pine chimneypiece, with eared top, the later frieze carved with a panel of Pegasus flanked by fluted panels, the jambs formed as fluted columns with composite capitals, 57in (145cm) wide.
£400-600 *C*

A mahogany fire surround, the inverted breakfront pediment with Greek key and blind fret carving over a plain panel within a beaded frame, all over a plain overmantel and outlined fire surround, the sides with carved double column mount with fluted stems, 75in (190.5cm).
£350-400 *DDM*

A Regency giltwood overmantel mirror, with eared moulded ball encrusted cornice, the parcel ebonised frieze applied in relief, the bevelled plate flanked by cluster columns and applied lion masks, 57½in (146cm).
£3,500-4,000 *C*

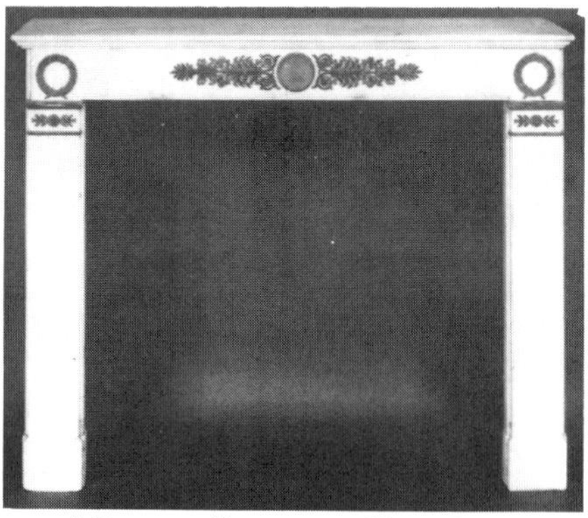

A Regency Carrara marble and bronze mounted chimneypiece, with moulded shelf above a plain frieze centred by an applied anthemion leaf motif flanked by wreaths, the conforming jambs with foliate capitals, 53in (134.5cm).
£1,700-2,200 *CSK*

Fire Grates

A cast iron and brass mounted fire grate, the serpentine railed front above a waved apron flanked by square section standards with spherical finials, the concave backplate in the form of a phoenix rising from the flames, 19thC, 36in (92cm).
£600-1,000 *CSK*

A late Georgian brass and cast iron fire grate in the Adam style.
£1,300-1,500 *GIL*

A Victorian cast iron and brass mounted fire grate, the railed front on paw feet with urn finials below an arched backplate, 21½in (55cm).
£700-900 *CSK*

A brass and iron serpentine fronted fire grate, incised with scrolling foliage and mythical beasts flanking an urn, the tapering standards with urn shaped finials, part 18thC, 31½in (80cm).
£450-650 *CSK*

Georgian iron and brass fire ate, the railed front flanked by plied bats' wing paterae above a erced fret, on tapering, lobed and g turned legs below an arched ckplate, 31in (79cm).
,200-1,600 *CSK*

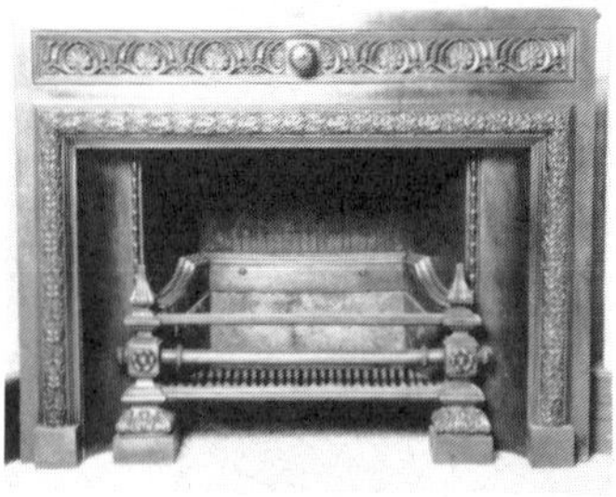

A cast iron Adam style register grate, decorated with swags and bell flowers, c1840.
£1,000-1,200 *ASH*

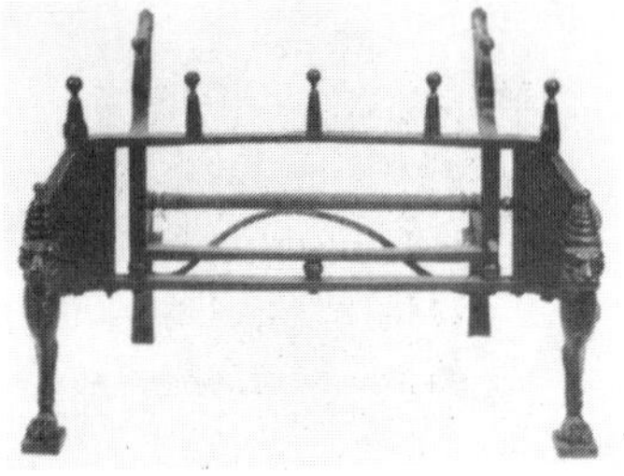

A cast iron fire grate, with inverted barred front flanked by lion monopodia standards with conical shaped finials, 35in (89cm).
£600-700 *CSK*

iron fire grate, the barred front ove a pierced fret flanked by ering column standards with ngated urn finials, 30½in (77cm), hC, with associated ash fender.
000-2,500 *CSK*

An Edwardian fireplace with cast iron surround.
£450-500 *WEL*

A Victorian iron and brass fire grate, with pierced fret flanked by stylised lion monopodia standards, the arched backplate cast with C-scrolls, 26in (66cm).
£900-1,200 *CSK*

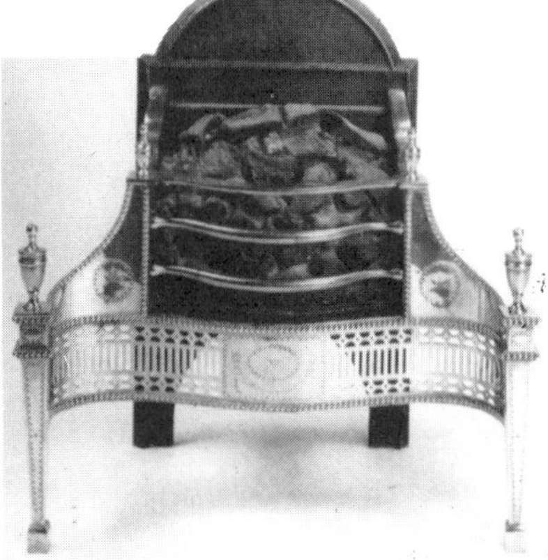

An engraved pierced brass and steel serpentine basket grate, with urn finials and square tapering legs, fitted for electricity, 27in (68.5cm).
£1,000-1,500 *C*

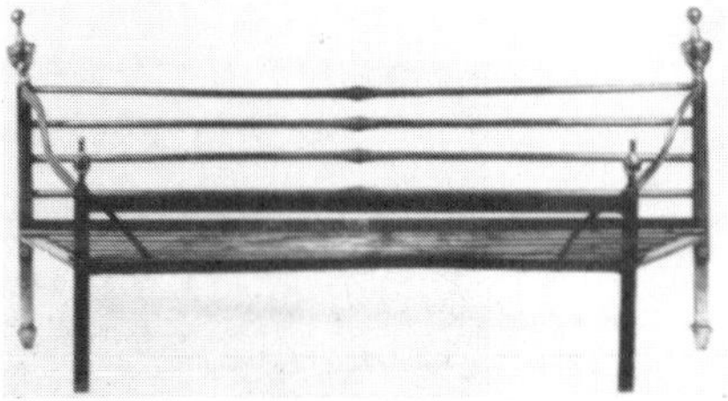

An iron log grate, the barred front flanked by plain standards with applied navette shaped bosses, surmounted by urn shaped finials, 44in (111.5cm).
£700-900 *CSK*

A brass and steel serpentine basket grate, with pierced frame and scrolled supports, fitted for electricity, 21in (53cm).
£300-500 *C*

A polished steel and cast iron basket grate, with arched backplate flanked by scrolling serpents above drapery swags on square stepped base with pierced ash drawer, 22in (56cm).
£600-900 *C*

A Victorian cast iron and brass fi grate with serpentine railed front, the fret pierced with Vitruvian scrolls flanked by baluster column standards on fluted tapering supports, the arched backplate wi raised swags, 24in (62cm).
£500-700 *CSK*

An iron and brass grate, the barred front above a pierced fret incised with dragons and foliage, the square section standards with urn shaped finials below an arched back plate, 28in (71cm).
£1,200-1,500 *CSK*

A Victorian iron and brass fire grate, with serpentine barred front above a pierced fret flanked by tapering standards with applied beaded mouldings, surmounted by urn finials, 27½in (70cm).
£900-1,200 *CSK*

An iron fire basket, 30in (77cm).
£400-450 *DRU*

A brass and iron grate, with finial and pierced fret frieze with pierced fret surmounted supports with cabriole legs, on paw feet, 18thC, 29in (74cm).
£800-1,200 *WW*

Garden Statuary

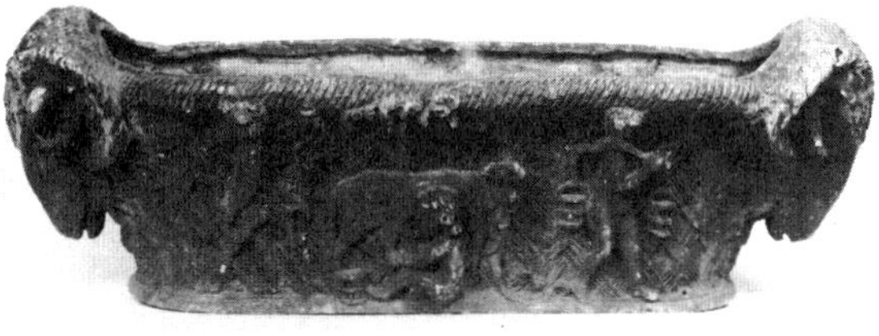

A pair of lead jardinières, with rams' masks terminals and rope twist border above running frieze depicting Bacchanalian scenes, early 19thC, 32in (81cm) wide.
£4,000-5,000 *C*

A terracotta urn, c1880, 26in (66cm) diam.
£80-90 *HUN*

A lead urn, with lid surmounted by a pineapple finial, on foliate capped lower half and foliate capped socle with wreath border, 18thC, 49in (124.5cm) high.
£4,000-5,000 *C*

A pair of Sicilian marble urns, c1830, 34in (86cm) diam.
£14,500-15,000 *HUN*

set of 3 Compton pottery
rracotta jardinières, one bearing
ottery stamp and registration
umber, designed by Gertrude
ekyll, early 20thC, 53in (59cm)
igh.
,000-5,000 *C*

A Victorian cast iron urn on base, 57in (144.5cm) high.
£600-800 *DRU*

A pair of white painted cast iron urns, the gadrooned bodies on fluted spreading shafts and square bases raised on plain square stepped plinths, 19thC, 32½in (83cm) high.
£1,200-1,500 *CAm*

A pair of Victorian lead urns, with lion cast scroll handles, on gadrooned plinths, 31in (79cm) wide.
£700-800 *Bon*

white painted cast iron
o-handled garden urn, the
destal decorated with wreaths of
urel, 19thC, 44½in (112cm) high.
,200-1,500 *CAm*

white marble torchère, the bowl
rved with acanthus leaf scrolls
d flowerheads with 4 grotesque
asks at the corners, on foliate
aped baluster support, on plain
nth, 69½in (176.5cm) high.
000-4,000 *C*

A pair of glazed stoneware garden urns, with egg-and-dart rims, on fluted socles and square bases, raised on square plinths with stepped moulded bases, the sides moulded with rosettes, 41½in (105.5cm) high.
£800-1,000 *C*

A pair of black painted cast iron urns, of campana form, decorated with a Bacchanalian and a scene from the Iliad, 19thC, 21½in (55cm).
£2,500-3,000 *CAm*

A pair of sandstone urns and lids, with waisted leaf carved bodies, 31in (79cm) high.
£300-400 *Bon*

A stone urn, the bulbous body with entwined double handles, on moulded socle with paw feet, 32in (81cm) diam.
£1,700-2,000 *C*

A pair of cast iron garden urns, with egg-and-dart rims, on circular fluted socles and square bases, mid-19thC, 44½in (113cm) diam.
£3,000-4,000 *C*

A composition urn, c1880.
£500-550 *HUN*

A pair of French garden urns, with fluted covers, repaired, 82in (208cm) high.
£3,500-4,000 *WW*

A pair of lead urns with covers, of Adam design, the lids with urn finials, mask side handles, 22in (56cm) high.
£3,500-4,000 *C*

A simulated granite urn, c1920, 33in (84cm) high.
£1,200-1,300 *HUN*

A pair of hardstone garden urns, c campana form, 32½in (82cm).
£1,200-1,500 *CAm*

A pair of stone urns, 21in (53cm) diam.
£350-450 *Bon*

A pair of Bath stone urns.
£4,500-5,000 *WRe*

white marble urn, the bowl with
oulded rim and foliate carved
dy, on cast iron fluted socle and
uare stepped base, 29½in (75cm)
am.
,000-1,500 *C*

A pair of Sicilian marble urns, base modern, damaged handles, c1800, 37in (94cm) high.
£5,500-6,000 *HUN*

An Egyptian terracotta pot, 50in (127cm) high.
£500-600 *WRe*

air of French ormolu urns, the
sted bodies chased with
orting amoretti beneath bocages
uiting vines with fluted bases,
hC, 9in (23cm) high.
0-700 *CSK*

A French cast iron bulb planter in Louis XV style, c1875, 16½in (42cm) wide.
£150-200 *UC*

lead fountain figure, with urn
nder her arm incorporating the
pout, on circular base and stone
linth, 19thC, 47½in (120.5cm)
igh.
2,000-2,500 *C*

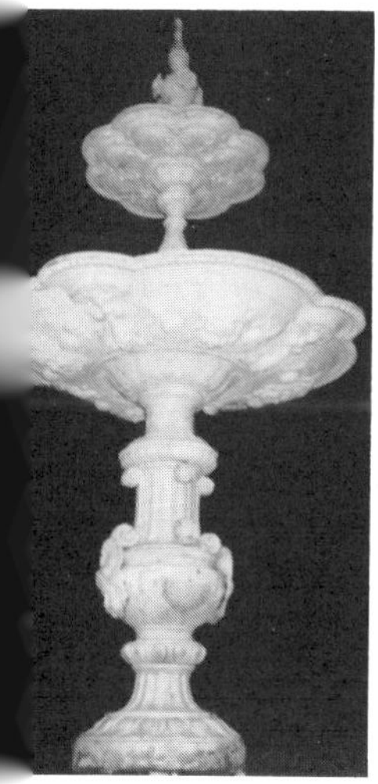

A cast iron fountain, with central baluster column support, the foliate capped spout above flowerhead motifs, the undersides cast with cherubs and foliate motifs, 19thC, 83in (211cm) high.
£2,500-3,000 *C*

A composition fountain, c1850, 62in (157cm) high.
£4,000-4,500 *HUN*

A bronze fountain modelled as a carp, with arched back, resting on its fins, 20thC, 59in (150cm) long.
£2,000-2,500 *C*

A stone carved fountain, 78i (198cm) high.
£4,500-5,000 *WRe*

An Italian stone fountain in the shape of a lion's mask, 20in (51cm) high.
£1,000-1,500 *WRe*

A cast iron fountain of a putto holding a fish, standing on 3 white painted shells on a shaft in the shape of 3 dolphins, on white painted hexagonal shaped base, 19thC, 49½in (126cm) high.
£2,500-3,000 *CAm*

A set of 10 sandstone garden gnomes, 18thC, 25in (64cm) high.
£4,000-4,500 *HUN*

A lead fountain figure, formed as figure of Cupid, holding a fish, w spout, standing on domed octago base, 25½in (65cm) high.
£750-800 *C*

A Vicenza limestone fountain, possibly 20thC, 62in (157cm) high.
£5,500-6,000 *HUN*

A Regency stone sundial, 38in (96.5cm) high.
£3,000-3,500 *DRU*

A composition boar, c1850, 42in (106.5cm) high.
£5,000-5,200 *HUN*

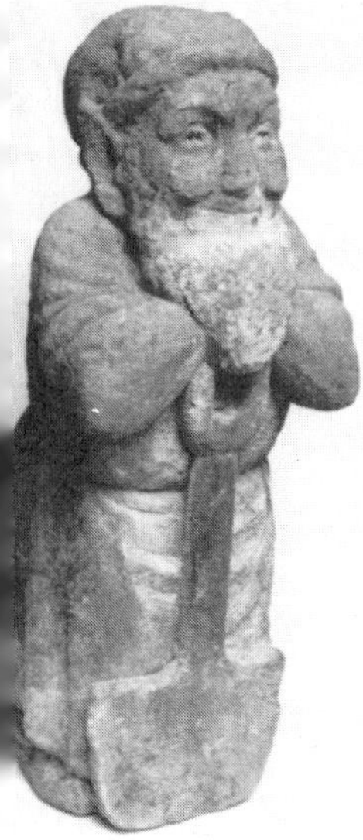

carved sandstone gnome, 'Welsh warf', 26in (66cm) high.
00-900 *WRe*

A pair of composition lions, c1860, 36in (92cm) wide.
£1,400-1,500 *HUN*

A pair of Jacobean sandstone caryatid statues of Summer and Autumn, both standing scantily draped, holding fruit and foliage, 37½in (95cm).
£2,000-3,000 *C*

These are 2 of a set of 17thC figures representing the Four Seasons, which stood on top of No. 42 Northbrook Street, Newbury, until the 1950s. The other 2 figures were destroyed on their removal from the house.

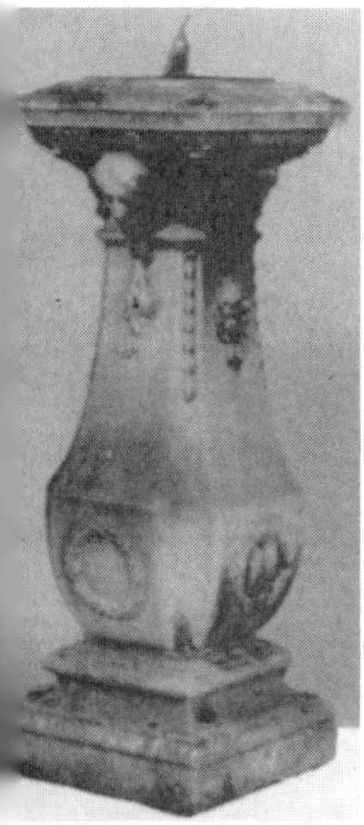

tone sundial, with masks icting The Four Seasons, hung h fruits, with bell husks at the gles, and wreath roundels below, square stepped base, with square nze sundial with inscription, the mon cast as a dolphin, late hC/early 19thC, 51in (129cm) h.
000-3,500 *C*

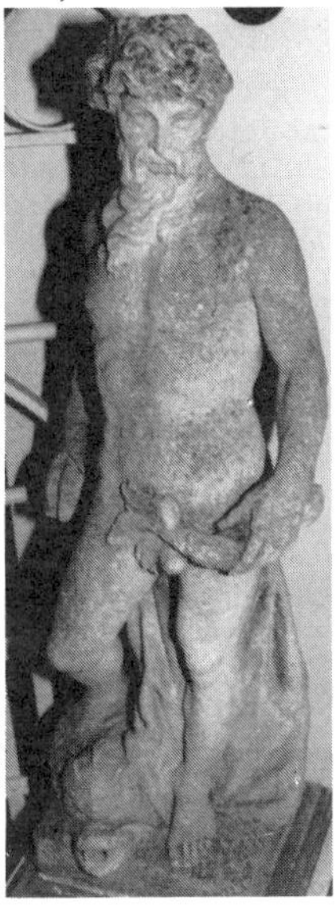

An Italian stone fountain of a sea god, 45in (114cm) high.
£1,500-2,000 *WRe*

A stone statue of a soldier with sword, 90in (228.5cm) high.
£2,500-3,000 *WRe*

one statue of a scholar, (228.5cm) high.
500-3,000 *WRe*

An Italian stone figure, 64in (162.5cm) high.
£2,500-3,000 *WRe*

A bronze fountain, the shaft with 3 addorsed musical putti, on gadrooned cylindrical spreading base, 20thC, 65½in (166.5cm) high.
£3,000-5,000 *C*

A terracotta stoneware figure of Samuel Viscount Hood, 43in (109cm) high.
£600-650 *DRU*

A terracotta group of 3 playing putti, on a cylindrical plinth decorated with a garland of foliage and flowerheads, 19thC, 85in (216cm) high.
£5,500-6,000 *CAm*

A lead figure of Mercury standin on a sphere, after Giambologna, 43½in (110cm) high.
£700-800 *CAm*

A stone statue, 80in (203cm) high.
£2,000-2,500 *WRe*

A sandstone figure of a nude boy, leaning against a ledge, the neck restored, 36in (92cm) high.
£550-600 *CAm*

A Scottish limestone sundial, c1840, 68in (172.5cm) high.
£11,000-12,000 *HUN*

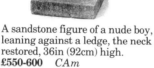

A lead figure of a heraldic lion, seated on its haunches, supporting a cabochon, on square base with cut corners, 17½in (44.5cm) high.
£200-250 *C*

A pair of sandstone figures of recumbent lions, on rock shape bases, 19thC, 36½in (93cm) hig
£2,000-2,500 *CAm*

A cast bronze fountain, in the for of a winged putti holding a dolph with a water spout in its mouth, marble plinth, 30in (76cm) high.
£700-750 *Bon*

A lead figure of a boy gardener, in the style of John Cheere, on stepped base, late 18th/early 19thC, 53in (134.5cm) high.
£2,000-3,000 *C*

A pair of stone eagles, reconstituted stone.
£700-900 *DRU*

. lead figure of a hawk, the head to exter, on a rock shaped base, 25in 4cm).
1,000-1,500 *CAm*

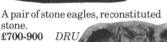

A lead statue of Pluto.
£800-900 *WRe*

A lead dwarf, c1800, 40in (101.5cm) high.
£650-800 *HUN*

A pair of lead lion masks, 10in (25cm) high.
£450-500 *C*

An Irish marble font, 18thC.
£4,000-4,500 *HUN*

ı alabaster font, with 8 columns low surrounding a central pport, on octagonal foot, one face th the Holy monogram in a ıciform shape, the alabaster ıcked and with some losses, thC, 40in (101.5cm) high.
00-800 *CSK*

Victorian lead figure, 26in (66cm) gh.
00-900 *WRe*

A lead cistern, dated 1883, 67½in (171cm) wide.
£3,000-3,500 *HUN*

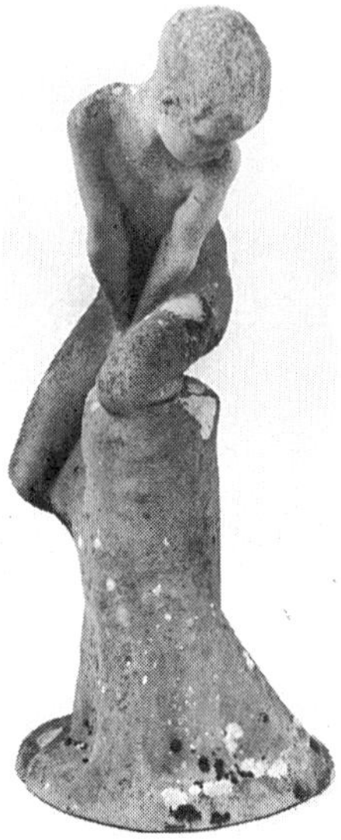

A stone figure of a boy, 38in (96cm) high.
£500-600 *Bon*

A lead cistern, moulded with rosettes and a tap on the bottom, early 19thC, 22in (56cm) wide.
£800-1,200 *Bon*

A terracotta Herm statue of winter, damaged, 18th/19thC, 180in (457cm) high.
£1,500-2,000 *C*

A group of 3 composition putti, o limestone base, c1840, 88in (223.5cm) high.
£7,500-8,000 *HUN*

A sandstone bird bath, the top with fluted frieze, on a spiral fluted column carved with bumble bees, and an oak leaf carved capital, with a faceted square plinth, 23in (58cm) wide.
£1,500-2,000 *Bon*

A sandstone figure of a female, the body partly shrouded in drapery, the right hand holding a cornucopia with corn, a smiling putto at her feet, 19thC, 67in (170cm) high.
£8,000-9,000 *CAm*

A pair of rustic planters, with frog in bird bath base, c1880, 32in (81cm) high.
£700-800 *HUN*

A brass and metal étagère, c184 36in (92cm) high.
£400-500 *HUN*

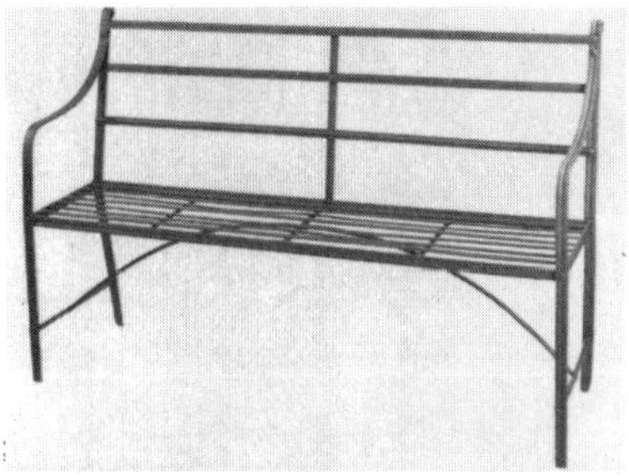

A reeded wrought iron garden seat, with down curved armrests and straight feet, the supports joined by a curved stretcher, early 19thC, 60½in (133cm) wide.
£600-1,000 *C*

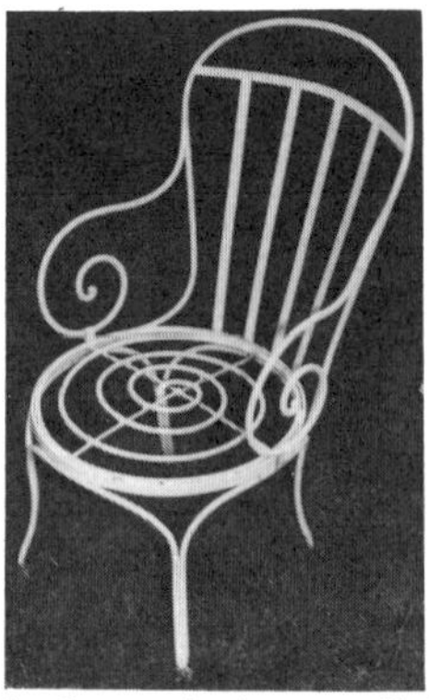

A pair of wrought iron scrolled design armchairs, 37in (94cm) high.
£400-450 *HUN*

A cast iron Coalbrookdale garden bench, sweet chestnut design, c1865, 73½in (186cm) wide.
£2,500-2,800 *HUN*

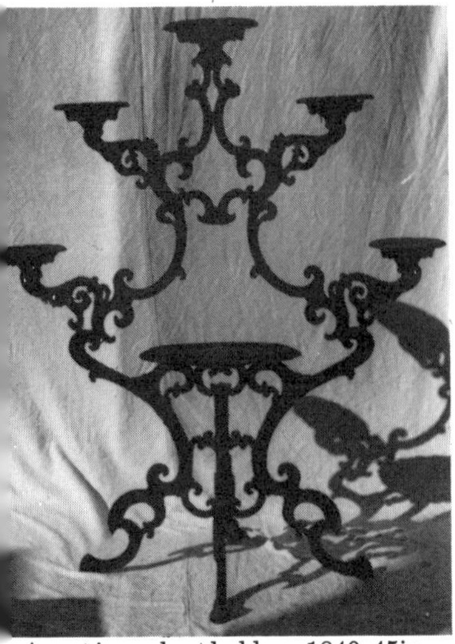

A cast iron plant holder, c1840, 45in (114cm) high.
£400-500 *HUN*

A pair of giltwood plant stands, with caned baskets decorated with laurel garlands, on cabriole legs carved with stylised foliage, 40in (101cm) high.
£2,500-3,000 *CAm*

A pair of wrought iron basket plant stands, 34in (86cm) high.
£650-700 *HUN*

A pair of Coalbrookdale garden seats, with Victorian registration mark, 44½in (113cm) wide.
£5,000-6,000 *C*

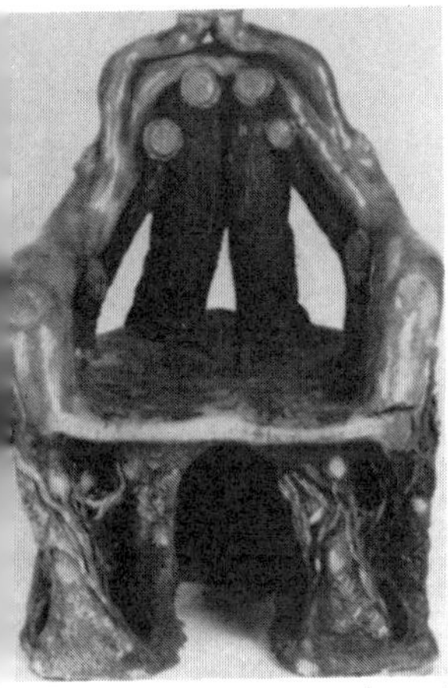

wo glazed stoneware rustic seats, ith pierced arched branch backs ıd arms, on tree stump seats, one amped Hurlford, Fireclay Works, ilmarnock.
,700-2,000 *C*

A set of 4 cast iron garden chairs, :1880, 32½in (82cm) high.
£1,800-2,000 *HUN*

white painted cast iron garden at, the pierced bowed back cast ith fern leaves on naturalistic ıpports, with later wooden slatted at, 45in (114cm) wide.
300-400 *Bon*

A cast iron chair, the pierced and cast back decorated with foliate scrolls, above oval drop-in seat and foliate scrolled legs with cross stretchers, mid-19thC.
£400-500 *C*

A pair of sandstone planters, 24in (62cm) high.
£1,500-1,800 *HUN*

A German parcel gilt and white painted cast iron garden seat, in the manner of Schinkel, the pierced toprail with twin lyres and scrolling winged putti, with re-railed seat and ram's mask and iron supports on chanelled X-frame legs and hoof feet, early 19thC, redecorated, 41in (104cm) wide.
£5,000-6,000 *C*

A cast iron garden table, with dolphin tripod, 28in (71cm) high.
£300-350 *HUN*

A white painted cast iron garden seat, the arched pierced back cast with foliate scrolls and rustic motifs, on down curved arm rests, wooden slatted seat and scroll feet, 49in (125cm).
£600-800 *C*

A pair of wrought iron gates, c1830, 62½in (158cm) high.
£600-650 *HUN*

A suite of rustic garden furniture, stamped J Hayward Phoenix Foundry Derby, c1850, bench 49in (124.5cm) wide.
Two chairs. **£1,400-1,600**
Two benches. **£2,400-2,600** *HUN*

A white marble garden bench, the moulded top with scrolled frieze centred by grotesque mask, on addorsed lion mask monopodia end supports and rectangular bases, 55in (139.5cm) wide.
£4,000-4,500 *C*

A Regency reeded wrought iron garden seat, c1790, 70½in (178cm) wide.
£7,300-7,500 *HUN*

A pair of wrought-iron sprung garden seats, and a matching armchair, 32in (81cm) high.
Armchair: **£200-250**
Pair of chairs: **£200-250**
HUN

A garden table, with marble top and cast iron base, c1850, 27in (69cm) high.
£500-550 *HUN*

Miscellaneous

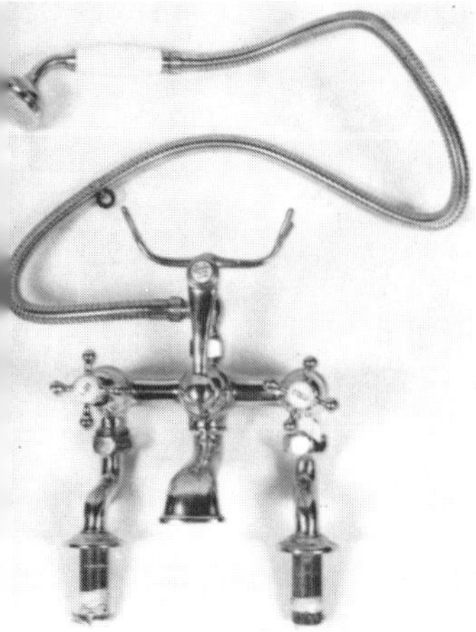

A brass shower unit, 14in (36cm).
£200-250 *DRU*

A pair of brass taps, 7½in (19cm).
£40-50 *DRU*

A canopy bath, restored and stove enamelled, c1902.
£5,500-7,500 *DRU*

A stone glazed bath with original paint and ledge feet. **£450-500** *WEL*

A cast and wrought iron window, complete with original glass, 18thC.
£45-60 *WEL*

A carved oak door, in need of some restoration, 80in (203cm) high.
£700-800 Restored *DRU*

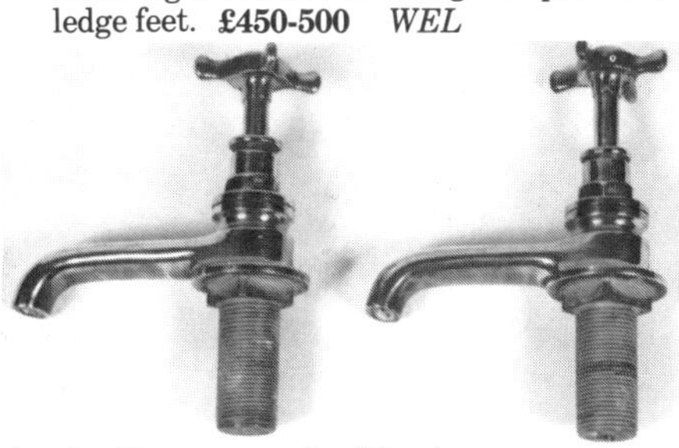

A pair of brass taps, 8in (20cm).
£70-85 *DRU*

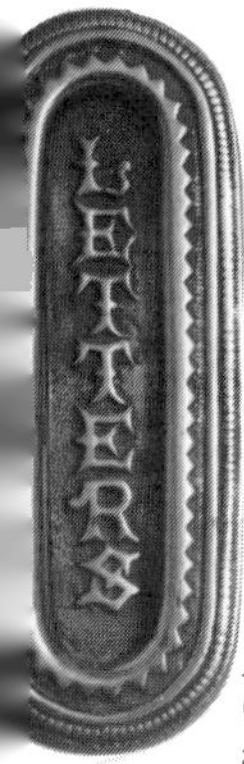
LETTERS

A small brass letter box cover, 6in (15cm).
£15-20 *WRe*

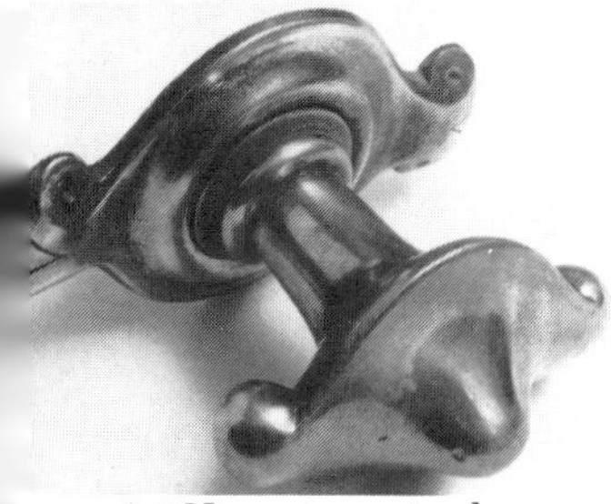

brass Art Nouveau centre door
5in (13cm). **£60-70** *WRe*

pair of nickel taps, 8in (20cm).
0-80 *DRU*

LETTERS

A brass letter box, 6½in (16cm).
£20-30 *WRe*

An iron letter plate knocker, in the form of a bull's head, 11in (28cm) wide.
£140-170 *DRU*

A small brass letter box cover, 6[…] (15cm).
£15-20 *WRe*

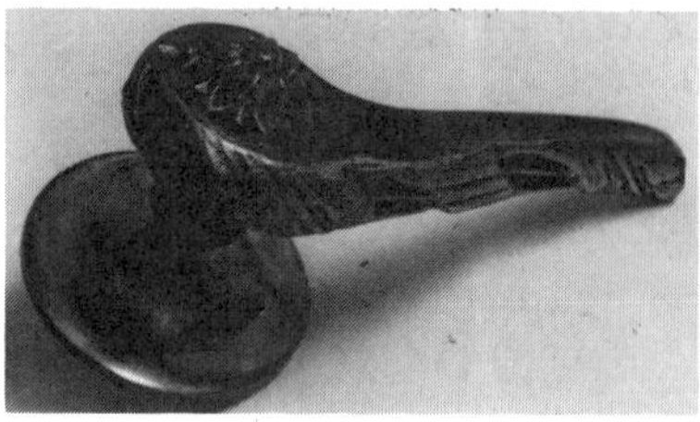

A brass door handle.
£45-55 *WRe*

A china washbasin with brackets and brass taps.
£225-250 *DRU*

A solid copper lion door knocker, 5in (13cm).
£80-100 *WRe*

A brass lion's head bell pull, 4[…] (11cm).
£90-120 *WRe*

A cast iron door handle.
£20-30 *WRe*

A brass door handle, 3in (8cm).
£20-40 *WRe*

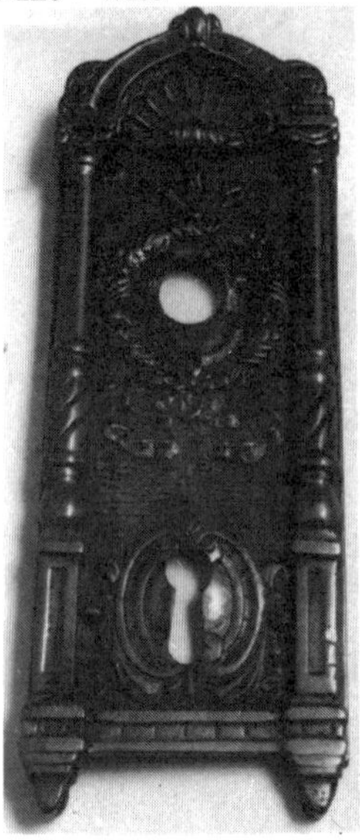

A brass keyhole cover and doo[…] plate, 7½in (19cm).
£30-40 *WRe*

A pair of brass door pulls, 8in (20cm).
£60-80 *WRe*

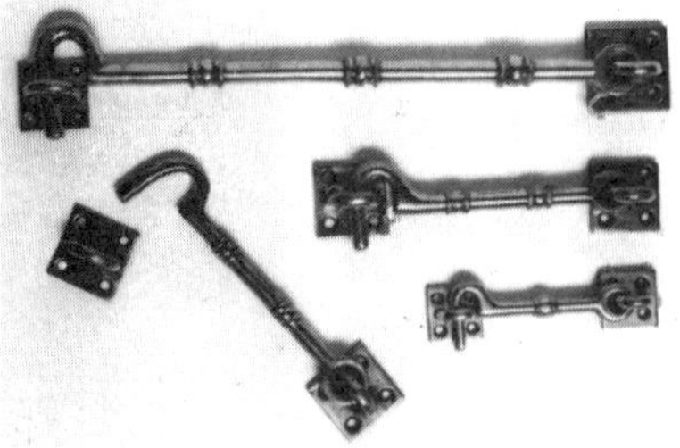

Four brass door hooks, 3 to 13in (8 to 33cm).
£10-20 each *WRe*

A brass door latch, 11in (28cm).
£70-90 *WRe*

Two oak locks.
£10-20 each *WEL*

A pair of brass and turned wooden handles, 14in (36cm).
£70-80 *DRU*

A pair of copper door handles, 3in (8cm).
£20-35 *WRe*

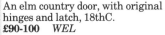

A brass bell pull, with face of Christ.
£60-70 *WRe*

A set of hand painted door furniture.
£10-15 *DRU*

A brass and copper door knocker letterbox, 10in (25cm).
£60-80 *WRe*

A set of brass door knobs, finger plates and escutcheons.
£35-40 *WRe*

A brass fox door knocker, 6in (15cm).
£40-60 *WRe*

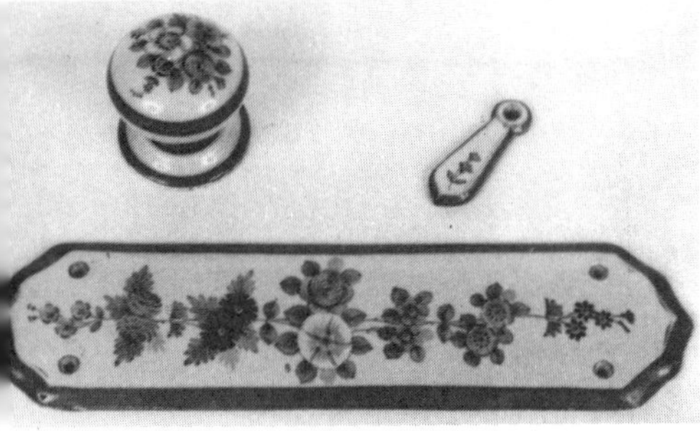

A set of Continental hand painted door furniture, c1900.
£50-70 *THA*

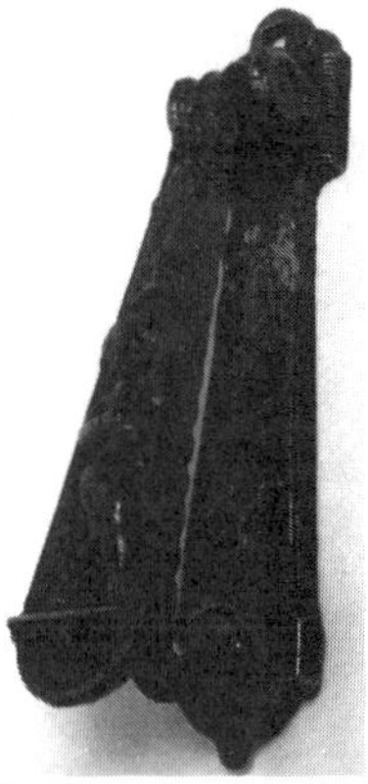

A cast iron door knocker, 9in (23cm).
£70-100 *WRe*

An elm country door, with original hinges and latch, 18thC.
£90-100 *WEL*

A ceramic and brass door handle.
£20-40 *WRe*

›rass bell pull, 6in (15cm).
5-85 *WRe*

A brass door bell pull on marble, 10in (25cm).
£90-120 *WRe*

A pair of ceramic bell pushes, 3in (8cm).
£50-60 *WRe*

A cast iron door knocker, 9in (23cm).
£40-60 *WRe*

A brass door knocker, 7in (18cm).
£90-120 *WRe*

A pair of large brass door knockers, 12in (31cm).
£100-140 *WRe*

A metal door knocker, 6i (15cm).
£35-45 *DRU*

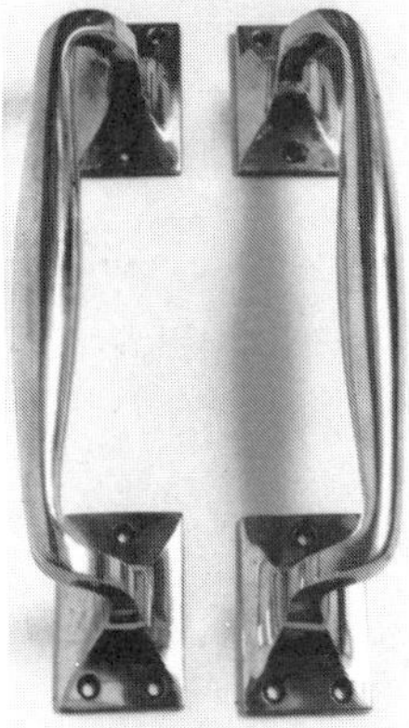

A pair of brass door pulls, 9in (23cm).
£30-50 *WRe*

A pair of brass door plates, 8 and 12in (20 and 30.5cm).
£10-20 each *DRU*

A pair of ceramic and brass bell pulls, 6in (15cm).
£60-90 *WRe*

A large brass door handle, 5i (13cm).
£100-150 *WRe*

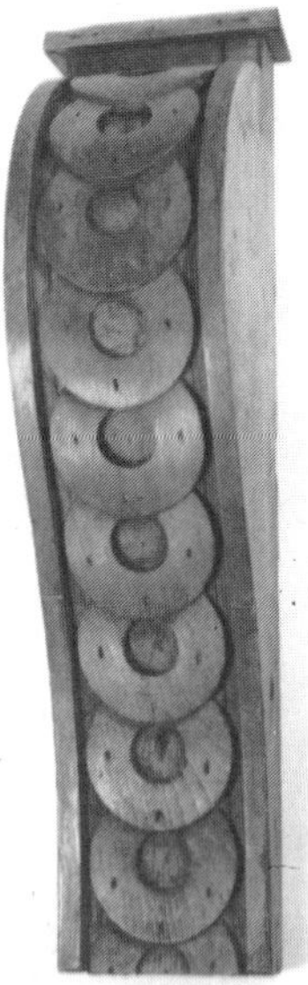

A pair of pine corbels, 9in (23cm).
£50-70 *ARC*

French stained glass church windows, St Corentin and St Edouard, 120in (304.5cm) high.
£2,000-2,500 each *ARC*

EDOUARD

LOUIS

French stained glass windows by G P Dagrant of Bordeaux, c1900, Joan of Arc, St Michel, St Louis, 43in (109cm) high.
£2,000-2,500 each *ARC*

A set of 11 mahogany corbels, 10in (25cm).
£350-400 *ARC*

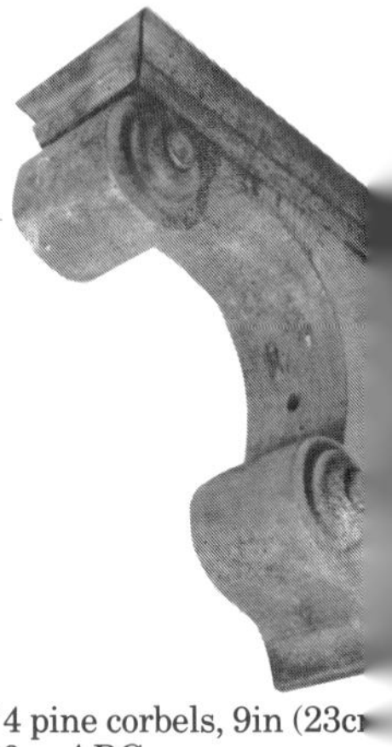

A set of 4 pine corbels, 9in (23c
£100-120 *ARC*

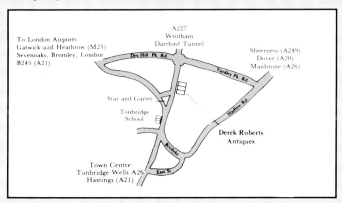

A George III flame mahogany Lancashire longcase clock, signed Henry Fisher, Preston, 101in (257cm) high.
£6,000-8,000
CNY

A George III mahogany longcase clock, signed Peter Fearnley, Wigan, 96in (244cm) high.
£8,000-10,000
C

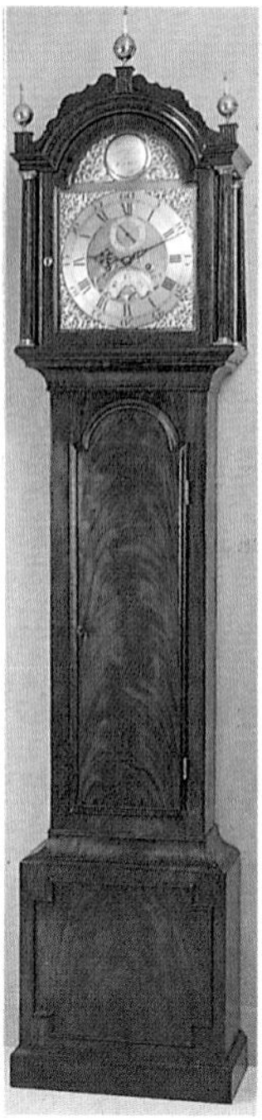

A mahogany 8-day longcase clock, by Wm. Hornsey, Exon, with a large date aperture, c1790.
£6,000-8,000
DRA

An 8-day longcase clock, east coast of Scotland, signed in the arch by John Memess Johnshaven, c1775, 87in (221cm) high.
£6,000-8,000
DRA

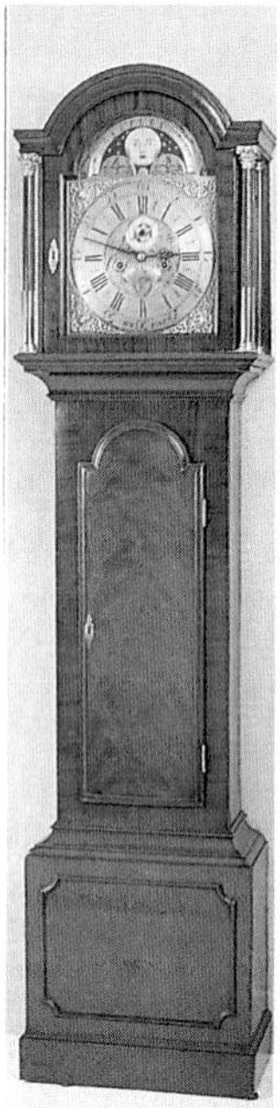

A small mahogany 8-day longcase clock, signed Dolly Rollisson of Halton, c1785, and numbered 479, 78in (198cm) high.
£6,000-8,000
DRA

An 8-day mahogany longcase cloc signed by Samuel Shep of Stockport, c1780, 82in (208cm) high
£7,000-9,000
DRA

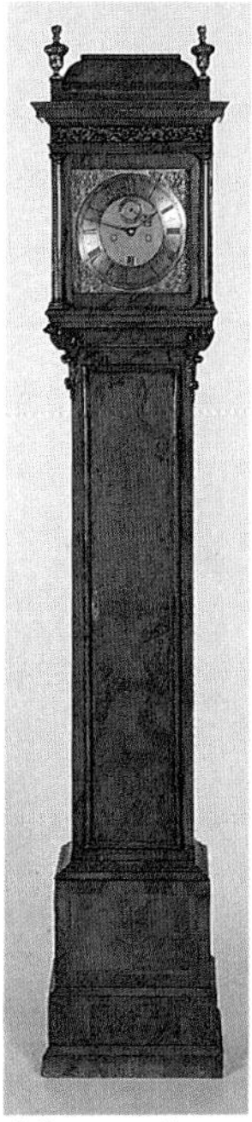

A burr walnut Queen Anne longcase clock, by Tho. Tompion, 92in (234cm) high.
£25,000-30,000
C

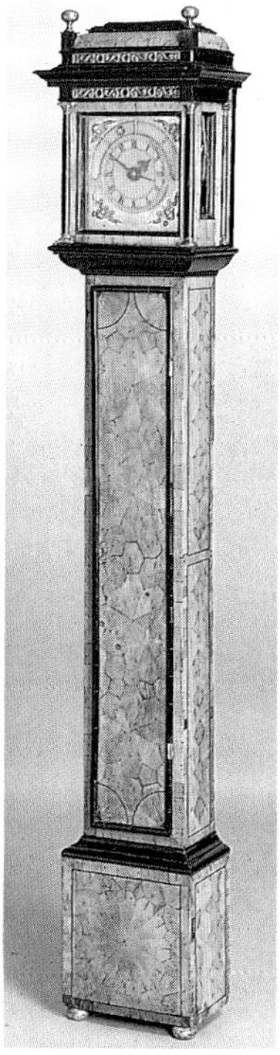

A boxwood and ebony parquetry, longcase clock, by Tho. Tompion, c1679, 73in high.
£800,000+ *C*

A Federal inlaid mahogany longcase clock, signed by Andrew Billings, New York, c1805, some repairs and minor in-painting to dial.
£9,000-11,000
CNY

A Federal inlaid cherrywood longcase clock, dial signed Caleb Davis, Virginia, with restored feet, dial chipped, c1804.
£5,000-7,500
CNY

A Chippendale mahogany longcase clock, by Thomas Harland, Connecticut, c1780, 92in (234cm) high.
£4,500-6,000
CNY

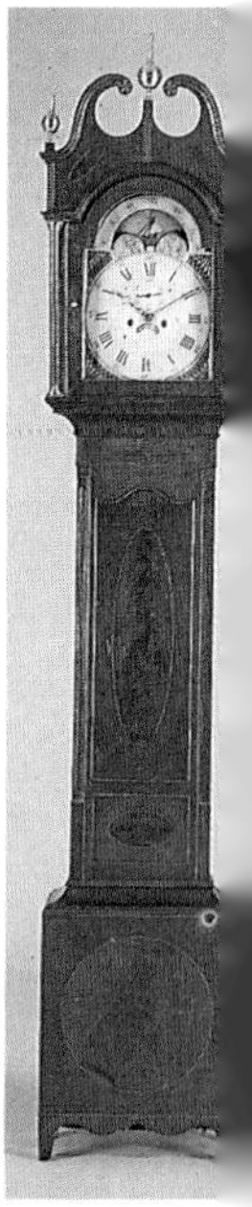

A Federal mahogany longcase clo signed by Joakim Hill New Jersey c1805, 101ir (256cm) hig
£10,000-15,
CNY

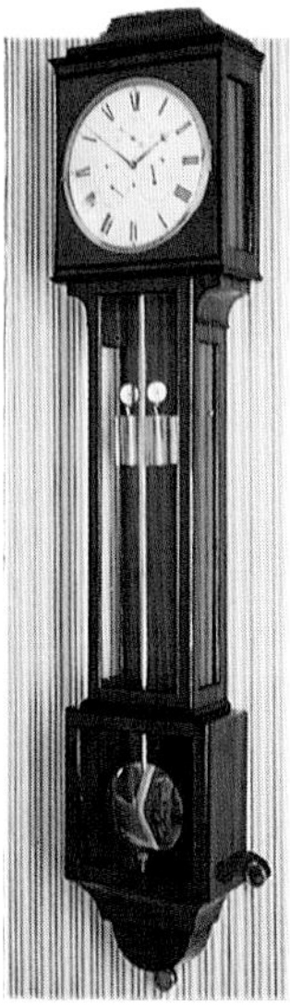

A striking Viennese regulator, by Brandl in Wien, c1811, 57in (144.5cm) high.
£30,000-40,000 *GeC*

Three Viennese regulators, c1835,
l. **£4,000-5,000,** r. **£20,000-25,000** *GeC*
c. **£2,500-3,500,**

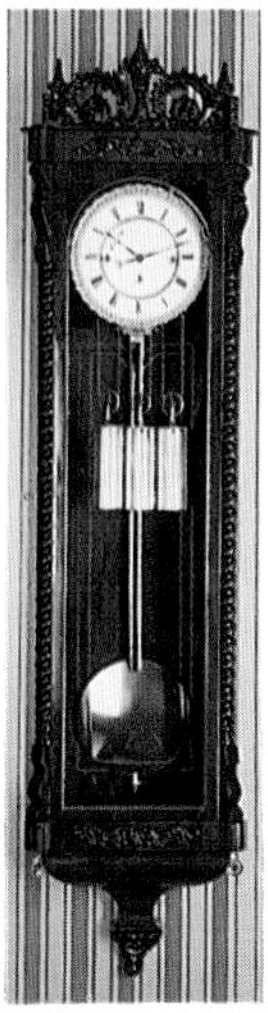

l. A Viennese grande sonnerie striking regulator, c1850, 50in high. **£5,500-6,500** *GeC*

l. A George IV longcase regulator, by Brownbill, Liverpool.
£10,000-12,000

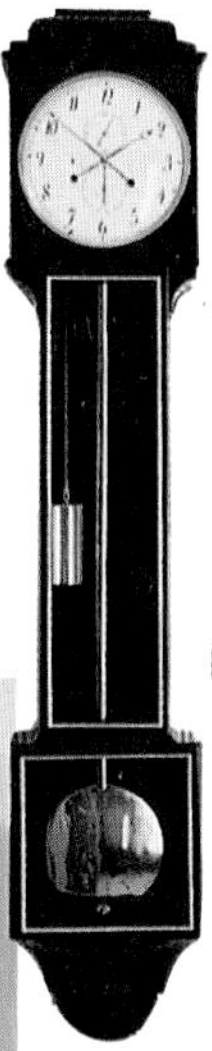

r. A Viennese regulator, by Brandl in Wien, c1811, 57in (144.5cm) long.
£25,000-30,000 *GeC*

r. A Charles II month-going longcase clock, some alteration, 84in (213cm).
£12,000-15,000 *C*

A panelled marquetry longcase clock, with 8-day count wheel striking movement with latched pillars, by Wm. Garfoot, c1690.
£20,000-25,000 *CLC*

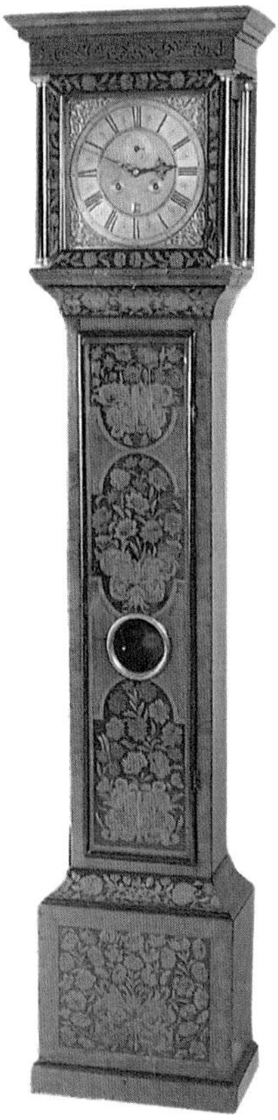

A walnut and panelled floral marquetry longcase clock, by Stephen Asselin, c1705, 85in (216cm) high.
£14,000-18,000 *DRA*

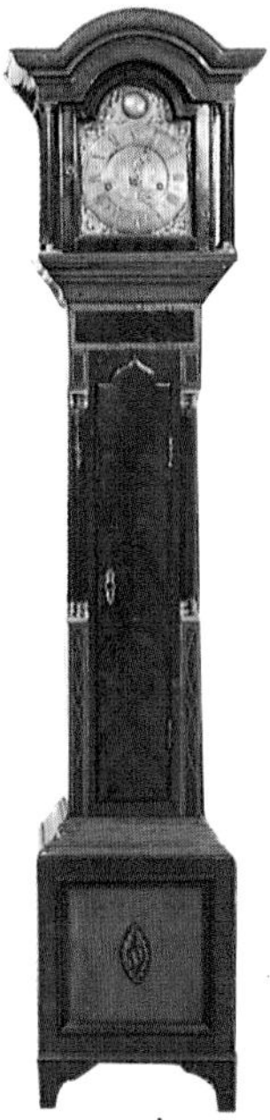

An oak longcase clock by William Wall, Richmond, late 18thC. **£2,500-3,500** *CLC*
Above r. A grandmother clock by John Carter of London, 1775, 69½in (176cm). **£9,500-10,500** *AH*
r. A longcase clock by Robert Dingley of London, late 17thC, 81in (205.5cm). **£6,000-7,000** *AH*

Rochester Fine Arts

Specialists in Fine Clocks, Furniture and Objets d'Art

88 High Street, Rochester, Kent ME1 1JT.

Telephone: (0634) 814129

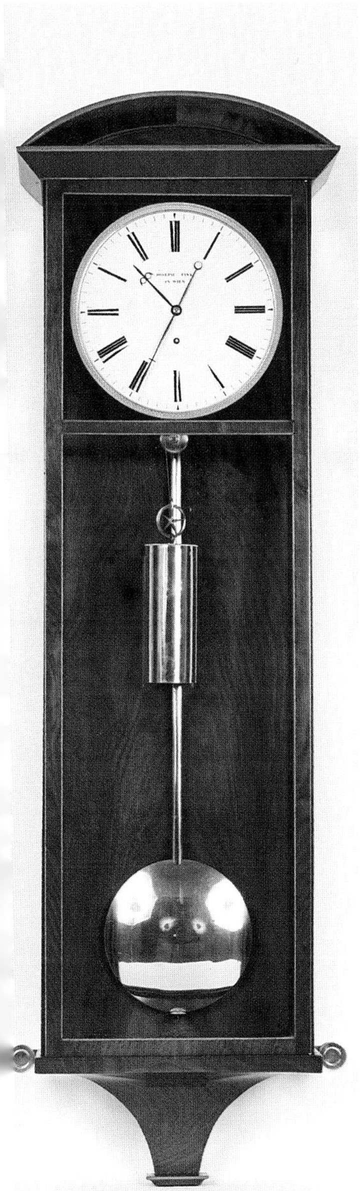

Finest quality walnut Vienna Regulator of month duration by Joseph Fink. Superb original condition circa 1830.

Superb musical Bracket Clock by Ellicott, playing one of eight tunes every third hour circa 1770.

Sublime and ridiculous horological artifacts, furniture, paintings and objets d'art

We specialize in early, precision, long duration or just plain interesting clocks, etc.

"We buy, price no object. We sell fine things of any subject."

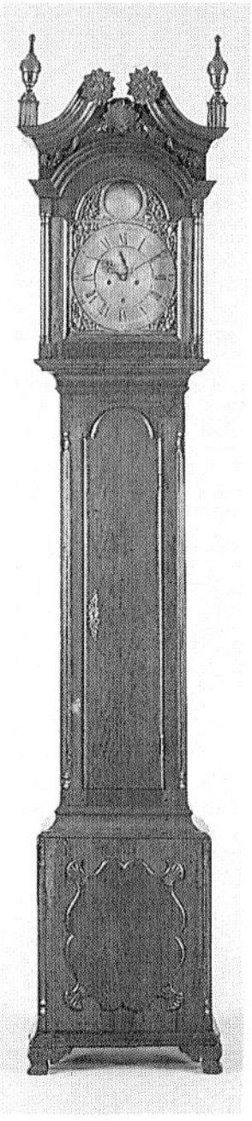

A Chippendale carved cherry-wood longcase clock, c1770, restorations.
£15-18,000 *CNY*

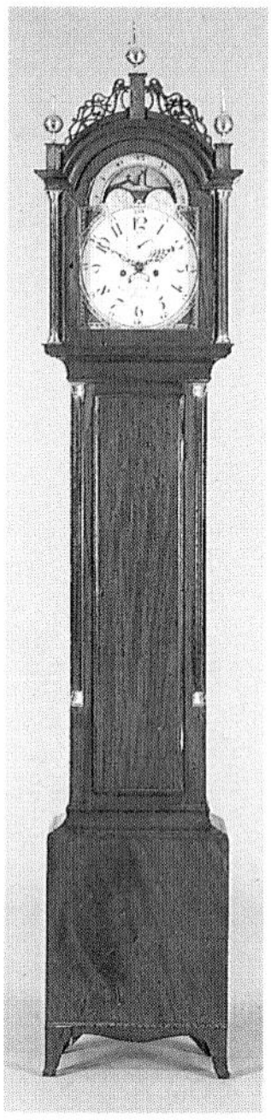

A Federal inlaid mahogany long-case clock, by Aaron Willard Jr., Boston, c1805, 100½in (255cm).
£15-18,000 *CNY*

A Federal inlaid mahogany long-case clock, by Aaron Willard Jr., Boston, slight damage, restored, c1805, 91in (231cm).
£28-30,000 *CNY*

A Federal inlaid mahogany long-case clock by Simon Willard, Roxbury, Mass., c1810, 92in (233.5cm) high.
£35-40,000 *CNY*

A Dutch burr walnut longcase clock with planisphere, slight damage, mid-18thC, 116in (294.5cm).
£40-45,000 *CNY*

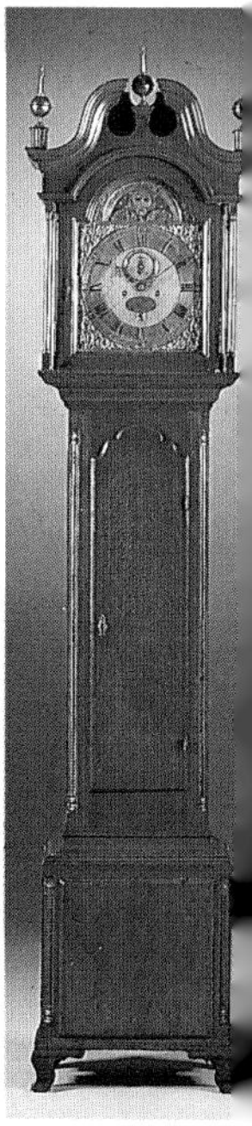

A Chippendal carved mahog longcase clock by John Wood Philadelphia, paint heighter on lunar dial, c1770, 96in (243.5cm) higl
£12-15,000 *C*

A Scandinavian longcase clock dated 1811.
£1,500-2,000 *RYA*

A Regency bronze and ormolu mounted clock, by George Bullock, 16in (40cm) high.
£14,000-16,000 *C*

Above. A Regency mantel clock by Vulliamy, in later case, inscribed Vulliamy, London 863, 16in (41cm) high.
£2,000-2,500 *C*

A Louis XV ormolu mantel clock, signed Charles Voisin à Paris, mid-18thC, 15½in (40cm) high.
£15,000-20,000 *C*

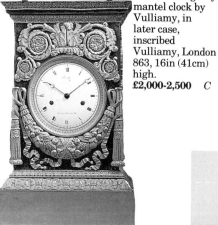

An Empire mantel clock, c1810. **£8,000-10,000** *CNY*
l. An Empire mantel clock, signed Knab à Paris, 22in (56cm) wide.
£6,000-10,000 *C*
r. A Louis XVI mantel clock, 14½in (37cm) high. **£10,000-15,000** *C*

George III musical
:acket clock.
,000-9,000 *C*

A late George III
mahogany and ebony
quarter chiming
and Dutch hour
striking calendar
equation bracket
clock.
£5,000-8,000 *C*

A Louis XIV
cartel clock,
17½in (44cm) high.
£5,000-8,000 *C*

A French gilt metal
mantel clock, late 19thC,
20in (51cm) high.
£300-400 *SWO*

Neuchatel musical calendar
acket clock.
2,000-14,000 *C*

A Dutch ebony veneered
striking bracket clock,
15½in (39cm) high.
£6,000-8,000 *C*

r. A Louis XV bracket
clock and bracket,
signed Gudin À Paris.
£3,000-4,500 *CNY*

An early Louis XV
bracket clock.
£4,000-6,000 *C*

Far l. A Charles II
longcase clock.
£11,000-14,000 *C*

l. A panelled
marquetry long-
case clock.
£17,000-20,000 *CLC*

A Règence bracket
clock, G. I. Champion.
£10,000-15,000 *C*

l. A Louis XV
bracket clock.
£5,000-7,000 *C*

A George III ebonised striking bracket clock, signed, 17in (43cm) high.
£4,500-5,000 *C*

A fusee bracket clock, early 19thC.
£3,000-3,500 *CLC*

l. A Regency mahogany brack clock, the dial inscribed Wasbrough Hale and Co., Bristol.
£1,000-1,500 *SW*

r. An Edwardian oak mantel clock, 3 train movement with Westminster chimes on 8 bells and gong, 25in (64cm) high.
£1,000-1,500 *SWO*

A George III mahogany striking bracket clock, 19½in (50cm) high.
£3,500-4,000 *C*

A George III scarlet japanned musical bracket clock, by Wm. Kipling, London, 25in (64cm) high.
£28,000-32,000 *C*

A Charles II ebony striking bracket clock, by Joseph Knibb, London, signed, restored, 15in (38.5cm) high. **£15,000-20,000** *C*

A Charles II ebony bracket clock by Joseph Knibb, London, signed, escapement rebuilt, 11½in (29cm) high.
£18,000-20,000 *C*

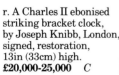

r. A Charles II ebonised striking bracket clock, by Joseph Knibb, London, signed, restoration, 13in (33cm) high.
£20,000-25,000 *C*

A George III tortoiseshell musical bracket clock by Markwick Markh London, 13in (33cm) high.
£15,000-20,000 *C*

A Regency mantel clock by Vulliamy, marked, 9½in (24cm). **£4,000-5,000** *C*

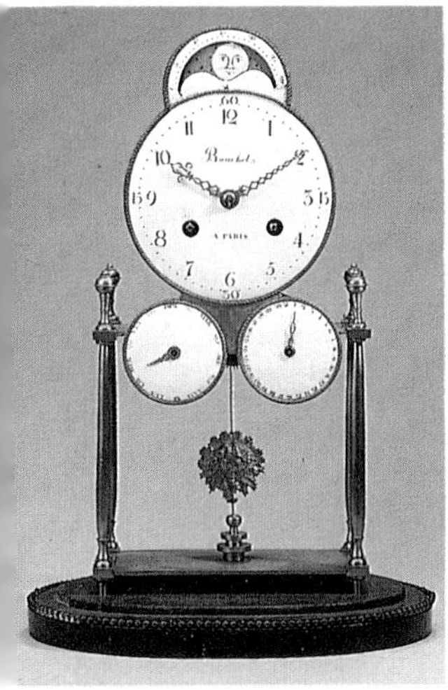

Louis XVI calendar clock, igned Bouchet à Paris. **4,500-5,000** *CNY*

A Napoleon III ormolu and bronze mantel clock, the movement within a blue enamelled globe, 23in (58.5cm). **£2,000-2,500** *C*

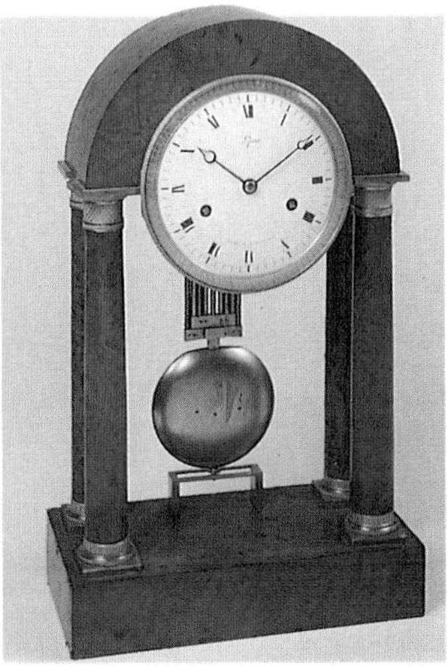

An Empire ormolu mounted burr elm portico clock, dial and backplate signed, 18in (46cm). **£2,500-3,000** *C*

l. A George II giltwood cartel clock, the dial signed, later movement, cover and eagle, 34½in (88cm) high. **£2,000-2,500** *C*

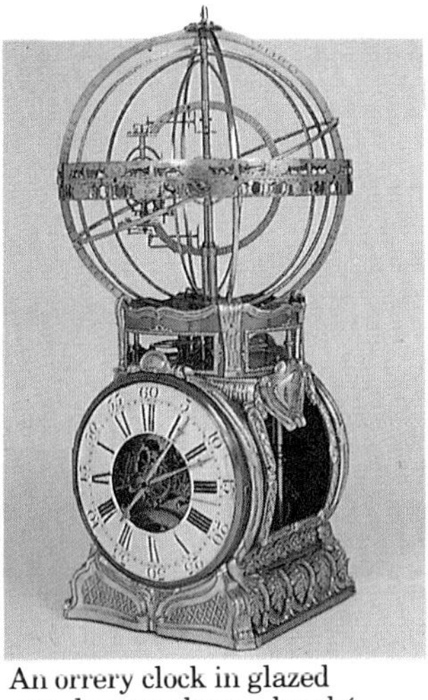

An orrery clock in glazed ormolu case above a bombé kingwood stand, c1770, 95in (241cm) high overall. **£600,000+** *C*

l. An 'Around the World' clock. **£650-750** *SBA*

A Louis Philippe portico mantel clock, signed Hry Marc À Paris, 17in (43cm) high. **£2,000-2,500** *C*

A French 'swinging clock', the dial signed Breguet et Fils, 22½in (57cm) high. **£8,500-9,000** *DRA*

An automaton magician in giltwood case below clock, 33in (84cm) high. **£4,500-5,500** *CSK*

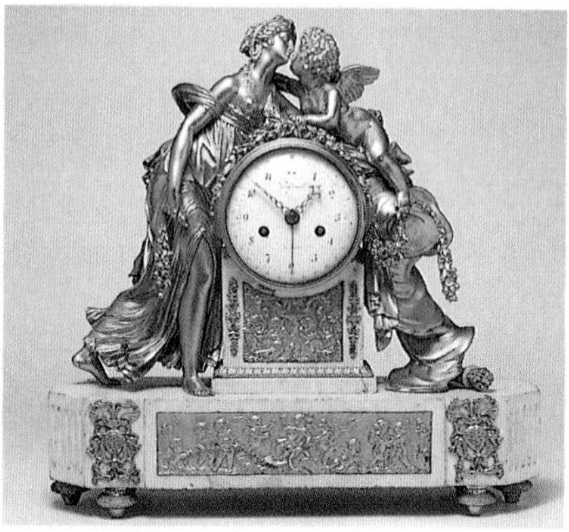

A Louis XVI ormolu and white marble clock, the dial signed, re-gilded. **£3,000-5,000** *C*

r. A Louis XVI ormolu mounted porcelain mantel clock, the porcelain French, 19thC, 17½in (44.5cm) high.
£40,000-45,000 *C*

A French spelter figural clock, 22½in (57cm).
£350-450 *JL*

A Charles X ormolu and bronze mantel clock, 1827, 26½in (68cm) high.
£2,000-3,000 *C*
r. A Napoleon III ormolu mantel clock, 21in (53cm).
£2,000-3,000 *C*

An ormolu mounted and Chinese porcelain mantel clock, 19thC, later movement. **£3,500-4,500** *C*

An ormolu and marble mantel clock, with restorations, early 19thC, 18½in (47cm) high.
£1,200-1,500 *C*

A neo-classical urn clock, 19thC, 23in (59cm) high.
£18,000-20,000 *C*

An ormolu bronze table clock of Louis XVI design, 30in (76c
£3,500-4,000 *C*
l. A French ormolu an bronze matched clock garniture, mid-19thC the clock 16in (41cm).
£5,500-6,500 *C*

A Louis XVI ormolu urn clock, the pedestal inset with marble, 16in (41cm) high.
£20,000-25,000 *C*

n enamelled gold keyless
ıronograph with perpetual
ılendar, signed J.W.
enson, London, No. 25069,
381, 5.5cm diam.
0,000-45,000 *CNY*

A gold pair case
quarter repeating watch,
1773, later dial, 5cm.
£4,500-6,500 *CNY*
l. A minute repeating,
full calendar keyless
hunter pocket watch,
small chips to enamel.
£5,000-10,000 *CSK*

presentation gold hunter
sed 5-minute repeating
ronograph, 5.5cm.
,500-7,500 *CNY*

A gold minute
repeating watch, signed
Patek Philippe, 1888.
£70,000-75,000 *CNY*
l. A Swiss gold hunter
chronograph, c1880.
£20,000-25,000 *CNY*

. enamelled half
nter gem set watch.
0,000-12,000 *CNY*
\ pendant watch and
ıin by Patek Philippe.
500-3,000 *CNY*

JULES JÜRGENSEN
Watch maker
Chronometer and
JULES JÜRGENSEN

l. An enamelled world
time watch, signed Patek
Philippe & Co.
£43,000-48,000 *CNY*
r. A presentation set of
chronograph and small
minute repeating watch.
£28,000-30,000 *CNY*

A rare early gold chronograph, by Patek Philippe, Genève, No. 860358, 18ct gold case, inscribed 1938. **£20,000-25,000** *CNY*

Three circular wristwatches, one in 14ct gold case, the others gold filled, all signed Otto K. Kramer, Chicago. **£400-500** *CNY*

An 18ct gold wrist chronograph with perpetual calendar, by Patek Philippe Genève, No. 863678 18ct strap, c1945. **£70,000-90,000** *C*

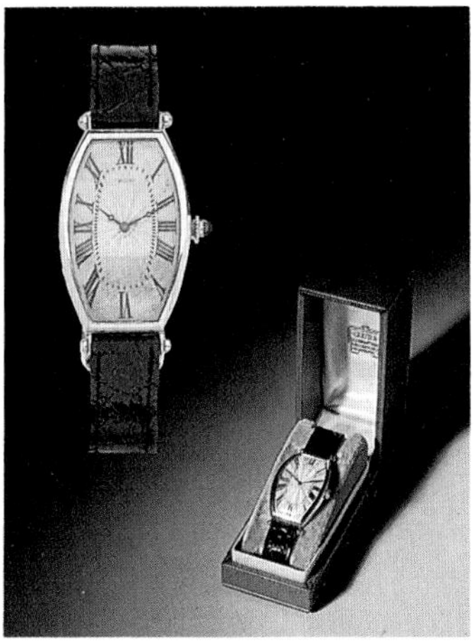

A gold jump hour time-zone wristwatch, signed Patek Philippe, Genève, No. 729422, 18ct case and buckle to leather strap, c1960. **£45-55,000** *CNY*
r. A rare 18ct gold gentleman's curved wristwatch, with sapphire winding crown, signed Cartier, 24112/25881, c1933. **£15,000-16,000** *CNY*

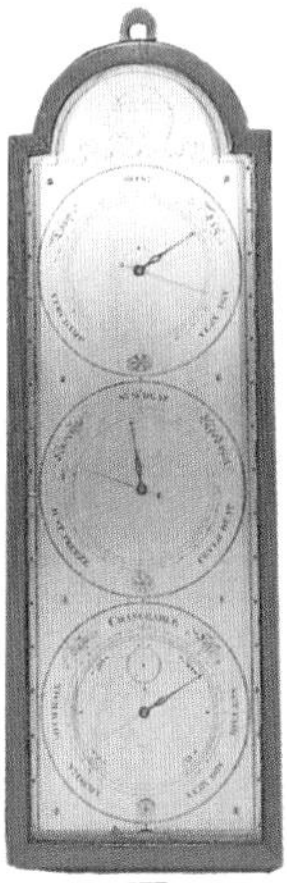

A George III mahogany baromet by George Adams with glazed door enclosing an engraved silver dial, inscribed, 37in (94.5cm). **£16,000-18,000** *C*

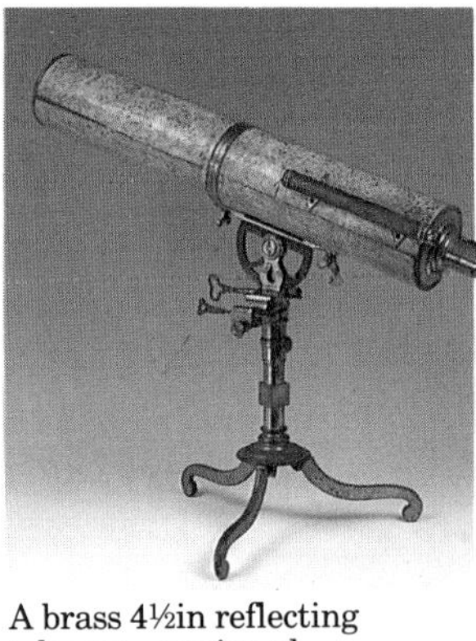

A brass 4½in reflecting telescope, unsigned, mahogany case, 18thC, 27in (73cm). **£2,500-3,500** *CSK*

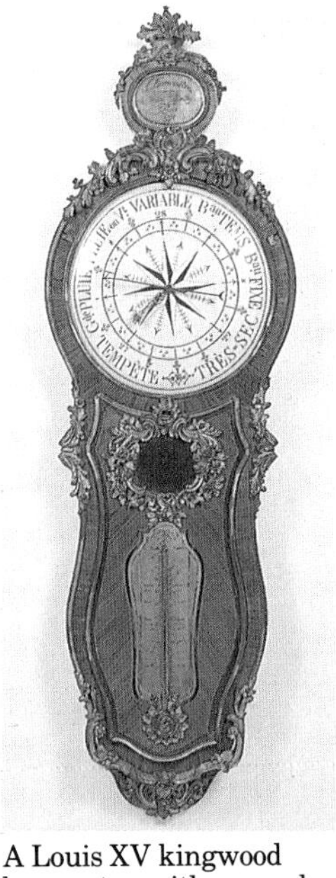

A Louis XV kingwood barometer, with enamel dial, signed C. Bousson, the case and thermometer inscribed J. Bettally, restorations, c1771, 46in (117cm) high. **£18,000-20,000** *C*

A French ormolu mounted mahogany barometer and clock, inscribed, 61in (155cm). **£12,000-14,000** *C*

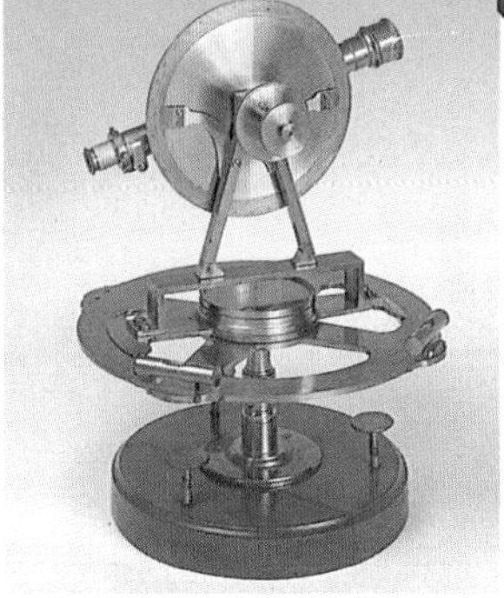

r. A Dutch brass theodolite signed J.M Kleman & Zoon Fecerunt, Amsterdam, c1800, 14½in (36.8cm). **£4,000-5,000** *CSK*

A rare French lacquere brass 'Achromatique Universal' horizontal microscope of Charles Chevalier pattern but signed Lerebours et Secretan à Paris, with original accessories in fitted mahogany cabin 19thC, 17in (43.2cm) w **£9,000-11,000** *CSK*

\ Persian brass astrolabe,
igned 'Made by Hājjī
Alī', c1790, 3½in (8cm)
iam.
'13,000-15,000 *CSK*

DAVID
CROMAE

l. A mariner's brass astrolabe, the scale divided into 4 quadrants, the alidade with 2 pin-hole sights, 17thC, 9in (23cm) diam. **£2,000-2,500** *CSK*

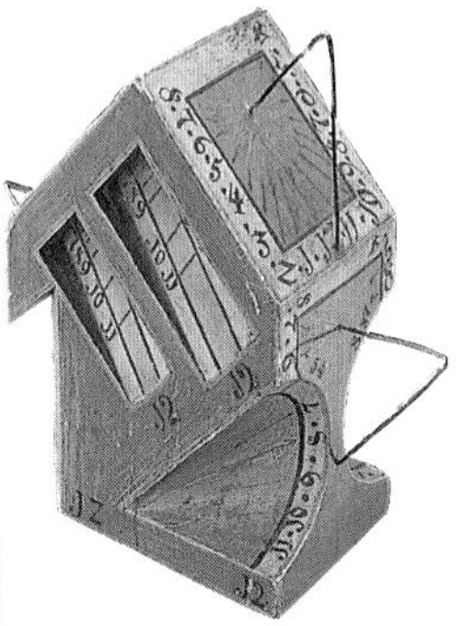

A German painted fruitwood polyhedral dial, with 3 wire gnomons and 12 dials, 18thC, 8in (20cm) high.
£2,000-3,000 *CSK*

French silver
ial, signed Butterfield,
aris, 18thC, 3½in (8.5cm),
ı fish skin case.
1,500-2,000 *CSK*

An Italian Copernican armillary sphere.
£3,500-4,500 *CSK*

Below. A large twin-plate machine.
£1,500-2,000 *CSK*

An English and gilded brass equinoctial ring dial, signed, late 18thC.
£25,000-30,000 *CSK*

A pair of George III mahogany framed library terrestrial and celestial globes, with brass scales, 42in (106.5cm) high.
£25,000-30,000 *C*

A pair of table globes, early 19thC.
£3,500-4,000 *CSK*

German silver and gilt
'ass horizontal dial,
gned, 3in (8cm).
3,500-5,000 *CSK*

A pair of Regency table globes, by Cary, the terrestrial globe dated 1820, celestial globe 1815, 13½in (34cm) high.
£6,500-8,500 *C*

lecture galvanometer,
thC, 10½in (26cm),
fitted case.
50-800 *CSK*

r. A pair of terrestrial and celestial globes, both signed Cary, the terrestrial dated 1812, the celestial dated 1799, some damage.
£50,000-60,000 *MN*

A Victorian parcel gilt copy of The Howard ewer and basin, by Frederick Elkington, Birmingham, 1875, basin 18in (46cm) diam, 85oz.
£5,000-10,000 *CNY*
r. A German parcel gilt tankard, indistinct marks, c1600, 1,160kg.
£65,000-70,000 *C*

A George II bread basket, engraved with coat-of-arms, by Robert Brown, 1740, 11½in (29.5cm) diam, 50oz.
£15,000-20,000 *C*

A rare cake basket by van Voorhis & Schanck, New York, c1792, 13½in (35cm) wide, 34oz.
£35,000-45,000 *CNY*

A George II shaped oval bread basket, by Eliza Godfrey, 1744, 13½in (34cm) long, 53oz.
£13,000-15,000 *C*

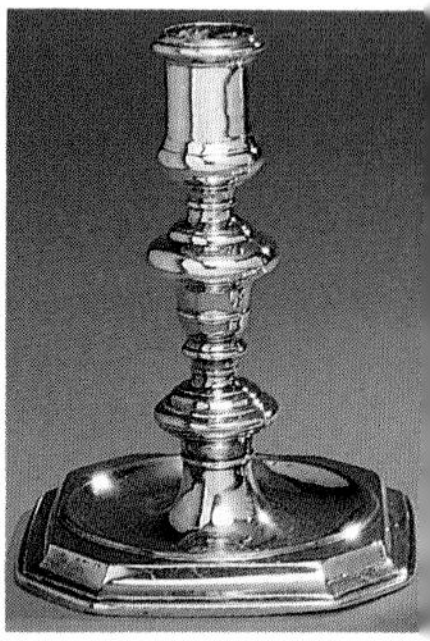

A pair of William III candlesticks, by Philip Rollos, 1697, 5in (12cm), 14oz.
£12,000-15,000 *C*

A silver and glass punch bowl, Gorham, Providence, marked, 1893, 16in (41cm) diam, 352oz gross.
£15,000-18,000 *CNY*

A Queen Anne monteith by Robert Timbrell, 1705, repairs, 13in (33cm) diam, 92oz. **£20,000-25,000** *C*

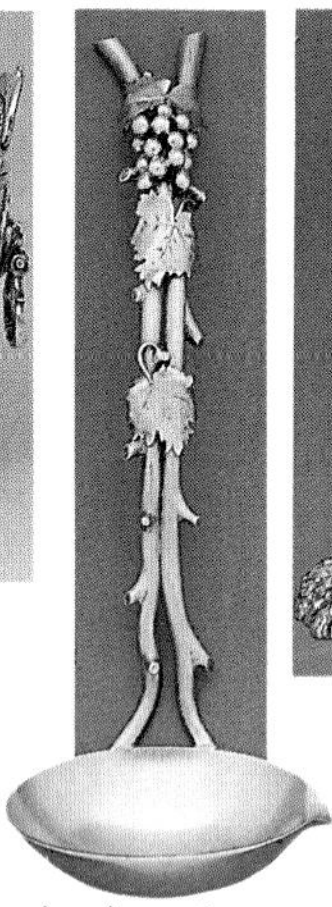

An American punch ladle, marked sterling, c1855, 11in (28cm), 7½oz.
£1,500-2,000 *CNY*

A pair of Georg II candlesticks with detachabl nozzles, engraved twice with a crest, by Peter Taylo 1741, 8½in (21.5cm), 45oz.
£20,000-25,00

A George I monteith, with detachable rim, by John East, 1718, 10in (25cm) diam, 52oz.
£16,000-20,000 *C*

A set of 12 George IV dinner plates, by Paul Storr, 1820, 10in (26.5cm) diam, 284oz.
£25,000-30,000 *C*

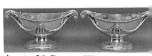

A set of 6 George III sauceboats, by Sir William Chambers, 1768, 169oz.
£20,000-25,000 *C*

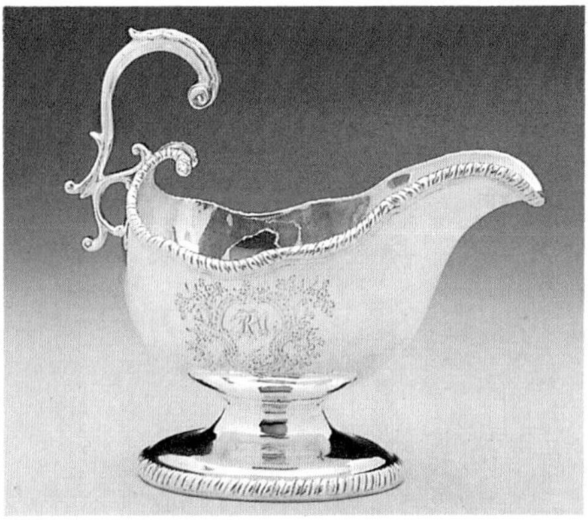

A sauceboat by Joseph Lownes, c1785. **£10,000-12,000** *CNY*

l. A William and Mary snuffer stand with a pair of matching candle snuffers. **£20,000-25,000** *C*

A George III silver presentation wine cooler, 1806, 144oz.
£15,000-20,000 *CNY*

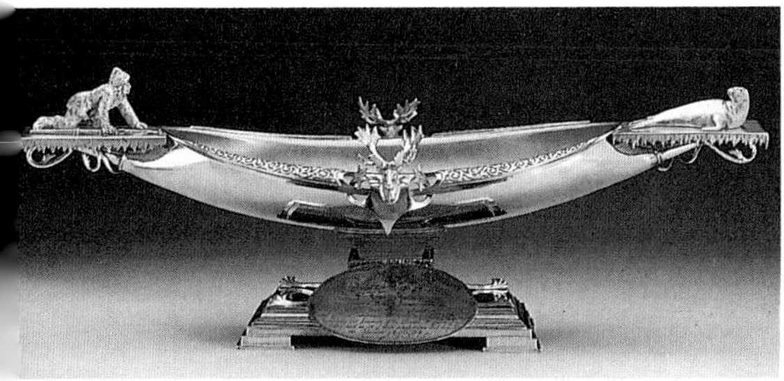

. silver presentation centrepiece, by Whiting Ianufacturing Company, marked, c1873, 4½in (62cm) wide, 78oz.
11,000-12,000 *CNY*

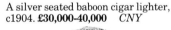

A silver tureen and stand.
£16,000-18,000 *CNY*

l. A George III silver tea urn, by Paul Storr, London, fully marked, c1809, 14in (35cm) high, 126oz.
£11,000-15,000 *CNY*

A silver seated baboon cigar lighter, c1904. **£30,000-40,000** *CNY*

A set of 4 George II silver salt cellars.
£20,000-25,000 *CNY*

A pair of George II silver two-handled soup tureens and covers, 1752, 13in (33cm) long, 196oz.
£25,000-30,000 *C*

l. A pair of William IV silver wine coolers, with removable liners, c1830, Sheffield, marked, 14in (35cm) high, 176oz. **£25,000-30,000** *CNY*

A set of 4 George III silver sauce tureens, 6in (15cm) high, 93oz.
£15,000-20,000 *C*

l. A Continental shaving set, comprising: 6 razors, a mirror, comb, stone strop and pair of later scissors, c1740.
£4,000-6,000 *C*

A George III Irish epergne, by Joseph Jackson, Dublin, 1791, fitted with 8 cut glass ewers, 4 casters with pierced covers, 1 broken, a central and 4 smaller baskets, 1 repaired, wood base on casters, fully marked, 23in (58cm) wide, 72oz.
£8,000-10,000 *CNY*

A cup and cover J. Garrard, 1882, 28in (72cm), 448oz.
£11,000-15,000 *C*

A George III tea urn, by Paul Storr, 1816, engraved with coat-of-arms and crest, tap with fluted ivory knob, fitted with liner and cover, 15in (38cm) high, 200oz gross.
£13,000-15,000 *C*

A George III epergne, by Thomas Pitts, London, 1765, 3 hanging baskets 1767 and one 1769, marked on frame, central dish, baskets and four branches, 31in (79cm) wide, 229oz. **£22,000-25,000** *CNY*

A George II Irish four-branch epergne, by Robert Calderwood, Dublin, c1750, 14in (35.5cm) high, 155oz. **£20,000-25,000** *C*

l. A George III epergne, by Thomas Pitts, 1781, 15in (38cm) high, 111oz.
£7,000-9,000 *C*
r. A Danish soup tureen, cover and stand by Julius Diderichsen, Copenhagen, 1864, 18in (47cm), 190oz.
£7,500-9,500 *CNY*

A rare teapot, the base engraved "EPL" probably initials of original owners Philip Lansing and Elsje Hun, married Albany 1757, and "IAH", unmarked, New York, c1750, 8in (21cm) high, 24.5oz gross.
£10,000-11,000 *CNY*

A George II coffee pot, by John Swift, London, 1739, marked, 11½in (29cm), 54oz gross. **£35,000-40,000** *CNY*

A George II kettle, stand and lamp, by Christian Hillan, 1740, 82oz gross.
£4,000-6,000 *C*

An enamelled and stone set gold match safe, by Tiffany for the 1889 Paris Exposition, marked, 1.2oz.
£6,000-7,000 *CNY*

r. An 18ct gold statue of Henri IV of France, 19thC, 4in (10cm) long, gold, 394gr.
£5,500-6,000 *C*

ASCOT
1901

A late Victorian 18ct gold cup and cover, by Sebastian Garrard, inscribed 'Won by Santoi, Ascot 1901', 25½in (65cm) high, 143oz.
£45,000-50,000 *C*

A set of 4 Victorian silver gilt candlesticks, by Robert Garrard, London, 1846, marked, 9in (22.5cm) high, 101oz.
£20,000-22,000 *CNY*

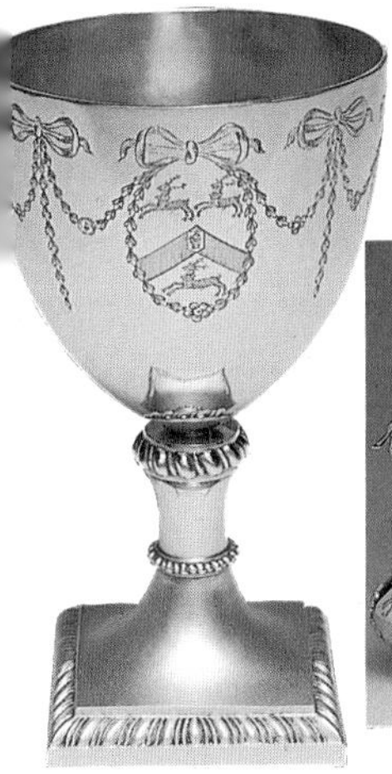

A George III inscribed goblet, mark 'R.B.' may be Robert Burton, c1780, 5½in (14cm), 7oz. 218gr.
£60,000-65,000 *C*

A Napoleon III silver gilt tea and coffee service, mark PQ, Paris 1860, 71oz gross.
£12-15,000
CNY

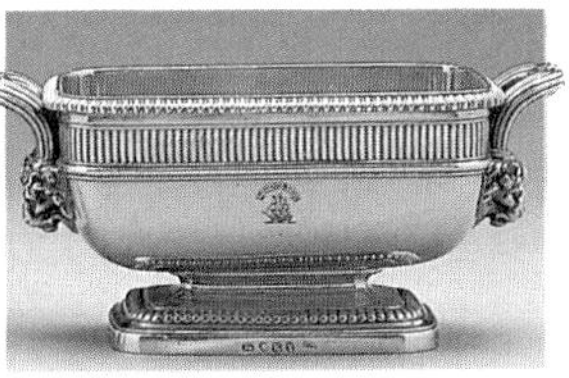

A pair of George III silver-gilt tureens by Paul Storr, 1805, 52oz.
£9,000-11,000 *CNY*

A French parcel gilt tray, c1860, 39in (99cm) long, 9886gr.
£10,000-15,000 *C*

A silver-gilt vase by Tiffany, small repair, marked, c1885, 8in (20cm) high, 10oz.
£4,000-6,000 *CNY*

. parcel gilt presentation punch bowl and ladle, ıscribed, by Gorham, Providence, 1871, marked Sterling', 12in (30cm) high, 103oz.
15,000-18,000 *CNY*

A set of 12 parcel gilt butter dishes, by Gorham, Providence, 1879, marked, each 3in (8cm) square, 13oz. **£6,500-7,500** *CNY*

A pair of Louis XVI style ormolu chenets, mid-19thC, 26in (66.5cm) high.
£12,000-15,000 *CNY*

l. A pair of Louis XVI style ormolu and rose agate covered urns, 19thC, 17½in (44.5cm) high.
£4,500-5,000 *CNY*

A pair of Empire ormolu urns, attributed to Gérard-Jean Galle, c1820, 22½in high.
£28-30,000 *CNY*

An Empire ormolu surtout-de-table, stamped Thomire à Paris, 117in (297cm) long.
£25,000-30,000 *C*

A pair of Louis XVI style chenets, signed Henri Dasson 1885, 9in (22.5cm) high.
£6,500-9,500 *CNY*

An ormolu inkstand, mid-19thC, 17½in (44cm) wide.
£1,500-2,000 *C*

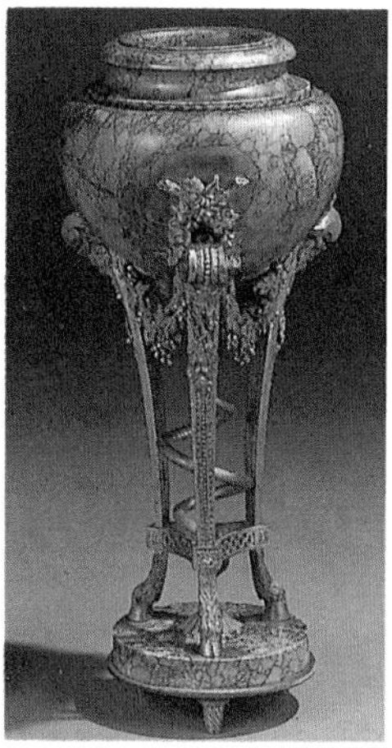

l. A pair of Napoleon III tazzas, 10in (25cm) high.
£3,000-4,000 *C*

A pair of Louis XIV style pedestals, restorations, 53½in. **£17,000-20,000** *CN*

A pair of ormolu and marble brûle parfums, 20in (51cm) high.
£10,000-15,000 *C*

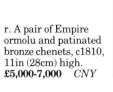

r. A pair of Empire ormolu and patinated bronze chenets, c1810, 11in (28cm) high.
£5,000-7,000 *CNY*

An Empire ormolu surtout-de-table, 25in (63.5cm) diam.
£9,000-12,000 *C*

. Paduan bronze Judith
ith head of Holophernes,
om the Workshop of
evero da Ravenna, early
6thC, 7½in (19cm).
9,000-12,000 *C*

A Venetian bronze
figure of
Bacchus, c1600,
12½in (32cm).
£20,000-25,000 *C*

A Neapolitan bronze of
Narcissus, with removable
fig leaf, signed and
inscribed, c1887, 24½in
(63cm). **£25,000-30,000** *C*

A Venetian bronze
allegory of peace,
base damaged,
16thC, 21in (54cm).
£13,000-15,000 *C*

bronze cast of a nymph and satyr,
fter Giambologna, heavily cast,
ctangular marble pedestal, 17thC,
by 12in (20 by 30cm).
10,000-12,000 *C*

A French bronze,
Rape of Proserpine,
damaged, 18thC,
23in (59cm).
£9,000-12,000 *C*

A pair of Empire
candelabra,
45½in (116cm).
£120-130,000 *C*

A pair of bronze
urns, with twin
swan's mask
scrolling foliate
handles, signed
Heizler,
21in (53cm).
£5,000-6,000 *C*

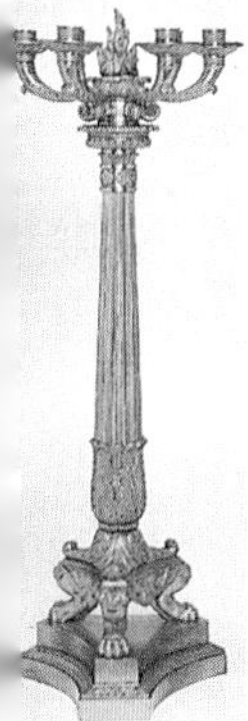

pair of Charles X
x-light ormolu
ındelabra, with flaming
nials, 30½in (77.5cm).
,000-6,000 *C*
bove r. A pair of
molu candlesticks, after
-D. Dugourc, 13in
3cm). **£10,000-12,000** *C*

A Venetian
darwood torchère, by
alentino Besarel, signed,
te 19thC, 69in (174cm).
17,000-20,000 *C*

A Florentine ebony and
pietra dura casket, mid-
19thC, 20½in (52cm)
wide. **£30,000-35,000** *C*

A French bronze bust of an Egyptian harem girl, mid-19thC, 14½in (38cm) high.
£5,000-8,000 *C*

Laurent, a Susse Frères 2-coloured bronze bust, signed, 23in (59cm).
£2,000-3,000 *MAG*

A Florentine bronze group, early 18thC. **£12,000-15,000**

l. A Roman gilt bronze figure of St John the Baptist, mid-17thC.
£15,000-20,000 *C*

BEETHOVEN

Gaudez, a bronze figure of a sword mender, 21in high.
£1,000-2,000 *MAG*

Muller, a bronze figu
£1,500-2,500 *MAG*

A French bronze figure, by Christophe-Gabriel Allegrain, 18thC.
£40,000-50,000 *CNY*

Above l. Picault, a bronze figure. **£1,500-2,500** *MAG*

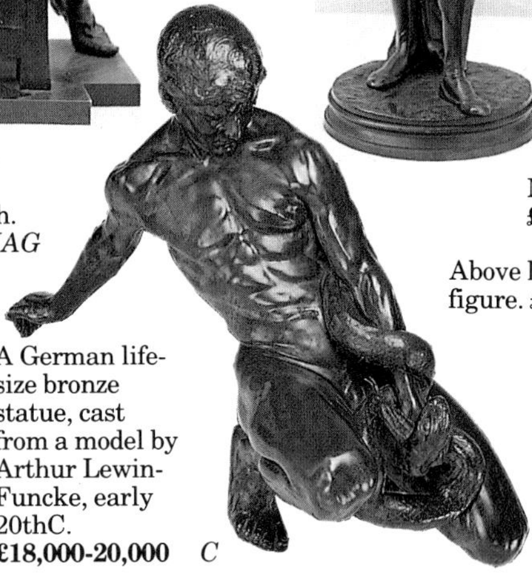

A German life-size bronze statue, cast from a model by Arthur Lewin-Funcke, early 20thC.
£18,000-20,000 *C*

r. A pair of bronze figures of athletes, after Pompeiian originals, raiser on later plinths, 45in (114cm). **£10,000-12,000** *CSK*

Boucharel, a bronze group of 2 seated bulldogs, signed, 19½in (49cm) high.
£2,000-3,000 *MAG*

l. A French bronze model of the setter named 'Cora', cast from a model by Isidore Bonheur, 19thC, 12½in (32cm) high
£4,000-6,000 *C*

n Isnik tile panel, comprising 4 les of different sizes, some storation, c1725, 21 by 16in 4 by 42.5cm). **£4,500-6,000** *C*

A Safavid dish and deep bowl in the Chinese kraak style, repaired, 17thC, dish 19½in (49.5cm) diam. **£1,500-2,500 each** *C*

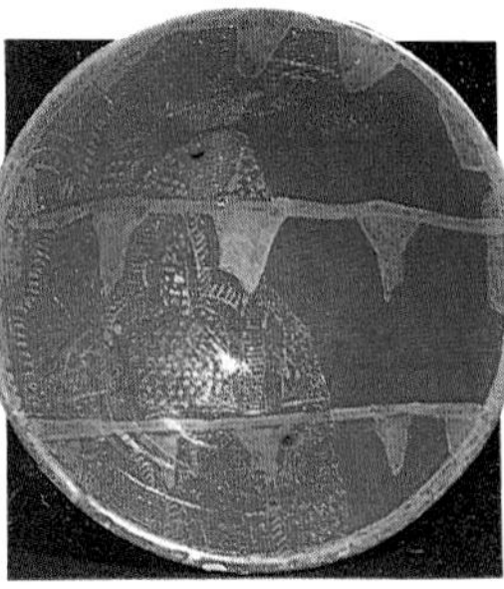

A rare fragmentary Abbasid red ground lustre bowl, restored, 9thC, 7½in (19.5cm). **£18,000-20,000** *C*

Kashan moulded cobalt d lustre inscription e, minor restoration, thC, 14 by 13¼in 5.5 by 33.5cm). **,000-5,000** *C*

A Kashan moulded cobalt and lustre inscription tile, minor chipping, 13thC, 18 by 5in (45.5 by 12.5cm). **£4,500-5,500** *C*

r. An amber wheel cut glass bottle, very slight surface iridescence, Nishapur, 10thC, 5in (12.5cm) high. **£5,000-7,000** *C*

A French inlaid octagonal islamic table, slight damage, late 19thC, 31½in 80cm) wide. **£1,500-2,000** *C*

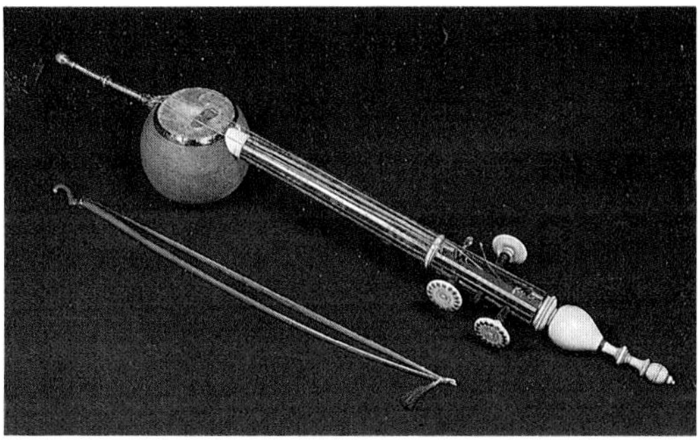

An Ottoman rebab of turned wood with a skin covering, the neck inlaid with ivory, ebony and tortoiseshell, horsehair strung bow, minor restoration, 18thC, 37in (94cm). **£5,000-6,500** *C*

An Ottoman gilt copper incense burner on tray, damaged, early 17thC, 9½in (24cm) high. **£3,000-5,000** *C*

l. A Persian silver inlaid brass pen box, minor damage, signed and inscribed, c1200, 12in (30.7cm) long. **£14,000-16,000** *C*

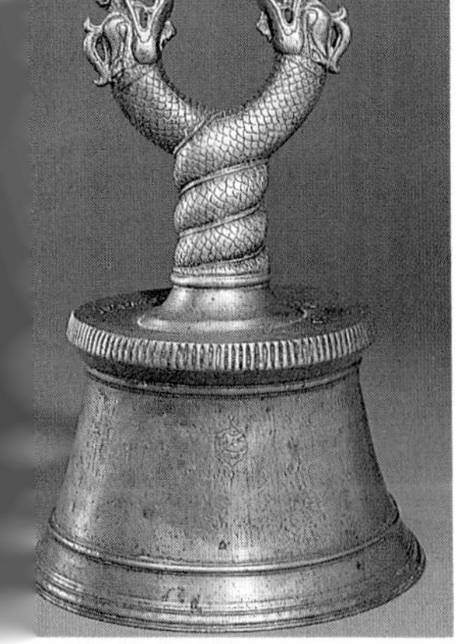

early Safavid brass dlestick, inscribed, hC, 10½in (27cm). **,000-30,000** *C*

A Mesopotamian silver inlaid brass casket, 13thC, Jazira, 7½in (19cm). **£250,000+** *C*

An Ottoman voided velvet and metal thread cushion cover, backed and stretched, slightly worn, one band of repair, 17thC, 43 by 25½in (110 by 65cm). **£4,000-6,000** *C*

A carved oak and painted coat-of-arms of His Majesty King William III, late 17thC, 19in (49cm) high.
£2,000-2,500 *AH*

A German boxwood group, after Albrecht Durer, damaged, early 17thC, 5½in (14cm). **£10,000-12,000** *C*

r. A Flemish oak relief, damaged, early 16thC, 48in (122cm). **£7,500-8,000** *C*

A pine Angel Gabriel weathervane, American, 19thC, 41½in (105cm). **£1,500-2,000** *CNY*

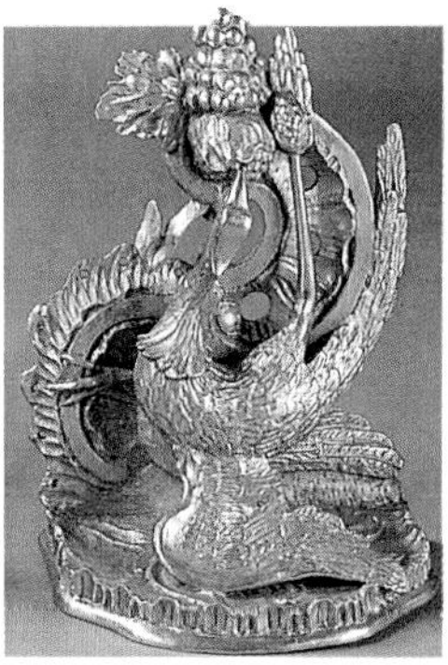

l. A set of 4 giltwood wall brackets, 21in (54cm) high. **£6,000-6,500** *C*

A carved and painted soldier whirligig, some paint loss, one arm lacks axe, American, 19thC, 20in (51cm). **£19,000-20,000** *CNY*

l. A set of 4 fruitwood candlesticks, c1800. **£6,000-7,000** *C*

A parrot, 10in (25cm). **£4,500-5,000** *CNY*

An oak figure of the seated Goddess 'Cer
by Sir Charles Whe
61in (155cm).
£6,000-6,500 *C*

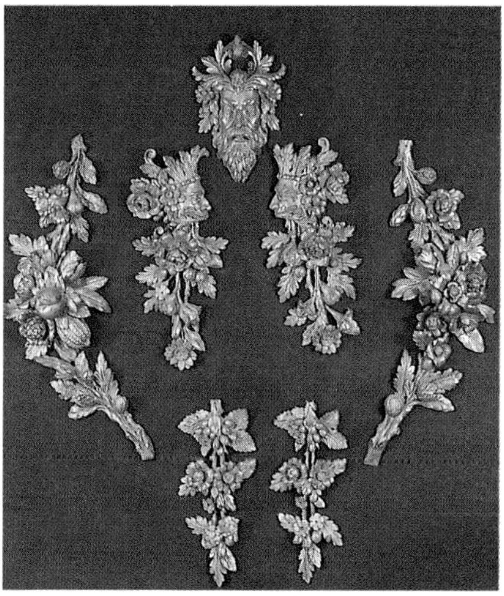

Twelve sections of giltwood carving, masks 24in (61cm). **£3,000-3,500** *C*

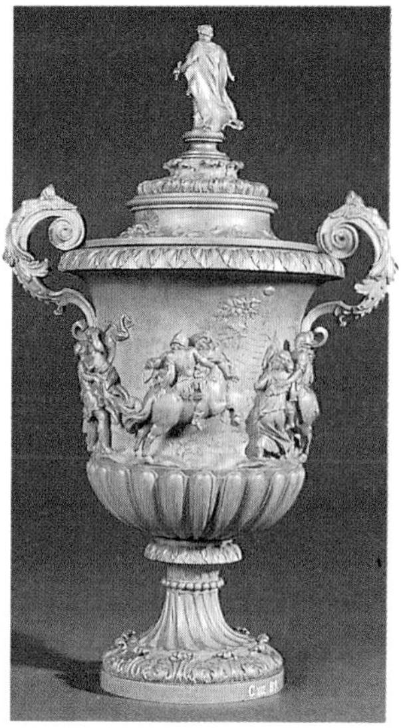

r. A German boxwood cup and cover, minor damage, early 18thC, marked CIII.89, 14½in (37cm). **£26,000-30,000** *C*

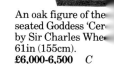

A lignum wassail with 3 brass taps, 18thC, 20in (51cm). **£1,500-2,000**

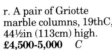

set of 4 white marble garden
ns, 19thC, 40in (101cm) high.
2,000-15,000 *CSK*

A pair of Code stone urns, early 19thC, 40½in (102cm) high.
£4,500-5,500 *C*

Above r. A pair of Napoleon III marble urns, 17in. **£1,500-2,000** *C*

Above l. A set of 4 lead urns, early 19thC, 31½in (80cm). **£12,000-15,000** *C*

r. A pair of Griotte marble columns, 19thC, 44½in (113cm) high.
£4,500-5,000 *C*

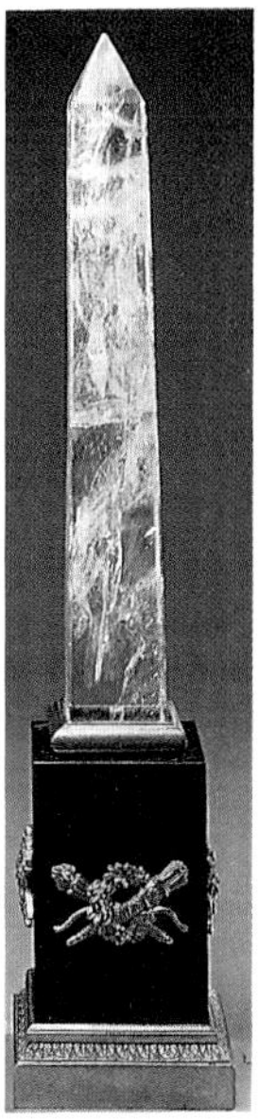

ɪair of ormolu mounted
ɪttled liver and grey-
ɪen marble vases after
uthière, 15in (38cm).
,000-10,000 *C*

A pair of French white marble urns, one with oak and laurel leaves, one with palm and olive leaves, some minor damage, c1700. **£50,000-55,000** *C*

Above r. A red and brown marble column, early 19thC, 36in (91.5cm) high.
£2,000-3,000 *C*

r. A pair of Empire style ormolu, marble and rock crystal obelisks, 18½in (47cm).
£5,500-6,500 *CNY*

English marble bust of Venus by
eph Wilton, signed J. Wilton
ɪlp. 1782, late 18thC, 28½in
cm).
,000-50,000 *C*

DANTE
IL PARADISO

An alabaster bust of a young lady in pre-Raphaelite headdress, signed E. Fiaschi, 50in (127cm).
£1-1,500 *SWO*

A carved marble lamp with matching shade, 25in (64cm). **£600-800** *JL*

l. An Italian marble statue of Pauline Borghese after Canova, some damage, mid-19thC, 35½in (90cm) high.
£6,000-7,000 *C*

A Victorian 18ct gold almondine garnet brooch, 4in (10cm) wide.
£750-850 *SBA*
r. A Victorian gold and garnet bracelet, set with almondine garnets and one cabochon in the centre.
£900-1,200 *SBA*

A diamond set floral spray brooch.
£2,500-3,000 *WW*

A French enamelled gol locket, some restoration, c1650, 1in (2.5cm) high.
£2,500-3,000

An important cushion shaped Fa Light Yellow 35.03 carat diamon single stone pendant, on a flattened curb link chain, 14½in (36.8cm) long.
£150,000-200,000 *C*

A pearl and diamond diadem, by Cartier, Paris, 1908, No. 1743, 5½in (14.2cm) wide. **£50,000-60,000** *C*
l. An Edwardian diamond bow brooch, 5in (12.6cm) high.
£45,000-50,000 *C*

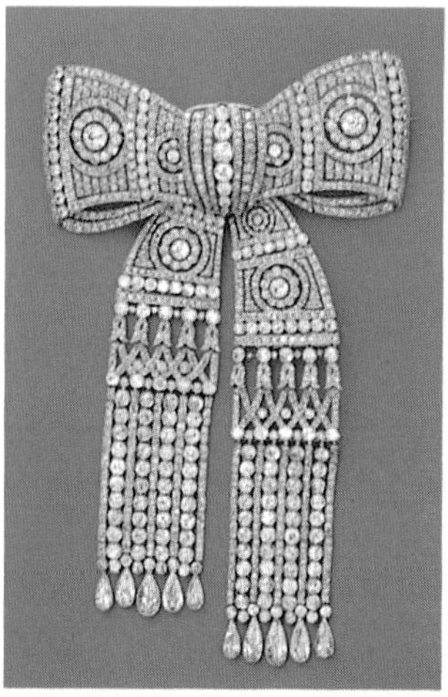

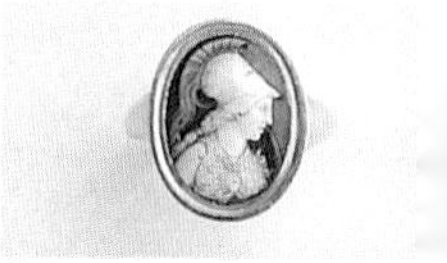

A sardonyx cameo wit the head of Pallas Athene, inscribed 'LAV.R.MED.' in gold setting, cameo 18thC, mount early 19thC.
£25,000-30,000 *C*

A necklace, comprising 19 gold mounted memori and love jewels with rock crystal covers, the central locket 2in (5cm) high. **£20,000-25,000** *C*

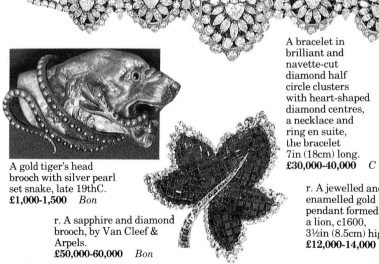

A bracelet in brilliant and navette-cut diamond half circle clusters with heart-shaped diamond centres, a necklace and ring en suite, the bracelet 7in (18cm) long.
£30,000-40,000 *C*

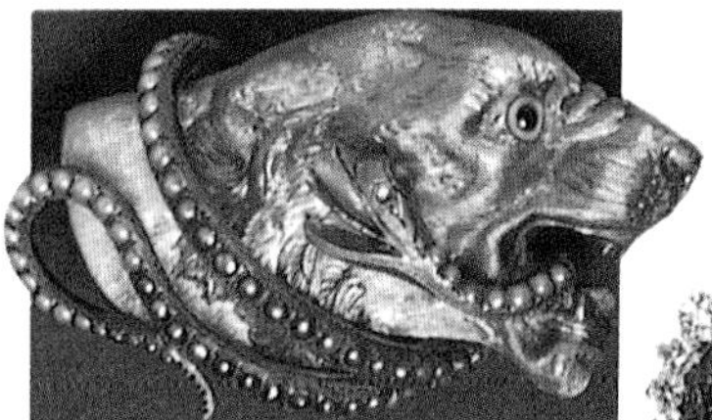

A gold tiger's head brooch with silver pearl set snake, late 19thC.
£1,000-1,500 *Bon*

r. A sapphire and diamond brooch, by Van Cleef & Arpels.
£50,000-60,000 *Bon*

r. A jewelled and enamelled gold pendant formed as a lion, c1600, 3½in (8.5cm) high.
£12,000-14,000 *C*

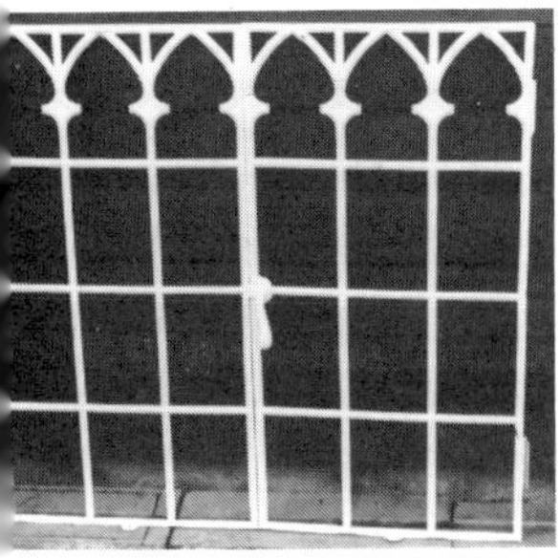

iron window frame, 34in (86cm)
e.
0-250 *DRU*

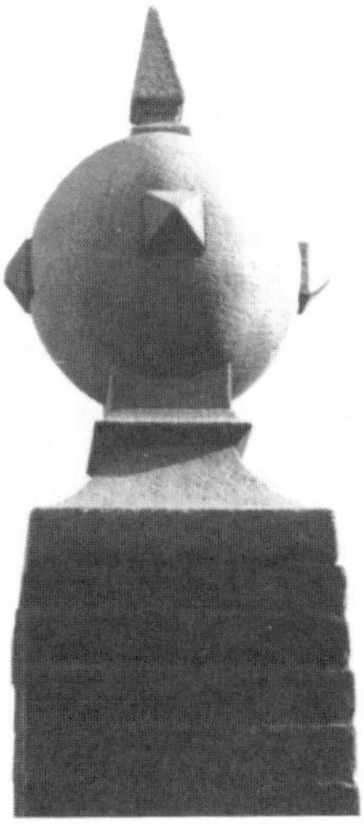

A set of 4 stone finials.
£3,000-3,500 *DRU*

A French bottle trolley, 39in (99cm) long.
£100-125 *DRU*

A Japanese stone lantern.
£350-450 *DRU*

1910

A cast iron drain, c1910, 26in (66cm) high.
£75-85 *HUN*

YE
OLD GATE
HOUSE

A wrought iron house sign with copper letters, 53in (134.5cm) wide.
£250-270 *AL*

ctorian wrought iron arbour.
00-2,200 *HUN*

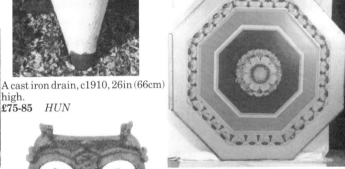

A dance hall ceiling from the German liner HV Columbus, c1903, each panel 74in (188cm) wide.
£12,000-14,000 complete *DRU*

An English cast iron boot scraper, c1870.
£60-70 *UC*

A pair of Victorian ormolu and brass curtain tie backs.
£50-70 *HF*

A miniature cannon, c1800, 15in (38cm) long.
£190-200 *HUN*

A pair of cast iron door stops, c1880, 10in (25cm).
£200-250 *HUN*

A Victorian wrought iron extending lamp standard.
£250-300 *DRU*

A lead pump head, c1800, 3-
(86cm) high.
£120-130 *HUN*

A lead pump head, c1800, 42in (106.5cm).
£150-160 *HUN*

A pair of Continental ormolu rococo design chenets, c1775.
£650-700 *HUN*

A spirit percolator, 13½in (35cm).
£90-120 *WRe*

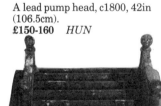

A mahogany stick stand, c1890.
£145-175 *HUN*

An iron boot scraper, 17½in (44cm) wide.
£85-95 *HUN*

A decorative cast iron finial, 19thC, 63in (160cm).
£300-400 *DRU*

A large wooden cog, 25in (64cm).
£65-75 *WRe*

A Victorian cog or casting mould, 16in (41cm).
£45-55 *WRe*

A hanging lamp, 27in (69cm).
£250-280 *WRe*

Four York stone balls, 10in (25cm).
£100-130 *WRe*

bell, 10in (25cm).
0-50 *WRe*

A wooden thermometer, 12in (31cm). **£5-10** *WRe*

Four brass and ceramic light switches.
£20-30 each *WRe*

A set of 4 brass casters, 4in (10cm).
£80-100 *WRe*

wrought iron lantern with
aseline glass shade, c1885, 34in
7cm) high.
00-450 *HUN*

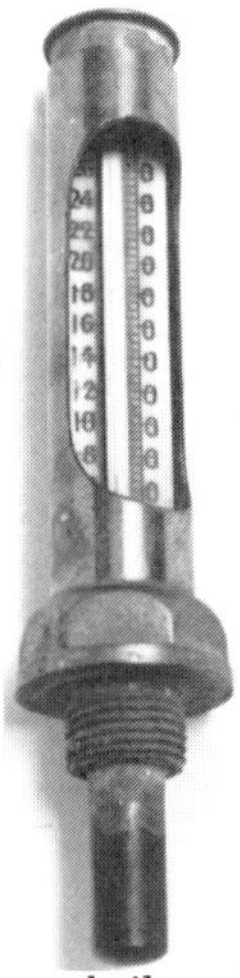

BOX

An elm country door, 18thC.
£90-100 *WEL*

A brass letter box cover, 7in (18cm).
£25-35 *WRe*

pair of iron troughs and feeder,
800, 46in (116.5cm) wide.
50-750 *HUN*

A brass boiler thermometer, 7in (18cm).
£12-15 *WRe*

pair of oak woodcarvings from a Renaissance
eplace, 25in (64cm) wide.
00-350 *HUN*

Two Victorian water closets, Activus and Waterfall, 16in (41cm) high.
£325-400 each *DRU*

A gas flare brass dragon, 5in (13cm).
£50-70 *WRe*

A set of 2 Edwardian red terracotta chimney pots.
£95-120 *WEL*

A Victorian cast iron stove.
£200-250 *WEL*

A pestle and mortar, 6in (15cm) high.
£75-100 *WRe*

A Victorian terracotta Tudor Rose design wall decoration.
£15-20 *WEL*

A set of 2 stone plaques, 17thC.
£180-200 *WEL*

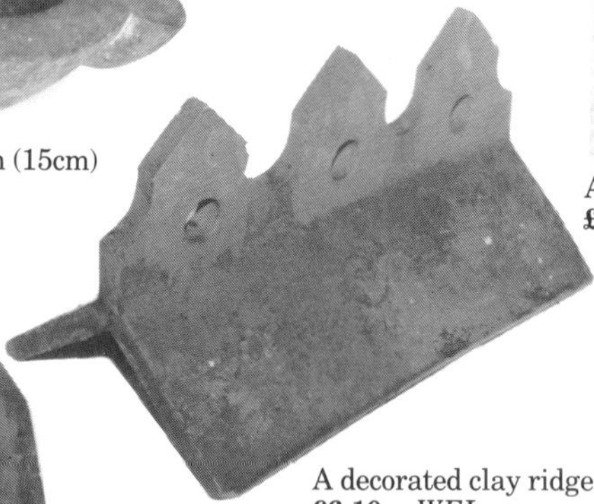

A decorated clay ridge tile.
£6-10 *WEL*

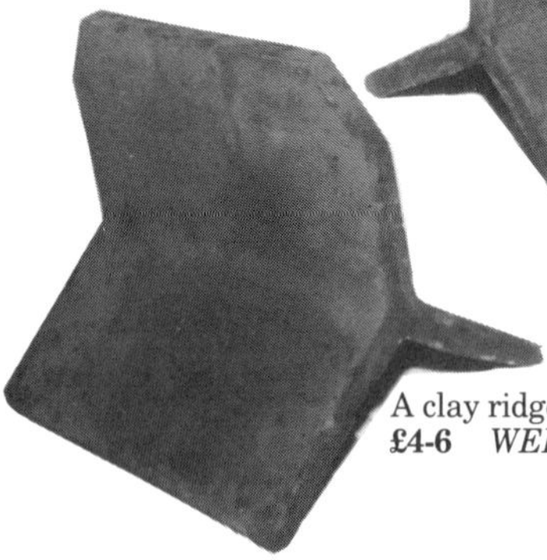

A clay ridge tile.
£4-6 *WEL*

A chimney pot, 16in (41cm) high.
£60-75 *WRe*

A set of 3 Victorian terracotta chimney pots.
£100-125 *WEL*

A set of 4 Italian relief moulded terracotta wall plaques, each depicting groups of classical musicians with children at their feet, each panel 34in (87cm) wide.
£400-500 *Bon*

A Bath stone carving with a Got cross.
£35-45 *WEL*

:LOCKS

.ongcase :locks

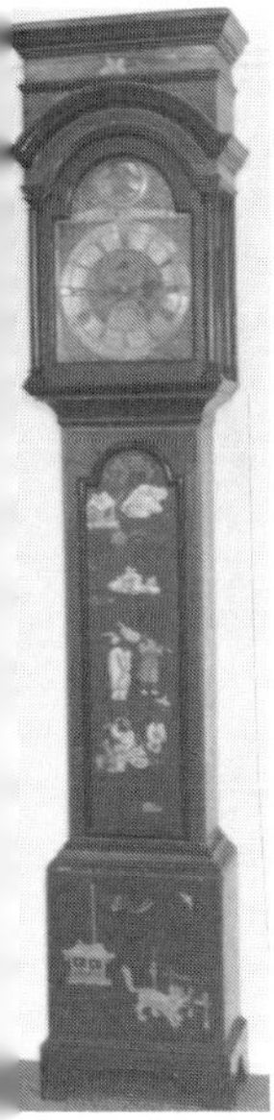

George II scarlet
.cquered
.inoiserie
.ngcase clock,
.ith arched brass
.al by Moses
.braham, Frome,
'in (221cm) high.
:,500-3,000
GM

A mahogany longcase clock, Wm. Aitken, Haddington, early 19thC.
£4,000-5,000 *CLC*

A mahogany longcase clock, by John Duffett, Bristol, with 'High water at Bristol Key' (sic), c1770.
£7,500-8,000 *OX*

A longcase clock with arabesque marquetry, John Barron, London, early 18thC.
£9,500-10,000 *CLC*

A mahogany North Country 8-day longcase clock, with lunar painted dial, the case with swan-neck pediment, ropetwist columns and Gothic arched door, on plinth base, 90in (230cm).
£750-1,000
MGM

.acquer longcase
.ck, by John
.rry, London, the
.ay 5-pillar
.vement with
.ss dial showing
.onds, date and
.h strike/silent,
. case with
.noiseries of
.iental design on
.rtoiseshell
.kground, c1750,
.n (218.5cm)
h.
500-5,000 *OX*

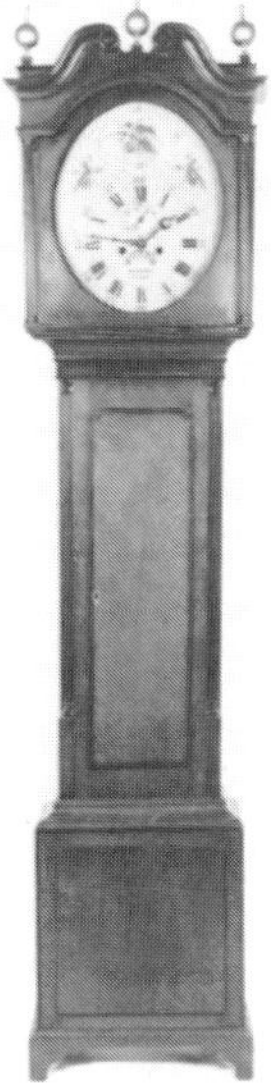

An oak and mahogany longcase clock, Thos. Bembow, Newport, late 18thC, 94in (238cm).
£1,500-2,000
P(M)

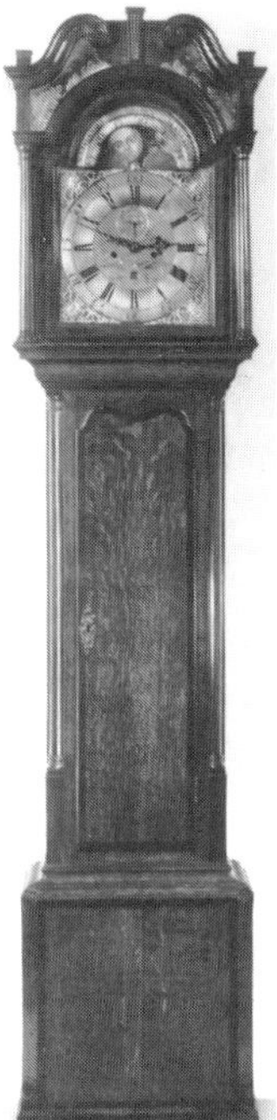

An oak longcase clock, Nat. Brown, Manchester, late 18thC.
£4,000-5,000 *CLC*

A George III oak and mahogany longcase clock, by John Warrone, Kirby Moorside, 96in (243.5cm).
£2,000-2,500
P(M)

A George III oak 8-day longcase clock, with brass dial inscribed Jn. Agar & Son, York, 84in (213cm) high.
£600-650 *GSP*

A late Georgian Scottish longcase clock, with 8-day movement and brass dial, the mahogany case with shell motif inlay, satinwood stringing and fluted pilasters, inscribed J Ramage, Edinburgh, 84in (213cm).
£2,600-3,000
RBB

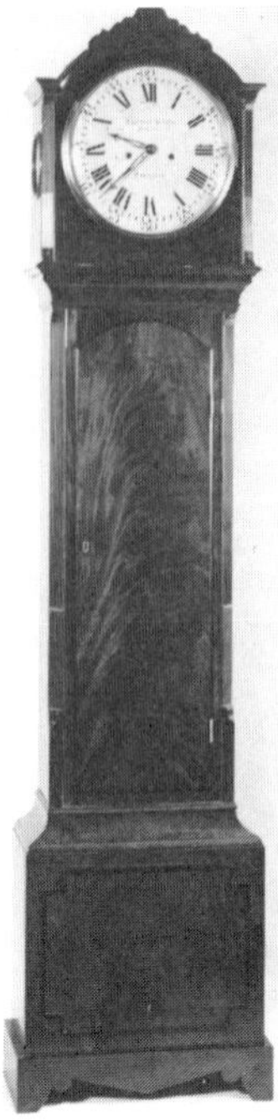

A mahogany longcase clock, c1815.
£3,000-4,000
HOL

An important walnut longcase clock, with hourly strike on a bell, 14in (35cm) arch brass dial, 5-pillar movement, 8-day duration, strike/silent in arch, by Joseph Bosley, London, c1720, 96in (243.5cm).
£12,800-13,500
SBA

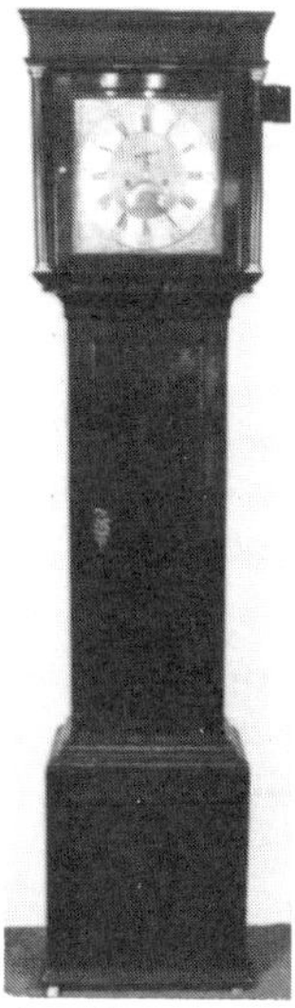

A mahogany longcase clock, with 8-day duration, hourly strike on a bell, by Joseph Brown, Worcester, c1780, 79in (200.5cm).
£3,500-4,000
SBA

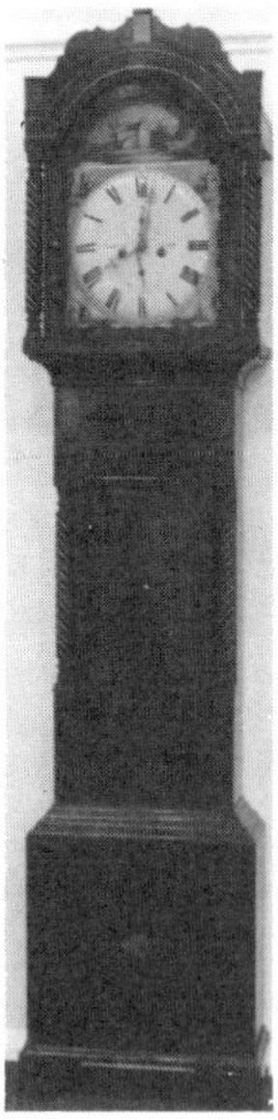

A mahogany 8-day longcase clock, with arched painted dial, boxwood strung case flanked with ropetwist columns, maker Neath, early 18thC, 86in (218cm).
£1,500-2,000
MGM

A mahogany longcase clock, by W B Cornforth, Macclesfield, early 19thC, 93in (236cm).
£1,500-2,000
P(M)

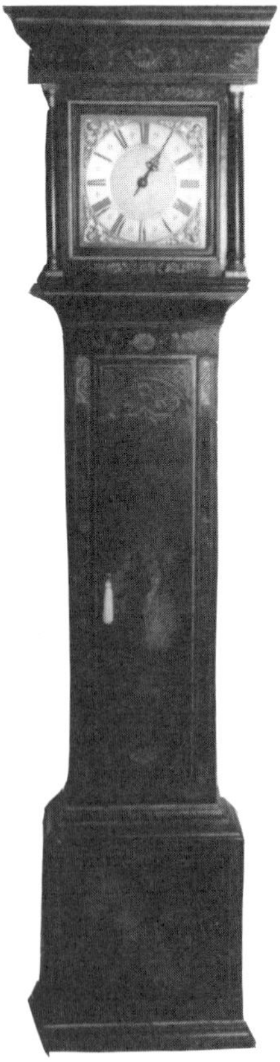

A Victorian 30-hour longcase clock, with original case and movement, Vernis Martin oil painting on door.
£1,300-1,700
RFA

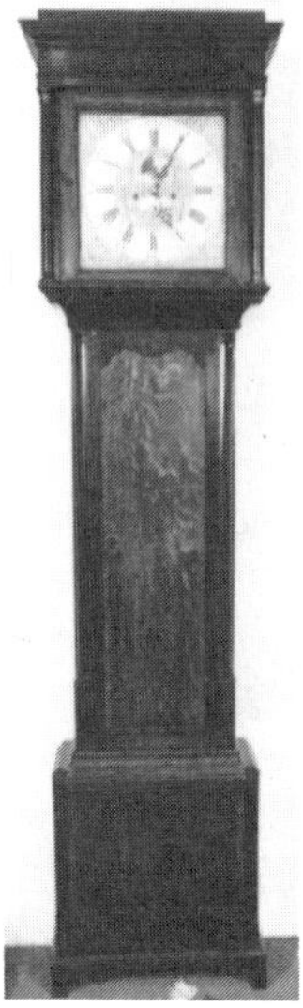

An oak longcase clock, 8-day duration, unusual bell aperture for the moon, by S Collier of Eccles, 80in (203cm).
£3,700-4,200
SBA

An early Georgian japanned 8-day longcase clock, with silvered ring dial and gilt vase spandrels with moving ship in the arch, inscribed The Duke of Cumberland, with seconds hand and date aperture inscribed Jno. Carter, London, the case with chinoiserie and scrolls on a dark ground, 96in (243.5cm).
£1,200-1,700 *GSP*

A Georgian mahogany and shell inlaid longcase clock, with arched brass dial, with pergoda style pediment, inscribed James Garvis, Darlington, 95in (241cm).
£3,000-3,500 *BWe*

. oak and hogany ssbanded gcase clock, the ½in (29cm) ıare brass dial h subsidiary onds and date scent, 4-pillar ay rack striking vement with hor apement, by hardson, averham, ied to the frieze ndrews, binet Maker, avering, late nC, 80in 3cm).
0-1,200 *P(M)*

An oak longcase clock, Rob Murray Lauder.
£3,000-3,500 *CLC*

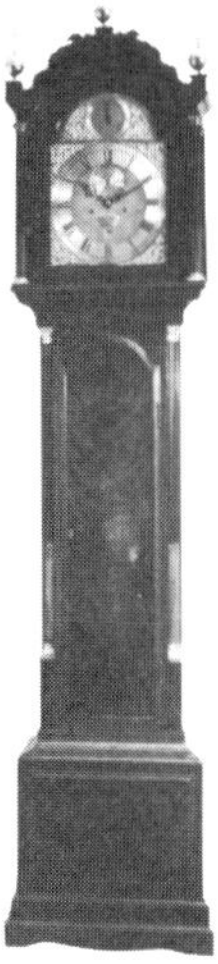

A walnut longcase clock, with 8-day duration, detachable caddy top, by Francis Dorrol, London, c1730, 94in (238cm).
£7,000-8,000 *SO*

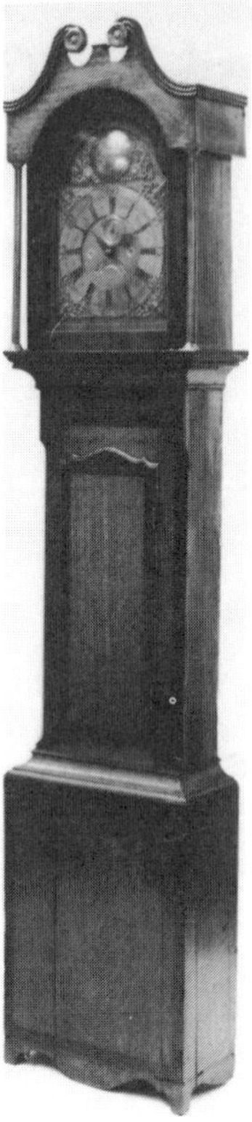

An oak longcase clock, with swan neck pediment and plain pillars to the hood, the case with mahogany crossbanding, the brass dial inscribed Thos Hanxnell, Brampton, with pierced spandrels, seconds and date dials, 30-hour movement, late 18thC, 83in (210.5cm).
£550-650 *DDM*

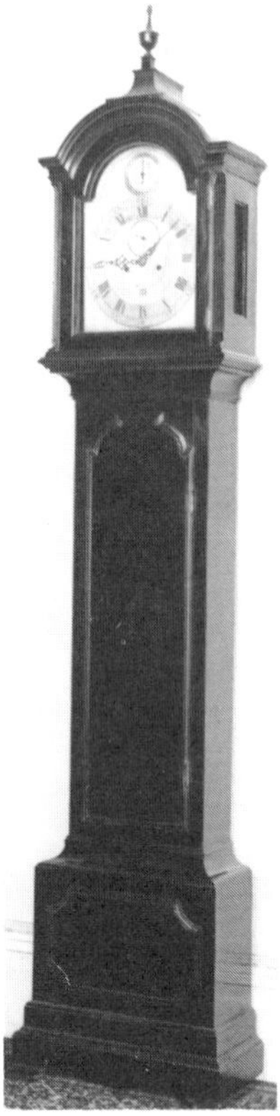

A George III longcase clock, in London mahogany style case, by Thomas Grignon, 95in (241cm).
£6,000-7,000
RBB

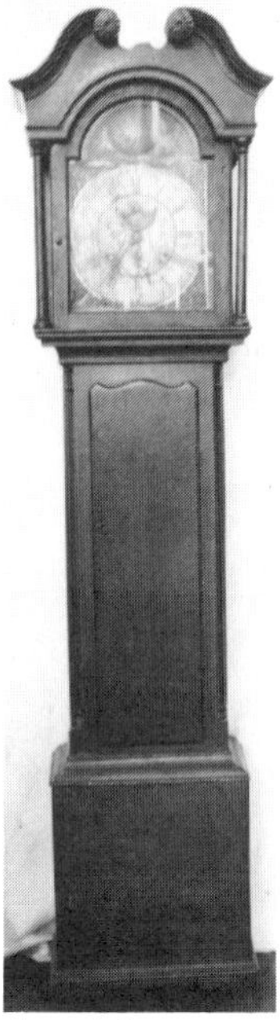

An oak longcase clock, with brass arched dial, with date and lunar ring and seconds dial, inscribed John Varley, mid-18thC, 82in (208cm).
£450-500 *HCH*

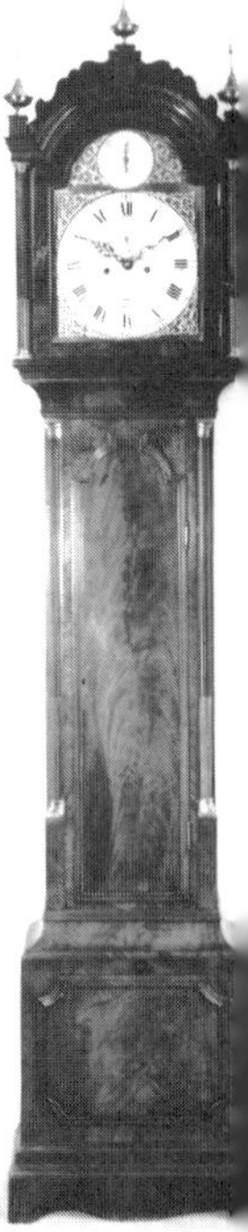

A mahogany longc clock, Henry Danie London, late 18th
£7,500-8,000 *C*

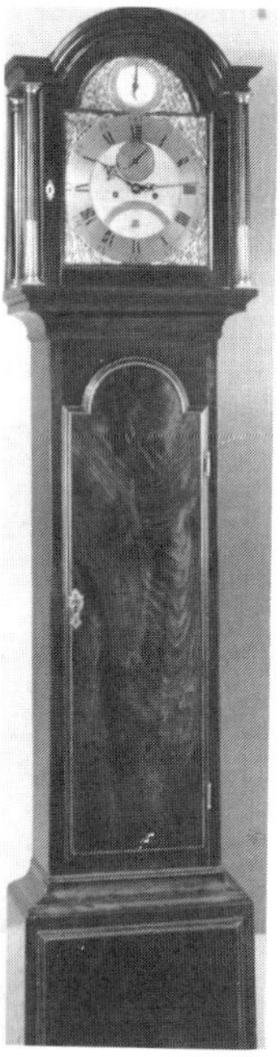

A mahogany longcase clock, c1765.
£6,000-7,000
HOL

A Scottish longca clock, in original case, 8-day brass dial, by John Kirkwood, Melrose, c1770, 87in (221cm).
£5,000-6,000 *S*

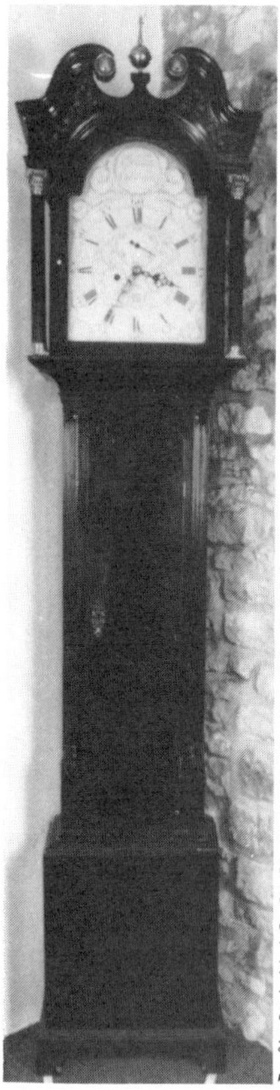

A mahogany longcase clock, with swan arch pediment and blind fretwork to trunk, 12in (30.5cm) arch silvered dial, 8-day duration, hourly strike on a bell, subsidiary dial for seconds, 31-day calendar, by John Durwood of Edinburgh, c1800, 89½in (227cm).
£5,500-6,000
SBA

A mahogany longcase clock, the painted movement of 8-day duration, 31-day calendar, subsidiary dial for seconds, hourly strike on a bell, by Colin Salmon, Dundee, c1811, 84in (213cm).
£5,000-6,000
SBA

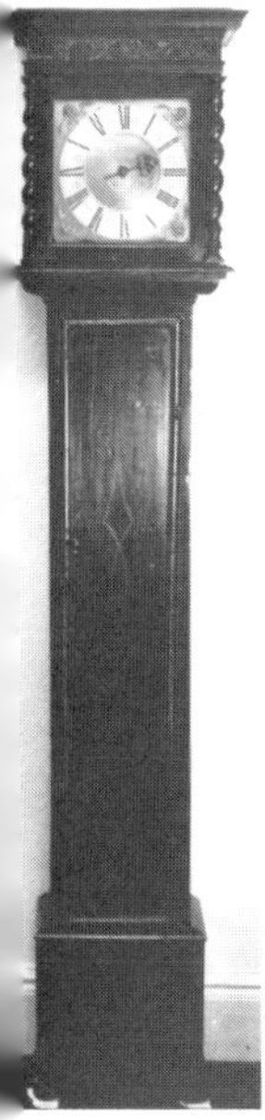

30-hour verge
›ngcase clock
ade by
Iumphrey
larke
f Hartford,
1680.
5,500-6,000
AAW

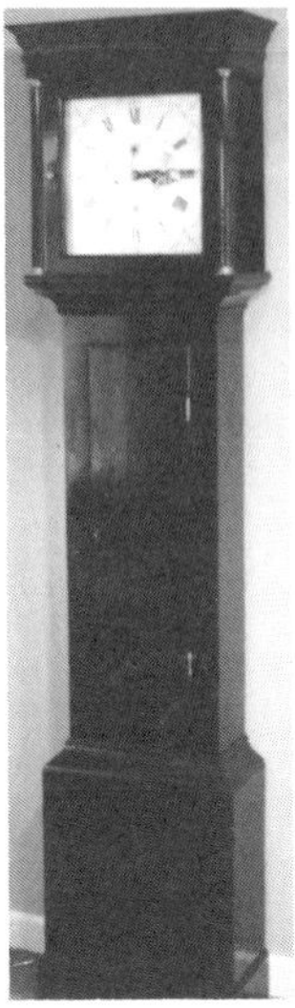

A mahogany longcase clock, by John Bullock, Bishops Waltham, the 8-day movement striking the hours on a bell, with engraved silvered brass dial, c1790, 78in (198cm) high.
£3,000-3,500 *OX*

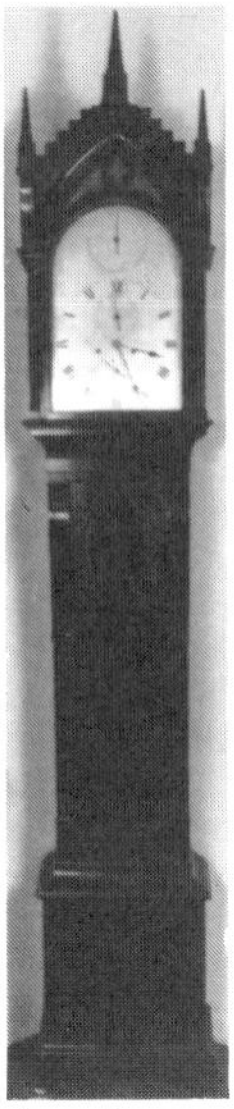

A mahogany longcase clock, with silvered dial, 8-day duration, hourly strike on a bell, subsidiary dial for seconds and 31-day calendar strike/silent by James Thwaites of London, c1808.
£7,500-8,000
SBA

A mahogany longcase clock, with swan arch pediment, the 12in (30.5cm) arched brass dial showing the phases of the moon, aperture for 31-day calendar and subsidiary dial for seconds, 8-day duration, hourly strike on a bell, by Richard Peyton, Gloucester, c1760, 94in (240cm).
£8,500-9,500
SBA

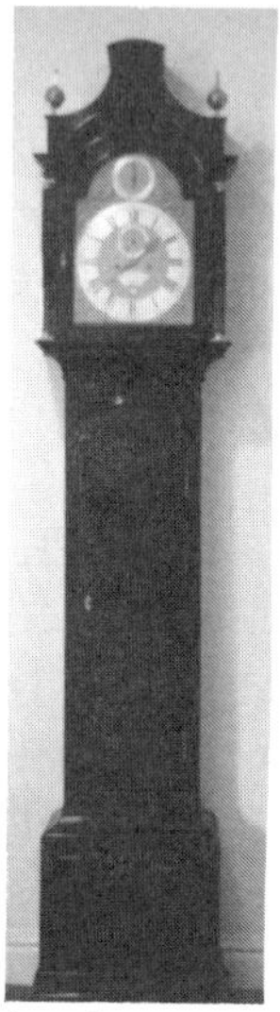

A mahogany longcase clock, by William Hughes, London, the 8-day movement striking the hours on a bell, the brass dial with seconds, date and strike/silent to the arch, c1765, 93in (236cm).
£5,500-6,000 *OX*

An oak longcase clock, the hood with a shaped and broken pediment, gilt brass scale panels and turned pillars at the corners, the arched brass dial with an oscillating ship in an engraved harbour surrounded by a semi-circular band, gilt brass rococo spandrels, silvered chapter ring, the centre with date aperture, engraved seconds dial, bell striking 8-day movement, inscribed Richd. Lear Pinhey Plymouth Dock, 94in (238cm).
£1,500-2,000
P(S)

A George III oak longcase clock, with 12in (30.5cm) brass dial, signed, with subsidiary seconds, date aperture and ringed winding holes, 8-day movement with inside count wheel, 4-finned pillars and anchor escapement, by Thomas Bridge, Wigan, 80in (203cm).
£1,000-1,500
P(M)

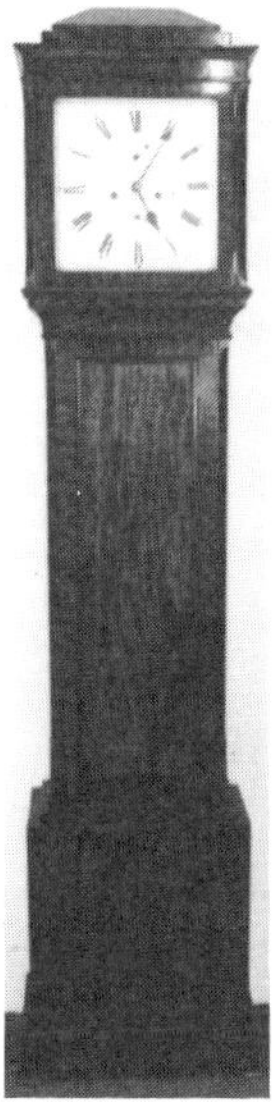

A mahogany longcase clock, with painted dial, subsidiary dial for seconds, 31-day calendar, hourly strike on a bell, by John Todd, Glasgow, c1825, 78in (198cm).
£3,500-4,500
SBA

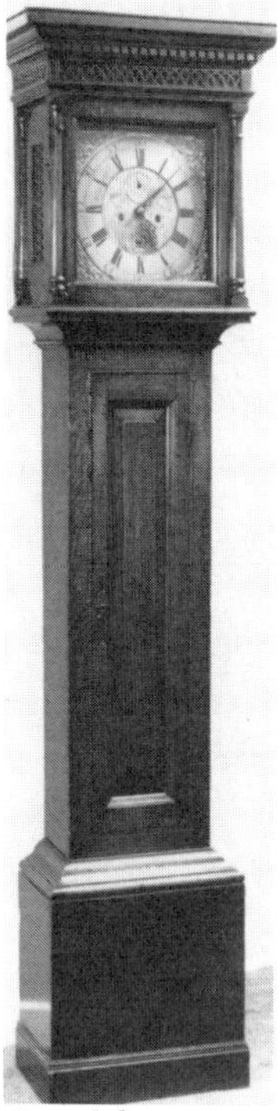

An oak longcase clock, with 11in (28cm) brass dial, with subsidiary seconds, date aperture, 8-day bell striking movement and a pair of brass cased weights, inscribed Peter Horner, Ripon, 18thC, 81in (205.5cm).
£1,500-2,500
MJB

An oak longcase clock, with painted arched dial movement, 8-day duration, 31-day calendar, subsidiary dial for seconds, hourly strike on a bell, by P Miller-Alloa, c1800, 85in (216cm).
£2,000-2,500
SBA

An oak and mahogany longcase clock, with swan neck pediment, rosewood decorated trunk and shaped door, the white dial inscribed Count Sleaford, with second dial and 8-day movement, 19thC, 85in (216cm).
£750-800 *DDM*

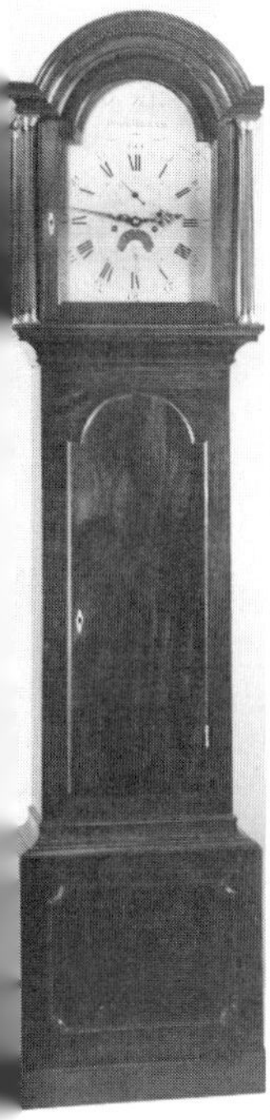

A mahogany longcase clock, c1770.
£3,500-4,000
HOL

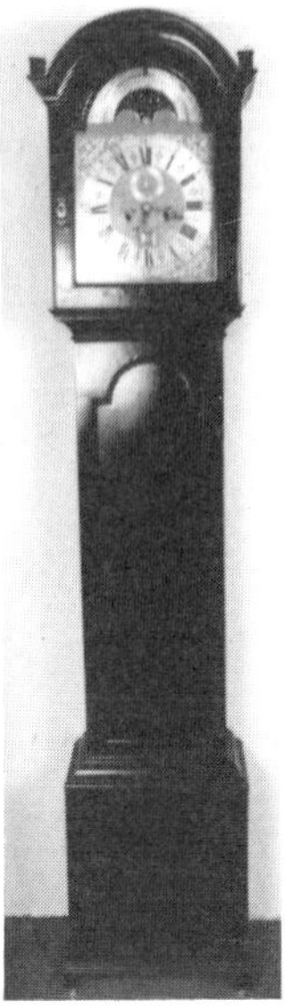

A Scottish red walnut longcase clock, with brass moon phase movement, sunburst inlay to the trunk, 8-day duration, 31-day calendar, subsidiary dial for seconds, hourly strike on a bell, by John Mearns, Aberdeen, c1760, 82in (208cm).
£6,500-7,500
SBA

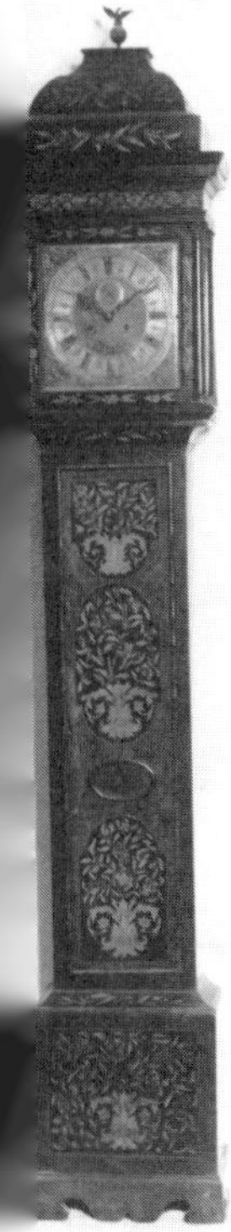

A walnut and marquetry longcase clock, with 12in (30.5cm) brass dial and silvered chapter ring, date aperture and seconds dial, late 17thC, the movement perhaps early 18thC, and Victorian alterations, 100in (254cm).
£4,000-4,500
GSP

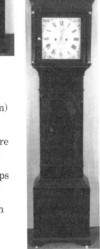

A mahogany longcase clock with 8-day duration, by Rowden, Stapleford, c1820, 78in (198cm).
£2,500-3,000 *SO*

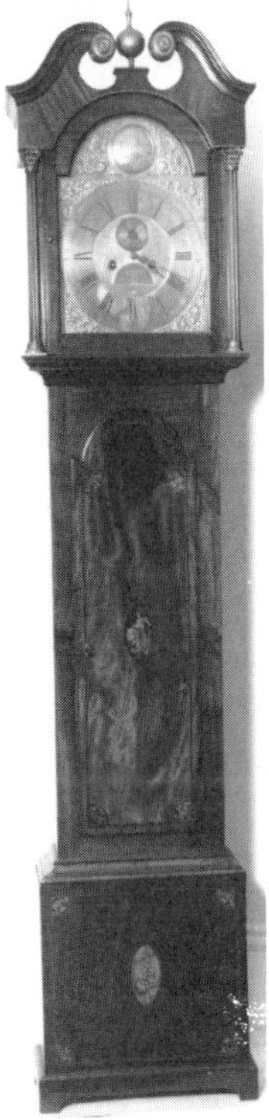

A George III Scottish 8-day longcase clock, with brass and silvered dial, seconds dial and date aperture, in mahogany case with swan neck pediment, Corinthian columns and door with marquetry Britannia and lion and plumes in angles, inscribed Will Morvat, Aberdeen and motto 'Keep your end in view', 83½in (211cm).
£2,500-3,000
GSP

A George III musical longcase clock, playing one tune of 7 bells every 4 hours, 8-day duration, hourly strike on a bell, subsidiary dial for seconds, in a mahogany case, inlaid with Sheraton shells, by James Pike, Newton Abbot, c1790, 83in (210.5cm).
£8,500-9,000
SBA

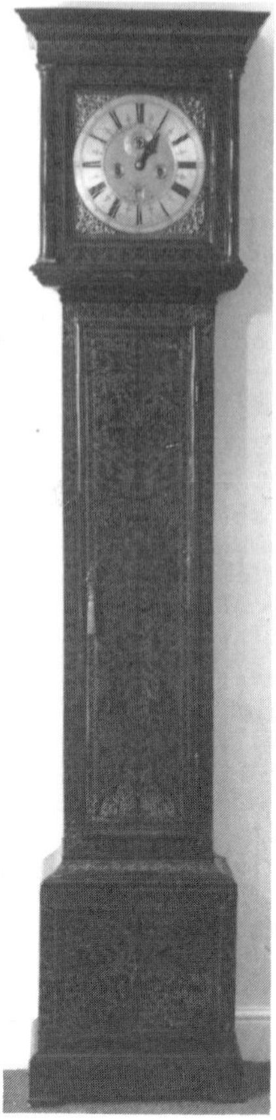

A marquetry longcase clock, with Transitional hood moulding and original frets, movement with internal count wheel and single latched pillar, by J Wiles, c1695, 88in (223.5cm).
£10,000-15,000
RFA

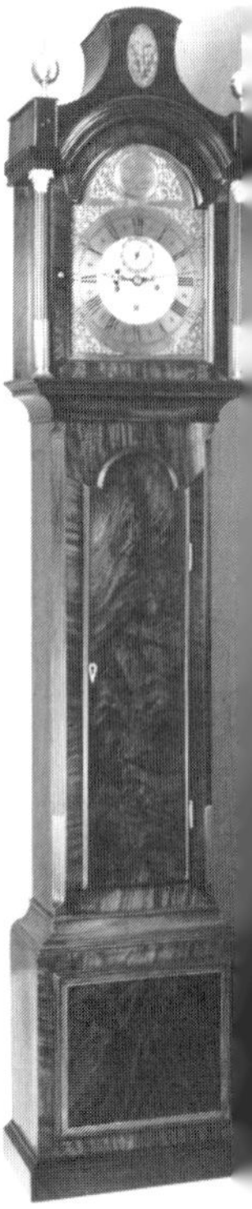

A mahogan
longcase clo
c1790.
£4,500-5,50
HOL

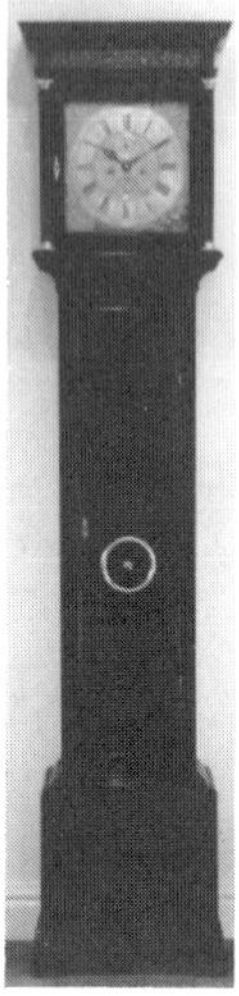

An ebonised longcase clock, by William Simes, London, the 8-day movement striking the hour on a bell, the movement with 5-plate pillars and rack striking, the brass dial with seconds and date, c1720.
£4,000-4,500 *OX*

A mahogany longcase clock with inlay, Wm. Bullock, Bath.
£4,000-5,000 *CLC*

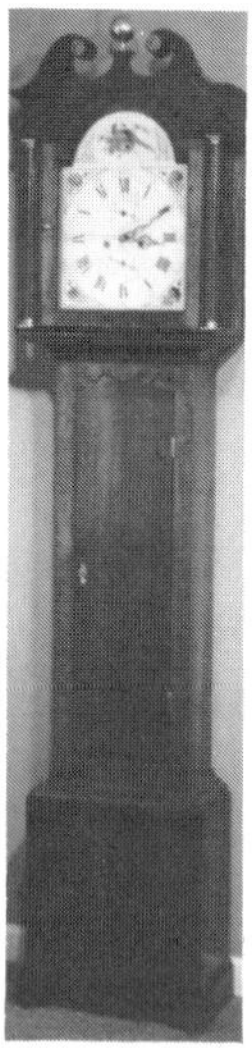

A Scottish oak longcase clock, by Walter Scott, the 8-day movement striking the hour on a bell and with seconds and date, with painted dial, c1780, 87in (221cm).
£2,000-3,000 *OX*

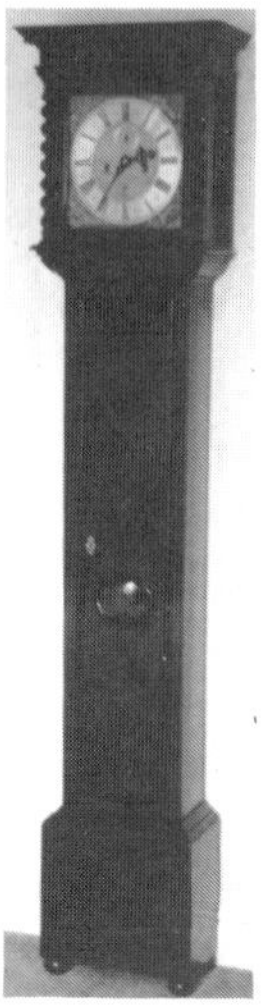

A walnut marquetry longcase clock, by Joseph Windmills, London, the 8-day movement with inside count wheel striking on a bell and 6 latched pillars, c1690, 80in (203cm).
£28,000-30,000
OX

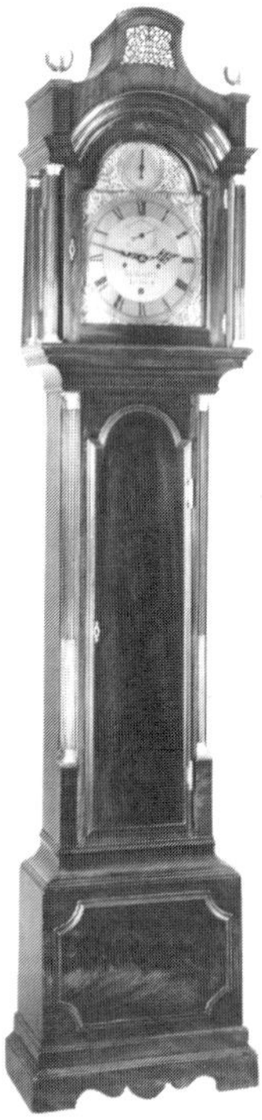

A mahogany longcase clock, c1770.
£5,500-6,500
HOL

An oak longcas
clock, the 8-day
movement with
anchor escapem
and Dutch strik
on 2 bells, the
5-pillar movem
with a verge al
and strike/silen
with plaque to
centre inscribe
Vincent Menil,
Amsterdam, la
18thC, 92in
(233.5cm).
£3,500-4,500
P(S)

₹egulators

walnut case
ring driven
ısical Vienna
gulator, c1860,
in (48cm).
50-550 *SBA*

A walnut case spring driven movement miniature Vienna regulator, 8-day duration, c1880, 18in (46cm).
£1,500-2,000
SBA

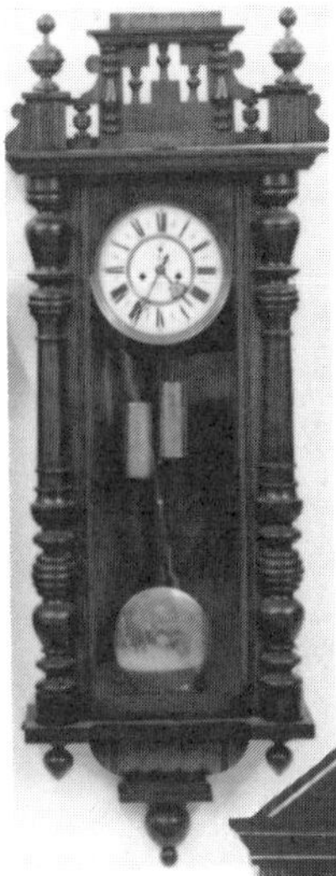

A walnut cased Vienna wall clock, with bobbin turned finial, ringed turned decoration to the case, enclosing a white dial and 8-day, 2-weight striking movement, late 19thC, 47½in (120cm).
£400-500 *DDM*

A Vienna regulator and ebonised spring wall clock, with gold inlay, late 19thC.
£450-500 *SBA*

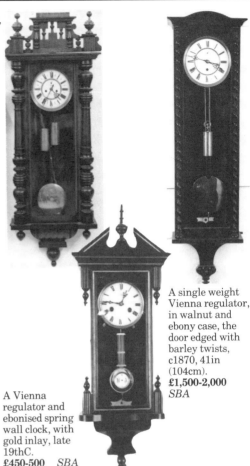

A single weight Vienna regulator, in walnut and ebony case, the door edged with barley twists, c1870, 41in (104cm).
£1,500-2,000
SBA

Three Vienna regulators.
£1,200-1,500 each *MAW*

A double weight Vienna regulator in walnut case, 44in (111.5cm).
£1,500-2,000
SBA

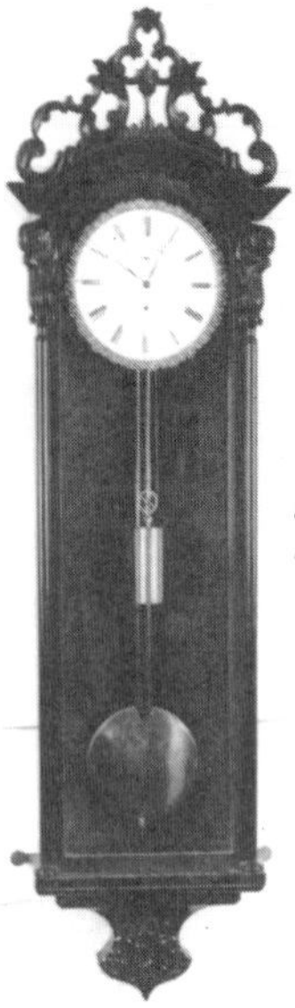

A single weight Vienna regulator in rosewood veneers edged with boxwood stringing, 8-day duration, maintaining pow dead beat escapement, G Becker, c1860, 42in (106.5cm).
£2,700-3,200
SBA

Bracket Clocks

An ebonised bracket clock, repeating on 6 bells, by Benj. Cotton, c1760, 22½in (57cm).
£3,500-4,000 *RFA*

A George III scarlet japanned striking bracket clock, with pierced wood quarter frets and gilt patterned glazed side frets, the florally painted dial signed Dollif Rollison Halton 472 on disc to the arch, brass chapter ring, the 5-pillar, centre pillar latched, twin fusee, wire lines, movement with verge escapement, foliate engraved backplate, 23in (58.5cm).
£2,500-3,000 *C*

A George III bracket clock by Francis Dorrell, London, the 8-day movement striking and repeating the hour on a bell, with verge escapement and engraved backplate, the dial with date aperture and strike/silent in the arch, in ebonised case with brass carrying handle, c1765.
£3,500-4,000 *OX*

A blue lacquered bracket clock, with original movement, finely engraved backplate and original verge, by Joshua Herring, c1750, 20in (51cm).
£5,000-6,000 *RFA*

A George III mahogany striking balloon bracket clock, with satinwood crossbanded case with gilt ball and eagle finial to bell top, white painted dial signed Evans Royal Exchange, London, with pierced gilt hands, 5-ringed pillar twin fusee movement, wire lines, with anchor escapement and pendulum holdfast, the similarly signed backplate with securing brackets to case, 33in (83.5cm).
£3,000-4,000 *C*

\ Regency mahogany bracket clock, he white enamel dial inscribed ;ibbs, London, 8-day bell striking usee movement, 20in (51cm).
:1,500-2,000 *P(S)*

\ Georgian ebonised bracket clock ith 3½in (8.5cm) white enamel ial, with 2 subsidiary dials in the rch for strike/silent and regulation, rass fret work side panels, bracket et and handles, and hole for repeat hord, missing, movement and dial ıscribed Grant, Fleet Street, ondon No. 210, 10in (25cm).
10,000-12,000 *GSP*

bracket clock, c1850.
4,000-5,000 *CLC*

A William IV mahogany bracket clock, with ring handles and brass mounts, the white dial with Roman numerals inscribed Henderson, Brigg, enclosing a brass 8-day single fusee non-striking movement, 19½in (49cm).
£500-700 *DDM*

An ebonised bracket clock, with silent escapement, by Wm. Hatton, 12in (31cm).
£2,500-3,000 *SBA*

A bracket clock, with web engraved back plate, by J Lawson of London, c1800. 16½in (42cm).
£2,500-3,000 *RFA*

A mahogany fusee bracket clock, by John Kemp, Yoxford, strikes the hour on a bell and repeats same at will, the original verge movement with engraved backplate and silvered brass dial incorporating strike/silent in the arch, c1790.
£4,500-5,000 *OX*

A mahogany bracket clock, with painted dial, 8-day duration, by S Norris, London, c1820, 15in (38cm).
£3,500-4,000 *SBA*

A George III mahogany bracket clock, the arched brass dial signed on a silvered cartouche, John Newton, London, subsidiary strike/silent ring to the arch, applied gilt metal rococo spandrels, the movement with verge escapement and bob pendulum, with glazed rear door, together with an associated oak bracket, c1790, 16½in (42cm).
£4,000-5,000 *N*

A Regency mahogany bracket clock, the case with gilded metal ring handles and pineapple finial, fluted pediment, brass inlaid dial surround on platform base, the white painted dial with Roman numerals, signed Hyman Bass & Co Louth, enclosing a single fusee non-striking 8-day movement, together with a mahogany wall bracket, 18½in (47cm).
£600-800 *DDM*

A Gothic style double fusee bracket clock in bronze case, Peter Hay, Edinburgh, c1840, 16in (41cm).
£1,000-1,200 *SBA*

A Regency mahogany bracket clock the chamfered top with gilt brass pineapple finial, brass beaded panels and canted corners, brass ball feet, the dial inscribed Thomas Reid, Edinburgh, bell striking fusee movement, 17in (43cm).
£1,500-2,000 *P(S)*

A late Regency rosewood striking bracket clock, with brass inlaid side angles, on wood bun feet, the engraved silvered dial signed in the arch G. Philcox Patentee London No 13, with blued Breguet hands, the 4-pillar twin fusee movement with shaped plates and anchor escapement, brackets to case, 11½in (30cm).
£1,700-2,500 *C*

A Georgian mahogany bracket clock, with repeating movement in lancet case, the silvered dial inscribed Recordon late Emery, London, with inlaid motifs and brass grilles and feet, on contemporary bracket with sliding front and secret key compartment, 17½in (45cm).
£1,500-2,000 *GSP*

A Georgian style mahogany bracke clock, with stepped pediment and base, the silvered dial enclosing a double fusee movement with strike on a single bell, 19in (49cm).
£400-500 *DDM*

An ebonised musical repeating bracket clock, made for the Turkish market, the silvered chapter ring with Turkish numerals, date aperture, the arch with subsidiary strike and chime, silent dial and tune selection dial flanking a shaped silvered panel signed Edward Pistor, London, the 3-train movement with verge escapement, striking the hours on a single bell and the quarters on 10 bells with 17 hammers operated from a pin barrel, together with an ebonised bracket with brass gallery and turned pendants, 18thC, 22½in (57cm).
£3,500-4,000 *P(S)*

An Edwardian bracket fusee clock.
£2,500-3,000 *CLC*

. George III mahogany striking
racket clock, with mock pendulum
nd calendar apertures, signed on a
laque W Turnbull, Darlington,
ith silvered chapter ring, twin
hain fusee movement with scroll
ngraved backplate also signed,
ith vertical rack and pinion rise
nd fall, pull quarter repeat,
rackets to case, 19½in (49cm).
4,500-5,000 *C*

A Louis XV ormolu mounted polychrome boulle bracket clock, with glazed enamel dial, the bracket with a floral spray and pierced foliate boss, stamped A G Peridiez, 42½in (108cm).
£1,200-1,500 *C*

A rosewood and inlaid bracket or mantel clock, with a rounded arch pediment having four brass urn finials, brass mounted fluted columns at the corners, brass bracket feet and side grilles, inlaid with a classical and foliate design, circular silvered dial, wire gong striking movement, late 19thC, 14½in (37cm).
£200-250 *P(S)*

A bracket clock in a mahogany case, the brass and silvered dial signed Wm Smith, London, c1770.
£9,000-12,000 *HOL*

A keyhole shaped mahogany bracket clock, by Simmons, London, the shaped 8-day movement striking the hour on a bell and with engraved border to the backplate, finely chased bezel to the dial, c1835, 15in (38cm) high.
£2,500-3,000 *OX*

A mahogany bracket clock with applied gilded embellishment, 8-day duration, hourly strike on a bell/pull repeat strike, by Vulliam of London, c1830, 15in (38cm).
£6,500-7,500 *SBA*

A George III fruitwood striking bracket clock, the dial signed Joseph Trattle Newport, on a shaped silvered chapter ring, pierced blue hands, scroll spandrels, strike/silent to the arch, the 4-pillar twin fusee, wire lines, movement with verge escapement, trip repeat, foliate engraved backplate, brackets to case, 16in (40.5cm).
£4,500-5,000 *C*

A mahogany bracket clock, by Edward Scales, London, the 8-day movement with verge escapement, engraved backplate, striking the hour on a bell, the brass dial with date and strike/silent, c1765.
£5,500-6,000 *OX*

A Regency mahogany striking bracket clock, with brass lined quarter mouldings, the glazed painted dial signed James McCab Royal Exchange London 1410, wi pierced Breguet hands and strike/silent above XII, 19½in (50cm).
£1,700-2,000 *C*

A Regency mahogany bracket clock in Egyptian style, by John Wakefield, London, with sphinx caryatids to the front and engraved brass bezel to the face, the 8-day fusee movement with anchor escapement and striking the hours on a bell, c1820.
£3,500-4,000 *OX*

A bracket clock, by Joseph Windmills, case restored, c1720.
£6,500-7,000 *RFA*

Did you know

MILLER'S Antiques Price Guide builds up year by year to form the most comprehensive photo-reference system available

Carriage Clocks

A satinwood English 4 glass carriage clock, chain fusee movement, by Barwise London, c1830, 9in (23cm).
£2,000-2,500 *SO*

A reproduction silver striking carriage clock, with uncut balance to lever platform, strike/repeat on bell on backplate signed Charles Frodsham London, similarly signed white dial with Roman numerals and blued spade hands within a florally engraved silver mask, anglaise case, base numbered 0012, 6½in (17cm).
£500-700 *C*

A gilt brass carriage clock, with strike repeat movement, with white enamelled dial and filigree dial surround, early 20thC, 8½in (21cm), with leather outer case.
£600-700 *GD*

A brass repeating carriage clock, in corniche case with white enamel dial and striking movement, 6½in (17cm), in morocco covered carrying case.
£350-400 *HCH*

Clocks
All clock measurements refer to height unless otherwise stated

A carriage clock, with repeating movement in engraved brass one-piece case, with lion's mask handle terminals, the white dial inscribed Martin Baskett & Cie, Paris, 5in (13cm).
£700-900 *GSP*

A brass carriage clock, striking a gong, c1880, 5in (13cm).
£650-700 *SBA*

A miniature carriage clock, 8-day duration, in serpentine case with cloisonné decoration, 3in (8cm).
£500-600 *SO*

A brass case repeating alarm carriage clock, with white enamel dials on a silvered ground, 6in (15cm), in leather travelling case.
£450-500 *GSP*

A French striking carriage clock, signed Soldano, c1870, 5½in (15cm).
£700-900 *SO*

A gilt brass striking carriage clock, with cut bimetallic balance to silvered lever platform strike/repeat/alarm on gong, white enamel dial signed Le Roy & Fils 57, New Bond Street, Made in France Palais-Royal Paris, with blued spade hands, subsidiary alarm ring below VI, corniche case, 5½in (15cm), leather travelling case.
£500-700 *C*

A gilt brass striking carriage clock with uncut bimetallic balance to silvered lever platform, strike/repeat on gong, white enamel dial indistinctly signed, with blued Breguet hands, 5½in (15cm), leather travelling case.
£700-800 *C*

An early satinwood striking carriage clock, with plain 3 arm balance to gilt lever platform, strik on bell, backplate stamped Hy Ma Paris, similarly signed white enamel dial with blued Breguet hands within engraved gilt bevell surround, one-piece satinwood cas with carrying handle to top, 6in (15.5cm).
£500-600 *C*

A gilt brass one-piece striking carriage clock, with compensated 3 arm balance to lever platform strike/repeat on bell, backplate wit stamp of Japy Frères, white enam dial signed Brevet D'Invention S G D G, with blued Breguet hanc 5½in (15cm).
£900-1,200 *C*

A gilt brass grande sonnerie striking carriage clock, with later platform lever escapement, strike/repeat on 2 gongs, backplate with stamp of Richard & Cie, 3 position selection lever to base, the white enamel dial signed Smith & Sons, with Roman numerals and blued spade hands, corniche case, 6in (16cm).
£800-900 *C*

A French repeating alarm carriage clock, striking the hours and half hours, with enamel chapter ring and alarm dial within a floral fret work panel, all set in a gilt brass case with hobnail style decoration, 6½in (16cm).
£1,000-1,200 *GSP*

A miniature carriage clock, c1870, 3in (8cm).
£450-500 *RFA*

A French cloisonné carriage clock, 4½in (11cm).
£550-650 *RFA*

\ gilt brass striking carriage clock, vith uncut bimetallic balance to ilvered platform level escapement, trike/repeat on gong, white enamel lial with blued Breguet hands, 5½in 15cm).
'550-650 *C*

A gilt brass striking carriage clock, with uncut bimetallic balance to silvered lever platform, strike on gong, backplate with stamp of Jacot, white enamel dial, blued spade hands, corniche case, 5½in (15cm).
£600-700 *C*

\ French carriage clock, the noulded case with fine decoration, ever escapement, 8-day duration, ıourly and half-hourly strike on a ell, by Lucien, Paris, c1840, 5in 14cm).
:950-1,200 *SBA*

A German miniature carriage clock, with lever escapement, 8-day duration, c1890, 2½in (6cm).
£400-450 *SBA*

An Austrian carriage clock with date, month, days and full grande sonnerie strike alarm/strike/silent, c1870, 7in (18cm).
£1,500-1,800 *SO*

Mantel Clocks

A Regency satinwood mantel clock, fusee time piece with alarm by Robert Ward, London, 13½in (34cm).
£5,000-6,000 *SO*

A mantel timepiece with silvered dial inscribed Jas Brown, London, with screw adjusting locking pendulum, in brass inlaid ebonized case, early 19thC, 9½in (24cm).
£350-450 *GSP*

A Gothic brass mantel clock, with enamel dial, 8-day duration, hourl strike on a gong, c1860, 9½in (24cm
£850-950 *SBA*

A mantel clock, with timepiece movement, c1820.
£1,200-1,500 *HOL*

An ebonised mantel calendar timepiece, the engine turned gilt dial with Roman numerals and engraved arch below, numbered from the centre with mechanical day dial, with simple fusee movement, early 19thC, 7in (18cm).
£1,000-1,500 *GSP*

An early Victorian satinwood veneered case mantel timepiece, th 8-day fusee movement with an engraved silvered dial and backplate inscribed Birch Fenchurch St., London, bevelled glass panels, the ogee frieze to a plinth base, 8½in (21cm).
£1,200-1,500 *WW*

A late Regency rosewood mantel timepiece, the case with ball finial to stepped gadrooned top and on wood bun feet, the arched engraved silvered dial with Roman numerals and signed Thos. Cox Savory 47 Cornhill London 762, blued steel Breguet hands, the 4-pillar single chain fusee movement with anchor escapement, 12in (30cm).
£1,200-1,500 *C*

A small gilt clock, 8-day duration, c1870, 4in (10cm).
£300-400 *SO*

An Edwardian mantel clock, by J W Benson of Ludgate Hill, London, th 8-day movement with quarter strike, the brass dial and silvered chapter ring within an architectura rosewood case with classical inlay and stringing, with ogee pediment and faceted pilasters.
£600-700 *MN*

An English brass desk clock, c1870, in (15cm).
300-400 *SO*

A gilt spelter and alabaster cased mantel clock, the white dial enclosing a French brass movement with strike, late 19thC, 14½in (37cm).
£90-120 *DDM*

A gilt metal and white marble mantel timepiece, surmounted by Cupid, 8in (20cm).
£400-450 *GSP*

mahogany clock, 9in (23cm).
50-750 *SBA*

A French balloon clock inlaid with satinwood, c1900, 10in (25cm).
£200-300 *SO*

A grey spelter cased mantel clock, with classical figure finial over a tapering case with mask mounts, on a rectangular stepped base and marble plinth, the French brass 8-day movement striking on a single bell, late 19thC, 17in (44cm).
£70-100 *DDM*

A French 4-glass mantel clock, 11in (28cm).
£800-900 *SO*

An English fusee clock, by Frodsham, with gilded and engraved dial, 19thC, 9½in (24cm). **£600-650** *RFA*

A Victorian black marble clock, with female mask designs to the sides, striking French movement, Japy Frères.
£100-200 *GAK*

A Louis XVI ormolu and cream marble portico mantel clock, the enamel dial signed Piolaine A Paris.
£1,700-2,000 *C*

A French rosewood and marquetry mantel clock, striking on a bell, 8-day duration, c1850, 13½in (34cm).
£1,100-1,200 *SO*

A French gilt clock, with Sèvres panels, c1860, 17in (43cm).
£1,500-2,000 *SBA*

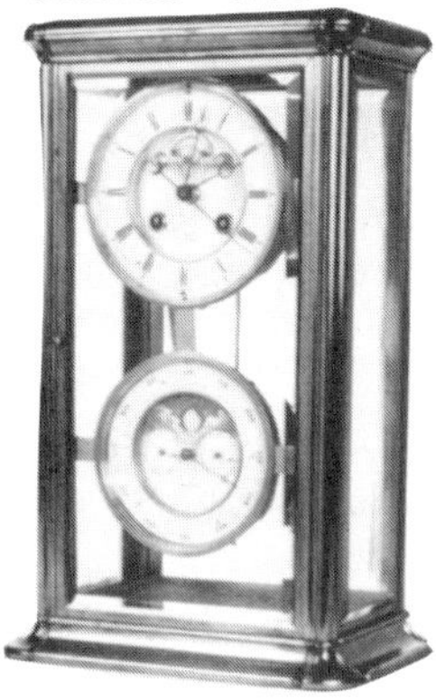

A gilt brass 4-glass striking mantel clock, with perpetual calendar dial below the chapter ring with jewelled visible Brocot escapement in the recessed centre, signed Steward Glasgow, with blued Breguet hands, the movement with twin going barrels striking on a bell on backplate, gorge type case, later plinth base, 17in (43cm).
£2,500-3,000 *C*

A small French boulle clock, 8-day duration, tortoiseshell case with brass inlay, c1860, 8in (20cm).
£900-1,200 *SO*

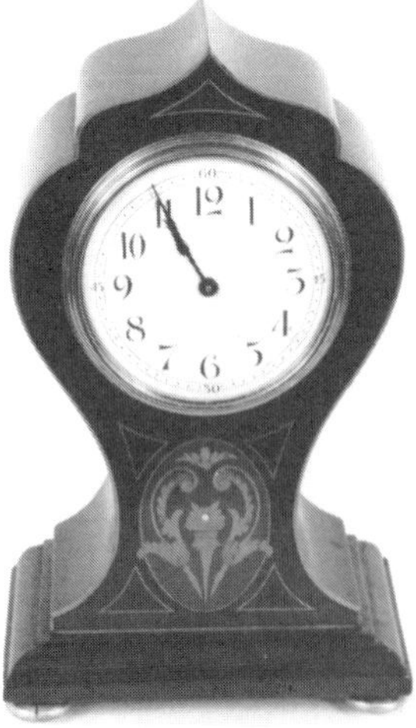

A French balloon clock, c1900, 10 (25cm).
£200-250 *SO*

A French Empire mantel clock, b B P & F No. 4618, with 4½in (11.5cm) gilt dial to the 8-day striking movement, supported in bird's-eye maple veneered case w arched and moulded top, on 4 columns with gilt mounts, 19th 22½in (57cm).
£700-900 *GA(W)*

A French clock, by Morgan Paris, 8-day duration, boulle case with tortoiseshell, c1870, 13½in (34cm).
£800-900 *SO*

A French ormolu ebonised and boulle mantel clock, with French striking movement, 19thC.
£450-500 *GAK*

A French gilt brass and porcelain mantel clock, the porcelain dial with Roman numerals, the movement striking the hours and half-hours on a gong, with giltwood stand, pendulum and winding key, late 19thC, 17½in (44cm).
£550-600 *Bea*

A mahogany cased mantel clock, with fusee movement, the dial inscribed LNWR, 13in (33cm).
£200-300 *ONS*

A French horseshoe mantel clock c1910, 5in (13cm).
£200-250 *SO*

A Charles X French gilt bronze mantel clock, with engine turned gilt dial flanked by a dog and a classical figure playing a flute, surmounted by a 2-handled urn, with 2-train spring driven movement with count wheel mechanism striking on a bell, 17in (43cm).
£500-700 *P(M)*

An oak balloon clock, 8-day French movement, c1910, 10in (25cm).
£100-150 *SO*

A French mantel clock, the movement stamped S Marti, with 4½in (11.5cm) white enamel dial, in ormolu mounted tortoiseshell veneered case, 13½in (34cm).
£550-600 *GSP*

A French mantel clock, 8-day striking with gilt case, c1900, 15in (38cm).
£400-500 *SO*

A French mantel clock, silk suspension, outside count strike on a bell, 8-day duration, by F C Paris, c1860.
£800-900 *SO*

An ebony clock, with enamel decoration, Laine A Paris, 14in (36cm).
£370-420 *SBA*

A French ormolu and ebony clock, c1840, 26in (66cm).
£6,000-6,500 *RFA*

A similar clock is in the Royal apartments in Windsor Castle, and there is reason to believe that this piece has Royal connections.

Lantern Clocks

A miniature winged brass lantern clock, with verge escapement and pendulum bob in the form of an anchor, the dial centre engraved with tulips, the front and wing frets also engraved, the arrow shaped steel hand indicating hours only, iron backplate fitted hoop and spikes, 9½in (24cm).
£1,500-2,000 *P(S)*

A lantern clock, half ting tang fusee movement, 19thC, 23in (59cm).
£2,800-3,000 *SBA*

A brass lantern clock, with anchor escapement, seconds pendulum and brass cased weight hoop and spikes to the rear, the chapter ring inscribed Danl. Hoskins, the single steel hand indicates hours only, lacking side and back doors, 15½in (39cm).
£550-600 *P(S)*

A brass lantern clock, 10in (25cm).
£400-450 *SBA*

A silver lantern timepiece, perhaps German, the movement with verge escapement and verge alarm, the dial plate with a central alarm setting dial, the single steel hand indicating minutes only on the chapter ring, the case surmounted with engraved dolphin frets, two brass weights and counter weights, modern wooden wall bracket, 9in (23cm).
£2,700-3,000 *P(S)*

A French lantern clock, 8-day duration, c1900, 9in (23cm).
£200-300 *SO*

Skeleton Clocks

skeleton clock by Read of Ipswich, 1½in (29cm).
700-800 *RFA*

A Victorian brass frame skeleton timepiece, with single fusee and chain movement, subsidiary seconds dial with star, pierced centre by Dwerrihouse, Ogston and Bell, on oval mahogany base, no dome, 13½in (34cm).
£2,500-3,000 *GSP*

A Walter Scott Memorial skeleton clock, with brass inlaid rosewood base, c1851, 20in (51cm).
£2,000-2,500 *SBA*

A Walter Scott Memorial Skeleton clock, striking on a gong, on a marble base, c1851, 19in (49cm).
£1,700-2,000 *SBA*

Clocks
All clock measurements refer to height unless otherwise stated

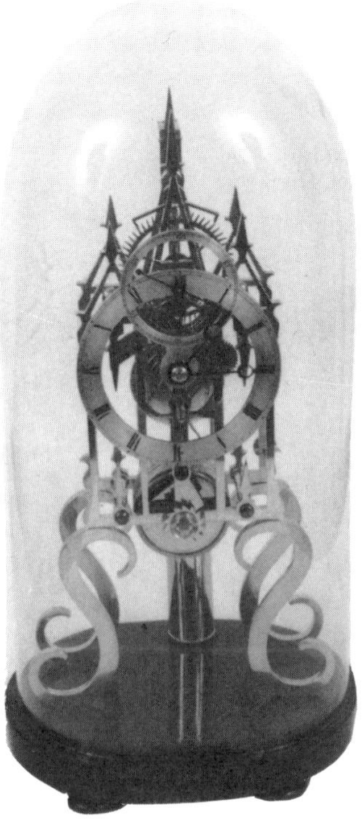

A rare English skeleton clock, Grant scope wheel and seconds dial, semi dead beat.
£1,200-1,500 *RFA*

Wall Clocks

A lacquer wall clock with alarm, c1730, 18in (46cm).
£2,700-3,000 *SBA*

A Swedish wall clock by Carl Bergstein, striking 8-day duration, with silk work suspension, and giltwood case, c1790, 30in (76cm).
£2,000-2,500 *SO*

H & E. GAYDON
BRENTFORD

An English single fusee dial clock, convex dial cast bezel 8-day duration, by H & E Gaydon of Brentford, London, c1830.
£550-600 *SBA*

Hastings

An English 12-hour fusee dial clock, 8-day duration, mahogany case, by Dobell, Hastings, c1880, 15½in (39cm) diam.
£400-450 *SO*

A mahogany clock with brass bezel, 8-day duration, c1830.
£400-500 *SBA*

A mahogany clock with brass bezel, 8-day duration, Fontana, High Wycombe, c1830.
£700-800 *SBA*

LEWES

A mahogany and inlaid wall clock, c1840, 20in (51cm).
£450-500 *RFA*

An English mahogany wall clock, with dial spring movement, c1860
£250-300 *SBA*

HALEY
LONDON

An apprentice mahogany wall clock, with fusee movement, 8-day duration, c1840, 14in (36cm).
£2,000-2,500 *SO*

A brass English ship's clock, early 20thC, 9in (23cm).
£325-375 *RFA*

A single fusee clock in mahogany case, inlaid with brass stringing, c1830.
£850-900 *SBA*

mahogany wall clock, 20in (51cm).
:50-500 *RFA*

LONDON
801SE

traditional railway clock, from
e South East Region, each part
amped with No. 801, 20in (51cm).
:50-500 *RFA*

English verge wall timepiece
h alarm, with silvered chapter
g, signed on a plaque in the arch,
Graham, London, the
vement with knife-edge verge
apement, the alarm with
arate pulley and operating on a
mounted on the shaped top
te, restoration, 5in (13cm).
)00-4,500 *C*

A small ship's bulkhead clock by Hughes, chromium plated and keyless winding, 6in (15cm).
£50-80 *RFA*

De La Salle
London

A rare striking Regency drop dial wall clock, double fusee movement, by De La Salle, London, 21in (53cm).
£2,000-2,400 *SO*

A carved walnut Gothic design wall clock, with single fusee, 8-day duration, c1850, J Brunner of Birmingham.
£950-1,000 *SBA*

A mahogany surround hanging wall clock, 6in (15cm). **£500-600** *SBA*

A French cartel clock, with gilt case, 8-day striking on bell, by Japy Frères, c1870, 20in (51cm).
£1,100-1,200 *SO*

A mahogany trunk wall clock, with shaped glass panel showing the pendulum, the convex glass enclosing a painted dial and single fusee movement, 19thC, 21in (54cm).
£300-400 *DDM*

Make the Most of Miller's

In Miller's we do NOT just reprint saleroom estimates. We work from realised prices either from an auction room or a dealer. Our consultants then work out a realistic price range for a similar piece. This is to try to avoid repeating freak results – either low or high

A rosewood and brass inlaid wall clock, made in Germany, retailed in Exeter by S F Hettish, c1840, 27in (69cm).
£500-600 *RFA*

A mahogany cased trunk wall clock, with inlaid decoration, carved and fretwork design, the white dial enclosing a striking American movement, late 19thC, 28in (71cm).
£120-170 *DDM*

A Vienna wall clock, the case with rearing horse and ring turned pediment, turned pillar sides, enclosing a white dial with strikir 8-day movement, 42in (106.5cm).
£150-200 *DDM*

A Georgian wall dial, the convex glazed engraved silvered 8in (20cm) dial, with mock pendulum aperture and pierced hands, the 4-pillar single gut fusee movement with knife-edge verge escapement and short bob pendulum, in later purpose made pegged mahogany case with side door, signed Thomas Harvey, London, 7½in (11cm).
£2,000-3,000 *C*

A Zaandam clock of typical form, the brass posted frame movement with Tuscan angle columns, Dutch strike on 2 bells above the velvet covered dial, signed Cornelis van Rossen on the chapter ring, 36in (91cm).
£2,000-4,000 *C*

Garnitures

A French 3-piece clock set with 8-day striking movement, the clock surmounted by Nymphe de Torrent, by A Quintrand.
£200-250 *MGM*

A French garnitu c1870, 12½in (32cm).
£2,000-2,500 *S*

A pink marble and ormolu cloc garniture, the clock with enam dial, inscribed Made in France Jas Crighton & Co., Edinburgh surmounted by an urn on a flut column and canted plinth, the candlesticks with beaded festoo nozzles on fluted columns, the 8½in (22cm).
£600-800 *C*

A French 3-piece mantel clock set, with 8-day striking movement, surmou by swan and girl, o marble base.
£100-150 *MGM*

Table clocks

An ormolu mounted ebony table clock, made for the Turkish market, the movement with verge escapement striking the hours on a bell and fitted with a six-bell repeater, the backplate engraved with scrolling foliate designs, the numerals changed from Turkish to Roman, engraved in the arch Geo. Prior London, 18thC, 20in (51cm).
£6,500-7,000 *P(S)*

A French table clock, 8-day duration, c1890, 5½in (14cm).
£300-350 *SO*

A Germanic table clock, with steel frontplate and pillars, brass backplate, chain fusee for the going with spring balance verge escapement, resting barrels for the hour and quarter strike on 2 bells in the hinged base, going barrel alarm, copper gilt dial with brass chapter ring, on winged paw and alternating toupie feet, signed Charleson London, initially early 17thC, extensively reconstructed mid-18thC, 6in (15cm) diam.
£3,000-3,500 *C*

A Germanic brass table clock, with chain fusee for the going with spring balance, verge escapement, pierced square footed cock, resting barrels for hour strike and alarm on bell in hinged base, signed Wenzl Wachter in Gaya, No. 151, basically 18thC, 3½in (8cm) diam.
£2,000-2,500 *C*

An English bird's-eye maple table clock, with fusee movement, 8-day duration, by William Hardy, c1830, 11in (28cm).
£1,500-1,800 *SO*

A boudoir clock, with engraved dial bezel, late 19thC, 8in (20cm).
£475-525 *RFA*

Miscellaneous

A carriage or desk clock, by Howell & Jones, 7in (18cm).
£675-725 *RFA*

NB. This was given by Disraeli to his private secretary, Sir Charles Wilson, who later became the President of the Grand Trunk Railway of Canada and thereafter to his descendents.

A Dutch walnut veneer longcase organ clock, numerous wood pipes, in need of restoration, early 19thC, 118in (300cm).
£850-900 *IM*

A dark brass Gravity clock, made in USA, 10in (25cm).
£350-450 *SBA*

An English organ clock, attributed to George Ryke, London, the engraved brass dial set in an elaborate cartouche flanked by Diana and Mercury, 2 subsidiary dials above for tune selection and lock/unlock for music, the timepiece fusee movement with verge escapement and a separate fusee organ movement driving a pinned wood barrel operating 15 valves and 44 pipes with 3 stops playing a choice of 9 tunes, c1750.
£20,000-25,000 *OX*

A brass alarm clock, with stainless steel surround, 4in (10cm).
£250-300 *SBA*

A musical clock, playing any one c 8 tunes every four hours or at will by Ellicot, c1770, 19thC, 27½in (70cm).
£7,000-7,500 *RFA*

A decorative silver front clock, wi lizard skin sides and pine back, 4i (10cm).
£350-400 *SBA*

A brass clock, 3in (8cm).
£200-300 *SBA*

A Gravity clock, with 30-hour duration, by Kee Less Clock Co, England, c1900, 10½in (26cm).
£200-300 *SO*

A small silver clock, top lift reveal a compass, by Mappi Webb, c1904, 7in (18cm).
£600-700 *RFA*

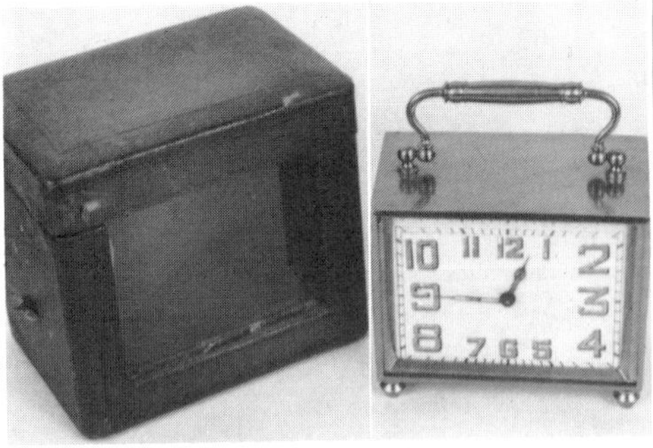

A travelling clock and case, c1920, 3in (8cm).
£150-200 *SO*

A Marjaine miniature clock, 2½in (6cm).
£500-600 *RFA*

A French automaton windmill clock, with timepiece, aneroid barometer and 2 thermometers in naturalistic gun metal case, with revolving sails worked from separate motor turned through front door, 17in (43cm).
£750-850 *GSP*

An American ship's clock, 8-day platform movement, by Waterbury, c1910, 8in (20cm).
£300-400

A ship's clock, by Seth Thomas, made in USA, 10½in (26cm).
£300-400 *RFA*

A mercury pendulum 400-day clock with glass dome, c1890, 11½in (29cm).
£600-650 *RFA*

400 day-clock with glass dome, 390, 11½in (29cm).
50-300 *RFA*

gilt metal strut timepiece, graved silvered dial and e, numbered 971 by Thomas le, retailers Tessier & Son, thC, 6in (15cm).
00-800 *GSP*

Price

Prices vary from auction to auction – from dealer to dealer. The price paid in a dealer's shop will depend on:
1) what he paid for the item
2) what he thinks he can get for it
3) the extent of his knowledge
4) awareness of market trends
It is a mistake to think that you will automatically pay more in a specialist dealer's shop. He is more likely to know the 'right' price for a piece. A general dealer may undercharge but he could also overcharge

Watches

A silver pair case verge pocket watch by Lampe, London, with silver champlevé dial, blued steel beetle and poker hands, signed by the maker on a cartouche, the frosted gilt fusee movement with pierced cock and foot to the edge of the top plate, the pillars decorated with unusual pierced Royal Crest of King George I, the inner and outer cases bearing the mark TB surmounted by a crown, possibly Thomas Bamford, London, early 18thC, 5.5cm.
£2,000-2,500 *CSK*

A white gold and diamond pendant watch, 4cm.
£350-450 *RFA*

An English silver pocket watch, c1880, 3cm.
£80-100 *RFA*

A Victorian gold watch, with flow engraved dial, 4cm.
£250-300 *RFA*

A Victorian ladies gold fob watch, with cylinder movement, 3cm.
£110-125 *RFA*

An engraved silver pocket watch, with enamel flower decoration, 4cm.
£100-130 *RFA*

A Dine 18 carat gold hunter case minute repeating centre seconds keyless chronograph, the white enamelled dial with black Romar numerals and Arabic minute rin enclosing a subsidiary seconds di with centre seconds, the jewelled lever escapement striking on 2 gongs, with dust cap, in a plain cas
£800-1,200 *HSS*

A Victorian ladies Swiss silver fob watch, 3cm.
£30-50 *RFA*

A pink gold two-train independent seconds keyless hunter pocket watch, in rubbed engine turned case with engraved monogram to the front cover, with white enamel dial, decorative gold hands and sweep centre jumping seconds hand operated by a button in the band, 5.5cm.
£500-1,000 *CSK*

MICKEY
INGERSOLL

keyless open face Mickey Mouse
›cket watch, by Ingersoll, the
ıbsidiary seconds indicated by
volving disc with 3 Mickeys, the
me indicated by Mickey's arms,
ıe signed three-quarter plate
ovement stamped P69, c1930,
:m.
300-500 *CSK*

'ristwatches

Rolex Oyster gentleman's
istwatch, with subsidiary seconds
ıl, in stainless steel case, with
er bracelet.
00-350 *GSP*

Rolex Oyster perpetual
istwatch, the dial inscribed
ıppin and Chronometre, with
minous hands and numerals and
bsidiary seconds dial, in stainless
el case.
00-450 *GSP*

A Rolex Oyster gentleman's perpetual wristwatch, in stainless steel case.
£150-200 *GSP*

A Rolex gentleman's square faced wristwatch, in 9ct. gold case, inscribed 'The Alex Clarke Co., London', glass missing.
£400-450 *GSP*

> **Make the Most of Miller's**
>
> ***Every care has been taken to ensure the accuracy of descriptions and estimated valuations. Price ranges in this book reflect what one should expect to pay for a similar example. When selling one can obviously expect a figure below. This will fluctuate according to a dealer's stock, saleability at a particular time, etc. It is always advisable to approach a reputable specialist dealer or an auction house which has specialist sales***

BAROMETERS
Stick

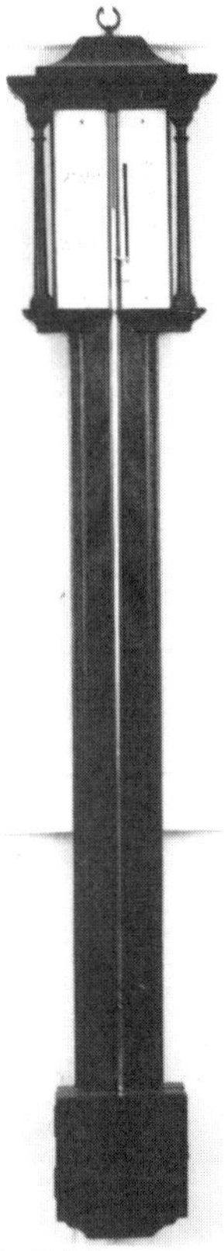

A walnut stick barometer, with silver scale, early 19thC, 37in (94cm).
£1,000-1,200 *SBA*

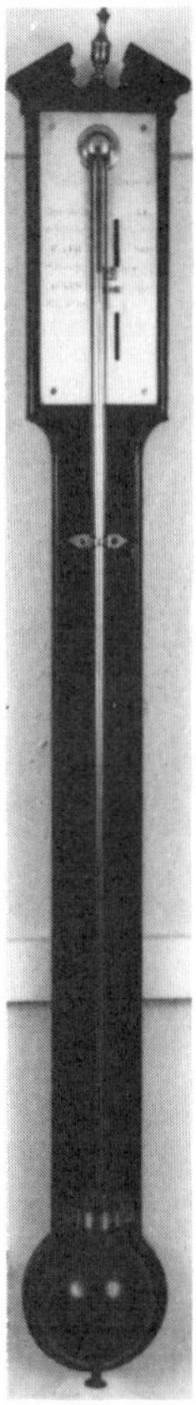

A mahogany stick barometer by Dollond of London, c1810.
£2,500-3,000 *SBA*

A mahogany stick barometer, by Edward Nairne, London, c1765.
£1,500-2,000 *OX*

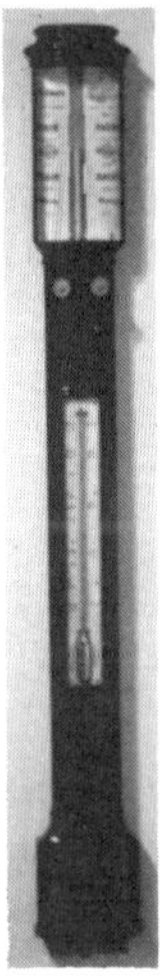

A bowfronted mercurial barometer, in an ebony veneered case, by Samuel Chare, Taunton, the ivory scales engraved and incorporate 2 setting verniers for a.m. and p.m., with a thermometer set into the front of the case, c1840.
£2,500-3,000 *OX*

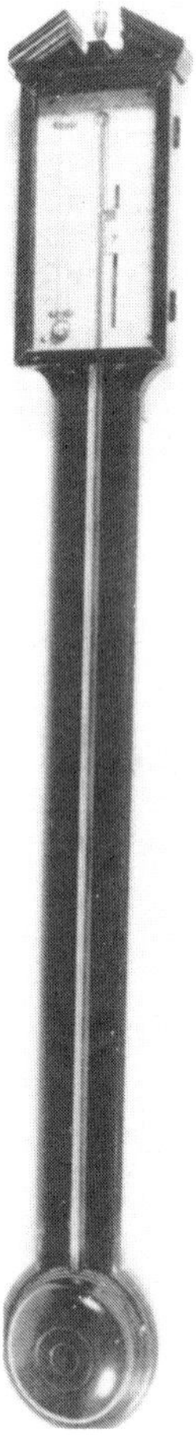

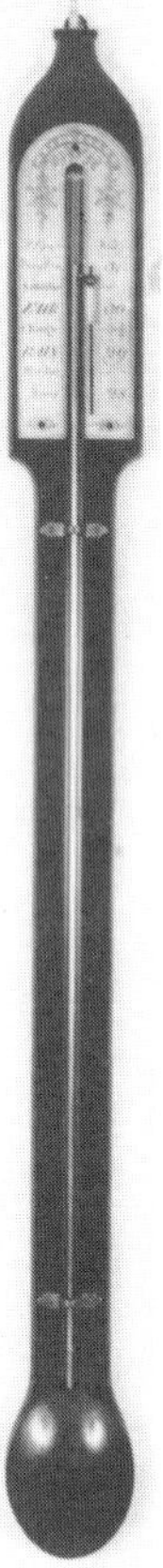

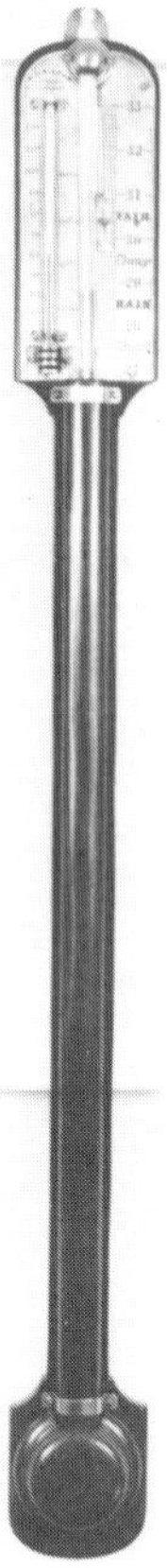

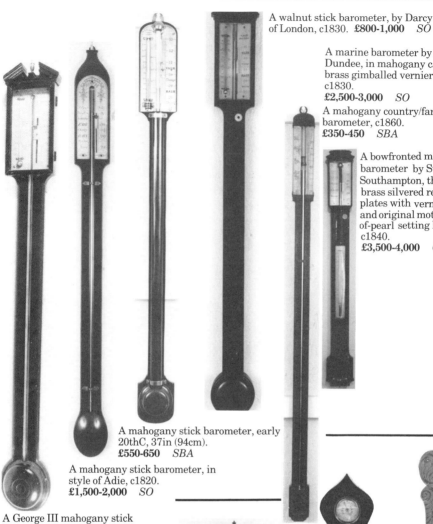

A walnut stick barometer, by Darcy of London, c1830. **£800-1,000** *SO*

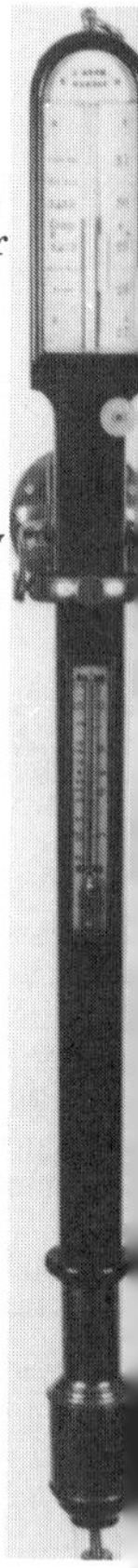

A marine barometer by Adam Dundee, in mahogany case with brass gimballed vernier adjuster c1830.
£2,500-3,000 *SO*

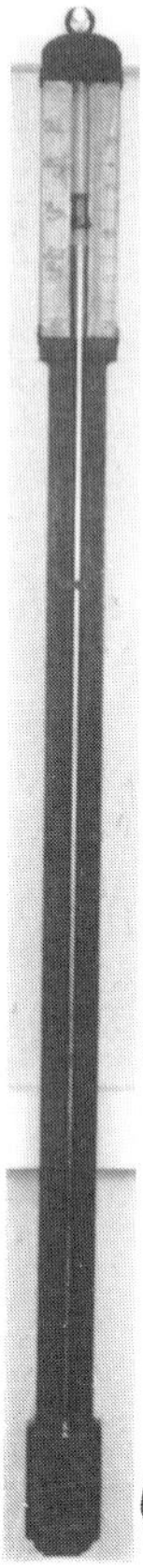

A mahogany country/farmers barometer, c1860.
£350-450 *SBA*

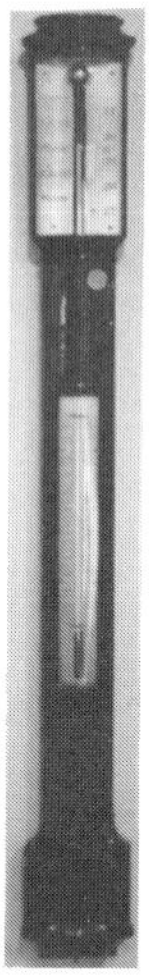

A bowfronted mahogany barometer by Stebbing, Southampton, the brass silvered register plates with vernier and original mother-of-pearl setting key, c1840.
£3,500-4,000 *OX*

A mahogany stick barometer, early 20thC, 37in (94cm).
£550-650 *SBA*

A mahogany stick barometer, in style of Adie, c1820.
£1,500-2,000 *SO*

A George III mahogany stick barometer/thermometer, with silvered scale plate inscribed with maker's name Tagliabue Torre and Co, 294 Holborn, London, with broken apex pediment centred by a brass urn finial, the stick with chevron banded veneer, 38in (97cm).
£600-700 *HSS*

Wheel

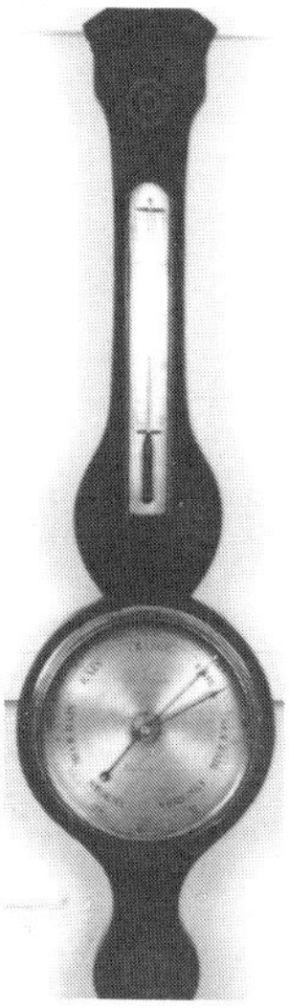

A mahogany banjo barometer inlaid with shell, 38in (97cm).
£700-800 *SBA*

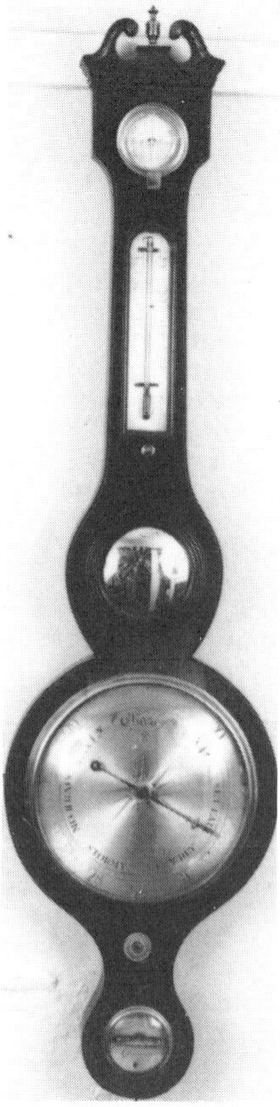

A mahogany banjo barometer by Girletti of Glasgow.
£500-600 *SBA*

A rosewood mercury barometer and thermometer, with a picture of original owners set within, c1840.
£400-500 *SO*

STORMY RAIN CHANGE FAIR VERY DRY
28
29
30
31
27
26

A miniature ornamental br aneroid barometer and thermometer, 7in (17.5cm).
£50-70 *PCh*

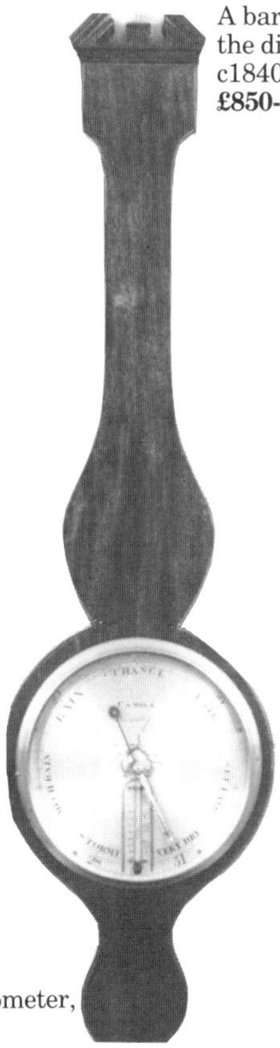

A barometer with thermometer in the dial, by Camble of Oswestry, c1840, 36in (90cm).
£850-950 *SBA*

nahogany banjo barometer, 360, 39in (99cm).
50-650 *SBA*

A mahogany barometer with boxwood stringing, by Nicholson of Kircudbright, c1860.
£550-650 *SBA*

A Victorian rosewood wheel barometer with onion styled pediment, hygrometer, thermometer, 8in (20cm) register and level, with mother of pearl banding to the case, 38in (97cm).
£350-450 *P(M)*

hronometers

A 2-day marine chronometer, the movement with Earnshaw spring, detent escapement compensation balance, blue steel helical spring maintaining power fusee, up-and-down winding dial dead beat, mahogany case, Barraud, No. 3422, 7in (17.5cm) square.
£2,000-2,500 *SO*

A 'Hertfordshire' 8-day mantel chronometer, the dial signed Thomas Mercer Ltd, St Albans, England, No. 794, 11½in (29cm).
£2,500-3,000 *C*

A one-day marine chronometer, brass bezel to the white enamel dial, no up-and-down dial, all hands of gold, convex glass, top plate engraved Brockbank's, number 836, London, one-day Earnshaw escapement, Brockbank's steel three-armed balance, bimetallic three segment balance rim, the movement protected by outer drum cover, in brass bowl with gimbal, mounted in 3-tier mahogany brass bound box with drop handles, complete with outer guard box, 3in (8.3cm) dial diam.
£2,000-2,500 *C*

Use the Index!

Because certain items might fit easily into any of a number of categories, the quickest and surest method of locating any entry is by reference to the index at the back of the book.
This has been fully cross-referenced for absolute simplicity

Miscellaneous

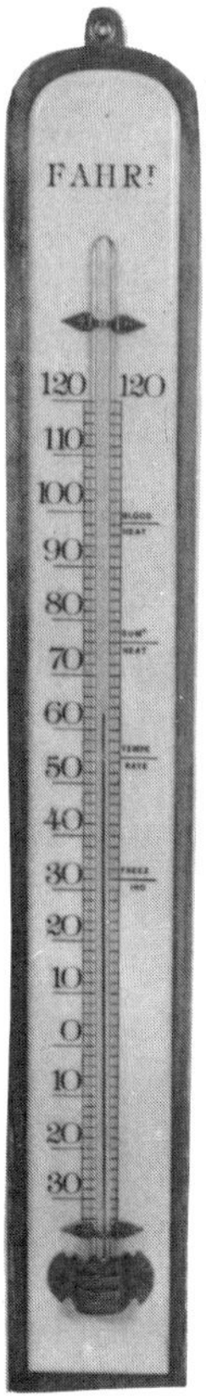
FAHR
120 120
110
100
90
80
70
60
50
40
30
20
10
0
10
20
30

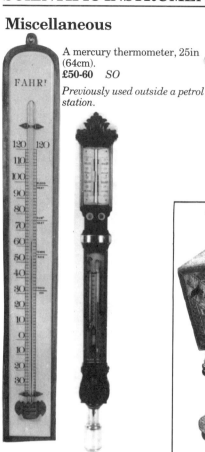

A mercury thermometer, 25in (64cm).
£50-60 *SO*

Previously used outside a petrol station.

A Victorian rosewood stick cased ship's system barometer/ thermometer, 39in (99cm).
£600-700 *HSS*

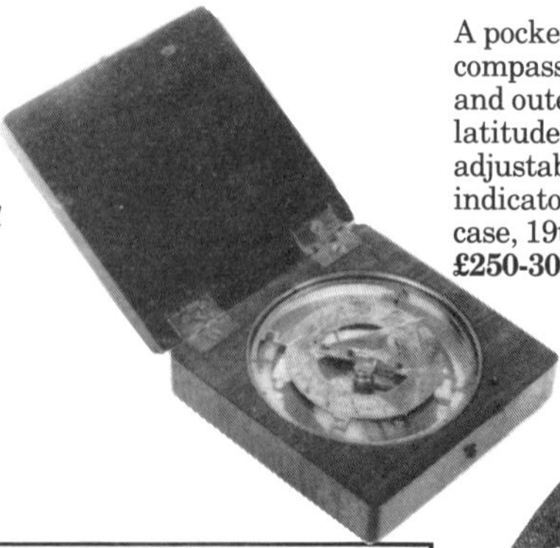

A pocket sundial with copper compass rose, with silvered scale and outer brass hour scale for latitudes 46° and 49°, with hinged adjustable small gnomon and bird indicator, contained in a mahogan case, 19thC, 3in (6.5cm).
£250-300 *HSS*

A German cube dial, inscribed HE1: FRANK, all faces with hand coloured engraved paper dials decorated with flowers, putti and geometric designs, string with plummet brass gnomons, on ball and socket joint over the base with compass and a table of latitudes for 38 Continental cities, on 4 bun feet, unsigned, 18thC, 7½in (19cm) high.
£800-1,000 *CSK*

An Augsburg-type gilt and silve brass universal equinoctial dial, signed Johan Schrettegger in Augsburg on the underside of th compass box, with silvered dial, blued needle on pivot with brass c 18thC, 2in (5.5cm).
£300-350 *C*

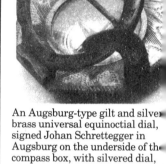

A French silver dial, signed Butterfield A Paris, the upper surface engraved with hour scal for 43°, 46°, 49° and 52°, with ins compass and spring loaded bird gnomon, with a degree scale for latitudes 40°-60°, supplemented with scrolls and foliage, 18thC, 2 (5.5cm).
£600-650 *C*

SCIENTIFIC INSTRUMENTS
Dials

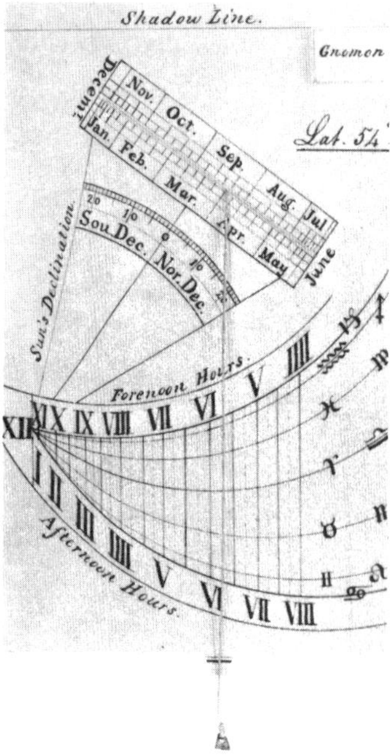
Shadow Line.
Gnomon
Lat. 54
Decem.
Nov.
Oct.
Sep.
Aug.
Jul.
Jan.
Feb.
Mar.
Apr.
May
June
Sou. Dec.
Nor. Dec.
Sun's Declination.
Forenoon Hours.
Afternoon Hours.

A paper rectilinear Capuchin dial, with sheet of written instructions forming the outer envelope, unsigned, 19thC, 4½in (11cm) high.
£150-250 *CSK*

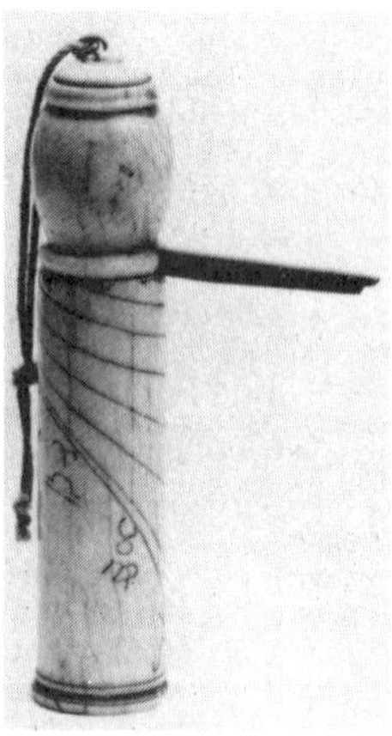

A bone-ivory pillar dial, incised for lines of hours, zodiac signs, with folding brass gnomon, bobbin turned cap with suspension loop and cord, unsigned, 18thC, 4½in (11.5cm).
£700-750 *CSK*

COLL. CAN'TAB. MDCCLV
DIVI JOHANN.
EX DONO SHAN

A brass universal equinoctial rin dial, engraved on one side, Robt. Fletcher, the other side Ex Dono Shan Divi Johann. Coll, Cantab. MDCCLV, the bridge with slidin pin hole sight and engraved with calendar and declination scales, unsigned, 18thC, 4½in (11.5cm) diam.
£500-550 *C*

brass universal equinoctial
npass dial, signed Newton & Co.
Fleet Street, London, with
npass box, late 19thC, 4in (9.5cm)
de.
50-450 *C*

lobes

3in (15cm) world time globe, the
ass drum shaped base stamped
ade in France No. 637, and
ntaining the time clock
chanism, with equatorial hour
g, sun and hour pointer, the gores
oured and with the international
ole route marked in red, 11½in
.5cm) high.
00-900 *C*

in (10cm) instructional star
be, mounted on twin oxydised
ss supports with scale 20°–0°
° and vernier arm, on circular
hogany base stamped S & A.D.,
h 3 adjustable brass feet, late
hC, 9½in (24cm) high.
0-250 *CSK*

A German silver and gilt brass universal equinoctial dial, signed Johan Martin In Augsburg-48, the underside of the compass box with the names and latitudes of 23 European cities and towns, the plate engraved with scrolls and fitted with 3 bun feet, late 17thC, 2in (5cm) long.
£2,200-2,600 *CSK*

A mechanical orrery with 2½in (6cm) diam. globe, zodiac circle candle socket with reflector, on shaped iron steel, 19thC, the arm 19½in (49.5cm) long.
£850-950 *CSK*

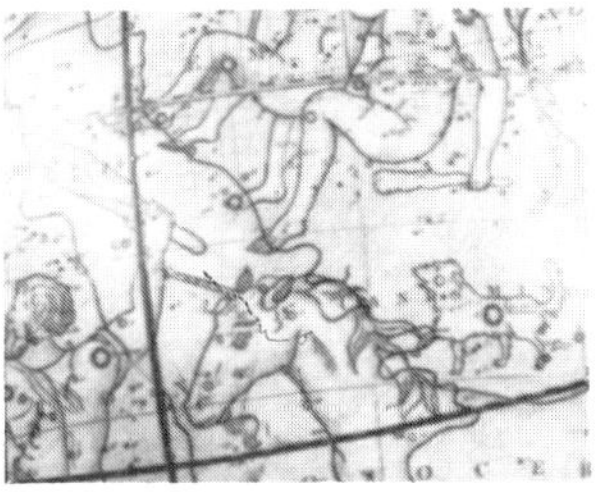

An 18in (45.5cm) diam celestial globe, the label inscribed Smith's Celestial Globe, Containing all the principal Stars Compiled from the Works of Wollaston, Flamsted, De La Caille, Havelius, Mayer, Bradley, Herschel, Maskelyne, the Transactions of the Astronomical Society of London & Co., Made in Great Britain, G. Phillip & Son Ltd 32 Fleet Street, London E.C., 22in (56cm) high.
£2,000-2,500 *C*

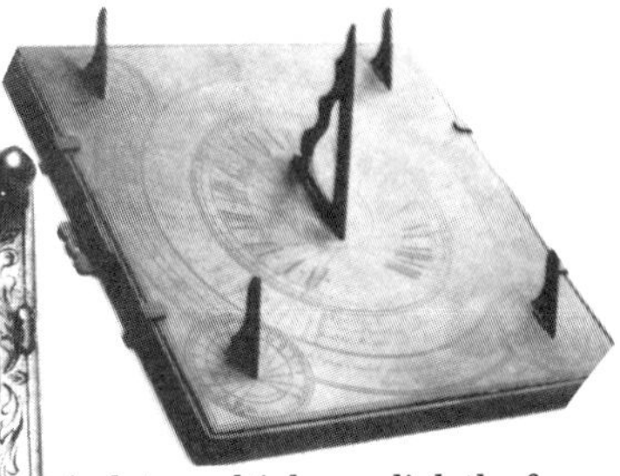

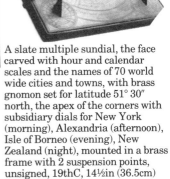

A slate multiple sundial, the face carved with hour and calendar scales and the names of 70 world wide cities and towns, with brass gnomon set for latitude 51° 30″ north, the apex of the corners with subsidiary dials for New York (morning), Alexandria (afternoon), Isle of Borneo (evening), New Zealand (night), mounted in a brass frame with 2 suspension points, unsigned, 19thC, 14½in (36.5cm) square.
£1,200-1,500 *CSK*

A Philips 19in (48.5cm) terrestrial globe, with brass support and turned oak stand, 28½in (72cm) high overall.
£250-350 *C*

An 8¼in (21cm) terrestrial globe, by Peter Bauer, Nürnberg, with brass meridian circle, mounted on horizon ring, printed with zodiac and calendar scales, on 4 quadrant supports, with inset compass on base, 19thC, 14½in (37cm) high.
£750-850 *CSK*

Surveying

THE HYDROGRAPH

A lacquered brass hydrograph with steel square, the quadrant engraved 0°-90°, unsigned, in mahogany case 10in (25cm) wide.
£150-200 *C*

An oxydised brass surveying level, the silvered compass dial signed Troughton & Simms, London, with rack and pinion focusing, bubble level, ray shade and dust slide, on 4 screw tripod mounting, in fitted mahogany case, 19thC, 19½in (49.5cm) long.
£200-250 *C*

A lacquered brass box sextant, signed Allan London, with silvere scale divided each 30 mins from 0°-150°, the index arm with vernie tangent screw fine adjustment an magnifier, the drum shaped cover forming the base, early 19thC, 4½ (11cm) diam.
£400-500 *CSK*

An oxydised and lacquered brass surveying level, signed Troughton & Simms, London, with graduated level and cross bubble, rack and pinion focusing and fine vertical adjustment, on 4 screw tripod mounting in mahogany case, 20in (51cm) wide.
£120-200 *CSK*

An aluminium and brass miniature simple theodolite, signed Stanley London, with enclosed compass and cross bubble, the telescope with rack and pinion focusing, level and half circle engraved in 2 quadrants with staff mounting, 6in (15cm) long.
£300-350 *CSK*

A brass and aluminium transit theodolite, by Cooke, Troughton Simms Ltd., No. Y2946, with silvered scales, levels, twin verni and magnifiers on 3 screw tripod mounting, in mahogany case, 15½ (40cm) wide.
£420-500 *CSK*

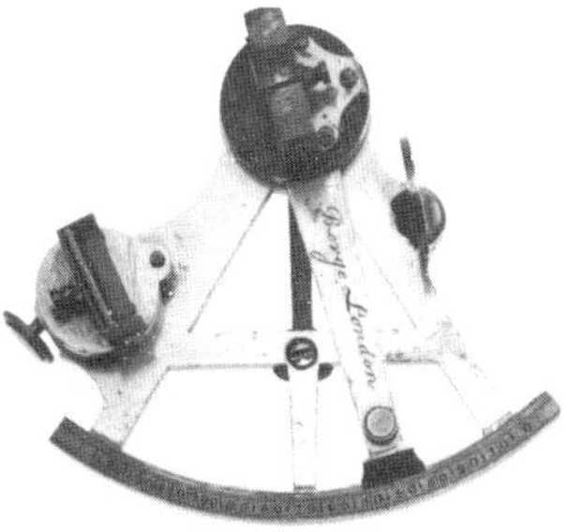
Berge London

A lacquered brass miniature sextant, signed on the index arm Berge London, the frame with pin hole sight adjustable mirrors, index arm with vernier scale, the arc divided 0°-130° radius 2in (5cm), in plush lined leather covered case.
£3,000-3,500 *CSK*

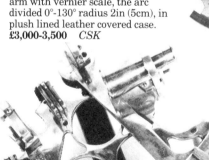

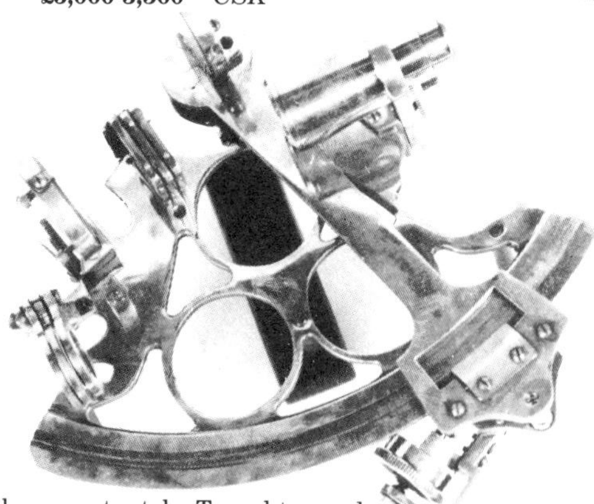

A brass sextant, by Troughton and Simms Ltd., with white metal degree scale, the index arm with dog clip clamp, and with 2 sets of coloured filters, in stained wood box, late 19thC.
£300-350 *HSS*

A sextant compendium, compri a sextant of small size, signed B London, with vernier, magnifie telescope and shades, the arc wi silvered scale, 4in (10cm) radiu additional tube, folding artifici horizon trough and mercury jar brass bound mahogany case, ea 19thC, 10in (25.5cm) wide.
£2,000-2,500 *CSK*

A pocket sextant, late 19thC.
£150-200 *GIL*

Telescopes

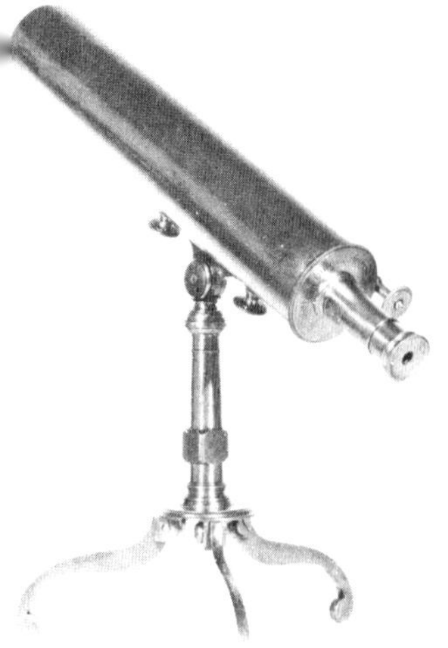

A 2½in (6cm) lacquered brass reflecting telescope, signed James Short London No. 211/1377 = 12, with screw rod focusing adjustment on tapering pillar support and tripod stand, in a fitted mahogany case, 18thC, 18½in (46.5cm) wide.
£1,500-2,000 *CSK*

James Short (1710-68) signed and engraved his reflecting telescopes with a coded numbering system where in this case 211 equals the serial number of the telescope for this size, 1377 indicates the number of telescopes constructed, and 12 equals the focal length of the large speculum mirror in inches.

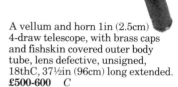

A 'Ramsden' pattern 2¾in (7cm) reflecting telescope, the 45in (115cm) long body tube with rack and pinion focusing, dust cap and located on the alt/azimuth trunnion by wedge and slot and 2 telescopic steadying bars, early 19thC.
£1,000-1,200 *CSK*

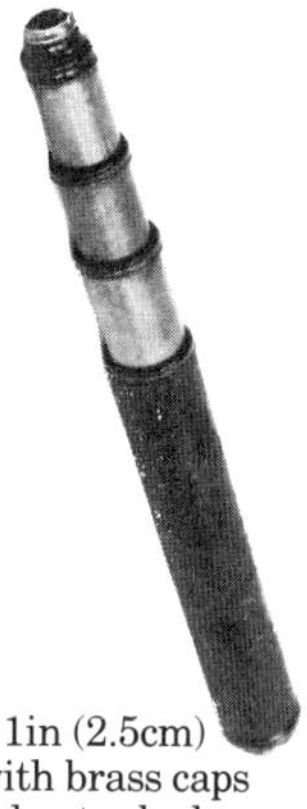

A vellum and horn 1in (2.5cm) 4-draw telescope, with brass caps and fishskin covered outer body tube, lens defective, unsigned, 18thC, 37½in (96cm) long extended.
£500-600 *C*

A 6in (15cm) Newtonian reflector telescope, on an alt/azimuth stand, in teak case.
£6,000-7,000 *WW*

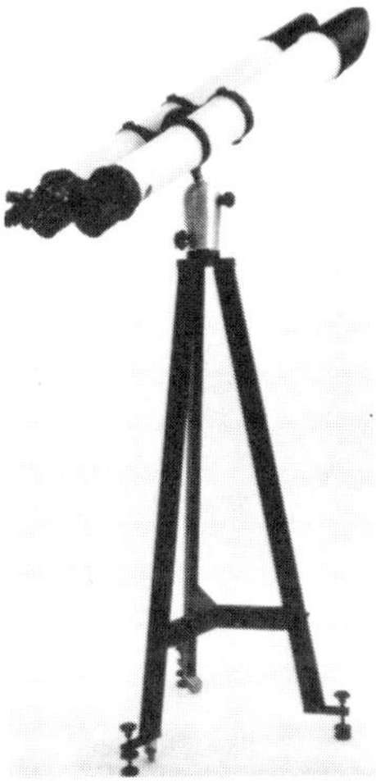

A binocular telescope, by Carl Zeiss Jena, the white painted body tubes 41¼in (104.8cm) long, the objectives 4½in (11cm) diam. clear aperture, with image erecting prism system with triple ×33, 53 and 72 magnifications, 5 screw adjustment and focusing, arranged for binocular observation for 1 person and monocular observation for 2 persons, in steel bound case, 62in (157.5cm) long, with a later steel tripod and mounting.
£3,000-3,500 *CSK*

A 2in (5cm) brass 4-draw refracting telescope, signed James Mann, Norwich, with dust cap and eye-piece slide, 3-eye pieces, mounted by a screw clamp on a tapering pillar support with folding tripod, the cabriole legs terminating in pad feet, in fitted mahogany case, 12½in (31.5cm) wide, with 2 clips and inset plaque to lid engraved John Harvey.
£800-900 *CSK*

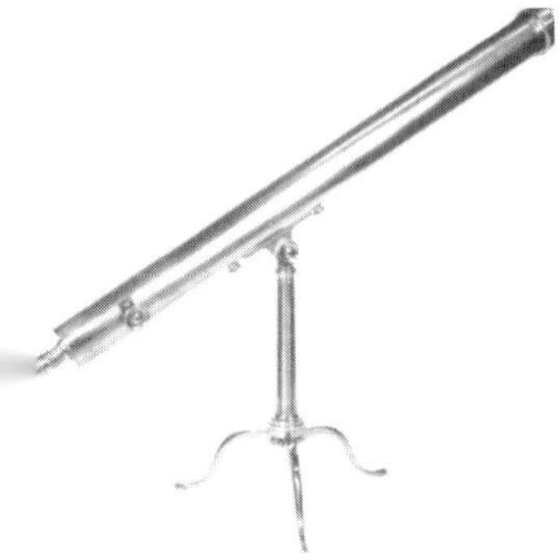

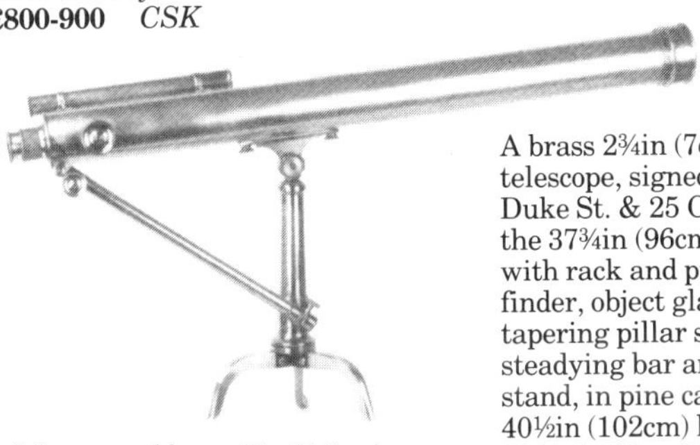

A lacquered brass 3in (7.5cm) refracting telescope, signed Watson & Son, 313 High Holborn, London, with rack and pinion focusing and dust cap, in a Broadhurst & Clarkson case with 2 eye-pieces, 45in (115cm) long.
£900-1,200 *CSK*

A brass 2¾in (7cm) refracting telescope, signed Wm. De Silva, 126 Duke St. & 25 Chapel St. Liverpool, the 37¾in (96cm) long body tube with rack and pinion focusing, star finder, object glass dust cap, on tapering pillar support with steadying bar and folding tripod stand, in pine carrying case, 19thC, 40½in (102cm) long.
£900-1,200 *C*

Microscopes

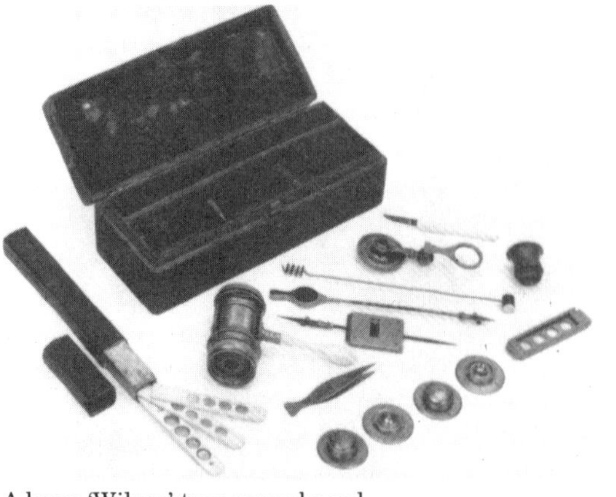

A brass 'Wilson'-type screw barrel and simple microscope compendium, with accessories, including 6 objectives, ivory sliders, specimen viewer, forceps and other items, unsigned, in fishskin covered case, 18thC, 7½in (18.5cm) wide.
£1,000-1,500 *CSK*

A brass microscope lamp, the case with cast signature Swift & Son, London, W.C. with the glass reservoir, lamp and shade, height adjustment, in stained pine case with brass carrying handle, late 19thC, 12in (31cm) high.
£120-150 *CSK*

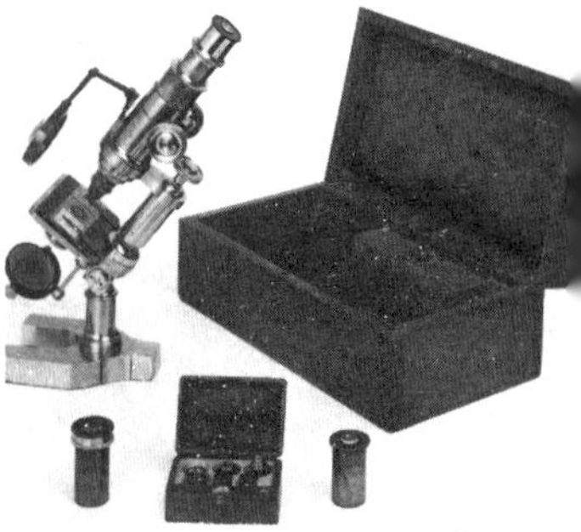

A lacquered brass compound monocular microscope, signed on the body tube E. Hartnack & A. Prazmowski, Rue Bonaparte, 7 Paris, complete with accessories and slides in the original fitted mahogany case, stamped 18140, 19thC, 11in (28cm) wide.
£400-450 *CSK*

A lacquered brass aquatic microscope, signed on the stage W&S Jones, 30 Holborn, London, the tubular pillar with rack and pinion focusing, the arm with objective adjustable both in the horizontal and vertical planes, the stage with forceps, the lower pillar with concave swivel mirror, with some accessories, in plush lined leather covered case, the lid with mounting ferrule, early 19thC, 5½in (13.5cm) wide.
£300-350 *CSK*

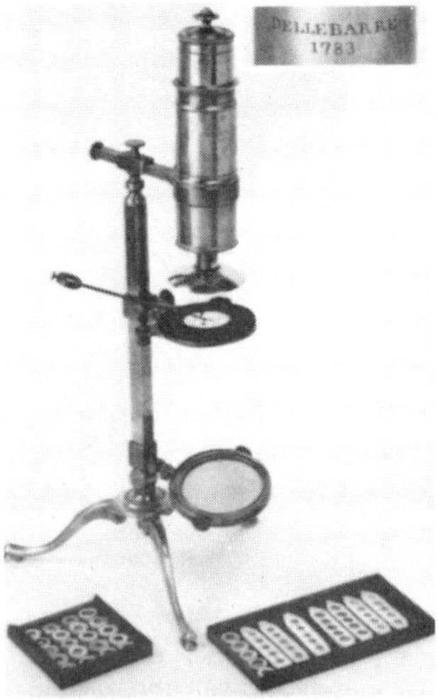
DELLEBARRE
1783

A brass compound monocular microscope, signed on the body tube Dellebarre 1783, located on an arm by friction leather band, now missing, on tripod stand, with a lieberkuhn, set of 5 objectives and other items including a case of ivory sliders and another with ivory specimen cups, in fitted walnut case, 12½in (32.5cm) wide.
£3,000-3,500 *CSK*

A black enamelled and lacquered brass monocular microscope, by Carl Zeiss Jena, No. 161198, with rack and pinion coarse focusing an micrometer fine adjustment, quadruple nose-piece, mechanical circuit stage, substage condenser and plane concave mirror, with a range of accessories including a binocular attachment, 2 cases, the largest 14½in (37.5cm) high.
£650-700 *CSK*

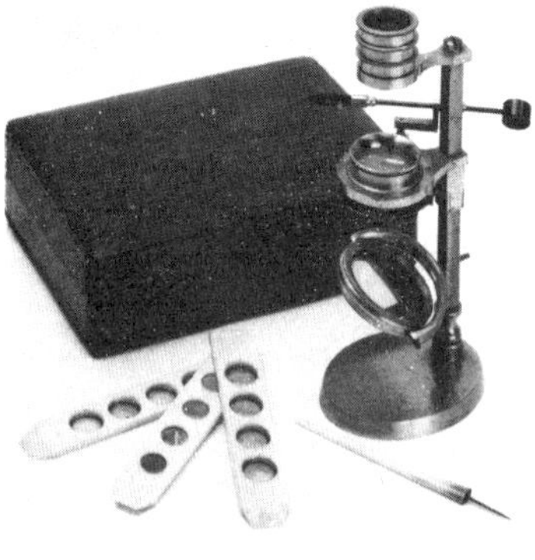

A lacquered brass aquatic pocket microscope, the pillar with arm for objectives, stage with forceps live box and swivel mirror, on oval base, unsigned, in fitted plush lined leather covered case with sliders and trade label inscribed Hawes, 95 Cheapside. From Dollonds, 19thC, the case 4½in (11.5cm) wide.
£250-300 *CSK*

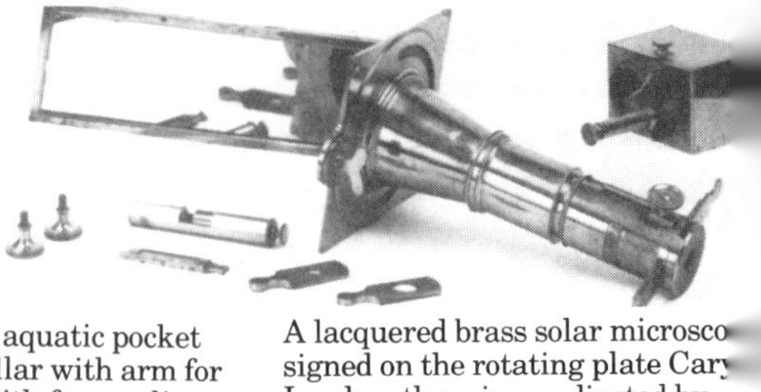

A lacquered brass solar microsco signed on the rotating plate Car London, the mirror adjusted by worm drive screw and enclosed r and pinion, with a bead glass objective carrier 1-6, spring load specimen clamp and other accessories, in mahogany case, li missing, 19thC, 15½in (40cm) w
£800-900 *CSK*

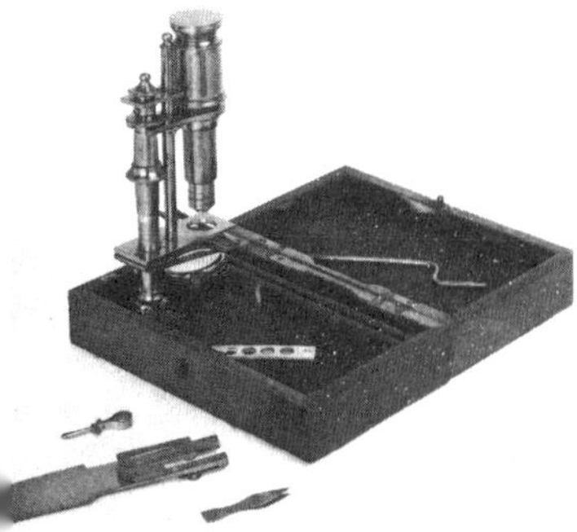

A lacquered brass compound nonocular microscope, unsigned with 'quick thread' focusing, the stage with sprung slide holder, the pillar mounted on swivel attachment with mirror, forceps, frogplate and other accessories in fitted crossbanded mahogany case, early 19thC, 9in (22.5cm) wide.
:550-600 *CSK*

A lacquered and oxidised brass microscope by W. Watson and Sons, with rack and pinion focusing, triple nose-piece, fully mechanical adjustable stage, sub-stage condenser and swivel mirror and various accessories, in mahogany case, late 19thC, 13in (33cm) high.
£200-250 *CSK*

A medical saw, the blade secured by rivet and wing nut, and with tapering octagonal section walnut handle, 18thC, 9½in (24.5cm) long.
£150-200 *CSK*

Medical Instruments

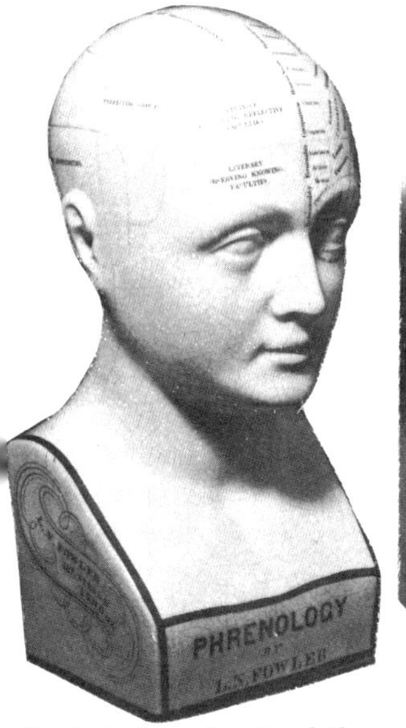
PHRENOLOGY
L.N.FOWLER

A Fowler's phrenology head, the cranium printed with the areas of the sentiments, the base with maker's label and title, crackle glaze finish, 11½in (29.5cm) high.
:600-700 *CSK*

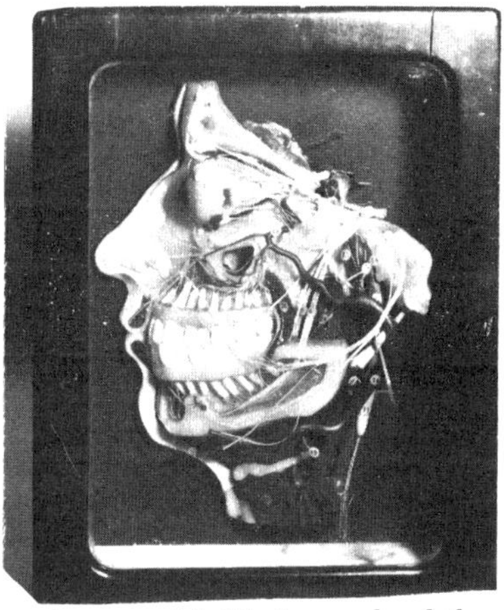

A wax model of the human head, the veins and arteries with numbered labels, in glazed ebonised case, 10in (25cm) high.
£270-300 *CSK*

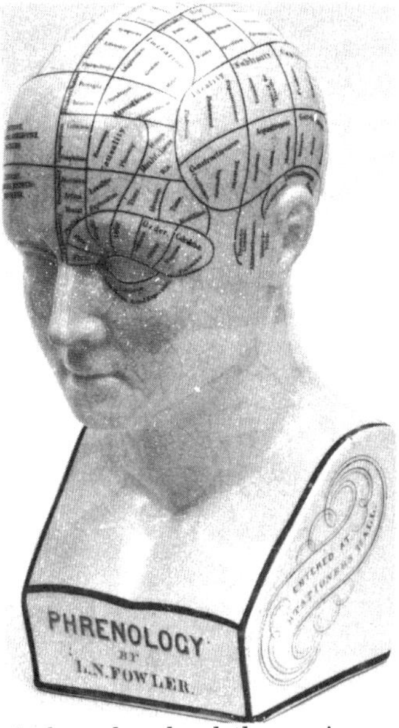
PHRENOLOGY
BY
L.N.FOWLER.

A phrenology head, the cranium printed with the areas of the sentiments, trade label, scroll and citation, by L. N. Fowler, 11½in (29.5cm) high.
£500-600 *C*

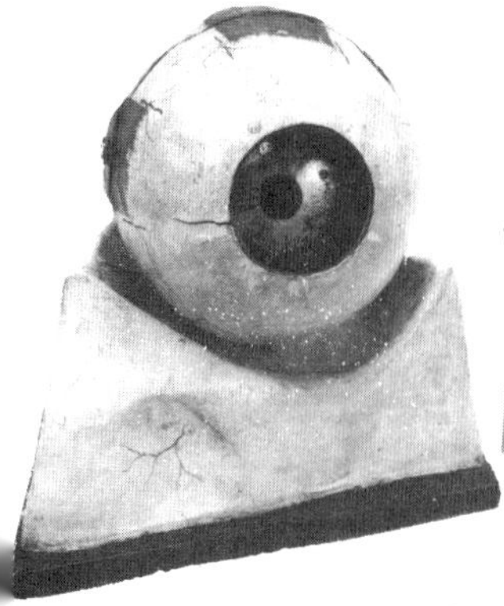

plaster model eye, signed on the base, 54 Anotomie Clostique Dr uioux 1949, the stand 7½in 9.5cm) wide.
:250-300 *CSK*

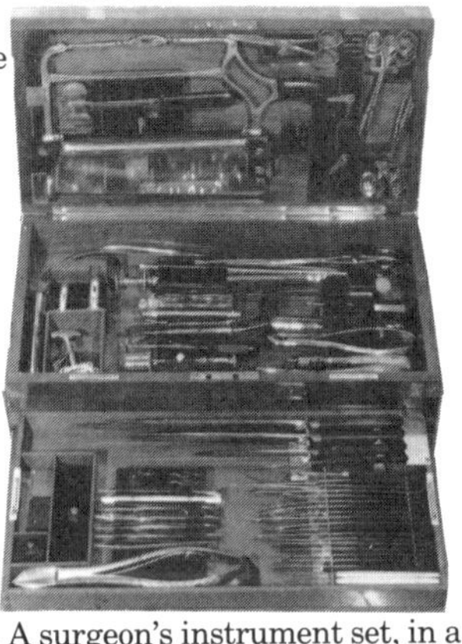

A surgeon's instrument set, in a mahogany and brass banded folding case with inner tray, virtually complete with 75 items each stamped with the maker's mark and in original condition, by S. Mawson & Thompson, Aldersgate, London, 19thC.
£3,000-3,500 *MAT*

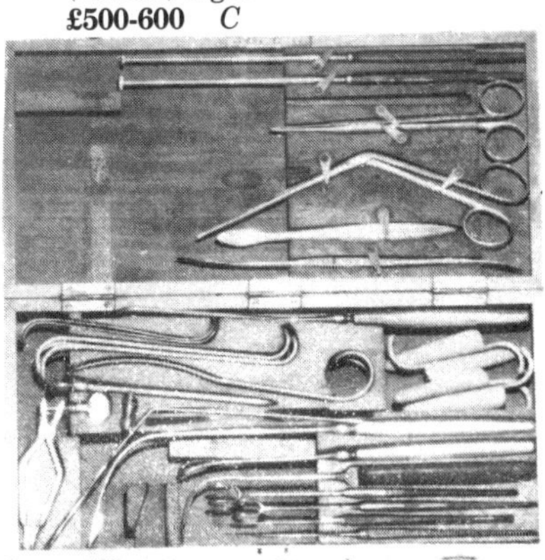

A mahogany cased set of surgical instruments, and a part set of ivory handled optician's instruments, by Weiss, 13in (33cm) wide.
£250-300 *CSK*

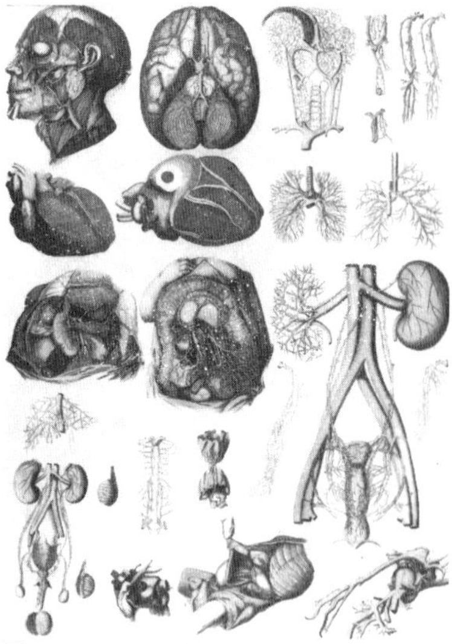

EX CATHOL
P MERCVRIA
P ANTE CIBUM
ET FUMARIÆ

A set of 4 Dutch blue and white drug jars, 18thC, 7½in (19cm) high.
£850-950 *CSK*

Four anatomical instructional prints, signed Impensis J. & P. Knapton Londini 1740, 1749 & 1750, J.S Müller Sculp and G. Grignion Sculp, 18thC, framed and glazed, 22½in (57cm) by 16in (40.5cm).
£600-700 *CSK*

A brass binocular telescope, with range of lenses and fittings, in mahogany case with brass handle, by Broadhurst Clarkson & Co, London, 19thC, 23in (59cm) high.
£800-1,000 *AH*

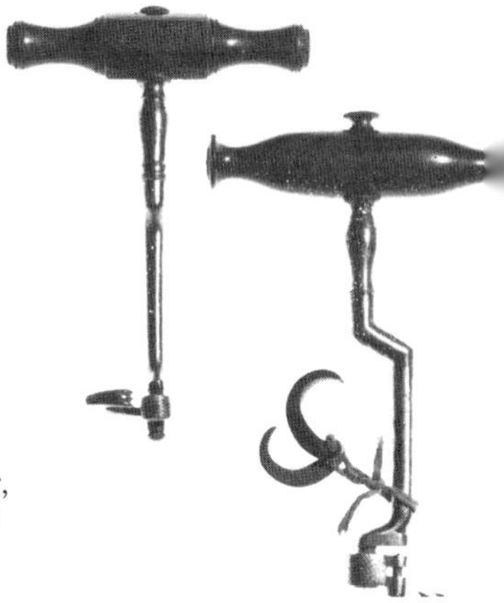

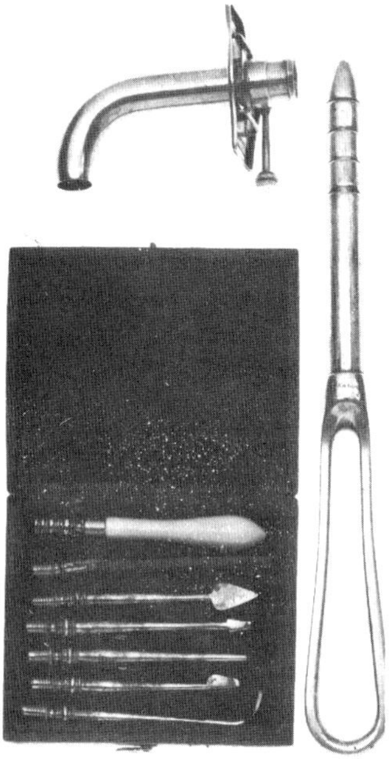

A burnished steel tooth key, with single claw and ebony handle with chequered grip, 5½in (13.5cm) long, and another tooth key with 2 spare claws, early 19thC.
£220-250 *C*

A leather covered domestic medicine casket, with chased silver mounts, the mansard lid with suspension loop rising to reveal 6 bottles, cup, funnel and scissors, 18thC, 7½in (19cm) wide.
£750-850 *CSK*

A label found with this casket says: Belonging to Adm. Sir Charles Cotton and taken by him on board ship when ever he went to sea.

A silver metal tracheotomy cannulae with lobster tail, 6½in (16cm) long, and a set of 6 dental instruments with ivory combination handle, in plush lined case with mirror, 19thC, 3in (7.5cm) wide.
£200-250 *C*

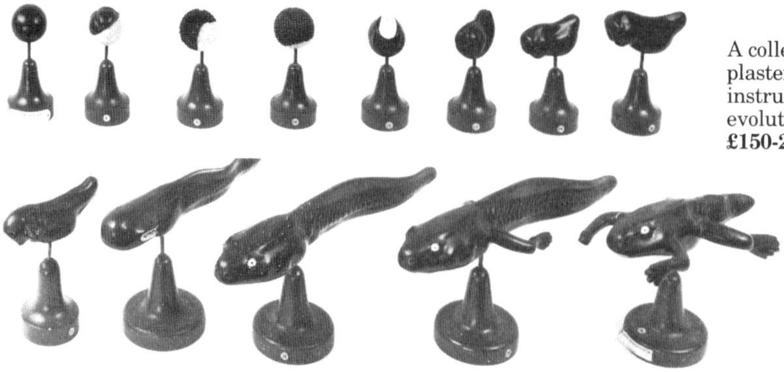

A collection of numbered coloured plaster demonstration and instructional models of the evolution of the common frog.
£150-200 *C*

A plaster model eye, painted in colours with numbers corresponding to the nervous system, on wood base, by van de Knip, Utrecht, 15½in (40cm) wide.
£200-300 *CSK*

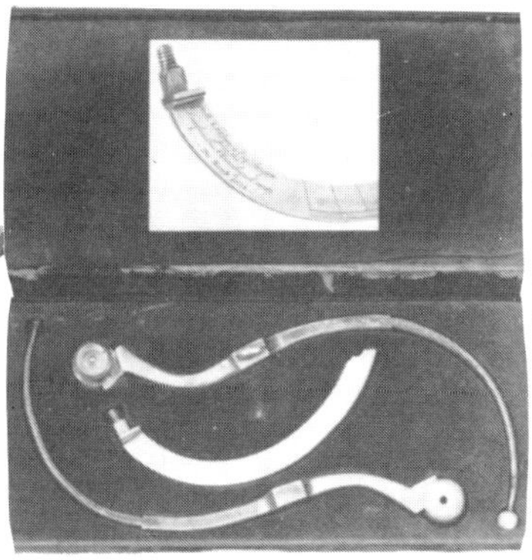

A silver cranium measure, signed and engraved in the quadrant arm to W.A.F. Brown Esqr. Surgeon, from the Dunfermline Phrenological Society 20 March 1834, in a plush lined leather case, 10½in (26.5cm) wide.
£1,500-2,000 *CSK*

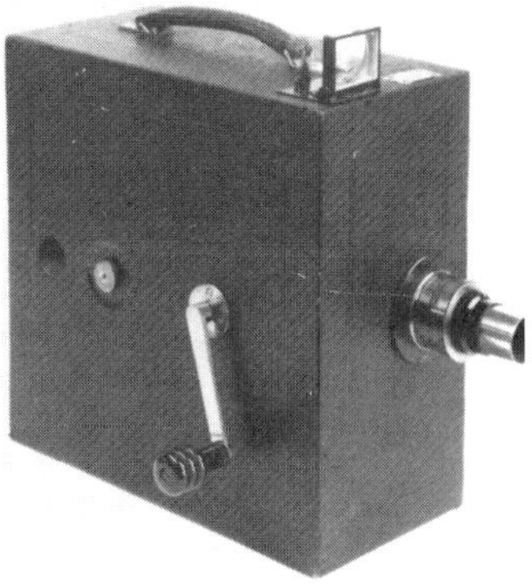

A 35mm 'Ensign cinematograph' camera, by Houghton-Butcher Mfg. Co. Ltd., England, with hand-crank and a brass bound Carl Zeiss, Jena Tessar f.3.5 5cm lens No. 241252, all in maker's leather case.
£400-450 *CSK*

A Victorian trepanning set by Wood, in red plush lined brass bound mahogany case containing common ebony handle, 3 crown trephines, bone brush, 2 Heys cranium saws, double ended forceps, double ended elevator and a scalpel, with 2 associated tortoiseshell mounted lancets, one stamped Gray, the other Wood & Co., mid-19thC, case 11½in (29cm) wide.
£650-750 *N*

A half-plate brass and mahogany tailboard camera, by W. I. Chadwick, Manchester, with a brass bound R. and J. Beck 5 by 4in (12.5 by 10cm) rectilinear 7in (17.5cm) focus lens No. 3945.
£250-300 *CSK*

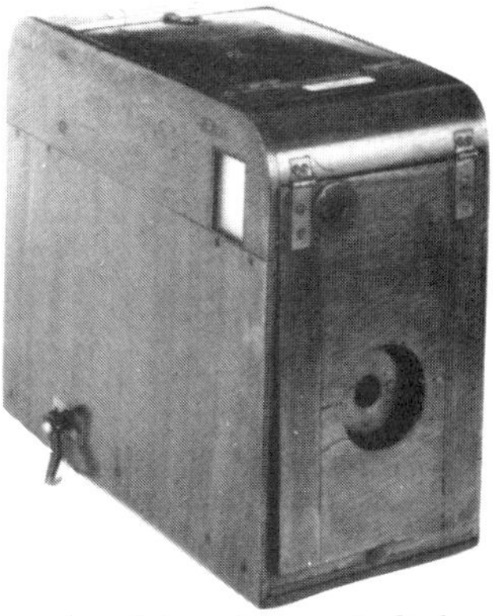

A quarter-plate mahogany bodied 'Rover' camera by J. Lancaster & Son, Birmingham, set into a 'Lancaster' patent See Saw shutter, in maker's original fitted leather case.
£400-450 *CSK*

Cameras

. 5 by 4in (12.5 by 10cm) ransitional wet-plate/dry-plate ahogany bodied studio camera, by . H. Dallmeyer, London, with brass ttings, rising and falling front, emovable repeating back with 2 eparate masks, mahogany single ark slide and a brass bound J. H. allmeyer Triple achromatic lens o. 5135 set into a non-original utter mechanism.
1,000-1,500 *CSK*

A postcard 'Xit' camera, by J. F. Shew and Co., London, with a C. P. Goerz Dogmar Series III 150mm f.6.8 lens No. 209149, in a leather case.
£120-200 *CSK*

A Telyt f.4.8 280mm lens No. 2713954, by Leitz, Canada, with integral lens hood and front and back lens caps.
£250-500 *CSK*

A 12cm diam. film 'Kinokam Style A' camera, with swinging taking and viewing lens, internal removable film holder and handle all contained in maker's original cardboard box, with paper label, by The Kinokam Co., London.
£1,500-2,000 *CSK*

The Kinokam camera was the subject of patent No. 17347 dated August 9, 1904, and taken out by S. H. Crocker. The specification described an apparatus for viewing or photographing moving pictures. The combined camera/viewer used a disc to hold the sensitised film or processed pictures and a revolving section mounted on the front of the camera carried a viewing lens, photographic lens and a view-finder. The apparatus could also be used for viewing transparencies.

The Kinokam produced 24 images on a circular disc of film. The subsequent paper print was viewed using the camera but with the lens section rotated 180 degrees bringing a magnifying lens into position.

A 6 by 9cm Ontoflex twin lens reflex camera, by Cornu, Paris, with a Berthiot Ontar f.3.5 viewing lens No. 316153 and a Berthiot Stellor f.3.5 90mm taking lens No. 257750 set into a Compur Rapid shutter and revolving roll film back, all in maker's case.
£200-250 *CSK*

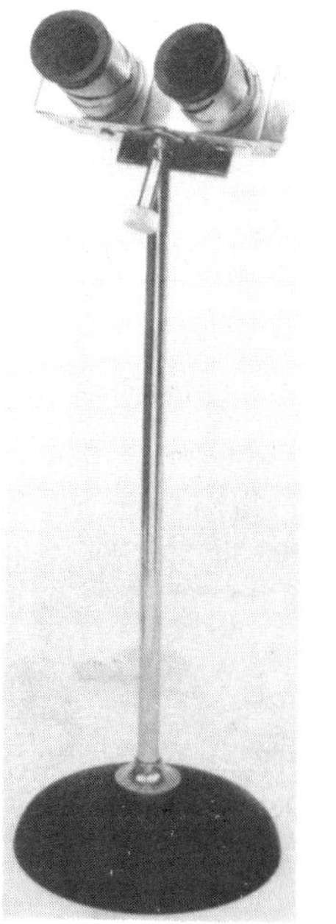

A Votra stereo transparency viewe by E. Leitz, Wetzlar, with rear film holder for a 35mm mounted stereo transparency and with a very rare Votiv stand.
£800-1,000 *CSK*

A 5 by 4in (12.5 by 10cm) Micro-Technical Mk. VI camera with a Carl Zeiss, Jena Tessar f.4.5 13.5cm lens No. 2549254 set into a Compur shutter, a Kodak Ektar f.7.7 203mm lens set into a Prontor-SVS shutter, 3 double dark slides and a Polaroid 545 Land film holder, all in a fitted leather case, and a Gandolfi tripod.
£550-650 *CSK*

Illingworth's
FILMS
STOCKED HERE
FILMS DEVELOPED & PRINTED

A metal enamelled advertising sign in the form of a film spool, by T. Illingworth and Co. England, 20 by 7in (50 by 18cm).
£170-200 *CSK*

A mahogany bodied, sliding box reflex camera obscura with 5 by 4in (12.5 by 10cm) ground glass focusing screen, 2½in (6cm) diam. lens with mahogany lens cap and hinged ground glass screen cover.
£2,500-3,000 *CSK*

A black painted cast iron photographer's head clamp, with adjustable height and neck clamp and cast maker's mark 'Johnson's Patent Leeds', and a photographer' birdie in mahogany box.
£200-250 *CSK*

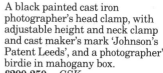

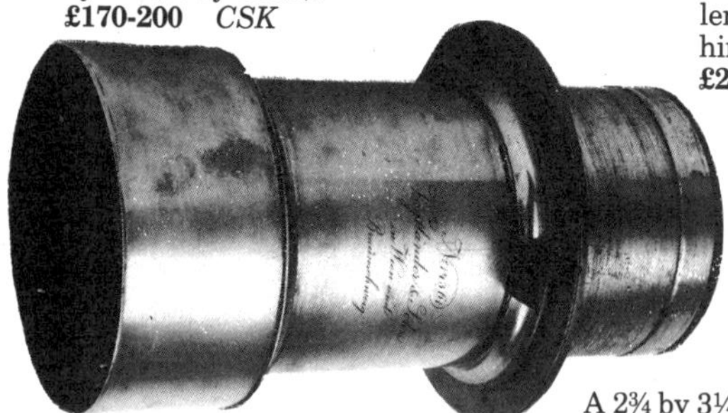

A brass bound portrait lens No. 14361, by Voigtlander & Son, Braunschweig, Germany, with brass mounting flange and Waterhouse stop, with engraved lens barrel.
£500-550 *CSK*

A 2¾ by 3¼in (7 by 8cm) mahogany bodied wet-plate camera, by A. Ross, London, with rising front, a brass bound A. Ross, London, lens No. 3892, with rack and pinion focusing and one wet-plate dark slide.
£4,500-6,000 *CSK*

A 35mm cream enamelled and alloy K. I. Monobar technical camera, by Ilford/Kennedy Instruments Ltd., England, with a sliding viewfinder, a Schneider Angulon f.6.8 90mm lens No. 4805934 set into a Synchro-Compur-P shutter, two cream-enamelled K. I. Monobar film magazines and a shutter all in maker's original fitted box.
£700-900 *CSK*

"TICKA"
PRINTING
BOX
4/6

A metal bodied 'Ticka' camera, by Houghtons Ltd., London, with lens cap and film spool in a cloth pouch with instruction booklets, all contained in maker's original box, and a wooden 'Ticka printing box' with 'Ticka pictures' instruction booklet, all in maker's original box.
£400-450 *CSK*

"Ensignette"
CAMERA

A rare 3 by 2in (8 by 5cm) 'Ensignette No. 2' camera, by Houghtons Ltd., London, Silver Plated model No. 2892 with a time and instantaneous shutter, in maker's original box with paper label 'Silver Plated Ensignette P/A1235/1/2/12' standard box label.
£900-1,200 *CSK*

A 10 by 8in (25.5 by 20cm) nahogany and brass field camera No. 7148, by G. Hare, London, with nset brass binding strips, red quare cut bellows and a brass ound J. H. Dallmeyer patent 3.D ens with rack and pinion focusing nd aperture for Waterhouse stops, nd a mahogany and brass fitted Morgan and Kidd patent roll film older No. 144, in a fitted leather ase.
900-1,200 *CSK*

A quarter-plate brass and mahogany bodied 'The Sanderson' camera, by Houghtons Ltd., London, No. 11.938, lacks focusing back, with a lens.
£150-200 *CSK*

LEITZ WETZLAR GERMANY

n Elmarit-R f.2.8 35mm lens o. 1995370, with a 12564K lens ood, by E. Leitz, Wetzlar, all in aker's plastic case.
150-200 *CSK*

Contarex

A 35mm Contarex camera No. T92434, by Zeiss Ikon, Germany, with a Carl Zeiss Planar f.2.5mm lens No. 2368376, all in maker's leather ever ready case.
£200-250 *CSK*

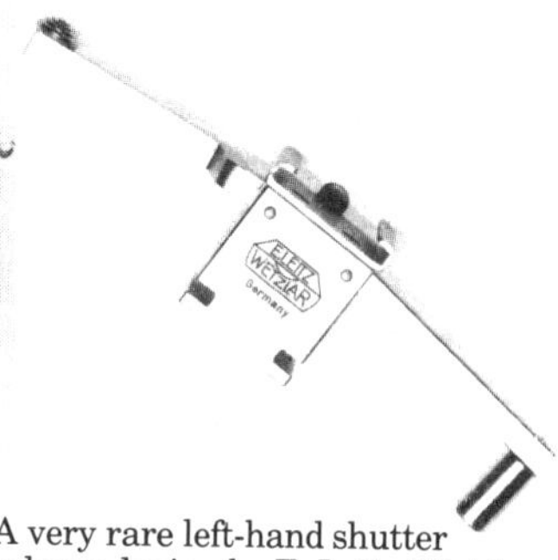
LEITZ
WETZLAR
Germany

A very rare left-hand shutter release device, by E. Leitz, Wetzlar, for use with the M-series Leica camera.
£600-700 *CSK*

A rare 35mm Esco camera with a Steinheil Cassar f.6.3 3.5cm lens No. 168632 set into a dial-set Pronto shutter, by Seischab, Germany.
£3,000-3,500 *CSK*

The Esco camera was made by Otto Seischab of Nuremburg from 1926. It could take up to 400 exposures on standard 35mm cine film. The enlarged film chambers were copied by Leitz in their 250 exposure Reporter camera of 1933.

A very rare hand held magnesium-ribbon flash unit with hand-crank magnesium-ribbon chamber and detachable reflector, all in original box.
£300-400 *CSK*

A 35mm mahogany cased, hand-cranked, cinematographic camera No. 50, by A. Darling and Son, Brighton, England, with brass binding strips, 2 internal mahogany W.K. Co. Ltd., film magazines, film transport mechanism and casing marked 'AD' and claw mechanism marked 'A 221. Pat. 21787-08', a Carl Zeiss, Jena Tessar f.3.5cm lens No. 236088 set into a brass focusing lens mount, hand crank, camera body stamped.
£900-1,200 *CSK*

A Leica IIIc camera No. 376411, with a Leitz Summar 5cm f.2 lens No. 424100, red shutter blind and Third Reich National Socialist insignia on camera front.
£900-1,200 *CSK*

The camera body dates to 1941-42.

A quarter-plate box-form wet-plate camera, with removable focusing screen, a pair of brass strips on each side panel, quarter inch tripod bush on base and side panel, internal tripod bush covers and an unusual brass bound collapsible three-section lens with rack and pinion focusing front section and front mounted wheel stops and 2 mahogany double dark slides each with internal yellow paper divider.
£1,800-2,500 *CSK*

The lens design is unusual in being in sections. These each unscrew and reverse around so that the lens is securely contained within the camera body. This method of storage explains the cut-off focusing knob. Without the knob being cut-off the front lens section will not fit within the camera.

A 7½ by 5in (19 by 12.5cm) Transitional mahogany bodied tailboard camera, by W. W. Rouch, London, with brass fittings, rising and cross front, swinging back, screw-focusing back standard, red leather bellows, removable ground glass screen, a brass bound Wray, London 5 by 4in (12.5 by 10cm) len No. 3792, a mahogany single wet-plate dark slide contained within the camera body and two mahogany dry-plate double dark slides with each plate holder numbered consecutively from 1 to and 3 containing a mahogany quarter-plate reducing mask, camera with maker's plaque.
£350-450 *CSK*

CARL ZEISS
JENA
PHOTO LENSES

Two Carl Zeiss Jena catalogues comprising 'Photo lenses. Referenc P. 185' dated 1910 and 'Photo Objective. P. 185' dated 1910.
£100-150 *CSK*

An 8 by 8in (20 by 20cm) mahogan wet-plate camera with black bellows, brass locking clips, a sturd brass handle, removable focusing screen, a brass bound Jamin a Par lens with rack and pinion focusing and a mahogany wet-plate dark slide.
£400-600 *CSK*

\ 35mm 'Rectaflex' Standard 1300
amera No. 29927, shutter
efective, with a Kilfitt Tele-Kilar
5.6 300mm lens No. 208-2488 all
ıounted on a Dawe rifle stock.
300-400 *CSK*

A very rare Thompson revolver
amera No. 48, with a polished
nahogany handle, lacquered brass
ody with upper rear mounted
iewing tube with sprung sliding
ront section, front lens element
igned in pencil 'AF', opening back
ection with rotating wheel and
otating internal section with
23mm diameter windows and
ront mounted internal shutter
nechanism, defective, camera base
ngraved '25' and front section
ngraved 'Thompson, Invt. Brevete
.G.D.G.' A. Briois, 4 Rue de la
Jouane, Paris No. 43'.
20,000-25,000 *CSK*

'hompson's revolver camera was atented in France on 20 January 862. No. 52,713. Although lesigned by Englishman John 'hompson the camera was nanufactured by A. Briois of Paris. : was demonstrated to the Société 'rançaise de Photographie on July, 1862.

'he camera had a number of new eatures including the taking of circular exposures on a single ircular plate. The exposure was nade via a rotary shutter. The front ns had a combined use as a viewing ns which dropped into position as he taking lens. The process of eleasing the lens and dropping it ıto position activated the shutter. 'his procedure allowed 4 exposures be made in rapid succession.

nly 3 other Thompson revolver ımeras have been traced.

A half-plate mahogany and brass studio camera, by Ross, London, with rising front, swinging and rotating back, red leather bellows, rack and pinion focusing back section, a repeating back and a brass bound A. Ross, London, lens No. 3782, camera with inset plaque 'Ross, London'.
£400-600 *CSK*

Viewers

A burr walnut Brewster pattern stereoscope, with rack and pinion focusing, shaped lens hood mounted on hinged lens section, opening top plate and inset ivory plaque 'London Stereoscopic Company, 54 Cheapside'.
£200-300 *CSK*

A 12in (31cm) diameter black painted Zoetrope, on turned wood base and a quantity of picture strips, each with a printed title and 'Entered at Stationer's Hall'.
£300-350 *CSK*

A 5 by 4in (12.5 by 10cm) wooden bodied View camera No. 115, with lens mounted behind a sector shutter, with screw focusing and one wooden double darkslide.
£200-240 *CSK*

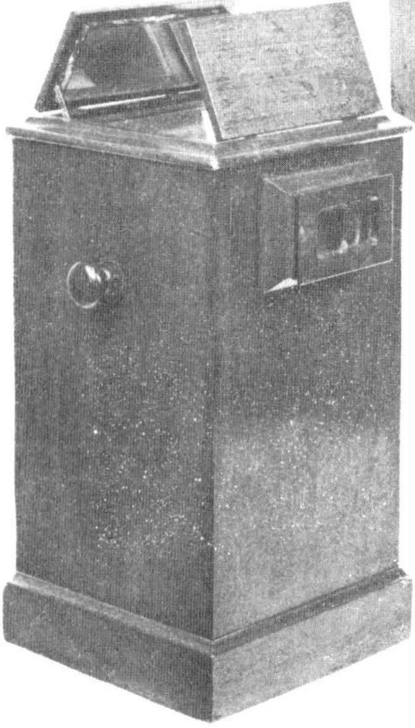

A mahogany pedestal dual-viewer stereoscope, with split hinged lid and hinged wood mounted glass cover containing a quantity of stereocards, including South Coast views by S. F. Mann, Hastings, and others, and a Brewster pattern stereoscope with brass strengthening screws.
£300-400 *CSK*

ART NOUVEAU

Ceramics

A jug and basin set, with green and pink embossed design, jug 12½in (32cm) high.
£120-140 *PAR*

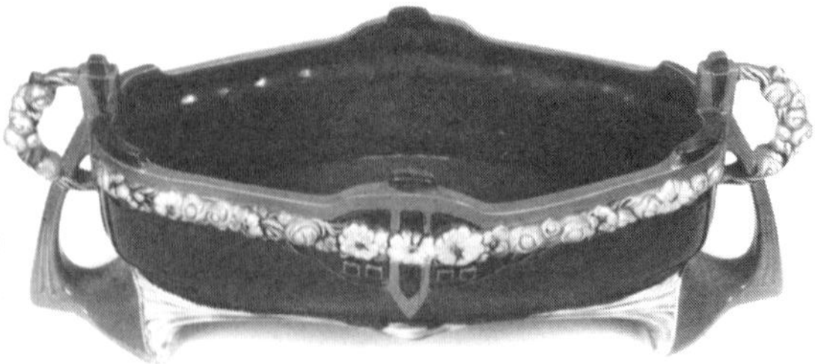

A Continent green boat vase, 16in (41cm) wide.
£60-80 *TH*

A Foley plate, produced for the American market, signed F Micklewright, c1893, 9in (23cm) diam.
£100-200 *AJ*

Two Foley Intarsio Toby jugs, John Bull and Scotsman, 7½in (19cm) high.
£250-350 each *AJ*

An Eichwald tazza, c1920, 11in (28cm).
£180-200 *BEV*

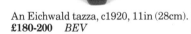

Two early E. Radford, Burslem. vases, tallest 6½in (16cm).
£40-60 each *MA*

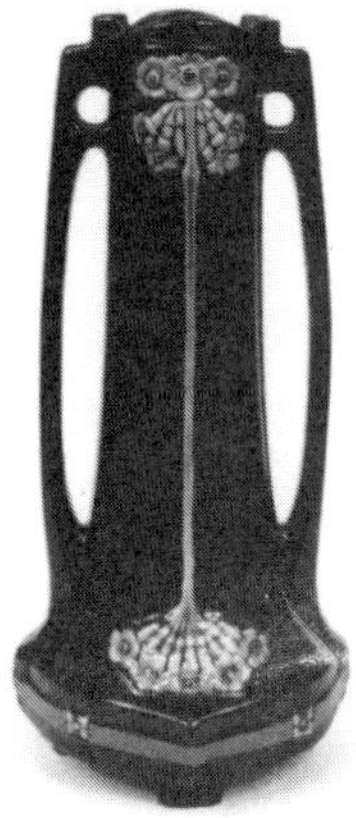

A pair of Eichwald vases, 12in (31cm).
£90-120 *BEV*

An E. Radford jug, Anemone pattern, 6½in (16cm).
£40-50 *MA*

An E. Radford vase, Strawberry pattern, 9in (22cm).
£50-60 *MA*

A large early E. Radford ju Ranunculus pattern.
£90-120 *MA*

An early E. Radford vase, Anemone pattern.
£75-85 *MA*

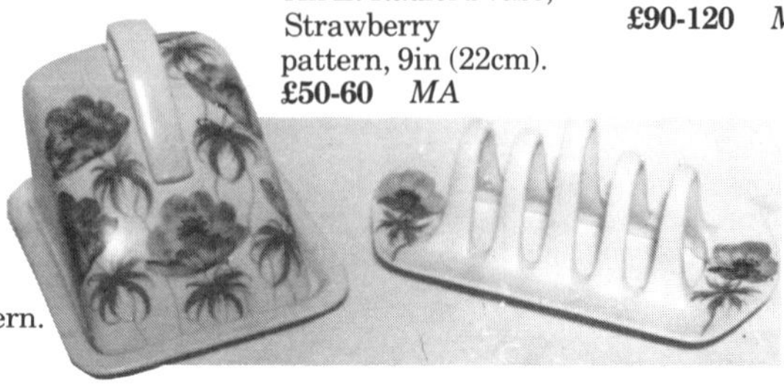

An E. Radford cheese dish and toast rack Anemone patt
£55-75 each

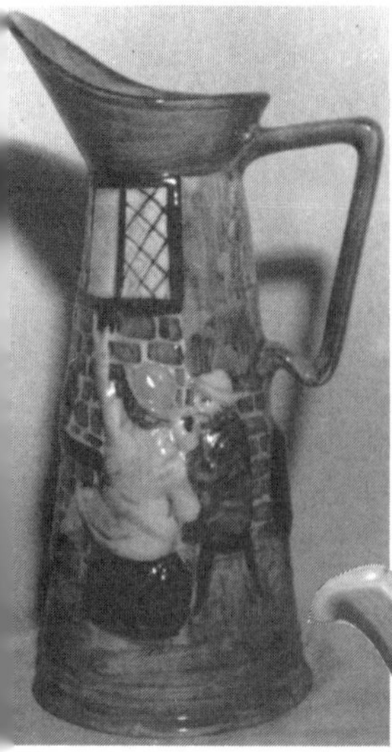

ın E. Radford 'coaching' jug, 0½in (27cm).
100-125 *MA*

Three pieces of Radford ware, Ranunculus pattern.
£25-100 each *MA*

An early E. Radford, Burslem, teapot, 5½in (14cm).
£80-100 *MA*

An E. Radford moulded vase, Rose pattern, 6in (15cm).
£50-70 *MA*

large E. Radford moulded jug, ıdian Tree pattern, 8½in (21cm) gh.
ŝ0-80 *MA*

Two E. Radford vases, Anemone pattern, 7½in (19cm) and 10in (25cm) high. **£40-60 each** *MA*

An early E. Radford, Burslem, jug, 7in (17cm) high.
£70-90 *MA*

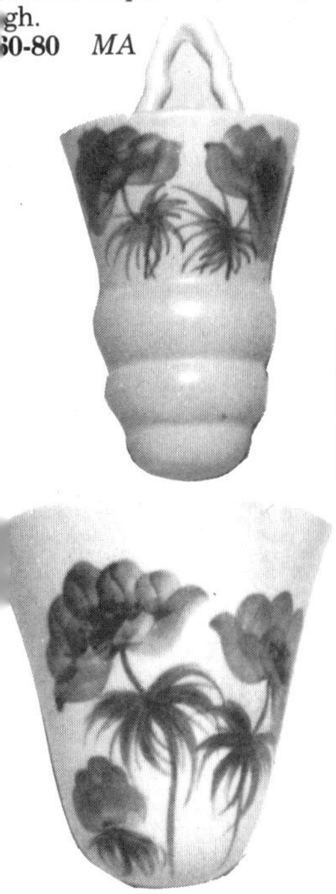

vo E. Radford wall pockets, ıemone pattern, 4½in (11cm).
0-60 each *MA*

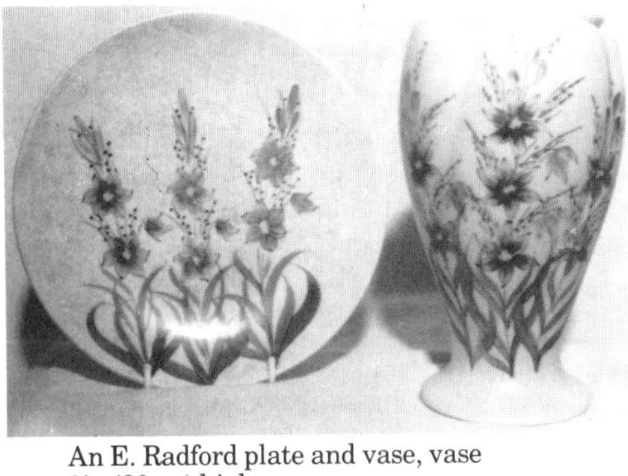

An E. Radford plate and vase, vase 8in (20cm) high.
£40-60 each *MA*

An early E. Radford, Burslem, table lamp base.
£70-80 *MA*

Two early E. Radford, Burslem, vases. **£70-90 each** *MA*

Two early E. Radford, Burslem, jugs. **£40-60 each** *M*

A collection of E. Radford Anemone ware.
£25-70 each *MA*

Two E. Radford pieces with the Anemone patter plate 10in (25cm) diameter. **£40-60 each** *M.*

Figures

A Royal Dux figure group, The Dolly Sisters, c1920, 16½in (42cm).
£1,500-2,000 *BEV*

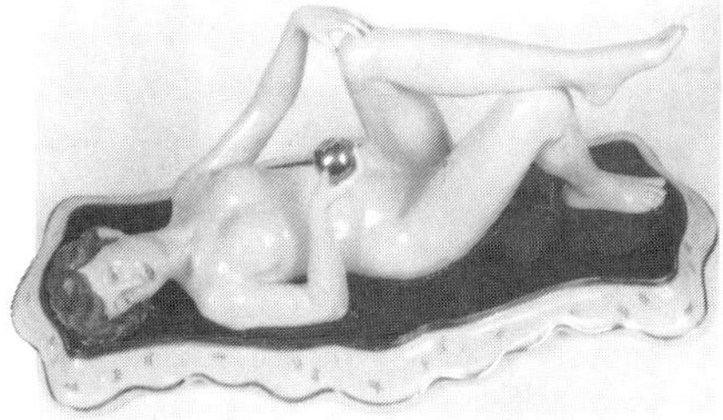

A Royal Dux figure, The girl with the Golden Apple, c1920, 22in (56cm) wide.
£1,400-1,600 *BEV*

A Rosenthal figure, child with b Liebermann, c1920, 9in (23cm).
£325-375 *BEV*

A Royal Dux figure, Pierette, Schaff design, c1920, 14½in (37cm).
£400-600 *BEV*

A Rosenthal figure of an Eastern lady, Holzer de Fanti design, c1920, 18½in (47cm).
£700-800 *BEV*

A Rosenthal figure, by Boehs, c1920, 9in (23cm).
£300-375 *BEV*

A Goldscheider earthenware fig of a woman, wearing pink and g skirt, the rose bodice with pink halter neck, restored, printed wi factory mark, 'Made in Austria', signature and impressed numbe 6126 42 6, 15in (39cm) high.
£270-350 *HSS*

Goldscheider earthenware figure, wearing a green skirt, painted in black with brief green spotted bodice, on a black painted base, printed with factory mark, 'Made in Austria', facsimile signature and impressed number '7195 570 11', 14in (36.5cm) high.
£400-450 *HSS*

Furniture

A mahogany table, probably Liberty, 27½in (71cm) square.
£400-600 *ARF*

An Art Nouveau set of 6 chairs and 1 carver, 45in (18in).
£700-800 *ARF*

A Thonet bentwood newspaper rack, with printed paper label, Thonet, Wien, 23in (60cm) high.
£600-800 *C*

A gold painted bentwood chair, style attributed to Hoffman, 37in (94cm) high.
£25-50 *ARF*

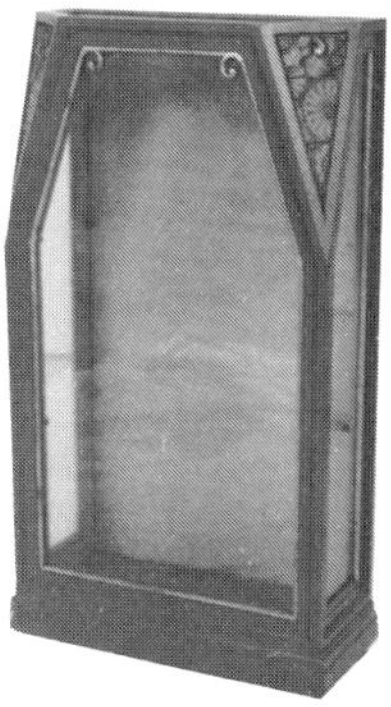

An Art Nouveau display cabinet, 31in (79cm) high.
£250-350 *ARF*

A Heals wardrobe, c1898, 41½in (105cm).
£700-850 *ARF*
Illustrated in A History of Heals.

A Thonet chair, No. 4 from their catalogue, 35in (89cm).
£60-90 *ARF*

A Georges De Feure carved cherrywood armchair, the carved apron and legs decorated with scrolling foliate motifs.
£2,000-2,500 *C*

An Art Nouveau desk, 20in (51cm). **£700-800** *ARF*

An Art Nouveau hall stand, 22in (56cm).
£145-175 *DH*

An Art Nouveau style oak and inlaid cabinet, 65in (165cm).
£850-950 *AH*

An Art Nouveau sideboard, c1900, 54in (137cm).
£2,000-2,500 *Wai*

An Aesthetic Movement easel, 52in (132cm) high.
£300-400 *ARF*

A bentwood nest of tables, by Thonet, 23½in (60cm).
£350-550 *ARF*

A bentwood table, with baize top, 27½in (70cm) high.
£300-400 *ARF*

A Morris screen, 46in (116.5cm).
£400-500 *ARF*

Glass

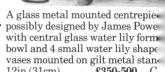

A glass metal mounted centrepie possibly designed by James Powe with central glass water lily form bowl and 4 small water lily shape vases mounted on gilt metal stan 12in (31cm). **£350-500** *C*

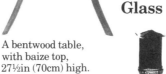

A James Powell engraved glass decanter, on domed foot, the green tinted glass engraved with sprigs of flowers, with silver stopper stamped J & P and London hallmarks for 1912, 10½in (27cm).
£700-900 *C*

An Art Nouveau green iridescent glass inkwell, overlaid with a silv and gilt Art Nouveau design.
£90-120 *GAK*

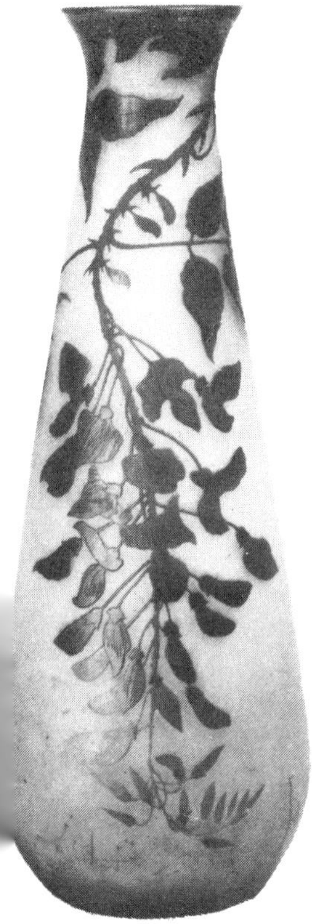

Gallé acid etched and carved
meo vase, the pale grey glass
erlaid in purple with trailing
isteria blossom, cameo signature
allé, with a star, 19in (48cm).
,700-3,000 *CSK*

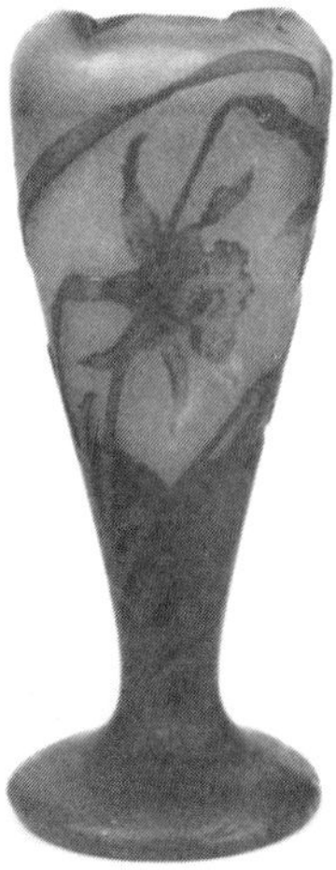

A Gallé vase with daffodils, 10½in (27cm).
£2,500-3,500 *ABS*

A Daum glass vase, c1900, 11in (28cm).
£4,000-5,000 *ABS*

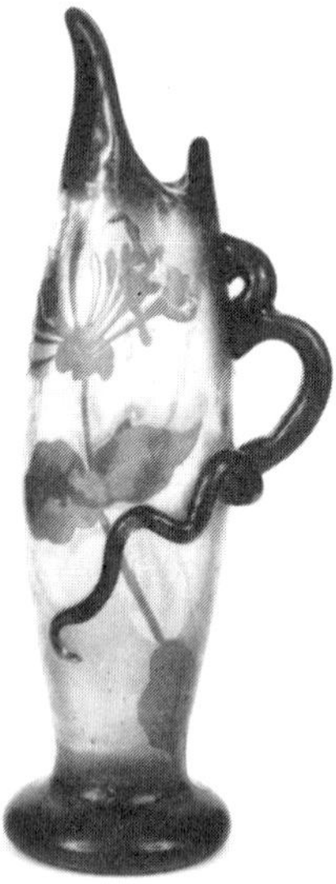

A Gallé jug, 11in (28cm).
£3,000-4,000 *ABS*

A Gallé vase, c1900, 8½in (22cm).
£5,000-6,000 *ABS*

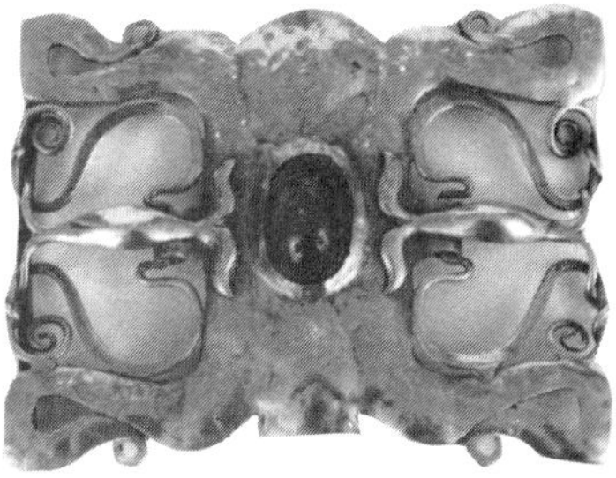

A Liberty buckle, Oliver Parker, 1902.
£450-500 *DID*

ewellery

Art Nouveau pendant/brooch
th gold, emerald and enamel
coration, made by John
rdman, Birmingham, design by
gin, c1880.
,200-3,500 *DID*

A German Art Nouveau pendant, in gold, with ruby, pearls and diamonds, signed F. Mahla Pforzheim.
£425-450 *DID*

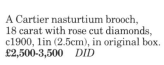

An Austrian golfer brooch in platinum, black onyx and diamonds, by Ernst Paltscho, c1925. **£2,500-3,500** *DID*

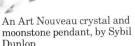

An Art Nouveau crystal and moonstone pendant, by Sybil Dunlop.
£450-500 *DID*

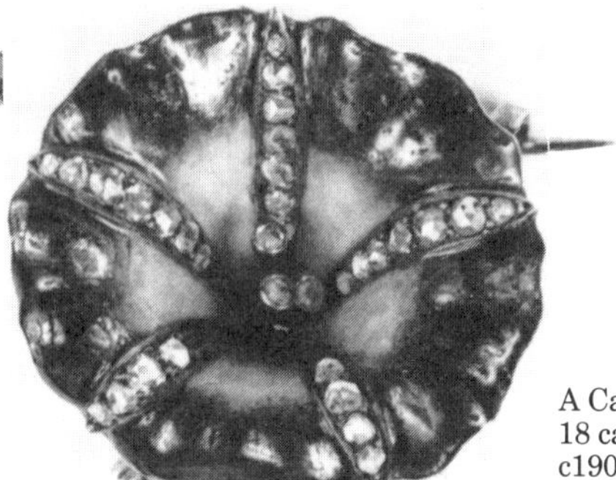

A Cartier nasturtium brooch, 18 carat with rose cut diamonds, c1900, 1in (2.5cm), in original box.
£2,500-3,500 *DID*

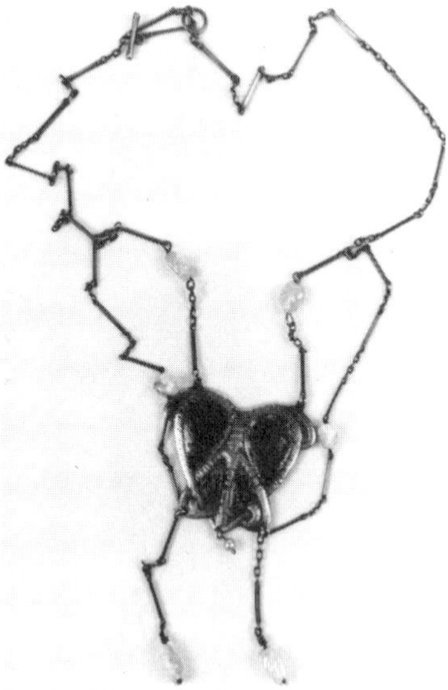

An Art Nouveau silver, enamel and pearl necklace by Mürlle Bennett & Co.
£330-350 *DID*

An Art Nouveau necklace made by Mürlle Bennett, in enamel and silver, c1900.
£500-600 *DID*

A German Art Nouveau 15 carat pendant, with ruby, diamond and pearl, Pforzheim in the style of Kleeman.
£500-600 *DID*

An Art Nouveau carved horn pendant of a butterfly, on woven silk cord with 2 blue glass beads between wooden spacers, 3in (8cm) long.
£200-250 *CSK*

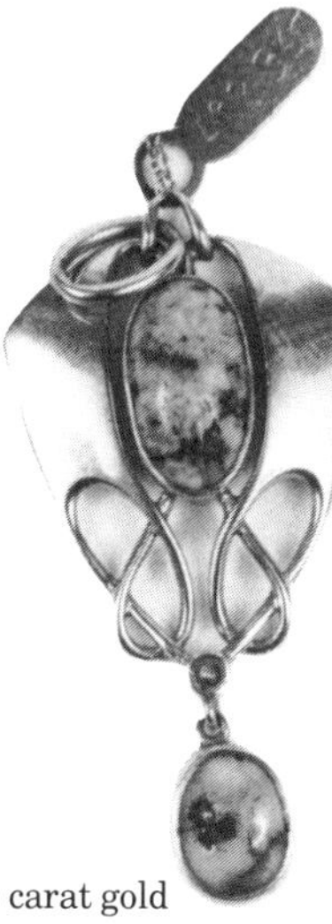

A 15 carat gold pendant, with turquoise, by Mürlle Bennett.
£350-400 *DID*

An acid etched and cut glass cameo table lamp, the clear glass overlaid in blue with flowers and foliage on a multi-faceted and textured surface, minor chips round the base, 20½in (51cm).
£1,600-2,500 *CSK*

An Art Nouveau tortoiseshell comb, in silver and olivine, by Wm. Soper, 5½in (13cm).
£400-500 *DID*

Lamps

An American copper table lamp in the form of a Doric column, with two lamp holders, the shade in leaded green glass, the stepped base marked "Gorham Co., Q497" and trademark, 19in (48cm).
£550-600 *P(S)*

A 'Le Verre Français' cameo glas and wrought iron table lamp, designed by Schneider, the pale green ground overlaid and etchec with thorny berry-laden branche striped cane signature on base, 15½in (39.5cm).
£2,500-3,000 *C*

A Muller Frères acid etched cameo table lamp, with three-branch gilt metal mount, the mottled orange glass overlaid in dark brown with continuous river landscape and grazing deer, cameo signature Muller Frères, Luneville, in the base, 19in (48.5cm).
£6,000-6,500 *CSK*

A set of 3 Art Nouveau gilt metal twin branch wall lights, with pineapple glass shades and one extra shade.
£350-400 *P*

Martin Bros

A Martin Brothers stoneware vase, with ovoid body decorated with large flowers and leaves on a turquoise ground, 1891, 9in (23cm).
£450-500 *GSP*

A Martin Brothers stoneware vase, with ovoid body decorated with flowers, grasses and insects on a golden ground, 1892, 8½in (22cm).
£900-1,200 *GSP*

A Martin Brothers stoneware vase, with ovoid body decorated with monkeys amidst foliage with various expressions on their faces, 1893, 9½in (24cm).
£1,700-2,000 *GSP*

Metal

An Art Nouveau W. M. F. bottle holder, 7in (17.5cm).
£250-300 *DSA*

A silver coffee pot, Sheffield, 1899, 10in (25cm), 27oz.
£500-525 *DSA*

A W. M. F. electroplated pewter three-piece coffee set, comprising: a coffee pot, a cream jug and sugar basin on trestle feet, each stamped with usual WMF marks, coffee pot 8in (19.5cm) high.
£450-650 *C*

A mixed metal sugar bowl and cream jug, applied with copper castings of foliage, birds and insects, the sugar bowl with 2 bronze handles and the cream jug with one, each cast in the form of a stylised elephant's head, with traces of gilding on the interiors, by Gorham Providence, both marked, 1882, sugar bowl 4in (10cm) diam, 11.5oz gross.
£3,000-4,000 *CNY*

A Liberty muffin dish, designed by Archibald Knox, 11½in (29cm) diam.
£400-500 *ABS*

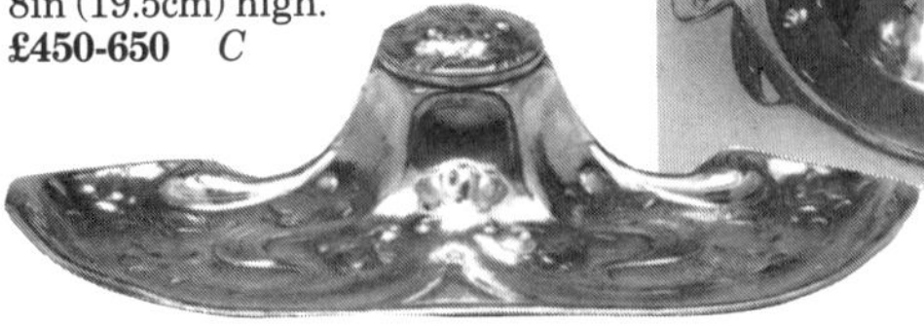

A Martele inkstand with removable glass liner, the stand repoussé and chased with serpentine ribs and flowers, on three ball feet, by Gorham, Providence, marked Martele.9584, c1905, 10in (25.5cm) wide, 9.5oz.
£1,200-1,500 *CNY*

A Tiffany fruit bowl, of fluted circular form on spreading base with lightly hammered surface, mid-20thC, 10½in (27cm) diam.
£2,000-2,500 *CNY*

An Art Nouveau silver photo frame, Birmingham, 1902.
£275-300 *DSA*

A Mappin and Webb Art Nouveau silver and enamelled frame, on easel support, cast in relief with shamrocks, enamelled in green and pale turquoise, stamped M & W, Sheffield, 1904, 8in (20cm) high.
£700-800 *CSK*

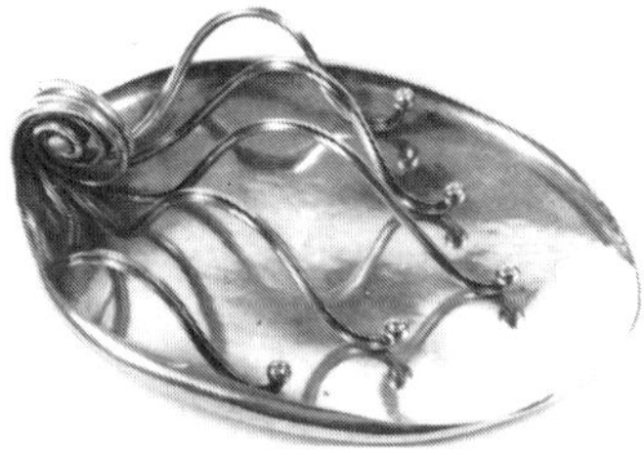

A silver toast rack, by Georg Jensen, c1930, 6in (15cm) wide.
£1,200-1,300 *DID*

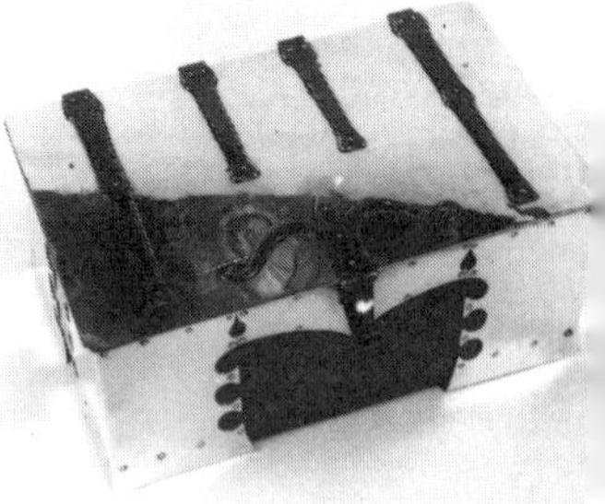

A silver and copper box, by Birmingham Guild of Handicraft signed B.G.H., c1900, 8½in (22cm wide.
£1,700-1,800 *DID*

A W. M. F. candelabrum, with 2 urn shape sconces on brassed stems, the centre pewter figure of a young scantily clad girl wearing a long flowering dress, 10in (25cm) high.
£1,000-1,500 *DDM*

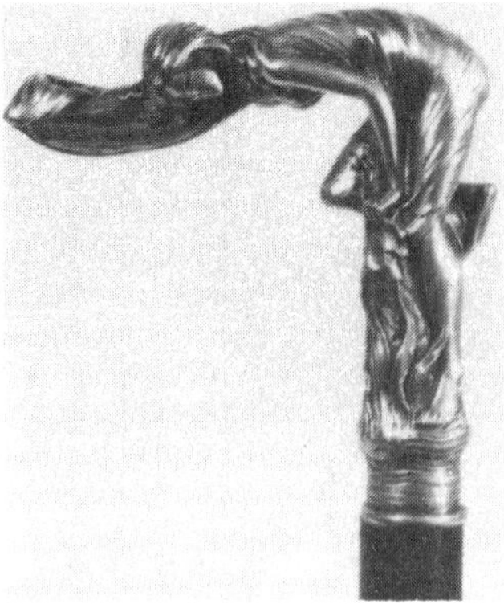

An Art Nouveau style malacca walking stick, the white metal handle modelled with a figure of a young woman kneeling amidst reeds.
£250-400 *CSK*

A hammered silver raised bowl, by A. E. Jones, the frieze cast with foxes chasing geese, on raised foot, Birmingham, 1915, 4in (10.5cm) diam.
£300-350 *P(M)*

A pair of W. M. F. gilded pewter
vases, moulded with rushes and
rocks in a stream and adorned with
water sprites and cherubim,
stamped with WMF marks, 11½in
(29.5cm) high.
£300-500 *C*

A set of 4 copper
and brass
candlesticks.
£300-350 *DID*

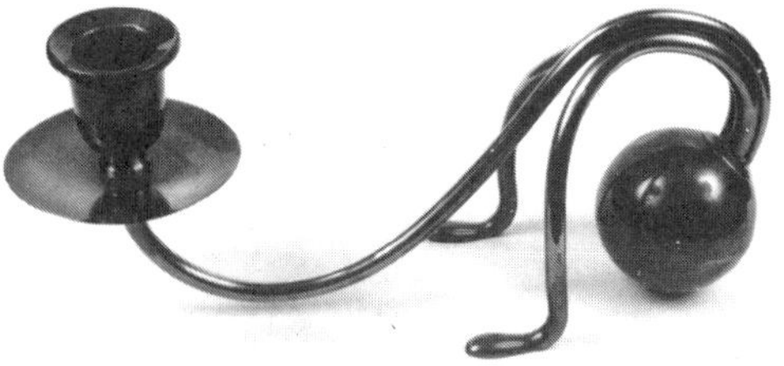

Two Art Nouveau cast
iron fire surrounds,
72in (182.5cm) high.
£3,000-3,500 *LRG*

Moorcroft

A Moorcroft pottery bowl, decorated
in shades of red, green, blue and
yellow with the Orchid pattern on
an inky-blue ground, impressed
Moorcroft Made in England,
signature in blue, 9in (23cm) diam.
£200-250 *HSS*

A Moorcroft pottery vase, the ovoid
body boldly painted with a lily
design on a cream and green
ground, impressed marks, Walter
Moorcroft initials and paper label,
13in (33.4cm).
£550-700 *Bea*

An Art pottery baluster vase,
decorated with bulrushes in
polychrome enamels, by Moorcroft.
£250-300 *GD*

l. & r. A pair of Moorcroft baluster
shaped vases painted with
pomegranates on dark blue
grounds, 13in (33.5cm) high.
£750-1,000

c. A Moorcroft pottery tazza, painted
with pomegranates on a mottled
blue ground, raised on circular foot,
10in (25cm) diam.
£150-200 *P(M)*

A Moorcroft Pottery three-piece
garniture, decorated in purple and
green with the Pansy pattern on a
mottled green/inky blue ground,
some hairline cracks to rims,
impressed Moorcroft, Burslem,
England, with green painted
signature, early 20thC, tallest 12in
(31cm).
£500-600 *HSS*

Miscellaneous

A set of 8 Richards tiles, 6in (15cm) square.
£75-125 *THA*

An Art Nouveau brass and wood punch set, comprising: circular tray on stand, with glass lined brass two-handled punch bowl, and 7 brass cups with glass liners, with embossed decoration of grape laden vines, the brass-mounted stand cast with linear motifs, the cups stamped CDE between crossed swords, 46in (116.5cm) high.
£250-300 *CSK*

A collection of 13 Goebels ceramic glass-eyed lights, comprising: monkey, cat, black mammy, orange gnome, spaniel, frog, googly-eyed girl, a pair of Dutch boys, fish, Turkish gentleman, owl, and elephant, 7 to 8in (17.5 to 20cm) high.
£4,500-5,000 *BIZ*

Doulton

A Doulton miniature mug, 1in (2.5cm) high.
£40-50 *THA*

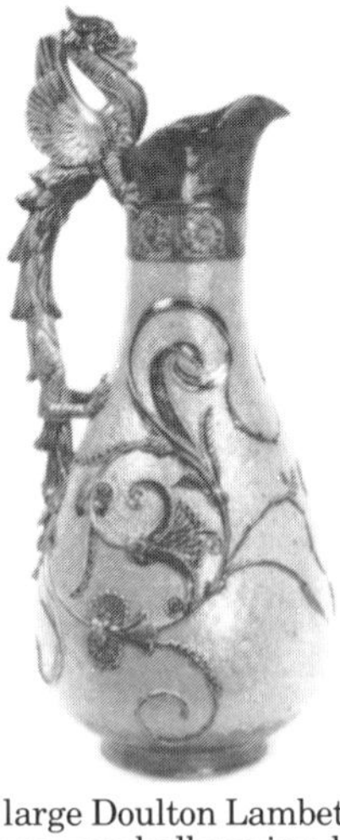

A large Doulton Lambeth stoneware bulbous jug, by Mark V Marshall with incised and applied foliate decoration glazed in shades of brown, the undulated rim glazed in blue and brown, damage to dragon, impressed marks, 24in (61.5cm) high.
£600-1,000 *CSK*

A pair of Doulton vases, initialled E.B., c1910, 12in (30.5cm) high.
£175-225 *THA*

A Doulton Burslem porcelain figu of a jester sitting on a pedestal, painted in pastel shades of salmo pink and mint green with gilt motifs, minor restorations, printe marks, 9½in (24cm) high.
£700-900 *CSK*

ı Doulton Lambeth
ɿase with
.ncised band of cattle,
ɔy Hannah Barlow,
lated 1888,
7½in (19cm) high.
£370-400 *TVA*

A Doulton Lambeth pottery lemonade jug, by Emily J Parrington, with silver plated hinged cover and thumbpiece, decorated in low relief within oval buff reserve panels, on flower decorated green and blue ground, impressed mark and initials, 9in (23cm) high.
£500-600 *AH*

A pair of Doulton Burslem blue and white transferware soup plates, Madras pattern, 10in (25cm) diam.
£15-20 *OD*

A Doulton Lambeth plaque, decorated by Hannah Barlow, dated 1874, 9in (23cm) square.
£400-500 *Wai*

Royal Doulton

A Royal Doulton flambé model of a seated fox, c1930, 5in (12.5cm) high.
£275-325 *TVA*

Royal Doulton tea service, D5104,
ıtitled 'Fox-hunting', comprising:
ɛapot and lid, 6 cups, saucers and
.ates, and a cake plate.
170-200 *P*

The Henley Teddy, limited edition of 250, 1989, 9in (22.5cm) high.
£110-140 *TP*

Shareholder, limited edition of 1,500, 1988, 9in (22.5cm) high.
£95-100 *TP*

The Cavalier with goatee beard, c1939, 6in (15cm) high.
£1,650-1,950 *TP*

hurchill, a limited
lition of 750,
990, 9in (22.5cm) high.
110-120 *TP*

.urchill, a limited
ition of 5,000,
39, 9in (22.5cm) high.
00-130 *TP*

Lord Nelson, No. D6336, 1952-69, 6in (15cm) high.
£200-250 *TP*

Margaret Thatcher, limited edition of 1,000, 1989, 9in (22.5cm) high.
£110-130 *TP*

The Gardener, No. D6630, 1973-81, 7in (17.5cm) high.
£110-145 *TP*

White-haired Clown, No. D6322, 1951-55, 6in (15cm) high.
£450-650 *TP*

The Vicar of Bray, No. D5615, 1936-60, 6in (15cm) high.
£110-130 *TP*

Old King Cole, No. D6036, 1939-60, 6in (15cm) high.
£110-135 *TP*

Miller's is a price Guide not a price List

The price ranges given reflect the average price a purchaser should pay for similar items. Condition, rarity of design or pattern, size, colour, provenance, restoration and many other factors must be taken into account when assessing values. When buying or selling, it must always be remembered that prices can be greatly affected by the condition of any piece. Unless otherwise stated, all goods shown in Miller's are of good merchantable quality, and the valuations given reflect this fact. Pieces offered for sale in exceptionally fine condition or in poor condition may reasonably be expected to be priced considerably higher or lower respectively than the estimates given herein

The Town Crier, No. D6530, 1960-73, 6in (15cm) high.
£140-170 *TP*

The Collector, No. D6796, limited edition of 5,000, 1988, 6in (15cm) high.
£90-120 *TP*

The Golfer, limited edition of 1,000, 1989, 9in (22.5cm) h
£110-130 *TP*

Mr. Pickwick, 1940-60, 6in (15cm) high.
£110-130 *TP*

Farmer John, No. 5788, 1938-60, 6in (15cm) high.
£65-85 *TP*

GEORGE ROBEY

George Robey, with removable ha
c1925, 10½in (26cm) high.
£2,000-2,250 *TP*

Che Antique Dealer, No. D6807, imited edition, 1988, 6in (15cm) iigh.
:70-80 *TP*

Sam Weller, No. D6064, 1940-60, 5½in (14cm) high.
£65-85 *TP*

The Auctioneer, No. D6838, limited edition of 5,000, 1989, 6in (15cm) high.
£70-80 *TP*

'he Fortune Teller, No. D6497, 959-67, 6in (15cm) high.
200-250 *TP*

Queen Victoria, No. D6788, limited edition of 3,000, made for China Guild 1988, 6in (15cm) high.
£75-95 *TP*

The Cardinal, No. D5614, 1936-60, 6in (15cm) high.
£65-85 *TP*

A Royal Doulton cabinet plate, painted and signed by W. E. J. Dean, dated 1916, 9in (23cm) diam.
£250-300 *TVA*

A Royal Doulton figure, 'The Curtsey', HN 334.
£400-450 *GSP*

A Royal Doulton boxed set of napki rings, comprising the Dickens figures, Mr. Pickwick, Mr. Micawber, Fat Boy, Tony Weller, Sam Weller and Sairey Gamp, printed marks.
£800-1,200 *CSK*

A Royal Doulton flambé model of a seated rabbit, restoration, c1925, 4in (10cm) high.
£125-175 *TVA*

A Royal Doulton porcelain figure, 'Matador and Bull', designed by M. Davies, HN 2011, printed and painted marks, 15½in (38cm) high
£2,300-3,000 *CSK*

A Royal Doulton Lambeth stoneware figure of Samuel, by George Tinworth, on oval moulded base, with impressed initials, 6in (15cm) high.
£450-500 *AH*

A Royal Doulton jug, 'The Pied Piper', number 252 of a limited edition of 600 by H. Fenton, 10in (25cm) high.
£170-250 *P(M)*

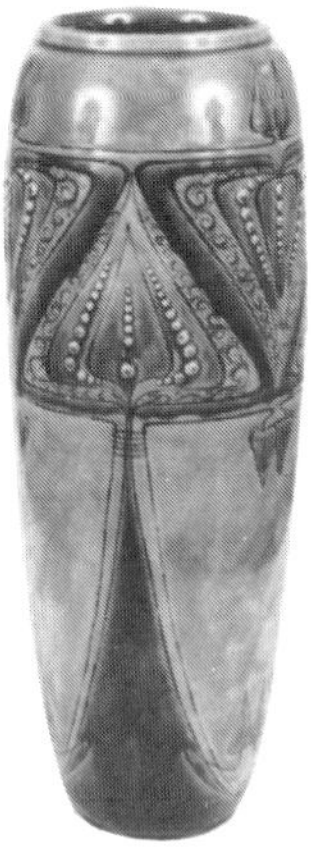

A Royal Doulton Art Nouveau vase, Artists' monogram Eliza Simmance and Bessie Newberry, incised date code for 1909, 15in (38.5cm) high.
£220-250 *TVA*

A Royal Doulton blue and white chamber pot, c1900.
£40-45 *OD*

A Royal Doulton Holbein ware pottery vase, decorated by W. Nunn, in colours with 2 men seated drinking at a table, signed, impressed Doulton Ivory, 1920B and printed mark in green, 9½in (24cm) high.
£200-250 *HSS*

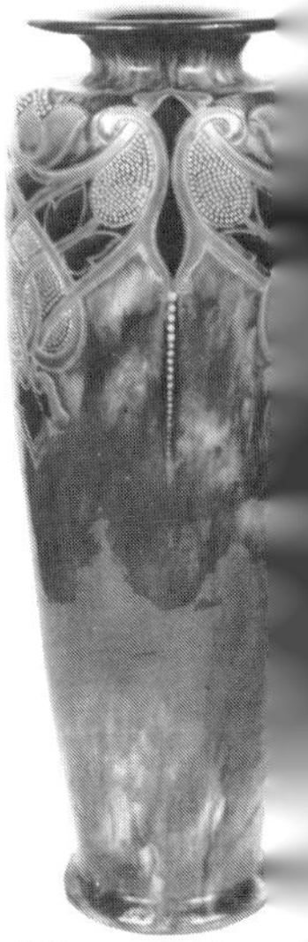

A Royal Doulto vase, restored, 14in (36cm) hig
£50-60 *OD*

Arts & Crafts

ʀoyal Doulton figure, 'The Jester',
: 702, one ball on tunic stuck, one
ssing. **£300-350** *GSP*

A Royal Doulton ovoid vase, by Eliza Simmance, with flared rim, the stylised flower decoration on brushed grey green ground with blue and brown banding, 15in (38.5cm) high.
£250-300 *AH*

DEPÔT
THE FOLEY CHINA
ENGLANDS
FINEST PORCELAIN

A Foley plaque, 10 by 8in (25 by 20cm), c1880.
£900-1,200 *AJ*

A very rare piece.

A Barum ware bottle vase, with blue bird and floral decoration on a cream ground, incised mark and dated 1890, 13½in (35cm) high.
£90-120 *PCh*

ʌ Foley Intarsio tray, with typical
ʌrt Nouveau design, c1880, 10½ by
·in (25 by 20cm).
'300-400 *AJ*

A Foley Intarsio bowl with geese, c1880, 8in (20.5cm) diam.
£300-400 *AJ*

·oley Intarsio bowl with scenes
ı Hamlet, c1900, 11½in (29cm)
ı.
·0-600 *AJ*

A French Longwy charger, c1900, 17in (43.5cm) diam.
£150-200 *BEV*

A Frederick Rhead Intarsio bowl, c1900, 11½in (30cm) diam.
£250-300 *BEV*

ıskin amethyst shaded bowl,
ʌ applied embossed flowers, high
ɪ, marked.
·-600 *PC*

A Ruskin grey and white mottled bowl, impressed mark, c1927, 8in (20cm) diam.
£400-500 *PC*

A Ruskin dark green bowl, on three feet, 8in (20cm) diam.
£75-95 *PC*

ARTS & CRAFT

A Sèvres Art Pottery bowl, in blue tones sponged with yellow, c1930, 11in (28cm) diam.
£50-100 *HOW*

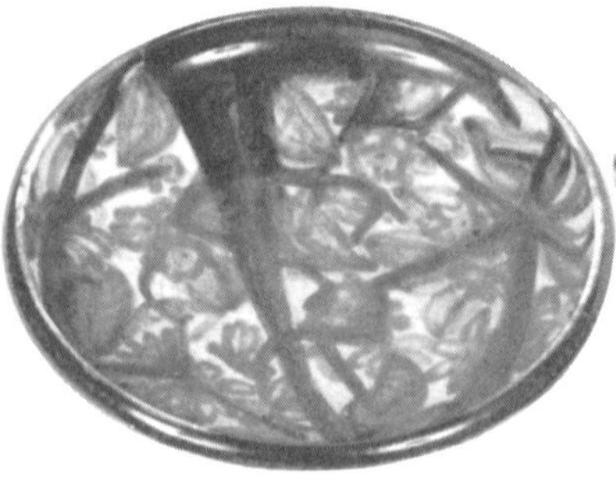

A Sèvres Art Pottery dish in red, green and brown, 7in (17.5cm) diam.
£40-65 *HOW*

A Brannam pink dog with toothache, 6½in (16.5cm) hi
£55-60 *BLO*

A Brannam green owl jar with lid, made for Liberty, 5in (12.5cm) high.
£50-80 *BLO*

A Brannam cat, green with black markings, 11in (28.5cm) high.
£200-220 *BLO*

An Upchurch pottery bowl with three handles, in blue and grey, (17.5cm) diam.
£50-70 *BLO*

A Brannam flower holder, initialled 'B W', c1900, 10in (25cm) wide.
£175-200 *BLO*

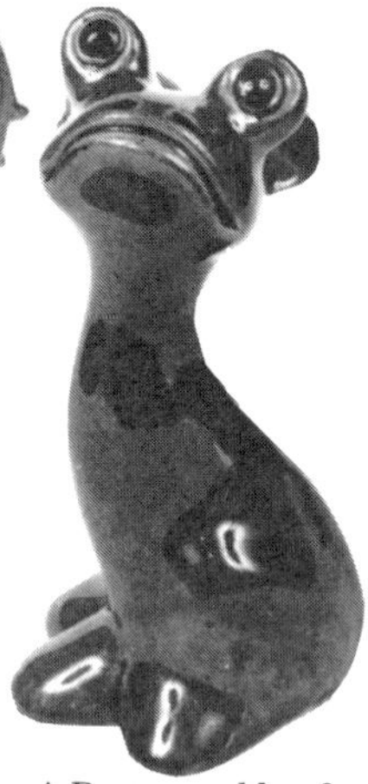

A Brannam blue frog, 2½in (6cm) high.
£60-80 *BLO*

A Brannam chamber stick, initialled 'S W', 4in (10cm) hig
£120-150 *BLO*

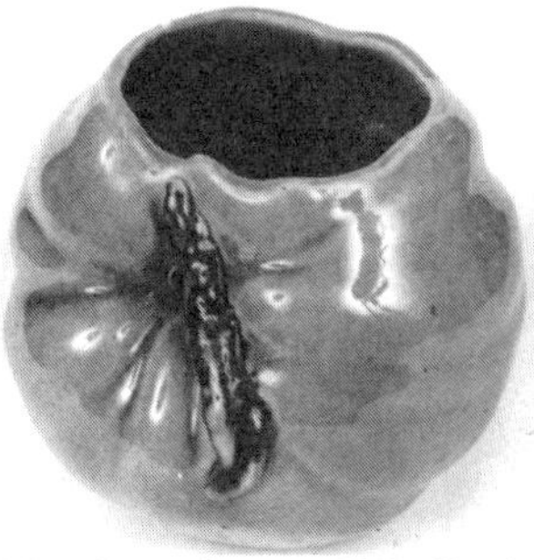

A Bretby apple vase, 3½in (9cm) high.
£30-45 *BLO*

A Ruskin green cup and saucer, with decoration, 3½in (9cm) diam.
£60-80 *PC*

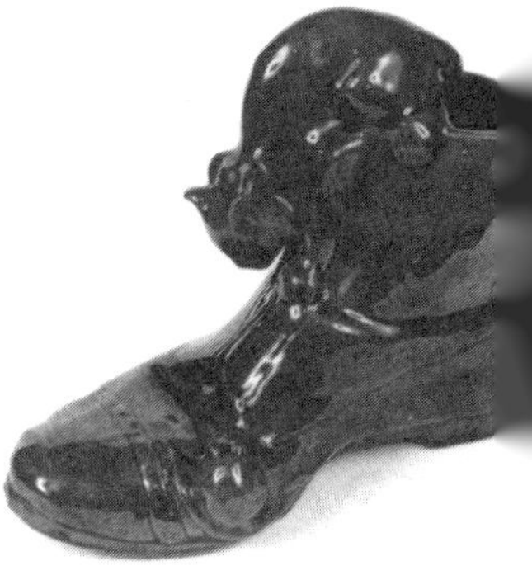

A Brannam blue boot, 8½in (21cm) long.
£130-150 *BLO*

to you my
all wealth
and
that is
thankful

Brannam beaker/mug, part of a emonade set, with inscription.
80-100 *BLO*

A Quimper cup and saucer, c1905, saucer 7in (18cm) diam.
£40-60 *VH*

An Elton ware loving cup, c1890, 8½in (21cm) high.
£300-375 *SAI*

A Ruskin green cup and saucer, 5½in (14cm) diam.
£70-90 *PC*

Brannam blue Toby jug, 4in 0cm) high.
30-50 *BLO*

not to spill
of your skill

A Barum blue puzzle jug, with inscription, 5in (12.5cm) high.
£35-40 *BLO*

A Ruskin dark green cup and saucer, from the Ferneyhough collection, saucer 6in (15cm) diam.
£90-110 *PC*

Barum jug, inscribed 'The Lundy arrot', 5in (12.5cm) high.
0-90 *BLO*

A Brannam puffin jug, c1900, 8in (20cm) high.
£80-100 *BLO*

A pair of Frederick Rhead Foley Intarsio ewers, c1880, 11in (28cm) high.
£800-900 *BEV*

A Brannam jug, with inscription, initialled 'F B', 1901, 5½in (14cm) high.
£130-145 *BLO*

Did you know

MILLER'S Antiques Price Guide builds up year by year to form the most comprehensive photo-reference system available

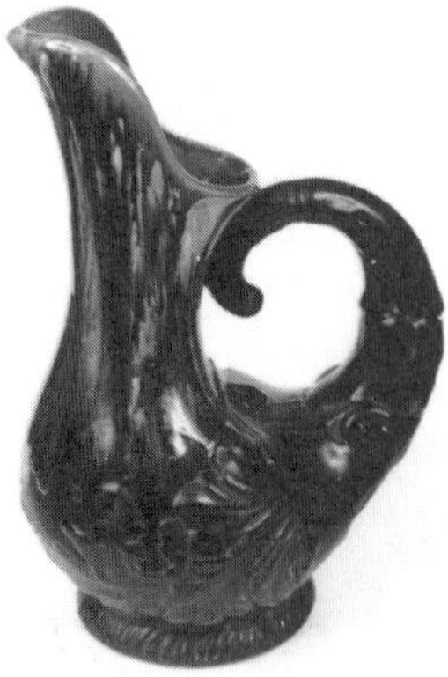

A Bretby jug, with flowing glaze spout, copperette handle and body, 12in (30.5cm) high.
£140-160 *BLO*

REG
13:

A Louis Desmant, Normandy, jug with scenes from the Bayeux Tapestry, 5½in (14cm) high.
£40-60 *BLO*

A Lauder green jug, 8in (20cm) hig
£100-110 *BLO*

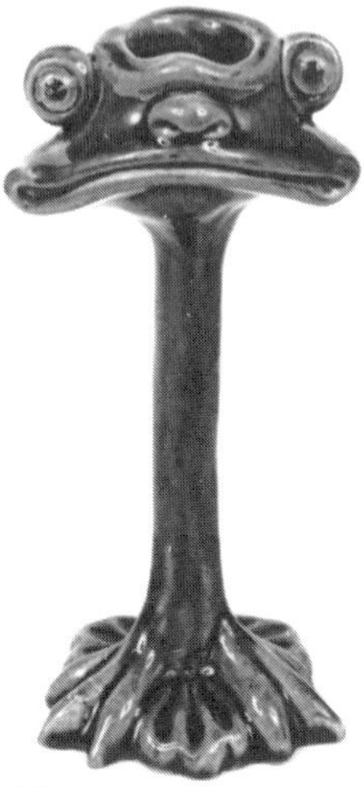

A Barum green frog candle holder, 6in (15cm) high.
£90-100 *BLO*

A Belgian pottery candle holder, 11½in (29cm) high.
£50-60 *BLO*

A Gouda ceramic candle holder, c1920, 8½in (21cm) high.
£70-80 *BEV*

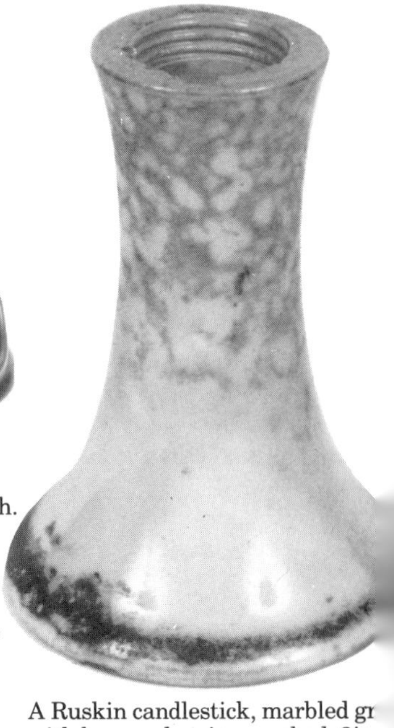

A Ruskin candlestick, marbled gr with burgundy trim, marked, 3in (7.5cm) high.
£150-200 *PC*

A Wardle mauve candle holder, 9in (22.5cm) high.
£40-60 *BLO*

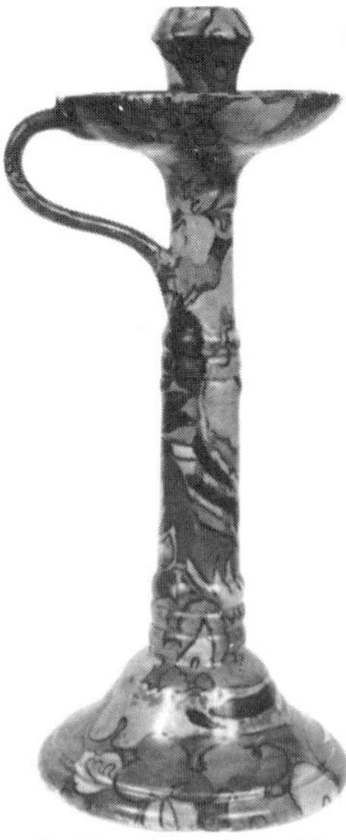

A Frederick Rhead candle holder, 15in (38cm) high.
£250-300 *BEV*

A Chameleon ware container w lid, 8½in (21cm) high.
£70-80 *BEV*

A Ruskin framed tile in shades of blue, 12 by 7in (30.5 by 17.5cm).
£50-60 *PC*

\ Barum ware jardinière, green
round with fish decoration, some
lamage, late 19thC, 9in (22.5cm)
iigh.
:70-100 *PCh*

A Della Robbia vase, marks include 'AB' and 'CEMB', 9in (22.5cm) high.
£170-190 *BLO*

A pair of Brannam vases, with sgraffito design in brown and blue on a cream ground, initialled 'W B' and dated 1889, 10in (25cm) high.
£500-600 *BLO*

. Lauder vase, with sgraffito
sh design, 6½in (16cm) high.
30-90 *BLO*

A Gouda vase, c1920, 7½in (19cm) high.
£50-60 *BEV*

A Gouda vase, c1925, 13in (33cm) high.
£150-200 *BEV*

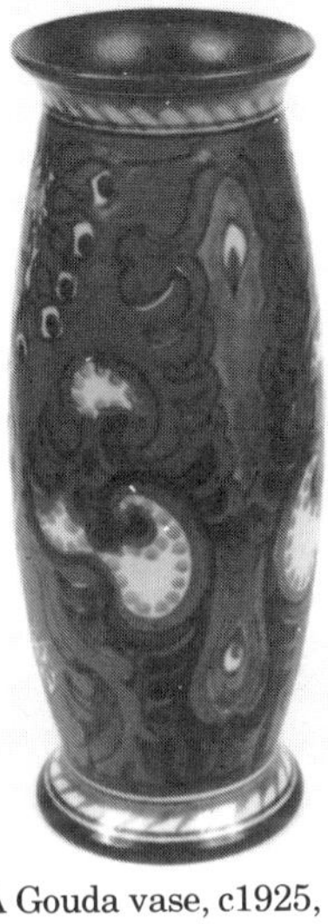

A Gouda vase, c1925, 10in (25cm) high.
£70-80 *BEV*

A Barum vase with lizard in relief, 7in (17.5cm) high.
£90-110 *BLO*

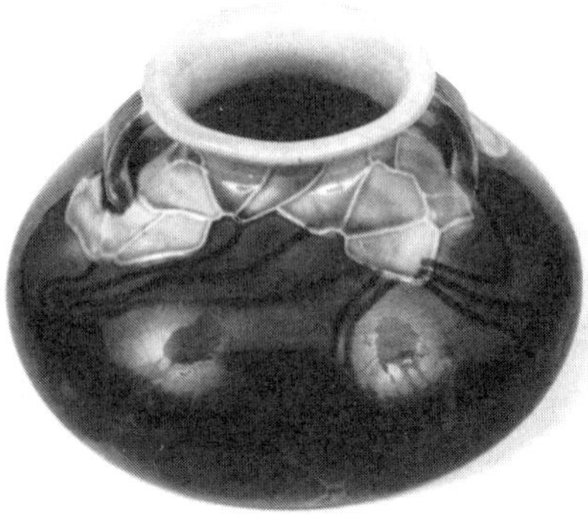

A Minton Secessionist vase, with water lily design, 1903, 8in (20cm) diam.
£140-160 *BLO*

A Charlotte Rhead vase, c1930, 12½in (32cm) high.
£350-450 *BEV*

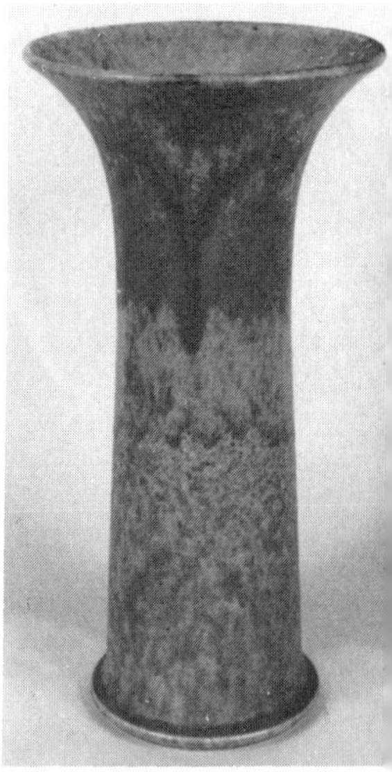

A Ruskin blue and ochre vase, marked 12in (30.5cm) high.
£110-130 *PC*

A Frederick Rhead Foley Intarsio vase, with fish decoration, 8½in (21cm) diam.
£350-450 *BEV*

A Charlotte Rhead vase, c1930, 10in (25cm) high.
£250-300 *BEV*

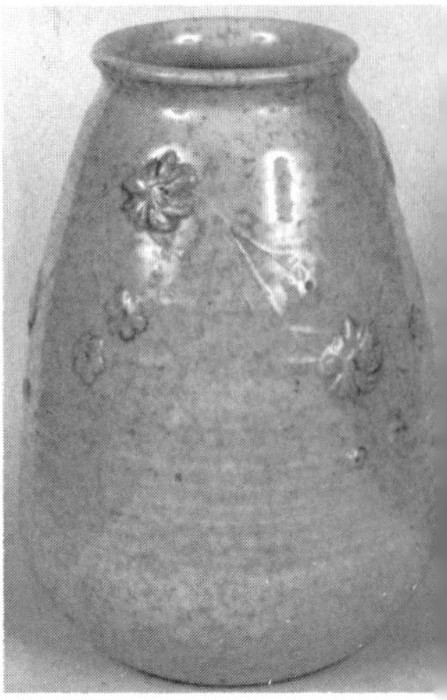

A Ruskin vase, with applied embossed decoration, impresse mark, dated 1927, 11in (28cm)
£80-100 *PC*

A Ruskin blue and beige vase from the Ferneyhough Collection, ex W. Howson Taylor collection, impressed mark, dated 1927, 9in (22.5cm) high.
£700-900 *PC*

A Royal Winton ware vase, c1920, 8½in (21cm) high.
£200-250 *RO*

A Royal Winton vase, c1920, 9½ (24cm) high.
£180-200 *RO*

A Gouda vase, c1900, 10in (25cm) high.
£80-100 *BEV*

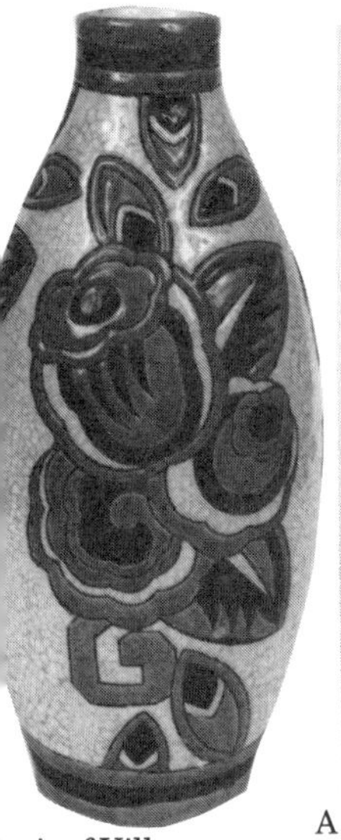

pair of Villeroy
d Boch vases,
½in (26cm) high.
00-350 *BEV*

A Boch blue and white vase, c1930,
12in (30.5cm) high.
£200-250 *BEV*

A Gouda vase, c1900,
14in (36cm) high.
£125-150 *BEV*

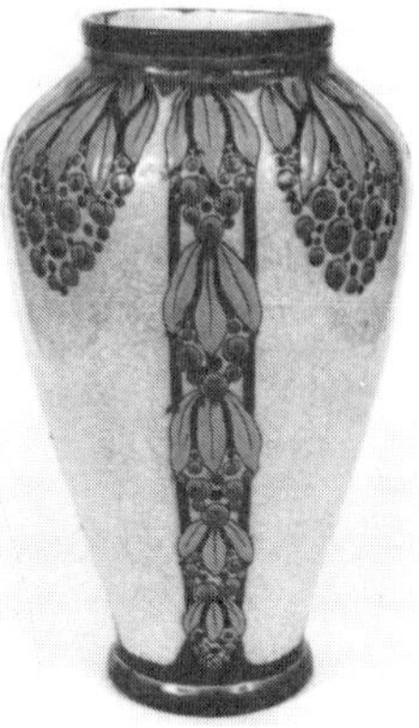

A Gouda vase, c1930,
4in (10cm) high.
£80-100 *BEV*

An E. B. Fisher vase,
8½in (21cm).
£270-320 *BLO*

early Frederick Rhead vase,
n (25cm) high.
00-350 *BEV*

A Maw's pink Art
Nouveau vase,
c1900, 12½in (32cm).
£120-140 *THA*

A majolica vase, c1880,
6in (15cm).
£60-70 *HOW*

An Upchurch pottery vase, in
pink/grey, 10in (25cm).
£70-80 *BLO*

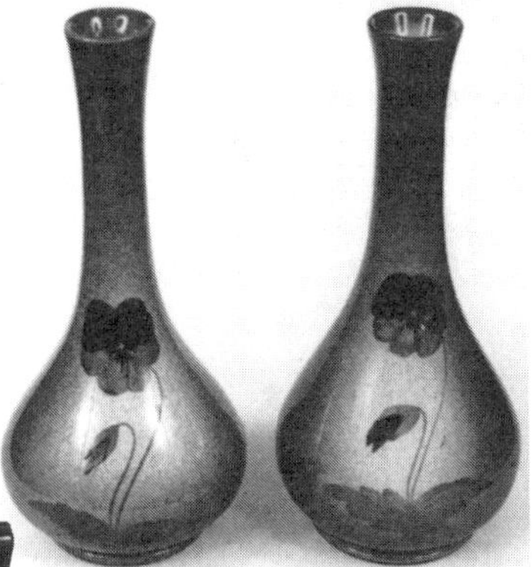

A pair of Ault vases with pansy
decoration, one signed by William
Ault, 9½in (24cm).
£80-100 *BLO*

retby deep
e vase.
-90 *BLO*

A pair of Bretby vases, painted with
ships on a chocolate coloured field,
13½in (34cm).
£100-120 *BLO*

An Ashby Potters'
Guild pink vase,
8in (20cm).
£100-120 *BLO*

Two Arts and Crafts armchairs with 4 matching side chairs.
£950-1,200 *ARF*

An Arts and Crafts tub chair.
£250-300 *ARF*

An Arts and Crafts carver chair.
£150-200 *ARF*

A set of 8 Arts and Craft rush seated chairs, including 2 carvers.
£800-900 *ARF*

A set of 6 Arts and Crafts chairs.
£700-800 *ARF*

A Gothic chair.
£130-150 *ARF*

Set of 4 Arts and Crafts chairs.
£400-450 *ARF*

A set of 8 Arts and Crafts chairs, by William Birch.
£800-900 *ARF*

An Arts and Crafts pot cupboard, 32½in (82cm) high.
£150-200 *ARF*

A Gothic style bedroom suite comprising: pot cupboard, wardrobe and dressing table.
£2,500-3,000 *ARF*

A pair of Arts and Crafts adjustable book shelves, 36in (92cm).
£250-350 each *ARF*

A pair of Gothic o pillars, with painted decoratio 49in (124.5cm).
£650-750 *ARF*

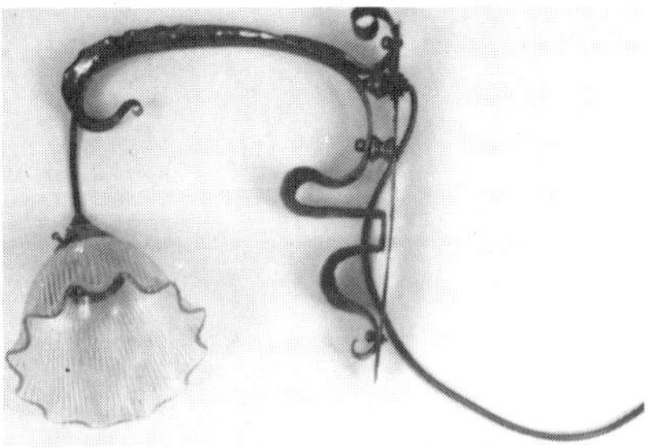

An Arts and Crafts copper wall light.
£60-70 *ARF*

A Newlyn copper repoussé tray, 17½in (44.5cm).
£150-180 *BLO*

ın Arts and Crafts
opper hanging
antern, 28in (71cm) high.
200-300 *ARF*

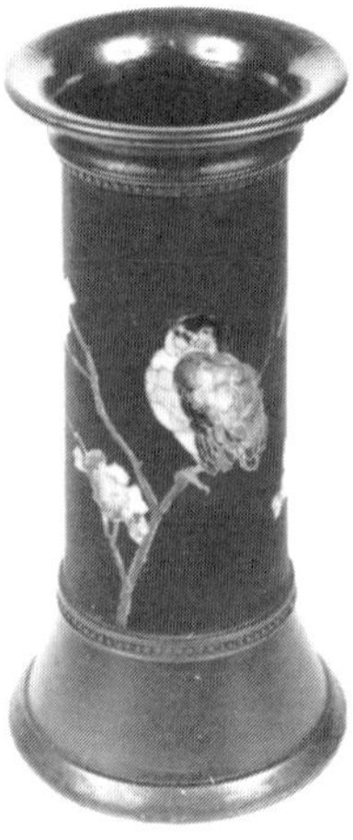

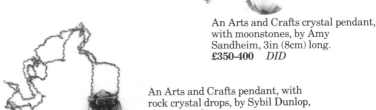

A Bretby cloisonné
ware vase, 7½in
(19cm) high.
£30-50 *BLO*

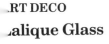

An Arts and Crafts buckle, by
Ramsden & Carr, 3in (8cm) wide.
£300-400 *DID*

An Arts and Crafts
crystal pendant,
2in (5cm) long.
£400-500 *DID*

An Arts and Crafts crystal pendant,
with moonstones, by Amy
Sandheim, 3in (8cm) long.
£350-400 *DID*

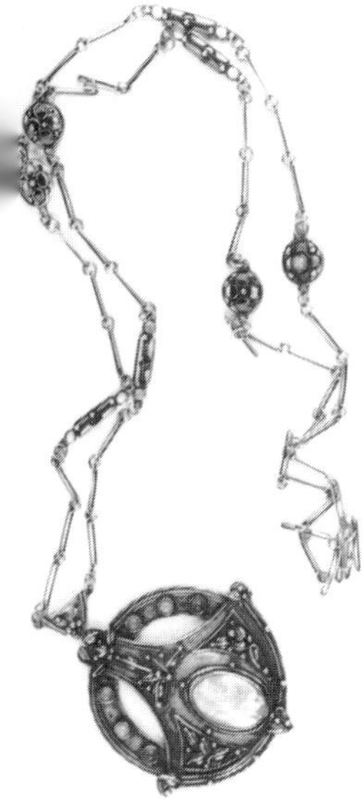

n Arts and Crafts pendant, in
lver and mother-of-pearl, 2in
cm) diam.
400-500 *DID*

An Arts and Crafts pendant, with
rock crystal drops, by Sybil Dunlop,
3½in (9cm) long.
£400-500 *DID*

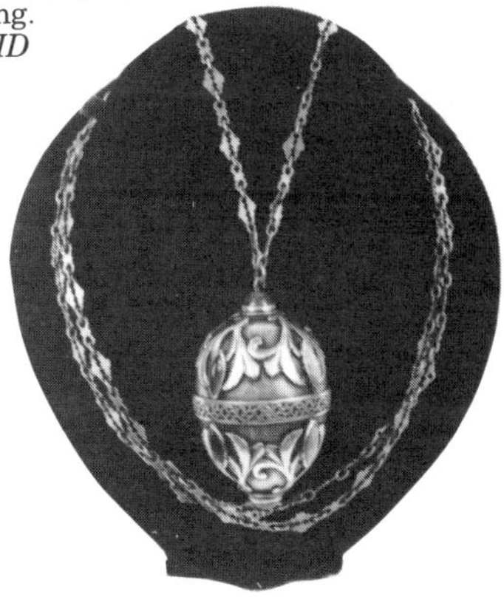

An Arts and Crafts pendant
enclosing a small compact, set with
coloured stones, possibly by Sybil
Dunlop.
£500-600 *DID*

An Arts and Crafts brooch in
amethyst and silver, 3½in (9cm)
diam.
£400-430 *DID*

RT DECO

ɪalique Glass

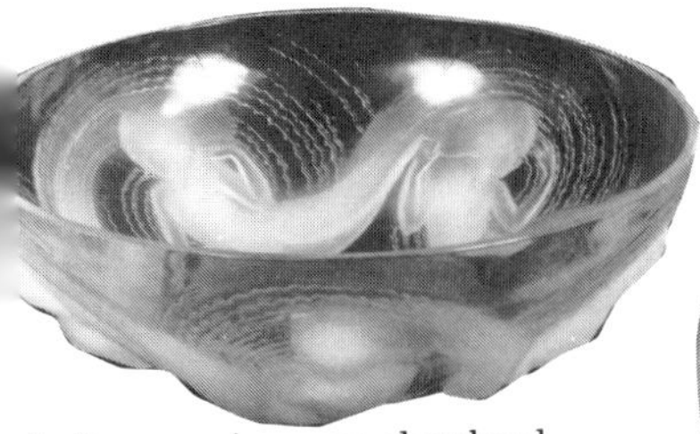

Lalique semi-opaque glass bowl,
shallow flared circular form,
oulded with continuous bands of
ermaids amidst waves, etched 'R.
alique', 12in (30cm) diam.
2,500-3,000 *HSS*

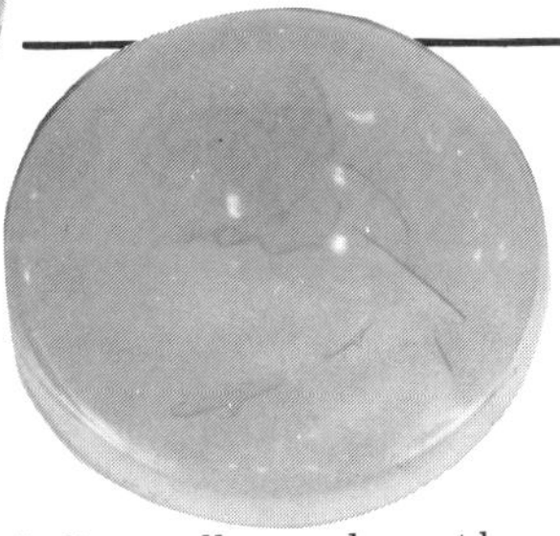

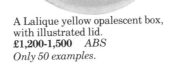

A Lalique yellow opalescent box,
with illustrated lid.
£1,200-1,500 *ABS*
Only 50 examples.

A Lalique blue bracelet, c1930.
£1,500-1,800 *ABS*

A Lalique opalescent glass bowl, moulded with an encircling band of budgerigars and blossom, etched 'R. Lalique, France', 9½in (24cm) diam.
£1,600-1,800 *Bea*

A Lalique opalescent table clock 'Inseparables', moulded R. Lalique, 4½in (11cm) high.
£800-1,000 *Bea*

A Lalique black necklace, on silk cord, c1930.
£1,000-1,200 *ABS*

Ceramics

A Quimper basket, signed, 4in (10cm) wide.
£140-160 *VH*

A Maling ware plate, with daffodils design, c1930, 11in (28cm) diam.
£150-200 *BEV*

A Maling ware plate, c1930
£150-200 *BEV*

A set of 6 Fornasetti '12 Mesi, 12 Soli' ceramic plates, each with painted polychrome decoration of the sun against differing landscapes, with printed signature '12 Mesi 12 Soli, Fornasetti Milano Made in Italy', 10½in (25.5cm).
£450-600 *C*

A Shelley plate, Iris pattern, c1930, 10in (25cm) wide.
£25-30 *THA*

A Goldscheider terracotta wall mask of a young woman, with gr curled hair, white face and yello shoulder, slight damage, 10in (25cm) high.
£270-350 *GSP*

A Crown Devon bowl painted wi galleon, c1930, 13in (33.5cm) wi
£120-140 *TVA*

Shelley lustre ware bowl, signed
· Walter Slater, c1920, 12in
).5cm) diameter.
30-80 *AJ*

A Shelley Harmony ware strainer, c1930, 8in (20cm) diam.
£40-60 *AJ*

A Quimper cup, Pecheur pattern, signed, 2in (5cm).
£15-20 *VH*

A Carlton ware Apple Blossom breakfast set, c1930.
£300-350 *RO*

Make the Most of Miller's

CONDITION is absolutely vital when assessing the value of an antique. Damaged pieces on the whole appreciate much less than perfect examples. However a rare, desirable piece may command a high price even when damaged

wall mask by Leonardi, with
ushroom coloured face and green
arf, Reg. No. 825795, c1930,
½in (52cm) high.
'50-300 *AW*

A Shelley ginger jar, in orange and yellow, c1930, 8½in (22cm) high.
£100-150 *AJ*

A Shelley Regent shape tea service, Mimosa pattern.
£350-450 *AJ*

Robj earthenware bowl and cover,
rmed as a Red Indian's head, with
rk red glazed feather headdress,
th impressed mark Robj Paris
ade in France, 8in (20cm) high.
00-500 *C*

A Lenci bust, Essevi Samdo Vachetti, 8½in (21cm) high.
£220-260 *BEV*

A Lenci bust, Essevi Samdo Vachetti, c1938, 7in (17.5cm) high.
£230-260 *BEV*

A Shelley 22 piece tea service with teapot, English Cottage design, low Queen Anne shape.
£500-600 *AJ*

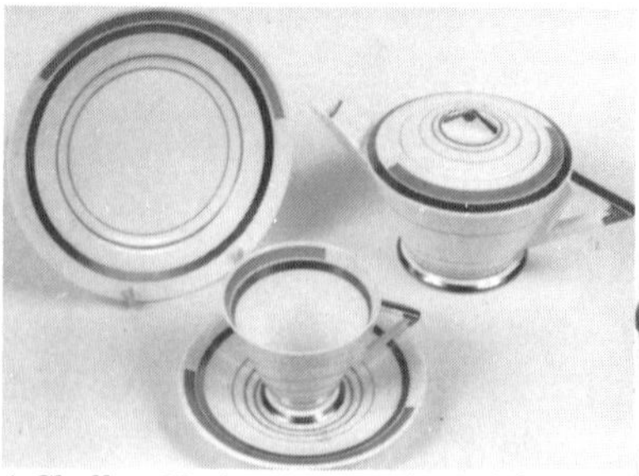

A Shelley 22 piece tea service, with green and silver pattern, c1933.
£450-550 *AJ*

A Wedgwood stoneware vase, designed by Keith Murray, of globular form with cylindrical n
and ribbed body, covered in an emerald green glaze, inscribed w
a facsimile signature Keith Mur
and Wedgwood, Made in Englan
7½in (18.5cm) high.
£250-450 *C*

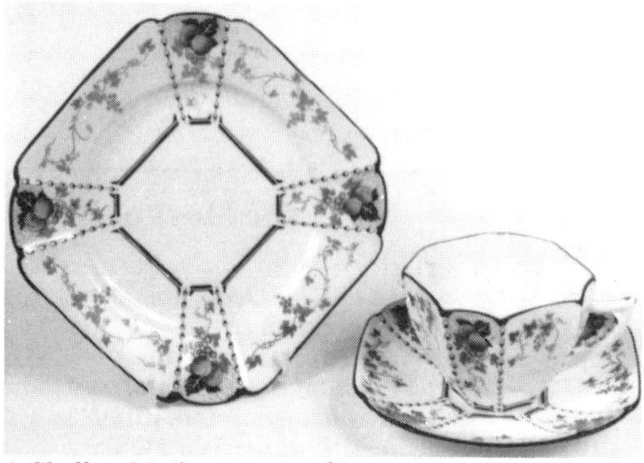

A Shelley 21 piece tea service, including teapot, low Queen Anne shape, with peaches and grapes design, c1920.
£350-400 *AJ*

A pair of Wedgwood bookends, designed by Keith Murray, each
right angle form, covered in a gre
glaze, and with fluted decoration
stamped Wedgwood, 5½in (14.5c
high.
£400-600 *C*

A Shelley afternoon tea service, decorated with The Apple Blossom Pattern comprising: 12 teacups, 12 saucers, 12 square tea plates, a pair of bread plates, teapot, hot water jug, cream jug, sugar bowl and a circular teapot stand, pattern No. 12287, Reg. No. 756533.
£450-550 *AG*

A Shelley 21 piece tea servic
Sunburst pattern, c1931.
£900-950 *RO*

A Wiener Keramik coffee service, decorated by Ida Schwetz, the cream ground decorated in grey and black with scalloped borders and handles, and flower patterns, with impressed Wiener Keramik marks and decorator's monogram IS, coffee pot 8in (19cm) high.
£450-650 *C*

Clarice Cliff

A plate by John Armstrong for Clarice Cliff, 9in (22.5cm) diam.
£320-360 *BEV*

A Fantasque Bizarre flower bowl, modelled as a Viking longboat, decorated in the Trees and House pattern of orange cottage in a wooded landscape, painted in green, orange and black, lithograph marks, tiny chip to foot, 13in (33.5cm) long.
£1,200-1,500 *CSK*

A Clarice Cliff Fantasque Bizarr
single handled Lotus jug, with
reeded decoration painted with t
Summerhouse pattern, 11in (28c
high.
£550-600 *AG*

.n Ernest Proctor, for Clarice Cliff, esigner plate, with a bride and room on horseback, in pale green ith silver lustre, 9in (23cm) diam.
250-350 *BEV*

A Clarice Cliff Fantasque charger, with coloured star-like motifs on a bubble ground within an orange border, 17in (43.5cm) diam.
£1,500-2,000 *GSP*

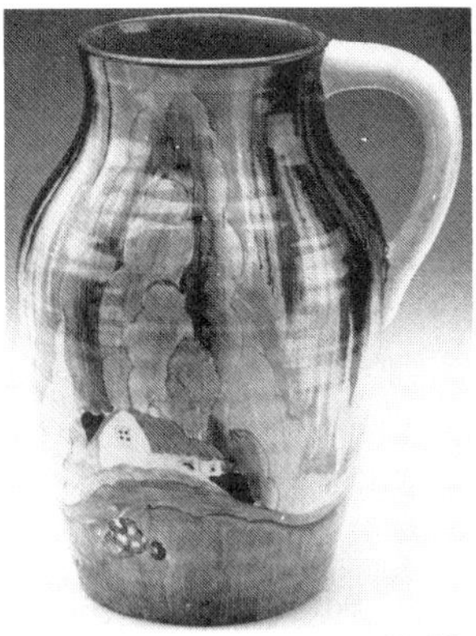

A Clarice Cliff single handled Isis jug, painted with the Forest Glenn pattern in bright, warm enamel colours, 10in (25cm) high.
£900-1,200 *Bea*

A Fantasque sandwich plate, decorated in the 7 colour version of the Trees and House pattern of cottage in a wooded landscape, painted in orange, yellow, blue, purple, green, rust and brown, minor wear, rubber stamp mark, 11½in (29cm) wide.
£450-500 *CSK*

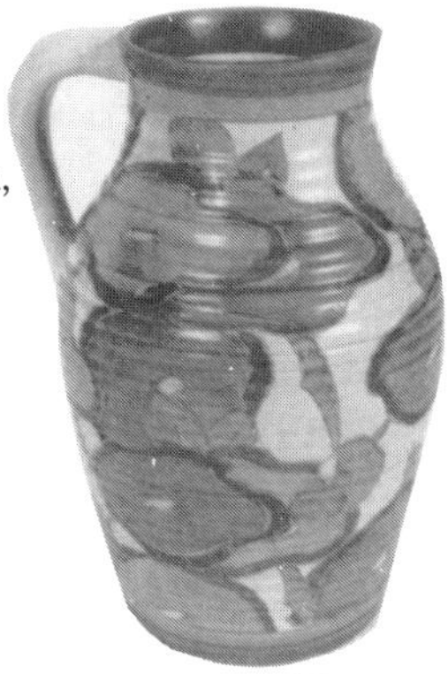

A Clarice Cliff Fantasque Bizarre pottery single handled Lotus jug, decorated in shades of blue, green and pink on a cream ground with the Blue Chintz pattern, cracked, printed mark, 11½in (29cm) high.
£50-70 *HSS*

Clarice Cliff Fantasque Bizarre ootball pattern, pottery two ındled Lotus jug, decorated in ıades of orange, yellow, blue, ırple, green and black, printed ark, 11½in (29cm) high.
,500-2,000 *HSS*

A charger decorated to a design by Sir Frank Brangwyn, printed and painted in colours with a procession of figures of various nationalities in a tropical garden, hand painted inscription, 17in (43.5cm) diam.
£3,500-4,500 *CSK*

pair of Clarice Cliff candlesticks, ½in (9cm) high.
50-170 *SAI*

A Fantasque Bizarre bon bon set, shape No. 471, decorated in the Windbells pattern of blue foliate tree in stylised garden, painted in green, orange, yellow and blue, comprising: oval dish with overhead handle and 6 triangular dishes, minor wear, lithograph mark.
£850-900 *CSK*

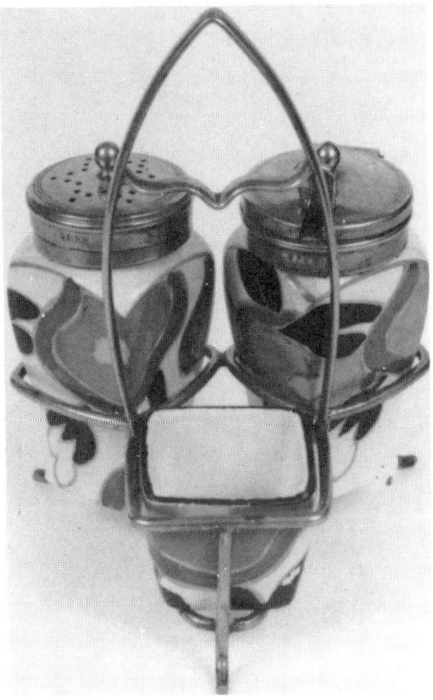

A Clarice Cliff cruet, Orange Chintz, 3½in (9cm) high.
£200-220 *BEV*

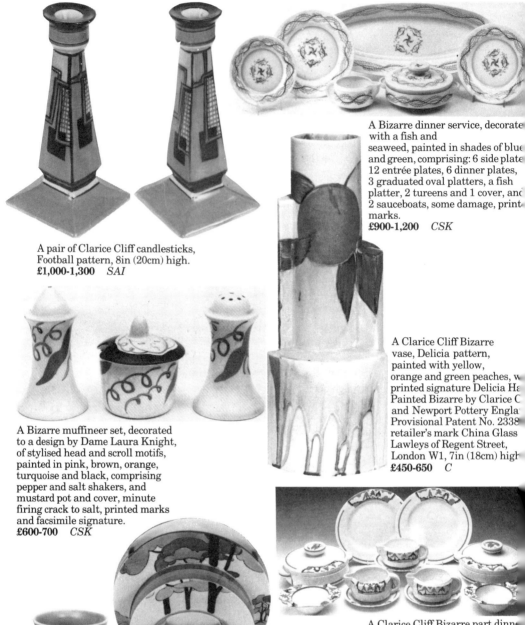

A pair of Clarice Cliff candlesticks, Football pattern, 8in (20cm) high.
£1,000-1,300 *SAI*

A Bizarre dinner service, decorate with a fish and seaweed, painted in shades of blu and green, comprising: 6 side plate 12 entrée plates, 6 dinner plates, 3 graduated oval platters, a fish platter, 2 tureens and 1 cover, an 2 sauceboats, some damage, print marks.
£900-1,200 *CSK*

A Clarice Cliff Bizarre vase, Delicia pattern, painted with yellow, orange and green peaches, w printed signature Delicia Ha Painted Bizarre by Clarice C and Newport Pottery Engla Provisional Patent No. 2338 retailer's mark China Glass Lawleys of Regent Street, London W1, 7in (18cm) high
£450-650 *C*

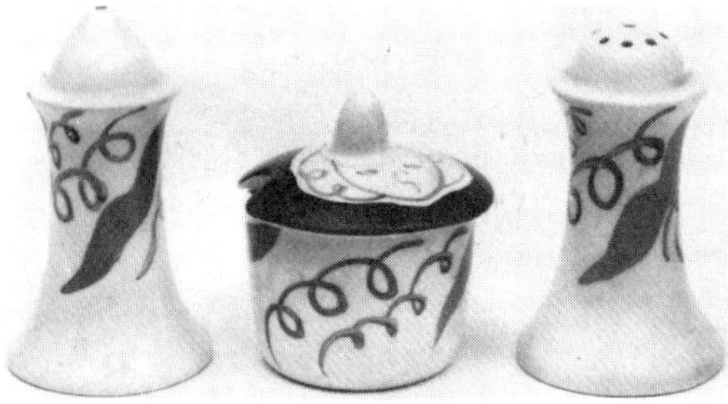

A Bizarre muffineer set, decorated to a design by Dame Laura Knight, of stylised head and scroll motifs, painted in pink, brown, orange, turquoise and black, comprising pepper and salt shakers, and mustard pot and cover, minute firing crack to salt, printed marks and facsimile signature.
£600-700 *CSK*

A Clarice Cliff Bizarre part dinn service, with Kew pattern of a red-roofed pagoda in parkland scenery, comprising: 3 tureens a 2 covers, 3 sauceboats and stands 6 grapefruit dishes and 8 stands, 5 meat dishes, 12 dinner plates, 8 dessert plates, and 7 small plat some damage.
£700-900 *Bea*

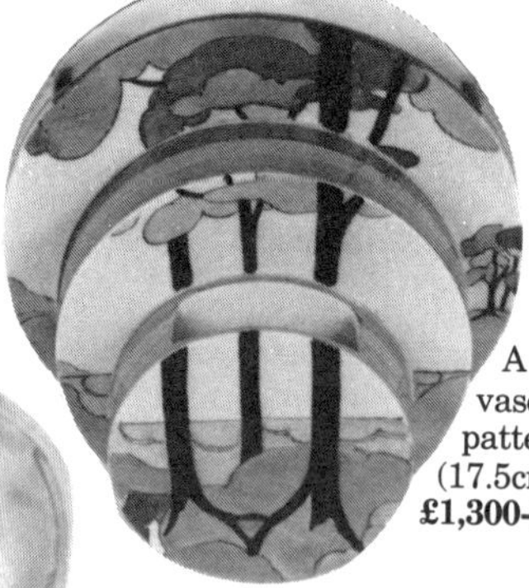

A Clarice Cliff vase in Blue Firs pattern, 7in (17.5cm) high.
£1,300-1,500 *SAI*

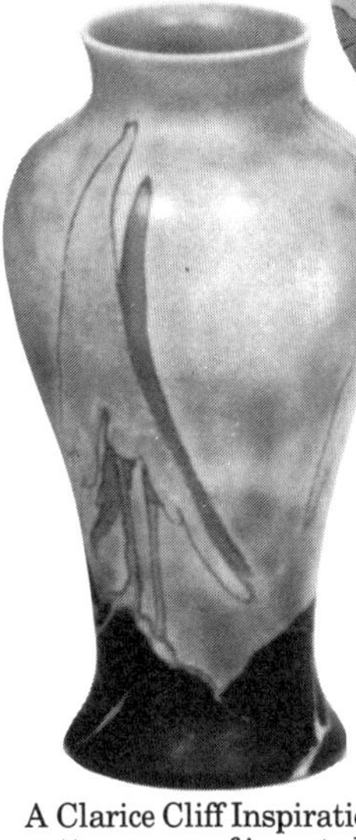

A Clarice Cliff Inspiration Caprice pattern vase, of inverted baluster form with pink and mauve trees on a turquoise ground, 9in (22.5cm) high.
£1,200-1,500 *GSP*

A Clarice Cliff Summer House pattern vase, Isis shape, 10in (25cm) high.
£2,000-2,200 *RO*

Make the Most of Miller's

In Miller's we do NOT just reprint saleroom estimates. We work from realised prices either from an auction room or a dealer. Our consultants then work out a realistic price range for a similar piece. This is to try to avoid repeating freak results – either low or high

Figures – Ceramics

A Goldscheider group designed by Lorenzl, of Harlequin and Columbine embracing, wearing polychrome enamelled elaborate costume, on domed base, with printed facsimile signature Goldscheider Wien Made in Austria Hand decorated, and impressed Lorenzl, 16in (40cm) high.
£500-700 *C*

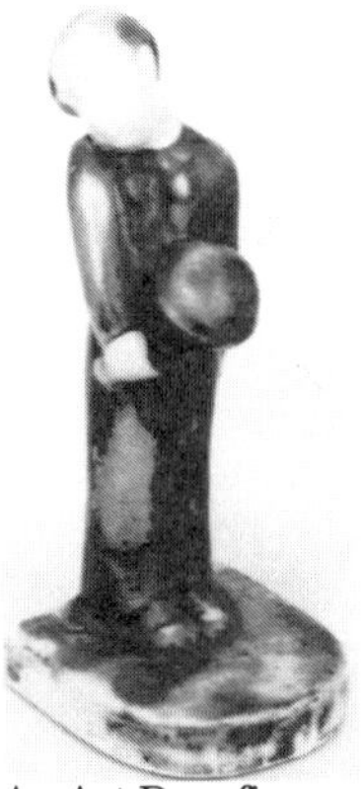

An Art Deco figure, 7½in (19cm) high.
£8-10 *OD*

An Art Deco plaster figure of Diana the Huntress.
£150-250 *LRG*

Figures – Metal

An Art Deco spelter figure of a kneeling lady holding a bird of paradise, on marble plinth.
£190-220 *LRG*

A gold and silver patinated bronze and ivory figure 'Liseuse', cast and carved from a model by A. Carrier-Belleuse, on bronze plinth, signed in the bronze A. Carrier-Belleuse and with plaque inscribed Liseuse, par Carrier Belleuse, Grand-Prix du Salon, 23½in (60cm) high.
£3,000-3,500 *C*

A bronze figure 'Young Girl', cast from a model by Dêmetre Chiparus, on an amber-coloured onyx plinth, the base damaged, signed in the onyx Chiparus, 11½in (29.5cm) high.
£1,500-2,000 *C*

A bronze figure of a lady by Bruno Zack, in green swimsuit holding beachball, on oval green marble base, 14in (35.5cm) high.
£550-650 *AH*

Bronze & Ivory Figures

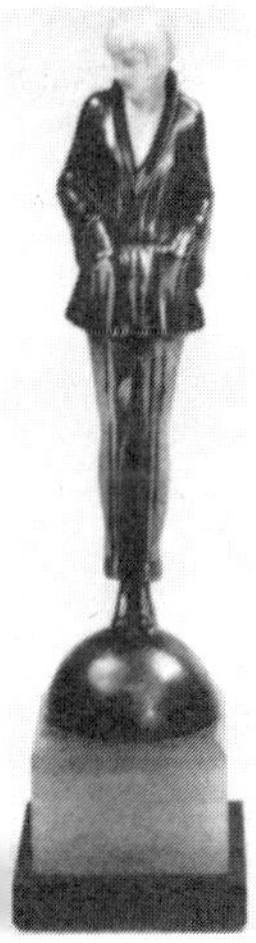

A bronze figure, 'Dancer with Thyrsus', cast from a model by Pierre Le Faguays, on a stepped, black striated marble base, signed Le Faguays, 22½in (56cm) high.
£3,000-3,500 *C*

A silvered bronze and ivory figure, cast and carved from a model by Lorenzl, on square stepped green onyx and marble base, bronze inscribed 'Lorenzl', 11in (28cm) high.
£500-700 *CSK*

A gilt, bronze and ivory group of a little girl and a baby snuggled up in an armchair, signed A. Croisy, the reverse with studio stamp on mink onyx base, entitled 'Le Nid', early 20thC, 7in (17.5cm).
£1,500-2,000 *WW*

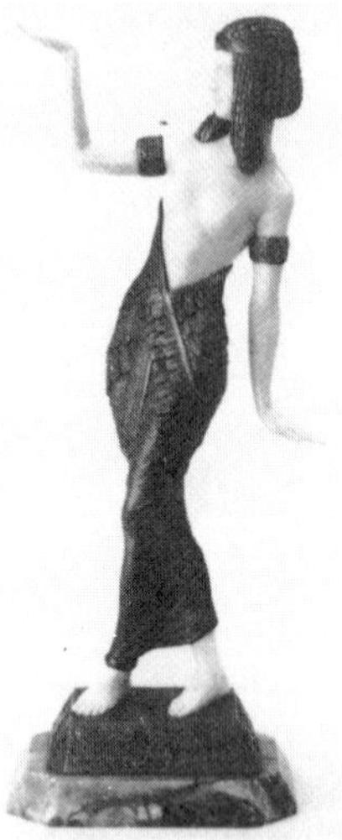

A silver patinated bronze figure, 'Amazon', by Marcel Bouraine, the stylised nude female warrior kneeling on a dark patinated base, signed in the bronze Bouraine, 7in (16.5cm) high.
£1,000-1,500 *C*

An Art Deco gilt bronze and ivory figure, cast and carved from a model by E. Monier, wearing armbands and tight fitting feathered skirt, on rectangular base cast in relief with eagles, on yellow onyx base, bronze inscribed E. Monier, 14½in (37cm) high.
£1,700-2,000 *CSK*

An F. Preiss figure of a naked boy, seated on a tree stump, removing a splinter from his foot, raised upon a tapered square onyx base with malachite edge, inscribed F Preiss, 4½in (11cm) high.
£400-500 *HSS*

A French bronze figure of the Pie Piper playing a flute, with ivory fa and hands, signed E. Barillot, on slate socle, 10in (25cm).
£700-800 *GSP*

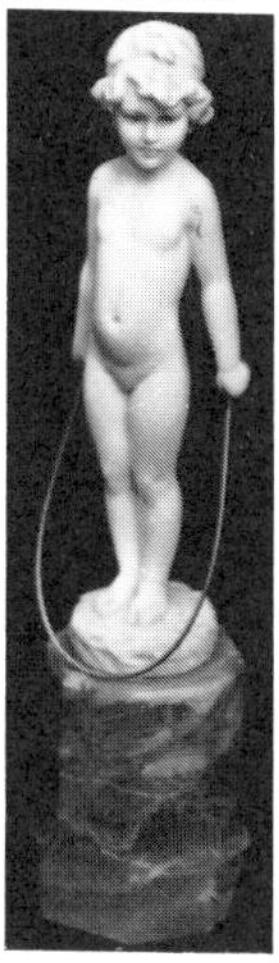

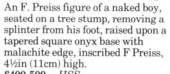

A bronze and ivory figure cast and carved from a model by A. Brandel, of a figure on tip-toe, dressed in a red and black cold-painted Oriental costume, on shaped repainted base indistinctly signed A. Brandel, 10½in (26.5cm) high.
£500-800 *C*

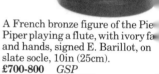

A Marquet gilt bronze and ivory figure, 'Draped Piper', in Egyptian costume, on veined black marble base, hand damaged, 17in (43.5cm) high.
£1,500-2,000 *GSP*

An F. Preiss carved ivory figure 'Girl with a skipping rope', signed.
£850-950 *GIL*

A French bronze and ivory figure of a jester holding a hand mirror, with an owl on his shoulder, signed E. Barillot, on a slate socle, 10½in (27cm).
£750-800 *GSP*

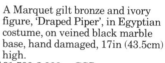

An Austrian bronze draped female by J. Benk, 1907, 11in (28cm) high.
£900-1,200 *ASA*

A bronze 'Hoop Girl' by D. H. Cheparus, 11in (28cm) high. **£1,800-2,600** *ASA*

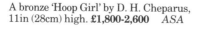

A figure lamp by le Verrier, c1930, 19in (48.5cm) high. **£5,000-7,000** *ASA*

A silvered bronze 'Messenger of Love' by Pierre le Fagnay, c1930, 30½in (78cm) hig
£4,000-5,500 *ASA*

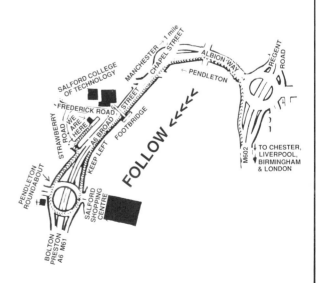

A bronze and ivory figure of Mephistopheles, on onyx base, polished, c1925, 8½in (21.5cm) high.
£210-250 *GSP*

A bronze and ivory figure of a lady dancer in a tunic, on onyx base, by Lorenzl, signed Renz, patination polished, 7in (17.5cm) high.
£300-350 *GSP*

A bronze and ivory figure table lamp, 'The Stile', the young woman wearing a green shirt and bronze trousers, standing between 2 pillars supporting a lamp, on black base, signed F. Preiss, with shade, 22in (56cm) high.
£3,500-4,000 *GSP*

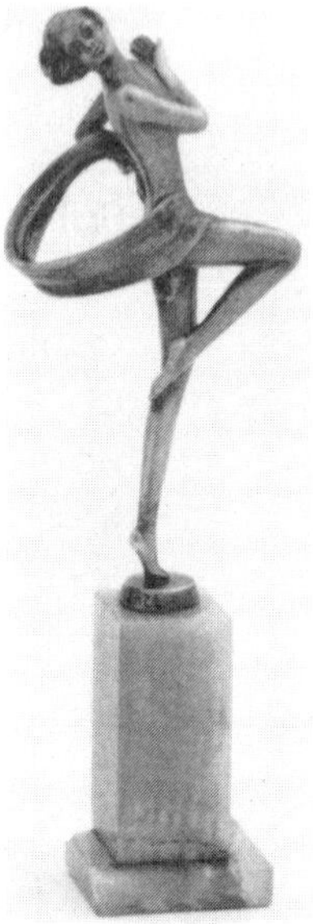

A gilt bronze figure of a female dancer, cast from a model by Lorenzl, standing on a green onyx base, base damaged, bronze inscribed Lorenzl, 8½in (21cm) high.
£300-400 *DDM*

Furniture

A pair of 'Barcelona' chairs, designed by Mies van der Rohe, with chromed steel 'X'-shaped frames strung with leather strap supports, with detachable black leather buttoned seat and cushions.
£500-550 *C*

A pair of chrome chairs, 33in (84cm) high.
£200-300 *ARF*

A cream leather three-piece suit
by Heal's.
£1,800-2,000 *ARF*

Illustrated in Heal's catalogue.

A Heal's oak adjustable lounge chair, with solid back and seat flanked by arm forming two-tier shelf and drop-leaf table, with upholstered cushions.
£250-300 *C*

A pair of Heal's limed oak adjustable armchairs, the solid panelled backs and seats supported on rounded rectangular trestle ends with plank supports, with original fabric upholstered cushions.
£600-700 *C*

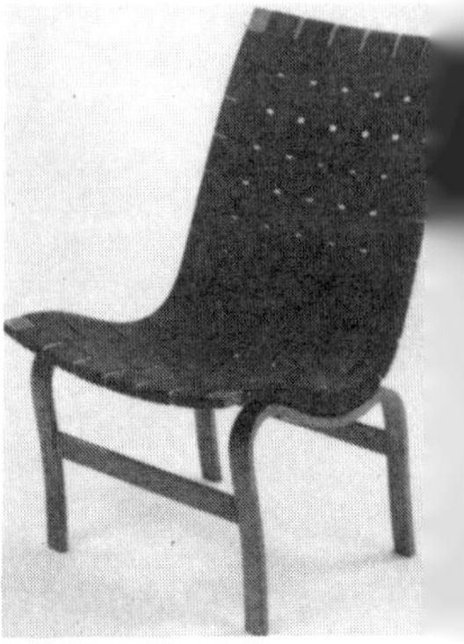

A set of 3 laminated beech side chairs, designed by Bruno Mathsson, the back and seat fram
woven with brown hessian, each
moulded trestle ends joined by pl
stretchers, paper label printed Designed by Bruno Mathsson, rubber stamped Made in Sweden.
£350-600 *C*

A Robert Thompson 'Mouseman' oak chest of drawers, the adze-finished top above 2 short and 3 long drawers, with panelled sides and back, on shaped feet, with carved mouse signature, 35½in (90.5cm).
£1,200-1,500 *C*

A Heal's oak dresser, designed by Ambrose Heal, slight restoration, 54in (137cm).
£1,500-2,000 *C*

A Wickerwork suite, chair 31in (79cm) high, table 28in (71cm) high.
£650-1,000 *ARF*

Complete suites including a settee are very sought after, especially made by Lloyd Loom.

A Robert Thompson 'Mouseman' oak dressing table, the adze-finished top above arched kneehole flanked on each side by 3 short drawers, with panelled sides and back, on shaped feet, with carved mouse signature, 54in (137cm) wide.
£1,200-1,500 *C*

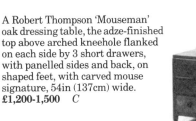

An Art Deco burr elm dining room suite, comprising: 6 single dining chairs, with leatherette upholstery, a matching dining table on curving platform base, and sideboard, 67in (170cm).
£3,000-3,500 *DDM*

A Lloyd Loom gold painted chair and table, c1934.
Chair **£70-90**
Table **£90-140** *ARF*

An Art Deco cabinet, 24in (61.5cm).
£150-200 *ARF*

A dressing table from an Art Deco bedroom suite, comprising: dressing table, bedside cupboard and large cupboard in oyster maple, 48in (122cm) wide. **£800-1,000** *ARF*

A Gordon Russell chestnut wardrobe, the top with chamfered finials above 2 panelled cupboard doors, on octagonal section legs wit printed paper label 'Design No 101/1283, Designer Gordon Russell, Foreman F. Shilton Cabinet Maker P. Wade, Timber used chestnut, Date 27.11.30', stamped 'E.A. Dorley', 76in (193.5cm) high.
£850-900 *C*

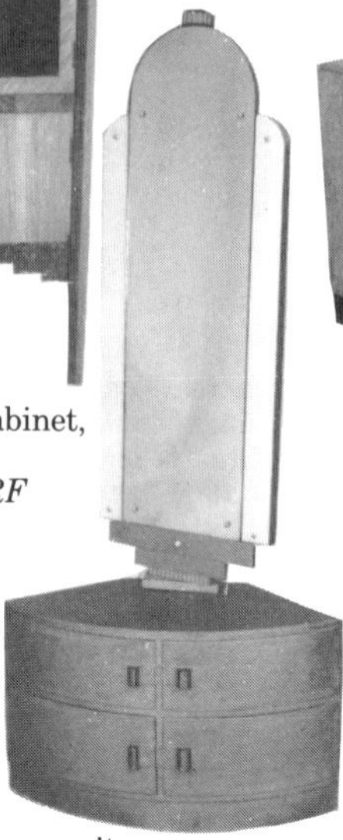

A Rowley bedroom suite, comprising: dressing table, stool, chest and bedhead, with illuminated side panels, dressing table 34in (86cm).
£600-800 *ARF*

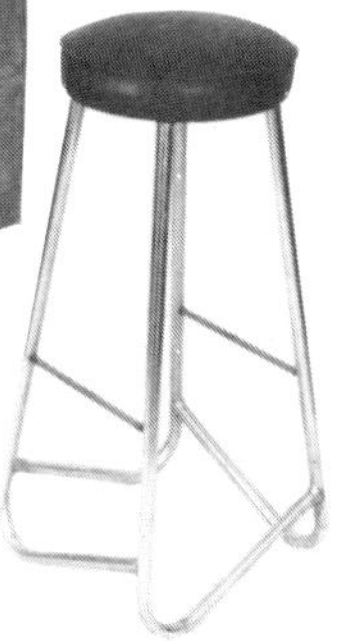

A chrome bar stool made by PEL, c1930, 30in (76cm) high.
£60-80 *ARF*

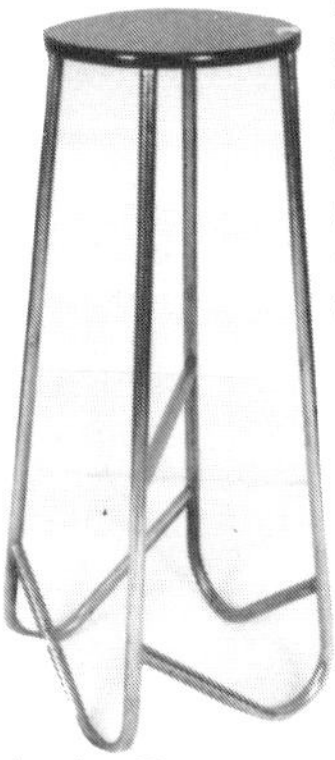

An Art Deco chrome stool, 37in (94cm) high.
£40-50 *ARF*

A Robert Thompson 'Mouseman' oak wardrobe, with beaten iron fittings, on short square section legs with mouse signature carved in intaglio, 48in (122cm).
£2,500-3,000 *C*

An Art Deco chrome and maroon glass cocktail trolley, 25½in (65cm) high.
£125-185 *ARF*

A Rowley Gallery corner unit, with inset picture of lion killing a deer, 44in (111.5cm) wide.
£200-300 *ARF*

An occasional table designed by Piero Fornasetti, with wooden top covered in black lacquer and decorated with a transfer printed sun and ray motif, on tripod steel legs modelled with nodules, with printed paper label, 29½in (75cm) high. **£900-1,200** *C*

An Art Deco French table, c1930, 24in (61.5cm) high.
£150-200 *ARF*

An Art Deco rosewood and burr-maple walnut centre table, in the style of Emile Ruhlmann, inla with ivory lattice stringing above plain frieze and chamfered legs, 33in (84cm).
£1,000-1,500 *C*

An occasional table, designed and labelled by Waring and Gillow, 21in (53cm) high.
£200-250 *ARF*

An Art Deco table, 32in (81.5cm) diam.
£500-600 *ARF*

An Art Deco nest of tables, 30in (76cm) diam.
£250-350 *ARF*

An Art Deco vitrolite occasional table by PEL, 29in (74cm) high.
£50-100 *ARF*

An Art Deco circular table, 36in (91.5cm) diam.
£800-900 *ARF*

An Art Deco glass and walnut coffee table, 21in (53cm) high.
£150-200 *ARF*

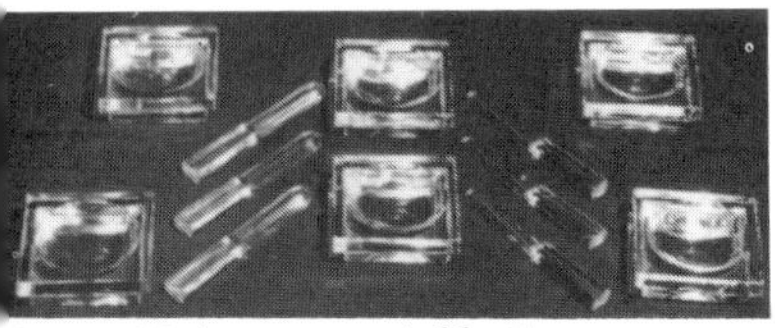

A set of 6 Asprey crystal butter dishes and knives, in original fitted box, marked Asprey 166 Bond Street London, butter knife 4in (10cm) long.
£500-600 *C*

Glass

An Orrefors 'Ariel' vase designed by Ingeborg Lundin, the thick clear glass decorated internally with a blue geometric pattern and air bubbles, with engraved signature Orrefors Ariel Nr 177-E7 Ingeborg London, 6½in (15.5cm) high.
£700-900 *C*

A Degué Art Deco acid-etched cameo vase, the acid-textured clear ground overlaid in high relief with mottled pink diamond pattern and chevron borders, with cameo signature Degué and acid-etched Made in France, 14in (35.5cm) high.
£1,000-1,500 *C*

A Venini bottle vase, the clear glass internally decorated with yellow diagonal lines, acid-stamped signature 'Venini Murano Italia', 14in (35.5cm) high.
£300-500 *C*

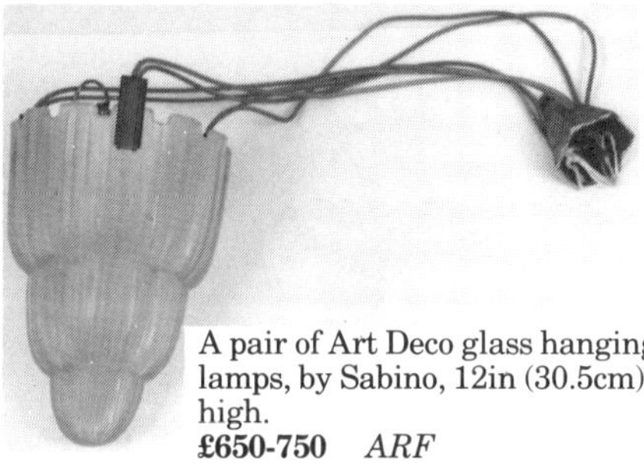

A pair of Art Deco glass hanging lamps, by Sabino, 12in (30.5cm) high.
£650-750 *ARF*

Jewellery

A lacquer, crystal and paste on silver bangle, c1920.
£300-600 *ABS*

An 18 carat gold ladies cocktail watch with synthetic rubies and diamonds, c1940.
£500-600 *ABS*

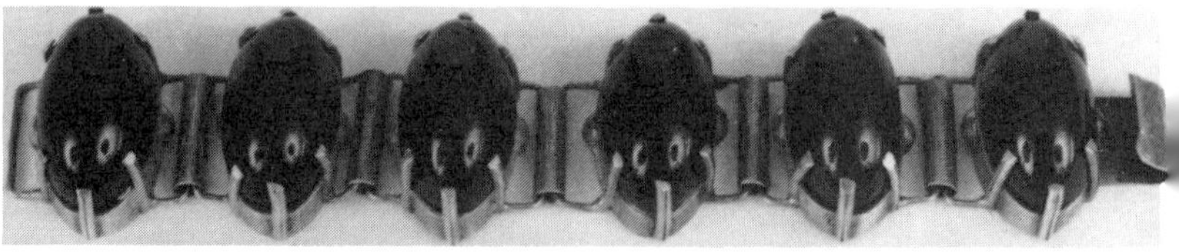

A Mexican silver and semi-precious stone bracelet, c1945, 7in (17.5cm) long.
£200-300 *ABS*

A Mexican silver and inlaid semi-precious stone necklace, designed by Ladesma, c1945.
£150-200 *ABS*

A silver, enamel and paste brooch/clip, c1920.
£150-200 *ABS*

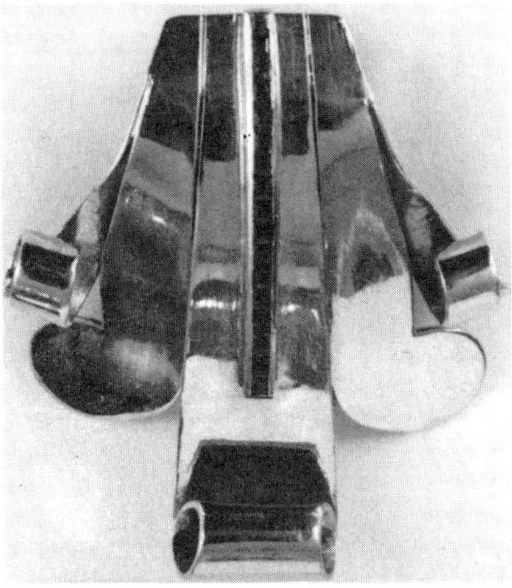

An 18 carat gold clip with rubies, c1940.
£400-500 *ABS*

An 18 carat gold watch ring, with cabochon sapphires, in original box, c1940.
£400-500 *ABS*

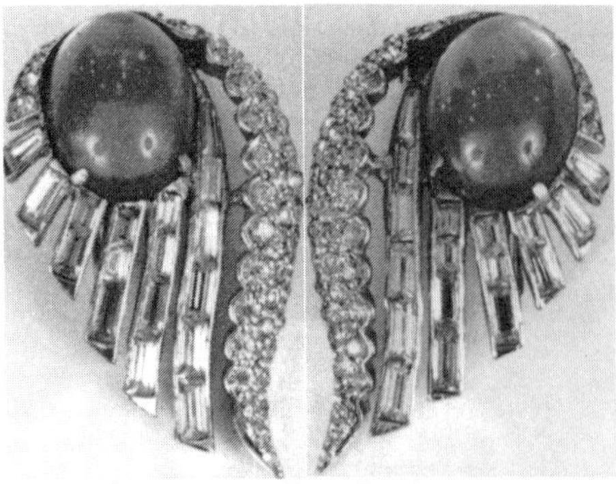

A pair of costume jewellery clips by Boucher, c1940.
£120-150 *ABS*

Metal

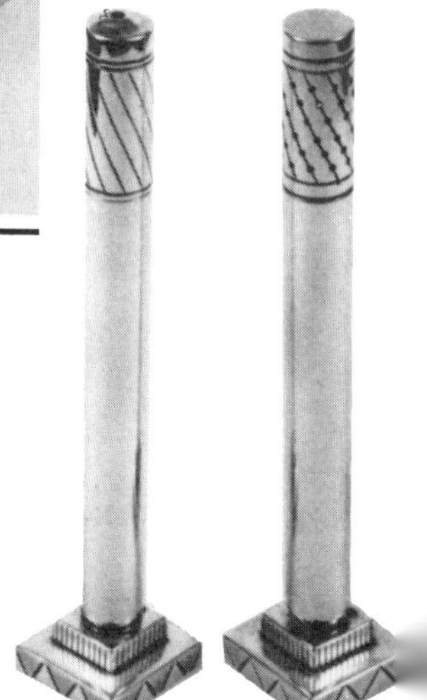

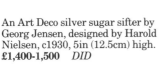

An Art Deco silver pepper and sa
by Georg Jensen, design by Jorge
Jensen, c1930, 4½in (11cm) high.
£1,250-1,500 *DID*

An Art Deco silver sugar sifter by Georg Jensen, designed by Harold Nielsen, c1930, 5in (12.5cm) high.
£1,400-1,500 *DID*

\n Art Deco lamp, with a silver and
old plaster figure of a lady.
:140-170 *LRG*

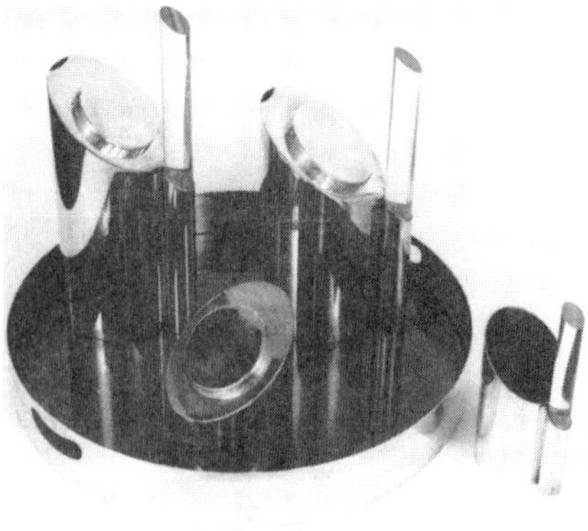

A silver plated teaset and tray, with French transparent Bakelite handles, c1960, 15in (38cm) diam.
£1,500-2,000 *ABS*

A silver inkstand, Birmingham, 1915, 7½in (19cm) wide.
£225-250 *DSA*

. hammered silver bowl and cover,
ith a stepped everted rim, gently
omed cover and ring finial,
amped with German silver marks,
1930, 4in (10cm) high.
1,700-2,000 *CAm*

A Danish 3-piece demitasse service by Georg Jensen, comprising: coffee pot, sugar bowl and cream pitcher, with side bone handles and knop finials with beaded joins, c1945, 18.5oz gross.
£800-1,000 *CNY*

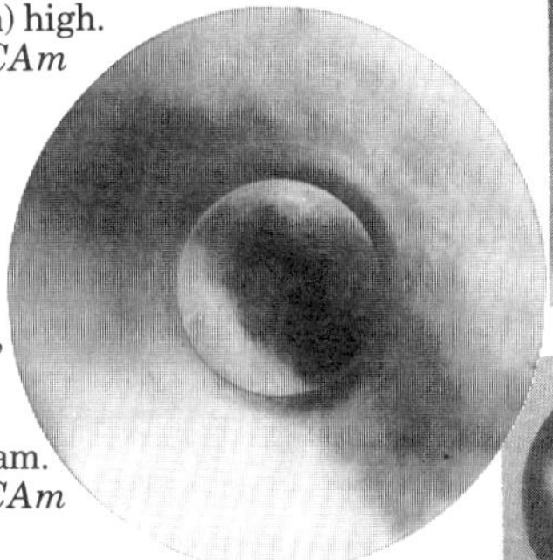

chrome plated
ass fruit bowl,
ith slightly
omed centre
id flaring well,
amped
auhaus, 1929,
½in (29cm) diam.
,000-3,500 *CAm*

A pair of Asprey chromium plated cocktail shakers, each dumb-bell shaped, with strainer, one end forming the lid, one dented, stamped mark A & Co. Asprey London 6333 Made in England, 10½in (25.5cm) high.
£500-700 *C*

Hagenauer brass bowl, the
allow hammered bowl on a
pering foot with openwork
coration of horses, stamped mark
Iw Hagenauer Wien Made in
istria, 12½in (32.5cm) diam.
,500-2,000 *C*

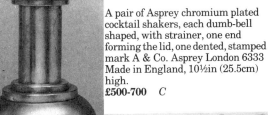

hree-piece Art Deco style silver
service, Birmingham, 1935, 20oz
ss.
50-400 *GAK*

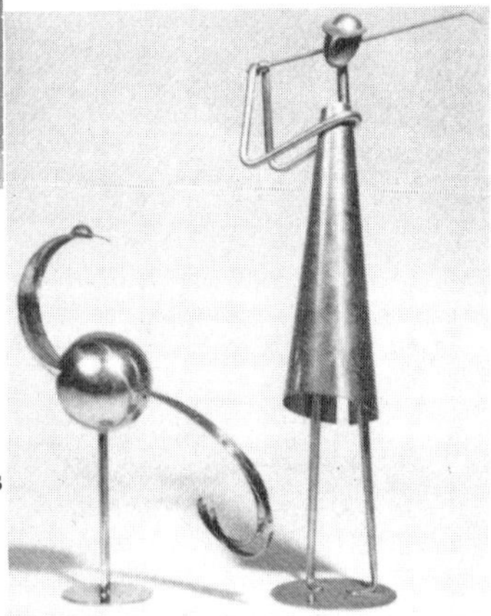

A Hagenauer brass sculpture of a bird and a golfer, the stylised forms on circular bases, stamped Hagenauer wHw Made in Austria, golfer 15in (38.5cm).
£700-900 each *C*

A Hagenauer brass hanging mirror, the frame decorated with stylised animals, birds and a geometric motif, stamped on the reverse wHw Hagenauer Wien, Made in Austria, 16½in (42cm) high.
£2,200-2,600 *C*

An Art Deco four-piece fluted rounded oblong tea service, with polished wood handles, the domed hinged covers with carved wood finials, hot water jug 8in (20cm), 56.5oz gross.
£1,800-2,000 *CSK*

An Art Deco plated tea service, marked, teapot 5in (12.5cm) high.
£260-300 *THA*

Miscellaneous

An Art Deco marble clock set, with a spelter panther figure and urns.
£250-300 *LRG*

An Art Deco marble clock set with spelter figure of a kneeling lady 'Time Flies'.
£300-350 *LRG*

An Art Deco marble clock set with brass decoration in the Epstein styl
£300-350 *LRG*

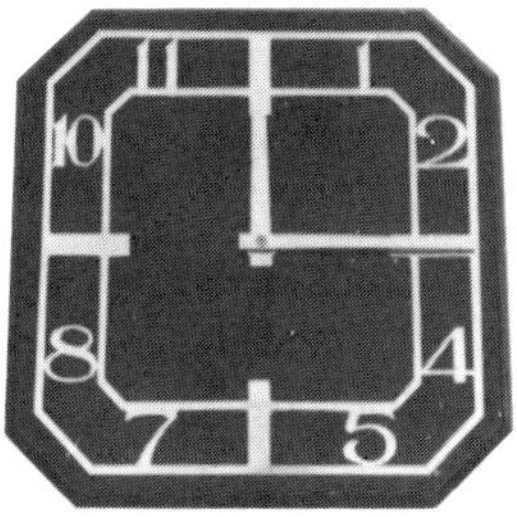

An Art Deco wall clock, 12in (30.5cm) square.
£100-150 *ARF*

A copper wall clock, c1930, with ne quartz movement, 13½in (35cm) diam.
£100-150 *ARF*

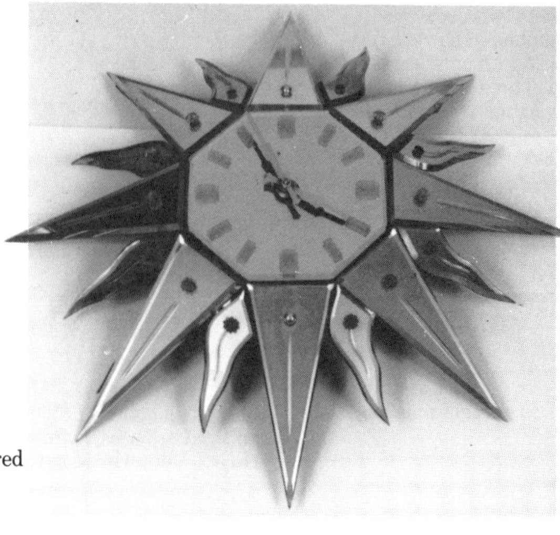

An Art Deco Sunburst mirrored clock, 26in (66cm) diam.
£250-300 *ARF*

An Art Deco chrome extractor fan.
£180-200 *ARF*

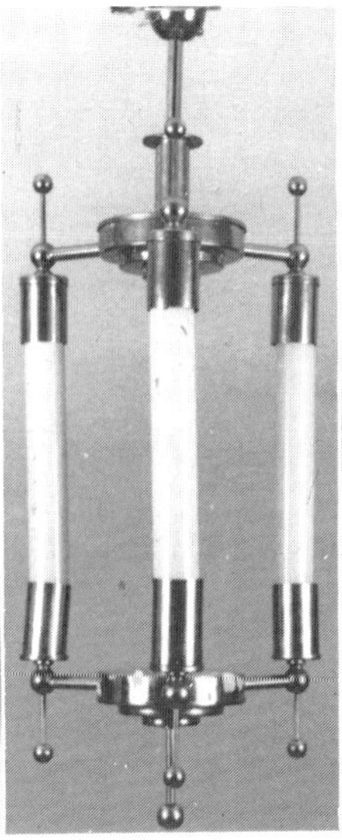

An Art Deco chrome hanging lamp.
£250-350 *ARF*

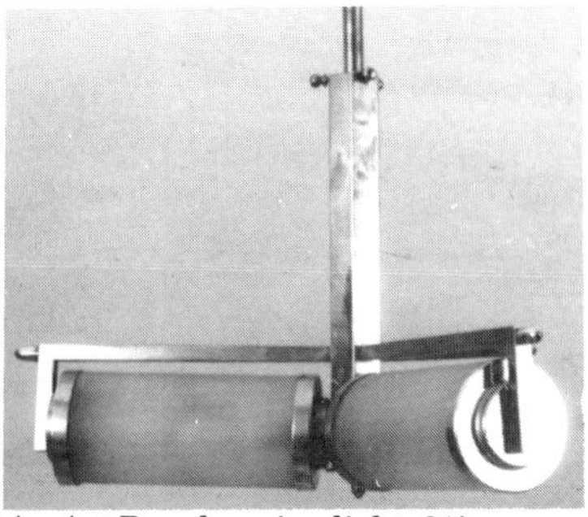

An Art Deco hanging light, 31in (79cm) high.
£100-200 *ARF*

An Art Deco brass wall light, 17in (43.5cm) high.
£80-120 *ARF*

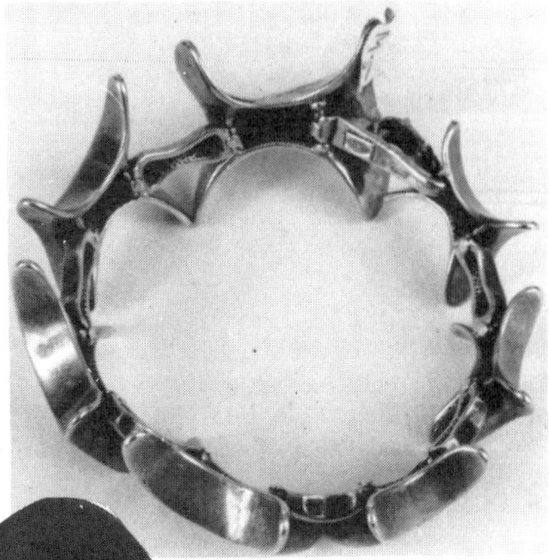

A Danish silver and enamel bracelet, c1960.
£150-200 *ABS*

Post-War Design

A James Powell ewer, with ovoid body on domed base, the tall neck with flaring trefoil rim, with applied elongated handle, milky vaseline glass, 14in (35.5cm) high.
£600-800 *C*

A Dino Martens vase, with pinched figure-of-eight shaped rim, the clear glass internally decorated with polychrome geometric fields and patterns, 7in (17.2cm) high.
£1,800-2,000 *C*

A chrome and vinyl settee and chair, c1945, 27in (68.5cm) high.
£650-800 *ARF*

Two pieces of Italian enamelled metal jewellery, design by Ettore Sotsass, c1980.
£25-50 *ABS*

A Hille plywood dining room suite, designed by Robin Day, comprising: rectangular table on tubular steel legs, sideboard with 2 smoked glass sliding doors enclosing shaped single shelves, on tubular steel legs, and 6 chairs with shaped plywood back and arm rests above upholstered seats, on tubular steel legs, with ivorine plaques Hille London, c1955.
£600-800 *C*

SILVER

Baskets

A George IV fruit basket, by John, Henry and Charles Lias, 1828, 13½in (34cm) diam, 53oz.
£1,800-2,200 *C*

A George III sugar basket, by Solomon Hougham, London, 1795, 3½in (9cm) high.
£600-700 *TG*

A George III bread basket, engraved with a coat-of-arms within an oval cartouche, by Richard Morton & Co., Sheffield, 1784, 15in (38cm) long, 27oz.
£2,200-2,800 *C*

A George III cake basket, pierced and engraved with foliage, by Robert Breading, Dublin, 1794, 15½in (39.5cm) long, 38oz.
£3,000-4,000 *C*

A George IV cake basket, engraved with the Royal arms, by Paul Storr, 1829, stamped Storr & Mortimer, 16½in (42cm) wide, 38oz.
£8,000-9,000 *C*

Beakers

A pair of George III goblets, engraved with crest, maker C.H., London, 1808, 20oz.
£1,500-2,000 *RBB*

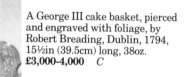

A George IV gilt lined campana shaped goblet with a contemporary presentation inscription, Langlands & Robertson, Newcastle, 1823, 7in (18cm), 12.75oz.
£550-650 *CSK*

A late Victorian part oxydised rose bowl, the cartouche with later inscription, by Henry Wilkinson & Co. Ltd., London, 1900, 10in (25cm), 37.75oz.
£800-1,000 *CSK*

Bowls

A George II Irish bowl, by Andrew Goodwin, Dublin, c1740, 6in (15.5cm) diam, 9oz.
£1,600-2,000 *C*

An Edwardian rose bowl with later presentation inscription, Birmingham, 1908, 11in (28.5cm), 32oz.
£1,000-1,200 *CSK*

A fruit bowl fitted with a glass liner, Birmingham, 1930, 9in (22.5cm), 29.75oz free.
£900-1,100 *CSK*

An Edwardian sugar bowl and tongs, London, 1905, 5in (12.5cm) diam.
£150-180 *TG*

៱ Victorian silver gilt bowl, on
urned wood plinth, by C. F.
Iancock, 1866, 10in (25.5cm) high,
ɜ1oz.
'3,000-3,500 *C*

Victorian rosebowl, engraved
ith a coat-of-arms and monogram,
ᵥ Joseph Clarke, 1896, 14in
5.5cm) diam, 79oz.
ɫ,000-5,000 *C*

A George II sugar bowl and cover, both engraved with a slightly later monogram, fully marked on base and cover, by Ralph Maidman, London, 1733, 3in (8cm) high, 7.5oz.
£2,500-3,800 *CNY*

A George III bowl, cover and stand, engraved with a crest, monogram and presentation inscription, by John Emes, the bowl and cover 1803, the stand 1807, the bowl 6in (15cm) diam, 28oz.
£3,000-4,000 *C*

An embossed and pierced silver bowl, London, 1900, 6in (15cm) wide, 8.25oz.
£280-360 *PCh*

A silver box, Chester, 1904, 2in (5cm) diam.
£70-80 *HF*

oxes

Queen Anne tobacco box and
ver, with inscription on base,
ıker's mark indistinct, 4in (10cm)
ıg, 3oz.
,700-2,000 *C*

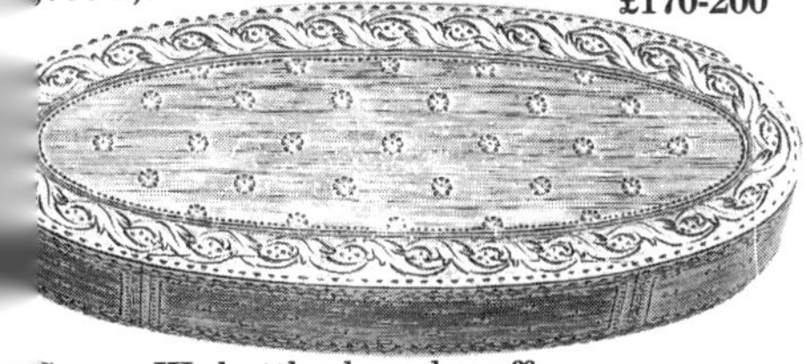

George III shuttle-shaped snuff
ᶜ, with concealed hinged cover, by
rnelius Bland, maker's mark
y struck 3 times, c1775, 4in
cm) long.
,000-1,300 *C*

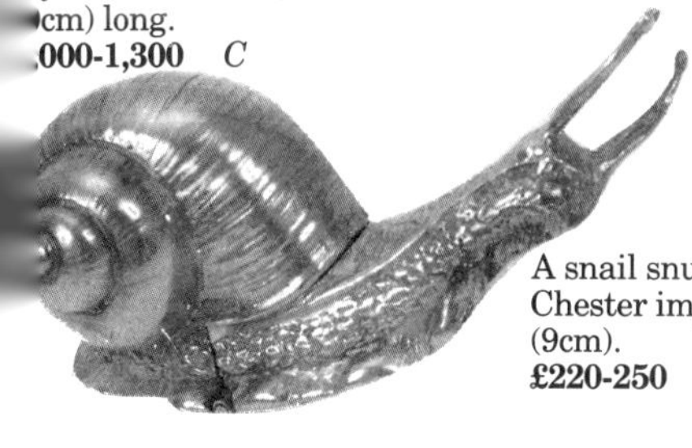

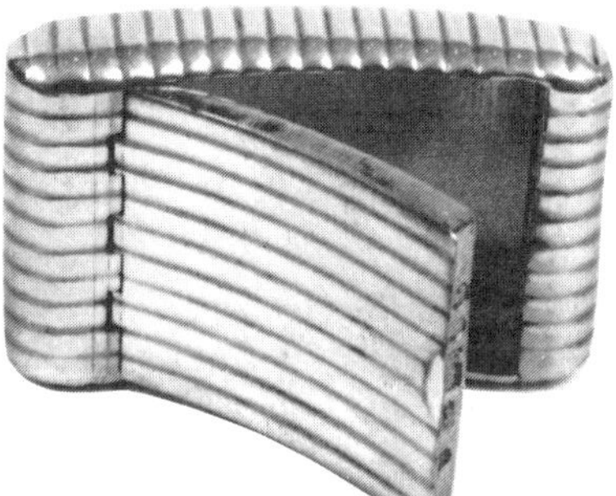

A George III snuff box inscribed 'Robt. Batchelor', by William Bingley (?), Birmingham, 1808, 2½in (6cm) long.
£170-200 *TG*

A snail snuff box by B. Muller, Chester import mark, 1900, 3½in (9cm).
£220-250 *WW*

A George III rectangular vinaigrette, c1812, 1½in (3.5cm) long.
£160-190 *TG*

A George I trefoil spice box, with detachable cover, the sides later engraved, maker's mark T.S. struck twice only, possibly for Thomas Steed, c1720, 1½in (4cm) high.
£2,800-3,200 *C*

An Edwardian scroll engraved vesta case, Chester 1903, 2 by 1½in (5 by 4cm).
£4-6 *TVA*

A Continental gilt lined toilet box, the lid inset with a circular ivory plaque carved with bust portraits of Louis XVI and Marie Antoinette, by Berthold Muller, bearing import marks for Chester, 1907, 6½in (17cm), 16.5oz. gross.
£800-1,000 *CSK*

A late Victorian brazil nut shape box, 2in (5cm) long.
£400-500 *TG*

A Victorian vesta case, Birmingham, 1896, 1½in (4cm) high.
£30-40 *TVA*

An American vesta case, by Gorham Manufacturing Co., c1900, 2½ by 2in (6 by 5cm).
£25-35 *TVA*

A hen on nest box, gilt to the interior, Chester import mark, 5½in (14cm), 10oz.
£650-750 *WW*

A George III Irish Freedom box, the detachable slightly domed cover engraved with the arms of Cork, the base with presentation inscription, dated 12 July 1780, the side with a crest and Earl's coronet, the maker's mark I.H., struck twice in the cover only, Cork, 3½in (9cm) diam, 5oz.
£3,700-4,000 *C*

The crest is that of Meade for the Right Hon. Sir John Meade, first Earl of Clanwilliam.

A Continental vesta case, the front enamelled with a bust portrait of a flaxen haired beauty on a blue ground, import marks for London 1907, 2in (5cm).
£300-350 *CSK*

A George III silver gilt mounted cowrie shell snuff box, the lid engraved with ornate initials within a beaded border, Phipps and Robinson, London 1789, 4in (10cm).
£500-550 *CSK*

A Continental gilt lined cigarette case, the front enamelled with a three-quarter length portrait of a lady holding a closed fan, 3½in (9cm).
£300-350 *CSK*

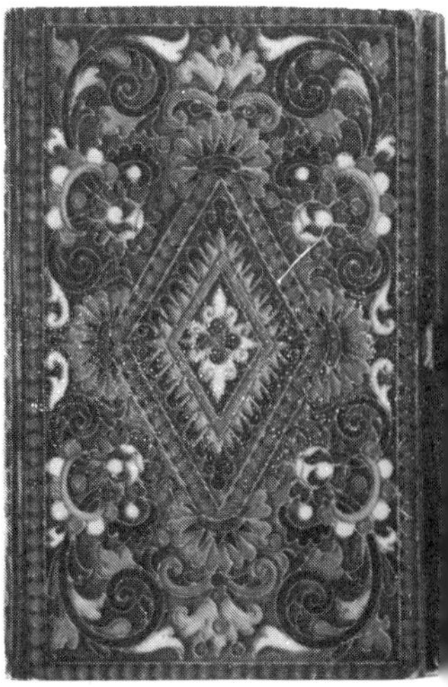

A Russian silver gilt box in the forn of a book, the 'covers' and the 'spin polychrome cloisonné enamelled with scroll work and flowers in shades of blue, red and white with blue beadwork borders, with fastening clip attached, 4in (11cm
£550-600 *CSK*

A George III vinaigrette by Josepl Willmore, Birmingham, 1816, 4ir (10cm) long.
£90-120 *TG*

An Edwardian card case, Birmingham 1902, 3½in (9cm) lon
£120-140 *TVA*

A French embossed snuff box, possibly Rheims, import mark London, 1890, 2½in (7cm) long.
£220-250 *TVA*

Candelabra

A pair of George II style two-light candelabra, 1968, 8½in (21.5cm), 46oz.
£1,500-2,000 *C*

Candlesticks

A pair of George II cast silver candlesticks, with shaped bases decorated with angels, fluted, spiral fluted, and knopped stems and spool-like nozzles, by John Perry, c1752, 34oz.
£1,700-2,200 *GSP*

A pair of George III silver candlesticks, Sheffield 1813, 12in (31cm).
£1,750-1,800 *DSA*

A Dutch gilt lined jewel casket, on caryatid scroll feet, the sides and the hinged cover chased with carousing figures in the style of Tenniers, the underside with 2 presentation inscriptions, 19thC, 10in (26cm), 31oz.
£1,300-1,500 *CSK*

A pair of Victorian beaded four-light candelabra, by Frederick Elkington, Birmingham 1880, 23in (59cm), 180oz.
£4,000-4,500 *CSK*

A pair of early George III candlesticks with cast shaped and stepped square bases decorated with shell motifs, fluted stem and corded spool-shape sconces, by William Cafe, c1763, 36.5oz.
£2,000-2,500 *GSP*

An Edwardian miniature card case London, 1901, 2in (5cm) high.
£45-55 *TVA*

A pair of candelabra, fitted for electricity, the knopped panelled baluster stems with spool shaped candleholders, on welled square bases with concave corners, the to with a central baluster ornamenta candleholder, the detachable nozzl with a pineapple finial and with 3 scroll branches, the candleholde with drip pans, by Hawksworth Eyre & Co., 22½in (57cm).
£600-700 *WW*

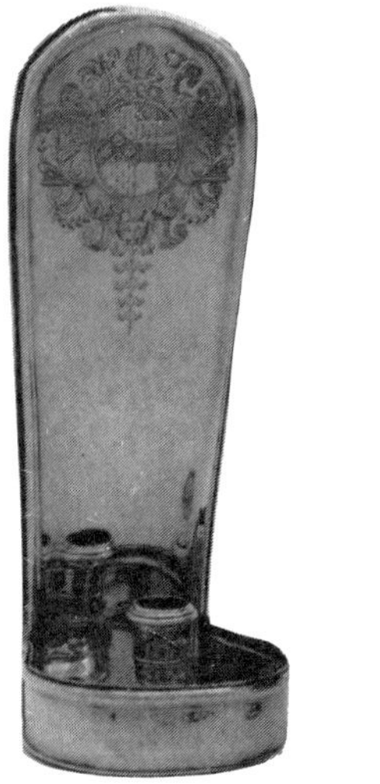

A pair of wall mounted candleholders, each with plain tapering backs and reeded urn shape candlesticks, engraved wit an ornate armorial, Britannia Standard, London 1919, 11½in (30cm), 30oz.
£2,500-3,000 *DDM*

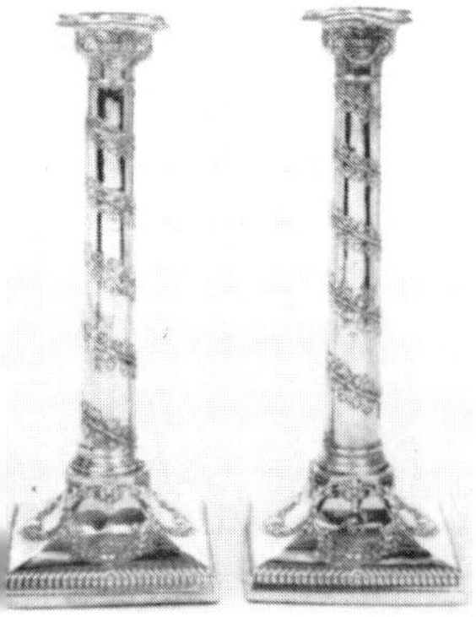

A pair of George III candlesticks, chased with a continuous band of trailing vines, the moulded sockets with detachable shaped square nozzles, each engraved with 2 crests, by Tudor and Leader, Sheffield, c1775, 12½in (32cm).
£2,200-2,600 *C*

A pair of George III cast silver table candlesticks of baluster form, the knopped stems gadrooned and spiral fluted detachable sconces, gadrooned stepped square bases, by Ebenezer Coker, London 1766, 11in (28cm), 41½oz.
£2,000-2,500 *P(S)*

A pair of William IV candlesticks, by Henry Wilkinson, Sheffield 1836, 9in (23cm) high.
£1,500-2,000 *TG*

Four George III chamber candlesticks, with gadrooned borders and foliage capped scroll handles, with detachable nozzles and extinguishers, by Matthew Boulton and Co., Birmingham 1807 35oz.
£4,000-4,500 *C*

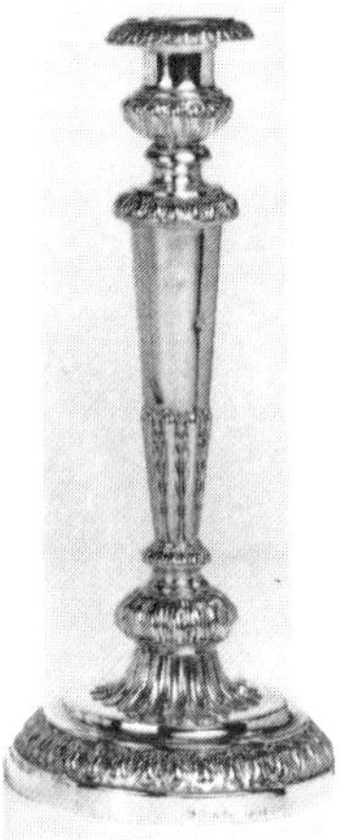

'our large table candlesticks, with ›artly fluted vase shaped sockets ınd detachable nozzles, engraved vith a crest, 2 by Matthew Boulton ınd Plate Co., Birmingham 1826, ınd 2 by R. E. Atkins, Birmingham 844, 14in (36cm) high.
:4,200-4,600 *C*

A pair of George II cast silver candlesticks, the bases, knops and sconces with corner shell moulding, maker John Cafe, London 1756, 8½in (21cm), 30oz.
£2,100-2,500 *P(S)*

A pair of silver pillar candlesticks, London 1904, 6in (16cm).
£90-120 *PCh*

;asters

. pair of William III casters and a ırger caster made to match, engraved with initials, by Thomas ›rydon, 1701, the larger caster 916, 6 and 8in (15 and 20cm), 20oz.
3,600-4,000 *C*

Miller's is a price Guide not a price List

The price ranges given reflect the average price a purchaser should pay for similar items. Condition, rarity of design or pattern, size, colour, pedigree, restoration and many other factors must be taken into account when assessing values.

A Queen Anne plain pear-shaped caster, or moulded foot, with a rib round the body and bayonet fitting cover pierced with stylised foliage and with baluster finial, by Charles Adam, probably 1708, marks worn, 8in (20cm), 9oz.
£600-900 *C*

A George II two-tier cruet stand, on 4 shell feet and with leaf capped scroll handle and applied rococo cartouche, fitted with 3 plain vase shaped casters in 2 sizes, each with pierced detachable domed cover with baluster finial and 3 silver mounted clear glass bottles, by Samuel Wood, the stand 1739, the casters 1740, 1742 and 1749, the bottle mounts unmarked, the larger bottle mounts engraved with a crest, largest caster 6in (15cm), 37oz.
£3,000-4,000 *C*

A mid-18thC style gadrooned and part spiral fluted vase shaped sugar caster, applied with rococo shell and scroll decoration and on a gadrooned rising circular foot, the spiral fluted cover with chased baluster finial, Goldsmiths and Silversmiths Co. Ltd., London 1915, 9in (22.5cm), 16oz.
£450-600 *CSK*

A Victorian coffee pot, in mid-18thC taste, with a leaf capped panelled rising curved spout, ebonised wood scroll handle, and panelled domed hinged cover with octagonal baluster finial, engraved with a crest, the interior fitted with a detachable filter, by W.H., London 1888, 9in (23cm), 18.25oz gross.
£650-750 *CSK*

Coffee & Chocolate Pots

A Victorian pear shaped coffee pot, chased with the signs of the zodiac in the Indian taste, and with several chased friezes of foliage, with a rising curved spout, double scroll handle and flat hinged cover with fluted finial, Houles & Co., London 1874, 9½in (24cm), 27oz.
£450-500 *CSK*

A George II coffee pot, on moulded foot with leaf capped curved spout, hinged domed cover and baluster finial, maker's mark indistinct, possibly John Lampfert, the cover unmarked, c1750, 9in (23cm), 21oz gross.
£1,500-2,000 *C*

A George II coffee pot, the domed hinged lid with turned finial, having a crested cartouche and wooden scroll handle, later engraved with scrolling acanthus and latticework, by Paul Crespin, London 1736, 8in (21cm), 30.5oz gross.
£4,700-5,000 *P*

A George II coffee pot, on moulded foot, with curved spout and shaped domed cover with baluster finial, engraved with a crest, by R. Gurney and T. Cooke, 1742, 8½in (21cm), 19oz gross.
£2,000-2,500 *C*

A George II baluster coffee pot, on gadrooned foot and with leaf capped bird's head spout, and hinged domed cover with spirally fluted vase shaped finial, by Fuller White, 1757, 11in (28cm), 33oz gross.
£3,000-4,000 *C*

George II coffee pot, with leaf ɩpped curved spout, later ivory ındle, hinged domed cover and ɩluster finial, later engraved with crest, by Richard Gurney and Co., '47, the cover unmarked, 8½in 1cm), 18oz gross.
ɩ,200-1,500 *C*

An urn shaped coffee pot, with half bead decoration to spout, dated 1789.
£2,000-2,500 *MGM*

A Victorian coffee pot, by Garrard, London 1862, 12in (31cm).
£900-1,200 *TG*

A George III coffee pot, with leaf capped spout, hinged domed cover, partly fluted baluster finial and gadrooned borders, later engraved with a coat-of-arms, the interior of the cover with a crest, maker's mark C.B., 1771, 11½in (29cm), 28oz gross.
£2,500-3,000 *C*

Maltese coffee pot, on 3 hoof feet, ɩker's mark indistinct, c1770, in (21cm), 611gr.
700-3,000 *C*

ɩeorge III coffee pot, with ɩering angular spout, polished ɩd scroll handle and gadrooned ɩned hinged cover with ball finial, ɩ the body and the cover ɩraved with a crest, William ɩwash and Richard Sibley, ɩdon 1806, 7in (18cm), 22.5oz ss.
ɩ00-1,200 *CSK*

Cups

A Commonwealth wine cup, on spreading trumpet shaped foot, the tapering cylindrical bowl punched with beading and chased with stylised flowerheads, engraved with an initial, maker's mark H.N., a bird and olive branch below, 1656, 3in (7.5cm), 1oz.
£5,000-5,500 *C*

A Queen Anne Irish cup, with a rib round the body and harp shaped handles, engraved with a coat-of-arms in plume mantling, by John Clifton, Dublin 1710, 6½in (16.5cm) high, 23oz.
£2,000-2,500 *C*

A contemporary gilt lined cast and chased stirrup cup modelled as the head of a bull dog wearing a studded collar, 4in (10cm), 22.75oz.
£1,200-1,500 *CSK*

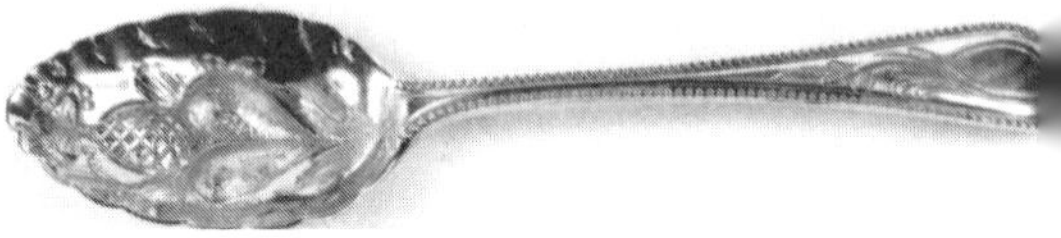

Three berry spoons, 7in (17.5cm) long.
£50-70 *HF*

Cutlery

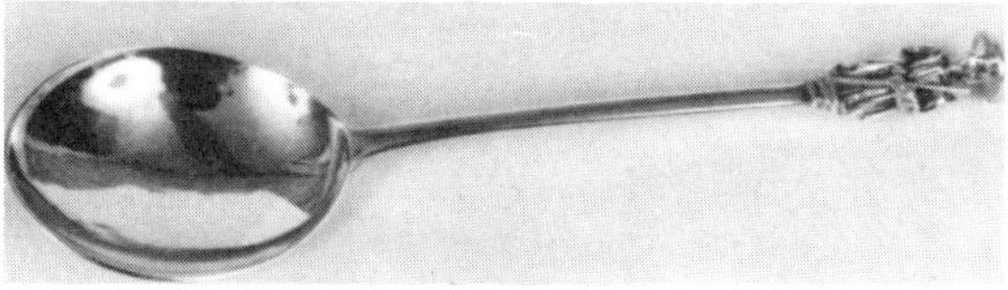

A George II silver Apostle spoon, London 1741, 7in (17.5cm).
£250-350 *TVA*

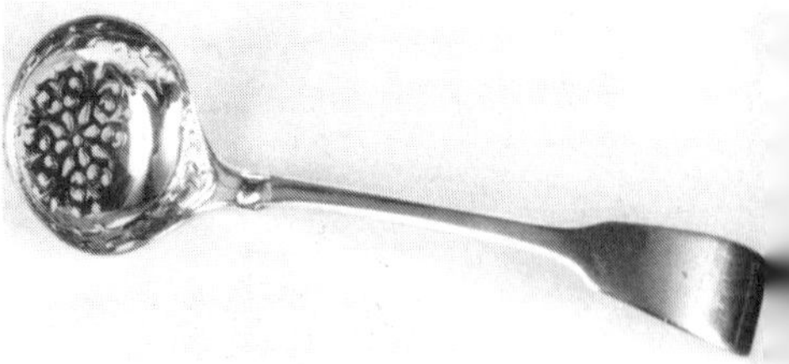

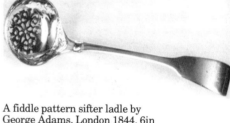

A fiddle pattern sifter ladle by George Adams, London 1844, 6in (15cm) long.
£70-100 *TVA*

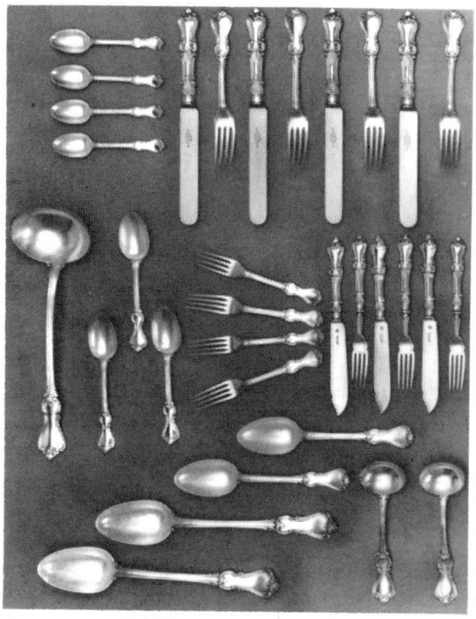

A canteen of Albert pattern cutlery comprising 205 pieces, with loaded husk pattern handles, London 1859, all fitted with either stainless steel or silver blades, various makers, London and Sheffield 1904-5, in a fitted mahogany case.
£6,000-7,000 *WW*

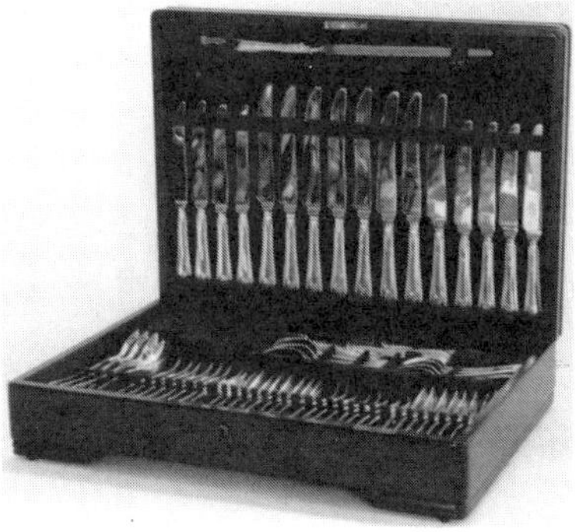

A flatware table service of 71 pieces, by Mappin and Webb, feather edge pattern, Sheffield assay, in stained oak canteen, 105oz excluding weighted items.
£1,700-2,000 *HCH*

A pair of George III Old English pattern sauce ladles, by Peter and William Bateman, London 1809, 6in (15cm) long.
£180-200 *TVA*

A Victorian fish slice, with crested and engraved blade, the handle cast and chased in the form of a fish.
£900-1,200 *Bea*

A pair of George III asparagus tongs, 10in (25cm) long.
£200-250 *TG*

Sheffco

PLATE & POLISH

A GUIDE TO THE RESTORATION, CARE AND PROTECTION OF YOUR SILVERWARE PRESENTED BY SHEFFCO

ilverware is a tradition of racious family living, its narm combines fine art and raftsmanship with the atchless beauty of a precious etal. Like any prized ossession it needs a little oughtful care.

OLID SILVER

he more often you care for our silver, the less effort is eeded to keep it looking its est. We recommend rtnightly dusting with olimit, the impregnated lver cleaning gloves (or any npregnated silvercloth). nis practice should ensure at you never need to use olish on your silver. If your lver is tarnished, then a mild ver polish must be used. The lver Maintenance Solution is eal for this purpose as it will ot destroy the patina – which the fine network of scratches at gives antique silver its autiful shine.

UTLERY

is important to rotate the use your cutlery, thereby giving ch piece equal wear. Rinse all od residue after every meal. it is left unwashed overnight may cause immediate rnishing and corrosion of the ver surface which will need ofessional restoration. For aning tarnished cutlery we commend The Polivit Plate, nich will remove dirt and idization from all crevices. nis process is far easier than lishing, completely non-rasive and prevents any ssibility of a bad taste arising m polish that becomes apped in the decoration and e fork prongs. After use keep a canteen, impregnated tlery roll or a closed drawer or pboard free from any oisture. Do not put away nile still warm from washing. your cutlery is silver ated follow the same structions, but polish once a month with The Silver Maintenance Solution to ensure that your silver-plating lasts forever.

ANTIQUE SHEFFIELD PLATE

The old items of fused plate are now becoming very valuable and it is important to know how to care for them. Over the years people have been polishing their Sheffield regularly with conventional abrasive polishes. Unfortunately, although this produces a nice shine, it in fact slowly destroys the piece as it removes a thin layer of the silver each time it is used, eventually uncovering the copper beneath the surface.

Remedy

Only The Silver Solution or The Silver Maintenance Solution should be used to clean your Sheffield as these products add pure silver, thereby ensuring that your pieces do not deteriorate any further. These solutions will also enhance the antique value, patina and appearance. If your Sheffield is already showing signs of copper wear stop using your abrasive polish immediately, you can only make it worse. Try The Silver Solution, which is now being used by antique dealers throughout the world – you'll be amazed at the difference. Continue use each time your item needs cleaning and you will never see the copper again.

Restoration by Electro-Plating

If your item is badly worn you must make the decision whether to have it professionally replated. This will almost certainly seriously affect the antique value and appearance as well as being very costly. Try The Silver Solution first, you may be very pleased with the result, although remember it is only a silver plating polish, not a silversmith in a bottle – it will not restore damaged or corroded items. Whatever your choice do not return to an abrasive polish once your piece has been restored. Electro plating is not as thick as Sheffield Plate and the problem will rapidly recur.

Lead Mounts

The borders and applied decoration of Sheffield items are normally made of lead and covered with a thin silver coat, these are the first to wear and the most difficult to restore. The Silver Solution Special Edition has been formulated for this purpose and is the most effective means (including electro plating) to replate lead mounts.

ELECTRO PLATE ON COPPER AND E.P.N.S.

The same basic rules apply as for Antique Sheffield except that nickel, which is the base metal for E.P.N.S., actually corrodes when exposed to the atmosphere and is far more difficult to restore than copper. Once again The Silver Solution will have a dramatic effect and with regular use your silver plate will never need to be restored.

ELECTRO PLATE ON LEAD AND E.P.B.M.

As stated before, lead and other soft base metals are very difficult to silver plate. The harsh chemicals used in electro plating can damage the surface beyond repair. Many antique restorers are now using The Silver Solution Special Edition as the only successful method of silver plating soft metals. We suggest you do the same, either as a prevention or a cure.

For further details about The Silver Solution and other Sheffco products, please see the advertisement on Page 577

Salvers

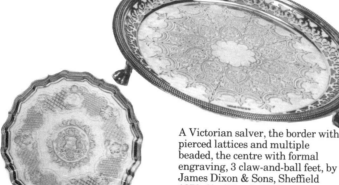

A George II salver, on 4 scroll feet, with moulded border, chased with a band of trellis-work, shells and scrolls enclosing a crest and engraved with a coat-of-arms within a baroque cartouche, by Augustine Courtauld, 1729, Britannia Standard, 13in (34cm) diam, 45oz.
£4,200-5,000 *C*

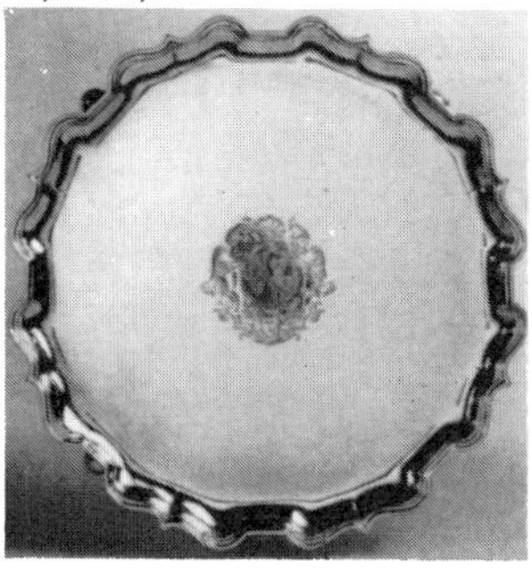

A George II salver, on 4 hoof feet, with waved moulded border, engraved with a coat-of-arms within a baroque cartouche, by Edward Cornock, 1734, 12½in (31.5cm) diam, 30oz.
£3,000-3,500 *C*

A George III salver, with perforated rim, on 4 feet, maker E.R., London 1764, 42oz.
£1,300-1,600 *IM*

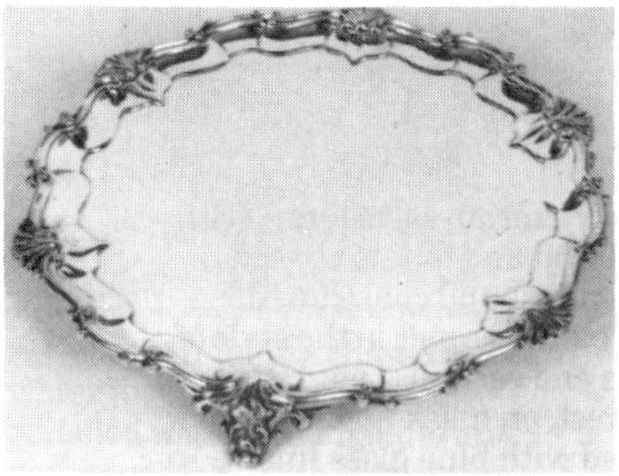

A Victorian hand-made salver, London 1900, 10in (25cm) diam, 21oz.
£500-550 *TVA*

A Victorian salver, the border with pierced lattices and multiple beaded, the centre with formal engraving, 3 claw-and-ball feet, by James Dixon & Sons, Sheffield 1879, 8in (20cm), 10.5oz.
£350-400 *P(S)*

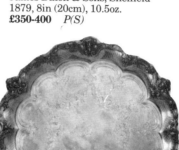

A Victorian salver, engraved with scrolls and floral festoons, with raised hatched border with cast scroll and mask rim, by The Barnards, 1889, 16in (40.5cm) diam, 49oz.
£900-1,200 *GSP*

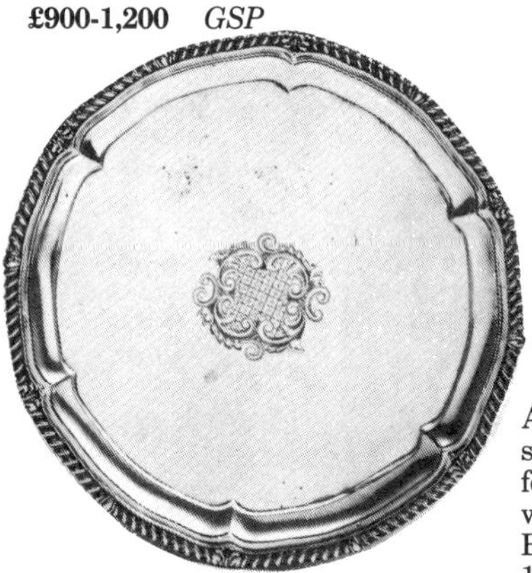

A Regency gadrooned salver, on foliate and floral capped pad feet, the ground engraved with a scrolling foliate cartouche containing an overall trellis design, by Paul Storr, London 1814, 12in (30.5cm), 26oz.
£700-750 *CSK*

A George III Irish salver, on satyr's mask feet, applied with a broad border die-stamped with trailing vines with egg-and-dart rim, the ground with later presentation inscription and facsimile signatures, I.S., Dublin 1808, 11in (28cm), 32.75oz.
£900-1,200 *CSK*

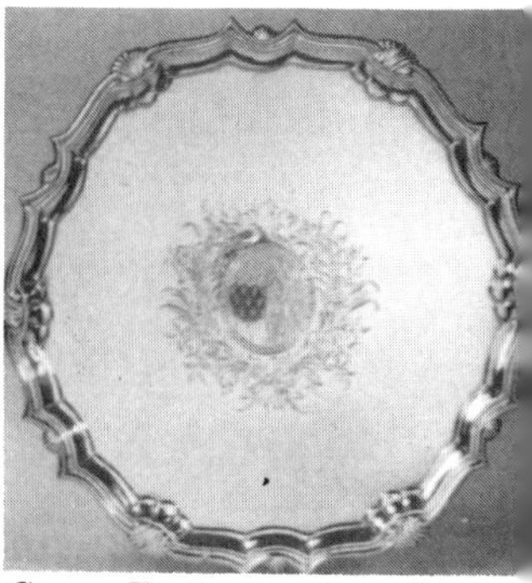

A George II salver, on 3 scroll hoof feet and with shell and scroll border, engraved with a coat-of-arms withir a floral cartouche, by Robert Abercrombie, 1739, 12in (30.5cm) diam, 27oz.
£2,000-2,500 *C*

A mid-18thC style salver on hoof feet, with a moulded rim and plai ground, by Elkington & Co., 12in (30.5cm) diam, 26oz.
£400-450 *CSK*

A George III salver, on 4 foliage a scroll feet, with moulded flower, foliage and scroll border, engrave with a coat-of-arms, by William Bennett, 1816, 24in (61.5cm) diar 178oz.
£4,000-5,000 *C*

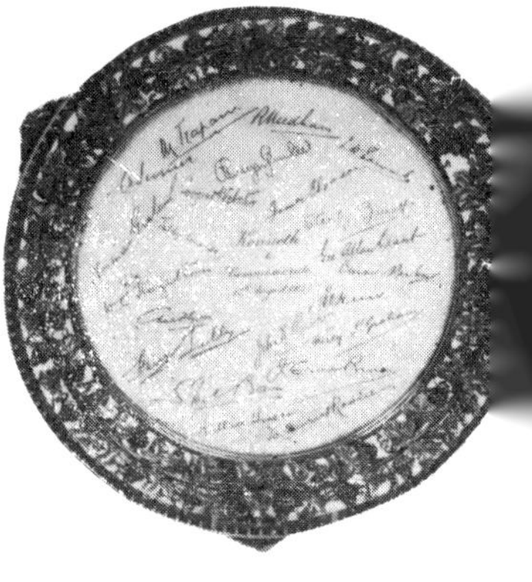

auceboats

George II plain brandy saucepan, ith turned wood handle and oulded lip, engraved with a crest, John Swift, 1757, 9in (22.5cm) ng overall, 9oz gross.
,200-1,700 *C*

A pair of Victorian sauceboats, with ovolo borders, the lower part of the body chased with vertical fluting, applied above with rams' masks and laurel festoons and wreaths within beaded borders, with reeded scroll foliage handles, by John S. Hunt, 1865, stamped Hunt & Roskell Late Storr & Mortimer, 48oz.
£7,000-7,500 *C*

A pair of George III sauceboats, with shaped gadroon and leaf decorated rims, acanthus leaf scroll handles and leaf and scroll feet, by Robert Garrard, London 1818, 9in (22.5cm) wide, 34.25oz.
£3,000-4,000 *AH*

pair of George III shell-shaped uceboats, each on cast foot, the dy and foot chased with alternate tes and foliage ribs, with drooned and foliage borders and uble scroll handles, engraved th a crest, by William Grundy and ward Fernell, 1779, 34oz.
,200-4,700 *C*

A George III sauceboat by Samuel Meriton, London 1753, 8in (20cm) wide.
£700-750 *TG*

A Victorian three-piece tea service, on open scroll feet, the milk jug and sugar basin gilt lined, each engraved with a crest and motto, by Reily and Storer, London 1850, teapot 8½in (21.5cm) high, 71oz.
£1,500-2,000 *CSK*

ervices

eorge III tea set, with everted drooned borders and leaf and ally engraved band to sides, the ap handles chased with flowers, lls and scrolls, on 4 lion mask cket feet, the teapot with long ped engraved handle, the domed ged cover with oval finial, nograms engraved to sides, by pthali Hart, London 1819, the ar bowl and cream jug 1818, z.
0-1,200 *Bon*

A George III York tea service, comprising teapot, cream jug and two-handled sugar basin, with decorative reeded handles on plain circular bases, makers James Barber and William Whitewell, York 1815, 35oz gross.
£1,200-1,500 *DDM*

The base of the teapot is inscribed 'This plate purchased with money won at Doncaster Agricultural Meeting 1816 by a subscription of two guineas each (thirteen subscribers) for the best shearling wether sheep'.

A five-piece tea and coffee service, all of half fluted bulbous form topped with bright cut floral decoration and ebony handles, by Walker & Hall, 3 pieces Birmingham 1921, 2 pieces Sheffield 1902, 83oz gross.
£1,500-2,000 *MN*

A four-piece tea and coffee service, each of bulbous form with gadrooned edges, angular handles, on ball supports, Sheffield, c1938, 64oz gross.
£700-800 *DDM*

Tea Caddies

A George III tea caddy, the sides and curved top finely engraved with riband ornament, festoons of husks and foliage, with feather-edge borders and oblong cover with flower finial, maker's mark I.L., 1772, 4½in (11cm) high, 6oz.
£2,000-2,500 *C*

A George III tea caddy, with hinged cover and wood finial, bright cut with bands of foliage, floral swags and oval cartouches, each enclosing initials, fitted with lock plate and key, by William Skeen, 1788, 5in (12.5cm) high, 13oz gross.
£2,500-3,000 *C*

A pair of Victorian bombé shaped tea caddies in the 18thC taste, on rococo shell and scroll feet and with chased rococo floral and foliate decoration incorporating scroll cartouches engraved with armorials, crests and mottos, the chased and fluted detachable covers with pagoda finials, by Elkington & Co., Birmingham, 7in (17.5cm).
£600-650 *CSK*

A George III fluted tea caddy, with hinged cover and stained ivory finial, bright cut with bands of rosettes and foliage and engraved with a monogram, by Henry Chawner, 1790, 6in (15cm) high, 12oz gross.
£3,600-4,000 *C*

A Victorian tea caddy and cover, maker F.A.P., London 1896, 3½in (9cm) high.
£225-275 *TVA*

Tea Kettles

A George II inverted pear shaped tea kettle, stand and lamp, the stand on 3 leaf capped shell and scroll feet, the kettle with bird's head curved spout, hinged domed cover, flower finial and scroll handle, chased with scrolls and foliage on a matted ground and engraved with a coat-of-arms and crest, each within a scroll cartouche, by William Shaw and William Priest, 1752, 14½in (37cm) high overall, 69oz gross.
£2,500-3,500 *C*

A Dutch silver gilt kettle stand, on 3 shell feet with openwork flower and scroll aprons between, the stand engraved with flowers, with reeded border and circular partly fluted lamp, by Hendrik Swierink, Amsterdam, 1768, 317gr.
£700-900 *C*

Teapots

A George III teapot, with tapering angular spout, hinged domed cover, wood finial and beaded borders, engraved with a coat-of-arms and monogram, by Hester Bateman, 1783, 5in (12.5cm), 13oz.
£1,800-2,200 *C*

A George IV compressed melon fluted teapot, on a rising foot, with a leaf capped rising curved spout, leaf capped scroll handle and domed hinged cover with fluted button finial, with later presentation inscription, I.W., London 1828, 5½in (14cm), 24oz.
£650-750 *CSK*

A George III teapot with wood scroll ıandle and ivory finial, by John Ēmes, London 1804, 19.25oz gross.
£500-600 *P(S)*

A George III teapot with scroll handle, allover embossed and engraved with rococo cartouches, flowers, mask, scrolls and foliage on a matted ground, maker's mark I pellet B, 24.75oz.
£500-600 *P(S)*

. George III teapot, with bright cut ngraved cartouches, floral swags nd decorative bands, beaded edges, traight spout, ivory scroll handle nd finial, by Hester Bateman, ondon 1784, 13.25oz gross.
800-1,200 *P(S)*

A George III reeded teapot, with rising curved spout, polished wood scroll handle and domed hinged cover with ivory pineapple finial, by Peter, Ann and William Bateman, London 1799, 6½in (16.5cm), 14.75oz gross.
£800-900 *CSK*

A George IV inverted pear shaped teapot, with repoussé rococo scroll decoration with foliage, vacant cartouches, cast fluted and leaf decorated swan neck spout, the raised hinged cover with a cast artichoke finial, scroll wood handle, on a collet foot, by Charles Fox, London 1825, 17oz gross.
£450-550 *WW*

George III teapot with domed, inged cover, bone finial and ırving handle, reeded edges and lain bulbous body, engraved with ıe Gilbert crest, maker's mark H/JT, London 1798, 11in (28cm) verall, 15oz gross.
300-400 *DDM*

A George III teapot, with fluted and chamfered corners, the body with engraved cartouches and bands of scrolls and foliage, ivory handle and finial, by Robert Hennell, London 1791, 15.75oz gross.
£600-700 *P(S)*

teapot with plain hinged cover, rdwood handle and finial, ythen fluted body and a plain out, engraved with the Gilbert est, maker's mark GL(?), London 83, 9in (22.5cm) overall, 14oz oss.
50-550 *DDM*

A George III moulded teapot, with a raised acorn finial and engraved foliate band, by John Emes, London 1801, 8in (20cm), 16oz gross, with a matching stand and a milk jug, 3½in (8cm), 3.5oz.
£1,500-2,000 *CSK*

A pair of Victorian tapersticks, of slender fluted column form, on animal tripods and concave sided platform bases, by Henry Wilkinson & Co., Sheffield 1870, 6½in (16cm), 8.25oz.
£450-550 *P(S)*

A Victorian cigar lighter formed as a lamp, the stem formed as entwined dolphins, the oval body similarly engraved to the foot, with bearded mask terminal and sphinx handle, the hinged cover with cone finial, by Charles and George Fox, 1842, 14oz.
£2,500-3,000 *C*

A tea urn of Classical proportions, on 4 reeded and tapered legs with claw feet on a gadrooned base on 4 ball feet, with lion masks carrying ring and a spherical finial on the domed lid, early 19thC.
£400-450 *WIL*

SILVER PLATE

Candlesticks

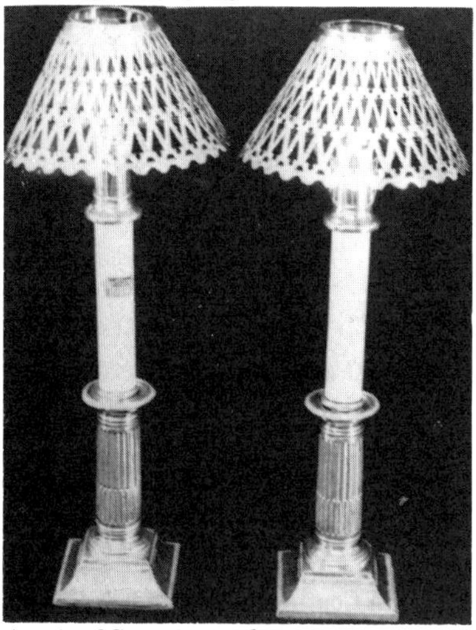

A pair of Georgian style candlesticks, with reeded column and square bases, having spring loaded candle feeds and with .1000 non-matching pierced shades.
£120-150 *GD*

A candelabrum, c1820, 26in (66.5cm) high.
£900-1,000 *DSA*

A set of 8 Victorian table candlesticks, of lobed baluster form with domed bases and detachable sconces, bell marks, 11in (28cm) high.
£600-800 *P(S)*

Services

A four-piece coffee set of demi-ribbed oval form comprising: coffee pot, hot water kettle, stand and burner, a sugar basin and creamer, by Mappin and Webb.
£300-400 *MN*

Tureens

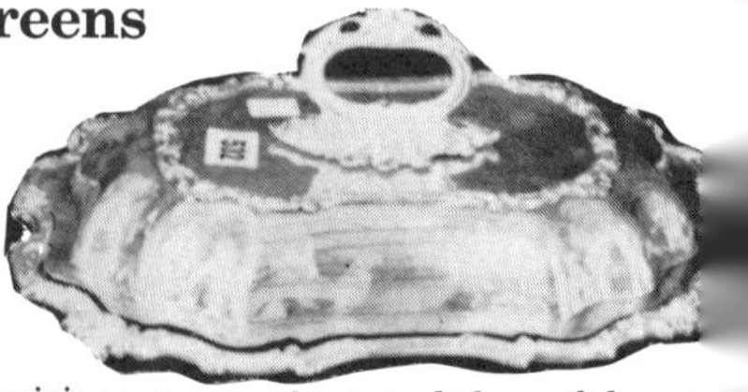

A pair of entrée dishes, of shaped oblong outline, having well cast handles and leaf scroll decoration.
£250-350 *GD*

A Victorian/Edward VII four-piece tea service, comprising: spirit kettle-on-stand, teapot, sugar basin and cream jug, semi-fluted design embossed with ribbon swags, engraved initials L.B., London, 1898, 1907, 1909 and Sheffield 1898.
£1,300-1,600 *RBB*

Miscellaneous

A sandwich box, by James Dixon & Son, c1880, 3 by 5in (7.5 by 12.5cm).
£50-60 *TVA*

Four egg cups on stand, 7½in (18.5cm) high.
£300-350 *TG*

An Old Sheffield plate plant stand, c1820, 8½in (21.5cm) high.
£15-25 *TG*

A sardine dish, late 19thC, 7 by 8in (17.5 by 20cm).
£100-140 *TVA*

An inkstand with cut glass and cranberry dipped bottle, heavy double mask finial to lid, by Elkington & Co.
£170-220 *GAK*

A parcel gilt electrotype inkstand, by Elkington & Co., c1810, 8in (20cm) diam.
£250-300 *TVA*

A hip flask, 6in (15cm) high.
£70-100 *HF*

Wine Antiques

A pair of English wine coasters, turned from single 'oysters' of laburnum wood, c1700.
£500-600 *RYA*

Four George III wine coasters, each on turned wood base, the sides pierced with slats and with beaded borders, by John Smith, Sheffield 1779.
£3,000-3,500 *C*

A pair of wirework wine coasters, c1790, 5in (12.5cm) diam.
£250-300 *TG*

A pair of William IV wine coasters, with ovolo borders and open wirework sides applied with vines, by John Edward Terrey, 1830.
£3,000-4,000 *C*

Four George IV wine coasters, wit shaped sides and gadrooned rims, engraved with a coat-of-arms and motto, by Charles Marsh, Dublin 1821, also with the mark of Brown as retailer.
£3,500-4,000 *C*

The arms are those of Ruxton.

A pair of Sheffield plate wine coasters, c1835, 6½in (16.5cm) diam.
£300-350 *TG*

A set of 4 William IV wine coaster the openwork sides cast with vine tendrils and grapes and with scrol borders, the turned wood bases inse with a silver print engraved with a crest, by Paul Storr, 1831.
£9,000-10,000 *C*

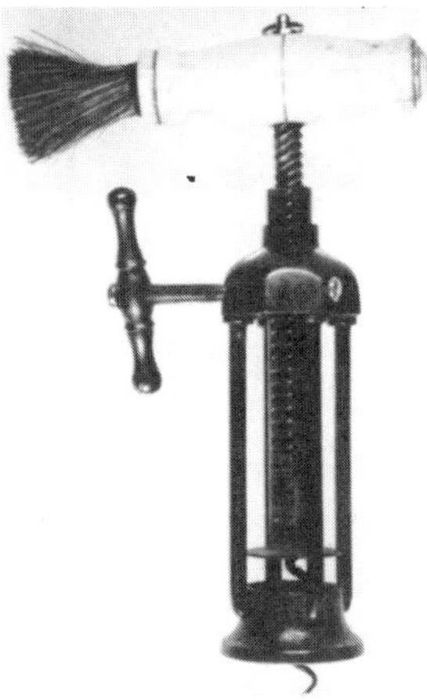

A King's Screw with 4 pillar open frame corkscrew, c1800.
£400-450 *CS*

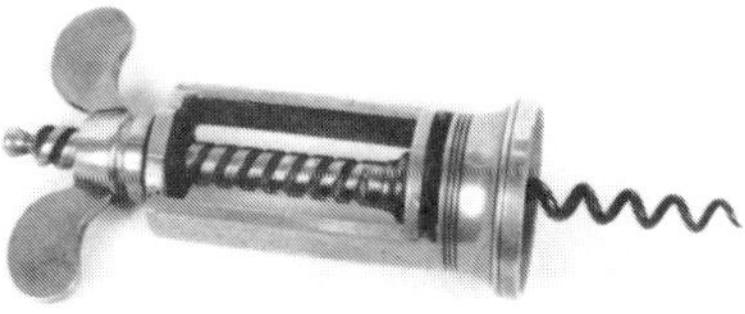

A Farrow and Jackson open barrel brass corkscrew, c1850.
£125-150 *HAR*

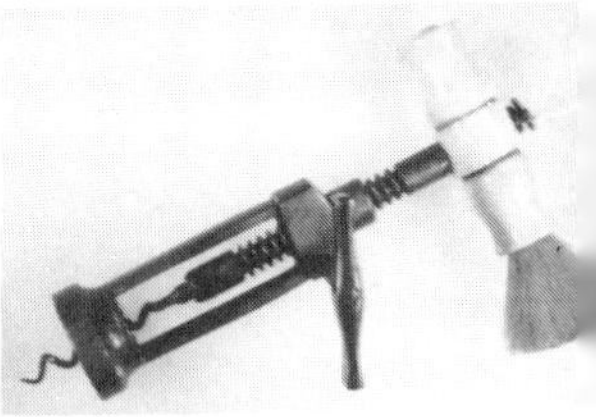

London Rack bronze corkscrew, with open frame and turned bo handle, c1855.
£250-270 *CS*

l. A turned wood corkscrew with brush, c1840.
£45-50

r. A gargantuan sized stag's horn handle corkscrew with 'diamant' mechanism.
£380-400 *CS*

An embossed double action corkscrew 'Autumnal Fruits', c1815.
£400-600 *CS*

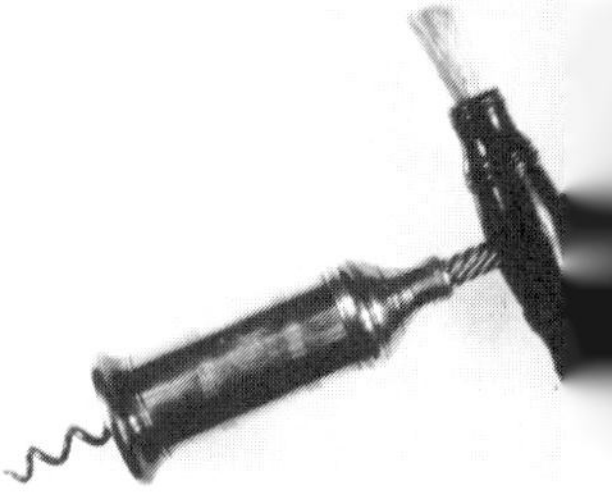

A 'J. Mabson' patent mechanic corkscrew, patented 1869.
£500-600 *CS*

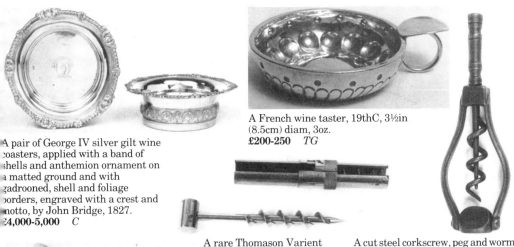

A pair of George IV silver gilt wine
:oasters, applied with a band of
shells and anthemion ornament on
a matted ground and with
gadrooned, shell and foliage
borders, engraved with a crest and
motto, by John Bridge, 1827.
:4,000-5,000 *C*

A French wine taster, 19thC, 3½in (8.5cm) diam, 3oz.
£200-250 *TG*

A cut steel corkscrew, peg and worm with seal and pipe tamper, 1800, 3in (7.5cm) long.
£640-660 *LEW*

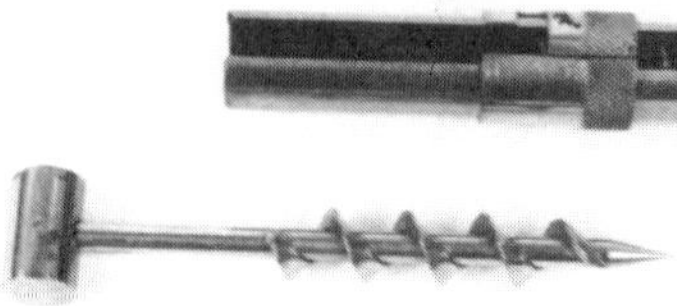

A rare Thomason Varient corkscrew, c1810.
£400-475 *HAR*

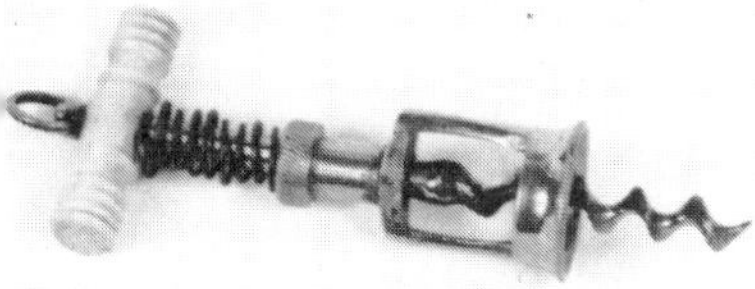

\ rare German miniature
corkscrew, c1820.
'225-275 *HAR*

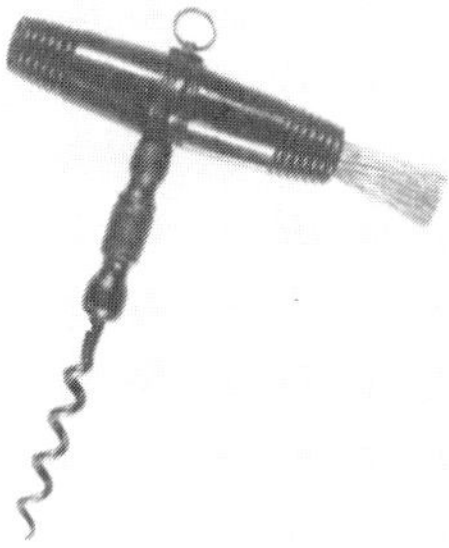

A turned wooden handle corkscrew with brush, c1850.
£30-50 *CS*

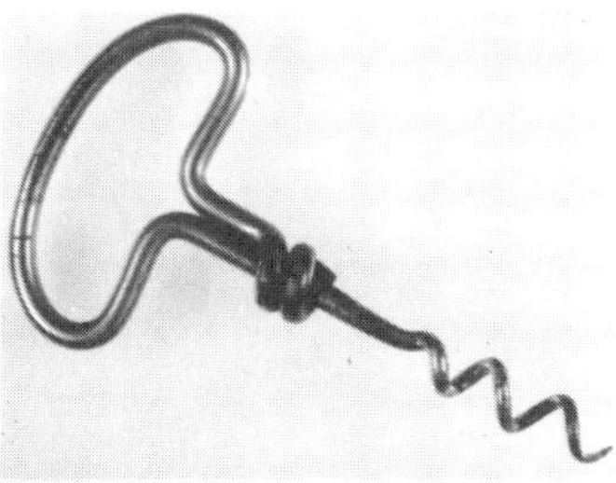

A single piece twisted wire corkscrew.
£10-20 *CS*

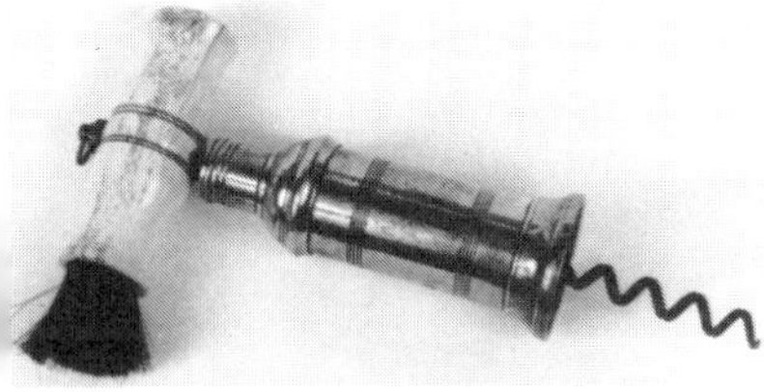

bone handled Thomason
orkscrew with black brush, c1820.
200-250 *HAR*

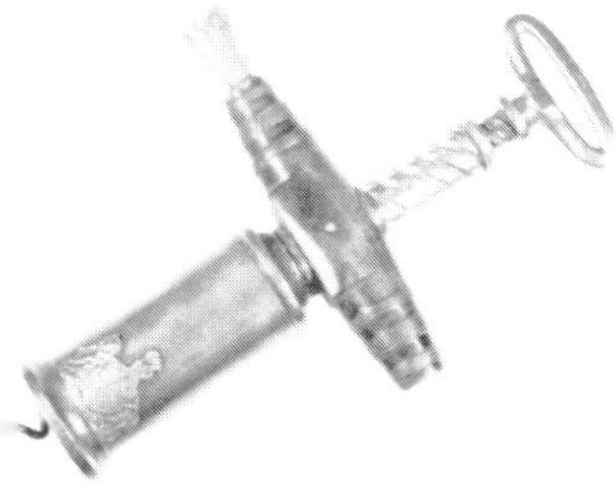

ir Edward Thomason's Varient
orkscrew.
350-650 *CS*

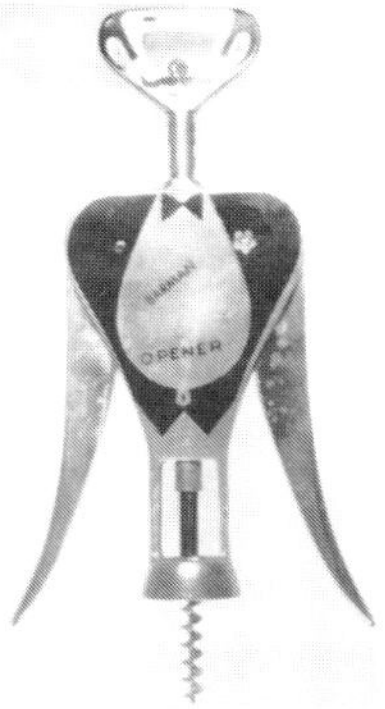
OPENER

A figural cast aluminium lever corkscrew, depicting a barman, Rosatis patent, c1955.
£45-75 *CS*

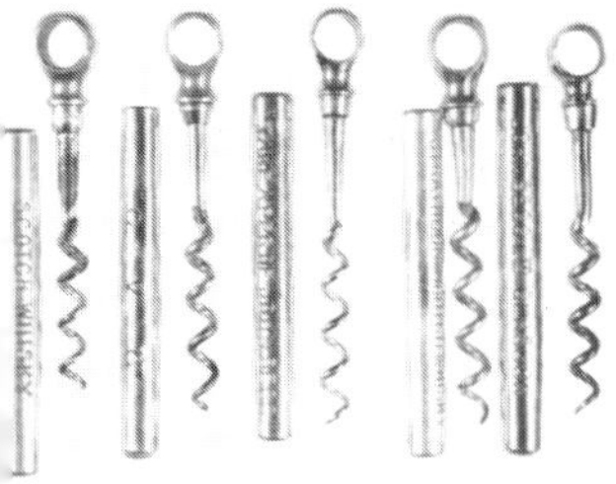

selection of picnic corkscrews with
dvertisements on their sheaths.
10-18 each *CS*

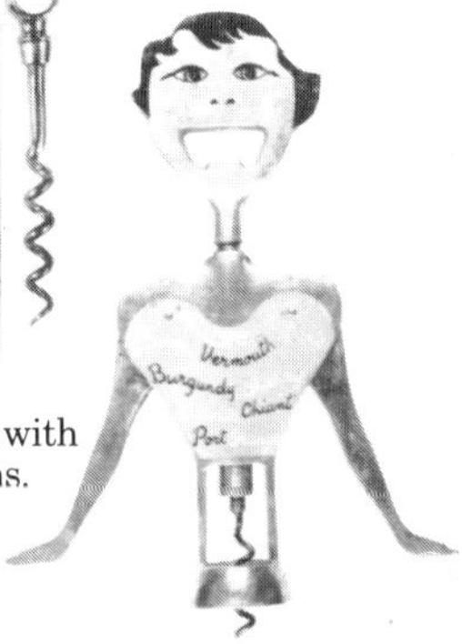
Vermouth
Burgundy
Chianti
Port

A barman's corkscrew in the form of a girl, 20thC.
£45-65 *CS*

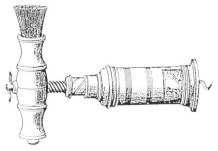

A cut steel corkscrew, peg and worm, c1820, 4in (10cm).
£80-90 *HAR*

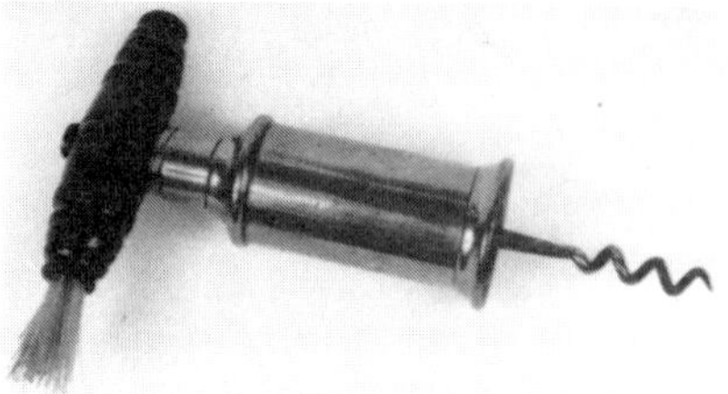

A Thomason type corkscrew, c1830.
£200-220 *HAR*

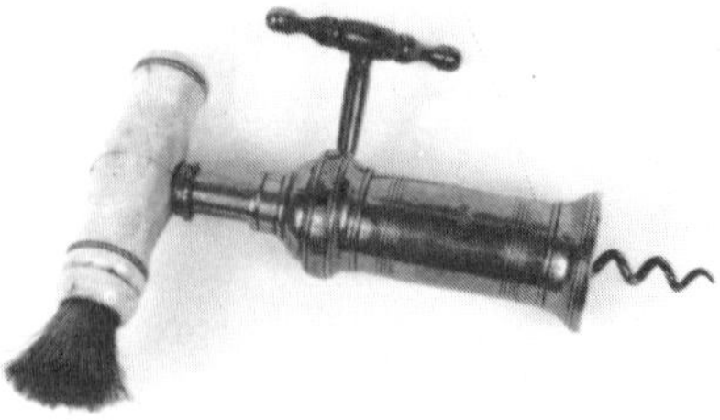

A bone handled Kemp corkscrew, with brass barrel and steel raising handle, c1830.
£350-400 *HAR*

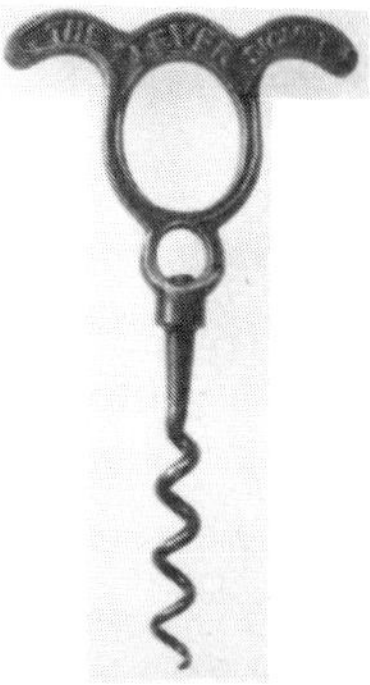

'The Lever Signet' cast steel corkscrew, c1880.
£35-50 *CS*

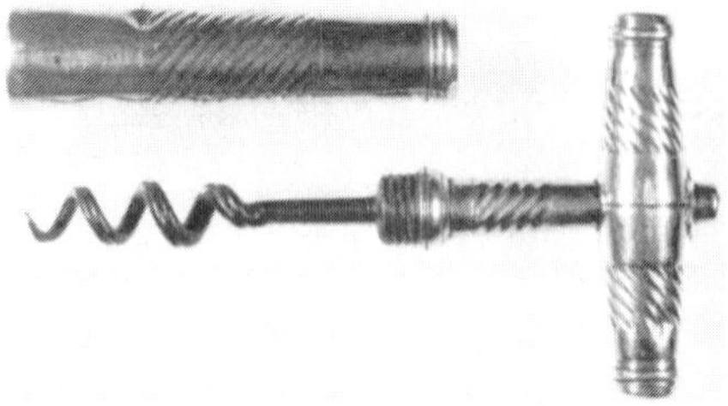

A silver pocket corkscrew, by Samuel Pemberton, 18thC.
£300-400 *CS*

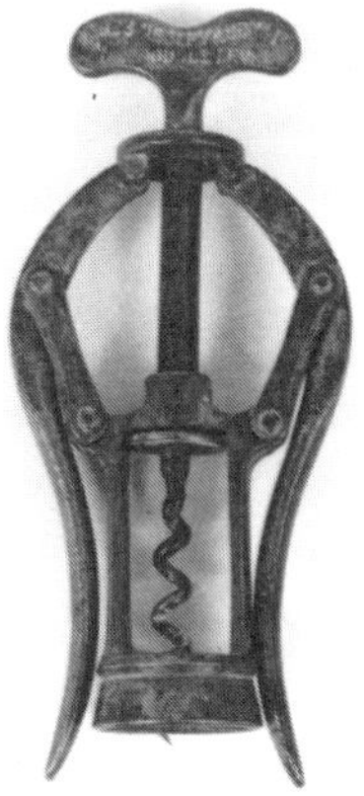

A Swiss corkscrew, with spring, c1920.
£100-130 *HAR*

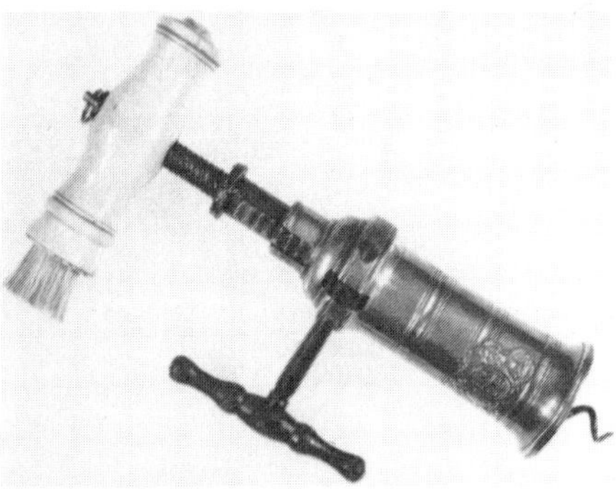

A brass barrel 'King's Screw', with royal coat-of-arms and bone handle.
£340-470 *CS*

A Heeley A1 double lever corkscrew, patent 1888, 6½in (16cm) long.
£75-80 *HAR*

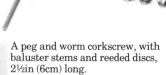

A Greely's cork extractor, patent March 6th, 1888.
£150-175 *HAR*

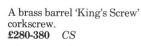

A corkscrew, by J Hedley & Sons, marked Weirs patent 25th Sept 1884, 13½in (34cm) long.
£80-90 *HAR*

A brass barrel 'King's Screw' corkscrew.
£280-380 *CS*

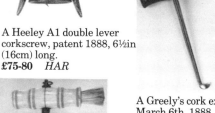

A peg and worm corkscrew, with baluster stems and reeded discs, 2½in (6cm) long.
£90-100 *HAR*

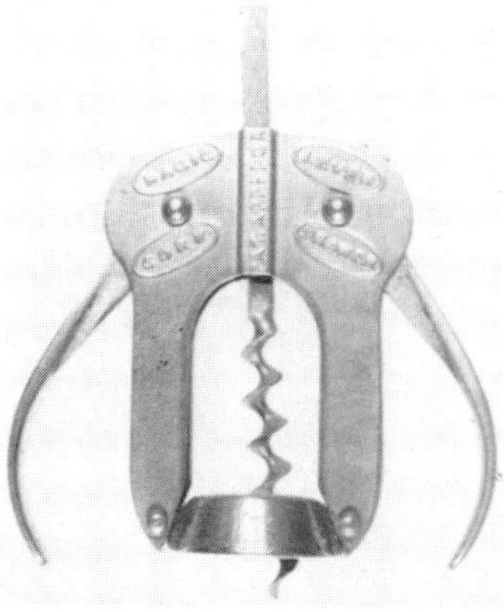

A 'Magic Lever' corkscrew.
£50-60 *CS*

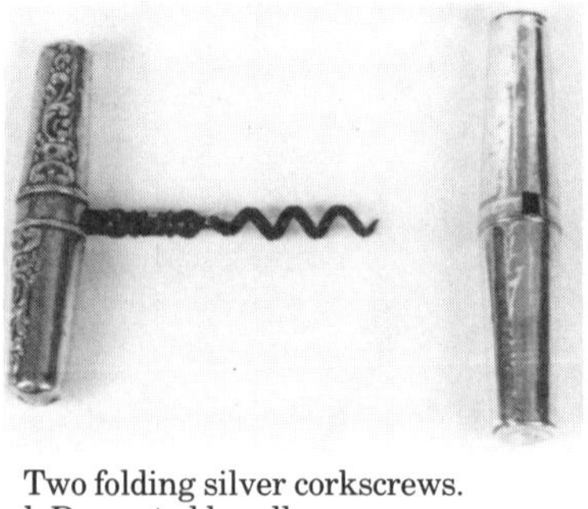

Two folding silver corkscrews.
l. Decorated handle.
£80-90
r. Unfolded corkscrew.
£120-130 *HAR*

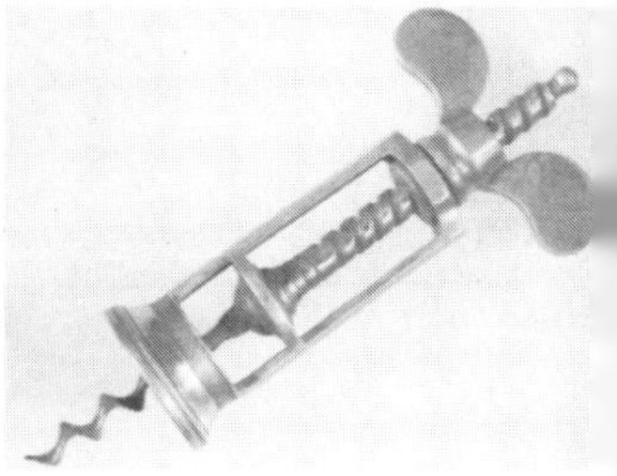

A brass Farrow and Jackson type wing nut corkscrew.
£170-240 *CS*

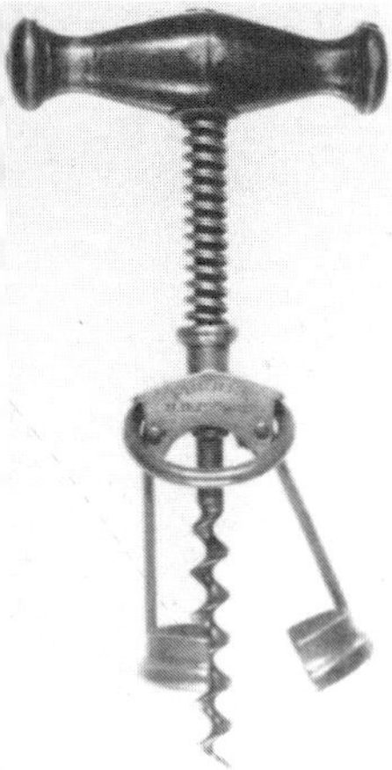

\ German 'Columbus' corkscrew.
:80-100 *CS*

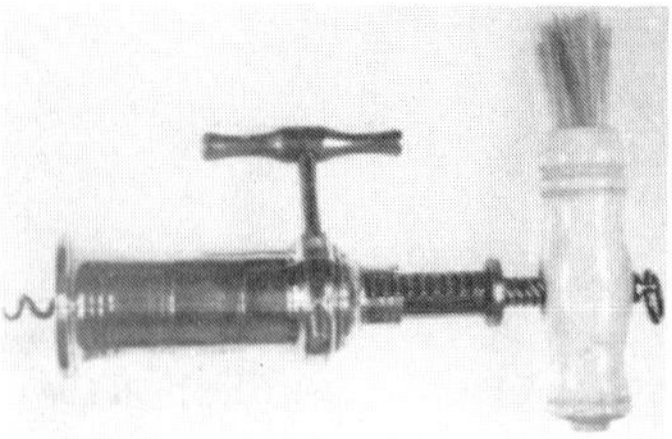

A brass barrel 'King's Screw' corkscrew.
£345-360 *CS*

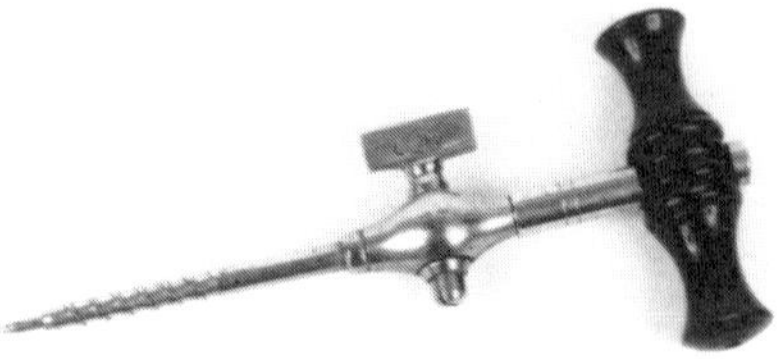

A C & G champagne tap, German, 3½in (9cm) long.
£45-55 *HAR*

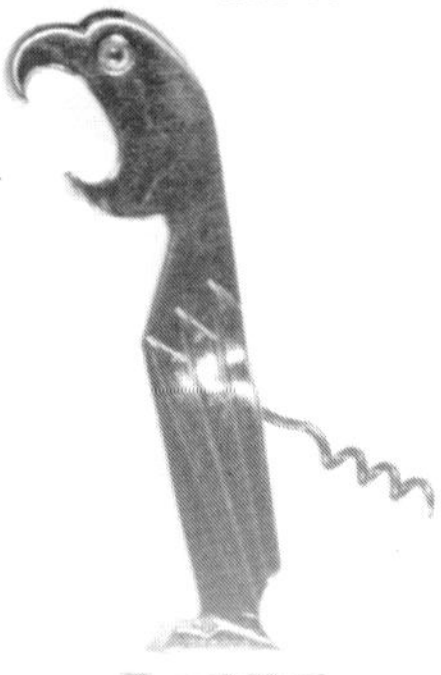

An American Negbaur parrot table corkscrew, chrome plated.
£120-140 *CS*

A George III wine ewer, in vase form with reeded borders and ball finial to slightly domed, hinged cover, with pear wood loop handle, on square pedestal base, by Henry Chawner, London 1798, 12½in (32cm) high, 22oz.
£450-600 *Bon*

A German corkscrew with shaped coiled spring, 19thC.
£30-40 *CS*

n American corking machine, ade of cast iron, c1885.
375-475 *CS*

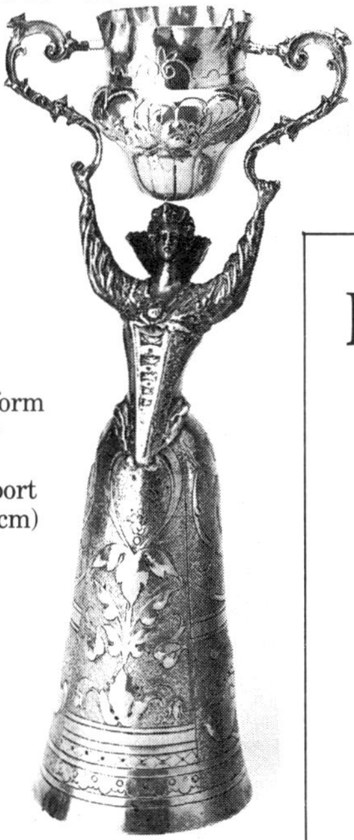

wager cup, in the traditional form a maid supporting a swinging ıp, lobed and engraved with rolls, by Bertholdt Müller, import arked Chester 1898, 10½in (27cm) gh, 10.5oz.
,000-1,200 *Bon*

bottle ticket, by Benjamin Tait, ıblin c1780, 1½in (4cm) wide.
20-130 *HAR*

French 'Zig Zag' concertina type rung corkscrew.
30-65 *CS*

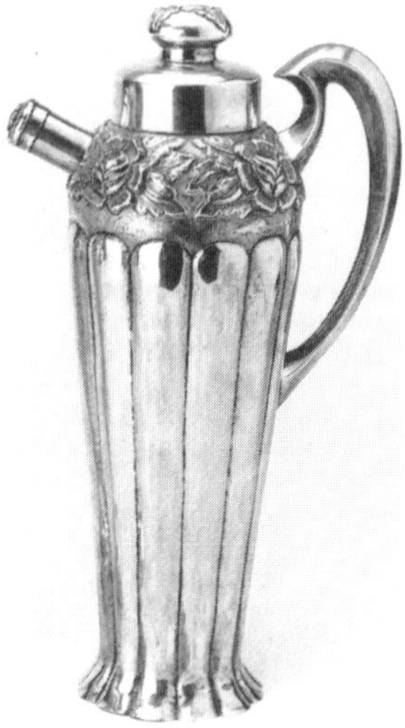

A Continental cocktail shaker, the fluted tapering cylindrical body with floral and leaf chased band to collar, scroll handle and angled spout, the pull off cover with floral finial and engraved monogram, 14in (36cm) high.
£350-400 *Bon*

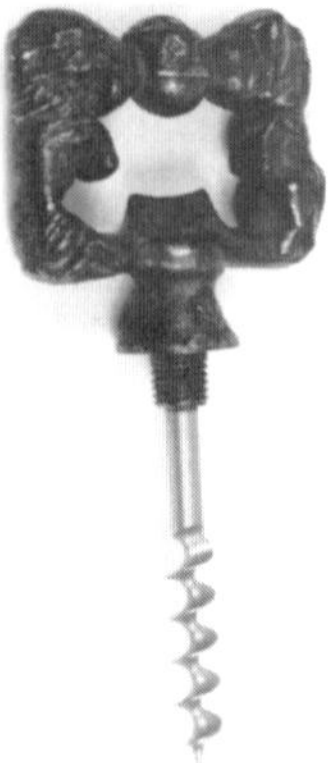

A decorative key corkscrew with a bottle opener handle, 5½in (14cm) long.
£85-95 *TG*

BRONTI

A Bronti label, Sheffield 1981, 2½in (7cm) wide.
£25-40 *TG*

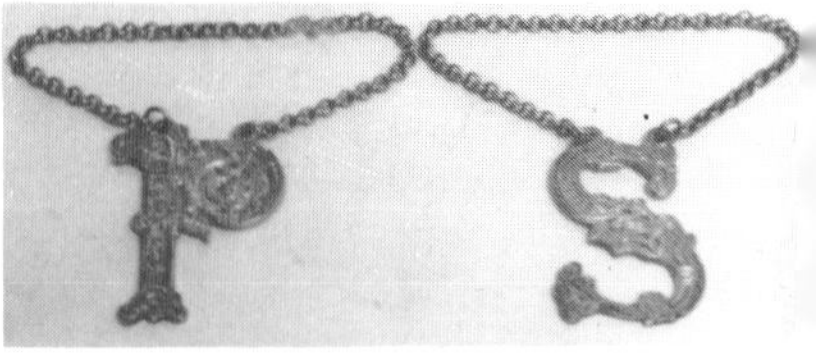
P
S

A pair of port/sherry labels, Edinburgh c1850, 2in (5cm) long.
£100-130 *TG*

An early George III wine funnel, by Hester Bateman, London 1770, 5in (13cm) high.
£450-550 *TG*

SOY

KETCHUP

A pair of sauce labels, London 1822 1in (3cm) wide.
£90-120 *TG*

A gin bottle ticket, by Taylor & Perry, c1845, 2in (5cm) wide.
£50-55 *HAR*

HOCK

A bottle ticket, by Hester Bateman, c1780, 2in (5cm) wide.
£175-185 *HAR*

A mahogany cellaret with domed top, square pilastered front, brass escutcheon and carrying handles, 2 doors below, moulded apron, ogee bracket feet and brass casters, late 18thC, 23in (59cm) wide.
£2,000-2,500 *AH*

A George III brass bound mahogany wine cooler, with hinged octagonal lid, the tapering body with carrying handles, on moulded square tapering legs, later brass liner, 18in (46cm) wide.
£3,000-3,500 *C*

A George III open tub wine cooler, without a stand or liner.
£1,500-2,000 *M*

PORT

A Minton port label, c1874, 5½in (14cm) wide.
£55-65 *HAR*

\ George IV mahogany wine cooler, ıf sarcophagus shape inlaid with ·bony lines with stepped canted top, nclosing a lead lined divided ıterior, the panelled tapering sides ıounted with lion mask ring ·andles, with reeded apron on paw eet, 29½in (75cm) wide.
1,500-2,000 *C*

pair of Old Sheffield plate ımpana shaped wine coolers, each ı spreading base and with shell ıd foliate scroll handles, plain ners and gadrooned, shell and liage collars, c1830, 9½in (24cm) gh.
2,500-3,500 *C*

ı early Victorian mahogany wine oler, the hinged coffered top closing a fitted interior, the pered sides with chamfered angles rved with acanthus volutes, on ff leaf scroll feet, 35in (90cm) de.
,000-5,500 *CSK*

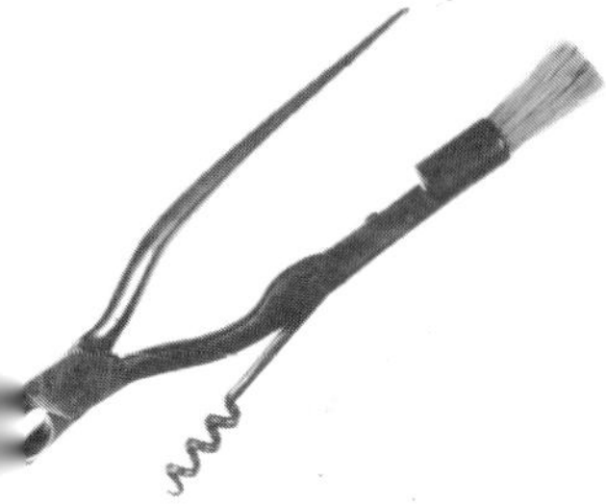

pair of steel champagne wire ppers combined with a fluted rm corkscrew, c1850.
30-250 *CS*

A George III brass bound mahogany wine cooler, with octagonal lid and carrying handles, the stand with fluted frieze and square tapering legs, 19½in (50cm) wide.
£3,000-3,500 *C*

Four Old Sheffield plate vase shaped wine coolers, the foot and lower part of the body chased with fluting, with foliage scroll handles and gadrooned borders, with detachable collars and liners, engraved with a crest, c1830, 10in (26cm) high.
£5,000-6,000 *C*

BORN

A brass bowls measure, advertising Johnny Walker, 1½in (4cm) diam.
£35-40 *HAR*

A cased champagne tap.
£50-60 *CS*

SHERRY

A Wedgwood creamware sherry label, c1830, 5½in (14cm).
£55-65 *HAR*

A George III style mahogany brass bound wine cooler, with fanned top centred by a turned handle, on square tapered legs, 28in (71cm) wide.
£850-1,200 *CSK*

A Regency fiddle back mahogany cellaret, of sarcophagus form, with rectangular hinged top, the sides applied with lion's mask and ring handles, on hairy paw feet, 29in (74cm) wide.
£1,200-1,600 *CSK*

A George III brass bound mahogany wine cooler, with hinged top and lined interior, on a stand with 4 square tapered legs, 17½in (45cm) wide.
£1,000-1,500 *CSK*

A pair of William IV style Warwick vase wine coolers, each with a moulded rim decorated with classical masks, vines and acanthus leaves and with an egg-and-dart and bead rim, fitted with detachable liners and collars, 10½in (27cm), 231.5oz.
£4,500-5,000 *CSK*

A late Regency mahogany sarcophagus wine cooler, inlaid with boxwood with original interior and raised on carved hairy paw feet, 24in (62cm) wide.
£1,500-2,000 *DEN*

A mahogany cellaret, the top with ovolo moulded edge, hinged and opening to reveal a lift-out tray and fitted interior, with 4 dummy drawers to the fascia, brass baluster tied loop handles to the sides, raised upon gadroon carved ogee bracket feet, the whole strung with box and with fan shaped rosettes, early 19thC, 16½in (42cm) wide.
£2,500-3,000 *HSS*

A pair of Old Sheffield plate tapering wine coolers, moulded with ribbed hoops and engraved with simulated staves, each with 2 handles and with a detachable liner and collar, engraved with crests and mottos within garter cartouches, c1815, 9in (23cm).
£3,500-4,000 *CSK*

A George III mahogany and brass bound wine cooler, of octagonal form with partitioned lead lined interior, the stand with moulded square section legs, 18½in (47cm) wide.
£2,500-3,000 *Bon*

A Continental ewer and basin, with gadroon swirl band decoration, 18thC, the basin 12½in (32cm) diam.
£120-160 *P(M)*

METALWARE

Pewter

A pedestal punch bowl, with pricked inscription 'The London Punch House, 1760', 10in (25cm) diam.
£450-500 *GSP*

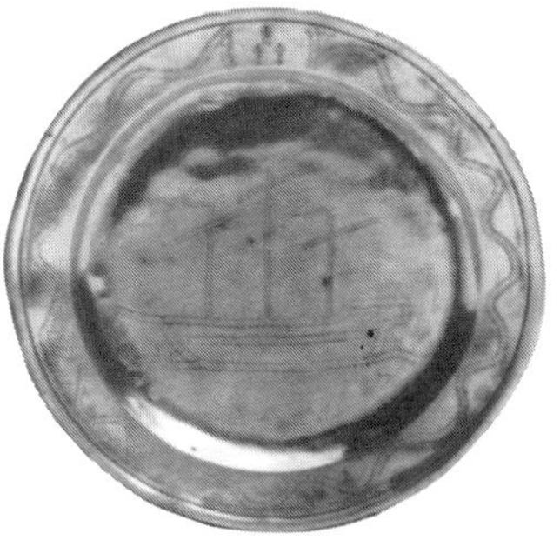

An English wriggle-work plate, c1710, 8½in (21.5cm) diam.
£100-150 *KEY*

A Continental alms dish, c1700, 12in (30.5cm) diam.
£350-400 *KEY*

Three English pewter salts, c1780.
£50-100 each *KEY*

A coffee pot, 19thC, 9½in (24cm) high.
£60-70 *RFA*

An inkstand with removable ink and pounce pots, centre taperstick and wax drawer, engraved 'For y use of y Great Vestry Room — Samuel Cooper (?) Vestry Clerk, 1743', 11in (28cm).
£800-1,000 *GSP*

Believed to be from Shoreham Old Church.

A pewter measure, Jersey, 18thC, 8in (20cm) high.
£150-180 *KEY*

A Scottish laver, the tapering banded body with scroll handle and twin lobed thumbpiece, late 18thC, 10½in (26.5cm) high.
£250-350 *CSK*

3rass

. pair of George II candlesticks, the ylindrical shafts with lobed knops n petal bases, 8in (20cm) high.
400-600 *CSK*

A Dutch chamber candlestick, c1700, 11in (28cm) long.
£100-150 *KEY*

A candlestick with heavy ribbed column, central reeded drip pan, on broad moulded circular foot, 17thC, 8in (20cm) high.
£4,000-4,500 *P(M)*

A pair of candlesticks, with knopped baluster stems on shell cast petal bases, 18thC, 8½in (21.5cm) high.
£550-650 *P(M)*

pair of candle lamps, 8½in 1.5cm) high.
350-400 *SBA*

A pair of chambersticks, 19thC.
£120-150 *PCA*

Dutch jardinière, with repoussé enes of drinking men, the sides ith lion masks, previously with ngs, 17in (43.5cm) wide.
400-450 *C*

A mid-Victorian brass and ormolu miniature frame in the form of a five-bar double gate, inscribed 'Please shut these gates' centred by a miniature oval frame and flanked by trees, opening to reveal 4 miniature oval frames, the reverse engraved 'R. Betjeman & Sons' with registration mark for 1867 and 'Registration No. 34' and bracket engraved 'Toulmin & Gale, 7, New Bond Street, and 85 & 86 Cheapside'.
£600-700 *C*

A heavily patinated lantern bracket, 32in (81cm) high.
£900-1,100 *WHB*

A pair of candlesticks, with segmented cylindrical columns and narrow everted rims, wide drip pans and spreading bases, 17thC, 7in (17.5cm) high.
£3,500-4,000 *Bea*

A French cast brass candlestick, 16thC, 10½in (26.5cm).
£300-350 *KEY*

A cast brass oil lamp, the boat shaped reservoir applied with masks in the Renaissance style, supported upon a circular base with green tinted shade, 19thC, 22½in (57cm) high.
£500-550 *HSS*

A Continental candlestick, repaired, c1600, 7in (17.5cm) high.
£400-600 *SBA*

A pair of Flemish repoussé sconces, each with scrolled candle branch and oval backplate, one with a figure holding a tulip, the other with an old man before a fire, traces of silvering, 13in (33cm) high.
£1,800-2,000 *C*

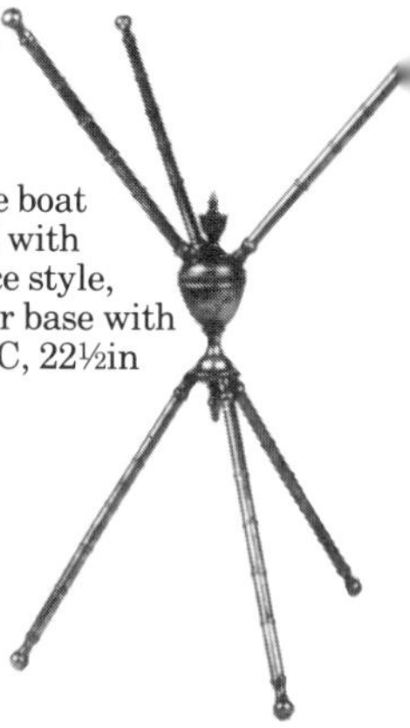

A brass cat, the ring turned support and legs around a central urn, early 19thC, 15½in (39.5cm) high.
£300-350 *C*

Cats were made of metal or wood and were used for keeping food or dishes warm beside a fire.

A pair of Adam and Eve chargers, 14in (35.5cm) diam.
£450-500 *SBA*

A gilt brass curfew of typical form, repoussé decorated with portraits, animals and figure subjects and pseudo coats-of-arms, surmounted by a carrying handle, 18thC, 17in (43.5cm) wide.
£750-800 *CSK*

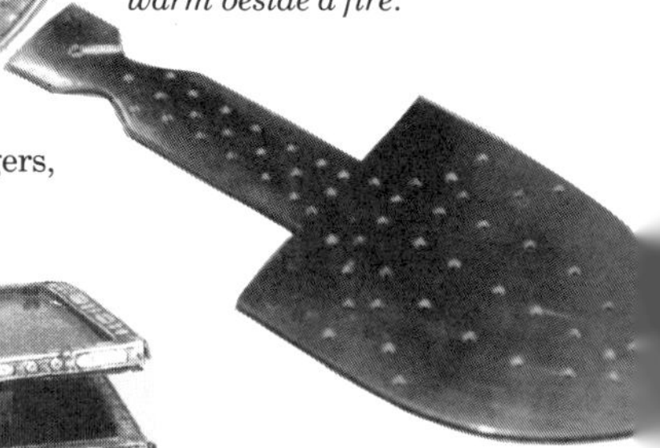

A trivet, 19thC, 12in (30.5cm) long.
£30-40 *PCA*

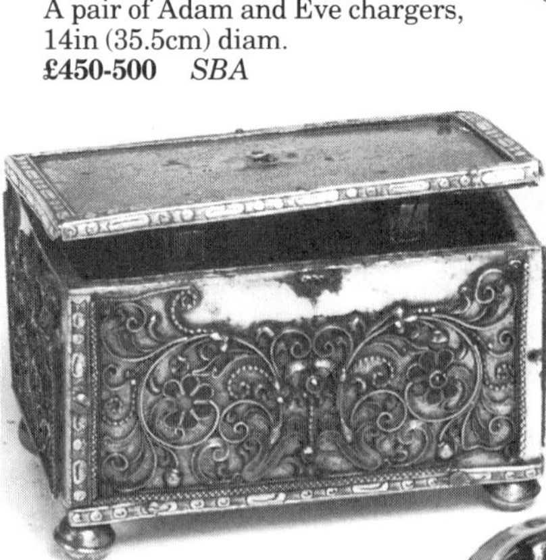

A Nuremberg minnekästchen, in the manner of Michael Mann, the base engraved inside and out, the sides with pierced silver, enamel and gem set appliques, applique from lid missing, minor damage to lock, minor losses, associated key, early 17thC, 2 by 3in (5 by 7.5cm).
£1,800-2,000 *C*

A desk ink stand with glass liner, 19thC.
£100-140 *PCA*

A down hearth, 20½in (52cm) long.
£220-280 *SBA*

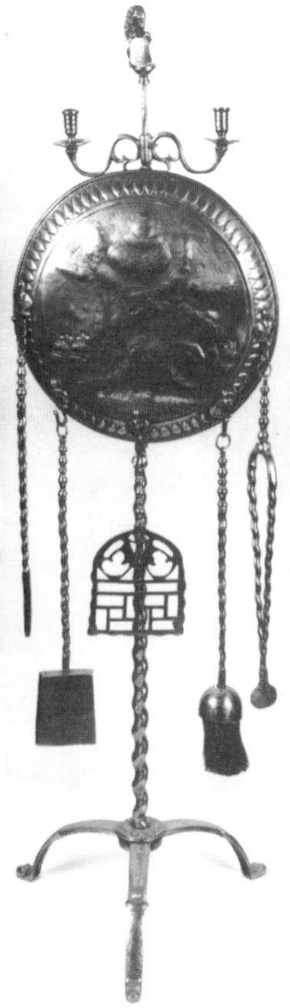

A standing fireside compendium, originally given as a gift to a member of staff from Maresfield Manor House, handmade, 1820, 56in (142cm) high.
£800-1,000 *SO*

An English bronze skillet, early 17thC, 13½in (35cm) long.
£150-180 *KEY*

Bronze

A French bronze bust of Beethoven, cast from a model by Pierre Félix Masseau, signed Fix Masseau, on a hardwood plinth, early 20thC, 10½in (27cm) high.
£1,700-2,000 *C*

Pierre Félix Masseau known as Fix Masseau exhibited at the Paris Salon from 1899 onwards. He first exhibited his bust of Beethoven at the Salon in 1902 and in Venice in 1907.

A French bronze group of Venus and Cupid, cast from a model by Moreau, the base signed Moreau, 19thC, 12½in (32cm) high.
£900-1,200 *C*

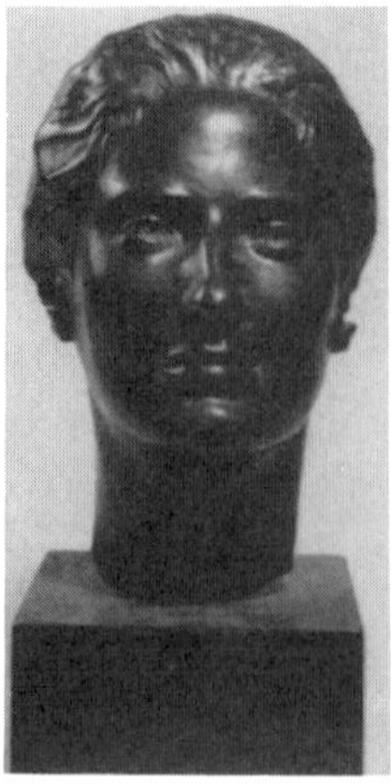

An English bronze mask of Mary Swainson, cast from a model by Alphonse Legros, pedestal chipped, late 19thC, 11½in (30cm) high.
£1,500-2,000 *C*

Mary Swainson was Legros' pupil at the Slade School from 1880 to 1883. Legros modelled the mask during one of his lessons and gave the original plaster mould to the sitter. A marble version was exhibited at the Grosvenor Gallery in 1884 and a bronze cast was made in Paris in 1890. The present mask is one of 3 bronzes cast.

A French bronze bust of the pensive Venus, signed J. Clessinger, Rome 1860, the integral socle stamped F. Barbedienne Fondeur, 19thC, 9½in (24cm) high.
£420-460 *CSK*

A French bronze bust of a lady, cast from a model by S. Salmson in Louis XVI costume, signed on one shoulder S. Salmson 1873 and inscribed on the other shoulder P. Baur, on turned marble socle, socle repaired, 19thC, 20½in (52cm) high.
£1,500-2,000 *C*

A French parcel gilt bronze figure of a recumbent bacchante, 19thC, 13 by 25½in (34 by 65cm).
£1,500-2,000 *C*

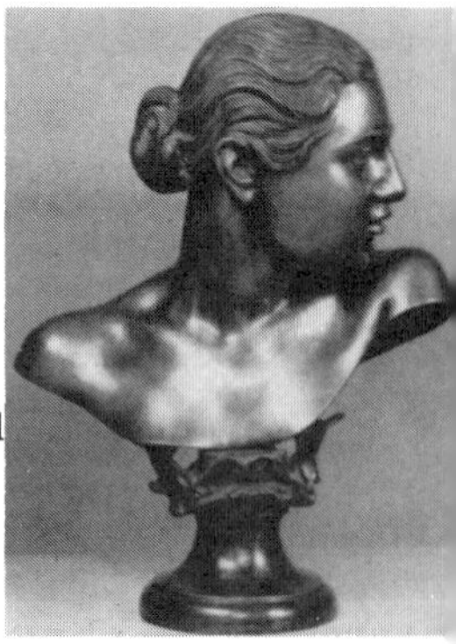

An Italian bronze bust of woman from Capri, cast from a model by Vincenzo Gemito, the base cast with twin dolphins, signed Gemito and with foundry stamp, early 20thC, 18½in (48cm) high.
£4,200-4,700 *C*

A French bronze figure, cast from a model by Eugene Aizelin, inscribed 'Conseils d'une mere a ses enfants', signed Aizelin, on marble base, 19thC, 14½in (36.5cm) high.
£900-1,200 *C*

A French bronze figure of a fisherboy, cast from a model by M. de Vasselot, the base inscribed 'Paris 1882, mon petit Charlot, M. de Vasselot', 19thC, 48½in (124cm) high.
£6,000-7,000 *C*

An Italian bronze heroic bust of Napoleon, cast from a model by A. Pandiani, the reverse signed A. Pandiani and dated Milano 1890, on rouge marble columnar base applied with bronze N, 19thC, 21in (54cm) high.
£2,500-3,000 *C*

A French bronzed metal group of 2 putti riding on the back of a giant tortoise, 10in (26cm) high.
£500-700 *CSK*

A French bronze figure of an animal trainer, cast from a model by Christopher Fratin, a self portrait caricature head of Fratin, the base stamped Fratin, mid-19thC, 8in (20cm) high.
£1,700-2,500 *C*

A pair of French statuettes of Painting and Sculpture, cast from models by Salmson, the bases signed Salmson, with ormolu pedestals with bronze reliefs of putti, with supports for candle holders behind, tops missing, mid-19thC, 15in (38.5cm) high.
£2,000-2,500 *C*

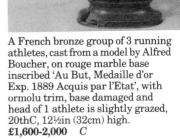

A French bronze group of 3 running athletes, cast from a model by Alfred Boucher, on rouge marble base inscribed 'Au But, Medaille d'or Exp. 1889 Acquis par l'Etat', with ormolu trim, base damaged and head of 1 athlete is slightly grazed, 20thC, 12½in (32cm) high.
£1,600-2,000 *C*

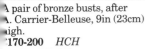

\ pair of bronze busts, after
\. Carrier-Belleuse, 9in (23cm)
ıigh.
'170-200 *HCH*

Three bronze mortars, 1 Spanish and 2 English, 17th & 18thC, 3½ and 4in (8.5 and 10cm).
£80-100 each *KEY*

pair of French bronze classical
gures of a fiddler and companion
laying bagpipes, inscribed
·regoire, on Siena marble bases,
9thC, 15in (38cm) high.
,500-2,000 *GSP*

A Venetian bronze model of an Arab reading on a carpet, c1900, 4½in (12cm) wide.
£350-450 *Ba*

A Venetian bronze, The carpet seller, c1900, 3½in (9cm) high.
£250-350 *Ba*

Venetian bronze model of a
ıncing lady, c1900, 10½in (27cm)
gh.
300-900 *Ba*

A large French bronze figure of Venus, after the antique, base stamped 'Reductions Sauvage', 19thC, 40½in (103cm) high.
£2,500-3,000 *C*

A Venetian bronze model of a pair of jockeys, c1900, 8in (21cm) high.
£800-900 *Ba*

An Italian bronze group of 2 dancing bacchantes, cast from a model by F. de Luca, on turned green marble socle and serpentine marble column with entwined dolphins, 19thC, 71in (180cm) high.
£3,500-4,000 *C*

A Venetian bronze, The water seller, c1900, 7½in (19cm) high.
£450-550 *Ba*

A Venetian bronze model of a small mechanical owl, opening to reveal a figure, c1900, 5½in (14cm) high.
£150-250 *Ba*

A Venetian bronze model of a mechanical owl on tree trunk, opening to reveal a figure, 5½in (14cm) high.
£1,000-1,500 *Ba*

A Venetian bronze, Bacchus and a nymph, c1900, 4½in (12cm) wide.
£900-1,000 *Ba*

A Venetian bronze, an ashtray with camel, c1900, 7½in (19cm) diam.
£800-900 *Ba*

A Venetian bronze model of a large Egyptian dancer, c1900, 10½in (27cm) high.
£1,600-2,000 *Ba*

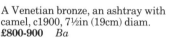

A bronze depicting a fat pig being ridden by the devil, 1½in (4cm).
£230-270 *MN*

A Rheinhold bronze, The Philosophical Chimpanzee, the animal seated on a pile of books and contemplating a skull, on a square base, signed, 13in (34cm) high.
£600-700 *WHB*

An English bronze model of a stalking panther, cast from a mode by I. M. Swan, the panther shown or a tall naturalistic rock, signed and dated I.M. Swan 1905, and stampe C Valsuani cire perdue, green brown patina, early 20thC, 8½in (22cm) high.
£2,200-2,500 *C*

A Venetian bronze model of 2 small dogs, c1900, 3½in (9cm) wide.
£200-300 *Ba*

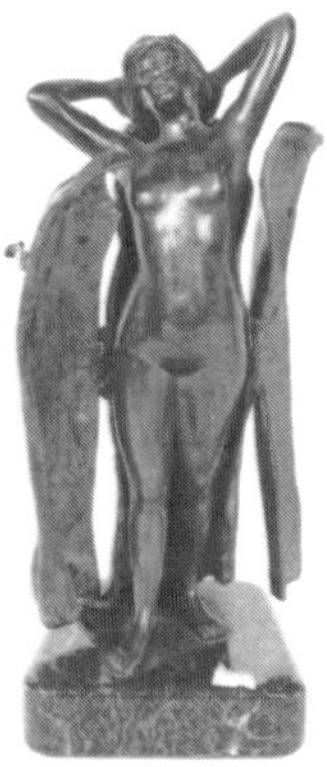

A Venetian bronze model of a mechanical cloaked lady, c1900, 8in (21cm) high.
£900-1,000 *Ba*

A Venetian bronze model of dogs frolicking, c1900, 3½in (9cm) wide
£300-400 *Ba*

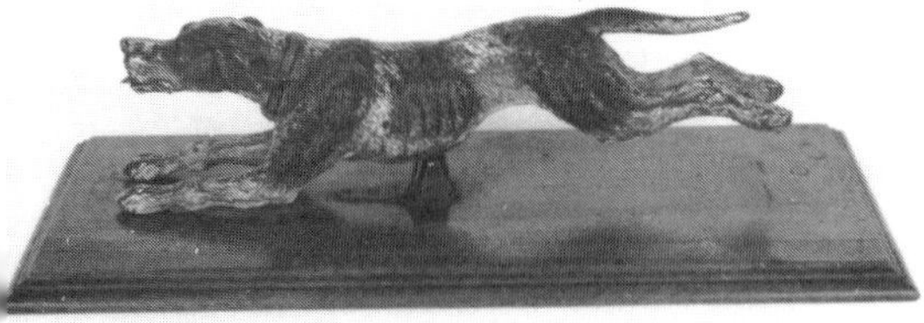

\ Venetian bronze model of a large
log paper holder, c1900, 12½in
32cm) wide.
:700-800 *Ba*

A Venetian bronze, The arms seller, c1900, 4½in (12cm) wide.
£500-600 *Ba*

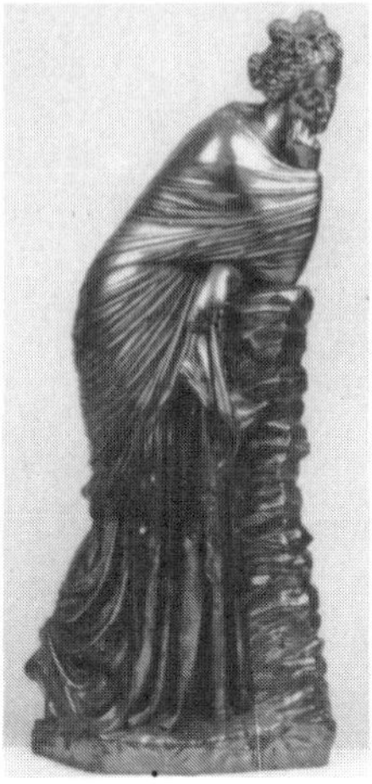

A French bronze statuette of Polyhymnia, after the antique, cast by Barbedienne, marked F. Barbedienne Fondeur, polished, 19thC, 29½in (75cm) high.
£1,500-2,000 *C*

. Venetian bronze, The elephant
ısk seller, c1900, 8in (21cm) high.
1,800-2,000 *Ba*

A Venetian bronze model of a fox pin holder, c1900, 7½in (19cm) wide.
£300-400 *Ba*

An Italian bronze figure of a classical nude youth, signed 'Amodio Naples', late 19thC, 24in (62cm) high.
£500-550 *DDM*

Venetian bronze model of a pug
·g, c1900, 3½in (9cm) wide.
00-200 *Ba*

A bronze depicting a cat holding her kitten in her mouth, 2½in (7cm).
£320-360 *MN*

A Venetian bronze model of a large tiger, c1900, 7in (18cm) wide.
£550-650 *Ba*

ɔronze horse's head, after the
tique, with arched neck, open
uth and flared nostrils, 20thC,
½in (78cm) high.
,500-3,000 *C*

e bronze horse's head is a copy of
original excavated at
itavechia near Rome, it was
quired by the Medici family, who
nost certainly commissioned
ambologna or his studio to adapt
s a fountain in the courtyard of
Medici Palace.

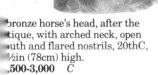

A French bronze model of a stag, cast from a model by Antoine-Louis Barye, on naturalistic base, signed Barye and stamped F. Barbedienne, Fondeur, the underside marked No. 640 and 43, 19thC, 7in (18cm) high.
£1,200-1,700 *C*

A French bronze model of a setter carrying a pheasant, cast from a model by Jules Moigniez, on naturalistic base signed J. Moigniez and stamped Exposition Paris 1900 M.D. Mlle d'or H.V., 19thC, 16in (40.5cm) high.
£3,000-4,000 *C*

A North Indian provincial bronze figure of Kali, standing with the principal hands holding patra and khadga handle, the secondary with staff and skull, slight corrosion, khadga blade and staff finial missing, 18thC, 19in (49cm) high.
£21,000-23,000 *C*

A Venetian bronze, a tent light fixture, c1900, 10½in (27cm) high.
£900-1,000 *Ba*

A bronze figure of the inventor Ambroise Pare, in 16thC costume, the base signed P.J. David, with Barbedienne foundry stamp, inscribed Ambroise Pare, 19thC, 19in (49cm) high.
£500-700 *CSK*

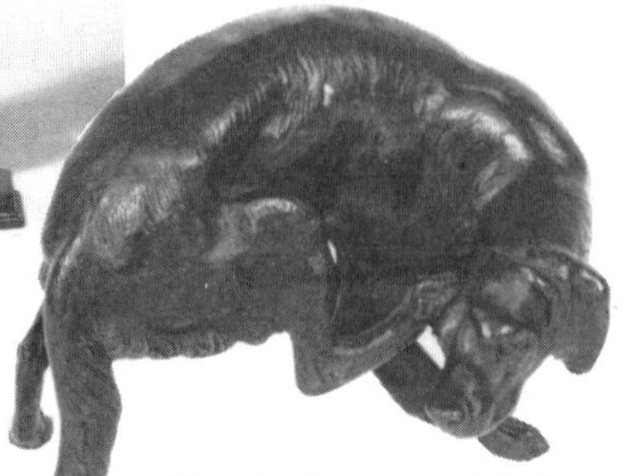

A Venetian bronze model of a scratching dog, c1900, 4½in (12cm) high.
£500-600 *Ba*

A French bronze group of a panther seizing a stag, cast from a model by Antoine-Louis Barye, on naturalistic base, signed Barye and inscribed Susse frères editeurs à Paris, late 20thC, 13in (33cm) high.
£2,000-3,000 *C*

A bronze model of a terrier dog fitted with a saddle being mounted by a cat wearing a jockey hat, slight chipping to body, 2in (6cm).
£400-450 *MN*

A bronze group of 2 dancing maidens, after Clodion, the infant Bacchus at their feet, on naturalisti base, incised Clodion and dated 1762, stamped 1937, 15½in (40cm) high.
£850-950 *P(W)*

A French bronze group, by Louis Sauvageau, on plain base, dark patination, signed, mid-19thC, 31½in (80cm) high.
£1,700-2,000 *N*

A bronze figure of a lion, signed Kenworthy '65 and numbered 6/10, on marble plinth, 14½in (37cm) wide.
£550-650 *P(S)*

An Austrian bronze model of a buffalo, with painted eyes, 19thC, 12in (31cm) long.
£1,200-1,500 *CSK*

A set of 6 bronze bell shaped standard weights, by Sewell & Young, Makers, London, each engraved Rygate 1795, 5616-216, each stamped with various George III proof marks, late 18thC.
£2,000-3,000 *C*

Victorian gilt bronze and brass ıounted four-piece desk set, with ardstone bosses, comprising an ıkstand, blotter, pentray and older, and a pen.
300-700 *CSK*

gilt bronze inkstand, with central ndle holder supported by a ıssical female figure, the 2 lotus st ink pots on dolphin supports d shell base, 19thC, 12in (31cm) ıg.
50-400 *P(M)*

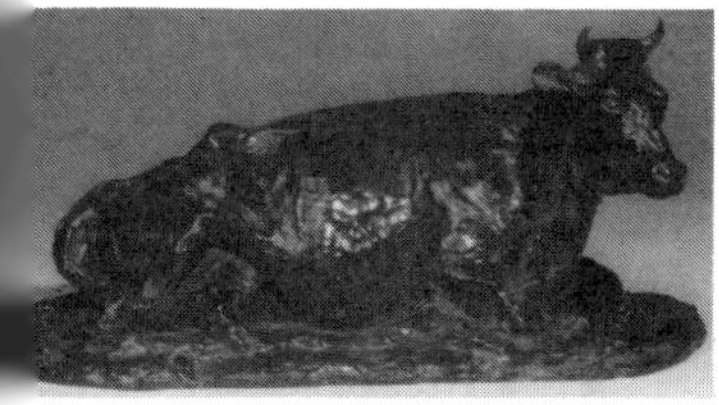

Italo-Russian bronze model of a umbent cow, cast from a model Prince Paul Troubetskoy, on a turalistic base, signed Troubetskoy 1914, and with the e perdue stamp of the Valsuani ndry, and No. 10, early 20thC, ½in (38cm) long.
500-3,500 *C*

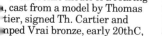

'rench bronze model of a roaring ı, cast from a model by Thomas tier, signed Th. Cartier and ıped Vrai bronze, early 20thC, ı (46cm) high.
0-1,200 *C*

A French bronze figure of the Cheval Turc, the base signed Barye, with gold F.B. stamp and F. Barbedienne Fondeur, the underside of the base stamped A.A. 45, 19thC, 7½in (19cm) high.
£3,000-5,000 *C*

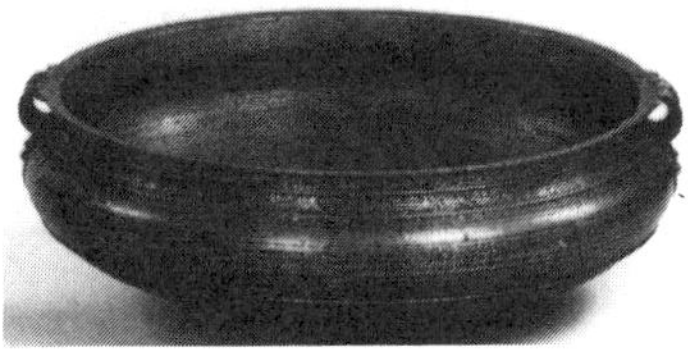

A large South Indian cast bronze ritual eating vessel, with rounded base and inturned mouth with small everted lip, the loop handle at each side with 3 ridges, an applied heart motif below, a brief Tamil inscription on the rim and shoulder below, Kerala, 18thC, 32½in (83cm) diam.
£1,000-1,500 *C*

The inscription on the rim states 'This belongs to the Panakel family', that on the shoulder gives the family house name 'Paramaswan' and another states that it has been disposed of by the family.

A pair of French bronze ornamental urns, from the Barbedienne foundry, with classical scenes on the bodies between anthemia with elegant handles and small heads each side of the tall necks, on black marble plinths, mid-19thC, 25in (64cm) high.
£1,700-2,000 *CSK*

A French table bronze and ormolu lamp, modelled with putti, 19thC.
£1,200-1,600 *LRG*

A pair of French bronze urns, after Clodion, the neck, handle and foot with foliate motifs, a musician putto seated on the handle, bearing the signature Clodion, on turned marble socles, 19thC, 19in (49cm) high.
£900-1,200 *C*

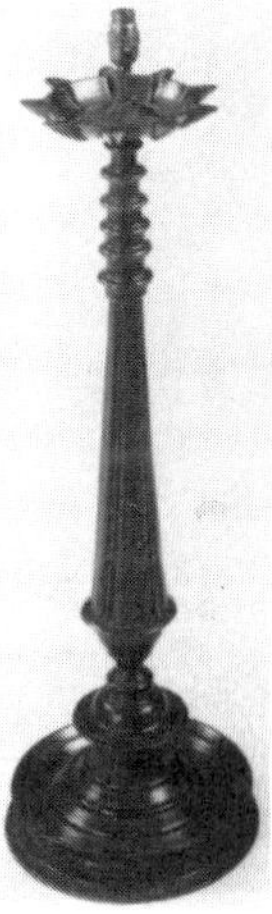

A bronze candlestick with spreading reeded stem, surmounted by a sun shaped dish, 17thC, fitted for electricity, 29in (73cm) high.
£2,500-3,000 *C*

A French bronze relief of Spring, cast from a model by Croisy, Spring shown as a seated naked nymph adorning herself with roses, with a putto holding a looking glass, signed Croisy and inscribed 'Printemps', within an ornate walnut frame with foliate brass inlay, late 19thC, with frame, 31½in (80cm) square.
£2,000-2,500 *C*

A copper preserving pan, with 2 carrying handles, c1820.
£75-125 *PCA*

Copper

A copper pan and lid, 19thC.
£100-150 *PCA*

A Tibetan gilt copper figure of a red hat lama, seated in dhyanasana, the left hand in dhyana, the right in abhaya, on double lotus base, sealed, 17thC, 7in (17.5cm) high.
£800-1,000 *C*

A copper jug, 15in (38cm) high.
£240-270 *RFA*

A English coffee pot, c1830, 7in (17.5cm) high.
£100-150 *KEY*

A copper chocolate pot, 7½in (18.5cm) high.
£300-350 *SBA*

A pair of German cold painted copper-electrotype busts of a Nubia chief and his wife, cast from mode by Rudolph Thiele, signed under th truncation R. Thiele, some chips t paint, late 19thC, 22in (55cm) hig
£3,000-4,000 *C*

A Nepalese gilt copper figure of a Dakini, the head with dharmapala crown and flaming nimbus behind, on 2 prostrate figures, on large double lotus base, scarf damaged, slight pitting, 17thC, 13½in (34.5cm) high.
£2,500-3,500 *C*

A Tibetan gilt copper figure of Vajrapani, the hair flaming behind, on double lotus base, vajra missing, 18thC, 8in (20cm) high.
£1,200-1,700 *C*

Firemarks

LONDON ASSURANCE
INCORPORATED
A.D. 1720

The London Assurance Co., c1890.
£20-25 *KEY*

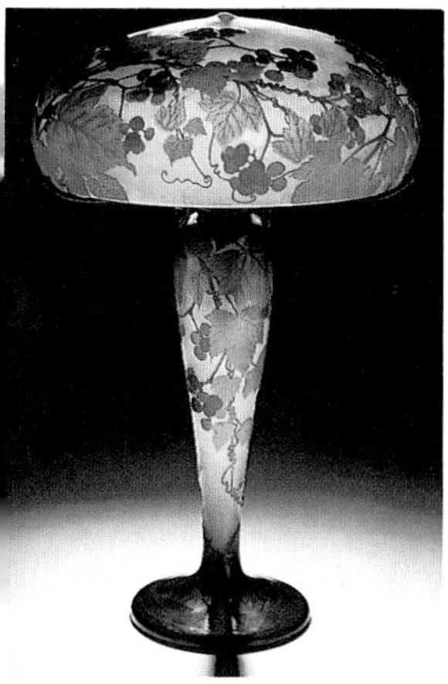

\ Gallé double overlay and
tched table lamp, shade
nd base signed, 21in (54cm).
28,000-30,000 *CNY*

A flowering dogwood leaded glass and bronze table lamp, stamped Tiffany Studios New York, 29½in (75cm) high.
£55,000-60,000 *CNY*

A Venetian leaded glass and gilt bronze table lamp, stamped Tiffany Studios New York 515, 20in (51cm).
£22,000-25,000 *CNY*

linenfold leaded glass and
onze table lamp, the 12-sided
ade stamped Tiffany Studios New
ork Pat. Appld. For 1927, the base
ffany Studios New York 370, 23in
9cm). **£10,000-12,000** *CNY*

A peony leaded glass and bronze table lamp, the shade stamped Tiffany Studios New York 1475-66, the pineapple bronze base stamped Tiffany Studios New York 366, 26in (66cm).
£55,000-60,000 *CNY*

A Tyler leaded glass and bronze table lamp, stamped Tiffany Studios New York 1440-5, 22in (56cm) high.
£8,000-9,500 *CNY*

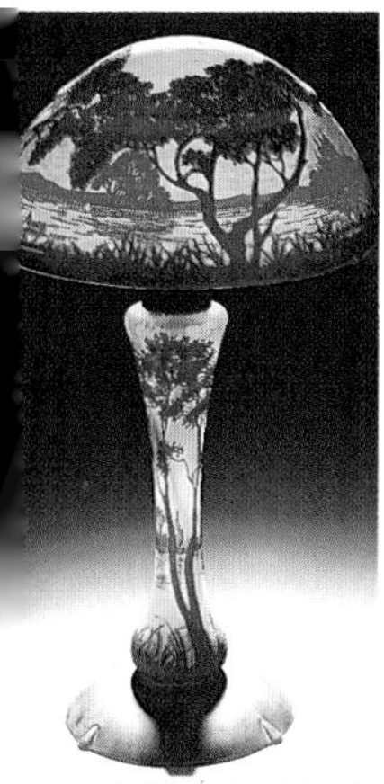

overlaid and etched glass table lamp, by
um, cameo signature Daum Nancy on shade
d base, 21in (54cm) high.
,000-18,000 *CNY*
ove r. An internally decorated glass lamp,
Daum, etched signature Daum Nancy France,
n (46cm) high.
,000-15,000 *CNY*
Gallé carved and acid etched double
rlay table lamp, with carved signature
llé, 14½in (37cm) high.
,000-14,000 *C*

A glass table lamp by Emile Gallé, the shade and base within a yellow and white frosted ground overlaid with purple-blue and etched to represent chrysanthemums, cameo signature Gallé on shade and base, 12½in (32cm) high.
£25,000-30,000 *CNY*

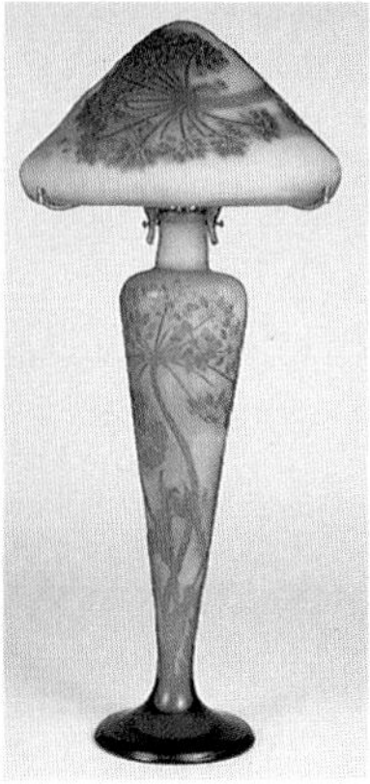

A Gallé carved and acid etched double overlay table lamp, carved signature Gallé, 25½in (65cm) high.
£15,000-20,000 *C*

A Gallé carved, acid etched and fire polished, double overlay table lamp, 23in (59cm) high.
£30,000-32,000 *C*

A double overlay and etched glass table lamp and shade, both parts signed Gallé in the overlay, 10½in (27cm) high.
£30,000-40,000 *HFG*

A double overlaid and etched glass table lamp, cameo signature Gallé, 22in (56cm) high.
£20,000-25,000 *CN*

An overlaid and etched glass table lamp, cameo signature on shade and base Gallé, 20in (51cm) high.
£30,000-40,000 *CNY*

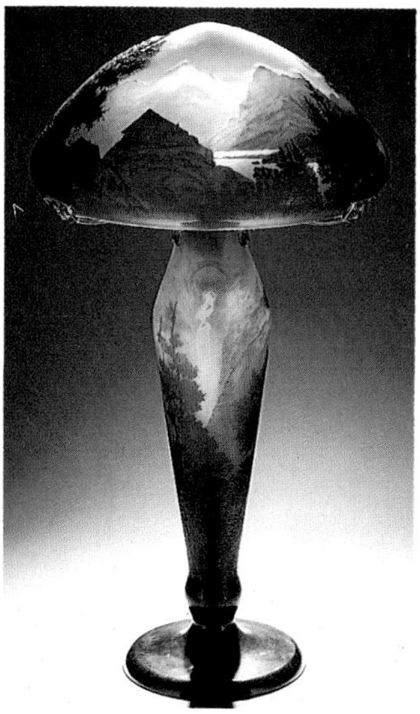

A double overlaid and etched glass table lamp, with original bronze mounts, cameo signature on shade and base Gallé, 30in (77cm) high.
£250,000+ *CNY*

A 'dragonfly' leaded glass and bronze table lamp, both shade an base stamped Tiffany Studio 18in (46cm) high.
£30,000-50,00
CNY

A 'geranium' leaded glass and bronze table lamp, stamped Tiffany Studios New York, 16½in (42cm) high.
£30,000-50,000 *CNY*

A favrile glass and metal table lamp, stamped under fuel canister Tiffany Studios, 20½in (52cm) high.
£9,000-10,000 *CNY*

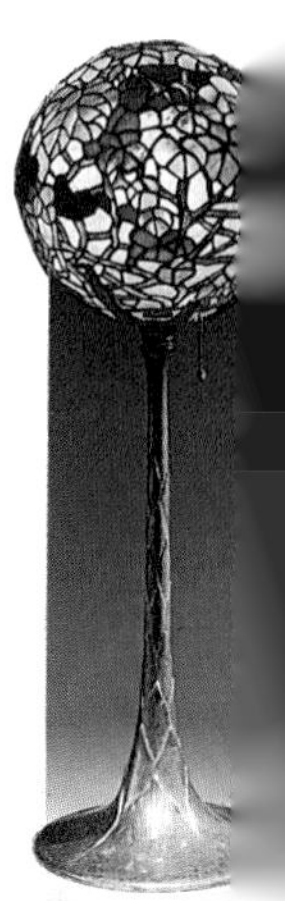

r. An 'autumn leaf' leaded glass and bronze table lamp, by Tiffany Studios, 31in (79cm) high.
£35,000-40,000 *CNY*

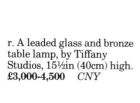

r. A leaded glass and bronze table lamp, by Tiffany Studios, 15½in (40cm) high.
£3,000-4,500 *CNY*

\ bronze base
vater lily
amp, with 10
ridescent
shades,
signed
Tiffany Studios.
:7,500-8,500 *JL*

A favrile lily 10-light glass and gilt bronze table lamp, by Tiffany Studios, 20½in (52cm) high. **£18,000-25,000** *CNY*

r. 'L'Orchidée', a lamp, from a model by Louis Chalon, French, early 20thC, 29in (74cm) high. **£4,500-5,500** *CNY*

A Cypriot glass hanging lantern, by Tiffany Studios, 18in (46cm) high. **£8,000-10,000** *CNY*

. geometric leaded glass and
ronze lamp shade, by Tiffany
tudios, 12½in (32cm) high.
5,500-6,500 *CNY*

l. A geometric leaded glass and metal chandelier, by Tiffany Studios, the shade suspended from 6 link chains, 14in (36cm) high. **£10,000-11,000** *CNY*

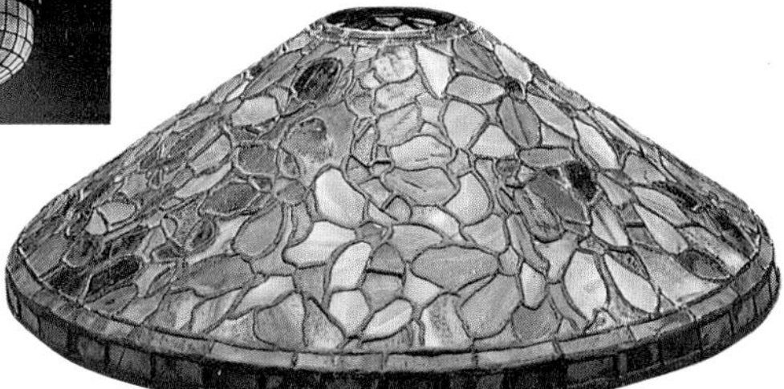

A 'Clematis' leaded glass shade, by Tiffany Studios, 18in (46cm) diam. **£25,000-30,000** *CNY*

An 'Iris' leaded glass and bronze chandelier, attributed to Tiffany Studios, 22½in (57cm) high. **£6,500-8,000** *CNY*

stained and leaded glass
ome light shade, decorated
ith grapes and leaves,
3in (71cm) diam.
500-700 *JL*

geometric 'Turtleback' chandelier,
' Tiffany Studios, 22in (56cm) high.
,000-10,000 *CNY*

A geometric 'Turtleback' tile and
aded glass hanging lantern, by
ffany Studios. **£17,000-20,000** *CNY*

An iridescent glass and brass chandelier, attributed to Kolo Moser, c1902, 25in (64cm) high. **£5,000-7,500** *CNY*

A wrought iron and glass chandelier, stamped E. Brandt.
£5,000-6,500 *CNY*

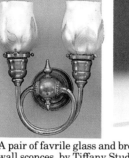

A pair of wrought iron and glass sconces, by Edgar Brandt and Daum.
£4,000-5,000 *CNY*

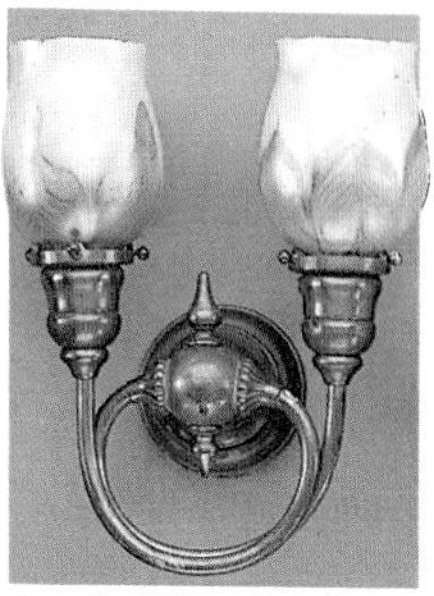

A pair of favrile glass and bronze wall sconces, by Tiffany Studios, inscribed L.C.T., 12in (31cm) high.
£4,000-5,000 *CNY*

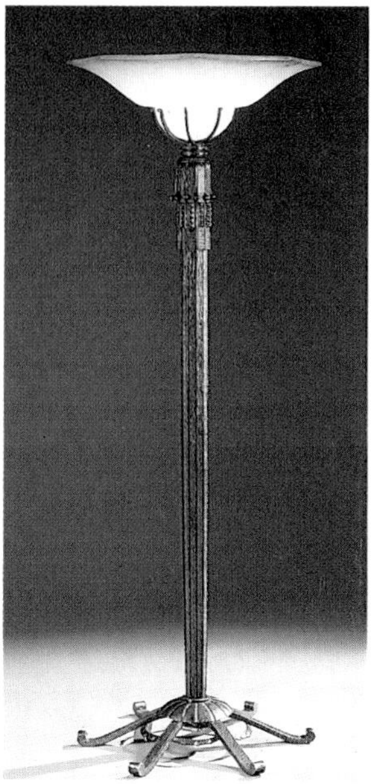

A pair of wrought iron and earthenware sconces, by the Roycrofters for Elbert Hubbard II.
£1,200-2,000 *CNY*

l. A wrought iron and alabaster floor lamp, by Raymond Subes, c1925, 70½in (179cm) high.
£15,000-20,000 *CNY*

A bronze and favrile glass mirror, by Tiffany Studios, 18in (46cm) high.
£17,000-20,000 *CNY*

A favrile glass and gilt bronze candelabra, by Tiffany Studios, fitted for electricity.
£7,500-9,000 *CNY*

A cast and wrought iron door gate, by Louis Sullivan, c1895.
£15,000-18,000 *CNY*

r. A wrought iron fire screen, by Edgar Brandt, c1925.
£20,000-25,000 *CNY*

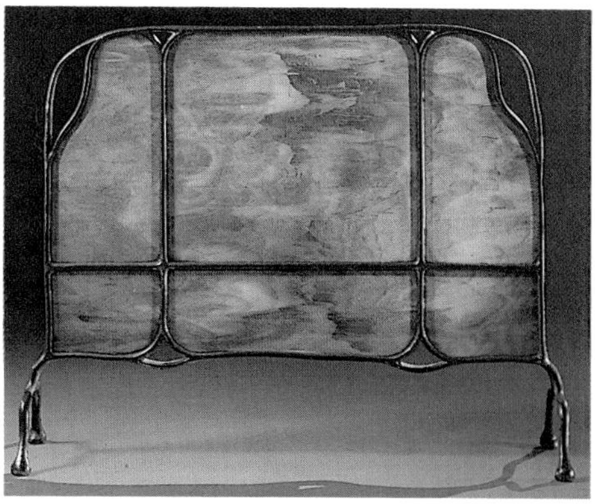

A bronze and favrile glass firescreen, by Tiffany Studios, 47in (119cm) wide. **£14,000-16,000** *CNY*

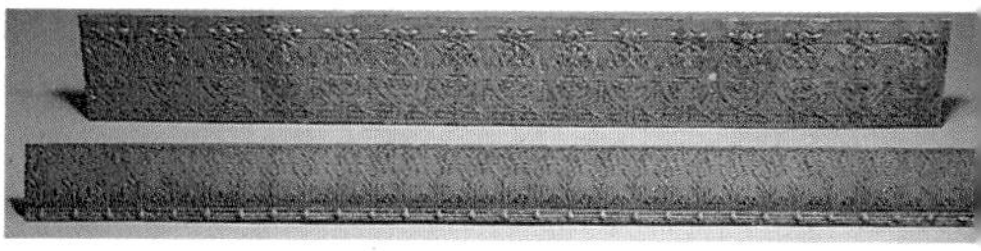

Two cast iron frieze panels, by Louis Sullivan, c1895. **£1,500-2,000** *CNY*

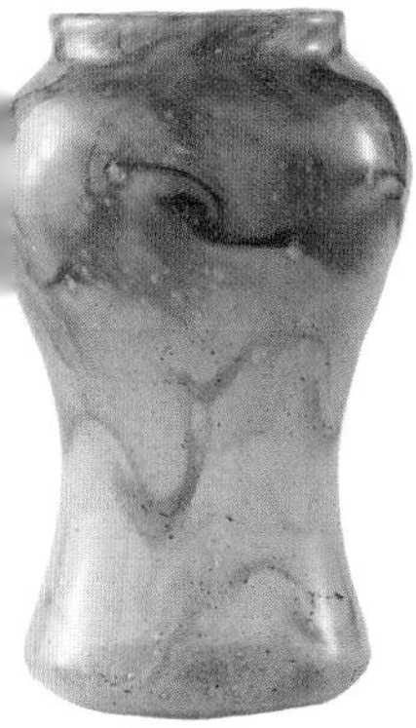

A Monart vase, blue and ochre, with whorls, 9in (23cm) high. **£200-230** *FA*

A Monart vase, the surface decorated in yellow and lustred white stripes, c1925, 8in (20cm) high. **£1,000-2,000** *FA*

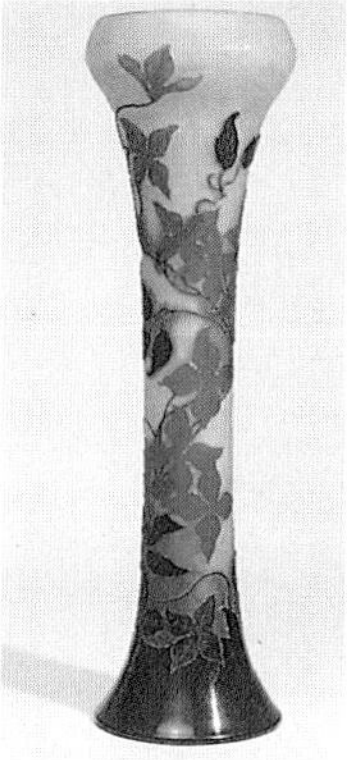

A Gallé carved, acid etched and partially fire polished vase. **£6,000-6,500** *C*

A Gallé carved and acid etched, double overlay vase, with carved signature, 12½in (32cm) high. **£6,000-7,500** *C*

. Daum martelé acid textured and arved vase. **£5,000-6,000** *C*
ıbove r. A Daum two-coloured lass vase. **£16,000-17,000** *C*

A frosted green glass vase, 'Perruches', by Rene Lalique et cie, with bronze stand, 10½in (26cm). **£10,000-11,000** *CNY*

An amber glass vase by Rene Lalique et cie, 'Serpent', 10in (25cm) high. **£10,000-11,000** *CNY*

l. A frosted amber glass vase, by Rene Lalique et cie, 'Languedoc'. **£9,000-10,000** *CNY*

r. A paperweight favrile glass vase, by Tiffany Studios, 6in (15cm). **£9,000-10,000** *CNY*

A Müller glass vase, c1900, 11in (28cm) high. **£4,000-5,000** *ABS*

l. An overlaid and etched glass vase, by Daum, Nancy, France, 15in (38cm) high. **£14,000-15,000** *CNY*

r. A gold favrile glass jack in the pulpit vase, by Tiffany Studios, 20in (51cm) high. **£9,500-11,000** *CNY*

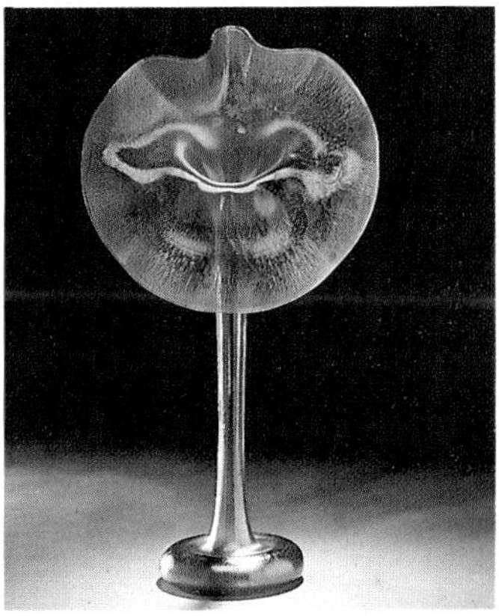

A double overlay and etched glass vase, signed Gallé, 22½in (57cm) high.
£20,000-25,000 *HFG*

A Gallé double overlay glass vase, 8in (20cm) high.
£16,000-20,000 *HFG*

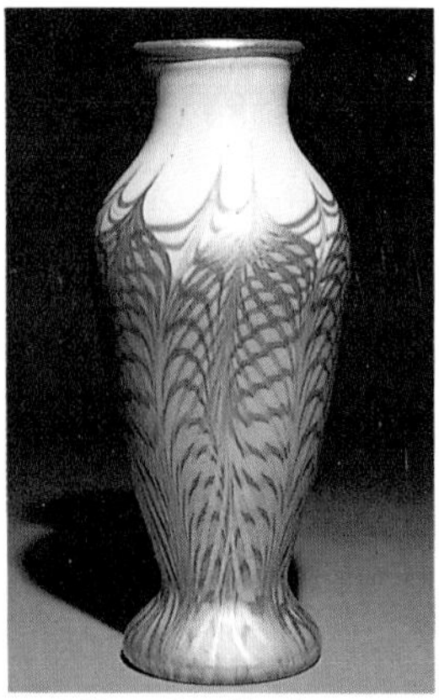

A Tiffany favrile glass vase with engraved signature L.C. Tiffany Favrile, 12½in (32.5cm) high.
£2,000-2,500 *C*

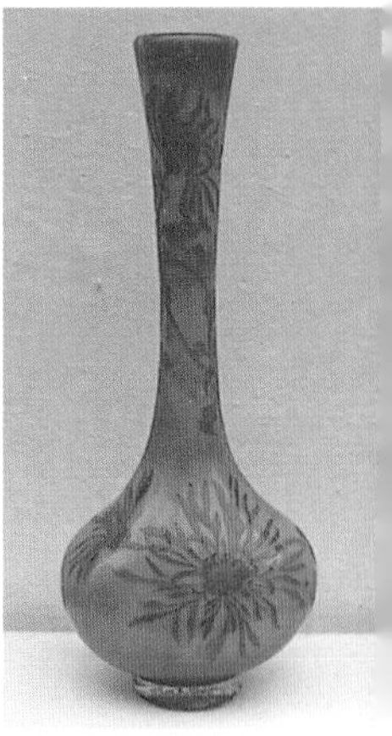

A cameo glass vase, engraved Gallé, 16in (41cm) high.
£5,000-6,000 *PSG*

A cameo glass vase, amethyst overlaid on amber, signed Gallé, 8in (20cm) high.
£3,500-4,000 *PSG*

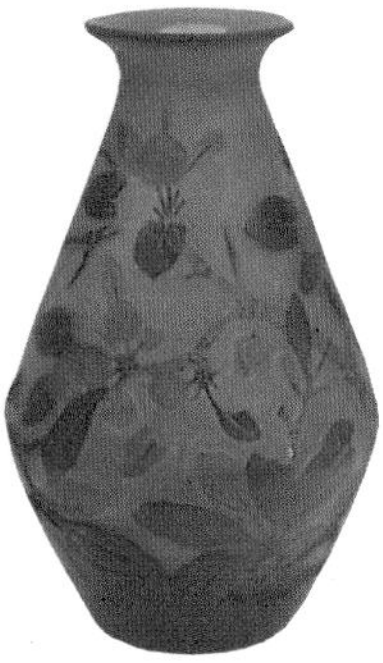

A cameo glass vase, signed Gallé, 6½in (16.5cm) high.
£1,700-2,000 *PSG*

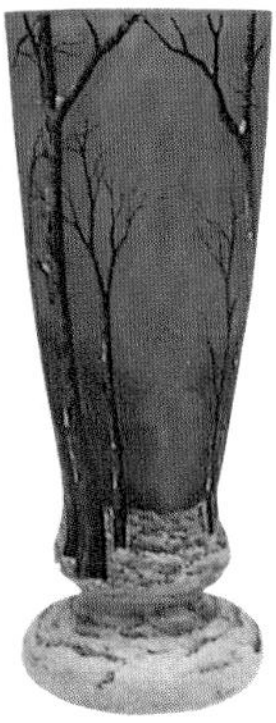

An etched and enamelled cameo glass vase, by Daum and with enamelled signature, 9in (22.5cm) high.
£2,700-3,000 *PSG*

A cameo glass landscape vase, etched and enamelled, by Daum with enamelled signature, 5in (12.5cm) high.
£2,000-2,500 *PSG*

A Monart vase, in red, black and gold, rare colour, 5½in (14cm) high.
£400-450 *FA*

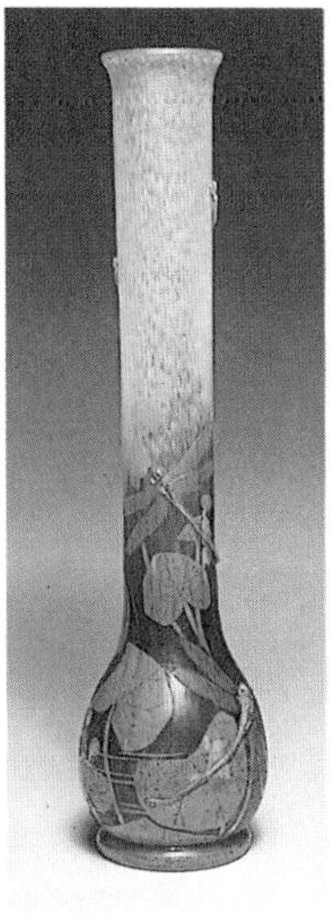

'Grand Vase Libellules', carved, acid-etched and applied, carved signature Daum Nancy, 23½in (60cm) high.
£60,000-65,000 *C*

A cameo glass vase, probably Thomas Webb, 6in (15cm) high.
£550-600 *SWO*

Two Lalique vases, 'Sophora' and 'Vases Davos', both signed, tallest 11½in (29cm).
l. **£5,500-6,000**
r. **£4,000-4,500** *C*

r. A Daum étude vase 'Anemones', engraved Daum Nancy, 9½in (23.5cm) high.
£14,000-16,000 *C*

An acid-etched, carved, enamelled and gilt decorated landscape vase, signed Daum Nancy, 11in (28cm) high.
£7,000-8,000 *C*

Gallé

A paperweight favrile glass bowl, by Tiffany Studios, inscribed 1333E L.C. Tiffany-Favrile, 8in (20cm) diam.
£4,500-5,000 *CNY*

A Le Verre Français cameo glass bowl, signed, 9in (22.5cm) high.
£900-1,000 *MAG*

A favrile glass plaque by Tiffany Studios, inscribed L.C.T., 19in (48cm). **£4,000-6,000** *CNY*

An internally decorated and engraved glass coupe, 'La Vague', engraved Daum Nancy, 6½in (16cm) high.
£20,000-25,000 *HFG*

A mould blown, overlaid and etched glass bowl, signed Gallé, 12½in (32cm) diam. **£25,000-30,000** *HFG*

A 'Grand vase de Tristesse', by Gallé for the Parish Exposition, 1889, base cracked, signed, 14in (36cm) high. **£5,500-7,500** *CNY*

A glass vase, signed Daum.
£18,000-22,000 *CNY*

A triple overlaid and etched glass vase, cameo signature Gallé, 28½in (72cm).
£15,000-18,000 *CNY*

A double overlaid and etched glass vase, cameo signature Gallé, 26in (66cm) high.
£12,000-15,000 *CNY*

An overlaid and etched glass vase, cameo signature Gallé, 15½in (40cm) high.
£5,500-7,500 *CNY*

A cameo glass vase, signed Le Verre Français.
£800-1,000 *MAG*

A cameo glass vase, signed Le Verre Français.
£800-1,000 *MAG*

r. An internally decorated glass vase, marked Gallé.
£50,000-60,000 *HFG*

l. A cameo glass vase, signed Le Verre Français, 19in (48cm). **£600-800** *MAG*

Three Powell guitar style vases, in tangerine, green and blue, c1965, 7in (18cm) high.
£20-40 each *SWa*

Three Powell 'log' vases, the coloured glass cased in clear, c1965, 6 to 9in (15 to 23cm) high. **£15-45 each** *SWa*

A Concetta Mason blown glass bowl, entitled Blue Fire, engraved marks, c1987, 12in (30.5cm).
£600-1,200 *CNY*

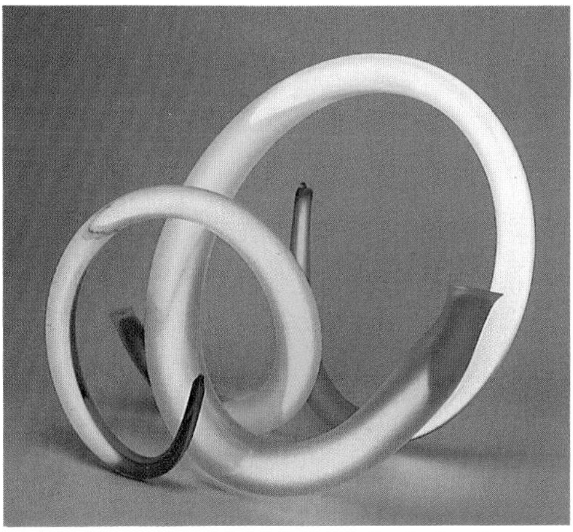

A Paul Seide frosted spiral radio light, complete with base and transmitter, 1 glass element engraved Seide, c1987. **£1,200-2,500** *CNY*

A Paul Ysart crown weight, in pink, blue, green and white, original label, c1970. **£450-550** *FA*

A Paul Ysart paperweight, red and green salamander, very rare, c1970.
£1,000-2,000 *FA*

Monart jug, in blue, ack and gold, 10in 5cm) high.
50-450 *FA*

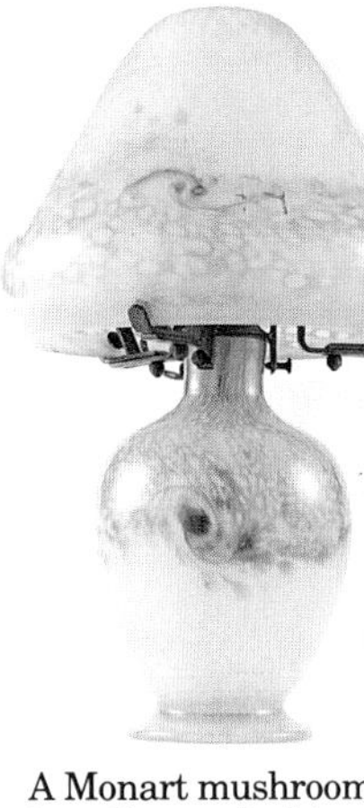

A Monart mushroom lamp, in yellow and white, probably post-war, with original label.
£1,500-2,500 *FA*

A Whitefriars lemonade set, comprising 6 glasses and jug, c1938, jug 6½in (17cm) high.
£75-80 *SWa*

An exotic bird series bowl form, by Toots Zynsky, 1987, 7½ by 16in (19 by 41cm).
£650-750 *CNY*

A clear glass vessel form, with surface application, by Joel Philip Myers, 1987. **£350-400** *CNY*

l. An enamelled and metal vase, by Camille Faure, in abstract designs, 7in (18cm) high.
£1,000-1,700 *CNY*

A Clarice Cliff plate with painted scene, Rock of Gibraltar, 9in (23cm).
£600-800 *BEV*

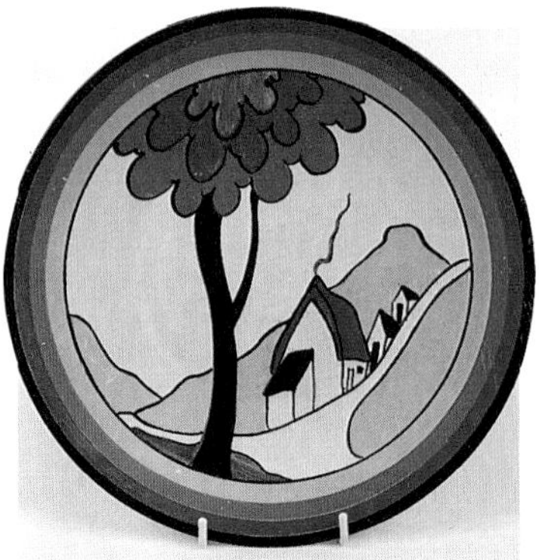

A Clarice Cliff painted plate, House and Tree, 9in (23cm).
£500-700 *BEV*

A Clarice Cliff painted plate, Crinoline Lady, 9in (23cm).
£300-500 *BEV*

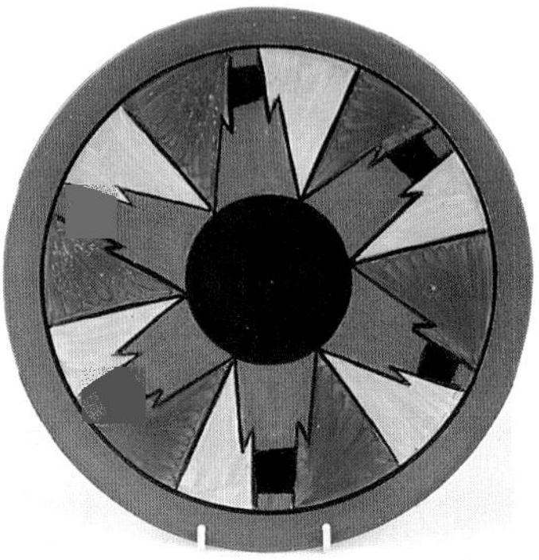

A Clarice Cliff plate, early geometric, by C. Cliff, c1925, 10½in (26cm). **£450-600** *BEV*

A Clarice Cliff painted plate, 'Gardenia', 9½in (24cm).
£400-600 *BEV*

A Clarice Cliff blue and yellow un-named plate, 9in (23cm).
£400-600 *BEV*

A Clarice Cliff painted plate, Orange tree cottage, 9in (23cm). **£600-800** *BEV*

A Clarice Cliff early geometric painted plate, 7in (18cm).
£200-300 *BEV*

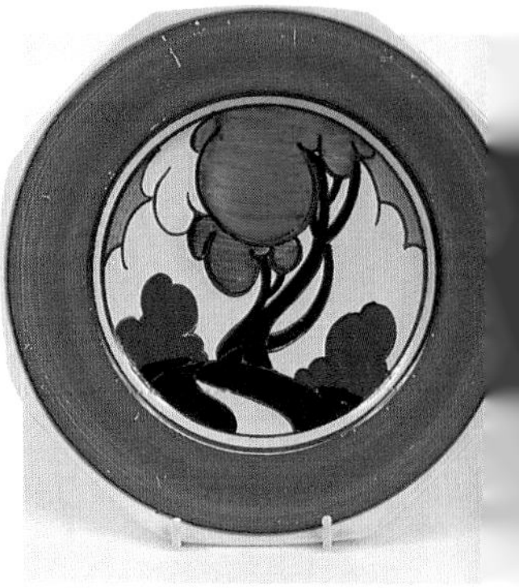

A Clarice Cliff painted plate, Autumn, 9in (23cm).
£400-600 *BEV*

A Clarice Cliff painted plate, Solitude, 9in (23cm).
£400-600 *BEV*

A Maling ware charger, c1930, 16in (41cm).
£400-450 *PC*

A Maling ware plate with an embossed design, Irises, 11in (28cm).
£150-200 *BEV*

A William de Morgan plate, 'Panthers', decorated on reverse, 9½in (24cm). **£900-1,200** *BLO*

A Foley Intarsio tea caddy, c1900, 6in (15cm) high.
£300-400 *AJ*

A 21-piece Shelley Deco tea service, in a blue, black and silver block pattern, c1931. **£800-900** *AJ*

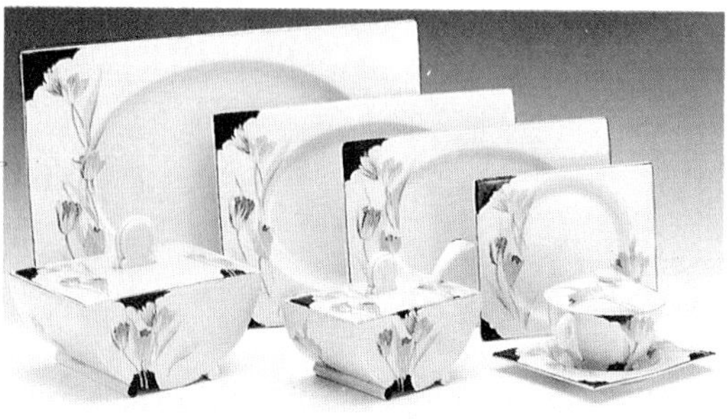

A Clarice Cliff 50-piece painted dinner service.
£2,000-2,500 *Bea*

A Shelley Deco 21-piece Orange J pattern tea service, no teapot, c1931. **£800-900** *AJ*

A Quimper cup and saucer, Deco period, signed, saucer 7½in (19cm), cup 4½in (11cm). **£25-30** *VH*

A Clarice Cliff Patina tea set, comprising: milk jug, sugar bowl, cup, saucer and plate, teapot 5in (13cm) high.
£900-1,000 *BEV*

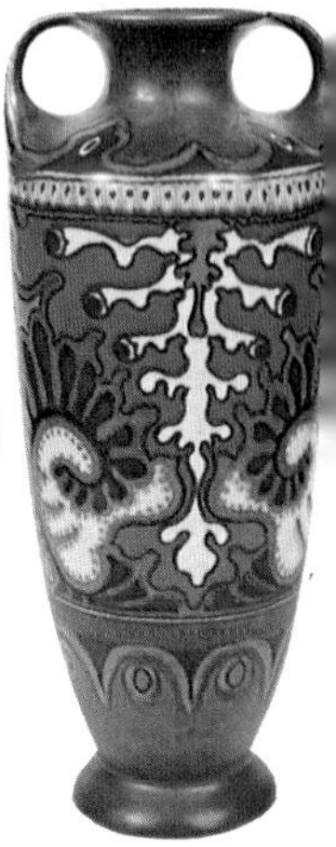

A pair of Villeroy and Boch vases, Dutch, c1900.
£350-450 *BEV*

A pair of Villeroy and Boch jars, c1900, 7in (18cm) high.
£250-350 *BEV*

A Minton vase, brown with gold decorations, Aesthetic influence, c1886, 12in (31cm) high.
£550-650 *BLO*

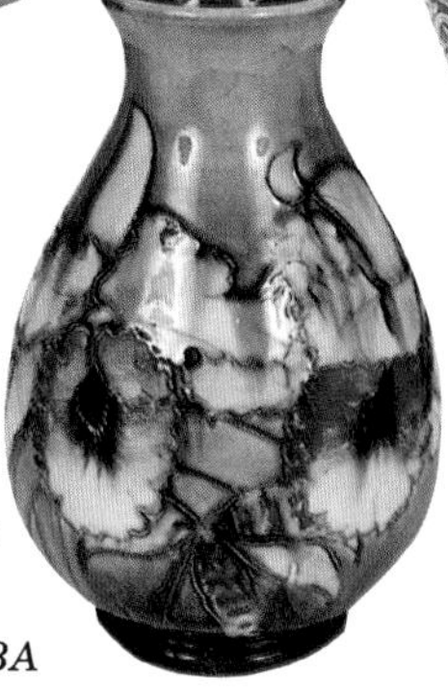

r. A Moorcroft vase, 9½in (24cm) high.
£450-500 *SBA*

A Foley Intarsio vase, Frederick Rhead design, chicken and hens, 9in (23cm) high.
£600-800 *PC*

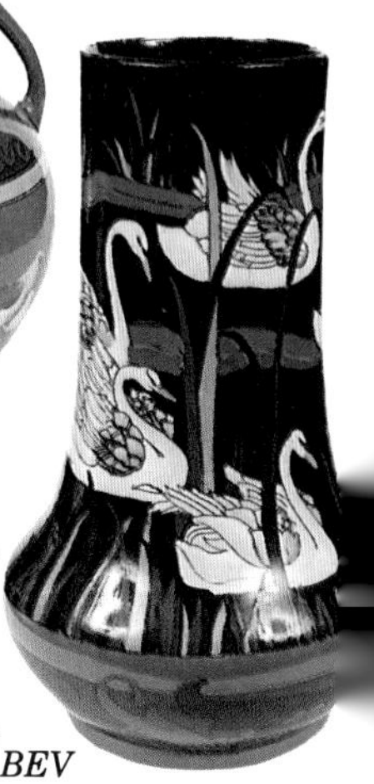

r. A Frederick Rhead swan design vase, 12½in (32cm) high. **£850-950** *BEV*

A Foley Intarsio bowl with Shakespeare scene, c1900, 11½in (29cm). **£500-600** *AJ*

A Clarice Cliff bowl with Kandina pattern, 8in (20cm). **£450-500** *BEV*

A Shelley lustre bowl, signed by Walter Slater, c1920, 7in (18cm) high. **£150-200** *AJ*

A Bernard Moore bowl, initialled by Cicely Jackson, 9in (22.5cm). **£250-300** *BLO*

An Austrian amphora blue and white flower holder, 9in (22.5cm) high. **£180-200** *BLO*

An Ault Grotesque jug, 7in (17.5cm) high. **£300-350** *BLO*

A Clarice Cliff Lotus jug with the Inspiration Caprice pattern, rim cracked, 12in (30.5cm). **£1,000-1,200** *SWO*

\ porcelain Limousine vater jug, 8in (20cm) ıigh. **80-100** *BLO*

A Foley Intarsio jardinière in the Goose pattern, c1900, 4½in (11cm) high. **£300-400** *AJ*

l. A Foley Intarsio jardinière on stand by Frederick Rhead. **£2,000-2,500** *PC*

A Clarice Cliff step jardinière, 3½in (8.5cm) high. **£200-250** *BEV*

. pair of Liberty & Co. toneware jardinières, esigned by Archibald .nox, 16in (41cm) high. **2,500-3,000** *C*

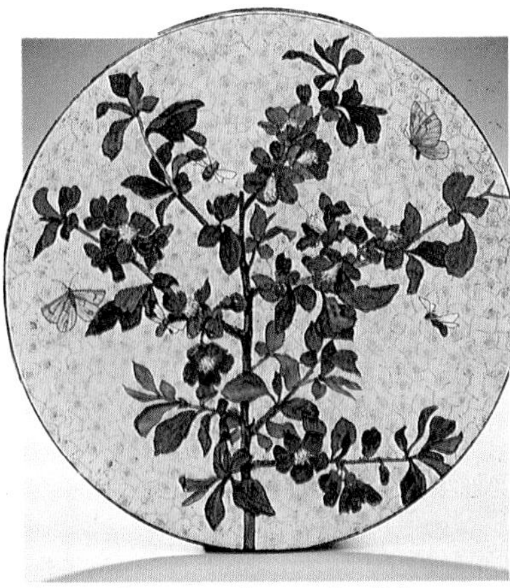

An earthenware charger by John Bennett, signed, 1878, 14½in (37cm). **£3,000-3,500** *CNY*

A Minton blank painted by an amateur painter, exhibited in 1883, 10in (25cm). **£100-150** *BLO*

A Clarice Cliff early geometric vase, 8in (20cm) high. **£550-600** *BEV*
Above r. A Clarice Cliff umbrellas and rain vase, 10in (25cm). **£800-1,000** *BEV*

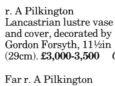

r. A Pilkington Lancastrian lustre vase and cover, decorated by Gordon Forsyth, 11½in (29cm). **£3,000-3,500** *C*

Far r. A Pilkington Royal Lancastrian lustre vase, decorated by William S. Mycock, 11in (28cm). **£900-1,000** *C*

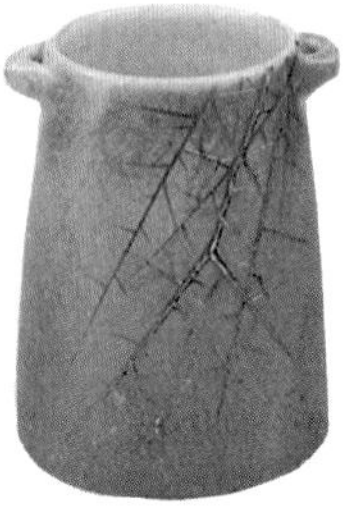

l. A Clément Massier vase, painted by Lucien Levy-Dhurmer, 4in (10cm) high. **£80-100** *BLO*

A Goebels ceramic glass-eyed gnome, 8in (22cm).
See below.

A Goldscheider figure, 15½in (39cm) high. **£800-1,000** *BEV*

A Continental majolica vase, in yellow, blue and lime, 5in (13cm). **£60-80** *BLO*

A Bernard Moore vase, initialled, 7½in (19cm). **£250-280** *BLO*

A set of 13 Goebels ceramic glass-eyed lamps. **£4,500-5,000** *BIZ*

r. A Goldscheider figure, 15in (38.5cm) high. **£900-1,000** *BEV*

An Intarsio clock, by Frederick Rhead, 13½in (35cm) high. **£450-480** *BEV*

Puff Puff
Toff-Toff

A pair of bisque porcelain figures, c1910, 7½in (19cm) high. **£200-250** *IW*

A Goldscheider figure, 12in (30.5cm) high. **£600-800** *BEV*

r. A Goldscheider figure, 17in (43.5cm) high. **£1,200-1,500** *BEV*

A Moorcroft brown chrysanthemum vase, signed W. Moorcroft, retailer's mark Spalding & Company, c1910, 12in (30.5cm). **£3,000-4,000** *C*

A Pilkington Royal Lancastrian lustre vase, decorated by Gordon Forsyth, impressed, signed and dated 1911, 25in (63cm). **£4,000-4,500** *C*

A porcelain centrepiece, by Adelaide Alsop Robineau, carved with artist's monogram and incised 1926, damaged in the firing, 13in (33cm) diam. **£23,000-25,000** *CNY*

l. A Goldscheider figure of a skier, 11in (28cm). **£600-650** *BEV*
r. A Goldscheider figure, 11in (28cm). **£400-450** *BEV*

\ Goldscheider figure ased on the Ballet Russe, designed by Lestial, 17½in (44cm). **2,500-3,000** *BEV*

A Goldscheider golfing figure, 9in (23cm). **£350-400** *BEV*

A Goldscheider figure by Clare Weiss, 13in (34cm). **£500-550** *BEV*

A Daum etched and enamelled cameo glass bowl, etched signature, 6in (15cm) diam. **£1,000-1,200** *PSG*

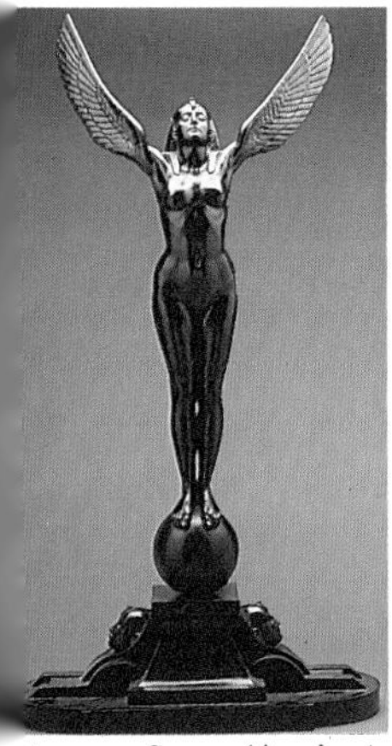

bronze figure 'Ancient istory' by Haig Patigian aris, 1907, signed and npressed with foundry al, 38in (96.5cm). **,000-7,000** *CNY*

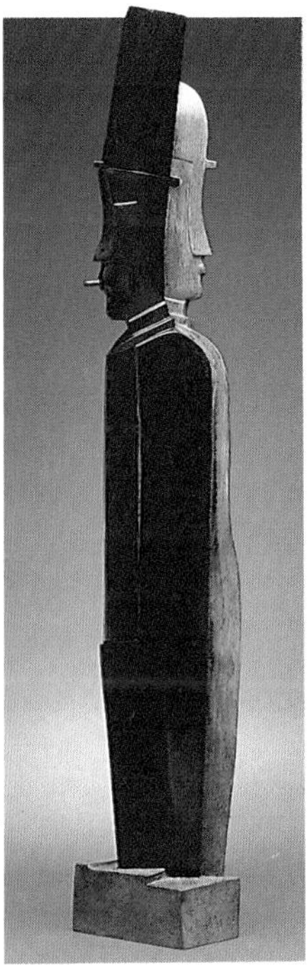

A polychrome bronze oup 'Les Noctambules' Jean Lambert-Rucki, 925, signed, 29in (75cm). **0,000-25,000** *CNY*

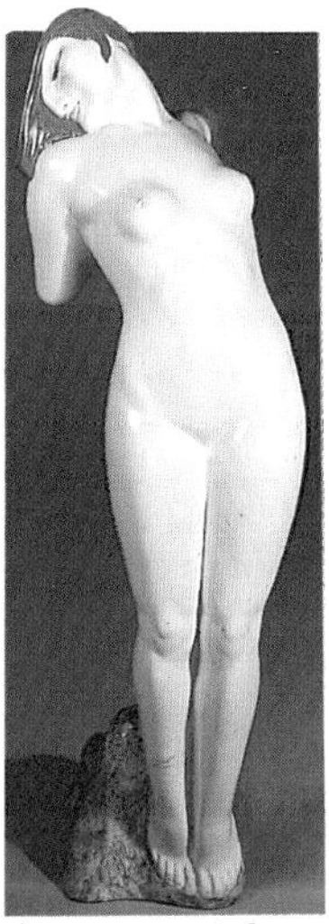

A monumental Lenci ceramic figure, with impressed signature Gnni Riva, 39in (99cm). **£6,500-8,500** *C*

A Gallé cameo glass bowl, signed in cameo, 6in (15cm) diam. **£1,700-2,000** *PSG*

A Daum etched and enamelled cameo glass bowl, signed in enamel, 6in (15cm) diam. **£1,700-2,000** *PSG*

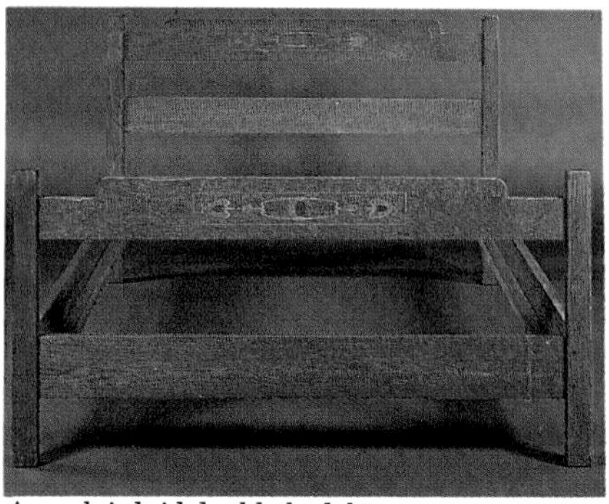

An oak inlaid double bed, by Gustav Stickley and used in his home at Morris Plains, New Jersey, c1909, 58in (147cm) wide.
£12,000-15,000 *CNY*

An oak double bed by Gustav Stickley, c1901, 58in (147cm) wide.
£8,000-9,000 *CNY*

A pair of oak beds by Gustav Stickley, c1909, 45in (114cm) wide.
£2,000-2,500 *CNY*

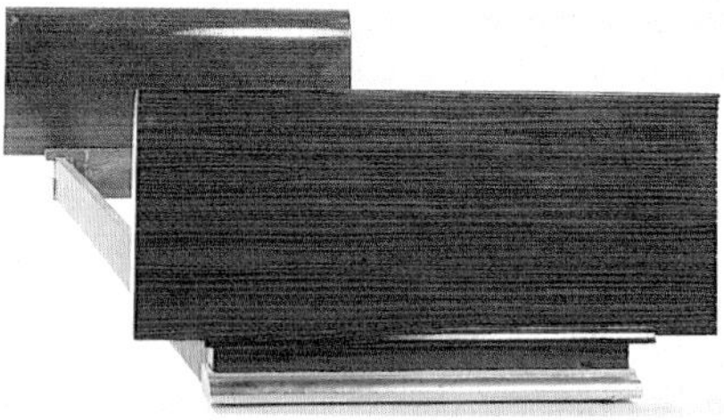

l. An Ebène de Macassar bed, by Emile Jacques Ruhlmann, 43in (109cm) wide.
£2,500-3,000 *C*
r. A walnut and ebonised bedroom suite, designed by Gio Ponti.
£3,000-3,500 *C*

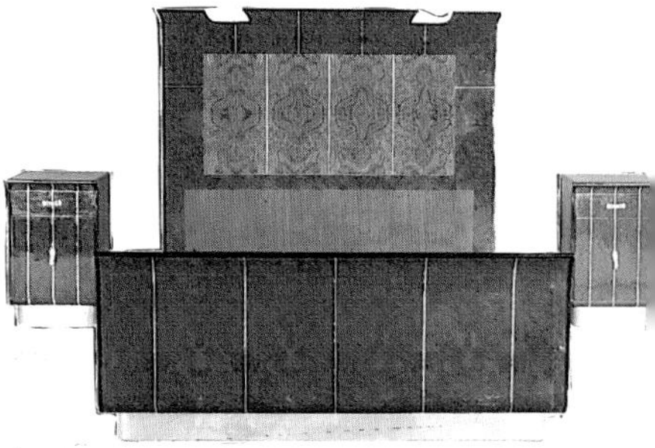

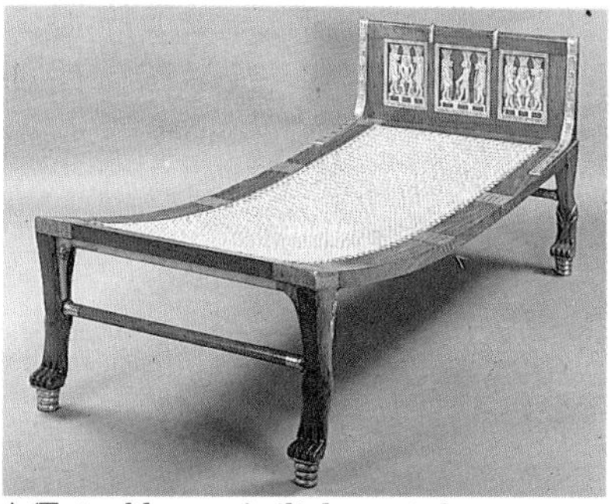

A 'Tutankhamun' gilt decorated mahogany daybed, in the style of J. Moyr-Smith, with cushion and bolsters, 69½in (176cm) long.
£3,000-3,500 *C*

An oak bookcase, by Gustav Stickley for the interior of his Craftsman Farms home, Morris Plains, New Jersey, c1909, 62in (157cm) wide.
£2,500-3,000 *CNY*

A chestnut bookcase in 2 sections, with adjustable shelves, by Gustav Stickley, c1909, 94½in (239cm) wide.
£3,000-4,000 *CNY*

r. An oak book rack, by Gustav Stickley, c1909, 33in (84cm) wide.
£2,500-3,500 *CNY*

A rare oak book shelf and cabinet by Gustav Stickley, with 3 adjustable shelves, c1904, 38in (96.5cm) wide. **£4,000-5,000** *CNY*

A Continental carved mahogany china cabinet, c1900, 81in (205.5cm) high.
£12,000-15,000 *CNY*
l. An oak armoire, by Gustav Stickley for the interior of his Craftsman Farms home, Morris Plains, New Jersey, c1909, 77in (195.5cm) high.
£5,500-6,500 *CNY*

An inlaid mahogany music cabinet, designed by Harvey Ellis, by Gustav Stickley, c1904, 48in (122cm) high.
£5,000-6,000 *CNY*

A burr walnut and marquetry, desk by Oscar Kaufmann, 1918, 102½in (260cm) wide. **£12,000-15,000** *C*
l. An oak drop front desk by Charles Rohlfs, 1902, 54in (137cm) high. **£14,000-17,000** *CNY*
r. An oak mirror, by Gustav Stickley, c1909. **£1,200-1,500** *CNY*

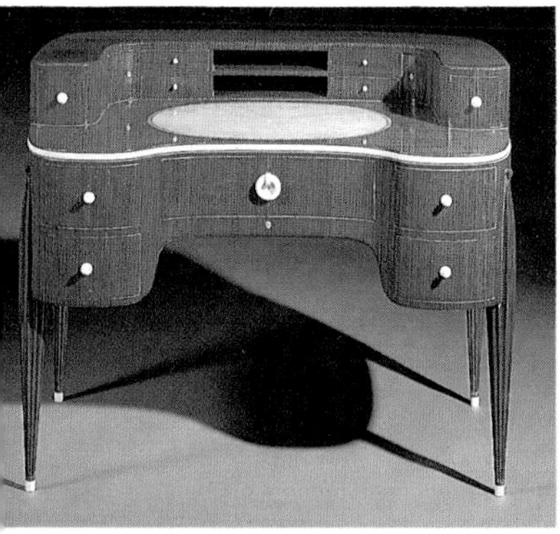

l. A palissandre and ivory desk, by Jacques-Emile Ruhlmann, 1927, 47in (119cm) wide.
£100,000+ *CNY*
r. An oak legged sideboard, by Gustav Stickley, c1902, 70in (178cm) wide.
£3,000-3,500 *CNY*

A carved mahogany and marquetry sideboard, by Louis Majorelle, with inset marble top, 65in (165cm) wide. **£22,000-25,000** *CNY*
l. A rare oak serving board, by Gustav Stickley, c1902, 60in (152cm) wide.
£8,000-9,000 *CNY*

A carved and marquetry vitrine, by Louis Majorelle, 68½in (174cm) high.
£7,000-8,000 *HFG*

l. A rosewood and walnut coffee table, by George Nakashima, 70½in (178cm) long.
£4,000-5,000 *CNY*
r. A table by Jacques-Emile Ruhlmann, c1932, 134in (342cm).
£35,000-40,000 *CNY*

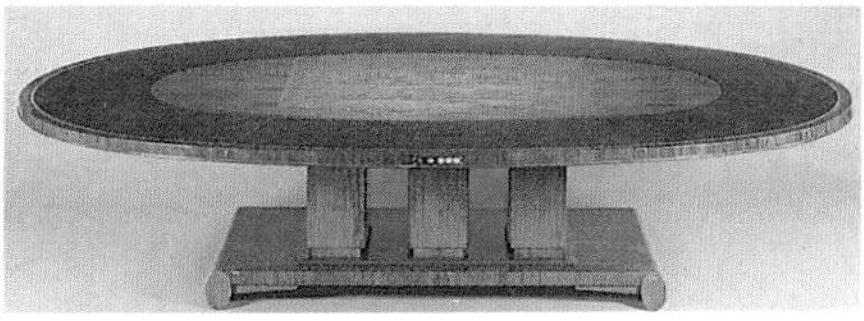

l. An oak dining table by Gordon Russell, labelled and dated 1923, 66in (167.5cm).
£3,000-3,500 *C*
r. A coffee table, by Jacques-Emile Ruhlmann, 31½in (80cm) diam.
£16,000-18,000 *CNY*

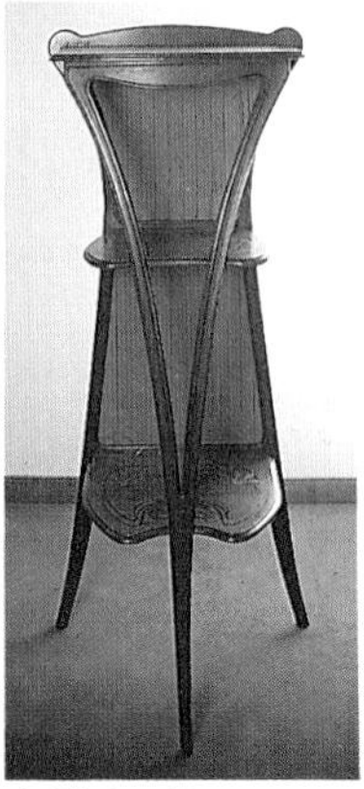

A Majorelle walnut and marquetry etagère, 48½in (123cm) high.
£2,000-2,500 *C*

A marquetry two-tier table, inlaid with flowers and leaves, signed Gallé Nancy, 17in (43cm) wide.
£3,000-4,000 *CNY*

An oak director's table, by Gustav Stickley, with branded mark, c1912, 72in (182.5cm).
£6,500-7,500 *CNY*

A burr walnut and marquetry centre table, designed by Oskar Kaufmann, 41½in (105cm) diam.
£4,000-5,000 *C*

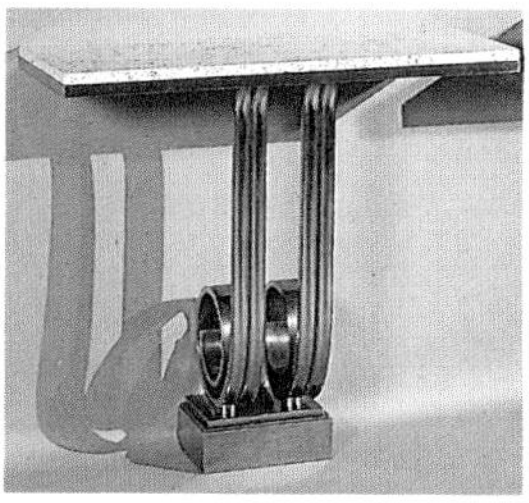

A pair of steel and marble consoles, 32in (81cm) high.
£9,000-10,000 *CNY*

r. A carved mahogany side table, by Louis Majorelle, 39in (99cm) high.
£4,000-5,000 *CNY*

An oak two-drawer library table, by Gustav Stickley, the drawers with hand forged oval pulls, model No. 461, c1905, 54in (137cm) wide. **£500-1,000** *CNY*

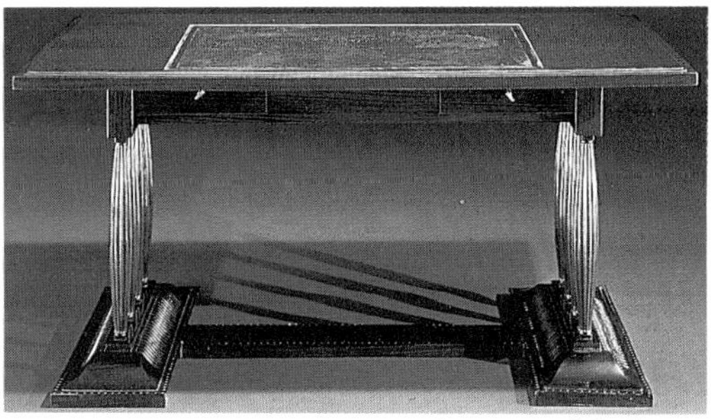

A rosewood desk, by Jacques-Emile Ruhlmann, the top inset with a leather panel, fitted with 2 drawers, branded, c1925, 60in (152cm) wide.
£120,000-150,000

l. An oak and brass dinner gong, by Gustav Stickley, c1909, 24in (61cm) wide.
£4,500-6,500 *CNY*

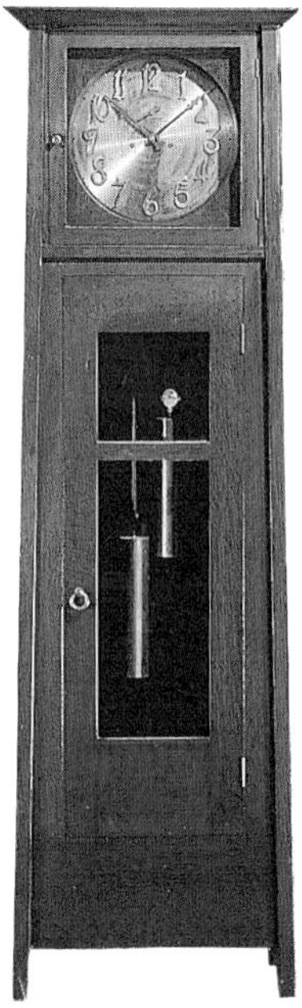

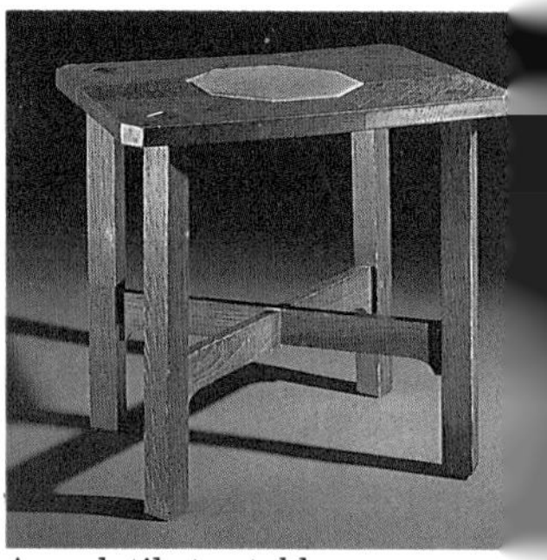

An oak tile top table, by Gustav Stickley, labelled, c1905, 24in (61cm) wide.
£9,000-11,000 *CNY*

l. A longcase clock, by Gustav Stickley, labelled, Model No. 3, 72in (183cm) high.
£30,000-40,000 *CNY*

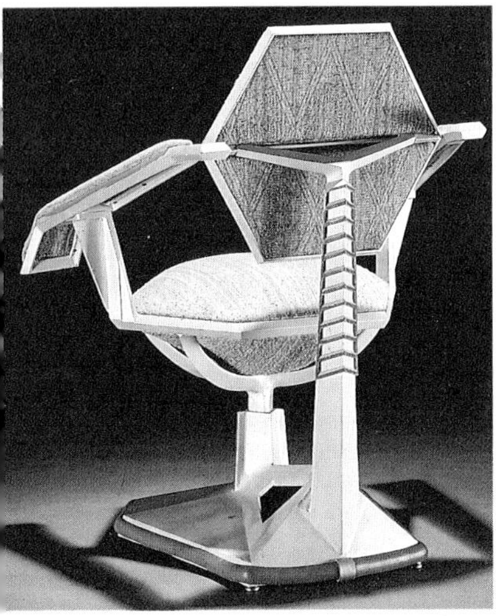

An aluminium chair, designed by Frank Lloyd Wright for the H. C. Price Co. Tower, Bartlesville, Oklahoma, c1954, 32½in (85cm) high.
£28,000-30,000 *CNY*

A Tidewater cypress end table, designed by Frank Lloyd Wright for the Misses Austin, Greenville, Carolina, c1951, 26in (66.5cm) high.
£17,000-20,000 *CNY*

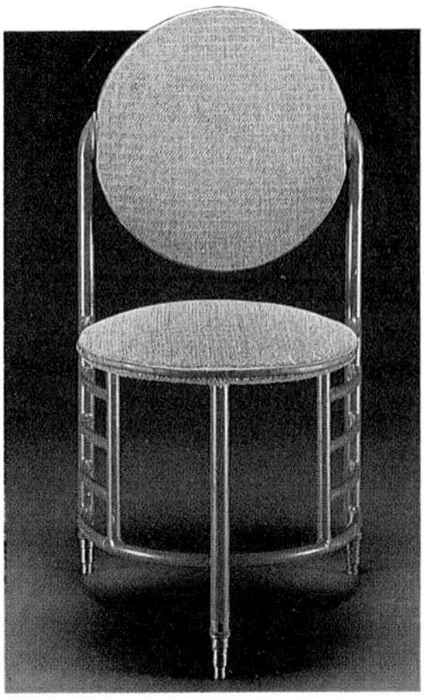

A tubular steel desk chair, designed by Frank Lloyd Wright for the S. C. Johnson Building, Racine, Wisconsin, c1936, 35in (89cm) high.
£45,000-50,000 *CNY*

Two Tidewater cypress dining tables ınd 6 chairs, by Frank Lloyd Wright or the Misses Austin, c1951.
:17,000-20,000 *CNY*

. A leaded glass window, by Frank .loyd Wright for the J. J. Walser ıouse, Chicago, Illinois, c1903, 5in (165cm) high. **£3,000-6,000** *CNY*

A gilt bronze and glass table lamp, by Frank Lloyd Wright for the Susan Lawrence Dana house, Springfield, Illinois, c1903, 10in (25cm) high.
£14,000-16,000 *CNY*

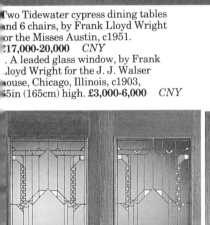

pair of leaded glass doors, by Frank loyd Wright for the Francis W. ittle house, Wayzata, Minnesota, .913, each 79in (200.5cm) high.
15,000-20,000 *CNY*

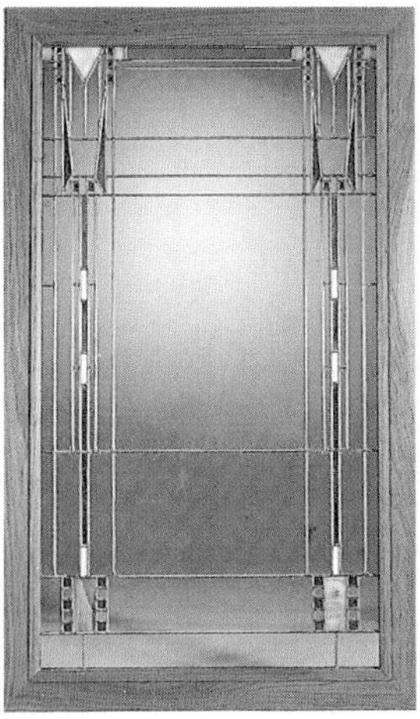

A leaded glass window, by Marion Mahony for the Gerald Mahony house, Elkhardt, Indiana, c1905, 47in (119cm) high framed.
£2,500-5,000 *CNY*

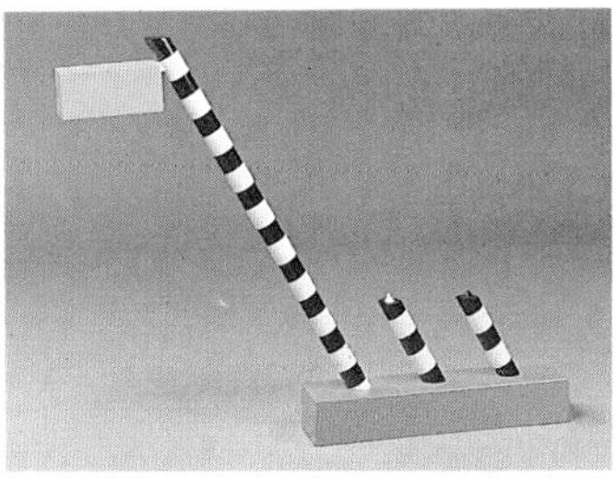

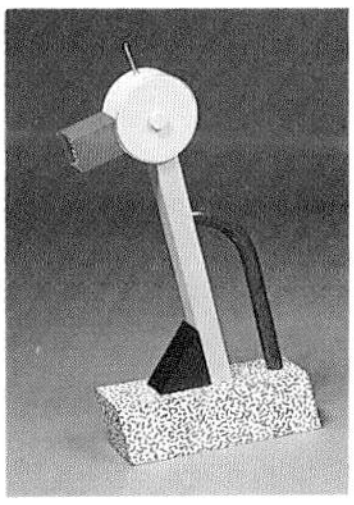

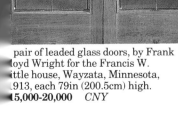

A Memphis lacquered metal table lamp, by Michele de Lucchi, 1981, 29in (74cm) high. **£600-800** *C*

l. A table lamp by Ettore Sottsass, 1981, 27½in (69.5cm) high.
£1,000-1,500 *C*

An Art Deco maple 3-piece suite, the design attributed to Maurice Adams, the sofa with waved padded back, rounded upholstered seat and scroll end arms on platform base, comprising a sofa and 2 armchairs, sofa 71½in (181cm) wide. **£6,000-8,000** *C*

r. A Carlo Bugatti ebonised, inlaid and painted vellum side chair.
£3,000-4,000
and table.
£7,000-8,000 *C*

l. An Edwin Lutyens 'Napoleon' chair, 38½in (98cm) wide.
£6,000-8,000 *C*

A carved mahogany dining table and a set of 12 dining chairs, by the firm of Louis Majorelle, the table with 3 additional leaves, 117in (297cm) extended. **£15,000-19,000** *CNY*

A set of 6 carved mahogany 'clematis' sidechairs, by the firm of Louis Majorelle, 37in (94cm) high. **£2,500-3,500** *CNY*
l. A beechwood and mahogany 'Sitz Machine' chair, c1912, 39in (99cm) high. **£25,000-30,000** *CNY*

A set of 4 mahogany dining chairs, from the oceanliner 'Normandie', 35in (89cm) high. **£12,000-15,000** *CNY*

A chair, model No. MR 90, known as the 'Barcelona Chair', designed by Ludwig Mies Van Der Rohe, Director of the Bauhaus, c1931. **£80,000-90,000** *CAm*
l. An inlaid oak armchair, designed by Harvey Ellis, c1904. **£7,500-11,000** *CNY*

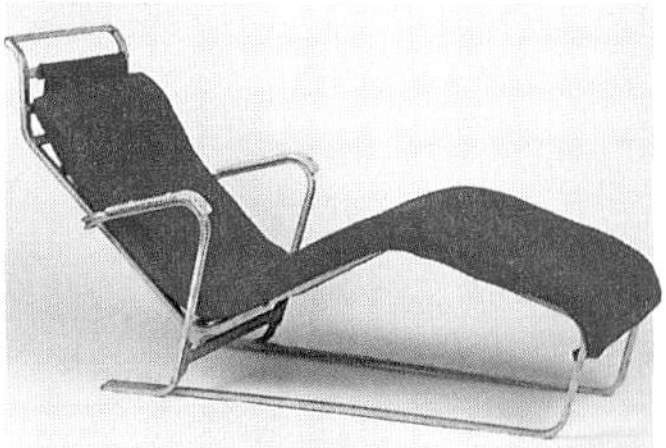

An aluminium chaise longue, designed by Marcel Breuer, Director of Bauhaus furniture workshop 1925-28, the arm supports set with wooden handles, c1935, 53in (134cm) long.
£10,000-12,000 *CAm*

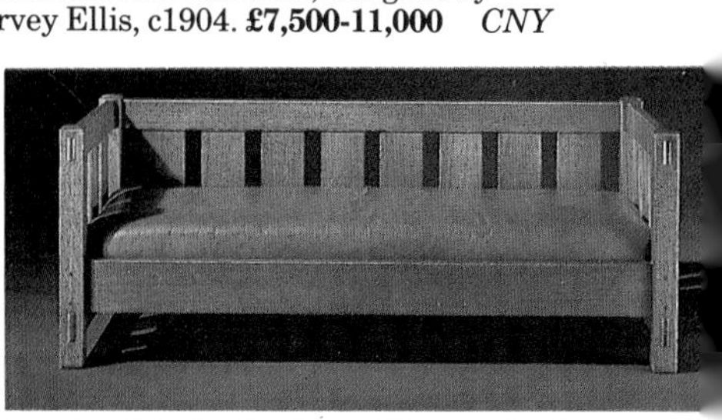

An oak settle, by the firm of Gustav Stickley, with branded mark, model No. 208, c1912, 76in (193cm) long. **£7,500-9,000** *CNY*
l. A walnut stool, designed by Pierre Chareau, the top moulded and shaped in a delicate scroll, 18in (46cm) high.
£10,000-11,000 *CNY*

ʌn ashtray, executed at
he Bauhaus metal
vorkshop, stamped
Bauhaus, c1924,
2½in (6cm) high.
£8,000-9,000 *CAm*

'Tee Extraktkannchen', a silver and ebony Bauhaus teapot, fitted with a tea strainer, by Marianne Brandt, c1924, 3in (7.5cm).
£120,000-125,000 *CAm*

A hand wrought hammered silver and ebony Bauhaus coffee pot, sterling and 925 silver mark, 8½in (21cm) high.
£9,000-11,000 *CAm*

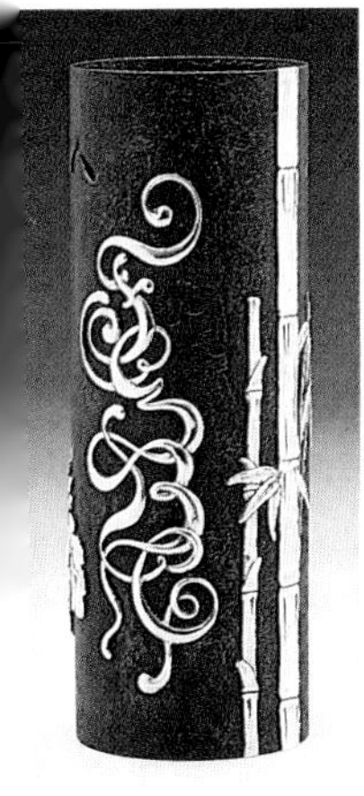

silver mounted
on cylindrical
ase, by Tiffany
Co., New York,
1880, 9in (23cm)
igh.
,000-7,500 *CNY*

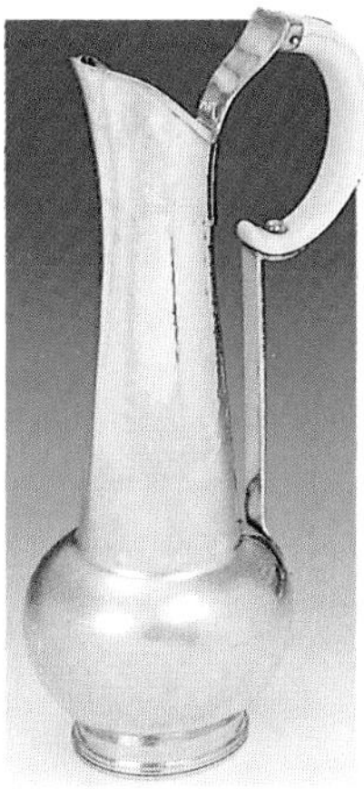

A metal plated brass tea caddy, stamped Bauhaus, c1925, 8½in (20cm) high. **£12,000-13,000** *CAm*

Above r. A hand wrought hammered silver and ivory wine jug, with applied shaped strap handle, interrupted by a crescent shaped ivory grip, stamped with maker's monogram CD, with 800 silver mark, 11½in (30cm) high. **£23,000-25,000** *CAm*

A hand wrought hammered silver and ebony, Bauhaus coffee pot, stamped CD and 900 silver mark, 9in (23cm) high. **£30,000-35,000** *CAm*

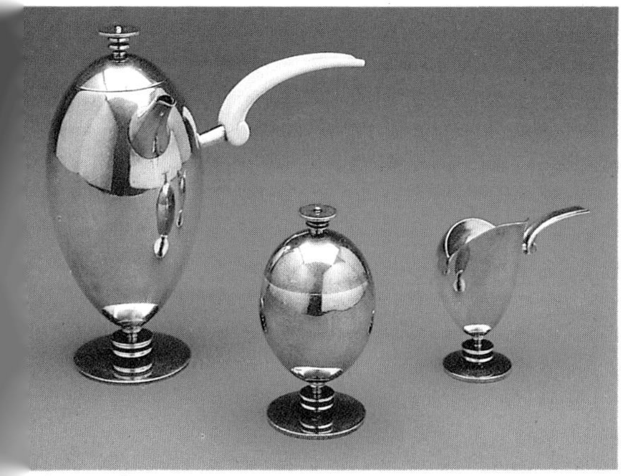

silver and
ory espresso
rvice, and
demi-tasse
oons, for
eorg Jensen,
935, 22oz
oss.
,000-5,000 *CNY*

A silver espresso service, designed by Johan Rohde for Georg Jensen silversmithy, comprising: a coffee pot, cream pitcher, and sugar bowl, and a tray, maker's marks, coffee pot 7in (18cm) high.
£5,500-6,500 *CNY*

silver plated,
a and coffee
rvice, W.M.F.
,000-3,000 *CNY*

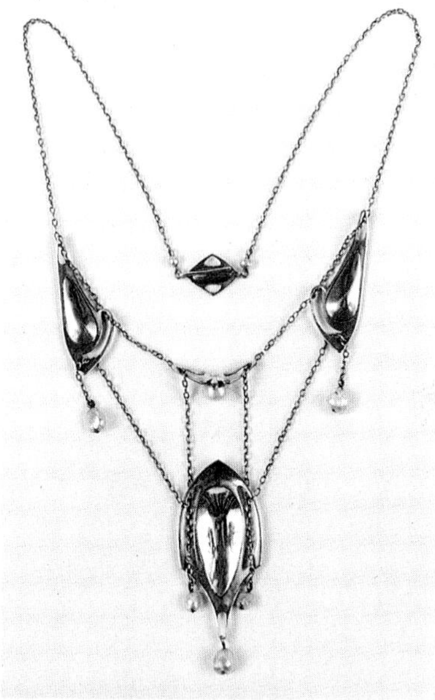

A Liberty gold, mother-of-pearl and pearl necklace, designed by Archibald Knox.
£3,000-3,500 *DID*

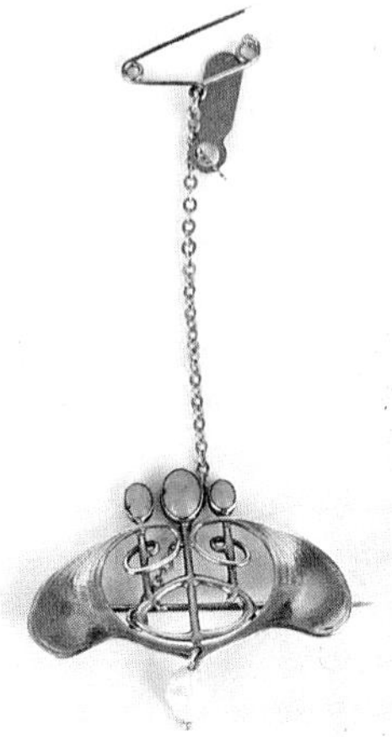

An Art Nouveau 15ct gold turquoise and pearl brooch by Murlle Bennett & Co., c1910.
£400-450 *DID*

A Liberty Art Nouveau opal pendant, possibly designed by Oliver Baker.
£1,200-1,500 *DID*

A Liberty gold and opal ring designed by Archibald Knox, marked.
£900-1,200 *DID*

A Liberty gold, opal and pearl pendant, designed by Archibald Knox.
£2,500-3,000 *DID*

A gold, opal and pearl necklace, designed by Archibald Knox.
£2,500-3,000 *DID*

A gold and turquoise pendant, designed by Archibald Knox.
£2,500-3,000 *DID*

A Liberty gold and turquoise pendant, by Archibald Knox.
£5,500-6,000 *DID*

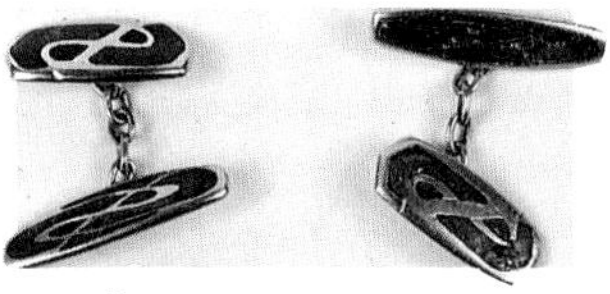

Above and l. A pair of Liberty cuff links and a Liberty pendant designed by Archibald Knox.
Cuff links, **£2-2,500** *DID*
Pendant, **£1-1,500** *DID*

A Liberty platinum pendant by Archibald Knox.
£4,000-4,500 *DID*

A Liberty gold and mother-of-pearl bracelet by Archibald Knox.
£2,000-2,500 *DID*

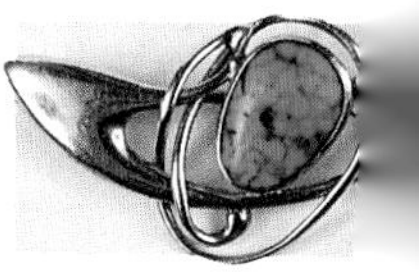

r. A Liberty gold and turquoise brooch, designed by Archibald Knox.
£1,200-1,500 *DID*

ι stoneware bowl by Lucie Rie, white
ınd blue pitted glaze, impressed LR
eal, c1982, 10½in (26cm) diam.
6,000-8,000 *Bon*

A stoneware bowl by Lucie Rie, c1983. **£4,000-4,500** *Bon*
l. A stoneware bowl by Lucie Rie, c1969.
£5,000-7,000 *Bon*

deep pink porcelain bowl
y Lucie Rie, impressed LR
eal, c1979, 9in (23cm).
4,000-5,000 *Bon*

A shiny green porcelain bowl, with golden bronze 'running' rim, by Lucie Rie, impressed LR seal, c1980, 8in (20cm) diam. **£3,000-4,000** *Bon*

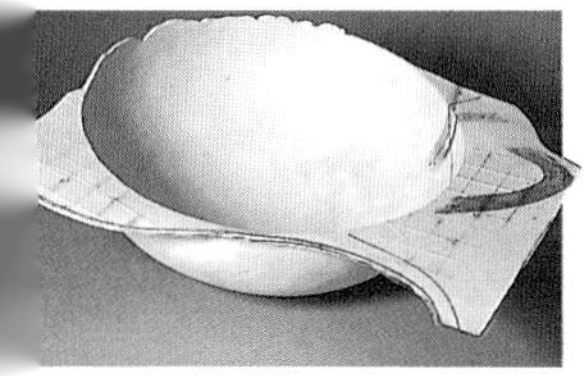

white bowl form, by
ordon Baldwin, signed
B 80, 20in (50cm) diam.
300-1,000 *Bon*

A large stoneware bowl by Bernard Leach, c1960.
£800-1,000 *Bon*

A porcelain bowl by Bernard Leach, white with blue Chinese landscape, small repaired kiln crack, c1925. **£4,000-5,000** *Bon*

stoneware bowl
Lucie Rie,
ıpressed LR,
984.
,000-4,000 *Bon*

l. A stoneware cup form, by Hans Coper, on drum foot with ochre and matt manganese blistering, c1972, 6in (15cm) high.
£17,000-19,000 *C*

vin candleholders,
Hans Coper,
ıck and bronze,
pressed HC
ıls and 1966.
0,000-90,000 *Bon*

A large bowl by Katherine Pleydell-Bouverie, impressed KPB seal, c1955, 13½in (34cm) diam.
£500-800 *Bon*

r. A white stoneware cup form by Hans Coper, impressed HC seal, c1970, 7in (17cm) high.
£12,000-14,000 *Bon*

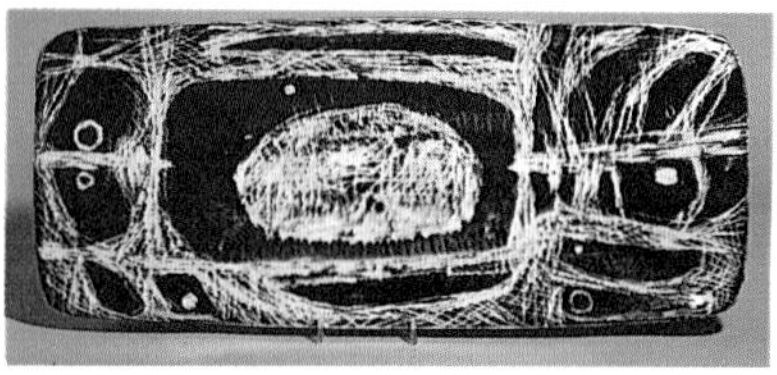

An earthenware shallow rectangular dish, by James Tower, inscribed J. Tower 1953, 22in (56cm) wide.
£1,500-2,000 *C*
r. A handbuilt stoneware irregular dish, by Ewen Henderson, 23½in (60cm) wide. **£700-1,000** *C*

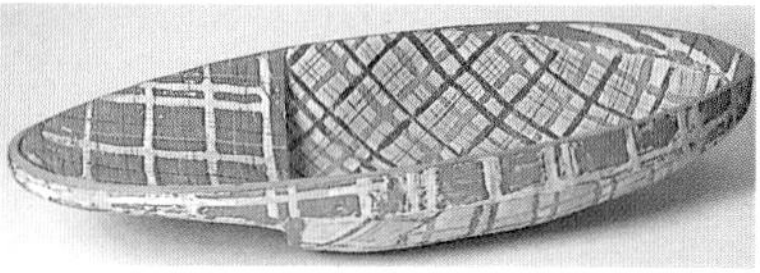

An eliptical boat vessel, by Jacqueline Poncelet, 23in (58cm) long.
£900-1,100 *Bon*

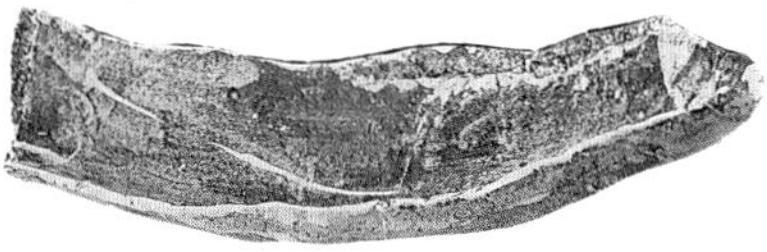

An earthenware dish by John Piper.
£600-800 *Bon*

A stoneware dish, by Hans Coper, impressed HC seal, c1952, 8in (20cm) wide.
£15,000-20,000 *C*

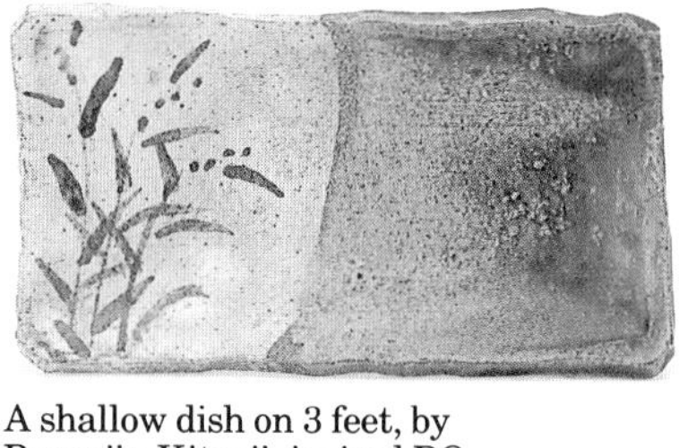

A shallow dish on 3 feet, by Rosanjin Kitaoji, incised RO signature, 8½in (21.5cm) wide.
£3,500-4,000 *Bon*

A stoneware charger, by Michael Cardew, marked MC
£2,000-2,500 *C*

A stoneware spout pot, by Elizabeth Fritsch, 7in (17.5cm) high.
£3,000-3,500 *Bon*

A stoneware spout pot, by Elizabeth Fritsch, with undulating rim, c1974.
£4,000-4,500 *Bon*

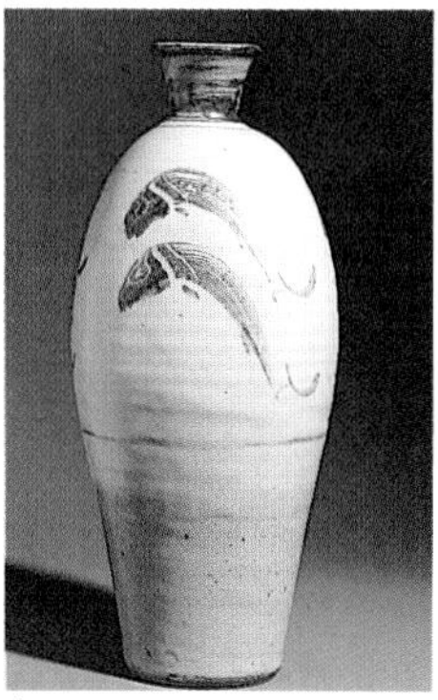

A stoneware vase, by Bernard Leach, impressed BL and St. Ives seals.
£4,500-5,000 *C*

A stoneware vase, by Lucie Rie, marked LR seal, c1960, 16in (41cm).
£7,000-10,000 *Bo*
l. A 'volcanic glazed' vase, by Hugh Cornwall Robertson for Dedham Pottery, marked by the artist and the Pottery, 8in (20cm) high.
£2,500-3,000 *CN*

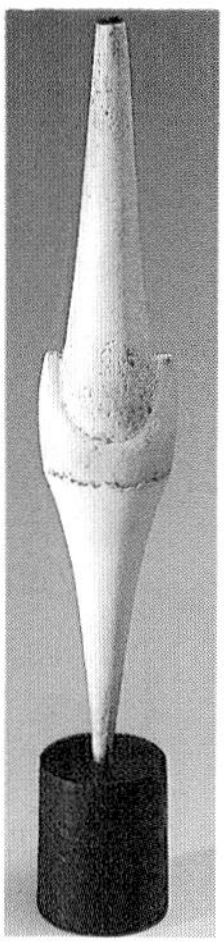

Above l. A porcelain vase by Lucie Rie, marked LR seal, c1980, 9½in (24cm). **£3,500-4,000** *Bon*
Above r. A 'Cycladic' vessel form, by Hans Coper, 1976. **£25-30,000** *Bon*

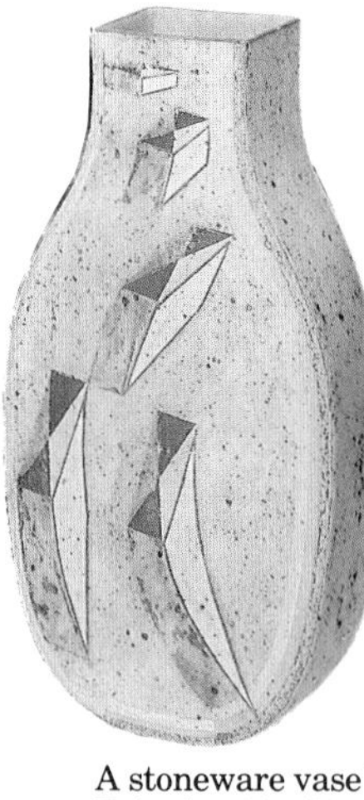

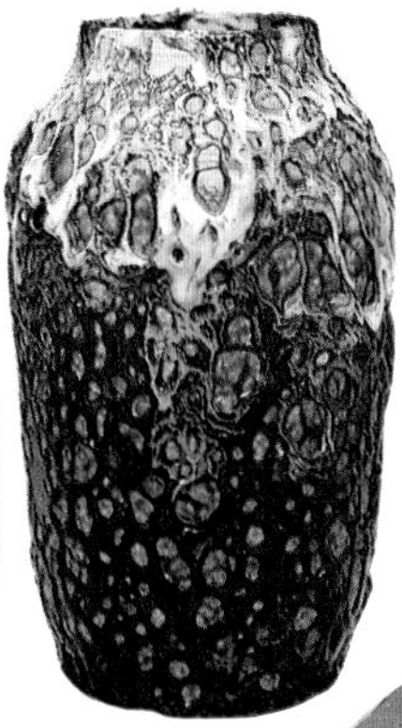

A stoneware vase by Elizabeth Fritsch, 13in (33cm).
£3,000-4,000 *Bon*
r. A vase by Shoji Hamada, c1950, 10in (25cm). **£6,000-7,000** *Bon*

ıe Yorkshire Fire and Life ɜurance Co., copper, c1860, 9½in ɫcm).
0-80 *KEY*

The Farmers and General Fire and Life Insurance Institution, copper, c1850, 10½in (26cm).
£50-80 *KEY*

The Royal Insurance Co., copper, c1850, 12in (30cm).
£40-50 *KEY*

The Royal Exchange Assurance, lead, c1830, 9in (22cm) high.
£60-70 *KEY*

ron

iron bed head, 46in (116.5cm) h.
0-130 *AL*

l. A plain hogscraper candlestick, c1800, r. a hogscraper rushnip, c1790, c. a wedding band hogscraper candlestick, c1800, 7½in (18.5cm) high.
£50-150 each *KEY*

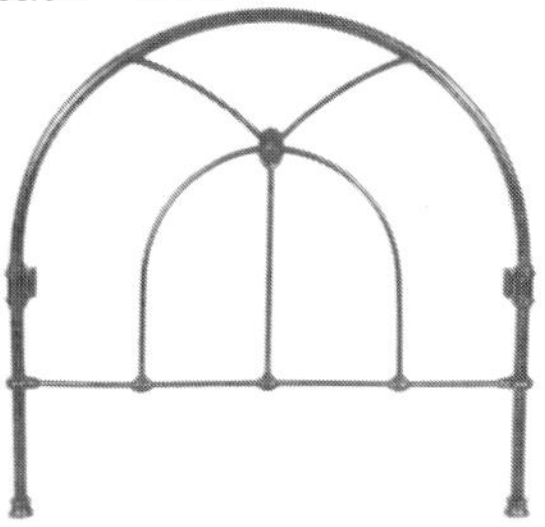

An iron bed foot, 32½in (82cm) high.
£100-120 *AL*

roup of keys dating from 1680 to).
20 each *KEY*

An English wrought iron rushnip, 18thC, 6in (15cm).
£160-190 *KEY*

A pair of gold painted cast iron figures of recumbent lions, their front paws crossed, 19thC, 31in (79cm) long.
£800-900 *C*

A pair of wrought iron wafering irons, with blacksmith's tong handles, the 2 flat discs engraved with the Pascal Lamb and a coat-of-arms, both within foliate cartouche surrounds, inscribed 1750, 30in (76.5cm) long.
£450-500 *CSK*

Wafer irons, which are certainly known from the mid-14thC, were used in making wafer bread for the Mass and other religious ceremonies. Their use, however, was not entirely confined to the ecclesiastical.

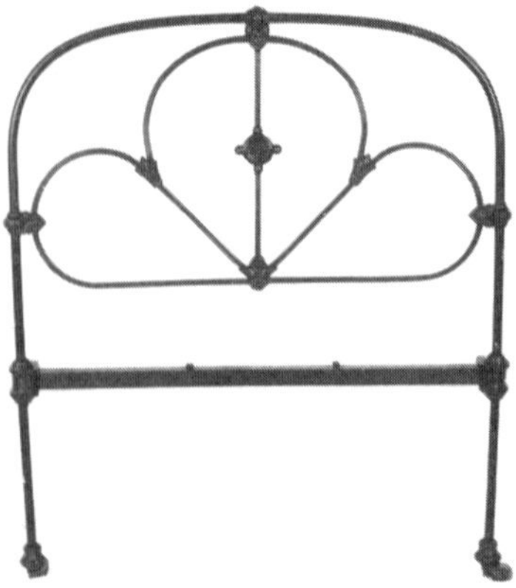

An iron bed head.
£100-140 *AL*

A rocking cradle, 37in (94cm) lon
£170-200 *AL*

Lead

A pair of Continental figures of a youth and girl in a dancing pose, the girl with a tambourine, 19thC, 38½ and 40in (97 and 101.5cm) high.
£2,000-2,500 *P(S)*

Ormolu

A pair of ormolu and glass tazzas, each with fluted moulded shaped dish supported by foliate S-scrolls emerging from a column flanked by 3 putti, on concave sided triangular plinth, 16in (41cm) high.
£3,500-4,500 *C*

A pair of Sèvres pattern assemble ormolu mounted 3-light candelab with turquoise ground porcelain bodies painted within gilt floral a hatched cartouches and applied with ormolu goat's mask and folia scroll handles, on spreading flute ormolu feet above royal blue porcelain cylindrical plinths and square ormolu bases, late 19thC, 19in (48.5cm) high.
£1,500-2,000 *C*

An ormolu and enamel toilet mirror, with bevelled plate enclosed by a double door with amethyst enamel floral cartouches and mirrored back, the frame with cresting of ribbon tied trophies with garlands of roses and banded with laurel, on easel stand, late 19thC, 15 by 10in (38 by 25cm).
£1,800-2,200 *C*

A pair of Louis XVI design candlesticks, the fluted bodies hung with swags, on circular beadwork and foliate chased circular bases, 11½in (29cm) high.
£550-650 *CSK*

An ormolu-mounted opaline vase, the lid pierced with scrolls, the sides with winged caryatids on circular spreading base, 12½in (32cm) high.
£800-1,000 *C*

A French 13-light floor standing candelabrum, the stepped variegated grey marble stand terminating in quadruped feet, late 19thC, 48in (122cm) high.
£2,000-2,500 *CSK*

An Empire caryatid of a putto, in the style of Thomire, supporting a stylised capital on his head, the rouge marble pedestal base with ormolu mounts, head loose, 13in (33cm) high.
£1,000-1,500 *C*

A pair of gilt metal and ivory stands, the chased and applied surmounts supported on 6 classical columns, on ball feet, 5½in (14cm) high.
£600-900 *CSK*

Miscellaneous

A cold painted spelter figure of a Moorish dancing girl, cast from a model by Louis Hottot, base signed 'L Hottot', 19thC, 30½in (78cm) high.
£1,500-2,000 *C*

A Regency painted tôle tray, painted with a scene depicting the death of General Wolfe at Quebec, after Benjamin West, on a blue ground, pierced with 2 handles underneath, with label inscribed 'The Hon. Mrs Adams Bradfield', 28½in (72.5cm) wide.
£800-1,000 *C*

A red and gilt tôle coal scuttle and cover, with scrolling decoration and a coat-of-arms, with lion mask and ring handles on claw feet, detachable liner, re-decorated, 16in (41cm) wide.
£2,000-3,000 *C*

An early Victorian black painted metal coal box and cover, with domed lid and tapering body and lion ring handles, on scrolling feet, 23in (59cm) high.
£600-800 *C*

VORY

vory/Shell

ı Italian Embriachi bone casket, e roof shaped lid with intarsia and nels of confronting angels, the les with scenes from the life of a nale saint, 4 ivory ball feet, feet placed, some restoration, late thC, 6 by 5in (14.5 by 13cm).
,500-3,000 *C*

A sailor's Valentine, the octagonal mahogany case opening to reveal an arrangement of brightly coloured sea shells, 19thC, 9½in (24cm).
£600-700 *RBB*

A French ivory statuette of Joan of Arc, opening to reveal a triptych with Joan of Arc pleading before the King, Bishop and courtiers, flanked by guards, 19thC, 6in (14.5cm) high.
£700-1,000 *C*

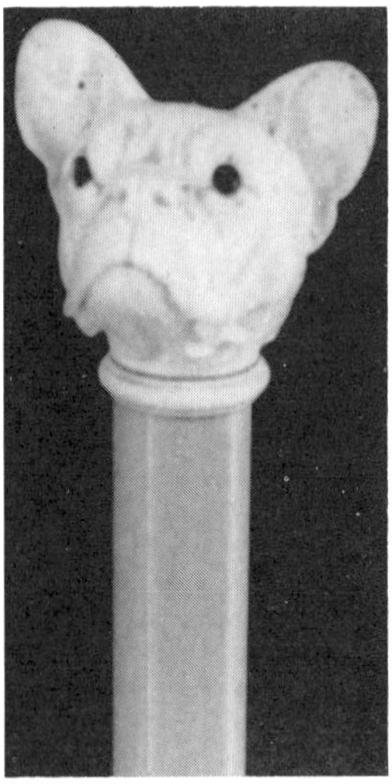

An umbrella, the handle finial of carved ivory in the form of a pug dog.
£200-250 *DEN*

A carved ivory figure of Mary Queen of Scots, opening to reveal a triptych with figures depicting a marriage ceremony, a Royal Pardon and a prison visitor, on a circular base, late 19thC, 9in (22.5cm) high.
£600-700 *HSS*

A German turned ivory box, the base and sides with wavy decoration, the screw-on lid with lobed border and flowerhead in centre, minor repair to lid, late 17thC, 4in (10cm) diam.
£1,200-1,700 *C*

An Anglo-Indian ivory inlaid wood cabinet, the doors opening to reveal 2 shelves with 2 small drawers below, surmounted by a cusped pediment, within chevron and floral lozenge borders, very slight damages to inlay, 19thC, 22in (55.5cm) high.
£600-900 *C*

Tortoiseshell

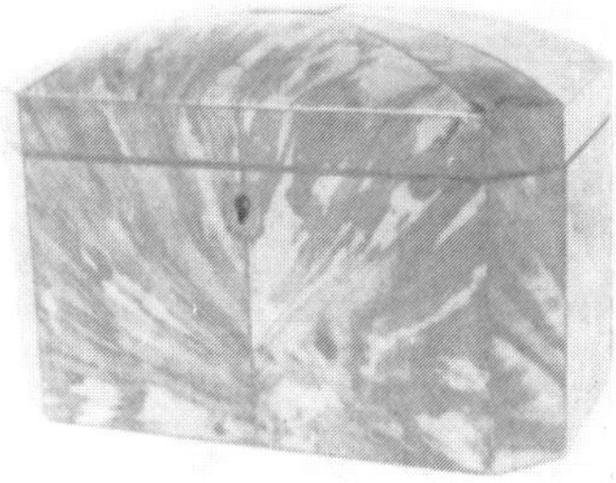

A Georgian pale tortoiseshell tea caddy, the domed top with segmented veneers, opening to reveal 2 caddies to the interior, 7in (18cm) wide.
£450-550 *HSS*

A Georgian tortoiseshell tea caddy, with sphere knop, the interior with 2 fitted compartments and supported upon sphere feet, 7in (18cm) wide.
£550-650 *HSS*

Marble

An English marble bust of Queen Victoria, signed L A Malempre 1887, on turned marble socle, 19thC, 19½in (50cm) high.
£600-700 *C*

A white marble relief of a youth, bust length and holding his hair in one hand, framed, probably English 19thC, 22 by 17½in (56 by 45cm).
£1,000-1,500 *C*

An Italian marble bust, 19th(25in (64cm) high.
£4,000-5,000 *DRU*

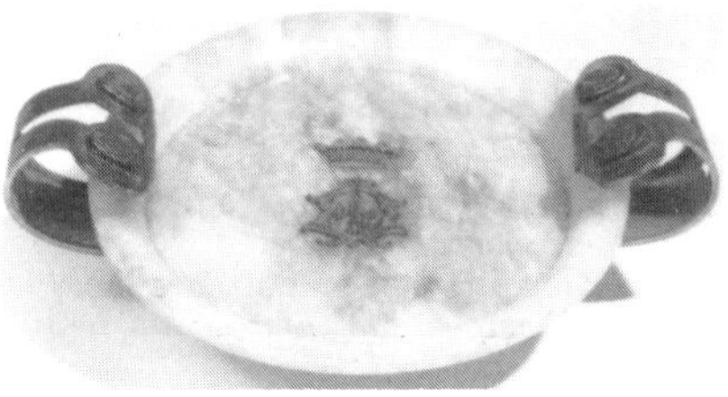

A gilt mounted alabaster tazza, the shallow bowl with the monogram DL beneath a crown, the pierced handles mounted with confronting silver plate portrait medallions of Roman style, on spreading base, the base signed Mon. Alph. Giroux, Paris, late 19thC, 18in (46cm) diam.
£600-900 *C*

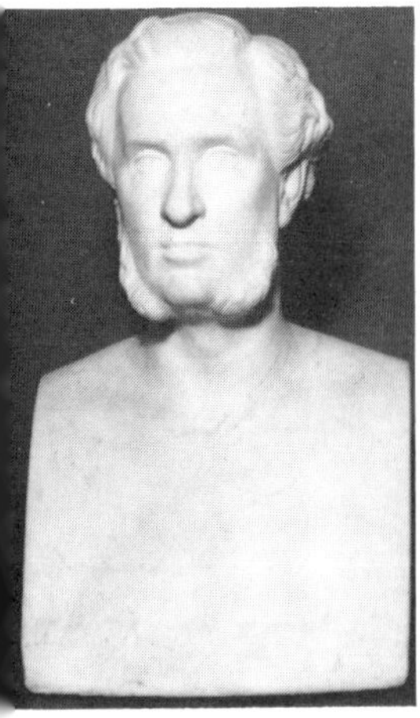

A white marble bust of Sir Joseph Hawley, 3rd Baronet, inscribed Joseph Henry Hawley, Bart, 26in (67cm) high.
£450-550 *WHB*

Sir Joseph Hawley (1813-75) was a patron of the Turf winning the Oaks in 1847, the 2,000 Guineas in 1858, the Derby in 1858, 1859 and 1868 and the St Leger in 1869. He also built a considerable library at his home at Leybourne Grange, Maidstone.

A pair of Italian marble busts of smiling and solemn children, wearing Roman togas, on turned socles, one repaired at neck with minor chips, 19thC, 10in (26cm) high.
£3,000-3,500 *CSK*

An English white marble figure of a recumbent bacchante, after Bartolini, lying on her discarded cloak, holding a tambourine and with a snake entwined around her right wrist, 19thC, 22in (56cm) long.
£2,000-2,500 *C*

A sculpted alabaster model of a snarling lion, with inset glass eyes, its head turned to dexter, on a naturalistic rocky base, 22in (56cm) long.
£600-700 *CSK*

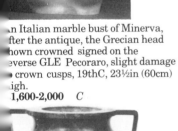

n Italian marble bust of Minerva, fter the antique, the Grecian head hown crowned signed on the everse GLE Pecoraro, slight damage crown cusps, 19thC, 23½in (60cm) igh.
1,600-2,000 *C*

An English plaster relief of 'Bluebell', cast from a model by Sir Richard Westmacott Jr, a winged fairy seated amidst bluebell flowers and tendrils, signed Westmacott Jun Scp and dated Feby 1836, framed and glazed, 25½ by 19in (65 by 48cm).
£1,600-2,000 *C*

A variegated rouge marble twin-handled urn, 18thC, 16in (41cm) high.
£3,000-4,000 *CSK*

An Ashford-in-the-water black marble occasional table by Samuel Birley, inlaid with various coloured marbles, the underside bearing a label inscribed 'This table was made from black marble quarried at Ashford, Derbyshire, it was turned and inlaid by Samuel Birley at Ashford about 1899, this work is now a lost art and the black marble is no longer quarried', 18½in (47cm) wide.
£3,500-4,000 *HSS*

An Italian white marble Medici vase, the urn carved with classical figures and handles, on a fluted socle, raised on an ebonised plinth, the sides decorated with gilt wreaths, 19thC, 48in (121.5cm) high overall.
£7,000-9,000 *C*

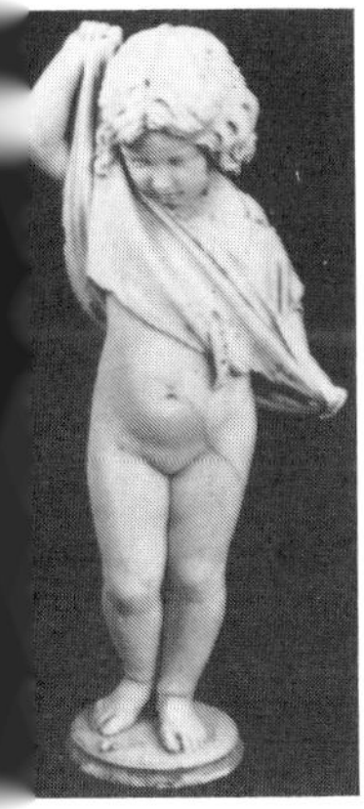

An Italian white marble figure of a young girl, the shy child raising her nightdress, signed P. Dal Nelro, Sculp, Milano, 1873, some damage, 19thC, 35in (90cm) high.
£2,000-2,500 *C*

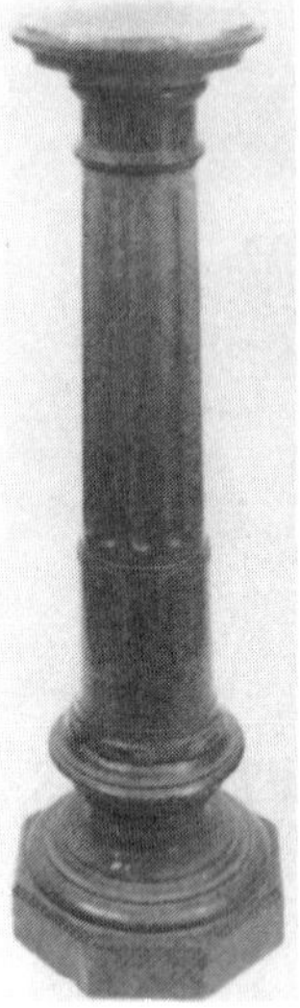

A verde antico marble column, the circular revolving top with fluted shaft and stepped hexagonal base, 19thC, 44in (111.5cm) high.
£350-450 *CSK*

A pair of French white marble urns, in the style of Clodion, carved with putti harvesting corn and fruit, with twin ram's head handles and fluted feet, one foot repaired in 2 places, 19thC, 16½in (41.5cm) high.
£3,500-5,000 *C*

A pair of Italian alabaster seated putti, one reading an alphabet book, the other writing Canova on a slate, both on naturalistic bases, minor damages to extremities, late 19thC, 16½in (42cm) high.
£2,000-2,500 *C*

A grey veined marble pedestal urn mounted in ormolu, the cover cast with fruiting vines, with ram's mask handles, garlands, swags and formal foliage, supported upon a square base, 24½in (63cm) high.
£650-750 *HSS*

A marble statue of a lady, 49in (124.5cm) high.
£3,000-3,500 *DRU*

An English marble portrait medallion of a young girl in profile, by S Terry, signed on the truncation S Terry, in walnut frame, late 19thC, 21in (54cm) high.
£1,000-1,500 *CSK*

Terracotta/Stone

A soapstone lotus bowl on stand, c1880, 9in (22.5cm) diam.
£60-80 *THA*

A South Indian granite figure of Nandi, kneeling with the right leg slightly raised, wearing jewellery and a backcloth, Vijayanagar, 15thC, 24in (61cm) high.
£5,000-6,000 *C*

A French terracotta bust of the 'Chanteuse Mauresque', by Charles-Henri-Joseph Cordier, the Moorish singer in folk costume, inscribed on the integral base and signed on the right side Cordier, 19thC, 18in (45cm) high.
£4,000-5,000 *C*

An English terracotta relief of a nymph, after a model by Alexander Munro, shown bust length in a stream with rushes crowning her long hair, within an integral square frame, mid-19thC, 22½ by 20in (56.5 by 51.5cm).
£1,500-1,800 *C*

An Italian terracotta relief, with the introduction, on the battlefield, of a commander to a young boy, minor damages and repair, 16thC, 7in (17cm) diam.
£600-800 *C*

French terracotta bust of a young ›y, after Pajou, bearing the gnature Pajou and the date 1780 ıder right shoulder, painted ›oden socle, 15in (37.5cm) high.
,500-3,000 *C*

A Sicilian terracotta group of a peasant family, on oval base with giltwood stand and glass dome, signed with label by Giacomo & Giuseppe Bongiovannie Vaccaro, Caltagirone, 19thC, 17in (43cm) wide.
£800-850 *GSP*

ı Indian red sandstone bracket in e form of a peacock, a small bird at e breast, 3 pendant banded cones low, very slight damages, c17thC, in (48.5cm) high.
00-800 *C*

An Austrian polychrome terracotta figure of a robed Arab, the base with the Goldscheide label, 19thC, 16½in (42cm) high.
£200-250 *CSK*

A red sandstone arched jali, the central panel pierced with a delicate octagonal lattice around a central rectangular opening, the spandrels carved with lilies and flowering vine, in a plain border, the reverse similar but simpler, slight weathering, reverse limed, 18th/19thC, 38 by 27½in (96.5 by 70cm).
£400-500 *C*

'oodcarvings

pair of carved oak figures of Roman soldiers, sword blade nissing from one, tallest 40in 101.5cm) high.
1,500-2,000 *C*

A South German polychrome wood group of Anna Selbdritt, St. Anne shown seated, holding the Virgin within her left arm and the Christ Child seated on her right knee, the integrally carved base dated 1519, all with damaged noses, the Virgin and the Child with arms lacking, other minor damages, early 16thC, 25½in (65cm) high.
£4,500-5,500 *C*

A pair of English oak carvings, c1660, 8in (20cm) high.
£250-300 *SBA*

A set of German carved wood and polychrome figures of itinerant musicians and peasants, on stepped bases, 18thC, tallest 12in (30.5cm) high.
£900-1,200 *CSK*

A set of 4 South German painted pinewood figures, the 2 women and 2 men in contemporary costume, emblematic of The Four Seasons, minor losses, 18thC, 12in (31cm) high.
£2,500-3,000 *C*

A Netherlandish boxwood relief of the Crucifixion, attributed to Albert Vinckenbrinck, carved in high relief on a naturalistic mound, signed with the monogram 'ALVB', 17thC, in contemporary but associated renaissance style ebonised wood frame, 10½in (26cm) high.
£6,000-7,000 *C*

A pair of wood appliqués, in the manner of Grinling Gibbons, carved and pierced with dead birds suspended amidst fruit and foliage, each attached to later backing, late 18thC, 75in (190.5cm) high.
£7,000-8,000 *C*

A German turned wood cup and cover, the ovoid cup gadrooned, with screw thread into the bulbous knop below, on a spreading foot, enriched allover with bone studs, screw to joint loose, c1700, 14in (36cm) high.
£1,700-2,500 *C*

Miscellaneous

An English bas relief medallion o young girl, by C Pibworth, in a wreath with a stylised flower at t top and ribbons below, on voluted plinth, late 19th/early 20thC, 28½ (73cm) high.
£5,000-6,000 *CSK*

A wax portrait relief bust of a gentleman, inscribed J.L. Elliot, early 19thC, 7in (18cm), in a glazed giltwood frame.
£200-300 *CSK*

ANTIQUITIES

Marble

A marble relief panel, with head of a bearded male deity in relief, possibly Zeus Serapis, wearing crown with leaves around its base, and grape cluster earrings, mounted, 1st-2nd Century A.D., 18in (46cm) high.
£4,500-5,500 *C*

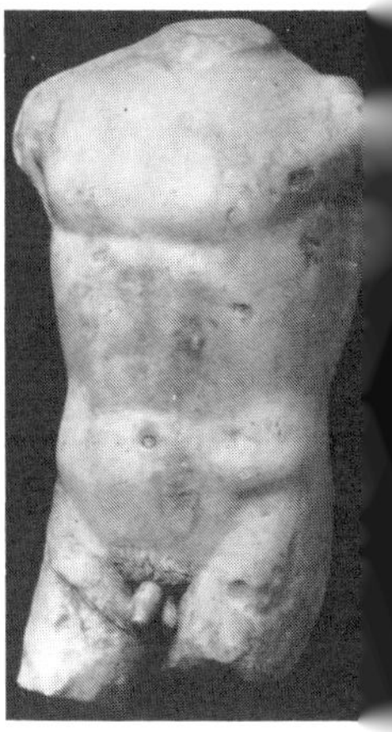

A marble torso of a youth, possibly copied from a 5th Century BC Greek original, lacking all extremities and surface marked and pitted, 1st-2nd Century A.D., 51in (129.5cm) high overall, on rectangular modern bronze base.
£12,000-14,000 *CSK*

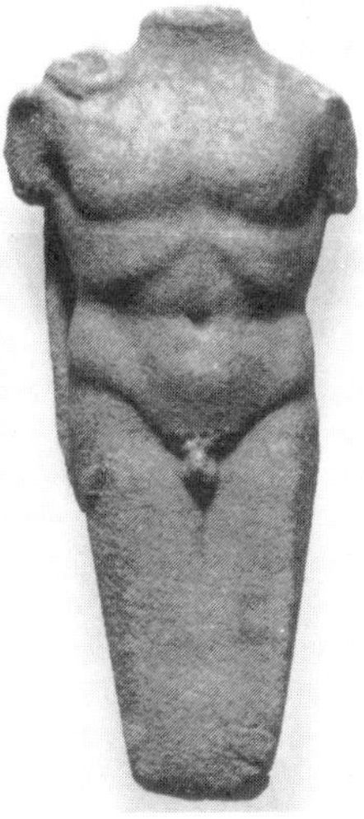

A Greek marble figure of a herm, showing strong muscular detail, incised pubes and cloak draped over right shoulder, head missing, Hellenistic, c3rd Century B.C.
£1,500-2,000 *C*

A Roman marble double head of a herm, on one side the head of a bearded satyr, on the other the head of a youth, both wearing ivy wreaths around their heads, mounted, 1st-2nd Century A.D., 5½in (14cm) high.
£5,000-6,000 *C*

Metalware

A bronze figure of Oriris, wearing atef crown and holding crook and flail, with detailed collar and wrist bands, mounted, c4th Century B.C., 10in (25cm) high.
£2,000-3,000 *C*

A bronze furniture attachment, in the form of the front part of a shrine, the cavetto cornice chased with a winged sun disc, each side bearing a dedication to Ptolemy II Philadelphus (?), the 4 tenons at the back pierced for attachment, Ptolemaic, 5in (13cm) high.
£1,700-2,000 *C*

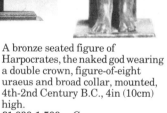

A Greek bronze figure of a rabbit or hare, with head turned to the right, 2 tangs below feet, mounted on perspex stand, 5th Century B.C., 2in (5cm) high.
£3,500-4,500 *C*

A bronze appliqué of the bust of a child, with wavy locks, the top plaited and tied in a bunch at the front, mounted, 2nd-3rd Century A.D., 2in (5cm) high.
£600-700 *C*

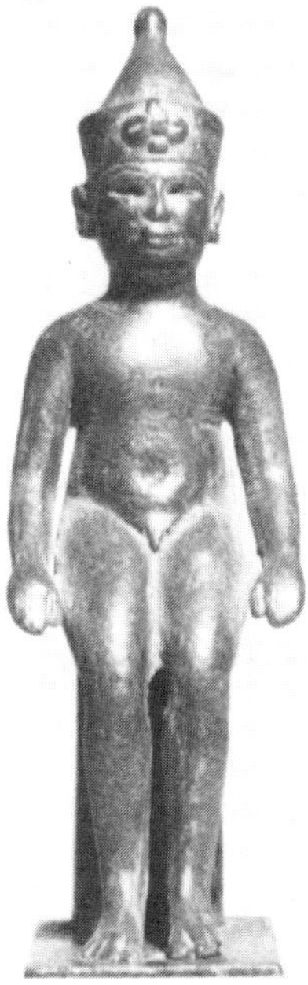

A bronze seated figure of Harpocrates, the naked god wearing a double crown, figure-of-eight uraeus and broad collar, mounted, 4th-2nd Century B.C., 4in (10cm) high.
£1,000-1,500 *C*

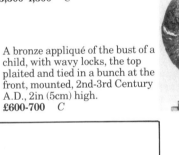

A set of 5 silver hairpins, each with plain shaft and elaborate finial, 1st-3rd Century A.D., 5½in (14cm) long.
£1,500-2,000 *C*

Many Roman hairstyles involved the use of elaborate tight curls made with hot tongs and arranged, rather than held, in place with the aid of such hairpins.

Pottery

A miniature Attic black figure hydria, the body with 3 naked komasts dancing between ivy border to each side, second half 6th Century B.C., 4½in (12cm) high.
£1,200-1,600 *C*

A Syrian pottery chariot or wagon, with 4 solid wheels, with incised decoration consisting of stylised branches and sunbursts or rosettes, and a pottery animal, 3rd Millennium B.C., 5½in (14cm) long.
£1,500-2,000 *C*

An Attic head flask, in the form of a female head with tightly fringed curls, handle repaired with some repainting, c460 B.C., 8in (20cm) high.
£2,500-3,500 *C*

A Gnathia ware black gloss hydria, with vertical ribbing, decorated with ovolo on the rim and a pendant chain on the neck, repaired at neck and handle, c300 B.C., 14in (36cm) high.
£2,000-3,000 *C*

An Etruscan Bucchero ware kyathos, with well preserved surface, decorated with 2 fine incised lines around rim on exterior, the high handle with moulded head in relief at its base in interior and applied decoration, 6th Century B.C., 5½in (14cm) high.
£300-500 *C*

A South Italian red figure Lekythos, depicting unusual scene of 2 actors in female dress, with dotted hatched band below, 4th Century B.C., 8½in (21cm) high.
£500-700 *C*

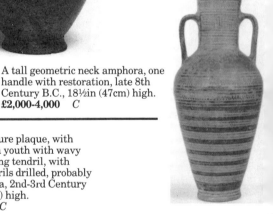

A tall geometric neck amphora, one handle with restoration, late 8th Century B.C., 18½in (47cm) high.
£2,000-4,000 *C*

Miscellaneous

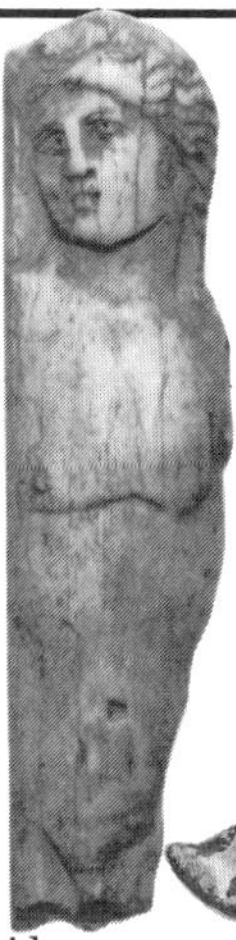

An ivory furniture plaque, with relief figure of a youth with wavy hair and escaping tendril, with pupils and nostrils drilled, probably from Alexandria, 2nd-3rd Century A.D., 5in (12cm) high.
£1,000-1,500 *C*

A Hellenistic terracotta pig rattle the pig of naturalistic form, c3rd-2nd Century B.C., 4in (10cm long.
£450-650 *C*

A terracotta bust of a nereid, mounted, c3rd Century B.C., 7½in (19cm) high.
£2,000-2,500 *C*

l. A terracotta figure of an actor, possibly representing a metic or Jew, his exaggerated features with tragic expression, wearing long garment, skull cap and earring in right ear, 4th-3rd Century B.C., 6in (15cm) high.
r. A terracotta grotesque figure of a dwarf as Mercury, holding caduceus in left arm and purse in right, conical hat and short tunic beneath which protrudes large phallus, one foot missing, c1st Century B.C., 5½in (14cm) high.
£2,000-2,500 *C*

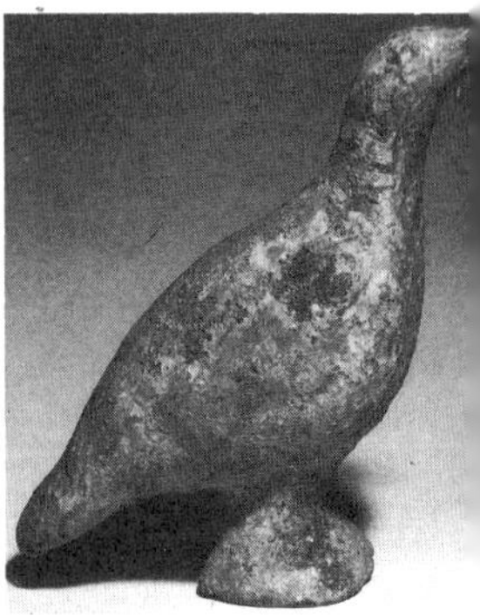

A Greek terracotta model of a cockerel and another bird, c5th Century B.C., cockerel 4in (10cm) high.
£300-400 *C*

A complete bun shaped schoolboy's tablet, with 3 lines of text on each side, an extract from a lexical composition with river names including the Tigris, Old Babylonian, early 2nd Millennium B.C., 3½in (9cm) diam.
£1,700-2,000 *C*

The skills of reading and writing were not widespread in ancient Mesopotamia. Scribes had to train from an early age to master their craft, first learning how to shape the clay tablets on which they wrote, practising individual characters and gradually learning to write the script. On these round bun shaped tablets the teacher would typically write out 3 lines on one side, the schoolboy would carefully examine these then try to reproduce exactly the same text on the reverse of the tablet.

A Palmyran limestone portrait head of a man, with powerful features, mounted on variegated green base, 3rd-4th Century A.D., 9in (23cm) high.
£5,000-6,000 *C*

A terracotta figure of a woman and child, the woman wearing a long garment seated on a stool, holding naked child in both her hands, the child on her knees, traces of yellow white and red pigment, Boeotian, 5th Century B.C., 5in (13cm) high.
£13,000-15,000 *C*

Rugs & Carpets

A Heriz carpet, the red field with an allover design of brightly coloured stylised flowering vines within a dark blue floral border, 135 by 109in (342.5 by 276.5cm).
£1,000-1,500 *CSK*

A Chi Chi rug, the black field with multi-coloured patterns, a short kilim strip at each end, partly replaced selvedges, slight corrosion, 76 by 46in (193 by 116.5cm).
£4,000-5,000 *C*

A Chinese carpet, in ivory and royal blue stripes, areas of slight wear and staining, 138 by 110in (350.5 by 279cm).
£2,000-2,500 *C*

A Bidjar rug, the indigo field with fox brown, turtle palmette and flowering vine border between medium blue floral stripes, inner zig-zag stripe, slight overall wear, fringes replaced, 77 by 57in (196 by 145cm).
£2,500-3,000 *C*

A Kazak carpet, the red field with 3 red, ivory and blue medallions, in turquoise, blue and red border stripes with stylised flowerheads and serrated leaves, 144 by 96in (365.5 by 243.5cm).
£800-1,000 *CSK*

An Iranian Sarouk rug, the shaded brick red field with a blue medallion and ivory spandrels, within an indigo palmette border, 56 by 39in (142 by 99cm).
£400-500 *CSK*

An Armenian rug, with 5 indigo gabled and hooked medallions with pink floral panels surrounded by similar dart motifs, in a broad ivory floral border between shaded blue, yellow, rust red flowerhead floral and baton stripes, 133 by 56in (337 by 142cm).
£2,000-2,500 *C*

A Heriz carpet, with lozenge shaped brick field, large indigo centre jewel pendant medallion, inner medallions in rose, pale blue, ivory and indigo, 223 by 149in (566.5 by 378cm).
£14,000-16,000 *WW*

A pair of part silk Isfahan rugs in ivory, tomato red, indigo, blue and sandy yellow, 91 by 58in (231 by 147cm).
£7,500-8,500 *C*

A Karadjar runner, the indigo field with stepped rows of alternately facing boteh in an ivory flowering vine border between brick red floral stripes, 196 by 42in (497.5 by 106.5cm).
£1,700-2,000 *C*

A Chinese silk rug, the apricot field with 5 imperial 5-clawed dragons surrounded by stylised clouds, within a stylised wave and mountain border, an inscribed panel above, areas of slight wear, 94 by 61in (238 by 155cm).
£900-1,200 *C*

A Chinese carpet, with golden yellow field and blue border between seed pearl and plain blu[e] stripes, 120 by 69in (304.5 by 175cm).
£3,500-4,500 *C*

A European carpet, with raspberry red, sandy yellow, ivory, brown an[d] pistachio green stripes in an ivory border, slight staining and colour run, 111 by 86in (282 by 218.5cm).
£2,500-3,000 *C*

A Khotan carpet, the shaded lilac and blue field with stylised floral motifs around 3 blue shaded lilac floral roundels, plain outer lilac stripe, slight overall wear, 136 by 66in (345 by 167.5cm).
£2,500-3,500 *C*

A Chinese carpet, the ivory field with an indigo flowering vine border with light blue flowering vine and plain blue stripes, a few minor stains, 143 by 110in (363 by 279cm).
£3,000-4,000 *C*

A Kerman carpet with pink and blue Tree of Life pattern on a faw[n] field with a blue flowered border, 120 by 82in (304.5 by 208cm).
£1,600-2,000 *AH*

\ Kazak rug, the tomato red field vith hooked lozenges, floral motifs ınd human figures in blue, indigo, nustard yellow and chocolate rown, slight overall wear, repaired, .10 by 75in (279 by 190.5cm).
:1,800-2,200 *C*

. Kirman carpet, the indigo field ·ith a large flowering tree with erching birds, 127 by 89in (322 by 26cm).
3,000-4,000 *C*

n Ushak carpet, the ivory field ithin a salmon pink border of ternate ivory and sea blue floral rtouches divided by floral bands, tween sea blue floral and zig-zag ripes, slight overall wear, 214 by .0in (543.5 by 533cm).
,500-2,000 *C*

Savonnerie carpet, on shaded ive green field with double narrow nk and white plain striped border, eas of wear and repair, backed, i1 by 48in (384 by 122cm).
,500-5,000 *C*

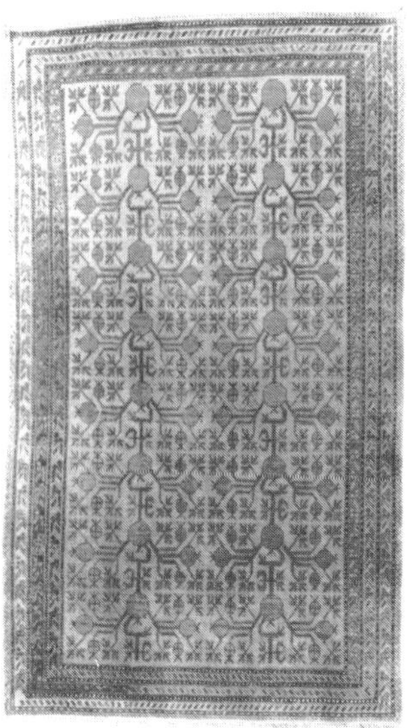

A Samarkand rug, with faded blue field with allover pomegranate design in soft brick with brown and brick fruiting branches, brick, faded blue, celadon green and pale gold narrow floral borders, 101 by 57in (256.5 by 144.5cm).
£1,000-1,500 *WW*

A central Anatolian kilim, in indigo, ivory, brick and pale green, with an allover design of various hooked medallions, rosettes and 'S' motifs, ivory fret outer border, 19thC, 110 by 44in (279 by 111.5cm).
£250-350 *WW*

A Tabriz carpet in blue, brick red and ivory, 267 by 174in (677 by 442cm).
£5,000-6,000 *C*

A Qashqai tribal rug, the blue field with an overall Herati-type design, with dark ivory spandrels, surrounded by brick red, ivory and dark mustard stripes, 90 by 57in (228.5 by 144.5cm).
£1,000-1,200 *CSK*

A Kazak rug, the tomato red field with 2 indigo floral medallions, in a light blue stylised flowering vine border between ivory boteh and brick red flowering vine stripes, slight overall wear, 83 by 59in (210.5 by 149.5cm).
£600-800 *C*

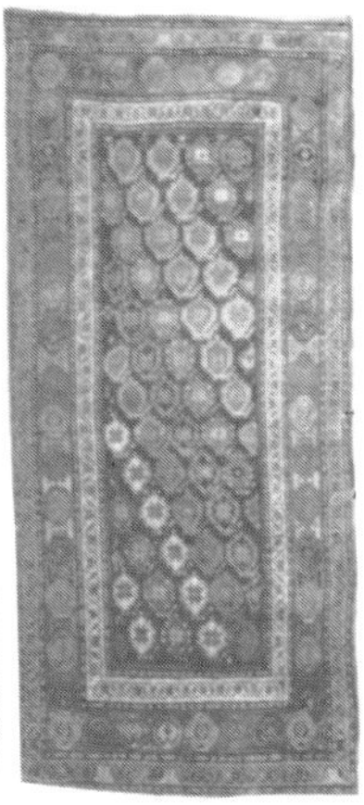

A Kazak-Gendje rug, the indigo field with columns of diagonal multi-coloured boteh, surrounded by ivory and mustard yellow inner and outer stripes with flowering vines and a brick red lozenge border, 106 by 50in (269 by 127cm).
£800-1,000 *CSK*

A Tabriz rug, in tan, ivory, indigo and brick red, very slight wear, 77 by 55in (195.5 by 139.5cm).
£1,700-2,200 *C*

TEXTILES
Costume

A young girl's dress of egg shell blue wool and silk, with a tiered skirt and short pleated cap sleeves, trimmed with lace, c1878.
£300-400 *CSK*

A complete highlander's outfit, comprising: green facecloth jacket and waistcoat, Gordon tartan kilt, shorts and sash, matching socks and sock tabs, tam-o'shanter, skhein dhu and sporran stamped R W Forsythe, Glasgow and Edinburgh.
£300-350 *CSK*

A Christening robe of Carrickmacross lace, the skirt threaded with ivory satin ribbons, the bodice worked with scrolling foliage, c1907.
£400-500 *CSK*

This robe was purchased in 1907 after it had won 1st prize in an exhibition in Chicago of Irish lace.

A dress of red grosgrain silk, the bodice of rust coloured velvet trimmed with large bows and blue chiffon, with gigot sleeves, 1893.
£200-250 *CSK*

A wedding gown of ivory tamboured net, with a frilled lace yoke, leg of mutton sleeves, an ivory satin sash and orange blossom wreath, 1905.
£450-550 *CSK*

A densely embroidered jack with Chinese scrolling embroidery with a sea wave border, the back worked with a phoenix, labelled Molyneux, 1937.
£250-300 *CSK*

A child's matador fancy dress outfit, comprising black velvet breeches, trimmed with white satin and metal braid, a waistcoat and bolero similarly trimmed, a hat, cummerbund and pair of ivory silk stockings, early 20thC.
£90-120 *CSK*

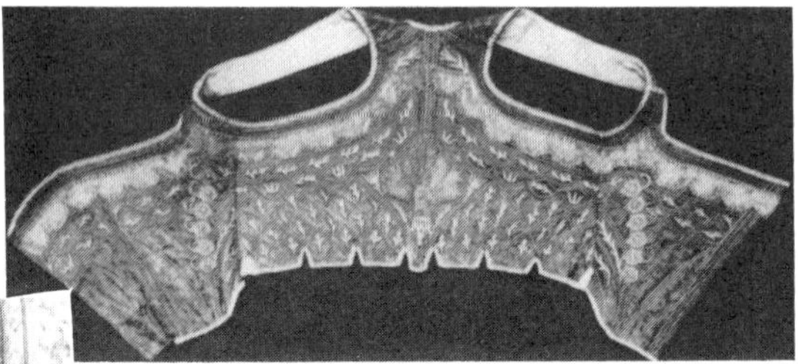

A corset of burgundy figured silk, lined with glazed printed cotton and embroidered with metal thread flowers and white metal hooks, regional, c1810. **£400-500** *CSK*

A dress of red chiffo with a wrap-over bodice of red chiffon over cream net, trimmed with gilt bugle beads at the neck and sleeves, knotted at the hem the back to show a Brussels lace applic underskirt, c1910.
£200-250 *CSK*

A Chinese lady's informal robe, of pink silk damask, embroidered in coloured silks in Peking knot stitch, the sleeve bands and elaborate collar trimmed with ivory embroidered silk, lined with blue silk, 19thC.
£1,000-1,200 *CSK*

A Chinese robe, of midnight blue silk embroidered with baskets of flowers and butterflies, the wide sleeve bands embroidered with large flowerheads, some in Peking knot on an ivory ground.
£150-250 *Bon*

A Chinese robe of ivory silk, richly embroidered in various coloured silks, with a wave border worked in Peking knots.
£900-1,200 *Bon*

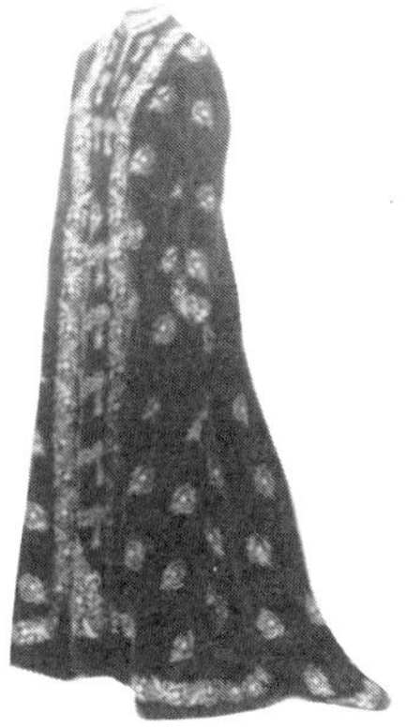

A Turkish robe of purple velvet, densely embroidered with beaten silver gilt wire arabesques, sprigged with ribboned sprays of flowers, 19thC.
£400-450 *CSK*

A cope of red velvet, the orphreys and hood finely embroidered in coloured silks and gilt threads, the hood with the Crucifixion, the orphreys with arched recesses framing scenes of the Passion, lined with crimson damask, the embroidery probably Flemish, late 15th/early 16thC.
£2,000-3,000 *CSK*

Cope: a long cloak worn in processions.

A Japanese furisode, of ivory silk, printed in black and rust to resemble tie-dyed patterns, embroidered in green, red and pink silk, and gilt threads, with padded hem, lined with red silk, early 19thC.
£900-1,200 *CSK*

A Chinese informal jacket, of red silk damask, with trimmings of ivory silk, embroidered in coloured silks, lined with fur, 19thC.
£300-400 *CSK*

A Chinese lady's informal coat of silver-green silk, embroidered in coloured silks, trimmed with black silk embroidered ribbon, lined with pink silk, late 19thC.
£450-500 *CSK*

A Chinese robe of red silk, embroidered mainly in shades of blue and white, with a pair of civil rank badges, worked with the seventh-rank mandarin duck, lined with blue silk, 19thC.
£400-500 *CSK*

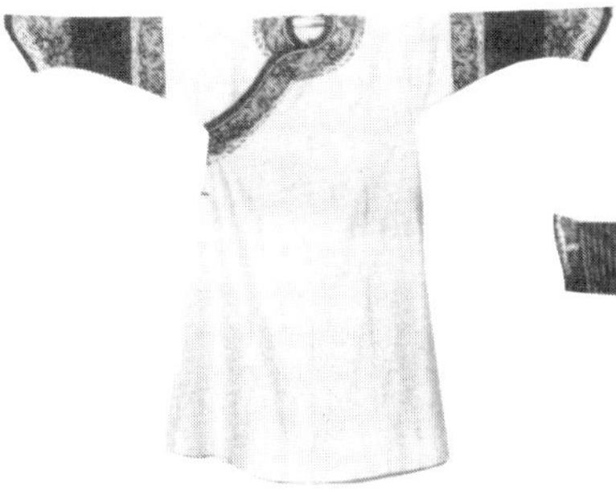

A Chinese robe of yellow silk, trimmed with blue kossu silk, woven in many colours, the kossu from an earlier robe, late 18th/early 19thC.
£1,000-2,000 *CSK*

The robe made-up before 1860, when it was brought to England by Colonel John Desborough from the Summer Palace.

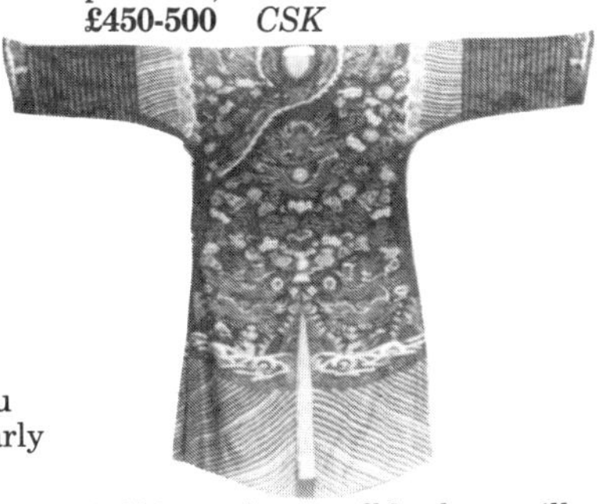

A Chinese dragon of blue kossu silk, woven in many colours, lined with pale blue silk, 19thC.
£650-1,000 *CSK*

A knitted waistcoat, of burgundy coloured silk, knitted with gold lace patterns at the borders and seams, with ball-shaped buttons of gold thread, repairs, 17thC.
£1,000-1,500 *CSK*

A waistcoat, of strawberry pink silk woven 'a disposition' in silver thread and pink, brown, green and blue silk, slight wear under arms, 2 buttons missing, one small hole, c1740.
£1,800-2,000 *CSK*

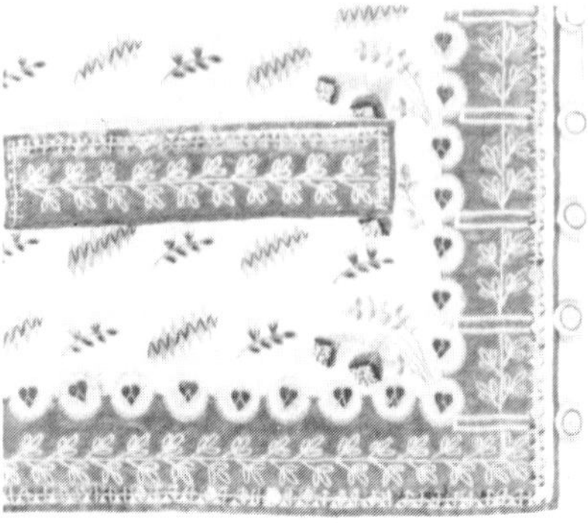

A waistcoat, of ivory satin embroidered with sprigs of flowers and zig-zag motifs, the borders applied with olive green satin and decorated with chenille work, paste and cut steel hearts, c1780.
£600-700 *CSK*

The lining stamped 'Sir. Tho: Cave'.

A pair of lady's beaded evening shoes, c1935.
£40-60 *Bon*

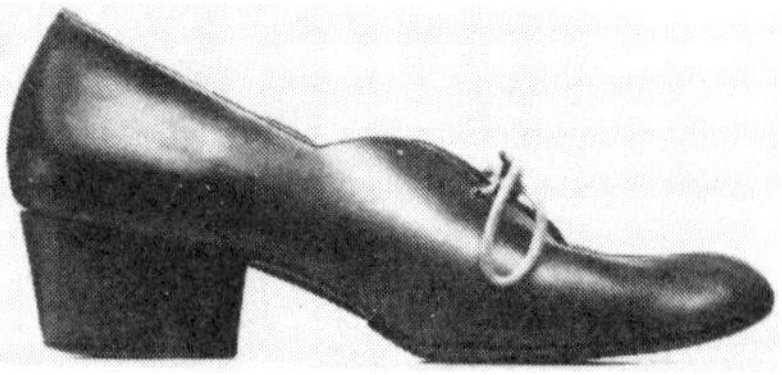

A pair of cherry red leather lace-up shoes, with circular heels labelled Ferrina, Created by Ferragamo, Made in England, and Harvey Nichols and Eros.
£40-60 *CSK*

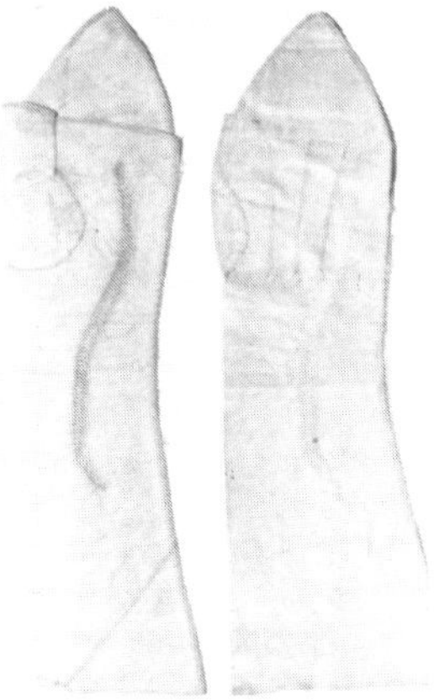

A pair of ivory silk mittens, with a long sinuous insertion at the inner wrists embroidered in pink silk, the borders also embroidered in pink silk, the tips lined in pink silk, c1770.
£500-800 *CSK*

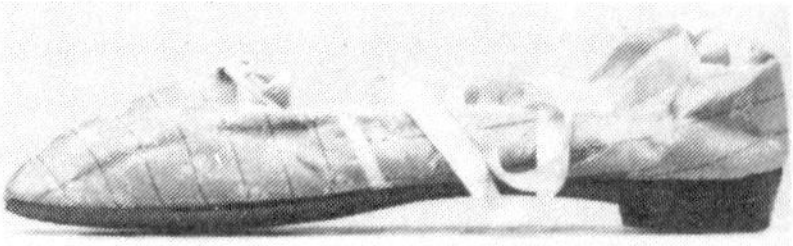

A pair of mauve brocade slippers, woven with a thin green stripe with white scrolling flowers, trimmed with white silk ribbons and bows, with a low stepped heel, c1865.
£120-160 *CSK*

A Victorian Lord Chancellor's bourse, of honey coloured velvet, worked with metallic threads and sequins, with the Royal coat-of-arms and motto, surmounted by the royal coat-of-arms, with the initials VR, the border with putti, the corners with large tassels, 2 loose, with bag, 17in (43cm) square.
£900-1,200 *CSK*

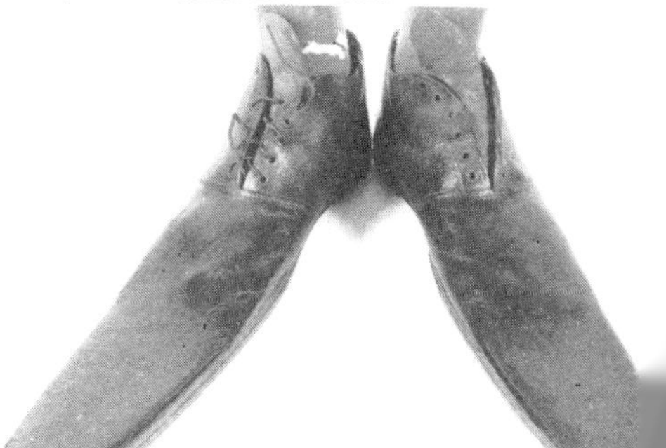

A pair of black leather clown's shoes, with square cut toes and wooden soles, contained in a brown leather carrying case, late 19thC, 18in (46cm) long.
£200-250 *HSS*

A Canton fawn silk shawl, embroidered with figures from Chinese life, with ivory painted faces, 60in (152cm) square.
£300-500 *CSK*

A Kashmir rumal shawl, with floral arches, with an indistinct description in pink silk, c1840, 72in (182.5cm) square.
£950-1,200 *CSK*

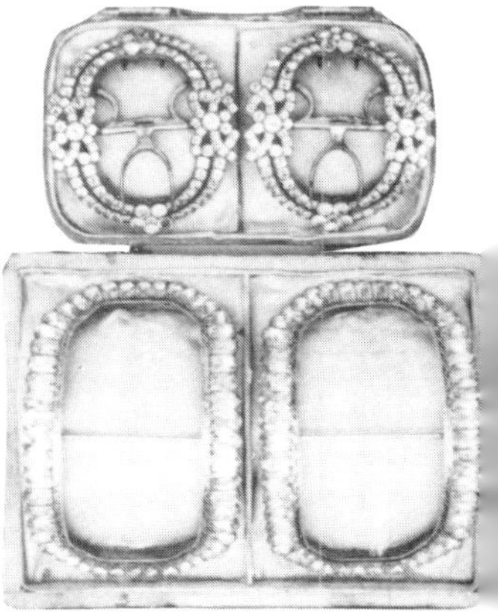

A pair of paste shoe buckles, with gold stamped trim, chapes missing, in fitted box, late 18thC; and another pair of oval shoe buckles, set with paste bows, with forked tongues, also late 18thC, in fitted box.
£500-600 *CSK*

\ Kashmir shawl, with complex
›road hashiya woven with S-motifs,
he palla woven with 3 circular
aurel wreaths and stylised sacred
nountains, the boteh reserved in
ellow, pink and blue, the dhor
imilar, with a black field, c1830,
ikh period, 130 by 56in (330 by
42cm).
1,200-1,500 *CSK*

double-sided Paisley shawl,
oven with bright colours, the
rders of palmette motifs, the field
oven with swirling leafy cones
ranged in informal columns, with
inges, c1860, 70 by 66in (177.5 by
57.5cm).
450-550 *CSK*

Paisley shawl, woven in fresh
ours with curled tipped cones
ming a central medallion, c1860,
by 128in (162.5 by 325cm).
00-900 *CSK*

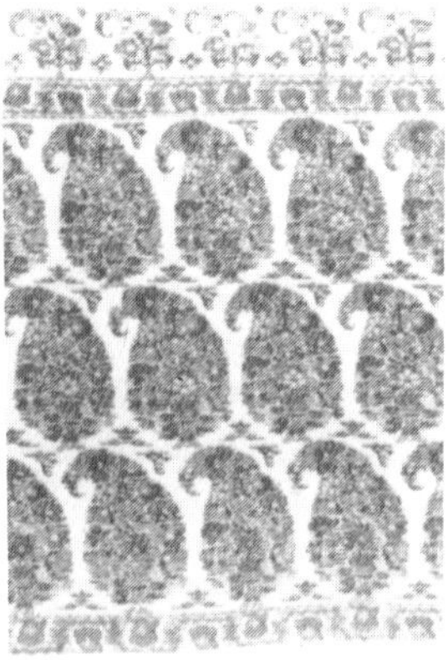

A shawl of ivory wool, the hashiya woven with an angular meandering vine with blue flowers, the palla woven with 3 rows of small mosaic boteh on ideogramme roots, woven in shades of red, blue and yellow, Afghan period, joined, c1820, 48 by 100in (122 by 254cm).
£700-750 *CSK*

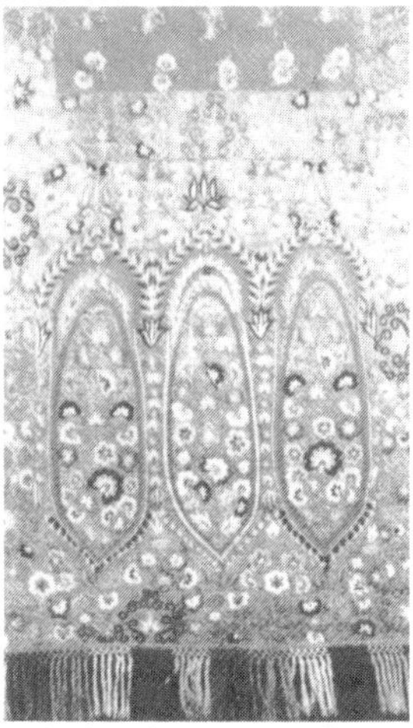

An Indian ivory net stole, embroidered with brightly coloured floss silks, the ends worked with 3 cones against a floral background, the field sprigged with flowers, c1835, 20 by 100in (50.5 by 254cm).
£200-250 *CSK*

A turnover shawl, with red field and attached borders woven with flower filled cones amid angular trees, with a floral border, c1845.
£350-400 *CSK*

A double sided Paisley shawl, woven with an intricate design of palmettes and mihrabs in green, black, red and ivory, 69½ by 65in (176 by 165cm).
£400-450 *Bon*

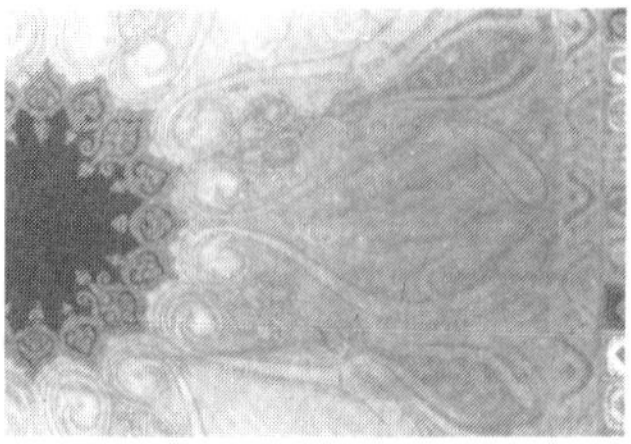

A rumal shawl, Doghra, c1850, 80in (203cm) square. **£650-750** *CSK*

A Paisley shawl woven predominantly in burgundy and blue, with cones flanking 4 central cartouches, 2 ivory, 2 blue, c1858, 64 by 130in (162.5 by 330cm).
£400-450 *CSK*

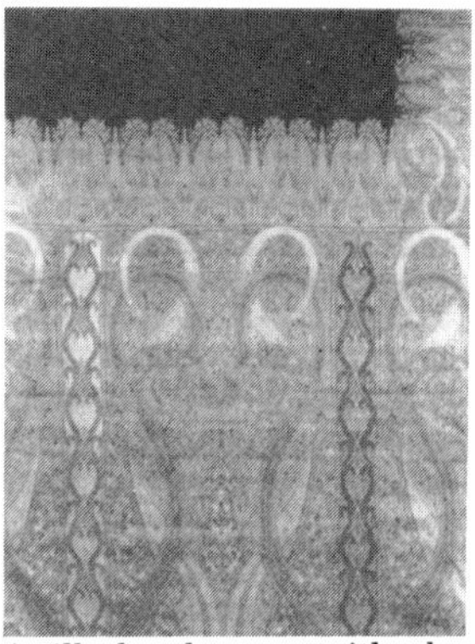

A silk shawl, woven with a border composed of serpentine cones separated by green and blue columns, with a twisted red silk fringe and black silk field, c1850, 70 by 140in (177.5 by 355cm).
£400-450 *CSK*

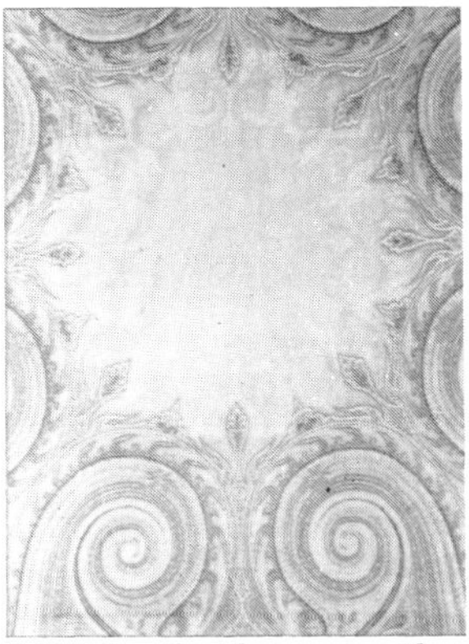

A Paisley shawl, woven with 2 spiral tipped opposing cones at either corner framing a red silk central medallion, c1855, 74in (188cm) square.
£400-500 *CSK*

A Paisley shawl, woven with a central palmette column flanked by cones and beneath a prayer arch, with a black silk residual field, c1860, 64 by 142in (162.5 by 360.5cm).
£1,200-1,500 *CSK*

A double sided shawl, woven with columns of bent tipped cones, c1865, 64 by 70in (162.5 by 177.5cm).
£400-500 *CSK*

A Paisley shawl, woven with elongated leafy columns, c1865, 12 by 64in (325 by 162.5cm).
£550-600 *CSK*

Embroidery

An embroidered panel from a chair back, worked in coloured wools against a sky blue ground, trimmed with later braid, made up into a cushion, French, late 17th/early 18thC, 15 by 20in (39 by 51cm).
£400-600 *CSK*

An embroidered picture, worked in coloured silks, 18thC, 18 by 16in (46 by 41cm), framed and glazed.
£700-750 *CSK*

A pair of 17thC style crewelwork curtains, embroidered in shades of green, blue, brown and red wool, 18thC, 82 by 34in (208 by 87cm), and a matching pelmet.
£1,200-1,500 *CSK*

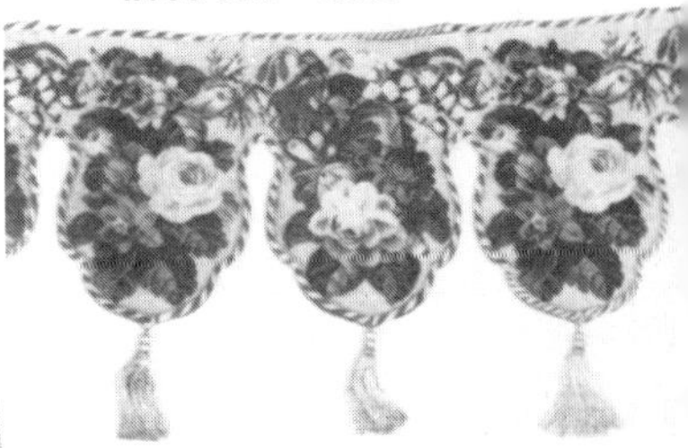

An embroidered scalloped pelmet, worked in coloured wools and whi beads, highlighted with silks, against a white beaded ground, c1840, 37 by 11in (94 by 29cm).
£350-400 *CSK*

An embroidered picture, worked in coloured silk, depicting an interior with children playing blind man's buff, late 18th/early 19thC, 13 by 18in (34 by 46cm), framed in black and gold glass.
£1,500-2,000 *CSK*

An embroidered silk chenille and gauze puffwork picture, of a spray of flowers on an ivory silk ground, early 19thC, 18 by 15½in (46 by 40cm).
£200-250 *Bon*

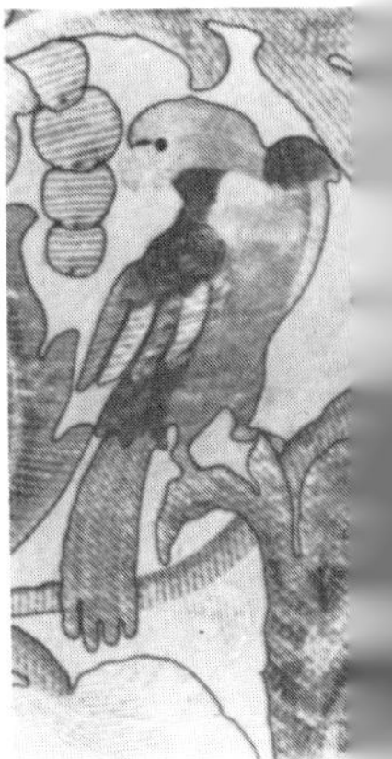

An embroidered panel, worked in coloured floss silks and couched black cord and gilt thread, with an early 18thC style pattern, c1880, 29 by 112in (74 by 284.5cm).
£450-550 *CSK*

An embroidered bag, worked in coloured silks with a swan and a lyre among flowers, the reverse with a spray of roses, the embroidery c1840, 8 by 6in (21 by 16cm).
£90-120 *CSK*

An embroidered picture, worked in coloured wools, highlighted with silks, with a spaniel sitting on a red cushion with large tassels at each corner, mid-19thC, 10 by 16in (26 by 41cm), framed and glazed.
£700-800 *CSK*

A pair of Japanese black silk hangings, embroidered in coloured silks, late 19thC, 120 by 45in (304.5 by 114cm).
£450-600 *CSK*

A Victorian embroidered and beadwork panel of an Imari pattern coffee cup, milk jug and sugar bowl on a tray, surrounded by a vitruvian scroll border.
£150-200 *Bon*

A Syrian silk and silver thread embroidered panel, the ivory field with a large baluster flowering vase within a golden yellow, ice blue and ivory scrolling frame with outer burgundy stripe, areas of repair and staining, 84 by 71in (213 by 180cm).
£1,700-2,000 *C*

Lace

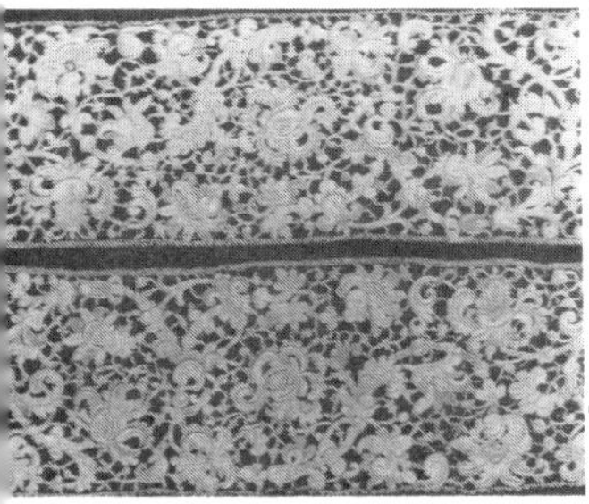

A flounce of gros point de Venise, 17thC, 112 by 7in (284.5 by 18cm).
£170-200 *Bon*

A collection of Italian lace, including 2 lengths of Punto in Aria, worked with bellflowers and flowers alternating with sunburst roundels, edged with bellflowers, 17thC.
£200-300 *CSK*

Two lengths of Venetian rose point lace, fragments of Venetian tape lace and another piece similar, late 17thC.
£50-100 *Bon*

A collection of lace, including 2 flounces of filet, worked with pomegranates, lilies and honeysuckle, probably 18thC, 8 by 92in (21 by 233.5cm) and 60in (152cm).
£200-250 *CSK*

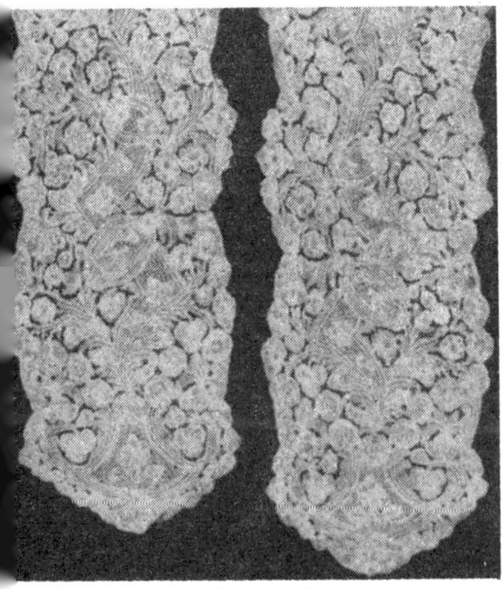

A pair of Brussels bobbin lace lappets, worked with a zig-zagging ribbon against a floral ground, mid-18thC, 4 by 23in (10 by 59cm).
£600-700 *CSK*

A flounce of fine Alençon needlelace, worked with flower filled cartouches above a scalloped border, late 19thC, 156 by 13in (396 by 33cm).
£900-1,000 *CSK*

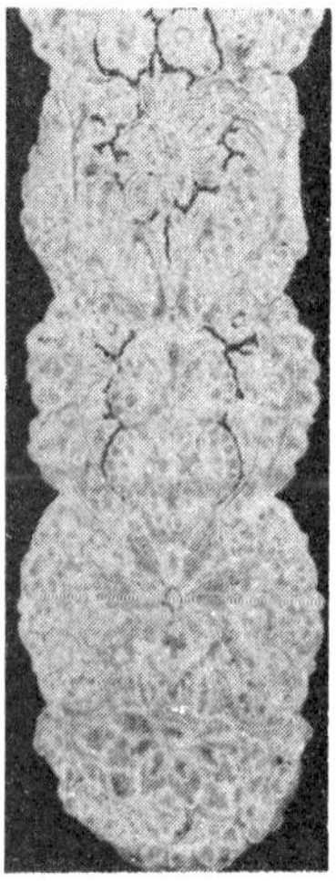

A pair of Brussels lace lappets, worked with a scalloped edge, with an orchid-like flower at either end, with various flowers above framed by informal garlands, c1730, 4 by 23in (10 by 59cm).
£350-500 *CSK*

A collection of lace, including a fine flounce of point de gaze, with shaped ends, worked with butterflies and birds, 18in (46cm) deep.
£1,200-1,500 *CSK*

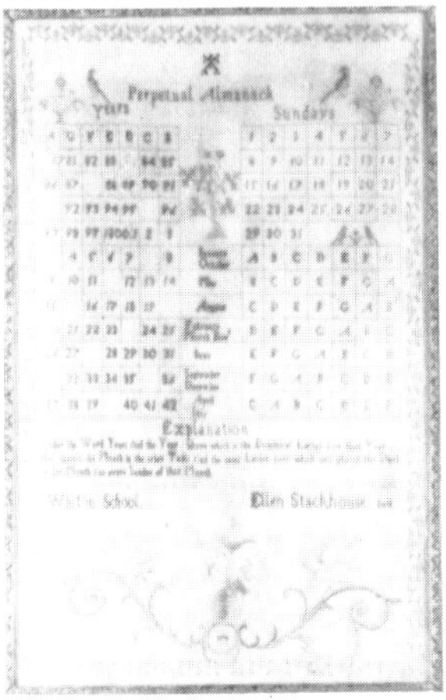

A perpetual almanack sampler, by Ellen Stackhouse, 1781, Walton School, the table and explanation in black silk, with a naturalistic pot of flowers and scrolling motifs worked beneath in coloured silks, with a trailing floral border, 16 by 11in (41 by 28cm), framed and glazed.
£300-400 *CSK*

A sampler by Marthe Le Patuorel, 1827, worked in coloured silks with a French verse, Channel Islands, 19 by 22in (49 by 56cm), framed and glazed.
£550-600 *CSK*

Samplers

A map sampler of England and Wales, worked in long and short stitch, and fine black cross stitch, with a border of entwining leaves and flowers, signed Mary Sutton, Cheadle School, Stoke 1797, Britannia is seated in the top right hand corner, late 18thC, 25 by 22in (64 by 56cm).
£300-400 *Bon*

A sampler, by E. B, embroidered in coloured silks, with a verse 'Let Gratitude', c1835, 14 by 12in (36 by 31cm), framed and glazed.
£500-600 *CSK*

A sampler, by Elizabeth Rennie, 1811, worked in coloured silks with a verse 'stretched on the cross', the verse framed by a garland of naturalistic flowers, with a border of trailing flowers, 17 by 13in (43 by 33cm), framed and glazed.
£500-600 *CSK*

A sampler by Ellen Greaves, 1846, worked in coloured wools, with a verse 'Jesus permit', 26 by 27in (67 by 69cm), mounted on a stretcher.
£200-300 *CSK*

Lord search oh search my inmost heart
And life and light and joy impart
From guilt and error set me free
And guide me safe to heav'n and thee

A sampler by Matilda Andrews, 1837, worked in coloured silks with a verse 'Lord search, oh search', also with a picture of St Pauls Chapel New York, with a formalised floral border, 15 by 12in (39 by 31cm), framed and glazed.
£800-900 *CSK*

A needlework sampler by Sarah Hemsley, of Bexley Heath, Kent, dated April 21 1894, worked in fine coloured silks, unframed, late 19thC, 16½ by 13in (43 by 34cm).
£600-700 *Bon*

A needlework sampler, by Elizabeth Lloyd aged 11 years, dated 1800, of Adam and Eve flanking the Tree of Knowledge beneath rows of alphabets, small animals, winged putti, and a 3 lined text, 18 by 15in (46 by 39cm). **£300-400** *Bon*

Tapestries

A tapestry border, woven in many colours, with a central roundel depicting one of the Labours of Hercules, with a centurion and grotesque above, 16thC, 110 by 13in (279 by 34cm).
£1,200-1,500 *CSK*

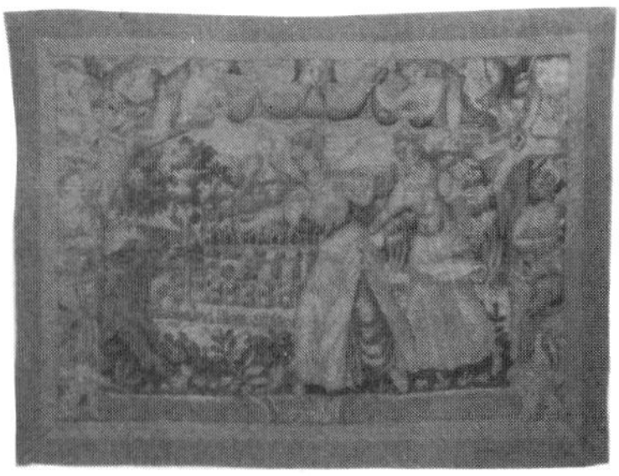

A tapestry panel woven in wools and silks, depicting 2 ladies hunting a fire breathing dragon within a landscape, flanked by centaurs, plain borders, restorations, 17thC, 30 by 22in (77 by 56cm).
£600-700 *C*

A French verdure tapestry panel, woven in shades of green, blue and brown, with leafy trees and foliage in the background and a small pavilion in the foreground, restored, Aubusson, late 17thC, 60 by 28in (152 by 72cm).
£500-600 *CSK*

A Louis XVI tapestry panel, woven in many colours depicting a scene after Oudry, against a cream ground, 22 by 18in (56 by 46cm).
£400-500 *CSK*

French tapestry border, woven ainly in shades of cream, blue, ·own and yellow, with a pale blue ·rder woven with a yellow trailing ıttern, restored, 17thC, 40 by 13in ·01.5 by 34cm).
:00-250 *CSK*

A pair of Louis XVI Aubusson tapestry cushion covers, woven in many colours, backed with crimson damask, 14 by 16in (36 by 41cm).
£700-800 *CSK*

An Aubusson tapestry, woven in shades of brown, cream, green and yellow, 19thC, 80 by 22in (203 by 56cm). **£2,700-3,000** *CSK*

A French tapestry, woven in muted colours, possibly the Aubusson Factory, 19thC, 49 by 67in (124.5 by 170cm).
£1,600-1,800 *GA(W)*

An Aubusson tapestry hanging, woven in many colours, within a frame entwined with roses, 19thC, 106 by 54in (269 by 137cm).
£2,500-3,000 *CSK*

Miscellaneous

A needlework mirror, with ivory satin frame, worked in coloured silks and gilt threads with raised work animals in each corner, the embroidery English, c1660, 22 by 20in (56 by 51cm), framed and glazed. **£3,500-4,000** *CSK*

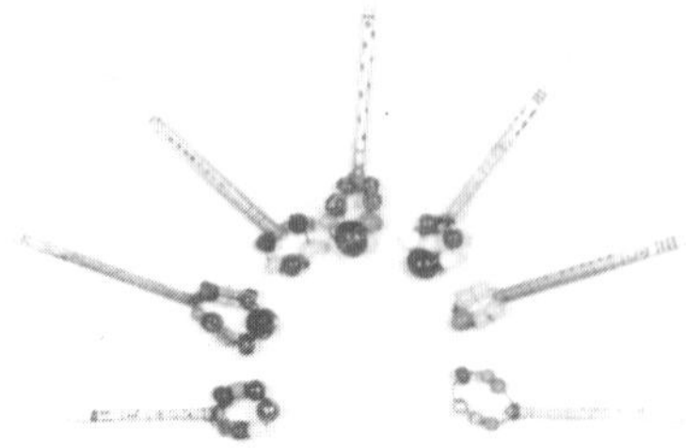

A collection of 7 named and initialled bone bobbins, including David Headland, Ann Gammons, David.
£70-100 *Bon*

A pair of George III needlework pictures by Ellen Foster, 1812, each with watercolour features on an ivory silk ground, 11 by 9in (29 by 23cm) with Victorian giltwood and gesso frames.
£1,000-1,500 *N*

A needlework panel, the ivory field with an acanthus oval enclosing a large bouquet, in a scrolled grey and green lattice with border bouquets in each corner, backed, 75 by 56in (190.5 by 142cm).
£1,000-1,500 *C*

A needlework picture, worked in coloured silks, late 18thC, 18 by 16in (46 by 41cm), framed and glazed.
£200-300 *CSK*

A pair of olive green velvet chair backs, woven to reveal a dark red silk ground, 19thC, 64 by 22in (162.5 by 56cm) each.
£600-700 *CSK*

A pair of cream cord tie backs, with elaborate tasselled heads trimmed with blue, red, green and cream silk and a pair of tie backs of cream and peach coloured cord with matching tassells decorated with gilt threads and 3 other tie backs.
£300-400 *CSK*

A needlework panel, the ivory ground divided into 4 groups of mustard yellow, green, raspberry red and blue open floral leafy palmettes, in a turquoise and mustard yellow plain striped border, backed, 91 by 60in (231 by 152cm).
£3,600-4,000 *C*

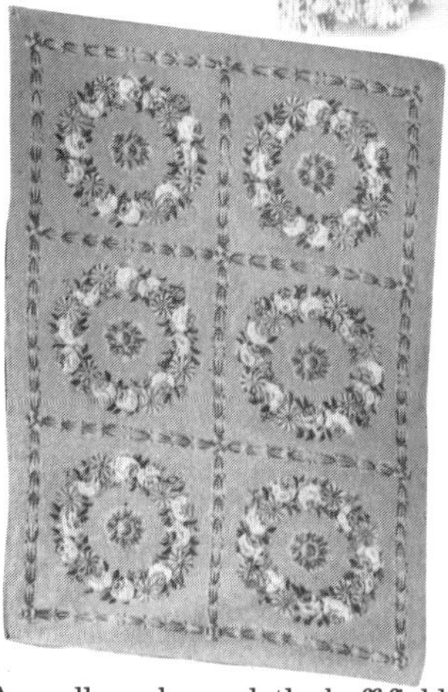

A needlework panel, the buff field divided by golden yellow floral strips into 6 panels, each with a floral wreath around a central golden flowerhead, backed, 62 by 42in (157 by 106.5cm).
£1,700-2,000 *C*

An early Georgian needlework panel, worked in tent stitch, of a lady and gentleman dressed as a shepherd and shepherdess tending their flock in a rural landscape, 23 by 17in (58.5 by 43cm).
£700-800 *Bon*

A Tulip and Rose hanging, woven i shades of blue, green, red and yello wool, with a repeating pattern of flowerheads among curling leave against a dark blue ground, designed by William Morris, late 19thC, 91 by 80in (231 by 203cm)
£1,800-2,200 *CSK*

This pattern was registered as a fabric on 20 January 1876.

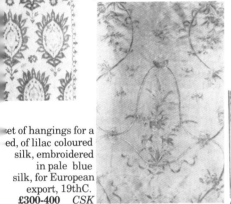

A hanging, composed of 3 panels of natural embroidered linen framed with a border of blue arabesques, the field worked with 4 columns of bold palmettes in blue or red, with serpent motifs, Ottoman, 17th/18thC, 56 by 88in (142 by 223.5cm).
£4,500-5,500 *CSK*

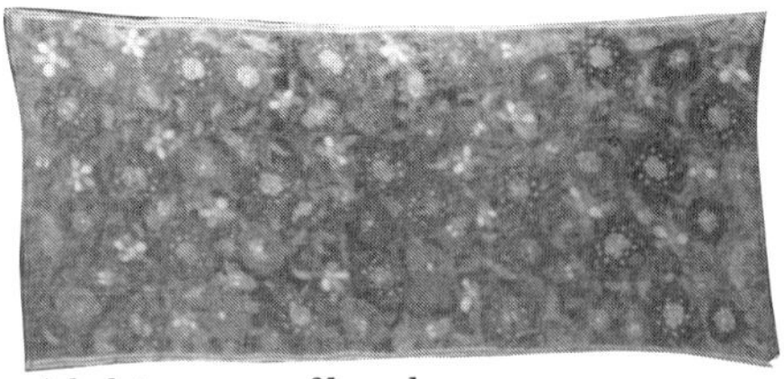

A bolster cover of loosely woven natural linen, embroidered with 2 arching flower sprays, worked with blue spikey florets, terracotta roses and pale green leaves and buds, 18thC, 21 by 47in (53.5 by 119cm).
£700-900 *CSK*

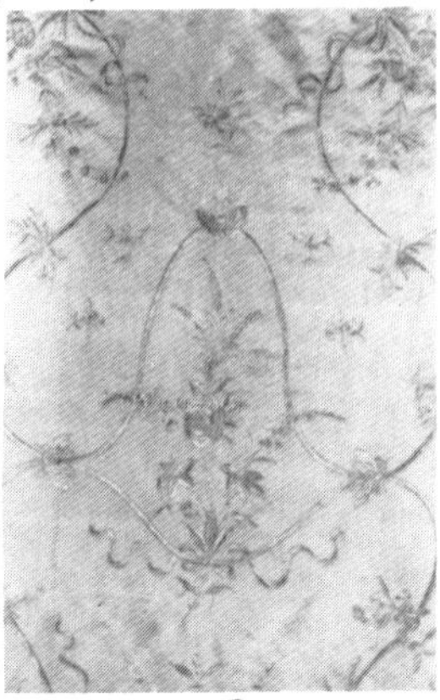

set of hangings for a ed, of lilac coloured silk, embroidered in pale blue silk, for European export, 19thC.
£300-400 *CSK*

A Turkish bolster cover, worked on ivory silk, embroidered with a border of alternating sky blue striped tents and trees, the field sprinkled with flowerbuds in silk and metal thread, 18thC, framed under polythene, 25 by 50in (64 by 127cm).
£350-500 *CSK*

A patchwork quilt, composed of various patterned chintzes, including some printed to commemorate Nelson's victories, against a cream coloured ground, backed with blue cotton, c1800, 114 by 126in (289.5 by 320cm).
£450-600 *CSK*

pair of cushions, incorporating thC verdure tapestry panels, oven in wools and silks depicting gures among pillars and arches, by 16in (66.5 by 40.5cm).
00-1,200 *C*

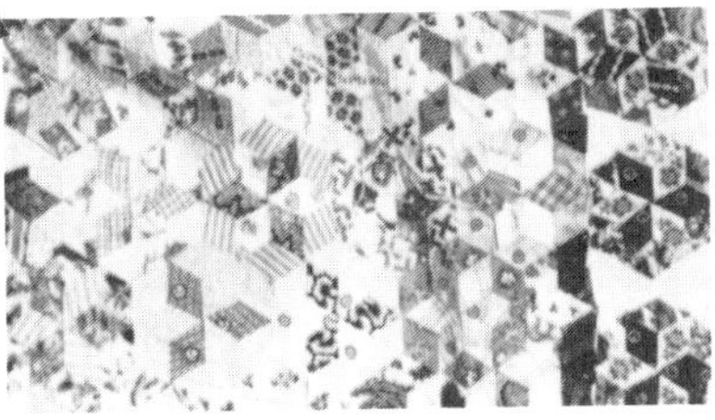

A diamond patchwork coverlet, composed of 19thC cottons dating from c1810, 90in (228.5cm) square.
£400-500 *CSK*

A Victorian taffeta patchwork quilt with geometric designs, 82in (208cm) square.
£300-400 *HCH*

framed patchwork coverlet, mposed of various plain and tterned silks, the central panel th 3 ovals woven with ladies in ts and the title 'Coventry anufacturers', c1850, 96 by 82in 43.5 by 208cm).
00-300 *CSK*

A fragment of an English quilt, the border embroidered in coloured silks depicting exotic birds, flowering shrubs, small butterflies and leaves, early 18thC, 41 by 33in (104 by 84cm).
£120-150 *Bon*

arge woolwork hanging, worked coloured wools, with a central sh stitch spaniel, with a tree in background and framed by iling plush stitch flowers, against olive green ground, mid-19thC, by 86in (142 by 218.5cm).
000-1,500 *CSK*

Fans

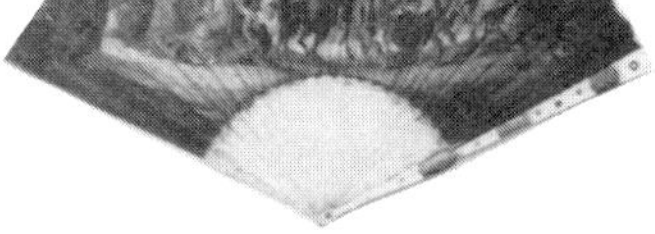

A fan, the leaf painted with the triumphal arrival of Alexander, with ivory sticks, the guardsticks clouté with mother-of-pearl and piqué with silver, c1700, 11in (29cm).
£1,500-2,000 *CSK*

A fan, the leaf painted with a shepherd and shepherdess, the verso painted with sprigs of brightly coloured roses, carnations and tulips, the ivory sticks piqué with silver, possibly English, leaf slightly rubbed, c1690, 11in (29cm).
£2,500-3,000 *CSK*

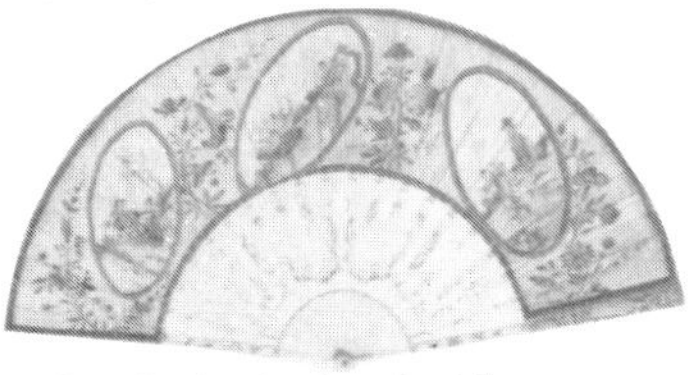

A fan, the leaf painted with a trompe l'oeil of 3 chinoiserie scenes against a pink and white striped ground strewn with flowers, the ivory sticks carved, pierced and painted, c1760, 10in (26cm).
£350-500 *CSK*

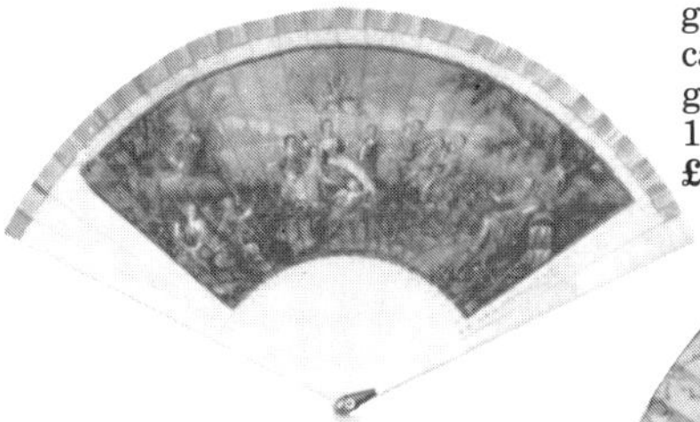

An ivory brisé fan, painted with Pan and Syrinx, the guardsticks carved with a portrait of a lady, early 18thC, 8½in (22cm).
£1,000-1,500 *CSK*

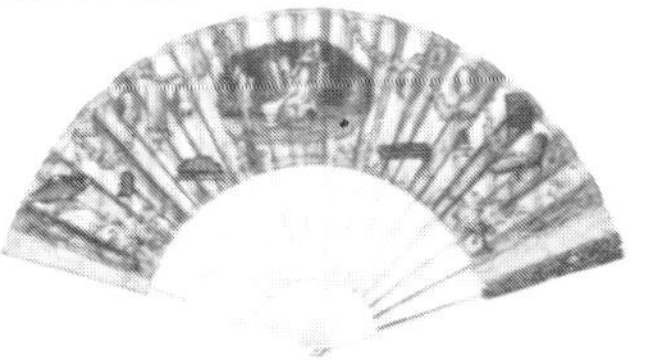

A fan, the leaf painted against a silver and green striped ground, the verso with a figure in a landscape, the ivory sticks gilt, worn and repaired, c1775, 10½in (27cm).
£400-500 *CSK*

A printed fan, with allegorical map of the Track of Youth to the Land of Knowledge, the leaf a hand coloured etching engraved by V. Woodthorpe, 27 Fetter Lane, and published by John Wallis June 25, 1796, 36 Ludgate Street, with wooden sticks, c1796.
£1,200-1,500 *CSK*

A fan, the leaf painted with Judith with the Head of Holofernes, the ivory sticks piqué with silver, the guardsticks clouté with tortoiseshell and mother-of-pearl, 2 pieces of mother-of-pearl missing, early 18thC, 10½in (28cm).
£1,500-2,000 *CSK*

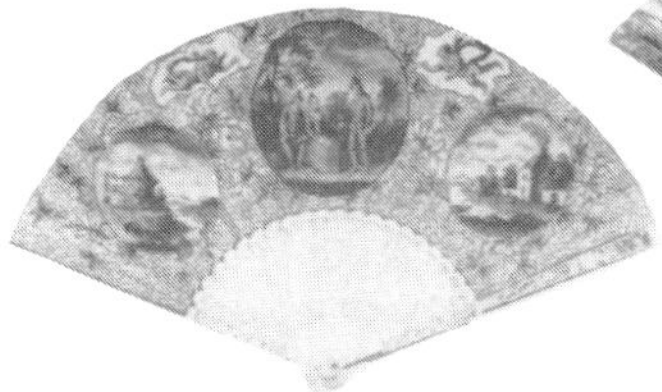

A fan, the leaf painted in tones of green with figures, the ivory sticks carved and pierced with figures, guardsticks damaged, mid-18thC, 11in (29cm), in contemporary box.
£900-1,200 *C*

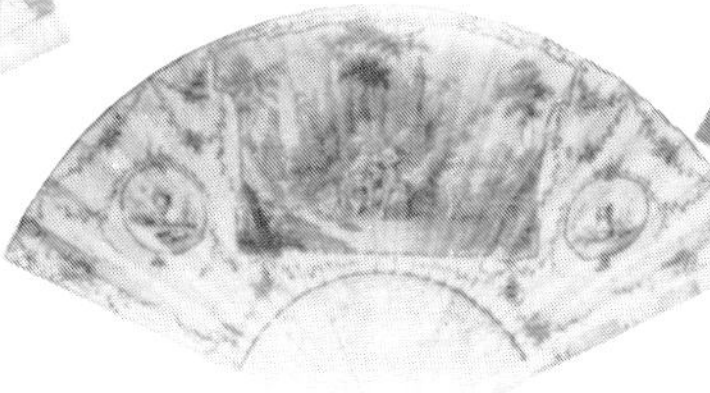

A fan, the ivory sticks clouté with mother-of-pearl, piqué with a trellis of silver and carved with a huntsman, c1770, the sticks c1730, 11½in (30cm).
£500-700 *CSK*

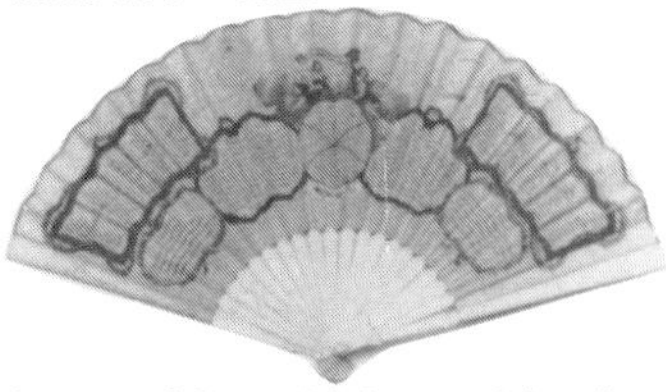

A printed fan, with bone sticks, the publication line overpainted but it is probably by John Cock, J. P. Crowder & Co., 21 Wood St., Cheapside, although in a contemporary fan box by Stunt, Fanmaker, 191 Strand, the old established shop late Sudlow, c1800, 9in (23cm).
£400-500 *CSK*

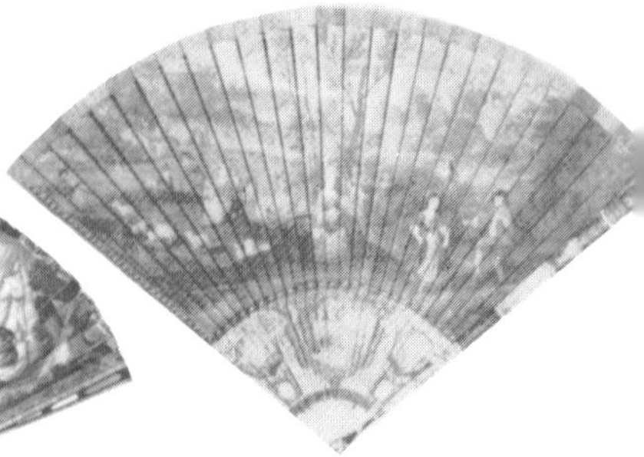

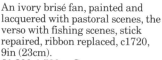

An ivory brisé fan, painted and lacquered with pastoral scenes, the verso with fishing scenes, stick repaired, ribbon replaced, c1720, 9in (23cm).
£1,200-1,500 *C*

A fan, the chickenskin leaf painted with a classical scene, the sticks lacquered in red, green and gold, the guardsticks clouté with mother-of-pearl, early 18thC, 11½in (30cm).
£700-900 *CSK*

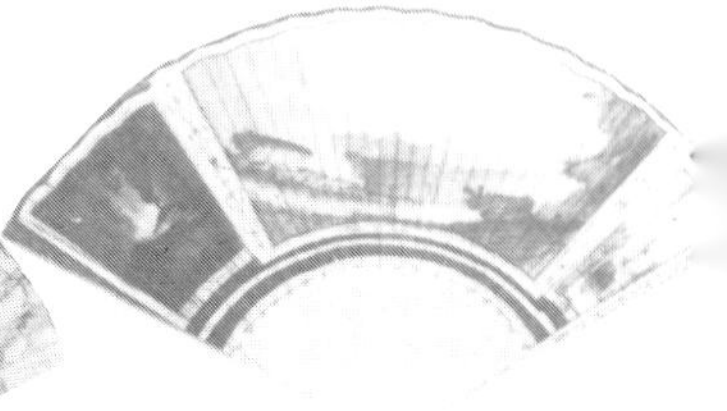

A fan, the chickenskin leaf painted with 3 views of Vesuvius, including the eruption of 1767, the ivory sticks pierced, leaf torn, c1770, 10½in (27cm).
£900-1,200 *CSK*

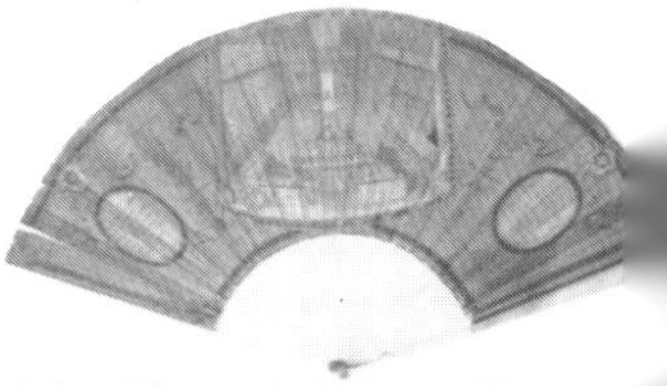

A fan, The trial of Warren Hastings, the leaf a hand coloured line engraving of Westminster Hall printed in brown and edged with sequins, with bone sticks, English, c1788.
£600-800 *CSK*

A pierced bone fan, early 19thC.
£200-250 *GIL*

A fan, the verso signed Alexandre, the mother-of-pearl sticks carved and pierced with putti and gilt with sunbursts, 3 sticks broken, the leaf c1860, the sticks 18thC, in glazed fan case.
£200-300 *CSK*

Rimmel's Cassolette fan, a hand coloured lithographic fan with bone sticks, 1 guardstick set with a gilt metal pomander, c1875, 11in (29cm).
£200-250 *CSK*

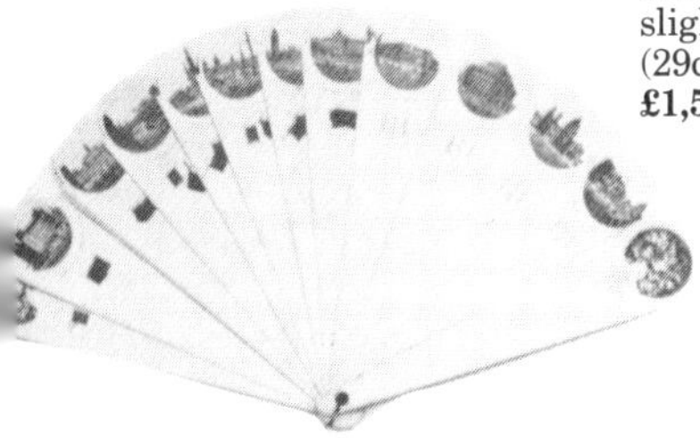

A card brisé fan, printed with views of London, c1870, 8in (21cm).
£120-150 *CSK*

A North European fan, the leaf painted with a central vignette of Moses striking the rock and 2 smaller vignettes of Moses with the Tablets and staff, the verso with a Medieval castle and classical ruins from the sea, the ivory sticks carved and pierced, the guardsticks backed with red foil, c1740, 11½in (30cm).
£600-900 *CSK*

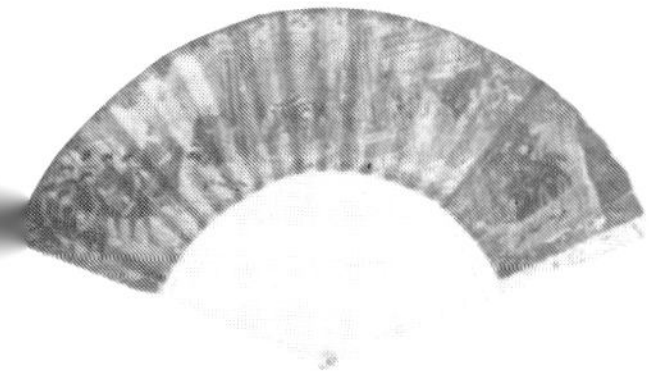

A Swedish fan, the leaf painted with a Court scene, the ivory sticks pierced, the guardsticks carved with a king, c1750, 10in (26cm).
£600-800 *CSK*

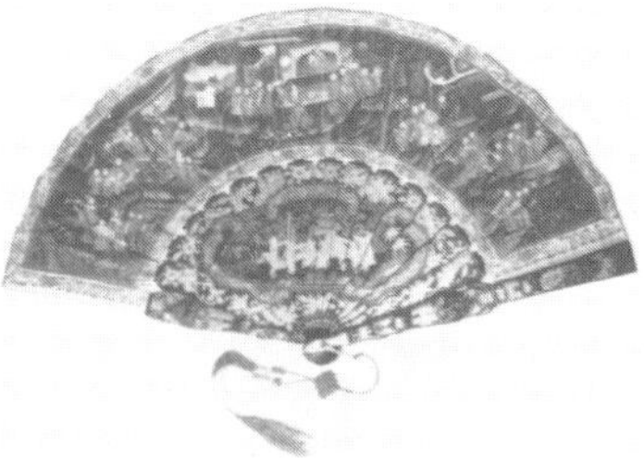

A Canton fan, the leaf painted with figures on a terrace, their faces of ivory, their clothes of silk, with lacquered sticks, c1860, 11in (29cm), in fitted lacquer box.
£500-600 *CSK*

An Austrian printed fan, the leaf an etching of a battle scene, with a key below, the verso with Joseph II and Turkish prisoners, published by Leonard Schielling, Vienna, with wooden sticks and bone fillet, slightly damaged, c1788, 11in (29cm).
£1,500-2,000 *CSK*

A Canton tortoiseshell parasol cockade fan, finely carved and pierced with roundels of buildings, figures and flowers, and slotted with blue and white ribbon, 2 sticks repaired, c1800, 9in (23cm).
£1,500-2,000 *CSK*

A Canton ivory brisé fan, carved and pierced with figures, animals and buildings and initials J.T., labelled J Threasher, c1820, 8in (21cm).
£500-600 *CSK*

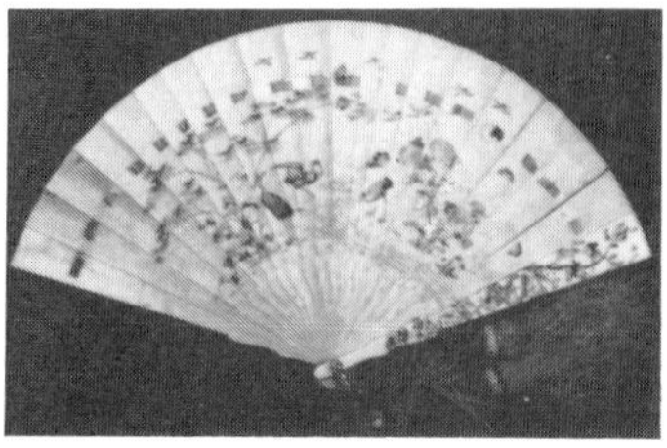

A Japanese ivory brisé fan, lacquered in gold on each side with storks, the guardsticks decorated with shibayama work, late 19thC, 10in (26cm).
£2,000-2,500 *CSK*

A Flemish fan with painted leaf, the mother-of-pearl sticks carved, pierced and silvered gilt and backed, with German sticks, c1750, 11½in (30cm), in later glazed carved wood fan-shaped frame.
£450-550 *C*

A note on the back of the frame states: Marie Elizabeth A. Cartwright, née Sandigell. In the year 1833 this fan came into my possession at the death of Amelia, Duchess of Pflaz Zewybruken (sic) Duchess of Neubourg, Bavaria née Princess of Saxony with my group of old Saxon china . . . the Duchess Amelia died in 1833 aged 86 she was a dear friend of my family.

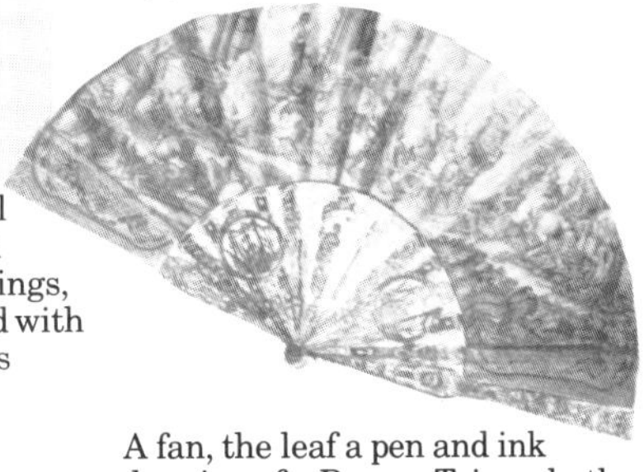

A fan, the leaf a pen and ink drawing of a Roman Triumph, the verso inscribed, the smokey grey mother-of-pearl sticks carved and pierced with figures and gilt, the leaf early 18thC, the verso and sticks mid-19thC.
£1,500-2,000 *CSK*

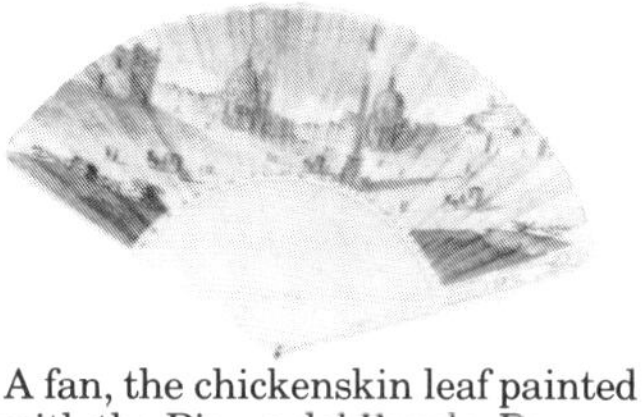

A fan, the chickenskin leaf painted with the Piazza del Popolo, Rome, the verso with a ruin, the ivory sticks pierced with a trellis, the guardsticks carved with figures and Chinese scenes, Italian with Chinese sticks, c1780, 10½in (27cm).
£1,500-2,000 *CSK*

A painted paper fan, on a gold sprinkled ground, the silk tassel with an ivory ojime, the ivory guards carved to simulate bamboo stalks with gold takamakie, shibayama and various flowering branches, signed Kunine, sealmark, Meiji period, 16in (41cm).
£600-800 *Bon*

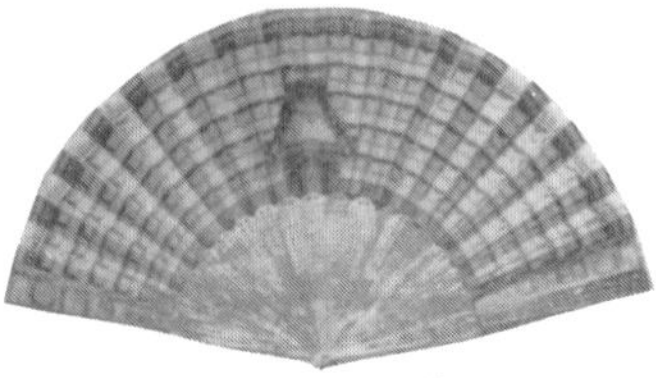

A fan commemorating the centenary of the Grand Theatre Royal de Turin, the leaves painted with the seating plan of the theatre in 1732 and 1782, decorated with garlands, with pierced and gilded mother-of-pearl sticks, 1832, 10in (26cm), in late 19thC box by A. Rodien, Eventailliste, 48 Rue Cambon Ancienne Rue de Luxembourg.
£1,500-2,000 *C*

A French fan, the leaf painted with a court scene, possibly Naples, the ivory sticks pierced and silvered, c1770, 11in (29cm), in glazed fan case.
£800-1,000 *CSK*

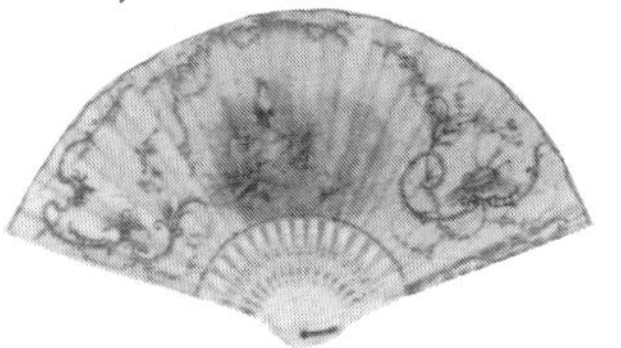

A French fan, the cream silk leaf hand painted in colours applied with gilt sequins, the ivory sticks decorated with stylised flowers and leaves, the guard stick carved and painted, 10in (24.5cm) long, in original box, upholstered in foliate fabric and inscribed in gilt J. Duvelleroy, Paris, By Appointment.
£120-170 *HSS*

An Italian fan, the chickenskin leaf painted with a view of Naples, the bone sticks pierced, c1780, 10½in (27cm), in 18thC fan case labelled Clarke, Fan Maker No 27, near Hungerford Street, Strand, London.
£1,000-1,500 *C*

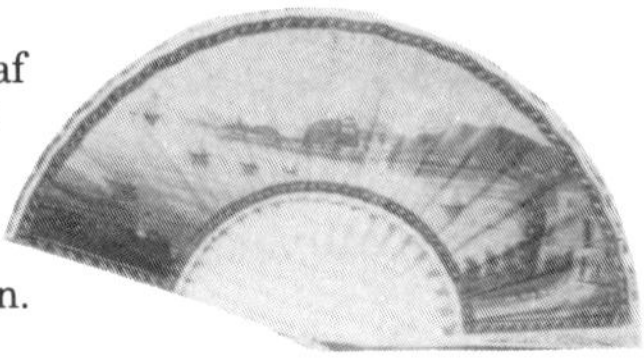

A Canton white metal filigree brisé fan, worked with a deer, butterflies and plants and partly gilt, 19thC, 7½in (19cm), in box labelled Wang sin kee fan shop 727 Nanking Road, Shanghai, established 1875.
£900-1,200 *CSK*

An Italian fan, the chickenskin leaf painted with the Triumph of Aurora, the ivory sticks carved and pierced, in glazed case, repaired, late 18thC.
£1,200-1,500 *CSK*

A Souvenir de l'Exposition Universelle de 1867 fan, the leaf a hand coloured lithograph with a bird's eye plan of the exhibition, lithographed by Truillot, 21, rue Grange-aux-belles, with wooden sticks, 10in (26cm).
£600-700 *CSK*

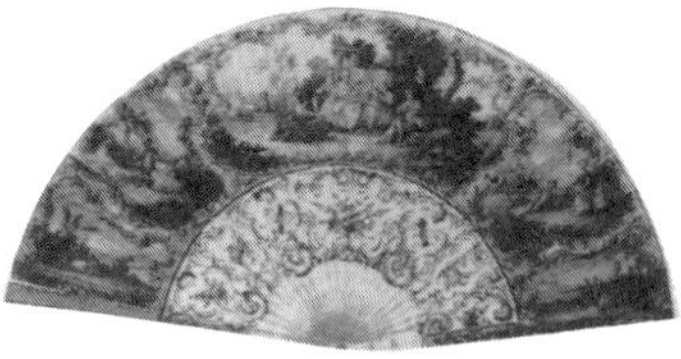

A French fan, the leaf painted with an 18thC pastiche, the ivory sticks carved, pierced and painted with trophies of love, leaf slightly torn and splitting at folds, mid-19thC, 11in (28cm).
£350-450 *CSK*

A Dutch fan, the leaf painted with a Dutch fishing scene, and baskets of flowers, the verso with a bunch of flowers, the ivory sticks pierced and silvered, c1770, 11in (29cm).
£300-400 *CSK*

A fan, the canepin leaf painted with a trompe l'oeil of genre scenes and portraits against a wooden ground, signed A. Gomez, Madrid, with ivory sticks, c1880.
£300-400 *CSK*

A French fan, the leaves painted with figures and a windmill in a landscape, the ivory sticks carved with a cabriolet, painted and gilt with chinoiserie, 2 sticks damaged, leaf split at folds, c1750.
£1,700-2,000 *CSK*

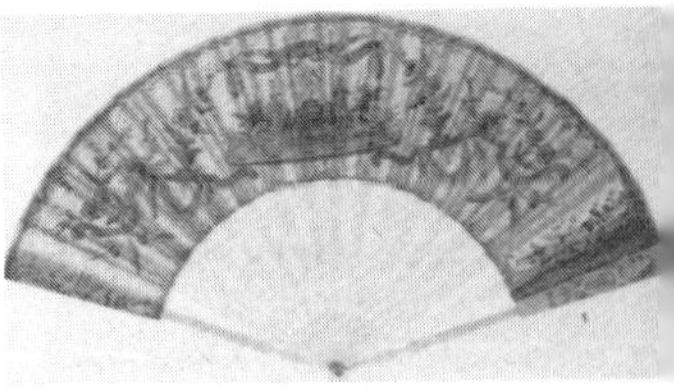

A French fan, the silk leaf painted with figures at the Altar of Love, and embroidered with gold braid and sequins, the ivory sticks carved and pierced with putti, c1760, 10in (26cm).
£350-450 *CSK*

A printed fan, the leaf a hand coloured etching of Cupid burning his wings inscribed, with gilt metal sticks, the guardsticks set with miniature vignettes of doves in red and white paste frames, repaired, c1820, 7in (18cm), in glazed case.
£150-200 *CSK*

An Indian fan, the ivory guards carved in low relief with trailing roses, the sticks pierced with keywork and roundels and with the name 'Elizabeth', with white feather and ostrich feather leaf, with gilt metal loop and white silk tassel, late 19thC, sticks 10in (26cm) high, boxed.
£70-100 *HSS*

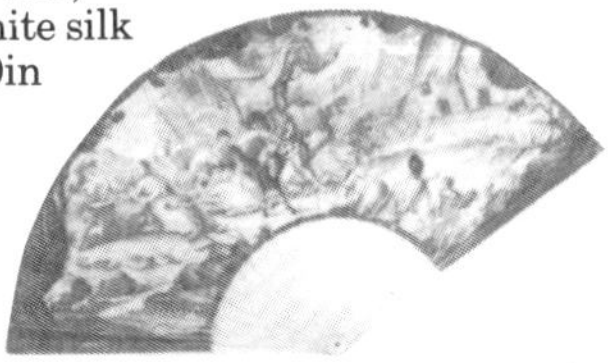

An Italian fan, the chickenskin leaf painted with the Birth of Jupiter, with ivory sticks, split at folds, c1730, 10½in (27cm).
£1,200-1,500 *CSK*

An Italian fan, the chickenskin leaf painted with a view of St Peter and the Vatican, the ivory sticks pierced and silvered, worn, c1780, 11in (29cm).
£1,500-2,000 *CSK*

)OLLS

Vooden Dolls

. George III wooden doll, with black nd white enamelled eyes, pink nouth, jointed pine legs, sculptured noes, fabric upper arms and ooden lower arms terminating in ng fork like digits, wearing an arly 19thC red and brown and hite lace bonnet, hair missing and ight damage, c1780, 23in (59cm) igh.
700-800 *HSS*

carved, turned and painted oden doll, with rouged cheeks, rk enamel eyes, stitched brows d lashes and carved ears, the nite painted wooden body with ms attached at shoulders with th, dressed as a child in ntemporary 18thC silk frock with ck back, blue silk calash.
,000-8,000 *CSK*

A George III wooden doll, the carved ovoid head with the remains of a styled ginger wig, black and white enamelled eyes, dot painted eyebrows and eyelashes, pink mouth and cheeks, jointed pine legs and primitively carved feet, wearing a 19thC crimson silk bodice, cream skirt, pantaloons and woven stockings, some damage, c1800, 26in (67cm) high.
£1,700-2,000 *HSS*

Wax

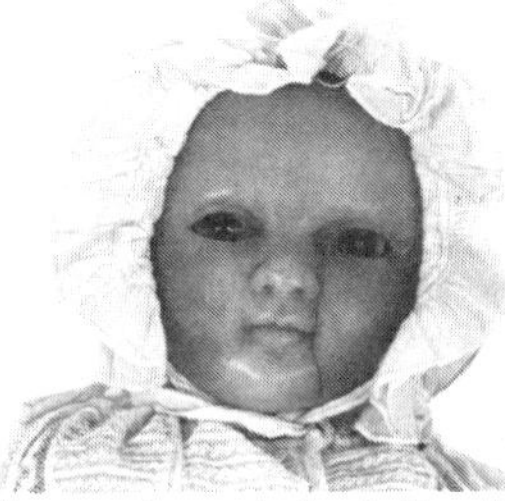

A poured wax baby doll, with blue sleeping eyes, blonde mohair wig, the stuffed body with wax limbs, dressed in original whitework gown, cracked face and damage to feet, eye mechanism lacks wire, c1820, 23in (59cm) high.
£400-500 *C*

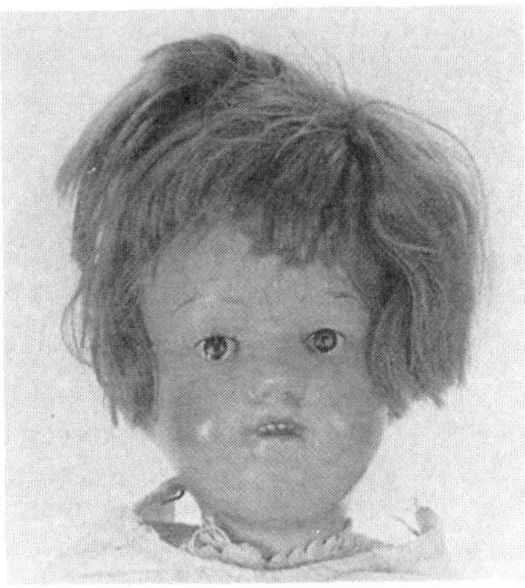

A wooden child doll, painted with brown eyes, 4 teeth and with blonde wool wig, the spring jointed body wearing original combinations and contemporary underclothes, including a liberty bodice, with oval transfer mark reading Schoenhut Doll Pat. Jan. 17th 1911, U.S.A., 15in (39cm) high.
£300-350 *C*

A wax over composition headed doll, with dark sleeping eyes, brown moulded hair, the composition body in original Highland outfit, c1850, 10½in (26.5cm) high.
£200-300 *CSK*

A wax doll, all original, c1830, 7in (18cm) high.
£200-300 *SP*

A wax over composition doll, 'Eliza', with wired eye mechanism, brown mohair ringlets, the stuffed body with wax over composition limbs, in contemporary cotton print dress, white quilted cotton sun bonnet and underwear, wax cracked, c1845, 22in (56cm) high.
£500-600 *C*

A wax over papier mâché headed doll, with fixed bright blue eyes an hair wig, the stuffed body with waxed arms, wearing original cream gauze dress trimmed with lace, flowers and ribbons, standing on a red painted doll's house chair, c1840, 14in (35.5cm) high, in glaze case.
£200-300 *C*

A wax over papier mâché headed doll, with fixed eyes, the cloth body with pink kid arms, in contemporary black satin dress, with separate white collar, ribbon, lace bonnet and underclothes, extra clothes including a green silk dress, a white muslin flounced dress, 2 coloured printed wool dresses, a woven blue patterned wool dress and a green and white checked cotton frock, c1848, 14in (35.5cm) long. **£800-1,000** *C*

A wax over composition doll, with dark eyes, brown mohair ringlets and stuffed body with wax over composition limbs in contemporary cotton print dress and straw hat, wax cracked, c1840, 25in (64cm) high.
£250-350 *C*

A wax over papier mâché heade doll, the dark sleeping eyes wir from the waist, the brown ringl set into a slit in the crown, the stuffed body with blue kid arms wearing muslin frock with pink sash and straw hat decorated w flowers, c1840, 28in (72cm) hig
£400-500 *C*

A wax over composition headed doll, with fixed blue eyes and blonde ringlets, the stuffed body dressed as a child in original white silk and lace frock, with artificial flowers in her hair, hands and bosom, carrying a banner embroidered with the message 'Forget me not', mid-19thC, 12in (30.5cm) high, in glazed case.
£400-500 *C*

A wax headed doll, with bead ey painted short hair, cloth body an wax arms, original blue wool ski white ribbed silk jacket, wired flower trimmed hat and underclothes, c1840, 7½in (19cm high.
£500-600 *C*

A poured wax headed doll, with dark eyes, the stuffed body with wax limbs, dressed in regional costume from Hamburg with wooden yoke and 2 baskets, broken at neck, c1850, 21in (53.5cm) high, with a letter written in German which accompanied the doll in 1850.
£600-700 *CSK*

A wax over papier mâché shoulder headed doll, with fixed pale blue eyes, fair hair ringlets, cloth body and waxed legs and arms with separate fingers, some cracking, old repair to eyelid, c1850, 34in (86.5cm) high.
£1,000-1,500 *C*

. poured wax doll, all original,
1880, 21in (53.5cm) high.
300-450 *SP*

A wax over composition headed doll, with dark eyes, moulded blonde hair with paper hair decoration, the stuffed body with composition limbs including blue boots with red tassels, original cotton print frock trimmed with purple braid and medallion marking the centenary of the founding of Sunday Schools in 1880, c1880, 15in (38.5cm) high, in glazed case.
£200-300 *CSK*

These medallions were given to children attending Sunday School in the centenary year.

A wax over composition headed doll, with black sleeping eyes operated with a wire, dark brown ringlets, the stuffed body with waxed limbs, dressed in original cream watered silk frock, mauve silk jacket, cream silk wired bonnet, underwear, shoes and socks, c1845, 30in (76.5cm) high.
£900-1,200 *CSK*

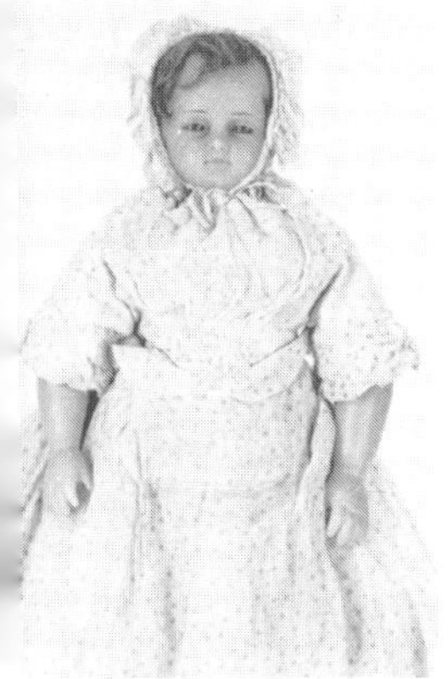

poured wax headed baby doll,
ith blue eyes, fair hair inset in
ashes, the stuffed body with wax
nbs in blue spotted muslin dress
d lace trimmed bonnet, probably
Pierotti, 16in (40.5cm) high.
00-700 *C*

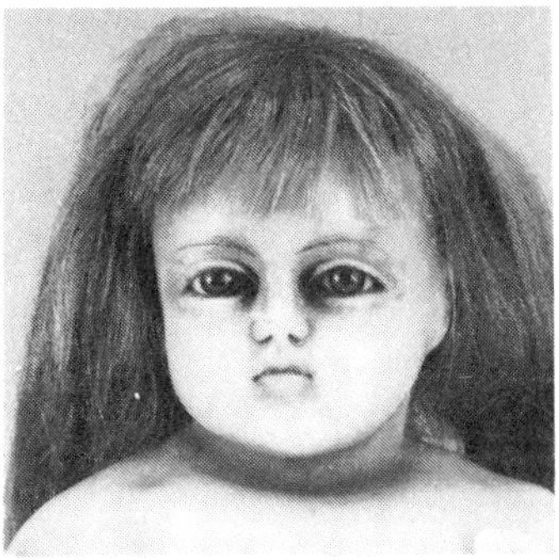

A poured wax headed child doll with pale grey eyes outlined in blue, with long blonde mohair inserted wig, the stuffed body with wax limbs, wearing original underclothes and knitted and beaded bootees, marked in ink on body 'B–/S', leg damaged, c1880, 17in (43.5cm) high.
£200-300 *CSK*

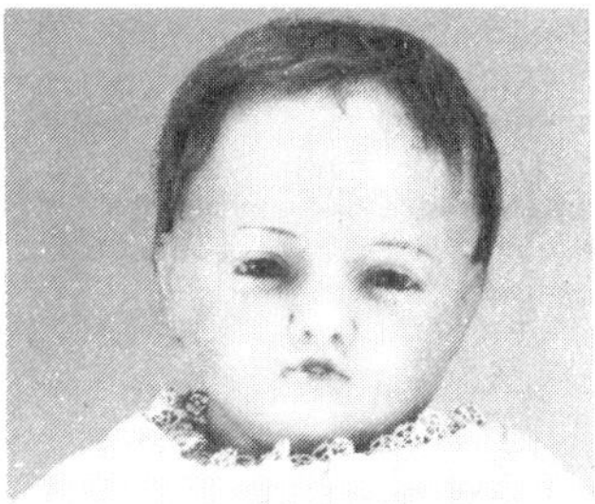

A poured wax headed doll modelled as a baby, with blue eyes, inset hair and eyelashes, the stuffed body with wax limbs dressed in white lace trimmed gown and underwear, probably by Pierotti, slight damage to forehead, 22in (55.5cm) high.
£700-800 *CSK*

A wax bride doll, c1925, 19in (48.5cm) high.
£80-100 *SP*

Bisque & Papier Mâché

A bisque headed character baby doll, with open closed mouth, blue sleeping eyes, short blonde wig and baby body dressed in cream silk robe and hat with tucks and lace insertions, marked 'D.I.P. 5' and stamped in green Geschutz, Germany S. & Co. for Swaine & Co.
£700-800 *CSK*

A bisque headed bébé, with fixed blue yeux fibres, pierced ears, blonde wig and jointed composition body, dressed in white, firing crack behind left ear, stamped in red 'Le Parisien' and on the body in purple Bebe 'Le Parisien' Medaille d'Or Paris, and impressed '11 Paris', 18in (45.5cm) high.
£900-1,200 *C*

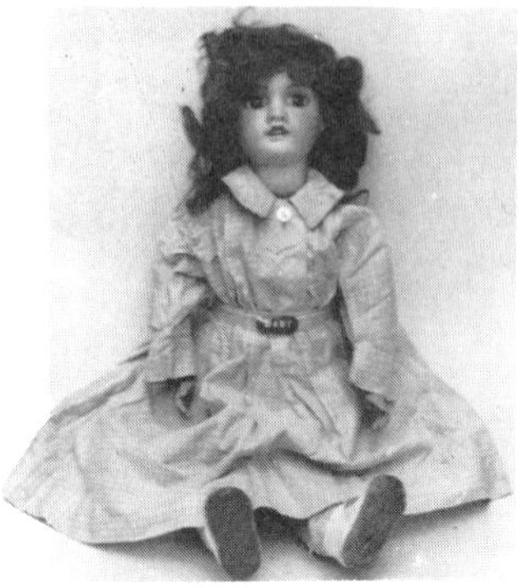

A French Liane bébé bisque doll, by J. Verlingue.
£250-350 *GIL*

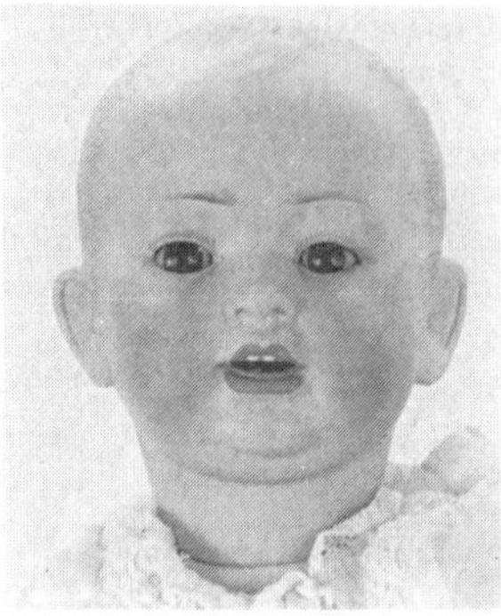

A bisque headed character baby doll, with brown sleeping eyes, painted brush strokes for hair and composition baby's body, dressed in cream, tiny chip to neck and eye, marked 151, 18in (45.5cm) high.
£300-350 *C*

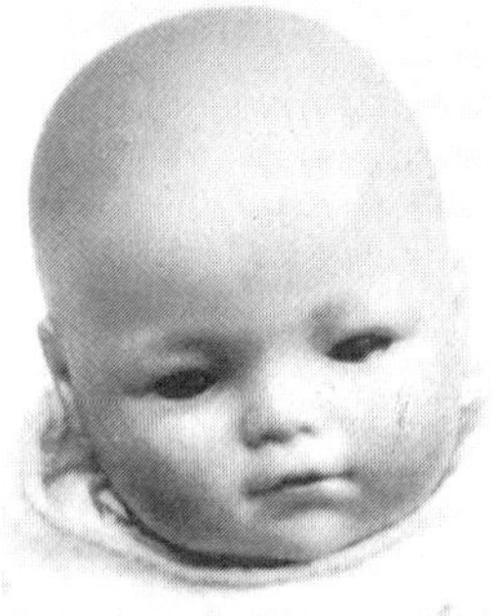

A bisque headed baby doll, with closed mouth, blue sleeping eyes, the stuffed body with composition arms and voice box, dressed in white, marked S PB in star H, N O B, 12in (30.5cm) high.
£400-500 *CSK*

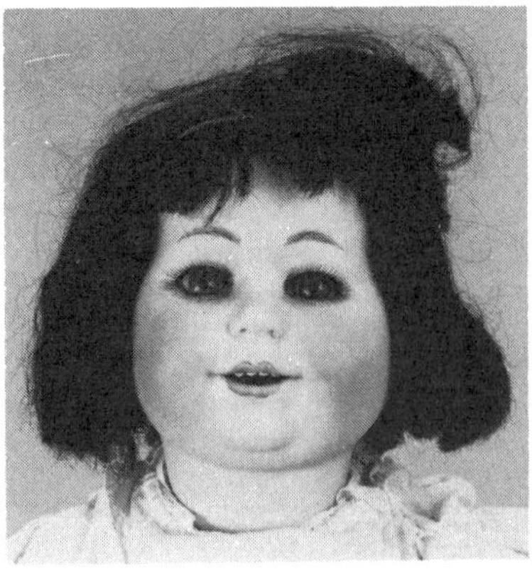

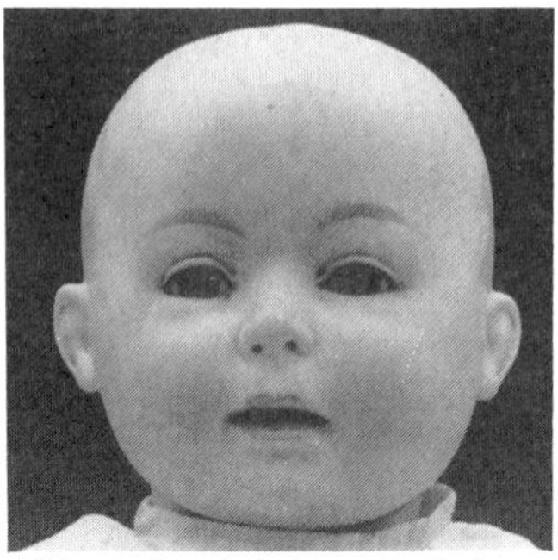

A bisque headed character baby doll, with blue sleeping eyes, moulded and painted hair, the bent limbed composition body dressed in white, marked D. Lori 1 and stamped S & Co., 23in (58.5cm) high.
£1,200-1,500 *CSK*

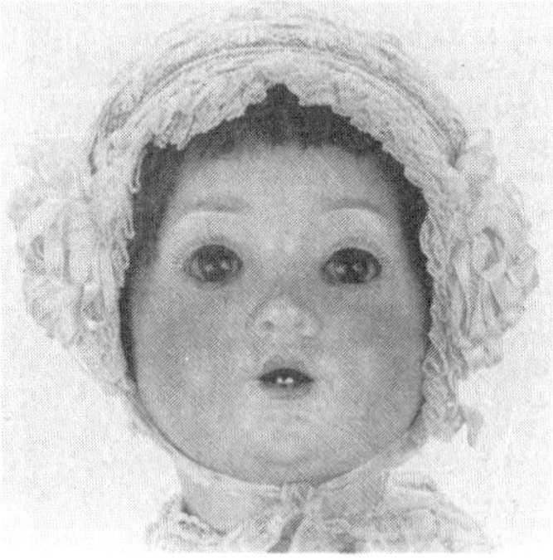

A bisque headed character baby doll, with brown lashed sleeping eyes, brown mohair wig, the bent limbed composition body in lace trimmed cream silk gown and bonnet, marked B & O B–3 3/4 by Bruckner & Och, 18in (45.5cm) high.
£200-300 *C*

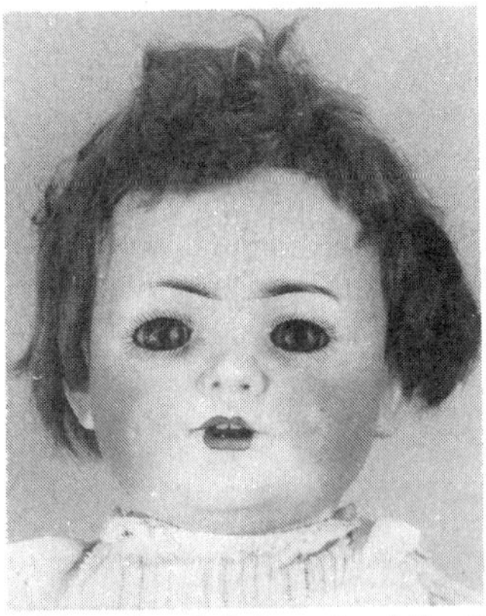

A bisque headed character doll, with blue sleeping eyes, feathered brows, dimples, light brown mohair wig, the jointed wood and composition toddler body in whitework dress and underwear, marked Harmus 660-10, 19in (48.5cm) high.
£400-500 *CSK*

A bisque headed character baby doll, with smiling mouth, blue lashed sleeping eyes, feathered brows and bent limbed composition body in whitework dress and underwear, marked WG B1 – 8, 19in (48.5cm) high.
£500-600 *CSK*

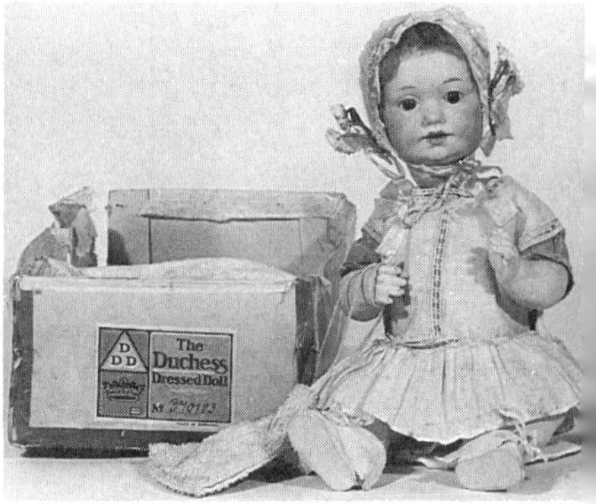
The
Duchess
Dressed Doll

A bisque headed character baby doll with brown sleeping eyes, light brown mohair wig and bent limbed composition body in original blue and white cotton dress, lace bonnet, shoes and socks, marked 971 A.3/OM, in original box marked 'The Duchess Dressed Doll', 12in (30.5cm) high.
£700-800 *C*

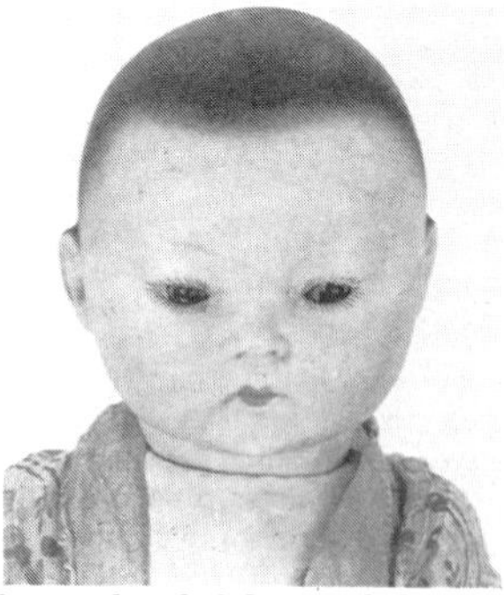

A bisque headed Oriental characte baby doll, with closed sleeping eyes the toddler body wearing a kimono marked '2', 12in (30.5cm) high.
£600-800 *C*

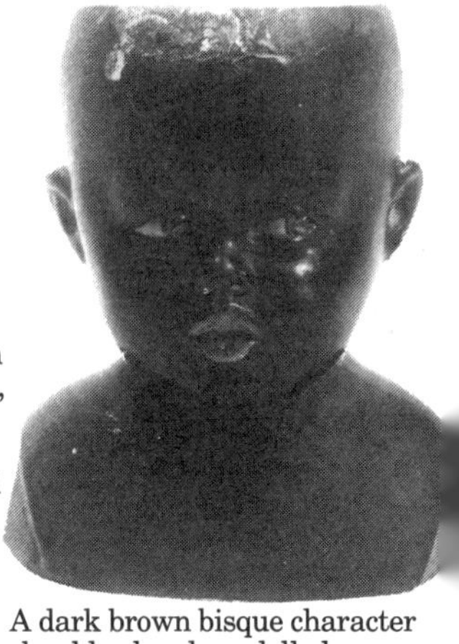

A dark brown bisque character shoulder-head, modelled as a frowning negro child, with open/closed mouth and brown intaglio eyes glancing to the left, impressed 93, Heubach Square 3 probably the shoulder head wigg version of mould 7671, 3½in (9cr high.
£300-400 *CSK*

A bisque headed character doll, with sleeping googlie eyes, closed mouth and bent limbed composition body dressed in sailor suit and hat, marked 323 A.O.M, 12½in (32cm) high.
£900-1,200 *CSK*

bisque headed bébé, with fixed lue eyes, pierced ears and jointed ody wearing a wedding dress, etticoat and underclothes, shoes nd socks, marked 3, the shoes tamped 3 Paris Deposé with the ee trademark, 12½in (32cm).
1,000-1,500 *C*

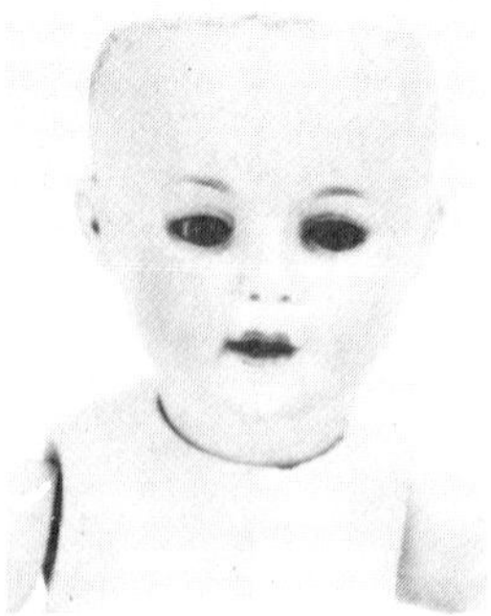

A rare bisque headed character baby doll, with blue lashed sleeping eyes and bent limbed composition body, probably the wigged version of Lori by Swaine & Co., tiny chip to neck, marked 233 7, 16in (40.5cm) high.
£700-800 *CSK*

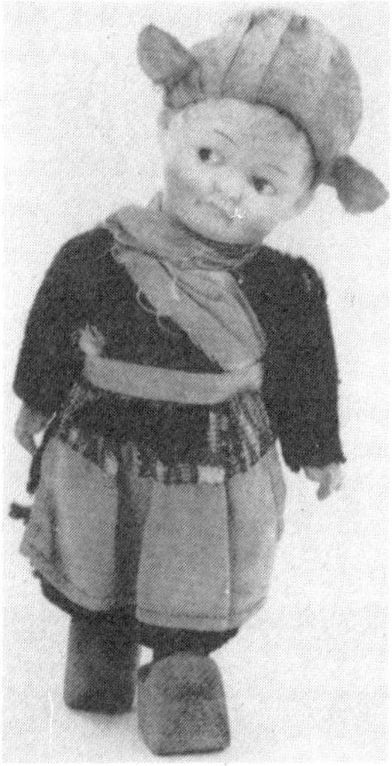

A bisque headed character doll, with googlie eyes, closed mouth with teeth over bottom lip, moulded and painted hair, the straight limbed composition body dressed in original Dutch regional costume, marked EH 262, 7½in (18.5cm) high.
£300-400 *CSK*

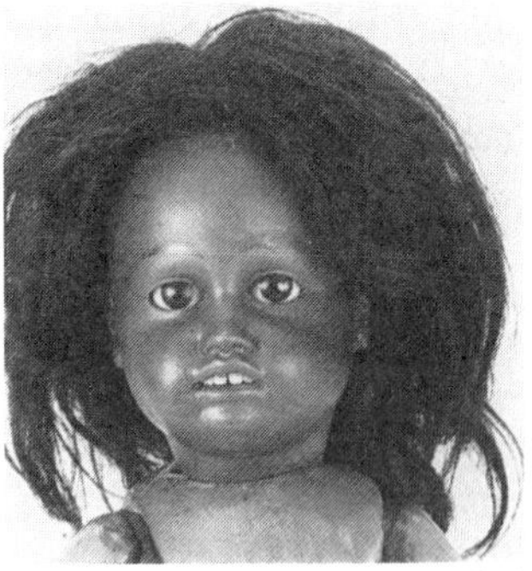

A rare dark brown bisque headed character doll, modelled as a negress with brown sleeping eyes, black wool wig and brown jointed body, marked 34-27, possibly Gebruder Kühnlenz, restored hands, 16in (40.5cm) high.
£1,500-2,000 *C*

A bisque headed character doll, with closed mouth, blue fixed eyes, feathered brows and brown wig, the jointed wood and composition body dressed in blue velvet with leather shoes, wig pulls and overpainted body, marked BSW in Heart for Bruno Schmidt of Waltershausen, 27in (68.5cm) high.
£600-1,000 *C*

bisque headed character doll, with ue lashed sleeping eyes and onde mohair wig, the composition ddler body in original frilled dress d underwear and blue felt hat, arked Porzellan fabrik Burggrub incess Elizabeth 3 1/2, 17in 3.5cm) high.
00-800 *C*

A pair of bisque headed twin dolls, by Max Handwerck, 21in (53.5cm) high.
£500-700 *P(M)*

A large bisque headed doll by C. M. Bergmann, Whershaven, Germany, 1916.
£300-400 *MGM*

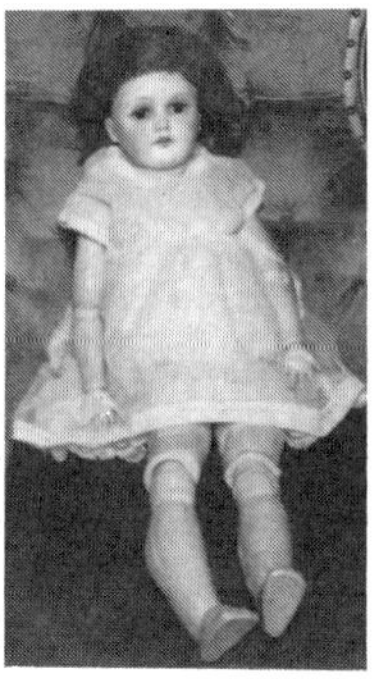

A bisque headed doll 'Queenie', with blue lashed sleeping eyes, moulded brows and brown wig, the jointed wood and composition body in sea green light woollen dress, underwear and blue leather shoes, hand overpainted, marked ABG 13641/214, 26in (66.5cm) high.
£700-800 *C*

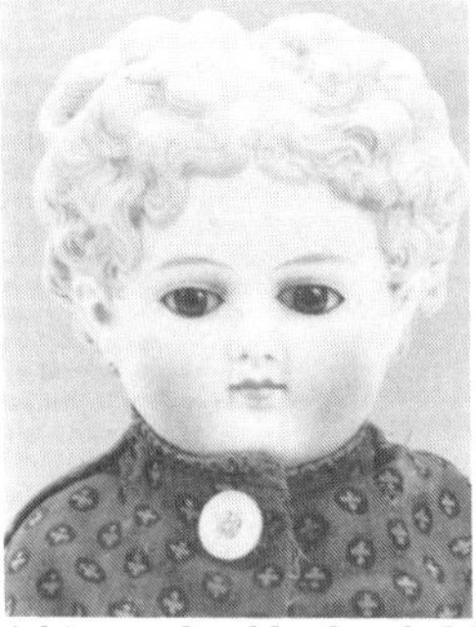

A bisque shoulder headed doll with fixed blue eyes, moulded and painted blonde hair, the stuffed body with kid arms in cotton print dress and underwear, 19½in (49.5cm) high.
£400-500 *CSK*

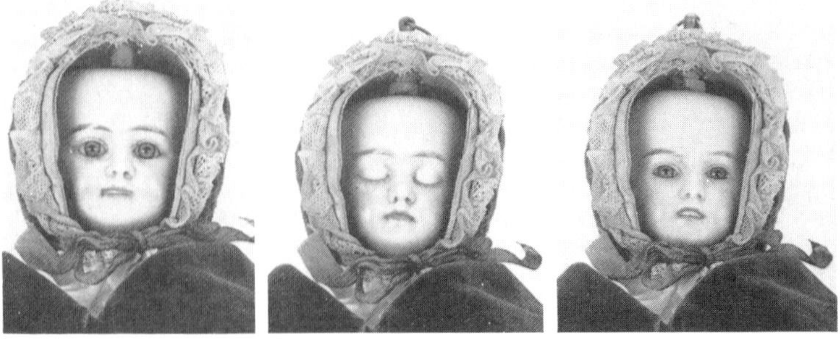

A bisque headed 3-faced doll, the faces smiling, crying and sleeping, under lace trimmed carton hood, the jointed wood and composition body dressed in corded silk coat, damaged hands, by Carl Bergner, c1900, 14in (35.5cm) high.
£800-1,000 *C*

A bisque swivel headed Parisienne, with fixed deep blue eyes, pierced ears, blonde wig and gusseted kid body, filled firing crack above left ear, 16½in (42cm) high.
£700-900 *C*

An all bisque doll with closed mouth, blue fixed eyes and blonde mohair wig, the body with moulded and painted shoes and socks in elaborate original cream silk dress with train, tiny chip to neck, silk distressed, 7in (17.5cm) high.
£600-700 *CSK*

A bisque headed Parisienne, with blue eyes, feathered brows, white cotton wig, stock and stuffed body with wooden limbs dressed in French Officer's uniform of blue and red jacket and pillbox hat, white breeches and high leather boots, toes of one foot missing, 13in (33.5cm) high.
£800-1,000 *CSK*

A Victorian papier mâché doll, all original, 16in (40.5cm) high.
£150-250 *SP*

Bru

A bisque swivel headed Parisienne with smiling mouth, pale blue paperweight eyes, feathered brows, pierced ears, fair mohair wig, and gusseted kid body with individually stitched fingers, dressed in blue woollen skirt and jacket, marked 'G', probably Bru, 18in (45.5cm) high. **£4,000-5,000** *C*

A bisque swivel-headed Parisienne, with fixed blue eyes, pierced ears and gusseted kid body, wearing original peacock green silk dress with matching sleeveless jerkin, with spare flower printed wool dress trimmed with orange and yellow silk fringing, large flat chip to front shoulder plate, marked on head and shoulder D, by Bru, c1862, 15in (38cm) high. **£1,300-1,700** *C*

A bisque headed Bébé Teteur, with brown eyes, feathered brows, pierced ears and blonde mohair wig with original cork pate, with kid body, bisque hands and composition legs, with drinking mechanism, dressed in original white muslin over pale blue, tucked and lace trimmed baby gown and bonnet, baby feeding bottle and dummy, in wicker moses basket with hood, draped in blue and white cotton, lace trimmed, one finger chipped, marked Bru Jne, 13in (33.5cm) high.
£4,000-6,000 *CSK*

Gebruder Heubach

\ Heubach Koppelsdorf character
loll, c1919, 15in (38.5cm) high.
:350-400 *BEB*

A large bisque headed doll, by Heubach Koppelsdorf.
£150-200 *MGM*

Jumeau

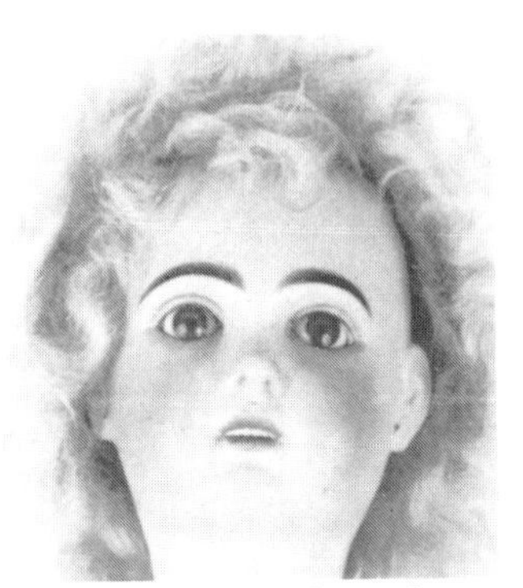

A bisque headed mechanical walking doll with fixed blue glass eyes, pierced ears and blonde mohair wig, the mechanical jointed body clothed in cotton dress and underclothes, mechanical train in need of restoration, stamped in red Tête Jumeau and marked 10, 24in (61.5cm) high. **£700-800** *Bon*

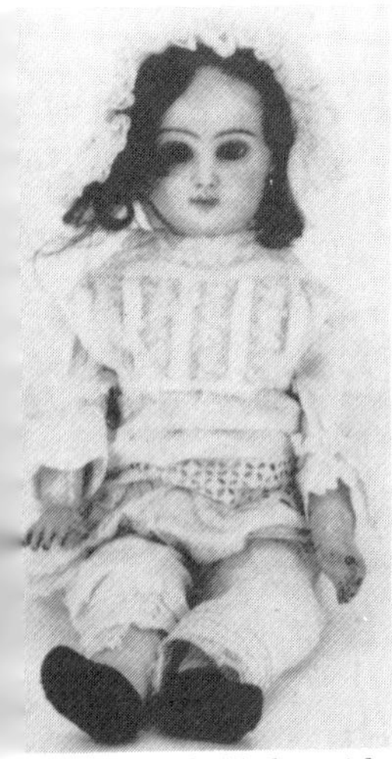

bisque headed bébé, with
:erced ears, fixed blue eyes
nd fixed wrist papier
ıâché body, stamped in red
épосé Tête Jumeau
te S.G.D.G. 7
nd impressed 7,
6½in (42cm) high.
3,000-3,500 *CSK*

A bisque headed bébé, 'Percy', with fixed brown eyes, closed mouth, pierced ears, short light brown wig and fixed wrist composition and papier mâché body, dressed as a boy in check plus-fours, Norfolk jacket and velvet Scots bonnet, impressed Déposé E 6 J and with red painter's marks, stamped on the body Jumeau Medaille D'or Paris, and the shoes stamped in gold Bébé Jumeau med.or 1878 Paris Déposé, 18in (45.5cm) high. **£2,500-3,500** *C*

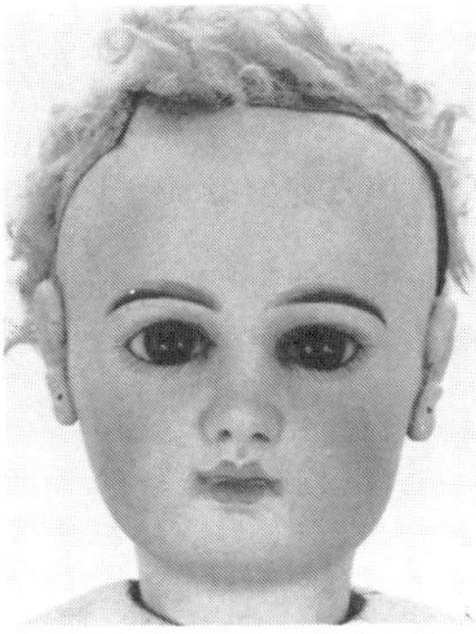

A bisque headed bébé, with fixed blue eyes, shaded lids, pierced ears and fixed wrist papier mâché and ball jointed body, 1 lower leg section missing, impressed Déposé Jumeau 10 painters red marks M8, 22in (56cm) high.
£3,000-3,500 *C*

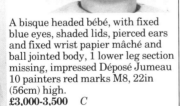

A bisque headed bébé, with fixed blue eyes, heavy brows, pierced ears and blonde hair wig, the jointed wood and composition body wearing printed cotton frock, hairline crack on forehead, stamped in red Déposé Tete Jumeau 12, impressed 2 and with painter's marks and blue stamp on body Bébé Jumeau Bte S.G.D.G. Déposé, 26in (67cm) high.
£1,800-2,500 *C*

J. D. Kestner

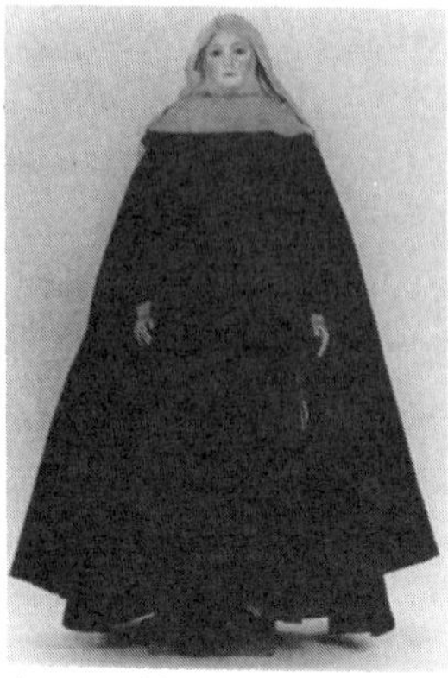

A pressed bisque swivel headed lady doll, with fixed sky blue eyes with grey brows, pink nostrils, chin and cheeks, pierced ears and cork pate, the shoulder plate with adult figure, the kid body wearing original novice's habit of the Augustinian order, comprising voile fin, veil, bandeau, wimple, serre-tête, choir cloak, habit, fichu, black serge waist petticoat, linen petticoat, chemise, laced bodice, knitted cotton stockings, garters and black kid slippers, by Jumeau, c1875, 31in (78.5cm) high, with original stand.
£4,000-6,000 *C*

This figure was kept in the roberie in the Convent des Oiseaux, a house of the Canonesses of Saint Augustine in Paris, as a model of how a Novice should dress. It seems probable, as this was a well endowed Convent, that the doll was ordered especially, as there are no gussets in the body; the hands, which would not be seen, are of poor quality, and there is no wig.

A Kestner 192 doll, in original clothes, c1915, 7½in (19cm) high.
£300-350 *BEB*

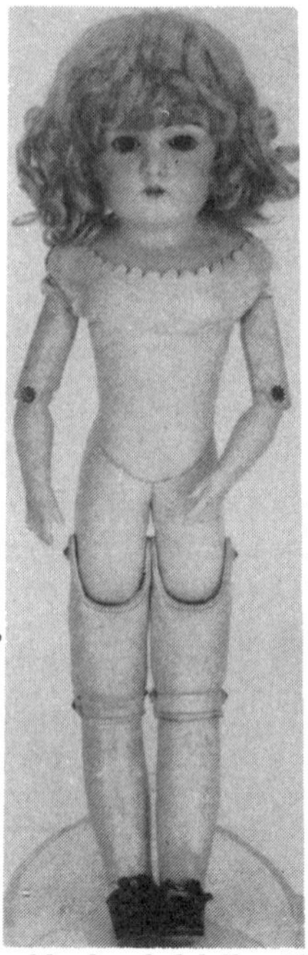

A bisque shoulder headed doll, with brown sleeping eyes, heavy feathered brows and blonde curly mohair wig, the pink jointed kid body with bisque arms, marked S 147, by Kestner, 16½in (42cm) high.
£1,000-1,500 *CSK*

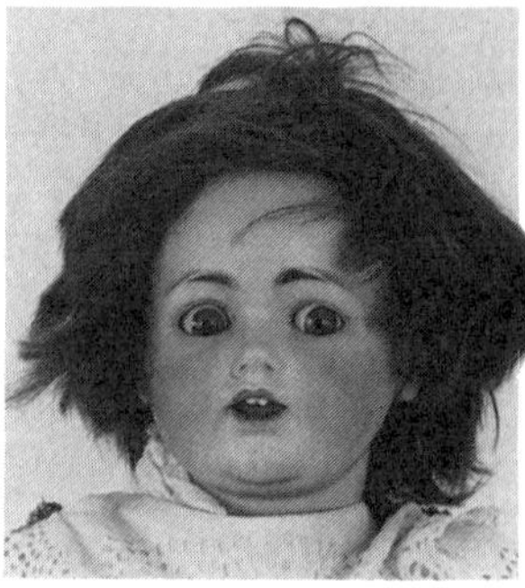

A bisque headed, flirty eyed, character baby doll, with blue eyes, trembling tongue, brown wig and bent limbed composition body dressed in white, hairline at neck, marked J.D.K. 257, 25½in (65cm) high.
£350-500 *C*

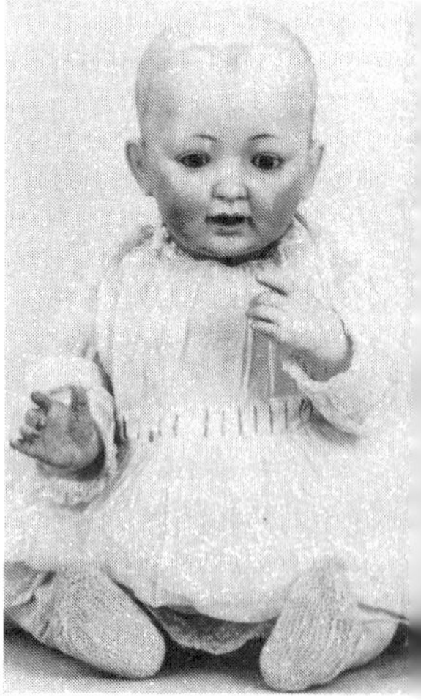

A bisque headed character baby doll, 'Peter', with blue sleeping eyes, feathered brows, painted hair with brushstrokes, the bent limbed composition body in white lace trimmed dress and underclothes, marked J.D.K., 25in (64cm) high.
£350-700 *CSK*

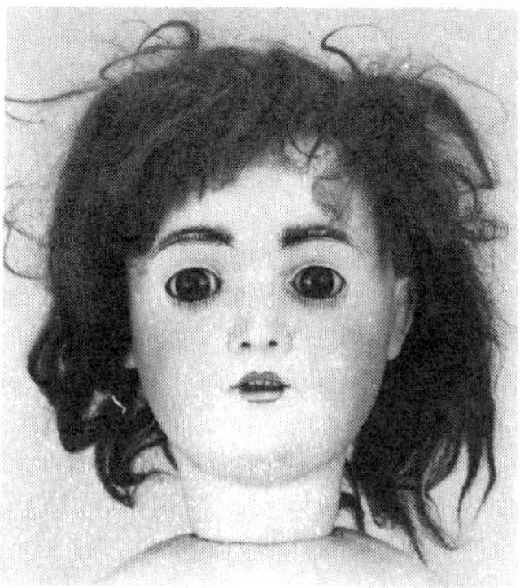

A large bisque headed doll, with blue sleeping eyes, moulded and feathered brows, brown mohair wig and jointed wood and composition body, marked 136 15 by Kestner, 30in (77cm) high.
£500-550 *CSK*

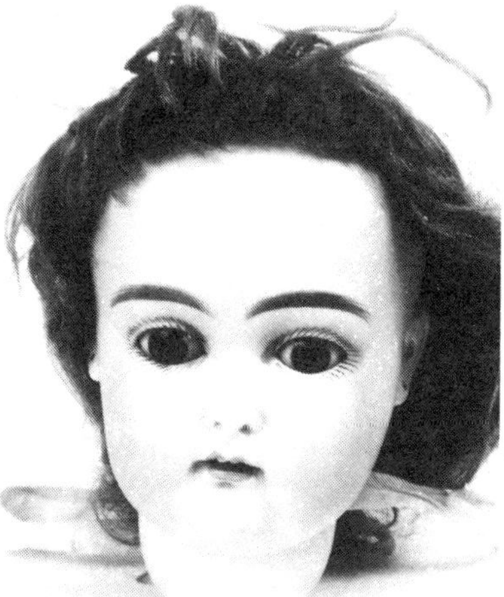

A bisque headed child doll, with brown sleeping eyes, pierced ears, light brown wig and jointed fixed wrist composition body, marked 192 10, Kestner, the head 5in (13cm) high.
£700-800 *CSK*

An all bisque googlie eyed doll, with blue painted eyes glancing to the left, closed watermelon mouth and moulded blue socks and black shoes, jointed at shoulder and hip, chips to legs at top, marked on the legs 310, by Kestner, 5½in (14cm) high.
£350-450 *C*

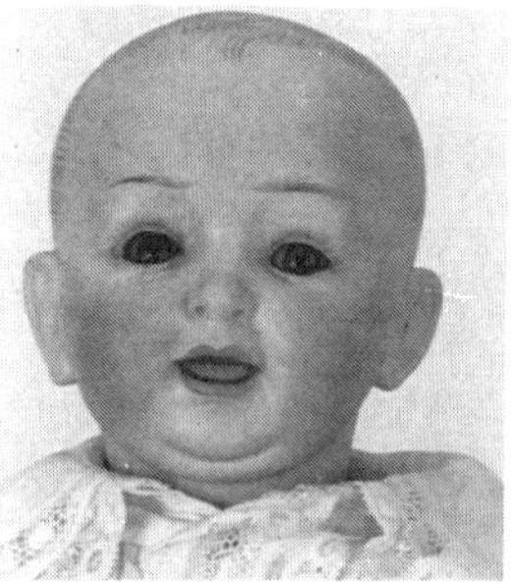

A bisque headed character baby doll, with blue sleeping eyes, moulded and painted hair, open/closed mouth and baby's body dressed in white, impressed 6 142, by Kestner, 14in (36cm) high.
£350-500 *C*

\n all bisque child doll, with closed
nouth, fixed brown eyes and
noulded socks and grey tasselled
ooots, jointed at neck shoulder and
iip, by J. D. Kestner, 6in (16cm)
iigh. **£400-450** *C*

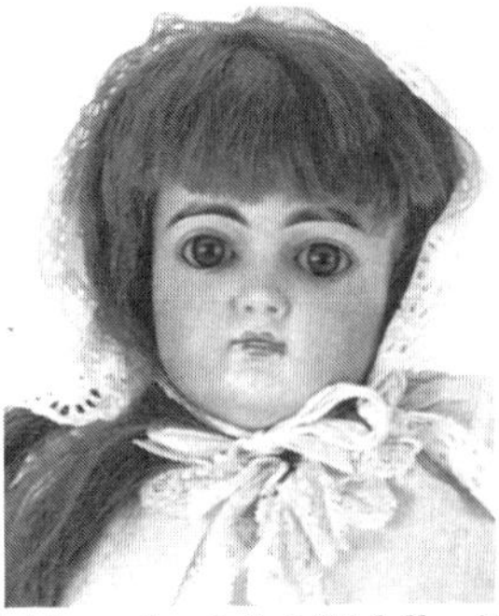

A bisque headed child doll, with fixed blue eyes, pierced ears, long fair hair wig and fixed wrist jointed composition body dressed in cream silk and wool, impressed 192 14, probably Kestner, 23in (59cm).
£2,000-2,500 *C*

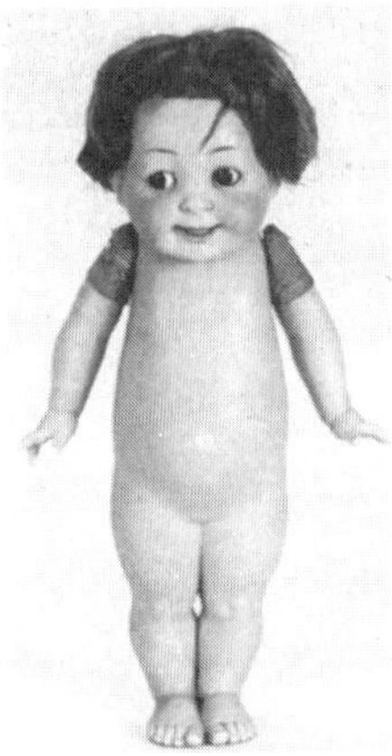

An all bisque googlie eyed doll, with open/closed watermelon mouth, brown sleeping eyes glancing to the side, light brown mohair wig, and all bisque body with arms jointed at shoulders and turned out hands, and a quantity of dolls clothes, damage at shoulders, marked 222 28 by Kestner, 11in (29cm) high.
£1,700-2,500 *C*

A pair of all bisque character dolls, modelled as Max and Moritz, with painted black and ginger hair, blue eyes glancing to the left and right, smiling watermelon mouths and moulded shoes, jointed at neck, shoulder, and hip, with bisque loops at shoulder and hip, by J. D. Kestner, 5in (13cm) high.
£1,500-2,000 *C*

Lenci

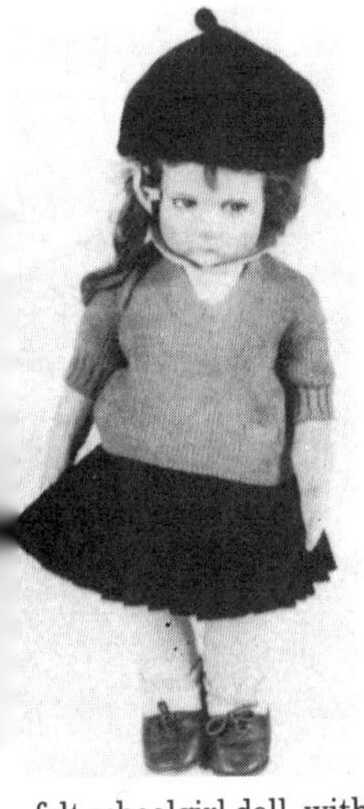

. felt schoolgirl doll, with long
rown hair, painted moulded facial
eatures, and moving limbs, with
itched fingers, wearing a blue felt
eret, a white felt short sleeved
louse, pleated navy blue felt skirt,
nitted orange wool short sleeved
umper, white ankle socks and
rown kid shoes, stamped Lenci in
lack on both feet, c1930, 18in
15.5cm) high.
450-550 *HSS*

A painted brown felt character doll, with black mohair wig, modelled as an American Indian with swivel waist, original orange and tan felt skirt and bolero, some moth damage to neck, bolero and feet, No. 104 by Lenci, c1920, 16½in (42cm) high.
£600-700 *CSK*

Armand Marseille

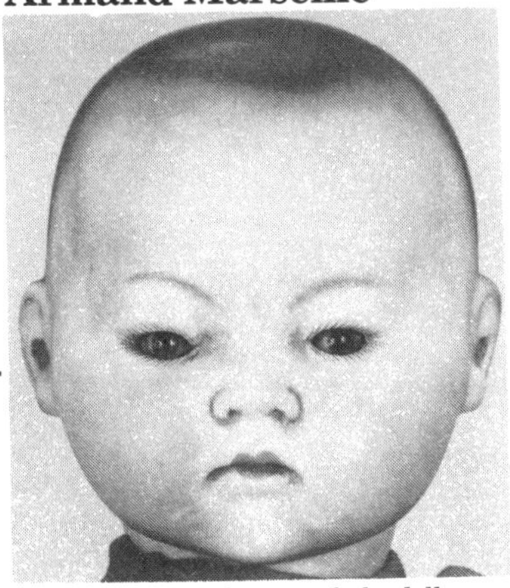

A bisque headed character baby doll modelled as an Oriental, with brown sleeping eyes and bent limbed composition body dressed in original shift, marked A.M. 353/3K, 13in (34cm) high.
£600-700 *CSK*

A bisque headed child doll, with blue sleeping eyes, brown wig and jointed body, in contemporary Scottish outfit, impressed 390 A 7 M, 24in (62cm) high.
£500-600 *CSK*

S.F.B.J.

A bisque headed character baby doll, with sleeping eyes, open/closed mouth with 2 teeth, and bent limbed composition toddler body, marked SFBJ 236-2, 9½in (24cm) high.
£300-400 *CSK*

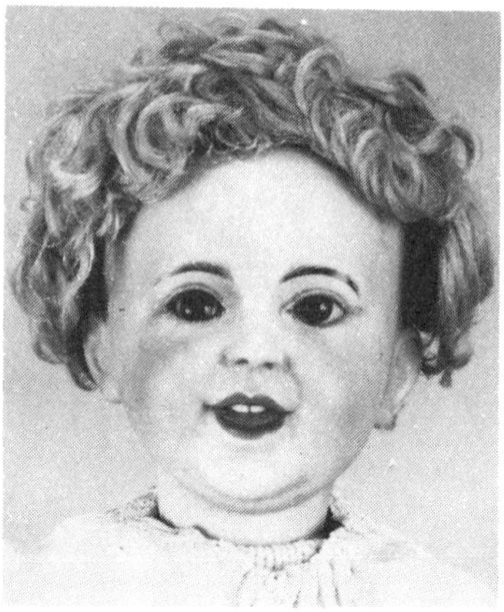

A bisque headed character baby doll, with brown sleeping eyes, open/closed mouth, curly blonde wig and bent limbed composition body dressed in cream baby gown, some damage to fingers, roughly moulded rim to head, marked SFBJ 236 10, 18in (46cm) high.
£500-600 *CSK*

Simon & Halbig/ Kammer & Reinhardt

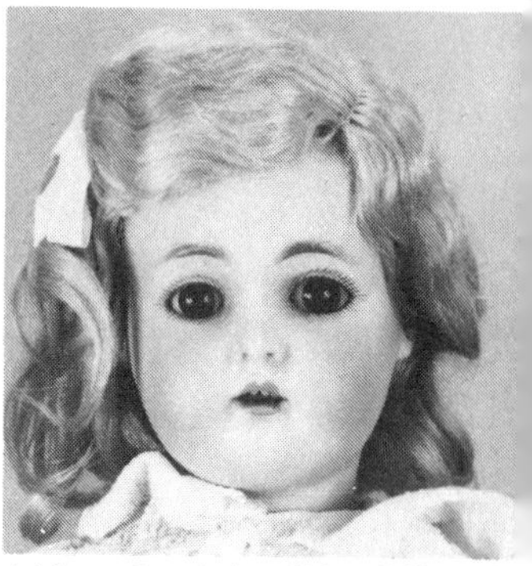

A bisque headed walking doll, with brown sleeping eyes, pierced ears, blonde mohair wig and rigid legs turning the head from side-to-side, marked Halbig K * R, 18in (46cm).
£600-700 *CSK*

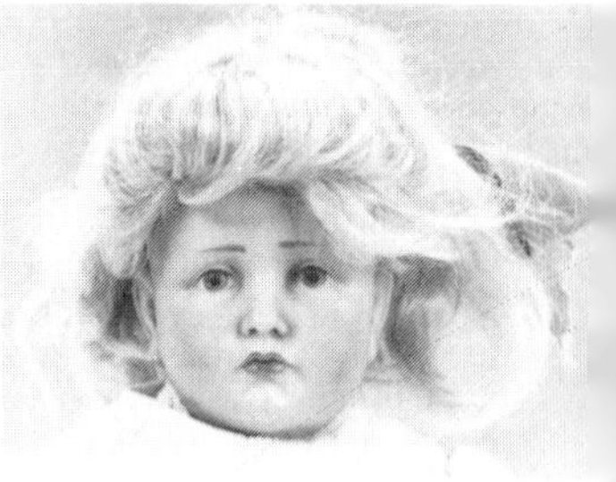

A bisque headed character doll, with closed mouth, painted features and blonde mohair wig, the jointed wood and composition toddler body in cotton print dress and underwear, wig pulls, marked K * R 114 34, 13in (34cm) high.
£800-1,000 *CSK*

A Simon and Halbig doll, all original, 15in (39cm) high.
£200-250 *SP*

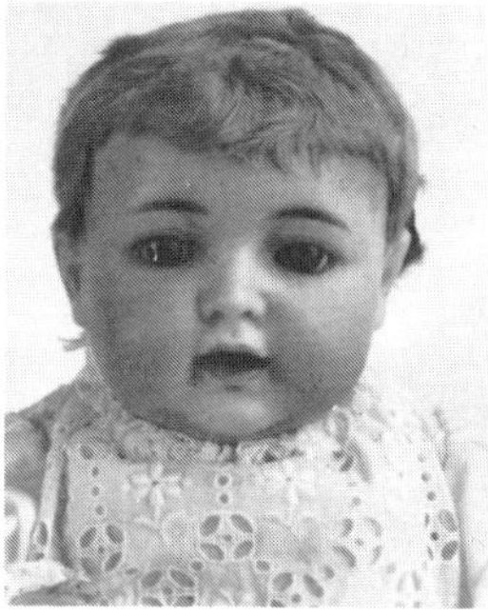

A bisque headed character doll, with blue sleeping eyes and baby's body dressed in white, marked K * R Simon & Halbig 122 28, 11in (29cm) high.
£500-600 *C*

A Simon & Halbig doll, K * R 46, 18in (46cm) high.
£750-850 *BEB*

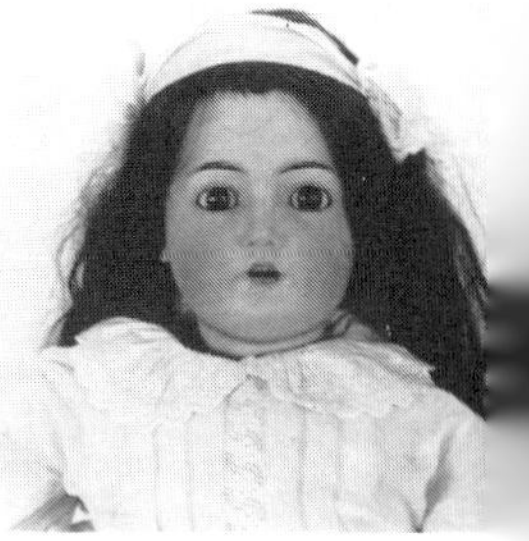

A bisque headed child doll, with brown sleeping eyes, jointed composition body dressed in pink cotton frock, impressed Simon & Halbig K * R 85, 34in (87cm) high.
£500-800 *C*

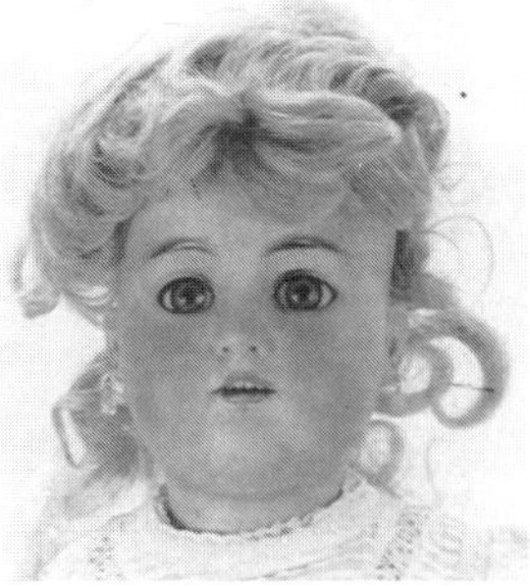

A bisque headed child doll, with blue sleeping eyes, pierced ears and jointed body dressed in white, marked Halbig K * R70, 27in (69cm) high.
£450-600 *C*

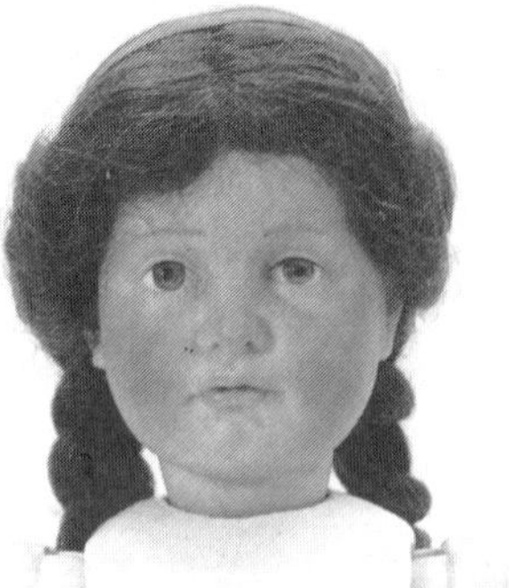

A bisque headed character doll, with painted blue eyes, auburn mohair wig, jointed wood and composition body, dressed in navy gym slip and pink blouse, marked K*R 114 49, 19in (49cm) high.
£2,500-3,000 *CSK*

A Simon and Halbig bisque head doll, with applied hair, sleeping eyes, open mouth and composition body with jointed limbs, stamped Simon and Halbig SH8, 19in (49cm) high.
£300-350 *DDM*

bisque headed child doll, with
ue sleeping eyes, pierced ears and
onde wig, the composition jointed
dy wearing robe with lace
sertions and wool cape and
nnet, marked Simon & Halbig
*R50, 19in (49cm) high.
00-700 *C*

A bisque headed child doll, with blue sleeping eyes, pierced ears and jointed body dressed in cream silk, marked Simon & Halbig K * R76, 30in (77cm) high.
£500-600 *C*

A bisque headed child doll, with blue sleeping eyes, pierced ears, blonde wig and jointed body wearing bronze kid boots with 3 ankle straps, marked S & H L.L. & S6½, 18in (46cm) high.
£350-450 *C*

A Simon & Halbig doll, early 20thC, 28in (72cm) high.
£450-550 *SP*

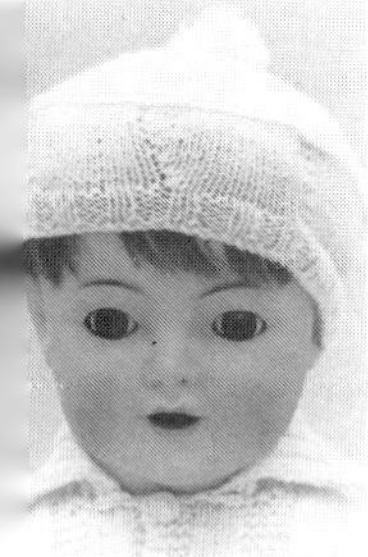

bisque headed character baby
l, with lidded flirting blue eyes,
athered brows and brown mohair
g, the bent limbed composition
dy with voice box, dressed in
itted suit, marked 1296 F.S.&Co.
non & Halbig, 20in (51cm) high.
00-600 *CSK*

Jules Steiner

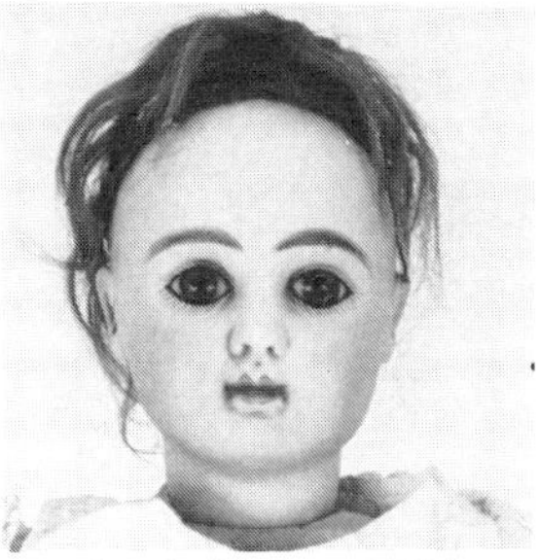

A bisque headed bébé, with blue yeux fibres, closed mouth, and pierced ears, the jointed composition body dressed in white shoes and socks, marked J. Steiner Paris A7, 14½in (37cm) high.
£3,000-3,500 *C*

A bisque headed Bébé Premier Pas, the solid pâté with fixed blue eyes and blonde, curly wig, the composition body with walking mechanism, wearing earlier embroidered linen dress, by J. Steiner, 20in (51cm) high.
£1,500-2,000 *C*

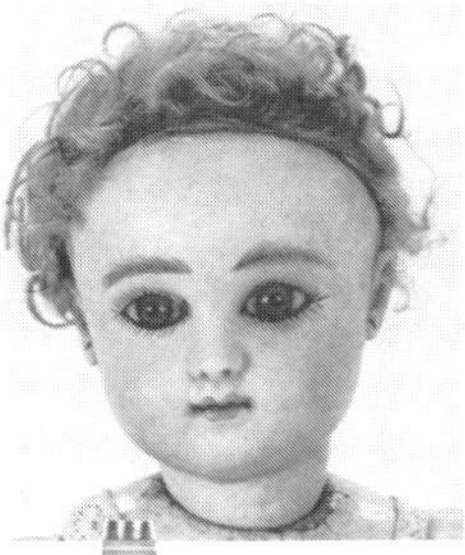

A bisque headed bébé, with closed mouth, pierced ears, fixed bright blue eyes, skin wig and papier mâché fixed wrist body, wearing a petticoat, impressed Ste CO, and with grey Jules Nicholas Steiner trademark stamp on the body, 13½in (35cm) high.
£3,500-4,000 *C*

olls Houses

nock Tudor style dolls house,
sibly Triang, c1930.
0-400 *GIL*

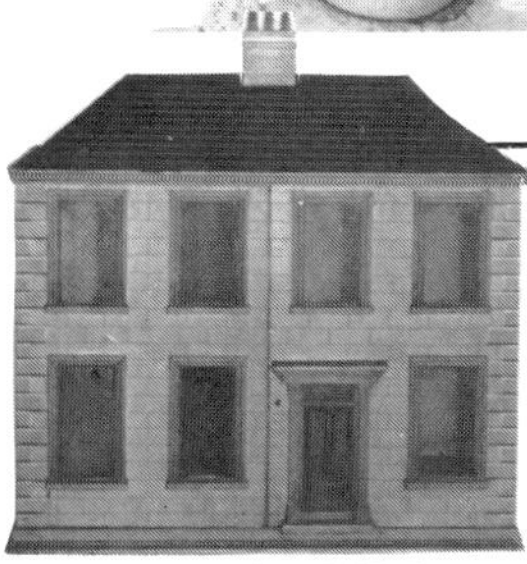

A painted wooden dolls house, simulating yellow stone with trompe l'oeil coining, dentil portico and imitation slate roof, opening at the front to reveal 7 rooms with original papers, on later stand, 37½in (95cm) high.
£1,500-2,000 *CSK*

A printed paper and wood dolls house, opening to reveal 4 rooms, each with fireplace, by G & J Lines Bros. DH/17, c1910, 25in (64cm) high. **£350-450** *CSK*

A painted wooden dolls house, opening at the front to reveal 9 rooms, 55in (139.5cm) high.
£600-700 *CSK*

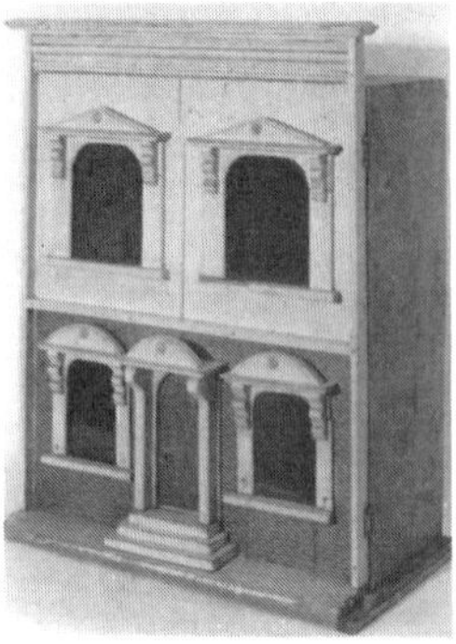

A box type wooden dolls house, the façade with brick paper ground floor and original cream paintwork with remains of gilt lines, opening to reveal 4 rooms, with varnished white wood pelmets, teak window sills and original papers on the inside of the façade, by G & J. Lines, c1910, 24in (62cm) high.
£500-600 *CSK*

A wooden dolls house, painted to simulate brickwork with grey roof and scalloped eaves, opening to reveal 4 fully furnished rooms, on shaped base, c1900, 50in (127cm) high.
£2,500-3,000 *C*

A printed paper on wood dolls house, with printed green slate roof, the door and windows with painted architectural details opening at the front and with roof removing to show 2 rooms with original floor, and wallpapers, the underside of the roof with paint and transfer decorations, stamped on the base Schutsmarke and C.H. in a monogram below a crown, for Christian Hacker, also inscribed in pencil R138/1, 20in (51cm) high.
£600-800 *CSK*

A group of dolls house furniture, including 2 soft metal chairs, a conversation seat and a cradle, and 3 printed paper on wood pieces, late 19thC.
£600-800 *C*

A Bing plated and tinplate child's live steam kitchen stove, with 5 burners, 3 ovens, adjustable rings, filling pipe and extra copper based utensils, not complete, some rusting, c1920, 19in (48cm) wide.
£500-600 *C*

A German painted wood toy grocer's shop, coloured cream with blue lines, the drawers with enamel content labels in English, 2 drawers missing, 21in (54cm) high.
£500-600 *CSK*

A Staffordshire child's china tea service for 6, painted with yellow and green tulips and gilt rims, c1840. **£350-400** *CSK*

Dolls bentwood furniture, with cane seats, 4 chairs, a settee and a table, 19thC, settee 14in (36cm) wide.
£380-420 *VH*

A Waltershausen gilt transfer decorated extending dining room table of serpentine shape, 6½in (17cm) long, a gilt transfer decorated writing desk, 4in (10cm) high, and a mantel clock with turned supports 3½in (9cm).
£300-400 *CSK*

Miscellaneous

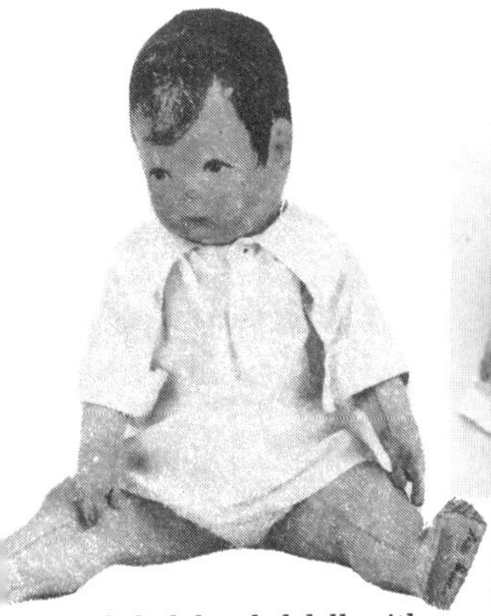

painted cloth headed doll, with
rown eyes, with wide hipped cloth
ody and separately sewn thumbs,
ressed in white cotton smock,
arked on foot Kathe Kruse, Doll 1,
7in (43cm).
400-600 *CSK*

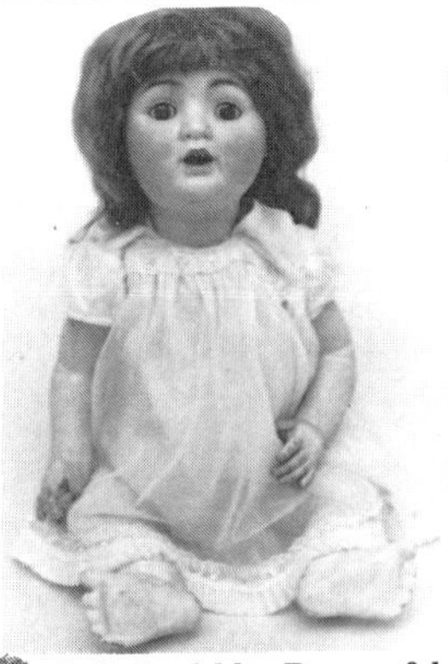

A Catierfelder Puppenfabrik doll, c1922.
£300-400 *GIL*

A pair of red leather doll's shoes, trimmed with red silk and with high pointed fronts and cross over straps, late 18thC, 3in (8cm) long.
£200-250 *C*

. swivel head doll, wearing original
othes, c1915, 7½in (19cm) high.
200-250 *BEB*

A Deans rag book doll, in good condition, c1945.
£50-60 *SP*

A Victorian china doll, 20in (50.5cm) high.
£250-350 *SP*

German Cuno
to dressed doll,
ginal, early 20thC,
in (50.5cm) high.
)0-300 *SP*

A Chad Valley felt doll, c1940, 16in (40.5cm) high.
£50-80 *SP*

Jerman doll,
n (53.5cm) high.
i0-450 *SP*

A French open mouth Julien doll, in original clothes, 19in (48.5cm) high.
£600-800 *SP*

TOYS

Automata

A hand operated musical automaton of a violin player, the bisque head with closed mouth and light brown wool wig, in original red and white suit, with wood hands, feet and violin, 7½in (19cm) high.
£400-500 *C*

A hand-operated musical automaton, of 3 bisque headed dolls seated at a table under an arbour, distressed, 11in (28cm) wide.
£1,000-1,500 *CSK*

A fur covered bear automaton with walking, turning head, and jaw mechanism, ivory teeth and wooden feet, inoperative, tail missing, probably number 77 in the Roullet and Decamps catalogue of 1878, 7in (17.5cm) high.
£250-300 *C*

A clockwork fur covered rabbit automaton, with pink glass eyes, emerging from a carton and cloth cabbage, turning his head and raising his ears, by Roullet and Decamps, 7½in (19cm) high.
£900-1,200 *C*

Teddy Bears

An early golden plush covered teddy bear, with boot button eyes, hump, excelsior stuffing and elongated limbs, wearing tortoiseshell rimmed spectacles, hole on left paw, replaced pads, appendix scar squeaker inoperative, lacks stuffing, small blank Steiff button in ear, c1903, 20in (50.5cm) high.
£400-600 *C*

A golden short plush covered teddy bear with boot button eyes, hump, low set ears, horizontally stitched nose, felt pads, firm stuffing and long straight legs, one pad recovered, some moth in paws, probably early American, 29in (73.5cm) high.
£800-900 *CSK*

An Edwardian gold plush teddy bear with black stitched snout, black and brown glass eyes, hump back, long arms, cloth pads to feet and paws, partly straw filled, with squeaker, 19in (48.5cm) high.
£300-350 *HCH*

A bear muff, c1920.
£200-250 *SP*

Two Schuco perfume bottle bears, 5in (12.5cm) high. **£250-300 each** *SP*

A long blonde plush covered teddy bear, with small hump, large feet and growler, 20in (50.5cm) high.
£400-500 *C*

An English Chilter teddy bear, c1950, 18in (45.5cm) high.
£60-80 *SP*

..n early teddy bear, in mint
..ndition, 18in (45.5cm) high.
180-200 *SP*

An English teddy bear, c1955, 18in (45.5cm) high.
£40-50 *SP*

A long plush mohair covered teddy bear, with boot button eyes, wide apart ears, hump and elongated limbs, pads replaced, 22in (55.5cm) high. **£3,000-3,500** *C*

An early English teddy bear, 15in (38cm) high.
£180-200 *SP*

..rman bear, c1950,
..in (50.5cm) high.
..0-100 *SP*

A Chad Valley teddy bear, c1939, 18in (45.5cm) high.
£50-60 *SP*

A cinnamon plush covered teddy bear, with boot button eyes, wide apart ears, elongated limbs, hump and cut muzzle, with Steiff button in ear, 13in (33cm) high.
£2,500-3,000 *C*

..teiff teddy bear,
..50, 10in
..cm) high.
..-80 *SP*

A Chad Valley teddy bear in good condition, c1939, 24in (61.5cm) high.
£180-200 *SP*

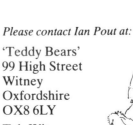

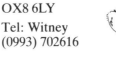

..teiff teddy bear,
.. (43cm) high.
..00-1,200 *SP*

A Steiff teddy bear, in mint conditon, 26in (66cm) high.
£3,000-3,500 *SP*

Lead Soldiers

BRITISH SOLDIERS
LIFEGUARDS

A set of 6 mounted Royal Life Guards by Britains, number 4284 from a limited edition of 7000, contained in original box together with a certificate of authenticity.
£50-70 *HSS*

A military marching band by Britains, comprising 12 figures, bass drum and mace missing, c1939.
£2,500-3,000 *WAL*

Money Banks

STUMP SPEAKER

A cast iron mechanical moneybox, 'Stump Speaker', with movable right arm, opening bag and unusual counterbalanced 'talking' mouth, in original paintwork, Pat. June 8 1886, 10in (25cm) high.
£900-1,200 *CSK*

A cast iron mechanical moneybox, 'Jolly Nigger Bank', with movable right arm, cast iron base, in original paintwork, with patent details, by Shepard Hardware Co., Buffalo, N.Y., c1883, 7in (17.5cm) high.
£200-250 *C*

Tinplate

A clockwork motorcycle, c1935.
£75-80 *COB*

LYONS TEA

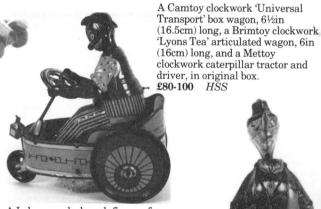

A Camtoy clockwork 'Universal Transport' box wagon, 6½in (16.5cm) long, a Brimtoy clockwork 'Lyons Tea' articulated wagon, 6in (16cm) long, and a Mettoy clockwork caterpillar tractor and driver, in original box.
£80-100 *HSS*

A Gama fire engine with turntable, 9in (23cm) long, and a clockwork Red Cross van, slight damage, 8in (20cm) long.
£45-60 *HSS*

A Hessmobile, the clockwork automobile in crimson livery lined in black and white, the chauffeur in dark navy blue uniform with peaked cap, bearing the trade mark of John Leonard Hess, c1908, 9in (22.5cm) long.
£350-400 *Bea*

A Lehmann clockwork figure of a negro driving a 3-wheeled vehicle, with lithographed detail and concentric back wheels, c1925, 5in (12.5cm) long.
£320-370 *HSS*

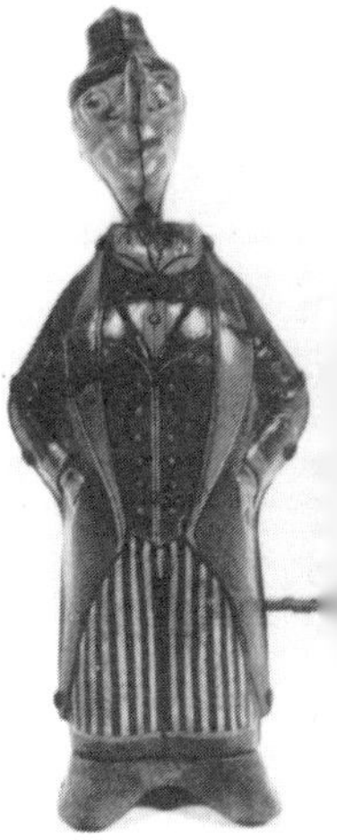

A German clockwork clown by H. Fischer, standing with upturned nose and moving head, early 20thC, 8in (20cm) high. **£150-200** *HSS*

A Mettoy clockwork racing car, 12½in (32cm) long, and a Mettoy clockwork yellow plated express delivery van, 6in (15cm) long.
£100-120 *HSS*

A painted hansom cab, with clockwork mechanism, 'Li La Hansom Cab', spoked wheels, driver with steering wheel and brake, 2 lady passengers, a dog, in original paintwork, EPL No. 520, by Lehmann, c1910, 5in (12.5cm).
£900-1,200 *C*

KADI

A printed and painted teabox with 2 Chinese coolies, 'Kadi', clockwork mechanism concealed in box, one arm missing, box supports broken, EPL No. 723, by Lehmann, c1910, 7in (17.5cm) long.
£400-500 *C*

A clockwork camouflaged ›bservation vehicle, with a driver ınd 3 figures to the flat back, ›perating a spot light, one figure nissing, 14in (35.5cm) long.
€100-150 *HSS*

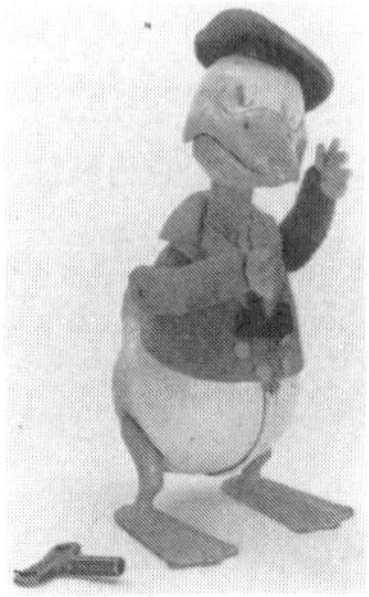

A felt covered and painted tinplate toy, 'Donald Duck', in sailor's uniform, with clockwork mechanism, slightly worn, by Schuco, c1936, 6in (15cm) high.
£250-350 *C*

A lithographed tinplate dancing negro, 'Oh My', EPL 690, with hand cranked clockwork mechanism concealed in base, in original paintwork, with stand, original lid with instructions, lid torn, by Lehmann, c1912, 10in (25cm) high.
£400-450 *C*

An Alfa Romeo P2 Racing Car, C.I.J., painted tinplate, finished in ›lue, with cloverleaf insignia, ›perating steering and handbrake, lummy shock absorbers and drum ›rakes, and narrow tread tyres, ›arly type, c1926. **£2,000-2,500** *CSK*

DINKY TOYS
60
G-A BTI

A Dinky set No. 60, Aeroplanes, 2nd Issue, with markings and instructions, in original box, some damage, pre-war, G, box F.
£500-600 *C*

ı German painted tinplate steam iverboat, in red and white, blue and ed lined, yellow funnel with red tar, single cylinder engine with ›ainted flywheel and brass boiler riving 3-screw propeller, c1905, 1½in (30cm) long.
400-500 *CSK*

DINKY TOYS
901
FODEN DIESEL
8-WHEEL WAGON

hree Dinky Supertoys, No. 901 oden Diesel 8-Wheel Wagon, 'o. 903 Foden Flat Truck and 'o. 905 Foden Flat Truck with hains, all in original boxes, E, ›xes E.
300-700 *C*

A German painted and lithographed tinplate clockwork pusher biplane, finished in cream, with front stabiliser, rear tailplane and 3-wheel under carriage, in the style of Gunthermann, propeller blades missing, c1910, 7in (18cm) long.
£700-800 *CSK*

A Carette painted pulley driven platen printing press, with operating mechanism, fly wheel, fount and tray of rubber type, finished in maroon, Cat. Ref. 634/1, c1911, 5in (12.5cm) wide.
£450-500 *CSK*

DINKY TOYS

A Dinky original set 39 box containing green 39a Packard Super 8 Sedan, black 39b Oldsmobile, 6 Sedan and yellow 39f Studebaker State Commander Coupe, pre-war F-G, box G, no insert.
£600-700 *CSK*

DINKY SUPERTOYS
986

A Dinky 977 Commercial Servicing vehicle, in original box, M, box E.
£200-250 *CSK*

FRYS
COCOA
Mackintosh's
TOFFEE

Two Dinky 28 series delivery vans, one No. 28s Frys van, 1 No. 28f Mackintosh's van, and a No. 22c Motor Truck, 2nd types, damage, pre-war, F-G.
£150-200 *C*

DINKY TOYS
922
BIG BEDFORD LORRY

Six Dinky Supertoys, No. 981 Horse Box, No. 982 Pullmore Transporter and 994 Loading Ramp, No. 932 Comet Wagon, No. 922 Big Bedford Lorry and No. 933 Leyland Comet Wagon, all in original boxes, E, boxes E.
£500-550 *C*

Miscellaneous

A child's wicker gig, with skin covered horse mounted over the front wheel, simulating a galloping motion as the pram is pushed, with whip and pram handle, restored, 63in (160cm) long.
£1,200-1,500 *CSK*

Advertised in Harrods Christmas Catalogue for 1911, priced 5gns.

Victorian dapple grey rocking horse.
£1,500-2,000 *GIL*

A Merrythought monkey, post war, 20in (51cm).
£40-50 *SP*

A set of Britains painted diecast figures of Snow White and the Seven Dwarfs, c1938.
£70-90 *HSS*

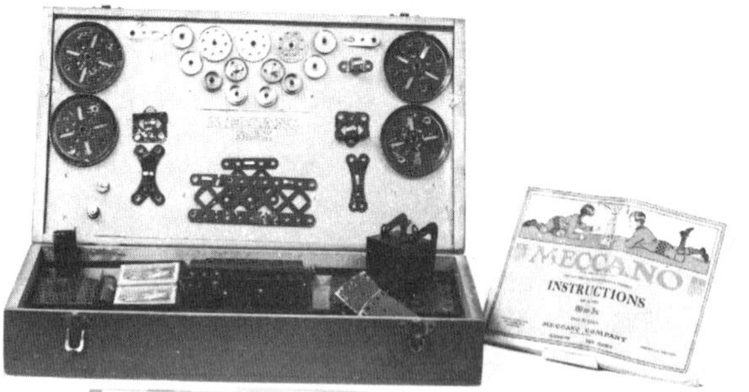
MECCANO
INSTRUCTIONS

A Meccano outfit No. 3X, red and green with electric motor, with manuals, in original wood box, good condition, c1928.
£250-300 *CSK*

MECCANO
ACCESSORY PARTS

A Meccano Dealers display cabinet, red and green, six drawers, original velvet card, c1928.
£1,700-2,000 *CSK*

Roma

A coloured plastic one-armed bandit, 1962. **£75-80** *COB*

A German toy wooden grocer's shop, stencilled and lined in brown with printed paper labelled drawers, wooden canisters and cash and ledger books, c1930, 21in (54cm) wide.
£500-600 *CSK*

MODELS

Air

G-EAGS

A detailed 1in:1ft scale static lisplay model of the prototype Austin Whippet biplane, constructor's No. AUI registration etter G-EAGS, built by P. Veale, Barcombe, wingspan 21½in (54cm).
£1,000-1,500 *C*

G-EAGS was first given the emporary registration number K-158 in 1919 and the model represents the prototype in its final form when owned by C. P. B. Ogilvie at Hendon in 1920-21. In all five Austin Whippets were built.

A radio controlled flying model ighwing monoplane 'Majestic Mayar', built by R. Golding, ingspan 90½in (227cm).
£200-300 *C*

late Victorian gilt painted paper nd cardboard scale model of a erris wheel, raised upon a canted quare plinth with scroll brackets to e corners, in a glazed stained wood splay cabinet, gilding worn in aces, 22in (55cm) high.
£200-300 *HSS*

Land

A Richardson and Allwin painted wood and metal model Bullnose Morris pedal car, with folding hood, and painted metal Shell oil can, 45in (114cm) long.
£4,000-4,500 *HCH*

LONG DISTANCE HAULAGE
C G THOMAS & SONS
7

A 3in scale model Foden 'C' type twin cylinder steam lorry Patricia, having welded steel boiler, Ackerman steering, hand and foot brakes, wooden cab, opening doors, 29 by 72in (74 by 182.5cm).
£3,200-3,600 *HCH*

A Mamod steam driven lorry.
£40-70 *WW*

A 3½in gauge model of the Shay 0–4–0 + 0–4–0 geared logging locomotive No. 2, with silver soldered copper boiler, hydraulic tested to 200 p.s.i., steam tested to 150 p.s.i., with fittings, finished in grey, red and polished brightwork, the tank sides lettered Renhold Timber Co, built by P. Higgins, Renhold, carrying box, 11 by 27½in (28 by 70cm).
£2,500-3,000 *C*

This model is new and has not been steamed.

10637

An exhibition standard 5in gauge model of the L.M.S. 2–4–2 side tank locomotive No. 10637, built to the designs of Don Young by Major F. R. Pearce, West Byfleet, with brazed superheated copper boiler built by R. R. Chambers, Poole, finished in L.M.S. red livery and lining, with showtrack, 14 by 39½in (35.5 by 99.5cm).
£4,000-4,500 *C*

METROPOLITAN

A Hornby Electric gauge 0 tinplate 0–4–0 Metropolitan locomotive and 4 Hornby tinplate gauge 0 accessories and track, in wooden box.
£150-200 *HCH*

A steam engine on a wood base.
£300-400 *WW*

A well detailed wood and metal model of Orbel Mill, with sails and angle adjustment mechanism, wooden driving gears, internal rollers, chains, shoots, mill stones, ladders and much detailing, built by A. Williams, some old damage, c1805, 65in (165cm) high.
£600-1,000 *C*

Sea

A brass and wood one-twelfth scale model of a marine 32lb cannon of c1850, built by V. Pentecost, Falmouth, 8 by 19in (20 by 48cm).
£900-1,200 *C*

GAMES

Chess Sets

A set of boxwood chessmen.
£150-200 *PCh*

A Chinese red and white ivory chess set, each piece carved as a member of the court or a warrior, the knights mounted, with castellated elephant rooks, on waisted oval bases, 2 to 4in (5 to 10cm), displayed in a later mahogany box together with a wooden chess board and a volume of A History of Chess by Harry Golombek, 1976.
£350-400 *P(S)*

MUSICAL

Musical Instruments

A chamber barrel organ, by G. Astor & Co., 79 Cornhill, with 3 of 4 ten-air barrels, 4 ranks of pipes, drum, triangle, 6 stops, 18 keys and mahogany case with chequer stringing, oval simulated false-pipe panel, storage for 2 barrels in base and maker's label and later tune sheet in lid, 59in (149.5cm) high, the case stamped 588.
£2,000-2,500 *CSK*

An Italian violin attributed to Cesare Candi, labelled Enrico Rocca . . . 1906, with red-orange varnish over a golden ground, length of back 14in (35.5cm).
£8,000-10,000 *C*

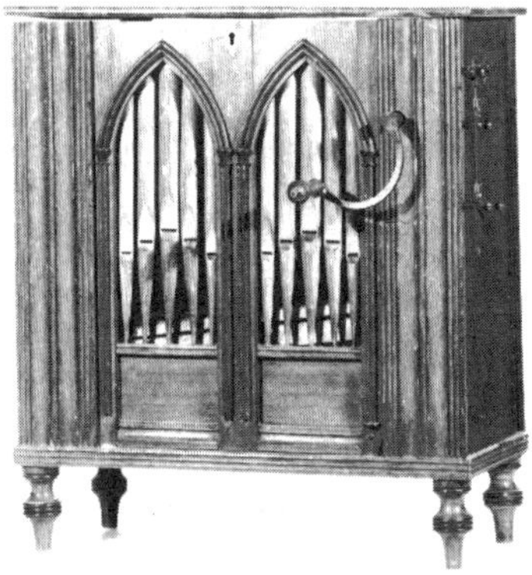

A mahogany 14-key table barrel organ with 10-air barrel, simulated pipes in 2-lancet Gothic front, list of tunes and trade label of J. Fentum, Music Printer & Publisher, early 19thC, 18½in (47cm) high.
£500-600 *C*

A ten-air street barrel piano, in varnished wood case with incised decoration and glazed upper panel, with trade labels of A. O. Wintle, Lawshall, Bury St. Edmunds, on painted cart, 99in (251.5cm) long overall.
£2,000-2,500 *C*

A street barrel piano by Keith Prowse & Co. Ltd., with ten-air barrel pinned by Tomasso with popular tunes of c1900, the case with typical incised name and decoration, Tomasso transfer, modern colour prints and detached pediment with typed Tomasso tune sheet, in traditional handcart with leaf-sprung wheels, 83in (210.5cm) long overall.
£3,000-3,500 *CSK*

An English violoncello by Lockey Hill, labelled L. Hill/Violin & Violoncello/Maker/Boro'/London, with golden-brown varnish, length of back 29in (73.5cm).
£12,000-15,000 *C*

The fingerboard is numbered H 34.

A Kessels 61-note automatic piano in ebonised case with roll mechanism in cupboard below keyboard, driven by hand crank or electric motor, wood tracker bar, pneumatic action and electro-pneumatic controls, with 31 rolls, 59in (149.5cm) wide.
£400-600 *CSK*

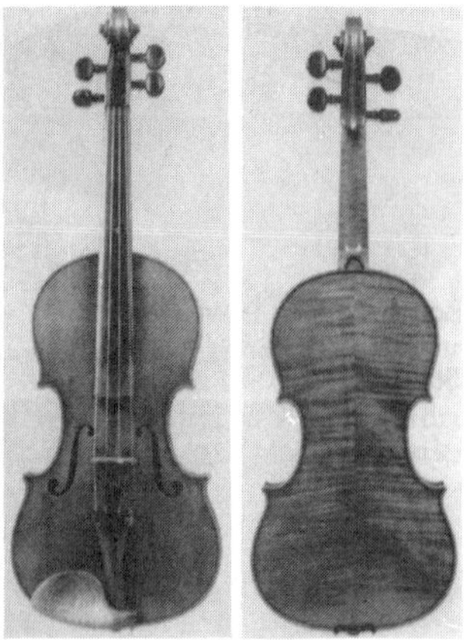

A Spanish violin by Mariano Ortega, labelled Marianus Ortega filius Silberi/fecit Matriti anno 1844, length of back 14in (35.5cm), in case.
£17,000-19,000 *C*

Sold with the certificate of W. E. Hill & Sons dated 11 September 1905.

A cabinet roller organ, in gilt stencilled walnut case, with instructions in rear lid and 1887 Patent date, 17in (43.5cm), with 12 'cobs'.
£900-1,000 *C*

A Bechstein boudoir grand piano, Model A, No. 108650, the mahogany case with 3 pairs of tapering square legs joined by stretchers and on brass casters, 72in (182.5cm).
£2,500-3,000 *Bea*

Musical Boxes

A Swiss gilt metal musical casket, the hinged lid containing singing bird mechanism with enamel cover, the base with timepiece and musical movement playing 4 airs listed underneath, early 20thC, 5in (12.5cm) wide.
£2,500-3,000 *C*

A 15⅝in (39.5cm) table Polyphon disc musical box, with double movement in panelled walnut case with carved mouldings, with 20 discs in storage case, with Nicole Freres index list, part lid missing.
£3,000-3,500 *C*

A Symphonion Eroica triple disc musical box, in walnut case with clock-backed fretwork door, small disc storage chute in base and balustraded top, with 16 sets of discs, 80in (203cm) high.
£12,000-13,000 *C*

A Lochmann's original 17in (43.5cm) table disc musical box, 40in (101.5cm).
£7,500-8,500 *CSK*

Gramophones

A Thorens No. 17 folding portable gramophone, in the form of a folding camera, in brown and yellow crackled enamel casing, 11in (28cm) wide.
£200-250 *AH*

An early E.M.G. Mark X hand-made gramophone, with gooseneck tone-arm, later E.M.G. soundbox, oak case, electric motor and papier-mâché horn, 29in (73.5cm) diam, a Davey fibre cutter, a B.C.N. thorn sharpener, and a Davey dry-air jar for fibre needles, c1930.
£1,500-2,000 *CSK*

Miscellaneous

A musical automaton tableau, with 3 pairs of bisque headed doll dancers on rotating turntable, in a rustic setting with waterfall, wooded background painted on glass dome, 2-train clock and ebonised wood base, 23½in (60cm) high.
£1,700-2,500 *C*

A folding fishing stool, 15in (38cm) high.
£15-25 *AL*

A table mat, with glass cover to hold one gut-eyed salmon fly, plus 4 smaller, 6in (15cm) square.
£4-6 *JMG*

A 123in Hardy Halford The Priceless rod, handle made with light and dark timber, the top joint pentagonal, made of 5 splices of cane rather than normal 6, extremely rare.
£80-100 *JMG*

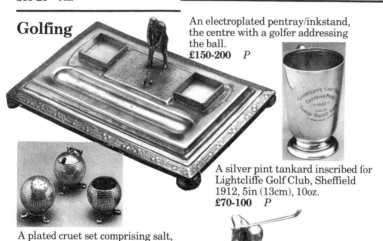

Golfing

An electroplated pentray/inkstand, the centre with a golfer addressing the ball.
£150-200 *P*

A silver pint tankard inscribed for Lightcliffe Golf Club, Sheffield 1912, 5in (13cm), 10oz.
£70-100 *P*

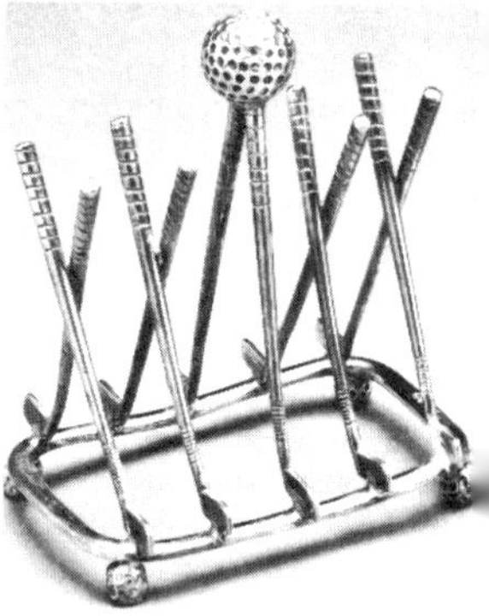

A silver five-bar toast rack, modelled from clubs and ball, London 1930, 4½in (11cm) tall
£370-420 *P*

A plated cruet set comprising salt, pepper and mustard pot, two with blue glass containers.
£180-220 *P*

An electroplated pentray/inkstand, the centre with a golfer playing a shot, club loose, on scrolled maskhead feet.
£200-250 *P*

A chrome and silver plate cocktail shaker, c1930, 7½in (19cm) high.
£80-100 *THA*

Cricket

A model of a cricketer in early 19thC dress, using a still earlier curved bat, on wood plinth, late 19thC, 13in (33cm).
£250-300 *P*

A Victorian silver smoker's condiment set, formed as a wicket with crossed bats, some damage, London, c1886, hallmark slightly rubbed, 5½in (14cm) long.
£300-350 *P*

A miniature model setting of a 19thC cricket match with glass wickets, 6 milk glass figures on flocked green pitch, in glazed case, 3 figures damaged, case 11in (28cm) wide.
£100-120 *P*

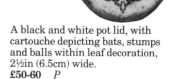

A black and white pot lid, with cartouche depicting bats, stumps and balls within leaf decoration, 2½in (6.5cm) wide.
£50-60 *P*

Boxes

A Regency tortoiseshell veneered two-division tea caddy with turned bone finial, 5½in (14cm) high.
£850-950 *P(M)*

A tortoiseshell, ivory and mother-of-pearl inlaid tea caddy, with concave corners, on bun feet, early 19thC, 4in (10cm) wide.
£500-600 *CSK*

A pair of brass tea caddies, 6in (15cm) high.
£35-50 each *RFA*

A Louis XV tortoiseshell and gold snuff box piqué overall with vari-colour gold stripes, chased with a guilloche, by Jean-Louis Capette, Paris, c1772, with the charge and décharge of Julien Alaterre, 3in (7.5cm) diam.
£1,700-2,000 *C*

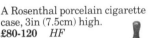

A Victorian coromandel games box, the cover with cruciform cut brass mount and agate bosses, the interior with bezique and whist markers, bearing the trade label of Carlisle & Watts, 49 Hanover Street, Edinburgh, 7in (17.5cm) square.
£350-450 *CSK*

A Rosenthal porcelain cigarette case, 3in (7.5cm) high.
£80-120 *HF*

A mahogany humidor with heavy brass hinges, handles and fittings, complete with key, 19thC, 10in (25cm) wide.
£300-350 *PCh*

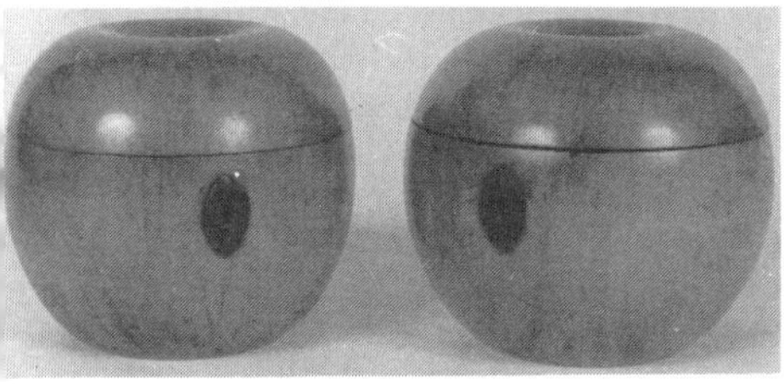

A pair of fruitwood tea caddies modelled as apples, the hinged covers opening to reveal a zinc lined interior, with oval metal lock escutcheons, one damaged and repaired, traces of red staining, 4in (10cm) high.
£2,500-3,000 *HSS*

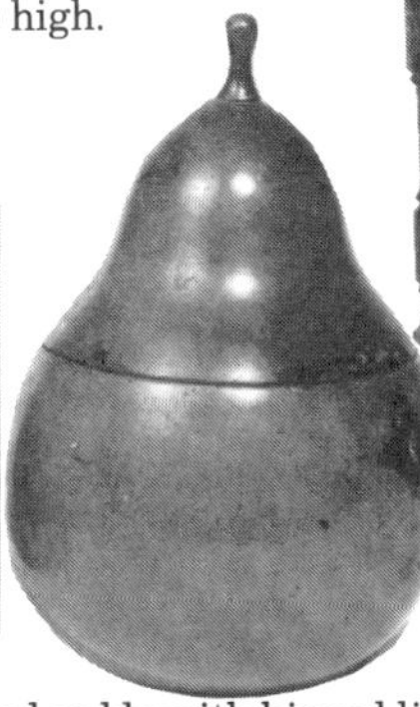

A fruitwood caddy with hinged lid, 19thC, 6½in (16.5cm) high.
£1,500-2,000 *C*

An Anglo-Indian micro-mosaic ebony and ivory stationery box, the lid enclosing a cedar divided interior, late 18th/early 19thC, 8in (20cm) wide.
£600-700 *C*

A Regency scarlet japanned 'coal box', the domed cover finely gilt with a band of wild roses and foliage outlined in black, with conforming painted cast iron loop handles and resting on bold paw feet, c1820, 19in (48.5cm) high.
£3,000-4,000 *N*

A George II gold mounted shagreen necessaire, containing a gold mounted agate patch box, a pair of glass scent bottles, tweezers, manicure stick, scissors and ivory tablets and a gold pencil holder, bodkin, spoon, ear pick and thimble and an ivory cotton reel, the base re-glued, c1755, 2½in (6.5cm) high.
£2,500-3,000 *C*

A Regency rosewood miniature lap desk, with brass inlaid decoration and fitted interior.
£270-300 *MGM*

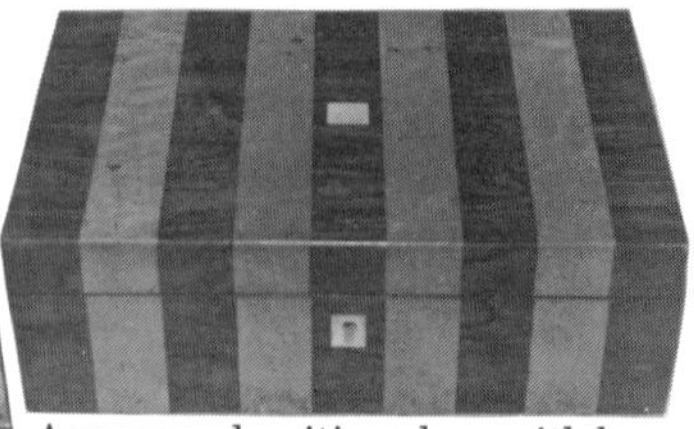

A rosewood writing slope with burr wood banding, 19thC.
£170-200 *PCA*

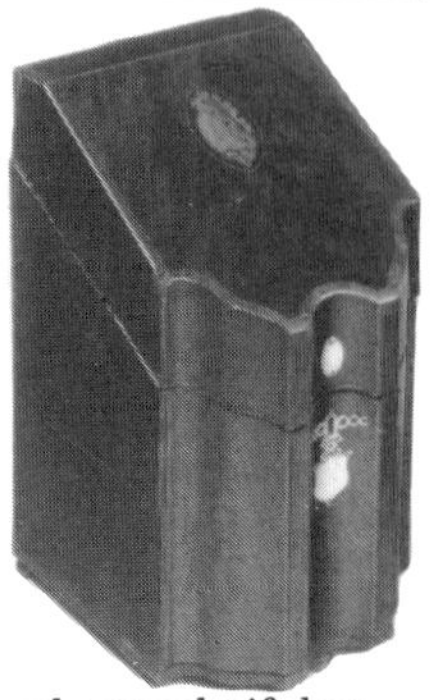

A George III mahogany knife box, later inlaid with a conch shell, with enclosed cutlery compartment, the front with later inlaid flutes, 9in (22.5cm) high.
£450-500 *C*

A walnut tantalus, with ivory and brass banding, 3 glass jars and stoppers, 7in (17cm) wide.
£280-320 *HF*

A Swedish mahogany, rosewood and marquetry inlaid spice cabinet, with brass knob handles, early 19thC, 8in (20cm) wide.
£270-300 *AH*

A finely carved Welsh love token snuff box, 18thC.
£350-400 *RYA*

An Edwardian silver and tortoiseshell dressing table box, or fluted tapering column legs with ball feet, inlaid with musical trophies, flowers and scrolling foliage and with stamped friezes o paterae, with 2 domed hinged covers, by William Comyns, London, 1905, 6in (15cm).
£1,500-2,000 *CSK*

An Anglo-Indian horn tea caddy, with ivory and ebony interior, fitted with 2 hinged zinc-lined caddies and a cut glass bowl, on ribbed bun feet, 15in (38cm) long.
£450-600 *C*

An Indian painted wooden box with hinged top, opening to reveal various compartments, inlaid with panels of ivory, and brass mounts, areas of slight damage and restoration, Rajasthan, 18thC, 21in (53cm) wide.
£400-500 *C*

A George III satinwood and scrolled paper tea caddy, the sides set with stamped white paper classical figures laid on a pine ground, decorated in original bright colours and gilt edged, opening to reveal an inner satinwood lid set with a walnut panel and chequered stringing, 6½in (16.5cm) wide, complete with its original protective wood carrying case of hexagonal form, the hinged cover with brass swan neck handle, 9in (22cm) wide.
£2,500-3,000 *HSS*

A casket with gilt brass ring and foliate handles, and with small drawers enclosed by a pair of panelled doors, the whole decorate with applied red wax seals, 19thC 10½in (27cm) wide.
£350-400 *HSS*

A Birmingham enamel casket, with gilt metal mounts, c1758, 10½in (27cm) long.
£2,000-3,000 *C*

A red damask covered casket, with domed hinged lid, enclosing a later marbled paper interior, 12in (31cm) wide.
£60-100 *C*

A brass snuff box with fleur-de-lys design, 2½in (6.5cm).
£40-60 *HF*

A yew and pine inlaid Killarney ware box, 19thC.
£150-200 *PCA*

A yew and pine Killarney box, 19thC.
£170-200 *PCA*

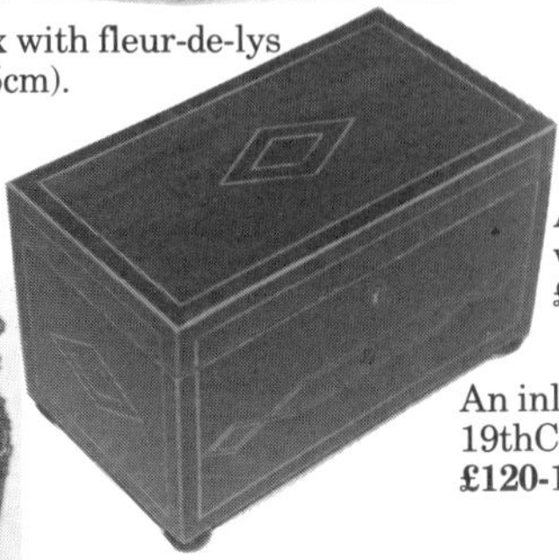

An inlaid mahogany tea caddy, 19thC.
£120-140 *PCA*

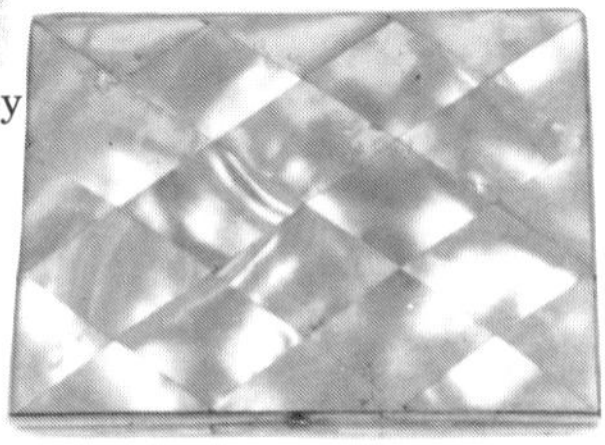

A Victorian mother-of-pearl card case, 4in (10cm) long.
£60-70 *HF*

A mid-Victorian ormolu and porcelain mounted kingwood jewel box, crossbanded with rosewood and inlaid à quatre faces with cabochons and foliate border, the interior lined in green velvet, 27½in (70cm) high.
£1,500-2,000 *C*

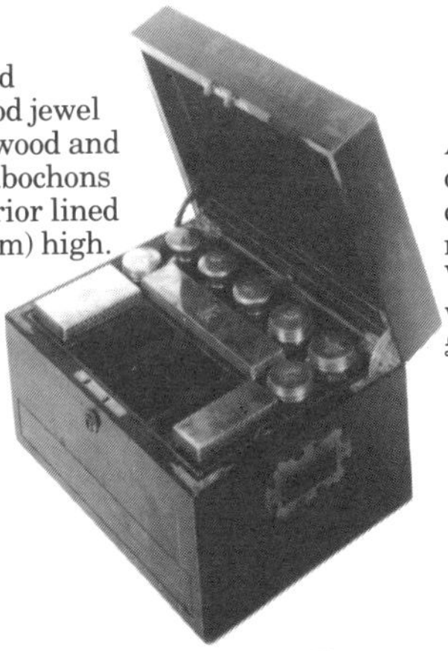

A Victorian crossbanded coromandel and brass inlaid toilet case, the lined interior with silver mounted fittings, maker's mark W.N., London 1871, 12in (30.5cm) wide.
£450-550 *GC*

pair of George III mahogany knife oxes, carved with a shield ontaining Prince of Wales' Plumes, pening to reveal the original fitted nterior.
650-700 *HSS*

A French wood and cuir bouilli missal box, with iron bands, hasp and lock, key missing, 15thC, 1 by 3½in (6 by 9cm).
£1,500-2,000 *C*

A burr walnut humidor, lined with cedarwood, with lock and handles, c1850, 9in (22.5cm) high.
£450-550 *RFA*

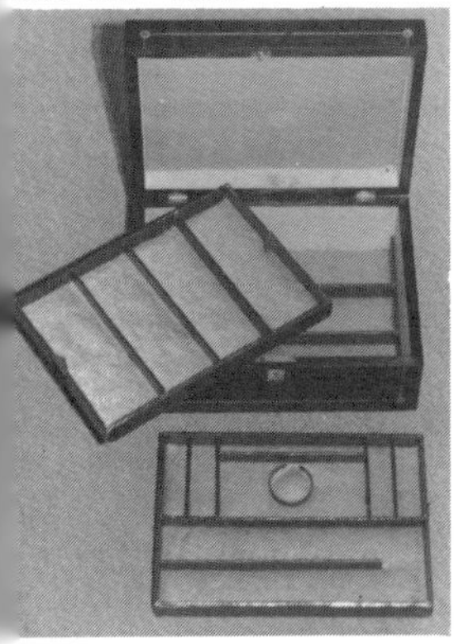

A rosewood jewellery box, with 3 trays, 19thC.
£100-150 *PCA*

A tortoiseshell veneered and ivory line inlaid tea caddy, the interior with 2 lidded compartments, early 19thC, 7in (17.5cm) wide.
£400-500 *CSK*

A tortoiseshell and silver box, London 1918, 2in (5cm) diam.
£60-80 *HF*

collage box, 12in (30.5cm) long.
70-100 *HF*

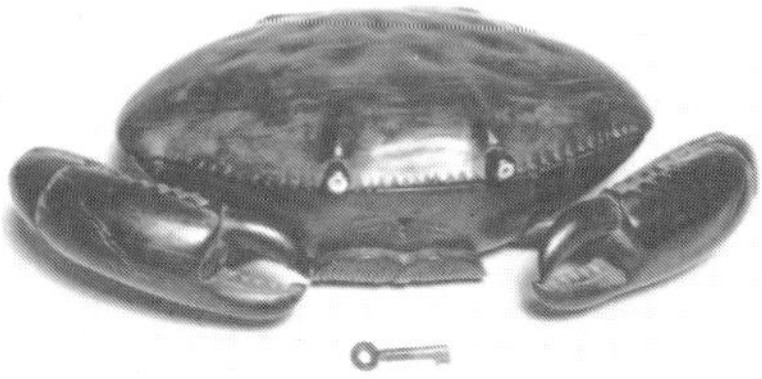

An unusual coromandel crab with central locking compartment.
£450-500 *MGM*

Transport

A Victorian child's horsedrawn carriage, the wicker seat lined with buttoned leatherette cushions, with brown leather restraining straps and green concertina action hood, 'pulled' by a pair of painted and carved wood figures of prancing horses, each with stitched leather harness and horse hair tail, 2 wheels replaced, 59in (150cm) long.
£2,000-2,500 *HSS*

An Edwardian governess cart, fitted with shaped bench seats and hinged access door to the rear, with 2 carriage lamp brackets, spoked wheels 36in (91.5cm) diam.
£500-600 *P(M)*

An Austin 10/4 saloon car, 1141c.c., originally registered 1st March 1933, re-registered under new number , with maroon and black paintwork.
£2,000-3,000 *DDM*

An English child's tricycle, c1910, 25in (64cm) high.
£170-200 *UC*

Car Mascots

A large green patinated bronze statue of a female archer on detachable marble base, one silver plated plaque inscribed 'Junior Car Club, International Trophy Race, 1938, presented by The Autocar', the other inscribed 'Group 2, won by H.W. Cook (E.R.A.), speed 84.34 M.P.H., driven by Raymond Mays', bow missing, slight damage to marble at foot of archer, 21½in (55cm) high overall.
£500-550 *P*

A chrome car mascot, c1930.
£75-85 *COB*

Miscellaneous

FENTON

A Fenton L.M.S. maroon enamelled totem.
£170-200 *C*

Fenton was the next station to Stoke-on-Trent on the N. Staffordshire Railway. Opened 7th August 1848, closed 6th February 1961, demolished shortly afterwards.

THE
PYTCHLEY

A London and North Eastern Railway cast brass nameplate, The Pytchley, being the left hand side plate removed from the D.49 Hunt Class 4-4-0 locomotive No. 62750, 33in (83cm) long.
£6,500-7,500 *C*

By Royal Letters Patent
No 3665
AVELING & PORTER
LIMITED
ROCHESTER
KENT
England

Two brass traction engine maker's plates, inscribed No. 2987 and No. 3665 Aveling & Porter Limited Rochester, Kent, England, 10in (26cm) wide.
£200-300 *C*

EX UNITATE VIRES

A Western Australian Government Railways coats-of-arms transfer on wood panel.
£50-80 *C*

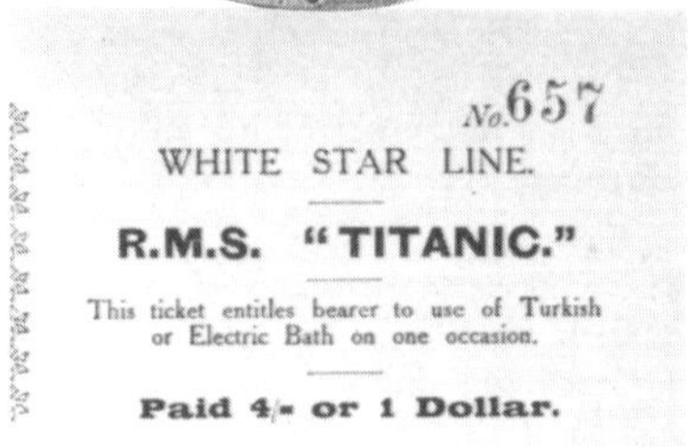
No. 657
WHITE STAR LINE.
R.M.S. "TITANIC."
This ticket entitles bearer to use of Turkish or Electric Bath on one occasion.
Paid 4/- or 1 Dollar.

A White Star Line, RMS Titanic, Turkish Bath ticket No. 657, 2 by 3in (5 by 8cm), together with letter of provenance.
£1,000-1,200 *ONS*

An Emile Monier bronze plaque cast in relief with the figure of a motorist at the steering wheel of car, c1920, 7½in (19cm) diam.
£120-150 *C*

Miscellaneous

A Lalique car mascot 'Archer', of flattened spherical form the clear glass moulded in intaglio with a kneeling archer, fitted onto an illuminated mount with cracked, green glass, moulded R. Lalique, wheelcut France, 8in (20cm) high.
£800-1,000 *P*

A bronze statue of a runner in action, wearing modern athlete's vest and shorts, the base inscribed F. Fraisse, 21in (53cm) high.
£400-500 *P*

A billiards scene in unglazed Continental porcelain, realistically coloured inscribed 'B. Merlin' on the ground, slight damage to underside, red ball and cues loose, 9in (23cm) high.
£350-450 *P*

A clock, the spelter mount containing raised depiction of a football match, c1930, 7in (18cm) high.
£100-150 *P*

A bronze trophy statue of a cyclist raising his cap, damaged, early 20thC, 12in (31cm) high.
£300-350 *P*

A Staffordshire creamware alphabet tea plate, with a sepia print of a man scoring a try despite opposition, decorated in colours, c1875, 7½in (18.5cm) diam.
£100-120 *P*

A silver cigarette box, with enamelled panel showing a racing scene just after the finish, the narrow raised border with incised decoration, Birmingham 1951, 4in (9cm) wide.
£250-300 *P*

A blue printed plate and a mug, commemorating Webb being the first man to swim the Channel.
£100-120 *P*

Crafts

A large stoneware bowl, by Ruth Duckworth, the interior covered in a celadon glaze, over a mottled and poured olive green and brown glaze, the exterior covered in a matt amber and olive green glaze, 18in (46cm) diam.
£2,000-2,500 *C*

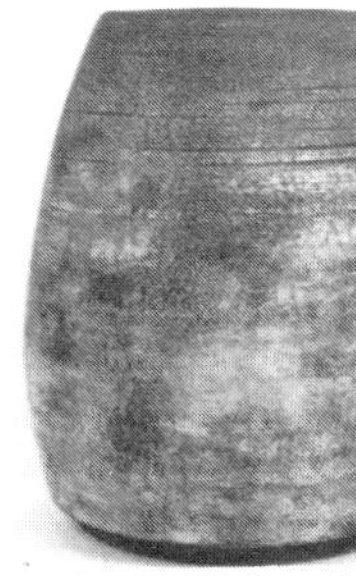

A stoneware cylindrical form by Hans Coper, covered in a matt buff slip heavily burnished to reveal areas of matt manganese, c1961, 18in (45cm) high.
£2,500-3,000 *C*

A stoneware footed vase by Ruth Duckworth, covered with a poured amber glaze over a celadon glaze, inscribed RDW, 6½in (16.6cm) high.
£1,200-1,500 *C*

A perforated stoneware bowl, by Ian Godfrey, the interior with an incised foliate design, black glazed, the fluting copper, 12½in (31cm) high.
£350-450 *Bon*

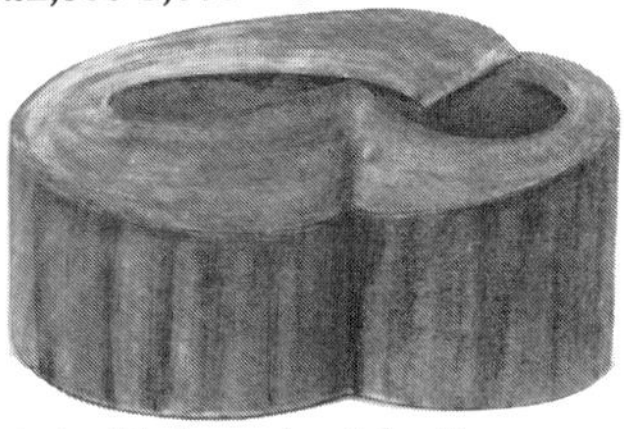

A double looped pot, by Ken Eastman, with grey brushed exterior, pale blue interior, painted Eastman signature, Number 5789, 20in (51cm) diam.
£450-500 *Bon*

A stoneware cylindrical form by Hans Coper, incised with spiral, covered in a matt buff slip burnished towards the base to reveal areas of matt manganese, c1961, 17½in (45cm) high.
£3,000-4,000 *C*

A stoneware hot water flask, by Sven Bayer, incised with foliate decoration, covered in a lustrous iron glaze with olive green splashes, impressed SB and Wenford Bridge seals, 12in (30.5cm) high.
£120-150 *C*

A slab with thrown vase, by Adam Sutherland, with painted head of a youth, in blue, green, pink, beige, black, potter's painted signature, 9in (23cm) high.
£170-200 *Bon*

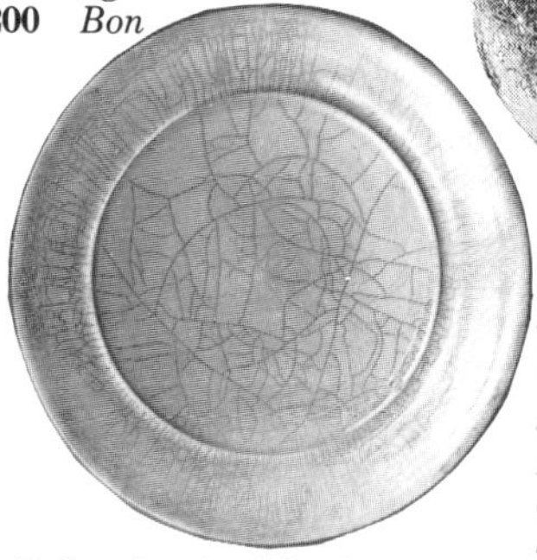

A large Raku plate by John Dunn, with cracked white glaze, impressed potter's seal, 23in (59cm) diam.
£70-100 *Bon*

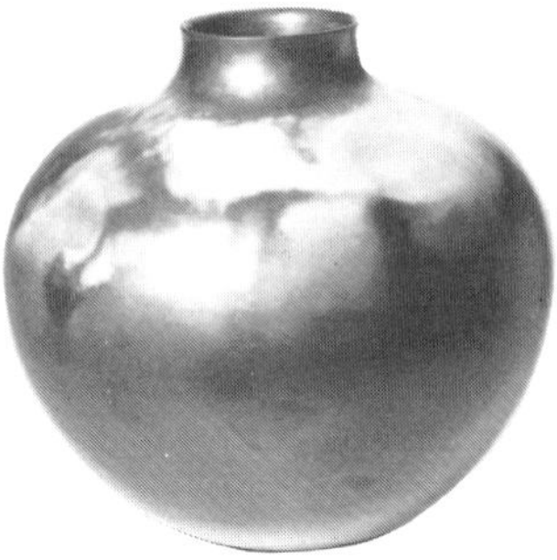

A spherical porcellaneous Form, by Gabriele Koch, in tones of burnished grey, incised Gabriele Koch, 15in (38cm) high.
£500-600 *Bon*

An earthenware ovoid pot, by Elspeth Owen, with irregular inverted rim, smoked and burnished, 7in (17cm) high.
£250-300 *Bon*

A covered Raku pot, by Mike Saul, in mottled grey and pink with twin vertical grey lines, signed M. Saul, 81, 7in (17cm) high.
£250-300 *Bon*

A Raku bowl, by Mike Saul, covered with a pink glaze, with red line below rim, signed M. Saul, 81, 10½in (27cm) diam.
£350-400 *Bon*

Mike Saul studied with Lucie Rie and Hans Coper at Camberwell School of Art together with Ewen Henderson and John Ward. Over the last 10 years he has devoted himself to establishing a major teaching college in Sunderland.

A Bernard Leach stoneware bowl, 8in (20.5cm) diam.
£200-250 *HSS*

A 'Neptune' stoneware vase, by Abdo Nagi, with bands in tones of blue, impressed potter's seal, 12in (31cm).
£400-450 *Bon*

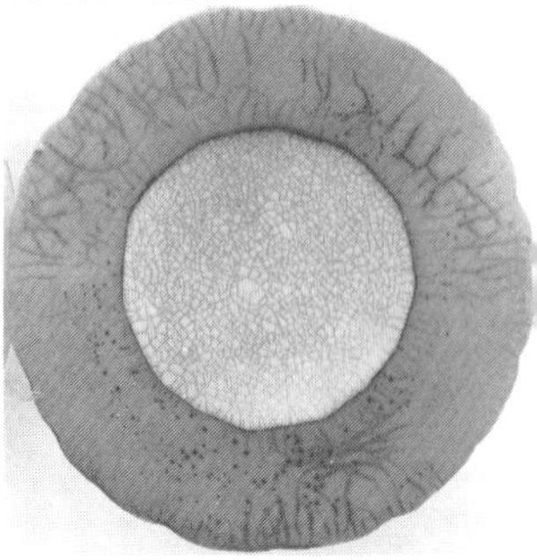

A large Raku bowl, by David Roberts, the interior well white with grey crackling, unglazed rim, impressed DR seal, 21½in (55cm) diam.
£250-350 *Bon*

A curved slab vase, by Adam Sutherland, with painted heads in blue, black and pink, potter's painted signature, 11½in (29cm).
£250-300 *Bon*

Adam Sutherland (b. 1958). After studying pottery with Colin Kellam and taking a B.A. in Fine Arts, Adam Sutherland studied at the Ecole des Arts Decoratifs, Paris. Since 1985 he has been teaching ceramics and printmaking at the Almond Road Workshops in North London, together with Ken Eastman

A stoneware bowl, by William Staite Murray, with prominent potting rings, on shallow foot, covered in a mottled olive brown and green glaze, the interior with a pale mushroom glaze thinning to reveal glaze beneath, impressed M seal, 7½in (20cm) diam.
£300-400 *C*

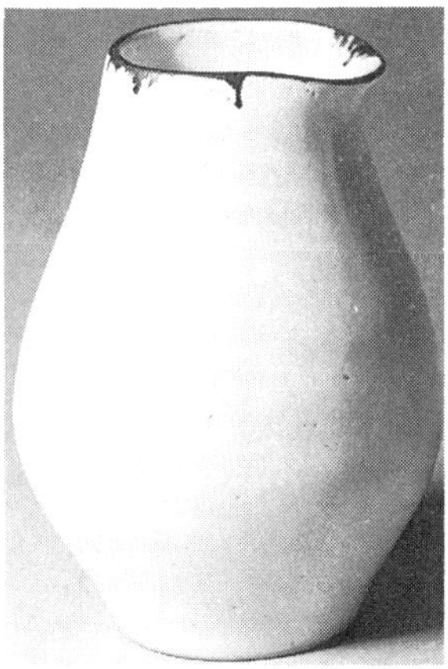

A white stoneware cream jug, by Lucie Rie, impressed LR seal, c1956, some restoration to rim, 4in (10cm).
£350-400 *Bon*

A stoneware goblet shaped vase by James Tower, the interior covered in a translucent black glaze, the exterior in a mottled brown and green glaze over white, inscribed Tower, 8in (20cm) high.
£300-500 *C*

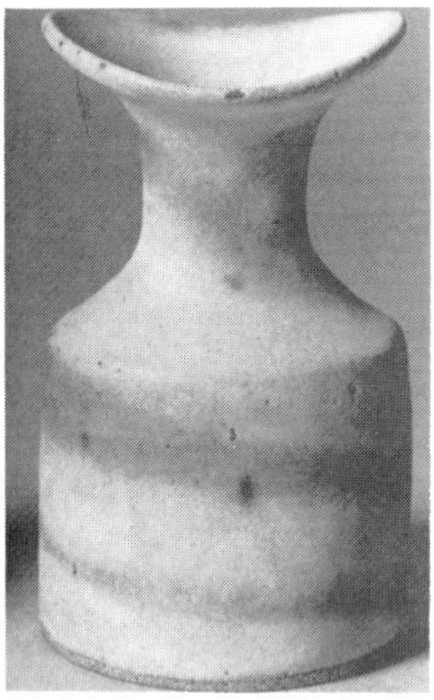

A Raku vase, by Lorraine Robinson, black with splashed white glaze, incised potter's signature, 10in (25cm) high.
£100-120 *Bon*

An Abuja stoneware candlestick by Bawa Ushafa, covered in a mottled lavender blue glaze thinning to reveal areas of lustrous iron brown, impressed B.U.A. seal, 14½in (37.5cm) high.
£200-250 *C*

A stoneware vase, by Lucie Rie, white with brown spiral, impressed LR seal, c1970, 5in (13cm) high.
£1,200-1,500 *Bon*

Tribal Art

A Nootka whalebone club, of spatulate form, the butt carved as a bird's head, the eyes as grooved circlets, the back of the head pierced 4 times, dark patina, 19thC, 22½in (57cm).
£3,500-4,000 *CSK*

A Maori greywacke hand club, the butt with 4 carved ridges and pierced for wrist thong, chipped, 15in (37.5cm) long.
£600-800 *CSK*

A small kero, painted with a central band of 2 monkeys and a parrot within foliage, old repairs, 6½in (15.5cm) high.
£500-550 *CSK*

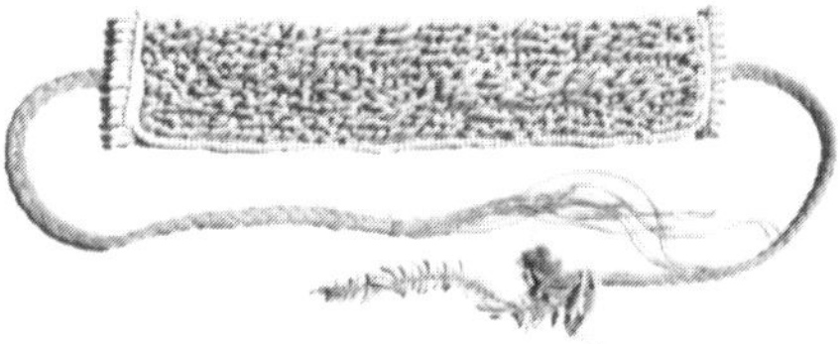

A Solomon Islands ornament, of twisted fibre sewn with 10 rows of porpoise teeth between bands of white trade beads, white bead border, nassa shells to each end, plaited fibre ties, one with tooth tassels, 8½in (22cm) long.
£1,500-2,000 *CSK*

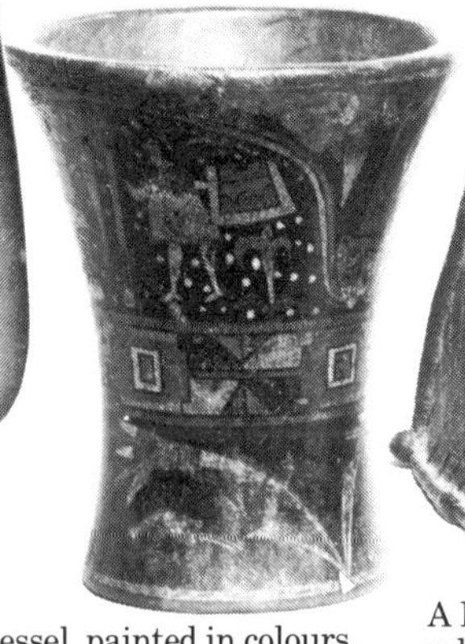

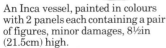

An Inca vessel, painted in colours with 2 panels each containing a pair of figures, minor damages, 8½in (21.5cm) high.
£1,000-1,500 *CSK*

A Benin bronze bell, cast in high relief, white painted collector's mark BC3, 19thC, 7in (18cm) high.
£200-300 *CSK*

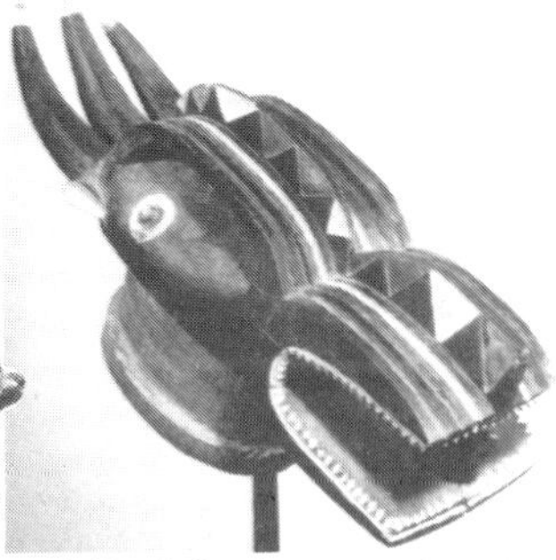

A Baule bush cow mask, 24in (61cm) long.
£400-600 *CSK*

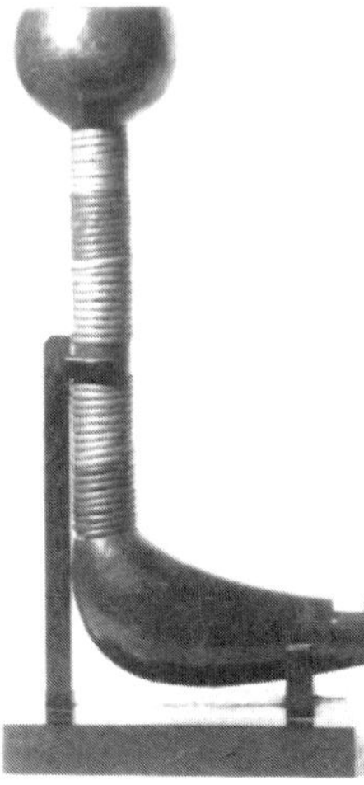

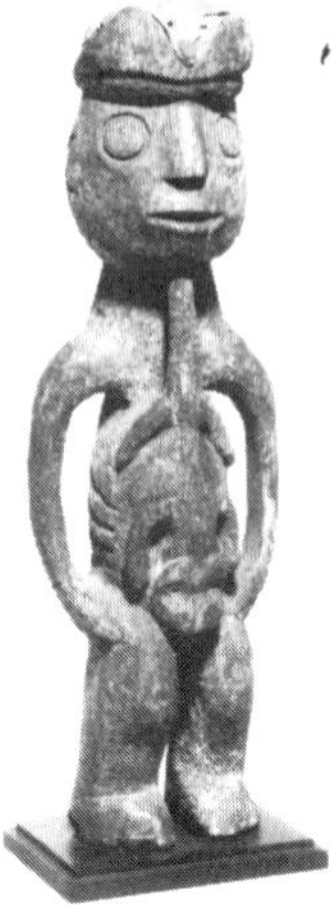

A rare Northwest coast bone figure, the spine and ribs carved in high relief, vestiges of applied skin remaining on the head with iron nails, Coastal Salish or Nootka, late 19thC, 9in (23cm) high.
£1,500-2,000 *CSK*

A Luba/Songye mask, with projecting square mouth and pierced eyes, the eyelids, nose and central band blackened, the remainder of the surface grooved and whitened, 18in (45cm) high.
£2,700-3,000 *CSK*

An unusual pipe, the stem bound with dark and pale copper strips, curved plump base to mouthpiece, on Inagaki stand, 12in (30cm) high.
£500-600 *CSK*

A fine Senufo wood mask, the concave cheeks carved in relief, triple incisions on forehead, the cresting with 3 rows of raised knobs, dark brown partially crusty patina, 11½in (29.5cm) high.
£4,000-6,000 *CSK*

A Guro female figure, the coiffure dressed as 5 lobes, white beaded waistband with small gold nugget, the crack at the back with some native filler, reddish brown patina, 13in (33cm) high.
£3,000-5,000 *CSK*

A Seneca moccasin, of tanned and smoked skin, decorated in coloured quillwork ornament in blue, red and white, the dark brown silk borders edged with white seed beads, minor damages, 8in (20cm) long.
£900-1,000 *CSK*

A Baga female figure, with red glass beads about neck, loins and ankles, circular base, Inagaki wood stand, 18½in (47cm) high.
£4,000-5,000 *CSK*

Three Ibeji, 2 males and a female, with pierced and pointed blued coiffure, smoothly worn faces, necklaces of fine dark blue beads and larger beads about the wrists and ankles, one with repaired base, from the Shaki area, 9½in (23.5cm) high.
£450-600 *CSK*

A rare Hungana male figure, encrusted red patina, termite erosion to left side, on Inagaki wood stand, 20½in (52cm) high.
£2,000-3,000 *CSK*

A Makonde staff, the finial carved as a head wearing rounded cap with incised band of circles, the face with large upper lip and incised scarification, the shaft with panels of incised geometrics, dark glossy patina, 58½in (148cm) long.
£500-600 *CSK*

A pair of Ibeji, male and female, each with blued coiffure, long strands of cowries suspended from one leg, coconut shell beads about the waists, the female with black bead necklace, dark glossy patinas from Shaki, 10in (25cm) high.
£200-250 *CSK*

A pair of Yoruba female twin figures, with necklace of large black beads, one with red and blue beads about the wrists, dark glossy patinas, from Baba Magba, 10½in (26cm) high.
£200-300 *CSK*

A Northern Northwest coast bowl, each end incised with the mask of a beaver, the rim with upholstery nails, 3 missing, dark glossy patina, 19thC, 14in (35cm) long.
£1,500-2,000 *CSK*

A Benin bronze head, for the altars of the Queen Mother, dark brown and black patina, mid-19thC, 19½in (49.5cm) high.
£12,000-15,000 *CSK*

A Baule mask, the eyes pierced with slits beneath narrow brows, the small mouth pierced at the centre, lower lip chipped, glossy brown patina, 8in (20cm) high.
£1,500-2,000 *CSK*

EPHEMERA

Pop Ephemera

A three quarter length signed photograph of Tina Turner, 8 by 10in (20 by 26cm).
£30-40 *VS*

THE BEATLES

Three Beatles twin track mono tapes.
£12-15 each *RTT*

JOHNNY FINGERS

A Canadian presentation gold disc to The Boomtown Rats, inscribed 'Presented to Johnny Fingers to commemorate the sale of over 50,000 units of the Mercury album "The Fine Art of Surfacing" December 10th, 1979', 20 by 16in (51.5 by 41cm), framed.
£200-300 *CSK*

A pair of black leather gloves, and a certificate of authenticity from the Elvis Presley Museum confirming that the gloves were worn by Elvis when riding his horses and motorcycles at Graceland.
£550-650 *CSK*

Exhibited at the Elvis Presley Museum for several years.

A souvenir concert programme for The Beatles/Mary Wells tour, signed on the cover by each member of the group and inscribed 'love Paul McCartney xxx', 1964.
£1,500-2,000 *CSK*

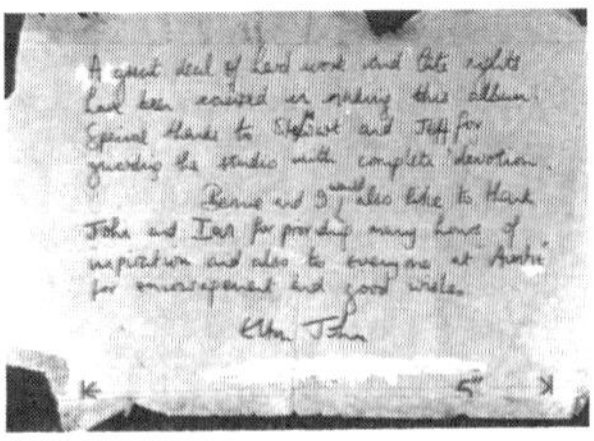

A great deal of hard work and late nights have been invested in making this album. Special thanks to [illegible] and Jeff for guarding the studio with complete devotion.
Bernie and I would also like to thank John and Ian for providing many hours of inspiration and also to everyone at [illegible] for encouragement and good wishes.
Elton John

An autograph note signed by Elton John, the note reproduced on the reverse of the album cover 'Empty Sky', 1969.
£650-750 *CSK*

A black and white portrait photograph of Eric Clapton, signed and inscribed Eric Clapton 89, 10 by 8in (25 by 20cm).
£200-220 *CSK*

A pair of tan leather zip-up boots, made by Verde, accompanied by an affidavit confirming that the boots were owned and worn regularly by Elvis, c1970.
£1,500-2,000 *CSK*

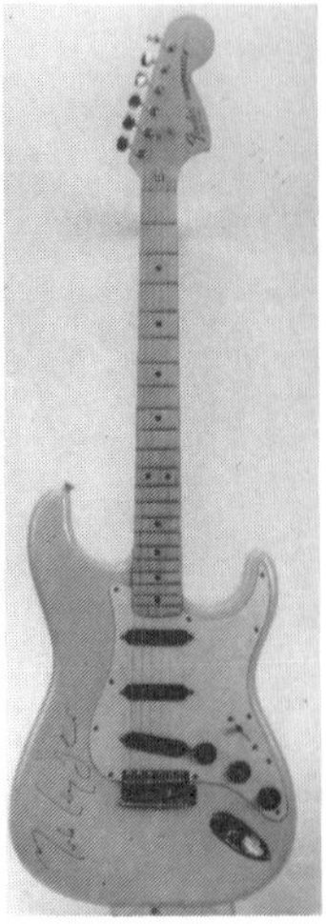

A Fender Stratocaster guitar, Serial No. S 981810 on 'ivory', bleached rosewood neck, signed by Mark Knopfler, 38½in (97cm) long.
£1,500-2,000 *CSK*

SLOW TRAIN COMING
BOB DYLAN

An album cover Slow Train Coming and a programme for European Concert Tour 1981, both signed by Bob Dylan in black felt pen.
£400-500 *CSK*

A custom-made ring, the mouth and eyes set with navette cut rubies, accompanied by a certificate of authenticity from the Elvis Presley Museum stating that Elvis bought the ring from Schwartz and Ableser fine jewellery store.
£4,500-5,000 *CSK*

THE
MELODY MAKER
THE LIDO
NORWICH
WINNING BAND
1934-1935

An embroidered banner for the winning band, 24 by 12in (61 by 30.5cm).
£35-40 *COB*

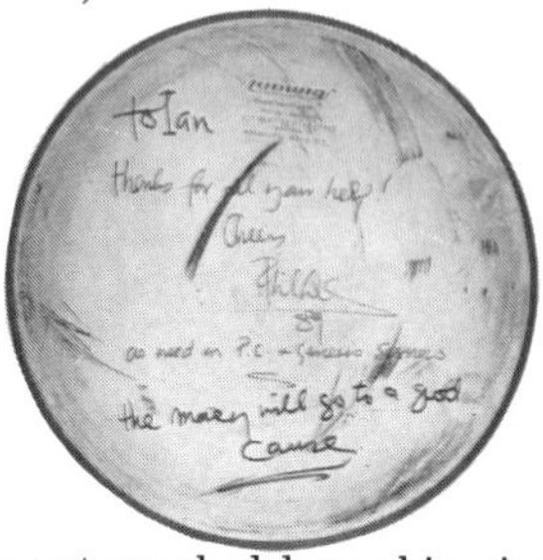

An autographed drum skin, signed and inscribed 'To Ian thanks for all your help, Cheers Phil Collins 89, as used on P.C. and Genesis sessions, the money will go to a good cause', in black felt pen, 13½in (34.5cm) diam.
£600-700 *CSK*

AMI
AMI

An A.M.I. JBJ 120 jukebox, Serial No. 461081, 45 r.p.m., finished in silver and black, 59½in (151cm) high.
£1,000-1,500 *CSK*

It is believed that the machine belonged to Malcolm MacLaren and was used by The Sex Pistols when miming for auditions.

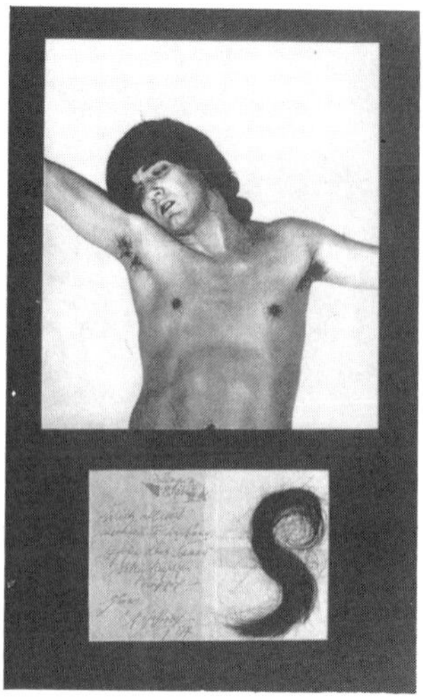

An autographed letter signed from P. J. Proby to a fan, inscribed 'With all best wishes to you Mary, hope this small token keeps you happy — from P. J. Proby xxx', in common mount with a lock of hair 9in (22.5cm) long, and a David Bailey portrait photograph of P. J. Proby, taken from 'David Bailey's Box of Pin-Ups', 1965, 28½ by 18½in (72.5 by 47cm) overall.
£100-200 *CSK*

A rare single-sided acetate 'Good Rockin Tonight', Memphis Recording Service label stamped 'W.H.B.Q. Memphis', accompanied by a certificate of authenticity from The Elvis Presley Museum stating that 'this Elvis Presley's 2nd recording for the Sun label is the original first copy made on the night it was recorded . . .'.
£3,000-3,500 *CSK*

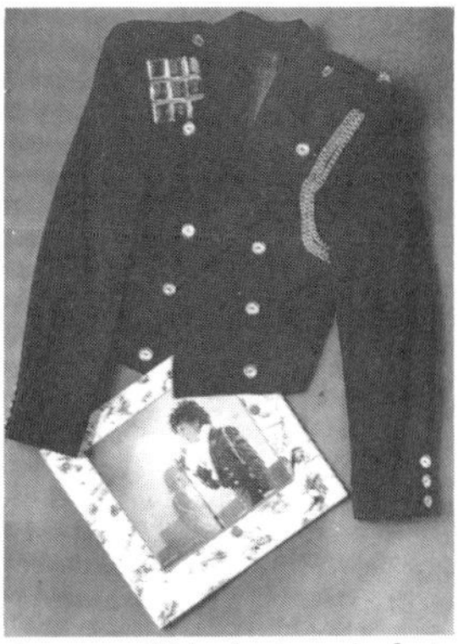

A cropped black stage jacket trimmed with metal buttons, decorated at the shoulders with imitation precious stones and a long curb link chain, accompanied by a souvenir programme showing Prince wearing the jacket in the 1984 Warner Bros. film Purple Rain, and a letter of authenticity from co-star Appollonia Kotero.
£3,000-3,500 *CSK*

The Rolling Stones

Two promotional posters signed by each member of The Rolling Stones, c1964, 22 by 17in (56 by 44cm), a machine print photograph of Jagger playing the maracas and a piece of paper both signed and inscribed by subject, two souvenir concert programmes, 1964, and two order forms for a Stones concert at the Guildford Odeon.
£550-650 *CSK*

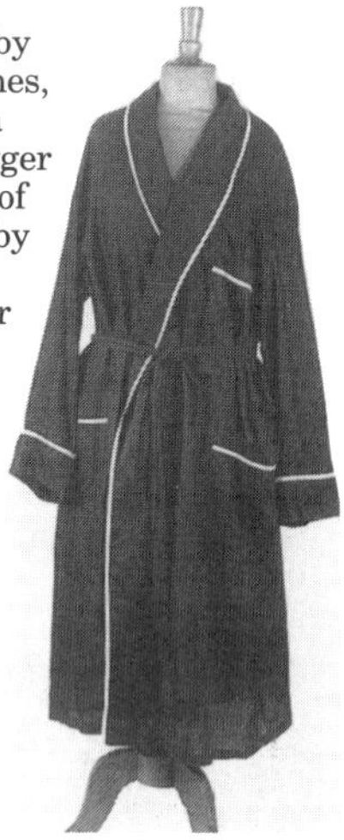

A dressing gown of maroon mixed fibre trimmed in white, with woven Amcrest label stitched inside, and a certificate of authenticity from the Elvis Presley Museum confirming that the robe was worn by Elvis.
£750-850 *CSK*

A presentation gold disc The Rolling Stones, 'Let It Bleed', the album mounted above a reduction of the cover and a plaque bearing the R.I.A.A. Certified Sales Award and inscribed 'Presented to Charlie Watts to commemorate the sale of more than one million dollars worth of the London Records long playing record album 'Let It Bleed', 21 by 17½in (54 by 44.5cm), framed.
£3,000-3,500 *CSK*

Postcards & Posters

JANE
RUSSELL
MARILYN
MONROE
HOWARD HAWKS'
Gentlemen Prefer Blondes
Colour by TECHNICOLOR
CHARLES
COBURN

A polychrome film poster Gentlemen Prefer Blondes, printed by The Haycock Press, London, 30 by 40in (76 by 101.5cm).
£200-250 *CSK*

A half length publicity postcard of Vivien Leigh in Gone With The Wind, signed by subject, and an autographed publicity postcard of Laurence Olivier.
£450-500 *CSK*

FRANKENSTEIN'S MONSTER
WOLF MAN
DRACULA
MAD DOCTOR
TOGETHER in the
HOUSE OF FRANKENSTEIN

Eight English polychrome horror posters, c1960, 30 by 40in (76 by 101.5cm).
£100-200 *CSK*

EDGAR ALLAN POES overwhelming tale of EVIL & TORMENT
THE FALL OF THE House of Usher
VINCENT PRICE

A polychrome film poster The Fall Of The House of Usher, featuring Vincent Price, 30 by 40in (76 by 101.5cm).
£50-100 *CSK*

STAN LAUREL AND OLIVER HARDY
THE DANCING MASTERS
TRUDY MARSHALL
BAILEY
MATT BRIGGS
DUMONT
ALLAN LANE

A Laurel and Hardy polychrome half sheet film poster The Dancing Masters, printed by Stafford & Co. Nottingham, 22 by 28in (56 by 72cm).
£50-70 *CSK*

EVEREST FILMS
CHARLOT

An August Leymarie Everest Film présente Charlot lithograph, in colours printed by L'Affiche d'Art, Paris, c1920, 62½ by 46½in (158 by 118cm), framed.
£450-650 *CSK*

FRANKENSTEIN MEETS THE WOLF MAN
ILONA MASSEY
PATRIC KNOWLES
BELA LUGOSI · LIONEL ATWILL
MARIA OUSPENSKAYA
LON CHANEY

Eighteen English polychrome horror posters, various titles, 1960s and 1970s, 30 by 40in (76 by 101.5cm).
£100-200 *CSK*

Campbell's
BEEF NOODLE SOUP
CHICKEN SOUP

A colour postcard Campbell's Soup Cans, signed Andy Warhol, 6 by 4in (15 by 10cm), mounted and framed.
£700-750 *CSK*

CREATURE FROM THE BLACK LAGOON
RICHARD CARLSON
JULIA ADAMS

Eleven English polychrome horror posters, largest 30 by 40in (76 by 101.5cm), and a collection of press, campaign books and related material.
£100-150 *CSK*

CIGARETTES
ANIC

A French advertisement for Anic cigarettes, by Dransy, slight corner crease.
£40-80 *VS*

HOE'S SAUCE

A Raphael Tuck Hoe's Sauce poster, 1505.
£20-30 *VS*

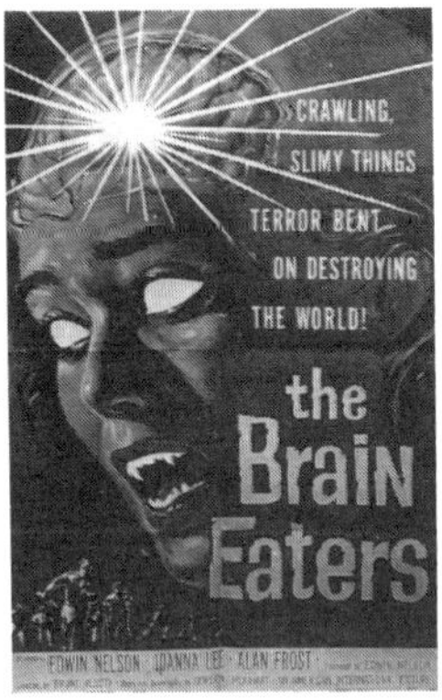
CRAWLING, SLIMY THINGS
TERROR BENT ON DESTROYING THE WORLD!
the Brain Eaters

Five polychrome English and American horror posters, c1960, largest 30 by 40in (76 by 101.5cm).
£70-100 *CSK*

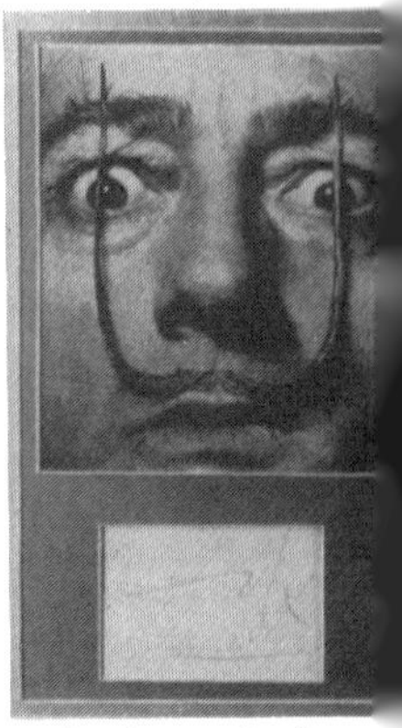

A signed reproduction portrait photo of Salvador Dali, overmount in gold, silver and ivory, framed an glazed.
£120-200 *VS*

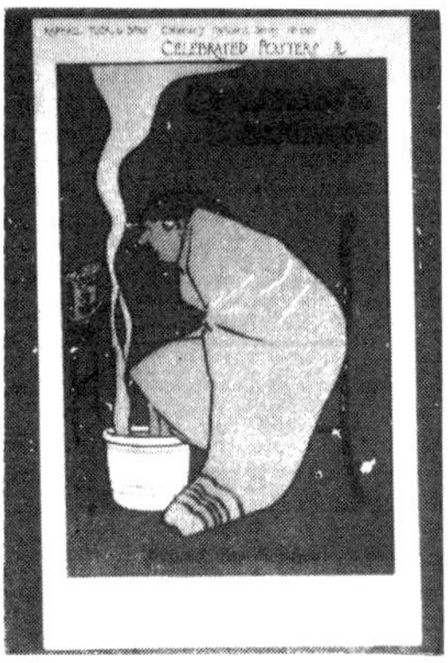
CELEBRATED POSTERS

A Raphael Tuck, Celebrated Posters, Colman's Mustard, Returned from Klondyke poster, 1500, by Hassall, UB, album corner marks.
£30-50 *VS*

Photographs

Eight publicity stills by Clarence Sinclair Bull of subject in the title role of the 1933 M.G.M. film Queen Christina, each with photographer's ink credit on reverse, 10 by 8in (25 by 20cm).
£350-450 *CSK*

Six 35mm colour transparencies of Marilyn Monroe, 5 with corresponding colour prints, largest 14 by 11in (36 by 28cm), sold with copyright.
£2,000-2,500 *CSK*

One of the above was used by William Carroll for his counter display card in 1945.

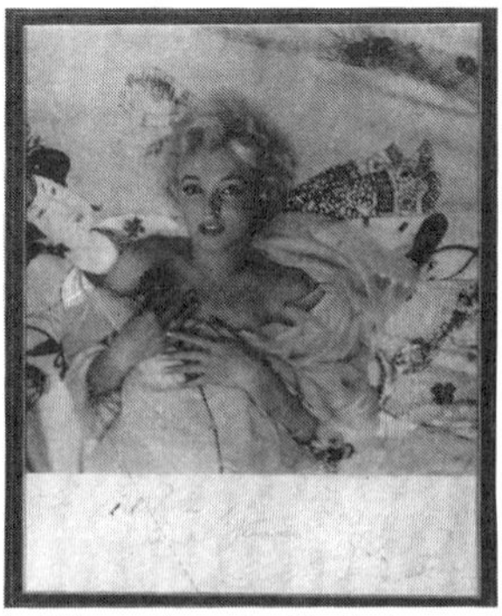

A half-length portrait photograph by Cecil Beaton, signed and inscribed on margin 'To Bridette (sic) Love & Kisses, Marilyn Monroe', 9 by 7½in (23 by 19cm), window mounted, framed, and a letter of authenticity on reverse.
£1,500-2,000 *CSK*

A colour publicity still of the Dynamic Duo, signed and inscribed, 10 by 8in (25 by 20cm).
£200-300 *CSK*

Disneyalia

The SEASON'S GREETINGS and all Good Wishes for the COMING YEAR

A Mickey and Minnie Mouse Christmas card, signed Walt Disney, 4 by 5in (10 by 13cm), and a biro sketch of Mickey Mouse.
£450-550 *CSK*

Walt Disney Studios, Snow White And The Seven Dwarfs, 1937, Dopey And Woodland Animals, gouache on celluloid with airbrush background, 5½in (14cm) square, window mounted and framed.
£1,300-1,500 *CSK*

Valt Disney Productions, Foul Iunting, a T.V. Production, Goofy nd a Friend Duck Hunting, ouache on celluloid on watercolour ackground, 8 by 10in (20 by 25cm), indow mounted.
450-550 *CSK*

BEST WISHES
WALT DISNEY

A piece of 'Cunard White Star R.M.S., Queen Elizabeth' headed paper, illustrated with a pencil drawing of Mickey Mouse, signed and inscribed 'Best Wishes, Walt Disney', 7 by 5½in (18 by 14cm).
£3,000-4,000 *CSK*

Walt Disney Studios, Alice in Wonderland, 1951, 4 celluloids, Red Rose, Red Rose and Rocking HorseFly, White Sleeping Rose and White Rose Awakes, each flower characterised with facial features, gouache on celluloid, largest 10 by 12in (25 by 31cm).
£700-800 *CSK*

Walt Disney Studios, Snow White And The Seven Dwarfs, 1937, 'Doc With A Lantern In His Hand Tells Bashful And Sneezy To Keep Quiet', gouache on multi-cel set up applied to a Courvoisier airbrush background, 9in (23cm) square, window mounted and framed.
£3,000-3,500 *CSK*

A piece of paper illustrated with a crayon drawing of Mickey Mouse, signed Walt Disney, 8 by 6½in (20 by 17cm).
£2,000-3,000 *CSK*

Walt Disney Studios, Snow White And The Seven Dwarfs, 1937, 'The Seven Dwarfs' gouache on celluloid with wood veneer background, 10½ by 14in (27 by 36cm), window mounted.
£1,000-2,000 *CSK*

Film & Theatre

An ornate Elizabethan style dress of figured silver lame trimmed with silver gilt braid, and lace, with petticoat and slashed sleeves of oyster satin, and 'Warner Bros.Pic.Inc.', embroidered label stitched inside, accompanied by a film still of Olivia de Havilland wearing the dress as Lady Penelope Gray in the 1939 Warner Bros. film 'The Private Lives of Elizabeth And Essex', 8 by 10in (20 by 26cm).
£450-550 *CSK*

DRESSING ROOM
24
CLARK
GABLE

A brass key ring, one side inscribed with the M.G.M. lion trade mark, the other inscribed 'Dressing Room 24 CLARK GABLE', 2½in (6cm) diam.
£300-350 *CSK*

Roger Furse, 'Ulyses', Mr Torin Thatcher, armed costume, tunic BCC 71' signed, watercolour and pencil costume design for the Warner film 'Helen Of Troy', 1955, 18½in by 13in (47 by 35cm), window mounted and framed.
£200-250 *CSK*

A photograph from 'It Happened in Brooklyn', showing Frank Sinatra and Kathryn Grayson and signed by Frank Sinatra only, 8 by 10in (20 by 26cm).
£50-80 *VS*

A half length colour photograph, signed by Adam West and Burt Ward, as Batman and Robin.
£70-80 *VS*

ORIENTAL

Cloisonné & Enamel

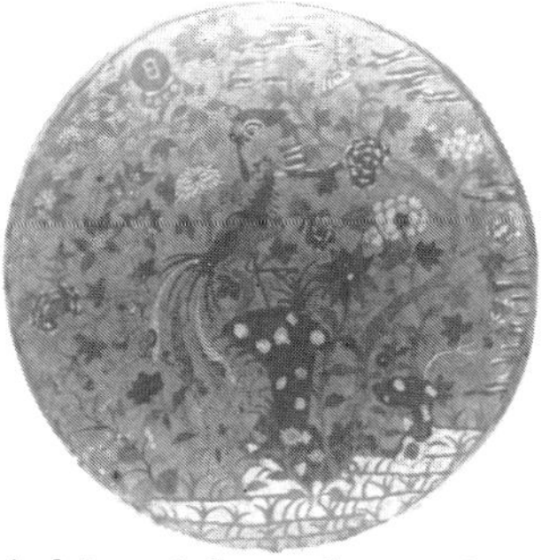

A cloisonné plaque, decorated on a turquoise ground, early 19thC, 23in (59cm).
£350-450 *Bon*

A Chinese cloisonné jardinière, decorated on a yellow ground of formal scrolling lotus flowers, 10in (26cm).
£250-350 *CSK*

A Chinese cloisonné teapot, with 8 Buddhistic emblems, c1800, 6in (16cm) high.
£350-400 *KOT*

A pair of Chinese cloisonné moon flasks, with gilt decoration on a flowerhead cell pattern ground, the necks with butterflies and stiff leaves, 14½in (37cm) high.
£700-800 *CSK*

Furniture

A Chinese ebonised wood desk and chair, on dragon carved cabriole legs, 52in (132cm) wide.
£450-650 *Bea*

A Japanese red lacquer cabinet and stand, some chipping, 18in (46cm) h
£300-400 *CSK*

A Hans Eberl limousine, with clockwork motor, opening doors, adjustable brake and steering, near mint condition, c1907, 15in (38cm). **£4,000-5,000** *MIN*

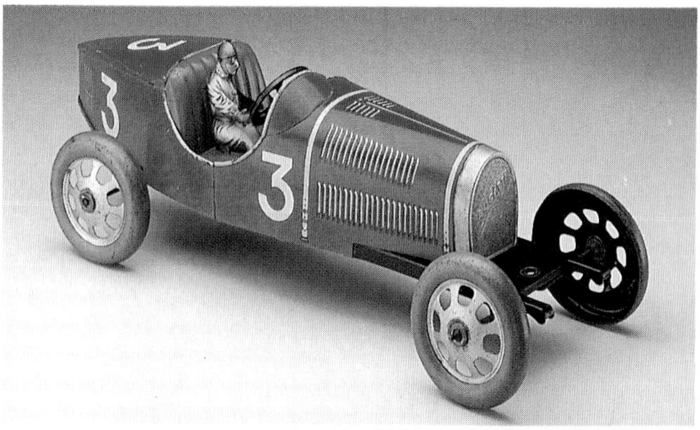

A very rare JEP Bugatti clockwork racer, near mint condition, c1930, 13in (33cm). **£20,000-25,000** *MIN*

A Hans Eberl clockwork limousine, adjustable steering and opening doors, near mint condition, c1908, 11in (28cm). **£5,500-5,750** *MIN*

A Mettoy Police Patrol motor cycle and rider, clockwork mechanism, mint condition, c1938, 8in (20cm). **£900-1,100** *MIN*

A Karl Bub 4-seat tourer, clockwork mechanism and adjustable steering, near mint condition, 10½in (27cm). **£3,000-3,500** *MIN*

A Bing hand painted lorry, trailer and load, near mint condition, c1908, 19in (48cm). **£16,000-16,500** *MIN*

A German clockwork open tourer, very good condition, c1905, 8in (21cm). **£2,000-2,500** *MIN*

Elektrische Strassenbahn

Märklin hand painted tramcar ıd suede horse, c1898, ıin (28cm). **£15,00-16,000** *MIN*

A Gunthermann clockwork Town Sedan, mint condition, c1906, 6½in (16.5cm). **£3,000-3,250** *MIN*

A Hess 4 seater, mint condition, c1925, 8½in (22cm). **£2-3,000** *MIN*

rare Bing clockwork limousine, ınor paint damage, c1908, 11in 3cm). **£18,000-18,500** *MIN*

A French clockwork runabout, with adjustable front wheels, c1898, 8½in (22cm). **£9,000-9,500** *MIN*

A rare clockwork Moko open bullnosed Morris, c1930, 7in (18cm). **£3,000-3,500** *MIN*

A Lehmann No. 555 'Uhu', clockwork amphibious car, c1907.
£3,000-4,000 *MIN*

A Louis Roussy Michelin railcar, powered by a 20 volt electric motor four gauge '0' in 1933.
£4,000-5,000 *MIN*

A Hess limousine, with working flywheel mechanism, opening doors, glass windows and chauffeur, c1908. **£3,000-4,000** *MIN*

STANDARD

A Distler 'Standard' oil tanker, clockwork, with adjustable steering, c1935. **£5,500-6,500** *MIN*

A Gunthermann fire engine, with clockwork motor, 2 firemen and bell, c1907, 6½in (16cm).
£3,000-4,000 *MIN*

A Bing open 4-seater car, with rubber-tyred wheels, clockwork motor, chauffeur and adjustable steering, c1922. **£6,000-7,000** *MI*

A Lehmann No. 595 clockwork 'Ihi' grocery van, with mechanically operated roller curtains.
£4,500-5,500 *MIN*

Silver Bullet

A Gunthermann 'Silver Bullet', Sunbeam record car, with powerful clockwork motor and adjustable steering, with box, 22in (56cm).
£1,000-2,000 *MIN*

A Lehmann No. 350 'Mikado Family', operated by a flywheel mechanism, c1897, 7in (18cm).
£4,000-5,000 *MIN*

A clockwork ship by Bing, c1912, 32½in (83cm) long.
£5,000-6,000 *CSK*

A Märklin, 'The Rheinuferbahn Set', electric, c1929.
£10,000-12,000 *CS*

A hand enamelled tinplate clockwork, De Dion car, No. 13654, by Bing, c1904. **£2,000-3,000** *CSK*

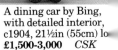

A clockwork ship by Bing, one lifeboat missing, c1908, 29in (74cm) long.
£3,000-4,000 *CSK*

A dining car by Bing, with detailed interior, c1904, 21½in (55cm) lo
£1,500-3,000 *CSK*

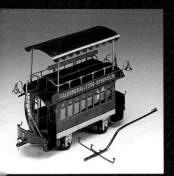

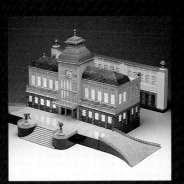

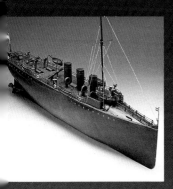

A Jumeau closed mouth doll, all original, c1880, 15in (38.5cm).
£1,700-2,000 *SP*

A Simon and Halbig lady doll, all original, c1900, 19in (48.5cm).
£1,200-1,500 *SP*

A pedlar doll, all original, c1836, 13½in (34.5cm).
£500-800 *SP*

A large Norah Wellings Dutch boy, 33in (84cm).
£250-350 *SP*

An English golliwog, post-war, 27in (69cm).
£15-25 *SP*

A pressed bisque headed bébé, by Emile Jumeau, marked, c1880, 16½in (42cm).
£5,000-6,000 *C*

A pair of poured wax headed character dolls, in original suits, some damage, c1880, 15in (38cm). **£1,500-2,000** *C*

A bisque heade bébé, c1885, 19 (48cm).
£4,500-5,500

A wax over papier mâché headed doll, with spare clothes, in original box, c1785, with later letter, 17½in (45cm) high.
£800-1,200 *C*

A Steiff plush teddy bear, with some wear, c1910, 20½in (52cm).
£3,000-4,000 *C*

A bisque headed bébé, rubbed body, marked BRU Jne.15.
£7,000-10,000 *CSK*

Above. A carved and painted wooden doll with some damage, c1740, 18in (46cm).
£10,000-15,000 *C*

r. A clockwork musical automaton, by Phalibois, c1885.
£3,000-5,000 *C*

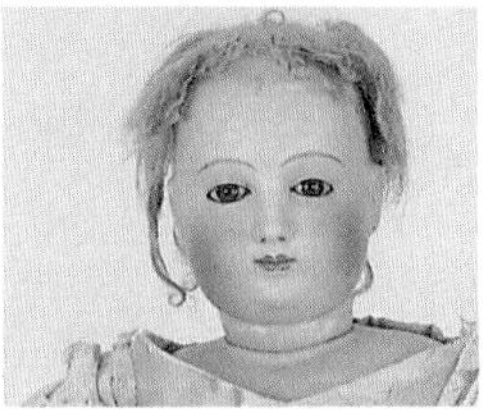

A bisque swivel headed Parisienne, probably Bru, 31½in (80cm).
£3,500-4,500 *C*

r. Two cloth headed character dolls, c1909.
£2,000-2,500 *CSK*

A fine Mycenaean chalice, painted with stylised lotus flowers around bowl with concentric bands below, part of foot restored, 1400-1200 BC, 7in (18cm) high. **£7,500-8,000** *C*

An Attic black-figure exaleiptron or plemochoe, black-glazed inside and out, edge of foot reserved, a band of rays between lines with dots around the rim of the knop handled lid, late 6th Century BC, 8in (21cm) high. **£7,500-10,000** *C*

An alabaster vase, with cuneiform inscription of Entemena, ruler of Lagash, 2404-2375 BC. **£8,000-12,000** *C*

Greek marble unerary stele, nscribed and nounted, 4th Century BC, 3in (83cm). **40,000-45,000** *C*

An Etruscan bronze helmet, 5th Century BC, 8in (20cm) high. **£140,000-150,000** *C*

l. A Greek marble head of a female, Hellenistic 2nd-1st Century BC, 6½in (16.5cm). **£9,000-12,000** *C*

A bronze handle, inlaid with gold and silver, c4th Century BC, 8½in (21.5cm). **£4,500-5,500** *C*

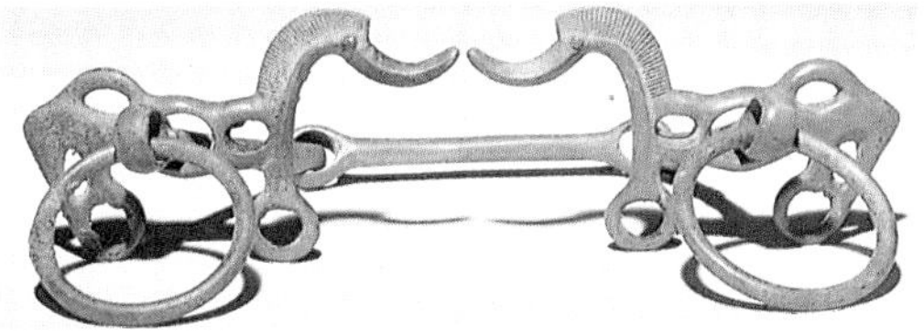

A Villanovan bronze horse bit, 8-7th Century BC, cheek-pieces, 4in (10cm). **£7,500-8,500** *C*

Celtic bronze terret, st Century AD, 3½in (8.5cm) vide. **£5,000-8,000** *C*

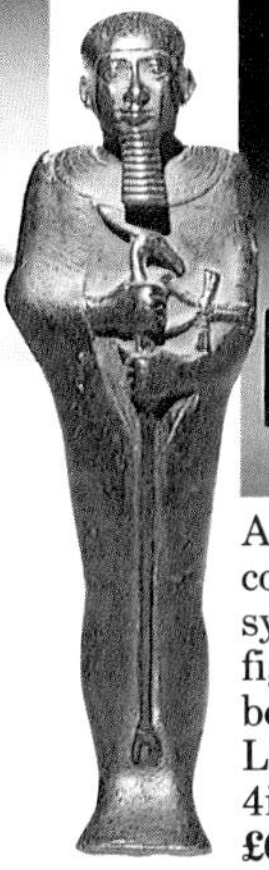

Above l. A bronze wagon attachment, c2nd Century AD, 4in (11cm) high. **£2,500-3,500** *C*

Above r. A Roman bronze figure of a gladiator, 1st Century AD, 3½in (9cm). **£3,500-4,500** *C*

l. A Greek bronze mirror cover, 4th Century BC, 6in (15cm). **£8,500-10,000** *C*

r. A bronze figure of Ptah, Late Period, 7½in (19cm). **£6,000-8,000** *C*

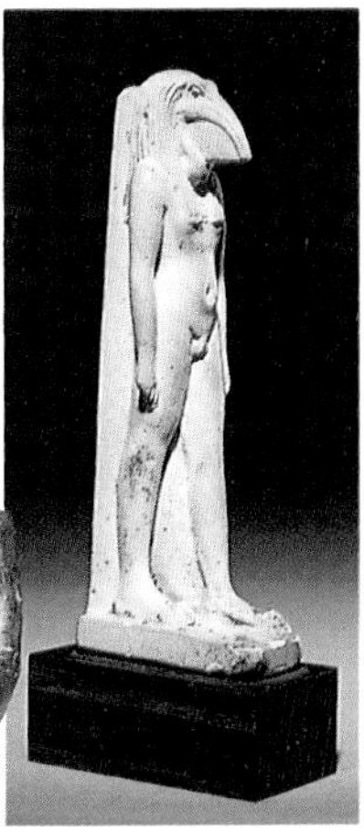

A glazed composition syncretistic figure of Thoth, beak restored, Late Period, 4in (10cm). **£6,500-8,500** *C*

A dragon dish, Daoguang seal mark and of the period, 6in (15cm) diam, fitted cloth box. **£600-950** *CNY*

大清光緒年製

A small café-au-lait glazed bowl, Guangxu mark and of the period, 4½in (11cm) diam. **£600-950** *CNY*

A Beijing glass carved bowl, Qianlong 4-character mark and of the period, 6in (15cm). **£9,500-12,000** *CNY*

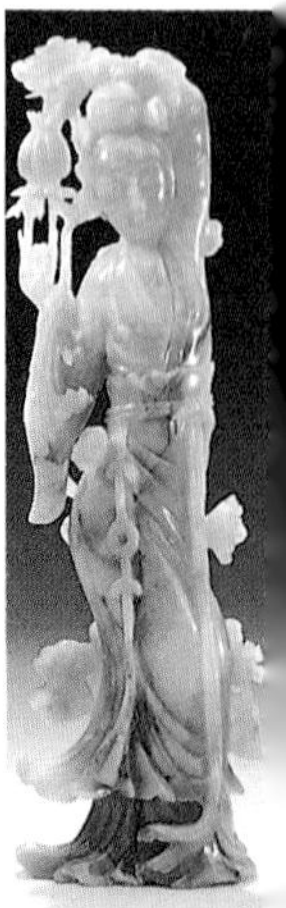

r. A mottled green jadeite figure of Lancaihe, some russet staining, 10in (25cm). **£20,000-25,000** *CNY*

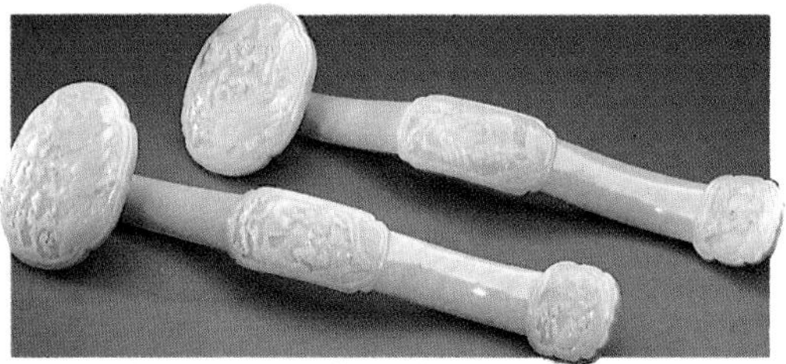

A pair of grey-green jade ruyi sceptres, 17½in (44.5cm) long. **£9,500-12,000** *CNY*

r. A carved, mottled jadeite group in green and russet, some damage, 8in (20cm) high. **£6,500-9,500** *CNY*

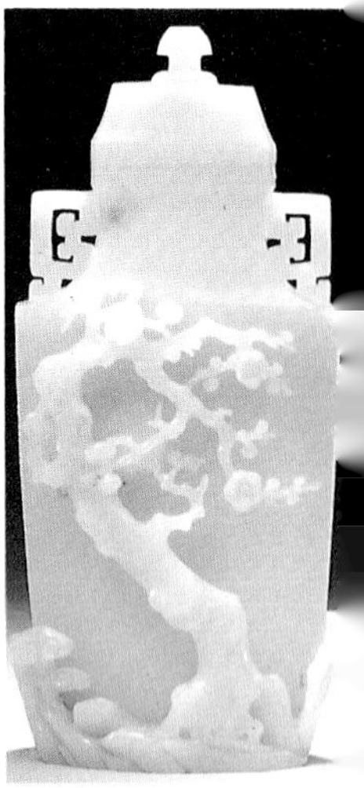

A jade vase and cover, c1800, 11in (28cm) high. **£9,500-12,000** *CNY*

A pair of jade bowls, 19thC, 8in (20cm). **£3,000-4,500** *CNY*

l. A jade beaker vase, c1700, 9in (23cm). **£9,500-11,000** *CNY*

Far l. A gilt decorated jade vase, c1800, 8in (20cm). **£3,000-5,000** *CNY*

A jade figure of a horse, Tang Dynasty or later, 2in (5cm) long. **£4,500-6,500** *CNY*

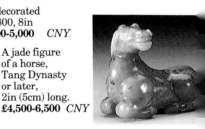

Above. A 2-colour jadeite goat group, 6½in (16cm) long. **£1,000-1,200** *CNY*

A jade figure of a camel, Song Dynasty, 3in (7.5cm) long, wi wood stand and box. **£5,000-7,000** *CNY*

Two jade figures, one male and one female, 19thC, 3in (7.5cm) high. **£1,500-2,000** *CNY*

A jade horse shown in the process of rolling, 3½in (8.5cm) long. **£2,500-3,000** *CNY*

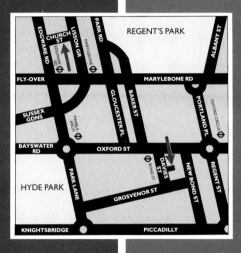

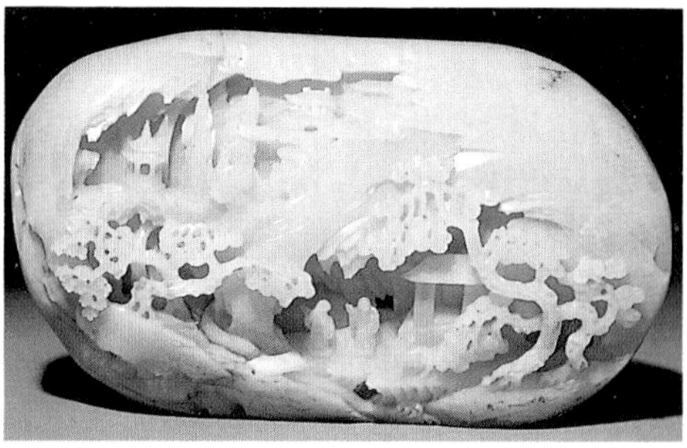

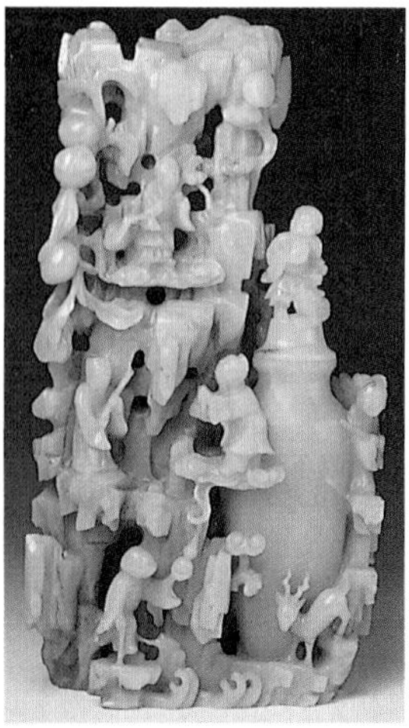

A jadeite flecked cylindrical box and cover, the base with shallow wide footring, 2½in (5.5cm) diam.
£1,000-1,500 *C*
r. A celadon jade mountain group, the stone flecked with russet inclusions, Kangxi, 11in (28cm) high. **£5,000-8,000** *C*

A Mughal jade ewer and cover, the stone of very even tones, 18thC, 8in (20cm) high.
£4,000-5,000 *C*

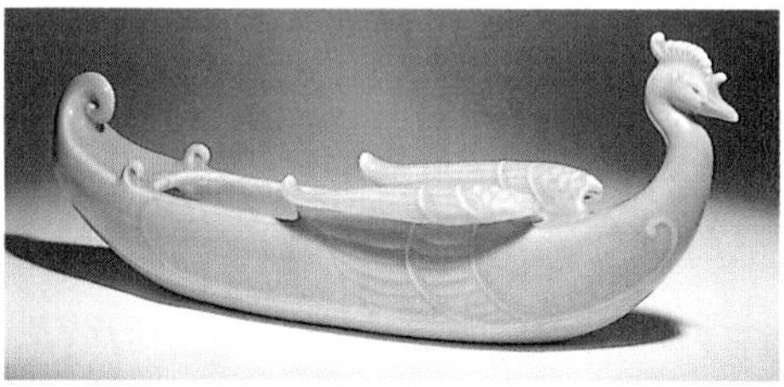

An ikebana vessel in the form of a celadon glazed boat, signed Makuzu Kozan, Meiji period, 17in (44cm) long. **£4,000-5,000** *C*

A silver and gilt inlaid bronze vase, minor dents, 17thC, 30in (76cm) high.
£4,000-5,000 *C*

A pair of black stone water buffalos, partially hollowed underside, late 17thC, 11½in (29cm) long.
£5,500-7,500 *CNY*

A pair of bronze vases, 19thC, 23in (59cm) high.
£7,000-8,000 *C*

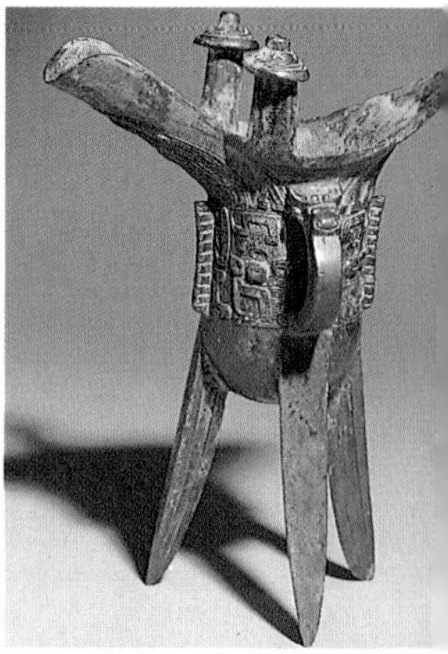

Two gilt splashed bronze censers and covers, mid Qing Dynasy, 10½in (27cm) and 12½in (32cm) high. **£2,500-3,500** *C*
Above l. A Japanese bronze vase, marked, 9½in (24cm).
£3,500-4,000 *Bea*
Above r. An archaic bronze wine vessel, some malachite encrustation, Shang Dynasty, 8in (21cm) high. **£11,000-13,000** *C*
l. An archaic bronze 2-handled vessel, some damage and malachite encrustations, Shang Dynasty, 10in (25.5cm) wide. **£3,000-4,000** *C*
r. A large archaic bronze food vessel, worn in places, Shang Dynasty, 14in (36cm) diam.
£13,000-14,000 *CNY*

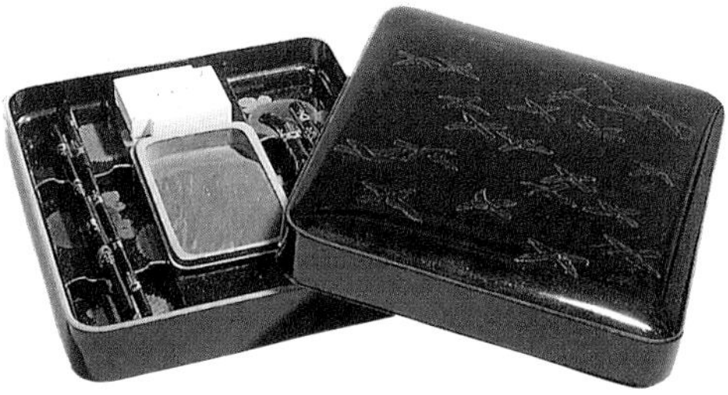

l. A roironuri cylindrical box and cover, Meiji period, 3½in (8.4cm). **£3,000-3,500** *C*

Above. A roironuri suzuribako and bundai, minor chips to bundai, Meiji period, bundai 23in (58.5cm) wide. **£4,000-5,000** *C*

A rare gold almond shaped openwork plaque, Five Dynasties, 3½in (9cm) high. **£13,000-15,000** *C*

A Chinese ormolu mounted crackle-glazed celadon vase, with twin lion mask handles, 14in (35.5cm) wide. **£7,000-8,000** *C*

A pair of gold fundame kobako, modelled as male and female mandarin ducks, both with some damage, late 19thC, 7½in (18.4cm) long. **£4,500-5,500** *C*

..n enamelled silver teapot and cover, ..e body worked in gold and silver ..ire, minor restoration, triangular ..ark with S.M., Meiji period, 7in ..7cm) high. **£4,000-5,000** *C*

Above. An archaistic silver and gold inlaid bronze wine pot, central finial missing, Song Ming Dynasty, 9½in (24.5cm) high. **£9,500-10,500** *CNY*

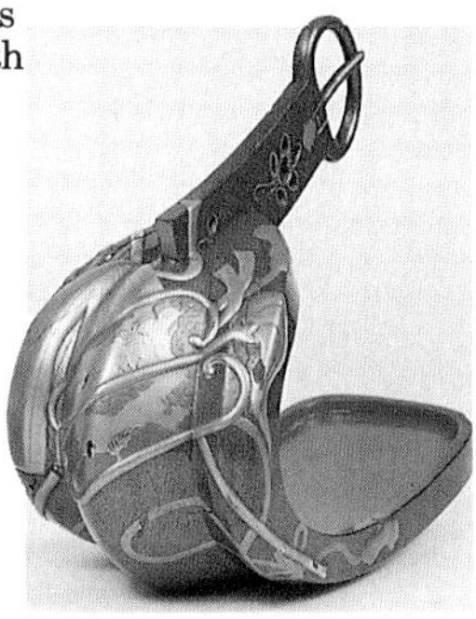

A pair of iron stirrups, 19thC, 11½in (29cm) long. **£3,000-4,000** *C*

An ostrich egg decorated in hiramakie, Meiji period, 6in (15cm) long. **£4,000-4,500** *C*

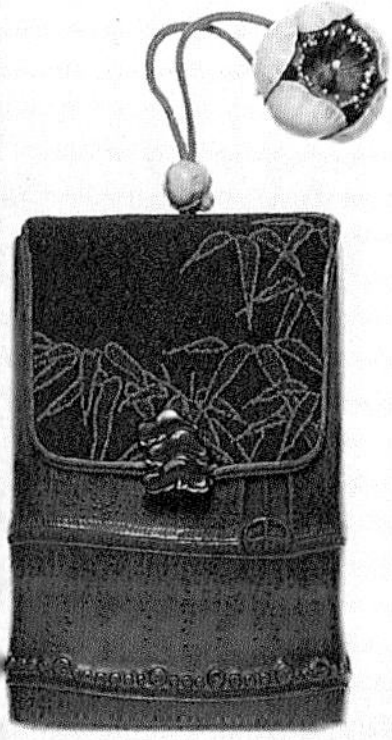

..lacquered tonkotsu, ..signed, with ivory ..tsuke and ojime signed ..ogyoku, late 19thC. **..,500-3,500** *C*

A flat inkstone with bamboo box and lid, 17th/18thC, 4in (10cm). **£11,000-12,000** *CNY*

r. A model signed Shoun, Meiji period, 18in (45cm) long. **£6,000-7,000** *C*

A late Ming gilt bronze seated figure of Guandi, his robe bordered with peony, 17thC, 14in (35.5cm) high, fitted box.
£15,000-16,000 *CNY*

An enamelled and gilt bronze model of a Buddhistic lion, on layered rock with peony flowers, some restoration, 18thC, 10in (25.5cm) wide. **£10,000-12,000** *CNY*

A pair of cloisonné enamel quail censers and covers, minor bruising, feet damage, Qianlong, 6in (14.5cm) high. **£9,000-10,000** *C*

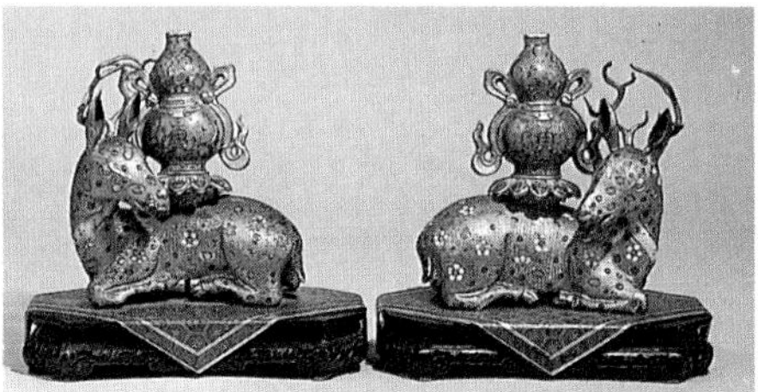

A pair of cloisonné enamel deer, each supporting a detachable double gourd vase, Qianlong, 9½in (24.6cm) high.
£8,000-10,000 *C*

A pair of cloisonné enamel moon flasks, with gilt kui dragon handles, slight damage, 19thC, 26in (66cm) high. **£5,500-7,500** *C*

A Ming gilt bronze polychrome cloisonné enamel beaker vase, vajra on base, 15thC, 7in (18.5cm).
£90,000-100,000 *CNY*

A group of 4 cloisonné enamel tripod incense burners and covers and 2 vases, Qianlong, largest 11in (28cm) high. **£8,000-10,000** *C*
r. A miniature lacquer kodansu, with fitted interior, 19thC, 5in (12.5cm) high.
£10,500-12,500 *C*

A silver rimmed shell box, damage, signed, 19thC, 6½in (16cm) wide. **£3,500-4,500** *C*

l. A silver rimmed box and tray, presented by Prince Hirohito, slight damage to tray, 19thC, box 6in (14.5cm) wide.
£6,500-7,000 *C*
r. A pewter rimmed bunko, brocade lined, worn, 18thC, 13in (33cm) wide.
£4,000-5,000 *C*
l. A kobako with 3 hishigata on a nashiji tray, slight damage, 19thC, 4½in (12cm).
£10,000-12,000 *C*
r. A lacquer box, minor damage, 19thC, 10in (25cm).
£2,500-3,000 *C*

A jewelled, silver and nephrite ashtray, marked Fabergé, Moscow, c1910, 6½in (16cm) diam.
£5,500-6,500 *CG*

A large shaded enamel silver-gilt kovsh, by Vasilii Agafanov, Moscow, c1910, enamelled overall in peonies and tulips, engraved with various donors' signatures under the handle, 13in (33cm) long.
£8,000-9,000 *CG*

A Fabergé picture frame, c1890, 4½in (11.5cm).
£12,000-15,000 *CNY*

A Fabergé gold and guilloche enamel frame, c1900.
£15-20,000 *CG*

A vodka service by the Imperial Glass Factory, Russian proverb on flask, 8 glasses and tray, dated 1875, flask 10in (25cm) high. **£3,000-4,000** *C*

A five-piece shaded enamel desk set, some surface wear, with Imperial warrant of Pavel Ovchinnikov, Moscow, c1910, stand 8½in (21.5cm) wide.
£10,000-12,000 *C*

An enamel silver gilt beaker, by Khlebnikov, c1910.
£1,500-2,000 *C*

An ormolu mounted lapis lazuli and marble commemorative plaque, by Count Fedor Tolstoi, inscribed, 1824, 11in (28cm) square.
£4,500-6,500 *C*

A silver mounted hardstone lamp and matching glue pot, the mounts marked Fabergé, c1890, lamp 6in (15cm).
£12,000-15,000 *CNY*

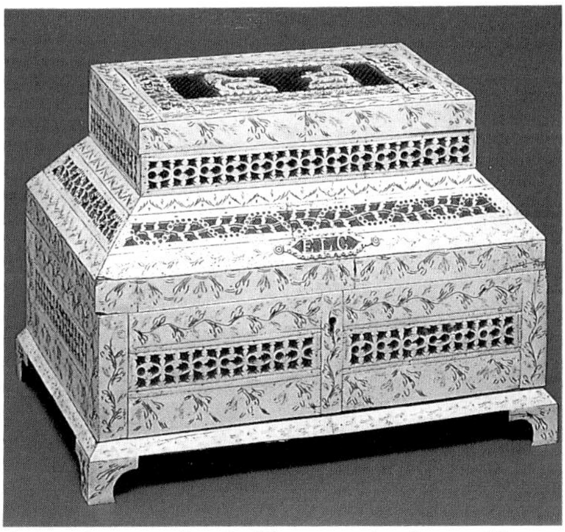

A Russian neo-classical bone sewing box, with lidded compartments, probably Arkhangelsk, c1775, 8in (20cm) high.
£2,500-3,000 *CNY*

Mother of God Eleousa of Kykkos, 18thC, 17in (43cm).
£4,000-4,500 *C*

l. The Virgin Kazanskaya in silver-gilt cloisonné enamel, marked Borisov, c1890, 12½in (32cm) high.
£4,000-5,000 *CNY*

A pair of shaded enamel silver gilt tea caddies, marked Fabergé, c1910, 5in (13cm) high.
£14,000-16,000 *CNY*

A pair of panels of Archangels Michael and Gabriel for an Iconastas, repainted, 16thC, 30½in (77.5cm) high.
£5,500-6,000 *C*

A gilt metal 10-branch chandelier, late 19thC, 33in (84cm) high.
£3,000-4,000 *C*

Above l. A pair of Empire bronze and ormolu candelabra, 34in (86cm) high.
£10,000-12,000 *C*

Above r. A pair of Louis XVI bronze and ormolu candelabra, 31in (79cm) high. **£7,000-10,000** *C*

Above. A set of 4 ormolu and bronze candlesticks, mid-19thC, 11in (28cm) high.
£6,000-8,000 *C*

l. A pair of Empire ormolu and patinated bronze candelabra, drilled for electricity, restorations, early 19thC, 34½in (87cm).
£15,000-18,000 *CNY*

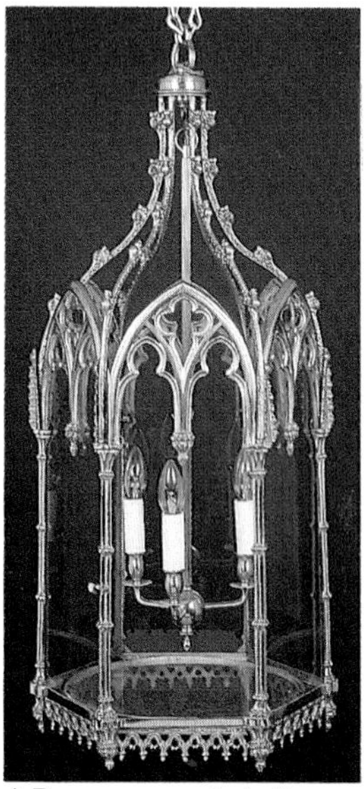

A Regency ormolu hall lantern, fitted for electricity, 37½in (95cm) high. **£20,000-25,000** *C*

A pair of Louis Philippe ormolu and patinated bronze wall lights, drilled for electricity, mid-19thC, 36in.
£5,500-7,500 *CN*

Above. A Continental gilt brass and copper hall lantern, fitted for electricity, late 19thC, 51in (129.5cm) high.
£4,000-6,000 *CNY*

l. A set of 6 ormolu wall lights, mid-19thC, 36½in (93cm) high.
£10,000-15,000 *C*

A pair of ormolu wall lights, mid-19thC, 43½in (110cm).
£1,500-2,000 *C*

l. A pair of Continental ormolu mounted rock crystal and malachite urns, fitted for electricity, 30in (76cm) high.
£5,000-7,000 *CN*

A pair of Regency ormolu, bronze and cut glass 3-light candelabra, 1 drip pan replaced, 21½in (54cm) high.
£8,000-10,000 *C*

A pair of Empire ormolu and patinated bronze 3-light candelabra, early 19thC.
£8,000-10,000 *CNY*

A matched pair of Empire ormolu and bronze 5-light candelabra, c1810, 33in (84cm).
£9,000-10,000 *CNY*

A pair of Empire ormolu 3-light candelabra, c1810, 17in (43cm).
£7,000-8,000 *CNY*

A pair of ormolu mounted Sèvres bleu nouveau 5-light candelabra, some cracks, 35in (89cm) high.
£7,000-9,000 *C*

\ Louis XVI ormolu 6-light handelier, drilled for lectricity, c1780, 33½in 35cm) high.
7,500-11,000 *CNY*

A Regency cut glass 21-light chandelier, restorations, 84in (213cm) high.
£30,000-35,000 *C*

A pair of ormolu and rock crystal 12-branch chandeliers, 19thC, 38in (97cm) high.
£15,000-20,000 *C*

Regency ormolu hanging sh light, 25in (64cm) am.
,000-10,000 *C*

An ormolu hall lantern, mid-19thC, 32in (82cm) high.
£8,000-10,000 *C*

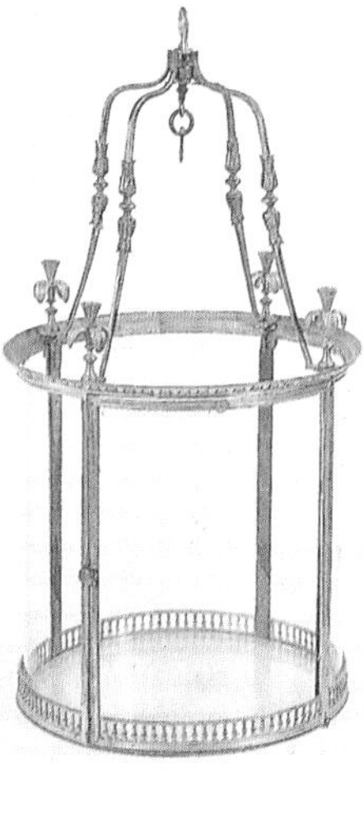

A pair of mahogany and painted copper wall lanterns, restorations, 29in (74cm) high.
£11,000-13,000 *C*

l. A Louis XVI ormolu hall lantern, 44in (112cm) high.
£30,000-35,000 *C*

A pair of early Victorian ormolu mounted, ivory and ebonised candlesticks, inset with precious stones. **£1,500-2,000** *C*

A pair of Regency ormolu, cut glass and Wedgwood porcelain candlesticks, 12in (31cm) high. **£1,500-2,000** *C*

A pair of candlesticks. **£2,000-3,000** *C*

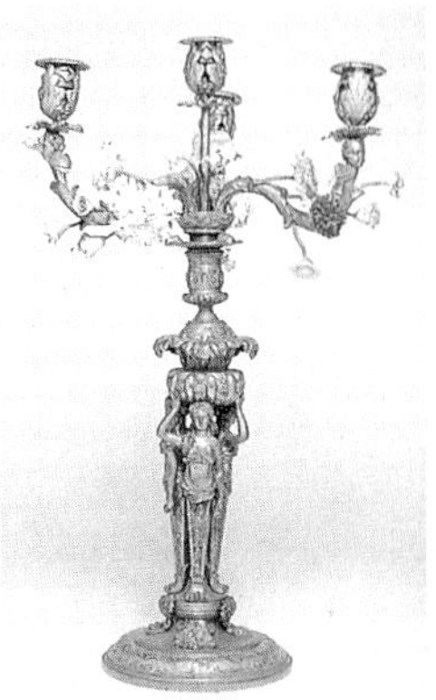

A pair of ormolu and porcelain candelabra, late 19thC, 20½in (52cm) high. **£1,500-2,000** *C*

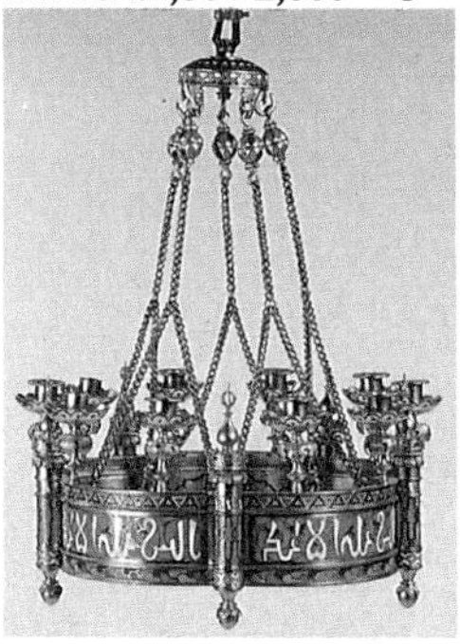

A gilt brass and enamel 10-light chandelier, fitted for electricity. **£2,000-3,000** *C*

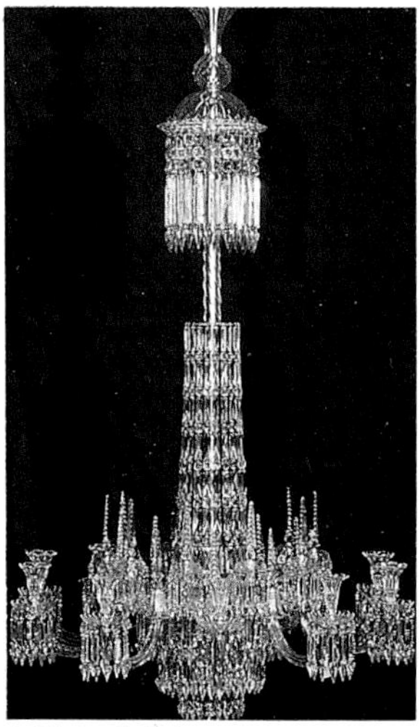

A Victorian cut glass 10-light chandelier, restorations, 42in (107cm) diam. **£5,000-7,000** *C*

A Danish ormolu and cut glass 6-light chandelier. **£4,000-5,000** *C*

An Empire bronze and ormolu 6-branch hanging light, drilled for electricity, 40in (101.5cm) high. **£4,500-6,000** *C*

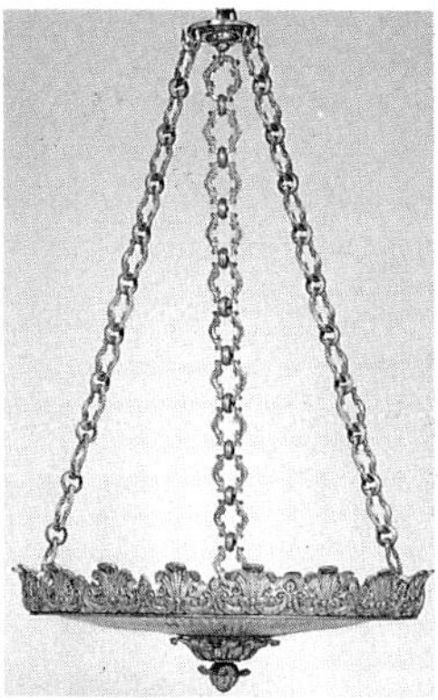

A George IV ormolu and cut glass dish light, 27in (69cm) diam. **£8,000-10,000** *C*

A pair of Empire bronze and ormolu tripod brûle parfums. **£11,000-12,000** *C*

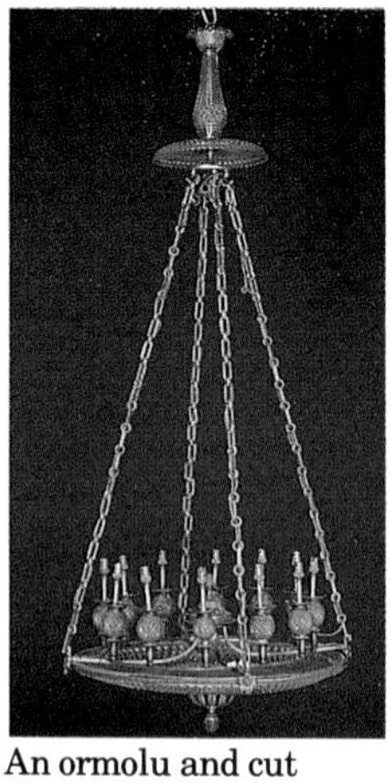

An ormolu and cut glass 12-light hanging light, part early 19thC. **£8,000-10,000** *C*

An ormolu and steel lampe bouillotte, 27in (69cm) high. **£1,000-2,000** *C*

l. An ormolu mounted, sang de boeuf vase, fitted for electricity. **£5,000-5,500** *C*

A pair of parcel gilt mahogany, wall lanterns, 12in (31cm) wide. **£8,000-9,000** *C*

l. A pair of ormolu mounted and 'famille noire' vases, fitted for electricity, 16in (41cm) high excluding fitments. **£3,000-3,500** *C*

An etched Italian Infantry half armour, probably Milanese, some damage and restoration. **£20,000-25,000** *CSK*

A relic Iberian dagger with scabbard. **£1,000-1,500** *ASB*

A British Life Guards helmet and cuirass, c1870. **£1,400-1,800** *ASB*

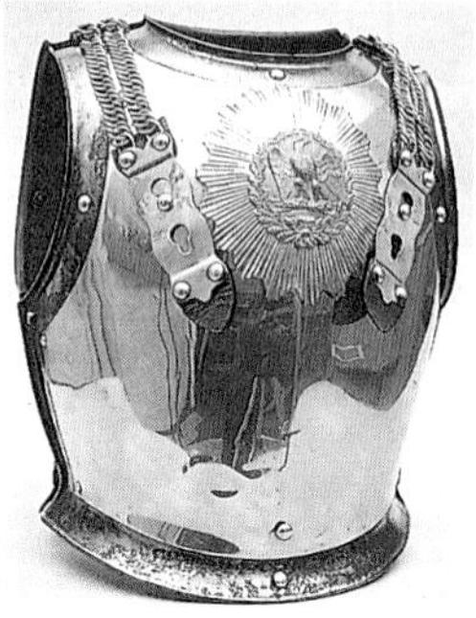

A French Caribinier trooper's brass faced cuirass, some cleaned rust, dated 1864. Est. **£1,500-1,750** *WAL*

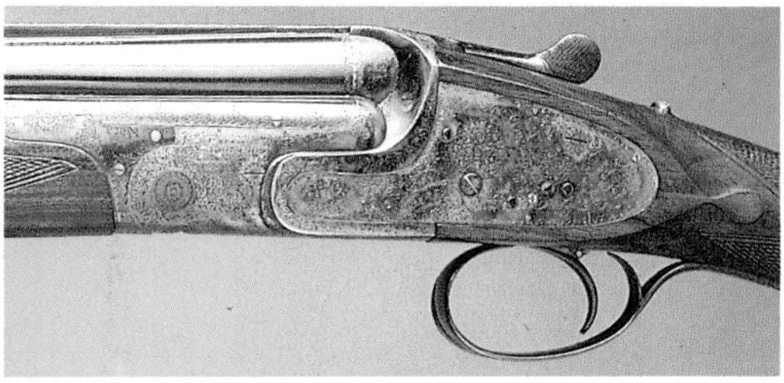

A 20-gauge double barrelled single trigger over-and-under hammerless sidelock ejector gun, by Boss, No. 9098, c1958. **£22,000-25,000** *CNY*

A German seige weight helmet, c1600. **£2,000-2,200** *ASB*
l. A lobster tail helmet, probably Polish, c1650. **£600-700** *ASB*

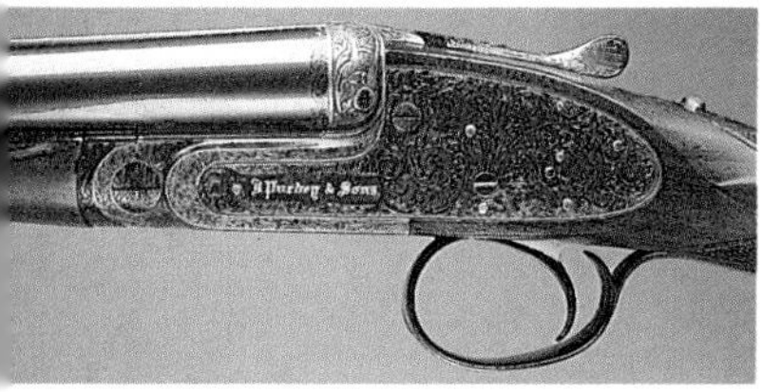

20-gauge double barrelled single rigger hammerless sidelock ejector un by J. Purdey, No. 26166, c1959. **15,000-18,000** *CNY*

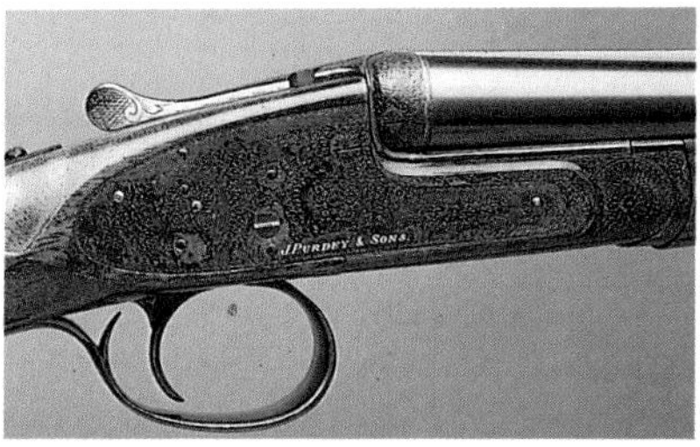

r. A .410 double barrelled single trigger hammerless sidelock ejector gun by J. Purdey, c1983. **£22,000-25,000** *CNY*

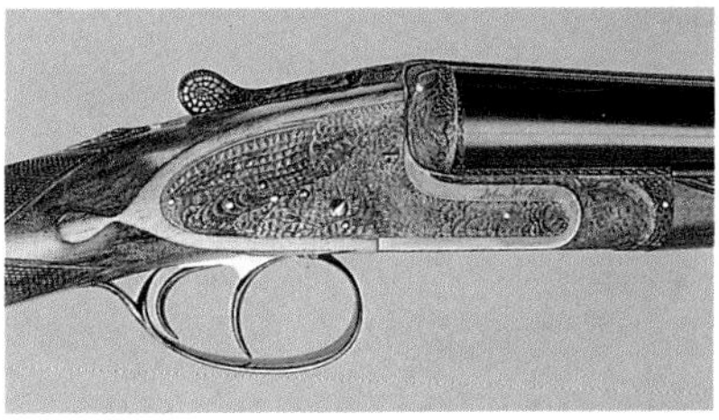

r. An Appleby engraved 12-gauge sidelock ejector gun by J. Wilkes, No. 15124. **£17,000-19,000** *CNY*

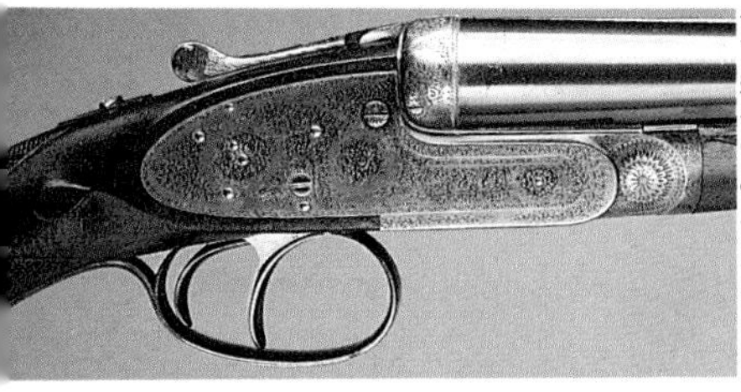

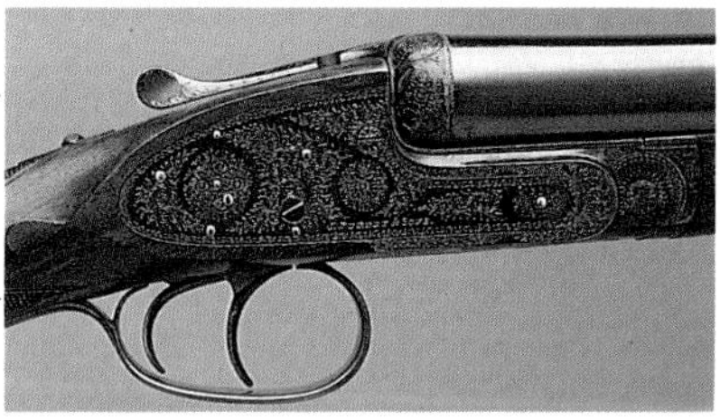

l. A pair of 12-gauge d.b. hammerless ejector guns by J. Purdey, c1925. **£19,000-22,000** *CNY*
r. A 12-gauge d.b. ejector gun by J. Purdey, c1965. **£10,000-15,000** *CNY*

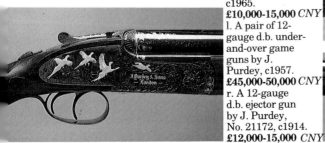

l. A pair of 12-gauge d.b. under-and-over game guns by J. Purdey, c1957. **£45,000-50,000** *CNY*
r. A 12-gauge d.b. ejector gun by J. Purdey, No. 21172, c1914. **£12,000-15,000** *CNY*

HONI·SOIT·QUI·MAL·Y·PENSE

The Most Noble Order of the Garter, Lesser George sash badge, chips to cameo border, early 19thC, in fitted case.
£10,000-12,000 *C*

The Most Noble Order of the Garter, Lesser George sash badge, some chips to enamel.
£23,000-25,000 *C*

HONI·SOIT·QUI·MAL·Y·PENSE

The Most Noble Order of the Garter, Lesser George sash badge, early 19thC, in case.
£11,000-12,000 *C*

HONI·SOIT·QUI·MAL·Y·PENSE

The Most Noble Order of the Garter, Lesser George sash badge, some damage to enamel, early 19thC.
£18,000-20,000 *C*

HONI·SOIT·QUI·MAL·Y·PENSE

The Most Noble Order of the Garter sash badge, c1800.
£22,000-25,000 *C*

The Most Noble Order of the Garter sash badge, mid-18thC.
£40,000-45,000 *C*

HONI·SOIT·QUI·MAL·Y·PENSE

The Most Noble Order of the Garter badge.
£18,000-20,000 *C*

The Most Noble Order of the Garter badge, mid-17thC.
£30,000-35,000 *C*

A pre-1914 Imperial Austrian Artillery officer's shako, in its original case. **£900-1,500** *WAL*
and a Bavarian General officer's pickelhaube, with original lining.
Est. **£1,000-1,250** *WAL*

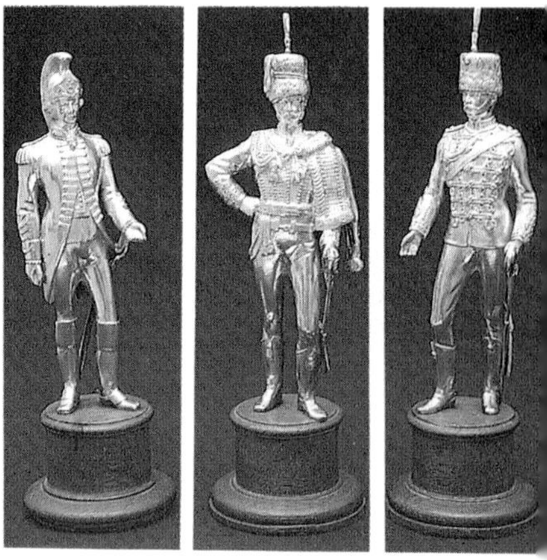

A set of 3 H.M. silver, London, military officer figures, 7in (18cm) high. **£1,000-2,000** *WAL*

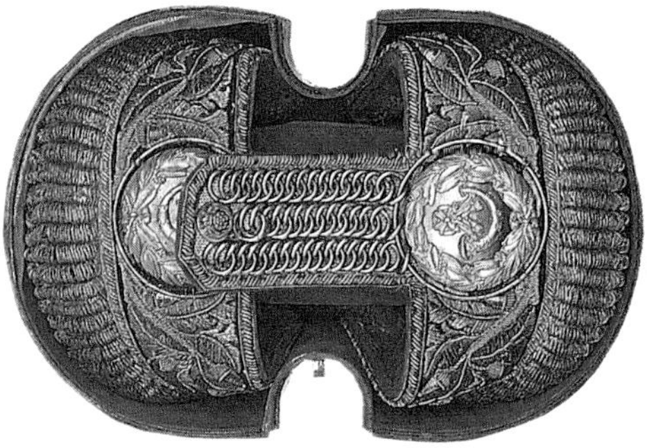

A pair of pre-1855 Light Company officer's dress wings. Est. **£250-300** *WAL*

A bronze figure of Edward, Prince of Wales, 1936.
£1,000-2,000 *WAL*

l. An Edward VII trumpet banner.
£600-700 *WAL*

A Spanish bronze cannon, barrel inscribed and dated 1639, on later carriage.
£4,500-5,000 *ASB*

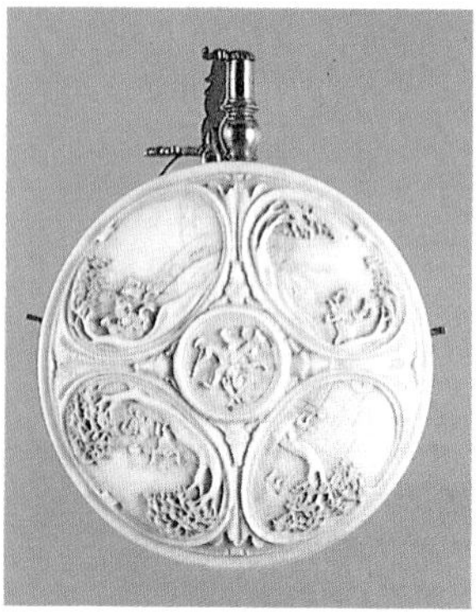

A German carved ivory powder flask, late 17thC, 5½in (14cm) high.
£10,000-12,000 *CSK*

A Partisan head of the Yeoman of the Guard with Edward VIII cypher, both sides etched, blued and gilt, with lined wooden case, c1936, 24½in (62cm) overall. **£1,500-2,000** *WAL*

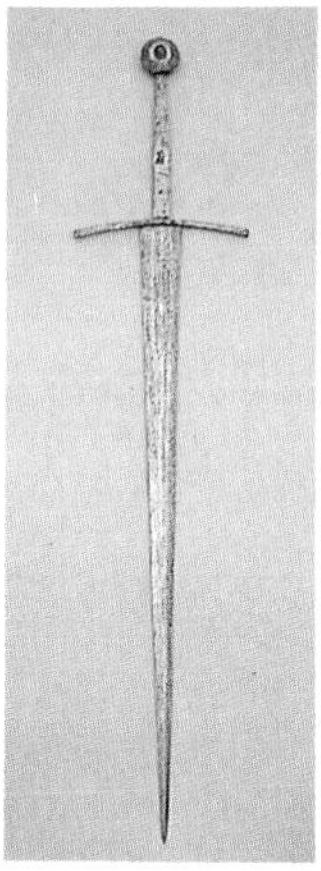

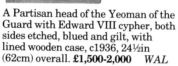

An Italian knightly sword, with double edged blade, c1400, 32in (81cm) blade.
£10,000-12,000 *CSK*

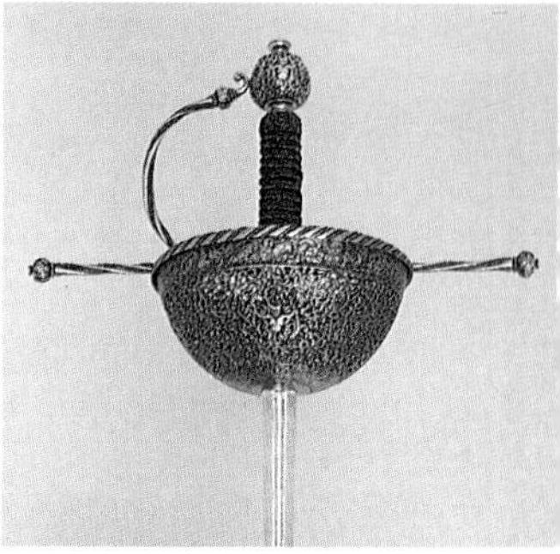

An Italian cup hilt rapier, with original wire bound wooden grip, c1660, 40½in (103cm) blade.
£8,000-12,000 *CSK*

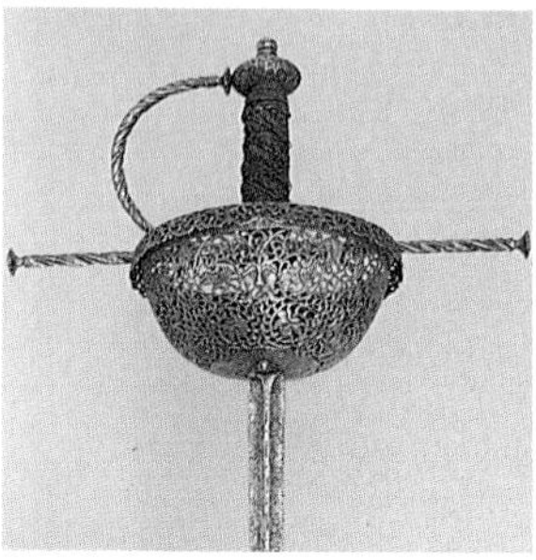

A Neapolitan cup hilt rapier, c1660, 44½in (113cm) blade.
£8,000-10,000 *CSK*

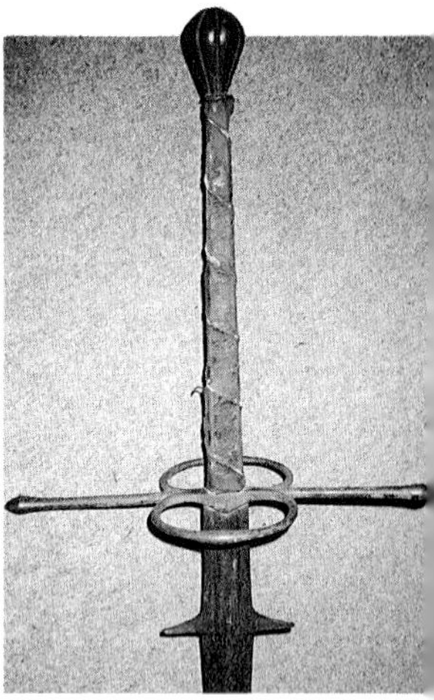

A German two-handed sword, c1500.
£1,500-2,000 *ASB*

An engraved gold medal, 1st Volunteer Movement, c1804.
£2-3,000 *C*

The Most Noble Order of the Garter Registrar's badge in gold and enamel, in original red leather case with riband, c1816.
£10,000-11,000 *C*

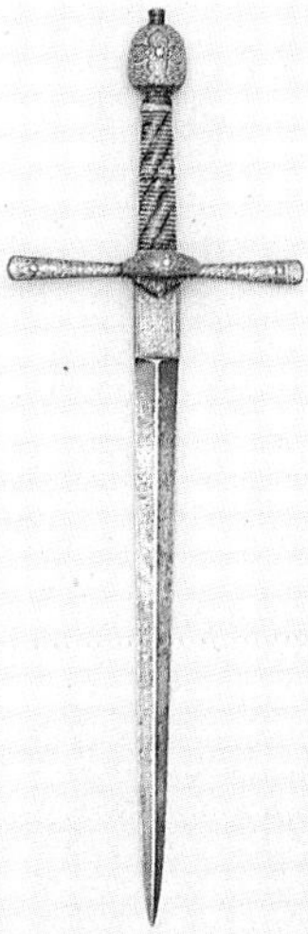

A left-hand dagger, with spirally fluted wooden grip, late 16thC, 18in (46cm). **£9,000-10,000** *CSK*
Above r. A German main gauche dagger, c1620. **£1,200-1,500** *ASB*

A German rapier, the hilt covered in silver, c1620.
£6,000-8,000 *ASB*
Above r. A basket hilt sword, c1740. **£350-400** *ASB*

The Most Noble Order of the Garter breast stars, mid-19thC.
£3,000-4,000 each *C*

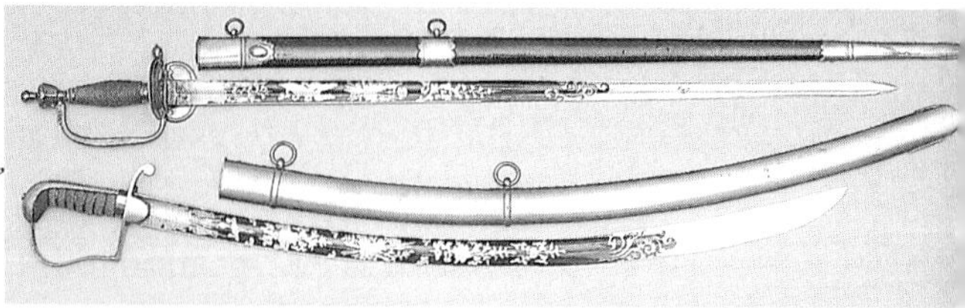

A Georgian 1796 pattern Light Cavalry officer's sabre with curved blade, 33in (84cm), steel scabbard.
£1,500-2,500 *WAL*
A Georgian 1796 pattern Infantry officer's sword, engraved 'Fras. Deakin Birmn', blade 32in (81cm). **£500-1,000** *WAL*

A pair of French silver mounted double barrelled flintlock pistols by Chasteau à Paris, 1749 Paris silver marks, 14½in (37cm).
£9,000-10,000 *CSK*

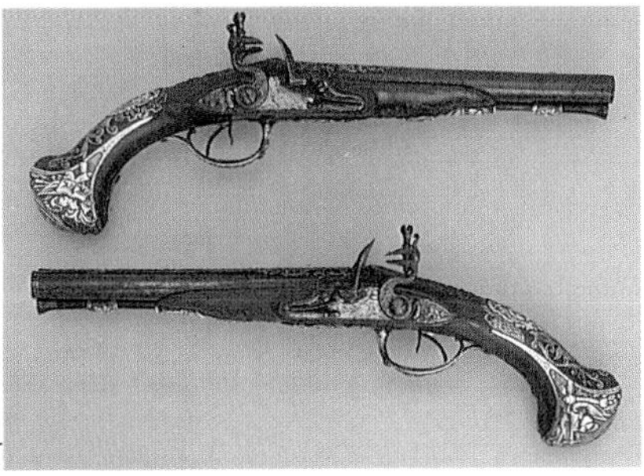

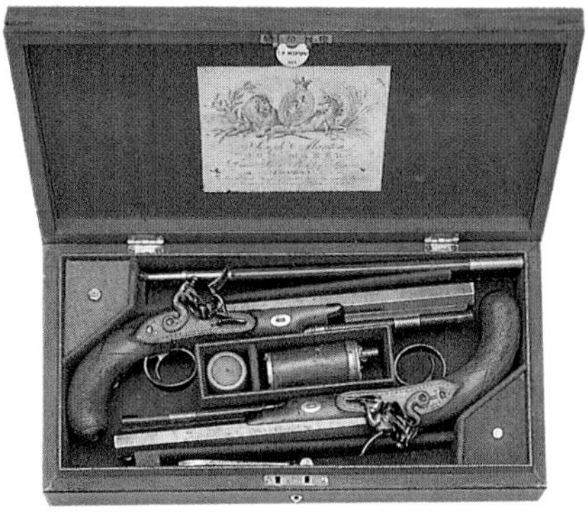

A pair of flintlock duelling pistols, by Joseph Manton, London, No. 4532 for 1805.
£6,000-10,000 *CSK*

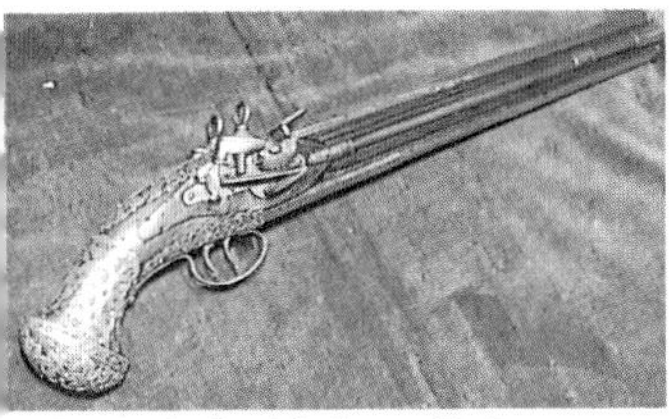

A Spanish double barrelled miquelet pistol, the stock overlaid with brass, c1740.
£800-1,000 *ASB*

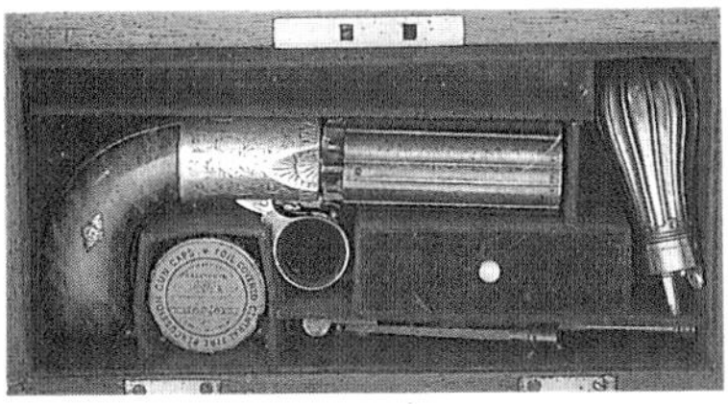

l. A 6-shot 120 bore revolver, by F. Barnes & Co. and engraved.
£800-1,000 *WAL*

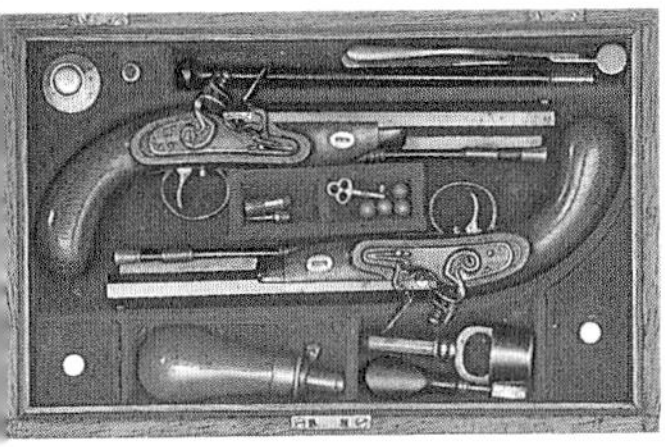

l. A pair of miniature flintlock duelling pistols, in the style of c1810.
£900-1,200 *WAL*
r. A pair of saw-handled flintlock officer's pistols, early 19thC.
£7,000-10,000 *CSK*

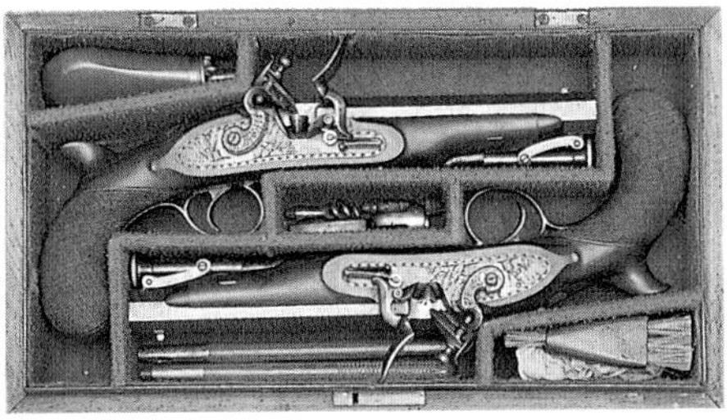

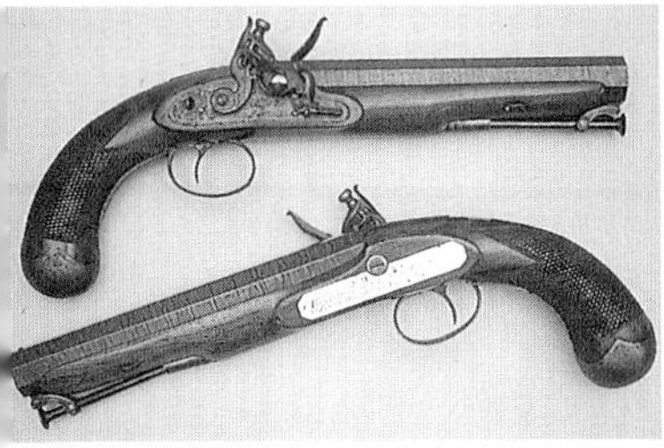

A pair of presentation 10 bore flintlock holster pistols by Westley Richards, 1832.
Est. **£3,000-4,000** *WAL*

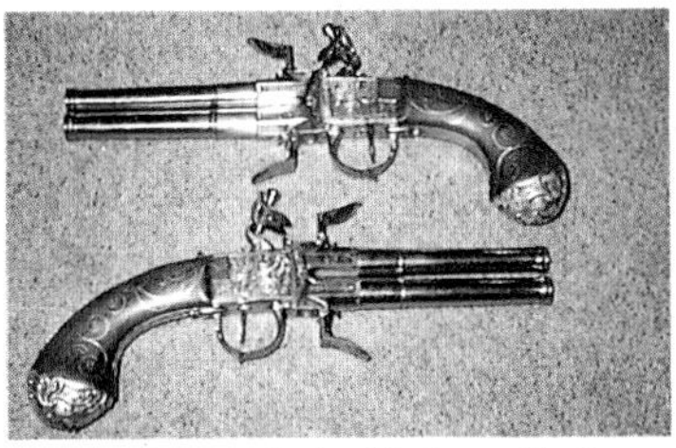

A pair of French double barrelled flintlock pistols, c1740.
£3,000-3,500 *ASB*

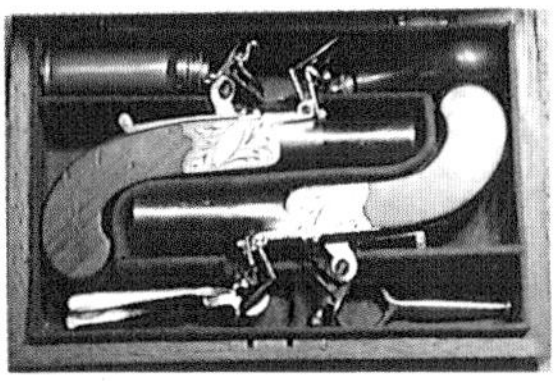

A pair of flintlock boxlock pocket pistols, complete in case, c1780.
£600-700 *ASB*

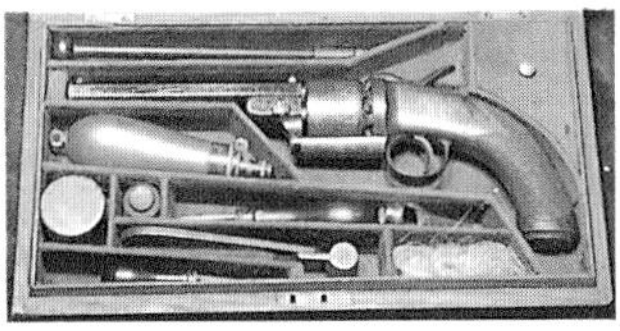

A Webley 'Longspur' percussion revolver with all accessories, c1840.
£800-900 *ASB*

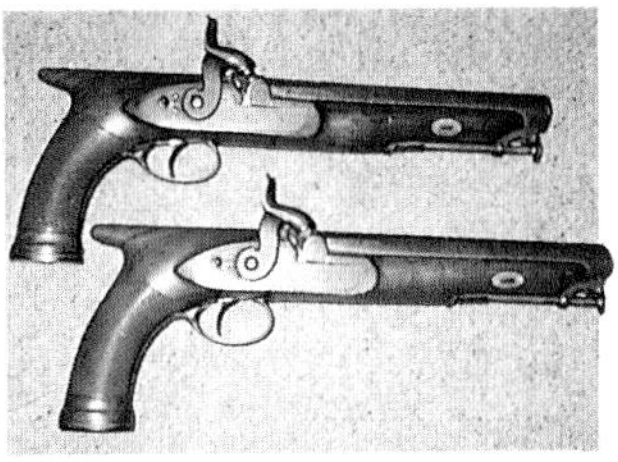

A pair of percussion saw handled pistols, c1840.
£1,800-2,000 *ASB*

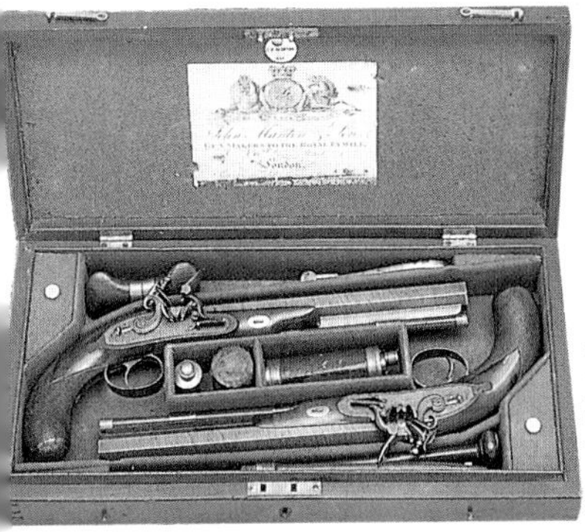

A pair of flintlock duelling pistols by John Manton, 1831, 15in (38cm).
£9,000-12,000 *CSK*

A prototype-experimental Colt open top single action revolver, 'N.M. Navy 1871'.
£10,000-12,000 *CNY*

A Colt pocket percussion revolver, No. 102789, 1849, 9in (22.5cm).
£3,000-4,000 *CSK*

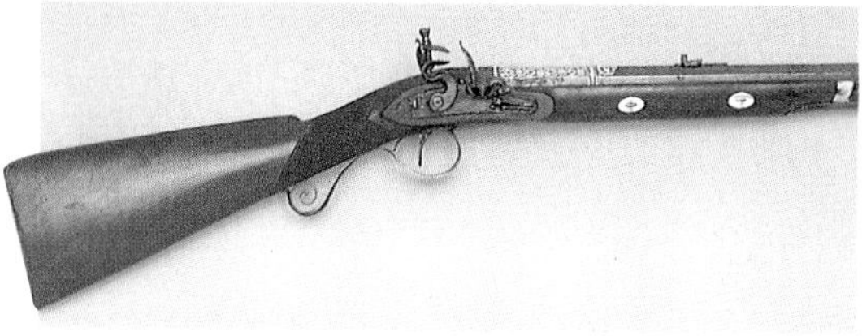

A 16-bore flintlock sporting rifle, with earlier Turkish browned etched twist octagonal barrel, by Bate, London proof marks, c1790, 32in (81cm) barrel. **£3,000-3,500** *CSK*

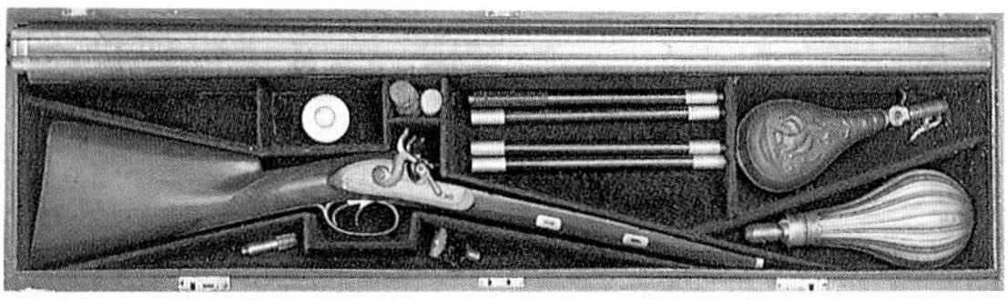

An 8-bore double barrel silver mounted tubelock fowling gun, original silver tipped ebony ramrod and much original finish, silver hallmarks for 1845, 42½in (108cm) barrels. **£5,000-5,500** *CSK*

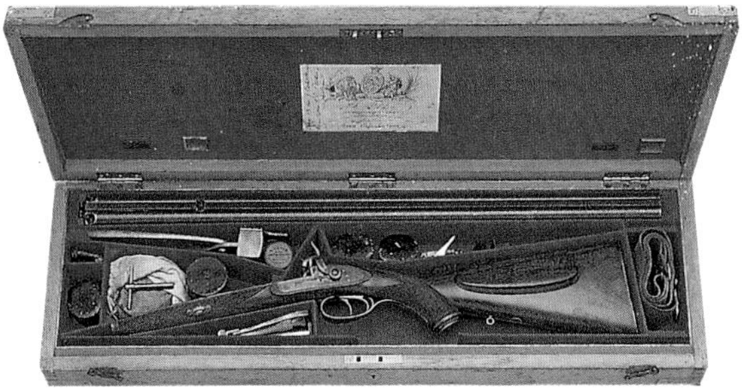

A 40-bore double barrel percussion sporting rifle, in its original oak case with London proof marks No. 6806 for 1864. **£5,000-6,000** *CSK*

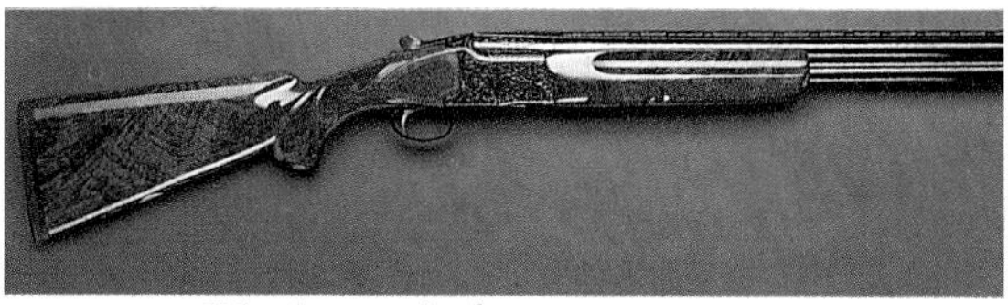

A 12-gauge Winchester single trigger, over/under gun, 28in (71cm) barrels. **£2,000-2,200** *CNY*

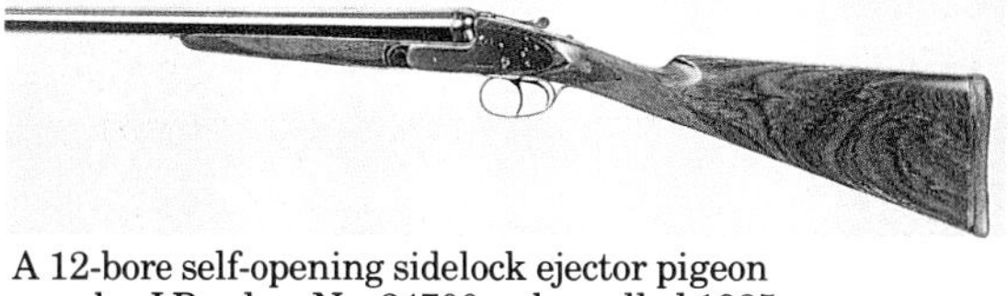

A 12-bore self-opening sidelock ejector pigeon gun, by J Purdey, No. 24700, rebarrelled 1985. **£6,000-8,000** *CSK*

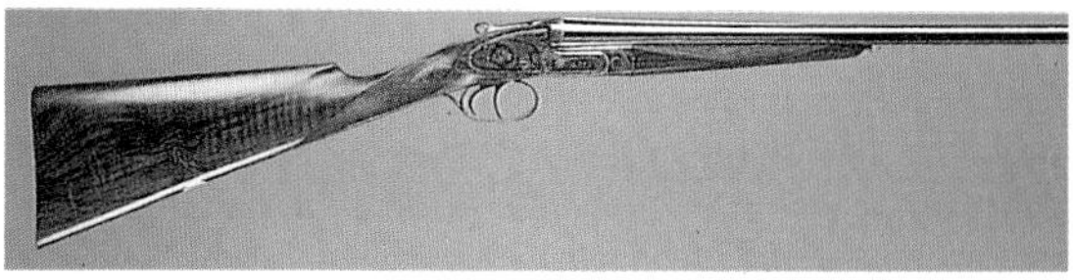

A Casbard engraved 28-gauge double barrel hammerless self-opening sidelock ejector gun, by Peter Chapman, No. 0029/28. **£11,000-12,000** *CNY*

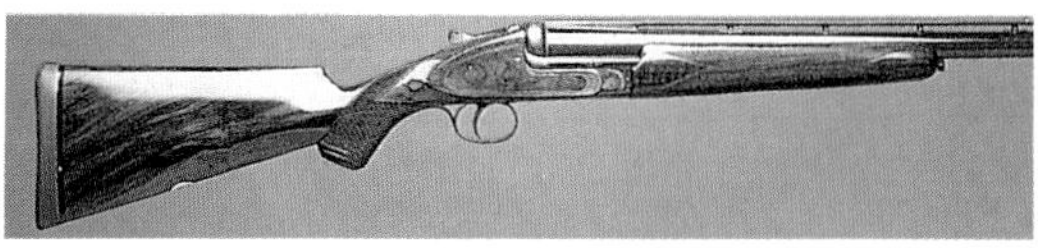

A 12-gauge single barrel hammerless self-opening sidelock ejector trap gun, by J. Purdey, No. 23870, c1930, 32in (81cm) barrel. **£5,000-6,000** *CNY*

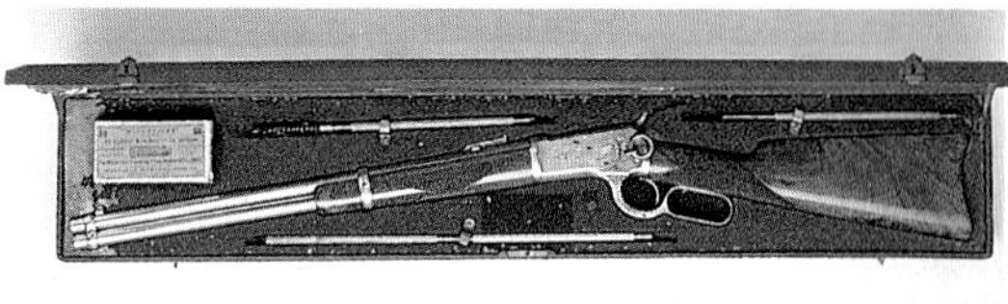

A factory engraved and cased Winchester model 1892 lever action carbine, No. 60909, .44-40 calibre, maker and calibre markings on the barrel, in excellent condition, case interior with some damage, 20in (51cm) barrel. **£20,000-25,000** *CNY*

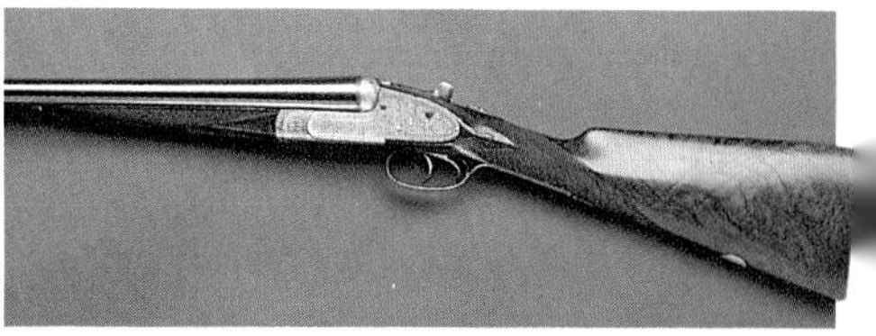

A light 12-gauge 'Royal' double barrel hammerless sidelock ejector gun, by Holland & Holland, No. 16567, the barrels possibly shortened, 28in (71cm) barrels. **£4,500-5,500** *CNY*

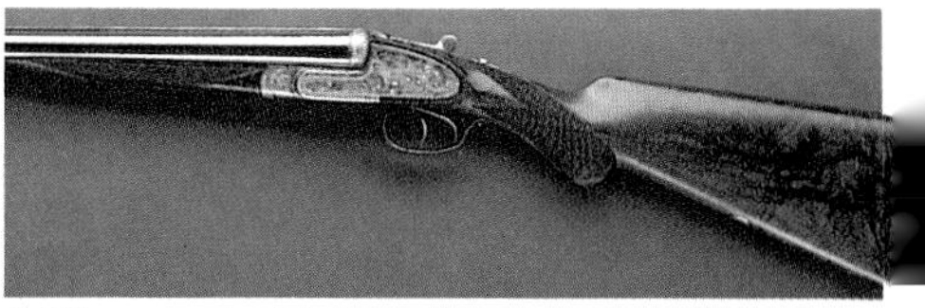

A 12-gauge double barrel hammerless sidelock ejector gun, by W. Evans, No. 15448, 30in (76cm) barrels. **£3,000-4,000** *CNY*

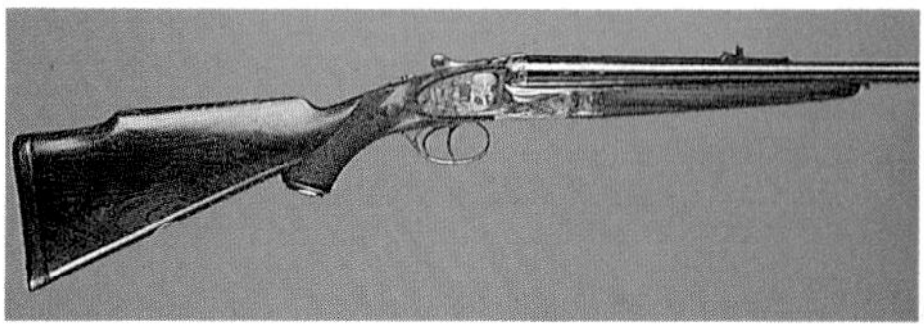

A Preater engraved .458 magnum 'modele de luxe' double barrel hammerless sidelock ejector rifle, by Holland & Holland, No. 35518, in oak and leather case, 24in (61cm) barrels. **£25,000-30,000** *CNY*

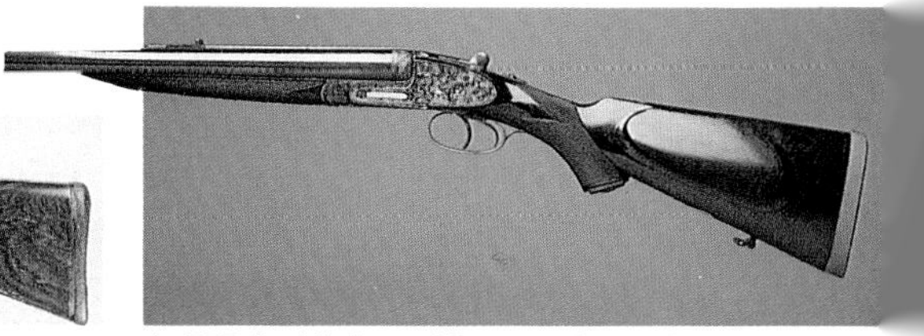

A .577 double barrel hammerless sidelock ejector rifle, by Holland & Holland, No. 19270, converted to ejector, with later goldwork by Philippe Grifnée, the rifle built c1900 and re-chambered and re-embellished in 1983, 26in (66cm) barrels. **£11,000-12,000** *CNY*

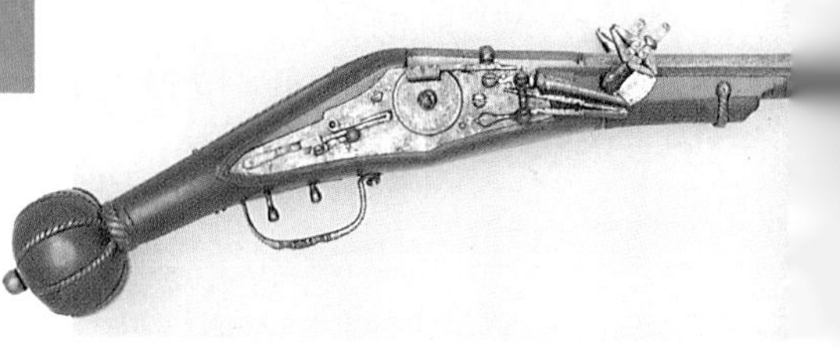

A Saxon double barrel wheel lock holster pistol, piece of stock and ramrods missing, late 16thC, 20in (51cm). **£15,000-16,000** *CSK*

A Lori Pambak rug, areas of wear and tear, 100 by 63in (254 by 160cm).
£4,000-6,000 *C*

A Ladik prayer rug, shows wear and repair, c1800, 72 by 47in (183 by 120cm). **£2,000-2,200** *CNY*

A Lenkoran long rug, late 19thC, 92in (234cm).
£3,500-5,000 *CNY*

An Ottoman embroidered cotton bokshe, late 18thC, 46 by 33in (117 by 84cm).
£1,500-2,500 *CNY*

A Mahal carpet, with an allover pattern of meandering vines and palmettes and a primary border of palmettes and rosettes, some wear, c1900, 126 by 94in (320 by 239cm).
£4,000-5,500 *CNY*

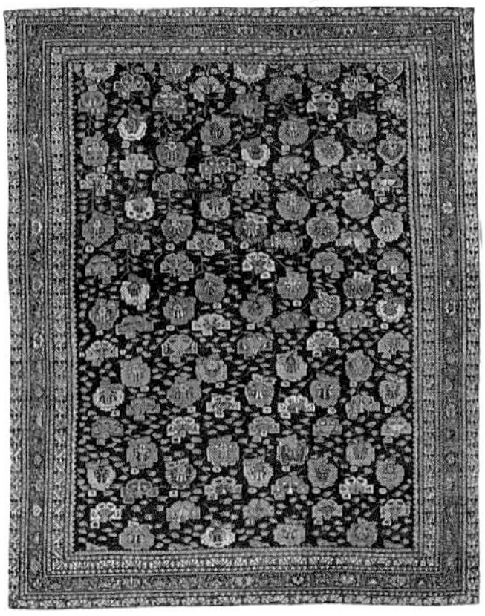

A Malayir carpet, the indigo field with a lattice of floral lozenges, surrounded by flowering vine, ends trimmed and rebound selvedges, 173 by 139in (439 by 354cm).
£5,000-6,000 *C*

A Malayer prayer rug, the deep rust ground covered by a floral Tree of Life flanked by cypress trees leading to the prayer arch, 89 by 67in (226 by 170cm). **£2,500-4,000** *CNY*

n antique Qashqai double bag, the ilim back with panels of multi-loured lappets, minor damage, 5in (114cm) long. **£4,000-5,000** *C*
bove r. A Qashqai rug, very slight ear, 88 by 48in (224 by 122cm).
2,000-2,500 *C*

A Serapi carpet, the rust ground covered by an allover pattern of floral vines with interconnecting spandrels, surrounded by a border, loss to ends and repaired, late 19thC, 134 by 110in (341 by 280cm). **£6,000-7,000** *CNY*

A Marasali Shirvan rug, the midnight blue ground covered by flaming botehs, surrounded by an inner reciprocal trefoil border, 3 brown borders and 2 reciprocal latchhook borders with web ends, 51 by 47in (130 by 119cm).
£1,700-2,000 *CNY*

A Heriz carpet, with pink field, areas of wear, repair and tinting, 148 by 116in (376 by 295cm). **£5,000-6,000** *C*

An Isfahan rug, 91 by 59in (231 by 150cm). **£2,000-3,000** *C*

A silk Kashan pictorial rug, depicting a cartoon by George McManus, entitled 'Bringing up Father', 71 by 61in (180 by 155cm). **£11,000-13,000** *C*

A silk Kashan prayer rug, a few areas of slight wear, 78 by 53in (198 by 135cm). **£8,000-10,000** *C*

A Kashan pictorial rug, with 2 registers of a seated Shah with womenfolk and courtiers, in a border, replaced fringes, 78 by 55in (198 by 140cm). **£3,000-4,000** *C*

A Chelaberd Karabagh rug, some repairs, mid-19thC, 78 by 50in (198 by 127cm). **£5,500-7,500** *CNY*

Above r. A Kuba runner, corrosi browns, c1880, 138 by 36in (351 by 92cm). **£4,000-5,000** *CNY*

A Kazak rug, the brick field with 2 ivory and 2 mid blue medallions, with inner brick hooked motifs, 85 by 47in (216 by 120cm). **£600-700** *WW*

A Kuba rug, with indigo floral field in a red vine border, repairs, 127in (322cm) long. **£3,000-4,000** *C*

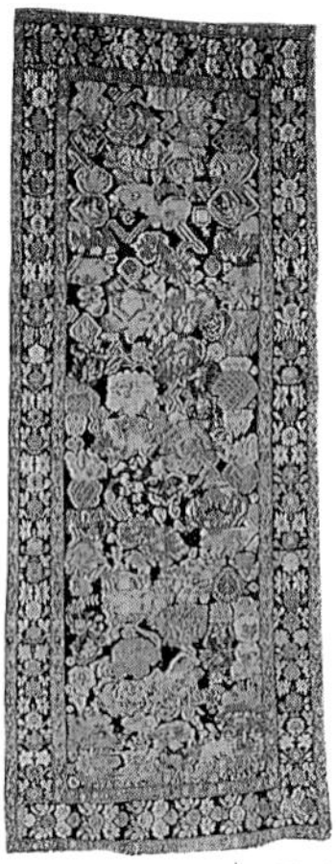

A Karabagh Kelleh rug, with indigo field and border, 180 by 61in (456 by 155cm). **£3,000-3,500** *C*

A Karatchoph Kazak rug, shows some wear, crease wear and slightly reduced end guard borders, late 19thC, 86 by 74in (219 by 188cm). **£2,500-4,000** *CN*

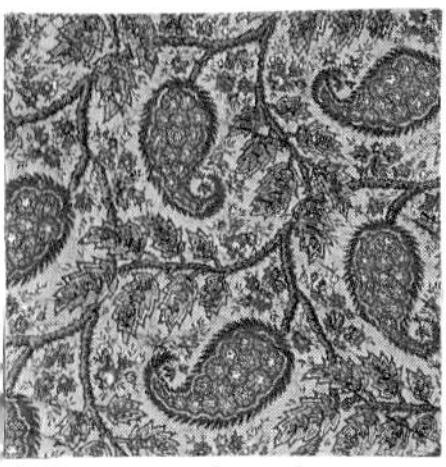

A Provençal quilt,
early 19thC,
new lining.
£350-450 *VH*

A reversible
Provençal quilt.
£320-350 *VH*

A reversible
Provençal quilt.
£250-300 *VH*

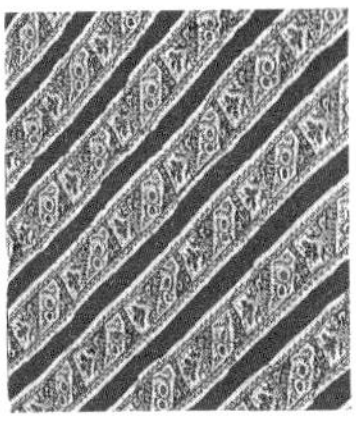

Above l. A Provençal quilt, red
reverse, c1800, 58in (147cm)
square. **£350-450** *VH*
Above r. A Provençal quilt, c1915,
83in (210.5cm) long. **£230-280** *VH*

A pair of Beauvais
tapestry pillows, late
18thC, 18in (45cm) square.
£4,000-5,000 *CNY*

r. A Brussels late baroque
mythological tapestry,
signed Behaegle, late
17thC, 86 by 182in
(219 by 461cm).
£20,000-25,000 *CNY*

A European
ıeedlework
ɔanel,
stained,
103in (261cm)
ong.
£3,500-4,000 *C*

A French embroidered silk panel,
19thC, 77 by 80in (196 by 203cm).
£2,000-2,500 *CNY*

A Brussels baroque mythological
tapestry, lacking borders, early
18thC, 117 by 141in (297 by
356cm).
£14,000-18,000 *CNY*

Brussels tapestry in silks and wools, with
weavers' marks and Brussels town mark, early
18thC, 135 by 168in (342 by 427cm).
£30,000-35,000 *C*

A needlework carpet,
backed, 147 by 87in
(373 by 221cm).
£4,000-4,500 *C*

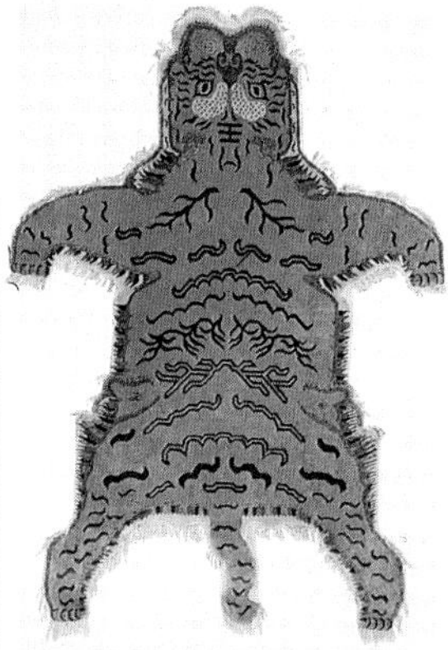

A Tibetan tiger shaped
rug, 96in (243.5cm) long.
£15,000-20,000 *C*

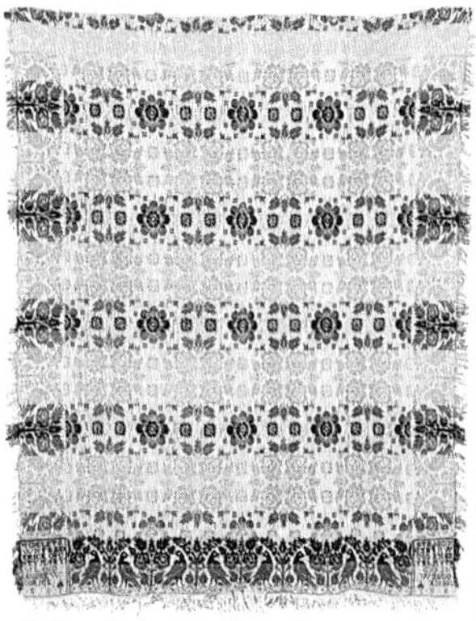

A 4-colour wool and cotton Jacquard coverlet, by Andrew Corick, Maryland, with self fringe, mid-19thC, 68 by 56in (172 by 142cm). **£1,200-2,000** *CNY*

Who can find a virtuous woman
for her price is far above rubies

A needlework sampler, by Alice Mather, Norwich, Connecticut, dated 1774, 14 by 11½in (36 by 30cm). **£30,000-50,000** *CNY*

An appliqued and pieced album quilt, slight staining, Maryland, mid-19thC, 85 by 95in (216 by 241cm). **£4,000-5,000** *CNY*

l. An appliqued cotton and quilted coverlet, slightly stained, American, c1850, 88in (223cm) square. **£3,000-3,500** *CNY*

r. An appliqued and stuffed cotton quilt, Pennsylvania, c1845, 79½in (202cm) square. **£2,500-3,000** *CNY*

A painted fireboard, Maine or New Hampshire, early 19thC. **£11,000-15,000** *CNY*

r. A wool and cotton double woven Jacquard coverlet, attributed to James Alexander, c1830. **£1,200-3,000** *CNY*

A needlework sampler, by Sarah Doubt, Massachusetts, 1765. **£4,000-5,500** *CNY*

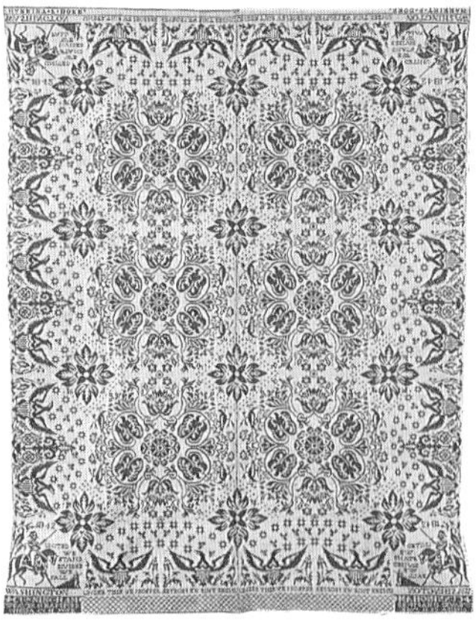

l. A wool and cotton double woven Jacquard coverlet, by James Cunningham, New York, 1842. **£2,000-3,000** *CNY*

r. A wool and cotton double woven Jacquard coverlet, inscribed 'Delhi New York', 1845. **£1,000-2,000** *CNY*

Chinese lac burgaute standing nest of boxes, the interior lacquered red, the exterior lacquered black, inlaid in mother-of-pearl, small faults, late 18thC, 19in (49cm) high.
£3,000-3,500 *P(S)*

A Chinese redwood table cabinet with 2 sliding doors, decorated with applied hard stones, ivory and mother-of-pearl, the corners with silver mounts, hallmarked London 1894, 12½in (32cm) wide.
£1,500-2,000 *AH*

An Oriental carved hardwood jardinière stand, of barrel shape with inset marble top, 19thC.
£400-500 *GD*

Glass

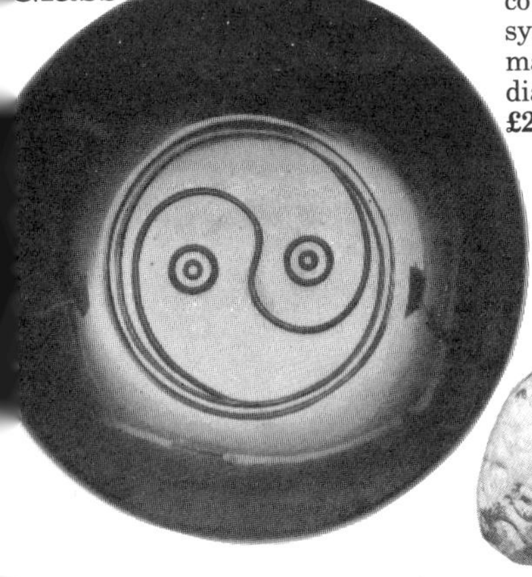

A deep red Peking glass box and cover, incised with the yinyang symbols, Qianlong 4-character mark and of the period, 5in (13cm) diam.
£2,000-2,500 *CSK*

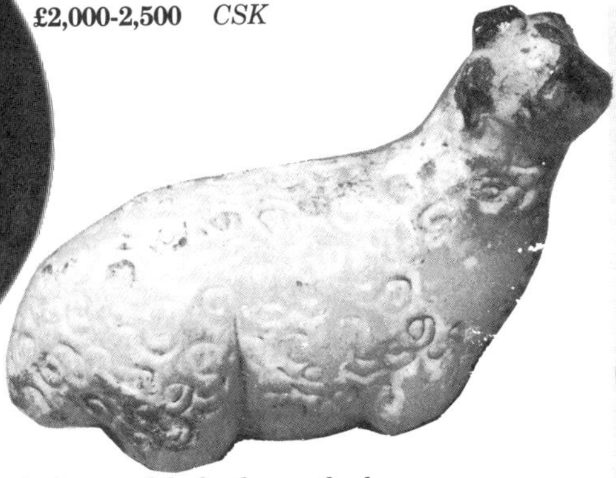

A glass model of a sheep, of pale celadon tone with amethyst coloured head, a whitish slightly degraded patination to most parts incised underneath with small curls imitating wool, chips, probably Han Dynasty, 2½in (7cm) wide.
£2,000-3,000 *C*

A pair of Chinese overlay glass vases, decorated in relief with birds in flight and perched on flowering prunus issuing from pierced rockwork, 9½in (24cm) high.
£250-400 *CSK*

nros

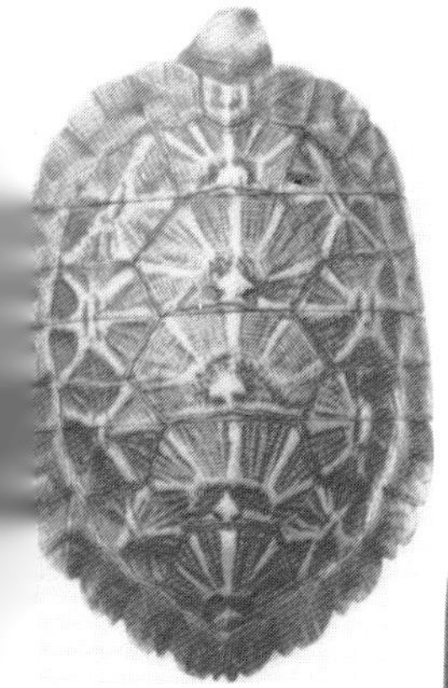

A three-case wood inro modelled as a turtle, the details well delineated, with inset eyes, unsigned, 4in (11cm) long.
£700-800 *CSK*

A four-case jidai inro, worked in gold and coloured takamakie with the legend of the 4 sleepers, the interior of nashiji, 18thC, 4in (11cm) long.
£500-800 *CSK*

A four-case wood inro, decorated with peony flowers issuing from pierced rockwork, the reverse with a butterfly, in gold takamakie, the interior black lacquered, signed Gyokushunsai, 3½in (9cm).
£400-500 *CSK*

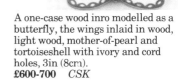

A four-case gold lacquer inro, with a fundame ground decorated within shaped panels with the front and reverse of a hawk tethered to a tasselled perch, in grey, black and gold takamakie, the interior of nashiji, chips, signed Nikkosai, 3½in (9cm).
£1,200-1,500 *CSK*

A one-case wood inro modelled as a butterfly, the wings inlaid in wood, light wood, mother-of-pearl and tortoiseshell with ivory and cord holes, 3in (8cm).
£600-700 *CSK*

Ivory

A Japanese ivory group of musicians, 3½in (9cm) high.
£300-400 *CSK*

A Cantonese ivory box and hinged cover on paw feet, deeply carved with figures on bridges and terraces before buildings, trees and rockwork, 12in (31cm) wide.
£1,500-2,000 *CSK*

A set of 4 ivory counter boxes, by Mariaual le Jeune, tinted for the 4 suits in green, yellow, white and red, the lids with revolving markers, complete with counters and in original fishskin case accompanied by notes of 'Rewards a Preference' in Quadrille, some counters replaced, 18thC, 7½in (18.5cm) wide.
£1,600-2,000 *C*

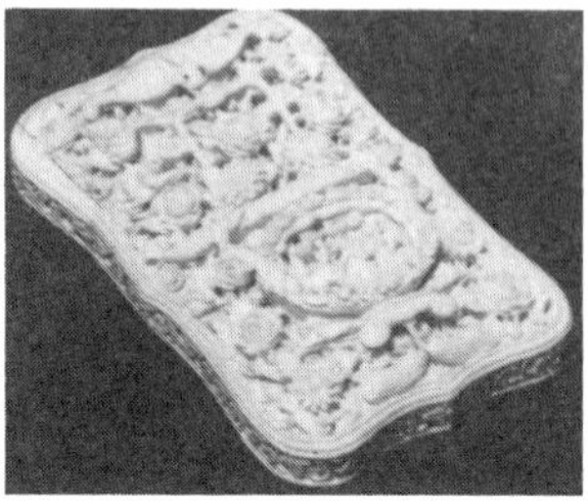

A Cantonese ivory card case, minor damage, 4in (10cm) long.
£300-400 *CSK*

An ivory figure of a Buddha, seated on a lotus throne, cracks, signed, Meiji period, 8½in (22cm), wood stand.
£1,000-1,200 *Bon*

A fine ivory tusk carving, on a pierced hardwood stand, 19thC, 18½in (47cm) long.
£650-750 *Bon*

Jade & Amber

A spinach green jade bowl, flecked with black inclusions and streaked with white areas, rim polished, small chips, Jiaqing, 7in (17.5cm) diam.
£1,500-2,000 *Bon*

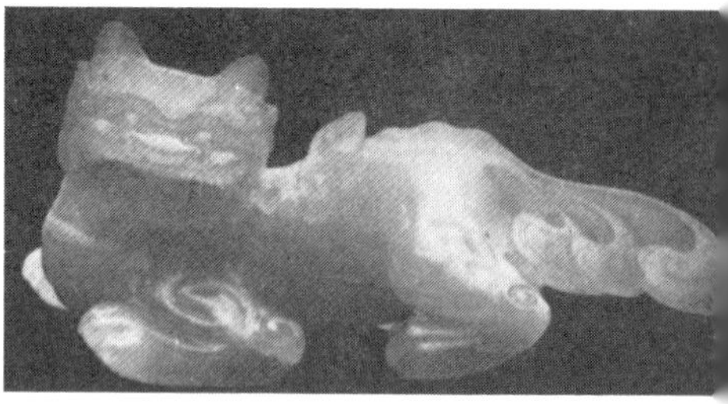

A Chinese jade carving of a crouching Buddhistic lion, grasping a lingzhi fungus in its mouth, its head turned to the left, 18thC, 3in (8cm) long.
£600-700 *CSK*

Amber group of the Virgin and Child, her cloak engraved with foliate decoration, Child's face restored, minor restorations, later base, late 17th/early 18thC, 5in (12.5cm) high.
£800-1,200 *C*

A Chinese dark green and mottled jade vase, modelled as a tree section and carved with pine and lingzhi, 4½in (11.5cm) high.
£350-450 *CSK*

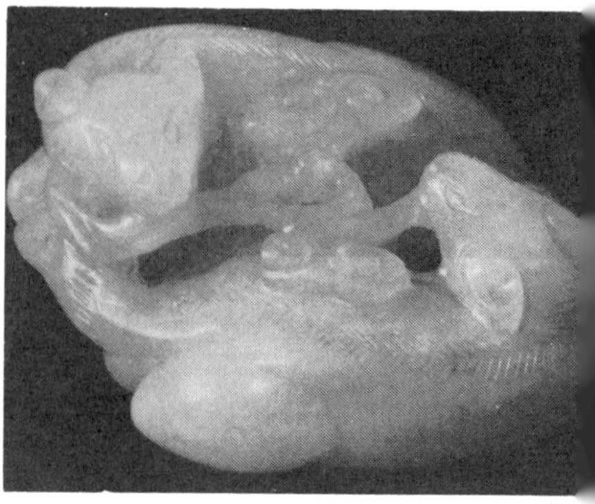

A Chinese pale celadon jade carving of 2 recumbent animals grasping a lingzhi fungus, 18thC, 2in (5cm) wide.
£200-300 *CSK*

Lacquer

A Chinese export lacquer games box and domed cover, on paw feet, decorated and heavily gilt, with approx. 100 monogrammed mother-of-pearl counters, 14½in (37cm) wide.
£2,500-3,000 *CSK*

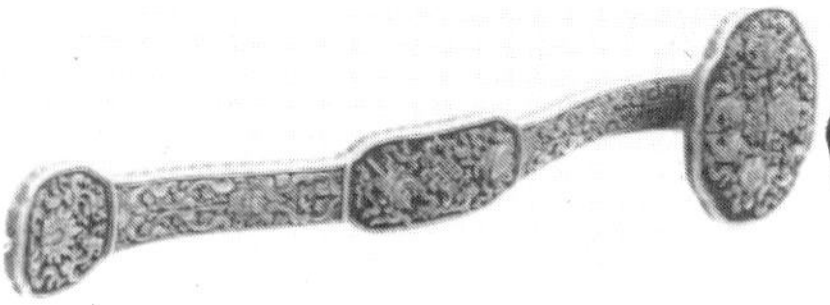

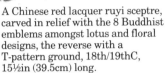

A Chinese red lacquer ruyi sceptre, carved in relief with the 8 Buddhist emblems amongst lotus and floral designs, the reverse with a T-pattern ground, 18th/19thC, 15½in (39.5cm) long.
£450-500 *CSK*

An Oriental lacquered brush box, the gold speckled ground inset with gold leaf, with a pair of metal ring handles with flowerhead backplates, 9½in (24cm) long.
£60-80 *HCH*

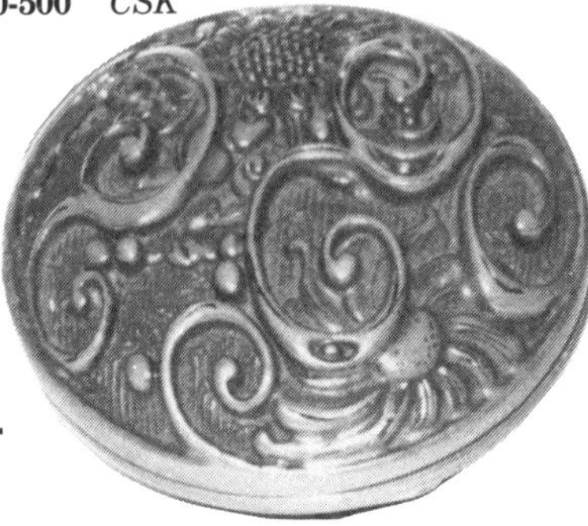

A Japanese red lacquer box and cover with black interior, carved in relief with flowerheads and foaming wave design, 2in (5cm) diam.
£60-90 *CSK*

Metal

A Chinese Han-style bronze head of a horse, 8in (20cm) high.
£700-800 *CSK*

A Chinese bronze ewer with a shallow domed cover, the spout with a dragon head, 16th/17thC, 9in (22.5cm) high.
£600-700 *CSK*

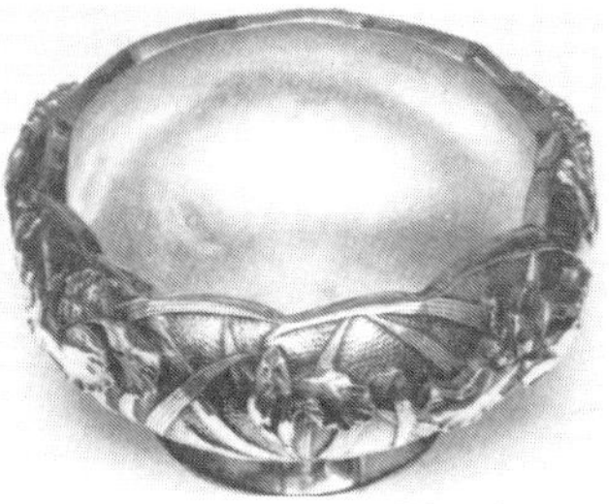

A Japanese white metal bowl, decorated with irises on a stippled ground, the interior plain, 7in (17.5cm) diam.
£600-650 *CSK*

. bronze figure of a sage, holding a earl in one hand, his robes cast vith dragon, cloud and floral esigns, 19thC, 10in (25cm) high.
250-350 *Bon*

A Chinese silver tripod lobed teapot and domed cover, decorated in relief with butterflies among flowerheads, the handle with ivory insets, signed, 7in (17.5cm) long.
£600-700 *CSK*

A Japanese bronze dish inlaid in brass with a writhing dragon, the details in black and red, signed Inove and Ariake, 11in (28cm) diam.
£400-450 *CSK*

Chinese white metal inlaid ronze tripod flattened censer, gned Shisou and with a Xuande character mark, probably 18thC, n (12.5cm) diam.
00-600 *CSK*

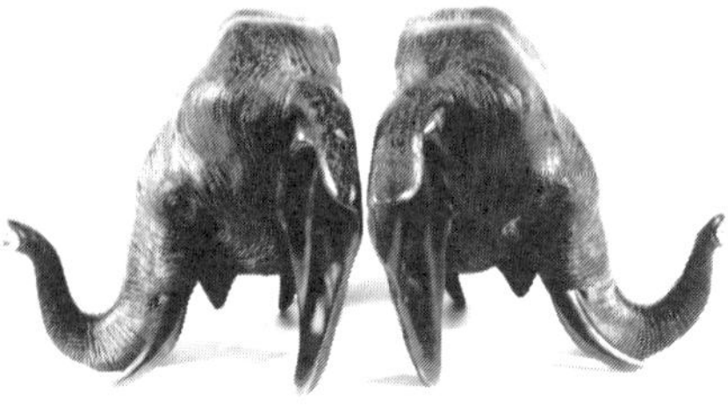

A pair of Japanese bronze elephant-head bookends, with deep red patinated decorated ears, undersides of trunks, and tusks, signed, late 19thC, 6in (15cm) high.
£450-500 *GC*

Netsuke

A Japanese wood tobacco pouch, ojime and netsuke, the eyes inlaid in dark horn, the pouch signed and the netsuke signed, the pouch 4in (10cm) long.
£1,000-1,500 *CSK*

A bone netsuke of a bearded Chinese sage, wearing robes and leaning on a stick, age cracks, late 18thC, 4in (10cm) long.
£120-180 *CSK*

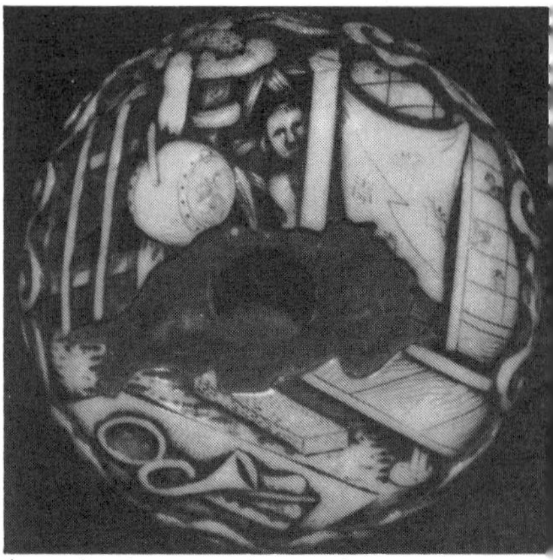

A marine ivory manju netsuke, signed Mitsu, 2in (5cm) diam.
£200-250 *CSK*

A set of 3 ivory netsuke, carved as the Three Mystic Apes, Iwazaru, Kikazaru and Mizaru, 2 signed in oval reserves 'Masatami' (Shomin), late 19thC, 1½in (3.5cm).
£1,500-2,000 *C*

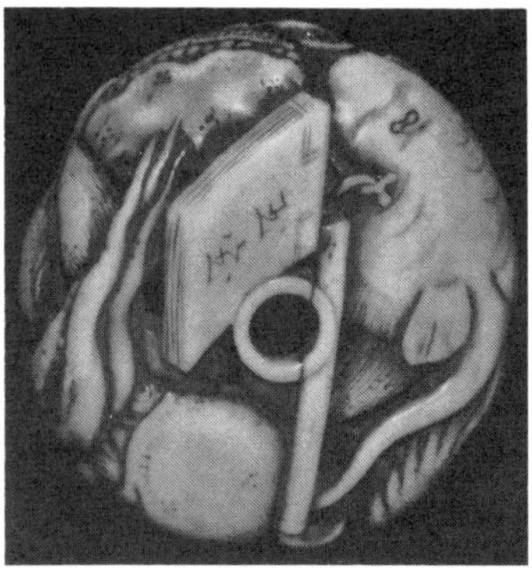

An ivory manju netsuke modelled with a variety of fish, shells and squid around a boat hook, signed Gyokuko, 2in (5cm) wide.
£450-500 *CSK*

An ivory netsuke of a man and boy completing a model of a karashishi and brocade ball with hammer and chisel, signed Gyokoku, 2in (5cm) long.
£270-300 *CSK*

Snuff Bottles

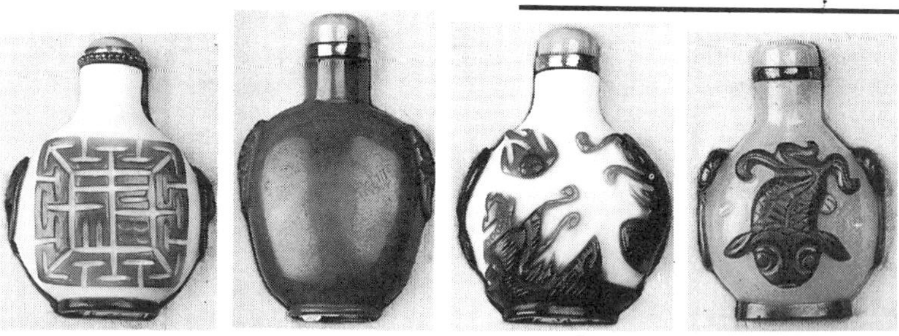

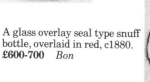

Four glass snuff bottles with jadeite stoppers, some damage, one 18thC.
£450-500 *Bon*

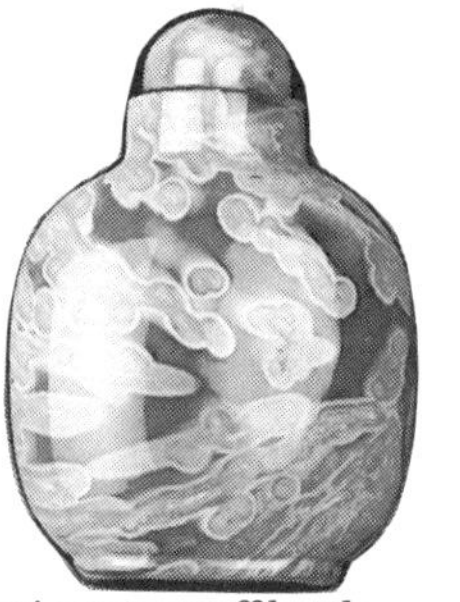

A macaroni agate snuff bottle, supported on a flattened footrim, c1825.
£300-350 *Bon*

An enamelled glass snuff bottle, the turquoise ground painted in coloured enamels, with coral stopper, c1850.
£170-200 *Bon*

An amber snuff bottle, 18thC.
£450-500 *Bon*

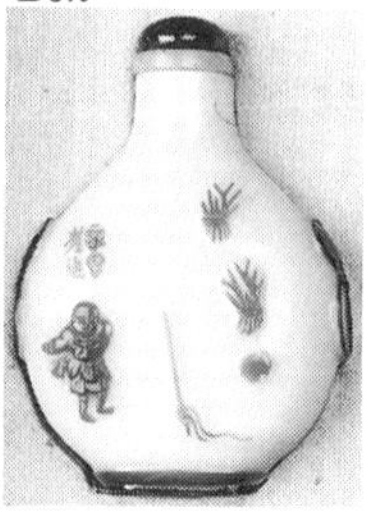

A glass overlay seal type snuff bottle, overlaid in red, c1880.
£600-700 *Bon*

A chalcedony snuff bottle, with an ochre inclusion in the front, carved in deep relief with a camel, monkey and lynx, yellow metal and jadeite stopper, c1830.
£720-750 *Bon*

An agate snuff bottle, the smoky stone with brown inclusions, c1800.
£100-120 *Bon*

An agate snuff bottle, with ochre and brown inclusions in the front, carved in deep relief with a cat below a butterfly, c1830.
£350-500 *Bon*

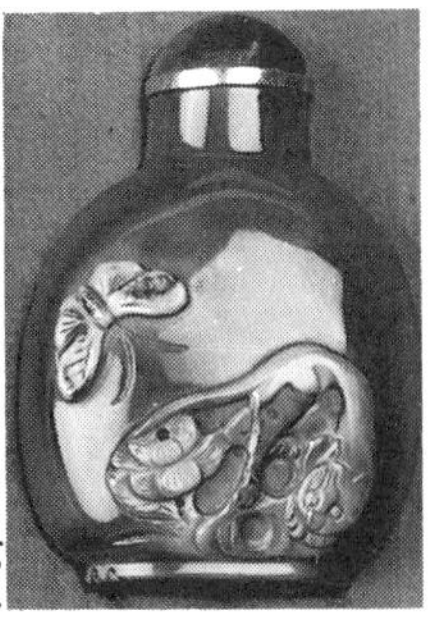

An agate snuff bottle, the reverse with pomegranates picked out using the ochre colours in the stone, c1830.
£70-100 *Bon*

A rock crystal snuff bottle, highlighted by brown inclusions in the stone, the reverse incised with bamboo stems, c1840.
£100-120 *Bon*

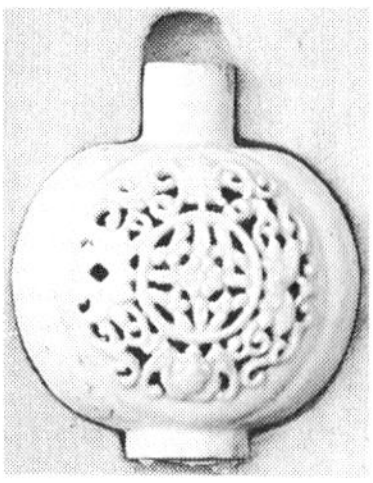

A porcelain snuff bottle, covered in a white glaze, foot and rim chipped, c1840.
£70-100 *Bon*

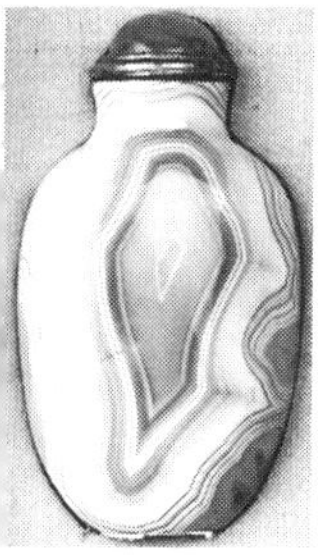

A porcelain snuff bottle, painted in underglaze blue with a 5-clawed dragon chasing the flaming pearl, silver jadeite stopper, 19thC.
£600-700 *Bon*

A rare porcelain snuff bottle, painted in iron red and gilt with dragons on each side, jadeite stopper, Daoguang 2-character mark, and period.
£650-750 *Bon*

An agate snuff bottle, with russet thumb print patterns, c1830.
£250-300 *Bon*

An amethyst snuff bottle, of ovoid form incised with Buddhist emblems, 19thC.
£150-200 *Bon*

A glass overlay and inside painted snuff bottle, overlaid in black with bands at the foot and neck and with mask ring handles at the shoulders, 19thC.
£50-100 *Bon*

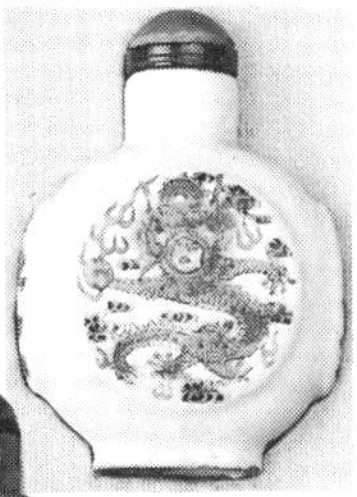

A porcelain snuff bottle, painted in 'famille verte' enamels, Daoguang mark, and period.
£120-160 *Bon*

An agate snuff bottle, supported on a neatly finished footrim, 19thC.
£200-250 *Bon*

An agate snuff bottle carved with dragons, the reverse with an inscription, 19thC.
£120-150 *Bon*

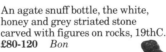

An agate snuff bottle, the white, honey and grey striated stone carved with figures on rocks, 19thC.
£80-120 *Bon*

Wood

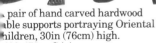

A pair of hand carved hardwood table supports portraying Oriental children, 30in (76cm) high.
£400-450 *SAA*

A lacquered wood and ivory figure of a female immortal, seated in an aubergine coloured spoon shaped vessel, the robes painted with floral pattern, the mounted head and hands of ivory, mid-Qing Dynasty, 7in (17cm) wide, on wood stand.
£1,200-1,500 *C*

A polychromed wood Bodhisattva's head in the Song style, Qing Dynasty, 31in (79cm) high, mounted on metal base.
£2,000-2,500 *C*

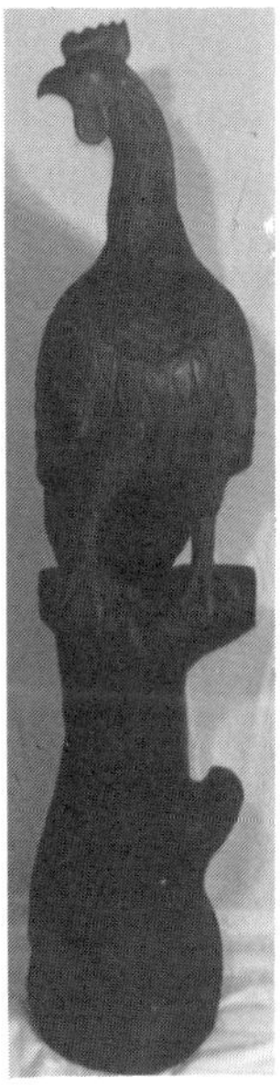

A hand carved hardwood peahen, 48in (122cm) high.
£280-320 *SAA*

LIGHTING

Four Regency mirror-backed double branch wall lights, with Wedgwood green and chinoiserie painted frames, with gilt shell and acanthus cresting.
£1,200-1,700 *P(Ch)*

A pair of Victorian lacquered brass oil lamp brackets, with cranberry reservoirs and cranberry tinted and etched glass shades.
£450-500 *CDC*

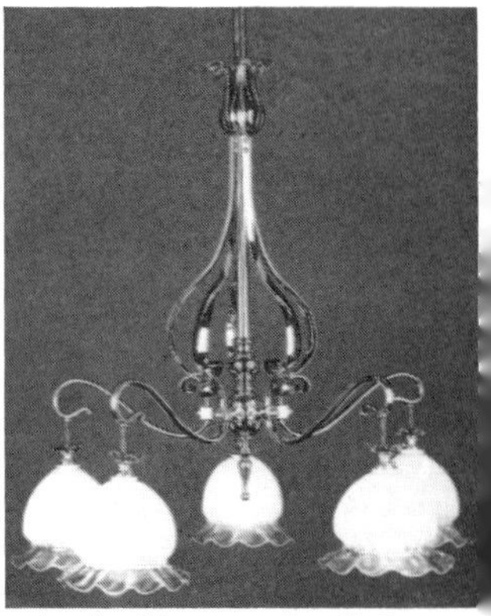

An Art Nouveau five-light electrolier with vaseline glass shades, c1905.
£750-850 *FF*

A Dutch style brass twelve-light chandelier, the scrolling branches fitted with twin tiered nozzles and drip pans, 23½in (60cm) high.
£600-1,000 *CSK*

An Edwardian fringed ceiling electric light, c1906.
£235-285 *FF*

A pair of porcelain vase lamps with ormolu branches, 43in (109cm) high.
£2,500-3,000 *LRG*

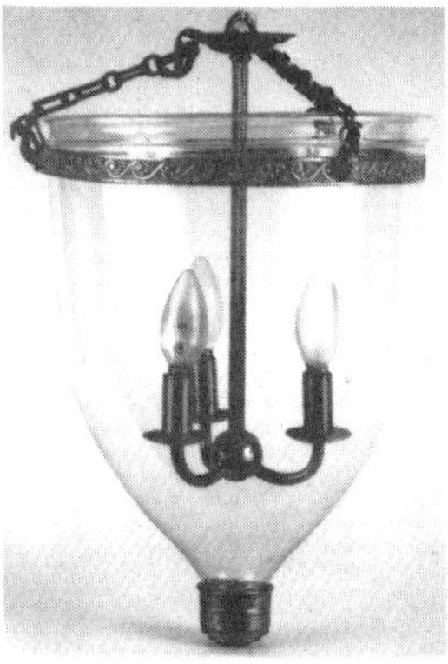

A gilt metal and moulded glass basket shaped hanging lantern, with vitruvian scroll banding and flowerhead boss, with later three-light fitment, 17in (43.5cm) high.
£600-800 *CSK*

A pair of wall lights, of wrought metal and white porcelain flowers with electric candle lights, some flowers missing, late 19thC, 20in (50.5cm) high.
£550-600 *WIL*

A brass ornamental table lamp supported on 4 paw feet, 17in (43.5cm) high.
£170-200 *PCh*

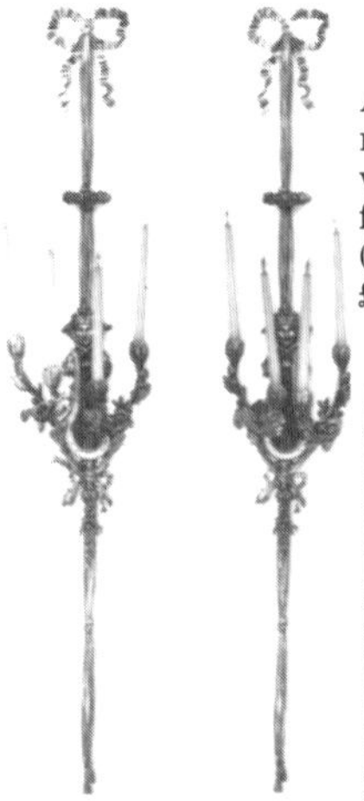

A pair of French ormolu four-light wall appliqués, decorated with female masks, with ribboned extensions surmounted by bows and terminating in tassels, 59½in (151cm) high.
£1,500-2,000 *CSK*

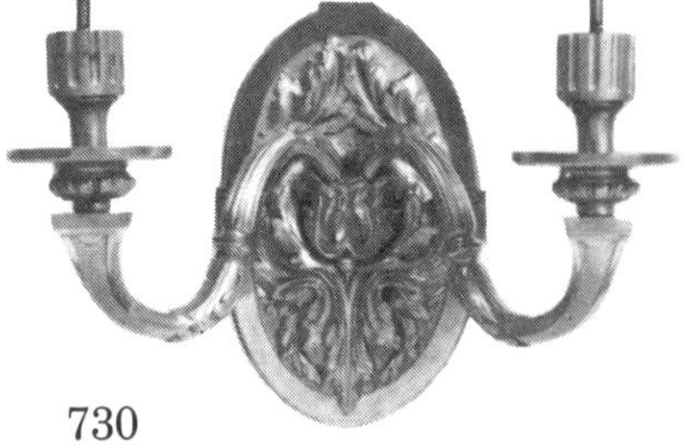

A pair of gilt brass twin-light wall appliqués, the scrolling branches emanating from oval backplates boldly chased with acanthus leaves, 14in (35.5cm) high.
£500-550 *CSK*

A brass three-light pendant, witl white satin bell shades, early 20tl
£135-155 *FF*

PAPIER MÂCHÉ

Miscellaneous

A papier mâché tray, painted with :hinoiserie figures and rococo gilt scrolls in an Oriental landscape, early 19thC, 31in (78.5cm) wide.
£750-800 *LAY*

A papier mâché comport in excellent condition, c1920, 14in (35.5cm) diam.
£80-120 *UC*

A pair of papier mâché lacquer bulbous flared neck vases, 33in (83.5cm) high.
£1,500-2,000 *CSK*

ι papier mâché collar box, c1900, ½in (14cm) high.
70-100 *UC*

A set of 3 graduated papier mâché tea trays, painted in shades of blue, green, red and purple with flowering saxifrage with large gilt leaves and hairy stems, slight damage, 19thC, largest 31½in (80cm) wide.
£1,800-2,200 *HSS*

A Regency papier mâché tray, painted and heightened in gilt with peonies and clematis with stylised leaves, 22 by 30in (55.5 by 76.5cm).
£700-750 *CSK*

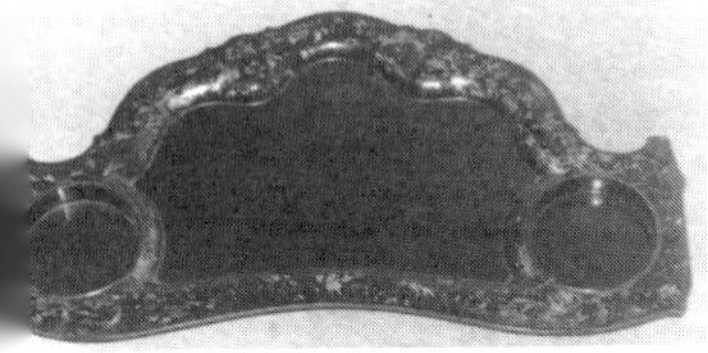

ι papier mâché butler's tray, 19thC.
250-300 *PCA*

A papier mâché blotter, 19thC.
£70-100 *PCA*

EWING

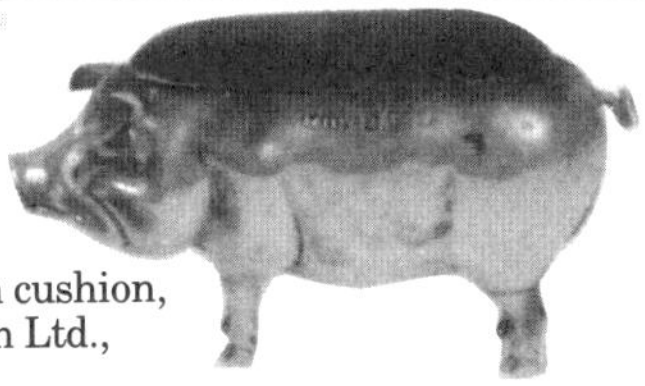

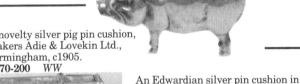

A novelty silver pig pin cushion, makers Adie & Lovekin Ltd., Birmingham, c1905.
£170-200 *WW*

bloodstone and gilt metal etui, the ιount bright cut engraved, the ιinged cover opening to reveal a ιenknife, a cylindrical needle ιolder, folding scissors and folding ιory rule, 2 panels damaged, early)thC, 4in (9.5cm) high.
400-500 *HSS*

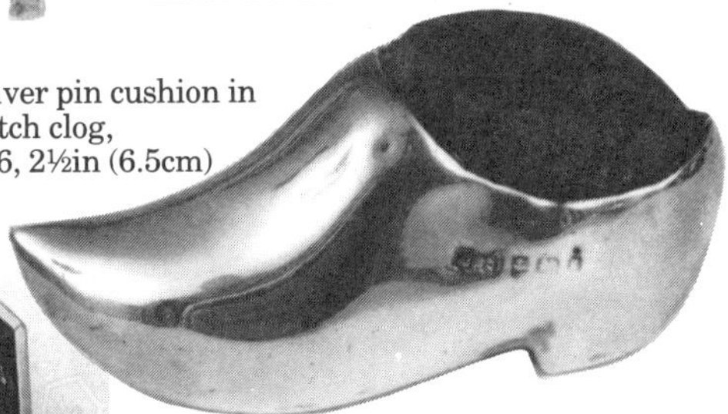

An Edwardian silver pin cushion in the shape of a Dutch clog, Birmingham 1906, 2½in (6.5cm) long.
£100-130 *TVA*

A lacquered work box, with fitted interior and some original ivory fittings and bobbins.
£100-150 *COG*

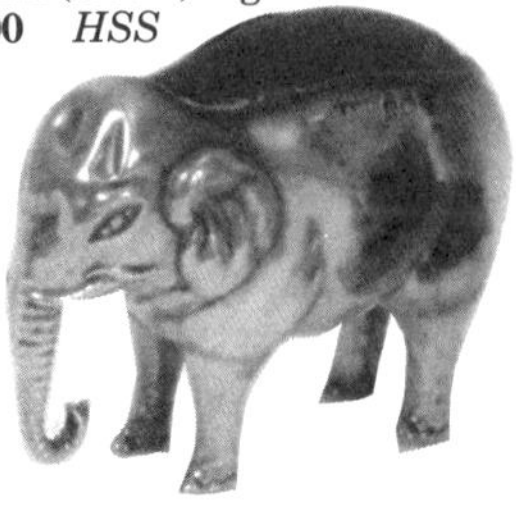

n elephant novelty silver pin ıshion, makers Adie & Lovekin td., Birmingham 1905, 3in (7.5cm).
200-250 *WW*

An Edwardian silver elephant pin cushion, by A. L. Davenport Ltd., Birmingham, c1907, marks rubbed, 3in (7.5cm) long.
£200-250 *TVA*

MINIATURES

A gentleman, in plum coloured coat with pearl buttons, white cravat, powdered hair en queue, gilt metal frame with blue enamel rim and simulated split-pearl border, slight damage, by Richard Cosway, R.A. 1742-1821, 2in (5cm) high.
£1,400-1,600 *C*

A lady, in lace trimmed décolleté red dress with brooch at corsage and gold pendant earrings, chased gold brooch clasp frame, attributed to Simon Jacques Rochard, 1788-1872, 1½in (4cm) high.
£600-700 *C*

Mrs. Robinson, in white dress trimmed with blue ribbon, white bandeau in her powdered hair, in gold frame, the reverse with plaited hair, by Frederick Buck, 1771-1840, 2½in (6.5cm) high.
£350-400 *C*

A lady, in lace bordered white dress with matching bonnet, trimmed with a large blue ribbon, gilt mounted rectangular black papier mâché frame, by John Barry, 1784-1827, 2in (5cm) high.
£1,000-1,200 *C*

A young lady, wearing a décolleté white dress with blue sash, gilt metal mount in square giltwood frame, by Louis Lié Périn-Salbreux, 1753-1817, 2½in (6.5cm) diam.
£2,000-2,500 *C*

A young girl, believed to be H. J. Dunlop, in white dress with frilled collar and matching large hat, within fitted leather case, by Nicholas Francois Dun, 1764-1832, 3in (7.5cm) high.
£800-900 *C*

A lady, in décolleté yellow dress with white underslip, wearing a re cloak on vellum, gold frame with pierced spiral cresting, School of Christian Friedrich Zincke 1683-1767, 2½in (6.5cm) high.
£400-600 *C*

A lady, in gold trimmed white dre and shawl, matching turban headgear, drop pearl earrings, unframed, by Charles Shirreff, c1750, 3in (7.5cm) high.
£350-400 *C*

A gentleman, believed to be Col. William Wasey, 1733-1817, of the Lifeguards, in white lined scarlet coat and grey cravat, powdered ha en queue, in gold frame, by Richa Cosway, R.A., 1742-1821, 1in (2.5cm) high.
£900-1,200 *C*

A lady, in décolleté white dress an a blue and yellow cloak gathered with a brooch on her right should enamel on gold, unframed, by the Huaud Brothers, c1700, 1in (2.5cn high.
£850-900 *C*

A lady, in white dress with pearl brooch at her corsage, green bordered red shawl draped over her shoulders, fitted red leather case, lid missing, attributed to Andrew Robertson 1777-1845, 3in (7.5cm) high.
£450-600 *C*

A lady, in surcoat with frilled border, a dress with ribbon at corsage, lace stole, pearl studded choker and lace bonnet trimmed with ribbon, by James Fergusson 1710-1776, plumbago turned black wood frame, 2½in (6.5cm) high.
£450-600 *C*

A staff officer, in scarlet uniform with blue collar, gold embroidered loops, epaulette and black stock, in gilt metal frame, the reverse with plaited hair, by Thomas Richmond, 1771-1837, 2½in (6.5cm) high.
£700-800 *C*

Three Russian miniatures, of Elizabeth I, Paul I, her son, and Catherine I, his wife, in ormolu frames with Russian eagle emblem, 5in (12.5cm) high.
£3,000-3,500 *BHA*

A gentleman, in black habit with lace bordered lawn collar, embroidered cross sash, black bow on shoulder, oil on copper contemporary tortoiseshell case, Dutch School, c1660, 2in (5cm) high.
£1,200-1,500 *C*

A miniature of a lady's right eye, with blue iris and brown lashes, in gold frame formed as a serpent, brooch clasp reverse, English School, late 18thC, ½in (1.5cm) diam.
£1,000-1,500 *C*

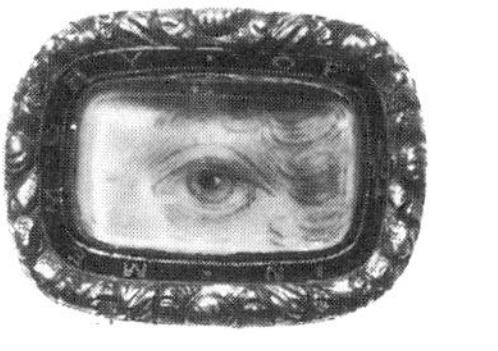

A miniature of a lady's left eye, with blue iris and blonde lock of hair, in chased gold frame with black enamel inscribed 'In Memory Of', the reverse inscribed GCI/WY/1839, English School, 1839, ½in (1.5cm) high.
£450-500 *C*

An Infantry officer, in scarlet uniform, buff facings and frilled white shirt, silver epaulette, in gold frame, by Abraham Daniel, c1780, 2in (5cm) high.
£1,500-2,000 *C*

A gentleman, in maroon coloured coat, white waistcoat and cravat, powdered hair, in gold frame, the reverse with plaited hair within blue glass border, by James Green, 1771-1834, 2in (5cm) high.
£2,500-3,000 *C*

A father and son, the father in blue coat, white waistcoat and cravat, the son in white and yellow gown, in gilt metal frame, ribbon cresting mounted with rubies and seed pearls, by James Nixon, A.R.A., c1741-1812, 2½in (6.5cm) high.
£1,200-1,500 *C*

PINE FURNITURE

Beds

Early pine rocking cradle, c1830, 39in (99cm) long.
£250-300 *AL*

A pine doll's cradle, c1850, 18½in (47cm) long.
£60-70 *AL*

Bookcases

An Irish pine glazed dresser/ bookcase, c1840, 80in (203cm) high.
£630-660 *BH*

A Victorian pine bookcase, c1860, 82in (208cm) high.
£470-520 *BH*

A Victorian original painted pine bookcase, Cumbrian, c1850, 83in (210.5cm) high.
£600-650 *BH*

A pine bookcase with adjustable shelves, original handles, c1860, 76½in (194cm) high.
£700-750 *AL*

A pine bookcase, c1860, 77in (195.5cm) high.
£500-600 *AL*

Chairs

A pine child's chair, 19in (49cm) high.
£30-50 *AL*

A Victorian elm child's chair, fr the village school at Preston, K 24in (62cm) high.
£40-50 *SAD*

A beechwood armchair, with r seat, 36in (92cm) high.
£200-250 *AL*

A pine child's school chair, 24in (62cm) high.
£30-50 *AL*

A pine child's chair, 30½in (78cm) high.
£30-50 *AL*

A set of 4 pine chairs, pegged, 34½in (88cm) high.
£50-80 each *AL*

A beech corner chair, with rush seat, 27in (69cm).
£150-200 *AL*

Chests

A pine chest of drawers with replacement handles, c1850, 46in (116.5cm) wide.
£400-500 *AL*

A painted pine child's folding chair, 22in (56cm) high.
£30-50 *AL*

A pine chair, c1840, 41in (104cm) high.
£120-150 *AL*

An English Regency pine and sycamore chest of drawers, with original feet and brasses, Suffolk, c1810, 37in (94cm) wide.
£900-1200 *UC*

A Scottish pine chest of drawers, original cock beading and handles, c1830, 42½in (108cm) wide.
£500-600 *AL*

An English two part chest-on-chest, with original ebonised handles, Yorkshire, c1860, 40in (101.5cm) wide.
£1,000-2,000 *UC*

A Scottish pine chest of drawers, c1850, 46in (116.5cm) wide.
£450-500 *AL*

An English pine five-drawer narrow chest, the top drawer containing 3 secret drawers, Lincolnshire, c1850, 41½in (105cm) high.
£750-800 *UC*

An Austrian pine domed top joined chest, 34in (86cm).
£300-350 *UC*

A Danish pine four-drawer chest, with replaced brassware, c1870, 36½in (92cm).
£550-650 *UC*

An English metal bound pine deed box, Sussex, c1860, 21in (54cm) wide. **£100-200** *UC*

A Spanish pine coffer, with original ironwork, c1840, 43in (109cm).
£275-350 *UC*

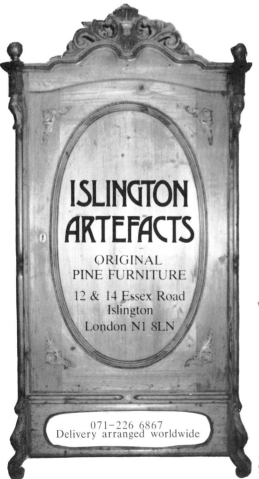

Commodes

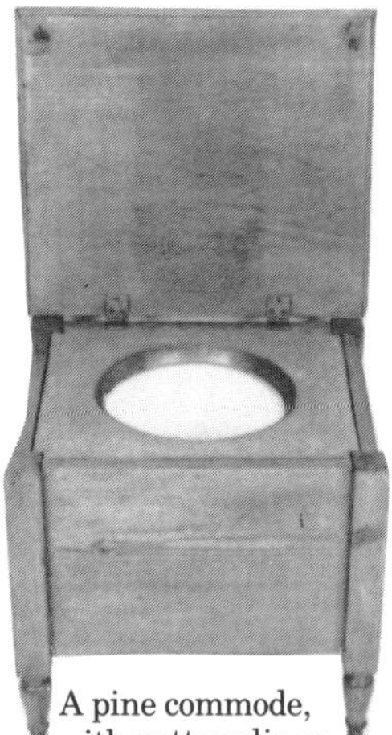

A pine commode, with pottery liner, c1860, 19in (48cm).
£100-150 *AL*

A pine commode with liner, 18½in (47cm) high.
£100-150 *AL*

Cupboards

A pine hanging corner cupboard, c1840, 36in (92cm) high. **£170-200** *AL*

A pine corner cupboard, wit hand made 'butterfly' hinge c1800, 21in (54cm) high.
£100-150 *AL*

A pine cupboard with shelves and drawer in base, c1800, 74in (188cm) high.
£550-650 *AL*

A George III Cumbrian corner cupboard, 76in (193cm) high.
£720-775 *BH*

A Scottish pine corner cupboard, 16in (41cm) wide.
£70-100 *BH*

A pine glazed corner cupboard, c1860, on a new base, 84in (213cm) high.
£700-750 *AL*

A Scottish pine linen press, late 18thC, 77½in (196cm) high.
£720-800 *BH*

A Scottish pine linen press, with 2 interior drawers and a secret drawer, c1780, 72in (182.5cm) high.
£750-800 *BH*

A bowfronted pine corner cupboard, with original handles, 12½in (32cm) high.
£120-150 *AL*

A Danish panelled pine two-part double armoire, on 2 drawer base, c1870, 73½in (186cm) high.
£950-1,200 *UC*

A pine linen press, with new feet, c1860, 78½in (199cm) high. **£650-750** *AL*

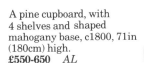

A pine cupboard, with 4 shelves and shaped mahogany base, c1800, 71in (180cm) high.
£550-650 *AL*

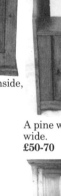

A pine cupboard with shelves inside, 40in (101.5cm) high.
£250-300 *AL*

A pine wall cupboard, 15in (38cm) wide.
£50-70 *AL*

A pine panelled cupboard with a new top c1840, 60in (152cm). **£570-820** *AL*

A pine chiffonier, c1860, 42in (106.5cm) wide.
£600-650 *AL*

An Austrian pine storage cupboard, Linz, c1860, 36½in (92cm) wide.
£700-800 *UC*

An Irish pine food press, c1840, 72in (182.5cm) high.
£670-730 *BH*

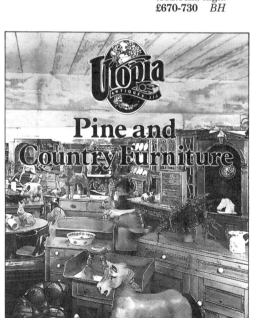

A French pine two-door raised panel pantry cupboard, Burgundy, c1840, 43in (109cm).
£1,000-1,200 *UC*

A pine desk with cupboards under, 44½in (113cm) wide.
£750-820 *AL*

A painted pine bedroom suite, pot cupboard, 32in (82cm) high.
£2,000-2,500 complete *AL*

A glazed pine cupboard with adjustable shelves c1860, 39½in (99cm) high.
£175-225 *AL*

Desks

A pine desk.
£30-50 *AL*

A pine clerk's desk, with cupboards at the back and 2 shelves, a china ink well with brass cover, c1850, 47in (119cm) high.
£250-350 *AL*

A pine clerk's desk with slide, pegged construction, c1860, 43½in (110cm) high.
£100-200 *AL*

Dressers

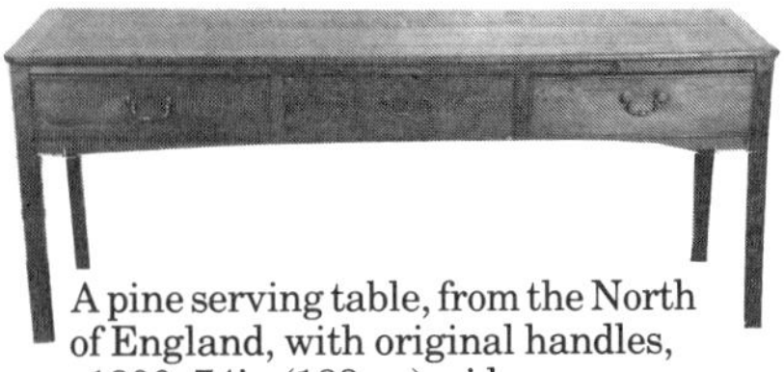

A pine serving table, from the North of England, with original handles, c1800, 74in (188cm) wide.
£400-450 *BH*

An English pine low dresser base, Lincolnshire, c1870, 52in (132cm) wide.
£800-900 *UC*

A West Country pine dresser, c1790, 88½in (225cm) wide.
£1,200-1,700 *BH*

An Austrian pine dresser base, Linz, c1860, 39½in (100cm).
£650-720 *UC*

A pine dresser base, c1840, 44in (111.5cm) wide. **£150-250** *AL*

A Cumbrian pine cabinet-on-stand, 19thC, 50in (127cm) wide.
£500-600 *BH*

A Scottish pine dresser, with spice drawers, c1850, 70in (177.5cm) high. **£550-600** *BH*

A Victorian pine breakfront dresser.
£1,500-2,000
WEL

Dressing Tables

A pine dressing table, with original paint, 36in (92cm) wide.
£250-320 *AL*

A pine dressing table, with new handles, 36in (92cm) wide.
£250-300 *AL*

A pine dressing table, with new handles, 36in (92cm) wide.
£300-350 *AL*

A pine dressing table with elm top, 34in (87cm) wide.
£220-250 *AL*

Mirrors

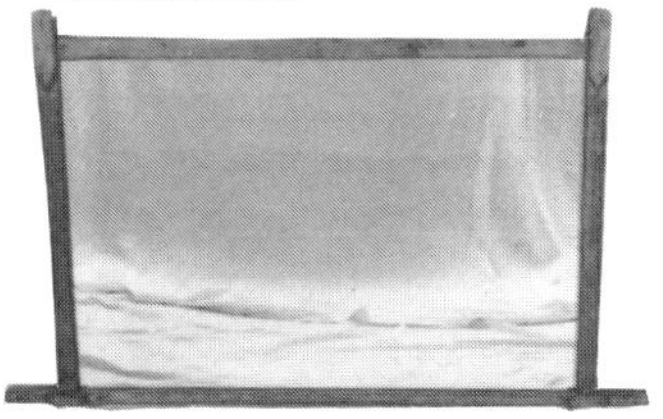

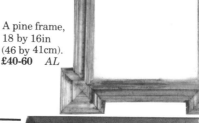

A pine overmantel with mirror and white china feet, c1860, 28in (71cm) high.
£80-100 *AL*

A pine mirror, 44 by 30in (111.5 by 77cm).
£120-150 *AL*

A pine frame, 18 by 16in (46 by 41cm).
£40-60 *AL*

Settles

A Georgian barrel-back settle, with cupboard, c1830, 81in (205.5cm) wide.
£650-750 *BH*

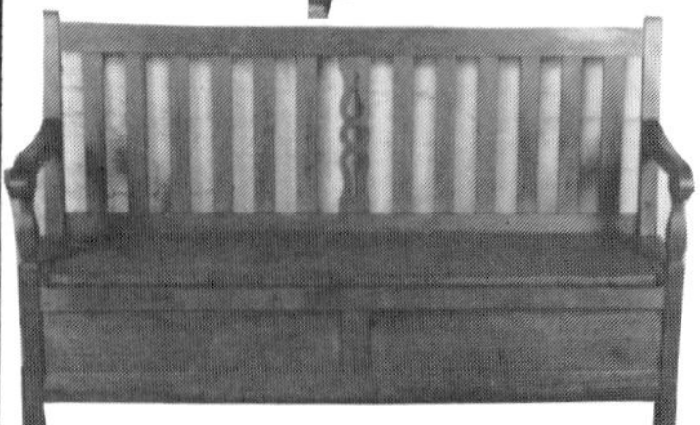

A Welsh pine box settle, c1840, 66in (167.5cm) wide.
£450-550 *BH*

A pine settle, c1850, 39in (99cm) wide.
£550-650 *AL*

Stools

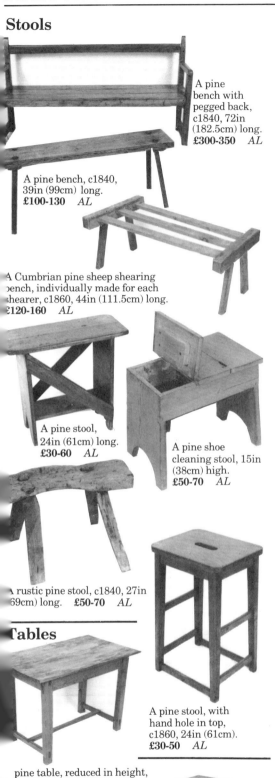

A pine bench with pegged back, c1840, 72in (182.5cm) long.
£300-350 *AL*

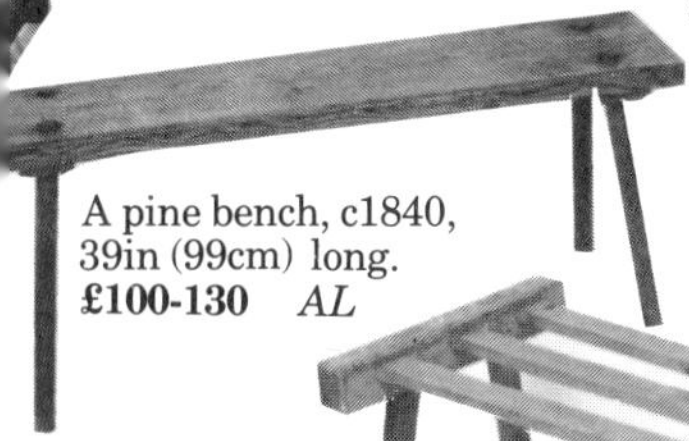

A pine bench, c1840, 39in (99cm) long.
£100-130 *AL*

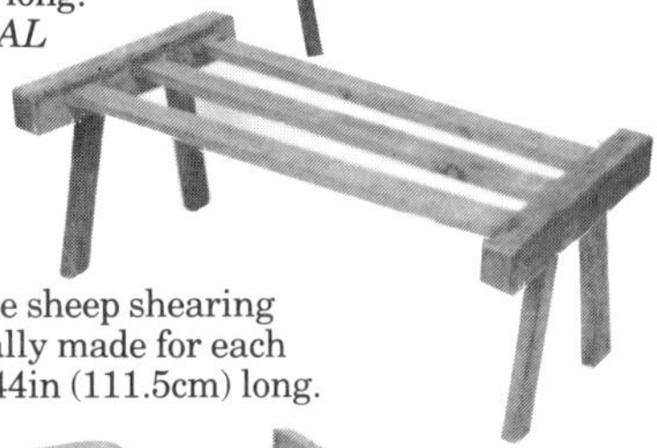

A Cumbrian pine sheep shearing ›ench, individually made for each ›hearer, c1860, 44in (111.5cm) long.
:120-160 *AL*

A pine stool, 24in (61cm) long.
£30-60 *AL*

A pine shoe cleaning stool, 15in (38cm) high.
£50-70 *AL*

› rustic pine stool, c1840, 27in 59cm) long. **£50-70** *AL*

A pine stool, with hand hole in top, c1860, 24in (61cm).
£30-50 *AL*

'ables

pine table, reduced in height, 800, 36in (91.5cm) long.
.00-130 *AL*

An English writing table, with carved supports, c1860, 50in (127cm) wide.
£450-500 *BH*

A pine gateleg table, c1850, 29in (74cm) high.
£270-320 *AL*

A pine table with drawer, c1840, 48in (122cm) wide.
£150-200 *AL*

A pine writing table, c1860, 42½in (107cm) wide.
£120-150 *AL*

An Irish pine bobbin leg 3-tier cake table, c1860, 27in (69cm) high.
£200-250 *BH*

A pine writing table, c1860, 36in (91.5cm) wide.
£170-220 *AL*

A pine drop-leaf table, c1860, 50in (127cm) wide extended.
£170-220 *AL*

A pine draw leaf table, c1870, 70in (177.5cm) wide extended.
£275-350 *AL*

A pine work table, c1860, 60in (152cm) long.
£250-300 *AL*

A pine table, with single drop leaf, c1860, 35in (89cm) wide.
£120-150 *AL*

Wardrobes

A pine wardrobe, with drawers under, 76in (193cm) high.
£550-575 *AL*

A pine wardrobe, c1860, 81in (205.5cm) high.
£570-600 *AL*

A pine wardrobe, 77in (195.5cm) high.
£270-350 *AL*

Washstands

A pine washstand, panelled all round, with towel rail, c1840, 33in (84cm) high.
£200-250 *AL*

A pine washstand in original condition, c1860, 22in (56cm) wide.
£100-150 *AL*

A pine double washstand, 40½in (102cm) wide.
£170-250 *AL*

A pine washstand, with original paintwork, 32in (82cm) wide.
£150-250 *AL*

Miscellaneous

Pine shelves, c1860, 34in (87cm) wide.
£70-90 *AL*

Pine hanging shelves, c1860, 22in (56cm) wide.
£40-60 *AL*

Pine shelves, 36in (91.5cm) wide.
£100-130 *AL*

A pine towel rail, 34in (87cm) high. **£40-80** *AL*

A pine salt box, carved 'Home Sweet Home' on box, W. J. Bothwell, 18in (46cm) high.
£80-100 *AL*

A pine plant stand, c1850, 30in (76cm) high.
£40-70 *AL*

n English ine offertory box, c1900, 9½in (75cm) wide. **£60-80** *UC*

A pine brick hod, 48in (122cm) high.
£40-60 *AL*

pine box, 860, 35in 9cm) wide.
140-170 *AL*

KITCHENALIA

A Scandinavian beechwood and lathe band flour barrel, with locking cover, c1900, 13½in (34cm) high.
£100-150 *UC*

An Austrian poplarwood dough trough, c1860, 31½in (80cm) long.
£70-100 *UC*

A Dutch original painted metal milk churn, 25½in (65cm) high.
£100-200 *UC*

An Austrian wicker linen basket and lid, Linz, c1920.
£120-160 *UC*

A lignum vitae treen pestle and mortar, 18thC, 9in (23cm).
£500-600 *WW*

A French wicker grape harvester's basket, Burgundy, c1920.
£120-150 *UC*

A pair of scales, minus weights, 26in (66cm) wide.
£40-60 *AL*

A pair of brass letter scales, by Stevens & Son, London, 14in (45.5cm) wide.
£30-50 *AL*

A set of scales and weights for butter or cheese, porcelain and brass pans, with mirror both sides, 28in (71cm) high.
£200-270 *AL*

A pair of brass and iron parce scales, 18in (45.5cm) wide.
£50-70 *AL*

A treen nutcracker, shaped as a squirrel, c1840, 7in (18cm) long.
£130-200 *LEW*

An English beechwood bath rack, c1910, 30 by 10in (77 by 26cm).
£20-60 *UC*

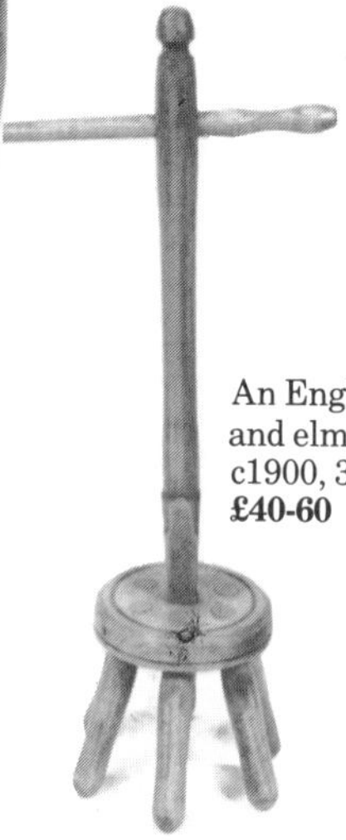

An English ash and elm dolly stick, c1900, 35in (89cm) high.
£40-60 *UC*

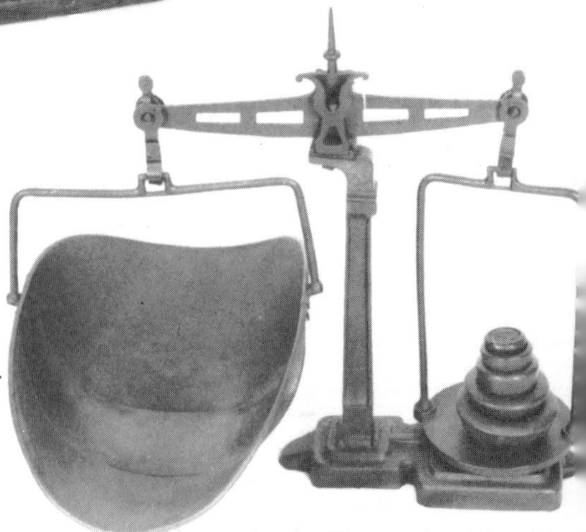

A pair of iron scales with weight 20in (51cm) high.
£80-100 *AL*

Walking Sticks & Canes

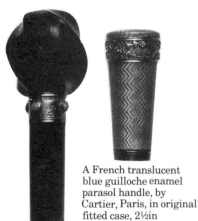

A French translucent blue guilloche enamel parasol handle, by Cartier, Paris, in original fitted case, 2½in (6cm) long.
£2,000-2,500 *C*

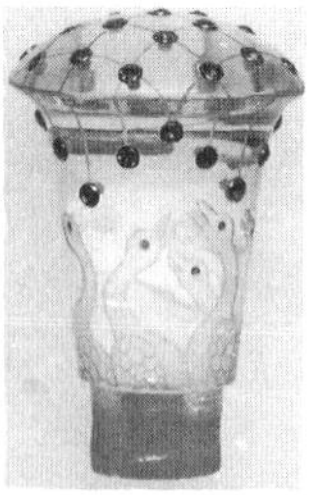

A jewelled rock crystal parasol handle, set with trellis of rubies in gold collets, in fitted case stamped with the retailer's name J.C. Vickery, Regent St., late 19thC, 2in (5cm) high.
£800-1,200 *C*

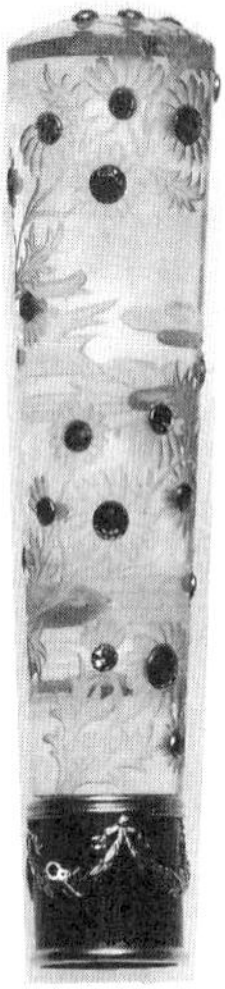

A gold mounted silver and rock crystal parasol handle, set with sapphires in gold collets, the silver collar enamelled in translucent blue and set with gold swags within reeded borders, by Tiffany and Co., in fitted case, late 19thC, 4½in (11cm).
£1,700-2,000 *C*

An Edward VII jewelled gold mounted tortoiseshell parasol handle, with a collar of matted gold set with diamonds and demantoid garnets, with spherical pommel, by Charles Cooke, 1906, in original fitted case stamped Brigg & Son, of London and Paris, 11in (28cm) long.
£800-1,200 *C*

An Edward VII jewelled gold mounted tortoiseshell parasol handle, with collar of matt gold set with turquoise, with writhen spherical pommel, by Charles Cooke, 1906, also stamped with retailer's name Brigg, in original fitted case, 6½in (16cm) long.
£700-800 *C*

Smoking & Snufftaking

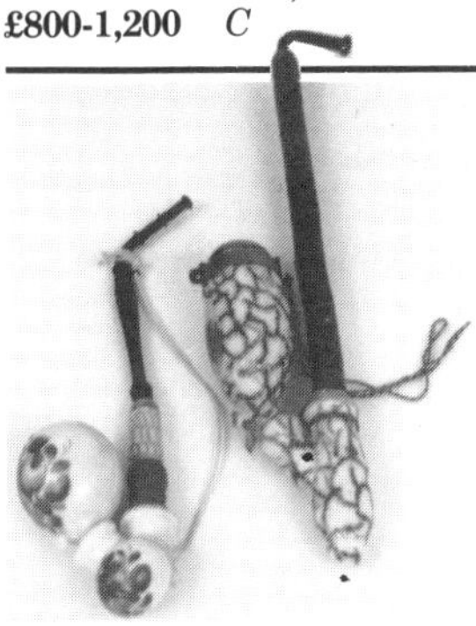

A small pipe, with two-piece porcelain bowl, the stem constructed of sections of ivory and ebony, a two-piece porcelain pipe depicting a dog, textured glaze, blue and gold pattern, natural fruitwood stem.
£120-160 *P(Ba)*

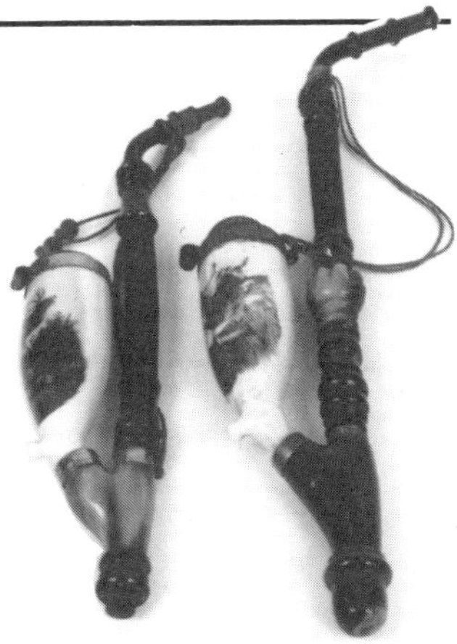

Two German two-piece porcelain pipes with rural scenes turned horn to stems, another similar of a stag.
£80-120 *P(Ba)*

A collection of 3 pipes and 6 porcelain bowls.
£280-320 *P(Ba)*

A comic clay pipe entitled 'The Whole Dam Family', 2 entitled 'The Arrest' and 'Victory', 3 RAOB's, a fish, an eagle claw, and a small black clay, contained in a pine box.
£120-150 *P(Ba)*

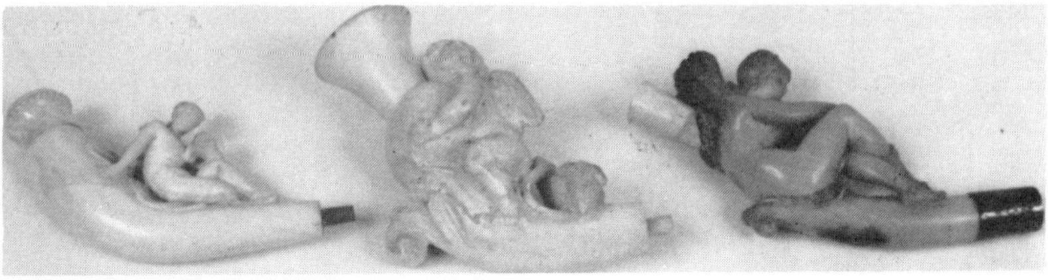

n Austrian meerschaum heroot of a cherub lutching the holder, with ase and no mouthpiece, ½in (9cm), another arved as a reclining lady, nother pipe bowl.
100-120 *P(Ba)*

JEWELLERY

Four garnet brooches.
£150-300 each *SBA*

Top. An 18ct ruby and diamond wing brooch.
£900-1,000

Bottom. An 18ct garnet and diamond brooch.
£800-900 *SBA*

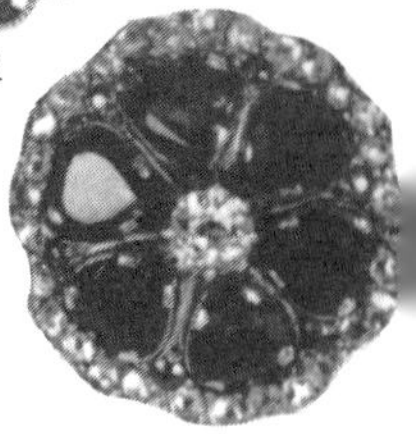

An 18ct gold pendant, inset with garnets and emeralds, 1½in (4cm) long.
£500-600 *SBA*

Four pearl surrounded brooches:
Top l. A small 18ct gold pearl pendant, for photograph.
£150-200

Top r. An 18ct gold pearl rectangular shaped brooch, for photograph or hair, c1820.
£500-600

Bottom l. An 18ct gold pearl locket, with picture of Victorian girl.
£300-400

Bottom r. An 18ct gold graduated pearl locket.
£300-400 *SBA*

Make the Most of Miller's

In Miller's we do NOT just reprint saleroom estimates. We work from realised prices either from an auction room or a dealer. Our consultants then work out a realistic price range for a similar piece. This is to try to avoid repeating freak results – either low or high

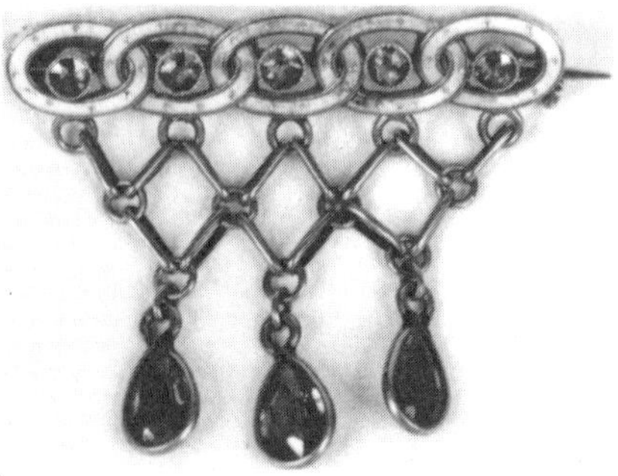

A garnet, enamel and gold brooch, 1½in (4cm) wide.
£275-320 *SBA*

A mother-of-pearl shell brooch, inset with pearl and gold flowers.
£400-500 *SBA*

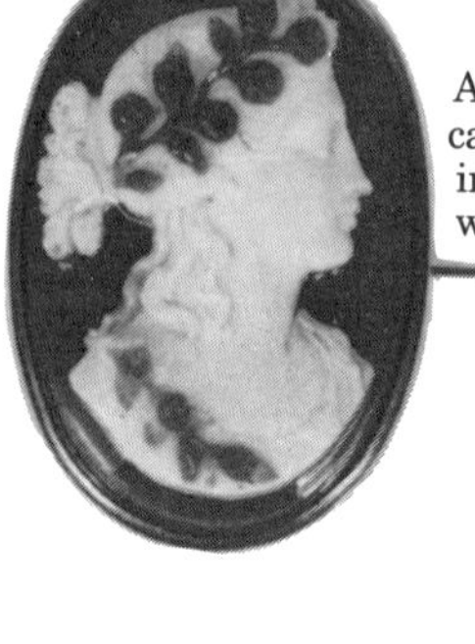

An 18ct gold deeply carved agate cameo, in green, brown and white, 1½in (4cm) long.
£1,200-1,500
SBA

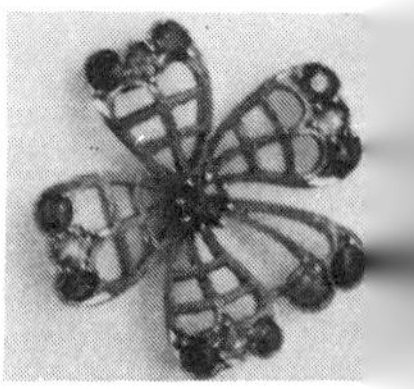

A demantoid garnet and sapphi openwork quatrefoil brooch.
£300-400 *CSK*

A 15ct gold butterfly brooch, 1½in (4cm) high.
£250-300 *SBA*

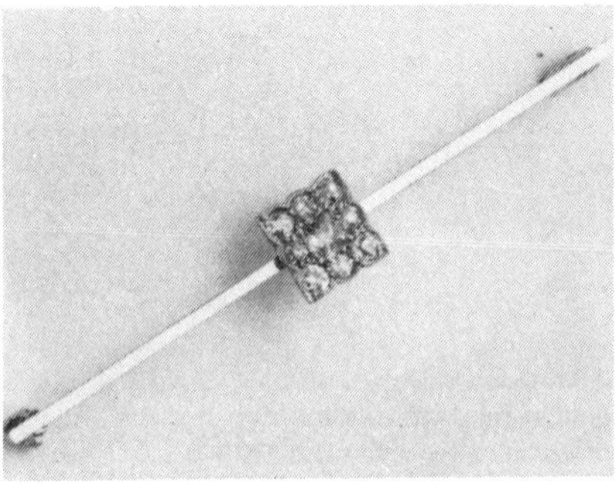

A diamond 9 stone cluster bar brooch.
£250-300 *CSK*

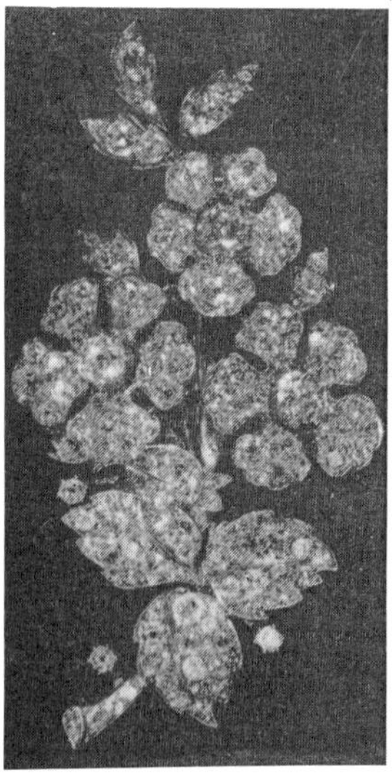

A Victorian gold floral and leaf trembler spray brooch, with approximately 168 diamonds set in silver.
£3,200-3,700 *P(S)*

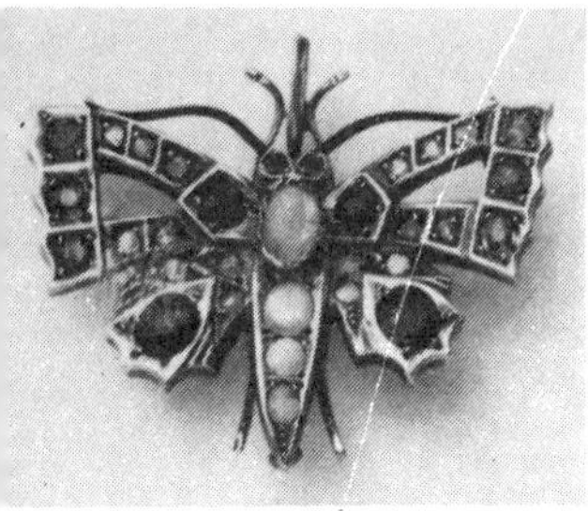

A rose diamond, opal, sapphire and garnet winged insect brooch.
£600-700 *CSK*

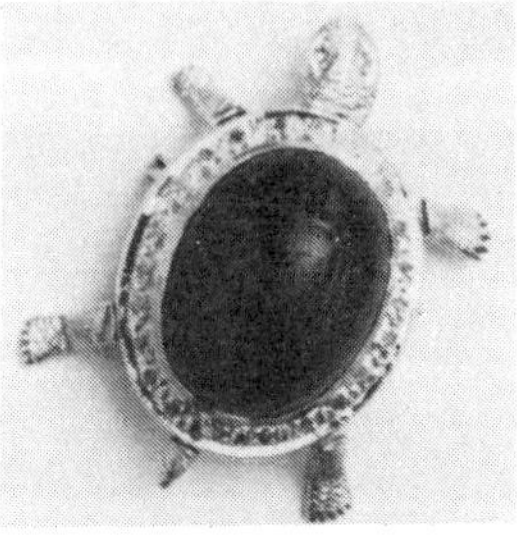

A cabochon sapphire and diamond turtle brooch with articulated limbs and diamond set eyes.
£350-400 *CSK*

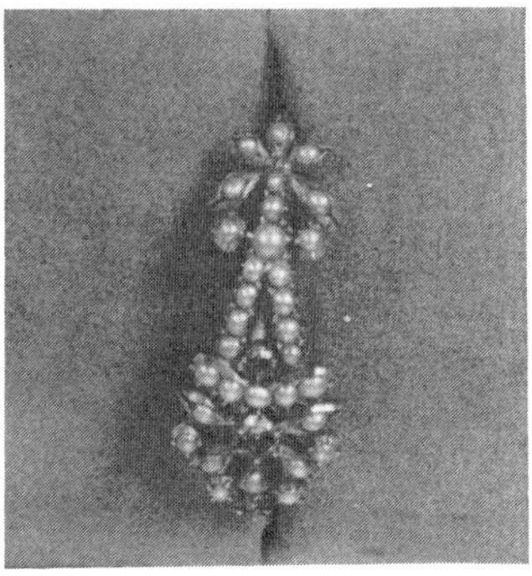

An 18ct gold Haley's comet style brooch, inset with pearls, rubies and emeralds.
£300-400 *SBA*

A 15ct gold bar brooch with pendant and monkey on a swing.
£400-500 *SBA*

A diamond, rose diamond and green guilloche enamel clover leaf brooch, with diamond centre.
£550-650 *CSK*

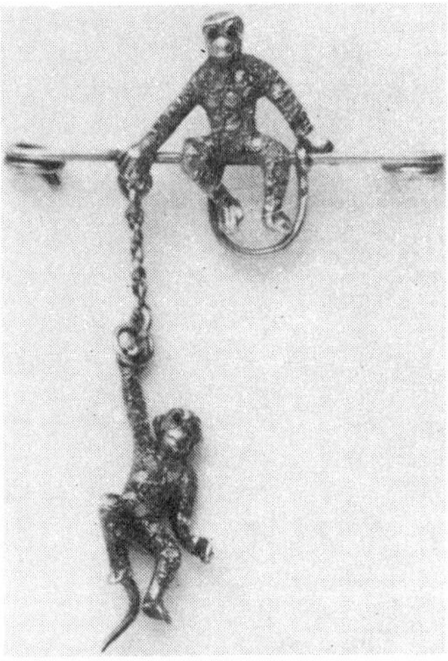

A rose diamond twin monkey bar brooch, 1 seated upon a bar, the other suspended beneath.
£500-600 *CSK*

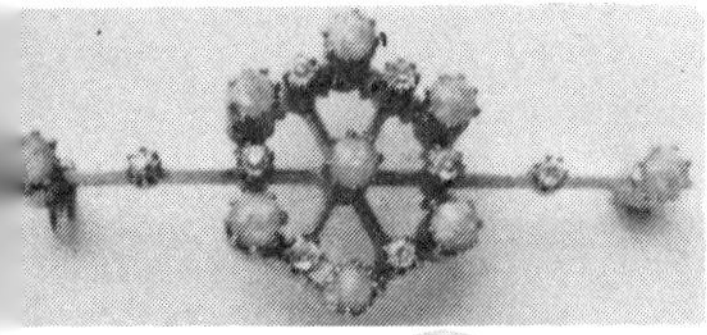

An opal and diamond openwork cluster bar brooch.
£300-400 *CSK*

A rose diamond, half pearl and gem bee brooch.
£400-500 *CSK*

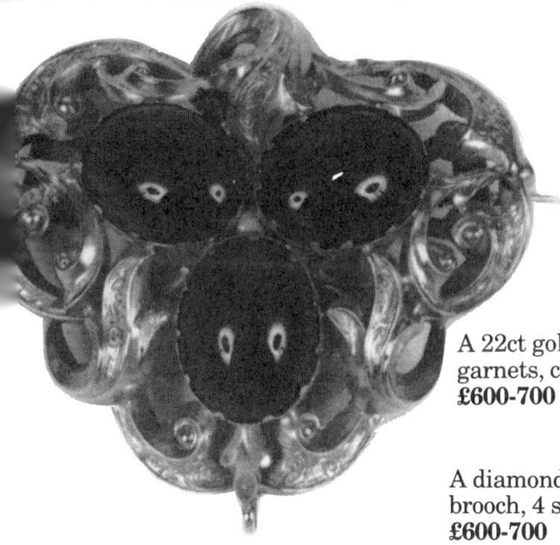

A 22ct gold brooch inset with garnets, c1840, 2in (6cm) wide.
£600-700 *SBA*

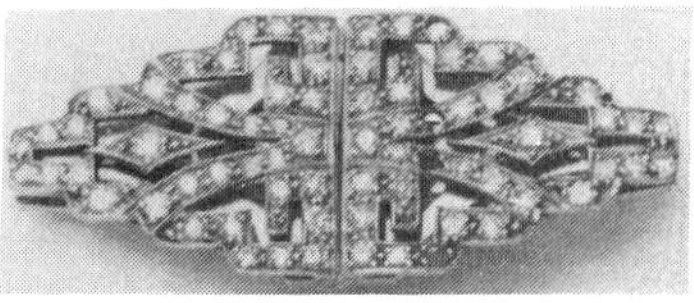

A diamond openwork double clip brooch, 4 stones damaged.
£600-700 *CSK*

An 18ct gold Georgian necklace, inset with pink topaz and turquoise.
£2,500-3,000 *SBA*

A gold, seed pearl and foliate pendant on a gold chain necklace.
£300-350 *HCH*

A drop cut ruby solitaire pendant with diamond border and suspension to an S-link integral necklet.
£1,500-2,000 *CSK*

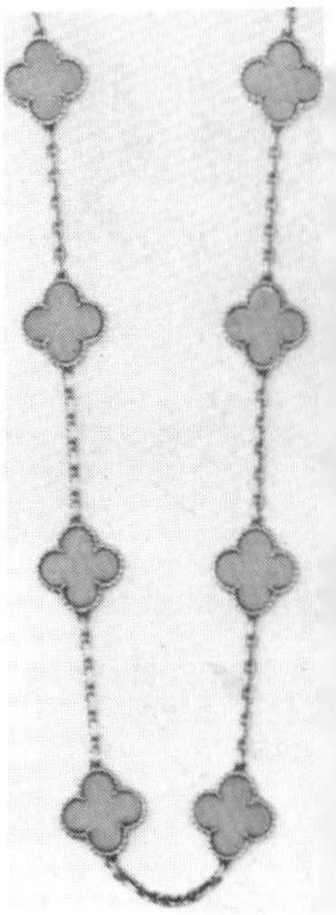

A French quatrefoil coral link necklace by Van Cleef and Arpels Paris, with chain link connections in maker's case.
£1,200-1,500 *CSK*

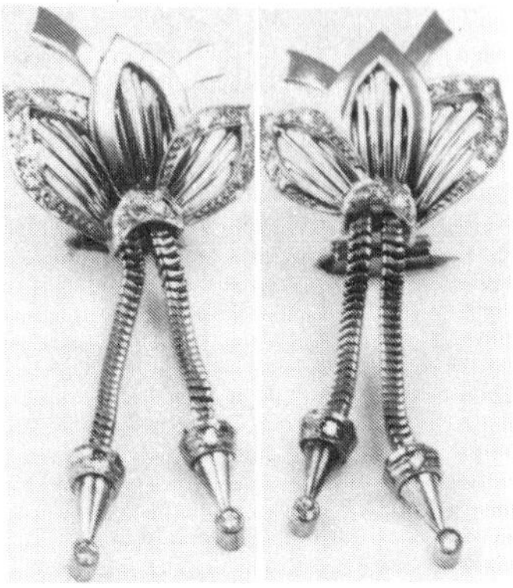

A pair of diamond set 1940s style bow design ear clips, with twin Brazilian link drops to diamond set terminals.
£600-700 *CSK*

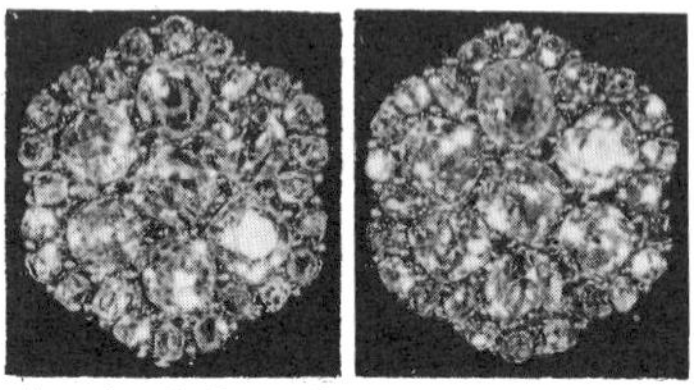

A pair of silver cluster ear studs, each set with 31 diamonds in closed settings.
£3,000-3,500 *P(S)*

A pair of diamond, calibre sapphire and yellow diamond line and drop earrings.
£1,500-2,000 *CSK*

A rose diamond pendant seal, modelled as a sphinx, set with a blister pearl forming the body, engraved with the legend 'Remember the Tangible Now'.
£350-400 *CSK*

An emerald single stone ring with baguette diamond single stone shoulders.
£800-1,200 *CSK*

A scroll and foliate design paste se pendant with centre oval blistered pearl, 19thC.
£20-50 *PCh*

A diamond, cultured pearl, half pearl and blue enamel boat shaped cluster ring with scrollwork shoulders.
£250-300 *CSK*

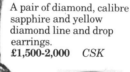

A diamond circular cluster ring.
£350-400 *CSK*

A diamond triple flower cluster ha hoop ring.
£600-700 *CSK*

A gold oval turquoise intagl ring, depicting the profile he of an Egyptian Pharaoh, 19thC.
£550-600 *CSK*

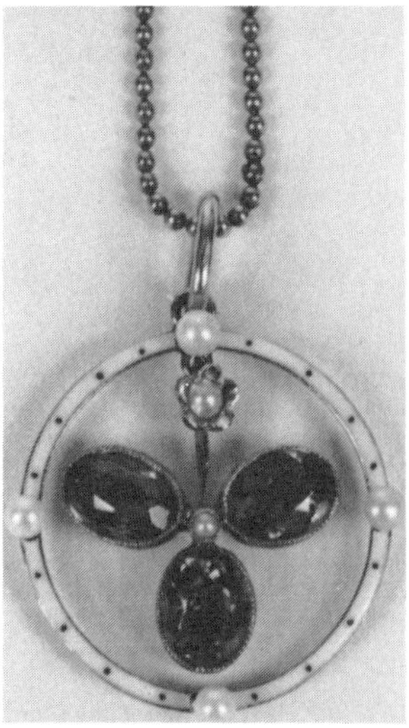

An Indian enamel, pearl and peridot pendant.
£400-500 *SBA*

A gold ring set with 3 step cut emeralds.
£1,200-1,500 *P(S)*

An 18ct gold ring set with a brilliant cut diamond, split shoulders.
£400-600 *P(S)*

A gold ring set with a sapphire and 2 brilliant cut diamonds, 18thC.
£250-300 *P(S)*

An 18ct white gold diamond cluster ring.
£500-800 *CSK*

A diamond 5 stone half hoop ring.
£250-300 *CSK*

ARMS & ARMOUR
Armour

A Victorian full suit of armour.
£3,000-4,000 *WAL*

An early suit of armour.
£9,500-11,000 *B*

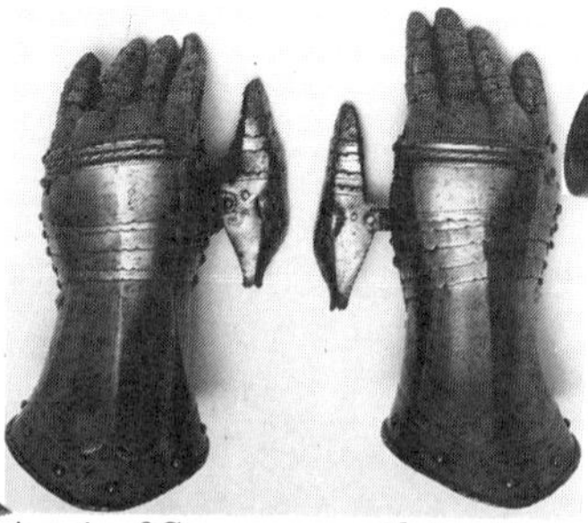

A pair of German gauntlets, of bright steel, with overlapping finger-plates with cusped edges bordered by incised lines, riveted to the original leathers, one damaged, separate hinged thumb guards, and original leather lining gloves (damaged), one retaining its original iron buckle for a wrist-strap, late 16thC, 11in (28cm).
£3,000-4,000 *CSK*

Cannon

A bronze signal carronade.
£500-600 *WAL*

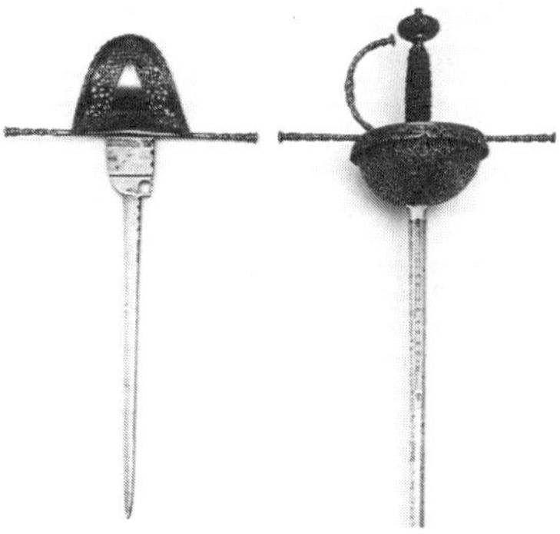

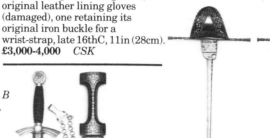

A Spanish cup hilt rapier and left-hand dagger, stamped respectively 'Antonio Picinio' and 'En Toledo', knuckle guard, cast and partly pierced, 41in (104cm) and 19in (48.5cm).
£2,000-2,500 *CSK*

Daggers

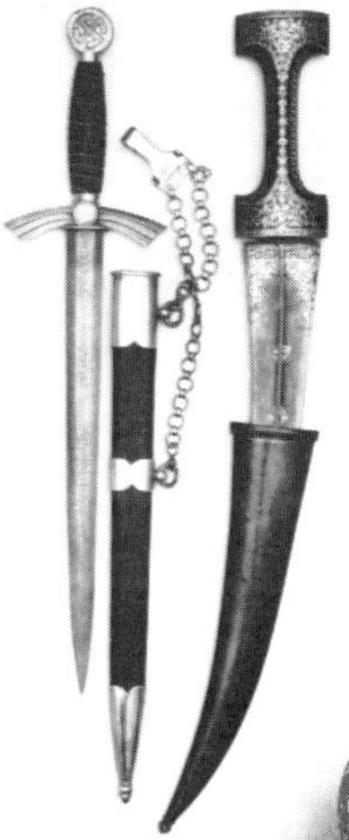

A Third Reich Luftwaffe 1934 pattern presentation dagger.
£2,000-2,500

r. A Balkan dagger, jambiya.
£800-1,000 *WAL*

A Scottish silver mounted dirk with tapering hollow-ground single-edged blade back-edged towards the point and with incised device on each face, silver-mounted rootwood handle, and silver pommel-cap engraved with later owner's crest and motto, in original leather scabbard with silver locket and chape, the blade of the by-knife stamped 'Paton' on one side, some damage, c1745, 19in (48.5cm).
£1,000-1,500 *CSK*

The crest and motto are of Macadam.

A Singhalese gold and silver mounted kastana, the hilt comprising knuckle guard and downturned quillons each terminating in a dragon's head, large pommel with gold tongue and eyes set with red stones, in original decorated silver scabbard, and 4 rings for suspension, together with its original gold brocade sash, 24in (61.5cm).
£1,200-1,500 *CSK*

A rare Swiss 'Holbein' dagger, with double-edged blade of flattened diamond section struck on both sides with a mark, a dagger, the hilt of characteristic form with hardwood grip of slightly swollen diamond section, and brass lined iron mounts, in gilt bronze mounted scabbard covered in leather, repairs, iron parts pitted throughout, the dagger late 16thC, 15½in (39.5cm).
£2,700-3,200 *CSK*

A Scottish Highland dirk, with straight fullered single-edged blade, the pommel-plate engraved with initials 'IC', in brass-mounted leather scabbard with side-pockets for the by-knife and fork each with flat pewter mounted cow horn handle, some damage, early 18thC, 15½in (39.5cm).
£900-1,200 *CSK*

A Tibetan miniature gilt brass mounted ritual dagger, the terminal in the form of the head of a hawk with open beak, 17thC, 4½in (11.5cm).
£1,000-1,500 *C*

Knives

A German Bowie style hunting knife, probably made in Solingen for the American market, the grips of vulcanised rubber, decorated with a winged mythical beast and scrolling foliage, the nickel silver guard with scalloped edges, straight, unfullered single edged blade, in its black leather bayonet style scabbard with nickel silver mounts, the locket with frog stud, some flaking of leather glaze, mid-19thC, blade 10in (25cm).
£350-450 *WD*

Swords

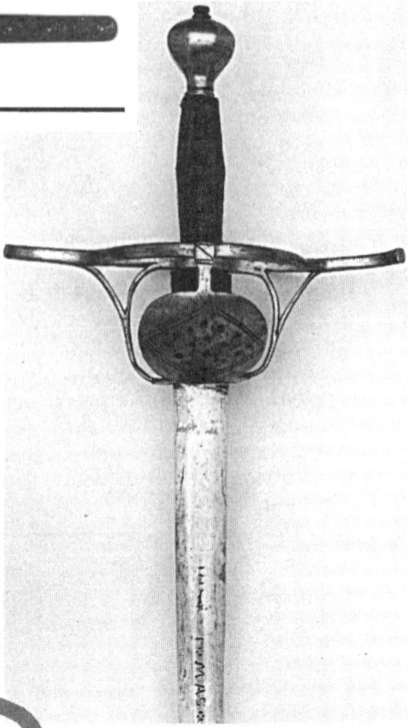

A composite riding sword, with broad straight double-edged blade with central fuller on each face at the forte stamped respectively 'Th(e)sus Maria' and '(To)mas Deaiala', leather-covered ricasso, faceted fig-shaped pommel, and later wire-bound wooden grip, early 17thC, blade 34in (86cm).
£700-800 *CSK*

A Polish sabre with leather covered wooden hilt, flattened iron quillons with button finials, one pierced for the knuckle-chain, and long slender langets, in original leather-covered wooden scabbard with embossed and pierced brass mounts, some damage, the hilt and scabbard painted black, early 17thC, blade 29in (73.5cm).
£600-800 *CSK*

An English rapier, c1630.
£350-400 *ASB*

Muskets

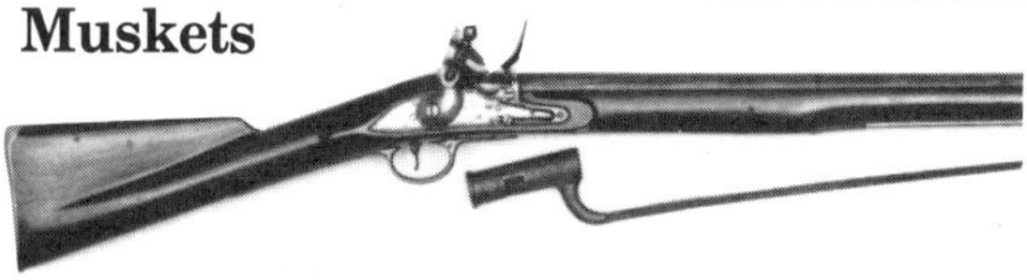

An India pattern Brown Bess flintlock musket of the Royal Fusiliers.
£1,500-2,000 *WAL*

An Austrian military repeating air rifle, with carved figured walnut full stock, leather-covered butt reservoir, brass mounts engraved behind the breech, owner's crest and initials, and stamped with a small maker's mark, solid side-plate engraved with a trophy of arms and foliage, trigger-guard matching and brass fore-end cap, ramrod missing, in original lined and fitted wooden case with trade label and accessories including pump, spanner, bullet mould and spare reservoirs, one with leather covering missing, finished by Mortimer, 21 St. James's Strt., London, c1820, 33in (83.5cm) barrel.
£2,500-3,500 *CSK*

Sporting

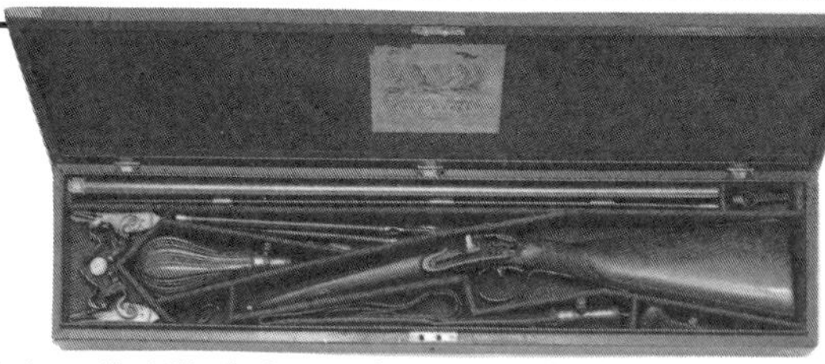

A 20-bore double barrelled flintlock sporting gun, with rebrowned twist sighted barrels, with gold-lined maker's stamp, gold lines and vents, engraved case-hardened tang, signed border engraved flat locks with rollers, one cock and mainspring replaced, one steel damaged, figured walnut half-stock, chequered grip, repaired, in lined and fitted brass mounted mahogany case, lock replaced, with trade label and some accessories including Sykes patent leather shot-belt, by Joseph Manton, London, No. 615 for 1794, 32in (81.5cm) barrels. **£3,500-4,500** *CSK*

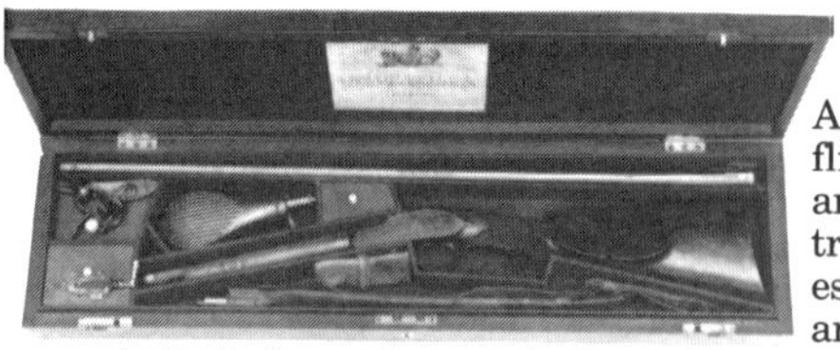

A flintlock sporting gun by Patrick, c1820.
£1,700-2,000 *WAL*

Pistols

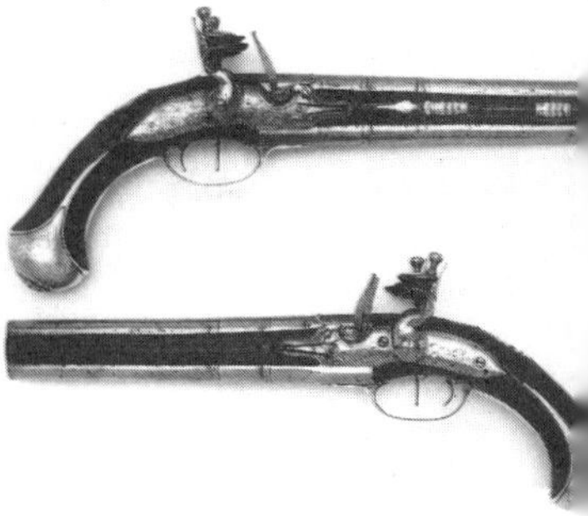

A rare pair of over-and-under flintlock holster pistols, with cast and chased silver mounts, trigger-guards, vacant grotesque escutcheons pierced with foliage, and later wooden ramrods, iron parts pitted throughout, some replacements, by I. Steward, late 17thC, 17in (43.5cm).
£2,000-2,500 *CSK*

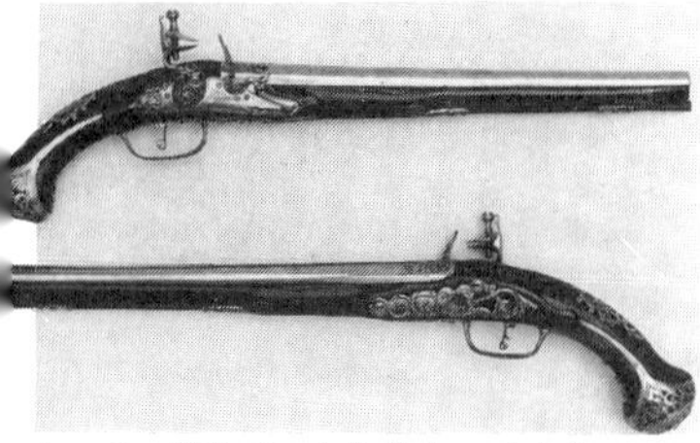

A pair of flintlock holster pistols, inscribed 'Johann Breidenfelder CB' in silver on the top flat, with horn fore-end caps, and horn-tipped wooden ramrods, the metal parts polished bright throughout, late 17th/early 18thC, 20½in (52cm).
£3,000-3,500 *CSK*

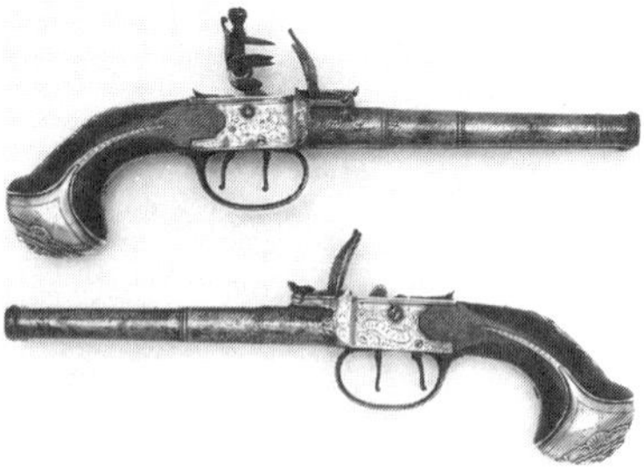

An unusual pair of silver-mounted double barrelled flintlock box-lock pistols, with 3-stage turn-off cannon barrels numbered from 1 to 4 and engraved at the breech, signed brass actions engraved with foliage, both cocks on one pistol incomplete, one top jaw and screw missing, by Joseph Griffin, London, c1760, 11½in (29.5cm).
£5,000-5,500 *CSK*

r. A pair of flintlock pocket pistols, with wirework inlaid hardwood stocks, the side plate inscribed 'T. Jordan', late 18thC.
£550-650 *WW*

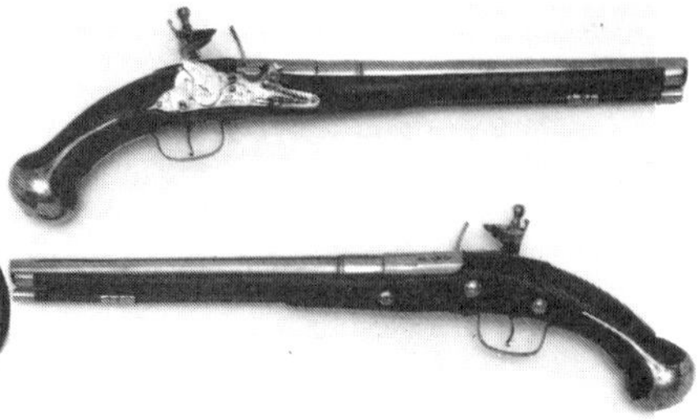

A pair of Spanish miquelet lock belt pistols, inlaid with silver foliate scrolls and 'Fabricao En Eibar', struck with gold-filled maker's stamp of Antonio Guisasola of Eibar (New Stockel 7541), engraved steel mounts, trigger-guards struck with maker's mark, and original wooden ramrods, belt hooks missing, c1820, 13in (33.5cm).
£2,200-2,500 *CSK*

A rare pair of flintlock holster pistols with lengthened 4-stage barrels, octagonal breeches struck with maker's mark 'EN' below a sun, trigger-guards with punched decoration, and later steel-tipped wooden ramrods, by Edward Nicholson, London proof marks, late 17thC, 21in (53.5cm).
£2,000-2,500 *CSK*

Edward Nicholson was elected Master of the Gunsmiths' Company in 1697.

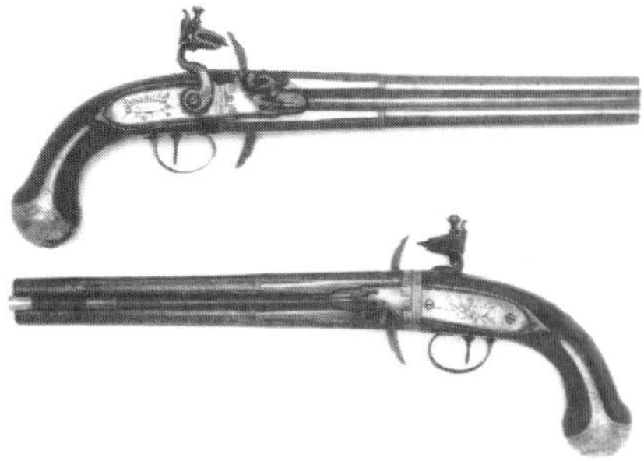

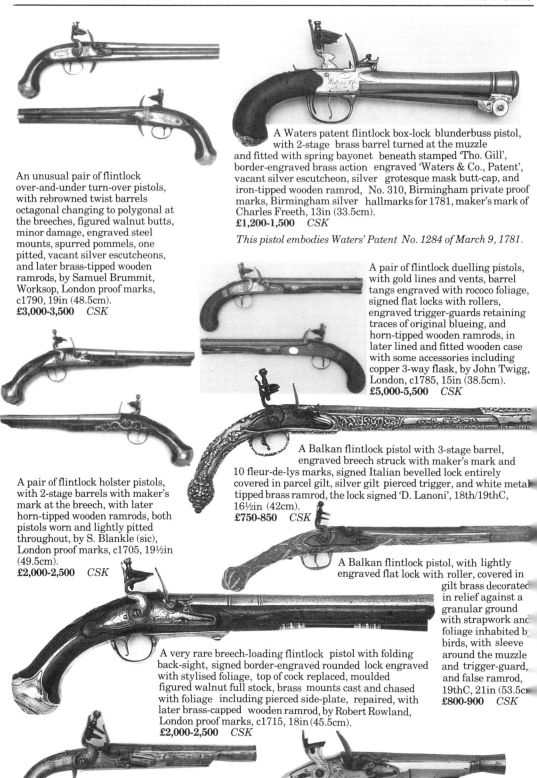

An unusual pair of flintlock over-and-under turn-over pistols, with rebrowned twist barrels octagonal changing to polygonal at the breeches, figured walnut butts, minor damage, engraved steel mounts, spurred pommels, one pitted, vacant silver escutcheons, and later brass-tipped wooden ramrods, by Samuel Brummit, Worksop, London proof marks, c1790, 19in (48.5cm).
£3,000-3,500 *CSK*

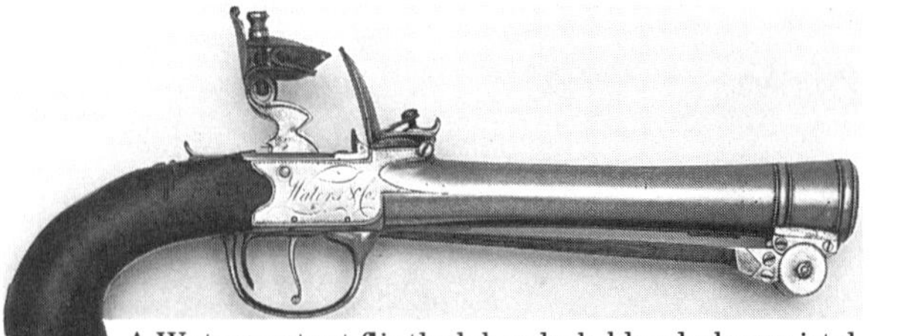

A Waters patent flintlock box-lock blunderbuss pistol, with 2-stage brass barrel turned at the muzzle and fitted with spring bayonet beneath stamped 'Tho. Gill', border-engraved brass action engraved 'Waters & Co., Patent', vacant silver escutcheon, silver grotesque mask butt-cap, and iron-tipped wooden ramrod, No. 310, Birmingham private proof marks, Birmingham silver hallmarks for 1781, maker's mark of Charles Freeth, 13in (33.5cm).
£1,200-1,500 *CSK*

This pistol embodies Waters' Patent No. 1284 of March 9, 1781.

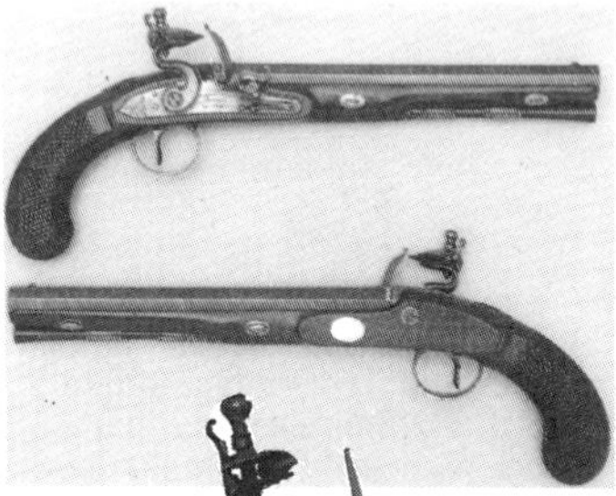

A pair of flintlock duelling pistols, with gold lines and vents, barrel tangs engraved with rococo foliage, signed flat locks with rollers, engraved trigger-guards retaining traces of original blueing, and horn-tipped wooden ramrods, in later lined and fitted wooden case with some accessories including copper 3-way flask, by John Twigg, London, c1785, 15in (38.5cm).
£5,000-5,500 *CSK*

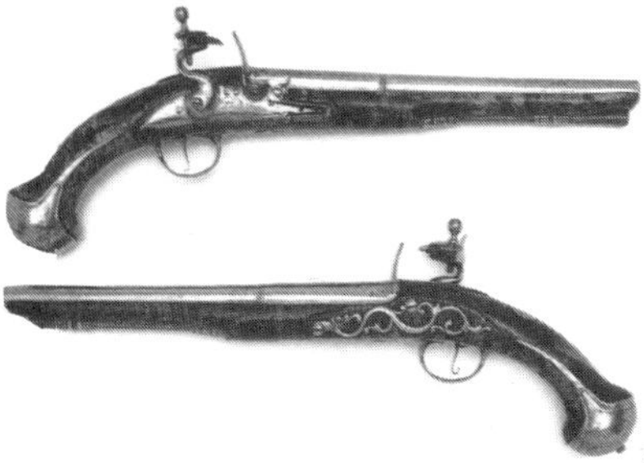

A pair of flintlock holster pistols, with 2-stage barrels with maker's mark at the breech, with later horn-tipped wooden ramrods, both pistols worn and lightly pitted throughout, by S. Blankle (sic), London proof marks, c1705, 19½in (49.5cm).
£2,000-2,500 *CSK*

A Balkan flintlock pistol with 3-stage barrel, engraved breech struck with maker's mark and 10 fleur-de-lys marks, signed Italian bevelled lock entirely covered in parcel gilt, silver gilt pierced trigger, and white metal tipped brass ramrod, the lock signed 'D. Lanoni', 18th/19thC, 16½in (42cm).
£750-850 *CSK*

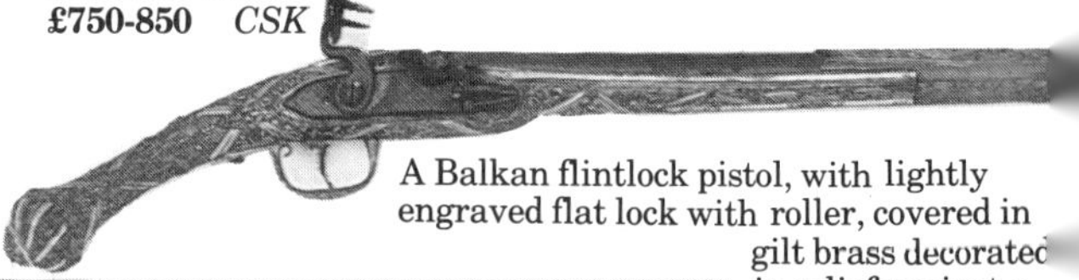

A Balkan flintlock pistol, with lightly engraved flat lock with roller, covered in gilt brass decorated in relief against a granular ground with strapwork and foliage inhabited by birds, with sleeve around the muzzle and trigger-guard, and false ramrod, 19thC, 21in (53.5cm).
£800-900 *CSK*

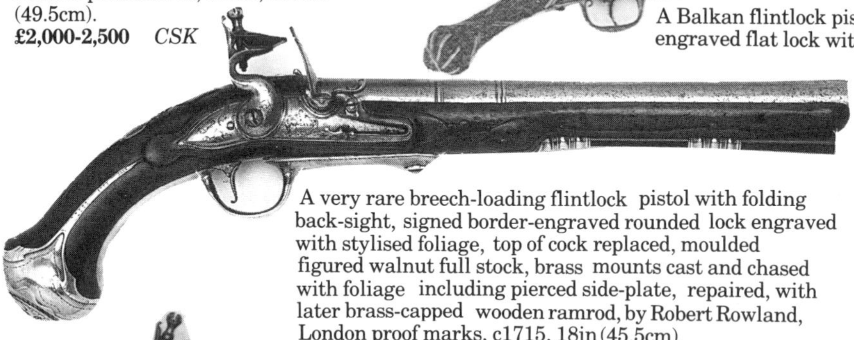

A very rare breech-loading flintlock pistol with folding back-sight, signed border-engraved rounded lock engraved with stylised foliage, top of cock replaced, moulded figured walnut full stock, brass mounts cast and chased with foliage including pierced side-plate, repaired, with later brass-capped wooden ramrod, by Robert Rowland, London proof marks, c1715, 18in (45.5cm).
£2,000-2,500 *CSK*

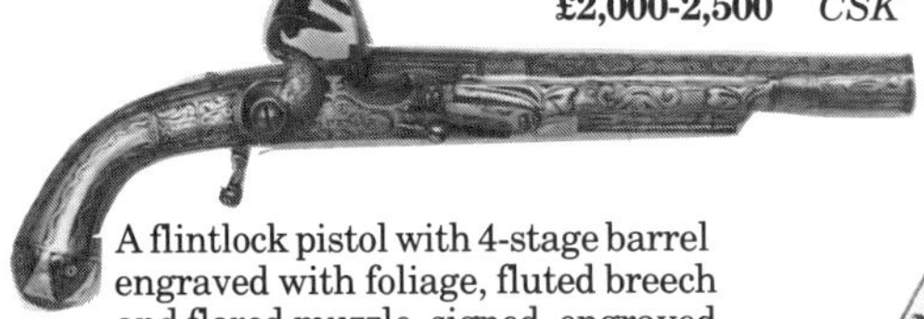

A flintlock pistol with 4-stage barrel engraved with foliage, fluted breech and flared muzzle, signed, engraved lock, action defective, lobe butt engraved with later owner's crest and motto, turned iron trigger, 3 engraved silver panels on the underside of the stock, and engraved steel belt hook, ramrod missing, by Thomas Murdoch, late 18thC, 12½in (32.5cm).
£1,800-2,200 *CSK*

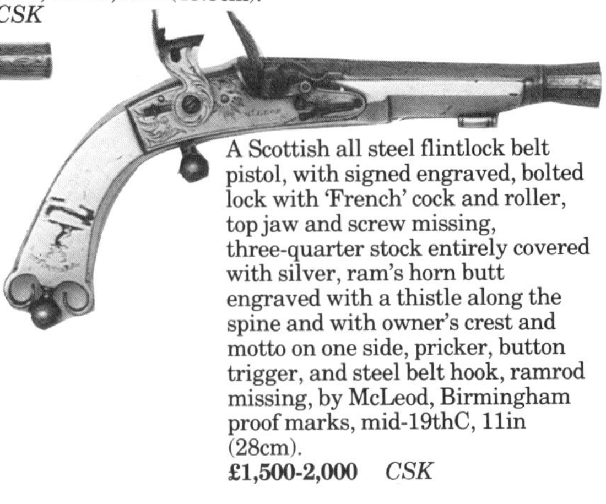

A Scottish all steel flintlock belt pistol, with signed engraved, bolted lock with 'French' cock and roller, top jaw and screw missing, three-quarter stock entirely covered with silver, ram's horn butt engraved with a thistle along the spine and with owner's crest and motto on one side, pricker, button trigger, and steel belt hook, ramrod missing, by McLeod, Birmingham proof marks, mid-19thC, 11in (28cm).
£1,500-2,000 *CSK*

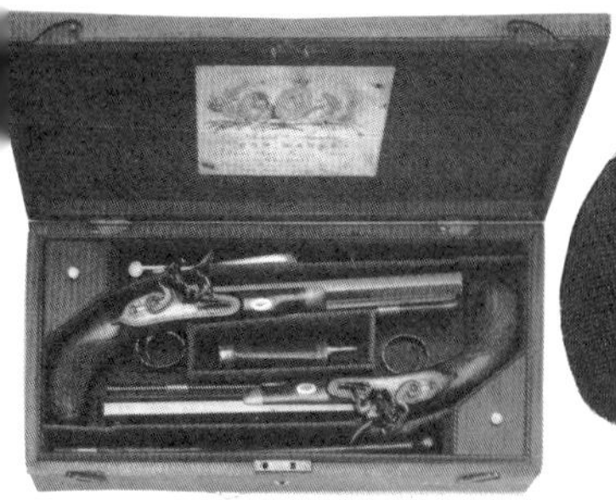

A rare pair of flintlock duelling pistols with rebrowned twist sighted rifled barrels, case-hardened breeches, platinum line and vent, case-hardened tangs, signed engraved case-hardened bolted locks with rollers and rainproof pans, the steels engraved 'Joseph Manton patent' and numbered 7525 and 7526, in original lined and fitted mahogany case, lid cracked, cleaned off, with trade label and accessories including red leather-covered flask, by Joseph Manton, London, No. 6862 for 1815.
£5,000-5,500 *CSK*

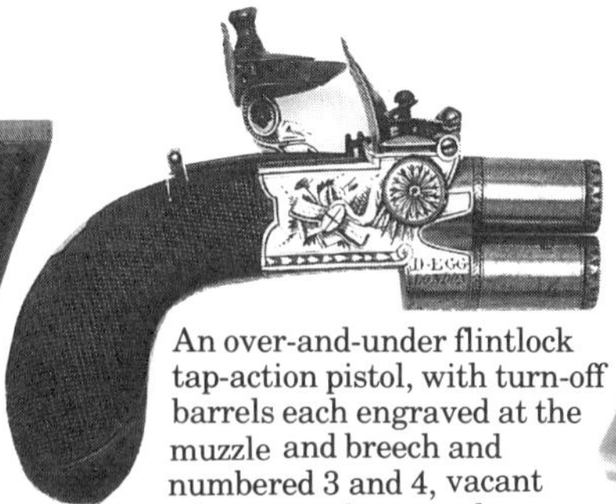

An over-and-under flintlock tap-action pistol, with turn-off barrels each engraved at the muzzle and breech and numbered 3 and 4, vacant silver escutcheon, and chequered figured walnut butt, signed 'D. Egg, London', Birmingham proof marks, early 19thC, 4½in (11.5cm).
£1,500-2,000 *CSK*

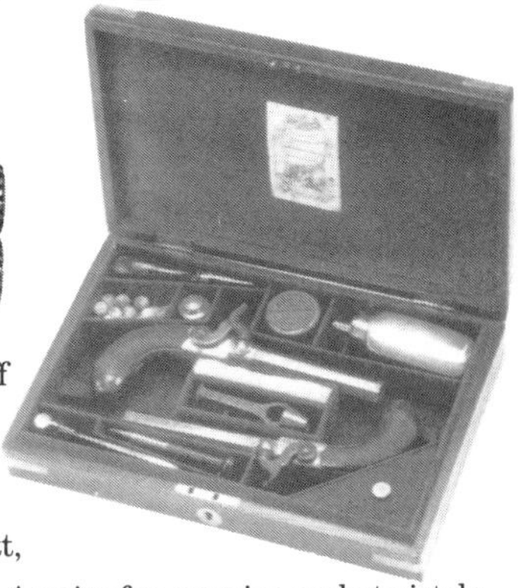

A pair of percussion pocket pistols, plated lock plates engraved with scrolling foliage, similarly engraved hammers and chequered butts, contained in a fitted mahogany box with accessories bearing the label of W. Pritchard of Birmingham, c1840, 4in (10cm) barrels.
£650-750 *Bea*

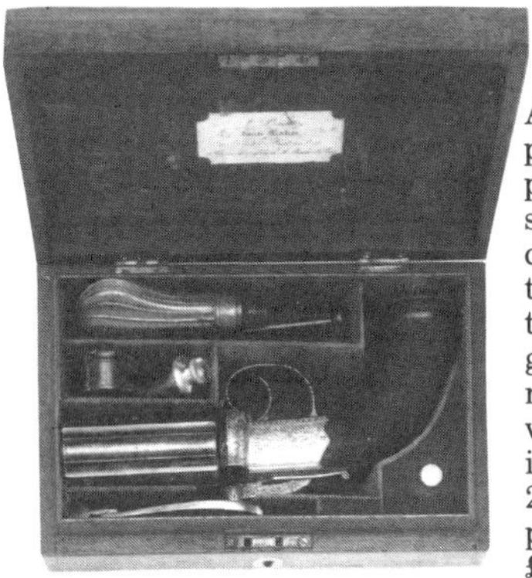

A self-cocking 6-shot percussion pepperbox revolver, with signed plated action engraved with scrolling foliage, engraved case-hardened bar-hammer and thumbpiece safety-catch, blued trigger, case-hardened trigger-guard and butt-trap, in original mahogany case lined in plum velvet with trade label and accessories including flask, by J. Beattie, 223 Regent St., London, London proof marks, c1845, 9½in (24cm).
£4,000-4,500 *CSK*

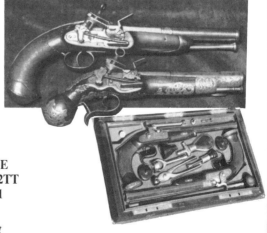

Revolvers

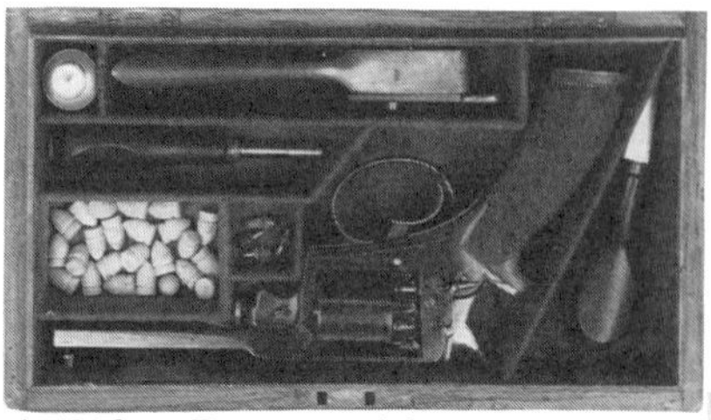

A 120-bore Beaumont-Adams double-action percussion revolver, with blued sighted rifled barrel stamped 'L.A.C.', blued cylinder, blued border engraved frame with safety-stop, blued rammer, chequered figured walnut butt, blued trigger-guard and butt-plate, No. 32239.R, in original lined and fitted oak case with accessories including bullet mould, London proof marks, 10in (25cm).
£1,000-1,500 *CSK*

Medals & Orders

A second World War Distinguished Flying Cross group, dated 1945, with ribbon, awarded to Flight Lieutenant Gretkiercwicz, who was shot down twice in the Battle of Britain.
£700-800 *HSS*

Companion of the Order of St. Michael and St. George neck badge.
£200-225 *RMC*

Union of South Africa medal 1910, un-named as issued.
£130-150 *RMC*

Distinguished Conduct Medal group, Edward VII, Q.M.Sgt. W. Dobbs, G. Coy., Royal Engineers.
£300-400 *RMC*

Order of The British Empire, for Meritorious Service, George V.
£55-65 *WIN*

1914-15 Star, British War medal, Victory medal, Pte. C. H. Bourne, C. of London Yeomanry.
£25-35 *RMC*

Badges & Plates

A shoulder belt plate of The 57th (West Middlesex) Regiment, pre-1855.
£400-450 *WAL*

A Boer War badge of the Commander in Chief's Yeomanry Escort.
£200-250 *WAL*

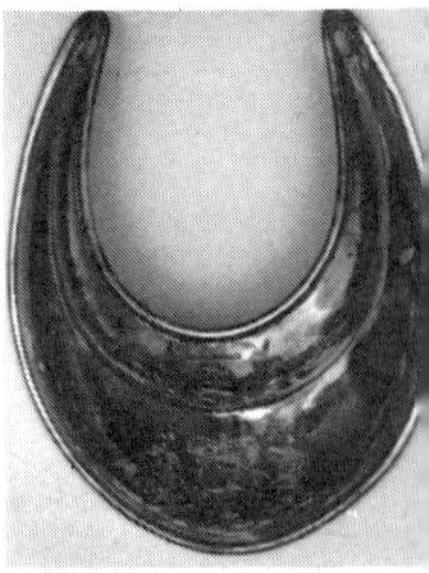

A Georgian gorget of th
Royal Marines, c1795.
£550-600 *WAL*

A Victorian officer's special pattern waist belt plate, The Essex Regiment.
£200-250 *WAL*

Drums

A German military side-drum, with copper hoops painted red and white, iron rod tension and copper shell stamped 'J.R. 141' and '59.L.J.R. 2.B.', probably dating from the Great War, 15in (38.5cm) diam.
£100-150 *CSK*

The stamps probably indicate use by Infantry Regiment No. 141 (a West Prussian unit based on Kulm) and later by the 59th Landwehr Infantry Regiment, 2nd Battalion (nearby at Posen). Prussian drum hoops were red and white as far back as 1857.

A rope-tension side-drum of a Sudanese battalion with bufftabs and drag-robes, the brass shell retaining some elements of its decoration including Egyptian crown, star and crescent flag, the honours and maker's details Hawkes & Son, London.
£200-250 *CSK*

Helmets

A lobster-tailed pot probably German, mid-17thC, 11in (28cm) high.
£800-850 *CSK*

A Persian chiselled and damascened steel kulah khud, the skull with 3 plume holders damascened in gold with invocations to Allah, gold damascened central spike, the base with gold foliage and pierced with Qur'anic script, the base of the skull profusely gold damascened with a religious verse, a dedication to Shah Abbas (1587-1628), the maker's name 'Aqa Hassan', and the date corresponding to 1626, 10in (25cm) high.
£4,000-4,500 *CSK*

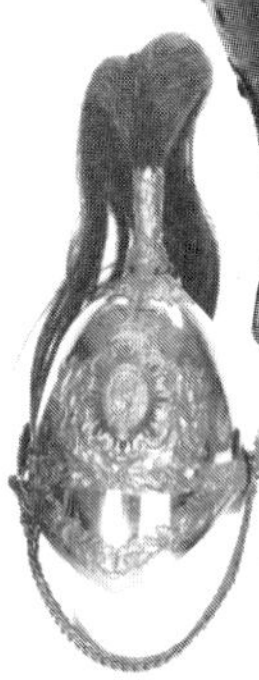

A Victorian gilt brass trooper's helmet of the King's Dragoon Guards, with 'gem' cut steel and gilt brass helmet plate, hair plume and rosette, in black japanned metal carrying box with brass shield-shaped trade plate of 'Cutler & Sons, Army Clothiers, 8 Hanover Square, London'.
£1,200-1,500 *N*

An officer's blue cloth spiked helmet by Barteld, Hanover Square, bearing a composite K.C. helmet plate of the South Wales Borderers and now fitted with a chin chain with white lining.
£350-400 *CSK*

Jniforms

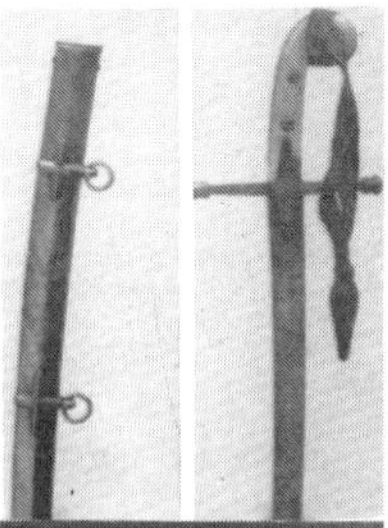

A pair of Field Marshal's gold houlder-cords in a velvet-lined glazed case with a card inscribed Robert Cornelius Napier, 1st Baron Magdala' and with details of his areer on the back of the case, and a General Officer's Victorian sword with 30½in (77.5cm) blade, by Andrews, 9, Pall Mall, with crown VR' and crossed sword and baton, arge ivory grips and old Bazaar-made replacement rosspiece of General's pattern with sword-knot, in gilt brass scabbard, he sword and shoulder-cords are elieved to have belonged to Napier.
450-500 *CSK*

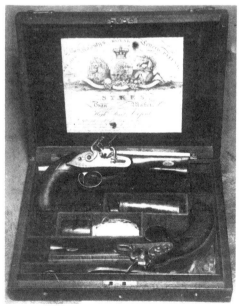

AUCTIONEERS

DAVID LAY A.S.V.A.

Fine Art and Antiques Valuers, Auctioneers and Consultants

The Penzance Auction House
CORNWALL'S MOST PRESTIGIOUS SALEROOMS

Specialist sales of Antiques, Collectors Items, Art — in particular the Newlyn and St Ives Schools, Books, Coins and Stamps, and monthly general sales

The Penzance Auction House, Alverton, Penzance, Cornwall TR18 4RE
Telephone: (0736) 61414 Fax: 0736 60035

MICHAEL NEWMAN

FINE ART AUCTIONEERS AND VALUERS

The Central Auction Rooms, Kinterbury House
St. Andrew's Cross, PLYMOUTH, Devon PL1 2DG

Regular Monthly Collective Sales
of 1000 Lots (approx.) and Specialist Sales
Subscription List for Illustrated Catalogues.

Telephone: (0752) 669298
Fax: (0752) 226124

Miller

FINE ART AUCTIONEERS IN CORNWALL

Weekly Victorian, Edwardian and Household Sales

Monthly Antiques, Furniture, Ceramics, Silver, Objects d'Art, etc., Sales

Monthly Picture Sales

Monthly Collector's and Sporting Sales

Monthly Property Auction

And where appropriate Sales on Site

Collection and Clearances arranged nationwide

Valuations prepared for probate, insurance and family division purposes

LEMON QUAY AUCTION ROOMS
TRURO
Tel: (0872) 74211 Fax: (0872) 561101

Michael J Bowman A.S.V.A.

Auctioneer & Valuer of Fine Art & Chattels

MONTHLY SALES OF ANTIQUES & FINE ART AT CHUDLEIGH

COLOUR ILLUSTRATED CATALOGUES

FREE HOME CONSULTATIONS

6 Haccombe House, Nr Netherton
Newton Abbot, Devon TQ12 4SJ
Tel Shaldon (0626) 872890

SPENCER-THOMAS & WOOLLAND

Auctioneers and Valuers

Church Street Auction Rooms
Exmouth, Devon

Our services include:

AUCTION SALES
Frequent sales of antique and later furniture and effects held at our salerooms in Exmouth.
Sales at regular intervals of government surplus, commercial and industrial goods at Andover.

VALUATIONS
Valuations for probate, insurance and family division, etc.

REMOVAL AND STORAGE
A local and countrywide removal service is available with the benefit of long or short term storage facilities.

Free catalogue mailing list to serious trade and buyers.

Verbal advice given free of charge.

TEL: EXMOUTH (0395) 267403

Kingsbridge Auction Sales

(J.A.S. HAWKINS)

incorporating CHARLES HEAD & SON (Auctions)

85 Fore Street, Kingsbridge, Devon TQ7 1AB

Regular Auctions of Antiques & Modern Household Furniture & Effects — Valuations — House Clearance undertaken.

TEL: KINGSBRIDGE (0548) 856829

Frome Market Auction Rooms — Cooper & Tanner

Regular Monthly Fine Art & Furniture Auction.
Second Friday in every month, viewing Thursday 2.00 - 7.30 pm.

* Purpose built New Saleroom.
* Ample Free Parking.
* Cafeteria.
* Easy Access for loading/unloading.
* Close to Major Trunk Roads.

Complete House Clearances Undertaken.
Valuations for Insurance, Probate and Family Division Purposes.

Cooper & Tanner, Frome Market,
Frome, Somerset BA11 2PY Tel: 0373-831010

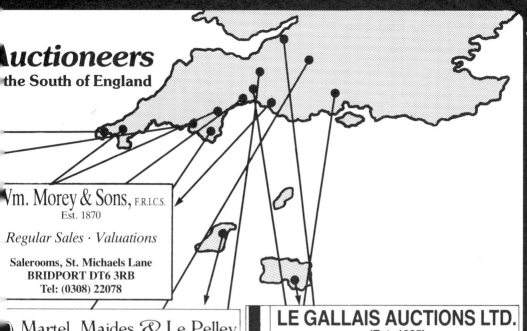

Auctioneers
the South of England

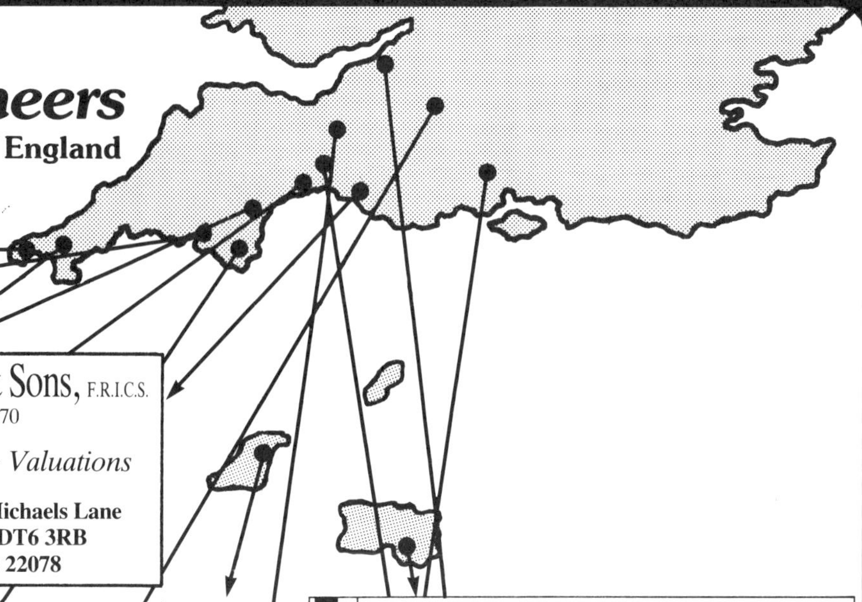

Wm. Morey & Sons, F.R.I.C.S.
Est. 1870

Regular Sales · Valuations

Salerooms, St. Michaels Lane
BRIDPORT DT6 3RB
Tel: (0308) 22078

Martel, Maides & Le Pelley
Auctioneers, Estate Agents, Surveyors, Valuers

50 High Street, St Peter Port, Guersney
Tel (0481) 713463

Quarterly Auctions of Antique Furniture, Porcelain, Silver, Jewellery, Pictures, Clocks, Miscellanea, etc.
Fortnightly Auctions of Victorian and ...er Furniture and Effects, Collectors' Items, etc.

5% BUYERS' PREMIUM. NO V.A.T.

LE GALLAIS AUCTIONS LTD.
(Est. 1825)

FINE ART AUCTIONEERS AND VALUERS in The Channel Islands

Services include: Weekly quality Modern Sales, Collectors Items, Victoriana etc.
Quarterly Fine Art Sales, Valuations undertaken, no V.A.T., no Buyers Premium, Weekly Shipping Service to and from U.K. Payment two weeks after sale (subject to our normal conditions of business).

36 Hilgrove Street
St. Helier
Jersey
(0534) 58789

GA **FINE ARTS & CHATTELS**

Romsey Auction Rooms

Monthly General Antique Sales
Monthly Silver, Jewellery & Plate Sales
Periodic 'Special' & Outside Sales

At: 86 The Hundred, Romsey
Hampshire SO51 8BX
Tel: (0794) 513331

BONHAMS

WEST COUNTRY

Sales of English and Continental Furniture, Oil Paintings, Silver, Jewellery, Clocks, Porcelain and Works of Art are held throughout the year.

Regular fortnightly sales of Furnishings, Decorative and Household Items.

For full details of our Auction Programme Please contact:

Bonhams West Country,
Dowell Street,
Honiton,
Devon.
Fax: 0404 43137
Tel: 0404 41872

Hunts FURNITURE AND FINE ART

MAGDALENE HOUSE,
...RCH SQUARE, TAUNTON,
SOMERSET TA1 1SB

TEL: (0823) 332525

...MONTHLY CATALOGUED FINE ART SALES

...urniture; Ceramics and Glass;
...r and Plate; Paintings and Prints;
Jewellery and Objets Vertu;
...llectors Items; Objets D'Art etc

PLUS

FORTNIGHTLY SALES

...rian Furniture and Shipping Goods
...s Quality Modern Furnishings

Clevedon Salerooms
(1M Junction 20, M5)

BI-MONTHLY SPECIALIST ANTIQUE SALES
FORTNIGHTLY GENERAL SALES
FREE ADVICE ON RESERVE AND SALE
FORMAL VALUATIONS FOR INSURANCE, PROBATE AND FAMILY DIVISION
CATALOGUES AVAILABLE FOR ALL SALES

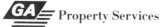

GA Property Services

Hoddel Pritchard, Six Ways, Clevedon
Avon BS21 7NT. Telephone: (0272) 876699

Auctioneers
n the South of England

HOBBS PARKER
1850
ANTIQUE & FINE ART AUCTIONEERS & VALUERS
AGRICULTURAL ESTATE AGENTS

ESTABLISHED 1850

Romney House, Ashford Market, Elwick Road
Ashford, Kent TN23 1PG
Tel: (0233) 622222

gular Auction sales of Antiques, Fine Art and Collector's Items held in the Amos Hall, hford Market, Ashford, Kent. Valuations for Insurance, Probate, Family Division and le by Auction. Collection service available. Sale calendar on request.

B. J. NORRIS
Auctioneers
YOUR LOCAL AUCTION PEOPLE

Regular twice monthly sales of Antique and Modern Furnishings and Effects held at:-
The Agricultural Hall, Maidstone, Kent.
Always a good selection of **Pine** and **Shipping Goods.**
See local press for dates or write direct to:-
B. J. Norris Auctioneers
The Quest, West Street, Harrietsham, Kent
Tel. Maidstone (0622) 859515.

DESMOND JUDD, Associates
Wealden Auction Galleries, Cranbrook, Kent)

800 Lot Monthly Evening Auction Sales:
Jewellery, Silver, Country Pursuits,
Weapons, Fine Paintings, Ceramics,
Furniture.

Telephone: Cranbrook (0580) 714522
(9.00 am – 8.00 pm)

Nationwide Anglia Estate Agents **Fine Art & Furniture**

New Forest Auction Rooms
Emsworth Road,
Lymington, Hants SO41 9BL
Tel: (0590) 677225

Midhurst Auction Rooms
Bepton Road,
Midhurst, Sussex
Tel: (073081) 2456

Bourne Auction Rooms
Spalding Road
Bourne, Lincs PE10 9LE
Tel: (0778) 422686

Amersham Auction Rooms
125 Station Road,
Amersham, Bucks HP7 0AH
Tel: (0494) 729292

Malton Auction Rooms
Milton Rooms, The Square,
Malton, Yorks
Tel: (0653) 695581

Whitby Auction Rooms
West End Saleroom, The Paddock,
Whitby, West Yorks
Tel: (0947) 603433

Isle of Wight Auction Rooms
50/52 Regent Street,
Shanklin, Isle of Wight PO37 7AE
Tel: (0983) 863441

Wotton Auction Rooms
Tabernacle Road, Wotton-Under-Edge,
Gloucestershire GL12 7EB
Tel: (0453) 844733

Frome Auction Rooms
Frome Market, Standerwick,
Nr. Frome, Somerset
Tel: (0373) 831010

A Network of Regional Salerooms

Auctioneers
the South of England

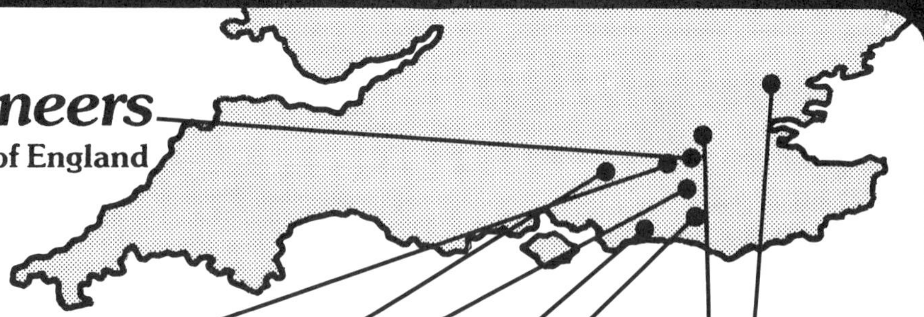

ROBIN ELLIOTT FRICS, IRRV
CHARTERED SURVEYORS
TIONEERS · VALUERS · SURVEYORS · MANAGEMENT · RATING

duct monthly sales of Antique Furniture, paintings, prints, rugs, metal and silverware, china and glass etc.

Dates for 1990
October 29th October 26th November

Dates for 1991
to be announced

uations for Insurance, Probate etc. undertaken

High St., Ascot, Berkshire SL5 7HG
☎ Ascot (0344) 872588
Fax (0344) 24700

COOPER HIRST AUCTIONS
Chartered Surveyors
Auctioneers and Valuers

- ★ REGULAR ANTIQUE SALES
- ★ HOUSEHOLD FURNITURE AND EFFECTS - Every TUESDAY at 10.00am (Viewing from 8.30am)
- ★ TIMBER, BUILDING MATERIALS, DIY, PLANT, MACHINERY AND VEHICLES. Every FRIDAY at 10.00am (Viewing from 8.30am)
- ★ BANKRUPTCY AND LIQUIDATION SALES ★
- ★ VALUATIONS OF ANTIQUES, FINE ART AND OTHER CHATTELS FOR ALL PURPOSES
- ★ HOUSE CLEARANCES, REMOVALS AND LONG/SHORT TERM STORAGE

THE GRANARY SALEROOM
VICTORIA ROAD, CHELMSFORD
Tel: 0245 260535

SOUTHGATE AUCTION ROOMS

London's premier suburban salerooms

Charge:

10% COMMISSION (plus VAT)

£4 (plus VAT) per lot as administration charge (sold or unsold)

10% (plus VAT) BUYERS PREMIUM

NO handling charge **NO** insurance charges **NO** hidden charges

Every Thursday, 6.30 p.m.

(Open for viewing 9.00 a.m. Thursday)

England's finest lady auctioneer sells at least 150 lots per hour, averaging 500 lots per sale.

Sales every week of up to £30,000

No children under 18 years of age admitted on sale day

No NEW reproduction accepted for sale

Munro House, Munro Drive, Cline Road
New Southgate, N11
Telephone: 081-886 7888 Fax: 081-368 6921

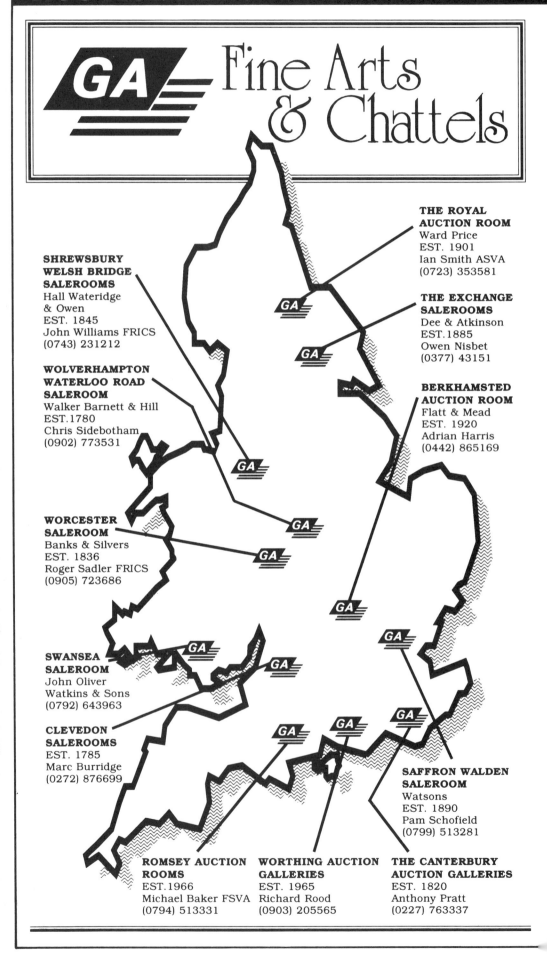

Auctioneers

the South of England

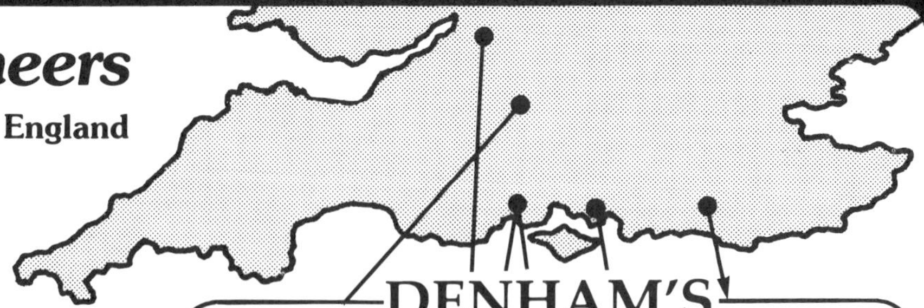

DENHAM'S

THE SUSSEX AUCTIONEERS — FOUNDED 1884

FINE ART, ANTIQUES AND COLLECTORS' ITEMS

Specialist sales held over two days in each month
Also Secondary Antiques and General Effects monthly

☆ FREE PRE-SALE VALUATIONS
☆ TRANSPORT SUBSIDISED OVER LONG DISTANCES

Regular collections from Sussex, Surrey, Hants and Kent

EXCELLENT FACILITIES INCLUDING
☆ Easy access and substantial free parking
☆ On-site restaurant and refreshments

HORSHAM AUCTION GALLERIES (On the A24 two miles north of Horsham)
WARNHAM, NR. HORSHAM, SUSSEX. Tel: (0403) 55699 & 53837

MAY & SON

(Established 1925)

Auctioneers & Estate Agents
long established Family Firm. Well experienced in Auctioneering and property matters.

Regular Monthly Auctions

ridge Street, Andover (0264) 23417

HOBBS & CHAMBERS

A PROPERTY LEEDS SERVICE

Regular Antique Furniture Sales with specialist sections of Silver, Jewellery, Paintings, Prints, Toys, Dolls, Ceramics and Collectables.

The Bingham Hall
Cirencester

Chapel Walk Saleroom
Cheltenham

For an auction calendar contact the auction offices

Market Place
Cirencester
Glos. GL7 1QQ
Tel: (0285) 654736

15 Royal Crescent
Cheltenham
Glos. GL50 3DA
Tel: (0242) 513722

Valuations undertaken for Probate, Insurance and Tax

FINE ART AUCTIONEERS

D.M. NESBIT & Company

CHARTERED SURVEYORS
AUCTIONEERS & VALUERS

Monthly sales to include furniture, porcelain, pottery, glassware, silver, jewellery, paintings and collectors' items. Valuations for insurance probate and family division.

Fine Art and Auction Department, Southsea Salerooms,
7 Clarendon Rd., Southsea, Hants. PO5 2ED
Tel: (0705) 864321 Fax: (0705) 295522

REGULAR SALES
OF COLLECTABLES

STAMPS	CIGARETTE CARDS
POSTAL HISTORY	COINS
POSTCARDS	BANK NOTES
AUTOGRAPHS	TOYS
STAGE AND SCREEN	EPHEMERA
MILITARIA	SMALL ANTIQUES
MEDALS	

Sample catalogue on request
Buying or selling it will pay you to contact

Garnet Langton Auctions

AUCTIONEERS • VALUERS

RLINGTON ARCADE, BOURNEMOUTH
TELEPHONE (0202) 22352

Established 1879

RIDDETTS

OF BOURNEMOUTH

Auctioneers and Valuers of Antiques and Fine Art

Fortnightly Sales of Antiques Porcelain, etc. and Regular Specialist Auctions

Offices and Auction Galleries – Richmond Hill, Bournemouth
Telephone: Bournemouth (0202) 25686

AUCTIONEERS

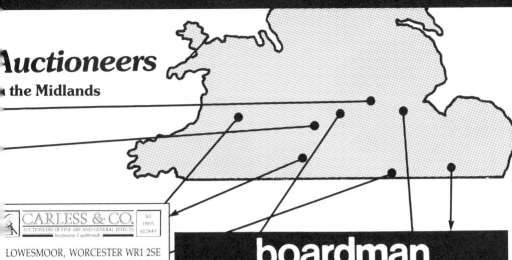

SPENCER'S

HENRY SPENCER & SONS

Fine Art Auctioneers & Valuers

1840

HALIFAX ESTATE AGENCIES LTD.

Principal Saleroom
RETFORD — 20 The Square, Retford, Nottinghamshire DN22 6BX. (0777) 708633

Regional Salerooms
NANTWICH — Victoria Gallery, Market Street, Nantwich, Cheshire CW5 5DG. (0270) 623878
ROSS-ON-WYE — The Georgian Rooms, Old Gloucester Road, Ross-on-Wye, Herefordshire HR9 5PB. (0989) 762227
CARMARTHEN — 19 King Street, Carmarthen, Dyfed SA31 1BH. (0267) 233456

Offices
ALTRINCHAM — 22 Railway Street, Altrincham, Cheshire WA14 2RE. (061) 929 0101
BRISTOL — 18-20 The Mall, Clifton, Bristol BS8 4DR. (0272) 738083
CAMBRIDGE — 65 Regent Street, Cambridge CB2 1AB. (0223) 327592
HARROGATE — 1 Princes Square, Harrogate, North Yorkshire HG1 1ND. (0423) 500566
LINCOLN — 42 Silver Street, Lincoln LN2 1TA. (0522) 536666
LONDON — 69 Walton Street, Knightsbridge, London SW3 2HT. (071) 584 0920
LYTHAM ST ANNES — 21 St Annes Road West, Lytham St Annes, Lancashire FY8 1SB. (0253) 712224
NOTTINGHAM — 4 Regent Street, Nottingham NG1 5BQ. (0602) 508833
SHEFFIELD — 1 St James' Row, Sheffield S1 1WZ. (0742) 728728
SHREWSBURY — 10 High Street, Shrewsbury, Shropshire SY1 1SP. (0743) 272183
YORK — Bell Hall, Escrick, York YO4 6HL. (0904) 87531

FINE ART
AUCTIONEERS & VALUERS

AYLSHAM SALEROOMS

SALES OF
★ ANTIQUES (3 WEEKLY)
★ PICTURES (BI-MONTHLY)
★ BOOKS (QUARTERLY)
WEEKLY HOUSEHOLD FURNITURE ETC

AYLSHAM (0263) 733195
8 MARKET PLACE, AYLSHAM, NORFOLK NR11 6EH

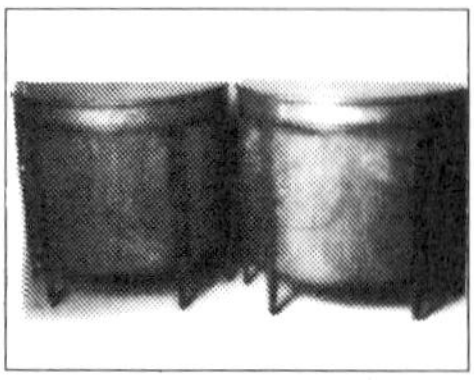

Pair of Sheraton Commodes sold at Aylsham Salerooms for £135,000

G. A. KEY

VALUATIONS FOR SALE INSURANCE & PROBATE PURPOSES

MORGAN EVANS & CO LTD.

GAERWEN, ANGLESEY NORTH WALES

Monthly Sales of Antique Furniture, Collectables and Paintings. (Saleroom 1)
Fortnightly Sales of Household and General Goods. (Saleroom 2)

Head Office: 30 Church Street, Llangefni Anglesey. (0248) 723303
Saleroom: (0248) 77582 Fax: (0248) 750146

Established 1846
Monthly Specialist Sales

RUSSELL, BALDWIN & BRIG

FURNITURE
WORKS of ART
PORCELAIN & POTTERY
SILVER
PEWTER
CLOCKS
MUSICAL BOXES
BRONZES
BOOKS and PICTURES
BYGONES
ORIENTAL CARPETS

VALUATIONS for all purposes carried out by our qualified staff.
SALES by AUCTION of the contents of Town and Country Houses conducted throughout th
West Midlands and Wales
Enquiries to: The Fine Art Saleroom, Ryelands Rd. Leominster, Herefordshire. HR6 8NZ (0568)61

Gilding's

◆AUCTIONEERS AND VALUERS◆

★ Regular Fine Art, Antique and Specialist Sales.
★ Fortnightly Victoriana and Collectable Sales.
★ Valuations for Insurance, Probate, and Family Division.
★ Confidential Valuation service in your own home.
★ Specialists available at all times, for free verbal Valuations and Consultations.
★ From a single item to a full house clearance.

A comprehensive service to suit your needs.

Roman Way, Market Harborough, Leicestershire, LE16 7PQ
Telephone: (0858) 410414

uctioneers
the Midlands

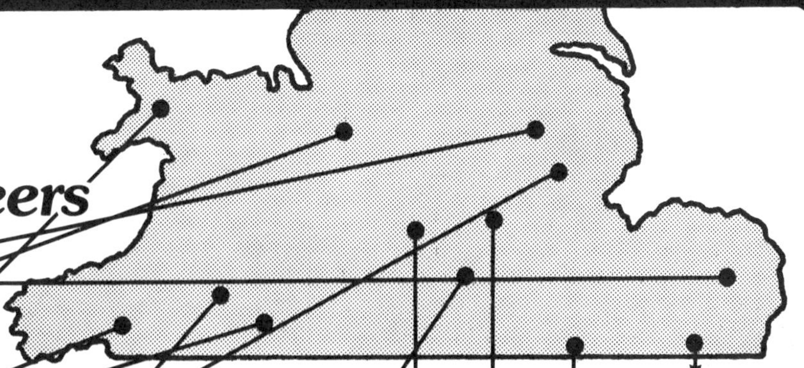

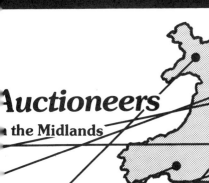

AUCTIONEERS

CUMBRIA AUCTION ROOMS
Fine Art, Antiques and Furniture Auctioneers and Valuers
Regular Catalogue Sales of Antiques and Works of Art
Weekly Sales of General Furniture and Effects
12 LOWTHER STREET, CARLISLE, CUMBRIA CA3 8DA
Telephone: Carlisle (0228) 25259

Anderson & Garland
The Fine Art Sale Rooms
Marlborough House, Marlborough Crescent
Newcastle upon Tyne NE1 4EE
Telephone: (091 232) 6278

Robert I. **Heyes** & ASSOCIATES
Fine Art Auctioneers and Valuers
WE OFFER A COMPLETE SERVICE THROUGHOUT THE NORTH WEST
Valuations for Probate and Insurance
Regular Specialist Auctions
Complete Contents Cleared
Hatton Buildings
Lightfoot Street
Chester
Tel (0244) 328941

A.E. Dowse & Son Sheffield
AUCTION CALENDAR
SPECIALIST AUCTIONS
Diecast, Tin Plate and Collectors' Toys, Stamps, Coins, Postcards and Cigarette Cards
QUARTERLY AUCTIONS
Fine Art and Antiques
MONTHLY AUCTIONS
General Antiques and Collectors' Items
FORTNIGHTLY AUCTIONS
Shipping Goods, Bric-a-brac, Modern Furniture and Effects
FINE ART AND ANTIQUE AUCTIONEERS
A.E. DOWSE & SON, CORNWALL GALLERIES SCOTLAND STREET, SHEFFIELD TEL: (0742) 725858

Lithgow Sons & Partners
(Established 1868)
North East Auctioneers
Antique House
Station Road, Stokesley
Middlesbrough
Cleveland TS9 7AB
Tel: 0642 710158
Fax: 0642 712641

H.C.CHAPMAN & SON
Chartered Surveyors **Established 1903**
MEMBERS OF THE SOCIETY OF FINE ART AUCTIONEERS
INDEPENDENT AUCTIONEERS & VALUERS
offering
MONTHLY SALES OF FINE ART & ANTIQUES
SALES EVERY WEEK OF VICTORIAN AND LATER HOUSEHOLD FURNISHINGS & COLLECTABLES
VALUATIONS FOR INSURANCE, PROBATE & FAMILY DIVISION
H.C.CHAPMAN & SON
Estate Office & Salerooms:
The Auction Mart, North St.
Tel: Scarborough (0723) 372424

ANDREW.
HILDITCH & Son Ltd
T. Spencer Andrew
Auctioneers, Valuers Surveyors.
Hanover House
1A, The Square, Sandbach
Tel: (0270) 767246, 762048
SALE EVERY WEDNESDAY
FINE ART AND ANTIQUE AUCTIONS

Boulton & Cooper Ltd
Founded in 1801
Fine Art Auctioneers
Estate Agents
Auctioneers
SOFAA
St. Michael's House, Market Place
Malton, North Yorkshire
Tel: (0653) 692151

uctioneers

;cotland and the North of England

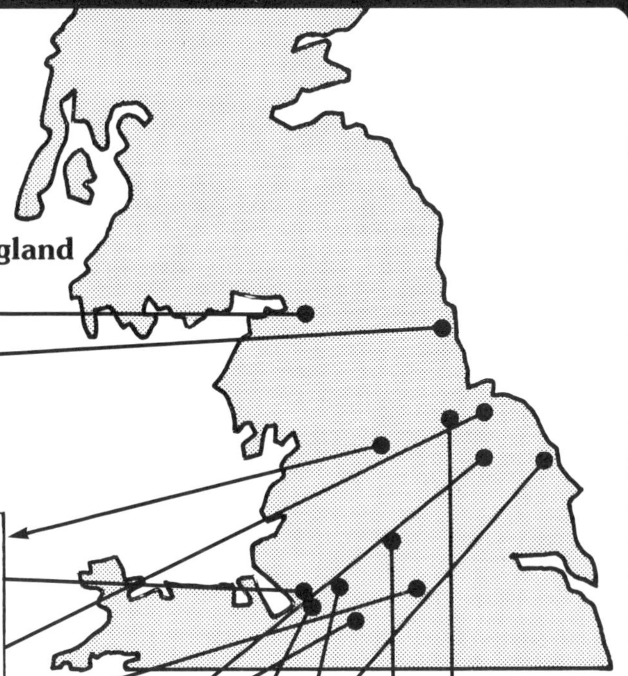

Tennants
of Yorkshire

e are a third generation family business and hold fortnightly ›0,000—£70,000 non-catalogue Saturday Sales at our Middleham aleroom of Antique and Later Residual House Contents. Important -annual Catalogue Sales are held at our Richmond Saleroom.

'e clear entire estates and smaller consignments, from throughout the U.K., and look forward to being of service to you.

All enquiries to:
27 Market Place, Leyburn, North Yorkshire, DL8 5AS
Telephone: Wensleydale (0969) 23780

Thomas Watson & Son
Est 1840

Fine Art – Chattels
Auctioneers – Valuers
NORTHUMBERLAND STREET
DARLINGTON DL3 7HJ
TEL. No. (0325) 462555

J R Parkinson Son and Hamer Auctions
Auctioneers
Fine Art, Antique & Modern Furnishings
THE AUCTION ROOMS, ROCHDALE ROAD (KERSHAW STREET), BURY, LANCS.
Tel: (061) 761 1612 & 761 7372
Fax: (061) 762 9310

Wright-Manley
Beeston Sales Centre, Near Tarporley, Cheshire CW6 9NJ
legular Furniture and Fine Art Sales
Fortnightly Collective Sales of Antique and Modern Furniture
Information: Gerald Tilston
Tel: (0829) 260318

Andrew Hartley Fine Arts
Victoria Hall Salerooms
Little Lane, Ilkley, West Yorkshire LS29 8EA
(Tel 0943 816363)

Independent
Furniture and Fine Arts Auctioneers for three generations. Now fully extended and computerised premises with two salerooms and carefully graded general and specialist sales every week.

DIRECTORY OF SPECIALISTS

This directory is in no way complete. If you wish to be included in next year's directory or if you have a change of address or telephone number, please could you inform us by April 1st 1991. Entries will be repeated in subsequent editions unless we are requested otherwise. Finally we would advise readers to make contact by telephone before a visit, therefore avoiding a wasted journey, which nowadays is both time consuming and expensive.
Any entry followed by (R) denotes a specialist who undertakes restoration work.

ANTIQUITIES DEALERS

London

Astarte Gallery,
Britannia Hotel, Grosvenor Square, W1
Tel: 071-409 1875

City Forum Auctions,
108 Belsize Avenue, NW3
Tel: 071-433 1305

Charles Ede,
37 Brook Street, W1
Tel: 071-493 4944

Faustus Fine Art,
Upper Gallery, 90 Jermyn Street, SW1
Tel: 071-930 1864

Diana Foley,
L 18-21 Grays in the Mews, Davies Mews, W1

Hadji Baba,
36 Davies Street, W1
Tel: 071-499 9363/9384

Thomas Howard Sneyd,
35 Furscroft, George Street, W1
Tel: 071-723 1976

Khalili Gallery,
15c Clifford Street, Bond Street, W1
Tel: 071-734 40202

Jonathan Mankowitz,
C 29 Grays in the Mews, Davies Street, W1

C J Martin,
85 The Vale, Southgate, N14
Tel: 081-882 1509

Nigel Mills,
51 Crescent Road, South Woodford, E18
Tel: 081-504 2569

Pars Antique,
H 16/17 Grays in the Mews, Davies Street, W1
Tel: 071-629 3788/081-399 8801

Simmons & Simmons,
K 37/38 Grays in the Mews, Davies Street, W1
Tel: 071-629 9321

Surena,
Grays Mews Antique Market, Davies Mews, W1
Tel: 071-493 6762

Annie Trotter and Ian Parsons,
A 10 Davies Mews, W1
Tel: 071-629 2813

Nicholas Wright,
42A Christchurch Avenue, NW6
Tel: 081-459 7123

Dorset

Centurion Coins,
Stour House, 11 Stour Road, Christchurch
Tel: (0202) 478592/474462

Glos

Brian L Carter,
25 Park Street, Cirencester
Tel: (045 36) 6719

Hants

Phil Goodwin,
3 Apollo Drive, Crookhorn, Portsmouth
Tel: (0705) 266866/452001

Michael Harrison,
Truelocke Antiques,
109 High Street, Odiham
Tel: (025671) 2387

Herts

David Miller,
51 Carlisle Avenue, St Albans
Tel: (0727) 52412

Kent

C J Denton,
PO Box 25, Orpington
Tel: (0689) 73690

Lancs

H & M J Burke,
Old Packet House Building, South Worsley

Middx

M & H Kashden,
19 The Lawns, Pinner
Tel: 081-421 3568

Somerset

Fox & Co,
30 Princes Street, Yeovil
Tel: (0935) 72323

Sussex

Agora,
18 Regent Arcade, East Street, Brighton
Tel: (0273) 26663

Yorks

Wilton House Gallery,
95 Market Street, Pocklington
Tel: (07592) 4858

ARCHITECTURAL ANTIQUES

London

Antique Fireplace Warehouse,
194-196 Battersea Park Road, SW11
Tel: 071-627 1410

Nigel Bartlett,
67 St Thomas Street, SE1
Tel: 071-378 7895

H Crowther Ltd,
Garden Leadwork (R),
5 Chiswick High Road, W4
Tel: 081-994 2326

Davis & Davis,
Architectural Antiques, Arch 266, Urlwin Street, Camberwell
SE5 0NF
Tel: 071-703 6525

Fortress,
23 Canonbury Lane, Islington, N1
Tel: 071-359 5875

Lassco,
Market Street, EC2
Tel: 071-739 0448

Lamont Antiques,
151 Tower Bridge Road, SE1
Tel: 071-403 0126

Miles D'Agar Antiques,
533 Kings Road, SW10
Tel: 071-352 6143

H W Poulter & Son,
279 Fulham Road, SW10
Tel: 071-352 7268

Westland Pilkington Antiques,
The Clergy House, Mark Street, EC2
Tel: 071-739 8094

Avon

David J Bridgwater,
14 Fountain Buildings, Lansdown Road, Bath
Tel: (0225) 69288/63652

Nigel Busek,
56 Stokes Croft, Bristol
Tel: (0272) 424257

Robert Mills,
Unit 3, Satelite Business Park, Blackswarth Road, Redfield, Bristol
Tel: (0272) 556542

Walcot Reclamation,
108 Walcot Street, Bath
Tel: (0225) 444404

Berks

The Fire Place (Hungerford) Ltd,
Old Fire Station, Charnham Street, Hungerford
Tel: (0488) 83420

Cheshire

Nostalgia,
61 Shaw Heath, Stockport
Tel: 061-477 7706

Cumbria

The Holme Firth Company,
Holme Mill, Holme, Nr. Carnforth
Tel: (0524) 781423

Derbyshire

Havenplan's Architectural Emporium,
The Old Station, Station Road, Killamarsh, Nr. Sheffield
Tel: (0742) 489972

Devon

Architectural Antiques,
Westley, Alswear Old Road, South Molton
Tel: (076 95) 3342

Ashburton Marbles,
Englands Antique Fireplaces,
6 West Street, Ashburton
Tel: (0364) 53189

Bellevue House Interiors,
Fort House, 36 East Street, South Molton
Tel: (07695) 3761

Cantabrian Antiques,
16 Park Street, Lynton
Tel: (0598) 53282

Dorset

Talisman Antiques,
The Old Brewery, Wyke, Gillingham
Tel: (074 76) 4423

Glos

Architectural Heritage,
Taddington Manor, Taddington, Nr. Cutsdean, Cheltenham
Tel: (0386) 73414

Hayes & Newby,
The Pit, 70 Hare Lane, Gloucester
Tel: (0452) 31145

Gt Manchester

Antique Fireplaces,
1090 Stockport Road, Levenshulme
Tel: 061-431 8075

Hants

Glover & Stacey Ltd,
Malthouse Premises, Kingsley, Nr Bordon
Tel: (042 03) 5754 or evenings (0420) 89067

Hereford & Worcester

Bailey's Architectural Antiques,
The Engine Shed, Ashburton Industrial Estate, Ross-on-Wye
Tel: (0989) 63015

Lancs

James Cook,
Barn House, Wigan Road, Cuerden, Preston
Tel: (0772) 321390

W J Cowell & Sons,
Church Hill House, Durdon Lane, Broughton, Preston
Tel: (0772) 862034

Leics

Britains Heritage,
Shaftesbury Hall, 3 Holy Bones, Leicester
Tel: (0533) 519592

Middx

Crowther of Syon Lodge,
London Road, Isleworth
Tel: 081-560 7978/7985

Oxon

Oxford Architectural Antiques
The Old Depot, Nelson Street, Jericho, Oxford
Tel: (0865) 53310

Shropshire

Architectural Antiques,
140 Corve Street, Ludlow
Tel: (0584) 6207

Somerset

Wells Reclamation Company,
The Old Cider Farm, Wells Road Coxley, Nr. Wells, Somerset
Tel: (0749) 77087 or evenings an weekends (0749) 77484

Sussex

Brighton Architectural Salvage,
33 Gloucester Road, Brighton
Tel: (0273) 681656

Yorks

Andy Thornton Architectural Antiques Ltd,
Ainleys Industrial Estate, Ellan
Tel: (0422) 75595

Cupid Architectural,
West Royd Cottage, West Royd Avenue, King Cross, Halifax
Tel: (0422) 63585

The Main Pine Co,
Grangewood, Green Hamerton, York
Tel: (0423) 330451

Manor House Fireplaces,
Bankgate Mills, Bankgate,
Slaithwaite, Huddersfield
Tel: (0484) 846055

Robert Aagaard Ltd,
Frogmire House, Stockwell Road,
Knaresborough
Tel: (0423) 864805

Wilts

Relic Antiques,
Brillscote Farm, Lea, Nr
Malmesbury
Tel: (0666) 822332

Wales

M & A Main Architectural
Antiques (R),
The Old Smithy, Cerrig-y-
Drudion, Corwen
Tel: (049 082) 491

Victorian Fireplaces (Simon
Priestley),
Saturdays only: Ground Floor,
Cardiff Antique Centre, 69-71 St
Mary Street, Cardiff
Tel: (0222) 30970
Any other time: Tel: (0222) 26049

ARMS & MILITARIA

London

Armada Antiques,
Gray's Antique Market, 58 Davies
Street
Tel: 071-499 1087

The Armoury of St James's,
17 Piccadilly Arcade, SW1
Tel: 071-493 5082

Colin C Bowdell,
Gray's Antique Market, 58 Davies
Street
Tel: 071-408 0176

Michael C German,
38b Kensington Church Street, W8
Tel: 071-937 2771

Rubens,
44 Honor Oak Park, Brockley
Tel: 081-291 1786

Tradition,
5a Shepherd Street, W1
Tel: 071-493 7452

Avon

Chris Grimes Militaria,
13 Lower Park Row, Bristol
Tel: (0272) 298205

Co. Durham

Matched Pairs Ltd,
20 High Street, Spennymoor
Tel: (0388) 819500 or (0740) 20667
evenings

Glos

HQ 84,
82-84 Southgate Street, Gloucester
Tel: (0452) 27716

Hants

Romsey Medal Centre,
112 The Hundred, Romsey
Tel: (0794) 512069

Lancs

Rod Akeroyd,
Woodcroft, 38 Todd Lane North,
Lostock Hall, Preston
Tel: (0772) 39321

Norfolk

Anglian Arms,
Market House, Harleston
Tel: (0379) 852184 or (09867) 5115

Northumberland

David A Oliver,
Pennystane, Church Lane,
Thropton, Nr. Morpeth
Tel: (0669) 20618

Surrey

Casque & Gauntlet Antiques,
55/59 Badshot Lea Road, Badshot
Lea, Farnham
Tel: (0252) 20745

Alan S Cook,
132 Rydens Road, Walton-on-
Thames
Tel: (0860) 334035
(0932) 228328 home

West Street Antiques,
63 West Street, Dorking
Tel: (0306) 883487

Sussex

Military Antiques (by
appointment only),
42 Janes Lane, Burgess Hill
Tel: (044 46) 3516 & 43088

Michael Miller,
The Lamb, 8 Cuckfield Road,
Hurstpierpoint
Tel: (0273) 834567

Wallis & Wallis,
West Street Galleries, Lewes
Tel: (0273) 480208

George Weiner,
2 Market Street, The Lanes,
Brighton
Tel: (0273) 729948

Worthing Gunshop,
80 Broadwater Street West,
Worthing
Tel: (0903) 37378

Warwickshire

Arbour Antiques Ltd,
Poet's Arbour, Sheep Street,
Stratford-upon-Avon
Tel: (0789) 293453

Yorks

The Antique & Bargain Store,
6 Sunny Bar, Doncaster
Tel: (0302) 344857

The Antique & Bargain Store,
20 Copley Road, Doncaster
Tel: (0302) 344857

The Antique Shop,
226 Harrogate Road, Leeds
Tel: (0532) 681785

Andrew Spencer Bottomley (by
appointment only),
The Coach House, Thongs Bridge,
Holmfirth
Tel: (0484) 685234

Wales

Hermitage Antiques,
10 West Street, Fishguard
Tel: (0348) 873037

ART DECO & ART NOUVEAU

London

Baptista Arts,
Stand D2/3, Chenil Galleries,
183 King's Road, SW3
Tel: 071-352 5799

Bizarre,
24 Church Street, NW8
Tel: 071-724 1305

Butler & Wilson,
189 Fulham Road, SW3
Tel: 071-352 3045

Chilton,
Stand A11/12, Chenil Galleries,
181-183 King's Road, SW3
Tel: 071-352 2163

Church Street Antiques,
8 Church Street, NW8
Tel: 071-723 7415

T Coakley,
Stand D13, Chenil Galleries,
181-183 King's Road, SW3
Tel: 071-351 2914

Cobra & Bellamy,
149 Sloane Street, SW1
Tel: 071-730 2823

Editions Graphiques Gallery,
3 Clifford Street, W1
Tel: 071-734 3944

The Facade,
196 Westbourne Grove, W11
Tel: 071-727 2159

Galerie 1900,
267 Camden High Street, NW1
Tel: 071-485 1001

Gallery '25,
4 Halkin Arcade, Motcomb Street,
SW1
Tel: 071-235 5178

Patrick & Susan Gould,
L17, Grays Mews, Davies Mews,
W1
Tel: 071-408 0129

Jazzy Art Deco,
67 Camden Road, Camden Town,
NW1
Tel: 071-267 3342/081-960 8988

John Jesse and Irina Laski Ltd,
160 Kensington Church Street, W8
Tel: 071-229 0312

Helen Lane,
212 Camden High Street, NW1
Tel: 071-267 6588

Lewis M Kaplan Associates Ltd,
50 Fulham Road, SW3
Tel: 071-589 3108

The Lamp Gallery,
355 New Kings Road, SW6
Tel: 071-736 6188

John & Diana Lyons Gallery,
47-49 Mill Lane, West Hampstead,
NW6
Tel: 071-794 3537

P & J,
K13-J28 Grays Mews, Davies
Mews, W1
Tel: 071-499 2719

Pruskin Gallery,
73 Kensington Church Street, W8
Tel: 071-937 1994

Paul Reeves,
32B Kensington Church Street,
W8
Tel: 071-937 1594

Simon Tracy,
18 Church Street, NW8
Tel: 071-724 5890

West Hampstead Trade Centre,
Blackburn Road, NW6
Tel: 071-328 2221

Ziggurat,
J 22 Grays Mews, Davies Mews,
W1
Tel: 071-629 3788

Berks

Lupin Antiques,
134 Peascod Street, Windsor
Tel: (0753) 856244

Cornwall

Judith Gunn,
25 Fore Street, Fowey, Cornwall
Tel: (072683) 2595

Dorset

Michael Howell,
912-914 Christchurch Road,
Boscombe, Bournemouth
Tel: (0202) 425435

Gt Manchester

AS Antiques,
26 Broad Street, Salford
Tel: 061-737 5938

Bizarre,
Unit 19, The Corn Exchange Hall,
Corn Exchange Buildings,
Hanging Ditch, Manchester
Tel: 061-835 2255/061-998 6106

Herts

Ziggurat,
2 Morley Cottages, Chells Manor,
Stevenage
Tel: (0438) 727084

Lancs

Decoroy,
105 New Hall Lane, Preston
Tel: (0772) 705371

Leics

Birches Antique Shop,
15 Francis Street, Stoneygate,
Leicester
Tel: (0533) 703235

Merseyside

Osiris Antiques (Paul & Carol
Wood),
24 Princes Street, Southport
Tel: (0704) 60418
(Closed Tues & Thurs)

Shropshire

Antiques on the Square,
2 Sandford Court, Church Stretton
Tel: (0694) 724111

Expressions,
17 Princess Street, Shrewsbury
Tel: (0743) 51731

Somerset

Decoration, Rosamund Morgan,
Taunton Antique Centre, Silver
Street, Taunton, every Monday
Tel: (0460) 40958 evenings

Suffolk

Victoria & Alan Waine,
Country Collectables, The Old
Surgery, Hall Street, Long Melford
Tel: (0787) 310140

Surrey

Galerie 39,
39 Kew Road, Richmond
Tel: 081-948 1633 & 3337

Peter & Debbie Gooday,
20 Richmond Hill, Richmond
Tel: 081-940 8652

Sussex

Armstrong-Davis Gallery,
The Square, Arundel
Tel: (0903) 882752

Le Jazz Hot,
14 Prince Albert Street, Brighton
Tel: (0273) 206091

Warwickshire

Castle Antiques,
1 Mill Street, Warwick
Tel: (0926) 498068

Yorks

Carlton Gallery,
60A Middle Street, Driffield
Tel: (0482) 443954

Dragon Antiques,
10 Dragon Road, Harrogate
Tel: (0423) 62037

Mr Muir Hewitt,
Halifax Antiques Centre, Queens
Road/Gibbet Street, Halifax
Tel: (0422) 366657

Scotland

The Rendezvous Gallery,
100 Forest Avenue, Aberdeen
Tel: (0224) 323247

Wales

Paul Gibbs Antiques,
25 Castle Street, Conway
Tel: (0492) 593429

West Midlands

Smithsonia,
15/16 Picadilly Arcade, New
Street, Birmingham
Tel: 021-643 8405

BOOKS

Staffs

The Old House,
47 High Street, Kinver
Tel: (0384) 872940

BOXES, TREEN & WOODEN OBJECTS

London

Simon Castle,
38B Kensington Church Street, W8
Tel: 071-937 2268

Halcyon Days,
14 Brook Street, W1
Tel: 071-629 8811

Alistair Sampson Antiques,
156 Brompton Road, SW3
Tel: 071-589 5272

Berks

Mostly Boxes,
92-52b High Street, Eton
Tel: (0753) 858470

Charles Toller,
Hall House, 20 High Street, Datchet
Tel: (0753) 42903

Bucks

A & E Foster (by appointment only),
Little Heysham, Forge Road, Naphill
Tel: (024 024) 2024

Hants

Gerald Austin Antiques,
2A Andover Road, Winchester
Tel: (0962) 69824 Ext 2

House of Antiques,
4 College Street, Petersfield
Tel: (0730) 62172

Millers of Chelsea,
Netherbrook House, 86 Christchurch Road, Ringwood
Tel: (0425) 472068

Leics

Stable Antiques,
35 Main Street, Osgathorpe
Tel: (0530) 222463

Oxon

Key Antiques,
11 Horse Fair, Chipping Norton
Tel: (0608) 643777

Sussex

Michael Wakelin & Helen Linfield,
10 New Street, Petworth
Tel: (0798) 42417

CAMERAS

London

Jessop Classic Photographica,
67 Great Russell Street, WC1
Tel: 071-831 3640

Vintage Cameras Ltd,
254/256 Kirkdale, Sydenham
Tel: 081-778 5416 & 5841

Essex

Cliff Latford,
91A East Hill, Colchester
Tel: (0206) 564474

Herts

P Coombs,
87 Gills Hill Lane, Radlett
Tel: (09276) 6949

CARPETS

London

David Black Oriental Carpets,
96 Portland Road, Holland Park, W11
Tel: 071-727 2566

Hindustan Carpets Ltd,
B Block, 53/79 Highgate Road, NW5
Tel: 071-485 7766

Mayfair Carpet Gallery,
6-8 Old Bond Street, W1
Tel: 071-493 0126/7

Swillet Rug Restorations (R),
(Warehouse), 8 Albert Wharf,
17 New Wharf Road, N1
Tel: 071-833 3529

Vigo Carpet Gallery,
6a Vigo Street, W1
Tel: 071-439 6971

Vigo Sternberg Galleries,
37 South Audley Street, W1
Tel: 071-629 8307

Bucks

Swillet Rug Restorations (R),
22 Lodge Lane, Chalfont-St-Giles
Tel: (024 04) 4776

Devon

Sheelagh Lewis,
5A High Street, Totnes
Tel: (0803) 863024

Dorset

J L Arditti (Old Oriental Rugs),
88 Bargates, Christchurch
Tel: (0202) 485414

Essex

Robert Bailey (by appointment only),
1 Roll Gardens, Gants Hill
Tel: 081-550 5435

Glos

Thornborough Galleries,
28 Gloucester Street, Cirencester
Tel: (0285) 2055

Kent

Persian Rugs, R & G King,
Ulnes Farm, Mathews Lane, W Peckham, Hadlow
Tel: (0732) 850228

Somerset

M & A Lewis,
Oriental Carpets & Rugs, 8 North Street, Wellington
Tel: (082 347) 7430

Sussex

Lindfield Galleries,
59 High Street, Lindfield
Tel: (04447) 3817

Yorks

Gordon Reece Gallery,
Finkle Street, Knaresborough
Tel: (0423) 866219/866502

London House Oriental Rugs & Carpets,
London House, High Street, Boston Spa By Wetherby
Tel: (0937) 845123

Omar (Harrogate) Ltd,
8 Crescent Road, Harrogate
Tel: (0423) 503675

Scotland

Whytock & Reid,
Sunbury House, Belford Mews, Edinburgh
Tel: 031-226 4911

CLOCKS WATCHES & BAROMETERS

London

Asprey PLC,
165-169 New Bond Street, W1
Tel: 071-493 6767

Bobinet Ltd,
102 Mount Street, W1
Tel: 071-408 0333/4

Aubrey Brocklehurst,
124 Cromwell Road, SW7
Tel: 071-373 0319

Camerer Cuss & Co,
17 Ryder Street, St James's, SW1
Tel: 071-930 1941

Chelsea Clocks,
479 Fulham Road
Tel: 071-731 5704

Also at:
69 Portobello Road
Tel: 071-727 5417

City Clocks,
31 Amwell Street, EC1
Tel: 071-278 1154

The Clock Clinic Ltd,
85 Lower Richmond Road, SW15
Tel: 081-788 1407

Philip & Bernard Dombey,
174 Kensington Church Street, W8
Tel: 071-229 7100

Gerald Mathias (R),
R5/8 Antiquarius, 136 King's Road, SW3
Tel: 071-351 0484

North London Clock Shop Ltd (R),
72 Highbury Park, N5
Tel: 071-226 1609

Pieces of Time,
1-7 Davies Mews, W1
Tel: 071-629 2422

R E Rose, FBHI,
731 Sidcup Road, Eltham, SE9
Tel: 081-859 4754

Strike One (Islington) Ltd,
51 Camden Passage
Tel: 071-226 9709

Temple Brooks,
12 Mill Lane, NW6
Tel: 081-452 9696

Avon

Smith & Bottrill,
The Clock House, 17 George Street, Bath
Tel: (0225) 22809

Berks

Richard Barder Antiques,
Crossways House, Near Newbury
Tel: (0635) 200295

Medalcrest Ltd,
Charnham House, Charnham Street, Hungerford
Tel: (0488) 84157

Times Past Antiques Ltd,
59 High Street, Eton
Tel: (0753) 857018

Bucks

The Guild Room,
The Lee, Great Missenden
Tel: (024 020) 463

The Old Town Clock Shop,
1-3 Aylesbury End, Beaconsfield
Tel: (049 46) 6783

Cambs

Rodney T Firmin,
16 Magdalene Street, Cambridge
Tel: (0223) 67372

Cheshire

Peter Bosson Antiques,
10B Swan Street, Wilmslow
Tel: (0625) 525250 & 527857

Coppelia Antiques
Holford Lodge, Plumley Moor Road, Plumley
Tel: (056 581) 2197

Derek Rayment Antiques (R),
Orchard House, Barton Road, Barton, Nr Farndon
Tel: (0829) 270429

Cumbria

Don Burns,
The Square, Ireby, Carlisle
Tel: (096 57) 477

Derbyshire

Derby Clocks,
974 London Road, Derby
Tel: (0332) 74996

Derbyshire Clocks,
104 High Street West, Glossop
Tel: (045 74) 62677

D J Mitchell,
Temple Antiques, Glenwood Lodge, Temple Walk, Matlock Bath
Tel: (0629) 4253

Devon

Musgrave Bickford Antiques,
6 The Village, Wembworthy, Chulmleigh
Tel: (083 78) 3473

Dorset

Good Hope Antiques,
2 Hogshill Street, Beaminster
Tel: (0308) 862119

Tom Tribe & Son,
Bridge Street, Sturminster Newton
Tel: (0258) 72311

Essex

It's About Time (R),
863 London Road, Westcliff-on-Sea
Tel: (0702) 72574 & 205204

Littlebury Antiques,
58/60 Fairycroft Road, Saffron Walden
Tel: (0799) 27961

Mark Marchant,
Market Square, Coggeshall
Tel: (0376) 61188

Tempus Fugit (appointment only),
c/o Trinity House, Trinity Street, Halstead
Tel: (0787) 475409

Trinity Clocks,
26 Trinity Street, Colchester
Tel: (0206) 46458

Glos

J & M Bristow Antiques,
28 Long Street, Tetbury
Tel: (0666) 52222

Gerard Campbell,
Maple House, Market Place, Lechlade
Tel: (0367) 52267

Montpellier Clocks Ltd,
13 Rotunda Terrace, Montpellier Street, Cheltenham
Tel: (0242) 242178

Colin Elliott,
4 Great Norwood Street, Cheltenham
Tel: (0242) 528590

Saxton House Gallery,
High Street, Chipping Camden
Tel: (0386) 840278

Southbar Antiques,
Digbeth Street, Stow-on-the-Wold
Tel: (0451) 30236

Hants

Charles Antiques,
101 The Hundred, Romsey
Tel: (0794) 512885

Evans & Evans,
40 West Street, Alresford
Tel: (096 273) 2170

Gerald E Marsh,
32A The Square, Winchester
Tel: (0962) 54505

Hereford & Worcester

G & V Taylor Antiques,
Winforton Court, Winforton
Tel: (054 46) 226

Herts

Country Clocks (R),
3 Pendley Bridge Cottages, Tring Station, Tring
Tel: (044 282) 5090

John de Haan,
12A Seaforth Drive, Waltham Cross
Tel: (0992) 763111 & (0920) 2534

Isle of Wight
Museum of Clocks,
Alum Bay
Tel: (0983) 754193

Kent
John Chawner Antiques,
44 Chatham Hill, Chatham
Tel: (0634) 811147 & (0843) 43309

Hadlow Antiques,
No. 1 The Pantiles, Tunbridge Wells
Tel: (0892) 29858

Henry Hall Antique Clocks,
19 Market Square, Westerham
Tel: (0959) 62200

The Old Clock Shop,
63 High Street, West Malling
Tel: (0732) 843246

Derek Roberts Antiques,
24/25 Shipbourne Road, Tonbridge
Tel: (0732) 358986

Malcolm G Styles (R),
Tunbridge Wells
Tel: (0892) 30699

Anthony Woodburn,
Orchard House, Leigh,
Nr Tonbridge
Tel: (0732) 832258

Lancs
Kenneth Weigh, Signwriting & Numbering,
9 Links Road, Blackpool
Tel: (0253) 52097

Leics
Bonington Clocks,
12 Market Place, Kegworth
Tel: (05097) 2900

Clock Replacements (R),
239 Welford Road, Leicester
Tel: (0533) 706190

G K Hadfield (R),
Blackbrook Hill House, Tickow Lane, Shepshed
Tel: (0509) 503014

C Lowe & Sons Ltd (R),
37-40 Churchgate, Loughborough
Tel: (0509) 217876

Lincs
George Clocks,
3 Pinfold Lane, Ruskington
Tel: (0526) 832200

Merseyside
T Brown Horological Restorers (R),
12 London Road, Liverpool 3
Tel: 051-709 4048

Norfolk
Delawood Antiques & Clock Restoration (R),
10 Westgate, Hunstanton
Tel: (048 53) 2903

Norfolk Polyphon & Clock Centre,
Wood Farm, Bawdeswell, Nr. East Dereham
Tel: (036 288) 230

Oxon
Laurie Leigh Antiques,
36 High Street, Oxford
Tel: (0865) 244197

Telling Time,
57 North Street, Thame
Tel: (084 421) 3007

Witney Antiques,
96-98 Corn Street, Witney
Tel: (0993) 3902

Somerset
Michael & Judith Avis (R),
The Barton, Simonsbath,
Minehead
Tel: (064383) 428

Shelagh Berryman,
15 The Market Place, Wells
Tel: (0749) 76203

Bernard G House,
Mitre Antiques, 13 Market Place, Wells
Tel: (0749) 72607

Edward A Nowell,
21-23 Market Place, Wells
Tel: (0749) 72415

Matthew Willis,
88 Bove Town, Glastonbury
Tel: (0458) 32103

Suffolk
AN Antiques,
Home Farm, South Green, Eye
Tel: (0379) 870367

Billivant Antiques (R),
White Gates, Elmswell Road,
Great Ashfield
Tel: (0359) 40040

R L Fryatt, Grad BHI (R),
10 Amberley Court, Oulton Broad,
Lowestoft
Tel: (0502) 560869

Surrey
BS Antiques,
39 Bridge Road, East Molesey
Tel: 081-941 1812

The Clock Shop,
64 Church Street, Weybridge
Tel: (0932) 4047 & 55503

Roger A Davis, Antiquarian Horologist,
19 Dorking Road, Great Bookham
Tel: (0372) 57655 & 53167

Douglas Dawes (by appointment only),
Antique Clocks, Linfield
Tel: (0342) 834965

Hampton Court Antiques,
75 Bridge Road, East Molesey
Tel: 081-941 6398

E Hollander Ltd,
The Dutch House, Horsham Road,
South Holmwood, Dorking
Tel: (0306) 888921

Horological Workshops,
204 Worplesdon Road, Guildford
Tel: (0483) 576496

R Saunders Antiques,
71 Queens Road, Weybridge
Tel: (0932) 42601

Geoffrey Stevens,
26-28 Church Road, Guildford
Tel: (0483) 504075

Surrey Clock Centre,
3 Lower Street, Haslemere
Tel: (0428) 4547

Sussex
Adrian Alan Ltd,
4 Frederick Place, Brighton
Tel: (0273) 25277

Michael J O'Neill,
Swan House, Market Square,
Petworth
Tel: (0798) 42616

Sam Orr Antique Clocks,
36 High Street, Hurstpierpoint
Tel: (0273) 832081

David & Sarah Pullen,
29/31 Sea Road, Bexhill-on-Sea
Tel: (0424) 222035

R W Wren, MBHI (R),
4 The Ridge, Hastings
Tel: (0424) 445248

Tyne & Wear
Hazel Cottage Clocks,
Eachwick, Dalton, Newcastle on Tyne
Tel: (06614) 2415

T P Rooney, Grad BHI (R),
191 Sunderland Road, Harton
Village, South Shields
Tel: 091-456 2950

Warwickshire
The Grandfather Clock Shop,
2 Bondgate House, Granville
Court, West Street, Shipston on Stour
Tel: (0608) 62144

Mason Antique Clocks,
Glympton House, 3 New Road,
Water Orton
Tel: (021 747) 5751

West Midlands
M Allen (R),
76A Walsall Road, Four Oaks,
Sutton Coldfield
Tel: 021-308 6117

Ashleigh House Antiques,
5 Westbourne Road, Birmingham
Tel: 021-454 6283

Osborne's (R),
91 Chester Road, New Oscott,
Sutton Coldfield
Tel: 021-355 6667

Wiltshire
Avon Antiques,
26-27 Market Street, Bradford-on-Avon
Tel: (022 16) 2052

P A Oxley,
The Old Rectory, Cherhill, Nr Calne
Tel: (0249) 816227

The Salisbury Clock Shop,
107 Exeter Street, Salisbury
Tel: (0722) 337076

Yorks
Brian Loomes,
Calf Haugh Farm, Pateley Bridge
Tel: (0423) 711163

Clocks & Gramophones,
11 Walmgate, York
Tel: (0904) 611924

The Clock Shop,
Hilltop House, Bellerby, Nr Leyburn
Tel: (0969) 22596

Haworth Antiques (R),
Harrogate Road, Huby, Nr Leeds
Tel: (0423) 74293
Also at:
26 Cold Bath Road, Harrogate
Tel: (0423) 521401

Keith Stones Grandfather Clocks,
5 Ellers Drive, Bessacarr,
Doncaster
Tel: (0302) 535258

Scotland
Browns Clocks Ltd,
203 Bath Street, Glasgow
Tel: 041-248 6760

Christopher Wood (appointment only),
Harlaw House, Kelso
Tel: (057 37) 321

DOLLS, TOYS & GAMES

London
Antique Dolls,
Stand L14, Grays Mews, W1
Tel: 071-499 6600

Dr Colin Baddiel,
Stand B24/B25, Grays Mews,
1-7 Davies Mews, W1
Tel: 071-408 1239

Jilliana Ranicar-Breese,
Martin Breese Ltd, 7A Jones
Arcade, Westbourne Grove (Sats only). Tel: 071-727 9378

Stuart Cropper,
Gray's Mews, 1-7 Davies Mews, W1
Tel: 071-499 6600

Donay Antiques,
12 Pierrepont Row, N1
Tel: 071-359 1880

Engine 'n' Tender,
19 Spring Lane, Woodside, SE25
Tel: 081-654 0386

Pete McAskie,
Stand D10-12 Basement, Grays
Mews Antiques, 1-7 Davies Mews, W1
Tel: 071-629 2813

The Dolls House Toys Ltd,
29 The Market, Covent Garden, WC2
Tel: 071-379 7243

The Singing Tree,
69 New King's Road, SW6
Tel: 071-736 4527

Yonna,
B19 Grays Mews, W1
Tel: 071-629 3644

Cornwall
Mrs Margaret Chesterton,
33 Pentewan Road, St Austell
Tel: (0726) 72926

Dorset
Hobby Horse Antiques,
29 West Allington, Bridport
Tel: (0308) 22801

Glos
Lilian Middleton's Antique Dolls' Shop & Dolls' Hospital,
Days Stable, Sheep Street,
Stow-on-the-Wold
Tel: (0451) 30381

China Doll,
31 Suffolk Parade, Cheltenham
Tel: (0242) 33164

Park House Antiques,
Park Street, Stow-on-the-Wold
Tel: (0451) 30159

Kent
Hadlow Antiques,
1 The Pantiles, Tunbridge Wells
Tel: (0892) 29858

Staffs
Multro Ltd,
10 Madeley Street, Tunstall,
Stoke-on-Trent
Tel: (0782) 813621

Surrey
Heather & Clifford Bond,
Victoriana Dolls
Tel: (073 72) 49525

Curiosity Shop,
72 Stafford Road, Wallington
Tel: 081-647 5267

Doll Shop (appointment only),
18 Richmond Hill, Richmond
Tel: 081-940 6774

Elizabeth Gant,
52 High Street, Thames Ditton
Tel: 081-398 0962

Sussex
Doll & Teddy Bear Restorer (R),
Wendy Foster, Minto, Codmore
Hill, Pulborough
Tel: (079 82) 2707

Rathbone Law,
7-9 The Arcade, Worthing
Tel: (0903) 200274

West Midlands
Woodsetton Antiques,
65 Sedgley Road, Woodsetton,
Dudley
Tel: (0384) 277918

Yorks
The Antique & Bargain Store,
6 Sunny Bar, Doncaster
Tel: (0302) 344857

The Antique & Bargain Store,
20 Copley Road, Doncaster
Tel: (0302) 344857

Andrew Clark,
12 Ingfield, Oakenshaw, Bradford
Tel: (0274) 675342

John & Simon Haley,
2 Lanehead Road, Soyland, Sowery Bridge
Tel: (0422) 822148/60434

Wales

Museum of Childhood Toys & Gift Shop,
1 Castle Street, Beaumaris, Anglesey, Gwynedd
Tel: (0248) 712498

EPHEMERA

London

Jilliana Ranicar-Breese, Martin Breese Ltd,
164 Kensington Park Road, Notting Hill Gate, W11
Tel: 071-727 9378 (by appointment only)
Also at:
7A Jones Arcade, Westbourne Grove (Sats only)
Also at:
Roger's Arcade, 65 Portobello Road (Sats only)

Gilda Conrich Antiques,
Tel: 071-226 5319
(by appointment only)

Dodo,
3 Denbigh Road, London, W11
Tel: 071-229 3132

Donay,
35 Camden Passage, N1
Tel: 071-359 1880

M & R Glendale,
Antiquarian Booksellers, 9A New Cavendish Street, W1
Tel: 071-487 5348

David Godfrey's Old Newspaper Shop,
37 Kinnerton Street, SW1
Tel: 071-235 7788

Jubilee,
1 Pierrepont Row, Camden Passage, N1
Tel: 071-607 5462

Pleasures of Past Times,
11 Cecil Court, Charing Cross Road, WC2
Tel: 071-836 1142

Danny Posner,
The Vintage Magazine Shop,
39/41 Brewer Street, W1
Tel: 071-439 8525

Avon

Michael & Jo Saffell,
3 Walcot Buildings, London Road, Bath
Tel: (0225) 315857

Bucks

Omniphil Ltd,
Germains Lodge, Fullers Hill, Chesham
Tel: (0494) 771851
Also at:
Stand 110, Gray's Antique Market, 58 Davies Street, W1
Tel: 081-629 3223

Essex

G K R Bonds Ltd,
PO Box 1, Kelvedon
Tel: (0376) 71138

Hants

Cobwebs,
78 Northam Road, Southampton
Tel: (0703) 227458

Kent

Mike Sturge,
39 Union Street, Maidstone
Tel: (0622) 54702

Notts

Neales of Nottingham,
192 Mansfield Road, Nottingham
Tel: (0602) 624141

T Vennett-Smith,
11 Nottingham Road, Gotham
Tel: (0602) 830541

Surrey

Richmond Antiquary,
28 Hill Rise, Richmond
Tel: 081-938 0583

FISHING TACKLE

Dorset

Yesterday Tackle & Books,
42 Clingan Road, Southbourne
Tel: (0202) 476586

Kent

Alan Clout,
36 Nunnery Fields, Canterbury
Tel: (0227) 455162

Sussex

N Marchant-Lane
Willow Court, Middle Street, Petworth
Tel: (0798) 43443

Scotland

Jamie Maxtone Graham,
Lyne Haugh, Lyne Station, Peebles
Tel: (07214) 304

Jess Miller,
PO Box 1, Birnam, Dunkeld, Perthshire
Tel: (03502) 522

FURNITURE

London

Asprey PLC,
165-169 New Bond Street, W1
Tel: 071-493 6767

F E A Briggs Ltd,
73 Ledbury Road, W1
Tel: 071-727 0909 & 071-221 4950

C W Buckingham,
301-303 Munster Road, SW6
Tel: 071-385 2657

Butchoff Antiques,
233 Westbourne Grove, W11
Tel: 071-221 8174

Rupert Cavendish Antiques (Biedermeir),
6-10 King Road, London, SW6
Tel: 071-731 7041/071-736 6024

John Creed Antiques Ltd,
3 & 5A Camden Passage, N1
Tel: 071-226 8867

Eldridge,
99-101 Farringdon Road, EC1
Tel: 071-837 0379 & 0370

Reindeer Antiques,
81 Kensington Church Street, W8
Tel: 071-937 3754

John Keil Ltd,
154 Brompton Road, SW3
Tel: 071-589 6454

C H Major (Antiques) Ltd,
154 Kensington Church Street, W8
Tel: 071-229 1162

Mallett & Son (Antiques) Ltd,
40 New Bond Street, W1
Tel: 071-499 7411

M & D Seligmann,
37 Kensington Church Street, W8
Tel: 071-937 0400

Michael Marriott Ltd,
588 Fulham Road, SW6
Tel: 071-736 3110

Murray Thomson Ltd,
141 Kensington Church Street, W8
Tel: 071-727 1727

Oola Boola Antiques,
166 Tower Bridge Road, SE1
Tel: 071-403 0794

Phelps Ltd,
133-135 St Margaret's Road, E Twickenham
Tel: 081-892 1778 & 7129

Alistair Sampson Antiques,
156 Brompton Road, SW3
Tel: 071-589 5272

Arthur Seager Ltd,
25a Holland Street, Kensington, W8
Tel: 071-937 3262

Stair & Co,
120 Mount Street, W1
Tel: 071-499 1784/5

Terry Antiques,
175 Junction Road, N19
Tel: 071-263 1219

William Tillman,
30 St James's Street, SW1
Tel: 071-839 2500

O F Wilson Ltd,
Queen's Elm Parade, Old Church Street, SW3
Tel: 071-352 9554

Robert Young Antiques,
68 Battersea Bridge Road, SW11
Tel: 071-228 7847

Zal Davar Antiques,
26a Munster Road, SW6
Tel: 071-736 1405 & 2559

Avon

Cottage Antiques,
The Old Post Office, Langford Place, Langford, Nr Bristol
Tel: (0934) 862597

Berks

Mary Bellis Antiques,
Charnham Close, Hungerford
Tel: (0488) 82620

Biggs of Maidenhead,
Hare Hatch Grange, Twyford
Tel: (073 522) 3281

The Old Malthouse,
Hungerford
Tel: (0488) 82209

Medalcrest Ltd,
Charnham House, Charnham Street, Hungerford
Tel: (0488) 84157

Charles Toller,
Hall House, 20 High Street, Datchet
Tel: (0753) 42903

Bucks

Jeanne Temple Antiques,
Stockwell House, 1 Stockwell Lane, Wavendon, Milton Keynes
Tel: (0908) 583597

A & E Foster (by appointment only),
Little Heysham, Forge Road, Naphill
Tel: (024 024) 2024

Lloyd Loom,
Western Turville
Tel: (0296 61) 5121 (R)

Cambs

Clover Antiques,
5-6 Soham Road, Fordham
Tel: (0638) 720250

Old School Antiques,
Chittering
Tel: (0223) 861831

Cheshire

Coppelia Antiques,
Holford Lodge, Plumley Moor Road, Plumley
Tel: (056 581) 2197

Derbyshire Antiques Ltd,
157-159 London Road South, Poynton
Tel: (0625) 873110

Christopher Howarth,
1 Chapel Road, Whaley Bridge, Stockport
Tel: (0663) 734774

Townwell House Antiques,
52 Welsh Row, Nantwich
Tel: (0270) 625953

Cornwall

Pydar Antiques & Gallery,
People's Palace, Off Pydar Street, Truro
Tel: (Michelle) (0872 51) 510485
(Newquay) (0637) 872034

Cumbria

Haughey Antiques,
Market Street, Kirkby Stephen
Tel: (0930) 71302

Fenwick Pattison,
Bowmanstead, Coniston
Tel: (0966) 41235

Shire Antiques,
The Post House, High Newton, Newton in Cartmel, Nr Grange-over-Sands
Tel: (0448) 31431

Townhead Antiques,
Newby Bridge
Tel: (0448) 31321

Jonathan Wood Antiques,
Broughton Hall, Cartmel, Grange-over-Sands
Tel: (044 854) 234

Derbyshire

Maurice Goldstone & Son,
Avenel Court, Bakewell
Tel: (062 981) 2487

Spurrier-Smith Antiques,
28B & 41 Church Street, Ashbourne
Tel: (0335) 43669 and (home) (077 389) 368

Yesterday Antiques,
6 Commercial Road, Tideswell, Nr Buxton
Tel: (0298) 871932

Devon

Robert Byles,
7 Castle Street, Bampton
Tel: (0398) 31515

Ian McBain & Sons,
Exeter Airport, Clyst Honiton, Exeter
Tel: (0392) 66261

Dorset

Dodge & Son,
28-33 Cheap Street, Sherborne
Tel: (0935) 815151

Johnsons of Sherborne Ltd,
South Street, Sherborne
Tel: (0935) 812585

Talisman Antiques,
The Old Brewery, Wyke, Gillingham
Tel: (074 76) 4423

Essex

F G Bruschweiler,
41-67 Lower Lambricks, Rayleigh
Tel: (0268) 773761

Stonehall Antiques,
Trade Warehouse, Down Hall Road, Matching Green, Nr Harlow
Tel: (0279) 731440

Glos

Baggott Church Street Ltd,
Church Street, Stow-on-the-Wold
Tel: (0451) 30370

Paul Cater,
High Street, Moreton-in-Marsh
Tel: (0608) 51888

Country Life Antiques,
Sheep Street, Stow-on-the-Wold
Tel: (0451) 30776
Also at:
Grey House, The Square, Stow-on-the-Wold
Tel: (0451) 31564

Gloucester House Antiques,
Market Place, Fairford
Tel: (0285) 712790

Huntington Antiques Ltd,
The Old Forge, Church Street,
Stow-on-the-Wold
Tel: (0451) 30842

Painswick Antiques & Interiors,
Beacon House, Painswick
Tel: (0452) 812578

Antony Preston Antiques Ltd,
The Square, Stow-on-the-Wold
Tel: (0451) 31586

Stone House Antiques,
St Mary's Street, Painswick
Tel: (0452) 813540

Studio Antiques Ltd,
Bourton-on-the-Water
Tel: (0451) 20352

Hants

C W Buckingham,
Twin Firs, Southampton Road,
Cadnam
Tel: (0703) 812122

Cedar Antiques,
High Street, Hartley Wintney
Tel: (025 126) 3252

Mark Collier Antiques,
24 The High Street, Fordingbridge
Tel: (0425) 52555

R C Dodson,
85 Fawcett Road, Southsea
Tel: (0705) 829481

House of Antiques,
4 College Street, Petersfield
Tel: (0730) 62172

Lita Kay of Lyndhurst,
13 High Street, Lyndhurst
Tel: (042 128) 2337

Millers of Chelsea Antiques Ltd,
Netherbrook House, 86
Christchurch Road, Ringwood
Tel: (0425) 472062

Truelocke Antiques,
109 High Street, Odiham
Tel: (0256) 702387

Hereford & Worcester

Gavina Ewart,
60-62 High Street, Broadway
Tel: (0386) 853371

Great Brampton House Antiques
Ltd,
Madley
Tel: (0981) 250244

Jean Hodge Antiques,
Peachley Manor, Lower
Broadheath, Worcester
Tel: (0905) 640255

Jennings of Leominster,
30 Bridge Street, Leominster
Tel: (0568) 2946

Lower House Fine Antiques (R),
Far Moor Lane, Winyates Green,
Redditch
Tel: (0527) 25117

Herts

C Bellinger Antiques
1 Wood Street, Barnet
Tel: 081-449 3467

John Bly,
0 High Street, Tring
Tel: (044 282) 3030

Collins Antiques,
Corner House, Wheathampstead
Tel: (058) 283 3111

Phillips of Hitchin (Antiques) Ltd,
The Manor House, Hitchin
Tel: (0462) 32067

Humberside

Geoffrey Mole,
00 Wincolmlee, Hull
Tel: (0482) 27858

Kent

Chislehurst Antiques,
7 Royal Parade, Chislehurst
Tel: 081-467 1530

Nigel Coleman Antiques,
High Street, Brasted
Tel: (0959) 64042

Conquest House Antiques,
Conquest House, 17 Palace Street,
Canterbury
Tel: (0227) 464587

Furnace Mill,
Lamberhurst
Tel: (0892) 890285

Garden House Antiques,
118 High Street, Tenterden
Tel: (058 06) 3664

John McMaster,
5 Sayers Square, Sayers Lane,
Tenterden
Tel: (058 06) 2941

The Old Bakery Antiques (Mr &
Mrs D Bryan),
St Davids Bridge, Cranbrook
Tel: (0580) 713103

Steppes Hill Farm Antiques,
Stockbury, Sittingbourne
Tel: (0795) 842205

Swan Antiques,
Stone Street, Cranbrook
Tel: (0580) 712720

Sutton Valence Antiques,
Sutton Valence, Maidstone
Tel: (0622) 843333 & 843499

Lancs

De Molen Ltd,
Moss Hey Garages, Chapel Road,
Marton Moss, Blackpool
Tel: (0253) 696324

West Lancs Exports,
Black Horse Farm, 123 Liverpool
Road, South Burscough, Nr
Ormskirk
Tel: (0704) 894634

Leics

Leicester Antiques Complex,
9 St Nicholas Place, Leicester
Tel: (0533) 533343

Lowe of Loughborough,
37-40 Church Gate, Loughborough
Tel: (0509) 217876

Lincs

Kirkby Antiques Ltd,
Kirkby-on-Bain, Woodhall Spa
Tel: (0526) 52119 & 53461

Geoff Parker Antiques Ltd,
Haltoft End, Freiston, Nr Boston
Tel: (0205) 760444

Laurence Shaw Antiques,
Spilsby Road, Horncastle
Tel: (06582) 7638 & (065888) 600

Middlesex

Binstead Antiques,
21 Middle Lane, Teddington
Tel: 081-943 0626

J W Crisp Antiques,
166 High Street, Teddington
Tel: 081-977 4309

Phelps Ltd,
133-135 St Margaret's Road,
E Twickenham
Tel: 081-892 1778

Norfolk

Joan Adams Antiques,
Rossendale, The Street,
Rickinghall, Diss
Tel: (0379) 898485

Arthur Brett & Sons Ltd,
40-44 St Giles Street, Norwich
Tel: (0603) 628171

Peter Howkins Antiques,
39, 40 & 135 King Street, Great
Yarmouth
Tel: (0493) 851180

Pearse Lukies,
Bayfield House, White Hart
Street, Aylsham
Tel: (0263) 734137

Rossendale Antiques (Ian Shaw),
Rossendale, The Street,
Rickinghall, Diss
Tel: (0379) 898485

Northants

Paul Hopwell Antiques,
30 High Street, West Haddon
Tel: (078 887) 636

Notts

Matsell Antiques Ltd,
2 & 4 Derby Street, off Derby Road,
Nottingham
Tel: (0602) 472691 & 288267

Oxon

David John Ceramics,
11 Acre End Street, Eynsham
Tel: (0865) 880786

Elizabethan House Antiques,
28 & 55 High Street, Dorchester-on-Thames
Tel: (0865) 340079

Key Antiques,
11 Horse Fair, Chipping Norton
Tel: (0608) 3777

Peter Norden Antiques,
High Street, Burford
Tel: (099 382) 2121

Manfred Schotten Antiques,
The Crypt, High Street, Burford
Tel: (099 382) 2302

Telling Time,
57 North Street, Thame
Tel: (084 421) 3007

Zene Walker,
The Bull House, High Street,
Burford
Tel: (099 382) 3284

Witney Antiques,
96-98 Corn Street, Witney
Tel: (0993) 3902

Shropshire

Castle Gate Antiques,
15 Castle Gate, Shrewsbury
Tel: (0743) 61011 (evenings)

R G Cave & Sons Ltd,
17 Broad Street, Ludlow
Tel: (0584) 3568

Dodington Antiques,
15 Dodington, Whitchurch
Tel: (0948) 3399

Doveridge House of Neachley,
Long Lane, Nr Shifnal
Tel: (090 722) 3131/2

F C Manser & Son Ltd,
53/54 Wyle Cop, Shrewsbury
Tel: (0743) 51120

Paul Smith,
The Old Chapel, Old Street,
Ludlow
Tel: (0584) 2666

M & R Taylor (Antiques),
53 Broad Street, Ludlow
Tel: (0584) 4169

White Cottage Antiques,
Tern Hill, Nr Market Drayton
Tel: (063 083) 222

Somerset

Grange Court Antiques,
Corfe, Nr Taunton
Tel: (082 342) 498

Peter Murray Antique Exports,
Station Road, Bruton
Tel: (0749) 812364

Edward A Nowell,
12 Market Place, Wells
Tel: (0749) 72415

Staffs

Richard Midwinter Antiques,
13 Brunswick Street, Newcastle
under Lyme
Tel: (0782) 712483

Suffolk

David Gibbins Antiques,
21 Market Hill, Woodbridge
Tel: (039 43) 3531

Hubbard Antiques,
16 St Margaret's Green, Ipswich
Tel: (0473) 226033

Michael Moore Antiques,
The Old Court, Nethergate Street,
Clare
Tel: (0787) 277510

Peppers Period Pieces (R),
22-24 Churchgate Street, Bury St
Edmunds
Tel: (0284) 68786

Randolph,
97 & 99 High Street, Hadleigh
Tel: (0473) 823789

Surrey

Churchill Antiques Gallery Ltd,
65 Quarry Street, Guildford
Tel: (0483) 506662

Richard Deryn Antiques,
7 Paved Court, The Green,
Richmond-upon-Thames
Tel: 081-948 5005

Dorking Desk Shop,
41 West Street, Dorking
Tel: (0306) 883327 & 880535

Hampshires of Dorking,
48-52 West Street, Dorking
Tel: (0306) 887076

J Hartley Antiques,
186 High Street, Ripley
Tel: (0483) 224318

Heath-Bullock,
8 Meadrow, Godalming
Tel: (048 68) 22562

Ripley Antiques,
67 High Street, Ripley
Tel: (0483) 224981

Swan Antiques,
62a West Street, Dorking
Tel: (0306) 881217

Anthony Welling Antiques,
Broadway Barn, High Street,
Ripley
Tel: (0483) 225384

Wych House Antiques,
Wych Hill, Woking
Tel: (048 62) 64636

Sussex

A27 Antiques Warehouses,
Chaucer Industrial Estate, Dittons
Road, Polegate
Tel: (032 12) 7167 & 5301

Bursig of Arundel,
The Old Candle Factory, Tarrant
Street, Arundel
Tel: (0903) 883456

Humphry Antiques,
East Street, Petworth
Tel: (0798) 43053

Richard Davidson,
Lombard Street, Petworth
Tel: (0798) 42508

The Grange Antiques,
High Street, Robertsbridge
Tel: (0580) 880577

Lakeside Antiques,
The Old Cement Works, South
Heighton, Newhaven
Tel: (0273) 513326

John G Morris Ltd,
Market Square, Petworth
Tel: (0798) 42305

The Old Mint House,
High Street, Pevensey, Eastbourne
Tel: (0323) 761251

David and Sarah Pullen,
29/31 Sea Road, Bexhill-on-Sea
Tel: (0424) 222035

Southey Gilbert Ward Ltd,
Units 5 & 6, Cliffe Industrial
Estate, Lewes
Tel: (0273) 474222

Village Antiques,
2 & 4 Cooden Sea Road, Little Common, Bexhill-on-Sea
Tel: (042 43) 5214

Tyne & Wear

Harold J Carr Antiques,
Field House, Rickleton, Washington
Tel: (091) 388 6442

West Midlands

John Hubbard Antiques,
224-226 Court Oak Road, Harborne, Birmingham
Tel: 021-426 1694

Rock House Antiques & Collectors Centre,
Rock House, The Rock, Tettenhall, Wolverhampton
Tel: (0902) 754995

Wilts

Avon Antiques,
26-27 Market Street, Bradford-upon-Avon
Tel: (022 16) 2052

Robert Bradley,
71 Brown Street, Salisbury
Tel: (0722) 333677

Combe Cottage Antiques,
Castle Combe, Nr Chippenham
Tel: (0249) 782250

Ian G Hastie, BADA,
46 St Ann Street, Salisbury
Tel: (0722) 22957

Robert Kime Antiques,
Dene House, Lockeridge
Tel: (067 286) 250

Melksham Antiques,
6A-8 King Street, Melksham
Tel: (0225) 707291

Monkton Galleries,
Hindon
Tel: (074 789) 235

Paul Wansbrough,
Seend Lodge, Seend, Nr Melksham
Tel: (038 082) 213

K & A Welch,
1a Church Street, Warminster
Tel: (0985) 214687 & 213433 (evenings)

Worcs

Gavina Ewart,
60-62 High Street, Broadway
Tel: (0386) 853371

Yorks

Robert Aagaard Ltd,
Frogmire House, Stockwell Road, Knaresborough
Tel: (0423) 864805
(Specialises in fireplaces)

Barmouth Court Antiques,
Abbeydale House, Barmouth Road, Sheffield
Tel: (0742) 582160 & 582672

Derbyshire Antiques Ltd,
27 Montpellier Parade, Harrogate
Tel: (0423) 503115/64242

Bernard Dickinson,
88 High Street, Gargrave
Tel: (075 678) 285

Jeremy A Fearn,
The Old Rectory, Winksley, Ripon
Tel: (076 583) 625

W F Greenwood & Sons Ltd,
2 & 3 Crown Place, Harrogate
Tel: (0423) 504467

Old Rectory Antiques,
The Old Rectory, West Heslerton, Malton
Tel: (094 45) 364

Robert Morrison & Son,
Trentholme House, 131 The Mount, York
Tel: (0904) 55394

R M S Precious,
King William House, High Street, Settle
Tel: (072 92) 3946

Scotland

John Bell of Aberdeen Ltd,
Balbrogie, By Blackburn, Kinellar, Aberdeenshire
Tel: (0224) 79209

Paul Couts Ltd,
101-107 West Bow, Edinburgh
Tel: 031-225 3238

Letham Antiques,
20 Dundas Street, Edinburgh
Tel: 031-556 6565

Roy Sim Antiques,
21 Allan Street, Blairgowrie, Perthshire
Tel: (0250) 3860 & 3700

Unicorn Antiques,
54 Dundas Street, Edinburgh
Tel: 031-556 7176

FURNITURE – PINE

London

Adams Antiques,
47 Chalk Farm Road, NW1
Tel: 071-267 9241

The Barewood Company,
58 Mill Lane, West Hampstead, NW6
Tel: 071-435 7244

Chest of Drawers,
281 Upper Street, Islington, N1
Tel: 071-359 5909

Islington Artefacts,
12-14 Essex Road, Islington, N1
Tel: 071-226 6867

Olwen Carthew,
109 Kirkdale, SW26
Tel: 081-699 1363

Princedale Antiques,
70 Princedale Road, W11
Tel: 071-727 0868

Remember When,
683-685 Finchley Road, NW2
Tel: 071-433 1333

Scallywag,
187-191 Clapham Road, Stockwell, London, SW9
Tel: 071-274 0300

This & That (Furniture),
50 & 51 Chalk Farm Road, NW1
Tel: 071-267 5433

Avon

Abbas Combe Pine,
4 Upper Maudlin Street, Bristol
Tel: (0272) 299023

Pennard House Antiques,
3/4 Piccadilly, London Road, Bath
Tel: (0225) 313791

Bucks

The Pine Merchants,
52 High Street, Gt Missenden
Tel: (024 06) 2002

Co Durham

Horsemarket Antiques,
27 Horsemarket, Barnard Castle
Tel: (0833) 37881

Devon

The Ark Antiques,
76 Fore Street, Topsham
Tel: (039287) 6251

Chancery Antiques,
8-10 Barrington Street, Tiverton
Tel: (0884) 252416/253190

Country Cottage Furniture,
The Old Smithy, Back Street, Modbury
Tel: (0548) 830888

Fine Pine,
Woodland Road, Harbertonford
Tel: (080 423) 465

Glos

Bed of Roses Antiques,
12 Prestbury Road, Cheltenham
Tel: (0242) 231918

Country Homes,
61 Long Street, Tetbury
Tel: (0666) 52342

Denzil Verey Antiques,
The Close, Barnsley House, Barnsley, Nr Cirencester
Tel: (028 574) 402

Gloucester House Antiques,
Market Place, Fairford
Tel: (0285) 712790

Hants

C W Buckingham,
Twin Firs, Southampton Road, Cadnam
Tel: (0703) 812122

Craftsman Furniture (Steve Hudson),
Castle Trading Estate, Portchester, Portsmouth
Tel: (0705) 219911

Millers of Chelsea Antiques Ltd,
Netherbrook House,
86 Christchurch Road, Ringwood
Tel: (0425) 472062

The Pine Cellars,
38 Jewry Street, Winchester
Tel: (0962) 67014

The Pine Co,
104 Christchurch Road, Ringwood
Tel: (042 54) 3932

Hereford & Worcester

The Hay Galleries Ltd,
4 High Town, Hay-on-Wye
Tel: (0497) 820356

Jennings of Leominster,
30 Bridge Street, Leominster
Tel: (0568) 2946

La Barre Ltd,
The Place, 116 South Street, Leominster
Tel: (0568) 4315

Marshall Bennett Restorations,
Eagle Lane, High Street, Cleobury Mortimer,
Nr Kidderminster, Worcester
Tel: (0299) 270553

Paul Somers Interiors incorporating Woodstock Interiors,
Unicorn Yard, Belle Vue Terrace, Malvern, Worcester
Tel: (068 45) 60297

Herts

Out of Town,
21 Ware Road, Hertford
Tel: (0992) 582848

Humberside

Bell Antiques,
68 Harold Street, Grimsby
Tel: (0472) 695110

The Hull Pine Co,
Bean Street, 253 Anlaby Road, Hull
Tel: (0482) 227169

Paul Wilson Pine Furniture,
Perth Street West, Hull
Tel: (0482) 447923 & 448607

Kent

Empire Antiques,
The Old Council Yard, Gazen Salts, Strand Street, Sandwich
Tel: (0304) 614474

Penny Lampard,
28 High Street, Headcorn
Tel: (0622) 890682

Andrée L Martin,
100 Sandgate High Street, Folkestone
Tel: (0303) 48560

The Old Bakery Antiques (Mr & Mrs D Bryan),
St Davids Bridge, Cranbrook
Tel: (0580) 713103

The Plough Pine Shop,
High Street, Eastry, Dover
Tel: (0304) 617418

Sissinghurst Antiques,
Hazelhurst Cottage, The Street, Sissinghurst, Nr Cranbrook
Tel: (0580) 713893

Traditional Furniture,
248 Seabrook Road, Seabrook, Hythe
Tel: (0303) 39931

Up Country,
The Old Corn Stores, 68 St John's Road, Tunbridge Wells
Tel: (0892) 23341

Lancs

Robert Sheriff,
Moss Hey Garages, Chapel Road, Marton Moss, Blackpool
Tel: (0253) 696324

Cottage Furniture,
Farnworth Park Industrial Estate, Queen Street, Farnworth, Bolton
Tel: (0204) 700853

Enloc Antiques,
Old Corporation Yard, Knotts Lane, Colne
Tel: (0282) 861417

Utopia Pine,
Holme Mills, Carnforth
Tel: (0524) 781739

Leics

Richard Kimbell Antiques,
Riverside, Market Harborough
Tel: (0858) 33444

Riverside Trading,
Riverside Industrial Estate, Market Harborough
Tel: (0858) 64110/64825

Lincs

Allens Antiques,
Moor Farm, Stapleford
Tel: (052 285) 392

J & J Palmer Ltd,
42/44 Swinegate, Grantham
Tel: (0476) 70093

Stowaway (UK) Ltd,
2 Langton Hill, Horncastle
Tel: (065 82) 7445

Norfolk

Rossendale Antiques (Ian Shaw),
Rossendale, The Street, Rickinghall, Diss
Tel: (0379) 898485

Northants

Acorn Antiques,
The Old Mill, Moat Lane, Towcester
Tel: (0327) 52788

The Country Pine Shop,
Northampton Road, West Haddor
Tel: (078887) 430

Oxon

Market Place Antiques,
35 Market Place, Henley-on-Thames
Tel: (0491) 57287

Julie Strachey,
Southfield Farm, Weston-on-the-Green
Tel: (0869) 50833/2

Somerset

Chalon,
Hambridge Mill, Hambridge, Ilminster
Tel: (0458) 252374

Crewkerne Antiques Centre,
42 East Street, Crewkerne
Tel: (0460) 76755

Grange Court Antiques,
Corfe, Taunton
Tel: (0823) 42498

Peter Murray Antique Exports,
Station Road, Bruton
Tel: (0749) 812364

Pennard House Antiques,
East Pennard, Shepton Mallet
Tel: (074 986) 266

Staffs

Anvil Antiques Ltd,
Cross Mills, Cross Street, Leek
Tel: (0538) 371657

Aspleys Antiques,
Compton Mill, Compton, Leek
Tel: (0538) 373396 & 373346

Directmoor Ltd,
The Coppice Farm, Nr Moorcourt, Oakamoor
Tel: (0588) 702419/387474

Gemini Trading,
Limes Mill, Abbotts Road, Leek
Tel: (0538) 387834

Johnsons,
Park Works, Park Road, Leek
Tel: (0538) 386745

Stone-wares,
The Stripped Pine Shop,
24 Radford Street, Stone
Tel: (0785) 815000

Suffolk

Michael Moore Antiques,
The Old Court, Nethergate Street, Clare
Tel: (0787) 277510

Surrey

Manor Antiques,
High Street, Old Woking
Tel: (048 62) 24666

Odiham Antiques,
High Street, Compton, Guildford
Tel: (0483) 810215

F & L Warren,
The Sawmills, Firgrove Hill, Farnham
Tel: (0252) 726713

Wych House Antiques,
Wych Hill, Woking
Tel: (048 62) 64636

Pine Warehouse at:–
34 London Road, Staines (off The Crooked Billet roundabout A30)
Tel: (0784) 65331

Sussex

Drummer Pine,
Hailsham Road, Herstmonceux
Tel: (0323) 833542/833661

Hillside Antiques,
Units 12-13, Lindfield Enterprise Park, Lewes Road, Lindfield
Tel: (044 47) 3042

Ann Lingard,
Ropewalk Antiques, Ropewalk, Rye
Tel: (0797) 223486

Peppers Antique Pine,
Crouch Lane, Seaford
Tel: (0323) 891400

Polegate Antique Centre,
Station Road, Polegate
Tel: (032 12) 5277

Graham Price Antiques Ltd,
A27 Antiques Complex, Unit 4, Chaucer Industrial Estate, Dittons Road, Polegate
Tel: (032 12) 7167 & 7681

Touchwood (Mervyn & Sue),
The Square, Herstmonceux
Tel: (0323) 832020

Michael Wakelin & Helen Lindfield,
10 New Street, Petworth
Tel: (0798) 42417

Wilts

Ray Coggins Antiques,
The Old Brewery, Newtown, Bradford-on-Avon
Tel: (02216) 3431

The Pine Dealer,
29 The Parade, Marlborough
Tel: (0672) 514967

Yorks

Daleside Antiques,
St Peter's Square, Cold Bath Road, Harrogate
Tel: (0423) 60286

Early Days,
7 Kings Court, Pateley Bridge, Harrogate
Tel: (0423) 711661

Michael Green,
Library House, Regent Parade, Harrogate
Tel: (0423) 60452

Manor Barn Pine,
Burnside Mill, Main Street, Addinsham, Ilkley
Tel: (0943) 830176

Pine Finds,
The Old Corn Mill, Bishop Monkton, Harrogate
Tel: (0765) 87159

Smith & Smith Designs,
58A Middle Street North, Driffield
Tel: (0377) 46321

Ireland

Alain Chawner,
The Square, Collon, Co Louth
Tel: (010 353 41) 26270

Patrick Bradley,
6 Shipquay Street, Londonderry
Tel: (0504) 263343

Albert Forsythe,
Mill Hall, 66 Carsontown Road, Saintfield, Co Down, Northern Ireland
Tel: (0238) 510398

Delvin Farm Galleries,
Gormaston, Co Meath
Tel: (0001) 412285

Luckpenny Antiques,
Kilmurray House, Shinrone, Birr, Co Offaly, Southern Ireland
Tel: (010 353 505) 47134

W J Somerville,
Shamrock Antiques Ltd,
Killanley, Ballina, Co Mayo
Tel: (096) 36275

Scotland

A & P Steadman,
Unit 1, Hatston Industrial Estate, Kirkwall, Orkney
Tel: (0856) 5040

Wales

Heritage Restorations,
Maes y Glydfa, Llanfair, Caereinion, Welshpool, Powys
Tel: (0938) 810384

Maclean,
Dudley & Marie Thorpe, Tiradda, Llansadwrn, Dyfed
Tel: (0550) 777-509

GLASS

London

Asprey PLC,
165-169 New Bond Street, W1
Tel: 071-493 6767

Phyllis Bedford Antiques,
3 The Galleries, Camden Passage, N1
Tel: 071-354 1332;
home 081-882 3189

Christine Bridge,
78 Castelnau, SW13
Tel: 081-741 5501

W G T Burne (Antique Glass) Ltd,
11 Elystan Street, SW3
Tel: 071-589 6074

Delomosne & Son Ltd,
4 Campden Hill Road, W8
Tel: 071-937 1804

East Gates Antiques,
Stand G006, Alfies Antique Market, 13-25 Church Street, NW8
Tel: 071-724 5650

Eila Grahame,
97C Kensington Church Street, W8
Tel: 071-727 4132

Lloyds of Westminster,
5A Motcomb Street, SW1
Tel: 071-235 1010

S W Parry (Old Glass),
Stand A4-A5 Westbourne Antique Arcade, 113 Portobello Road, W11 (Sat only)
Tel: 081-740 0248 (Sun to Fri)

J F Poore,
5 Wellington Terrace, W2
Tel: 071-229 4166

Pryce & Brise Antiques,
79 Moore Park Road, Fulham, SW6
Tel: 071-736 1864

Gerald Sattin Ltd,
25 Burlington Arcade, Piccadilly, W1
Tel: 071-493 6557

Mark J West,
Cobb Antiques Ltd,
39B High Street, Wimbledon Village, SW19
Tel: 081-946 2811

R Wilkinson & Son (R),
43-45 Wastdale Road, Forest Hill, SE23
Tel: 081-699 4420

Avon

Somervale Antiques,
6 Radstock Road, Midsomer Norton, Bath
Tel: (0761) 412686

Dorset

A & D Antiques,
21 East Street, Blandford Forum
Tel: (0258) 55643

Quarter Jack Antiques,
The Quarter Jack, Bridge Street, Sturminster Newton
Tel: (0258) 72558

Hants

Stockbridge Antiques,
High Street, Stockbridge
Tel: (0264) 810829

Todd & Austin Antiques & Fine Art
2 Andover Road, Winchester
Tel: (0962) 69824

Shropshire

Tiffany Antiques (Antique Glass & Pottery),
Unit 11, Shrewsbury Antique Centre, 15 Princess House, The Square, Shrewsbury
Tel: (Home) (0270) 257425

Somerset

Abbey Antiques,
51 High Street, Glastonbury
Tel: (0458) 31694

Suffolk

Maureen Thompson,
Sun House, Long Melford
Tel: (0787) 78252

Surrey

Shirley Warren (by appointment only),
42 Kingswood Avenue, Sanderstead
Tel: 081-657 1751

Shirley Warren (shop),
333B Limpsfield Road, Sanderstead
Tel: 081-651 5180

Sussex

Rusthall Antiques,
Chateaubriand Antique Centre, High Street, Burwash
Tel: (0435) 882535 & (0892) 20668 (evenings)

Warwickshire

Sharon Ball (Antique glass & collectables),
Unit 41, Stratford-on-Avon Antique Centre, Ely Street, Stratford-on-Avon
Tel: (0789) 204180

West Midlands

Sharon Ball,
6 Delrene Road, Shirley, Solihull
Tel: 021-745 9034

Scotland

Janet Lumsden,
51A George Street, Edinburgh
Tel: 031-225 2911

William MacAdam (appointment only),
86 Pilrig Street, Edinburgh
Tel: 031-553 1364

GRAMOPHONES, PHONOGRAPHS & RADIOS

Avon

The Vintage Wireless Co,
Tudor House, Cossham Street, Mangotsfield, Bristol
Tel: (0272) 565474

Devon

Brian Taylor Antiques,
24 Molesworth Road, Stoke, Plymouth
Tel: (0752) 569061

Somerset

Philip Knighton (R),
The Wellington Workshop,
14 South Street, Wellington
Tel: (082 347) 7332

West Midlands

Woodsetton Antiques,
65 Sedgley Road, Woodsetton, Dudley
Tel: (0384) 277918

Yorks

Clocks & Gramophones,
11 Walmgate, York
Tel: (0904) 611924

ICONS

London

Maria Andipa,
Icon Gallery, 162 Walton Street, SW3
Tel: 071-589 2371

Mark Gallery,
9 Porchester Place, Marble Arch, W2
Tel: 071-262 4906

JEWELLERY

London

Hirsh Fine Jewels,
Diamond House, Hatton Garden, EC1
Tel: 071-405 6080/071-404 4392

Glos

South Bar Antiques (Cameos),
Digbeth Street, Stow-on-the-Wold
Tel: (0451) 30236

Hereford & Worcester

Old Curiosity Antiques,
11 Tower Buildings, Blackwell Street, Kidderminster
Tel: (0562) 742859

Norfolk

Peter & Valerie Howkins,
39, 40 & 135 King Street, Great Yarmouth
Tel: (0493) 844639

Somerset

Edward A Nowell,
21-23 Market Place, Wells
Tel: (0749) 72415

Sussex

Rusthall Antiques,
Chateaubriand Antique Centre, High Street, Burwash
Tel: (0435) 882535 (0892) 20668 (evenings)

KITCHENALIA

Lancashire

Kitchenalia,
36 Inglewhite Road, Longridge, Nr Preston
Tel: (077 478) 5411

LIGHTING

London

Judy Jones,
194 Westbourne Grove, W11
Tel: 071-229 6866

The Lamp Gallery,
355 New Kings Road, SW6
Tel: 071-736 6188

Hereford & Worcester

Fritz Fryer,
27 Gloucester Road, Ross-on-Wye, Hereford
Tel: (0989) 64738 & 84512

Hertfordshire

J Marsden,
Magic Lanterns and Vestalia Antique Lighting Ltd, 23 George Street, St Albans
Tel: (0727) 65680 & 53032

LOCKS & KEYS

Notts

The Keyhole, Dragonwyck (R), Far Back Lane, Farnsfield, Newark
Tel: (0623) 882590

MARINE ANTIQUES

Devon

Temeraire,
63 Brownston Street, Modbury
Tel: (0548) 830317

Essex

Littlebury Antiques,
58/60 Fairycroft Road, Saffron Walden
Tel: (0799) 27961

METALWARE

London

Christopher Bangs (by appointment only),
Tel: 071-352 3384

Jack Casimir Ltd,
The Brass Shop, 23 Pembridge Road, W11
Tel: 071-727 8643

Arthur Davidson Ltd,
78-79 Jermyn Street, SW1
Tel: 071-930 6687

Robert Preston,
1 Campden Street, W8
Tel: 071-727 4872

Alistair Sampson Antiques,
156 Brompton Road, SW3
Tel: 071-589 5272

Avon

Cottage Antiques,
The Old Post Office, Langford Place, Langford, Nr Bristol
Tel: (0934) 862597

Beds

Christopher Sykes Antiques,
The Old Parsonage, Woburn, Milton Keynes
Tel: (052 525) 259/467

Berks

Rye Galleries,
60-61 High Street, Eton
Tel: (0753) 862637

Bucks

Albert Bartram,
177 Hivings Hill, Chesham
Tel: (0494) 783271

Cumbria

Stable Antiques,
Oakdene Country Hotel, Garsdale Road, Sedbergh
Tel: (0587) 20280

Glos

Country Life Antiques,
Sheep Street, Stow-on-the-Wold
Tel: (0451) 30776
Also at:
Grey House, The Square, Stow-on-the-Wold
Tel: (0451) 31564

Oxon

Robin Bellamy Ltd,
97 Corn Street, Witney
Tel: (0993) 4793

Elizabethan House Antiques,
28 & 55 High Street, Dorchester-on-Thames
Tel: (0865) 340079

Key Antiques,
11 Horse Fair, Chipping Norton
Tel: (0608) 3777

Lloyd & Greenwood Antiques,
Chapel House, High Street, Burford
Tel: (099 382) 2359

Suffolk

Brookes Forge Flempton (R),
Flempton, Bury St Edmunds, Suffolk
Tel: (028 484) 473 business
(0449) 781376 home

Sussex

Michael Wakelin & Helen Linfield,
10 New Street, Petworth
Tel: (0798) 42417

Wilts

Avon Antiques,
26-27 Market Street, Bradford-on-Avon
Tel: (022 16) 2052

Combe Cottage Antiques,
Castle Combe, Chippenham
Tel: (0249) 782250

Rupert Gentle Antiques,
The Manor House, Milton Lilbourne, Nr Pewsey
Tel: (0672) 63344

Yorks

Windsor House Antiques (Leeds) Ltd,
18-20 Benson Street, Leeds
Tel: (0532) 444666

MUSICAL INSTRUMENTS

London

Mayflower Antiques,
117 Portobello Road, W11
Tel: 071-727 0381
(Sats only 7am-3pm)

Essex

Mayflower Antiques,
2 Una Road, Parkeston, Harwich
Tel: (0255) 504079

Kent

David Bailey Pianos Warehouse,
Ramsgate Road, Sandwich
Tel: (0304) 613948

Glos

Vanbrugh House Antiques,
Park Street, Stow-on-the-Wold
Tel: (0451) 30797

Oxon

Laurie Leigh Antiques,
36 High Street, Oxford
Tel: (0865) 244197

Somerset

Shelagh Berryman,
Musical Boxes,
15 The Market Place, Wells
Tel: (0749) 76203

Suffolk

The Suffolk Piano Workshop,
The Snape, Maltings
Tel: (072 888) 677

Sussex

Sound Instruments,
Worth Farm, Little Horsted, Nr Uckfield
Tel: (082 575) 567

ORIENTAL

London

Kotobuki,
F100 Alfies Antique Market,
13-25 Church Street, NW8
Tel: 071-402 0723

Somerset

Ron & F Fairbrass,
48 West Street, Crewkerne
Tel: (0460) 76941

Sussex

Linda Loveland Fine Arts,
18-20 Prospect Place, Hastings
Tel: (0424) 441608

PORCELAIN

London

Albert Amor Ltd,
37 Bury Street, St James's, SW1
Tel: 071-930 2444

Antique Porcelain Co Ltd,
149 New Bond Street, W1
Tel: 071-629 1254

Susan Becker,
18 Lower Richmond Road, SW15
Tel: 081-788 9082

David Brower Antiques,
113 Kensington Church Street, W8
Tel: 071-221 4155

Cale Antiques,
24 Cale Street, Chelsea Green, SW3
Tel: 071-589 6146

Cathay Antiques,
12 Thackeray Street, W8
Tel: 071-937 6066

Belinda Coote Antiques,
29 Holland Street, W8
Tel: 071-937 3924

Craven Antiques,
17 Garson House, Gloucester Terrace, W2
Tel: 071-262 4176

Marilyn Delion,
Stand 7 (Basement), Portobello Road, W11
Tel: 071-937 3377

Delomosne & Son Ltd,
4 Campden Hill Road, W8
Tel: 071-937 1804

H & W Deutsch Antiques,
111 Kensington Church Street, W8
Tel: 071-727 5984

Miss Fowler,
1A Duke Street, Manchester Square, W1
Tel: 071-935 5187

Graham & Oxley (Antiques) Ltd,
101 Kensington Church Street, W8
Tel: 071-229 1850

Grosvenor Antiques Ltd,
27 Holland Street, Kensington, W8
Tel: 071-937 8649

Harcourt Antiques,
5 Harcourt Street, W1
Tel: 071-723 5919

Heirloom & Howard Ltd,
1 Hay Hill, Berkeley Square, W1
Tel: 071-493 5868

Hoff Antiques Ltd,
66A Kensington Church Street, W8
Tel: 071-229 5516

Klaber & Klaber,
2A Bedford Gardens, Kensington Church Street, W8
Tel: 071-727 4573

D M & P Manheim Ltd,
69 Upper Berkeley Street, Portman Square, W1
Tel: 071-723 6595

Mayfair Gallery,
97 Mount Street, W1
Tel: 071-499 5315

Mercury Antiques,
1 Ladbroke Road, W11
Tel: 071-727 5106

St Jude's Antiques,
107 Kensington Church Street, W8
Tel: 071-727 8737

Edward Salti,
43 Davies Street, W1
Tel: 071-629 2141

Gerald Sattin Ltd,
25 Burlington Arcade, Piccadilly, W1
Tel: 071-493 6557

Jean Sewell (Antiques) Ltd,
3 Campden Street, Kensington Church Street, W8
Tel: 071-727 3122

Simon Spero,
109 Kensington Church Street, W8
Tel: 071-727 7413

Aubrey Spiers Antiques,
Shop C5, Chenil Galleries, 183 King's Road, SW3
Tel: 071-352 7384

Constance Stobo,
31 Holland Street, W8
Tel: 071-937 6282

Earle D Vandekar of Knightsbridge Ltd,
138 Brompton Road, SW3
Tel: 071-589 8481/3398

Venner's Antiques,
7 New Cavendish Street, W1
Tel: 071-935 0184

Winifred Williams,
3 Bury Street, St James's, SW1
Tel: 071-930 4732

Avon

Andrew Dando,
4 Wood Street, Queen Square, Bath
Tel: (0225) 22702

Berks

Len's Crested China,
Twyford Antiques Centre, Nr Reading
Tel: (0753) 35162

The Old School Antiques,
Dorney, Windsor
Tel: (062 86) 3247

Cornwall

Mrs Margaret Chesterton,
33 Pentewan Road, St Austell
Tel: (0726) 72926

London Apprentice Antiques,
Pentewan Road, St Austell
Tel: (0726) 63780

Derbys
C B Sheppard Antiques
(appointment only),
Hurst Lodge, Chesterfield Road,
Tibshelf
Tel: (0773) 872419

Devon
David J Thorn,
2 High Street, Budleigh Salterton
Tel: (039 54) 2448

Glos
Gloucester House Antiques,
Market Place, Fairford
Tel: (0285) 712790

L Greenwold,
Digbeth, Digbeth Street,
Stow-on-the-Wold
Tel: (0451) 30398

Hamand Antiques,
Friday Street, Painswick
Tel: (0452) 812310

Pamela Rowan,
High Street, Blockley, Nr
Moreton-in-Marsh
Tel: (0386) 700280

Studio Antiques Ltd,
Bourton-on-the-Water
Tel: (0451) 20352

Wain Antiques,
45 Long Street, Tetbury
Tel: (0666) 52440

Hants
Gerald Austin Antiques,
2A Andover Road, Winchester
Tel: (0962) 69824 Ext 2

Goss & Crested China Ltd,
62 Murray Road, Horndean
Tel: (0705) 597440

Rogers of Alresford,
16 West Street, Alresford
Tel: (096 273) 2862

Hereford & Worcs
avina Ewart,
0-62 High Street, Broadway
el: (0386) 853371

abina Jennings,
Newcourt Park, Lugwardine
el: (0432) 850752

M Lees & Sons,
ower House, Severn Street,
Vorcester
el: (0905) 26620

ent
eaubush Antiques,
5 Sandgate High Street,
olkestone
el: (0303) 49099

he History in Porcelain Collector,
igh Street, Shoreham Village,
r Sevenoaks
el: (095 92) 3416

ent Cottages Antiques,
9 High Street, Rolvenden
el: (0580) 241719

teppes Hill Farm Antiques,
tockbury, Sittingbourne
el: (0795) 842205

Vakefield Ceramic Fairs (Fred
ynds),
Fountain Road, Strood,
ochester
el: (0634) 723461

V W Warner (Antiques) Ltd,
he Green, Brasted
el: (0959) 63698

ancs
urnley Antiques & Fine Arts Ltd,
36A Colne Road, Burnley
el: (0282) 20143/65172

Leics
Charnwood Antiques,
54 Sparrow Hill, Loughborough
Tel: (0509) 231750

Norfolk
T C S Brooke,
The Grange, Wroxham
Tel: (060 53) 2644

Margaret Corson,
Irstead Manor, Neatishead
Tel: (0692) 630274

Oxon
Castle Antiques,
Lamb Arcade, Wallingford, Oxon
Tel: (0491) 35166

David John Ceramics,
11 Acre End Street, Eynsham,
Oxford
Tel: (0865) 880786

Shropshire
Castle Gate Antiques,
15 Castle Gate, Shrewsbury
Tel: (0743) 61011 evenings

F C Manser & Son Ltd,
53-54 Wyle Cop, Shrewsbury
Tel: (0743) 51120

Teme Valley Antiques,
1 The Bull Ring, Ludlow
Tel: (0584) 4686

Tudor House Antiques,
33 High Street, Ironbridge
Tel: (095 245) 3237

Somerset
Ray Antonies Antiques,
86 Holyrood Street, Chard
Tel: (0460) 67163

Suffolk
Crafers Antiques,
The Hill, Wickham Market,
Woodbridge
Tel: (0728) 747347

Surrey
Elias Clark Antiques Ltd,
1 The Cobbles, Bletchingley
Tel: (0883) 843714

J P Raison (by appointment only),
Heathcroft, Walton Heath,
Tadworth
Tel: (073 781) 3557

Whittington Galleries,
22 Woodend, Sutton
Tel: 081-644 9327

Sussex
Barclay Antiques,
7 Village Mews, Little Common,
Bexhill-on-Sea
Tel: (0797) 222734 home

Geoffrey Godden,
Chinaman, 17-19 Crescent Road,
Worthing
Tel: (0903) 35958

William Hockley Antiques,
East Street, Petworth
Tel: (0798) 43172

Leonard Russell,
21 King's Avenue, Newhaven
Tel: (0273) 515153

Wilts
The China Hen,
9 Woolley Street, Bradford-on-Avon
Tel: (022 16) 3369

Mark Collier Antiques,
High Street, Downton
Tel: (0725) 21068

Melksham Antiques,
6A-8 King Street, Melksham
Tel: (0225) 707291

Yorks
Brian Bowden,
199 Carr House Road, Doncaster
Tel: (0302) 65353

Angela Charlesworth,
99 Dodworth Road, Barnsley
Tel: (0226) 282097/203688

David Love,
10 Royal Parade, Harrogate
Tel: (0423) 65797

Nanbooks,
Undercliffe Cottage, Duke Street,
Settle
Tel: (072 92) 3324

Wales
Brenin Porcelain & Pottery,
Old Wool Barn, Verity's Court,
Cowbridge, South Glamorgan
Tel: (044 63) 3893

Gwalia Antiques,
Main Street, Goodwick,
Fishguard, Dyfed
Tel: (0348) 872634

POTTERY

London
Britannia,
Stand 101, Gray's Market,
58 Davies Street, W1
Tel: 071-629 6772

Cale Antiques,
24 Cale Street, Chelsea Green,
SW3
Tel: 071-589 6146

Gerald Clark Antiques,
1 High Street, Mill Hill Village,
NW7
Tel: 081-906 0342

Belinda Coote Antiques,
29 Holland Street, W8
Tel: 071-937 3924

Marilyn Delion,
Stand 7 (Basement), Portobello
Road, W11
Tel: 071-937 3377

Richard Dennis,
144 Kensington Church Street, W8
Tel: 071-727 2061

Graham & Oxley (Antiques) Ltd,
101 Kensington Church Street, W8
Tel: 071-229 1850

Jonathan Horne,
66C Kensington Church Street,
W8
Tel: 071-221 5658

Valerie Howard,
131e Kensington Church Street,
W8 7PT
Tel: 071-792 9702

D M & P Manheim Ltd,
69 Upper Berkeley Street,
Portman Square, W1
Tel: 071-723 6595

J & J May,
40 Kensington Church Street, W8
Tel: 071-937 3575

Mercury Antiques,
1 Ladbroke Road, W11
Tel: 071-727 5106

Oliver Sutton Antiques,
34C Kensington Church Street,
W8
Tel: 071-937 0633

Rogers de Rin,
76 Royal Hospital Road, SW3
Tel: 071-352 9007

St Jude's Antiques,
107 Kensington Church Street, W8
Tel: 071-727 8737

Alistair Sampson Antiques,
156 Brompton Road, SW3
Tel: 071-589 5272

Constance Stobo,
31 Holland Street, W8
Tel: 071-937 6282

Earle D Vandekar of
Knightsbridge Ltd,
138 Brompton Road, SW3
Tel: 071-589 8481 & 3398

Cornwall
Mrs Margaret Chesterton,
33 Pentewan Road, St Austell
Tel: (0826) 72926

Cumbria
Kendal Studio Pottery,
2-3 Wildman Street, Kendal
Tel: (0539) 23291

Devon
David J Thorn,
2 High Street, Budleigh Salterton
Tel: (039 54) 2448

Hants
Goss & Crested China Ltd,
62 Murray Road, Horndean
Tel: (0705) 597440

Millers of Chelsea,
Netherbrook House, Christchurch
Road, Ringwood
Tel: (0425) 472062

Rogers of Alresford,
16 West Street, Alresford
Tel: (096 273) 2862

Kent
W W Warner (Antiques) Ltd,
The Green, Brasted
Tel: (0959) 63698

Lancs
Burnley Antiques & Fine Arts Ltd
(appointment only),
336A Colne Road, Burnley
Tel: (0282) 65172

Roy W Bunn Antiques,
34/36 Church Street,
Barnoldswick, Colne
Tel: (0282) 813703

Norfolk
Margaret Corson,
Irstead Manor, Neatishead
Tel: (0692) 630274

Suffolk
Crafers Antiques,
The Hill, Wickham Market,
Woodbridge
Tel: (0728) 747347

Surrey
Elias Clark Antiques Ltd,
1 The Cobbles, Bletchingley
Tel: (0883) 843714

Whittington Galleries,
22 Woodend, Sutton
Tel: 081-644 9327

Sussex
Ron Beech,
150 Portland Road, Hove
Tel: (0273) 724477

Leonard Russell,
21 King's Avenue, Newhaven
Tel: (0273) 515153

Warwickshire
Beehive Antiques,
Kenilworth
Tel: (0926) 55253

Wilts
Bratton Antiques,
Market Place, Westbury
Tel: (0373) 823021

Yorks
The Antique & Bargain Store,
6 Sunny Bar, Doncaster
Tel: (0302) 344857

The Antique & Bargain Store,
20 Copley Road, Doncaster
Tel: (0302) 344857

The Crested China Company,
The Station House, Driffield
Tel: (0377) 47042

Nanbooks,
Undercliffe Cottage, Duke Street, Settle
Tel: (072 92) 3324

Wales

Islwyn Watkins,
1 High Street, Knighton, Powys
Tel: (0547) 520145/528940

Isle of Man

Rushton Ceramics,
Tynwald Mills, St Johns
Tel: (0624) 71618

SCENT BOTTLES

Kent

Kent Cottage Antiques,
39 High Street, Rolvenden
Tel: (0580) 241719

SCIENTIFIC INSTRUMENTS

London

Jilliana Ranicar-Breese, Martin Breese Ltd,
164 Kensington Park Road, Notting Hill Gate, W11
Tel: 071-727 9378
(Optical Toys/Illusion)

Arthur Davidson Ltd,
78-79 Jermyn Street, SW1
Tel: 071-930 6687

Mariner Antiques Ltd,
55 Curzon Street, W1
Tel: 071-499 0171

Mayfair Microscopes Ltd,
64 Burlington Aracade, W1
Tel: 071-629 2616

Mayflower Antiques,
117 Portobello Road, W11
Tel: 071-727 0381
(Sats only 7am-3pm)

Arthur Middleton Ltd,
12 New Row, Covent Garden, WC2
Tel: 071-836 7042/7062

Trevor Philip & Sons Ltd,
75A Jermyn Street, St James's, SW1
Tel: 071-930 2954/5

David Weston Ltd,
44 Duke Street, St James, SW1
Tel: 071-839 1051-2-3

Harriet Wynter Ltd (by appointment only),
50 Redcliffe Road, SW10
Tel: 071-352 6494

Beds

Christopher Sykes Antiques,
The Old Parsonage, Woburn, Milton Keynes
Tel: (052 525) 259/467

Devon

Galaxy Arts,
38 New Street, Barbican, Plymouth
Tel: (0752) 667842

Essex

Mayflower Antiques,
2 Una Road, Parkeston, Harwich
Tel: (0255) 504079

Glos

Country Life Antiques,
Sheep Street, Stow-on-the-Wold
Tel: (0451) 30776
Also at:
Grey House, The Square, Stow-on-the-Wold
Tel: (0451) 31564

Kent

Hadlow Antiques,
No. 1 The Pantiles, Tunbridge Wells
Tel: (0892) 29858

Norfolk

Margaret Corson,
Irstead Manor, Neatishead
Tel: (0692) 630274

Humbleyard Fine Art,
Waterfall Cottage, Mill Street, Swanton Morley
Tel: (036 283) 793
Also at:
Coltishall Antiques Centre, Coltishall, Norfolk

Turret House (Dr D H Morgan),
27 Middleton Street, Wymondham
Tel: (0953) 603462

Surrey

Whittington Galleries,
22 Woodend, Sutton
Tel: 081-644 9327

SILVER

London

Asprey PLC,
165-169 New Bond Street, W1
Tel: 071-493 6767

N Bloom & Son (Antiques) Ltd,
40-41 Conduit Street, W1
Tel: 071-629 5060

Bond Street Galleries,
111-112 New Bond Street, W1
Tel: 071-493 6180

J H Bourdon-Smith,
24 Mason's Yard, Duke Street, St James's, SW1
Tel: 071-839 4714

H & W Deutsch Antiques,
111 Kensington Church Street, W8
Tel: 071-727 5984

Howard Jones,
43 Kensington Church Street, W8
Tel: 071-937 4359

London International Silver Co,
82 Portobello Road, W11
Tel: 081-979 6523

S J Phillips Ltd,
139 New Bond Street, W1
Tel: 071-629 6261/2

Gerald Sattin Ltd,
25 Burlington Arcade, Piccadilly, W1
Tel: 071-493 6557

S J Shrubsole Ltd,
43 Museum Street, WC1
Tel: 071-405 2712

Cheshire

Watergate Antiques,
56 Watergate Street, Chester
Tel: (0244) 44516

Hereford & Worcester

Lower House Fine Antiques (R),
Far Moor Lane, Winyates Green, Redditch
Tel: (0527) 25117

Kent

Ralph Antiques,
40A Sandwich Industrial Estate, Sandwich
Tel: (0304) 611949/612882

Steppes Hill Farm Antiques,
Stockbury, Sittingbourne
Tel: (0795) 842205

Oxon

Thames Gallery,
Thameside, Henley-on-Thames
Tel: (0491) 572449

Shropshire

F C Manser & Son Ltd,
53-54 Wyle Cop, Shrewsbury
Tel: (0743) 51120

Somerset

Edward A Nowell,
21-23 Market Place, Wells
Tel: (0749) 72415

Yorks

Georgian House,
88 Main Street, Bingley
Tel: (0274) 568883

TEXTILES

London

Act One Hire Ltd,
2a Scampston Mews, Cambridge Gardens, W10 6HX
Tel: 081-960 1456/1494

Matthew Adams,
A1 Rogers Antique Galleries,
65 Portobello Road, W11
Tel: 081-579 5560

Gallery of Antique Costume & Textiles,
2 Church Street, Marylebone, NW8
Tel: 071-723 9981

Linda Wrigglesworth,
Grays Inn, The Mews, 1-7 Davies Mews, W1
Tel: 071-408 0177

Kent

The Lace Basket,
1A East Cross, Tenterden
Tel: (05806) 3923

Norfolk

Mrs Woolston,
Design House, 29 St Georges Street, Norwich
Tel: (0603) 623181
Also at:
Long Melford Antique Centre

Sussex

Celia Charlotte's Antiques,
7 Malling Street, Lewes
Tel: (0273) 473303

WINE ANTIQUES

London

Brian Beat,
36 Burlington Gardens, W1
Tel: 071-437 4975

Graham Bell,
177/8 Grays Antique Market,
58 Davies Street, W1
Tel: 071-493 1148

Eximious Ltd,
10 West Halkin Street, W1
Tel: 071-627 2888

Richard Kihl,
164 Regent's Park Road, NW1
Tel: 071-586 3838

Avon

Robin Butler,
20 Clifton Road, Bristol
Tel: (0272) 733017

Beds

Christopher Sykes Antiques,
The Old Parsonage, Woburn, Milton Keynes
Tel: (052 525) 259 & 467

Cumbria

Bacchus Antiques,
Longlands at Cartmel
Tel: (044 854) 475

Warwickshire

Bigwoods Auctioneers,
The Old School, Tiddington, Stratford-upon-Avon
Tel: (0789) 69415

WRITING MATERIALS

London

Jasmin Cameron (R),
Stand J6 Antiquarius,
131-141 Kings Road, SW3 5ST
Tel: 071-352 4690
(after 9pm) (0474) 873875

FAIR ORGANISERS

London

KM Fairs,
58 Mill Lane, NW6
Tel: 071-794 3551

Philbeach Events Ltd,
Earl's Court Exhibition Centre, Warwick Road, SW5
Tel: 071-385 1200

Berks

Bridget Fraser,
Granny's Attic Antique Fairs,
Dean House, Cookham Dean
Tel: (062 84) 3658

Silhouette Fairs (inc Newbury Antique & Collectors' Fairs),
25 Donnington Square, Newbury
Tel: (0635) 44338

Cheshire

Antique & Collectors Fair,
The Guildhall, Watergate Street, Chester
(no telephone number)

Susan Brownson,
Antique Fairs North West,
Brownslow House, Gt Budworth, Northwich
Tel: (0606) 891267 &
(061962) 5629

Pamela Robertson,
8 St George's Crescent, Queen's Park, Chester
Tel: (0244) 678106

Cornwall

West Country Antiques & Collectors' Fairs (Gerry Mosdell),
Hillside, St Issey, Wadebridge
Tel: (084 14) 666

Richard Castle Fairs,
Bake Barton, Trerulefoot, Saltash
Tel: (05034) 694

Essex

Robert Bailey Antiques Fairs,
1 Roll Gardens, Gants Hill
Tel: 081-550 5435

Stephen Charles Fairs,
3 Leigh Hill, Leigh-on-Sea
Tel: (0702) 714649/556745 &
(0268) 774977

Heirloom Markets,
11 Wellfields, Writtle, Chelmsford
Tel: (0245) 422208

Hereford & Worcester

Unicorn Fairs,
PO Box 30, Hereford
Tel: (061 773) 7001

Herts

Bartholomew Fayres,
Executive House, The Maltings,
Station Road, Sawbridgeworth
Tel: (0279) 725809

Humberside

Seaclef Fairs,
78 Humberston Avenue, Humberston, Grimsby
Tel: (0472) 813858

Kent

Darent Fairs,
Whitestacks Cottage, Crockenhill Lane, Eynsford
Tel: (0474) 63992

Tudor Fairs,
59 Rafford Way, Bromley
Tel: 081-460 2670

Wakefield Ceramic Fairs (Fred Hynds),
1 Fountain Road, Strood, Rochester
Tel: (0634) 723461

Norfolk
Broadland Fayres,
Dakenham Hall, Salhouse, Norwich
Tel: (0603) 721360

Notts
Top Hat Exhibitions Ltd,
66-72 Derby Road, Nottingham
Tel: (0602) 419143

Oxon
Portcullis Fairs,
6 St Peter's Street, Wallingford
Tel: (0491) 39345

Staffs
Waverley Fairs,
at Kinver, Womburn, Bromsgrove, Bridgnorth
Tel: (021 550) 0309

Suffolk
Camfair (Ros Coltman),
Longlands, Kedington, Haverhill
Tel: (0440) 704632

Emporium Fairs,
Longlands, Kedington, Haverhill
Tel: (0440) 704632

Surrey
Antiques & Collectors' Club,
No. 1 Warehouse, Horley Row, Horley
Tel: (0293) 772206

Joan Braganza,
76 Holmesdale Road, Reigate
Tel: (073 72) 45587

Cultural Exhibitions Ltd,
8 Meadrow, Godalming
Tel: (048 68) 22562

Historic and Heritage Fayres
Tel: 081-398 5324

Sussex
Ron Beech,
1 Brambledean Road, Portslade
Tel: (0273) 423355

Brenda Lay,
Dyke Farm, West Chiltington Road, Pulborough
Tel: (079 82) 2447

Penman Antique Fairs,
Cockhaise Mill, Lindfield, Haywards Heath
Tel: (044 47) 2514

Yorks
Bowman Antique Fairs,
PO Box 37, Otley
Tel: (0532) 843333
Also in:
Cheshire, Cleveland, Lincs, Staffs and Yorks

SHIPPERS

London
Featherston Shipping Ltd,
24 Hampton House, 15-17 Ingate Place, SW8
Tel: 071-720 0422

Lockson Services Ltd,
29 Broomfield Street, E14
Tel: 071-515 8600

Stephen Morris Shipping,
89 Upper Street, N1
Tel: 071-359 3159

Phelps Ltd,
133-135 St Margaret's Road, E Twickenham
Tel: 081-892 1778/7129

Pitt & Scott Ltd,
20/24 Eden Grove, N7
Tel: 071-607 7321

Avon
A J Williams,
607 Sixth Avenue, Central Business Park, Petherton Road, Hengrove, Bristol
Tel: (0272) 892166

Dorset
Alan Franklin Transport,
Unit 8, 27 Black Moor Road, Ebblake Industrial Estate, Verwood
Tel: (0202) 826539 & 826394 & 827092

Essex
Victor Hall Antique Exporters,
The Old Dairy, Cranes Farm Road, Basildon
Tel: (0268) 289545/6

Hants
Colin Macleod's Antiques Warehouse,
139 Goldsmith Avenue, Hants
Tel: (0705) 816278

Humberside
Geoffrey Mole,
400 Wincolmlee, Hull
Tel: (0482) 27858

Lancs
GG Antique Wholesalers,
25 Middleton Road, Middleton, Morecambe
Tel: (0524) 51565

West Lancs Antique Exports,
Black Horse Farm, 123 Liverpool Road, South Burscough, Nr Ormskirk
Tel: (0704) 894634/35720

Lincs
Laurence Shaw Antiques,
Spilsby Road, Horncastle
Tel: (06582) 7638

Middx
Burlington Northern Air Freight,
Unit 8, Ascot Road, Clockhouse Lane, Feltham
Tel: (0784) 244152

Staffs
Aspleys Antiques,
Compton Mill, Compton, Leek
Tel: (0538) 373396

Sussex
British Antiques Exporters Ltd,
Queen Elizabeth Avenue, Burgess Hill
Tel: (0444) 245577

Graham Price Antiques Ltd,
A27 Antiques Complex, Unit 4, Chaucer Industrial Estate, Dittons Road, Polegate
Tel: (032 12) 7167 & 7681

Peter Semus Antiques,
The Warehouse, Gladstone Road, Portslade
Tel: (0273) 420154/202989

SJB Shipping,
Chewton High Street, Angmering
Tel: (0903) 770198/785560

Wiltshire
C&C Transport Services,
The White House, Winterbourne Monkton, Swindon
Tel: (06723) 375

Scotland
Mini-Move Maxi-Move (Euro) Ltd,
27 Jock's Lodge, London Road, Edinburgh
Tel: 031-652 1255

TRADE SUPPLIERS

London
Air Improvement Centre Ltd,
23 Denbigh Street, London, SW1
Tel: 071-834 2834

Green & Stone of Chelsea – Art Supplies, Framing Service,
259 King's Road, London, SW3
Tel: 071-352 6521/0837

Devon
Optimum Brasses,
7 Castle Street, Bampton
Tel: (0398) 31515

Kent
C & A J Barmby,
Fine Art Accessories, 68 Judd Road, Tonbridge, Kent
Tel: (0732) 356479

Lancs
GG Antique Wholesalers,
25 Middleton Road, Middleton, Morecambe
Tel: (0524) 51565

Sussex
Loveland Antiques,
18-20 Prospect Place, Hastings
Tel: (0424) 441608

Westham Desk Leathers,
High Street, Westham, Pevensey
Tel: (0323) 766483

West Midlands
Retro Products,
174 Norton Road, Stourbridge
Tel: (0384) 373332

Yorks
Stanley Tools Ltd,
Woodside, Sheffield, S Yorkshire
Tel: (0742) 78678

ANTIQUE CENTRES & MARKETS

London
Atlantic Antique Centres,
15 Flood Street, SW3
Tel: 071-351 5353

Alfies Antique Market,
13-25 Church Street, NW8
Tel: 071-723 6066

Antiquarius Antique Market,
135/141 King's Road, Chelsea, SW3
Tel: 071-351 5353

Bermondsey Antique Market & Warehouse,
173 Bermondsey Street, SE1
Tel: 071-407 2040

Bond Street Antique Centre,
124 New Bond Street, W1

Camden Passage Antique Centre,
357 Upper Street, Islington, N1
Tel: 071-359 0190

Chenil Galleries,
181-183 King's Road, SW3
Tel: 071-351 5353

Georgian Village,
Camden Passage, Islington, N1
Tel: 071-226 1571

Grays,
1-7 Davies Mews, 58 Davies Street, W1
Tel: 071-629 7034

Hampstead Antique Emporium,
12 Heath Street, NW3
Tel: 071-794 3297

London Silver Vaults,
Chancery House, 53-65 Chancery Lane, WC2
Tel: 071-242 3844

The Mall Antiques Arcade,
359 Upper Street, Islington, N1
Tel: 071-359 0825/3111

Avon
Bath Antique Market,
Guinea Lane, Paragon, Bath
Tel: (0225) 22510

Clifton Antiques Market,
26/28 The Mall, Clifton
Tel: (0272) 741627

Great Western Antique Centre,
Bartlett Street, Bath
Tel: (0225) 24243

Beds
Woburn Abbey Antiques Centre,
Woburn Abbey
Tel: (052 525) 350

Berks
Twyford Antiques Centre,
1 High Street, Twyford
Tel: (0734) 342161

Bucks
Great Missenden Antique Arcade,
76 High Street, Gt Missenden
Tel: (024 06) 2819 & 2330

Cambs
Collectors' Market,
Dales Brewery, Gwydir Street (off Mill Road), Cambridge

Cheshire
Chester Antique Centre (Antique Forum Ltd),
41 Lower Bridge Street, Chester
Tel: (0244) 314991

Cleveland
Mother Hubbard's Antiques Arcade,
140 Norton Road, Stockton-on-Tees
Tel: (0642) 615603

Cumbria
Cockermouth Antiques Market,
Main Street, Cockermouth
Tel: (0900) 824346

J W Thornton Antiques,
Supermarket, North Terrace, Bowness-on-Windermere
Tel: (0229) 88745 (0966) 22930 & 25183

Devon
Barbican Antiques Market,
82-84 Vauxhall Street, Barbican, Plymouth
Tel: (0752) 266927

New Street Antique Centre,
27 New Street, The Barbican, Plymouth
Tel: (0752) 661165

Sidmouth Antiques Market,
132 High Street (next to Fords), Sidmouth
Tel: (03955) 77981

Torquay Antique Centre,
177 Union Street, Torquay
Tel: (0803) 26621

Dorset
Antique Market,
Town Hall/Corn Exchange, Dorchester
Tel: (0963) 62478

Antique Market,
Digby Hall, Sherborne
Tel: (0963) 62478

Antiques Trade Warehouse,
28 Lome Park Road, Bournemouth
Tel: (0202) 292944

Barnes House Antiques Centre,
West Row, Wimborne Minster
Tel: (0202) 886275

Essex
Antique Centre,
Doubleday Corner, Coggeshall
Tel: (0376) 62646

Baddow Antiques & Craft Centre,
The Bringy, Church Street, Great Baddow
Tel: (0245) 71137 & 76159

Boston Hall Antiques Fair,
Boston Hall Hotel, The Leas,
Westcliff-on-Sea
Tel: (0702) 714649

Maldon Antiques & Collectors' Market,
United Reformed Church Hall,
Market Hill, Maldon
Tel: (078 75) 2826

Orsett Antiques Fair,
Orsett Hall, Prince Charles
Avenue, Orsett
Tel: (0702) 714649

Trinity Antiques Centre,
7 Trinity Street, Colchester
Tel: (0206) 577775

Glos

Antique Centre,
London House, High Street,
Moreton-in-Marsh
Tel: (0608) 51084

Cheltenham Antique Market,
54 Suffolk Road, Cheltenham
Tel: (0242) 29812/32615/20139

Cirencester Antique Market,
Market Place (Antique Forum Ltd), Cirencester
Tel: 071-262 1168 &
071-263 4045

Gloucester Antique Centre,
1 Severn Road, Gloucester
Tel: (0452) 29716

Tewkesbury Antique Centre,
78 Church Street, Tewkesbury
Tel: (0684) 294091

Hants

Winchester Craft & Antique Market,
King's Walk, Winchester
Tel: (0962) 62277

Hereford & Worcester

Kidderminster Antiques Market,
11 Towers Buildings, Blackwell
Street, Kidderminster
Tel: (0562) 742859

Leominster Antiques Market,
14 Broad Street, Leominster
Tel: (0568) 2189/2155

Herts

The Herts & Essex Antiques Centre,
The Maltings, Station Road,
Sawbridgeworth
Tel: (0279) 722044

St Albans Antique Market,
Town Hall, Chequer Street,
St Albans
Tel: (0727) 66100 & 50427

Kent

The Antiques Centre,
120 London Road, Sevenoaks
Tel: (0732) 452104

Canterbury Weekly Antique Market,
Sidney Cooper Centre, Canterbury
(No telephone number)

Hoodeners Antiques & Collectors' Market,
Red Cross Centre, Lower Chantry
Lane, Canterbury
Tel: (022 770) 437

Hythe Antique Centre,
The Old Post Office, 5 High Street,
Hythe
Tel: (0303) 69643

Noah's Ark Antique Centre,
King Street, Sandwich
Tel: (0304) 611144

The Old Rose Gallery (Antique Market),
152 High Street, Sandgate
Tel: (0303) 39173

Rochester Antiques & Flea
Market, Rochester Market,
Corporation Street, Rochester
Tel: 081-262 1168 &
081-263 4045

Sandgate Antiques Centre,
61-63 Sandgate High Street,
Sandgate (Nr Folkestone)
Tel: (0303) 38987

Westerham Antique Centre,
18 Market Square, Westerham
Tel: (0959) 62080

Lancs

Castle Antiques,
Moore Lane, Clitheroe
Tel: (0254) 35820

Eccles Used Furniture & Antique Centre,
325/7 Liverpool Road, Patricroft
Bridge, Eccles
Tel: 061-789 4467

Manchester Antique Hypermarket,
Levenshulme Town Hall,
965 Stockport Road, Levenshulme
Tel: 061-224 2410

North Western Antique Centre,
New Preston Mill (Horrockses
Yard), New Hall Lane, Preston
Tel: (0772) 798159

Leics

The Kibworth Antique Centre,
5 Weir Road, Kibworth
Tel: (053 753) 2761

Leicester Antique Centre Ltd,
16-26 Oxford Street, Leicester
Tel: (0533) 553006

Lincs

The Antique Centre,
1 Spilsby Road, Wainfleet
Tel: (0754) 880489

Lincolnshire Antiques Centre,
Bridge Street, Horncastle
Tel: (06582) 7794

Norfolk

Antique & Collectors Market,
St Michael at Plea, Bank Plain,
Norwich
Tel: (0603) 619129
Open 9.30-5pm

Coltishall Antiques Centre,
High Street, Coltishall
Tel: (0603) 738306

Fakenham Antique Centre,
Old Congregational Chapel,
14 Norwich Road, Fakenham
Tel: (0328) 2941 or home (0263)
860543

Holt Antiques Centre,
Albert Hall, Albert Street, Holt
Tel: (0362) 5509 & (0263) 733301

Norwich Antique & Collectors' Centre,
Quayside, Fye Bridge, Norwich
Tel: (0603) 612582

The Old Granary Antique & Collectors' Centre,
King Staithe Lane, off Queen's
Street, King's Lynn
Tel: (0553) 5509

Northants

Finedon Antiques Centre,
3 Church Street, Finedon
Tel: (0933) 680316

The Village Antique Market,
62 High Street, Weedon
Tel: (0327) 42015

Northumberland

Colmans of Hexham (Saleroom & Antique Fair),
15 St Mary's Chare, Hexham
Tel: (0434) 603812/605522

Notts

East Bridgford Antiques Centre,
Main Street, East Bridgford
Tel: (0949) 20540 & 20741

Newark Art & Antiques Centre,
The Market Place, Chain Lane,
Newark
Tel: (0636) 703959

Nottingham Antique Centre,
British Rail Goods Yard, London
Road, Nottingham
Tel: (0602) 54504/55548

Top Hat Antiques Centre,
66-72 Derby Road, Nottingham
Tel: (0602) 419143

Oxon

The Antique Centre,
Laurel House, Bull Ring, Market
Place, Deddington
Tel: (0869) 38968

Shropshire

Ironbridge Antique Centre,
Dale End, Ironbridge
Tel: (095 245) 3784

Ludlow Antiques Centre,
29 Corve Street, Ludlow
Tel: (0584) 5157

Shrewsbury Antique Market,
Frankwell Quay Warehouse
(Vintagevale Ltd), Shrewsbury
Tel: (0734) 50916

Stretton Antiques Market,
Sandford Avenue, Church Stretton
Tel: (06945) 402
also: (05884) 374

Somerset

Crewkerne Antiques Centre,
42 East Street, Crewkerne
Tel: (0460) 76755

Taunton Antiques Centre,
27/29 Silver Street, Taunton
Tel: (0823) 89327

Staffs

The Antique Centre,
7A The Digbeth Arcade, Walsall
Tel: (0922) 725163/5

Barclay House,
Howard Place, Shelton,
Stoke-on-Trent
Tel: (0782) 657674/274747

Bridge House Antiques & Collectors' Centre,
56 Newcastle Road, Stone
Tel: (0785) 818218

Rugeley Antique Centre,
161/3 Main Road, Rugeley
Tel: (088 94) 77166

Suffolk

Old Town Hall Antique Centre,
High Street, Needham Market
Tel: (0449) 720773

St John's Antique Centre,
31-32 St John's Street, Bury St
Edmunds
Tel: (0284) 3024

Waveney Antique Centre,
The Old School, Peddars Lane,
Beccles
Tel: (0502) 716147

Surrey

Antique Centre,
22 Haydon Place, Corner of Martyr
Road, Guildford
Tel: (0483) 67817

Andrew Cottrell Galleries,
7/9 Church Street, Godalming
Tel: (048 68) 7570

Farnham Antique Centre,
27 South Street, Farnham
Tel: (0252) 724475

Maltings Market,
Bridge Square, Farnham
Tel: (0252) 726234

The Old Forge Antiques Centre,
The Green, Godstone
Tel: (0883) 843230

The Old Smithy Antique Centre,
7 High Street, Merstham
Tel: (073 74) 2306

Victoria & Edward Antiques,
61 West Street, Dorking
Tel: (0306) 889645

Sussex – East

Antique Market,
Leaf Hall, Seaside, Eastbourne
Tel: (0323) 27530

Bexhill Antiques Centre,
Old Town, Bexhill
Tel: (0424) 210182

Chateaubriand Antique Centre,
High Street, Burwash
Tel: (0435) 882535

Heathfield Antiques Centre,
Heathfield Market, Heathfield
Tel: (042 482) 387

Lewes Antiques Centre,
20 Cliffe High Street, Lewes
Tel: (0273) 476148

Newhaven Flea Market,
28 South Way, Newhaven
Tel: (0273) 517207

St Leonards Antique Dealers,
Norman Road, St Leonards-on-Sea
Tel: (0424) 444592

Polegate Antique Centre,
97 Station Road, Polegate
Tel: (032 12) 5277

Seaford's 'Barn Collectors' Market',
The Barn, Church Lane, Seaford
Tel: (0323) 890010

Strand Antiques,
Strand House, Rye
Tel: (0797) 222653

Sussex – West

Antiques Market,
Parish Hall, South Street, Lancing
Tel: (0903) 32414

Arundel Antiques Market,
5 River Road, Arundel
Tel: (0903) 882012

Midhurst Antiques Market,
Knockhundred Row, Midhurst
Tel: (073 081) 4231

Mostyns Antiques Centre,
64 Brighton Road, Lancing
Tel: (0903) 752961

Petworth Antiques Market,
East Street, Petworth
Tel: (0798) 42073

Robert Warner & Son Ltd,
South Farm Road, Worthing
Tel: (0903) 32710

Treasure House Antiques Market,
Rear of High Street, in Crown
Yard, Arundel
Tel: (0903) 883101

Tyne & Wear

Newcastle Antiques Centre,
64-80 Newgate Street, Newcastle-upon-Tyne
Tel: (0632) 614577

Warwickshire

Antiques Etc,
22 Railway Terrace, Rugby
Tel: (0788) 62837

Bidford-on-Avon Antiques Centre
High Street, Bidford-on-Avon
Tel: (0789) 773680

Vintage Antique Market,
36 Market Place, Warwick
Tel: (0926) 491527

Warwick Antique Centre,
16-18 High Street, Warwick
Tel: (0962) 492482

West Midlands

Birmingham Thursday Antique Centre,
141 Bromsgrove Street,
Birmingham
Tel: 021-692 1414

The City of Birmingham Antique Market,
St Martins Market, Edgbaston Street, Birmingham
Tel: 021-267 4636

Rock House Antiques & Collectors Centre,
Rock House, The Rock, Tettenhall, Wolverhampton
Tel: (0902) 754995

Yorks – North

Grove Collectors' Centre,
Grove Road, Harrogate
Tel: (0423) 61680

Harrogate Antique Centre,
The Ginnel, Corn Exchange Building, Harrogate
Tel: (0423) 508857

West Park Antiques Pavilion,
20 West Park, Harrogate
Tel: (0423) 61758

York Antique Centre,
2 Lendal, York
Tel: (0904) 641445

Yorks – South

Treasure House Antiques and Antique Centre,
8-10 Swan Street, Bawtry
Tel: (0302) 710621

Yorks – West

Halifax Antique Centre,
Queen's Road/Gibbet Street, Halifax
Tel: (0422) 366657

Scotland

Bath Street Antique Centre,
203 Bath Street, Glasgow
Tel: 041-248 4220

Corner House Antiques,
217 St Vincent Street, Glasgow
Tel: 041-221 1000

The Victorian Village,
57 West Regent Street, Glasgow
Tel: 041-332 0808

Wales

Cardiff Antique Centre,
69-71 St Mary Street, Cardiff
Tel: (0222) 30970
(Open Thurs & Sat)

Graham H Evans, FRICS,
Auction Sales Centre,
Kilgetty, Nr Saundersfoot, Dyfed
Tel: (0834) 812793

RESTORATION

Sussex

Richard Davidson,
Lombard Street, Petworth
Tel: (0798) 42508/43354

Scotland

Traditional Antique Restoration,
The Stable, Altyre Estate, Forres, Moray
Tel: (0309) 72572

DIRECTORY OF AUCTIONEERS

This directory is by no means complete. Any auctioneer who holds frequent sales should contact us for inclusion in the next Edition. Entries must be received by April 1991. There is, of course, no charge for this listing. Entries will be repeated in subsequent editions unless we are requested otherwise.

London

Academy Auctioneers & Valuers,
Windsor Hall, Windsor Road, Ealing, W5
Tel: 081-992 2518/081-868 2812

Allen of Lee Ltd,
165 Lee High Road, SE13
Tel: 081-852 3145

Bethnal Green Auctions,
4-6 Ellsworth Street, E2
Tel: 071-739 7348

Bonhams, Montpelier Galleries,
Montpelier Street, Knightsbridge, SW7
Tel: 071-584 9161

Camden Auctions,
The Saleroom, Hoppers Road, Winchmore Hill, N21
Tel: 081-886 1550

Christie Manson & Woods Ltd,
8 King Street, St James's, SW1
Tel: 071-839 9060

Christie's Robson Lowe,
47 Duke Street, London, SW1
Tel: 071-839 4034/5

Christie's South Kensington Ltd,
85 Old Brompton Road, SW7
Tel: 071-581 7611

Colney Hatch Auctions,
54/56 High Street, Hornsey, N8
Tel: 081-340 5334

Forrest & Co,
79-85 Cobbold Road, Leytonstone, E11 Tel: 081-534 2931

Stanley Gibbons Auctions Ltd,
399 Strand, WC2
Tel: 071-836 8444

Glendining & Co,
Blenstock House, 7 Blenheim Street, New Bond Street, W1
Tel: 071-493 2445

Harmers of London Stamp Auctioneers Ltd,
1 New Bond Street, W1
Tel: 071-629 0218

Jackson-Stops & Staff,
4 Curzon Street, W1
Tel: 071-499 6291

Lots Road Chelsea Auction Galleries,
1 Lots Road, Worlds End, Chelsea, SW10
Tel: 071-351 7771

MacGregor Nash & Co,
Lodge House, 9-17 Lodge Lane, North Finchley, N12 8JH
Tel: 081-445 9000

Thomas Moore,
17-219 Greenwich High Road, E10 Tel: 081-858 7848

Newington Green Auctions,
55 Green Lanes, N16
Tel: 071-226 4442 & 0368

North West London Auctions,
Lodge House, 9-17 Lodge Lane, North Finchley, N12
Tel: 081-445 9000

Onslow's,
Metrostore, Townmead Road, SW6 2RZ.
Tel: 071-793 0240

Phillips,
Blenstock House, 7 Blenheim Street, New Bond Street, W1
Tel: 071-629 6602

Phillips,
10 Salem Road, London W2 4BU
Tel: 071-229 9090

Rippon Boswell & Co,
The Arcade, Sth Kensington Station, SW7
Tel: 071-589 4242

Rosebery's Fine Art Ltd,
Old Railway Booking Hall, Station Road, Crystal Palace, SE19 2A7
Tel: 081-778 4024

Sotheby's,
34-35 New Bond Street, W1
Tel: 071-493 8080

Southgate Antique Auction Rooms,
Munro House, Munro Drive, Cline Road, New Southgate, N11
Tel: 081-886 7888

Greater London

Chancellors,
Kingston upon Thames
Tel: 081-541 4139

Croydon Auctions Rooms (Rosan & Co)
144-150 London Road, Croydon
Tel: 081-688 1123/4/5

Parkins,
18 Malden Road, Cheam, Surrey
Tel: 081-644 6633 & 6127

Avon

Alder King, Black Horse Agencies,
The Old Malthouse, Comfortable Place, Upper Bristol Road, Bath
Tel: (0225) 447933

Aldridges, Bath,
The Auction Galleries, 130-132 Walcot Street, Bath
Tel: (0225) 62830 & 62839

GA Property Services,
Clevedon Salerooms, Sixways, Clevedon
Tel: (0272) 876699

Osmond Tricks,
Regent Street Auction Rooms, Clifton, Bristol
Tel: (0272) 737201

Phillips Auction Rooms of Bath,
1 Old King Street, Bath
Tel: (0225) 310609 & 319709

Phillips Fine Art Auctioneers,
71 Oakfield Road, Clifton, Bristol
Tel: (0272) 734052
also at:
Station Road, Weston-super-Mare
Tel: (0934) 33174

Taviner's Auction Rooms,
Prewett Street, Redcliffe, Bristol
Tel: (0272) 25996

Woodspring Auction Rooms,
Churchill Road, Weston-super-Mare
Tel: (0934) 28419

Bedfordshire

Peacock,
The Auction Centre, 26 Newnham Street, Bedford
Tel: (0234) 66366

Berkshire

Chancellors Fine Art,
32 High Street, Ascot
Tel: (0990) 872588

Dreweatt, Neate,
Donnington Priory, Donnington, Newbury
Tel: (0635) 31234

Holloway's,
12 High Street, Streatley, Reading
Tel: (0491) 872318

Martin & Pole,
5a & 7 Broad Street, Wokingham
Tel: (0734) 780777

Thimbleby & Shorland,
31 Great Knollys Street, Reading
Tel: (0734) 508611

Duncan Vincent Fine Art & Chattel Auctioneers,
105 London Street, Reading
Tel: (0734) 594748

Buckinghamshire

Hamptons,
10 Burkes Parade, Beaconsfield
Tel: (0494) 672969

Nationwide Anglia,
Amersham Auction Rooms,
125 Station Road, Amersham
Tel: (0494) 729292

Geo Wigley & Sons,
Winslow Sale Room, Market Square, Winslow
Tel: (029 671) 2717

Cambridgeshire

Cheffins Grain & Comins,
2 Clifton Road, Cambridge
Tel: (0223) 358721/213343

Phillips Fine Art Auctioneers,
The Saleroom, Market Square, St Ives, Huntingdon
Tel: (0480) 68144

Grounds & Co
2 Nene Quay, Wisbech
Tel: (0945) 585041

Hammond & Co,
Cambridge Place, off Hills Road, Cambridge
Tel: (0223) 356067

Maxey & Son,
1-3 South Brink, Wisbech
Tel: (0945) 583123/4

Cheshire

Andrew, Hilditch & Son,
19 The Square, Sandbach
Tel: (0270) 762048/767246

Bridgfords Ltd,
The Alderley Saleroom, 1 Heyes Lane, Alderley Edge
Tel: (0625) 585347

Robert I Heyes,
Hatton Buildings, Lightfoot Street, Hoole, Chester
Tel: (0244) 28941

Highams Auctions,
Waterloo House, Waterloo Road, Stalybridge
Tel: 061-303 2924/061-303 1091

Frank R Marshall & Co,
Marshall House, Church Hill, Knutsford
Tel: (0565) 53284/53461

Phillips in Chester,
New House,
150 Christleton Road, Chester
Tel: (0244) 313936

Phillips Fine Art Auctioneers,
Trinity House, 114 Northenden Road, Sale, Manchester
Tel: 061-962 9237

Sotheby's
Booth Mansion, 28-30 Watergate Street, Chester
Tel: (0244) 315531

Henry Spencer Inc. Peter Wilson,
Victoria Gallery, Market Street, Nantwich
Tel: (0270) 623878

Wright Manley,
Beeston Sales Centre, 63 High Street, Tarporley
Tel: (0829) 260318

Cleveland

Norman Hope & Partners,
2 South Road, Hartlepool
Tel: (0429) 267828

Lithgow Sons & Partners,
The Auction Houses, Station Road, Stokesley, Middlesbrough
Tel: (0642) 710158 & 710326

Cornwall

Eric Distin & Dolton,
7 New Road, Callington
Tel: (0579) 83322

Lambrays, incorporating R J Hamm ASVA,
Polmorla Walk, The Platt, Wadebridge
Tel: (020 881) 3593

W H Lane & Son,
St Mary's Auction Rooms,
64 Morrab Road, Penzance
Tel: (0736) 61447

David Lay,
Penzance Auction House,
Alverton, Penzance
Tel: (0736) 61414

Miller & Co,
Lemon Quay Auction Rooms,
Lemon Quay, Truro
Tel: (0872) 74211

Phillips Cornwall,
Cornubia Hall, Par
Tel: (072 681) 4047

Pooley and Rogers,
9 Alverton Street, Penzance and Regent Auction Rooms, Penzance
Tel: (0736) 63816/7 and (0736) 68814

Jeffery's
5 Fore Street, Lostwithiel
Tel: (0208) 872245

Cumbria

Mitchells,
Fairfield House, Cockermouth
Tel: (0900) 822016

Alfred Mossops & Co,
Loughrigg Villa, Kelsick Road, Ambleside
Tel: (09663) 3015

Phillips Fine Art Auctioneers,
2 Market Street, Ulverston
Tel: (0229) 55205

James Thompson,
64 Main Street, Kirkby Lonsdale
Tel: (0468) 71555

Thomson, Roddick & Laurie,
24 Lowther Street, Carlisle
Tel: (0228) 28939 & 39636

Tiffen, King & Nicholson,
12 Lowther Street, Carlisle
Tel: (0228) 25259

Derbyshire

Noel Wheatcroft & Son,
The Matlock Auction Gallery,
39 Dale Road, Matlock
Tel: (0629) 584591

Devon

Bearnes,
Avenue Road, Torquay
Tel: (0803) 296277

Bonhams West Country,
Devon Fine Art Auction House,
Dowell Street, Honiton
Tel: (0404) 41872/3137

Michael J Bowman,
6 Haccombe House, Nr Netherton, Newton Abbot
Tel: (0626) 872890

Eric Distin & Dolton,
2 Bretonside, Plymouth
Tel: (0752) 663046

Peter J Eley,
Western House, 98-100 High Street, Sidmouth
Tel: (0395) 513006

Robin A Fenner & Co
51 Bannawell Street, Tavistock
Tel: (0822) 4974

Kingsbridge Auction Sales,
113 Fore Street, Kingsbridge
Tel: (0548) 2352

Michael Newman,
Kinterbury House, St Andrew's Cross, Plymouth
Tel: (0752) 669298

Phillips,
Alphin Brook Road, Alphington, Exeter
Tel: (0392) 39025/6
and
Armada Street, North Hill, Plymouth
Tel: (0752) 673504

Potburys of Sidmouth,
High Street, Sidmouth
Tel: (039 55) 2414

Rendells,
Stone Park, Ashburton
Tel: (0364) 53017

G S Shobrook & Co,
20 Western Approach, Plymouth
Tel: (0752) 663341

John Smale & Co,
19 Cross Street, Barnstaple
Tel: (0271) 42000/42916

Spencer Thomas & Woolland,
Church Street Auction Rooms, Exmouth
Tel: (0395) 267403

Taylors,
Honiton Galleries, 205 High Street, Honiton
Tel: (0404) 2404

Ward & Chowen,
1 Church Lane, Tavistock
Tel: (0822) 2458

Whitton & Laing,
32 Okehampton Street, Exeter
Tel: (0392) 52621

Dorset

Cottees, Bullock & Lees,
The Market, East Street, Wareham
Tel: (09295) 2826

Hy Duke & Son,
Fine Art Salerooms, Weymouth Ave, Dorchester
Tel: (0305) 65080
also at:
The Weymouth Saleroom,
St Nicholas Street, Weymouth
Tel: (0305) 783488

Garnet Langton Auctions,
Burlington Arcade, Bournemouth
Tel: (0202) 22352

House & Son,
Lansdowne House, Christchurch Road, Bournemouth
Tel: (0202) 26232

John Jeffery & Son,
The Livestock Market, Christ's Lane, Shaftesbury
Tel: (0747) 52720

William Morey & Sons,
The Saleroom, St Michaels Lane, Bridport Tel: (0308) 22078

Phillips Fine Art Auctioneers,
Sturminster Newton
Tel: (0258) 72244

Riddetts of Bournemouth,
26 Richmond Hill, Bournemouth Square, Bournemouth
Tel: (0202) 25686

County Durham

Denis Edkins,
Auckland Auction Room,
58 Kingsway, Bishop Auckland
Tel: (0388) 603095

Thomas Watson & Son,
Northumberland Street, Darlington
Tel: (0325) 462559/463485

Wingate Auction Co,
Station Lane, Station Town, Wingate
Tel: (0429) 837245

Essex

Abridge Auction Rooms,
Market Place, Abridge
Tel: (037881) 2107/3113

Black Horse Agencies,
Ambrose, 149 High Road, Loughton
Tel: 081-508 2121/081-502 3951

William H Brown,
The Auction Rooms, 11-14 East Hill, Colchester
Tel: (0206) 868070

Cooper Hirst,
The Granary Saleroom, Victoria Road, Chelmsford
Tel: (0245) 258141/260535

GA Property Services,
1 Market Street, Saffron Walden
Tel: (0799) 513281

Grays Auction Rooms,
Ye Old Bake House, Alfred Street, Grays
Tel: (0375) 381181

Hamptons,
The Old Town Hall, Great Dunmow
Tel: (0371) 873014

John Stacey & Sons,
Leigh Auction Rooms, 86-90 Pall Mall, Leigh-on-Sea
Tel: (0702) 77051

Vosts' Fine Art Auctioneers,
Layer Marney, Colchester
Tel: (0206) 331005

Gloucestershire

Bruton, Knowles & Co,
111 Eastgate Street, Gloucester
Tel: (0452) 21267

Fraser Glennie & Partners,
The Old Rectory, Siddington, Nr Cirencester
Tel: (0285) 3938

Hobbs & Chambers,
Market Place, Cirencester
Tel: (0285) 654736
also at:
15 Royal Crescent, Cheltenham
Tel: (0242) 513722

Ken Lawson t/as Specialised Postcard Auctions,
25 Gloucester Street, Cirencester
Tel: (0285) 69057

Mallams,
26 Grosvenor Street, Cheltenham
Tel: (0242) 35712

Moore, Allen & Innocent,
33 Castle Street, Cirencester
Tel: (0285) 61831

Nationwide Anglia (Sandoes),
Wotton Auction Rooms,
Tabernacle Road, Wotton-under-Edge
Tel: (0453) 844733

Hampshire

Andover Saleroom,
41A London Street, Andover
Tel: (0264) 64820

Fox & Sons,
5 & 7 Salisbury Street, Fordingbridge
Tel: (0425) 52121

GA Fine Art & Chattels,
The Romsey Auction Rooms,
86 The Hundred, Romsey
Tel: (0794) 513331

Stanley Gibbons Auctions Ltd,
5 Parkside, Christchurch Road, Ringwood
Tel: (04254) 77107

Hants & Berks Auctions,
82, 84 Sarum Hill, Basingstoke
Tel: (0256) 840707
also at:
Heckfield Village Hall, Heckfield, Berks

Jacobs & Hunt,
Lavant Street, Petersfield
Tel: (0730) 62744/5

May & Son,
18 Bridge Street, Andover
Tel: (0264) 23417

D M Nesbit & Co,
7 Clarendon Road, Southsea
Tel: (0705) 864321

Nationwide Anglia,
New Forest Auction Rooms,
Emsworth Road, Lymington
Tel: (0590) 677225

Phillips Fine Art Auctioneers,
54 Southampton Road, Ringwood
Tel: (04254) 3333
also at:
The Red House, Hyde Street, Winchester
Tel: (0962) 62515

Hereford & Worcester

Carless & Co,
58 Lowesmoor, Worcester
Tel: (0905) 612449

Henry Spencer Inc. Coles, Knapp & Kennedy,
Georgian Rooms & Tudor House, Ross-on-Wye
Tel: (0989) 62227/63553/4

Andrew Grant,
St Mark's House, St Mark's Close, Worcester
Tel: (0905) 357547

Arthur G Griffiths & Son,
57 Foregate Street, Worcester
Tel: (0905) 26464

Hamptons,
71 Church Street, Malvern
Tel: (0684) 892314

Philip Laney & Jolly,
12a Worcester Road, Gt Malvern
Tel: (06845) 63121/2

Phipps & Pritchard,
Bank Buildings, Kidderminster
Tel: (0562) 822244/6 & 822187

Russell, Baldwin & Bright,
Fine Art Saleroom, Ryelands Road, Leominster
Tel: (0568) 611166

Sandoes,
41-43 High Street, Broadway
Tel: (0386) 852456

Village Auctions,
Sycthampton Community Centre, Ombersley
Tel: (0905) 421007

Hertfordshire

Bayles,
Childs Farm, Cottered, Buntingford, Herts
Tel: (076 381) 256

Brown & Merry,
41 High Street, Tring
Tel: (044 282) 6446

M & B Nesbitt,
The Antique Centre, 23 Hydeway Welwyn Garden City
Tel: (07073) 34901

Norris & Duvall,
106 The Fore Street, Hertford
Tel: (0992) 582249

Pamela & Barry Auctions,
The Village Hall, High Street, Sandridge, St Albans
Tel: (0727) 61180

Sworders,
Northgate End Salerooms, Bishops Stortford
Tel: (0279) 651388

Watsons,
Water Lane, Bishops Stortford
Tel: (0279) 757250

Humberside North

Gilbert Baitson, FSVA,
The Edwardian Auction Galleries,
194 Anlaby Road, Hull
Tel: (0482) 223355/645241/865831

Broader & Spencer,
18 Quay Road, Bridlington
Tel: (0262) 670355/6

H Evans & Sons,
1 Parliament Street, Hull
Tel: (0482) 23033

Humberside South

Dickinson, Davy & Markham,
10 Wrawby Street, Brigg
Tel: (0652) 53666

Isle of Man

Chrystals Auctions,
St James Chambers, Athol Street,
Douglas
Tel: (0624) 73986

Isle of Wight

Nationwide Anglia,
Isle of Wight Auction Rooms,
50/52 Regent Street, Shanklin
Tel: (0983) 863 441

Phillips Fine Art Auctioneers,
Cross Street Salerooms, Newport
Tel: (0983) 523812

Ways,
Town Hall Chambers, Lind Street,
Ryde
Tel: (0983) 62255

Kent

Albert Andrews Auctions & Sales,
Maiden Lane, Crayford, Dartford
Tel: (0322) 528868

Black Horse Agencies,
Geering & Colyer, Highgate,
Hawkhurst
Tel: (0580) 753463

Bracketts,
27-29 High Street, Tunbridge
Wells
Tel: (0892) 33733

County Group,
Butler & Hatch Waterman,
102 High Street, Tenterden
Tel: (05806) 2083/3233

GA Auction Galleries,
39-41 Bank Street, Ashford
Tel: (0233) 24321

GA Auction Galleries,
0 Station Road West, Canterbury
Tel: (0227) 763337

Stewart Gore,
100-102 Northdown Road,
Margate
Tel: (0843) 221528/9

Hobbs Parker,
Romney House, Ashford Market,
Elwick Road, Ashford
Tel: (0233) 622222

Ibbett Mosely,
125 High Street, Sevenoaks
Tel: (0732) 452246

Kent Sales,
Giffords', Holmesdale Road, South
Darenth
Tel: (0322) 864919

Lawrence Butler & Co, (inc. F W
Butler & Co),
Fine Art Salerooms, Butler House,
5 High Street, Hythe
Tel: (0303) 266022/3

J Norris,
The Quest', West Street,
Harrietsham, Nr Maidstone
Tel: (0622) 859515

Phillips,
1 Bayle Parade, Folkestone
Tel: (0303) 45555

Phillips Fine Art Auctioneers,
49 London Road, Sevenoaks
Tel: (0732) 740310

Halifax Property Services,
Fine Art Department, 53 High
Street, Tenterden
Tel: (05806) 3200
also at:
The Sandwich Saleroom,
The Drill Hall, The Quay,
Sandwich
Tel: (0304) 611044

Walter & Randall,
7-13 New Road, Chatham
Tel: (0634) 841233

Peter S Williams, FSVA,
Orchard End, Sutton Valence,
Maidstone
Tel: (0622) 842350

Lancashire

Artingstall & Hind,
29 Cobden Street, Pendleton,
Salford
Tel: 061-736 5682

Capes Dunn & Co,
The Auction Galleries, 38 Charles
Street, Manchester
Tel: 061-273 6060/1911

Entwistle Green,
The Galleries, Kingsway, Ansdell,
Lytham St Annes
Tel: (0253) 735442

Robt. Fairhurst & Son,
39 Mawdsley Street, Bolton
Tel: (0204) 28452/28453

Highams Auctions,
Southgate House, Southgate
Street, Rhodes Bank, Oldham
Tel: 061-626 1021/061-665 1881/
061-624 8580
also at:
Onward Buildings,
207 Deansgate, Manchester
Tel: 061-834 0068

Robert Maybin & Co (Auctions),
The Sale Rooms, 88 Stansfield
Street, Blackburn
Tel: (0254) 676976

McKennas, formerly Hothersall,
Forrest, McKenna & Sons,
Bank Salerooms, Harris Court,
Clitheroe
Tel: (0200) 25446/22695

Mills & Radcliffe,
101 Union Street, Oldham
Tel: 061-624 1072

J R Parkinson Son & Hamer
Auctions, The Auction Rooms,
Rochdale Road, Bury
Tel: (061 761) 1612/7372

Phillips,
Trinity House, 114 Northenden
Road, Sale, Manchester
Tel: 061-962 9237

John E Pinder & Son,
Stone Bridge, Longridge, Preston
Tel: (077478) 2282

Smythe, Son & Walker,
174 Victoria Road West, Cleveleys
Tel: (0253) 852184 & 854084

Warren & Wignall Ltd,
The Mill, Earnshaw Bridge,
Leyland Lane, Leyland
Tel: (0772) 453252/451430

Leicestershire

Churchgate Auctions,
The Churchgate Saleroom,
66 Churchgate, Leicester
Tel: (0533) 621416

Gildings,
64 Roman Way, Market
Harborough
Tel: (0858) 410 414

N H Noton & Associates,
4 Market Place, Oakham
Tel (0572) 722681

David Stanley Auctions,
Stordon Grange, Osgathorpe,
Loughborough
Tel: (0530) 222320

William H Brown,
The Warner Auction Rooms,
16/18 Halford Street, Leicester
Tel: (0533) 519777

Lincolnshire

William H Brown,
Fine Art Dept, Westgate Hall,
Westgate, Grantham
Tel: (0476) 68861

A E Dowse & Son,
89 Mary Street, Scunthorpe
Tel: (0724) 842039

James Eley & Son,
1 Main Ridge West, Boston
Tel: (0205) 61687

Henry Spencer & Sons,
42 Silver Street, Lincoln
Tel: (0522) 536666

Thomas Mawer & Son,
63 Monks Road, Lincoln
Tel: (0522) 524984

Nationwide Anglia,
Bourne Auction Rooms, Spalding
Road, Bourne
Tel (0778) 422686

John H Walter,
1 Mint Lane, Lincoln
Tel: (0522) 525454

Merseyside

Hartley & Co,
12 & 14 Moss Street, Liverpool
Tel: 051-263 6472/1865

Robert I Heyes & Associates,
9 Hamilton Street, Birkenhead
Tel: 051-647 9104

Kingsley Galleries,
3-4 The Quadrant, Hoylake,
Wirral
Tel: 051-632 5821

Outhwaite & Litherland,
Kingsway Galleries, Fontenoy
Street, Liverpool
Tel: 051-236 6561/3

Eldon E Worrall,
13-15 Seel Street, Liverpool
Tel: 051-709 2950

Norfolk

Ewings,
Market Place, Reepham, Norwich
Tel: (0603) 870473

Thos Wm Gaze & Son,
10 Market Hill, Diss
Tel: (0379) 651931

Glennie's,
Wensum Hall, Wensum Street,
Norwich
Tel: (0603) 633558

Nigel F Hedge,
28B Market Place, North
Walsham
Tel: (0692) 402881

Hilhams,
Baker Street, Gorleston, Great
Yarmouth
Tel: (0493) 662152 & 600700

James Norwich Auctions Ltd,
33 Timberhill, Norwich
Tel: (0603) 624817/625369

G A Key,
8 Market Place, Aylsham
Tel: (0263) 733195

Northamptonshire

T W Arnold Corby & Co,
30-32 Brook Street, Raunds
Tel: (0933) 623722

Goldsmiths,
15 Market Place, Oundle
Tel: (0832) 72349

Heathcote Ball & Co,
Albion Auction Rooms, Old Albion
Brewery, Commercial Street,
Northampton Tel: (0604) 22735

R L Lowery & Partners,
24 Bridge Street, Northampton
Tel: (0604) 21561

Southam & Sons,
Corn Exchange, Thrapston,
Kettering
Tel: (08012) 4486

H Wilford Ltd,
Midland Road, Wellingborough
Tel: (0933) 222760 & 222762

Northumberland

Louis Johnson & Co Ltd,
Morpeth
Tel: (0670) 513025/55210

Nottinghamshire

Arthur Johnson & Sons Ltd,
The Nottingham Auction Rooms,
The Cattle Market, Meadow Lane,
Nottingham
Tel: (0602) 869128

Neales of Nottingham,
192 Mansfield Road, Nottingham
Tel: (0602) 624141

John Pye & Sons,
Corn Exchange, Cattle Market,
London Road, Nottingham
Tel: (0602) 866261

C B Sheppard & Son,
The Auction Galleries, Chatsworth
Street, Sutton-in-Ashfield
Tel: (0773) 872419

Henry Spencer & Sons Ltd,
20 The Square, Retford
Tel: (0777) 708633

T Vennett-Smith,
11 Nottingham Road, Gotham,
Nottinghamshire
Tel: (0602) 830541

Oxfordshire

Green & Co,
33 Market Place, Wantage
Tel: (02357) 3561/2

Holloways,
49 Parsons Street, Banbury
Tel: (0295) 53197/8

Mallams,
24 St Michael's Street, Oxford
Tel: (0865) 241358

Messengers,
27 Sheep Street, Bicester
Tel: (08692) 52901

Phillips Inc Brooks,
39 Park End Street, Oxford
Tel: (0865) 723524

Simmons & Sons,
32 Bell Street, Henley-on-Thames
Tel: (0491) 571111

Shropshire

Cooper & Green,
3 Barker Street, Shrewsbury
Tel: (0743) 232244

John German,
43 High Street, Shrewsbury
Tel: (0743) 69661/4

Hall, Wateridge & Owen,
Welsh Bridge Salerooms,
Shrewsbury
Tel: (0743) 60212

Ludlow Antique Auctions,
29 Corve Street, Ludlow
Tel: (0584) 5157/3496

McCartneys,
25 Corve Street, Ludlow
Tel: (0584) 872636

Perry & Phillips,
Newmarket Salerooms,
Newmarket Buildings, Listley
Street, Bridgnorth
Tel: (07462) 2248

Somerset

Dores, The Auction Mart,
Vicarage Street, Frome
Tel: (0373) 62257

John Fleming,
4 & 8 Fore Street, Dulverton
Tel: (0398) 23597

W R J Greenslade,
13 Hamet Street, Taunton
Tel: (0823) 277121
also at:
Priory Saleroom, Winchester Street, Taunton

Gribble Booth & Taylor,
32 The Avenue, Minehead
Tel: (0643) 702281/3

King Miles,
25 Market Place, Wells
Tel: (0749) 73002

The London Cigarette Card Co Ltd,
Sutton Road, Somerton
Tel: (0458) 73452

Nationwide Anglia,
Frome Auction Rooms, Frome Market, Standerwick, Nr Frome
Tel: (0373) 831010

Nuttall Richards & Co,
The Square, Axbridge
Tel: (0934) 723969

Wellington Salerooms, Mantle Street, Wellington
Tel: (082347) 4815

Staffordshire

Bagshaws,
17 High Street, Uttoxeter
Tel: (08893) 562811

Hall & Lloyd,
South Street Auction Rooms, Stafford
Tel: (0785) 58176

Louis Taylor,
Percy Street, Hanley, Stoke-on-Trent
Tel: (0782) 260222

Wintertons,
St Mary's Chambers, Lichfield
Tel: (0543) 263256

Suffolk

Abbotts (East Anglia) Ltd,
The Hill, Wickham Market, Woodbridge
Tel: (0728) 746321

Boardman Fine Art,
Station Road Corner, Haverhill
Tel: (0440) 730414

Diamond, Mills & Co,
117 Hamilton Road, Felixstowe
Tel: (0394) 282281

Durrant's,
10 New Market, Beccles
Tel: (0502) 712122

Flick & Son,
Ashford House, Saxmundham
Tel: (0728) 603232

Lacy Scott,
Fine Art Department, The Auction Centre, 10 Risbygate Street, Bury St Edmunds
Tel: (0284) 763531

Neal Sons & Fletcher,
26 Church Street, Woodbridge
Tel: (03943) 2263/4

Olivers, William H Brown,
Olivers Rooms, Burkitts Lane, Sudbury
Tel: (0787) 880305

Phillips,
Dover House, Wilsey Street, Ipswich
Tel: (0473) 55137

Tuohy & Son,
Denmark House, 18 High Street, Aldeburgh
Tel: (072885) 2066

H C Wolton & Son,
6 Whiting Street, Bury St Edmunds
Tel: (0284) 61336

Surrey

Ewbank Fine Art,
Welbeck House, High Street, Guildford
Tel: (0483) 232134

Clark Gammon,
The Guildford Auction Rooms,
45 High Street, Guildford
Tel: (0483) 572266

Hamptons,
93 High Street, Godalming
Tel: (04868) 23567

Lawrences,
Norfolk House, 80 High Street, Bletchingley
Tel: (0883) 843323

Phillips Fine Art Auctioneers,
Millmead, Guildford
Tel: (0483) 504030

Wentworth Auction Galleries,
21 Station Approach, Virginia Water
Tel: (09904) 3711

P F Windibank,
18-20 Reigate Road, Dorking
Tel: (0306) 884556

Sussex – East

Ascent Auction Galleries,
11-12 East Ascent, St Leonards-on-Sea, E Sussex
Tel: (0424) 420275

Burstow & Hewett,
Abbey Auction Galleries and Granary Salerooms, Battle
Tel: (04246) 2374/2302

Clifford Dann Auction Galleries,
20-21 High Street, Lewes
Tel: (0273) 480111

Eastbourne Auctioneers,
10 Cornfield Lane, Eastbourne
Tel: (0323) 411315

Fryers Auction Galleries,
Terminus Road, Bexhill-on-Sea
Tel: (0424) 212994

Gorringes Auction Galleries,
15 North Street, Lewes
Tel: (0273) 472503

Graves, Son & Pilcher,
Fine Arts, 71 Church Road, Hove
Tel: (0273) 735266

Hove Auction Galleries,
115 Church Road, Hove
Tel: (0273) 736207

Raymond P Inman,
Auction Galleries, 35 & 40 Temple Street, Brighton
Tel: (0273) 774777

Lewes Auction Rooms (Julian Dawson),
56 High Street, Lewes
Tel: (0273) 478221

Phillips Fine Art Auctioneers,
Rye Auction Galleries, Cinque Ports Street, Rye
Tel: (0797) 222124

Michael Shortall,
120 Marina, St Leonards-on-Sea
Tel: (0424) 434854

Wallis & Wallis,
West Street Auction Galleries, Lewes
Tel: (0273) 480208

E Watson & Sons,
Heathfield Furniture Salerooms, The Market, Burwash Road, Heathfield
Tel: (04352) 2132

Sussex – West

T Bannister & Co,
Market Place, Haywards Heath
Tel: (0444) 412402

Peter Cheney,
Western Road Auction Rooms, Western Road, Littlehampton
Tel: (0903) 722264 & 713418

Denham's,
Horsham Auction Galleries, Warnham, Horsham
Tel: (0403) 53837/53699

R H Ellis & Sons,
44-46 High Street, Worthing
Tel: (0903) 38999

Nationwide Anglia,
Midhurst Auction Rooms, Bepton Road, Midhurst
Tel: (073081) 2456

Phillips Fine Art Auctioneers,
Baffins Hall, Baffins Lane, Chichester
Tel: (0243) 787548

Sotheby's in Sussex,
Summers Place, Billingshurst
Tel: (040381) 3933

Stride & Son,
Southdown House, St John's Street, Chichester
Tel: (0243) 780207

Sussex Auction Galleries,
59 Perrymouth Road, Haywards Heath
Tel: (0444) 414935

Tyne & Wear

Anderson & Garland,
The Fine Art Sale Rooms, Marlborough House, Marlborough Crescent, Newcastle-upon-Tyne
Tel: 091-232 6278

Boldon Auction Galleries,
24a Front Street, East Boldon
Tel: 091-537 2630

Thomas N Miller,
18-22 Gallowgate, Newcastle-upon-Tyne
Tel: 091-232 5617

Sneddons,
Sunderland Auction Rooms,
30 Villiers Street, Sunderland
Tel: 091-514 5931

Warwickshire

Bigwood Auctioneers Ltd,
The Old School, Tiddington, Stratford-upon-Avon
Tel: (0789) 69415

John Briggs & Calder,
133 Long Street, Atherstone
Tel: (0827) 718911

Locke & England,
18 Guy Street, Leamington Spa
Tel: (0926) 427988

West Midlands

Biddle & Webb,
Icknield Square, Ladywood Middleway, Birmingham
Tel: 021-455 8042

Cariss Residential,
20-22 High Street, Kings Heath, Birmingham 14
Tel: 021-444 5311

Ronald E Clare,
Clare's Auction Rooms, 70 Park Street, Birmingham
Tel: 021-643 0226

Codsall Antiques Auctions,
Codsall Village Hall, Codsall, Wolverhampton
Tel: (0902) 606728

Frank H Fellows & Sons,
Bedford House, 88 Hagley Road, Edgbaston, Birmingham
Tel: 021-454 1261 & 1219

Giles Haywood,
The Auction House, St Johns Road, Stourbridge
Tel: (0384) 370891

James & Lister Lea,
11 Newhall Street, Birmingham
Tel: 021-236 1751

Phillips,
The Old House, Station Road, Knowle, Solihull
Tel: (0564) 776151

K Stuart Swash, FSVA,
Stamford House, 2 Waterloo Road, Wolverhampton
Tel: (0902) 710626

Walker Barnett & Hill,
3 Waterloo Road, Wolverhampton
Tel: (0902) 773531

Walton & Hipkiss,
149a Worcester Road, Hagley
Tel: (0562) 885555

Weller & Dufty Ltd,
141 Bromsgrove Street, Birmingham
Tel: 021-692 1414

Wiltshire

Allen & Harris,
Saleroom & Auctioneers Dept,
The Planks (off The Square), Old Town, Swindon
Tel: (0793) 615915

Dennis Pocock & Drewett,
20 High Street, Marlborough
Tel: (0672) 53471

Hamptons,
20 High Street, Marlborough
Tel: (0672) 513471

Woolley & Wallis,
The Castle Auction Mart, Castle Street, Salisbury
Tel: (0722) 411422

Yorkshire – East

Dee & Atkinson,
The Exchange, Driffield
Tel: (0377) 43151

Yorkshire – North

Boulton & Cooper Ltd,
Forsyth House, Market Place, Malton
Tel: (0653) 692151

H C Chapman & Son,
The Auction Mart, North Street, Scarborough
Tel: (0723) 372424

M W Darwin & Sons,
The Dales Furniture Hall, Bedale
Tel: (0677) 22846

GA Fine Art & Chattels,
Royal Auction Rooms, Queen Street, Scarborough
Tel: (0723) 353581

Hutchinson Scott,
The Grange, Morton-Le-Moor, Ripon
Tel: (0423) 324264

Morphets of Harrogate,
4-6 Albert Street, Harrogate
Tel: (0423) 530030

M Philip H Scott,
Church Wynd, Burneston, Bedale
Tel: (0677) 23325

Nationwide Anglia,
Malton Auction Rooms, Milton Rooms, The Square, Malton
Tel: (0653) 695581

Stephenson & Son,
Livestock Centre, Murtom, York
Tel: (0904) 489731

G A Suffield & Co,
27 Flowergate, Whitby
Tel: (0947) 603433

Geoffrey Summersgill, ASVA,
8 Front Street, Acomb, York
Tel: (0904) 791131

Tennants,
26-27 Market Place, Leyburn
Tel: (0969) 23780

D Wombell & Son,
Bell Hall, Escrick, York
Tel: (090 487) 531

Yorkshire – South

Eadon Lockwood & Riddle,
Western Saleroom, Croomes, Sheffield
Tel: (0742) 686294

William H Brown,
Regent Street South,
Barnsley
Tel: (0226) 367766

William H Brown,
Stanilands Auction Room,
28 Nether Hall Road,
Doncaster
Tel: (0302) 67766

Roland Orchard,
Fine Art & Chattels Valuers & Auctioneers, 55 Copley Road,
Doncaster (Call Monday)
Tel: (0302) 340499

Henry Spencer & Sons Ltd,
1 St James Road, Sheffield
Tel: (0742) 728728

Wilkinson & Beighton,
Woodhouse Green, Thurcroft,
Nr Rotherham
Tel: (0709) 700005

Yorkshire – West

Bond Street Auctions,
23 Bond Street, Dewsbury,
Wakefield
Tel: (0924) 469381

Butterfield's,
The Auction Galleries, Riddings Road, Ilkley
Tel: (0943) 603313

Cornerstone,
Crown Court Salerooms (off Wood Street), Wakefield
Tel: (0924) 375301

Andrew Hartley,
Victoria Hall Salerooms, Little Lane, Ilkley
Tel: (0943) 816363

Ernest R de Rome,
12 New John Street, Bradford
Tel: (0274) 734116

Eddisons,
Auction Rooms, 4-6 High Street,
Huddersfield
Tel: (0484) 533151

W Mackay Audsley, FRVA,
11 Morris Lane, Kirkstall, Leeds 5
Tel: (0532) 758787

Malcolms No. 1 Auctioneers & Valuers,
3b Finkle Hill, Sherburn-in-Elmet,
Nr Leeds
Tel: (0977) 684971/685334
(24 hours)

Nationwide Anglia,
Whitby Auction Rooms, West End Saleroom, The Paddock, Whitby
Tel: (0947) 603433

Phillips,
17a East Parade, Leeds
Tel: (0532) 448011

John H Raby & Son,
Salem Auction Rooms,
21 St Mary's Road, Bradford
Tel: (0274) 491121

Windle & Co,
The Four Ashes, 535 Great Horton Road, Bradford
Tel: (0274) 572998

Channel Islands

Langlois Ltd,
Don Street, St Helier, Jersey
Tel: (0534) 22441
also at:
St Peter Port, Guernsey
Tel: (0481) 23421

Le Gallais Auctions Ltd,
36 Hillgrove Street, St Helier,
Jersey
Tel: (0534) 58789

Martel, Maides & Le Pelley,
50 High Street, St Peter Port,
Guernsey
Tel: (0481) 21203

Ireland

James Adam & Sons,
26 St Stephens Green, Dublin 2
Tel: 0001 760261

Morgans Auctions,
Dunroe Crescent, Dunroe Road,
Belfast
Tel: (0232) 771552

Frank Murphy Auctions,
Main Street, Abbeyleix, Co Laois
Tel: (0502) 01035 3502

Northern Ireland

Dunmurry Auctions,
Barbour Gardens, Dunmurry,
Belfast
Tel: (0232) 602815/6

Temple Auctions Limited,
133 Carryduff Road, Temple
Tel: (084 663) 777

Scotland

John Anderson,
33 Cross Street, Fraserburgh,
Aberdeenshire
Tel: (0346) 28878

Christie's Scotland,
164-166 Bath Street, Glasgow
Tel: (041 332) 8134

B L Fenton & Sons,
Forebank Auction Halls,
84 Victoria Road, Dundee
Tel: (0382) 26227

Frasers (Auctioneers),
28-30 Church Street, Inverness
Tel: (0463) 232395

J & J Howe,
24 Commercial Street, Alyth,
Perthshire
Tel: (08283) 2594

Thomas Love & Sons Ltd,
The Auction Galleries, 52 Canal Street, Perth
Tel: (0738) 33337

McTears (Robert McTear & Co),
Royal Exchange Salerooms,
Glasgow
Tel: 041-221 4456

John Milne,
9 North Silver Street, Aberdeen
Tel: (0224) 639336

Robert Paterson & Son,
8 Orchard Street, Paisley,
Renfrewshire
Tel: (041 889) 2435

Phillips in Scotland,
207 Bath Street, Glasgow
Tel: 041-221 8377
also at:
65 George Street, Edinburgh
Tel: 031-225 2266

L S Smellie & Sons Ltd,
Within the Furniture Market,
Lower Auchingramont Road,
Hamilton
Tel: (0698) 282007

West Perthshire Auctions,
Dundas Street, Cowie, Perthshire

Wales

T Brackstone & Co,
19 Princes Drive, Colwyn Bay,
Clwyd
Tel: (0492) 30481

Dodds Property World,
Victoria Auction Galleries,
Chester Street, Mold, Clwyd
Tel: (0352) 2552

Graham H Evans, FRICS, FRVA,
Auction Sales Centre, The Market Place, Kilgetty, Dyfed
Tel: (0834) 812793 & 811151

John Francis,
Curiosity Salerooms, King Street, Carmarthen
Tel: (0267) 233456

King Thomas,
Lloyd Jones & Company,
Bangor House, High Street,
Lampeter, Dyfed
Tel: (0570) 422550

Morgan Evans & Co Ltd,
28-30 Church Street, Llangefni,
Anglesey, Gwynedd
Tel: (0248) 723303/77582

Morris Marshall & Poole,
10 Broad Street, Newtown,
Powys
Tel: (0686) 25900

Phillips Fine Art Auctioneers,
56 Machen Place, Cardiff
Tel: (0222) 374320

Rennies,
1 Agincourt Street, Monmouth
Tel: (0600) 2916

Wingett's Auction Gallery,
29 Holt Street, Wrexham,
Clywd
Tel: (0978) 353553

INDEX

A

Abbasid 481
Abercrombie, Robert 586
Abraham, Moses 489
Adam, Charles 579
Adams, George 472, 582
Adie & Lovekin Ltd. 731
Aesthetic Movement 538
Agar, Jn., & Son 490
Aitken, Wm. 489
Aizelin, Eugene 606
alabaster 705
albarelli 55–7, 69
Alcock, Samuel 93, 126, 145, 154, 157
Alençon 655
Alla Candiana 70
Allan 524
Allegrain, Christophe-Gabriel 480
amber 89, 726
amethyst 89–90
amphora 646
Amstel 142
Andrews, J. 490–1
Angarano 70
Anglo-Indian 687
antiquities 644–6
  marble 644–5
  metalware 645
  miscellaneous 646
  pottery 645–6
arbours 485
Arcadian 167–9
architects' tables 403
architectural antiques 441–60, 485–8
  fenders 442–3
  fire grates 444–6
  fire irons 441
  fireplaces 443–4
  garden statuary 441–56
  miscellaneous 457–60, 485–8
Arita,
  bottles 78
  bowls 178, 185
  chamber pots 209
  chargers 189
  dishes 82, 187–8, 190–1, 193
  ewers 83
  figures 84, 181
  jars 198
  kendi 183
  vases 201, 205
armchairs 243–7, 286, 297–304, 337–47, 632
  Art Nouveau 538
  open 337–42
  upholstered 343–7
Armenian 648
armillary spheres 473
armoires 628
armour 715, 749
arms and armour 715–16, 718–20, 749–55
  armour 715, 749
  badges 716, 754
  cannon 716, 749
  daggers 715, 718, 749
  drums 755
  guns 715
  helmets 715, 755
  knives 750
  medals 718, 754
  muskets 750
  orders 716, 718, 754
  pistols 719, 750–3
  plates 754
  revolvers 719, 754
  rifles 720
  sporting 750
  swords 718, 750
  uniforms 755
Art Deco 557–73, 624–7
  cabinets 568
  ceramics 558–60
  Clarice Cliff 560–2
  dressing tables 568
  figures 563–5, 621–7
  furniture 561–9, 632
  glass 569
  jardinières 625
  jewellery 569–70
  Lalique glass 557–8
  metal 563, 570–2
  miscellaneous 572–3, 621–7
  tea services 560, 572
Art Nouveau 534–48
  armchairs 538
  ceramics 534–6
  chairs 537–8
  desks 538
  display cabinets 537
  Doulton 544–5
  figures 531–7
  furniture 537–8
  glass 538–9
  jewellery 539–40
  jugs 534–6, 548
  lamps 540–1
  Martin Bros 541
  metal 541–3
  miscellaneous 544
  Moorcroft 543
  Royal Doulton 545–8
  sideboards 538
  tables 537–8
  teapots 535
  tiles 544
  vases 534–6, 548
  wardrobes 538
Arts & Crafts 550–7
Ashby Potters' Guild 555
ashtrays 608, 633
Asprey 569, 571
Asselin, Stephen 464
Astor, G., & Co. 682
astrolabes 473
Atkins Brothers 588
Atkins, R.E. 579
Aubusson 657
Ault 555
automata 676, 704
Aynsley 169

B

Baccarat 231–9
Bacchus 237–9
badges 716, 754
Baga 694
bags 654
Baldwin, Gordon 635
bar stools 568
Barbedienne, F. 609–11
Barber, James 587
barber's bowls 178, 184
Barillot, E. 564
Barlow, Hannah 545
Barnards 586
Barnes, F., & Co. 719
barometers 472, 519–22
  stick 519–20, 522
  wheel 520–1
Baron 550
Barr, Flight & Barr 141, 162
barrel organs 682
Barron, John 489
Barry, John 732
Barum 549, 551–3
Barwise 503
Barye, Antoine-Louis 609–11
basalt 67–8, 101
basin sets 59
baskets,
  porcelain 118–19
  pottery 29, 103, 107, 558
  silver 574
Baskett, Martin, & Cie 504
Bass, Hyman, & Co. 500
Bate 524
Bateman, Ann 591
Bateman, Hester 590–1
Bateman, Peter 582, 591
Bateman, William 582, 591
Bates, Brown-Westhead and Moore 116
bath racks 744
baths 457
Bathwell and Goodfellow 71
Bauer, Peter 523
Bauhaus 571, 633
Baule 693
Bayer, Sven 692
Bayreuth 75
beakers,
  glass 211
  pottery 67
  silver 574
Beatles 695
Beaton, Cecil 699
Beattie, J. 753
Beaumont-Adams 754
Bechstein 683
bed heads 637–8
beds 261–2, 287, 628
  oak & country 242
  pine 734
bedside cupboards 371
Beilby 224, 233–4
bell pulls 459–60
bell pushes 459
bellarmines 116
Belleek 118
bells 92, 487
Bembow, Thos. 489
Benin 693, 695
Benk, J. 564
Bennett, John 625
Bennett, Murlle 540, 634
Bennett, William 586
Benson, J.W. 471, 506
Berettino 56
Berge 524
Bergner, Carl 668
Bergstein, Carl 512
Berlin 71, 75, 122, 135, 150
Berry, John 489
Besarel, Valentino 479
Bevington 54
Bidjar 647
Biedermeier 341
billiards tables 403
Billings, Andrew 462
Bing 701–2
Bingley, William 575
Birch 506
bird whistles 36
Birley, Samuel 641
Birmingham 571
Birmingham Guild of Handicrafts 542
Bizarre 562
blanc de chine 83
Bland, Cornelius 575
Blankle, S. 752
Bloor Derby 159
Boch 555
Bohemian 211, 215, 220, 228, 240–1
bolster covers 659
bone caskets 639
Bo'Ness 50
Bonheur, Isidore 480
bonheurs du jour 262, 312–13
book racks 628
bookcases 262–70, 287–8, 628
  breakfront 262–4
  bureau 242, 264–6
  dwarf 261–7
  library 267–8
  pine 330, 734
  secretaire 268–70
boot scrapers 485–6
Bosley, Joseph 490
Böttger 72, 76
bottle trolleys 485
bottles,
  glass 89, 212–13, 481
  oriental 78, 176
  pottery 29, 107
Boucharel 480
Boucher, Alfred 570, 607
Bouchet 469
Boulton, Matthew, and Co. 579
Bouraine, Marcel 564
bourses 652
Bousson, C. 472
Bovey Tracey 104
Bow 72, 71–7, 121, 125–8, 136
  chocolate pots 154
  mugs 147
  pots 150
  stands 175
  tureens 156
  vases 157
bowls,
  glass 213–16, 557–8, 621, 627
  oriental 78–9, 177–9, 182, 184–5
  porcelain 119–20, 550
  pottery 29–31, 50, 103, 107
  silver 574–5
  stoneware 691
boxes 687–9
  ivory 640
  oriental 81
  porcelain 120
  silver 542, 575–8
bracket clocks 467–8, 498–502
brackets 482
Brameld 50
Brandel, A. 564
Brandl 464
Brandt, E. 616
Brangwyn, Sir Frank 561
Brannam 550–1, 553
brass 481, 603–5, 633
bread baskets 474
breakfast tables 316, 326, 404–6
breakfront bookcases 262–4, 287–8
Breguet et Fils 469
Bretby 550, 552, 555, 557
brick hods 743
Bridge, John 589, 597
Bridge, Thomas 494
Brierley, S. & W. 89
Bristol 75, 89, 97, 99, 107–13
Broadhurst Clarkson & Co. 528
bronze 605–12
  figures 479–80, 563, 566, 705
brooches 484, 634, 746
Brown, Jas 506
Brown, Joseph 490
Brown, Robert 474
Brown, W.A.F. 529
Brownbill 464
Brownfield 95
Bru 668, 704
brûle parfums 478, 714
Brummit, Samuel 752
Brunner, J. 513
brush boxes 727
brush vases 105
Brussels 164
Brydon, Thomas 579
Bub 701
Buck, Frederick 732
buckets 270–1, 329
Buen Retiro 135
buffets 250
Bugatti 701
bulb bowls 178
bulb troughs 105
Bullock, George 466
Bullock, John 493
Bullock, Wm. 496
bureau bookcases 264–6
bureau cabinets 271–8, 289
bureaux 271–6, 293
  oak & country 242
Burmantofts 56
Burslem 544
Burton, Robert 477
Burwash, William 581
busts,
  bronze 480, 605, 607
  copper 612
  marble 483, 640–1
  terracotta 642–3, 646
butter dishes 107–8, 215, 477

butter tubs, porcelain 72, 156
Butterfield 473, 522

C

cabarets 75
cabinets,
  Art Deco 568
  bureau 271–8
  on chests 292
  display 278–81, 628
  oak & country 242
  side 283–4, 333–5
  on stands 242, 281–3, 290–2
cachepots 85
caddies, porcelain 121
Cafe, William 578
caisse à fleurs 77
cake baskets 474
Calderwood, Robert 476
calendar clocks 469
Caltagirone 57
Camble 521
cameos 484, 746
cameras 529–33
Camtoy 678
candelabra,
  glass 616
  ormolu 639, 712–14
  porcelain 121
  silver 542, 578
Candi, Cesare 682
candle holders 83
candle lamps 603
candle snuffers 121, 175, 475
candleboxes 332
candlesticks,
  brass 481, 603–4
  glass 216, 714
  iron 637
  ormolu 479, 638, 712, 714
  pottery 69
  silver 474, 477, 578–9
  silver plate 594
  wood 482
canes 745
cannon 716, 749
canterburies 335–6
Canton 87, 652
Cantonese,
  bowls 177, 184–5
  dishes 187, 194
  tureens 199
  vases 200–1, 203, 206, 208
car mascots 690
carafes 90, 217
card cases 689
card tables 316, 326, 401–10
Cardew, Michael 636
Carette 679
Carlton 167–8, 559
carpets 647–9, 721–4
carriage clocks 503–5
Carrier-Belleuse, A. 563
Carter, John 464, 491
Cartier 539, 745
Cartier, Thomas 611
Cary 473, 526
caskets 327, 329, 479, 481, 688
Castelli 70
casters, silver 487, 579–80
casting moulds 486
Catierfelder Puppenfabrik 675
Caughley,
  beakers 122
  bowls 119–20
  dishes 136
  jugs 145
  sauceboats 150
  tureens 156
celadons 177, 726
cellarets 328, 600–2
censers 182, 708, 727
centre tables 311–17, 322, 326, 410–12
centrepieces 122, 475
ceramics,
  Art Deco 558–60
  Art Nouveau 534–6
  figures 563
Chad Valley 675, 677
Chadwick, W.I. 529
chairs 286, 297–304, 337–59, 631–2
  arm 243–7, 286, 297–304, 337–47, 632
  Art Nouveau 537–8
  dining 243, 298–304, 347–55, 632
  hall 355–6
  oak & country 243–7
  pine 734–5
  side 301–4, 351–9
chalices 705
chamber pots 68, 548
Chamberlain 122, 146
Chamberlain's Worcester 124, 141–2, 145, 153, 157
Chambers, Sir William 474
chambersticks 121, 603
Chameleon 552
champagne taps 601
Champion, G.I. 467
chandeliers,
  brass 730
  glass 90, 92, 211–17, 616
  metal 712
  ormolu 713–14
Chantilly 77
Chapman, Peter 720
Chare, Samuel 519
Chareau, Pierre 632
chargers,
  Art Deco 622
  brass 604
  earthenware 625
  metal 604
  oriental 85–6, 190, 194
  pottery 50, 108–9, 112
Charleson 515
Chawner, Henry 590
cheese bells 69
cheese dishes 534
Chelaberd Karabagh 722
Chelsea,
  boxes 72
  dishes 137
  figures 74, 128
  plates 136
  tureens 76
  vases 77, 157–8
chenets 478, 486
Chenghua 80–1
chenilles 654
Cheparus, D.H. 564
chess sets 682
chests 307, 310, 312, 360–8
  on chests 312, 365–6
  oak & country 248–50
  pine 735–6
  small 360–5
  on stands 310, 312, 367–8
  Wellington 368
chests of drawers 310, 312, 330, 735–6
Chi Chi 647
chimney pots 488
Chinese 161, 647–8, 651
Chinese dynasties and marks pointer 210
Chinese export 84, 87
Chiparus, Demetre 563
chocolate pots 580–1, 612
Chongzhen 86
christening robes 650
Christian's 146
chronographs 471–2
chronometers 521
cigar lighters 475
cigarette boxes 691
cisterns 117, 453–4
Clapton, Eric 696
Clarke, Humphrey 493
Clarke, Joseph 575
Clews & Co. 52
Clichy 237–9
Cliff, Clarice 560–2, 622, 624–6
Clifton, John 582
clocks 102, 489–519
  bracket 467–8, 498–502
  carriage 503–5
  garnitures 514
  lantern 510
  longcase 462–7, 489–96, 630
  mantel 461–70, 501–10
  miscellaneous 515–17
  regulators 497–8
  skeleton 511
  table 515
  wall 512–14, 572
  watches 471–2, 518–19
  wristwatches 519
Clodion 610–11
cloisonné 700, 710
coal scuttles 639
Coalbrookdale 145, 454–5
Coalport,
  bowls 119
  chambersticks 121
  comports 122
  cups 123
  ewers 125
  figures 129
  garnitures 77
  jardinières 145
  mugs 147–8
  pin trays 175
  plates 137–8
  pots 150
  services 75, 151
  teapots 154
  vases 158–9
coats-of-arms 482
cocktail shakers 600, 686
cocktail trolleys 568
coffee pots,
  copper 612
  pottery 95–7
  silver 541, 580–1, 633
coffee services 477, 560
  silver 587–9
  silver plated 633
coffee tables 322
coffee urns 199
coffers 248–50, 286, 369
Coker, Ebenezer 579
colanders 195
Cole, Thomas 517
Collier, S. 490
columns 483
comb trays 105
commemorative 31, 691
commodes 307–10, 338, 369–71
  pine 736
comports 122, 143, 215, 731
condiment stands 117
console tables 320–1, 325, 412–13
Continental 131, 150
Cooke, Charles 745
Cooke, T. 580
Cooke, Troughton & Simms Ltd 524
Copeland 148, 152
Copenhagen 77, 154, 164
Coper, Hans 635–6, 691–2
copes 651
copper 612
corbels 460
Cordier, Charles-Henri-Joseph 642
corking machines 599
corkscrews 591–9
corner cupboards 330, 371–3, 731–7
corner units 568
Cornforth, W.B. 490
Cornock, Edward 586
Coronation mugs 31
corsets 650
costume 650–4
Cosway, Richard 732
cottages, pottery 32
Cotton, Benj. 498
Count 494
Courtauld, Augustine 586
coverlets 724
cow creamers, pottery 32
Craddock, Joseph 584
cradles 242, 638, 734
crafts 691–3
cream jugs 59–60, 91, 542
creamware,
  baskets 29
  bowls 31
  coffee pots 97
  condiment stands 117
  cow creamers 32
  figures 33, 35–6, 42
  flatware 50, 54
  jars 55–7
  jugs 58, 60–5
  mugs 65, 67
  sauceboats 69
  services 94
  tankards 66
  tea caddies 95
  teapots 97
  tureens 100
  vases 101
Crespin, Paul 580
crested china 167–70
cricket 686
Crighton, Jas, & Co. 514
Croisy, A. 563, 612
Crown Devon 558
cruet sets 686
cuff links 634
cuirasses 715
Cunningham, Daniel 585
Cuno Otto 675
cupboards 290, 371–4
  bedside 371
  corner 371–3
  linen presses 373–4
  oak & country 250–4
  pine 731–8
  wardrobes 374
cups,
  oriental 81, 182–3
  porcelain 122–5
  pottery 32–3, 551
  silver 582
curtain tie backs 485
cushion covers 481
cushions 659
cutlery 582

D

da Ravenna, Severo 479
daggers 715, 718, 749
Dal Belro, P. 641
Dali, Salvador 698
Dallmeyer, J.H. 529
Daniel, Abraham 733
Daniel, Henry 492
Daoguang 80, 82, 706, 729
Darcy 520
Daum 539, 613, 611–18, 620, 627
Davenport 93, 118, 123, 138–9, 145
Davenport, A.L., Ltd. 731
davenports 374–6
David, P.J. 610
Davis, Caleb 462
De Dissel 112
de Fanti, Holzer 536
De Feure, Georges 538
De Grieksche 107
De La Salle 513
De Silva, Wm. 525
Deans 675
Decantelle 685
decanters, glass 89–90, 217–20
decoys 332
Degue 569
delft 101–15
  Bristol 70, 107–13
  Dublin 111
  Dutch 70, 107–8, 112–15
  English 107–11, 115
  Lambeth 111–15
  Liverpool 107, 111, 114
  London 70, 107–14
  Southwark 70
Della Robbia 553
Dellebarre 526
Delpech 116
Derby,
  candlesticks 121
  cups 123
  dishes 138–40
  figures 128–30
  jugs 146
  mugs 148
  pots 150
  services 75, 151–2
  teapots 155
  tureens 156
  vases 159
Derbyshire 57, 101
Deruta 54, 56, 70
desk sets 117
desks 293, 312–13, 377–83, 629
  Art Nouveau 538
  kneehole 312–13, 377–83
  pine 739
Desmant, Louis 552

Devonia 167
diadems 484
dials 473, 522–3
Diderischen, Julius 476
Dillwyn 52, 116
dining chairs 243, 298, 300–4, 347–55
dining pedestals 310
dining tables 317, 322, 324, 414–17
dining-room suites 567
Dinky 679–80
dinner plates 474
dirks 749
dishes,
oriental 80–2
silver 584
Disneyalia 699
display cabinets 278–81, 296, 537, 628
display tables 418
Distler 702
Dixon, James, & Sons 586, 595
Dobell 512
Doccia 72, 125, 135
Dollond 519
dolls 663–75, 704
Armand Marseille 671
bisque 665–8, 704
Bru 668
dolls' houses 673–4
Gebrüder Heubach 669
Jules Steiner 673
Jumeau 669–70
Kammer & Reinhart 672
Kestner 670–1
Lenci 671
miscellaneous 675
papier mâché 665–8
S.F.B.J. 672
Simon & Halbig 672–3
wax 663–5, 704
wooden 663
dolls' houses 673–4
dolly sticks 744
door gates 616
door handles 458–60
door knockers 458–60
door plates 460
door stops 486
doors 631
Dorrell, Francis 492, 498
double gourd bottles 176
Doucai 80, 85–6, 183
dough troughs 744
Doulton 544–5
drains 485
drawleaf tables 259, 418
Dresden 121, 131–2, 166, 175
dress wings 716
dressers, oak & country 254–6, 739
dresses 650
dressing tables 324, 330, 418
Art Deco 568
pine 740
drinking glasses 221–34
drinking glasses pointer 223
dropleaf tables 418–19
drug jars 56, 112–13
drum tables 419
drums 755
Du Paquier 143–4
Dublin 111
Duckworth, Ruth 691
Duffett, John 489
Dugourc, J.D. 479
dumb waiters 325
Dundee, Adam 520
Dunlop, H.J. 732
Dunlop, Sybil 538, 557
Dunn, John 692
Durer, Albrecht 482
Durwood, John 492
dwarf bookcases 261–7
dwarf cabinets 294
Dwerrihouse, Ogston and Bell 511
Dylan, Bob 696

E
ear clips 748
ear studs 748
earthenware 39
East, John 474
Eastman, Ken 691
Eberl 701
Eberlein, J.F. 75
Edwards, James 585
egg cups 595
Egg, D. 753
Eichwald 534
Elkington & Co. 586, 589–90
Elkington, Frederick 474, 578
Ellicot 516
Elliot, J.L. 644
Elliott, William 585
Ellis, Harvey 628, 632
Elton 551
embroidered panels 654–5
embroidered pictures 654–5
embroidery 654–5
Emes, John 575, 591, 593
enamel 69, 700
English,
figures 121–7, 131
mugs 149
plates 142
scent bottles 151
services 154
vases 160, 163–4
English Chiltern 676
epergnes 476
ephemera 695–700
Disneyalia 699
film 700
photographs 698–9
pop 695–7
postcards 697–8
posters 697–8
theatre 700
Evans 498
Evans, W. 720
ewers,
bronze 727
oriental 83, 180, 183, 708, 727
pewter 602
porcelain 125
silver 474
eye baths 175

F
Fabergé 711
Faenza 54, 69
faience 31, 50, 62, 71, 73, 100
Fairyland Lustre 161
famille rose,
baskets 209
bottles 176
bowls 78–9, 177, 179, 184–5
candle holders 83
cups 183
dishes 190–1, 193
figures 186
flasks 187
jardinières 85, 86
jars 197–8
mugs 182
plates 191–3
spoon trays 192
tureen stands 199
tureens 87
vases 200, 202–4, 207–9
famille rose/verte 82
famille verte,
bottles 78–9, 176
bowls 178
dishes 80–2, 188–9
figures 181, 186
flasks 186
jardinières 195
plates 189
tea caddies 198
vases 202–3, 205–6, 208
fans 659–63
Fantasque 561
Fantasque Bizarre 560–1
Farlow 684
farmhouse dressers 330
Farquharson, Clyne 241
Farrow and Jackson 598
Faure, Camille 621
Fearnley, Peter 462
fenders 325, 442–3
Fentum, J. 682
Fergusson, James 733
Fiaschi, E. 483
figures,
animal 33–6, 69
Art Deco 563–5
Art Nouveau 531–7
bronze 479–80, 563, 566, 605–11, 645, 705, 716
ceramic 563
copper 612
iron 637
ivory 563–6
metal 563
oriental 83, 180–1, 186
people 31–49, 71, 108, 531–7, 548–9
porcelain 73, 125–36, 548–9
pottery 33–49, 71, 83–4, 108
silver 716
spelter 639
terracotta 643, 641–7
wood 643–4
film 700
finger plates 117
finials 485–6
fire grates 444–6
fire irons 441
fireboards 724
firemarks 612, 637
fireplaces 443–4
firescreens 327, 616
fireside compendium 605
Fischer, H. 678
Fisher, E.B. 555
Fisher, Henry 462
fishing 684–6
Fitzhugh 200
flagons 90
flasks,
glass 235
oriental 85, 186
pottery 49, 646
flatware,
oriental 187–95
porcelain 131–44
pottery 50–5
Fletcher, Robt. 522
Flight & Barr 153
Flight, Barr & Barr 157, 161
flounces 655
flour barrels 744
flower bricks 101, 115
Foley 534, 549
Foley Intarsio 549, 551, 624–5
Fontana 512
fonts 453
Fornasetti 558
Foster, Ellen 658
Fountain, William 584–5
fountains 449–52
Fox, Charles 591, 594
Fox, George 594
Frankenthal 72, 127
Fraser-Kilian 684
Fratin, Christopher 606
Freeth, Charles 752
French 134, 165, 240
frieze panels 616
Fritsch, Elizabeth 636
Frodsham, Charles 503, 508
Fukagawa 204
Fulda 73
furniture 261–440, 628–32
architects' tables 403
armchairs 286, 297–300, 302, 304, 337–47, 538
Art Deco 561–9
Art Nouveau 537–8
beds 261–2, 287, 628
bedside cupboards 371
billiards tables 403
bonheurs du jour 262, 312–13
bookcases 242, 262–70, 287–8, 330
breakfast tables 316, 326, 404–6
breakfront bookcases 262–4, 287–8
buckets 270–1, 329
bureau bookcases 264–6
bureau cabinets 271–8, 289, 292
bureaux 271–6, 293
cabinets on stands 242, 281–3, 290–2
canterburies 335–6
card tables 316, 326, 401–10
centre tables 311–17, 322, 326, 410–12, 630
chairs 286, 337–59, 631–2
chests 307, 310, 312, 330, 360–8
chests on chests 312, 365–6
chests on stands 310, 312, 367–8
coffers 286, 369
commodes 307–10, 338, 369–71
console tables 320–1, 325, 412–13, 630
corner cupboards 290, 330, 371–3
cupboards 290, 371–4
davenports 374–6
desks 293, 312–13, 377–83, 629–30
dining chairs 243, 298, 300–3, 347–55, 632
dining tables 317, 322, 324, 414–17, 629
display cabinets 278–81, 296, 537, 628
display tables 418
drawleaf tables 259, 418
dressing tables 324, 330, 418, 568
dropleaf tables 418–19
drum tables 317, 419
dwarf bookcases 261–7
games tables 317, 419–20
hall chairs 355–6
lamp tables 434
library bookcases 267–8
library tables 319, 420–1
linen presses 290, 373–4
loo tables 322, 421
lowboys 251–7, 383
mirrors & frames 314–15, 383–92, 629
miscellaneous 440
nests of tables 421–2, 538, 569
occasional tables 423, 568
open armchairs 337–42
oriental 700, 725
pedestal tables 423–4
Pembroke tables 324, 424–5
reading tables 425–6
screens 321–7, 392
secretaire bookcases 268–70, 288, 291
serving tables 319–21, 421–7
settees 301, 305, 393–5
side cabinets 283–4, 296, 333–5
side chairs 302–4, 351–9
side tables 260, 319–21, 324, 328, 427–8
sideboards 294, 296, 391–8, 538, 629
silver tables 428–9
small chests 360–8
sofa tables 319–20, 429–30
sofas 305
stands 398–400
steps 400
stools 305, 400–2, 632
Sutherland tables 430
tables 286, 311–29, 403–39, 537–8, 629–31
tallboys 310, 312, 366
tea tables 319, 326, 430–1
teapoys 439
tray tables 431–2
tripod tables 260, 320, 432–4
upholstered armchairs 343–7
wardrobes 374
washstands 330, 439–40
Wellington chests 368
whatnots 440
wine tables 434
work tables 325, 434–6
writing tables 319–20, 431–9
furniture rests 116
Furstenberg 72, 149

G
G & M 588
Gallé 69, 539, 613–14, 617–18

620, 627
galvanometers 473
Gama 678
games 682
games boxes 687
games tables 317, 419–20
garden seats 454–6
garden statuary 441–56, 483
Garfoot, Wm. 464
garnitures,
clocks 514
oriental 86
vases 101, 543
Garrard 581
Garrard, J. 476
Garrard, Robert 477, 587
Garrard, Sebastian 477
Garvis, James 491
gas flares 488
gateleg tables 251–8
gates 456
Gaudez 480
Gaydon, H. & E. 512
Gaze, Richard 585
Gebrüder Heubach 669
Gebrüder Kuhnlenz 667
Gemito, Vincenzo 606
Genroku 78, 81–7
German 134, 143, 150, 165–6, 170
Gibbons, Grinling 644
Gibbs 499
Gilbert 591
Girletti 520
Glamorgan 53
glass 211–41
Art Deco 569
Art Nouveau 538–9
beakers 211
bottles 89, 212–13, 481
bowls 213–16, 557–8, 621, 627
candlesticks 216
chandeliers 90, 92, 211–17, 616
decanters 217–20
drinking glasses 221–34
flasks 235
inkwells 241
jelly glasses 235
jugs 236
miscellaneous 241
oriental 725
panels 92
paperweights 231–9
plaques 620
scent bottles 91–2, 240
vases 92, 241, 617–21
globes 473, 523
goblets 222–30, 477
Godfrey, Eliza 474
Godfrey, Ian 691
Goebels 544, 626
Gold 477
Goldscheider 531–7, 556, 558, 621–7
Goldsmiths and Silversmiths Co. 580
golf 686
gongs 630
Goodwin, Andrew 574
Gorham 474, 477, 540, 542
Gorham Manufacturing Co. 576
goss china 171–4
Gouda 552–5
governess carts 690
Grafton 168
Graham, Geo 513
Grainger & Co. 161
Grainger, Lee & Co. 126
Grainger's Worcester 120, 126, 142, 155, 161–2
gramophones 683
grand pianos 328
Grant 499
grape harvester's baskets 744
Gray 529
Green, James 733
Griffnée, Philippe 720
Grignon, Thomas 492
Grue, Aurelio 70
Grundy, William 587
Guangxu 706
Gudin 467
guns 715
Gunthermann 701–2
Gurney, R. 580
Gurney, Richard, and Co. 581
Guro 694
Gyokoku 728

H
Hacker, Christian 674
Hagenauer 571–2
hall chairs 355–6
hall lanterns 712–13
Hall, Martin, & Co. 588
Hamada, Shoji 636
Han Dynasty 85
Hancock 148
Hancock, C.F. 574
Hancock, Sampson, & Sons 94
hanging lamps 487
hangings 655, 659
Hanxnell, Thos. 492
Hardy 684–6
Hare, G. 531
Harland, Thomas 462
Hart, Napthali 587
Hartnack, E. 526
Harvey, Thomas 514
Hatton, Wm. 499
Hauer, Bonaventura Gottlieb 76, 120
Hausmalerei 75, 125, 155
Hawes 526
Hawksworth, Eyre & Co. 578
Hay, Peter 500
Heal, Ambrose 567
Heal's 538, 561–7
Hearn, Louis 584
Heath & Middleton 593
Heizler 479
helmets 705, 715, 755
Henderson 499
Henderson, Ewen 636
Hennell, Robert 591
Heriz 647–8, 722
Herman 677
Herring, Joshua 498
Hess 701–2
Hessmobile 678
Hettne, Johann Georich 89
Heubach Koppelsdorf 669
Hicks & Meigh 160
Hill, Joakim 462
Hill, Lockey 682
Hillan, Christian 476
hip flasks 595
Hirado 180, 199
Hispano-Moresque 54–5, 70
Hochst 73, 156
Hodges, Edward 585
Hoffman 537
Holics 70
Holland & Holland 720
Horner, Peter 494
Hornsey, Wm. 462
Horoldt, J.G. 72
horse bits 705
Horton 684
Hoskins, Danl. 510
Hougham, Solomon 574
Houghtons Ltd. 531
Houles & Co. 580
Howell & Jones 515
Huaud Brothers 732
Hughes 513
Hughes, William 492, 494
humidors 687, 689
Hun, Elsie 476
Hungana 694
Hunt & Roskell 587
Hunt, John S. 587
hunting knives 750
hydria 646

I
Ibeji 694
ice pails 145
Illingworth, T., & Co. 530
Imari,
bottles 176
bowls 78, 178–9, 184–5, 190
chargers 86, 194
coffee urns 199
colanders 195
cups 183
dishes 82, 140, 193–4
jars 87, 197–8
jugs 183
plates 191
pots 85
services 151–2
trays 195
vases 201, 204–5
Imperial Porcelain Factory 75
Inca 693
incense burners 481
Ingersoll 519
inkstands 116, 595, 603, 686
brass 604
silver 584
inkwells 145, 241
inros 725
iron 637–8
Isfahan 648, 722
Islamic 481
Isnik 481
Istoriato 70
ivory 639–40, 646
figures 563–6
oriental 726

J
jackets 650
Jackfield 29, 33, 57, 66, 95
Jackson, Joseph 476
Jaco 66
Jacobite 231–2
Jacot 505
jade 706, 708, 726
jali 643
Japanese 651
Japy Frères 504, 513
jardinières,
Art Deco 625
brass 603
oriental 85, 195–6, 700
ormolu 329
porcelain 145
pottery 30, 56, 116
stoneware 625
jars 55–7, 112
oriental 87, 191–9
jasper 101
Jazira 481
jelly glasses 235
Jensen, Jorgen 570
Jenson, Georg 542, 570–1
jewel boxes 689
jewellery 741–8
Art Deco 569–70
Art Nouveau 539–40
Jiajing 79–81
Jiaqing 83
John, Elton 695
Jones, A.E. 542
Jones, W. & S. 526
jugs,
Art Nouveau 534–6
copper 612
glass 236
porcelain 145–7, 625
pottery 57–65, 108, 114
silver 584
jukeboxes 696
Jumeau, Emile 669–70, 704

K
K.P.M. 75, 166
Kadi 679
Kaga 206
Kakiemon,
bowls 78, 81, 178
dishes 74, 82, 189–90
figures 83
Kammer & Reinhart 672
Kändler, J.J. 73–6
Kangxi 78, 80, 82, 85, 202
Karabagh Kellch 722
Karadjar 648
Karatchoph Kazak 722
Kashan 481, 722
Kashmir 652–3
Kaufmann, Oscar 629–30
Kazak 647, 649, 722
Kazak-Gendje 649
Kee Less Clock Co. 516
Keeling & Co. 93
Kemp, John 499
kendi 83, 180, 183
Kerman 648
Kessels 682
Kestner, J.D. 671
kettles 476, 590
keys 637
Keyser, Cornelis 112
Khlebnikov 711
Khotan 648
Killarney 689
Kinkozan 194
Kipling, Wm. 468
Kirkwood, John 492
Kirman 649
Kitaoji, Rosanjin 636
kitchen chairs 330
kitchenalia 744
Kleman, J.M., & Zoon 472
Klokken 114
Knab 466
Knapton, J. & P. 528
kneehole desks 312–13, 377–83
Knibb, Joseph 468
knife boxes 688, 689
knife rests 117
knives 750
Knox, Archibald 625, 634
Ko-Imari 87
kobako 709, 710
Koch, Gabriele 692
Kocks, Pieter Adriaenszoon 115
koro 209
kovsh 711
Kramer, Otto K. 472
Kuba 722
Kurfursten Humpen 92
Kutani 78, 181, 195, 204, 207–9
kyathos 646
Kyo-Satsuma 179

L
lace 655–6
lacquer 727
Ladesma 570
Ladik 721
Lalique glass 557–8, 617–18, 691
Lambert-Rucki, Jean 627
Lambeth 111–15, 548
lamp brackets 730
lamp shades 615
lamp standards 486
lamp tables 434
Lampe 518
Lampfert, John 580
lamps, Art Nouveau 540–1
Lancaster, J., & Son 529
Langlands & Robertson 574
Lanoni, D. 752
Lansing, Philip 476
lantern clocks 510
lanterns 485, 487, 615
lappets 655
Laterza 57
Lauder 552–3
Laurel and Hardy 698
Lawson, J. 499
le Fagnay, Pierre 564
le Jeune, Mariaual 726
Le Roy & Fils 504
Le Verre Français 540, 620
Leach, Bernard 635–6, 692
lead 483, 638
lead soldiers 678
leather 684
Leeds 60, 100
Legros, Alphonse 606
Lehmann 678, 702
Leigh, Vivien 697
Leitz, E. 529–32
Lekythos 646
Lenci 559, 627, 671
Lenkoran 721
Leonardi 559
Lerebours et Secretan 472
Lessore, Emile 52
letter box covers 457–8
letter scales 744
Levy-Dhurmer, Lucien 626
Lewin-Funcke, Arthur 480

Lias, Charles 574
Liberty 537, 539, 542, 634
library bookcases 267–8
library cabinets 291
library steps 329
library tables 319, 420–1
light switches 487
lighting 730
Ligurian 57
linen baskets 744
linen presses 290, 373–4
Linz 738
Liverpool,
bottles 107
dishes 50, 111
flower bricks 101, 115
jugs 114, 146
mugs 65
tiles 97–8
Lladro 136
Lloyd Loom 567
Lochmann 683
lockets 484, 746
London 70, 98–9, 107–14
longcase clocks 462–7, 489–96, 630
Longquan 177–8
Longton Hall 76, 130, 160
Longwy 549
loo tables 322, 421
Lorenzl 563, 566
Lori Pambak 721
loving cups 33, 103
lowboys 251–7, 383
Lowestoft,
baskets 118
bowls 119
coffee pots 155
cups 123–4
dishes 139–40
jugs 145–6
mugs 147–8
teapots 156
Luba/Songye 694
Lucchi, Michele de 631
Lucien 505
Ludwigsburg 136
luggage 684
Luneville-Keller & Guerin 30
lustres 241
Lutyens, Edwin 632

M

McCabe, James 502
McLeod 752
Mahal 721
Mahla, F. 539
Mahony, Gerald 631
Maidman, Ralph 575
maiolica 55–6, 100
majolica 30, 69, 102, 131, 555, 626
Majorelle, Louis 629–30
Makonde 694
Malayir 721
Malicone 51
Maling 558, 622
Mann, James 525
mantel clocks 461–70, 501–10
Manton, John 719
Manton, Joseph 753
Maori 693
Mappin & Webb 220, 516, 542, 582, 593–4
Marasali 721
marble 483, 640–2, 644–5
Marc, Hry 469, 504
Marcolini 121, 166
Marjaine 516
Marklin 701–2
marriage boxes 328
Marseille, Armand 671
Martele 542
Marti, S. 509
Martin Bros 541
Martin, Johan 523
Martin, Vernis 490
Marwick 468
Masonic 218
Mason's 101–2
Mason's Ironstone 53, 59, 67, 94
Mathsson, Bruno 566
Maws 555
Mawson, S., & Thompson 527
Max Handwerck 667
Mearns, John 495
measures 603
medallions 116
medals 718, 754
medical instruments 527–9
Meiji 709, 726
Meissen,
bowls 120
busts 75
centrepieces 122
coffee pots 156
cups 125
dishes 143, 144
ecuelles 76
figures 73, 121–7, 132–4
groups 74
plates 74, 142–3
salts 73
sauceboats 75
services 153–4
tankards 72
tea canisters 121
teapots 76, 155
tobacco boxes 72
vases 166
Memess, John 462
Menil, Vincent 496
Mennecy 73
Mercer, Thomas Ltd. 521
Meriton, Samuel 587
Merrythought 680
Mesopotamian 481
metal,
Art Deco 563, 570–2
Art Nouveau 541–3
figures 563
oriental 727
metalware 602–12, 637–8
antiquities 645
brass 603–5
bronze 605–12
copper 612
firemarks 612, 637
iron 637–8
lead 638
miscellaneous 639
ormolu 638–9
pewter 602–3
Mettlach 68, 116
Mettoy 701
microscopes 472, 521–7
Milan 100
Miller, P. 494
Ming 79–82, 85–7, 201, 710
bottles 176
bowls 177
dishes 179, 187–8
ewers 180
figures 181
jars 191–7
plates 188
vases 201
miniatures 732–3
Minton,
bowls 119
chambersticks 121
dishes 139
figures 126, 130–1
frames 175
inkwells 145
jardinières 30
teapots 154–5
tiles 99
tureens 100
vases 101, 160, 554, 624
mirrors & frames 314–15, 383–92, 616
ormolu 638
pine 740
missal boxes 689
Mitsu 728
mittens 652
mocha 61
models 84, 681
Moigniez, Jules 609
Moko 701
Monart 89, 617–18, 621
money banks 678
money boxes 116, 332, 678
Monier, E. 564
Monier, Emile 690
Monobar, K.I. 531
Monroe, Marilyn 699
monteiths 474
Montelupo 55
moon flasks 186, 710
Moorcroft 543, 624, 627
Moore, Bernard 625–6
Morgan 509
Morgan, William de 624
Mororv, S. 112
mortars 607
Morton, Richards, & Co. 574
Morvat, Will 495
Moser, Kolo 615
muffin dishes 542
mugs,
porcelain 72, 147–9, 544
pottery 31, 65–7, 103, 691
silver 585
Muller 480
Muller, Berthold 575–6, 599
Muller Frères 541
Munro, Alexander 642
Murdoch, Thomas 752
Murray, Keith 89, 560
Murray, William Staite 693
music stools 305
musical 682–3
gramophones 683
musical boxes 683
musical instruments 682–3
muskets 750
mustard pots 68

N

Nagi, Abdo 692
Nailsea 91, 235, 240
Nakashima, George 629
Nantgarw 139–40
napkin rings 548
Naples 75–6
Neath 490
necessaires 687
necklaces 484, 634, 748
needlework panels 658
needlework pictures 658
Nekola, Joseph 104
nests of tables 421–2, 569
netsuke 728
Neuchatel 467
Nevers 50, 55
New Hall 123
Newcastle 222, 228–9
Newlyn 556
Newton & Co. 523
Newton, John 499
Nicholson 521
Niculoso, Francisco 56
Niderviller 153
Nielsen, Harold 570
Nixon, James 733
Nootka 693
Norris, S. 499
Northern Northwest 695
Northern Wei 83
Northwest 694
Nunn, W. 548
nutcrackers 744
Nymphenburg 73–4, 76

O

oak & country furniture 242–60
beds 242
bureaux 242
cabinets 242
chairs 243–7
chests 248–50
cupboards 250–4
dressers 254–6
miscellaneous 260
stools 256
tables 251–60
occasional tables 423, 568
offertory boxes 743
oil lamps 604
Old Sheffield plate 602
Olivier, Laurence 697
orders 754
oriental 700, 701–11, 725–9
amber 726
cloisonné 700
enamel 700
furniture 700, 725
glass 725
inros 725
ivory 726
jade 726
lacquer 727
metal 727
netsuke 728
snuff bottles 728–9
wood 729
oriental pottery and porcelain 171–209
bottles 78, 176
bowls 78–9, 177–9, 182, 184–5
censers 182
cups 81, 182–3
dishes 80–2
ewers 183
figures 83, 180–1, 186
flasks 186
flatware 187–95
garnitures 86
jardinières 85, 195–6
jars 87, 191–9
miscellaneous 209
services 199
tea and coffee pots 199
tureens 87, 199–200
vases 81–7, 200–9
ormolu 638–9
candelabra 479, 639
chandeliers 712–13
clocks 470
inkstands 478
jars 77
vases 92, 714
Orr, P., & Sons 589
Orrefors 569
Ortega, Mariano 683
Ottoman 481, 721
Ottweiler 74
Owen, Elspeth 692

P

Paisley 653–4
Pajou 643
Palermo 56
Palmyran 647
Paltscho, Ernst 538
Pandiani, A. 606
panels, glass 92
paperweights, glass 231–9, 621
papier mâché 664, 731
dolls 665–8
vases 731
Pare, Ambroise 610
parian ware 129, 131
Paris 121
Parrington, Emily J. 545
pastille burners 32
Patigian, Haig 627
pearlware,
figures 34–5, 42, 68
flatware 50, 54
jugs 57–8, 61–5
mugs 67
services 94
stirrup cups 33
teapots 91–7
pedestal cupboards 308
pedestal tables 423–4
pedestals 327, 329, 478
Pellatt, Apsley 240
pelmets 654
Pembroke tables 324, 424–5
Pembroke tables pointer 425
pen boxes 481
pendants 484, 634, 748
pepper pots 43
Peridiez, A.G. 501
Perin-Salbreux, Louis Lie 732
Perrin, La Veuve 71
Perry, John 578
pestles and mortars 488
Petit, Jacob 153, 164–5
pewter 60, 543, 602–3
Peyton, Richard 494
Philcox, G. 500
Philippe, Patek 471–2
photo frames 542
photographs 698–9
pianos 328, 682
Pibworth, C. 644
Picault 480
pier tables 321
Pike, James 496

- Pilkington 621–7
- pillows 723
- pin trays 175
- pine furniture 734–43
  - beds 734
  - bookcases 734
  - chairs 734–5
  - chests 735–6
  - commodes 736
  - cupboards 731–8
  - desks 739
  - dressers 739
  - dressing tables 740
  - mirrors 740
  - miscellaneous 743
  - settles 740
  - stools 741
  - tables 741–2
  - wardrobes 742
  - washstands 742
- Pinhey, Richd. Lear 494
- Pinxton 148
- Piper, John 636
- ›ipes 92, 745
- ›istols 719–20, 750–3
- Pistor, Edward 500
- Pitts, Thomas 476
- lant stands 455, 595, 743
- lanters 117
- laques,
  - bronze 690
  - glass 620
  - porcelain 149–50
  - pottery 67–8, 105, 115
  - stone 488
- lates, pottery 31, 560
- leydell-Bouverie, Katherine 635
- lummer, William 593
- lymouth 131
- olyphon 683
- oncelet, Jacqueline 636
- oole 99
- op ephemera 695–7
- orcelain 118–75
  - baskets 118–19
  - bowls 119–20
  - boxes 120
  - butter tubs 72, 156
  - caddies 121
  - candelabra 121
  - centrepieces 122
  - crested china 167–70
  - cups 122–5
  - ewers 125
  - figures,
    - animal 125–7
    - people 127–36
  - flatware 131–44
  - Goss china 171–4
  - ice pails 145
  - inkwells 145
  - jardinières 145
  - jugs 145–7, 625
  - miscellaneous 175
  - mugs 72, 147–9, 544
  - oriental 171–209
  - plaques 149–50
  - pots 150
  - sauceboats 150
  - scent bottles 151
  - services 151–4
  - sucriers 154
  - tankards 72
  - tea and coffee pots 154–6
  - tea services 545
  - tureens 151–7
  - vases 77, 157–66, 554
- rringers 31
- rt labels 600
- rtico clocks 469
- rtobello 41, 102
- sset pots 236
- st-war design 573
- stcards 697–8
- sters 697–8
- t lids 68, 93
- ts 68, 112, 150
- tschappel, Carl Thieme 122, 166
- ttery 29–117
  - ntiquities 645–6
  - askets 29, 103, 107
  - ottles 29, 107
  - owls 29–31, 50, 103, 107
  - offee pots 95–7
  - commemorative 31
  - cottages 32
  - cow creamers 32
  - cups 32–3
  - delft 101–15
  - figures,
    - animal 33–6
    - people 31–49, 83–4, 108
  - flasks 49
  - flatware 50–5
  - jardinières 30, 56, 116
  - jars 55–7, 112
  - jugs 57–65, 108, 114
  - miscellaneous 111–17
  - mugs 65–7, 103
  - oriental 171–209
  - plaques 67–8, 115
  - plates 31, 560
  - pot lids 68, 93
  - pots 68, 112
  - sauceboats 69
  - services 93–4
  - Staffordshire figures 44–9
  - tankards 31, 66, 103–4, 107
  - tea caddies 95, 107
  - teapots 95–7
  - tiles 97–9, 114–15
  - Toby jugs 62–5
  - tureens 71, 100
  - vases 101–2, 543, 548
  - Wemyss 103–5
- powder flasks 718
- Powell 621
- Powell, James 538
- Pratt ware,
  - cradles 116
  - figures 33, 35, 37
  - jugs 58, 64
  - money boxes 116
  - pots 68
- Prazmowski, A. 526
- Preiss, F. 564, 566
- preserving pans 612
- Presley, Elvis 695–6
- press cupboards 254
- Price, Vincent 698
- Priest, William 590
- Pritchard, W. 753
- Proctor, Ernest 561
- Provençal 723
- Prowse, Keith, & Co. Ltd. 682
- pudding boxes 332
- pump heads 486
- punch bowls 69, 78–9
  - oriental 178–9, 184–5
  - pewter 602
  - silver 474, 477
- punch ladles 474, 477
- punch sets 544
- Purdey, J. 715, 720
- Pyne, Benjamin 585

Q

- Qashqai 649, 721
- Qianlong 78–9, 82, 85–7, 706
- Qing 708, 729
- quilts 659, 723–4
- Quimper,
  - baskets 558
  - bowls 30
  - coffee pots 96
  - cups 32–3, 551, 559, 624
  - figures 39
  - jars 56
  - jugs 58, 62
  - knife rests 117
  - mugs 65
  - plates 51–2
  - pots 68
  - services 96
  - teapots 71
  - tureens 100
  - vases 102
- Quintrand, A. 514

R

- Radford, E. 534–6, 536
- Ramage, J. 490
- Ramsden & Carr 557
- Rankin & Co. 588
- rapiers 749–50
- Rasollo, Benedena 593
- Rauenstein 154
- reading chairs 300
- reading tables 425–6
- rebabs 481
- refectory tables 259–60
- regulator clocks 464, 497–8
- Reid, Thomas 500
- Reid, William K. 584
- Reily, Charles 592
- Reily, Mary Ann 592
- Reily and Storer 587
- repeating watches 471
- revolvers 719, 754
- Rhead, Charlotte 554
- Rhead, Frederick 549, 551–2, 554–5, 624, 626
- Richard & Cie 505
- Richards 544
- Richards, Westley 719
- Richmond, Thomas 733
- ridge tiles 488
- Ridgway 121, 140, 143, 152
- Rie, Lucie 635–6, 693
- rifles 720
- Riley 52
- Riley, John 29
- Riley, Richard 29
- rings 634, 748
- Riossen, Cornelis van 514
- Riva, Gianni 627
- Roberts, David 692
- Robertson, Andrew 733
- robes 650–1
- Robineau, Adelaide Alsop 627
- Robinson, Lorraine 693
- Robj 559
- Rochard, Simon Jacques 732
- Rockingham 118, 120, 156
- Rolex 519
- Rolling Stones 697
- Rollisson, Dolly 462
- Rollos, Philip 474
- Rose, John, & Co. 138
- Rosenthal 531–7
- Ross, A. 530, 533
- Rouch, W.W. 532
- Roullet and Decamps 676
- Roussy, Louis 702
- Rowden 495
- Rowland, Robert 752
- Rowley 568
- Royal Crown Derby 119, 151–2, 159
- Royal Doulton 545–9
- Royal Dux 536
- Royal Winton 554
- Royal Worcester 126
  - candle snuffers 175
  - cups 124–5
  - figures 126, 130–1
  - jugs 141–7
  - plates 141–3
  - services 153
  - tureens 157
  - vases 161–3
- Roycrofters 616
- rugs 647–9, 721–4
- Ruhlmann, Emile 568, 628–30
- rummers 227–8
- Ruskin 549–52, 554
- Russell, Gordon 568, 629
- Rye Pottery 58
- Ryke, George 516

S

- S.F.B.J. 672
- Sabino 569
- sabres 718, 750
- Sadler, John 50
- Safavid 481
- St Clement 165
- St Louis 234, 237–9
- Salmon, Colin 492
- Salmson, S. 606
- salt boxes 743
- salt cellars 475
- saltglaze,
  - figures 34
  - jardinieres 116
  - jugs 58, 61
  - mugs 65–6
  - pots 68
  - teapots 96
- salts 73, 117, 585
- salvers 586
- Samarkand 649
- samplers 651–7, 724
- Samson 126, 140–1, 160
- Sancai 83, 85, 177
- sandwich boxes 595
- sardine dishes 595
- Sarouk 647
- Satsuma,
  - bottles 176
  - bowls 178–9, 182, 185
  - chargers 194
  - dishes 194
  - jardinières 196
  - jars 199
  - koro 209
  - services 199
  - vases 200, 204–9
- sauceboats,
  - porcelain 75, 150
  - pottery 69
  - silver 474–5, 587
- Saul, Mike 692
- Sauvageau, Louis 610
- Savonnerie 649
- Savory, Thos. Cox 506
- scales 744
- Scales, Edward 502
- scent bottles 91–2, 151, 240
- sceptres 706
- Schaff 536
- Schmetterling 143
- Schrettegger, Johan 522
- Schuco 676
- scientific instruments 522–33
  - cameras 529–33
  - dials 522–3
  - globes 523
  - medical 527–9
  - microscopes 521–7
  - surveying 524
  - telescopes 525
  - viewers 533
- sconces 604, 616
- Scott, Walter 496, 511
- screens 326, 392
- secretaire bookcases 268–70, 288, 291
- Seide, Paul 621
- Seneca 694
- Senufo 694
- Serapi 721
- services,
  - Art Deco 624
  - oriental 199
  - porcelain 75, 151–4
  - pottery 93–4
  - silver 587–9
  - silver plate 594
- serving tables 319–21, 421–7
- settees 301, 305, 393–5
- settles 330, 740
- Sèvres,
  - bowls 550
  - caisse a fleurs 77
  - cups 125
  - figures 73, 127
  - jardinières 145
  - plates 74
  - services 154
  - trays 143–4
  - vases 77, 165–6
  - wine coolers 72, 175
- Sewell & Young 610
- sewing 731
- sewing tables 320
- Shang 708
- Shaw, William 590
- shawls 653–4
- Sheffield plate 61
- shell 639–40
- Shelley 558–60, 624–5
- Shelley Harmony 559
- shelves 743
- Shepley, Samuel 462
- Sherratt, Obadiah 37, 40, 42
- sherry labels 601
- Shew, J.F., & Co. 529
- Shino 178
- Shirreff, Charles 732
- shoes 652
- Shonzui 81
- Sibley, Richard 581
- Sicilian 55
- side cabinets 283–4, 296,

333–5
side chairs 302–4, 351–9
side tables 260, 319–21, 324, 328, 427–8
sideboards 294, 296, 391–8
Art Nouveau 538
silver 474–7, 574–94
baskets 574
beakers 574
bowls 574–5
boxes 575–8
candelabra 542, 578
candlesticks 578–9
casters 579–80
chocolate pots 580–1
coffee pots 476, 580–1, 633
coffee services 587–9
cups 582
cutlery 582
dishes 584
epergnes 476
ewers 474
figures 716
inkstands 584
jugs 584
miscellaneous 592–4
mugs 585
plates 474
salts 585
salvers 586
sauceboats 587
services 587–9
tankards 585
tea caddies 590, 711
tea kettles 590
tea services 587–9
teapots 476, 590–1, 633, 727
toys 592
tureens 475–6, 592
vases 477
wine coolers 475
silver plate 594–5
candlesticks 594
miscellaneous 595
services 594, 633
tureens 594
silver tables 428–9
Simes, William 496
Simmance, Eliza 549
Simmons 502
Simon & Halbig 672–3, 704
Sitzendorf 135
Skeen, William 590
skeleton clocks 511
skillets 605
Slater, Walter 625
slippers 652
slipware 53, 56, 66
small chests 360–8
Smith, Stephen 593
Smith, Wm. 502
smoking 745
snuff bottles 728–9
snuff boxes 72, 578, 687–9
snufftaking 745
sofa tables 319–20, 429–30
sofas 305
Soldano 504
Solomon Islands 693
Soper, Wm. 540
soup plates 191, 193
Southwark 70
spelter 470, 507, 639
spice cabinets 688
spice jars 332
spill vases 102, 163
Spilsbury, Francis 585
spinning wheels 325
spirit percolators 486
Spode,
baskets 118–19
cups 123–4
dishes 53–4, 71, 140–1, 143
jugs 58, 147
services 94
tureens 100
vases 160–1
wine coolers 175
spoon trays 192
sports 684–6
cricket 686
fishing 684–6
golf 686
Stafford & Co. 698
Staffordshire,
bowls 31
candlesticks 69
figures 33–49, 71
jugs 58–60, 62–4
mugs 65–6
pastille burners 32
plates 52
pots 68
teapots 95–7
tureens 71
vases 102
stands 398–400
Stanley 524
statuettes 639
Stebbing 520
Steiff 671–7, 704
Steiner, Jules 673
steles 705
Stephan, Pierre 41
steps 400
Steward 508
stick barometers 519–20, 522
stick stands 486
Stickley, Gustav 628–30
stirrup cups 33, 123
stirrups 709
stoles 653
stone 642–3
stone carvings 488
stoneware,
bottles 29
bowls 691
desk sets 117
jugs 57
vases 101, 541
stools 305, 400–2, 632
oak & country 256
pine 741
Storr & Mortimer 574, 587
Storr, Paul 474, 476, 574, 586, 592
stoves 488
Strasbourg 50
strongboxes 292
Subes, Raymond 616
sucriers 154
sugar basins 91, 215
sugar bowls 68, 542
Sullivan, Louis 616
Sultanabad 177
surtout-de-tables 478
surveying 524
Susse Frères 480
Sutherland tables 430
Swaine & Co. 667
Swan, I.M. 608
Swansea 52, 54, 60, 141
Swatow 177
Swierink, Hendrik 590
Swift & Son 526
Swift, John 476, 587
swords 718, 750

T

table cabinets 294, 296
table clocks 515
table lamps 175, 613–15, 621, 631
table mats 686
tables 403–39
architects' 403
Art Nouveau 537–8
billiards 403
breakfast 316, 326, 404–5
card 316, 326, 401–10
centre 311–17, 322, 326, 410–12, 630
console 320–1, 325, 412–13, 630
dining 317, 322, 324, 414–17, 629
display 418
drawleaf 259, 418
dressing 324, 330, 418, 568
dropleaf 418–19
drum 317, 419
French 568
games 317, 419–20
gateleg 251–8
lamp 434
library 319, 420–1
loo 322, 421
low 325
nests 421–2, 569
oak & country 251–60
occasional 423, 568
pedestal 423–4
Pembroke 324, 424–5
pier 321
pine 741–2
reading 425–6
refectory 259–60
serving 319–21, 421–7
side 260, 319–21, 324, 328, 427–8
silver 428–9
sofa 319–20, 429–30
Sutherland 430
tea 319, 326, 430–1
tray 431–2
tripod 260, 320, 432–4
wine 434
work 325, 434–6
writing 319–20, 431–9
Tabriz 649
Tagliabue Torre & Co. 520
Tait, Benjamin 599
Talavera 55
tallboys 310, 312, 366
Tang 83, 706
tankards,
porcelain 72
pottery 31, 66, 103–4, 107
silver 585
tantalus 688
tapestries 657, 723
taps 457, 601
tavern pots 66
Taylor, Peter 474
tazzas 70, 638, 640
tea caddies,
brass 633
horn 688
paperwork 328
porcelain 76
pottery 95, 107
silver 590, 711
tortoiseshell 640, 687
wood 332, 687
tea canisters 121
tea and coffee pots,
oriental 199
porcelain 154–6
pottery 95–7
tea kettles, silver 476, 590
tea services,
Art Deco 560, 572, 624
porcelain 545
silver 477, 587–9
silver plated 633
tea tables 319, 326, 430–1
tea urns 475–6
teabowls 81, 123–4
teapots,
Art Nouveau 535
cloisonné 700
porcelain 76
pottery 71, 95–7
silver 476, 590–1, 633, 727
teapoys 439
teddy bears 671–7, 704
telescopes 472, 525
Tenniers 578
terracotta 642–3, 646
terrets 705
Terrey, John Edward 592
Terry, S. 642
textiles 650–9
costume 650–4
embroidery 654–5
lace 655–6
miscellaneous 657–9
samplers 651–7
tapestries 657
theatre 700
theodolites 472
thermometers 175, 487, 522
Thomas, Seth 517
Thomason 597
Thomason Varient 597
Thompson, Robert 567–8
Thonet 537–8
Thorens 683
Thuringian 175
Thwaites, James 493
Tianqi 80, 86
Tiffany 542, 618, 633, 745
Tiffany Studios 613–17, 620
tiles 97–9, 114–15, 544
Timbrell, Robert 474
tinplate 678–80, 702
toast racks 534, 542
tobacco boxes 72
tobacco jars 113–14, 332
Toby jugs 62–5, 534
Todd, John 494
toilet cases 689
Tompion, Thos. 462
tonkotsu 709
torchères 325, 327
tortoiseshell 60, 640, 661, 687–9
towel rails 743
Tower, James 636, 693
toys 671–80, 701–2, 704
automata 676, 704
lead soldiers 678
miscellaneous 680
money banks 678
silver 592
teddy bears 671–7, 704
tinplate 678–80
Transitional 77, 188, 191–7, 200–1
transport 690
Trattle, Joseph 502
tray tables 431–2
trays 477, 639
tribal art 693–5
tricycles 690
tridarns 286
tripod tables 260, 320, 432–4
trivets 604
trophies 477
Troubetskoy, Prince Paul 611
troughs 487
Troughton & Simms 524
trumpet banners 716
Tuck, Raphael 698
Tudor and Leader 579
tulipières 115
tureen stands 199
tureens,
oriental 87, 199–200
porcelain 151–7
pottery 71, 100
silver 475–6, 592
silver plate 594
Turin 50
Turnbull, W. 501
Turton, Frederick W. 588
Twigg, John 752

U

umbrellas 640
uniforms 755
Upchurch 550, 555
upholstery pointer 344
urn clocks 470
urns 441–9, 478–9, 483, 611, 641
Ushafa, Bawa 693
Ushak 649

V

Van Cleef & Arpels 484
van de Knip 529
van der Briel, Pieter 108
van der Rohe, Mies 566
van Voorhis & Schank 474
Varley, John 492
vases 617–21
alabaster 705
Art Nouveau 534–6, 548
glass 92, 241, 617–21
jade 706
oriental 81–7, 200–9, 708–10
ormolu 714
papier mâché 731
pewter 543
porcelain 77, 157–66, 544, 554, 624–6
pottery 101–2, 543, 548
silver 477
stoneware 101, 541
Vasselot, M. de 606
Venice 76, 235
Venini 569
Verstelle, Geertruy 108, 115
vide poches 325
Vienna 135, 143–4, 150, 497
viewers 533
Villeroy and Boch 555, 624
vinaigrettes 575

Vincennes 74, 120
Vinckenbrinck, Albert 644
violins 683
violoncellos 682
Voigtlander & Son 530
Volkstedt 135–6
Vuitton, Louis 684
Vulliamy 469, 502

W

W.K. Co. Ltd. 532
W.M.F. 541–3
waistcoats 651–2
Wakefield, John 502
Walker & Hall 587, 589
walking sticks 542, 745
wall clocks 512–14, 572
wall lanterns 714
wall lights 712, 730
wall plaques 488
wall pockets 175, 535
Wall, William 464
Walton 35
Wanli 78–9, 81, 86
Ward, Robert 506
Wardle 552
wardrobes 374
  Art Nouveau 538
  pine 742
Warhol, Andy 698
Waring and Gillow 569
Warrone, John 490
Wasbrough, Hale & Co. 468
washstands 439–40
  pine 330, 742
wassails 482
watches 471–2, 518–19
water closets 457
Watson, W., & Sons 525, 527
Watteauszehen 156
weathervanes 482
Webb 89
wedding gowns 650
Wedgwood,
  bookends 560
  bowls 120
  candlesticks 714
  cups and saucers 33
  dishes 30, 52
  figures 36
  jugs 59
  lamp bases 116
  plaques 67
  plates 53
  pots 68
  services 94
  sucriers 154
  teapots 95
  tureens 100
  vases 101, 161
Wedgwood and Bentley 67, 101, 116
weights 610, 744
Wellings, Norah 704
Wellington chests 368
Wemyss 69, 71, 103–5
Wemyss Gordon 71, 104–5
Wenzl Wachter 515
Westerwald 66, 117
Westmacott 641
whatnots 440
wheel barometers 520–1
Wheeler, Sir Charles 482
Whieldon 40, 96
White, Fuller 580
Whitefriars 621
Whitewell, William 587
Wiles, J. 496
Wilkes-Osprey 685
Wilkinson, Henry 579, 584
Wilkinson, Henry, & Co. Ltd. 574, 594
Willard, Aaron 466
Willard, Simon 466
Willmore, Joseph 576
Willow 168, 170
Wilton, Joseph 483
Windmills, Joseph 496, 502
window frames 485
window seats 305
windows 631
Windsor chairs 286
wine antiques 591–602
wine coasters 596
wine coolers 72, 175, 328–9, 475, 600–2
wine ewers 599
wine glasses 91, 222–34
wine jugs 60
wine tables 434
wine tasters 597
wire nippers 601
wood, oriental 729
Wood & Co. 529
Wood, Enoch 36, 41
Wood, John 466
Wood, Ralph 40, 42
Wood, Samuel 580
woodcarvings 487, 643–4
Worcester,
  baskets 118–19
  bowls 120
  butter tubs 72
  centrepieces 122
  coffee pots 155
  cups 124–5
  dishes 140, 142
  figures 130–1
  jugs 147
  mugs 148–9
  plates 141
  services 153
  teapots 156
  tureens 157
  vases 102, 161, 163
Worcester First Period 146, 148, 157
work tables 325, 434–6
Wright, Frank Lloyd 631
wristwatches 472, 519
writing slopes 688
writing tables 319–20, 431–
Wucai 184, 186, 196, 201
Wurzburg 73, 135

Y

Yingqing 200
Yixing 199
Yongzheng 79, 81–2, 85–6
Yorkshire 35, 64–5, 97
Yoruba 695
Ysart, Paul 237, 239, 621
Yuan 177

Z

Zack, Bruno 563
Zeiss, Carl 525–6, 529–32
Zhengde 79
Zincke, Christian Friedrich 732

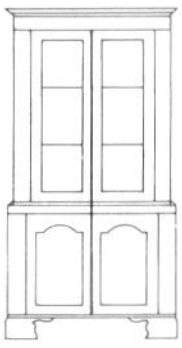

LAKESIDE
limited

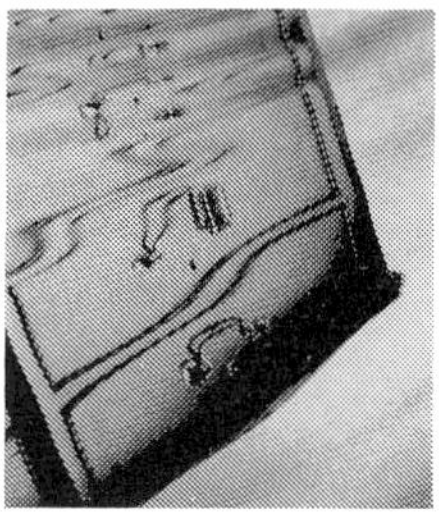

Quality

Lakeside's furniture features strong, classic designs and is made using only old or well seasoned materials. They're the collectors' items of the future, available today.

Craftsmanship

Our skilled tradesmen make each piece individually and to exacting standards. However, we are equipped to provide the considerable quantity of furniture which our success demands – we can manufacture customised designs too.

Design

Whether you choose from stock or specify custom furniture, our models will sit comfortably in any setting. It's an ideal service for interior designers as well as dealers in fine furnishings.

Availability

At Lakeside we always have a large stock of items ready for shipment. Orders can therefore be satisfied quickly.

The Corner Solution is a fine example of our custom built furniture.